A London Bibliography of the Social Sciences

BRITISH LIBRARY OF POLITICAL AND ECONOMIC SCIENCE

A London Bibliography of the Social Sciences

Eighth Supplement
1972-73

VOLUME XXXI

Rubber

—

Zuman

—

Index

MANSELL LONDON 1975

*This Bibliography has been reproduced from
cards forming the subject catalogue of the
British Library of Political and Economic Science by*
Mansell Information/Publishing Limited
3 Bloomsbury Place, London WC1A 2QA

ISBN 0 7201 0454 8
Library of Congress Card Number 31–9970

*The paper on which this Bibliography has
been printed is based on requirements established
by the late William J. Barrow for a permanent/
durable book paper. It is laboratory certified
to meet or exceed the following values:
Substance 89 gsm
pH cold extract 9·4
Fold endurance* (MIT ½ kg tension) 1200
Tear resistance (Elmendorf) 73 (or 67 × 3)
Opacity 90·3%.

Printed and bound in England
© 1975 *The British Library of Political and Economic Science*

Preface

The present supplement to *A London Bibliography of the Social Sciences* continues the use of the photographic method of reproduction, direct from the cards filed in the Subject Catalogue of the British Library of Political and Economic Science during 1972 and 1973. Entries listed are identical with those in the Library's author catalogue.

As with the two previous supplements, speed of publication has meant the omission of cross-references. Readers are, as a guide, referred to the 'List of subject headings used in the Bibliography arranged under topics', which is to be found at the end of the final volume of this supplement. This list also includes under the section *Geography, history and topography* a list of individual countries and places used as main headings.

D. A. Clarke   *October 1974*

Contents

VOLUMES I-XXXI

VOLUMES I–IV *Original Compilation*

Holdings up to 1929 of the
British Library of Political and Economic Science
Edward Fry Library of International Law
Goldsmith's Library of Economic Literature,
 University of London
National Institute of Industrial Psychology
Royal Anthropological Institute
Royal Institute of International Affairs
Royal Statistical Society

Special collections in the libraries of
The Reform Club (political and historical pamphlets)
University College, London (the Hume, Ricardo and other economic and political collections)
The University of London (works on economics and related subjects)

VOLUME V *First Supplement*

Additions from 1929 to 1931 to the collections included in Volumes I–IV

VOLUME VI *Second Supplement*

Additions from 1931 to 1936 to the
British Library of Political and Economic Science
Edward Fry Library of International Law
Goldsmith's Library of Economic Literature

VOLUMES VII–IX *Third Supplement*

Additions from 1936 to 1950, other than works in the Russian language, to the
British Library of Political and Economic Science
Edward Fry Library of International Law

VOLUMES X–XI *Fourth Supplement*

Additions from 1950 to 1955 in all languages, and also from 1936 to 1950 in Russian, to the
British Library of Political and Economic Science
Edward Fry Library of International Law

VOLUMES XII–XIV *Fifth Supplement*

Additions from 1955 to 1962 to the
British Library of Political and Economic Science
Edward Fry Library of International Law

VOLUMES XV–XXI *Sixth Supplement*

Additions from 1962 to 1968 to the
British Library of Political and Economic Science
Edward Fry Library of International Law
Volume XXI contains indexes to Volumes XV–XXI

VOLUMES XXII–XXVIII *Seventh Supplement*

Additions from 1969 to 1972 to the
British Library of Political and Economic Science
Edward Fry Library of International Law
Volume XXVIII contains an index to
Volumes XXII–XXVIII

VOLUMES XXIX–XXXI *Eighth Supplement*

Additions from 1972 to 1973 to the
British Library of Political and Economic Science
Edward Fry Library of International Law
Volume XXXI contains an index to
Volumes XXIX–XXXI

PERIODICALS LISTS

An alphabetical list of the periodicals in the British Library of Political and Economic Science in 1929 is given in Volume IV; supplementary lists up to 1936 are given in Volumes V and VI, after which they have been discontinued.

AUTHOR INDEX

Author indexes are given in Volumes IV (for Volumes I–III), V, and VI, but not in later volumes.
Volumes I–XIV were published by the
British Library of Political and Economic Science,
Houghton Street, London WC2

A LONDON BIBLIOGRAPHY OF THE SOCIAL SCIENCES

RUBBER INDUSTRY AND TRADE

CHEONG (KEE CHEOK) An econometric study of the world natural and synthetic rubber industry; (Ph.D. (London) thesis]. 1972. fo. 462. bibliogs. Typescript: unpublished. This thesis is the property of London University and may not be removed from the Library.

- Guatemala

GUATEMALA. Comision Nacional del Salario. 1967. Estudio economico para la determinacion del salario minimo en la industria de productos de caucho. Guatemala, 1967. fo. (38).

- Malaya

DRABBLE (JOHN H.) Rubber in Malaya, 1876-1922: the genesis of the industry. Kuala Lumpur, 1973. pp. 256. bibliog.

- Malaysia

LIM SWEE AUN. Rubber and the Malaysian economy: implications of declining prices. Athens, Ohio, 1969. fo. 31. (Ohio University. Center for International Studies. Papers in International Studies. Southeast Asia Series. No. 11)

- Nigeria

WELLS (JEROME C.) Benefit-cost analysis of government investment proposals: rubber. [Ibadan], 1967. pp. 14.

RUG AND CARPET INDUSTRY

- Syria

INTERNATIONAL LABOUR OFFICE. Development Programme: Technical Assistance Sector. [Syria]. R.15. Rapport au gouvernement de la République Arabe Syrienne sur la production de tapis en Syrie. (OIT/TAP/Syrie/R.15). Genève, 1970. pp. 21.

RUHR

- Economic conditions

SONNENSCHEIN (ULRICH) Das Ruhrgebiet: Struktur seiner Wirtschaft; Teil: Industrie. Düsseldorf, [1972]. pp. 118. bibliog. (Volks- und Betriebswirtschaftliche Vereinigung im Rheinisch-Westfälischen Industriegebiet. Schriften. Neue Folge. Hauptreihe. Heft 20)

- Economic history

MOENNICH (HORST) Aufbruch ins Revier, Aufbruch nach Europa: Hoesch 1871-1971. München, [1971]. pp. 444.

POTH (LUDWIG) Die Stellung des Steinkohlenbergbaus im Industrialisierungsprozess; unter besonderer Berücksichtigung des Ruhrgebietes. Berlin, [1971]. pp. 249. bibliog.

- History

ZIMMERMANN (LUDWIG) Frankreichs Ruhrpolitik von Versailles bis zum Dawesplan; herausgegeben von Walther Peter Fuchs. Göttingen, [1971]. pp. 299.

- Industries

SONNENSCHEIN (ULRICH) Das Ruhrgebiet: Struktur seiner Wirtschaft; Teil: Industrie. Düsseldorf, [1972]. pp. 118. bibliog. (Volks- und Betriebswirtschaftliche Vereinigung im Rheinisch-Westfälischen Industriegebiet. Schriften. Neue Folge. Hauptreihe. Heft 20)

RULE OF LAW

KENT (EDWARD) ed. Revolution and the rule of law: [selected essays]. Englewood Cliffs, [1971]. pp. 181. bibliog.

MEYER-CORDING (ULRICH) Die Rechtsnormen. Tübingen, 1971. pp. 164. bibliog.

- Czechoslovakia

LUKEŠ (ZDENĚK) Základy bezpečnostního práva. Praha, 1971. pp. 211. With Russian and German summaries.

- Russia

BLINOV (VLADIMIR MIKHAILOVICH) Zakonnost' i pravoporiadok v sovetskom obshchestve. Moskva, 1971. pp. 96.

CHECHINA (NADEZHDA ALEKSANDROVNA) Vospitatel'naia funktsiia sovetskogo grazhdanskogo protsessual'nogo prava. Leningrad, 1972. pp. 112.

IAVICH (LEV SAMOILOVICH) Sotsialisticheskii pravoporiadok. Leningrad, 1972. pp. 78.

NA strazhe sovetskikh zakonov. Moskva, 1972. pp. 454.

- Russia - Chuvash Republic

SHUTIN (MIKHAIL VASIL'EVICH) Obshchestvennost' Chuvashii v bor'be za ukreplenie sotsialisticheskoi zakonnosti. Cheboksary, 1964. pp. 96.

- South Africa

MATHEWS (ANTHONY S.) Law, order and liberty in South Africa. Berkeley, 1972. pp. 318. bibliog.

RUPPIN (ARTHUR)

RUPPIN (ARTHUR) Memoirs, diaries, letters; edited...by Alex Bein; translated from the German by Karen Gershon. London, [1971]. pp. 332.

RURAL CONDITIONS

NADEL' (SEMEN NAUMOVICH) Sotsial'naia struktura sovremennoi kapitalisticheskoi derevni. Moskva, 1970. pp. 192.

ASIAN REGIONAL SEMINAR ON THE CONTRIBUTION OF RURAL INSTITUTIONS TO RURAL DEVELOPMENT, PARTICULARLY EMPLOYMENT, NEW DELHI, 1971. Report...on the seminar... [held in] New Delhi, 3 - 16 November 1971. (ILO/TAP/AFE/R.19). Geneva, International Labour Office, 1972. pp. 137.

RURAL CONDITIONS - Underdeveloped areas
  See UNDERDEVELOPED AREAS -
Rural conditions

RURAL ELECTRIFICATION

- America, Latin

ROSS (JAMES E.) Cooperative rural electrification: case studies of pilot projects in Latin America. New York, 1972. pp. 343. bibliog.

RURAL ELECTRIFICATION (Cont'd.)

- Brazil - Pernambuco

MARQUES DE ALMEIDA (JOSE RILDO) Eletrificação rural de Pernambuco um problema de infra estrutura: (contributed to the] II Seminario Nacional de Distribuição de Energia Eletrica. [Recife], CODEPE, 1964. fo. 39. bibliog. With summaries in English and French.

- Mexico

ANDA GUTIERREZ (CUAUHTEMOC) The rural electrification of Mexico. Austin, 1972. fo. 162. bibliog.

RURAL SCHOOLS

- Ghana

GHANA. Committee appointed...to consider the Problem created by the Closure of Inefficient Schools. 1929. Report and recommendations; [W.J.A. Jones, chairman]. Sessional paper No. 21 of 1928-29. in GHANA. Legislative Council. Minutes (formerly Minutes...and sessional papers).

RURAL-URBAN MIGRATION

RITTER (ULRICH PETER) Siedlungsstruktur und wirtschaftliche Entwicklung: der Verstädterungsprozess...in den Ländern der Dritten Welt, vorwiegend exemplifiziert an Lateinamerika. Berlin, [1972]. pp. 177. bibliog.

- Bibliography

PRYOR (ROBIN J.) compiler. Internal migration and urbanisation: an introduction and bibliography. [Townsville], 1971. pp. 177. (James Cook University of North Queensland. Department of Geography. Monograph Series. No. 2)

- Mathematical models

PETTERSSON (ROLAND) Demographic forecasting models for rural-urban migration and Zipfian distributions. Lisboa, 1970. pp. 35-60. (From Arquivo do Instituto Gulbenkian de Ciência, Secção B, vol. 5, no.2)

OSAYIMWESE (IZEVBUWA) An application of control theory to rural-urban migration and urban unemployment. Ann Arbor, 1972. pp. 19. (Michigan University. Center for Research on Economic Development. Discussion Papers. No. 20)

- Africa

BJEREN (GUNILLA) Some theoretical and methodological aspects of the study of African urbanization. Uppsala, 1971. fo. 37. bibliog. (Uppsala. Universitet. Nordiska Afrikainstitutet. Research Reports. No. 9)

- Argentine Republic

MONTEAGUDO (PIO ISAAC) Migraciones internas en la Argentina y las utopias revolucionarias de L. de la Torre: problemas agrarios. Buenos Aires, 1956. pp. 187.

- Colombia

SEMINARIO NACIONAL SOBRE URBANIZACION, 2ND, [BOGOTA], 1969. Migracion y desarrollo urbano en Colombia; (memoria); editado por Ramiro Cardona Gutierrez [and others]. [Bogota], 1970. pp. 289,35.

CARDONA GUTIERREZ (RAMIRO) ed. Las migraciones internas. [Bogota, 1972?]. pp. 385.

- France

PITIE (JEAN) Exode rural et migrations intérieures en France: l'exemple de la Vienne et du Poitou-Charentes. Poitiers, 1971. pp. 750. bibliog.

- Germany

MEYER (KONRAD) Professor at Berlin University, and THIEDE (KLAUS) eds. Die ländliche Arbeitsverfassung im Westen und Süden des Reiches: Beiträge zur Landfluchtfrage. Heidelberg, 1941. pp. 410.

- Honduras

TELLER (CHARLES HEINROTH) Internal migration, socio-economic status and health: access to medical care in a Honduran city. [Ithaca], 1972. pp. 302. bibliog. (Cornell University. Latin American Studies Program. Dissertation Series. No. 41)

- Mexico

BATAILLON (CLAUDE) Ville et campagnes dans la région de Mexico. Paris, [1971]. pp. 442. bibliogs.

- Peru

VALDIVIA PONCE (OSCAR) Migracion interna a la metropoli: contraste cultural, conflicto y desadaptacion. Lima, 1970. pp. 469. bibliog.

- Russia

ZAIONCHKOVSKAIA (ZHANNA ANTONOVNA) Novosely v gorodakh: metody izucheniia prizhivaemosti. Moskva, 1972. pp. 164.

- Russia - White Russia - Mathematical models

MAKSIMOV (GENNADII TERENT'EVICH) Izuchenie sistemy gorodskikh poselenii BSSR metodami matematicheskoi statistiki. Minsk, 1972. pp. 159.

- Spain

SIGUAN SOLER (MIGUEL) El medio rural en Andalucia oriental. Barcelona, [1972]. pp. 255. bibliog.

- Yugoslavia

SIMIĆ (ANDREI) The peasant urbanites: a study of rural-urban mobility in Serbia. New York, 1973. pp. 180. bibliog.

RURAL YOUTH

- East (Far East)

FAR EAST RURAL YOUTH WORKSHOP, 2ND, TOKYO, 1959. The second Far East rural youth workshop, Tokyo, 1959. [Tokyo, 1959?]. pp. 52.

- France

ENQUETE O.R.L.E.C., région rurale Lyon-Sud, Vienne-nord: étude sociologique sur l'animation et les équipements sociaux-culturels de la région. [Vienne, 1964]. 4 pts. (in 1 vol.). 10 maps in end pocket.

- Poland

ALEKSANDER (TADEUSZ) Awans oświatowy młodzieży wiejskiej 1945-1970 na przykładzie Sądecczyzny. Olsztyn, 1972. pp. 234. bibliog.

KOLBUSZ (FRANCISZEK) and MOSKAL (STANISŁAW) Młodzież wiejska o swej sytuacji i dążeniach. [Olsztyn], 1972. pp. 155.

ŁOŚ (MARIA) Aspiracje a środowisko. Warszawa, 1972. pp. 300. With English and Russian summaries.

RUSH (BENJAMIN)

HAWKE (DAVID) Benjamin Rush: revolutionary gadfly. Indianapolis, [1971]. pp. 490. bibliog.

RUSSELL (BERTRAND ARTHUR WILLIAM) 3rd Earl Russell

KLEMKE (ELMER D.) ed. Essays on Bertrand Russell. Urbana, [1970]. pp. 458. bibliog.

AYER (Sir ALFRED JULES) Russell. London, 1972. pp. 152. bibliog.

JAGER (RONALD) The development of Bertrand Russell's philosophy. London, 1972. pp. 520. bibliog.

RUSSELL (BERTRAND ARTHUR WILLIAM) 3rd Earl Russell. The life of Bertrand Russell in pictures and in his own words; compiled by Christopher Farley and David Hodgson. Nottingham, 1972. pp. 95. bibliog.

HOROWITZ (DAVID) The fate of Midas, and other essays. San Francisco, [1973]. pp. 255.

RUSSELL (ELIZABETH ANNE) Lady William Russell

BLAKISTON (GEORGIANA) Lord William Russell and his wife, 1815-1846. London, [1972]. pp. 566. bibliog.

RUSSELL (Lord GEORGE WILLIAM)
See RUSSELL (Lord WILLIAM)

RUSSELL (JOHN) 1st Earl Russell

REID (STUART J.) Lord John Russell. rev. ed. London, 1895. pp. 380.

PREST (JOHN) Lord John Russell. London, 1972. pp. 558. bibliog.

RUSSELL (Lady WILLIAM)
See RUSSELL (ELIZABETH ANNE) Lady William Russell

RUSSELL (Lord WILLIAM)

BLAKISTON (GEORGIANA) Lord William Russell and his wife, 1815-1846. London, [1972]. pp. 566. bibliog.

RUSSIA

Here are entered works on the Russian Empire or the USSR as a whole. For works on the Russian Federative Republic see RUSSIA (R.S.F.S.R.). In previous volumes of the London Bibliography such material has been entered simply under RUSSIA.

La RUSSIE: géographique, ethnologique, historique, administrative, économique...; par L. Delavaud [and others]. 2nd ed. Paris, [1892?]. pp. 496. bibliog.

THIRTY years of the Soviet state: calendar, 1917xxx1947. Moscow, 1947. 1 vol. (unpaged).

- Annexation - Armenia

PRISOEDINENIE Vostochnoi Armenii k Rossii: sbornik dokumentov. Erevan, 1972 in progress.

- Annexation - Bessarabia

STRANITSY revoliutsionnoi bor'by i sotsialisticheskogo stroitel'stva v Moldavii: [sbornik statei]. Kishinev, 1966. pp. 183.

MEZHDUNARODNAIA podderzhka bor'by trudiashchikhsia Bessarabii za vossoedinenie s Sovetskoi Rodinoi, 1918-1940 gg.: sbornik dokumentov i materialov. Kishinev, 1970. pp. 391.

KOPANSKII (IAKOV MIKHAILOVICH) Nash drug - Gabriel' Peri: vystupleniia G. Peri v podderzhku bor'by trudiashchikhsia Bessarabii za vossoedinenie s Sovetskoi Rodinoi. Kishinev, 1971. pp. 124.

- Annexation - Estonia

RIANZHIN (VALENTIN ANATOL'EVICH) Krizis burzhuaznoi konstitutsionnoi zakonnosti i vosstanovlenie sovetskoi gosudarstvennosti v Estonii. Leningrad, 1971. pp. 71.

- Armed forces

BESKROVNYI (LIUBOMIR GRIGOR'EVICH) Russkaia armiia i flot v XIX veke: voenno-ekonomicheskii potentsial Rossii. Moskva, 1973. pp. 616.

- Armed forces - Bibliography

AZOVTSEV (NIKOLAI NIKOLAEVICH) compiler. Voennye voprosy v trudakh V.I. Lenina: annotirovannyi ukazatel' proizvedenii i vyskazyvanii V.I. Lenina po vazhneishim voprosam voiny, armii i voennoi nauki. Moskva, 1964. pp. 310.

AZOVTSEV (NIKOLAI NIKOLAEVICH) compiler. Voennye voprosy v trudakh V.I. Lenina: annotirovannyi ukazatel' proizvedenii i vyskazyvanii V.I. Lenina po vazhneishim voprosam voiny, armii i voennoi nauki. 2nd ed. Moskva, 1972. pp. 454.

- Armed forces - Mobilization

KIRSANOV (NIKOLAI ANDREEVICH) Partiinye mobilizatsii na front v gody Velikoi Otechestvennoi voiny; pod redaktsiei... N.I. Shatagina. Moskva, 1972. pp. 187.

- Armed forces - Officers

RUSSIA (U.S.S.R.). Ministerstvo Oborony. 1970. Sovetskii ofitser. Moskva, 1970. pp. 327.

- Armed forces - Political activity

RABINOVICH (S.E.) Bor'ba za armiiu v 1917 g.: ocherki partiino-politicheskoi bor'by i raboty v armii v 1917 godu. Moskva, 1930. pp. 160. bibliog.

KALASHNIK (MIKHAIL KHARITONOVICH) Politorgany i partiinye organizatsii Sovetskoi Armii i Voenno-Morskogo Flota: lektsiia, prochitannaia v Vysshei partiinoi shkole pri TsK KPSS. Moskva, 1963. pp. 89.

ANNANEPESOV (M.) Uchastie soldatskikh mass v revoliutsii 1905-1907 godov v Turkmenistane. Ashkhabad, 1966. pp. 171.

RIPA (EKATERINA IVANOVNA) Voenno-revoliutsionnye komitety raiona XII armii v 1917 g. na neokkupirovannoi territorii Latvii. Riga, 1969. pp. 65.

RUSSIA (U.S.S.R.). Ministerstvo Oborony. 1972. Partiino-politicheskaia rabota v Sovetskikh Vooruzhennykh Silakh: uchebnoe posobie dlia studentov grazhdanskikh vuzov. Moskva, 1972. pp. 286.

SENCHAKOVA (L.T.) Revoliutsionnoe dvizhenie v russkoi armii i flote v kontse XIX - nachale XX v., 1879-1904 gg. Moskva, 1972. pp. 216.

RUSSIA - Armed forces - Political activity (Cont'd.)

VAZHNYI faktor boegotovnosti: iz opyta moral'-no-politicheskoi i psikhologicheskoi podgotovki voinov. Moskva, 1972. pp. 216.

- Armed forces - Regulations

RUSSIA (U.S.S.R.). Ministerstvo Oborony. 1964. Obshchevoinskie ustavy - svod pravil povedeniia i deiatel'nosti voennosluzhashchikh; [by] I.F. Pobezhimov [and] D.N. Artamonov. Moskva, 1964. pp. 68.

RUSSIA (U.S.S.R.). Ministerstvo Oborony. 1972. Obshchevoinskie Ustavy Vooruzhennykh Sil SSSR, etc. Moskva, 1972. pp. 480.

- Army - History

POLOVTSOV (PETR A.) Dni zatmeniia: zapiski Glavnokomanduiushchego Voiskami Petrogradskogo Voennogo Okruga generala P.A. Polovtsova v 1917 godu. Paris, [1925?]. pp. 207.

ALEKSANDROVICH (V.) K poznaniiu kharaktera grazhdanskoi voiny: bunt v 5-m Severnom strelkovom polku 20 iiulia 1919 goda. Belgrad, 1926. pp. 28.

PODVOISKII (NIKOLAI IL'ICH) Krasnaia gvardiia v Oktiabr'skie dni: Leningrad i Moskva. Moskva, 1927. pp. 107.

PECHE (IA.) Krasnaia gvardiia v Moskve v boiakh za Oktiabr'. Moskva, 1929. pp. 187.

PRONIN (V.M.) Poslednie dni Tsarskoi Stavki. Belgrad, 1929. pp. 88. Title page missing. Cover dated 1930.

HELLIE (RICHARD) Enserfment and military change in Muscovy. Chicago, 1971. pp. 432. bibliog.

TAIRIAN (IVAN AGASIEVICH) XI Krasnaia Armiia v bor'be za ustanovlenie i uprochenie Sovetskoi vlasti v Armenii. Erevan, 1971. pp. 319. bibliog.

- Army - History - Sources

GRAZHDANSKAIA voina: materialy po istorii Krasnoi Armii. t.1. Moskva, 1923. pp. 509.

- Bibliography

KNIZHNIK-VETROV (IVAN SERGEEVICH) compiler. Chto chitat' po obshchestvennym naukam: sistematicheskii ukazatel' kommunisticheskoi i marksistskoi literatury, 1917-1923 g.g., etc. 2nd ed. Leningrad, 1924. pp. 491.

- Biography

GOLUBTSOV (VADIM SERGEEVICH) Memuary kak istochnik po istorii sovetskogo obshchestva. Moskva, 1970. pp. 114.

WHO was who in the USSR: a biographic directory containing 5,015 biographies of prominent Soviet historical personalities; compiled by the Institute for the Study of the USSR, Munich, Germany; edited by Heinrich E. Schulz [and others]. Metuchen, N.J., 1972. pp. 677.

- Boundaries

KLIMENKO (BORIS MIKHAILOVICH) Gosudarstvennye granitsy - problema mira. Moskva, 1964. pp. 138.

- Boundaries - China

JACKSON (WILLIAM ARTHUR DOUGLAS) The Russo-Chinese borderlands: zone of peaceful contact or potential conflict? 2nd ed. Princeton, N.J., [1968]. pp. 156. bibliog.

AN (TAI SUNG) The Sino-Soviet territorial dispute. Philadelphia, 1973. pp. 254.

- Census

RUSSIA (U.S.S.R.). Tsentral'noe Statisticheskoe Upravlenie. 1961. Chislennost', sostav i razmeshchenie naseleniia SSSR: kratkie itogi Vsesoiuznoi perepisi naseleniia 1959 goda. Moskva, 1961. pp. 64.

KOLPAKOV (BORIS TIMOFEEVICH) Vsesoiuznaia perepis' naseleniia 1970 goda. Moskva, 1969. pp. 62. bibliog.

RUSSIA (U.S.S.R.). Census, 1970. O predvaritel'nykh itogakh Vsesoiuznoi perepisi naseleniia 1970 goda: soobshchenie Tsentral'nogo statisticheskogo upravleniia pri Sovete Ministrov SSSR. Moskva, 1970. pp. 16.

RUSSIA (U.S.S.R.). Tsentral'noe Statisticheskoe Upravlenie. 1971. Chislennost', razmeshchenie, vozrastnaia struktura, uroven' obrazovaniia, natsional'nyi sostav, iazyki i istochniki sredstv sushchestvovaniia naseleniia SSSR: po dannym Vsesoiuznoi perepisi naseleniia 1970 goda. Moskva, 1971. pp. 34.

- Church history

MEL'GUNOV (SERGEI PETROVICH) Moskva i staraia vera: ocherk iz istorii religiozno-obshchestvennykh dvizhenii na rubezhe XVII-XVIII vv. Moskva, 1917. pp. 32.

- Civilization

KAIRIAN (VACHE MIKHAILOVICH) Preemstvennost' v razvitii kul'tury v usloviiakh sotsializma: filosofskie problemy kul'tury v trudakh V.I.Lenina. Moskva, 1971. pp. 212.

BARMICHEV (VITALII DMITRIEVICH) V edinom soiuze: istoriko-publitsisticheskii ocherk o razvitii mnogonatsional'noi sotsialisticheskoi kul'tury v SSSR; nauchnyi redaktor... I.M. Ignatenko. Minsk, 1972. pp. 247. bibliog.

GORBUNOV (VLADIMIR VLADIMIROVICH) Lenin i sotsialisticheskaia kul'tura: leninskaia kontseptsiia formirovaniia sotsialisticheskoi kul'tury. Moskva, 1972. pp. 340.

RUSSIA: essays in history and literature; [lectures delivered at Washington University, 1967-1969]; edited by Lyman H. Legters. Leiden, 1972. pp. 164.

THOMSON (BORIS) The premature revolution: Russian literature and society, 1917-1946. London, [1972]. pp. 325. bibliog.

- Civilization - Bibliography

SIMMONS (JOHN SIMON GABRIEL) compiler. Russian bibliography, libraries and archives: a selective list of bibliographical references for students of Russian history, literature, political, social and philosophical thought, theology and linguistics. Oxford, 1973. pp. 76.

- Civilization - Occidental influences

  MEDLIN (WILLIAM K.) and PATRINELIS (CHRISTOS G.) Renaissance influences and religious reforms in Russia: Western and post-Byzantine impacts on culture and education, 16th-17th centuries. Geneva, 1971. pp. 181. bibliog.

  PLATONOV (SERGEI FEDOROVICH) Moscow and the West; translated and edited by Joseph L. Wieczynski. Hattiesburgh, Miss., 1972. pp. 171.

  WITTRAM (REINHARD) Russia and Europe. London, [1973]. pp. 180. bibliog.

- Commerce

  LENINGRADSKII INSTITUT SOVETSKOI TORGOVLI. Sbornik trudov. vyp.24. Problemy sovershenstvovaniia protsessa obmena v narodnom khoziaistve SSSR. Leningrad, 1965. pp. 291.

  RUSSIA (U.S.S.R.). Ministerstvo vneshnei Torgovli. Sbornik normativnykh materialov po voprosam vneshnei torgovli SSSR. Moskva, 1970 (vyp.1) -

  ORLOV (IAKOV L'VOVICH) and SHIMANSKII (VSEVOLOD PAVLOVICH) Reforma i torgovlia. Moskva, 1970. pp. 240.

  FRERS (DIRK) Zur Frage ausserökonomischer Aktionen im sowjetischen Rohstoffhandel, dargestellt am Beispiel zweier Rohstoffmärkte. Göttingen, 1971. pp. 243, xxii. bibliog.

  KANEVSKII (EVGENII MARKOVICH) and MARGOLIN (LEONID GRIGOR'EVICH) U istokov sovetskoi torgovli. Moskva, 1971. pp. 199

  KATAL'NIKOV (IGNATII FEDOROVICH) Statistika sovetskoi torgovli. 4th ed. Moskva, 1971. pp. 238.

  McMILLAN (C.H.) Factor proportions and the structure of Soviet foreign trade. [Ottawa, 1971?]. fo. 26. bibliog. (Carleton University. Carleton Economic Papers)

  SOLOV'EV (BORIS ALEKSANDROVICH) Izuchenie sprosa na tovary dlitel'nogo pol'zovaniia. Moskva, 1971. pp. 69.

  ZAIDENVARG (VIKTOR ALEKSANDROVICH) Effektivnost' kreditovaniia torgovli. Moskva, 1971. pp. 158.

  BAIDAKOV (NIKOLAI FEDOROVICH) and others. Problemy razmeshcheniia torgovoi seti v sel'skoi mestnosti. Moskva, 1972. pp. 111.

  FONAREV (EVGENII NIKOLAEVICH) Finansovye problemy gosudarstvennoi torgovli. Moskva, 1972. pp. 176.

  LIUBEL'FEL'D (V.I.) and others. Fondy ekonomicheskogo stimulirovaniia v torgovle. Moskva, 1972. pp. 167.

  McMILLAN (C.H.) Soviet specialization and trade in manufactures. Ottawa, 1972. fo. 29. bibliog. (Carleton University. Carleton Economic Papers)

  MARER (PAUL) Soviet and East European foreign trade, 1946-1969: statistical compendium and guide; computer programs by Gary J. Eubanks. Bloomington, [1972]. pp. 408. bibliog. (Indiana University. International Development Research Center. Studies in Development. No. 4)

  NOVOSELOV (PAVEL IVANOVICH) and GOFMAN (GRIGORII ABRAMOVICH) Finansirovanie i kreditovanie torgovli. Moskva, 1972. pp. 272.

- Commerce - Europe

  La RUSSIE et l'Europe, XVIe-XXe siècles. Paris, 1970. pp. 326. bibliog. (Paris. École Pratique des Hautes Études. Section des Sciences Économiques et Sociales. Bibliothèque Générale)

- Commerce - Finland

  SUNI (L.) Finliandsko-russkie torgovye otnosheniia vo vtoroi polovine XIX veka, 1858-1885. Tartu, 1963. pp. 174. bibliog.

- Commerce - Germany

  KUCZYNSKI (JUERGEN) and WITTKOWSKI (GRETE) Die deutsch-russischen Handelsbeziehungen in den letzten 150 Jahren. 2nd ed. Berlin, [1948]. pp. 126.

  MAI (JOACHIM) Das deutsche Kapital in Russland 1850-1894. Berlin, 1970. pp. 255. bibliog. (Greifswald. Universität. Historisches Institut. Veröffentlichungen. Band 4)

  BREMEIER (EBERHARD) Westdeutsche Industrieanlagen-Exporte in die Sowjetunion: Entscheidungsrahmen und Entscheidung. Berlin, 1971. pp. 328. bibliog.

- Commercial policy

  KAGANOV (EFIM DAVYDOVICH) Sotsialisticheskoe vosproizvodstvo i rynok. Moskva, 1966. pp. 191.

  ALYMKULOV (SAGYNBEK) Vzaimootnosheniia organov Soiuza SSR i soiuznykh respublik v oblasti upravleniia sovetskoi torgovlei. Frunze, 1971. pp. 142. bibliog.

  ZASUKHIN (ANTONII TIKHONOVICH) Realizatsiia sredstv proizvodstva. Moskva, 1972. pp. 103.

  CLEMENT (HERMANN) Die Organisationsstruktur der sowjetischen Aussenwirtschaft. Hamburg, 1973. pp. 223. bibliog. (Hamburg. Hamburgisches Welt-Wirtschafts-Archiv. Veröffentlichungen)

  SCHNEIDER (HUBERT) Das sowjetische Aussenhandelsmonopol 1920-1925. Köln, [1973]. pp. 216. bibliog. (Bundesinstitut für Ostwissenschaftliche und Internationale Studien. Abhandlungen. Band 28)

- Constitution

  VOPROSY gosudarstva i prava. Minsk, 1960. pp. 160. Cover title ends...BSSR.

  KERIMOV (DZHANGIR ALI-ABASOVICH) and CHEKHARIN (EVGENII MIKHAILOVICH) Sotsialisticheskaia demokratiia i sovremennaia ideologicheskaia bor'ba. Moskva, 1970. pp. 253.

  MESTRE (ACHILLE) and GUTTINGER (PHILIPPE) Constitutionnalisme jacobin et constitutionnalisme soviétique. Paris, 1971. pp. 152. bibliogs. (Paris. Université. Faculté de Droit et des Sciences Economiques. Travaux et Recherches. Série "Science Politique". No. 22)

  SHABANOV (IURII VASIL'EVICH) Leninskie printsipy raboty gosudarstvennogo apparata. Minsk, 1971. pp. 294.

  GRIGOR'IAN (LEVON ARMENAKOVICH) Narodovlastie v SSSR. Moskva, 1972. pp. 296.

  KOZHOKHIN (BORIS IVANOVICH) Osnovnye tendentsii razvitiia demokraticheskoi sushchnosti sotsialisticheskogo gosudarstva. Leningrad, 1972. pp. 96.

RUSSIA - Constitution (Cont'd.)

SHEVTSOV (VIKTOR SERGEEVICH) Suverenitet Sovetskogo gosudarstva. Moskva, 1972. pp. 264.

SOIUZ SSR - sodruzhestvo ravnopravnykh respublik. Moskva, 1972. pp. 296.

TADEVOSIAN (EDUARD VRAMOVICH) Sovetskaia natsional'naia gosudarstvennost'. Moskva, 1972. pp. 232.

ARNOLD (JUERGEN) Die nationalen Gebietseinheiten der Sowjetunion: Staatlichkeit, Souveränität und Autonomie im Sowjetföderalismus. Köln, [1973]. pp. 176. bibliog. (Bundesinstitut für Ostwissenschaftliche und Internationale Studien. Abhandlungen. Band 27)

- Constitutional history

SUKHOMLIN (VASILII) Vserossiiskoe Uchreditel'noe Sobranie pervogo sozyva. N'iu Iork, [1919]. pp. 15.

RONIN (SAMUIL LAZAREVICH) K istorii Konstitutsii SSSR, 1924. Moskva, 1949. pp. 123.

GAL'PERIN (GRIGORII BORISOVICH) Forma pravleniia russkogo tsentralizovannogo gosudarstva XV-XVI vv. Leningrad, 1964. pp. 91.

IRKUTSK. Universitet. [Trudy]. tom 39. Seriia Istoricheskaia. vyp.7. Voprosy sovetskogo gosudarstva i prava. Irkutsk, 1965. 2 vols (in 1).

MAVRODIN (VLADIMIR VASIL'EVICH) Obrazovanie Drevnerusskogo gosudarstva i formirovanie drevnerusskoi narodnosti. Moskva, 1971. pp. 192.

AGZAMKHODZHAEV (ANVAR) and URAZAEV (SHAVKAT ZAKARIEVICH) SSSR - sotsialisticheskoe gosudarstvo sovetskikh narodov. Tashkent, 1972. pp. 339.

CHUGAEV (D.A.) and others, eds. Istoriia natsional'no-gosudarstvennogo stroitel'stva v SSSR. Moskva, 1972. 2 vols.

CHUGAEV (DMITRII AGEEVICH) Kommunisticheskaia partiia - organizator Soiuza Sovetskikh Sotsialisticheskikh Respublik. Moskva, 1972. pp. 412. bibliog.

DENISOV (ANDREI IVANOVICH) ed. Teoriia gosudarstva i prava. [rev. ed.]. Moskva, 1972. pp. 531. bibliog.

GILILOV (S.S.) V.I. Lenin - organizator Sovetskogo mnogonatsional'nogo gosudarstva. 2nd ed. Moskva, 1972. pp. 232.

IAKUBOVSKAIA (SOFIIA IOSIFOVNA) Razvitie SSSR kak soiuznogo gosudarstva, 1922-1936 gg. Moskva, 1972. pp. 227.

KURITSYN (VSEVOLOD MIKHAILOVICH) Perekhod k nepu i revoliutsionnaia zakonnost'. Moskva, 1972. pp. 216.

SSSR - velikoe sodruzhestvo narodov-brat'ev. Moskva, 1972. pp. 339.

STROITEL'STVO Sovetskogo gosudarstva: sbornik statei k 70-letiiu doktora istoricheskikh nauk, professora E.B. Genkinoi. Moskva, 1972. pp. 306. bibliog.

TARANOV (ANATOLII PAVLOVYCH) P"iatdesiat rokiv Soiuzu Radians'kykh Sotsialistychnykh Respublik: derzhavno-pravovyi narys. Kyïv, 1972. pp. 194.

ZLATOPOL'SKII (DAVID L'VOVICH) and CHISTIAKOV (OLEG IVANOVICH) Obrazovanie Soiuza SSR. Moskva, 1972. pp. 319.

HOSKING (GEOFFREY A.) The Russian constitutional experiment: government and Duma, 1907-1914. Cambridge, 1973. pp. 281. bibliog. (National Association for Soviet and East European Studies. Soviet and East European Studies)

- Constitutional history - Sources

OBRAZOVANIE i razvitie SSSR kak soiuznogo gosudarstva: sbornik zakonodatel'nykh i drugikh normativnykh aktov. Moskva, 1972. pp. 343.

OBRAZOVANIE Soiuza Sovetskikh Sotsialisticheskikh Respublik: sbornik dokumentov. Moskva, 1972. pp. 531.

SOVETSKOE sodruzhestvo narodov: ob"edinitel'noe dvizhenie i obrazovanie SSSR; sbornik dokumentov, 1917-1922. Moskva, 1972. pp. 336.

- Constitutional law

OSNOVIN (VIKTOR STEPANOVICH) Sovetskie gosudarstvennopravovye otnosheniia. Moskva, 1965. pp. 168.

MITSKEVICH (ALEKSEI VALENTINOVICH) Akty vysshikh organov Sovetskogo gosudarstva: iuridicheskaia priroda normativnykh aktov vysshikh organov gosudarstvennoi vlasti i upravleniia SSSR. Moskva, 1967. pp. 175.

IRKUTSK. Universitet. Trudy. t.57. Seriia Iuridicheskaia. vyp.9, ch.2. Voprosy gosudarstvennogo prava i sovetskogo stroitel'stva. Irkutsk, 1968. pp. 131.

LENINSKAIA teoriia sotsialisticheskogo gosudarstva i prava i sovremennost': nauchnaia konferentsiia iuridicheskikh fakul'tetov, posviashchennaia 100-letiiu so dnia rozhdeniia V.I. Lenina, 27-29 ianvaria 1970 goda. Kazan', 1970. pp. 275.

GRIGORIAN (LEVON ARMENAKOVICH) and DOLGOPOLOV (IURII) Fundamentals of Soviet state law; edited by B. Shchetinin. Moscow, 1971. pp. 324.

SHABANOV (MIKHAIL RODIONOVICH) Akty sel'skikh i poselkovykh Sovetov. Moskva, 1971. pp. 96.

OSNOVNYE zakonodatel'nye akty po sovetskomu gosudarstvennomu stroitel'stvu i pravu. Moskva, 1972 in progress.

SAZHIN (GRIGORII MAKSIMOVICH) Sovet deputatov trudiashchikhsia natsional'nogo okruga. Moskva, 1972. pp. 68.

VOEVODIN (LEONID DMITRIEVICH) Konstitutsionnye prava i obiazannosti sovetskikh grazhdan. Moskva, 1972. pp. 300.

- Defences

GALLAGHER (MATTHEW PHILIP) and SPIELMANN (KARL F.) Soviet decision-making for defense: a critique of U.S. perspectives on the arms race. New York, 1972. pp. 102.

- Description and travel

EINHEITSKOMITEE FÜR ARBEITERDELEGATIONEN. Was sahen 58 deutsche Arbeiter in Russland?: Bericht der deutschen Arbeiter-Delegation über ihren Aufenthalt in Russland vom 14. Juli bis zum 28. August 1925. Berlin, 1925. pp. 176

DUTCH (OSWALD) Das Räderwerk des roten Betriebes: eine Studienfahrt durch die Wirtschaft Sowjet-Russlands; von Otto Deutsch. Wien, 1929. pp. 112.

GRGURIĆ (HRVOJE) Kroz tamnice i crvenu maglu: doživljaji u zemlji nove ideologije. Zagreb, 1932. pp. 399.

NEARING (HELEN KOTHE) and NEARING (SCOTT) The brave new world. Harborside, Maine, [1958]. pp. 247.

BLANC (ANDRE) and CHAMBRE (HENRI) L'U.R.S.S. Paris, 1971. pp. 286. bibliog.

DEWDNEY (JOHN CHRISTOPHER) A geography of the Soviet Union. 2nd ed. Oxford, 1971. pp. 169. bibliog.

HAXTHAUSEN (AUGUST VON) Freiherr. Studies on the interior of Russia; edited and with an introduction by S. Frederick Starr; translated by Eleanore L.M. Schmidt. Chicago, 1972. pp. 328.

- Duma

TAGANTSEV (NIKOLAI STEPANOVICH) Perezhitoe. Petrograd, 1919. 2 vols. Xerographic reprint.

HOSKING (GEOFFREY A.) The Russian constitutional experiment: government and Duma, 1907-1914. Cambridge, 1973. pp. 281. bibliog. (National Association for Soviet and East European Studies. Soviet and East European Studies)

- Duma - Biography

FILIPPOV (P.O.) Pervoe ministerstvo svobodnoi Rossii: portrety i biografii chlenov Vremennogo Pravitel'stva. Moskva, 1917. pp. 31. Xerographic reprint.

- Economic conditions

ZAGORSKII (SEMEN OSIPOVICH) K sotsializmu ili k kapitalizmu. [Prague], Respublikansko-Demokraticheskii Soiuz, 1927. pp. 308.

DUTCH (OSWALD) Das Räderwerk des roten Betriebes: eine Studienfahrt durch die Wirtschaft Sowjetrusslands; von Ot o Deutsch. Wien, 1929. pp. 112.

KHABAROVSK. Gosudarstvennyi Pedagogicheskii Institut. Uchenye Zapiski. t.10. Kafedry obshchestvennykh nauk: ekonomicheskie nauki. Khabarovsk, 1962. pp. 61.

DZHAVADOV (GATAM AGALIEVICH) Dal'neishee sovershenstvovanie i postepennoe preobrazovanie sotsialisticheskikh proizvodstvennykh otnoshenii v kommunisticheskie. Moskva, 1963. pp. 92.

PROKHORENKO (IVAN DENISOVICH) Pererastanie sotsialisticheskikh proizvodstvennykh otnoshenii v kommunisticheskie. Moskva, 1963. pp. 132.

SOREVNOVANIE dvukh sistem: problemy ekonomicheskoi nauki. Moskva, 1963. pp. 304.

DEIAKI pytannia postupovoho pererostannia sotsializmu v komunizm. L'viv, 1964. pp. 128.

DOVGAN' (LEONTII IVANOVICH) O tempakh rosta dvukh podrazdelenii obshchestvennogo proizvodstva. Moskva, 1965. pp. 80.

MARKERT (WERNER) ed. Sowjetunion: das Wirtschaftssystem; (Osteuropa-Handbuch). Köln, 1965. pp. 587.

PESHEKHONOV (IURII VLADIMIROVICH) and SHATALIN (STANISLAV SERGEEVICH) Otraslevaia struktura obshchestvennogo proizvodstva: k analizu faktorov i struktury sootnosheniia I i II podrazdelenii. Moskva, 1965. pp. 82.

PROBLEMY formuvannia bazysu komunistychnoho suspil'stva: respublikans'kyi mizhvidomchyi zbirnyk. Kyïv, 1965. pp. 214. With Russian summaries and table of contents.

SOVETSKII Soiuz: geograficheskoe opisanie. Moskva, 1966-72. 22 vols. (in 23). bibliog.

VOPROSY marksistsko-leninskoi teorii i praktiki na sovremennom etape. Saratov, 1968. pp. 176.

POLITICHESKAIA ekonomiia: sotsializm - pervaia faza kommunisticheskogo sposoba proizvodstva. Moskva, 1969. pp. 374.

HORWITZ (BERTRAND) Accounting controls and the Soviet economic reforms of 1966. Evanston, Ill., 1970. pp. 74. (American Accounting Association. Studies in Accounting Research. 4)

PASHKOV (ANATOLII IGNAT'EVICH) Ekonomicheskie problemy sotsializma. Moskva, 1970. pp. 528. bibliog.

ABALKIN (LEONID IVANOVICH) Ekonomicheskie zakony sotsializma. Moskva, 1971. pp. 191.

BAGDASARIAN (ALEKSEI MUSHEGOVICH) Sovetskii opyt ekonomicheskogo vyravnivaniia natsional'nykh respublik. Groznyi, 1971. pp. 79. bibliog.

BLANC (ANDRE) and CHAMBRE (HENRI) L'U.R.S.S. Paris, 1971. pp. 286. bibliog.

DEWDNEY (JOHN CHRISTOPHER) A geography of the Soviet Union. 2nd ed. Oxford, 1971. pp. 169. bibliog.

KORIAGIN (ALEKSANDR GEORGIEVICH) Nauchno-tekhnicheskaia revoliutsiia i proportsii sotsialisticheskogo vosproizvodstva. Moskva, 1971. pp. 303.

KRITIKA burzhuaznykh kontseptsii ekonomiki sotsializma. Moskva, 1971. pp. 303.

KUZ'MINOV (IVAN IVANOVICH) Ocherki politicheskoi ekonomii sotsializma: voprosy metodologii. Moskva, 1971. pp. 349.

LIAPIN (ANDREI PAVLOVICH) Ekonomicheskie zakonomernosti pererastaniia sotsializma v kommunizm. Moskva, 1971. pp. 127.

MOISEENKO (NIKOLAI ANDREEVICH) Ocherki teorii individual'nogo vosproizvodstva pri sotsializme. Leningrad. 1971. pp. 95.

OSNOVY sotsialisticheskoi ekonomiki. Moskva, Molodaia Gvardiia, 1971. pp. 335.

POLITICHESKAIA ekonomiia sotsializma. 2nd ed. Moskva, 1971. pp. 575.

SHKAREDNYI (IVAN ILLICH) Protses sotsialystychnoho vyrobnytstva ta ioho efektyvnist'. Kyïv, 1971. pp. 181. bibliog.

STOIMOST' v usloviiakh sotsializma. Minsk, 1971. pp. 435. bibliog.

AGENTSTVO PECHATI NOVOSTI. USSR 50: Novosti Press Agency year book. Moscow, 1972. pp. 335.

ISTORIIA obshchestvennoi mysli: sovremennye problemy. Moskva, 1972. pp. 535.

ISTORIIA politicheskoi ekonomii sotsializma: ocherki. Leningrad, 1972. pp. 383.

KRUK (DAVID MOISEEVICH) Upravlenie obshchestvennym proizvodstvom pri sotsializme. Moskva, 1972. pp. 223.

RUSSIA - Economic conditions (Cont'd.)

KUNIAVSKII (MAKS SAMUILOVICH) Otnosheniia neposredstvennogo proizvodstva pri sotsializme: ocherk teorii. Minsk, 1972. pp. 342.

KUZ'MINOV (IVAN IVANOVICH) and others, eds. Osnovnoi ekonomicheskii zakon i razvitie sotsialisticheskogo proizvodstva. Moskva, 1972. pp. 293.

LAVRISHCHEV (ALEKSEI NIKITICH) Ekonomicheskaia geografiia SSSR: obshchaia chast', geografiia otraslei narodnogo khoziaistva soiuznykh respublik i ekonomicheskikh raionov. [rev.ed.] Moskva, 1972. pp. 687.

NOVOZHILOV (VIKTOR VALENTINOVICH) Voprosy razvitiia sotsialisticheskoi ekonomiki. Moskva, 1972. pp. 327. Selection of works published 1923-70.

OL'SEVICH (IULII IAKOVLEVICH) Effektivnost' ekonomiki sotsializma: kritika burzhuaznykh i revizionistskikh kontseptsii. Moskva, 1972. pp. 288.

OSNOVY ekonomicheskikh znanii dlia rabochikh. Moskva, 1972. pp. 335.

PARKER (WILLIAM HENRY) The superpowers: the United States and the Soviet Union compared. London, 1972. pp. 347.

PROBLEMY ekonomicheskoi nauki i praktiki: sbornik statei, posviashchennyi 95-letiiu akademika S.G. Strumilina. Moskva, 1972. pp. 311. bibliog.

PROKHORENKO (IVAN DENISOVICH) Razvitie sotsialisticheskikh proizvodstvennykh otnoshenii. Moskva, 1972. pp. 301.

PROTIV burzhuaznykh i melkoburzhuaznykh teorii sotsializma. Moskva, 1972. pp. 295.

SUKHAREVSKII (BORIS MIKHAILOVICH) O sovremennom etape razvitiia ekonomiki sotsializma v SSSR. Moskva, 1972. pp. 173.

SUVOROVA (GALINA TIKHONOVNA) and STEPANOV (ANATOLII IVANOVICH) Ekonomicheskaia geografiia SSSR. Moskva, 1972. pp. 311.

TOLKACHEV (ALEKSANDR SERGEEVICH) ed. Problemy teorii i analiza effektivnosti obshchestvennogo proizvodstva. Moskva, 1972. pp. 335.

VAL'TUKH (KONSTANTIN KURTOVICH) Mezhotraslevoi balans proizvodstvennykh moshchnostei. Moskva, 1972. pp. 183. bibliog.

- Economic conditions - Maps

KISH (GEORGE) Economic atlas of the Soviet Union. 2nd ed. Ann Arbor, [1971]. pp. 90. bibliog.

- Economic conditions - Mathematical models

MAEVSKII (IVAN VASIL'EVICH) and MAEVSKII (VLADIMIR IVANOVICH) Nekotorye voprosy izmereniia ekonomicheskoi effektivnosti. Moskva, 1970. pp. 147. bibliog.

ARKHANGEL'SKII (IURII SEMENOVICH) and KONOPLITSKII (VLADIMIR AVRAMOVICH) Modelirovanie narodnogo khoziaistva: modeli, tseny, kriterii optimal'nosti. Moskva, 1972. pp. 134. bibliog.

KATSENELINBOIGEN (ARON IOSIFOVICH) and others. Vosproizvodstvo i ekonomicheskii optimum. Moskva, 1972. pp. 152.

KOTOV (IVAN VASIL'EVICH) Primenenie matematicheskikh metodov v ekonomike i politicheskaia ekonomiia sotsializma. Leningrad, 1972. pp. 167.

- Economic conditions - Statistics

RUSSIA (U.S.S.R.). Tsentral'noe Statisticheskoe Upravlenie and others. 1965. Itogi vypolneniia narodnokhoziaistvennogo plana SSSR i soiuznykh respublik v 1964 godu: soobshcheniia TsSU SSSR i TsSU soiuznykh respublik. Moskva, 1965. pp. 255.

CLARKE (ROGER A.) Soviet economic facts, 1917-1970. London, 1972. pp. 151. bibliog.

- Economic history

FINN-ENOTAEVSKII (ALEKSANDR IUL'EVICH) Kapitalizm v Rossii, 1890-1917 gg. tom 1. 2nd ed. Moskva, 1925. pp. 400. 1st ed. entitled Sovremennoe khoziaistvo Rossii. Xerographic reprint.

STALINSKII (E.) Puti revoliutsii. Praga, 1925. pp. 309.

BOR'BA partii za vosstanovlenie i razvitie sotsialisticheskogo narodnogo khoziaistva v poslevoennyi period, 1945-1953 gody: konsul'tatsii, metodicheskie sovety. Moskva, 1963. pp. 136.

CHUNTULOV (VLADIMIR TIMOFEEVICH) Ekonomicheskaia istoriia SSSR. Moskva, 1969. pp. 464.

LENIN (VLADIMIR IL'ICH) Poagotovitel'nye materialy k knige "Razvitie kapitalizma v Rossii". Moskva, 1970. pp. 717.

MAI (JOACHIM) Das deutsche Kapital in Russland 1850-1894. Berlin, 1970. pp. 255. bibliog. (Greifswald. Universität. Historisches Institut. Veröffentlichungen. Band 4)

PROBLEMY istorii feodal'noi Rossii; sbornik statei k 60-letiiu prof. V.V. Mavrodina. Leningrad, 1971. pp. 271. bibliog.

FALKUS (MALCOLM E.) The industrialisation of Russia, 1700-1914. London, 1972. pp. 93. bibliog. (Economic History Society. Studies in Economic History)

FUHRMANN (JOSEPH T.) The origins of capitalism in Russia: industry and progress in the sixteenth and seventeenth centuries. Chicago, 1972. pp. 376. bibliog.

KUKIN (DMITRII MIKHAILOVICH) Leninskii plan postroeniia sotsializma v SSSR i ego osushchestvlenie. Moskva, 1972. pp. 223.

VORONTSOV (ALEKSEI GRIGOR'EVICH) and others. Kommunisticheskaia partiia v bor'be za vosstanovlenie i perestroiku narodnogo khoziaistva na osnove novoi ekonomicheskoi politiki, 1921-1925 gg. Moskva, 1972. pp. 216.

BRATSKOE sodruzhestvo soiuznykh respublik v razvitii narodnogo khoziaistva SSSR, 1917-1971. Moskva, 1973. pp. 555.

DAY (RICHARD B.) Leon Trotsky and the politics of economic isolation. Cambridge, 1973. pp. 221. bibliog. (National Association for Soviet and East European Studies. Soviet and East European Studies)

- Economic history - Historiography

TARNOVSKII (KONSTANTIN NIKOLAEVICH) Sovetskaia istoriografiia rossiiskogo imperializma. Moskva, 1964. pp. 244.

IGNATENKO (TAMARA ALEKSANDROVNA) Sovetskaia istoriografiia rabochego kontrolia i natsionalizatsii promyshlennosti v SSSR, 1917-1967 gg. Moskva, 1971. pp. 259. bibliog.

POTASHEV (F.I.) Leninskii plan postroeniia sotsializma v SSSR. in Kommunisticheskaia Partiia Sovetskogo Soiuza. Tsentral'nyi Komitet. Uchenye Zapiski Kafedr Istorii Kommunisticheskoi Partii Sovetskogo Soiuza Vysshikh Partiinykh Shkol. vyp 10. Moskva, 1971.

ZAK (LIUDMILA MARKOVNA) and others. Stroitel'stvo sotsializma v SSSR: istoriograficheskii ocherk. Moskva, 1971. pp. 318. bibliog.

- Economic history - Sources

BOL'SHAKOV (A.M.) and ROZHKOV (NIKOLAI ALEKSANDROVICH) compilers. Istoriia khoziaistva Rossii v materialakh i dokumentakh. Leningrad, 1926. 3 pts (in 1). Vyp.1 and 2 are of the 2nd ed. Xerographic reprint.

POKROVSKII (NIKOLAI NIKOLAEVICH) Aktovye istochniki po istorii chernososhnogo zemlevladeniia v Rossii XIV - nachala XVI v.; otvetstvennyi redaktor... M.N. Tikhomirov. Novosibirsk, 1973. pp. 231.

- Economic policy

AXELROD (ALEXANDER) Das wirtschaftliche Ergebnis des Bolschewismus in Russland. Olten, [1920]. pp. 111.

BUKHARIN (NIKOLAI IVANOVICH) Novyi kurs ekonomicheskoi politiki. Peterburg, 1921. pp. 15. Xerographic reprint.

SMILGA (IVAR TENISOVICH) Promyshlennost' v usloviiakh novoi ekonomicheskoi politiki. Moskva, [1924]. pp. 61.

MOSCOW. Gorodskoi Sovet Deputatov Trudiashchikhsia. Osnovnye voprosy sovetskogo i khoziaistvennogo stroitel'stva: lektsii, chitannye na kursakh vydvizhentsev pri Moskovskom Sovete R., K. i K. D. Moskva, 1926. pp. 139.

RUSSIA (U.S.S.R.). Gosudarstvennyi Planovyi Komitet. Tsentral'naia Komissiia po Piatiletnemu Planu. 1927. Perspektivy razvertyvaniia narodnogo khoziaistva S.S.S.R. na 1926-27/1930-31 gg.: materialy Tsentral'noi Komissii po piatiletnemu planu. Moskva, 1927. pp. 218. Xerographic reprint.

RUSSIA (U.S.S.R.). Gosudarstvennyi Planovyi Komitet. 1929. Kontrol'nye tsifry narodnogo khoziaistva SSSR na 1928/1929 god. Moskva, 1929. pp. 702. Xerographic reprint.

GARBUZOV (S.) In den Kampf für den Fünfjahrplan; ins Deutsche übertragen von E. Spitz. Moskau, 1931. pp. 63.

RUSSIA (U.S.S.R.). Gosudarstvennyi Planovyi Komitet. 1931. Narodno-khoziaistvennyi plan SSSR na 1931 god. [Moskva], 1931. pp. 287. Xerographic reprint.

RUSSIA (U.S.S.R.). Gosudarstvennyi Planovyi Komitet. 1935. Narodno-khoziaistvennyi plan na 1935 god. 2nd ed. Moskva, 1935. pp. 942. Xerographic reprint.

RUSSIA (U.S.S.R.). Gosudarstvennyi Planovyi Komitet. 1936. Narodnokhoziaistvennyi plan na 1936 god, chetvertyi god vtoroi piatiletki. 2nd ed. Moskva, 1936. pp. 648. Xerographic reprint.

RUSSIA (U.S.S.R.) Gosudarstvennyi Planovyi Komitet. 1939. Itogi vypolneniia vtorogo piatiletnego plana razvitiia narodnogo khoziaistva Soiuza SSR. Moskva, 1939. pp. 159. Xerographic reprint.

RUSSIA (U.S.S.R.). Gosudarstvennyi Planovyi Komitet. 1939. Tretii piatiletnii plan razvitiia narodnogo khoziaistva Soiuza SSR, 1938-1942 gg. Moskva, 1939. pp. 240. Xerographic reprint.

RUSSIA. Soviet Information Bureau. 1959. The great seven-year plan: album of diagrams on the economic development of the USSR in 1959-1965. [Washington], 1959. fo. (36).

KIEV. Universytet. Pytannia komunistychnoho budivnytstva na suchasnomu etapi: zbirnyk naukovykh prats' aspirantiv kafedr suspil'nykh nauk. Kyïv, 1962. pp. 139.

DZHAVADOV (GATAM AGALIEVICH) Dal'neishee sovershenstvovanie i postepennoe preobrazovanie sotsialisticheskikh proizvodstvennykh otnoshenii v kommunisticheskie. Moskva, 1963. pp. 92.

EKONOMICHNI problemy budivnytstva komunizmu. Kyïv, 1963. pp. 141.

GROMOV (E.A.) O faktorakh povysheniia effektivnosti obshchestvennogo proizvodstva. Moskva, 1964. pp. 118.

SMEKHOV (BORIS MOISEEVICH) Statistika i planirovanie. 2nd ed. Moskva, 1964. pp. 104.

CHEREDNICHENKO (ANATOLII PAVLOVICH) Ekonomicheskaia sluzhba i kadry. Moskva, 1965. pp. 111.

CHERKOVETS (VIKTOR NIKITICH) Planomernost' sotsialisticheskogo proizvodstva. Moskva, 1965. pp. 212.

GRADOV (GEORGII LEONT'EVICH) Spetsializatsiia i kompleksnoe razvitie Iuzhnogo ekonomicheskogo raiona SSSR. Kiev, 1965. pp. 160. bibliog.

OPYT i problemy stimulirovaniia v novykh usloviiakh. Moskva, 1966. pp. 112.

PETRAKOV (NIKOLAI IAKOVLEVICH) Nekotorye aspekty diskussii ob ekonomicheskikh metodakh khoziaistvovaniia. Moskva, 1966. pp. 126.

BUKHARIN (NIKOLAI IVANOVICH) Put' k sotsializmu v Rossii: izbrannye proizvedeniia; The path to socialism in Russia: selected works. N'iu Iork, 1967. pp. 415. Introduction and introductory notes in English and Russian.

KHOZIASTVENNAIA reforma i zadachi finansovo-bankovskikh, planovykh, statisticheskikh organov: materialy Permskoi oblastnoi konferentsii, 21-23 marta 1967 g. Perm', 1967. pp. 114.

NAUMENKO (MIKHAIL FEDOROVICH) V novykh usloviiakh khoziaistvovaniia. Moskva, 1967. pp. 112.

SOVERSHENSTVOVANIE upravleniia narodnym khoziaistvom: materialy nauchnoi konferentsii, posviashchennoi 50-letiiu Velikoi Oktiabr'skoi sotsialisticheskoi revoliutsii. Vil'nius, 1967. pp. 139.

BESEDY ob ekonomicheskoi reforme. 2nd ed. Moskva, 1968. pp. 208.

RUSSIA - Economic policy (Cont'd.)

SMEKHOV (BORIS MOISEEVICH) ed. Problemy sovershenstvovaniia planirovaniia. Moskva, 1968. pp. 130. (Moscow. Moskovskii Institut Narodnogo Khoziaistva Nauchnye Trudy. vyp.59)

EKONOMICHESKAIA effektivnost' proizvodstva i khoziaistvennaia reforma: materialy konferentsii. Leningrad, 1969. pp. 142. bibliog.

GRIGOR'IAN (GRIGORII SEMENOVICH) and ABALKIN (LEONID IVANOVICH) eds. Nekotorye voprosy razvitiia sovetskoi ekonomicheskoi nauki za 50 let Sovetskoi vlasti. Moskva, 1969. pp. 128. (Moscow. Moskovskii Institut Narodnogo Khoziaistva. Nauchnye Trudy. vyp.71)

KURSKII (ALEKSANDR DMITRIEVICH) La planification en U.R.S.S. et dans les autres pays socialistes;... traduit du russe par Jacqueline Portier. Paris, 1969. pp. 119. bibliog. (International Committee for Social Sciences Documentation. Confluence. vol.13) In French, with English summaries.

VOPROSY ekonomicheskoi teorii: ispol'zovanie rezervov proizvodstva. Saratov, 1969. pp. 109

1970

ABALKIN (LEONID IVANOVICH) Politicheskaia ekonomiia i ekonomicheskaia politika. Moskva, 1970. pp. 232.

MESTNAIA promyshlennost' v novykh usloviiakh khoziaistvovaniia. Moskva, 1970. pp. 176.

MOLEN (J.W. VAN DER) Economische hervormingen in de Sowjet-Unie, 1965-1969. Rotterdam, 1970. pp. 172. bibliog. With English summary.

ORLOV (IAKOV L'VOVICH) and SHIMANSKII (VSEVOLOD PAVLOVICH) Reforma i torgovlia. Moskva, 1970. pp. 240.

PASHKOV (ANATOLII IGNAT'EVICH) Ekonomicheskie problemy sotsializma. Moskva, 1970. pp. 528. bibliog.

PEROV (GEORGII VASIL'EVICH) and ZAGORODNEVA (ALEKSANDRA MIKHAILOVNA) eds. Voprosy planirovaniia otraslei narodnogo khoziaistva. Moskva, 1970. pp. 173.

TSIVADZE (DZHEMAL IUSUPOVICH) Razvitie ekonomicheskikh funktsii Sovetskogo gosudarstva. Moskva, 1970. pp. 341.

UPRAVLENIE narodnym khoziaistvom i problemy ego sovershenstvovaniia. Kiev 1970. pp. 172.

VOLUISKII (NIKOLAI MIKHAILOVICH) Svodnyi finansovyi plan: balans finansovykh resursov i narodnokhoziaistvennyi plan. Moskva, 1970. pp. 159. bibliog.

1971

ALLAKHVERDIAN (DERENIK AKOPOVICH) Finansy i sotsialisticheskoe vosproizvodstvo. Moskva, 1971. pp. 287.

OR (MIKHAIL ZAKHAROVICH) Osnovy planirovaniia narodnogo khoziaistva SSSR. Moskva, 1971. pp. 231.

CHISTIAKOV (MIKHAIL IVANOVICH) and MOROZOV (PETR TARASOVICH) Planirovanie v SSSR: organizatsiia i metody. Moskva, 1971. pp. 141

DRON' (PAVEL PETROVICH) V.I.Lenin o rukovodstve narodnym khoziaistvom. Minsk, 1971. pp. 183.

DZARASOV (SOLTAN SAFARBIEVICH) ed. Planomernaia organizatsiia i upravlenie proizvodstvom. Moskva, 1971. pp. 174.

IOFFE (OLIMPIAD SOLOMONOVICH) Plan i dogovor v sotsialisticheskom khoziaistve. Moskva, 1971. pp. 216.

KATORGIN (IVAN IVANOVICH) Istoricheskii opyt KPSS po osushchestvleniiu novoi ekonomicheskoi politiki, 1921-1925gg. Moskva, 1971. pp. 431. bibliog.

KOZLOVA (OLIMPIADA VASIL'EVNA) and LENSKAIA (SVETLANA ALEKSEEVNA) Za dal'neishee sovershenstvovanie sistemy upravleniia ekonomikoi. Moskva, 1971. pp. 101.

LENINSKIE printsipy planovogo rukovodstva narodnym khoziaistvom v deistvii: k 50-letiiu Gosplana i planovykh organov SSSR. Riga, 1971. pp. 155.

LIBERMAN (EVSEI GRIGOR'EVICH) Economic methods and the effectiveness of production. White Plains, N.Y., [1971]. pp. 183.

MAIMINAS (EFREM ZALMANOVICH) Protsessy planirovaniia v ekonomike: informatsionnyi aspekt. 2nd ed. Moskva, 1971. pp. 390. bibliog.

METODOLOGIIA prognozirovaniia ekonomicheskogo razvitiia SSSR. Moskva, 1971. pp. 343.

NAIDENOV (VIKTOR SERGEEVICH) and others. Tekushchii plan i ekonomicheskie stimuly. Moskva, 1971. pp. 141.

PETERSEN (JØRN HENRIK) Aspekter af den økonomiske problematik i en centraldirigeret økonomi. Odense, 1971. pp. 311. bibliog. (Odense Universitet. Studies in History and Social Sciences. vol. 2)

PETRAKOV (NIKOLAI IAKOVLEVICH) Khoziaistvennaia reforma: plan i ekonomicheskaia samostoiatel'nost'. Moskva, 1971. pp. 134.

ROBERTS (PAUL CRAIG) Alienation and the Soviet economy: toward a general theory of marxian alienation, organizational principles, and the Soviet economy. Albuquerque, [1971]. pp. 121.

SHEREMET (ANATOLII DANILOVICH) Razvitie teorii ekonomicheskogo analiza v usloviiakh khoziaistvennoi reformy. Moskva, 1971. pp. 164.

SOVETY i ekonomicheskaia reforma: v pomoshch' rabotnikam Sovetov deputatov trudiashchikhsia. Moskva, 1971. pp. 174.

SUMTSOV (ANATOLII IVANOVICH) Ekonomicheskaia reforma i voprosy teorii bukhgalterskogo ucheta. Moskva, 1971. pp. 288.

TOLKACHEV (ALEKSANDR SERGEEVICH) Ekonomicheskie problemy material'no-tekhnicheskoi bazy kommunizma v SSSR. Moskva, 1971. pp. 357. bibliog.

TSAGOLOV (NIKOLAI ALEKSANDROVICH) ed. Tovarno-denezhnye otnosheniia v sisteme planomerno organizovannogo sotsialisticheskogo proizvodstva. Moskva, 1971. pp. 373.

VOGEL (HEINRICH) Gesellschaftliche Konsumtionsfonds als Instrument der sowjetischen Wirtschaftspolitik. Berlin, [1971]. pp. 148. bibliog. (Osteuropa-Institut, München. Veröffentlichungen. Reihe: Wirtschaft und Gesellschaft. Heft 8)

ZHIGAREV (LEV VIKTOROVICH) Budushchee, stavshee deistvitel'nost'iu: zametki publitsista. Moskva, 1971. pp. 168.

1972

BELIK (IURII ANDREEVICH) Die Wirtschaft der UdSSR im neunten Planjahrfünft; (Übersetzung aus dem Russischen... [by] Ingrid Stolte). Berlin, 1972. pp. 91.

BOR (MIKHAIL ZAKHAROVICH) Effektivnost' obshchestvennogo proizvodstva i problemy optimal'nogo planirovaniia. Moskva, 1972. pp. 336

BOR (MIKHAIL ZAKHAROVICH) and IATSKOV (V.A.) eds. Upravlenie sotsialisticheskim vosproizvodstvom. Moskva, 1972. pp. 286.

DELLENBRANT (JAN ÅKE) Reformists and traditionalis a study of Soviet discussions about economic reform, 1960-1965. Stockholm, [1972]. pp. 163. bibliog. (Uppsala. Statsvetenskapliga Föreningen Skrifter. 63)

DEUTSCHES INSTITUT FÜR WIRTSCHAFTSFORSCHUNG. Sonderhefte. [Neue Folge]. Nr. 93. Wirtschaftsreform und Wirtschaftsentwicklung in der Sowjetunion 1965 bis 1975; ([by] Maria-Elisabeth Ruban und Heinrich Machowski). Berlin, 1972. pp. 32.

FASOLIAK (NIKOLAI DMITRIEVICH) Upravlenie proizvodstvennymi zapasami: ekonomicheskii aspekt problemy. Moskva, 1972. pp. 271.

FEDORENKO (NIKOLAI PROKOF'EVICH) and others, eds. Effektivität in der sozialistischen Wirtschaft; aus dem Russischen ([translated by] Karl Bauer). Berlin, 1972. pp. 270.

FEIWEL (GEORGE R.) The Soviet quest for economic efficiency: issues, controversies and reforms; expanded and updated edition. New York, [1972]. pp. 790. bibliog.

FINK (GERHARD) GOSSNAB SSSR: Planung und Planungsprobleme der Produktionsmittelverteilung in der UdSSR. Berlin, [1972]. pp. 123. bibliog. (Osteuropa-Institut, München. Veröffentlichungen. Reihe: Wirtschaft und Gesellschaft. Heft 10)

ISTORICHESKII opyt KPSS v osushchestvlenii novoi ekonomicheskoi politiki. Moskva, 1972. pp. 328.

JASNY (NAUM) Soviet economists of the twenties: names to be remembered. Cambridge, 1972. pp. 218.

KARPOV (PAVEL PROKOF'EVICH) Raspredelenie sredstv proizvodstva v novykh usloviiakh khoziaistvovaniia. Moskva, 1972. pp. 159.

KATZ (ABRAHAM) The politics of economic reform in the Soviet Union. New York, 1972. pp. 230. bibliog.

KIRILLOV (VIKTOR SERGEEVICH) Kurs, podtverzhdennyi zhizn'iu: k istorii ekonomicheskoi platformy bol'shevikov, aprel'-oktiabr' 1917 g. Moskva, 1972. pp. 334. bibliog.

KOMMUNISTY i ekonomicheskaia reforma. Moskva, 1972. pp. 357.

KOVAL (NIKOLAI STEPANOVICH) and MIROSHNICHENKO (BORIS PANTALEIMONOVICH) Fundamentals of national economic planning in the USSR. Moscow, 1972. pp. 344.

KURITSYN (VSEVOLOD MIKHAILOVICH) Perekhod k nepu i revoliutsionnaia zakonnost'. Moskva, 1972. pp. 216.

LEONT'EV (LEV ABRAMOVICH) Ekonomicheskie problemy razvitogo sotsializma. Moskva, 1972. pp. 207.

MAKAROV (STANISLAV PAVLOVICH) Tsentralizovannoe upravlenie proizvodstvom v usloviiakh reformy. Moskva, 1972. pp. 175.

NOVICHKOV (BORIS FEDOROVICH) Material'nye balansy: voprosy sovershenstvovaniia razrabotki. Moskva, 1972. pp. 126.

PROBLEMY ekonomicheskoi nauki i praktiki: sbornik statei, posviashchennyi 95-letiiu akademika S.G. Strumilina. Moskva, 1972. pp. 311. bibliog.

REFORMS in the Soviet and eastern European economies; [expanded version of the proceedings of a symposium sponsored by the Studiengesellschaft für Fragen mittel- und osteuropäischer Partnerschaft]; edited by L.A.D. Dellin and Hermann Gross. Lexington, [1972]. pp. 175.

RUSSIA (U.S.S.R.). Gosudarstvennyi Planovyi Komitet. 1972. Gosudarstvennyi piatiletnii plan razvitiia narodnogo khoziaistva SSSR na 1971-1975 gody. Moskva, 1972. pp. 455.

RUTGAIZER (VALERII MAKSOVICH) Regional'nye osobennosti obshchestvennogo vosproizvodstva: territorial'nye aspekty vzaimozameniaemosti proizvodstvennykh resursov. Moskva, 1972. pp. 191.

SHNIPER (RUVIN ISAKOVICH) Svodnoe planirovanie narodnogo khoziaistva oblasti i raiona. Moskva, 1972. pp. 191.

VORONTSOV (ALEKSEI GRIGOR'EVICH) and others. Kommunisticheskaia partiia v bor'be za vosstanovlenie i perestroiku narodnogo khoziaistva na osnove novoi ekonomicheskoi politiki, 1921-1925 gg. Moskva, 1972. pp. 216.

VYSHNEVETS'KYI (IOSYF ANTONOVYCH) and others. Ekonomichni problemy naukovoho upravlinnia sotsialistychnym vyrobnytstvom. Kyïv, 1972. pp. 187. With Russian summary and table of contents.

ZAITSEV (IGOR' FEDOROVICH) and IZIUMSKII (OLEG AL'BERTOVICH) Prirodnye resursy na sluzhbu ekonomicheskomu progressu. Moskva, 1972. pp. 157. bibliog.

ZIRKEL (REGINALD) Das System der materiellen Anreize als wirtschaftspolitisches Instrument in der Industrie der Sowjetunion nach den Wirtschaftsreformen von 1965. Hamburg, 1972. pp. 191. bibliog. (Hamburg. Hamburgisches Welt-Wirtschafts Archiv. Veröffentlichungen)

1973

CONYNGHAM (WILLIAM J.) Industrial management in the Soviet Union: the role of the CPSU in industrial decision-making, 1917-1970. Stanford, [1973]. pp. 378. bibliog. (Stanford University. Hoover Institution on War, Revolution and Peace. Hoover Institution Publications. 116)

DAY (RICHARD B.) Leon Trotsky and the politics of economic isolation. Cambridge, 1973. pp. 221. bibliog. (National Association for Soviet and East European Studies. Soviet and East European Studies)

DZARASOV (SOLTAN SAFARBIEVICH) ed. Nauchnye osnovy upravleniia sotsialisticheskoi ekonomikoi. Moskva, 1973. pp. 228.

RUSSIA - Economic policy (Cont'd.)

KOZLOV (IURII MARKOVICH) ed. Khoziaistvennaia reforma, upravlenie i pravo. Moskva, 1973. pp. 413.

STEPANOV (ARKHIP PETROVICH) Ekonomicheskie problemy planirovaniia narodnogo khoziaistva SSSR. Kiev, 1973. pp. 221.

- Economic policy - Bibliography

ZAGRANICHNAIA (V.I.) and others, compilers. Khoziaistvennaia reforma - perekhod predpriiatii na novuiu sistemu planirovaniia i ekonomicheskogo stimulirovaniia: ukazatel' literatury. Kiev, 1969. pp. 159.

- Economic policy - Matnematical models

KHAIKIN (VLADLEN PAVLOVICH) and others. Korreliatsiia i statisticheskoe modelirovanie v ekonomicheskikh raschetakh; pod redaktsiei...E.G. Libermana. Moskva, 1964. pp. 216.

ROGOVOI (MARK RAFAILOVICH) Matematicheskie metody v planirovanii. Moskva, 1964. pp. 117. bibliog.

DADAIAN (VLADISLAV SURENOVICH) Matematika v ekonomike. Moskva, 1965. pp. 59. (Akademiia Nauk SSSR. Nauchno-Populiarnaia Seriia)

DUDKIN (LEV MIKHAILOVICH) Optimal'nyi material'nyi balans narodnogo khoziaistva: modeli dlia tekushchego perspektivnogo planirovaniia. Moskva, 1966. pp. 183. bibliog.

GOLENKO (DMITRII ISAAKOVICH) Statisticheskie metody v ekonomicheskikh sistemakh. Moskva, 1970. pp. 203. bibliog.

KOZLOV (LEONARD ALEKSANDROVICH) Optimal'noe planirovanie razvitiia i razmeshcheniia otraslei promyshlennosti: voprosy metodologii i metodiki; otvetstvennyi redaktor... A.G. Aganbegian. Novosibirsk, 1970. pp. 176.

CHETYRKIN (EVGENII MIKHAILOVICH) Teoriia massovogo obsluzhivaniia i ee primenenie v ekonomike. Moskva, 1971. pp. 103. bibliog.

IOFFE (VLADIMIR MANAR'EVICH) and KHAZANOV (BORIS KHAIMOVICH) Metodologiia optimizatsii perspektivnogo otraslevogo planirovaniia: na primere promyshlennosti plastmass. Moskva, 1971. pp. 148. bibliog.

NAUCHNYE osnovy ekonomicheskogo prognoza. Moskva, 1971. pp. 424.

NEVELEV (ALEKSANDR MIKHAILOVICH) Razrabotka material'nykh balansov v soiuznoi respublike. Moskva, 1971. pp. 151. bibliog.

BELKIN (VIKTOR DANILOVICH) Ekonomicheskie izmereniia i planirovanie. Moskva, 1972. pp. 303.

DUDKIN (LEV MIKHAILOVICH) Sistema raschetov optimal'nogo narodnokhoziaistvennogo plana. Moskva, 1972. pp. 383. bibliog.

FEDORENKO (NIKOLAI PROKOF'EVICH) ed. Problemy optimal'nogo funktsionirovaniia sotsialisticheskoi ekonomiki. Moskva, 1972. pp. 566.

MIKHALEVSKII (BORIS NATANOVICH) Sistema modelei srednesrochnogo narodnokhoziaistvennogo planirovaniia: printsipy, obzor, opisanie verkhnego urovnia narodnokhoziaistvennogo planirovaniia. Moskva, 1972. pp. 475. bibliog.

NOVOZHILOV (VIKTOR VALENTINOVICH) Problemy izmereniia zatrat i rezul'tatov pri optimal'nom planirovanii. Moskva, 1972. pp. 434.

RAJECKAS (R.) Integrirovannaia sistema planirovaniia narodnogo khoziaistva soiuznoi respubliki. Vil'nius, 1972. pp. 236. bibliog. With English summary and table of contents.

RAJECKAS (RAIMUNDAS) and ŽEMAITAITITE (SALOMEJA) Informatsiia, prognoz, plan. Moskva, 1972. pp. 190. bibliog.

SEMENOV (AL'BERT KONSTANTINOVICH) Mezhotraslevoi balans respubliki. Moskva, 1972. pp. 103. bibliog.

TURCHINS (IANIS BOLESLAVOVICH) Optimizatsiia sotsialisticheskogo proizvodstva. Riga, 1972. pp. 340.

KOSSOV (VLADIMIR VIKTOROVICH) Mezhotraslevye modeli: teoriia i praktika ispol'zovaniia. Moskva, 1973. pp. 359.

VOLKONSKII (VIKTOR ALEKSANDROVICH) Printsipy optimal'nogo planirovaniia. Moskva, 1973. pp. 239. bibliog.

- Emigration and immigration

LEIBBRANDT (GEORG) Die Auswanderung aus Schwaben nach Russland 1816-1923: eine schwäbisches Zeit- und Charakterbild. Stuttgart, 1928. pp. 212. bibliog. (Stuttgart. Deutsches Ausland Institut. Schriften. Kulturhistorische Reihe. Band 21)

- Executive departments

VASIL'EV (RUSLAN FEDOROVICH) Pravovye akty organov upravleniia: uchebnoe posobie. Moskva, 1970. pp. 108.

ALYMKULOV (SAGYNBEK) Vzaimootnosheniia organov Soiuza SSR i soiuznykh respublik v oblasti upravleniia sovetskoi torgovlei. Frunze, 1971. pp. 142. bibliog.

LENINSKIE printsipy planovogo rukovodstva narodnym khoziaistvom v deistvii: k 50-letiiu Gosplana i planovykh organov SSSR. Riga, 1971. pp. 155.

PRAVOVOE polozhenie ministerstv SSSR. Moskva, 1971. pp. 296.

PRONINA (VERA SERGEEVNA) Tsentral'nye organy upravleniia narodnym khoziaistvom. Moskva, 1971. pp. 167.

VOLKOV (NIKOLAI ANDREEVICH) Vysshie i tsentral'nye organy gosudarstvennogo upravleniia SSSR i soiuznykh respublik v sovremennyi period. Kazan', 1971. pp. 144.

CHUGUNOV (ALEKSANDR IVANOVICH) Organy sotsialisticheskogo kontrolia RSFSR, 1923-1934 gg. Moskva, 1972. pp. 472. bibliog.

LAZAREV (BORIS MIKHAILOVICH) Kompetentsiia organov upravleniia. Moskva, 1972. pp. 280.

ORGANIZATSIIA raboty ministerstv v usloviiakh ekonomicheskoi reformy. Moskva, 1972. pp. 218.

ORLOV (EVGENII NIKOLAEVICH) Deiatel'nost' Moskovskoi kontrol'noi komissii - raboche-krest'ianskoi inspektsii v 1924-1934 gg.: v oblasti partiinogo stroitel'stva i sovershenstvovaniia gosapparata. Moskva, 1972. pp. 191.

TUMANOV (GENNADII ANISIMOVICH) Organizatsiia upravleniia v sfere okhrany obshchestvennogo poriadka. Moskva, 1972. pp. 232.

VISHNIAKOV (VIKTOR GRIGOR'EVICH) Struktura i shtaty organov sovetskogo gosudarstvennogo upravleniia. Moskva, 1972. pp. 278.

- Exploring expeditions

LEBEDEV (DMITRII MIKHAILOVICH) and ESAKOV (VASILII ALEKSEEVICH) Russkie geograficheskie otkrytiia i issledovaniia s drevnikh vremen do 1917 goda. Moskva, 1971. pp. 516.

- Fairs

BRODSKII (IOSIF L'VOVICH) and GAL'PERIN (LEV BORISOVICH) Optovye iarmarki v SSSR: pravovye voprosy. Moskva, 1972. pp. 102.

- Foreign economic relations

STEPANOV (VLADIMIR IL'ICH) Ekonomicheskie osnovy mirnogo sosushchestvovaniia; pod redaktsiei S.L. Vygodskogo. Moskva, 1964. pp. 156.

KAS'IANENKO (VASILII IGNAT'EVICH) Zavoevanie ekonomicheskoi nezavisimosti SSSR, 1917-1940gg. Moskva, 1972. pp. 335.

- Foreign economic relations - Finland

KORNILOV (GENRIKH DMITRIEVICH) Russko-finliandskie tamozhennye otnosheniia v kontse XIX- nachale XX v. Leningrad, 1971. pp. 220.

- Foreign economic relations - France

FRANKO-russkie ekonomicheskie sviazi. Moskva, 1970. pp. 433. With French table of contents.

- Foreign economic relations - India

DAGLI (VADILAL) ed. Indo-Soviet economic relations: a survey. Bombay, 1971. pp. 159. bibliog.

DATAR (ASHA L.) India's economic relations with the USSR and Eastern Europe, 1953 to 1969. Cambridge, 1972. pp. 278. bibliog.

- Foreign opinion.

VEL'TOV (NIKOLAI) Uspekhi sotsializma v SSSR i ikh vliianie na SShA; pod redaktsiei N.N.Iakovleva. Moskva, 1971. pp. 215. bibliog.

- Foreign relations

SLOAN (PATRICK ALAN) From the Russian revolution to Yalta: a review of Soviet foreign policy. Watford, 1945. pp. 24.

PONOMAREV (BORIS NIKOLAEVICH) and others, eds. Istoriia vneshnei politiki SSSR. Moskva, 1961-71. 2 vols.

KENNAN (GEORGE FROST) Russia and the West under Lenin and Stalin. Boston, Mass., [1961]. pp. 11.

BOGUSH (EVGENII IUL'EVICH) Mif ob "eksporte revoliutsii" i sovetskaia vneshniaia politika. Moskva, 1965. pp. 150.

KOVALEV (AN.) Azbuka diplomatii. Moskva, 1965. pp. 163.

LENINSKAIA diplomatiia mira i sotrudnichestva: ustanovlenie diplomaticheskikh otnoshenii mezhdu SSSR i kapitalisticheskimi stranami v 1924-1925 gg. Moskva, 1965. pp. 246.

SONKIN (MOISEI EVELEVICH) Kliuchi ot bronirovannykh komnat. Moskva, 1966. pp. 232.

STUDIENGESELLSCHAFT FÜR ZEITPROBLEME. Die sowjetische Deutschlandpolitik 1956-1960. Duisdorf bei Bonn, [1966]. pp. 174. (Staatspolitische Schriftenreihe)

STUDIENGESELLSCHAFT FÜR ZEITPROBLEME. Die sowjetische Deutschlandpolitik 1960-1963. Duisdorf bei Bonn, [1966]. pp. 144. (Staatspolitische Schriftenreihe)

AMALRIK (ANDREI ALEKSEEVICH) L'Union soviétique survivra-t-elle en 1984?; [translated from the Russian by] Michel Tatu; préface de Alain Besançon. [Paris, 1970]. pp. 118.

DUNCAN (W. RAYMOND) ed. Soviet policy in developing countries: (case studies in conflict-management). Waltham, Mass., [1970]. pp. 350. bibliogs.

GRUNDFRAGEN sowjetischer Aussenpolitik: [papers presented to a joint conference organized by the Deutsche Gesellschaft für Osteuropakunde with the Arbeitsgemeinschaft für Osteuropaforschung, Tübingen, 1969]; herausgegeben von Boris Meissner und Gotthold Rhode. Stuttgart, [1970]. pp. 175.

IVASHIN (I.F.) Leninskaia vneshniaia politika i ee vsemirnoe znachenie. in Kommunisticheskaia Partiia Sovetskogo Soiuza. Tsentral'nyi Komitet. Uchenye Zapiski Kafedr Istorii Kommunisticheskoi Partii Sovetskogo Soiuza Vysshikh Partiinykh Shkol. vyp. 9. Moskva, 1970.

MEYER (GERD) Die sowjetische Deutschland-Politik im Jahre 1952. Tübingen, 1970. pp. 182. bibliog. (Arbeitsgemeinschaft für Osteuropaforschung. Forschungsberichte und Untersuchungen zur Zeitgeschichte. Nr. 24)

MINASIAN (NIKOLAI MIKHAILOVICH) Pravovye osnovy leninskoi diplomatii. Rostov-na-Donu, 1970. pp. 231.

1971

ASPATURIAN (VERNON V.) ed. Process and power in Soviet foreign policy: [a reader]. Boston, [Mass., 1971]. pp. 939.

EICHWEDE (WOLFGANG) Revolution und internationale Politik: zur kommunistischen Interpretation der kapitalistischen Welt, 1921-1925. Köln, 1971. pp. 246. bibliog.

FRANTSOV (GEORGII PAVLOVICH) Bor'ba za mir: (izbrannye trudy). Moskva, 1971. pp. 512. bibliog.

FRERS (DIRK) Zur Frage ausserökonomischer Aktionen im sowjetischen Rohstoffhandel, dargestellt am Beispiel zweier Rohstoffmärkte. Göttingen, 1971. pp. 243, xxii. bibliog.

IBRAGIMBEILI (KHADZHI MURAT) Kavkaz v Krymskoi voine 1853-1856 gg. i mezhdunarodnye otnosheniia. Moskva, 1971. pp. 404.

MAISKII (IVAN MIKHAILOVICH) Vospominaniia sovetskogo diplomata, 1925-1945 gg. Moskva, 1971. pp. 711.

NALIN (IU.) and NIKOLAEV (A.) Sovetskii Soiuz i evropeiskaia bezopasnost'. Moskva, 1971. pp. 104.

TRUKHANOVSKII (VLADIMIR GRIGOR'EVICH) Leninskim vneshnepoliticheskim kursom. Moskva, 1971. pp. 159.

TUCKER (ROBERT CHARLES) The Soviet political mind: Stalinism and post-Stalin change. rev. ed. New York, [1971]. pp. 304.

RUSSIA - Foreign relations (Cont'd.)

1972

GEYER (DIETRICH) ed. Sowjetunion: Aussenpolitik...; (Osteuropa-Handbuch); unter Mitarbeit von Heinz Brahm [and others]. Köln, 1972 in progress.

ANTIVOENNYE traditsii mezhdunarodnogo rabochego dvizheniia. Moskva, 1972. pp. 556.

BABICH (IURII PAVLOVICH) and OGANIS'IAN (IULII STEPANOVICH) Sovetskaia programma mira. Moskva, 1972. pp. 86.

BREZHNEV (LEONID IL'ICH) KPSS v bor'be za edinstvo vsekh revoliutsionnykh i miroliubivykh sil. Moskva, 1972. pp. 303. Collected articles and speeches.

CHERKASSKII (LEONID IAKOVLEVICH) Strategiia mira: bor'ba SSSR protiv ugrozy iadernoi voiny i za razoruzhenie na sovremennom etape. Moskva, 1972. pp. 223. bibliog.

CHUBAR'IAN (ALEKSANDR OGANOVICH) V.I. Lenin i formirovanie sovetskoi vneshnei politiki. Moskva, 1972. pp. 315. bibliog.

FISCHER (LOUIS) The road to Yalta: Soviet foreign relations, 1941-1945. New York, [1972]. pp. 238. bibliog.

FOOTE (JAMES) Russian and Soviet imperialism. Richmond, Surrey, 1972. pp. 272. bibliog.

HANAK (HARRY) ed. Soviet foreign policy since the death of Stalin; [selected documents]. London, 1972. pp. 340. bibliog.

KNIAZHINSKII (VSEVOLOD BORISOVICH) Mezhdunarodnaia strategiia antikommunizma. Moskva, 1972. pp. 111.

KUZNETSOV (VALERII IVANOVICH) and others. Ot Dekreta o mire k Deklaratsii mira, etc. Moskva, 1972. pp. 144.

MUNTIAN (MIKHAIL ALEKSEEVICH) Bor'ba Sovetskogo Soiuza za priem v OON Bolgarii, Vengrii i Rumynii. Kishinev, 1972. pp. 191. bibliog.

ON the road to communism: essays on Soviet domestic and foreign politics; [mainly revised versions of papers read at the sixth annual Bi-State Slavic Conference (Kansas-Missouri), 1967]; edited by Roger E. Kanet and Ivan Volgyes. Lawrence. [1972]. pp. 209.

OSAKWE (CHRIS O.) The participation of the Soviet Union in universal international organizations: a political and legal analysis of Soviet strategies and aspirations inside ILO, UNESCO and WHO. Leiden, 1972. pp. 194. bibliog.

PROBLEMY istorii mezhdunarodnykh otnoshenii: sbornik statei pamiati akademika E.V. Tarle. Leningrad, 1972. pp. 427.

RUBINSTEIN (ALVIN ZACHARY) The foreign policy of the Soviet Union. 3rd ed. New York, [1972]. pp. 474. bibliogs.

SHVETSOV (LEONID ANDREEVICH) Internatsional'naia rol' KPSS v mirovom revoliutsionnom dvizhenii. Leningrad, 1972. pp. 79.

SKRZYPEK (ANDRZEJ) Związek Bałtycki: Litwa, Łotwa, Estonia i Finlandia w polityce Polski i ZSRR w latach 1919-1925. Warszawa, 1972. pp. 309. bibliog.

SOVETSKAIA vneshniaia politika i evropeiskaia bezopasnost': predislovie... A.P. Shitikova. Moskva, 1972. pp. 254.

SOVREMENNYE mezhdunarodnye otnosheniia i vneshniaia politika Sovetskogo Soiuza: uchebnoe posobie. Moskva, 1972. pp. 335.

V.I. Lenin i vneshniaia politika sotsialisticheskogo gosudarstva: sbornik statei istorikov Kievskogo Ordena Lenina Gosudarstvennogo Universiteta im. T.G. Shevchenko i Leiptsigskogo Universiteta im. Karla Marksa. Kiev, 1972. pp. 156.

VÄYRYNEN (RAIMO) Some bases of Soviet foreign policy: a review of western behavioral literature. Tampere, 1972. pp. 66-79. (Tampere Peace Research Institute. Offprint Series. 1972.3) (Reprinted from Politiikka, 1972, Special issue)

VNESHNIAIA politika SSSR: uchebnoe posobie. 4th ed. Moskva, 1972. pp. 383. bibliog.

The WORLD socialist system and anti-communism; [edited by A.P. Butenko]; translated from the Russian by A. Bratov. Moscow, 1972. pp. 284.

1973

EPSTEIN (FRITZ T.) Germany and the East: selected essays; edited... by Robert F. Byrnes. Bloomington, Ind., [1973]. pp. 234. bibliog.

FLETCHER (WILLIAM C.) Religion and Soviet foreign policy, 1945-1970. London, 1973. pp. 179. bibliog.

KULSKI (WŁADYSŁAW WSZEBÓR) The Soviet Union in world affairs: a documented analysis, 1964-1972. Syracuse, N.Y., 1973. pp. 526. bibliog.

- Foreign relations - Treaties

MARKERT (WERNER) and GEYER (DIETRICH) compilers. Sowjetunion: Verträge und Abkommen; Verzeichnis der Quellen und Nachweise, 1917-1962; (Osteuropa-Handbuch). Köln, 1967. pp. 611. bibliog.

GERMANY. Treaties. 1918-1941. Ostverträge...; zusammengestellt von Ingo von Münch. Berlin, 1971. 2 vols. (in 1).

RUSSIA - Foreign relations - Treaties
See also INDO-SOVIET TREATY OF PEACE, FRIENDSHIP, AND COOPERATION, 1971

- Foreign relations - Afghanistan

BABAKHODZHAEV (ABDUSAMAD KHANTURAEVICH) Ocherki po istorii sovetsko-afganskikh otnoshenii. Tashkent, 1970. pp. 91. bibliog.

RUSSIA (U.S.S.R.). Ministerstvo Inostrannykh Del. 1971. Sovetsko-afganskie otnosheniia, 1919-1969 gg.: dokumenty i materialy. Moskva, 1971. pp. 439.

TEPLINSKII (LEONID BORISOVICH) 50 let sovetsko-afganskikh otnoshenii, 1919-1969. Moskva, 1971. pp. 237. bibliog

- Foreign relations - Africa, Subsaharan

COHN (HELEN DESFOSSES) Soviet policy toward black Africa: the focus on national integration. New York, 1972. pp. 316. bibliog.

- Foreign relations - Arab countries

PENNAR (JAAN) The U.S.S.R. and the Arabs: the ideological dimension. London, 1973. pp. 180.

- Foreign relations - Arabia

   PAGE (STEPHEN) The USSR and Arabia: the development of Soviet policies and attitudes towards the countries of the Arabian peninsula, 1955-1970. London, 1971. pp. 149. bibliog.

- Foreign relations - Asia

   RUSSIA and Asia: essays on the influence of Russia on the Asian peoples; [papers read at a conference at Stanford University in 1967]; edited by Wayne S. Vucinich. Stanford, [1972]. pp. 521. (Stanford University. Hoover Institution on War, Revolution, and Peace. Hoover Institution Publications. 107)

   SCALAPINO (ROBERT A.) Asia and the major powers. Washington, 1972. pp. 117. (American Enterprise Institute for Public Policy Research and Stanford University. Hoover Institution on War, Revolution and Peace. AEI-Hoover Policy Studies. 3)

   JUKES (GEOFFREY) The Soviet Union in Asia. Sydney, 1973. pp. 304. bibliog. (Australian Institute of International Affairs. Countries Series)

- Foreign relations - Balkan States

   DOSTIAN (IRINA STEPANOVNA) Rossiia i balkanskii vopros: iz istorii russko-balkanskikh politicheskikh sviazei v pervoi treti XIX v. Moskva, 1972. pp. 368. bibliog. With French table of contents.

- Foreign relations - Bulgaria

   RUSSIA (U.S.S.R.). Ministerstvo Inostrannykh Del. 1969. Sovetsko-bolgarskie otnosheniia, 1944-1948 gg.: dokumenty i materialy. Moskva, 1969. pp. 507. Bulgarian documents in Bulgarian with Russian translation.

- Foreign relations - Caribbean area

   THEBERGE (JAMES DANIEL) ed. Soviet seapower in the Caribbean: political and strategic implications. New York, 1972. pp. 172. bibliog.

- Foreign relations - China

   DEMIDOVA (NATAL'IA FEDOROVNA) and MIASNIKOV (VLADIMIR STEPANOVICH) Pervye russkie diplomaty v Kitae: "Rospis'" I. Petlina i stateinyi spisok F.I. Baikova. Moskva, 1966. pp. 159.

   RUSSKO-kitaiskie otnosheniia v XVII veke. Moskva, 1969-72. 2 vols.

   CECCARINI (E.) Il PCI, il dissidio russo cinese e la questione della Conferenza internazionale. in Il comunismo da Budapest a Praga, 1956-1968. Roma, 1969.

   LEVESQUE (JACQUES) Le conflit sino-soviétique et l'Europe de l'Est: ses incidences sur les conflits soviéto-polonais et soviéto-roumain. Montréal, 1970. pp. 387. bibliog.

   ASIAN PEOPLES' ANTI-COMMUNIST LEAGUE. Pamphlets. No. 155. An analytical survey of Moscow-Peiping relations. [Taipei], 1971. pp. 81.

   GRIFFITH (WILLIAM E.) Cold war and coexistence: Russia, China, and the United States. Englewood Cliffs, [1971]. pp. 115.

   HINTON (HAROLD CLENDENIN) The bear at the gate: Chinese policymaking under Soviet pressure. Washington, 1971. pp. 112. bibliog. (American Enterprise Institute for Public Policy Research, and Stanford University. Hoover Institution on War, Revolution and Peace. AEI-Hoover Policy Studies)

   JOHNSON (A. ROSS) The Sino-Soviet relationship and Yugoslavia, 1949-1971. [Santa Monica], 1971. pp. 13. (Rand Corporation [Papers]. 4591)

   LEONG (SOW-THENG) Sino-Soviet relations: the first phase 1917-1920. Canberra, 1971. pp. 32. (Australian National University. Contemporary China Centre. Contemporary China Papers. No.1)

   MANCALL (MARK) Russia and China: their diplomatic relations to 1728. Cambridge, Mass., 1971. pp. 396. bibliog. (Harvard University. East Asian Research Center. Harvard East Asian Series. No. 61)

   YIN (JOHN) Sino-Soviet dialogue on the problem of war. The Hague, 1971. pp. 247. bibliog.

   AMBROZ (OTON) Realignment of world power: the Russo-Chinese schism under the impact of Mao Tse-tung's last revolution. New York, [1972]. 2 vols. bibliog.

   IURKOV (S.G.) Pekin: novaia politika? Moskva, 1972. pp. 270.

- Foreign relations - Czechoslovakia

   SVOBODA (LUDVÍK) President of Czechoslovakia. Izbrannye stat'i i rechi, [1968-1970]. Moskva, 1970. pp. 167. bibliog.

   HUSÁK (GUSTÁV) Ausgewählte Reden und Aufsätze, April 1969 - April 1971. Berlin, 1971. pp. 560.

   JANCAR (BARBARA WOLFE) Czechoslovakia and the absolute monopoly of power: a study of political power in a communist system. New York, 1971. pp. 330. bibliog.

   PETERS (IHOR ADRIANOVYCH) SSSR, Chekhoslovakiia i evropeiskaia politika nakanune Miunkhena. Kiev, 1971. pp. 189.

   RUSSIA (U.S.S.R.). Ministerstvo Inostrannykh Del. 1972. Sovetsko-chekhoslovatskie otnosheniia, 1945-1960 gg.: dokumenty i materialy. Moskva, 1972. pp. 556.

- Foreign relations - East (Near East)

   LANDMANN (KAMILLO) Die russische Judenfrage und die Nahost-Politik der Sowjetunion. Rothenburg ob der Tauber, 1970. pp. 104. bibliog.

   ZUERRER (WERNER) Die Nahostpolitik Frankreichs und Russlands 1891-1898. Wiesbaden, 1970. pp. 524. bibliog. (Osteuropa-Institut, München. Veröffentlichungen. Band 36)

   HIRSCHMANN (IRA) Red star over Bethlehem: the Soviet influence in the Middle East. London, 1971. pp. 192.

   BECKER (ABRAHAM S.) Oil and the Persian Gulf in Soviet policy in the 1970s. [Santa Monica], 1972. pp. 49. (Rand Corporation. [Papers]. 4743]

   BOSE (TARUN CHANDRA) The superpowers and the Middle East. London, [1972]. pp. 208.

   LAQUEUR (WALTER ZE'EV) The struggle for the Middle East: the Soviet Union and the Middle East, 1958-70. rev. ed. Harmondsworth, 1972. pp. 267. bibliog.

   LENCZOWSKI (GEORGE) Soviet advances in the Middle East. Washington, 1972. pp. 176. (American Enterprise Institute for Public Policy Research. Foreign Affairs Studies. 2)

RUSSIA - Foreign relations - East (Near East) (Cont'd)

    SELLA (AMNON) 'The second Baghdad Pact': Soviet political and military position in the Middle East. [Edinburgh, 1972]. pp. 26. (Edinburgh. University. Department of Politics. Waverley Papers. Series 4. Politico-Military Studies. Occasional Papers. 3)

    The U.S.S.R. and the Middle East; [papers read at a Conference on the Soviet Union and the Middle East, Tel Aviv University, 1971]; edited by Michael Confino and Shimon Shamir. New York, [1973]. pp. 437.

- Foreign relations - Europe

    La RUSSIE et l'Europe, XVIe-XXe siècles. Paris, 1970. pp. 326. bibliog. (Paris. École Pratique des Hautes Études. Section des Sciences Économiques et Sociales. Bibliothèque Générale)

    GRIFFITHS (FRANKLYN) Genoa plus 51: changing Soviet objectives in Europe. Toronto, 1973. pp. 68. (Canadian Institute of International Affairs. Wellesley Papers. 4)

- Foreign relations - Europe, Eastern

    LEVESQUE (JACQUES) Le conflit sino-soviétique et l'Europe de l'Est: ses incidences sur les conflits soviéto-polonais et soviéto-roumain. Montréal, 1970. pp. 387. bibliog.

    SCHWARTZ (HARRY) Eastern Europe in the Soviet shadow. London, [1973]. pp. 117. bibliog.

- Foreign relations - Finland

    PALM (THEDE) ed. The Finnish-Soviet armistice negotiations of 1944. Stockholm, [1971]. pp. 160. (Vetenskapssamhället i Uppsala. Acta Academiae Regiae Scientiarum Upsaliensis. 14)

    INGUL'SKAIA (LIDIIA ANTONOVNA) V bor'be za demokratizatsiiu Finliandii, 1944-1948. Moskva, 1972. pp. 279. bibliog.

- Foreign relations - France

    PANKRASHOVA (M.) and SIPOLS (VILNIS IANOVICH) Pochemu ne udalos' predotvratit' voinu: moskovskie peregovory SSSR, Anglii i Frantsii 1939 goda; dokumental'nyi obzor. Moskva, 1970. pp. 122.

    PALEOLOGUE (MAURICE) An ambassador's memoirs 1914-1917; translated [from the French] by Frederick A. Holt; [one-volume edition with a new] introduction by L.B. Schapiro. London, 1973. pp. 945.

- Foreign relations - Germany

    HITLER (ADOLF) Proklamation des Führers an das deutsche Volk und Note des Auswärtigen Amtes an die Sowjet-Regierung nebst Anlagen. [Berlin? 1941?]. pp. 79. Page 79 imperfect.

    ROSENKO (IVAN ARKHIPOVICH) Sovetsko-germanskie otnosheniia, 1921-1922 gg. Leningrad, 1965. pp. 159. bibliog.

    STUDIENGESELLSCHAFT FÜR ZEITPROBLEME. Die sowjetische Deutschlandpolitik 1956-1960. Duisdorf bei Bonn, [1966]. pp. 174. (Staatspolitische Schriftenreihe)

    STUDIENGESELLSCHAFT FÜR ZEITPROBLEME. Die sowjetische Deutschlandpolitik 1960-1963. Duisdorf bei Bonn, [1966]. pp. 144. (Staatspolitische Schriftenreihe)

    RUSSIA (U.S.S.R.). Ministerstvo Inostrannykh Del. 1968-71. Sovetsko-germanskie otnosheniia ot peregovorov v Brest-Litovske do podpisaniia Rapall'skogo dogovora. Moskva, 1968-71. 2 vols. bibliog.

    KRUMMACHER (F.A.) and LANGE (HELMUT) Krieg und Frieden: Geschichte der deutsch-sowjetischen Beziehungen von Brest-Litowsk zum Unternehmen Barbarossa. München, [1970]. pp. 565. bibliog.

    BAUMGART (WINFRIED) ed. Von Brest-Litovsk zur deutschen Novemberrevolution: aus den Tagebüchern... von Alfons Paquet, Wilhelm Groener und Albert Hopman, März bis November 1918. Göttingen, [1971]. pp. 750. bibliog. (Bayerische Akademie der Wissenschaften. Historische Kommission. Deutsche Geschichtsquellen des 19. und 20. Jahrhunderts. Band 47)

    CYCON (DIETER) Es geht um die Bundesrepublik: eine kritische Wertung der Aussenpolitik Willy Brandts; [articles previously published in German newspapers]. Stuttgart, [1971]. pp. 301.

    FABRY (PHILIPP WALTER) Die Sowjetunion und das Dritte Reich: eine dokumentierte Geschichte der deutsch-sowjetischen Beziehungen von 1933 bis 1941. Stuttgart, [1971]. pp. 485. bibliog.

    GUTTENBERG (KARL THEODOR VON UND ZU) Freiherr. Die neue Ostpolitik: Wege und Irrwege. 2nd ed. Osnabrück, 1971. pp. 82.

    WALSDORFF (MARTIN) Westorientierung und Ostpolitik: Stresemanns Russlandpolitik in der Locarno-Ära. Bremen, [1971]. pp. 326. bibliog.

    ASTAF'EV (I.I.) Russko-germanskie diplomaticheskie otnosheniia 1905-1911 gg.: ot Portsmutskogo mira do Potsdamskogo soglasheniia. Moskva, 1972. pp. 305. bibliog.

    WENGER (PAUL WILHELM) Die Falle: deutsche Ost-, russische Westpolitik. 2nd ed. Stuttgart, 1972. pp. 214.

    GOLDBACH (MARIE LUISE) Karl Radek und die deutsch-sowjetischen Beziehungen, 1918-1923. Bonn-Bad Godesberg, [1973]. pp. 163. bibliog. (Friedrich-Ebert-Stiftung. Forschungsinstitut. Schriftenreihe. Band 97)

    VOGEL (BARBARA) Deutsche Russlandpolitik: das Scheitern der deutschen Weltpolitik unter Bülow 1900-1906. Düsseldorf, [1973]. pp. 335. bibliog. (Hamburg. Hansisch. Universität. Studien zur Modernen Geschichte. Band 11)

- Foreign relations - Germany, Eastern

    NASHE edinstvo nerushimo: prebyvanie Pervogo sekretaria Tsentral'nogo Komiteta Sotsialisticheskoi edinoi partii Germanii, Predsedatelia Gosudarstvennogo soveta GDR tovarishcha V. Ul'brikhta v SSSR, 29 maia-13 iiunia 1964 goda. Moskva, 1964. pp. 206.

- Foreign relations - Hungary

    RUSSIA (U.S.S.R.). Ministerstvo Inostrannykh Del. 1969. Sovetsko-vengerskie otnosheniia, 1945-1948 gg.: dokumenty i materialy. Moskva, 1969. pp. 355.

    RADVÁNYI (JÁNOS) Hungary and the superpowers: the 1956 revolution and Realpolitik. Stanford, [1972]. pp. 197. bibliog. (Stanford University. Hoover Institution on War, Revolution and Peace. Hoover Institution Publications. 111)

- Foreign relations - India

    KAPUR (HARISH) The Soviet Union and the emerging nations: a case study of Soviet policy towards India. London, 1972. pp. 124. bibliog.

    NEELKANT (K.) Partners in peace: a study in Indo-Soviet relations. Delhi, [1972]. pp. 192.

- Foreign relations - Iran

    ABDULLAEV (FATKHULLA) Iz istorii russko-iranskikh otnoshenii i angliiskoi politiki v Irane v nachale XIX v. Tashkent, 1971. pp. 135. bibliog.

- Foreign relations - Japan

    LENSEN (GEORGE ALEXANDER) The strange neutrality: Soviet-Japanese relations during the Second World War, 1941-1945. Tallahassee, Fla., [1972]. pp. 332. bibliog.

- Foreign relations - Mediterranean.

    SALOMON (MICHEL) Méditerranée rouge: un nouvel empire soviétique? Paris, [1970]. pp. 399. bibliog.

- Foreign relations - Pakistan

    KOMPANTSEV (IGOR' MIKHAILOVICH) Pakistan i Sovetskii Soiuz. Moskva, 1970. pp. 199. bibliog.

- Foreign relations - Poland

    FLORIA (BORIS NIKOLAEVICH) Russko-pol'skie otnosheniia i baltiiskii vopros v kontse XVI - nachale XVII v. Moskva, 1973. pp. 223. bibliog.

- Foreign relations - Roumania

    BOLDUR (ALEXANDRE) La Bessarabie et les relations russo-roumaines: la question bessarabienne et le droit international. Paris, 1927; München, 1973. pp. 410.

- Foreign relations - United Kingdom

    BABAKHODZHAEV (ABDUSAMAD KHANTURAEVICH) Proval angliiskoi antisovetskoi politiki v Srednei Azii i na Srednem Vostoke v period priznaniia Sovetskogo gosudarstva de-fakto i de-iure, 1921-1924 gg. Tashkent, 1957. pp. 214. bibliog. For 2nd ed. see his Proval angliiskoi politiki v Srednei Azii i na Srednem Vostoke.

    PANKRASHOVA (M.) and SIPOLS (VILNIS IANOVICH) Pochemu ne udalos' predotvratit' voinu: moskovskie peregovory SSSR, Anglii i Frantsii 1939 goda; dokumental'nyi obzor. Moskva, 1970. pp. 122.

    IBRAGIMBEILI (KHADZHI MURAT) Kavkaz v Krymskoi voine 1853-1856 gg. i mezhdunarodnye otnosheniia. Moskva, 1971. pp. 404.

    NIEDHART (GOTTFRIED) Grossbritannien und die Sowjetunion 1934-1939: Studien zur britischen Politik der Friedenssicherung zwischen den beiden Weltkriegen. München, 1972. pp. 497. bibliog. (Mannheim. Universität. Historisches Institut. Veröffentlichungen. Band 2)

    EDWARDS (GEOFFREY RICHARD) Sir Austen Chamberlain's and Sir John Simon's conduct of Anglo-Soviet relations: a case study in the relationship between the House of Commons and the Foreign Secretary; [Ph.D.(London) thesis]. 1973. fo.306. bibliog. Typescript: unpublished. This thesis is the property of London University and may not be removed from the Library.

- Foreign relations - United States

    ZERI I POPULLIT. Soviet-U.S. alliance at work against the Czechoslovak people. Tirana, 1969. pp. 16.

    ALLISON (GRAHAM T.) Essence of decision: explaining the Cuban missile crisis. Boston, [Mass.], 1971. pp. 338.

    GRIFFITH (WILLIAM E.) Cold war and coexistence: Russia, China, and the United States. Englewood Cliffs, [1971]. pp. 115.

    ULAM (ADAM BRUNO) The rivals: America and Russia since World War II. New York, 1971. pp. 405.

    GADDIS (JOHN LEWIS) The United States and the origins of the cold war, 1941-1947. New York, 1972. pp. 396. bibliog.

    HOLSTI (OLE R.) Crisis, escalation, war. Montreal, 1972. pp. 290.

    LAFEBER (WALTER) America, Russia, and the cold war, 1945-1971. 2nd ed. New York, [1972]. pp. 339. bibliog.

    BOHLEN (CHARLES EUSTIS) Witness to history, 1929-969. London, 1973. pp. 562.

    HERRING (GEORGE C.) Aid to Russia, 1941-1946: strategy, diplomacy, the origins of the Cold War. New York, 1973. pp. 365. bibliog.

    JOXE (ALAIN) Socialisme et crise nucléaire. Paris, [1973]. pp. 561.

    ROSE (LISLE A.) After Yalta. New York, [1973]. pp. 216. bibliog.

    SLUSSER (ROBERT M.) The Berlin crisis of 1961: Soviet-American relations and the struggle for power in the Kremlin, June-November 1961. Baltimore, [1973]. pp. 509. bibliog.

    TSVETKOV (GLEB NIKOLAEVICH) Politika SShA v otnoshenii SSSR nakanune voiny. Kiev, 1973. pp. 192.

- Foreign relations - Vietnam

    USSR-Vietnam: a lasting solidarity. Moscow, 1972. pp. 100.

- Foreign relations - Yugoslavia

    JOHNSON (A. ROSS) The Sino-Soviet relationship and Yugoslavia, 1949-1971. [Santa Monica], 1971. pp. 13. (Rand Corporation [Papers]. 4591)

- Government property

    ZAMENGOF (ZOIA MIKHAILOVNA) Pravovoi rezhim imushchestva khoziaistvennykh organov. Moskva, 1972. pp. 183.

- Historical geography

    DROBIZHEV (VLADIMIR ZINOV'EVICH) and others. Istoricheskaia geografiia SSSR. Moskva, 1973. pp. 319.

- Historical geography - Maps

    GILBERT (MARTIN) Russian history atlas. London, [1972]. pp. 174. bibliog.

- History

    KOVALEVSKII (P.E.) Istoricheskii put' Rossii: sintez russkoi istorii po noveishim dannym nauki. 5th ed. Parizh, 1949. pp. 130. bibliog.

    PUSHKAREV (SERGEI GERMANOVICH) Obzor russkoi istorii. N'iu-Iork, 1953. pp. 509.

    ISSLEDOVANIIA po sotsial'no-politicheskoi istorii Rossii: sbornik statei pamiati Borisa Aleksandrovicha Romanova. Leningrad, 1971. pp. 399. bibliog. (Akademiia Nauk SSSR. Institut Istorii SSSR. Leningradskoe Otdelenie. Trudy. vyp. 12)

RUSSIA - History (Cont'd.)

PROBLEMY istorii feodal'noi Rossii; sbornik statei k 60-letiiu prof. V.V. Mavrodina. Leningrad, 1971. pp. 271. bibliog.

FEODAL'NAIA Rossiia vo vsemirno-istoricheskom protsesse: sbornik statei, posviashchennyi L'vu Vladimirovichu Cherepninu. Moskva, 1972. pp. 439.

FOOTE (JAMES) Russian and Soviet imperialism. Richmond, Surrey, 1972. pp. 272. bibliog.

RUSSIA: essays in history and literature; [lectures delivered at Washington University, 1967-1969]; edited by Lyman H. Legters. Leiden, 1972. pp. 164.

- History - Bibliography

OKTIABR': desiat' let bor'by i stroitel'stva, 1917-1927: katalog knig. Moskva, 1927. pp. 257.

SHOKINA (N.A.) compiler. Istoriia sovetskogo obshchestva: rekomendatel'nyi ukazatel' literatury dlia uchitelei; pod redaktsiei... I.B. Berkhina. Moskva, 1971. pp. 248.

ZAIONCHKOVSKII (PETR ANDREEVICH) ed. Spravochniki po istorii dorevoliutsionnoi Rossii: bibliografiia. Moskva, 1971. pp. 515.

SIMMONS (JOHN SIMON GABRIEL) compiler. Russian bibliography, libraries and archives: a selective list of bibliographical references for students of Russian history, literature, political, social and philosophical thought, theology and linguistics. Oxford, 1973. pp. 76.

- History - Historiography

POKROVSKII (MIKHAIL NIKOLAEVICH) Bor'ba klassov i russkaia istoricheskaia literatura; lektsii, chitannye v kommunisticheskom universitete imeni tov. Zinov'eva, 3-7 maia 1923 g. 2nd ed. Leningrad, [1926]. pp. 124. Xerographic reprint.

SOVETSKII narod - novaia istoricheskaia obshchnost' liudei: trudy mezhvuzovskoi nauchnoi konferentsii. Volgograd, 1969. pp. 558.

SKVORTSOV-STEPANOV (IVAN IVANOVICH) Izbrannoe. Moskva, 1970. pp. 254.

MAZOUR (ANATOLE GRIGOREVICH) The writing of history in the Soviet Union. Stanford, [1971]. pp. 383.

PASHUTO (VLADIMIR TERENT'EVICH) Revanshisty - psevdoistoriki Rossii. Moskva, 1971. pp. 160. bibliog.

PROBLEMY istorii obshchestvennogo dvizheniia i istoriografii. Moskva, 1971. pp. 471. bibliog.

ISTORIIA i istoriki: istoricheskaia kontseptsiia V.I. Lenina; metodologiia, laboratoriia: istoriograficheskii ezhegodnik, 1970. Moskva, 1972. pp. 568

KRITIKA burzhuaznoi istoriografii sovetskogo obshchestva. Moskva, 1972. pp. 412.

MARUSHKIN (BORIS IL'ICH) Istoriia v sovremennoi ideologicheskoi bor'be: stroitel'stvo sotsializma v SSSR skvoz' prizmu antikommunisticheskoi istoriografii SShA. Moskva, 1972. pp. 230.

PETROV (IURII PAVLOVICH) O kharaktere istoriko-partiinogo issledovaniia: o nekotorykh voprosakh metodologii i metodiki istoriko-partiinogo issledovaniia, etc. Moskva, 1973. pp. 64.

- History - Sources

GIPPIUS (ZINAIDA NIKOLAEVNA) Siniaia kniga: peterburgskii dnevnik, 1914-1918. Belgrad, 1929. pp. 234.

GOLUBTSOV (VADIM SERGEEVICH) Memuary kak istochnik po istorii sovetskogo obshchestva. Moskva, 1970. pp. 114.

LESURE (MICHEL) Les sources de l'histoire de Russie aux Archives Nationales. Paris, 1970. pp. 502. (Paris. Ecole Pratique des Hautes Études. Section des Sciences Économiques et Sociales. Études sur l'Histoire, l'Economie et la Sociologie des Pays Slaves. 15)

MOSKOVSKII GOSUDARSTVENNYI ISTORIKO-ARKHIVNYI INSTITUT. Trudy. t.28. [Sbornik statei]; pod redaktsiei... E.I. Berzina, L.S. Dmitrovskogo [i] N.P. Eroshkina. Moskva, 1970. pp. 573.

GOR'KII (MAKSIM) pseud. [i.e. Aleksei Maksimovich PESHKOV] Fragments from my diary; translated by Moura Budberg; [an expanded version of the English translation of 1940]. London, 1972. pp. 265.

VERNADSKII (GEORGII VLADIMIROVICH) and others, eds. A source book for Russian history from early times to 1917. New Haven, Conn., 1972. 3 vols. bibliogs.

PALEOLOGUE (MAURICE) An ambassador's memoirs 1914-1917; translated [from the French] by Frederick A. Holt; [one-volume edition with a new] introduction by L.B. Schapiro. London, 1973. pp. 945.

- History - Sources - Bibliography

ZAIONCHKOVSKII (PETR ANDREEVICH) ed. Spravochniki po istorii dorevoliutsionnoi Rossii: bibliografiia. Moskva, 1971. pp. 515.

- History - To 1533.

KLASSEN (EGOR') Novye materialy dlia drevneishei istorii slavian voobshche i slaviano-russov do riurikovskogo vremeni v osobennosti, s legkim ocherkom istorii russov do rozhdestva Khristova. Moskva, 1854. pp. various.

PRESNIAKOV (ALEKSANDR EVGEN'EVICH) Obrazovanie Velikorusskogo gosudarstva: ocherki po istorii XIII-XV stoletii. Petrograd, 1918. pp. 458.

MAVRODIN (VLADIMIR VASIL'EVICH) Obrazovanie Drevnerusskogo gosudarstva i formirovanie drevnerusskoi narodnosti. Moskva, 1971. pp. 192.

ZIMIN (ALEKSANDR ALEKSANDROVICH) Rossiia na poroge novogo vremeni: ocherki politicheskoi istorii Rossii pervoi treti XVI v. Moskva, 1972. pp. 453.

- History - 1533-1613

ZIMIN (ALEKSANDR ALEKSANDROVICH) Rossiia na poroge novogo vremeni: ocherki politicheskoi istorii Rossii pervoi treti XVI v. Moskva, 1972. pp. 453.

SHMIDT (SIGURD OTTOVICH) Stanovlenie rossiiskogo samoderzhavstva: issledovanie sotsial'no-politicheskoi istorii vremeni Ivana Groznogo. Moskva, 1973. pp. 359. bibliog.

- History - 1613-1689

BERKH (VASILII NIKOLAEVICH) Tsarstvovanie Tsaria Alekseia Mikhailovicha. Sanktpeterburg, 1831. 2 vols.

- History - 1773-1775, Pugachev uprising

ROZNER (IONAS GERMANOVICH) Kazachestvo v Krest'ianskoi voine 1773-1775 gg. L'vov 1966. pp. 200.

BELIKOV (TROFIM IVANOVICH) Uchastie kalmykov v Krest'ianskoi voine pod rukovodstvom E.I. Pugacheva, 1773-1775 gg. Elista, 1971. pp. 167. bibliog.

- History - 1825, Conspiracy of December

NASONKINA (LIDIIA IL'INICHNA) Moskovskii universitet posle vosstaniia dekabristov. Moskva, 1972. pp. 343.

OKUN' (SEMEN BENTSIANOVICH) Dekabristy. Moskva, 1972. pp. 104.

RUSSIA - History - 1825, Conspiracy of December
See also DECEMBRISTS

- History - 1825, Conspiracy of December -
Bibliography

CHENTSOV (I.M.) compiler. Vosstanie dekabristov: bibliografiia...; redaktsiia N.K. Piksanova. Moskva, 1929. pp. 794. Xerographic reprint.

- History - 1894-1917.

VINBERG (FEDOR VIKTOROVICH) Krestnyi put'. ch.1. Korni zla. 2nd ed. Miunkhen, 1922. pp. 375.

SHLIAPNIKOV (ALEKSANDR GAVRILOVICH) Kanun semnadtsatogo goda [1] Semnadtsatyi god. Moskva, [1923?]-27. 3 vols (in 1). Vol. 3 has title Semnadtsatyi god. The 1st ed. of vol.1 has title Nakanune 1917 goda. In this volume vol.1 is of the 3rd ed., vol.2 of the 4th.

IL'IN-ZHENEVSKII (ALEKSANDR FEDOROVICH) Iiul' 1917 goda. Moskva, 1927. pp. 46.

- History - 1905, Revolution of

LIADOV (MARTYN NIKOLAEVICH) pseud. [i.e. Martyn Nikolaevich MANDEL'SHTAM]. Iz zhizni partii nakanune i v gody pervoi revoliutsii: vospominaniia. Moskva, 1926. pp. 208. For 1956 ed. with abridgements see his Iz zhizni partii v 1903-1907 godakh. Xerographic reprint.

POZNER (SELIMA MARKOVNA) compiler. 1905: boevaia gruppa pri TsK RSDRP/b/, 1905-1907 g.g.: stat'i i vospominaniia. Moskva, 1927. pp. 284. Xerographic reprint.

SOKOL'SKII (VLADIMIR DMITRIEVICH) "Novorossiiskaia respublika": Sovet rabochikh deputatov Novorossiiska v 1905 godu. Moskva, 1963. pp. 136.

ANNANEPESOV (M.) Uchastie soldatskikh mass v revoliutsii 1905-1907 godov v Turkmenistane. Ashkhabad, 1966. pp. 171.

BAYLEN (JOSEPH O.) The tsar's "lecturer-general": W.T. Stead and the Russian revolution of 1905; with two unpublished memoranda of audiences with the Dowager Empress Marie Fedorovna and Nicholas II. Atlanta, 1969. pp. 91. bibliog. (Georgia State College. School of Arts and Sciences. Research Papers. No. 23)

ARUTIUNIAN (A.M.) Revoliutsionnoe dvizhenie v Armenii, 1905-1907 gg. Erevan, 1970. pp. 312.

LARSSON (REIDAR) Theories of revolution from Marx to the first Russian Revolution. Stockholm, [1970]. pp. 381. bibliog. (Uppsala. Statsvetenskapliga Föreningen. Skrifter. 53)

ONIANI (VASIL SARIIONISOVICH) Bol'shevistskaia partiia i intelligentsiia v pervoi russkoi revoliutsii. Tbilisi, 1970. pp. 447.

ZHUKOV (TIMOFII IVANOVYCH) Bil'shovyky u borot'bi za selianstvo u revoliutsii 1905-1907 rr.: na materialakh ievropeis'koi chastyny Rosii. L'viv, 1970. pp. 224.

PERVYI Sovet rabochikh deputatov: Ivanovo-Voznesensk, mai - iiul', 1905 g. 2nd ed. Iaroslavl', 1971. pp. 167. bibliog.

CHANIIA (VALERIAN KALISTRATOVICH) Sovety v pervoi russkoi revoliutsii. Sukhumi, 1972. pp. 230.

MEHLINGER (HOWARD D.) and THOMPSON (JOHN M.) Count Witte and the Tsarist government in the 1905 revolution. Bloomington, Ind., [1972]. pp. 434. bibliog.

TROTSKII (LEV DAVYDOVICH) 1905; translated by Anya Bostock. London, 1972. pp. 488.

- History - 1917, February Revolution

LOMONOSOV (IURII VLADIMIROVICH) Vospominaniia o martovskoi revoliutsii 1917 g. N'iu-Iork, 1919 g. pp. 86.

LOKOT' (TIMOFEI VASIL'EVICH) Zavoevaniia revoliutsii. Vena, 1921. pp. 53.

MASLOVSKII (SEMEN DMITRIEVICH) Gibel' tsarizma. Leningrad, 1927. pp. 134.

VISHNIAK (MARK VENIAMINOVICH) Dva puti - Fevral' i Oktiabr'. Parizh, 1931. pp. 287. Collected essays.

WITTRAM (REINHARD) Studien zum Selbstverständnis des 1. und 2. Kabinetts der russischen Provisorischen Regierung, März bis Juli 1917. Göttingen, 1971. pp. 158. (Göttingen. Akademie der Wissenschaften. Abhandlungen. Philologisch-Historische Klasse. 3. Folge. Nr. 78)

- History - 1917-1921, Revolution

ARGUNOV (ANDREI ALEKSANDROVICH) Mezhdu dvumia bol'shevizmami. [Paris, 1919]. pp. 47.

KUZ'MIN-KARAVAEV (V.D.) and others. Obrazovanie Severo-Zapadnogo Pravitel'stva: ob"iasneniia Chlenov Politicheskogo Soveshchaniia pri Glavnokomanduiushchem Severo-Zapadnogo fronta. [Helsinki], 1919. pp. 48.

KVASHA (G.I.) Ocherki russkoi revoliutsii. N'iu-Iork, [1919?]. pp. 80. 9 articles first printed in Di Naye welt.

RUSSIA - History - 1917-1921, Revolution
(Cont'd.)

GUTMAN (ANATOLII IA.) Rossiia i bol'shevizm: materialy po istorii revoliutsii i bor'by s bol'shevizmom. ch.1. 1914-1920; Russia and bolshewism. Shankhai, [1921]. pp. x, 83-356, various. Commencement of pagination at p.83 is erroneous: the entire text is present.

LOKOT' (TIMOFEI VASIL'EVICH) Zavoevaniia revoliutsii. Vena, 1921. pp. 53.

MALAKHOV (A.) Velikaia russkaia revoliutsiia i rol' v nei kommunistov. London, [1921]. pp. 56.

RADEK (KARL) Les questions de la révolution mondiale à la lumière du menchevisme. Pétrograd, 1921. pp. 39. (Éditions Françaises. No. 66)

L'VOV (VLADIMIR) Sovetskaia vlast' v bor'be za russkuiu gosudarstvennost': doklad, chitannyi v Salles des Sociétés savantes v Parizhe, 12 noiabria 1921 g. Berlin, 1922. pp. 32.

VISHNIAK (MARK VENIAMINOVICH) Chernyi god: publitsisticheskie ocherki. Parizh, 1922. pp. 294.

ANTANTA i Vrangel': sbornik statei. vyp.1. Moskva, 1923. pp. 260,11.

BERDIAEV (NIKOLAI ALEKSANDROVICH) Novoe srednevekov'e: razmyshlenie o sud'be Rossii i Evropy: [tri etiuda]. Berlin, 1924. pp. 143.

MEL'GUNOV (SERGEI PETROVICH) "Krasnyi terror" v Rossii, 1918-1923. 2nd ed. Berlin, 1924. pp. 312.

WILLIAMS (ALBERT RHYS) Ocherki russkoi revoliutsii. Moskva, 1924. pp. 203.

STALINSKII (E.) Puti revoliutsii. Praga, 1925. pp. 309.

ALEKSANDROVICH (V.) K poznaniiu kharaktera grazhdanskoi voiny: bunt v 5-m Severnom strelkovom polku 20 iiulia 1919 goda. Belgrad, 1926. pp. 28.

PIONTKOVSKII (SERGEI ANDREEVICH) Oktiabr'skaia revoliutsiia v Rossii: ee predposylki i khod; populiarno-istoricheskii ocherk. 3rd ed. Moskva, 1926. pp. 104.

MILIUKOV (PAVEL NIKOLAEVICH) Rossiia na perelome: bol'shevistskii period russkoi revoliutsii. t.2. Antibol'shevistskoe dvizhenie. Parizh, 1927. pp. 281.

BUBNOV (ANDREI SERGEEVICH) and others, eds. Grazhdanskaia voina, 1918-1921. Moskva, 1928-30. 3 vols. Xerographic reprint.

LISOVSKII (P.) Na sluzhbe kapitala: esero-men'shevistskaia kontr-revoliutsiia. Leningrad, 1928. pp. 142. bibliog.

SONKIN (MOISEI EVELEVICH) Kliuchi ot bronirovannykh komnat. Moskva, 1966. pp. 232.

IZ glubiny: sbornik statei o russkoi revoliutsii; S.A. Askol'dov [and others]; vstupitel'nye stat'i N. Poltoratskogo i N. Struve. 2nd ed. Paris, YMCA - Press, 1967. pp. 331. 1st ed. appeared clandestinely in Moscow in 1921.

50 años: revolucion socialista de octubre, 1917-7 de noviembre-1967; fundación del Partido Comunista de la Argentina, 1918-6 de enero-1968. Buenos Aires, 1968. pp. 269.

NABOKOV (VLADIMIR DMITRIEVICH) The provisional government...; edited by Andrew Field. [Brisbane, 1970]. pp. 147.

SERGE (VICTOR) pseud. [i.e. Viktor L'vovich KIBAL'CHICH.] L'an I de la révolution russe: les débuts de la dictature du prolétariat, 1917-1918; édition augmentée; suivi de La ville en danger. rev. ed. Paris, 1971. 3 vols (in 1).

VLADIMIRTSEV (VASILII SERGEEVICH) Partiia - organizator razgroma kontrrevoliutsii na Iuge. Moskva, 1971. pp. 303.

BRUEGMANN (UWE) Die russischen Gewerkschaften in Revolution und Bürgerkrieg, 1917-1919. Frankfurt am Main, [1972]. pp. 285. bibliog.

FERRO (MARC) The Russian revolution of February 1917; translated by J.L. Richards, etc. London, 1972. pp. 478. bibliog.

MELGUNOV (SERGEI PETROVICH) The Bolshevik seizure of power; edited...by Sergei G. Pushkarev in collaboration with Boris S. Pushkarev; translated by James S. Beaver. Santa Barbara, Calif., [1972]. pp. 260. bibliog.

PETHYBRIDGE (ROGER WILLIAM) The spread of the Russian revolution: essays on 1917. London, 1972. pp. 238. bibliog.

SCHULZ (GERHARD) Revolutions and peace treaties, 1917-1920...; translated by Marian Jackson. London, 1972. pp. 258. bibliog.

SERGE (VICTOR) pseud. [i.e. Viktor L'vovich KIBAL'CHICH] Year one of the Russian Revolution: translated from the French by Peter Sedgwick. London, 1972. pp. 436.

- History - 1917-1921, Revolution - Bibliography

DANISHEVSKII (S.L.) compiler. Opyt bibliografii Oktiabr'skoi revoliutsii; pod redaktsiei i s predisloviem S. Piontkovskogo. Moskva, 1926. pp. 276.

- History - 1917-1921, Revolution - Campaigns

POLOVTSOV (LEV VIKTOROVICH) Rytsari ternovogo ventsa: vospominaniia... o 1-om Kubanskom (ledianom) pokhode gen. M.V. Alekseeva, L.G. Kornilova i A.I. Denikina. [Praga, 1920?]. pp. 219.

DOBRYNIN (V.) Bor'ba s bol'shevizmom na Iuge Rossii: uchastie v bor'be Donskogo kazachestva, fevral' 1917 - mart 1920: ocherk. Praga, 1921. pp. 123.

GRAF (GARAL'D KARLOVICH) Na "Novike": Baltiiskii Flot v voinu i revoliutsiiu. Miunkhen, 1922. pp. 480.

VETLUGIN (A.) pseud. [i.e. Vladimir Il'ich RYNDZIUN] Geroi i voobrazhaemye portrety. Berlin, 1922. pp. 247.

GRAZHDANSKAIA voina: materialy po istorii Krasnoi Armii. t.1. Moskva, 1923. pp. 509.

POLOVTSOV (PETR A.) Dni zatmeniia: zapiski Glavnokomanduiushchego Voiskami Petrogradskogo Voennogo Okruga generala P.A. Polovtsova v 1917 godu. Paris, [1925?]. pp. 207.

PODVOISKII (NIKOLAI IL'ICH) Krasnaia gvardiia v Oktiabr'skie dni: Leningrad i Moskva. Moskva, 1927. pp. 107.

RUSSIA (U.S.S.R.). Armiia. Shtab. Nauchno-Ustavnoi Otdel. 1927. Kornilov: popytka voennogo perevorota; E.I. Martynov. [Leningrad], 1927. pp. 196.

GERONIMUS (A.) Razgrom Iudenicha: partiia, rabochii klass i Krasnaia Armiia v bor'be za Petrograd; voenno-politicheskii ocherk s 6 skhemami. Moskva, 1929. pp. 152. bibliog.

KHADZHIEV (RAZAK BEK) Velikii boiar. [Belgrad, 1929]. pp. 397.

VERTSINSKII (E.A.) God revoliutsii: vospominaniia ofitsera general'nogo shtaba za 1917-1918 goda. Tallinn, 1929. pp. 61.

CHAADAEVA (OL'GA NESTEROVNA) Kornilovshchina. Moskva, 1930. pp. 207.

SPIRIN (LEONID MIKHAILOVICH) Na Kolchaka! Moskva, 1962. pp. 79.

DIREKTIVY komandovaniia frontov Krasnoi Armii, 1917-1922 gg.: sbornik dokumentov v 4-kh tomakh. Moskva, 1971 in progress.

DAVIES (NORMAN) White eagle, red star: the Polish-Soviet war, 1919-20. London, [1972]. pp. 318. bibliog.

KRASTIŅŠ (JAN) ed. Istoriia latyshskikh strelkov, 1915-1920; [perevod s latyshskogo]. Riga, 1972. pp. 788. bibliog.

- History - 1917-1921, Revolution - Chronology

MAKSAKOV (VLADIMIR VASIL'EVICH) and NELIDOV (NIKOLAI VASIL'EVICH) Khronika revoliutsii. vyp.1. 1917 god. Moskva, 1923. pp. 143.

- History - 1917-1921, Revolution - Foreign participation

INTERNATSIONALISTY: trudiashchiesia zarubezhnykh stran - uchastniki bor'by za vlast' Sovetov na iuge i vostoke Respubliki. Moskva, 1971. pp. 288. bibliog.

- History - 1917-1921, Revolution - Foreign Participation, Czechoslovak

SYLLABA (THEODOR) T.G. Masaryk a revoluce v Rusku. Praha, 1959. pp. 265. bibliog. With 5 separate facsimiles.

- History - 1917-1921, Revolution - Foreign Participation, Hungarian

JÓZSA (ANTAL) Háború, hadifogság, forradalom: magyar internacionalista hadifoglyok az 1917-es oroszországi forradalmakban. Budapest, 1970. pp. 470.

- History - 1917-1921, Revolution - Foreign Participation, Latvian

KRASTIŅŠ (JAN) ed. Istoriia latyshskikh strelkov, 1915-1920; [perevod s latyshskogo]. Riga, 1972. pp. 788. bibliog.

- History - 1917-1921, Revolution - Foreign Participation, Latvian - Bibliography

PŪCE (O.) and STRAUMĪTE (O.) compilers. Latyshskie strelki: ukazatel' literatury. Riga, 1972. pp. 132. In Latvian and Russian.

- History - 1917-1921, Revolution - Foreign public opinion

IVASHIN (IVAN FEDOROVICH) Vsemirno-istoricheskoe znachenie Velikoi Oktiabr'skoi sotsialisticheskoi revoliutsii. Moskva, 1953. pp. 144.

KALENYCHENKO (PAVLO MYKHAILOVYCH) Velykyi Zhovten' i revoliutsiinyi rukh u Pol'shchi, lystopad 1917 - zhovten' 1919 r. Kyïv, 1971. pp. 343.

VEL'TOV (NIKOLAI) Uspekhi sotsializma v SSSR i ikh vliianie na SShA; pod redaktsiei N.N. Iakovleva. Moskva, 1971. pp. 215. bibliog.

ZORINA (ADELAIDA MIKHAILOVNA) Revoliutsionnoe dvizhenie na Kube, 1917-1925 gg. Moskva, 1971. pp. 112.

- History - 1917-1921, Revolution - Foreign public opinion - Bibliography

GOL'DBERG (ALEKSANDR L'VOVICH) compiler. Mezhdunarodnoe znachenie Velikoi Oktiabr'skoi sotsialisticheskoi revoliutsii: ukazatel' literatury. Moskva, 1967. pp. 128.

- History - 1917-1921, Revolution - Historiography

VISHNIAK (MARK VENIAMINOVICH) Dva puti - Fevral' i Oktiabr'. Parizh, 1931. pp. 287. Collected essays.

MEL'GUNOV (SERGEI PETROVICH) "Rossiiskaia kontrrevoliutsiia": metody i vyvody gen. Golovina; doklad v Akademicheskom Soiuze, 17 iiunia 1938 g. Parizh, [1938?]. pp. 23.

NAUMOV (VLADIMIR PAVLOVICH) Letopis' geroicheskoi bor'by: sovetskaia istoriografiia grazhdanskoi voiny i imperialisticheskoi interventsii v SSSR. Moskva, 1972. pp. 472. bibliog.

RUSSIA - History - 1917-1921, Revolution - Influence
See RUSSIA - History - Revolution - 1917-1921, - Foreign public opinion

- History - 1917-1921, Revolution - Influence on literature

ANDREEV (IURII ANDREEVICH) Revoliutsiia i literatura: otobrazhenie Oktiabria i grazhdanskoi voiny v russkoi sovetskoi literature i stanovlenie sotsialisticheskogo realizma, 20-30-e gody. Leningrad, 1969. pp. 431.

- History - 1917-1921, Revolution - Personal narratives

POLOVTSOV (LEV VIKTOROVICH) Rytsari ternovogo ventsa: vospominaniia... o 1-om Kubanaskom (ledianom) pokhode gen. M.V. Alekseeva, L.G. Kornilova i A.I. Denikina. [Praga, 1920?]. pp. 219.

CHERNOV (VIKTOR MIKHAILOVICH) Meine Schicksale in Sowjet-Russland; aus der russischen Handschrift übersetzt von Elias Hurwicz. Berlin, 1921. pp. 59.

KARABCHEVSKII (NIKOLAI PLATONOVICH) Chto glaza moi videli. Berlin, 1921. 2 vols [in 1].

NAZHIVIN (IVAN FEDOROVICH) Zapiski o revoliutsii. Vena, 1921. pp. 330.

PESHEKHONOV (ALEKSEI VASIL'EVICH) Pochemu ia ne emigriroval?. Berlin, 1923. pp. 77.

USTINOV (S.M.) Zapiski Nachal'nika kontr-razvedki, 1915-1920g. Berlin, 1923. pp. 144.

RUSSIA - History - 1917-1921, Revolution
- Personal narratives (Cont'd.)

    VARSHER (TATIANA S.) Vidennoe i perezhitoe v Sovetskoi Rossii. Berlin, 1923. pp. 155.

    VASILEVSKII (IL'IA MARKOVICH) Gen. A.I. Denikin i ego memuary. Berlin, 1924. pp. 176.

    KALININ (IVAN MIKHAILOVICH) Pod znamenem Vrangelia: zametki byvshego voennogo prokurora. Leningrad, 1925. pp. 273.

    IL'IN-ZHENEVSKII (ALEKSANDR FEDOROVICH) Bol'sheviki u vlasti: vospominaniia o 1918 gode. Leningrad, 1929. pp. 196.

    KHADZHIEV (RAZAK BEK) Velikii boiar. [Belgrad, 1929]. pp. 397.

    PYKHACHEVA (V.D.) Sem' let vo vlasti temnoi sily: vospominaniia, etc. Belgrad, 1929. pp. 89.

    VERTSINSKII (E.A.) God revoliutsii: vospominaniia ofitsera general'nogo shtaba za 1917-1918 goda. Tallinn, 1929. pp. 61.

    NIKITIN (B.V.) Rokovye gody: novye pokazaniia uchastnika. Parizh, [1937]. pp. 271.

    BAUMGART (WINFRIED) ed. Von Brest-Litovsk zur deutschen Novemberrevolution: aus den Tagebüchern... von Alfons Paquet, Wilhelm Groener und Albert Hopman, März bis November 1918. Göttingen, [1971]. pp. 750. bibliog. (Bayerische Akademie der Wissenschaften. Historische Kommission. Deutsche Geschichtsquellen des 19. und 20. Jahrhunderts. Band 47)

    PUTIATINA (OL'GA EVGEN'EVNA) Grafinia. War and revolution: excerpts from the letters and diaries of the Countess Olga Poutiatine; translated...by George Alexander Lensen. Tallahassee, [1971]. pp. 111.

    VON MOHRENSCHILDT (DIMITRI) ed. The Russian Revolution of 1917: contemporary accounts. New York, 1971. pp. 320.

    HEALD (EDWARD T.) Witness to revolution: letters from Russia, 1916-1919;...edited by James B. Gidney. Kent, Oh., [1972]. pp. 367.

- History - 1917-1921, Revolution - Pictorial works

    VOLKOV-LANNIT (LEONID FILIPPOVICH) Istoriia pishetsia ob"ektivom. Moskva, 1971. pp. 256.

- History - 1917-1921, Revolution - Sources

    GRAZHDANSKAIA voina: materialy po istorii Krasnoi Armii. t.1. Moskva, 1923. pp. 509.

    LISOVOI (IA.M.) ed. Belyi arkhiv: sbornik materialov po istorii i literature voiny, revoliutsii, bol'zhevizma, belogo dvizheniia i t.p., etc. Parizh, 1926-28. 3 vols. (in 2)

    AVRICH (PAUL HENRY) ed. The anarchists in the Russian revolution: [articles, manifestos, speeches, etc.]. Ithaca, N.Y., 1973. pp. 179. bibliog.

- History - 1918-1920, Allied intervention

    ANTANTA i Vrangel': sbornik statei. vyp.1. Moskva, 1923. pp. 260,11.

    GUKOVSKII (ALEKSEI ISAEVICH) Frantsuzskaia interventsiia na Iuge Rossii, 1918-1919 g. Moskva, 1928. pp. 268.

    IAKUSHKIN (EVGENII EVGEN'EVICH) and POLUNIN (S.) Angliiskaia interventsiia v 1918-1920 gg. Moskva, 1928. pp. 106.

    DENIKIN (ANTON IVANOVICH) Sprostowanie historji: odpowiedź Polakom; (translated from the Russian). Paryż, 1937. pp. 16.

    IZ istorii inostrannoi interventsii v Armenii v 1918 godu: dokumenty i materialy. Erevan, 1970. pp. 249.

    SURGULADZE (AKAKII NESTOROVICH) Zakavkaz'e v bor'be za pobedu sotsialistiheskoi revoliutsii. Tbilisi, 1971. pp. 470. With English summary.

RUSSIA - History - 1921, Kronstadt Revolt
  See KRONSTADT - History - 1921, Revolt

- History - 1941-1945 - German occupation

    IUDENKOV (ANDREI FEDOROVICH) Politicheskaia rabota partii sredi naseleniia okkupirovannoi sovetskoi territorii, 1941-1944 gg. Moskva, 1971. pp. 358.

    MUEHLEN (PATRIK VON ZUR) Zwischen Hakenkreuz und Sowjetstern: der Nationalismus der sowjetischen Orientvölker im Zweiten Weltkrieg. Düsseldorf, [1971]. pp. 256. bibliog. (Bonn. Universität. Seminar für Politische Wissenschaft. Bonner Schriften zur Politik und Zeitgeschichte. 5)

- History - 1953-

    SSSR na puti stroitel'stva kommunizma, 1959-1970 gg. Moskva, 1971. pp. 463.

- History, Military

    KRASNOZNAMENNYI Severo-Kavkazskii: ocherk istorii Krasnoznamennogo Severo-Kavkazskogo voennogo okruga. Rostov-na-Donu, 1971. pp. 408.

- Industries

    RUSSIA (U.S.S.R.). Tsentral'noe Statisticheskoe Upravlenie. Trudy. t.3, vyp.2-6. Vserossiiskaia perepis' promyshlennykh zavedenii 1920 g.: itogi po guberniiam, gruppam i klassam proizvodstv. Moskva, 1922-23. 5 vols.(in 1). Some matter in French.

    SMILGA (IVAR TENISOVICH) Promyshlennost' v usloviiakh novoi ekonomicheskoi politiki. Moskva, [1924]. pp. 61.

    EINHEITSKOMITEE FÜR ARBEITERDELEGATIONEN. Was sahen 58 deutsche Arbeiter in Russland?: Bericht der deutschen Arbeiter-Delegation über ihren Aufenthalt in Russland vom 14. Juli bis zum 28. August 1925. Berlin, 1925. pp. 176.

    GORBUNOV (EDUARD PETROVICH) Sotsialisticheskaia industrializatsiia SSSR i ee burzhuaznye kritiki. Moskva, 1962. pp. 131.

    SOKURENKO (GRIGORII MIKHAILOVICH) Partiinyi komitet i rukovodstvo promyshlennost'iu. Dnepropetrovsk, 1963. pp. 76.

    PLINER (MIKHAIL DAVYDOVICH) Vosproizvodstvo rabochei sily v promyshlennosti SSSR. Leningrad, 1964. pp. 116.

    PRIMENENIE matematiki pri razmeshchenii proizvoditel'nykh sil. Moskva, 1964. pp. 136.

    VAL'TUKH (KONSTANTIN KURTOVICH) Krugooborot i oborot fondov predpriiatii. Moskva, 1964. pp. 196.

GORBUNOV (EDUARD PETROVICH) Tempy, uroven' i struktura promyshlennogo proizvodstva v SSSR. Moskva, 1965. pp. 188.

MAL'TSEV (NIKOLAI ALEKSANDROVICH) Material'noe i moral'noe stimulirovanie truda v promyshlennosti. Moskva, 1965. pp. 96.

PLOKHOV (ALEKSANDR ALEKSANDROVICH) Normirovanie oborotnykh sredstv na predpriiatii. Moskva, 1965. pp. 68.

BYCHKOV (PETR SERGEEVICH) Oborotnye sredstva sotsialisticheskikh promyshlennykh predpriiatii. Moskva, 1966. pp. 151.

GUBIN (EVGENII PAVLOVICH) Puti formirovaniia agrarno-promyshlennykh ob"edinenii. [2nd ed.] Moskva, 1966. pp. 168.

KLEPIKOV (VASILII FEDOROVICH) Sotsialisticheskaia kooperatsiia truda. Moskva, 1966. pp. 112.

KOGAN (KIVA IZRAILEVICH) and KUZIAKOV (NIKITA VASIL'EVICH) Khoziaistvennyi raschet i ekonomicheskoe stimulirovanie na predpriiatii. Moskva, 1966. pp. 78.

LUKASHEVICH (SERGEI IVANOVICH) Effektivnost' upravlencheskogo truda i puti ee povysheniia. Minsk, 1966. pp. 166.

SLASTENENKO (VASILII ANTONOVICH) Sotsialisticheskii proizvodstvennyi kollektiv i effektivnost' proizvodstva. Moskva, 1966. pp. 44.

SLASTENENKO (VASILII ANTONOVICH) and others, eds. Sotsialisticheskii proizvodstvennyi kollektiv kak kategoriia politicheskoi ekonomii. Moskva, 1966. pp. 206.

UPRAVLENIE sotsialisticheskim proizvodstvom i metody khoziaistvovaniia. Saratov, 1966. pp. 222.

EREMENKO (STEPAN IVANOVICH) and ALEKSEENKO (MIKHAIL MAKSIMOVICH) Finansy promyshlennykh predpriiatii v novykh usloviiakh khoziaistvovaniia. Kiev, 1969. pp. 127.

KHOZIAISTVENNYI raschet i finansy predpriiatii. Moskva, 1969. pp. 111.

KUZ'MIN (VALENTIN IVANOVICH) Istoricheskii opyt sovetskoi industrializatsii. Moskva, 1969. pp. 180. bibliog.

MAMUTOV (VALENTIN KARLOVICH) ed. Khoziaistvenno-pravovye voprosy upravleniia promyshlennost'iu. Donetsk, 1969. pp. 297.

1970

BUDAVEI (VSEVOLOD IUR'EVICH) Problemy amortizatsii v promyshlennosti. Moskva, 1970. pp. 191.

KAPLAN (A.I.) Analiz balansa promyshlennogo predpriiatiia. Moskva, 1970. pp. 80.

KOGAN (LEV NAUMOVICH) Sotsial'noe planirovanie: rabota, obrazovanie, byt; o plane sotsial'nogo razvitiia kollektiva predpriiatiia. Moskva, 1970. pp. 87.

MESTNAIA promyshlennost' v novykh usloviiakh khoziaistvovaniia. Moskva, 1970. pp. 176.

NOVICHENKO (PETR PARAMONOVICH) Uchet i kal'kulirovanie sebestoimosti produktsii v vazhneishikh otrasliakh promyshlennosti. Moskva, 1970. pp. 191.

PESSEL' (MARK ABRAMOVICH) Effektivnost' kreditovaniia promyshlennosti. Moskva, 1970. pp. 176.

ROTSHTEIN (LEV ABRAMOVICH) Finansovoe planirovanie na promyshlennom predpriiatii: metodologiia sostavleniia balansa dokhodov i raskhodov. Moskva, 1970. pp. 255.

RYZHOVA (VALENTINA VADIMOVNA) and KUZNETSOVA (LARISA ARKHIPOVNA) Matematicheskie metody v analize khoziaistvennoi deiatel'nosti predpriiatii. Moskva, 1970. pp. 88.

SAVITSKAIA (G.V.) Analiz vzaimosviazei v khoziaistvennoi deiatel'nosti predpriiatiia. Moskva, 1970. pp. 80.

SOLODUKHIN (VLADIMIR ZAKHAROVICH) Ekonomicheskii analiz raboty promyshlennykh predpriiatii. Moskva, 1970. pp. 174.

UTENKOV (ANDREI IAKOVLEVICH) KPSS - organizator i rukovoditel' sotsialisticheskogo sorevnovaniia v promyshlennosti v poslevoennye gody, 1946-1950 gg. Moskva, 1970. pp. 164.

VASIL'EVA (EL'ZA FEDOROVNA) Fond razvitiia proizvodstva: sovershenstvovanie formirovaniia i puti povysheniia effektivnosti ispol'zovaniia. Moskva, 1970. pp. 141.

VZAIMOOTNOSHENIIA promyshlennosti s biudzhetom i kreditnoi sistemoi v novykh usloviiakh: materialy nauchnoi konferentsii. Moskva, 1970. pp. 192.

ZAOZERSKAIA (ELIZAVETA IVANOVNA) U istokov krupnogo proizvodstva v russkoi promyshlennosti XVI-XVII vekov: k voprosu o genezise kapitalizma v Rossii. Moskva, 1970. pp. 474.

1971

ARTEMOV (IU.M.) Problemy material'nogo pooshchreniia v usloviiakh intensifikatsii proizvodstva. Moskva, 1971. pp. 160.

CHERNOUDOV (NIKOLAI NIKOLAEVICH) and IUR'EV (NIKOLAI MIKHAILOVICH) Planirovanie i kal'kulirovanie sebestoimosti promyshlennoi produktsii. Moskva, 1971. pp. 183.

EVSEEV (PROKOFII VASIL'EVICH) and KHARABIBEROV (VIKTOR STEPANOVICH) Razvitie mestnoi promyshlennosti v 1971-1975 godakh. Moskva, 1971. pp. 168.

IGNATENKO (TAMARA ALEKSANDROVNA) Sovetskaia istoriografiia rabochego kontrolia i natsionalizatsii promyshlennosti v SSSR, 1917-1967 gg. Moskva, 1971. pp. 259. bibliog.

KAMENITSER (SOLOMON EFREMOVICH) Osnovy upravleniia promyshlennym proizvodstvom: printsipy, metody i problemy. Moskva, 1971. pp. 287.

KIPERMAN (GRIGORII IAKOVLEVICH) Sovershenstvovanie pokazatelei statistiki promyshlennosti. Moskva, 1971. pp. 208.

KLIMENKO (KONSTANTIN IVANOVICH) and PETROVA (ELIZAVETA VASIL'EVNA) Ekonomicheskaia effektivnost' tekhnicheskogo progressa v tiazheloi promyshlennosti SSSR. Moskva, 1971. pp. 240.

RUSSIA - Industries (Cont'd.)

KOROVUSHKIN (ALEKSANDR KONSTANTINOVICH) Sovershenstvovanie finansovykh otnoshenii v promyshlennosti. Moskva, 1971. pp. 191.

LIVSHITS (RAISA SOLOMONOVNA) Effektivnost' kontsentratsii proizvodstva v promyshlennosti SSSR. Moskva, 1971. pp. 327. bibliog.

MASLENNIKOV (VIACHESLAV NIKITICH) and KHEIFETS (SARRA BORISOVNA) Vzaimootnosheniia s biudzhetom predpriiatii mestnoi promyshlennosti i bytovogo obsluzhivaniia. Moskva, 1971. pp. 128.

MASLOVA (NADEZHDA SEMENOVNA) Voprosy ekonomicheskoi effektivnosti novoi sistemy material'nogo stimulirovaniia v promyshlennosti SSSR. Moskva, 1971. pp. 303.

MEZENTSEV (PAVEL VENEDIKTOVICH) Organizatsiia bukhgalterskogo ucheta v promyshlennosti. Moskva, 1971. pp. 127.

MOLIAKOV (DMITRII STEPANOVICH) Finansirovanie promyshlennosti. 3rd ed. Moskva, 1971. pp. 127.

OKAEV (KABI OKAEVICH) Polnyi khozraschet i osnovnye fondy v promyshlennosti. Alma-Ata, 1971. pp. 171. bibliog.

SAZONTOV (GENNADII ALEKSEEVICH) Sotsial'no-ekonomicheskie problemy kontsentratsii i razmeshcheniia promyshlennogo proizvodstva. Moskva, 1971. pp. 262. bibliog.

SHOKIN (NIKOLAI ALEKSEEVICH) Metodologicheskie problemy razmeshcheniia otrasli promyshlennosti. Moskva, 1971. pp. 327. bibliog.

VOROBEICHIKOV (ALEKSEI PETROVICH) and KAUFMAN (MOISEI ZEL'MANOVICH) Mezhzavodskoi ekonomicheskii analiz; pod redaktsiei...Novaka V.A. Moskva, 1971. pp. 104.

1972

AMBARTSUMOV (ALEKSANDR ARMENAKOVICH) Ekonomicheskie sviazi promyshlennosti i sel'skogo khoziaistva pri sotsializme. Moskva, 1972. pp. 236.

BOROVIK (FEDOR VASIL'EVICH) and PLASHCHINSKII (NIKOLAI ALEKSANDROVICH) Obrazovanie fonda proizvodstvennogo nakopleniia v promyshlennosti. Minsk, 1972. pp. 320.

FALKUS (MALCOLM E.) The industrialisation of Russia, 1700-1914. London, 1972. pp. 93. bibliog. (Economic History Society. Studies in Economic History)

FINANSOVYI mekhanizm vozdeistviia na proizvodstvo: na primere promyshlennosti SSSR i NRB. Moskva, 1972. pp. 239.

FUHRMANN (JOSEPH T.) The origins of capitalism in Russia: industry and progress in the sixteenth and seventeenth centuries. Chicago, 1972. pp. 376. bibliog.

GREKOV (LEONID IVANOVICH) Kachestvo produktsii i material'noe stimulirovanie. Moskva, 1972. pp. 147. bibliog.

IAKUB (VASILII IUR'EVICH) and MUKHINA (VALENTINA ALEKSANDROVNA) Osnovnye proizvodstvennye fondy v legkoi promyshlennosti. Moskva, 1972. pp. 212.

KALIAKIN (PAVEL VASIL'EVICH) and others. Povyshenie effektivnosti promyshlennogo proizvodstva. Moskva, 1972. pp. 199.

KALMYKOV (IURII KHAMZATOVICH) Khozraschet promyshlennogo predpriiatiia: pravovye voprosy. Moskva, 1972. pp. 184.

KHOZRASCHET v sovremennykh usloviiakh upravleniia promyshlennost'iu. Leningrad, 1972. pp. 132.

KOLESOV (NIKOLAI DMITRIEVICH) ed. Predpriiatie v sisteme narodnogo khoziaistva. Moskva, 1972. pp. 247.

KOROVINA (ZINAIDA PAVLOVNA) and IGOL'NIKOV (GRIGORII L'VOVICH) Udel'naia fondoemkost' produktsii. Moskva, 1972. pp. 183.

KOVALENKO (IURII NIKOLAEVICH) Tekhniko-ekonomicheskie i sotsial'nye problemy razmeshcheniia promyshlennykh predpriiatii. Kiev, 1972. pp. 255. bibliog.

KOZLOVSKAIA (L.V.) and PAVLOVA (A.D.) eds. Metodicheskie voprosy vnutriraionnogo razmeshcheniia promyshlennosti. Minsk, 1972. pp. 263.

MODIN (ANATOLII ANDREEVICH) and IAKOVENKO (EVGENII GEORGIEVICH) Organizatsiia i upravlenie proizvodstvennym protsessom na promyshlennom predpriiatii; pod redaktsiei... N.P. Fedorenko. Moskva, 1972. pp. 296. bibliog.

NOVAK (VASILII ANDREEVICH) Ekonomicheskii analiz effektivnosti proizvodstva. Moskva, 1972. pp. 96.

PETUKHOV (REM MIKHAILOVICH) and LAZUTKIN (ERMOLAI SEMENOVICH) Ekonomicheskaia effektivnost' i organizatsiia proizvodstva. Moskva, 1972. pp. 220.

SHUMOV (NIKOLAI SERGEEVICH) Effektivnost' ispol'zovaniia oborotnykh sredstv v promyshlennosti. Moskva, 1972. pp. 192.

SPRAVOCHNIK finansista promyshlennogo predpriiatiia. 2nd ed. Moskva, 1972. pp. 447. For 1st ed. see Aleksandrov (Aleksandr Mikhailovich) and others, eds.

TAKSIR (KIM ISAEVICH) Upravlenie promyshlennost'iu SSSR v sovremennykh usloviiakh. Moskva, 1972. pp. 280.

TSAGOLOV (NIKOLAI ALEKSANDROVICH) ed. Nauchnye osnovy upravleniia sotsialisticheskim proizvodstvom. Moskva, 1972. pp. 263.

VLADIMIRSKII (BORIS DAVIDOVICH) Ekonomicheskie zadachi promyshlennykh predpriiatii i pervichnykh proforganizatsii v novykh usloviiakh. Erevan, 1972. pp. 127.

VODARSKII (IAROSLAV EVGEN'EVICH) Promyshlennye seleniia tsentral'noi Rossii v period genezisa i razvitiia kapitalizma. Moskva, 1972. pp. 256.

- Industries - Classification

GUR'EV (VLADIMIR IL'ICH) Klassifikatsiia otraslei narodnogo khoziaistva SSSR. Moskva, 1971. pp. 124. bibliog.

- Industries - Mathematical models

KOZLOV (LEONARD ALEKSANDROVICH) Optimal'noe planirovanie razvitiia i razmeshcheniia otraslei promyshlennosti: voprosy metodologii i metodiki; otvetstvennyi redaktor... A.G. Aganbegian. Novosibirsk, 1970. pp. 176.

METODICHESKIE polozheniia optimal'nogo otraslevogo planirovaniia v promyshlennosti. 2nd ed. Novosibirsk, 1972. pp. 312. bibliog.

- **Intellectual life**

    POTRESOV (ALEKSANDR NIKOLAEVICH) Etiudy o russ-
    koi intelligentsii: sbornik statei, etc. S.-
    Peterburg, 1906. pp. 314.

    BERDIAEV (NIKOLAI ALEKSANDROVICH) Dukhovnyi kri-
    zis intelligentsii: stat'i po obshchestvennoi
    i religioznoi psikhologii, 1907-9 g. S.-Peter-
    burg, 1910. pp. 304. Xerographic reprint.

    BELOV (VADIM) Po novym vekham. Tallinnas, [1922].
    pp. 43.

    AVERBAKH (LEOPOL'D LEONIDOVICH) Kul'tur-
    naia revoliutsiia i voprosy sovremennoi
    literatury. Moskva, 1928. pp. 143.
    2 reports originally presented to MAPP
    and VAPP.

    AVERBAKH (LEOPOL'D LEONIDOVICH) Na
    putiakh kul'turnoi revoliutsii.
    3rd ed. Moskva, 1929. pp. 198.
    Xerographic reprint.

    AVERBAKH (LEOPOL'D LEONIDOVICH) Spornye vopro-
    sy kul'turnoi revoliutsii. Moskva, 1929. pp.
    217. Xerographic reprint.

    EL'SBERG (ZH.) Krizis poputchikov i nastroeniia
    intelligentsii. [Leningrad], 1930. pp. 253.
    Collected articles first published in Na li-
    teraturnom postu, 1926-29. Xerographic reprint.

    BUZLIAKOV (NIKOLAI IVANOVICH) and STEPANOV (NI-
    KOLAI IVANOVICH) Planirovanie razvitiia ot-
    raslei kul'tury; pod redaktsiei I.I. Tsvetko-
    va. Moskva, 1961. pp. 120.

    FEDONIUK (KONSTANTIN EVGEN'EVICH) Deiatel'nost'
    raionnogo Soveta po rukovodstvu narodnym ob-
    razovaniem i kul'turno-prosvetitel'noi rabo-
    toi; otvetstvennyi redaktor B.M. Babii. Mosk-
    va, 1962. pp. 72.

    ALLAKHIAROV (FEZAIL GESENOVICH) Sblizhenie kul'-
    tur sovetskikh sotsialisticheskikh natsii v pe-
    riod stroitel'stva kommunizma. Baku, 1966.
    pp. 137.

    FADEEV (ANATOLII VSEVOLODOVICH) Ideinye svia-
    zi i kul'turnaia zhizn' narodov doreformen-
    noi Rossii. Moskva, 1966. pp. 154.

    AMALRIK (ANDREI ALEKSEEVICH) L'Union soviétique
    survivra-t-elle en 1984?; [translated from the
    Russian by] Michel Tatu; préface de Alain Besançon.
    [Paris, 1970]. pp. 118.

    FUHRMANN (JOSEPH T.) and others. Essays on Russian
    intellectual history;...edited by Leon Borden
    Blair. Austin, [1971]. pp. 123. bibliogs.
    (Texas University. Walter Prescott Webb Memorial
    Lectures. 5)

    KABANOV (PAVEL IVANOVICH) Istoriia kul'turnoi
    revoliutsii v SSSR: kratkii ocherk. Moskva,
    1971. pp. 271.

    KAIRIAN (VACHE MIKHAILOVICH) Preemstvennost'
    v razvitii kul'tury v usloviiakh sotsializma:
    filosofskie problemy kul'tury v trudakh V.I.Lenina.
    Moskva, 1971. pp. 212.

    LEIKINA-SVIRSKAIA (VERA ROMANOVNA) Intelligen-
    tsiia v Rossii vo vtoroi polovine XIX veka.
    Moskva, 1971. pp. 367.

    PAPMEHL (K.A.) Freedom of expression in eighteenth
    century Russia. The Hague, 1971. pp. 166.
    bibliog.

    SLAVINSKY (MICHEL) and STOLYPINE (DIMITRI)
    La vie littéraire en U.R.S.S. de 1934 à nos
    jours. [Paris, 1971]. pp. 260.

    GORBUNOV (VLADIMIR VLADIMIROVICH) Lenin i so-
    tsialisticheskaia kul'tura: leninskaia kontsep-
    tsiia formirovaniia sotsialisticheskoi kul'tu-
    ry. Moskva, 1972. pp. 340.

    KPSS vo glave kul'turnoi revoliutsii v SSSR. Moskva,
    1972. pp. 376.

    LENIN i kul'turnaia revoliutsiia: khronika so-
    bytii, 1917-1923 gg. Moskva, 1972. pp. 496.

    PROBLEMY sovremennoi ideologicheskoi bor'by, raz-
    vitiia sotsialisticheskoi ideologii i kul'tu-
    ry: materialy nauchnoi konferentsii... 29 sen-
    tiabria - 1 oktiabria 1971 g. Moskva, 1972.
    pp. 207.

    THOMSON (BORIS) The premature revolution: Russian
    literature and society, 1917-1946. London, [1972].
    pp. 325. bibliog.

    SZAMUELY (TIBOR) Unique Conservative:
    three extracts from the works of Tibor
    Szamuely. London, 1973. pp. 28.
    (Conservative Political Centre. [Publications].
    No. 531)

- **Intellectual life - Bibliography**

    SIMMONS (JOHN SIMON GABRIEL) compiler. Russian
    bibliography, libraries and archives: a selective
    list of bibliographical references for students
    of Russian history, literature, political, social
    and philosophical thought, theology and linguistics.
    Oxford, 1973. pp. 76.

- **Intellectual life - Statistics**

    RUSSIA (U.S.S.R.). Tsentral'noe Statisticheskoe
    Upravlenie. 1971. Narodnoe obrazovanie, na-
    uka i kul'tura v SSSR: statisticheskii sbor-
    nik. Moskva, 1971. pp. 403.

- **Kings and rulers**

    VINBERG (FEDOR VIKTOROVICH) Krestnyi put'. ch.1.
    Korni zla. 2nd ed. Miunkhen, 1922. pp. 375.

    MASLOVSKII (SEMEN DMITRIEVICH) Gibel' tsarizma.
    Leningrad, 1927. pp. 134.

    SOLOV'EV (IURII BORISOVICH) Samoderzhavie i dvo-
    rianstvo v kontse XIX veka. Leningrad, 1973.
    pp. 383.

- **Languages**

    LAURAT (LUCIEN) Staline: la linguistique et l'im-
    périalisme russe. Paris, [1951]. pp. 93.

    TURNIANSKII (R. V.) Vzaimootnosheniia iazykov
    narodov SSSR. in Uchenye Zapiski Kafedr
    Obshchestvennykh Nauk Vuzov G. Leningrada.
    Problemy Nauchnogo Kommunizma. vyp. 2.
    Leningrad, 1968. pp. 144.

    BELODED (IVAN KONSTANTINOVICH) Lenins'ka teo-
    riia natsional'no-movnoho budivnytstva v so-
    tsialistychnomu suspil'stvi. Kyïv, 1969. pp.
    91.

    V.I. Lenin i rozvytok natsional'nykh mov. Kyïv,
    1971. pp. 207.

    BELODED (IVAN KONSTANTINOVICH) Leninskaia teo-
    riia natsional'no-iazykovogo stroitel'stva v
    sotsialisticheskom obshchestve. Moskva, 1972.
    pp. 214.

    LATVIISKII GOSUDARSTVENNYI UNIVERSITET. Uchenye
    Zapiski. t.154. Nekotorye sotsial'no-politi-
    cheskie voprosy teorii nauchnogo kommunizma.
    Riga, 1972. pp. 135.

RUSSIA - Languages (Cont'd.)

BAZIEV (AKHIIA TANAEVICH) and ISAEV (MAGOMET IZMAILOVICH) Iazyk i natsiia. Moskva, 1973. pp. 247. bibliog.

- Learned institutions and societies

AKADEMIIA NAUK SSSR. Geograficheskoe Obshchestvo SSSR. Geograficheskoe obshchestvo za 125 let. Leningrad, 1970. pp. 394.

- Manufactures

LOMAZOV (MIKHAIL EVSEEVICH) and SUL'POVAR (LEV BORISOVICH) Ekonomicheskaia effektivnost' standartizatsii tovarov narodnogo potrebleniia. Moskva, 1971. pp. 200. bibliog.

NEROSLAVSKAIA (BELLA ALEKSANDROVNA) and SALIMZHANOV (IN'IATULLA KATDUSOVICH) Tsena i problemy povysheniia kachestva produktsii. Moskva, 1971. pp. 160.

McMILLAN (C.H.) Soviet specialization and trade in manufactures. Ottawa, 1972. fo. 29. bibliog. (Carleton University. Carleton Economic Papers)

- Military policy

RUSSIA (U.S.S.R.). Ministerstvo Oborony. 1970. Voprosy taktiki v sovetskikh voennykh trudakh, 1917-1940 gg. Moskva, 1970. pp. 519.

STROKOV (ALEKSANDR ALEKSANDROVICH) V.I. Lenin o voine i voennom iskusstve. Moskva, 1971. pp. 183

WHETTEN (LAWRENCE L.) The Soviet presence in the eastern Mediterranean. New York, [1971]. pp. 49. bibliog. (National Strategy Information Center. Strategy Papers. No. 10)

GALLAGHER (MATTHEW PHILIP) and SPIELMANN (KARL F.) Soviet decision-making for defense: a critique of U.S. perspectives on the arms race. New York, 1972. pp. 102.

JUKES (GEOFFREY) The development of Soviet strategic thinking since 1945. Canberra, 1972. pp. 44. (Australian National University. Strategic and Defence Studies Centre. Canberra Papers on Strategy and Defence. No. 14)

RUSSIA (U.S.S.R.). Ministerstvo Oborony. 1972. Filosofskoe nasledie V.I. Lenina i problemy sovremennoi voiny; pod redaktsiei... Milovidova A.S. i... Kozlova V.G. Moskva, 1972. pp. 392.

SELLA (AMNON) 'The second Baghdad Pact': Soviet political and military position in the Middle East. [Edinburgh, 1972]. pp. 26. (Edinburgh. University. Department of Politics. Waverley Papers. Series 4. Politico-Military Studies. Occasional Papers. 3)

- Militia

PODVOISKII (NIKOLAI IL'ICH) Krasnaia gvardiia v Oktiabr'skie dni: Leningrad i Moskva. Moskva, 1927. pp. 107.

PECHE (IA.) Krasnaia gvardiia v Moskve v boiakh za Oktiabr'. Moskva, 1929. pp. 187.

- Moral conditions

PROKOF'EV (VASILII IVANOVICH) Kodeks kommunisticheskoi morali i religioznaia "nravstvennost'". Moskva, 1964. pp. 113.

MORAL'NYI oblik sovetskogo rabochego. Moskva, 1966. pp. 312.

AASAMAA (IINA) Kak sebia vesti; (perevod s estonskogo). Tallin, 1971. pp. 222.

REBRIN (VENIAMIN ALEKSEEVICH) Obshchestvennoe blago i obshchestvennyi dolg. Moskva, 1971. pp. 127.

CONNOR (WALTER D.) Deviance in Soviet society: crime, delinquency, and alcoholism. New York, 1972. pp. 327.

KHARCHEV (ANATOLII GEORGIEVICH) and IAKOVLEV (BORIS DMITRIEVICH) Ocherki istorii marksistsko-leninskoi etiki v SSSR. Leningrad, 1972. pp. 218.

- Nationalism

ZHORDANIIA (NOI NIKOLAEVICH) Nashi raznoglasiia. Parizh, 1928. pp. 48.

ARTSIUK (EVGENII) Mysli o griadushchei osvobozhdennoi Rossii i estestvennye zakony natsionalizma. [Paris, 1939?]. pp. 80.

DERZHAVNIK pseud. Rossiiskoe Narodnoderzhavie kak ideia novoi Rossii. Zheneva, 1944. pp. 104.

POREMSKII (V.D.) Problemy natsional'noi revoliutsii. Frankfurt-am-Main, Posev, 1952. pp. 103.

ABAKIROV (ANASH) Pechat' i nekotorye voprosy razvitiia bratskikh sviazei narodov SSSR. Frunze, 1965. pp. 63.

ALLAKHIAROV (FEZAIL GESENOVICH) Sblizhenie kul'tur sovetskikh sotsialisticheskikh natsii v period stroitel'stva kommunizma. Baku, 1966. pp. 137.

LEWYTZKYJ (BORYS) Polityka narodowościowa Z.S.S.R. w dobie Chruszczowa; przełożył z niemieckiego Mieczysław Zarzycki; posłowie Wsewołoda Hołubnyczego. Paryż, 1966. pp. 302.

NARYNBAEV (AZIS ISADZHANOVICH) and RISS (IAKOV ABRAMOVICH) Opyt razresheniia natsional'nogo voprosa v SSSR i ego istoricheskoe znachenie: v pomoshch' propagandistam. Frunze, 1967. pp. 73. bibliog.

SOVETSKII narod - novaia istoricheskaia obshchnost' liudei: trudy mezhvuzovskoi nauchnoi konferentsii. Volgograd, 1969. pp. 558.

STROITEL'STVO kommunizma i problemy sblizheniia natsii. Kiev, 1969. pp. 220.

DZHANDIL'DIN (NURUMBEK DZHANDIL'DINOVICH) Priroda natsional'noi psikhologii. Alma-Ata, 1971. pp. 304.

MUEHLEN (PATRIK VON ZUR) Zwischen Hakenkreuz und Sowjetstern: der Nationalismus der sowjetischen Orientvölker im Zweiten Weltkrieg. Düsseldorf, [1971]. pp. 256. bibliog. (Bonn. Universität. Seminar für Politische Wissenschaft. Bonner Schriften zur Politik und Zeitgeschichte. 5)

OSUSHCHESTVLENIE leninskoi natsional'noi politiki u narodov Krainego Severa. Moskva, 1971. pp. 344.

SOVIET nationality problems: [contributions to a research seminar at Columbia University]; editor, Edward Allworth. New York, 1971. pp. 296. bibliog.

AGADZHANIAN (GAIK SERGEEVICH) K voprosu o prirode i perspektivakh razvitiia sotsialisticheskikh natsii v SSSR: opyt teoreticheskogo analiza. Erevan, 1972. pp. 191.

AZIZIAN (ATYK KEGAMOVICH) Leninskaia natsional'naia politika v razvitii i deistvii. Moskva, 1972. pp. 381.

BARMICHEV (VITALII DMITRIEVICH) V edinom soiuze: istoriko-publitsisticheskii ocherk o razvitii mnogonatsional'noi sotsialisticheskoi kul'tury v SSSR; nauchnyi redaktor... I.M. Ignatenko. Minsk, 1972. pp. 247. bibliog.

GILILOV (S.S.) V.I. Lenin - organizator Sovetskogo mnogonatsional'nogo gosudarstva. 2nd ed. Moskva, 1972. pp. 232.

KULICHENKO (MIKHAIL IVANOVICH) Natsional'nye otnosheniia v SSSR i tendentsii ikh razvitiia. Moskva, 1972. pp. 564.

MALANCHUK (VALENTYN IUKHYMOVYCH) Istoricheskii opyt KPSS po resheniiu natsional'nogo voprosa i razvitiiu natsional'nykh otnoshenii v SSSR. Moskva, 1972. pp. 294. bibliog.

MIKOIAN (ANASTAS IVANOVICH) Sovetskomu Soiuzu piat'desiat let. Moskva, 1972. pp. 72.

MNOGONATSIONAL'NOE Sovetskoe gosudarstvo. Moskva, 1972. pp. 431.

SOVETSKII narod i dialektika natsional'nogo razvitiia. Baku, 1972. pp. 332.

SSSR - velikoe sodruzhestvo narodov-brat'ev. Moskva, 1972. pp. 339.

TADEVOSIAN (EDUARD VRAMOVICH) Sovetskaia natsional'naia gosudarstvennost'. Moskva, 1972. pp. 232.

ZEVELEV (ABRAM IZRAILEVICH) The nationalities question: how it was solved in the USSR. Moscow, 1972. pp. 60.

- Native races

KLESHCHENOK (IVAN PAVLOVICH) Istoricheskii opyt KPSS po osushchestvleniiu leninskoi natsional'noi politiki sredi malykh narodov Severa, 1917-935, etc. Moskva, 1972. pp. 239. bibliog.

SAZHIN (GRIGORII MAKSIMOVICH) Sovet deputatov trudiashchikhsia natsional'nogo okruga. Moskva, 1972. pp. 68.

- Navy

GRAF (GARAL'D KARLOVICH) Na "Novike": Baltiiskii Flot v voinu i revoliutsiiu. Miunkhen, 1922. pp. 480.

USTINOV (S.M.) Zapiski Nachal'nika kontr-razvedki, 1915-1920g. Berlin, 1923. pp. 144.

ELLER (ERNEST McNEILL) The Soviet sea challenge. [Chicago, 1971]. pp. 315. bibliog.

INTERNATIONAL INSTITUTE FOR STRATEGIC STUDIES. Adelphi Papers. No. 87. The Indian Ocean in Soviet naval policy; by Geoffrey Jukes. London, 1972. pp. 30.

POLMAR (NORMAN) Soviet naval power: challenge for the 1970s. New York, [1972]. pp. 106. bibliog.

THEBERGE (JAMES DANIEL) ed. Soviet seapower in the Caribbean: political and strategic implications. New York, 1972. pp. 172. bibliog.

- Navy - Officers

KONSTANTINOV (ALEKSANDR PETROVICH) F.F. Il'in-Raskol'nikov. Leningrad, 1964. pp. 155.

- Nobility

JONES (ROBERT E.) The emancipation of the Russian nobility, 1762-1785. Princeton, [1973]. pp. 326. bibliog.

SOLOV'EV (IURII BORISOVICH) Samoderzhavie i dvorianstvo v kontse XIX veka. Leningrad, 1973. pp. 383.

- Non-Russian territories

ABAKIROV (ANASH) Pechat' i nekotorye voprosy razvitiia bratskikh sviazei narodov SSSR. Frunze, 1965. pp. 63.

ALLAKHIAROV (FEZAIL GESENOVICH) Sblizhenie kul'tur sovetskikh sotsialisticheskikh natsii v period stroitel'stva kommunizma. Baku, 1966. pp. 137.

FADEEV (ANATOLII VSEVOLODOVICH) Ideinye sviazi i kul'turnaia zhizn' narodov doreformennoi Rossii. Moskva, 1966. pp. 154.

STROITEL'STVO kommunizma i problemy sblizheniia natsii. Kiev, 1969. pp. 220.

BAGDASARIAN (ALEKSEI MUSHEGOVICH) Sovetskii opyt ekonomicheskogo vyravnivaniia natsional'nykh respublik. Groznyi, 1971. pp. 79. bibliog.

AGADZHANIAN (GAIK SERGEEVICH) K voprosu o prirode i perspektivakh razvitiia sotsialisticheskikh natsii v SSSR: opyt teoreticheskogo analiza. Erevan, 1972. pp. 191.

AGZAMKHODZHAEV (ANVAR) and URAZAEV (SHAVKAT ZAKARIEVICH) SSSR - sotsialisticheskoe gosudarstvo sovetskikh narodov. Tashkent, 1972. pp. 339.

AZIZIAN (ATYK KEGAMOVICH) Leninskaia natsional'naia politika v razvitii i deistvii. Moskva, 1972. pp. 381.

BARMICHEV (VITALII DMITRIEVICH) V edinom soiuze: istoriko-publitsisticheskii ocherk o razvitii mnogonatsional'noi sotsialisticheskoi kul'tury v SSSR; nauchnyi redaktor... I.M. Ignatenko. Minsk, 1972. pp. 247. bibliog.

KHIDOIATOV (GOGA ABRAROVICH) Leninskaia natsional'naia programma i sovremennaia ideologicheskaia bor'ba. Tashkent, 1972. pp. 296.

KULICHENKO (MIKHAIL IVANOVICH) Natsional'nye otnosheniia v SSSR i tendentsii ikh razvitiia. Moskva, 1972. pp. 564.

MALANCHUK (VALENTYN IUKHYMOVYCH) Istoricheskii opyt KPSS po resheniiu natsional'nogo voprosa i razvitiiu natsional'nykh otnoshenii v SSSR. Moskva, 1972. pp. 294. bibliog.

MIKOIAN (ANASTAS IVANOVICH) Sovetskomu Soiuzu piat'desiat let. Moskva, 1972. pp. 72.

MNOGONATSIONAL'NOE Sovetskoe gosudarstvo. Moskva, 1972. pp. 431.

SOIUZ SSR - sodruzhestvo ravnopravnykh respublik. Moskva, 1972. pp. 296.

SOVETSKII narod i dialektika natsional'nogo razvitiia. Baku, 1972. pp. 332.

SOVETSKOE sodruzhestvo narodov: ob"edinitel'noe dvizhenie i obrazovanie SSSR; sbornik dokumentov, 1917-1922. Moskva, 1972. pp. 336.

RUSSIA - Non-Russian territories (Cont'd.)

SSSR - velikoe sodruzhestvo narodov-brat'ev. Moskva, 1972. pp. 339.

ZEVELEV (ABRAM IZRAILEVICH) The nationalities question: how it was solved in the USSR. Moscow, 1972. pp. 60.

BRATSKOE sodruzhestvo soiuznykh respublik v razvitii narodnogo khoziaistva SSSR, 1917-1971. Moskva, 1973. pp. 555.

- Non Russian territories - Verkhovnyi Sovet - Statistics

RUSSIA (U.S.S.R.). Verkhovnyi Sovet. Prezidium. Otdel po Voprosam Raboty Sovetov. 1967. Itogi vyborov i sostav deputatov Verkhovnykh Sovetov soiuznykh i avtonomnykh respublik, 1967 g.: statisticheskii sbornik. Moskva, 1967. pp. 87.

RUSSIA (U.S.S.R.). Verkhovnyi Sovet. Prezidium. Otdel po Voprosam Raboty Sovetov. 1971. Itogi vyborov i sostav deputatov Verkhovnykh Sovetov soiuznykh i avtonomnykh respublik, 1971 g.: statisticheskii sbornik. Moskva, 1971. pp. 94.

- Occupations

KORCHAGIN (VIKTOR PAVLOVICH) and SBYTOVA (LIDIIA SERGEEVNA) Sfera uslug i zaniatost' naseleniia. Moskva, 1970. pp. 172.

NAZIMOV (IGOR' NIKOLAEVICH) Proforientatsiia i profotbor v sotsialisticheskom obshchestve. Moskva, 1972. pp. 254.

- Officials and employees - Directories

INSTITUT PO IZUCHENIIU SSSR. Party and government officials of the Soviet Union 1917-1967;... edited by Edward L. Crowley [and others]. Metuchen, N.J., [1969]. pp. 214.

- Officials and employees - Travel regulations

ABRAMOVA (ALEKSANDRA AFANAS'EVNA) Komandirovki. Moskva, 1961. pp. 102. bibliog.

- Politics and government

SVIATOPOLK-MIRSKII (DMITRII NIKOLAEVICH) Prince. Chem ob"iasnit' nashe proshloe i chego zhdat' ot nashego budushchego?. Parizh, 1926. pp. 88.

PODVOISKII (NIKOLAI IL'ICH) God 1917. Moskva, 1958. pp. 190. Articles 1918-1933, together with unpublished MSS.

LODGE (MILTON C.) Soviet elite attitudes since Stalin. Columbus, Ohio, [1969]. pp. 135. bibliog.

AZAROV (NIKOLAI IVANOVICH) V.I.Lenin o politike kak obshchestvennom iavlenii. Moskva, 1971. pp. 240.

STAHL (ZDZISŁAW) Najazd od Wschodu. Londyn, 1971. pp. 256.

STRONG (JOHN W.) ed. The Soviet Union under Brezhnev and Kosygin: the transition years; [a collection of essays based on lectures given at Carleton University, Ottawa, 1968, sponsored by Carleton's Program of Soviet and East European Studies]. New York, [1971]. pp. 277.

AGENTSTVO PECHATI NOVOSTI. USSR 50: Novosti Press Agency year book. Moscow, 1972. pp. 335.

BELYKH (AKAT KALISTRATOVICH) Upravlenie i samoupravlenie: sotsialisticheskoe upravlenie: sushchnost' i perspektivy razvitiia. Leningrad, 1972. pp. 209.

PARKER (WILLIAM HENRY) The superpowers: the United States and the Soviet Union compared. London, 1972. pp. 347.

REVOLUTION and politics in Russia: essays in memory of B.I. Nicolaevsky; edited by Alexander and Janet Rabinowitch, with Ladis K.D. Kristof. Bloomington, [1972]. pp. 416. bibliog. (Indiana University. Russian and East European Institute. Russian and East European Series. vol. 41)

SHAKHNAZAROV (GEORGII KHOSROEVICH) Sotsialisticheskaia demokratiia: nekotorye voprosy teorii. Moskva, 1972. pp. 192.

TOPORNIN (BORIS NIKOLAEVICH) Politicheskaia sistema sotsializma. Moskva, 1972. pp. 232.

- Politics and government - Anecdotes, facetiae, satire, etc.

BRITAN (ILIIA) Ibo ia - bol'shevik!!.. Berlin, 1924. pp. 37.

ARPACHAISKII (T.) Oshibka partorga ili sluchai v gorakh Kavkaza: rasskaz iz vospominanii politemigranta. [Stuttgart?], 1948. pp. 62.

ANDREEVICH (EVGENII) Kreml' i narod: politicheskie anekdoty; The Kremlin and the people: political jokes. Miunkhen, 1951. pp. 134.

- Politics and government - Bibliography

ANTONOV (VLADIMIR VASIL'EVICH) compiler. Sovetskaia sotsialisticheskaia demokratiia: rekomendatel'nyi ukazatel' literatury. Moskva, 1971. pp. 87.

- Politics and Government - 1689-1800

JONES (ROBERT E.) The emancipation of the Russian nobility, 1762-1785. Princeton, [1973]. pp. 326. bibliog.

- Politics and government - 1800-1899

KENNAN (GEORGE) The last appeal of the Russian liberals. [New York, 1888]. pp. 50-63. (Extracted from The Century illustrated monthly magazine, vol. 35)

ISTORIKO-revoliutsionnyi sbornik; pod redaktsiei V.I. Nevskogo. Moskva, 1924-26. 3 vols. Xerographic reprint.

MEN'SHCHIKOV (LEONID PETROVICH) Okhrana i revoliutsiia: k istorii tainykh politicheskikh organizatsii v Rossii. ch.1,2, vyp, 1,2. Moskva, 1925-29. 2 vols. Pt.2 has subtitle:...organizatsii, sushchestvovavshikh vo vremena samoderzhaviia. Xerographic reprint. There is another copy of pt.2 vyp.1 at R(Coll.) Russ/D/126.

AMBLER (EFFIE) Russian journalism and politics, 1861-1881: (the career of Aleksei S. Suvorin). Detroit, 1972. pp. 239. bibliog.

KENNAN (GEORGE FROST) The Marquis de Custine and his Russia in 1839. London, 1972. pp. 145. (Oxford. University. All Souls College. Chichele Lectures. 1969)

KOROLENKO (VLADIMIR GALAKTIONOVICH) The history of my contemporary; translated and abridged by Neil Parsons. London, 1972. pp. 255.

SOLOV'EV (IURII BORISOVICH) Samoderzhavie i dvorianstvo v kontse XIX veka. Leningrad, 1973. pp. 383.

- Politics and government - 1894-1917

REISNER (MIKHAIL ANDREEVICH) Die russischen Kämpfe um Recht und Freiheit. Halle a.S., 1905. pp. 215.

MARTOV (IULII OSIPOVICH) and others, eds. Obshchestvennoe dvizhenie v Rossii v nachale XX-go veka. S.-Peterburg, 1909-11. 4 vols. Xerographic reprint.

SUVOROV (P.) The Finnish question: equal rights; the position of Russians in Finland and of Finns in the rest of the Russian Empire. St. Pétersbourg, 1910. pp. 60.

TAGANTSEV (NIKOLAI STEPANOVICH) Perezhitoe. Petrograd, 1919. 2 vols. Xerographic reprint.

KARABCHEVSKII (NIKOLAI PLATONOVICH) Chto glaza moi videli. Berlin, 1921. 2 vols [in 1].

ISTORIKO-revoliutsionnyi sbornik; pod redaktsiei V.I. Nevskogo. Moskva, 1924-26. 3 vols. Xerographic reprint.

MEN'SHCHIKOV (LEONID PETROVICH) Okhrana i revoliutsiia: k istorii tainykh politicheskikh organizatsii v Rossii. ch.1,2, vyp. 1,2. Moskva, 1925-29. 2 vols. Pt.2 has subtitle:...organizatsii, sushchestvovavshikh vo vremena samoderzhaviia. Xerographic reprint. There is another copy of pt.2 vyp.1 at R(Coll.) Russ/D/126.

SAVINKOV (BORIS VIKTOROVICH) Vospominaniia terrorista; predislovie Feliksa Kona. 2nd ed. [Khar'kov, 1926?]. pp. 375.

SHAKHOVSKOI (VSEVOLOD NIKOLAEVICH) Prince. "Sic transit gloria mundi", tak prokhodit mirskaia slava, 1893-1917 g.g. Parizh, 1952. pp. 218.

MOSKOVSKII GOSUDARSTVENNYI ISTORIKO-ARKHIVNYI INSTITUT. Trudy. t.27. Voprosy teorii marksizma-leninizma i istorii KPSS; pod redaktsiei... S.I. Murashova [i] D.I. Nadtocheeva. Moskva, 1970. pp. 417.

VOSTRIKOV (NIKOLAI IVANOVICH) Bor'ba za massy: gorodskie srednie sloi nakanune Oktiabria. Moskva, 1970. pp. 200.

KIR'IANOV (IURII IL'ICH) Rabochie Iuga Rossii, 1914-fevral' 1917 g. Moskva, 1971. pp. 307.

UCHENYE ZAPISKI KAFEDR OBSHCHESTVENNYKH NAUK VUZOV G. LENINGRADA. Istoriia KPSS. vyp.11. Nekotorye voprosy sotsialisticheskoi revoliutsii i sotsialisticheskogo stroitel'stva v SSSR. Leningrad, 1971. pp. 184.

BAZYLOW (LUDWIK) Ostatnie lata Rosji carskiej: rządy Stołypina. Warszawa, 1972. pp. 507.

COPELAND (WILLIAM R.) The uneasy alliance: collaboration between the Finnish opposition and the Russian underground, 1899-1904. Helsinki, 1973. pp. 224. bibliog. (Academia Scientiarum Fennica. Annales. Ser.B. Tom. 179)

- Politics and government - 1917-

RENAISSANCE du bolchévisme en U.R.S.S.: mémoires d'un bolchévik-léniniste. Paris, 1970. pp. 191.

DANILENKO (DMITRII IVANOVICH) Razvitie V.I. Leninym dialektiki v posleoktiabr'skii period. Moskva, 1971. pp. 286.

PERFIL'EV (MARAT NIKOLAEVICH) Sovetskaia demokratiia i burzhuaznaia "sovetologiia": kritika kontseptsii o politicheskikh i sotsial'nykh pravakh grazhdan SSSR. Moskva, 1971. pp. 71.

TUCKER (ROBERT CHARLES) The Soviet political mind: Stalinism and post-Stalin change. rev. ed. New York, [1971]. pp. 304.

UCHENYE ZAPISKI KAFEDR OBSHCHESTVENNYKH NAUK VUZOV G. LENINGRADA. Istoriia KPSS. vyp.11. Nekotorye voprosy sotsialisticheskoi revoliutsii i sotsialisticheskogo stroitel'stva v SSSR. Leningrad, 1971. pp. 184.

BARGHOORN (FREDERICK CHARLES) Politics in the U.S.S.R.: (a country study). 2nd ed. Boston, [Mass.], 1972. pp. 360.

NOGEE (JOSEPH L.) ed. Man, state, and society in the Soviet Union. London, 1972. pp. 599. bibliog.

ON the road to communism: essays on Soviet domestic and foreign politics; [mainly revised versions of papers read at the sixth annual Bi-State Slavic Conference (Kansas-Missouri), 1967]; edited by Roger E. Kanet and Ivan Volgyes. Lawrence, [1972]. pp. 209.

WESSON (ROBERT GALE) The Soviet Russian state. New York, [1972]. pp. 404. bibliogs.

WESSON (ROBERT GALE) The Soviet state: an aging revolution. New York, [1972]. pp. 222.

ROSITZKE (HARRY A.) The USSR today. London, [1973]. pp. 114.

- Politics and government - 1917-1953

ROMANOV (E.R.) Sily revoliutsii. [Frankfurt-m-Main, Possev, 1953?]. pp. 68. Lacks title page.

KHRUSHCHEV (NIKITA SERGEEVICH) Rech' Khrushcheva na zakrytom zasedanii XX s"ezda KPSS, 24-25 fevralia 1956 g. Miunkhen, 1956. pp. 57.

TROTSKII (LEV DAVYDOVICH) Writings of Leon Trotsky ...; (edited by George Breitman [and others]). New York, 1969 in progress.

ARSIĆ (DRAGINJA) Društveno-ekonomski koreni staljinizma. Beograd, 1972. pp. 283. bibliog. With English and Russian summaries.

DANIELS (ROBERT VINCENT) ed. The Stalin revolution: foundations of Soviet totalitarianism. 2nd ed. Lexington, Mass., [1972]. pp. 233. bibliog.

TROTSKII (LEV DAVYDOVICH) Writings of Leon Trotsky ...; (edited by George Breitman [and others]). 2nd ed. New York, 1973 in progress.

STALIN (IOSIF VISSARIONOVICH) The essential Stalin: major theoretical writings; 1905-52, edited and with an introduction by Bruce Franklin. London, 1973. pp. 511.

- Politics and government - 1917-1936

BELOV (VADIM) Po novym vekham. Tallinnas, [1922]. pp. 43.

NA ideologicheskom fronte bor'by s kontr-revoliutsiei: sbornik statei. Moskva, 1923. pp. 262.

ZHORDANIIA (NOI NIKOLAEVICH) Bol'shevizm. Berlin, [1923?]. pp. 85.

ARTSYBASHEV (MIKHAIL PETROVICH) Zapiski pisatelia. [Warsaw], 1925. pp. 104. Articles originally published in "Za svobodu".

RUSSIA - Politics and government - 1917-1936 (Cont'd.)

BUKHARIN (NIKOLAI IVANOVICH) Ob itogakh ob"edinennogo plenuma TsK i TsKK VKP/b/: doklad na sobranii partaktiva Leningradskoi organizatsii VKP/b/ 11 avgusta 1927 g. 2nd ed. Leningrad, 1927. pp. 62. Xerographic reprint.

MASLOV (SERGEI S.) Na revoliutsionnoi rabote v Rossii, 1.IV.1929 - 1.II.1930. [Belgrad?, 1930?]. pp. 68. Lacks title page.

BAZILI (NIKOLAI ALEKSANDROVICH) Rossiia pod Sovetskoi vlast'iu. Parizh, [1937]. pp. 382.

POTRESOV (ALEKSANDR NIKOLAEVICH) A.N. Potresov: posmertnyi sbornik proizvedenii; B. Nikolaevskii, A.N. Potresov: opyt literaturno-politicheskoi biografii. Parizh, 1937. pp. 368. bibliog.

HERBETTE (JEAN) Ein französischer Diplomat über die bolschewistische Gefahr: Berichte des Botschafters der französischen Republik in Moskau...aus den Jahren 1927-1931. Berlin, 1943. pp. 178. (Entstehung des Krieges von 1939, Die. 2. Schrift)

MOSKOVSKII GOSUDARSTVENNYI ISTORIKO-ARKHIVNYI INSTITUT. Trudy. t.26. [Sbornik statei]; pod redaktsiei... A.A. Abramova, ... Iu.F. Kononova [i] E.A. Lutskogo. Moskva, 1968. pp. 325.

MOSKOVSKII GOSUDARSTVENNYI ISTORIKO-ARKHIVNYI INSTITUT. Trudy. t.27. Voprosy teorii marksizma-leninizma i istorii KPSS; pod redaktsiei... S.I. Murashova [i] D.I. Nadtocheeva. Moskva, 1970. pp. 417.

NABOKOV (VLADIMIR DMITRIEVICH) The provisional government...; edited by Andrew Field. [Brisbane, 1970]. pp. 147.

ROSMER (ALFRED) Moscou sous Lénine. Paris, 1970. 2 vols. (in 1).

VOPROSY strategii i taktiki v trudakh V.I. Lenina posleoktiabr'skogo perioda. Moskva, 1971. pp. 311.

- Politics and government - 1936-

SUSLOV (MIKHAIL ANDREEVICH) Izbrannoe: rechi i stat'i. Moskva, 1972. pp. 695.

- Politics and government - 1936-1953

MEDVEDEV (ROI ALEKSANDROVICH) Let history judge: the origins and consequences of Stalinism. London, 1972. pp. 566, xviii.

- Politics and government - 1953-

MARKOVIĆ (ŽIVKO) Koncepcije KPSS o razvitku socijalističke demokratije. Beograd, 1970. pp. 359. bibliog. With English summary.

BREZHNEV (LEONID IL'ICH) Report of the CPSU Central Committee to the 24th Congress of the Communist Party of the Soviet Union; delivered... March 30, 1971. Moscow, 1971. pp. 124.

MAURACH (REINHART) and MEISSNER (BORIS) eds. Sowjetstaat und Sowjetrecht nach Chruschtschow: [papers presented to the 5th Ostrechtstagung, 1970, organised by the Deutsche Gesellschaft für Osteuropakunde, etc.]. Stuttgart, 1971. pp. 232.

GERSTENMAIER (CORNELIA) Die Stimme der Stummen: die demokratische Bewegung in der Sowjetunion. 3rd ed. Stuttgart, 1972. pp. 395. bibliog.

GILISON (JEROME MARTIN) British and Soviet politics: legitimacy and convergence. Baltimore, [1972]. pp. 186.

GITELMAN (ZVI Y.) The diffusion of political innovation: from Eastern Europe to the Soviet Union. Beverly Hills, [1972]. pp. 59.

SLUSSER (ROBERT M.) The Berlin crisis of 1961: Soviet-American relations and the struggle for power in the Kremlin, June-November 1961. Baltimore, [1973]. pp. 509. bibliog.

- Politics and government - 1964-

BREZHNEV (LEONID IL'ICH) Leninskim kursom: rechi i stat'i. Moskva, 1970-72. 3 vols. Originally planned in 2 vols.; vol. 3 was added later.

LEWYTZKYJ (BORYS) Die Marschälle und die Politik: eine Untersuchung über den Stellenwert des Militärs innerhalb des sowjetischen Systems seit dem Sturz Chruschtschews. Köln, [1971]. pp. 193. bibliog.

MARKO (KURT) Dogmatismus und Emanzipation in der Sowjetunion: Philosophie, Reformdenken, Opposition. Stuttgart, [1971]. pp. 224.

BREZHNEV (LEONID IL'ICH) Following Lenin's course: speeches and articles. Moscow, 1972. pp. 500.

GORBANEVSKAIA (NATAL'IA E.) Red Square at noon; translated [from the French] by Alexander Lieven. London, 1972. pp. 288.

- Population

SMULEVICH (BOLESLAV IAKOVLEVICH) Narodnoe zdorov'e i sotsiologiia. Moskva, 1965. pp. 232.

VALENTEI (DMITRII IGNAT'EVICH) and BURNASHEV (E.IU.) eds. Voprosy teorii i politiki narodonaseleniia. Moskva, 1970. pp. 163.

BRONER (DAVID L'VOVICH) and VENETSKII (IL'IA GRIGOR'EVICH) eds. Problemy demografii: voprosy teorii i praktiki. Moskva, 1971. pp. 214.

KABUZAN (VLADIMIR MAKSIMOVICH) Izmeneniia v razmeshchenii naseleniia Rossii v XVIII - pervoi polovine XIX v.: po materialam revizii. Moskva, 1971. pp. 191.

VLIIANIE sotsial'no-ekonomicheskikh faktorov na demograficheskie protsessy. Kiev, 1972. pp. 238. With brief English summary and table of contents.

ZAIONCHKOVSKAIA (ZHANNA ANTONOVNA) Novosely v gorodakh: metody izucheniia prizhivaemosti. Moskva, 1972. pp. 164.

TOMILIN (SERGEI ARKAD'EVICH) Demografiia i sotsial'naia gigiena: [sbornik statei]. Moskva, 1973. pp. 311. bibliog.

UCHENYE ZAPISKI PO STATISTIKE; [published by] Akademiia Nauk SSSR, Tsentral'nyi Ekonomiko-Matematicheskii Institut. tom spetsial'nyi [issued in conjunction with] tom 21. Statistika migratsii naseleniia. Moskva, 1973. pp. 365. bibliog. With English and French tables of contents.

- Population - Bibliography

BURNASHEV (E.IU.) and others, compilers. Bibliografiia po problemam narodonaseleniia: sovetskaia i perevodnaia literatura, 1965-1968 gg. Moskva, 1971. pp. 282.

- Population - Mathematical models

ZASLAVSKAIA (TAT'IANA IVANOVNA) and others, eds. Metodika vyborochnogo obsledovaniia migratsii sel'skogo naseleniia. Novosibirsk, 1969. pp. 167. bibliog.

- Relations (general) with Arab countries

YODFAT (ARYEH) Arab politics in the Soviet mirror. Jerusalem, [1973]. pp. 332. (Tel-Aviv. University. Shiloah Center for Middle Eastern and African Studies. Monograph Series)

- Relations (general) with Asia

RUSSIA and Asia: essays on the influence of Russia on the Asian peoples; [papers read at a conference at Stanford University in 1967]; edited by Wayne S. Vucinich. Stanford, [1972]. pp. 521. (Stanford University. Hoover Institution on War, Revolution, and Peace. Hoover Institution Publications. 107)

- Relations (general) with Bulgaria

POGLUBKO (KONSTANTIN ALEKSANDROVICH) Ocherki istorii bolgaro-rossiiskikh revoliutsionnykh sviazei, 60-70-e gody XIX veka. Kishinev, 1972. pp. 311. bibliog.

- Relations (general) with Czechoslovakia

SYLLABA (THEODOR) T.G. Masaryk a revoluce v Rusku. Praha, 1959. pp. 265. bibliog. With 5 separate facsimiles.

- Relations (general) with Eastern Germany

GESELLSCHAFT FÜR DEUTSCH-SOWJETISCHE FREUNDSCHAFT. Kongress, 1949. Freunde für immer!: (Kongressbericht). Berlin, 1949. pp. 238. (Neue Gesellschaft, Die: Monatszeitschrift der Gesellschaft für Deutsch-Sowjetische Freundschaft. Sondernummern. Kongressbericht, 1949)

FREUNDSCHAFT der Tat; wie die Sowjetunion hilft; herausgegeben vom Amt für Information der Regierung der Deutschen Demokratischen Republik. Berlin, 1952. pp. 333.

- Relations (general) with Europe

MEDLIN (WILLIAM K.) and PATRINELIS (CHRISTOS G.) Renaissance influences and religious reforms in Russia: Western and post-Byzantine impacts on culture and education, 16th-17th centuries. Geneva, 1971. pp. 181. bibliog.

- Relations (general) with Finland

COPELAND (WILLIAM R.) The uneasy alliance: collaboration between the Finnish opposition and the Russian underground, 1899-1904. Helsinki, 1973. pp. 224. bibliog. (Academia Scientiarum Fennica. Annales. Ser.B. Tom. 179)

- Relations (general) with France

CHERNIKOV (GENNADII PAVLOVICH) and CHERNIKOVA (DIANA ALEKSANDROVNA) Storonniki i protivniki franko-sovetskogo sotrudnichestva. Moskva, 1971. pp. 256.

ITENBERG (BORIS SAMUILOVICH) Rossiia i Parizhskaia Kommuna. Moskva, 1971. pp. 202.

- Relations (general) with Hungary

UKRAINS'KA RSR u radians'ko-uhors'komu spivrobitnytstvi, 1945-1970 rr. Kyïv, 1972. pp. 292.

- Relations (general) with Iran

SHAMIDE (ALI ISMAILOVICH) Lenin i Iran. Baku 1970. pp. 78. bibliog.

- Relations (general) with Israel

ANTIKOMMUNIZM i antisovetizm - professiia sionistov. Moskva, 1971. pp. 128. Collected newspaper articles.

SIONIZM - orudie imperialisticheskoi reaktsii. Moskva, 1971. pp. 79. Articles first published in various journals.

SEMENIUK (VLADIMIR ANDREEVICH) Zloveshchii al'ians. Minsk, 1972. pp. 134.

- Relations (general) with Latin America

SIZONENKO (ALEKSANDR IVANOVICH) Ocherki istorii sovetsko-latinoamerikanskikh otnoshenii, 1924-1970 gg. Moskva, 1971. pp. 204. bibliog.

KOROLEV (NIKOLAI VASIL'EVICH) Strany Iuzhnoi Ameriki i Rossiia, 1890-1917 gg.; pod redaktsiei... N.A. Mokhova. Kishinev, 1972. pp. 180.

- Relations (general) with Norway

MAURSETH (PER) Fra Moskvateser til Kristianiaforslag: Det norske Arbeiderparti og Komintern fra 1921 til februar 1923. Oslo, [1972]. pp. 215. bibliog.

- Relations (general) with other countries

OZEROV (LEONID STEPANOVICH) Stroitel'stvo sotsializma v SSSR i mezhdunarodnaia proletarskaia solidarnost', 1921-1937 gg. Moskva, 1972. pp. 236.

- Relations (general) with Scandinavia

DASHKOV (IURII FEDOROVICH) Po leninskim mestam Skandinavii: zhurnalistskii poisk. Moskva, 1971. pp. 239.

- Relations (general) with Spain

PROBLEMY ispanskoi istorii. Moskva, 1971. pp. 399.

- Relations (general) with the East (Near East)

IDEI Lenina i razvitie progressivnoi mysli narodov Vostoka: Iran, Turtsiia, Irak. Baku, 1970. pp. 193. Some articles in Azerbaijani.

- Relations (general) with the United States

VEL'TOV (NIKOLAI) Uspekhi sotsializma v SSSR i ikh vliianie na SShA; pod redaktsiei N.N.Iakovleva. Moskva, 1971. pp. 215. bibliog.

TSVETKOV (GLEB NIKOLAEVICH) Politika SShA v otnoshenii SSSR nakanune voiny. Kiev, 1973. pp. 192.

- Religion

MEL'GUNOV (SERGEI PETROVICH) Religiozno-obshchestvennye dvizheniia XVII-XVIII v.v. v Rossii. Moskva, 1922. pp. 194.

VALENTINOV (ALEKSANDR A.) compiler. Chernaia kniga "Shturm nebes": sbornik dokumental'nykh dannykh, kharakterizuiushchikh bor'bu sovetskoi kommunisticheskoi vlasti protiv vsiakoi religii, protiv vsekh ispovedanii i tserkvei;... s vvodnoi stat'ei Petra Struve, etc. Parizh, 1925. pp. 295.

PRICHINY sushchestvovaniia i puti preodoleniia religioznykh perezhitkov: na materialakh Moskvy i Moskovskoi oblasti. Moskva, 1963. pp. 195.

OKHRIMENKO (IURII MUSIIOVYCH) Krytyka khrystyians'kykh pohliadiv na osobu. Kyïv, 1964. pp. 174. With Russian summary.

RUSSIA - Religion (Cont'd.)

PROKOF'EV (VASILII IVANOVICH) Kodeks kommunisticheskoi morali i religioznaia "nravstvennost'" Moskva, 1964. pp. 113.

VOPROSY formirovaniia nauchno-ateisticheskikh vzgliadov. Moskva, 1964. pp. 108.

ANDRIANOV (NIKOLAI PAVLOVICH) and others. Osobennosti sovremennogo religioznogo soznaniia. Moskva, 1966. pp. 247.

OSIPOV (ALEKSANDR ALEKSANDROVICH) Zhenshchina pod krestom: stat'i, besedy, razmyshleniia. Leningrad, 1966. pp. 214.

SHTIUKA (VLADIMIR GEORGIEVICH) Byt i religiia. Moskva, 1966. pp. 62. bibliog.

SAFRONOV (IURII NIKOLAEVICH) Obshchestvennoe mnenie i religioznye traditsii. Moskva, 1970. pp. 144.

ATEIZM i sotsialisticheskaia kul'tura. Moskva, 1971. pp. 133.

LISAVTSEV (EMILII IVANOVICH) Kritika burzhuaznoi fal'sifikatsii polozheniia religii v SSSR. Moskva, 1971. pp. 278. bibliog.

MEDLIN (WILLIAM K.) and PATRINELIS (CHRISTOS G.) Renaissance influences and religious reforms in Russia: Western and post-Byzantine impacts on culture and education, 16th-17th centuries. Geneva, 1971. pp. 181. bibliog.

MOLODEZH' i ateizm. Moskva, 1971. pp. 148. bibliog.

ROTHENBERG (JOSHUA) The Jewish religion in the Soviet Union. New York, [1971]. pp. 242.

IABLOKOV (IGOR' NIKOLAEVICH) Metodologicheskie problemy sotsiologii religii. Moskva, 1972. pp. 132.

LASKOVAIA (MARINA PAVLOVNA) Bogoiskatel'stvo i bogostroitel'stvo prezhde i teper'. Moskva, 1972. pp. 110

LUNACHARSKII (ANATOLII VASIL'EVICH) A.V. Lunacharskii ob ateizme i religii: sbornik statei, pisem i drugikh materialov. Moskva, 1972. pp. 508.

VAKHABOV (ABDULA) Islam in the USSR. Moscow, 1972. pp. 139.

FLETCHER (WILLIAM C.) Religion and Soviet foreign policy, 1945-1970. London, 1973. pp. 179. bibliog.

- Rural conditions

SHCHEPETOV (KONSTANTIN NIKANOROVICH) Iz zhizni krepostnykh krest'ian Rossii XVIII-XIX vekov: po materialam Sheremetevskikh votchin. Moskva, 1963. pp. 100. bibliog.

LEKHOVA (ZINAIDA NAUMOVNA) Potrebitel'skaia kooperatsiia i sblizhenie urovnei zhizni sel'skogo i gorodskogo naseleniia. Moskva, 1969. pp. 128.

IAKUSHOV (ANTON IVANOVICH) Preodolenie sushchestvennykh razlichii mezhdu gorodom i derevnei. Moskva, 1971. pp. 231

SHKURKO (VALENTIN NIKOLAEVICH) Problemy formirovaniia vsestoronne razvitoi lichnosti kolkhoznika. Minsk, 1971. pp. 261.

EKONOMICHESKIE voprosy razvitiia byta na sele. Moskva, 1972. pp. 145.

LITVAK (BORIS GRIGOR'EVICH) Russkaia derevnia v reforme 1861 goda: chernozemnyi tsentr 1861-1895 gg. Moskva, 1972. pp. 423.

POTAPENKO (MIKHAIL SERGEEVICH) Partiinaia rabota v derevne, 1924-1925 gg. Moskva, 1972. pp. 95.

SAZONOV (NIKOLAI IVANOVICH) Zmina sotsial'noï pryrody selianstva SRSR: metodolohichni i teoretychni pytannia doslidzhennia zminy sotsial'noï pryrody i sotsial'noho oblychchia kolhospnoho selianstva. Kharkiv, 1972. pp. 250. bibliog.

· Social conditions

EVSEEV (V.P.) ed. Sotsial'no-klassovye problemy razvitiia sotsialisticheskogo obshchestva: sbornik statei. Moskva, 1969. pp. 188.

FILOSOFIIA ta sotsiolohiia: materialy naukovoï konferentsiï aspirantiv ta molodykh naukovtsiv Instytutu filosofiï. Kyïv, 1969. pp. 254.

SOTSIAL'NYE razlichiia i ikh preodolenie: sotsiologicheskie issledovaniia. vyp 3. Sverdlovsk, 1969. pp. 158.

AMALRIK (ANDREI ALEKSEEVICH) L'Union soviétique survivra-t-elle en 1984?; [translated from the Russian by] Michel Tatu; préface de Alain Besançon. [Paris, 1970]. pp. 118.

REDLIKH (ROMAN N.) Stalinshchina kak dukhovnyi fenomen: ocherki bol'shevizmovedeniia. kniga 1. [2nd ed.] Frankfurt-am-Main, Posev, [1970]. pp. 251. 1st ed. (of which this is the 2nd ed. of the 1st part) had title: Ocherki bol'shevizmovedeniia.

ANUFRIEV (EVGENII ALEKSANDROVICH) Sotsial'naia rol' i aktivnost' lichnosti. Moskva, 1971. pp. 152.

BAGMET (NIKOLAI STEPANOVICH) ed. V.I. Lenin i formuvannia komunistychnykh suspil'nykh vidnosyn. Kyïv, 1971. pp. 251.

CHIKHICHIN (I.N.) ed. Sotsial'no-klassovaia struktura i politicheskaia organizatsiia sotsialisticheskogo obshchestva. Saratov, 1971. pp. 143.

LEBEDEV (BORIS KONSTANTINOVICH) Sotsial'nyi tip lichnosti: teoreticheskii ocherk. Kazan', 1971. pp. 63.

AGENTSTVO PECHATI NOVOSTI. USSR 50: Novosti Press Agency year book. Moscow, 1972. pp. 335.

AMVROSOV (ANATOLII ALEKSEEVICH) Ot klassovoi differentsiatsii k sotsial'noi odnorodnosti obshchestva. Moskva, 1972. pp. 271.

BALLER (ELEAZAR ALEKSANDROVICH) Chelovek i svoboda. Moskva, 1972. pp. 283.

BUSLOV (KAZIMIR PAVLOVICH) Sotsial'noe edinstvo, protivorechiia, otvetstvennost'. Minsk, 1972. pp. 171.

HAXTHAUSEN (AUGUST VON) Freiherr. Studies on the interior of Russia; edited and with an introduction by S. Frederick Starr; translated by Eleanore L.M. Schmidt. Chicago, 1972. pp. 328.

MATTHEWS (MERVYN) Class and society in Soviet Russia. London, [1972]. pp. 366. bibliog.

MEISSNER (BORIS) ed. Social change in the Soviet Union: Russia's path toward an industrial society;...translated by Donald P. Kommers. Notre Dame, Indiana, [1972]. pp. 247. (Notre Dame. University. Committee on International Relations. International Studies)

NOGEE (JOSEPH L.) ed. Man, state, and society in the Soviet Union. London, 1972. pp. 599. bibliog.

PARKER (WILLIAM HENRY) The superpowers: the United States and the Soviet Union compared. London, 1972. pp. 347.

SHARIIA (KARL SPIRIDONOVICH) Nekotorye voprosy razvitiia sotsialisticheskikh obshchestvennykh otnoshenii v period stroitel'stva kommunizma. Tbilisi, 1972. pp. 75.

SPASIBENKO (SVETLANA GEORGIEVNA) Lichnost' i sotsializm. Moskva, 1972. pp. 182.

SUTIAGIN (VASILII SERGEEVICH) and SUTIAGIN (ANDREI SERGEEVICH) Osobennosti protivorechii v sotsialisticheskom obshchestve i puti ikh preodoleniia. Moskva, 1972. pp. 207.

HOLLANDER (PAUL) Soviet and American society: a comparison. New York, 1973. pp. 476. bibliog.

ROSITZKE (HARRY A.) The USSR today. London, [1973]. pp. 114.

- Social history

V.I. Lenin i nekotorye voprosy izmeneniia sotsial'noi struktury sovetskogo obshchestva v perekhodnyi period. Moskva, 1973. pp. 280.

- Social life and customs

DOMOSTROI; [reprint of the 1882 edition with] introduction by W.F.Ryan. Letchworth, 1971. pp. 202. A reprint of Imperatorskoe Obshchestvo Istorii i Drevnostei Rossiiskikh: text in original script.

AASAMAA (IINA) Kak sebia vesti; (perevod s estonskogo). Tallin, 1971. pp. 222.

GOR'KII (MAKSIM) pseud. [i.e. Aleksei Maksimovich PESHKOV] Fragments from my diary; translated by Moura Budberg; [an expanded version of the English translation of 1940]. London, 1972. pp. 265.

KENNAN (GEORGE FROST) The Marquis de Custine and his Russia in 1839. London, 1972. pp. 145. (Oxford. University. All Souls College. Chichele Lectures. 1969)

KULAZHNIKOV (MIKHAIL NIKITICH) Pravo, traditsii i obychai v sovetskom obshchestve. Rostov-na-Donu, 1972. pp. 175. bibliog.

PEN'KOV (EVGENII MIKHAILOVICH) Sotsial'nye normy - reguliatory povedeniia lichnosti: nekotorye voprosy metodologii i teorii. Moskva, 1972. pp. 198.

SOVETSKII etiket. Leningrad, 1972. pp. 158.

- Social policy

AVERBAKH (LEOPOL'D LEONIDOVICH) Na putiakh kul'turnoi revoliutsii. 3rd ed. Moskva, 1929. pp. 198. Xerographic reprint.

RUSSIA (U.S.S.R.) 1967. The Union of Soviet Socialist Republics. (ST/SOA/75). New York, United Nations, 1967. pp. 78. (Department of Economic and Social Affairs. Organization and Administration of Social Welfare Programmes: A Series of Country Studies)

AFANAS'EV (VIKTOR GRIGOR'EVICH) ed. Nauchnoe upravlenie obshchestvom. vyp.4. Moskva, 1970. pp. 351.

KOGAN (LEV NAUMOVICH) Sotsial'noe planirovanie: rabota, obrazovanie, byt; o plane sotsial'nogo razvitiia kollektiva predpriiatiia. Moskva, 1970. pp. 87.

NAUCHNO-ISSLEDOVATEL'SKII INSTITUT KOMPLEKSNYKH SOTSIAL'NYKH ISSLEDOVANII. Uchenye Zapiski. vyp.7. Chelovek i obshchestvo: problemy sotsial'nogo planirovaniia; pod obshchei redaktsiei...B.G. Anan'eva, etc. Leningrad, 1970. pp. 109.

ERMOLAEV (IVAN DMITRIEVICH) Zakony razvitiia obshchestva i stroitel'stvo kommunizma. Moskva, 1971. pp. 224.

IVANOV (VLADIMIR GEORGIEVICH) Kollektiv i lichnost'. Leningrad, 1971. pp. 120.

NOVIKOV (P.G.) ed. Obshchestvenno-politicheskie preobrazovaniia pri sotsializme. Moskva, 1971. pp. 148.

SMIRNOV (GEORGII LUKICH) Sovetskii chelovek: formirovanie sotsialisticheskogo tipa lichnosti. Moskva, 1971. pp. 376.

AFANAS'EV (VIKTOR GRIGOR'EVICH) ed. Nauchnoe upravlenie obshchestvom. vyp.6. Moskva, 1972. pp. 408.

GROMOV (IGOR' ALEKSANDROVICH) and others. Sotsiologicheskaia laboratoriia na predpriiatii: iz opyta raboty laboratorii sotsiologicheskikh issledovanii Kirovskogo zavoda. Leningrad, 1972. pp. 74.

LUZAN (PETR PAVLOVICH) Planirovanie sotsial'nogo razvitiia proizvodstvennogo kollektiva. Moskva, 1972. pp. 206.

ON the road to communism: essays on Soviet domestic and foreign politics; [mainly revised versions of papers read at the sixth annual Bi-State Slavic Conference (Kansas-Missouri), 1967]; edited by Roger E. Kanet and Ivan Volgyes. Lawrence, [1972]. pp. 209.

PROBLEMY sovremennoi ideologicheskoi bor'by, razvitiia sotsialisticheskoi ideologii i kul'tury: materialy nauchnoi konferentsii... 29 sentiabria - 1 oktiabria 1971 g. Moskva, 1972. pp. 207.

PUTI formirovaniia sotsial'noi aktivnosti lichnosti pri sotsializme. Moskva, 1972. pp. 141. bibliog.

RIABOV (DMITRII DMITRIEVICH) Sotsialisticheskoe gosudarstvo i vospitanie novogo cheloveka; pod redaktsiei... S.I. Nikishova. Moskva, 1972. pp. 202.

SOTSIAL'NI problemy upravlinnia sotsialistychnym suspil'stvom. Kyïv, 1972. pp. 315. With Russian summary and table of contents.

AFANAS'EV (VIKTOR GRIGOR'EVICH) Nauchnoe upravlenie obshchestvom: opyt sistemnogo issledovaniia. 2nd ed. Moskva, 1973. pp. 392.

RUSSIA - Social policy (Cont'd.)

SMIRNOV (GEORGII LUKICH) Soviet man: the making of a socialist type of personality; (translated from the Russian by Robert Daglish). Moscow, [1973]. pp. 306.

- Statistics

RUSSIA (U.S.S.R.). Tsentral'noe Statisticheskoe Upravlenie. 1969. Soviet Union 50 years: statistical returns. Moscow, 1969. pp. 343.

RUSSIA (U.S.S.R.). Tsentral'noe Statisticheskoe Upravlenie. 1970. SSSR i zarubezhnye strany posle pobedy Velikoi Oktiabr'skoi sotsialisticheskoi revoliutsii: statisticheskii sbornik. Moskva, 1970. pp. 319.

SOVIET economic statistics: [papers of a conference held at Duke University in November 1969]; (Vladimir G. Treml and John P. Hardt, editors). Durham, N.C., 1972. pp. 457.

MICKIEWICZ (ELLEN PROPPER) ed. Handbook of Soviet social science data. New York, [1973]. pp. 225.

- Statistics - Bibliography

RUSSIA (U.S.S.R.). Komitet po Pechati. 1971. Annotirovannyi katalog knig izdatel'stva "Statistika", 1966-1970 gg. Moskva, 1971. pp. 423.

- Statistics, Vital

DARSKII (LEONID EVSEEVICH) Formirovanie sem'i: demografo-statisticheskoe issledovanie. Moskva, 1972. pp. 208. bibliog.

- Territorial expansion

BASHARIN (GEORGII PROKOP'EVICH) Nekotorye voprosy istoriografii vkhozhdeniia Sibiri v sostav Rossii. Iakutsk, 1971. pp. 135.

PREOBRAZHENSKII (ALEKSANDR ALEKSANDROVICH) Ural i Zapadnaia Sibir' v kontse XVI - nachale XVIII veka. Moskva, 1972. pp. 392.

- Verkhovnyi Sovet

MITSKEVICH (ALEKSEI VALENTINOVICH) Akty vysshikh organov Sovetskogo gosudarstva: iuridicheskaia priroda normativnykh aktov vysshikh organov gosudarstvennoi vlasti i upravleniia SSSR. Moskva, 1967. pp. 175.

KRIVENKO (LIDIIA TARASOVNA) Postoiannye komissii Verkhovnykh Sovetov soiuznykh respublik. Moskva, 1970. pp. 142.

- Verkhovnyi Sovet - Biography

RUSSIA (U.S.S.R.). Verkhovnyi Sovet. 1970. Deputaty Verkhovnogo Soveta SSSR: vos'moi sozyv. Moskva, 1970. pp. 552.

- Verkhovnyi Sovet - Elections

GRIGOR'EV (VADIM KONSTANTINOVICH) Poriadok provedeniia vyborov v Verkhovnyi Sovet SSSR. Moskva, 1970. pp. 78.

- Verkhovnyi Sovet - Statistics

RUSSIA (U.S.S.R.). Verkhovnyi Sovet. Prezidium. Otdel po Voprosam Raboty Sovetov. 1970. Verkhovnyi Sovet SSSR vos'mogo sozyva: statisticheskii sbornik. Moskva, 1970. pp. 51.

- Yearbooks

EZHEGODNIK BOL'SHOI SOVETSKOI ENTSIKLOPEDIIA. a., 1957-1966 (vyp.[1]-10); 1972 (vyp.16)- Moskva.

RUSSIA (R.S.F.S.R.)

- Constitution

RUSSIA (R.S.F.S.R.). Constitution. 1971. Konstitutsiia (Osnovnoi Zakon) Rossiiskoi Sovetskoi Federativnoi Sotsialisticheskoi Respubliki: s izmeneniiami i dopolneniiami, priniatymi na vos'moi sessii Verkhovnogo Soveta RSFSR sed'mogo sozyva. Moskva, 1971. pp. 31.

- Description and travel

RUSSIAN Soviet Federative Socialist Republic. Moscow, 1972. pp. 126.

- Economic conditions

IUGO-Vostok Evropeiskoi chasti SSSR. Moskva, 1971. pp. 459. bibliog. (Akademiia Nauk SSSR. Institut Geografii. Prirodnye Usloviia i Estestvennye Resursy SSSR)

- Industries

KONIUKHOV (VASILII NIKOLAEVICH) Osushchestvlenie leninskoi idei industrializatsii v avtonomnykh respublikakh RSFSR; pod obshchei redaktsiei.. N.S. Shevtsova. Moskva, 1971. pp. 208.

- Politics and government

PARTIINO-gosudarstvennyi kontrol' v deistvii. Moskva, 1964. pp. 157.

RUSSIAN ESSAYS

NEKHAI (MIKHAIL VASIL'EVICH) Russkii demokraticheskii ocherk 60-kh godov XIX stoletiia: N. Uspenskii, V. Sleptsov, A. Levitov. Minsk, 1971. pp. 146. bibliog.

RUSSIAN LANGUAGE

SHVETS (ALLA VASIL'EVNA) Razgovornye konstruktsii v iazyke gazet. Kiev, 1971. pp. 95.

- Dictionaries

OZHEGOV (SERGEI IVANOVICH) compiler. Slovar' russkogo iazyka ...; pod redaktsiei ... N.Iu. Shvedovoi. 10th ed. Moskva, 1973. pp. 847. This 10th ed. is a new impression of the 9th rev. ed. of 1972.

- Dictionaries - English

WHEELER (MARCUS) The Oxford Russian-English dictionary. Oxford, 1972. pp. 918.

- Slang - Dictionaries

GALLER (MEYER) and MARQUESS (HARLAN E.) Soviet prison camp speech: a survivor's glossary, supplemented by terms from the works of A.I. Solženicyn. Madison, Wisc., 1972. pp. 216.

- Word frequency

SHTEINFELDT (E.) Russian word count: 2500 words most commonly used in modern literary Russian; guide for teachers of Russian. Moscow, [1969]. pp. 228.

RUSSIAN LANGUAGE IN ABKHAZIA

TARBA (BORIS GRIGOR'EVICH) Leninskaia natsional'naia politika i bilingvizm u abkhazov. Sukhumi, 1970. pp. 53.

RUSSIAN LETTERS

PIS'MA slavy i bessmertiia, 1905-1920 gody. Moskva, 1964. pp. 33-192.

RUSSIAN LITERATURE

- History and criticism

PANAEV (IVAN IVANOVICH) Literaturnye vospominaniia, i Vospominaniia o Belinskom. Sankt-peterburg, 1876. pp. 420.

AVERBAKH (LEOPOL'D LEONIDOVICH) Za proletarskuiu literaturu: o politike RKP/b/ v oblasti khudozhestvennoi literatury. Leningrad, 1925. pp. 91. Xerographic reprint.

AVERBAKH (LEOPOL'D LEONIDOVICH) Nashi literaturnye raznoglasiia. Leningrad, 1927. pp. 261. Xerographic reprint.

POLONSKII (VIACHESLAV PAVLOVICH) Marksizm i kritika: s prilozheniem stat'i G. Lelevicha "Otvet Viach. Polonskomu" i rezoliutsii TsK VKP/b/ o politike partii v ... khudozhestvennoi literature. Moskva, 1927. pp. 158. Xerographic reprint.

AVERBAKH (LEOPOL'D LEONIDOVICH) Kul'turnaia revoliutsiia i voprosy sovremennoi literatury. Moskva, 1928. pp. 143. 2 reports originally presented to MAPP and VAPP.

POLONSKII (VIACHESLAV PAVLOVICH) Literatura i obshchestvo: sbornik statei. Moskva, 1929. pp. 402. Xerographic reprint.

POLONSKII (VIACHESLAV PAVLOVICH) Ocherki literaturnogo dvizheniia revoliutsionnoi epokhi. 2nd ed. Moskva, 1929. pp. 339. bibliog. Xerographic reprint.

EL'SBERG (ZH.) Krizis poputchikov i nastroeniia intelligentsii. [Leningrad], 1930. pp. 253. Collected articles first published in Na literaturnom postu, 1926-29. Xerographic reprint.

S kem i pochemu my boremsia. Moskva, 1930. pp. 248. Articles from Na literaturnom postu. Xerographic reprint.

BUSH (VLADIMIR V.) Ocherki literaturnogo narodnichestva, 70-80 gg. Moskva, 1931. pp. 164. Xerographic reprint.

GLAGOLEV (NIKOLAI ALEKSANDROVICH) Problemy istorii russkoi demokraticheskoi kritiki. Moskva, 1966. pp. 142.

ANDREEV (IURII ANDREEVICH) Revoliutsiia i literatura: otobrazhenie Oktiabria i grazhdanskoi voiny v russkoi sovetskoi literature i stanovlenie sotsialisticheskogo realizma, 20-30-e gody. Leningrad, 1969. pp. 431.

RIURIKOV (BORIS SERGEEVICH) V.I. Lenin i voprosy literatury. Moskva, 1970. pp. 111.

VELENGURIN (NIKOLAI) Vsevolod Kochetov. Moskva, 1970. pp. 119.

CROSS (A.G.) N.M. Karamzin: a study of his literary career, 1783-1803. Carbondale, Ill., [1971]. pp. 306. bibliog.

SLAVINSKY (MICHEL) and STOLYPINE (DIMITRI) La vie littéraire en U.R.S.S. de 1934 à nos jours. [Paris, 1971]. pp. 260.

V.I. Lenin i khudozhestvennaia literatura. Minsk, 1971. pp. 253

VOLKOV (ANATOLII ANDREEVICH) A.M. Gor'kii i literaturnoe dvizhenie sovetskoi epokhi. 2nd ed. Moskva, 1971. pp. 575.

IDEOLOGICHESKAIA bor'ba v literature i estetike sbornik statei. Moskva, 1972. pp. 335.

LUKÁCS (GEORG) Marxist. Studies in European realism: a sociological survey of the writings of Balzac, Stendhal, Zola, Tolstoy, Gorki and others. London, 1972. pp. 277.

RUSSIA: essays in history and literature; [lectures delivered at Washington University, 1967-1969]; edited by Lyman H. Legters. Leiden, 1972. pp. 164.

THOMSON (BORIS) The premature revolution: Russian literature and society, 1917-1946. London, [1972]. pp. 325. bibliog.

TVARDOVSKII (ALEKSANDR TRIFONOVICH) Stat'i i zametki o literature. 3rd ed. Moskva, 1972. pp. 295.

RUSSIAN NEWSPAPERS

"POSLEDNIE novosti" 27 aprelia, 1920-1930 gg. [Paris, 1930]. pp 64, xxx.

AKBAROV (ADKHAM IBRAGIMOVICH) Rol' gazety "Pravda" v pobede sotsialisticheskoi revoliutsii v Turkestane. Tashkent, 1968. pp. 304. bibliog.

LENINSKAIA "Iskra" i mestnye partiinye organizatsii Rossii, 1900-1903 gg. Perm', 1971. pp. 530. bibliog.

SHVETS (ALLA VASIL'EVNA) Razgovornye konstruktsii v iazyke gazet. Kiev. 1971. pp. 95.

KUZNETSOV (IVAN VASIL'EVICH) and FINGERIT (EFIM MARKOVICH) Gazetnyi mir Sovetskogo Soiuza, 1917-1970 gg. Moskva, 1972 in progress.

LOGINOV (VLADLEN TERENT'EVICH) Leninskaia "Pravda", 1912-1914 gg. Moskva, 1972. pp. 408.

SALADKAŬ (TSIMAFEI ERAFEEVICH) Bol'shevistskaia gazeta "Pravda" v Belorussii, 1912-1917 gg. 2nd ed. Minsk, 1972. pp. 296. For 1st White Russian ed. see his Bal'shavitskaia hazeta "Pravda" ŭ Belarusi, 1912-1917 hh.

VERKHOVSKAIA (ALLA ISAAKOVNA) Pis'mo v redaktsiiu i chitatel'. Moskva, 1972. pp. 192.

- Bibliography

RUSSIA (U.S.S.R.). Vsesoiuznaia Knizhnaia Palata. 1970- Gazety SSSR, 1917-1960: bibliograficheskii spravochnik. Moskva, 1970 in progress.

RUSSIANS

See also NATIONAL CHARACTERISTICS, RUSSIAN

RUSSIANS IN BULGARIA

SLAVICH (VALERIAN VECHESLAVOVICH) Ispoved' smenovekhovtsa. Sofiia, 1924. pp. 152.

RUSSIANS IN CHINA

KAZANIN (MARK ISAAKOVICH) V shtabe Bliukhera: vospominaniia o Kitaiskoi revoliutsii 1925-1927 godov. Moskva, 1966. pp. 167.

KOZLOV (NIKOLAI GRIGOR'EVICH) V nebe Kitaia: vospominaniia letchika. Moskva, 1966. pp. 54.

KARTUNOVA (ANASTASIIA IVANOVNA) V.K. Bliukher v Kitae, 1924-1927 gg.: dokumentirovannyi ocherk; dokumenty. Moskva, 1970. pp. 184.

CHEREPANOV (ALEKSANDR IVANOVICH) Zapiski voennogo sovetnika v Kitae, 1925-1927. 2nd ed. Moskva, 1971. pp. 311.

VISHNIAKOVA-AKIMOVA (VERA VLADIMIROVNA) Two years in revolutionary China, 1925-1927;... translated by Stephen I. Levine. Cambridge, Mass., 1971. pp. 352. (Harvard University. East Asian Research Center. Harvard East Asian Monographs. 40)

RUSSIANS IN FINLAND

SUVOROV (P.) The Finnish question: equal rights; the position of Russians in Finland and of Finns in the rest of the Russian Empire. St. Pétersbourg, 1910. pp. 60.

RUSSIANS IN FOREIGN COUNTRIES

CHASTNOE SOVESHCHANIE CHLENOV VSEROSSIISKOGO UCHREDITEL'NOGO SOBRANIIA. Ispolnitel'naia Komissiia. Biulleten'. No.1. Parizh, 1921. pp. 43.

KARTASHEV (A.V.) Zadachi, kharakter i programma Russkogo Natsional'nogo Ob"edineniia: doklad S"ezdu Russkogo Natsional'nogo Ob"edineniia v Parizhe 5-12 iiunia 1921 g. Paris, 1921. pp. 32.

LOKHVITSKII (I.A.) To, chto bylo.... Berlin, 1922. pp. 63.

VETLUGIN (A.) pseud. [i.e. Vladimir Il'ich RYNDZIUN] Geroi i voobrazhaemye portrety. Berlin, 1922. pp. 247.

KHMAR (S.) ed. Otkrovennoe raskaianie. Shankhai, 1928. pp. 162. Cover has title: Avantiuristy-Operputy.

ZHORDANIIA (NOI NIKOLAEVICH) Nashi raznoglasiia. Parizh, 1928. pp. 48.

"POSLEDNIE novosti" 27 aprelia, 1920-1930 gg. [Paris, 1930]. pp. 64, xxx.

ARTSIUK (EVGENII) Mysli o griadushchei osvobozhdennoi Rossii i estestvennye zakony natsionalizma. [Paris, 1939?]. pp. 80.

ARONSON (GREGOR) Pravda o vlasovtsakh: problemy novoi emigratsii. N'iu Iork, 1949. pp. 95. Collected articles.

FEVR (NIKOLAI) Solntse voskhodit na zapade. [pt.1]. Buenos-Aires, 1950. pp. 287.

SOIUZ ANDREEVSKOGO FLAGA. Otchet informatsionnoi konferentsii V/politicheskoi organizatsii SAF, sostoiavsheisia 12 fevralia 1950 g. Münchеn, [1950?]. pp. 22.

SOIUZ BYVSHIKH POLITZAKLIUCHENNYKH IZ SSSR. Ne zabud' nas!: miting Soiuza... v g. Miunkhene 28 marta 1955 goda; kontslager' segodnia; rezul'taty amnistii 1953 g. [Miunkhen], 1955. pp. 32.

PAMIATKA emigranta kak uberech' sebia ot sovetskoi agentury. Miunkhen, 1956. pp. 20.

SOIUZ BOR'BY ZA OSVOBOZHDENIE NARODOV ROSSII. S"ezd, 4-yi, 1956. 4-yi s"ezd Soiuza Bor'by za Osvobozhdenie Narodov Rossii (SBONR), 17-22 fevralia 1956 goda. Miunkhen, [1956]. pp. 80.

SHATOV (MIKHAIL VASIL'EVICH) compiler. Materialy i dokumenty Osvoboditel'nogo Dvizheniia Narodov Rossii v gody Vtoroi mirovoi voiny, 1941-1965; Materials and documents of the Liberation Movement of the Peoples of Russia in World War II. N'iu Iork, 1966. pp. 176. (Russkaia Osvoboditel'naia Armiia. Arkhiv v N'iu Iorke. Trudy. t.2). Introduction and 2 documents in English.

ARSEN'EV (IURII MIKHAILOVICH) Lenin i sotsial-demokraticheskaia emigratsiia, 1900-1904 gg. Moskva, 1971. pp. 366.

NASHA dan' Bestuzhevskim kursam: vospominaniia byvshikh bestuzhevok za rubezhom. Parizh, 1971. pp. 175.

IAKUSHINA (ANTONINA PAVLOVNA) Lenin i zagranichnaia organizatsiia RSDRP, 1905-1917. Moskva, 1972. pp. 399.

- Bibliography

FOSTER (LUDMILA A.) compiler. Bibliografiia russkoi zarubezhnoi literatury, 1918-1968; Bibliography of Russian émigré literature, 1918-1968. Boston, Mass., 1970. 2 vols. Bibliography in Russian, editorial matter in English and Russian.

RUSSIANS IN FRANCE

MILIUKOV (PAVEL NIKOLAEVICH) Tri platformy Respublikansko-Demokraticheskikh Ob"edinenii, 1922-24 gg.: politicheskii kommentarii P.N. Miliukova, s prilozheniem sravnitel'nogo teksta platform 1924, 1923, 1922 gg. Paris, 1925. pp. 63.

KAGANOVA (RAISA IUL'EVNA) Lenin vo Frantsii, dekabr' 1908 - iiun' 1912: revoliutsioner, teoretik, organizator. Moskva, 1972. pp. 430. bibliog.

PAROT'KIN (I.V.) ed. Protiv obshchego vraga: sovetskie liudi vo frantsuzskom dvizhenii Soprotivleniia. Moskva, 1972. pp. 395.

- Bibliography

BEYSSAC (MICHELE) La vie culturelle de l'émigration russe en France: chronique, 1920-1930. Paris, 1971. pp. 339. (Clermont-Ferrand. Université. Faculté des Lettres et Sciences Humaines. [Publications]. 2e Série. Fasc. 32)

RUSSIANS IN GERMANY

WILLIAMS (ROBERT CHADWELL) Culture in exile: Russian émigrés in Germany, 1881-1941. Ithaca, N.Y., 1972. pp. 404. bibliog.

RUSSIANS IN HUNGARY

RUSSKIE internatsionalisty v bor'be za Vengerskuiu Sovetskuiu Respubliku 1919 g.: sbornik dokumentov. Moskva, 1972. pp. 255.

RUSSIANS IN ITALY

LO GATTO (ETTORE) Russi in Italia, dal secolo XVII ad oggi. Roma, 1971. pp. 332.

RUSSIANS IN KIRGHIZIA

DANIIAROV (SANZHARBEK SEITOVICH) O progressivnom znachenii russkoi kul'tury v razvitii kul'tury kirgizskogo naroda v kontse XIX i nachale XX vekov. Frunze, 1964. pp. 59.

RUSSIANS IN NORTH AMERICA

FEDOROVA (SVETLANA GRIGOR'EVNA) Russkoe naselenie Aliaski i Kalifornii, konets XVIII veka - 1867 g.; The Russian population in Alaska and California, late 18th century - 1867. Moskva, 1971. pp. 275. With English table of contents.

RUSSIANS IN YAKUTIA

BIRKENGOF (ANDREI L'VOVICH) Potomki zemleprokhodtsev: vospominaniia-ocherki o russkikh porechanakh nizov'ev i del'ty reki Indigirki. Moskva, 1972. pp. 222. bibliog.

RUSSIANS IN YUGOSLAVIA

DAVATTS (VLADIMIR KHRISTIANOVICH) Gody: ocherki piatiletnei bor'by; s prilozheniem polnogo spiska znamen i regalii Russkoi Armii, khraniashchikhsia v russkoi tserkvi v Belgrade. Belgrad, 1926. pp. 239.

RUSSO-TURKISH WAR, 1877-1878

ULUNIAN (AKOP ARUTIUNOVICH) Bolgarskii narod i russko-turetskaia voina 1877-1878 gg. Moskva, 1971. pp. 205. bibliog.

RUTHENIA

- History

SLYVKA (IURII IURIIOVYCH) Pidstupy mizhnarodnoï reaktsiï na Zakarpatti v 1938-1939 rr. L'viv, 1966. pp. 70.

- Politics and government

BIELOUSOV (VIKTOR IVANOVYCH) Roky vyprobuvan' i hart'u: z istoriï zakarpats'koï komunistychnoï orhanizatsiï 1929-1932 rr. Uzhhorod, 1962. pp. 87.

RYNDZIUN (VLADIMIR IL'ICH)

See VETLUGIN (A.) ps.

SAAR QUESTION

BALK (THEODOR) Hier spricht die Saar: ein Land wird interviewt. Zürich, [1934]. pp. 176.

SAARLAND

- Economic conditions

MUELLER (JOSEF HEINZ) and others. Problèmes de la structure économique de la Sarre. Luxembourg, [European Coal and Steel Community], 1967. pp. 194. (Collection d'Economie et Politique Régionale. 2. Programmes de Développement et de Conversion. 9)

- Economic policy

MUELLER (JOSEF HEINZ) and others. Problèmes de la structure économique de la Sarre. Luxembourg, [European Coal and Steel Community], 1967. pp. 194. (Collection d'Economie et Politique Régionale. 2. Programmes de Développement et de Conversion. 9)

- Industries

MUELLER (JOSEF HEINZ) and others. Problèmes de la structure économique de la Sarre. Luxembourg, [European Coal and Steel Community], 1967. pp. 194. (Collection d'Economie et Politique Régionale. 2. Programmes de Développement et de Conversion. 9)

- Officials and employees

SAARGEBIET. Statistisches Amt. Einzelschriften zur Statistik des Saarlandes. Nr. 37. Personalstrukturuntersuchung im öffentlichen Dienst 1968. Saarbrücken, 1972. pp. 273.

- Politics and government

BALK (THEODOR) Hier spricht die Saar: ein Land wird interviewt. Zürich, [1934]. pp. 176.

- Population

SAARGEBIET. Statistisches Amt. Einzelschriften zur Statistik des Saarlandes. Nr. 36. Gemeindestatistik 1970: Bevölkerung und Erwerbstätigkeit: Ergebnisse der Volks- und Berufszählung am 27. Mai 1970. Saarbrücken, 1972. pp. 135.

SABA

- Emigration and immigration

CRANE (JULIA GORHAM) Educated to emigrate: the social organization of Saba. Assen, 1971. pp. 269. bibliog.

- Social conditions

CRANE (JULIA GORHAM) Educated to emigrate: the social organization of Saba. Assen, 1971. pp. 269. bibliog.

- Social life and customs

CRANE (JULIA GORHAM) Educated to emigrate: the social organization of Saba. Assen, 1971. pp. 269. bibliog.

SABOTAGE

- Russia

MOLOTOV (VIACHESLAV MIKHAILOVICH) Die Lehren der Schädlingsarbeit... der japanisch-deutsch-trotzkistischen Agenten:... enthält den Bericht... auf dem Plenum des ZK der KPdSU(B) am 28. Februar 1937, etc. Strasbourg, [1937]. pp. 67.

SABREVOIS DE BLEURY (CLEMENT CHARLES)

[LEBLANC DE MARCONNAY (H.)] La petite clique dévoilée; [ou], Quelques explications sur les manoeuvres dirigées contre la minorité patriote, qui prit part au vote sur les subsides dans la session de 1835 à 1836, et plus particulièrement contre C.C. Sabrevois de Bleury, etc. Rome, N.Y., 1836; Montréal, 1969. pp. 50.

SACCO (NICOLA)

CANNON (JAMES PATRICK) Notebook of an agitator. 2nd ed. New York, 1973. pp. 369. A reprint of the 1st ed. with the addition of an index and illustrations.

SACRIFICE

GIRARD (RENE) La violence et le sacré. Paris, [1972]. pp. 453. bibliog.

SADE (DONATIEN ALPHONSE FRANÇOIS DE) Marquis

BARTHES (ROLAND) Sade, Fourier, Loyola. Paris, [1971]. pp. 191.

SAFETY EDUCATION, INDUSTRIAL

INDUSTRIAL TRAINING SERVICE. Safety training needs and facilities in one industry: an accident prevention survey commissioned by the Department of Employment and carried out in the paper and boardmaking industry. London, H.M.S.O., 1973. pp. 76. bibliog.

SAINT-ETIENNE

- Politics and government

LOIRE. Préfecture. Etude sur un regroupement des communes de la vallée de l'Ondaine: La Ricamarie, Le Chambon-Feugerolles, Firminy, Fraisses et Unieux. [Saint-Etienne], 1971. fo. 127.

MONTBRISON. Sous-Préfecture. Etude pour un projet de regroupement communal: Andrezieux-Bouthéon, Bonson, Saint Cyprien, Saint-Just-sur-Loire, Saint-Rambert-sur-Loire. [Montbrison], 1971. pp. 140.

SAINT-FONS

- Schools

GROUPE DE SOCIOLOGIE URBAINE. Evolution des effectifs scolaires de la commune de St. Fons, 1968-1985; [by] A. Chazalette [and] E. Lacoin. Lyon, 1971. fo. 16, (36).

ST. GALL (CANTON)

- Economic history

WALDER (EMIL) Die Geschichte des Handelsbankwesens in St. Gallen: Beitrag zur praktischen Bankpolitik. St.Gallen, 1913. pp. 260.

ST. JOHN, NEW BRUNSWICK

- Civic improvement

SAINT JOHN, NEW BRUNSWICK. Town Planning Commission. Comprehensive community plan, St. John, New Brunswick: implementation; [survey by] Proctor, Redfern, Bousfield and Bacon. [Toronto], 1970. pp. 55.

ST. LAWRENCE RIVER

RICHARDSON (RONALD E.) and others. Developing water resources: the St. Lawrence Seaway and the Columbia/Peace power projects. Toronto, [1969]. pp. 113. bibliog.

INTERNATIONAL JOINT COMMISSION, CANADA AND UNITED STATES. Pollution of Lake Erie, Lake Ontario and the international section of the St. Lawrence river. [Ottawa, Information Canada, 1970 or rather 1971]. pp. 105.

- Maps

SIMPSON (WENDY) Gulf of St Lawrence: water uses and related activities: a cartographic presentation; Golfe Saint-Laurent: utilisations des eaux et activités connexes: représentation cartographique. Ottawa, 1973. pp. 22. bibliog. (Canada. Lands Directorate. Geographical Papers. No.53) In English and French.

SAINT LUCIA

- Economic conditions

DISEASE and economic development: the impact of parasitic diseases in St. Lucia; [by] Burton A. Weisbrod [and others]. Madison, 1973. pp. 218. bibliog.

- Social conditions

DISEASE and economic development: the impact of parasitic diseases in St. Lucia; [by] Burton A. Weisbrod [and others]. Madison, 1973. pp. 218. bibliog.

SAKHALIN

- History

STEPHAN (JOHN J.) Sakhalin: a history. Oxford, 1971. pp. 240. bibliog.

SALAN (RAOUL)

FIGUERAS (ANDRÉ) L'affaire du bazooka: (1957; qui a voulu tuer Salan?). Paris, [1970]. pp. 207.

SALARIED EMPLOYEES

THOMAS (ALBERT) and others. Angestellte und Arbeiter: Wandlungen in Wirtschaft und Gesellschaft: drei Vorträge gehalten auf dem 3. AfA-Gewerkschaftskongress in Hamburg 1928. Berlin, 1928. pp. 83.

- Germany

SCHUSSER (WALTER H.) Ein empirischer Beitrag zur Diskussion um die Abgrenzung von Arbeitern und Angestellten. [Erlangen, imprint, 1970?]. pp. 428. bibliog.

KRACAUER (SIEGFRIED) Die Angestellten: aus dem neuesten Deutschland; mit einer Rezension von Walter Benjamin. 2nd ed. Frankfurt am Main, 1971. pp. 129. bibliog.

STEINEBACH (NIKOLAUS) Die Gehaltsstruktur der Angestellten in der Bundesrepublik Deutschland. Berlin, [1973]. pp. 314. bibliog.

- Japan

VOGEL (EZRA FEIVEL) Japan's new middle class: the salary man and his family in a Tokyo suburb. 2nd ed. Berkeley, Calif., 1971. pp. 313. bibliog.

- United Kingdom

TRADES UNION CONGRESS. The TUC and the non-manual worker, 1972-73. London, [1973]. pp. 30.

- United States

SNYDER (CARL DEAN) b. 1921. White-collar workers and the UAW. Urbana, Ill., [1973]. pp. 197. bibliog.

SALAZAR (ANTONIO DE OLIVEIRA)

CAETANO (MARCELLO) A man: speech broadcast on 27 July 1970, on radio and television [Lisbon?], Secretaria de Estado da Informação e Turismo, 1970. pp. 8.

SALCEDO (MANUEL MARIA DE)

ALMARÁZ (FÉLIX D.) Tragic cavalier: Governor Manuel Salcedo of Texas, 1808-1813. Austin, Texas, [1971]. pp. 206. bibliog.

SALERNO (PROVINCE)

- **Economic conditions**

  BONAZZI (GIUSEPPE) and others. L'organizzazione della marginalità: industria e potere politico in una provincia meridionale. Torino, [1972]. pp. 494. (Turin. Università. Scuola di Amministrazione Industriale. Centro di Ricerche sull'Impresa e lo Sviluppo. [Stato e Prospettive dello Sviluppo Industriale in Italia]. 7) With summaries in various languages.

SALES

- **United Kingdom**

  ATIYAH (PATRICK SELIM) The sale of goods. 4th ed. London, 1971. pp. 356.

  LOWE (ROBERT) Solicitor. Sale of goods and hire-purchase. 2nd ed. Harmondsworth, 1972. pp. 285.

SALES TAX

- **India - Andhra Pradesh**

  NATIONAL COUNCIL OF APPLIED ECONOMIC RESEARCH. Review of sales tax in Andhra Pradesh. New Delhi, [1971]. pp. 129.

- **Russia**

  ABRAMOVA (N.I.) and others. Ischislenie naloga s oborota v otrasliakh promyshlennosti. Moskva, 1972. pp. 175.

- **United Kingdom**

  BRITISH FEDERATION OF MASTER PRINTERS. Purchase tax on printing. London, 1958. pp. 38.

SALFORD

- **Poor**

  MANCHESTER AND SALFORD TRADES COUNCIL. What the Trades Council wants to know: the slow murder of the unemployed. [Manchester, 1932]. pp. (4).

- **Social conditions**

  WHITE (EMILY E.) A history of the Manchester and Salford Council of Social Service, 1919-1969. Manchester, 1969. pp. 56.

SALINE WATER CONVERSION

FRIED (JEROME J.) and EDLUND (MILTON C.) Desalting technology for Middle Eastern agriculture: an economic case. New York, 1971. pp. 113.

U.K. Water Resources Board. 1972. Desalination, 1972. London, 1972. pp. 48.

SALISBURY, RHODESIA

- **Politics and government**

  RHODESIA. Greater Salisbury Local Authority Commission. 1970. Report: [Brian Porter, chairman]. [Salisbury], 1970. pp. 98. (Rhodesia. [Command Papers]. 1970. Cmd. R.R. 1)

SALMON

MILLS (DEREK) Salmon and trout: a resource, its ecology, conservation and management. Edinburgh, 1971. pp. 351.

SALMON-FISHERIES

- **Ireland (Republic)**

  O'CONNOR (ROBERT) and WHELAN (B.J.) An economic evaluation of Irish salmon fishing. Dublin, 1973 in progress. (Economic and Social Research Institute. Papers. No. 68)

SALOMON (WALTER HANS)

SALOMON (WALTER HANS) One man's view: an account of an individualist's crusade over twenty years on inflation, taxation, capitalism and liberty in the speeches and writing of Walter Salomon. Enfield, 1973. pp. 129.

SALT DEPOSITS

- **United Kingdom**

  NOTHOLT (ARTHUR JOHN GEORGE) and HIGHLEY (D.E.) Salt. London, H.M.S.O., 1973. pp. 36. bibliog. (Mineral Dossiers. No. 7)

SALT INDUSTRY AND TRADE

- **Germany**

  FREYDANK (HANNS) Die Hallesche Pfännerschaft. Halle/Saale, 1927-30. 2 vols. bibliog.

  SCHREMMER (ECKART) ed. Handelsstrategie und betriebswirtschaftliche Kalkulation im ausgehenden 18.Jahrhundert: der süddeutsche Salzmarkt; zeitgenössische quantitative Untersuchungen u.a. von Mathias Flurl und Joseph Ludwig Wolf. Wiesbaden, 1971. pp. 503. bibliog. (Bayerische Akademie der Wissenschaften. Historische Kommission. Deutsche Handelsakten des Mittelalters und der Neuzeit. Band 14)

- **United Kingdom**

  NOTHOLT (ARTHUR JOHN GEORGE) and HIGHLEY (D.E.) Salt. London, H.M.S.O., 1973. pp. 36. bibliog. (Mineral Dossiers. No. 7)

SALT MINES AND MINING

- **Germany**

  SCHREMMER (ECKART) ed. Handelsstrategie und betriebswirtschaftliche Kalkulation im ausgehenden 18.Jahrhundert: der süddeutsche Salzmarkt; zeitgenössische quantitative Untersuchungen u.a. von Mathias Flurl und Joseph Ludwig Wolf. Wiesbaden, 1971. pp. 503. bibliog. (Bayerische Akademie der Wissenschaften. Historische Kommission. Deutsche Handelsakten des Mittelalters und der Neuzeit. Band 14)

SALVADOR

- **Description and travel**

  SQUIER (EPHRAIM GEORGE) Notes on Central America: particularly the states of Honduras and San Salvador, their geography, topography, climate, population, resources, productions, etc., etc., and the proposed Honduras interoceanic railway;...(reprinted from the edition of 1855).' New York, 1971. pp. 397. bibliog.

- **History**

  ANDERSON (THOMAS P.) Matanza: El Salvador's communist revolt of 1932. Lincoln, Neb., [1971]. pp. 175. bibliog.

SAMARA
See KUIBYSHEV

SAMBURU

SPENCER (PAUL) Nomads in alliance: symbiosis and growth among the Rendille and Samburu of Kenya. London, 1973. pp. 230. bibliog.

SAMOA

- Economic conditions

LOCKWOOD (BRIAN) Economic statistics of Samoan village households;...a supplement to Samoan village economy, etc. Canberra, 1970. fo. 46. bibliog.

LOCKWOOD (BRIAN) Samoan village economy. Melbourne, 1971. pp. 232. bibliog.

SAMPLING (STATISTICS)

TANGANYIKA. Treasury. Economics and Statistics Division. 1961. Pilot surveys of African agriculture: report. [Dar es Salaam, 1961]. pp. 24.

SANCHEZ-CRESPO (JOSE LUIS) Diseño de encuestas por muestreo probabilistico. Madrid, 1967. pp. 187. bibliog.

DRUZHININ (NIKOLAI KAPITONOVICH) Vyborochnyi metod i ego primenenie v sotsial'no-ekonomicheskikh issledovaniiakh. Moskva, 1970. pp. 104. bibliog.

ISRAEL. Central Bureau of Statistics. 1970. Sample surveys in Israel, 1966-1969: report prepared for the United Nations twelfth report on "Sample surveys of current interest". Jerusalem, 1970. pp. 32.

CHACKO (V.J.) and KPEDEKPO (G.M.K.) The use of interpenetrating sample designs in Ghana with special reference to demographic studies. Legon, 1971. fo. 47. (Ghana University. Institute of Statistical Social and Economic Research. Technical Publication Series. No. 16)

GRAY (SHEILA) The electoral register: practical information for use when drawing samples, both for interview and postal surveys. [London],1971. fo. 18. (U.K. Social Survey. [Papers. Methodological Series.] No. M. 151. New Sampling Series. No. 3)

INTERREGIONAL WORKSHOP ON THE METHODOLOGY OF DEMOGRAPHIC SAMPLE SURVEYS, COPENHAGEN, 1969. Methodology of demographic sample surveys: report of the Interregional Workshop...[held in] Copenhagen, Denmark, 24 September - 3 October 1969. (ST/TAO/SER.C/119)(ST/STAT/SEAM/51). New York, United Nations, 1971. pp. 311. (Statistical Office. Statistical Papers. Series M. No.51)

U.K. Social Survey. [Reports. New Series.] 477. Sample surveys in local authority areas, with particular reference to the handicapped and elderly; by Amelia I. Harris and Elizabeth Head; a guide commissioned by the Department of Health and Social Security. [London], 1971. pp. 69.

GEARY (ROBERT CHARLES) The social science percentage nuisance. Dublin, 1972. pp. 17. (Economic and Social Research Institute. Broadsheets. No. 6)

RAJ (DES) The design of sample surveys. New York, [1972]. pp. 390. bibliogs.

CAULCOTT (EVELYN) Significance tests. London, 1973. pp. 145. bibliogs.

PERRY (N.H.) Greater London recreation study: report on sampling procedures. [London], 1973. pp. 18. (London. Greater London Council. Department of Planning and Transportation. Research Memoranda. 407)

SAMUELSON (PAUL ANTHONY)

ROMIG (FRIEDRICH) Die ideologischen Elemente in der neoklassischen Theorie: eine kritische Auseinandersetzung mit Paul A. Samuelson. Berlin, [1971]. pp. 68. bibliog.

DIEWERT (W.E.) The Samuelson nonsubstitution theorem and the computation of equilibrium prices. Stanford, 1972. fo. 20. bibliog. (Stanford University. Institute for Mathematical Studies in the Social Sciences. Technical Reports. [New Series]. No.69)

SAN FRANCISCO

- 1906, Earthquake and fire

THOMAS (GORDON) and MORGAN-WITTS (MAX) Earthquake: the destruction of San Francisco. London, 1971. pp. 316. bibliog.

- Industries

GROVES (PAUL A.) Towards a typology of intrametropolitan manufacturing location: a case study of the San Francisco Bay area. Hull, 1971. pp. 89. bibliog. (Hull. University. Department of Geography. Occasional Papers in Geography. No.16)

- Transit systems

STUCKER (J.P.) Long run effects of an intraurban air transportation system on residential location and commuting in the San Francisco Bay Area; a report prepared for National Aeronautics and Space Administration. [Santa Monica], 1972. pp. 84.

SAN JOSE METROPOLITAN AREA

ALESCH (DANIEL J.) An outline for Rand urban policy research in the San Jose metropolitan area. [Santa Monica], 1972. pp. 10. (Rand Corporation. [Papers]. 4889)

SAN JUAN (PROVINCE OF THE ARGENTINE REPUBLIC)

- Historical geography

MARZO (MIGUEL) La conquista del espacio territorial sanjuanino. Mendoza, 1968. pp. 89. bibliog. (Mendoza. Universidad Nacional de Cuyo. Instituto de Investigaciones Politicas y Sociales. Cuadernos. No.15)

SAN LUIS POTOSI

- Rural conditions

ALEMAN ALEMAN (ELOISA) Investigacion socioeconomica directa de los ejidos de San Luis Potosi. Mexico, 1966. pp. 191. bibliog.

SANCHEZ CERRO (LUIS MIGUEL) President of Peru

UGARTECHE Y TIZON (PEDRO) Sanchez Cerro: papeles y recuerdos de un presidente del Peru. [Lima, 1969-70]. 4 vols.

SANCTIONS (INTERNATIONAL LAW)

MIKHEEV (IURII IAKOVLEVICH) Primenenie prinuditel'nykh mer po Ustavu OON. Moskva, 1967. pp. 207.

EISEMANN (PIERRE MICHEL) Les sanctions contre la Rhodésie. Paris, [1972]. pp. 154. bibliog.

SANCTIS (FRANCESCO DE)

SANCTIS (FRANCESCO DE) Lettere politiche, 1865-1880; [edited by] Gian Battista Gifuni. Milano, 1970. pp. 87.

SAND

- United Kingdom

NICKLESS (E.F.P.) The sand and gravel resources of the country south-east of Norwich, Norfolk: description of 1: 25 000 resource sheet TG 20. London, 1971. pp. 94. bibliog. (U.K. Institute of Geological Sciences. Reports. No. 71/20) (Assessments of British Sand and Gravel Resources. No.1) Map in end pocket.

ARCHER (A.A.) Sand and gravel as aggregate. London, H.M.S.O., 1972. pp. 29. bibliog. (Mineral Dossiers. No.4)

SAND, GLASS

WROBLICKI (J.) The Kapiri Mposhi glass sand: [with addendum]. [Lusaka, 1968]. pp. 159. bibliog. (Zambia. Geological Survey Department. Economic Reports. No.24) Maps in end pocket.

SANDINO (AUGUSTO CÉSAR)

MACAULAY (NEILL) The Sandino affair. Chicago, 1971. pp. 319. bibliog.

SANSCULOTTES

REVUNENKOV (VLADIMIR GEORGIEVICH) Parizhskie sankiuloty epokhi Velikoi frantsuzskoi revoliutsii. Leningrad, 1971. pp. 176.

SANTA CATARINA (STATE)

- Statistics

BRAZIL. Instituto Brasileiro de Estatistica. Grupo Executivo de Pesquisas Domiciliares. População, habitação, mão-de-obra, salario, instrução. Região 3: Parana, S[anta] Catarina, R[io] G[rande] do Sul. q., Ja/Mr 1968 - Ja/Mr 1969. Rio de Janeiro.

SANTO DOMINGO

- Social conditions

CORTEN (ANDRÉ) and CORTEN (ANDRÉE) Cambio social en Santo Domingo. Rio Piedras, 1968. pp. 180. (Puerto Rico University. Institute of Caribbean Studies. Special Studies. No.5)

SÃO FRANCISCO VALLEY

- Economic conditions

LEVANTAMENTO socioeconômico em áreas do Baixo e Médio São Francisco. Recife, [Instituto Joaquim Nabuco de Pesquisas Sociais], 1972. 2 vols.(in 1)

- Social conditions

LEVANTAMENTO socioeconômico em áreas do Baixo e Médio São Francisco. Recife, [Instituto Joaquim Nabuco de Pesquisas Sociais], 1972. 2 vols.(in 1).

SAO PAULO (CITY)

- Poor

CONN (STEPHEN) The squatters' rights of favelados. Cuernavaca, 1969. 1 vol. (various pagination). (Centro Intercultural de Documentacion. Cidoc Cuadernos. No. 32)

- Statistics

BRAZIL. Instituto Brasileiro de Estatistica. Grupo Executivo de Pesquisas Domiciliares. População, habitação, mão-de-obra, salario, instrução. Região 2: São Paulo. q., Ja/Mr 1968 - Ja/Mr 1969. Rio de Janeiro.

SARAGAT (GIUSEPPE)

INDRIO (UGO) La presidenza Saragat: cronaca politica di un settennio, 1965-1971. [Verona], 1971. pp. 294.

SARAWAK

SARAWAK. Information Service. 1960. Information on Sarawak (with additions and corrections, December, 1960). Kuching, [1960]. pp. 178, fo.(2). bibliog. Map in end pocket.

SARDINIA

- Economic conditions

Il PIANO di rinascita della Sardegna: leggi e programmi. Sassari, 1971. pp. 582.

PASTORE (GIULIO) Il piano di rinascita della Sardegna: discorso al Senato, 23 Novembre 1961. [Rome, 1962]. pp. 44.

PARTITO SOCIALISTA ITALIANO. [Sezione] di Nuoro. Il Meridione: punto nodale per la trasformazione del sistema economico italiano, etc. Milano, [1969]. pp. 14.

Il PIANO di rinascita della Sardegna: leggi e programmi. Sassari, 1971. pp. 582.

- History

SATTA (FRANCESCO SPANU) I problemi della Sardegna nelle sue vicende storiche. [Roma, 1962]. pp. 79. (Italy. Cassa per Opere Straordinarie di Pubblico Interesse nell'Italia Meridionale. Nuova Serie Monografica. 1)

BUFFA (DOMENICO) Il Regno di Sardegna nel 1848-1849 nei carteggi di Domenico Buffa; a cura di Emilio Costa. Roma, 1966-1970. 3 vols. (Istituto per la Storia del Risorgimento Italiano. Pubblicazioni. 2a Serie. Fonti. vols. 54, 58, 61)

SECHI (SALVATORE) Dopoguerra e fascismo in Sardegna: il movimento autonomistico nella crisi dello stato liberale, 1918-1926. Torino, 1969. pp. 504. (Fondazione Luigi Einaudi. Studi. 8)

SARDINIA (Cont'd)

- Politics and government

CONTINI (GIUSEPPE) ed. Lo statuto della Regione sarda: documenti sui lavori preparatori. Milano, 1971. pp. 808. (Cagliari. Università. Facoltà di Giurisprudenza. Pubblicazioni)

- Social history

BRIGAGLIA (MANLIO) Sardegna: perchè banditi. Roma, [1971]. pp. 382.

LEDDA (ALBERTO) La civiltà fuorilegge: natura e storia del banditismo sardo. Milano, [1971]. pp. 220.

SARKISOV (GRIGORII KHOSROVOVICH)

SARKISOV (GRIGORII KHOSROVOVICH) Za rabochee delo: vospominaniia. Baku, 1966. pp. 32.

SARTRE (JEAN PAUL)

ROZHIN (N.V.) V poiskakh gumanisticheskoi filosofii: k kritike ekzistentsializma Zh.P. Sartra. in Sikorskii (Vsevolod Mikhailovich) and Fricke (Dieter) eds. Protiv burzhuaznoi i reformistskoi ideologii: sbornik statei. Minsk, 1972. pp. 212. Some articles translated from German.

SARTRE (JEAN PAUL) Situations, IX: mélanges. [Paris, 1972]. pp. 365.

- Bibliography

BELKIND (ALLEN) compiler. Jean-Paul Sartre: Sartre and existentialism in English; a bibliographical guide. [Kent, Ohio, 1970]. pp. 234.

SASKATCHEWAN

- Population

DOWNING (JEAN C.) Preliminary report: population and land use; South Saskatchewan River development region. Regina, South Saskatchewan River Development Commission, 1960. fo. v,63.

SASSARI (CITY)

- Social history

CHERCHI (GIOVANNI MARIA) Togliatti a Sassari, 1908-1911: una provincia sarda nell'età giolittiana. Roma, 1972. pp. 140.

SATIRE, ENGLISH

ROGERS (PAT) Grub Street: studies in a subculture. London, 1972. pp. 430.

SAUCKE (KURT)

BRIEFE an Kurt Saucke. Hamburg, 1970. pp. 33.

SAVING AND INVESTMENT

DELEECK (HERMAN) Vermogensaanwasdeling en investeringsloon: een terreinverkenning. Antwerpen, 1967. pp. 208. bibliog. (Antwerp. Universitaire Faculteiten Sint Ignatius. Studiecentrum voor Economisch en Sociaal Onderzoek. Publikaties)

- Mathematical models

DIEWERT (W.E.) Walras' theory of capital formation and the existence of a temporary equilibrium. Stanford, 1972. pp. 79. bibliog. (Stanford University. Institute for Mathematical Studies in the Social Sciences. Technical Reports. [New Series]. No. 63)

SCHIMMELMANN (WULF VON) Ein aktivitätsanalytisches Sparmodell. Zürich, 1972. pp. 173. bibliog.

SOMERMEIJER (WILLEM HENDRIK) and BANNINK (R.) A consumption-savings model and its applications. Amsterdam, 1973. pp. 431. bibliog.

- Africa

AMORE (GIORDANO DELL') Politica bancaria e politica del risparmio nei paesi africani; relazione generale alla Conferenza...Milano, 20-23 settembre 1971. Milano, 1971. pp. 21. (Milan. Università Commerciale Luigi Bocconi. Istituto di Economia Aziendale. Serie Relazioni. N. 68)

CONFERENCE ON THE MOBILIZATION OF SAVINGS IN AFRICAN COUNTRIES, MILAN, 1971. Proceedings of a conference organized... by the International Savings Banks Institute and the Cassa di Risparmio delle Provincie Lombarde, etc. Milan, [1972]. pp. 441. (Cassa di Risparmio delle Provincie Lombarde. The Credit Markets of Africa.3)

- Africa, Subsaharan

ONOH (JAMES K.) Strategic approaches to crucial policies in economic development: a macro link study in capital formation, technology and money. Rotterdam, 1972. pp. 236. bibliog.

- Asia, Southeast

LAMBERT (RICHARD D.) and HOSELITZ (BERTHOLD FRANK) eds. The role of savings and wealth in southern Asia and the West. Paris, [1963]. pp. 432.

- Canada

BAUM (DANIEL JAY) The investment function of Canadian financial institutions. New York, 1973. pp. 264.

- Cyprus

CYPRUS. Statistics and Research Department. Capital formation survey in the manufacturing sector. a., 1971 [1st]- Nicosia.

- Europe

PROBLEME der Sparförderung in der OECD; von Horst Albach [and others]. Berlin, [1973]. pp. 192. (Bonn. Universität. Institut für das Spar-, Giro- und Kreditwesen. Untersuchungen über das Spar-, Giro- und Kreditwesen. Band 70)

ROBINSON (DEREK) Incomes policy and capital sharing in Europe; [collected papers]. London, 1973. pp. 223.

- France

L'HARDY (PHILIPPE) and HOFFMANN (GEORGES) Epargne des ménages et gestion du patrimoine, enquête 1967: [and] Les vacances des Français en 1969, par Pierre Le Roux. [Paris], 1970. pp. 152. bibliog. (France. Institut National de la Statistique et des Etudes Economiques. Collections de l'INSEE. Série. M. Ménages. 6) With summaries in English and Spanish.

FRANÇOIS (WILLIAM) Le capital sans capitalisme: essai d'actualité sur la formation du capital productif en France et sa circulation en Europe. [Paris, 1972]. pp. 260.

L'HARDY (PHILIPPE) Le comportement d'épargne des ménages de 1967 à 1969. [Paris, 1972]. pp. 125. (France. Institut National de la Statistique et des Etudes Economiques. Collections de L'INSEE. Série M. Ménages. 17) Summaries in English and Spanish.

- Germany

GERMANY (BUNDESREPUBLIK). Statistisches Bundesamt. 1971. Vermögensformen und -bestände privater Haushalte, 1969. Stuttgart, 1971. pp. 192. (Preise, Löhne, Wirtschaftsrechnungen. Reihe 18. Einkommens- und Verbrauchsstichproben. 2)

SAARBRUECKEN. Universität. Annales Universitatis Saraviensis. Rechts- und Wirtschaftswissenschaftliche Abteilung. Band 57. Pläne und Massnahmen zur Vermögensbildung: eine Analyse ihrer Ziele und Funktionselemente; von Michael Bitz. Köln, 1971. pp. 272. bibliog.

FRICKE (DIETER) Das Sparverhalten der privaten Haushalte in der Bundesrepublik Deutschland: eine empirische Überprüfung der Sparfunktion. Berlin, [1972]. pp. 159. bibliog.

- India

NATIONAL COUNCIL OF APPLIED ECONOMIC RESEARCH. All India household survey of income, saving and consumer expenditure, with special reference to middle class households. New Delhi, [1972]. pp. 130.

- Kenya

EAST AFRICA HIGH COMMISSION. East African Statistical Department. 1961. Capital formation in Kenya, 1954-1960. Nairobi, 1961. pp. 15.

- Netherlands

POST (J.G.) Besparingen in Nederland, 1923-1970: omvang en verdeling. Deventer, 1972. pp. 140. bibliog. (Nederlands Instituut voor het Banken Effectenbedrijf. Publikaties. No. 13) With English summary.

- Norway

STUDIER i sparing og sparebankvesen i Norge, 1822-1972; (redaksjonskomiteen: Arne Jensen [and others]). Oslo, 1972. pp. 314. bibliog.

- Spain

DATA, S.A. Comportamiento y actitudes de las economias domesticas hacia el ahorro y el consumo. Madrid, 1968. pp. 719. bibliog. (Confederacion Española de Cajas Ahorros. Fondo para la Investigacion Economica y Social. Publicaciones. 1)

- Sweden

KJUSE (JAN) Inkomstutveckling och förmögenhetsbildning: en undersökning av vissa yrkesgrupper, 1924-1959. Göteborg, 1970. pp. 245. bibliog. (Göteborgs Universitet. Ekonomisk-Historiska Institutionen. Meddelanden. 23) With English summary.

SAVING AND INVESTMENT: Underdeveloped areas
See UNDERDEVELOPED AREAS - Saving and investment

- United Kingdom

DAVIES (CHRISTIE) and DAVIES (DAVID RHYS) Incentive to invest. London, 1972. pp. 34. (Conservative Political Centre. [Publications]. No. 512)

NAYLOR (MARGOT) Margot Naylor's guide to money, savings and investment. London, 1972. pp. 202.

ORNSTIEN (EDWIN J.) The marketing of money. Epping, Essex, 1972. pp. 254.

- United States

KUZNETS (SIMON SMITH) National income and capital formation, 1919-1935: a preliminary report. New York, 1937. pp. 86. (National Bureau of Economic Research. Publications. No. 32)

JANEWAY (ELIOT) You and your money: a survival guide to the controlled economy. New York, [1972]. pp. 284.

LONGSTRETH (BEVIS) and ROSENBLOOM (H. DAVID) Corporate social responsibility and the institutional investor: a report to the Ford Foundation. New York, 1973. pp. 104. bibliog.

- United States - Mathematical models

GRAMLICH (EDWARD M.) and JAFFEE (DWIGHT M.) eds. Savings deposits, mortgages, and housing: studies for the Federal Reserve-MIT-PENN economic model. Lexington, [1972]. pp. 307.

SAVINGS-BANKS

AMORE (GIORDANO DELL') L'evoluzione strutturale e funzionale delle casse di risparmio mondiali. Milano, 1971. pp. 12. (Milan. Università Commerciale "Luigi Bocconi". Istituto di Economia Aziendale. Serie Relazioni. N.67)

MOBILIZATION of savings and local credits; report of an international seminar for experts from African countries and Pakistan... [held by the Deutsche Stiftung für Entwicklungsländer in 1972]. Berlin, 1972. pp. 309.

- Africa

CONFERENCE ON THE MOBILIZATION OF SAVINGS IN AFRICAN COUNTRIES, MILAN, 1971. Proceedings of a conference organized... by the International Savings Banks Institute and the Cassa di Risparmio delle Provincie Lombarde, etc. Milan, [1972]. pp. 441. (Cassa di Risparmio delle Provincie Lombarde. The Credit Markets of Africa.3)

- Denmark

ANDERSEN (EDV.) Sydfyns Sparekasse, 1870-1970; udgivet i anledning af Sparekassens 100 års jubilaem. Faaborg, [1970?]. pp. 47.

- Germany

SPITTEL (OSKAR) Die deutschen Sparcassen, deren Entstehung, Einrichtung, Aufgaben und Ziele; [reprint of work originally published in 1880]. [Frankfurt am Main], 1970. pp. 58.

KAVEN (JUERGEN PETER) Die besondere Wettbewerbsstellung der öffentlich-rechtlichen Sparkassen. [Erlangen, imprint, 1971?]. pp. 204. bibliog.

ROEPER (BURKHARDT) Die Wettbewerbsfunktion der deutschen Sparkassen und das Subsidiaritätsprinzip: eine wettbewerbspolitische Analyse. Berlin, [1973]. pp. 200.

- Norway

STUDIER i sparing og sparebankvesen i Norge, 1822-1972; (redaksjonskomiteen: Arne Jensen [and others]). Oslo, 1972. pp. 314. bibliog.

- Russia

CHETVERIKOV (P.A.) ed. Sberegatel'nye kassy SSSR za 50 let. Moskva, 1972. pp. 96.

SAVINGS - BANKS (Cont'd)

- Spain

    ARENAS GARCIA (JUAN FRANCISCO) El fomento de la propiedad privada como funcion socioeconomica de las cajas de ahorros. Madrid, 1971. pp. 347. bibliog. (Confederacion Española de Cajas de Ahorros. Fondo para la Investigacion Economica y Social. Publicaciones. 23)

- Sweden

    ANDERSSON (ROLF) and BJERKE (BJÖRN) Dynamisk kapitalplanering: ett system för planering av kapitalströmmarna i en sparbank. [Stockholm, 1971]. pp. 482. bibliog. With English summary.

- Switzerland

    ERSPARNISKASSE DER STADT SOLOTHURN. 150 Jahre Ersparniskasse der Stadt Solothurn. [Solothurn, 1971]. pp. 71.

SAVINKOV (BORIS VIKTOROVICH)

LOKHVITSKII (I.A.) To, chto bylo.... Berlin, 1922. pp. 63.

SAVINKOV (BORIS VIKTOROVICH) defendant. Delo Borisa Savinkova, so stat'ei B. Savinkova "Pochemu ia priznal Sovetskuiu vlast'"; s predisloviem Em. Iaroslavskogo, etc. Moskva, [1924?]. pp. 161.

SAVINKOV (BORIS VIKTOROVICH) Vospominaniia terrorista; predislovie Feliksa Kona. 2nd ed. [Khar'kov, 1926?]. pp. 375.

SAY (JEAN BAPTISTE)

GUILLAUMONT (PATRICK) La pensée demo-économique de Jean-Baptiste Say et de Sismondi. Paris, [1969]. pp. 144. bibliog.

SCALE ANALYSIS (PSYCHOLOGY)

MOKKEN (ROBERT J.) A theory and procedure of scale analysis: with applications in political research. The Hague, [1971]. pp. 353. bibliog.

SCANDICCI

- Economic policy

    SCANDICCI. Amministrazione Comunale. Per un piano quadriennale di sviluppo economico del Comune di Scandicci, etc. [Scandicci, 1968]. pp. 160.

SCANDINAVIA

- Biography

    DICTIONARY of Scandinavian biography; hon. general editor Ernest Kay...with the full text of the Treaty of Cooperation between Denmark, Finland, Iceland, Norway and Sweden. London, [1972]. pp. 467.

- Defences

    SKODVIN (MAGNE) Norden eller NATO?: Utenriksdepartementet og alliansespørsmålet, 1947-1949. Oslo, [1971]. pp. 355.

- Economic conditions

    FULLERTON (BRIAN) and WILLIAMS (ALAN F.) Scandinavia. London, 1972. pp. 374. bibliogs.

    PISKULOV (IURII VASIL'EVICH) and GRADOBITOVA (LIUDMILA DMITRIEVNA) Sever i integratsiia: ekonomicheskie problemy stran Severnoi Evropy. Moskva, 1972. pp. 215.

- Economic history

    LAFFERTY (WILLIAM M.) Economic development and the response of labor in Scandinavia: a multi-level analysis. Oslo, 1971. pp. 360. bibliog.

    VEREIN FÜR SOZIALPOLITIK. Schriften. Neue Folge. Band 63. Beiträge zu Wirtschaftswachstum und Wirtschaftsstruktur im 16. und 19. Jahrhundert; herausgegeben von Wolfram Fischer. Berlin, 1971. pp. 279. bibliog. In German or English.

- Economic policy

    NORWAY. Utenriksdepartementet. 1970. Traktat om opprettelse av organisasjonen for nordisk økonomisk samarbeid. [Oslo?, 1970]. pp. 212.

    BERNITZ (ULF) Konkurrens och priser i Norden: en komparativ studie av konkurrens- och prislagstiftningens syften och medel i de nordiska länderna. [Stockholm, 1971]. pp. 276. bibliog.

- Foreign economic relations - United Kingdom

    KENT (HEINZ SIGFRID KOPLOWITZ) War and trade in Northern seas: Anglo-Scandinavian economic relations in the mid-eighteenth century. Cambridge, 1973. pp. 240. bibliog.

- Foreign opinion

    ALKJAER (EJLER) and others. Scandinavian cooperation around the world. Oslo, 1973. pp. 77.

- Foreign relations - Treaties

    SWEDEN. Treaties. 1962. Treaty of cooperation between Denmark, Finland, Iceland, Norway and Sweden, entered into force on July 1, 1962. Stockholm, 1962. pp. 7.

- Industries

    ZENK (GUENTHER) Konzentrationspolitik in Dänemark, Norwegen und Finnland. Tübingen, 1971. pp. 187. bibliog.

- Population

    SCANDINAVIAN DEMOGRAPHIC SYMPOSIUM, 2ND, HÄSSELBY, 1970. [Papers presented at the Symposium]. Stockholm, 1970. pp. 134. (Scandinavian Demographic Society. Scandinavian Population Studies 2)

- Relations (general) with Russia

    DASHKOV (IURII FEDOROVICH) Po leninskim mestam Skandinavii: zhurnalistskii poisk. Moskva, 1971. pp. 239.

- Social policy

    NORDISKE SOCIALMINISTERMØDE, KØBENHAVN, 1955. Referat. [Copenhagen?, 1955?]. pp. 150. Variously in Swedish and Danish.

SCAVENIUS (ERIK)

SJØQVIST (VIGGO) Erik Scavenius: Danmarks udenrigsminister under to verdenskrige, statsminister 1942-1945. [Copenhagen, 1973]. 2 vols. bibliog.

SCHACHT (HORACE GREELEY HJALMAR)

MUELLER (HELMUT) Die Zentralbank, eine Nebenregierung: Reichsbankpräsident Hjalmar Schacht als Politiker der Weimarer Republik. Opladen, 1973. pp. 139. bibliog.

SCHAUENSTEIN (CARL FERDINAND VON BUOL-)
See BUOL-SCHAUENSTEIN (CARL FERDINAND VON) Graf

SCHAUMBURG-LIPPE

- **Economic history**

STEINKAMP (ARNO) Stadt- und Landhandwerk in Schaumburg-Lippe im 18. und beginnenden 19. Jahrhundert. Rinteln, 1970. pp. 182. bibliog. (Historische Arbeitsgemeinschaft für Schaumburg. Schaumburger Studien. Heft 27)

SCHEIDEMANN (PHILIPP)

SCHEIDEMANN (PHILIPP) Zwischen den Gefechten. Berlin, [1920]. pp. 152.

SCHELER (MAX FERDINAND)

ALTMANN (ALEXANDER) Die Grundlagen der Wertethik: Wesen, Wert, Person; Max Schelers Erkenntnis- und Seinslehre in kritischer Analyse. Berlin, 1931. pp. 113. bibliog.

SCHELLING (FRIEDRICH WILHELM JOSEPH VON)

NAUEN (FRANZ GABRIEL) Revolution, idealism and human freedom: Schelling, Hölderlin and Hegel and the crisis of early German idealism. The Hague, 1971. pp. 104. bibliog.

SCHEU (FRIEDRICH)

SCHEU (FRIEDRICH) Der Weg ins Ungewisse: Österreichs Schicksalskurve, 1929-1938. Wien, [1972]. pp. 320. bibliog.

SCHEURER (KARL)

SCHEURER (KARL) Bundesrat Karl Scheurer: Tagebücher, 1914-1929; herausgegeben und eingeleitet von Hermann Böschenstein. Bern, 1971. pp. 390.

SCHICK (ALLEN)

NOVICK (DAVID) and FISHER (GLENN WILLIAM) A review of Budget innovation in the States, by Allen Schick. [Santa Moniva], 1972. pp. 4. (Rand Corporation. [Papers]. 4834)

SCHINCKEL (MAX VON)
See SCHINCKEL (MAXIMILLIAN HEINRICH VON)

SCHINCKEL (MAXMILIAN HEINRICH VON)

ROHRMANN (ELSABEA) Max von Schinckel: hanseatischer Bankmann im Wilhelminischen Deutschland. Hamburg, 1971. pp. 340. bibliog. (Hamburg. Hamburgisches Welt-Wirtschafts-Archiv. Veröffentlichungen)

SCHISTOSOMIASIS

DISEASE and economic development: the impact of parasitic diseases in St. Lucia; [by] Burton A. Weisbrod [and others]. Madison, 1973. pp. 18. bibliog.

SCHIZOPHRENIA

COULTER (JEFF) Approaches to insanity: a philosophical and sociological study. London, 1973. pp. 170.

SCHIZOPHRENICS

- **Family relationships**

ESTERSON (AARON) The leaves of spring: a study in the dialectics of madness. Harmondsworth, 1970 repr. 1972. pp. 310. bibliog.

PARKER (BEULAH) A mingled yarn: chronicle of a troubled family. New Haven, 1972. pp. 333.

SCHLEIERMACHER (FRIEDRICH DANIEL ERNST)

DILTHEY (WILHELM) Gesammelte Schriften; [Bände 1-14 edited by Bernard Groethuysen and others; Bände 15- edited by Karlfried Grunder and others]. Leipzig, later Göttingen, 1923 in progress.

SCHLESWIG-HOLSTEIN

- **Economic history**

EHLERS (FRANZ) ed. Zoll- und Steuergeschichte Schleswig-Holsteins;... mit Beiträgen von Fritz Brinckmann [and others]. [Kiel, 1968]. pp. 549. bibliog.

- **History**

WETZEL (JUERGEN) Theodor Lehmann und die nationale Bewegung in Schleswig-Holstein, 1859-1862. Neumünster, 1971. pp. 256. bibliog. (Gesellschaft für Schleswig-Holsteinische Geschichte. Quellen und Forschungen zur Geschichte Schleswig-Holsteins. Band 61)

- **Politics and government**

ERHARDT-LUCHT (RENATE) Die Ideen der Französischen Revolution in Schleswig-Holstein. Neumünster, 1969. pp. 227. (Gesellschaft für Schleswig-Holsteinische Geschichte. Quellen und Forschungen zur Geschichte Schleswig-Holsteins. Band 56)

SAHNER (HEINZ) Politische Tradition, Sozialstruktur und Parteiensystem in Schleswig-Holstein: ein Beitrag zur Replikation von Rudolf Heberles: Landbevölkerung und Nationalsozialismus. Meisenheim am Glan, 1972. pp. 144. bibliog.

SCHLESWIG-HOLSTEIN QUESTION

FREDERIKSEN (BJARNE W.) Danmarks Sydslesvigpolitik efter det tyske sammenbrud i 1945: en analyse, etc. [Copenhagen, 1971]. pp. 210. bibliog. (Dansk Udenrigspolitisk Institut. Skrifter. 3)

SCHLESWIG-HOLSTEIN WAR, 1848-1850

HJELHOLT (HOLGER) Great Britain, the Danish-German conflict and the Danish succession, 1850-1852, etc. København, 1971. pp. 323. (Danske Videnskabernes Selskab. Historisk-filosofiske Meddelelser. Bind 45, Nr.1)

SCHMALKALDIC LEAGUE, 1530-1547

PRUESER (FRIEDRICH) England und die Schmalkaldener, 1535-1540; [reprint of work originally published in 1929]. New York, 1971. pp. 342. bibliog. (Verein für Reformationsgeschichte. Quellen und Forschungen zur Reformationsgeschichte. Band 11)

SCHMITT (CARL)

BENTIN (LUTZ ARWED) Johannes Popitz und Carl Schmitt: zur wirtschaftlichen Theorie des totalen Staates in Deutschland. München, [1972]. pp. 186. bibliog. (Munich. Universität. Institut für Politische Wissenschaft. Münchener Studien zur Politik. 19. Band)

RUMPF (HELMUT) Carl Schmitt und Thomas Hobbes: ideelle Beziehungen und aktuelle Bedeutung, etc. Berlin, [1972]. pp. 116. bibliog.

SCHNITZER (EDUARD) called Emin, Pasha

SMITH (IAIN R.) The Emin Pasha relief expedition, 1886-1890. Oxford, 1972. pp. 335. bibliog.

SCHOBER (JOHANNES)

HOCHENBICHLER (EDUARD) Republik im Schatten der Monarchie: das Burgenland, ein europäisches Problem. Wien, [1971]. pp. 183.

SCHOENLANK (BRUNO)

MAYER (PAUL) Bruno Schoenlank, 1859-1901: Reformer der sozialdemokratischen Tagespresse. Hannover, [1971]. pp. 158. bibliog. (Friedrich-Ebert-Stiftung. Forschungsinstitut. Schriftenreihe. Band 87)

SCHOLARLY PUBLISHING

- United States

NEMEYER (CAROL A.) Scholarly reprint publishing in the United States. New York, 1972. pp. 262. bibliog.

SCHOLARS

- Directories

ROCKEFELLER FOUNDATION. Directory of fellowships and scholarships, 1917-1970. New York, 1972. pp. 412.

INTERNATIONAL scholars directory; John Warwick Montgomery, general editor. Strasbourg, 1973. pp. 288.

SCHOLARS, AMERICAN

FORD FOUNDATION. Scholars' work and works. New York, [1963]. pp. 33.

SCHOLARS, RUSSIAN

KORNEEV (STEPAN GAVRILOVICH) Sovetskie uchenye - pochetnye chleny inostrannykh nauchnykh uchrezhdenii. Moskva, 1973. pp. 295.

SCHOLARSHIPS

- Directories

The GRANTS register, 1973-1975; editor, Roland Turner. London, 1973[or rather 1972]. pp. 685.

- United Kingdom - British Empire

SCHOLARSHIPS GUIDE FOR COMMONWEALTH POSTGRADUATE STUDENTS: scholarships, grants, assistantships, etc. open to graduates of Commonwealth universities...; [pd. by] the Association of Commonwealth Universities. bien., current issue only kept. London. Supersedes in part UNITED KINGDOM POSTGRADUATE AWARDS, which see also.

- United States

COLUMBIA UNIVERSITY. Russian Institute. Soviet Union and Eastern Europe: financial aid, exchanges, language and travel programs: a preliminary survey; compiled and edited by Constance A. Bezer. Ohio, 1971. pp. 122. bibliog.

SCHOLASTIC APTITUDE TEST

POWELL (JOHN L.) Selection for university in Scotland: a first report on the Assessment for Higher Education Project. London, [1973]. pp. 100. bibliog. (Scottish Council for Research in Education. Publications. 64)

SCHOOL, CHOICE OF

SOCIALIST EDUCATIONAL ASSOCIATION. Parental choice or neighbourhood schools?: (transfer from primary to secondary school in a comprehensive system). London, [1971?]. s.sh.

SCHOOL ADMINISTRATORS

SULLIVAN (NEIL VINCENT) and others. Walk, run, or retreat: the modern school administrator. Bloomington, [1971]. pp. 182.

SCHOOL ATTENDANCE

JACOBY (E.G.) Methods of school enrolment projection. [Paris, 1959]. pp. 43. (United Nations Educational, Scientific and Cultural Organization. Educational Studies and Documents. No. 32)

- United Kingdom

SHEARMAN (Sir HAROLD CHARLES) Exempting children from school: an examination of the new Education Bill. London, [1936]. pp. 12.

SCHOOL BOARDS

NEW YORK STATE SCHOOL BOARDS ASSOCIATION. Shared Services Committee. Cooperative boards: their present and future: a report to the Commissioner of Education of the State of New York on stewardship and future plans. Albany, N.Y., 1963. pp. 50.

SCHOOL BUILDINGS

HUTTON AND ROSTRON (ARCHITECTS) Comparative study of secondary school building costs. [Paris], United Nations Educational, Scientific and Cultural Organization, 1971. pp. 77. (Educational Studies and Documents. New Series. No. 4)

- United Kingdom

U.K. Department of Education and Science. 1972- Notes on procedures for the approval of school building projects in England; (with Amendments). London, 1972 in progress. 1 vol. (loose-leaf).

SCHOOL CHILDREN

- France

BABY (NICOLAS) and BERTIN (FRANCIS) Politique au lycée? Paris, [1970]. pp. 119.

BOIRAUD (HENRI) Contribution à l'étude historique des congés et des vacances scolaires en France du moyen-âge à 1914. Paris, 1971. pp. 269. bibliog.

SCHONFELD (WILLIAM R.) Youth and authority in France: a study of secondary schools. Beverly Hills, [1971]. pp. 77. bibliog.

- Netherlands

BAKKER (S.) and others. Het groene boekje: nuchter protest tegen het rode boekje voor scholieren. Apeldoorn, 1970. pp. 77.

DIEMER (WILLEM) Het rood-wit-blauwe boekje voor (niet-)scholieren, met als bovenste kwart(ier) een pe(n)dant 'rood boekje' voor collega's. Delden, 1970. pp. 96.

- Nigeria

PESHKIN (ALAN) Kanuri schoolchildren: education and social mobilization in Nigeria. New York, [1972]. pp. 156. bibliog.

- South Africa

GEBER (BERYL ANNE) Occupational aspirations and expectations of South African high school children; [Ph.D. (London) thesis]. 1972. fo. 433. bibliog. Typescript: unpublished. This thesis is the property of London University and may not be removed from the Library.

- Sweden

SVENSSON (ALLAN) Relative achievement: school performance in relation to intelligence, sex and home environment. Stockholm, [1971]. pp. 176. bibliog.

- United Kingdom

BARRY (MICHAEL KANETI) and others. 2,100 sixth formers: a study of sixth form boys and girls, with particular relevance to their subject specialisation, educational aims, vocational choice and career prospects. London, 1971. pp. 106. bibliog. (Brunel University. Brunel Further Education Monographs. 2)

FURNITURE INDUSTRY RESEARCH ASSOCIATION. British school population dimensional survey, 1971. London, 1972. pp. 61. (U.K. Department of Education and Science. Building Bulletins. 46)

SUMNER (R.) and WARBURTON (FRANCIS WILLIAM) Achievement in secondary school: attitudes, personality and school success. Windsor, 1972. pp. 208. bibliog.

- United Kingdom - London

HAMMOND (ALEC R.) The forecasting of pupil numbers. [London], 1972. pp. 5. bibliog. (London. Greater London Council. Department of Planning and Transportation. Research Memoranda. 392)

- United States

BIRMINGHAM (JOHN) ed. Our time is now: notes from the high school underground. New York, 1970. pp. 273.

- United States - California.

RACIAL AND ETHNIC SURVEY OF CALIFORNIA PUBLIC SCHOOLS: pt.1: Distribution of pupils; [pd. by] California State Department of Education. a., fall 1966 [1st issue]- Sacramento. The Library has no file of pt.2.

SCHOOL DISCIPLINE

NEWELL (PETER) ed. A last resort?: corporal punishment in schools; [including case-study material from the files of STOPP]. Harmondsworth, 1972. pp. 198. bibliog.

SCHOOL DISTRICTS

- United States

RUBIN (LILLIAN B.) Busing and backlash: white against white in a California school district. Berkeley, [1972]. pp. 248. bibliog.

SCHOOL EXCURSIONS

- United Kingdom

U.K. Department of Education and Science. Schools Council. 1972. Short-stay residential experience: residential work by secondary school pupils. London, 1972. pp. 59. (Pamphlets. 10)

SCHOOL FACILITIES

- France

GROUPE DE SOCIOLOGIE URBAINE. Evolution des effectifs scolaires de la commune de St. Fons, 1968-1985; [by] A. Chazalette [and] E. Lacoin. Lyon, 1971. fo. 16, (36).

SCHOOL INTEGRATION

In earlier volumes of the Bibliography similar works have been entered under SEGREGATION IN EDUCATION.

- United States

PETRONI (FRANK A.) and others. Two, four, six, eight, when you gonna integrate? New York, [1970]. pp. 258.

PELTASON (JACK WALTER) Fifty-eight lonely men: Southern Federal judges and school desegregation; (a new edition with epilogue by Kenneth N. Vines and bibliographic essay by Numan V. Bartley). Urbana, Ill., 1971. pp. 288. bibliog.

BAGWELL (WILLIAM) Professor of Social Sciences, Cheyney State College. School desegregation in the Carolinas: two case studies. Columbia, S.C., [1972]. pp. 341. bibliog.

- United States - California

BONACICH (EDNA) and GOODMAN (ROBERT F.) Deadlock in school desegregation: a case study of Inglewood, California. New York, 1972. pp. 107. bibliog.

SCHOOL MANAGEMENT AND ORGANIZATION

UNITED NATIONS EDUCATIONAL, SCIENTIFIC AND CULTURAL ORGANIZATION. 1962. The organization of the school year: a comparative study. Paris, [1962]. pp. 113. (Educational Studies and Documents. No.43)

SCHOOL MANAGEMENT AND ORGANIZATION (Cont'd)

DOORNBOS (K.) Opstaan tegen het zittenblijven. 's-Gravenhage, Staatsuitgeverij, 1969. pp. 103. bibliog.

WALKER (W.G.) and others, eds. Explorations in educational administration: [articles selected from the Journal of Educational Administration, 1963-1969]. St. Lucia, Queensland, [1973]. pp. 433. bibliog.

- Australia

SCHOOL, college, and university: the administration of education in Australia; [papers delivered at a conference at Armidale, January 1968]; edited by W.G. Walker. St. Lucia, [1972]. pp. 250.

- New Zealand

NEW ZEALAND. Department of Education. Public Relations Section. 1970. Education administration in New Zealand. Wellington, 1970. pp. 10.

- United Kingdom

IKIN (ALFRED EDWARD) Organization and administration of the education department. London, 1926. pp. 238.

BLACKIE (J.E.H.) Inspecting and the inspectorate. London, 1970. pp. 101. bibliog.

LAWRENCE (BERNARD) The administration of education in Britain. London, 1972. pp. 213. bibliog.

RANK AND FILE. Discussion Pamphlets. Democracy in schools. London, [1972]. pp. 23.

TOWNSEND (HERBERT ELLWOOD ROUTLEDGE) and BRITTAN (E.M.) Organization in multiracial schools. Slough, 1972. pp. 172. bibliog.

KING (RONALD) School organisation and public involvement: a study of secondary schools. London, 1973. pp. 256. bibliog.

KOGAN (MAURICE) and others. County hall: the role of the chief education officer; Maurice Kogan with Willem van der Eyken in conversation with Dan Cook, Claire Pratt and George Taylor. Harmondsworth, 1973. pp. 187.

- United Kingdom - Scotland

SCOTLAND. Scottish Education Department. 1972- Secondary schools staffing survey, 1970. [Edinburgh], 1972 in progress.

- United States

JOHN GUY FOWLKES INVITATIONAL SEMINAR, 1ST, 1970. Education, administration, and change: the redeployment of resources; seminar papers [by] Lanore A. Netzer [and others]. New York, [1970]. pp. 204. bibliogs.

ANDREE (ROBERT G.) The art of negotiation: roles, games, logic. Lexington, [1971]. pp. 239. bibliog.

SCHOOL SPORTS - Underdeveloped areas
See UNDERDEVELOPED AREAS - School sports

SCHOOLS

SHIPMAN (M.D.) The sociology of the school. London, 1968 repr. 1971. pp. 196. bibliog.

- Italy

LETTER to a teacher; by the School of Barbiana; translated by Nora Rossi and Tom Cole with an afterword by Lord Boyle of Handsworth. Harmondsworth, 1970. pp. 138.

PIACENZA (PROVINCE). Ufficio Studi. Documenti e Notizie. Le scuole medie superiori in provincia di Piacenza: situazione attuale e prospettive di sviluppo. [Piacenza], 1970. pp. 125.

- Russia

LEVIN (DEANA) Soviet schools today. London, 1944. pp. 11.

- Uganda

WEEKS (SHELDON GRISWOLD) An African school: a sociological case study of a day secondary school in Uganda. 1968. pp. xxii,500. Ed. D. (Harvard) thesis: unpublished. Microfilm of typescript: 1 reel.

- United Kingdom

The MULTI-racial school: a professional perspective; edited by Julia McNeal and Margaret Rogers. Harmondsworth, 1971. pp. 154. bibliogs.

SOCIALIST EDUCATIONAL ASSOCIATION. Parental choice or neighbourhood schools?: (transfer from primary to secondary school in a comprehensive system). London, [1971?]. s.sh.

EDUCATIONAL priority...; edited by A.H. Halsey [and others]...; report of a research project sponsored by the Department of Education and Science and the Social Science Research Council. London, H.M.S.O., 1972 in progress. bibliogs.

BENN (CAROLINE) Comprehensive schools in 1972: reorganization plans to 1975. [London, 1972]. pp. 64.

BENN (CAROLINE) and SIMON (BRIAN) Half way there: report on the British comprehensive school reform. 2nd ed. Harmondsworth, 1972. pp. 591.

CLEGG (Sir ALEC) Recipe for failure. London, 1972. pp. 79. (National Children's Home and Orphanage. Convocation Lectures. 1972)

- United Kingdom - Furniture, equipment, etc.

FURNITURE INDUSTRY RESEARCH ASSOCIATION. Furniture and equipment dimensions: further and higher education: 18 to 25 age group. London, 1970. pp. 31. (U.K. Department of Education and Science. Building Bulletins. No. 44)

FURNITURE INDUSTRY RESEARCH ASSOCIATION. British school population dimensional survey, 1971. London, 1972. pp. 61. (U.K. Department of Education and Science. Building Bulletins. 46)

- United States

FEIN (LEONARD J.) The ecology of the public schools: an inquiry into community control. New York, [1971]. pp. 170.

KATZMAN (MARTIN T.) The political economy of urban schools. Cambridge, Mass., 1971. pp. 235.

SCHOOLS and inequality; [by] James W. Guthrie [and others]. Cambridge, Mass., [1971]. pp. 253. bibliog.

SWIFT (DAVID W.) Ideology and change in the public schools: latent functions of progressive education. Columbus, Ohio, [1971]. pp. 214. bibliog.

POLK (KENNETH) and SCHAFER (WALTER E.) Schools and delinquency. Englewood Cliffs, [1972]. pp. 282.

STATE, school, and politics: research directions; [papers of a workshop sponsored by the Committee on Basic Research in Education; edited by] Michael W. Kirst. Lexington, Mass., [1972]. pp. 281. bibliogs.

REISCHAUER (ROBERT DANTON) and HARTMAN (ROBERT W.) Reforming school finance. Washington, [1973]. pp. 185. bibliog. (Brookings Institution. Studies in Social Economics)

SIZER (THEODORE RYLAND) Places for learning, places for joy: speculations on American school reform. Cambridge, Mass., 1973. pp. 167 bibliog.

SCHUECKING (WALTHER)

ACKER (DETLEV) Walther Schücking, 1875-1935. Münster in Westfalen, 1970. pp. 228. bibliogs. (Historische Kommission Westfalens. Veröffentlichungen. 18)

SCHUMACHER (KURT)

WINZER (OTTO) Sozialistische Politik?: eine kritische Stellungnahme zu Reden und Aufsätzen von Dr. Kurt Schumacher. Berlin, [1947]. pp. 112.

SCHUMAN (ROBERT)

KEYSERLINGK (ROBERT WENDELIN) Patriots of peace. Gerrards Cross, 1972. pp. 175. bibliog.

SCHWEITZER (ALBERT)

AL'BERT Shveitser - velikii gumanist XX veka: vospominaniia i stat'i. Moskva, 1970. pp. 238.

MARSHALL (GEORGE) Unitarian clergyman, and POLING (DAVID) Schweitzer: a biography. London, [1971]. pp. 342. bibliog.

ŚCIEGIENNY (PIOTR)

D'IAKOV (VLADIMIR ANATOL'EVICH) Revoliutsionnaia deiatel'nost' i mirovozzrenie Petra Stsegennogo, 1801-1890 gg. Moskva, 1972. pp. 330.

SCIENCE

DIÉGUEZ (MANUEL DE) Science et nescience. [Paris, 1970]. pp. 548.

BRUECKNER (PETER) and KROVOZA (ALFRED) Was heisst Politisierung der Wissenschaft und was kann sie für die Sozialwissenschaften heissen? Frankfurt am Main, [1972]. pp. 137. bibliog. (Hanover. Technische Hochschule. Psychologisches Seminar. Veröffentlichungen)

DINGLE (HERBERT) Science at the crossroads. London, 1972. pp. 256.

MEDAWAR (Sir PETER BRIAN) The hope of progress. London, 1972. pp. 133.

THIEL (CHRISTIAN) Grundlagenkrise und Grundlagenstr Studie über das normative Fundament der Wissenschaften am Beispiel von Mathematik und Sozialwissenschaft. Meisenheim am Glan, 1972. pp. 226. bibliog.

- History

INTERNATIONAL CONGRESS OF THE HISTORY OF SCIENCE AND TECHNOLOGY, 1931. Science at the cross roads: papers presented to the... Congress... by the delegates of the U.S.S.R.; with a new foreword by Joseph Needham, etc. London, 1971. pp. 235.

KEARNEY (HUGH FRANCIS) ed. Origins of the scientific revolution. London, 1964 repr. 1973. pp. 159. bibliog.

BASALLA (GEORGE) ed. The rise of modern science: external or internal factors? Lexington, [1968]. pp. 109. bibliog.

KUCZYNSKI (JUERGEN) Wissenschaft und Wirtschaft bis zur industriellen Revolution: Studien und Essays über drei Jahrtausende. Berlin, 1970. pp. 152.

HANSON (NORWOOD RUSSELL) What I do not believe, and other essays; edited by Stephen Toulmin and Harry Woolf. Dordrecht, [1971]. pp. 390.

INTERNATIONAL ECONOMIC ASSOCIATION. Conference, [1972?], St. Anton. Science and technology in economic growth: proceedings of a conference...; edited by B.R. Williams. London, 1973. pp. 446.

MANUEL (FRANK EDWARD) Freedom from history, and other untimely essays. London, [1971]. pp. 301.

PERSPECTIVES in the history of science and technology: [papers and commentaries presented at a symposium at the University of Oklahoma, April 8-12, 1969, sponsored by the University, the Midwest Junto, and the Society for the History of Technology]; edited by Duane H.D. Roller. Norman, Oklahoma, [1971]. pp. 307.

NYE (MARY JO) Molecular reality: a perspective on the scientific work of Jean Perrin. London, 1972. pp. 201. bibliog.

- History - Bibliography

ISIS cumulative bibliography: a bibliography of the history of science formed from ISIS critical bibliographies 1-90, 1913-65; edited by Magda Whitrow. London, 1971 in progress.

- History - Baltic States

IZ istorii estestvoznaniia i tekhniki Pribaltiki. t.4. Riga, 1972. pp. 412. With English table of contents.

- History - Europe

BRIDGES (JOHN HENRY) Essays and addresses. London, 1907. pp. 307.

- History - France

HAHN (ROGER) The anatomy of a scientific institution: the Paris Academy of Sciences, 1666-1803. Berkeley, 1971. pp. 433. bibliogs.

- History - Germany

MENDELSSOHN (KURT ALFRED GEORG) The world of Walther Nernst: the rise and fall of German science. London, 1973. pp. 191.

- History - Poland

JACZEWSKI (BOHDAN) Organizacja i finansowanie nauki polskiej w okresie międzywojennym. Wrocław, 1971. pp. 232. (Polska Akademia Nauk. Zakład Historii Nauki i Techniki. Monografie z Dziejów Nauki i Techniki. 70) With English and Russian summaries.

SCIENCE (Cont'd)

- History - Russia - Bibliography

GURKO (Z.V.) and others, compilers. Razvitie sovetskoi nauki za 50 let: ukazatel' iubileinoi literatury, 1967-1969 gg. Moskva, 1972. pp. 327.

- History - United Kingdom

MUSSON (ALBERT EDWARD) ed. Science, technology, and economic growth in the eighteenth century. London, 1972. pp. 211. bibliog.

SCIENCE and society, 1600-1900; by P.M. Rattansi [and others; based on lectures delivered in Cambridge in 1968]; edited by Peter Mathias. Cambridge, 1972. pp. 166.

- History - United Kingdom - British Empire

STEARNS (RAYMOND PHINEAS) Science in the British colonies of America. Urbana, [1970]. pp. 760. bibliog.

- History - United States

STEARNS (RAYMOND PHINEAS) Science in the British colonies of America. Urbana, [1970]. pp. 760. bibliog.

DANIELS (GEORGE H.) Science in American society: a social history. New York, 1971. pp. 390,x. bibliog.

- History - West Indies

STEARNS (RAYMOND PHINEAS) Science in the British colonies of America. Urbana, [1970]. pp. 760. bibliog.

- Information services

ORGANISATION FOR ECONOMIC CO-OPERATION AND DEVELOPMENT. Information Policy Group. 1971. Canada. Paris, 1971. pp. 161. bibliog. (Reviews of National Scientific and Technical Information Policy. [No.1.])

- International cooperation

ORGANISATION FOR ECONOMIC CO-OPERATION AND DEVELOPMENT. 1962. Scientific research and education for the future: international co-operation in research. [Paris, 1962]. pp. 36.

SALOMON (JEAN-JACQUES) and LORIDAN (GUY) compilers. International scientific organisations: catalogue; (with Supplement). Paris, Organisation for Economic Co-operation and Development, 1965-1966. 2 pts.

ORGANISATION FOR ECONOMIC CO-OPERATION AND DEVELOPMENT. Ministerial Meeting on Science. 1st, 1963. Ministers talk about science: a summary and review of the...Meeting...edited...by Emmanuel G. Mesthene. Paris. 1965. pp. 178.

COURTEIX (SIMONE) Recherche scientifique et relations internationales: la pratique française. Paris, 1972. pp. 287. bibliog. With folding table at end.

- Methodology

TROSHIN (DENIS MIKHAILOVICH) Metodologicheskie problemy sovremennoi nauki. Moskva, 1966. pp. 175.

ACKOFF (RUSSELL LINCOLN) Scientific method: optimizing applied research decisions;... with the collaboration of Shiv K. Gupta and J. Sayer Minas. New York, 1968. pp. 464. bibliogs.

MUELLER (JOHANNES) Writer on scientific method. Grundlagen der systematischen Heuristik. Berlin, 1970. pp. 233. bibliog. (Zentralinstitut für Sozialistische Wirtschaftsführung, and Arbeitskreis "Sozialistische Wirtschaftsführung". Schriften zur Sozialistischen Wirtschaftsführung)

NAUKOVEDENIE, prognozirovanie, informatika. Kiev, 1970. pp. 348.

WISSENSCHAFTSTHEORETISCHES KOLLOQUIUM, 5.-6., 1969-1970. Der Methoden- und Theorienpluralismus in den Wissenschaften: Vorträge und Diskussionen des 5. ... und des 6. ...Kolloquiums...(des Philosophischen Instituts der Universität Düsseldorf); herausgegeben von A. Diemer. Meisenheim am Glan, 1971. pp. 325. bibliogs. (Fritz Thyssen Stiftung. Neunzehntes Jahrhundert. Arbeitskreis Wissenschaftstheorie. Studien zur Wissenschaftstheorie. Band 6)

BITZ (ALLAN) Conformity and creativity: an application of theory to some problems in the sociology of science; [Ph.D. (London) thesis]. [1972] fo. 272. bibliog. Typescript: unpublished. This thesis is the property of London University and may not be removed from the Library.

FEIBLEMAN (JAMES KERN) Scientific method: the hypothetico-experimental laboratory procedure of the physical sciences. The Hague, 1972. pp. 246. bibliog.

FILOSOFIIA, metodologiia, nauka. Moskva, 1972. pp. 236.

PLATONOV (GRIGORII VASIL'EVICH) and PETRUSHEVSKII (S.A.) eds. Marksistsko-leninskaia filosofiia kak metodologiia obshchestvennykh i estestvennykh nauk. Moskva, 1972. pp. 196.

- Philosophy

The COMMUNIST answer to The challenge of our time; a reprint of the lectures by Dr. [John] Lewis [and others]. London, 1947. pp. 85.

SHVYREV (VLADIMIR SERGEEVICH) Neopozitivizm i problemy empiricheskogo obosnovaniia nauki. Moskva, 1966. pp. 215. bibliog.

INTERNATIONAL COLLOQUIUM IN THE PHILOSOPHY OF SCIENCE, LONDON, 1965. Problems in the philosophy of science; proceedings ... vol. 3; edited by Imre Lakatos [and] Alan Musgrave. Amsterdam, North-Holland Publishing Company, 1968. pp. ix, 448. 22½cm. (Studies in Logic and the Foundations of Mathematics)

SAMBURSKY (SHMUEL) Balfour's philosophy of science;...address...at the Weizmann Institute of Science, November, 1969. [Rehovot?, 1969?]. pp. 29. bibliog.

ROSSI (MARIO MANLIO) Da Hegel a Marx. [Milan, 1970 in progress].

HUSSERL (EDMUND) The crisis of European sciences and transcendental phenomenology: an introduction to phenomenological philosophy; translated, with an introduction, by David Carr. Evanston, 1970. pp. 405.

BRADLEY (JOHN) Mach's philosophy of science. London, 1971. pp. 226.

GESSEN (B.) The social and economic roots of Newton's 'Principia'; [first published in 1931 in Science at the Cross Roads: papers presented to the International Congress of the History of Science and Technology]; with a new introduction by Robert S. Cohen. New York, 1971. pp. 62.

HANSON (NORWOOD RUSSELL) Observation and explanation: a guide to philosophy of science. New York, 1971. pp. 84.

HANSON (NORWOOD RUSSELL) What I do not believe, and other essays; edited by Stephen Toulmin and Harry Woolf. Dordrecht, [1971]. pp. 390.

KORDIG (CARL R.) The justification of scientific change. Dordrecht, [1971]. pp. 119. bibliog.

MICHALOS (ALEX C.) The Popper-Carnap controversy. The Hague, 1971. pp. 124. bibliog.

PHILOSOPHY OF SCIENCE ASSOCIATION. Meeting. 1970. PSA 1970: in memory of Rudolf Carnap; proceedings of the...Meeting... [held in cooperation with the Boston Colloquium for the Philosophy of Science, Boston, 1970]; edited by Roger C. Buck and Robert S. Cohen. Dordrecht, [1971]. pp. 615. bibliogs. (Boston Colloquium for the Philosophy of Science. Boston Studies in the Philosophy of Science. vol. 8)

WISSENSCHAFTSTHEORETISCHES KOLLOQUIUM, 5.-6., 1969-1970. Der Methoden- und Theorienpluralismus in den Wissenschaften: Vorträge und Diskussionen des 5. ... und des 6. ...Kolloquiums...(des Philosophischen Instituts der Universität Düsseldorf); herausgegeben von A. Diemer. Meisenheim am Glan, 1971. pp. 325. bibliogs. (Fritz Thyssen Stiftung. Neunzehntes Jahrhundert. Arbeitskreis Wissenschaftstheorie. Studien zur Wissenschaftstheorie. Band 6)

WRIGHT (GEORG HENRIK VON) Explanation and understanding. Ithaca, 1971. pp. 230. bibliog.

BOLZANO (BERNARD PLACIDUS JOHANN) Theory of science: attempt at a detailed and in the main novel exposition of logic with constant attention to earlier authors; edited and translated by Rolf George. Oxford, 1972. pp. 399.

GRAHAM (LOREN R.) Science and philosophy in the Soviet Union. New York, 1972. pp. 584, xvi. bibliog.

HARRÉ (HORACE ROMANO) The philosophies of science: an introductory survey. London, 1972. pp. 191. bibliog.

LOSEE (JOHN) A historical introduction to the philosophy of science. London, 1972. pp. 218. bibliog.

HANSON (NORWOOD RUSSELL) Constellations and conjectures; edited by Willard C. Humphreys. Dordrecht, [1973]. pp. 282.

JEVONS (FREDERICK RAPHAEL) Science observed: science as a social and intellectual activity. London, 1973. pp. 186.

ZINOV'EV (ALEKSANDR ALEKSANDROVICH) Foundations of the logical theory of scientific knowledge (complex logic); revised and enlarged English edition; with an appendix, etc. Dordrecht, [1973]. pp. 301. (Boston Colloquium for the Philosophy of Science. Boston Studies in the Philosophy of Science. vol. 9)

- Social aspects

FULLER (RICHARD BUCKMINSTER) and others. Approaching the benign environment. [New York], 1970. pp. 160. (Auburn University. Franklin Lectures in the Sciences and Humanities. 1st Series)

ACQUAVIVA (SABINO SAMELE) Una scommessa sul futuro: sociologia e programmazione globale. Milano, 1971. pp. 193.

BEN-DAVID (JOSEPH) The scientist's role in society: a comparative study. Englewood Cliffs, [1971]. pp. 207.

DAINTON (Sir FREDERICK SYDNEY) Science: salvation or damnation. [Southampton], 1971. pp. 28. (Southampton. University. Fawley Foundation. Lectures. 1971)

ECKERT (ROLAND) Wissenschaft und Demokratie: Plädoyer für eine verantwortliche Wissenschaft. Tübingen, 1971. pp. 63. With summaries in English and French.

ORGANISATION FOR ECONOMIC CO-OPERATION AND DEVELOPMENT. Ad Hoc Group on New Concepts of Science Policy. 1971. Science, growth and society: a new perspective. Paris, 1971. pp. 113.

The SOCIAL responsibility of the scientist; [essays based on a course of lectures delivered at Berkeley, 1969 and organized by Science Students for Social Responsibility]; edited by Martin Brown. New York, [1971]. pp. 282. bibliog.

SPEAY (JACQUES) and others. Science for development: an essay on the origin and organization of national science policies. Paris, United Nations Educational Scientific and Cultural Organization, 1971. pp. 224. bibliog.

STEWART (BRUCE) A science of social issues. Metuchen, N.J., 1971. pp. 327.

BARNES (BARRY) ed. Sociology of science: selected readings. Harmondsworth, 1972. pp. 396. bibliogs.

CALDER (PETER RITCHIE) Baron Ritchie-Calder. How long have we got? Montreal, 1972. pp. 88. (McGill University. Beatty Memorial Lectures. 1971)

CIBA FOUNDATION. Symposia. Civilization and science: in conflict or collaboration? Amsterdam, 1972. pp. 227.

MAIZEL' (ISAAK ALEKSANDROVICH) Nauka, avtomatizatsiia, obshchestvo. Leningrad, 1972. pp. 280.

MULKAY (MICHAEL J.) The social process of innovation: a study in the sociology of science. London, 1972. pp. 64. bibliog. (British Sociological Association. Studies in Sociology)

RÁCZ (MIKLÓS) Universiteit en klassenstrijd: wetenschap, partijdigheid en samenleving. Amsterdam 1972. pp. 200.

SOCIOLOGICAL REVIEW, THE; [published by] University of Keele. Monographs. No. 18. The sociology of science; edited by Paul Halmos. Keele, 1972. pp. 226. bibliogs.

JEVONS (FREDERICK RAPHAEL) Science observed: science as a social and intellectual activity. London, 1973. pp. 186.

MULLINS (NICHOLAS C.) Science: some sociological perspectives. Indianapolis, [1973]. pp. 40. bibliog.

RICHTER (MAURICE NATHANIEL) Science as a cultural process. London, 1973. pp. 130.

SEMINAR ON SOCIAL ASPECTS OF SCIENCE AND TECHNOLOGY, UNIVERSITY OF EDINBURGH, 1970. Meaning and control: essays in social aspects of science and technology; edited by D.O. Edge and J.N. Wolfe. London, 1973. pp. 274. bibliogs.

SKLAIR (LESLIE ALLAN) Organized knowledge: a sociological view of science and technology. London, 1973. pp. 284. bibliog.

- Study and teaching - Statistics

FREEMAN (CHRISTOPHER) The measurement of scientific and technological activities: proposals for the collection of statistics on science and technology on an internationally uniform basis. Paris, United Nations Educational, Scientific and Cultural Organization, 1969. pp. 63. (Statistical Reports and Studies. [No. 15])

SCIENCE (Cont'd.)

- Study and teaching - Africa

SEMINAR ON THE TEACHING OF BASIC SCIENCES IN AFRICAN UNIVERSITIES, RABAT, 1962. The teaching of sciences in African universities: report, etc. Paris, 1964. pp. 112. (United Nations Educational, Scientific and Cultural Organization. Development of Higher Education)

- Study and teaching - France

SAINT MARTIN (MONIQUE DE) Les fonctions sociales de l'enseignement scientifique. Paris, 1971. pp. 258. (Paris. Ecole Pratique des Hautes Etudes. Section des Sciences Economiques et Sociales. Centre de Sociologie Européenne. Cahiers. 8)

- Study and teaching - Iceland

ORGANISATION FOR ECONOMIC CO-OPERATION AND DEVELOPMENT. Directorate for Scientific Affairs. 1972. Iceland. Paris, 1972. pp. 159. (Reviews of National Science Policy. [No. 15.])

- Study and teaching - Netherlands

ORGANISATION FOR ECONOMIC CO-OPERATION AND DEVELOPMENT. Directorate for Scientific Affairs. 1973. Netherlands. Paris, 1973. pp. 375. (Reviews of National Science Policy. [No. 16])

- Study and teaching - Russia

PLATONOV (GRIGORII VASIL'EVICH) and PETRUSHEVSKII (S.A.) eds. Marksistsko-leninskaia filosofiia kak metodologiia obshchestvennykh i estestvennykh nauk. Moskva, 1972. pp. 196.

- Study and teaching - Spain

ORGANISATION FOR ECONOMIC CO-OPERATION AND DEVELOPMENT. Directorate for Scientific Affairs. 1971. Spain. Paris, 1971. pp. 123. (Reviews of National Science Policy. [No. 13])

- Study and teaching - United Kingdom

ASSOCIATION OF SCIENTIFIC WORKERS. Science and adult education: a report, etc. [London, 1963]. pp. 11.

CARDWELL (DONALD STEPHEN LOWELL) The organisation of science in England. rev. ed. London, 1972. pp. 268. bibliogs.

RODERICK (GORDON W.) and STEPHENS (MICHAEL D.) Scientific and technical education in nineteenth-century England. Newton Abbot, [1972]. pp. 173.

- Study and teaching - United States

SCIENTIFIC manpower: a dilemma for graduate education: [report of a symposium held at the Massachusetts Institute of Technology, 1970]; edited by Sanborn C. Brown and Brian B. Schwartz. Cambridge, Mass., [1971]. pp. 180. bibliog. (Massachusetts Institute of Technology. M.I.T. Reports. No. 22)

SNELLING (W. RODMAN) and BORUCH (ROBERT F.) Science in liberal arts colleges: a longitudinal study of 49 selective colleges. New York, 1972. pp. 285. bibliog.

- Canada

CANADA. Ministry of State for Science and Technology. Annual report. a., 1971/72 [1st]- Ottawa. [In English and French]

- Communist countries

COUNCIL FOR MUTUAL ECONOMIC ASSISTANCE. Permanent Commission for the Coordination of Scientific and Technical Research. Teoriia i praktika prognozirovaniia razvitiia nauki i tekhniki v stranakh-chlenakh SEV. Moskva, 1971. pp. 407.

- Israel

ZAHLAN (ANTOINE B.) Science and higher education in Israel. Beirut, [1970]. pp. 153. (Institute for Palestine Studies. Monograph Series. No. 22.)

- Russia

AL'PEROVICH (IURII IZRAILEVICH) Na poliakh budushchego. Moskva, 1964. pp. 175.

CHEMODANOV (MARK PETROVICH) Prevrashchenie nauki v neposredstvennuiu proizvoditel'nuiu silu v protsesse stroitel'stva kommunizma. Moskva, 1966. pp. 92. Colophon gives author's name as Marki.

- Russia - Statistics

RUSSIA (U.S.S.R.). Tsentral'noe Statisticheskoe Upravlenie. 1971. Narodnoe obrazovanie, nauka i kul'tura v SSSR: statisticheskii sbornik. Moskva, 1971. pp. 403.

- Russia - Kirghizia

ASANGULOV (KUBAT) Kommunisticheskaia partiia Kirgizii v bor'be za nauchnyi progress, 1959-1965 gody. Frunze, 1972. pp. 127.

- Russia - Latvia

VALESKALN (PETR IVANOVICH) and RAMAN (M.) Puti nauchno-tekhnicheskogo progressa. Riga, 1965. pp. 77.

- Russia - Uzbekistan

ARIFOV (UBAI ARIFOVICH) Nauka Sovetskogo Uzbekistana. Tashkent, 1964. pp. 62.

- United Kingdom

CONFERENCE ON INDUSTRY AND SCIENCE, MANCHESTER, 1954. Report of the Conference on industry and science held on 9th July, 1954, [and sponsored by the Manchester Joint Research Council]. Manchester, 1955. pp. 64.

- United States

MENARD (HENRY W.) Science: growth and change. Cambridge, Mass., 1971. pp. 215.

TOBEY (RONALD C.) The American ideology of national science, 1919-1930. Pittsburgh, [1971]. pp. 263. bibliog.

MULLINS (NICHOLAS C.) Science: some sociological perspectives. Indianapolis, [1973]. pp. 40. bibliog.

SCIENCE AND CIVILIZATION

BASALLA (GEORGE) ed. The rise of modern science: external or internal factors? Lexington, [1968]. pp. 109. bibliog.

DANIELS (GEORGE H.) Science in American society: a social history. New York, 1971. pp. 390,x. bibliog.

SCIENCE and society, 1600-1900; by P.M. Rattansi [and others; based on lectures delivered in Cambridge in 1968]; edited by Peter Mathias. Cambridge, 1972. pp. 166.

SCIENCE AND ETHICS

RAMSEY (PAUL) Fabricated man: the ethics of genetic control. New Haven, 1970. pp. 174.

SCIENCE AND STATE

ORGANISATION FOR ECONOMIC CO-OPERATION AND DEVELOPMENT. Ministerial Meeting on Science. 1st, 1963. Ministers talk about science: a summary and review of the...Meeting...edited...by Emmanuel G. Mesthene. Paris, 1965. pp. 178.

PARLIAMENTARY AND SCIENTIFIC CONFERENCE, 2nd, 1964. Science and parliament: final report; presented by Pierre Piganiol. [Paris], 1965. pp. 177.

DOMIN (GEORG) and MOCEK (REINHARD) eds. Ideologie und Naturwissenschaft: Politik und Vernunft im Zeitalter des Sozialismus und der wissenschaftlich-technischen Revolution. Berlin, 1969. pp. 368. bibliog.

MAIER (HANS) and others, eds. Politik und Wissenschaft. München, [1971]. pp. 573. (Munich. Universität. Institut für Politische Wissenschaft. Münchener Studien zur Politik. 17. Band)

ORGANISATION FOR ECONOMIC CO-OPERATION AND DEVELOPMENT. Ad Hoc Group on New Concepts of Science Policy. 1971. Science, growth and society: a new perspective. Paris, 1971. pp. 113.

SPEAY (JACQUES) and others. Science for development: an essay on the origin and organization of national science policies. Paris, United Nations Educational, Scientific and Cultural Organization, 1971. pp. 224. bibliog.

SALOMON (JEAN JACQUES) Science and politics; translated by Noël Lindsay. London, 1973. pp. 277. bibliog.

- Canada

DOERN (G. BRUCE) Science and politics in Canada. Montreal, 1972. pp. 238.

SEMINAR ON GUIDELINES FOR SCIENTIFIC ACTIVITIES IN NORTHERN CANADA, MONT GABRIEL, QUEBEC, 1972. Science and the north: a seminar on guidelines for scientific activities in northern Canada, 1972. Ottawa, Information Canada, 1973. pp. 287. bibliogs.

- Germany

ROTH (KARL HEINZ) and KANZOW (ECKARD) Unwissen als Ohnmacht: Grundrisse einer Analyse der Wissenschafts- und Bildungspolitik des bundesrepublikanischen Herrschaftskartells. [Berlin, 1970]. pp. 377. bibliog.

HIRSCH (JOACHIM) Wissenschaftlich-technischer Fortschritt und politisches System: Organisation und Grundlagen administrativer Wissenschaftsförderung in der BRD. 2nd ed. Frankfurt am Main, 1971. pp. 306.

- Ireland, (Republic)

NATIONAL SCIENCE COUNCIL [EIRE]. Progress report, 1969-71. Dublin, Stationery Office, 1972. pp. 44.

- Russia

RASSUDOVSKII (VLADIMIR ALEKSANDROVICH) Gosudarstvennaia organizatsiia nauki v SSSR: pravovye voprosy. Moskva, 1971. pp. 246.

GRAHAM (LOREN R.) Science and philosophy in the Soviet Union. New York, 1972. pp. 584, xvi. bibliog.

- Russia - Georgia

OKROSTSVARIDZE (IVANE E.) Gosudarstvennyi biudzhet Gruzinskoi SSR na sluzhbe nauki. Tbilisi, 1970. pp. 104.

- United Kingdom

POOLE (J.B.) and ANDREWS (E. KAY) eds. The government of science in Britain. London, [1972]. pp. 358.

U.K. Central Office of Information. Reference Division. 1972. The promotion of the sciences in Britain. rev. ed. London, 1972. pp. 29. bibliog.

- United States

GREENBERG (DANIEL S.) The politics of American science. Harmondsworth, 1969. pp. 368.

WEINGART (PETER) Die amerikanische Wissenschaftslobby: zum sozialen und politischen Wandel des Wissenschaftssystems im Prozess der Forschungsplanung. Düsseldorf, [1970]. pp. 253. bibliog.

MURPHY (THOMAS P.) Science, geopolitics, and federal spending. Lexington, Mass., [1971] pp. 568.

The POLITICS of American science, 1939 to the present;...edited by James L. Penick [and others]. rev. ed. Cambridge, Massachusetts, 1972. pp. 453.

SCIENCE AND THE HUMANITIES

KREUZER (HELMUT) ed. Literarische und naturwissenschaftliche Intelligenz: Dialog über die "zwei Kulturen". Stuttgart, [1969]. pp. 273. bibliog.

MEILAKH (BORIS SOLOMONOVICH) Na rubezhe nauki i iskusstva: spor o dvukh sferakh poznaniia i tvorchestva. Leningrad, 1971. pp. 247.

SNOW (CHARLES PERCY) Baron Snow. Public affairs; [lectures and articles from 1959 to 1970]. London, 1971. pp. 224.

SCIENCE AS A PROFESSION

SAINT MARTIN (MONIQUE DE) Les fonctions sociales de l'enseignement scientifique. Paris, 1971. pp. 258. (Paris. Ecole Pratique des Hautes Etudes. Section des Sciences Economiques et Sociales. Centre de Sociologie Europeenne. Cahiers. 8)

SCIENCE TEACHERS

LINNÉ (OLGA) An evaluation of the Kenya Science Teachers College. Uppsala, 1972. pp. 67. bibliog. (Nordiska Afrikainstitutet. Research Reports. No. 10)

SCIENTIFIC SOCIETIES

SALOMON (JEAN-JACQUES) and LORIDAN (GUY) compilers. International scientific organisations: catalogue; (with Supplement). Paris, Organisation for Economic Co-operation and Development, 1965-1966. 2 pts.

- France

HAHN (ROGER) The anatomy of a scientific institution: the Paris Academy of Sciences, 1666-1803. Berkeley, 1971. pp. 433. bibliogs.

SCIENTISTS

PUBLIC OPINION INDEX FOR INDUSTRY. The conflict between the scientific mind and the management mind: research report. [Princeton], 1959. pp. 38, A 57.

UNITED NATIONS EDUCATIONAL, SCIENTIFIC AND CULTURAL ORGANIZATION. Statistical Reports and Studies. [No.17]. World summary of statistics on science and technology: results of experimental surveys of scientific and technical manpower and expenditures for research and experimental development. Paris, 1970. pp. 66. In English and French.

BEN-DAVID (JOSEPH) The scientist's role in society: a comparative study. Englewood Cliffs, [1971]. pp. 207.

MCKNIGHT (ALLAN) Scientists abroad: a study of the international movement of persons in science and technology. Paris, United Nations Educational, Scientific and Cultural Organization, 1971. pp. 147.

ROTBLAT (JOSEPH) Scientists in the quest for peace: a history of the Pugwash Conference. Cambridge, Mass., [1972]. pp. 399.

- Canada

KELLY (FRANK) Prospects for scientists and engineers in Canada. Ottawa, 1971. pp. 59. (Canada. Science Council of Canada. Special Studies. No.20)

- India

INDIA. Census. Papers. 1966. No. 1. 1961 census: scientific and technical personnel tables. [Delhi, 1966]. pp. 223.

- New Zealand

NEW ZEALAND. National Research Advisory Council. 1967. Some aspects of technical manpower in New Zealand: an interim report to the ... Council. Wellington, 1967. pp. 73. (Publications. No. 2)

- Russia

SOVIET science, 1917-1970...; edited by Paul K. Urban, Andrew I. Lebed; (compiled at the Institute for the Study of the USSR... by Melinskaya, S.I.). Metuchen, N.J., 1971 in progress.

LEBIN (BORIS DMITRIEVICH) and TSYPKIN (GENNADII ALEKSANDROVICH) Prava rabotnika nauki. Leningrad, 1971. pp. 226.

SCIENTISTS - Underdeveloped areas
See UNDERDEVELOPED AREAS - Scientists

- United Kingdom

U.K. Civil Service Commission. 1972. Scientists in government service. Basingstoke, 1972. pp. 103.

- United Kingdom - Biography

EDINBURGH. Royal Society. Year book. a., 1946- Edinburgh.

OBITUARY NOTICES OF FELLOWS OF THE ROYAL SOCIETY. a., 1952 (v.8, no.21), 1953 (v.8, no.22), 1954 (v.9); ceased pbln. London. Superseded by BIOGRAPHICAL MEMOIRS OF FELLOWS OF THE ROYAL SOCIETY, which see.

BIOGRAPHICAL MEMOIRS OF FELLOWS OF THE ROYAL SOCIETY. a., 1955-1972 (v.1-18). London. Supersedes OBITUARY NOTICES OF FELLOWS OF THE ROYAL SOCIETY, which see.

- United States

HARMON (LINDSEY R.) Profiles of Ph.D's in the sciences: summary report on follow-up of doctorate cohorts, 1935-1960. Washington, 1965 repr. 1968. pp. 123. (National Research Council. Career Patterns Reports. No. 1)

MENARD (HENRY W.) Science: growth and change. Cambridge, Mass., 1971. pp. 215.

MULLINS (NICHOLAS C.) Science: some sociological perspectives. Indianapolis, [1973]. pp. 40. bibliog.

SCIENTISTS, AMERICAN

SCIENTIFIC manpower: a dilemma for graduate education: [report of a symposium held at the Massachusetts Institute of Technology, 1970]; edited by Sanborn C. Brown and Brian B. Schwartz. Cambridge, Mass., [1971]. pp. 180. bibliog. (Massachusetts Institute of Technology. M.I.T. Reports. No. 22)

SCIENTISTS, GERMAN

HERGENROEDER (UDO) Männer, die Erfolg erfinden: Techniker und Wissenschaftler als Motoren der Wirtschaft. Düsseldorf, 1970. pp. 310. bibliog.

LASBY (CLARENCE G.) Project paperclip: German scientists and the cold war. New York, 1971. pp. 338. bibliog.

SCIENTOLOGY

VOSPER (CYRIL) The mind benders. London, [1971]. pp. 188.

SOUTH AFRICA. Commission of Enquiry into Scientology. 1973. Report; [G.P.C. Kotzé, chairman] (R.P.55/1973). in SOUTH AFRICA. Parliament. House of Assembly. Votes and proceedings; (with Printed annexures).

SCOTCH IN GERMANY

FISCHER (THOMAS ALFRED) The Scots in Germany: being a contribution towards the history of the Scot abroad; [reprint of the work first published in Edinburgh, 1902]. Edinburgh, [1973]. pp. 324.

SCOTLAND

- Biography

EDINBURGH. Royal Society. Year book. a., 1946- Edinburgh.

- Census

SCOTLAND. Census, 1971. Census, 1971: Scotland: county report[s]. Edinburgh, 1972 in progress.

SCOTLAND. Census, 1971. Census, 1971: Scotland: second preliminary report: advance analysis of computer-read data. Edinburgh, 1972. pp. 205.

SCOTLAND. Census, 1971. Census, 1971: Scotland: Scottish population summary: area populations, economic activity, households. Edinburgh, 1973. pp. 12.

- Commerce

LOCH (DAVID) A tour through most of the trading towns and villages of Scotland; containing notes and observations concerning the trade, manufactures, improvements, etc. Edinburgh, 1778. pp. 72.

- Constitution

    THIRTEEN TWENTY CLUB. An outline of a
        Scottish constitution. 2nd ed.
        Currie, Midlothian, [1969?]. pp. 11.

- Constitutional history

    MACNEILL (DUNCAN HARALD) The historical Scottish
        constitution. Edinburgh, [1971]. pp. 123.

- Description and travel

    MILLMAN (ROGER) Outdoor recreation in the High-
        land countryside: a study of rural management
        and access for public recreation in ten selected
        areas of the Highlands and Islands. [Cambridge?,
        1971]. 1 vol. (pagination varies). bibliog.

- Directories

    SCOTLAND [ ]; issued under the patronage of the
        Convention of Royal Burghs, the Association of
        County Councils in Scotland and the Scottish
        Counties of Cities Association: a comprehensive
        guide to local authorities and public bodies
        in Scotland pd. by the Scottish Council (Develop-
        ment and Industry). Irreg., 1971- Edinburgh.

- Economic conditions

    M'KILLOP (JAMES) Thoughts for the people. Stir-
        ling, 1898. pp. 186.

    JOHNSTON (THOMAS LOTHIAN) and others. Structure
        and growth of the Scottish economy. London,
        1971. pp. 356. bibliogs.

- Economic history

    YOUNGSON (ALEXANDER JOHN) After the Forty-five:
        the economic impact on the Scottish Highlands.
        Edinburgh, [1973]. pp. 246.

- Economic policy

    NORTH EAST SCOTLAND DEVELOPMENT AUTHORITY. Annual
        report. a., 1971/2- Aberdeen.

    SLESSER (MALCOLM) The politics of environment,
        including a guide to Scottish thought and action.
        London, 1972. pp. 176.

- History

    SINCLAIR (Sir JOHN) Analysis of the statistical
        account of Scotland; with a general view of the
        history of that country, and discussions on some
        important branches of political economy. London,
        1825-6; New York, 1970. 2 vols. Facsimile reprint.

    FERGUSON (WILLIAM) Ph.D. Scotland: 1689 to the
        present. Edinburgh, 1968. pp. 464. bibliog.

    REID (JAMES MACARTHUR) Scotland's progress: the
        survival of a nation. London, 1971. pp. 221.

- History - Sources

    SCOTLAND. Scottish Record Office. 1971-   . List
        of gifts and deposits. Edinburgh, 1971 in progress.

    SCOTLAND. Scottish Record Office. 1973. Reports
        on the annexed estates, 1755-1769; from the records
        of the forfeited estates preserved in the Scot-
        tish Record Office; edited by Virginia Wills.
        Edinburgh, 1973. pp. 116.

- Industries

    LOCH (DAVID) A tour through most of the trading
        towns and villages of Scotland; containing notes
        and observations concerning the trade, manufac-
        tures, improvements, etc. Edinburgh, 1778.
        pp. 72.

    NORTH EAST SCOTLAND DEVELOPMENT AUTHORITY. Annual
        report. a., 1971/2- Aberdeen.

    FORSYTH (DAVID JAMES CAMERON) U.S. investment
        in Scotland. New York, 1972. pp. 320. bibliog.

    SCOTTISH COUNCIL (DEVELOPMENT AND INDUSTRY). Inter-
        national Forum, 3rd, Aviemore, 1972. The changing
        pattern of industry and employment: Scotland's
        future. [Edinburgh, 1972]. pp. 169.

- Nationalism

    SCOTTISH NATIONAL PARTY. [Policy leaflets]. [Glasgow,
        193-?-196-?]. 11 parts (in 1 vol).

    REID (JAMES MACARTHUR) Scotland's progress: the
        survival of a nation. London, 1971. pp. 221.

    [GRIEVE (CHRISTOPHER MURRAY)] A political speech;
        [by] Hugh MacDiarmid [pseud.]; a transcription
        from a recording taken at the 1320 Club Sympo-
        sium, Glasgow University, 6th April 1968. Edin-
        burgh, 1972. pp. 15.

    SLESSER (MALCOLM) The politics of environment,
        including a guide to Scottish thought and action.
        London, 1972. pp. 176.

- Politics and government

    M'KILLOP (JAMES) Thoughts for the people. Stir-
        ling, 1898. pp. 186.

    KELLAS (JAMES G.) The Scottish political system.
        Cambridge, 1973. pp. 260. bibliog.

- Population

    SCOTLAND. Scottish Development Department. 1972.
        Projections of households for the regions and
        sub-regions of Scotland. Edinburgh, 1972. pp.
        22.

- Registers

    SCOTLAND. Scottish Record Office. Indexes. No.
        68. Index to particular register of sasines
        for sheriffdom of Lanark preserved in H.M. General
        Register House. vol. 2. 1721-1780. Edinburgh,
        1973. pp. 249.

- Social conditions

    M'KILLOP (JAMES) Thoughts for the people. Stir-
        ling, 1898. pp. 186.

    FRANCIS (JOHN) Physical scientist and SWAN (NORMAN)
        Scotland in turmoil: a social and environmental
        assessment of the impact of North Sea oil and
        gas on communities in the north of Scotland.
        Edinburgh, [1973]. pp. 108.

- Statistics

    SINCLAIR (Sir JOHN) Analysis of the statistical
        account of Scotland; with a general view of the
        history of that country, and discussions on some
        important branches of political economy. London,
        1825-6; New York, 1970. 2 vols. Facsimile reprint.

- Statistics, Medical

    LOCKWOOD (ERIC) Scottish hospital morbidity data,
        1961-1968. [Edinburgh], Scottish Home and Health
        Department, 1971. pp. 171. bibliog. (Scottish
        Health Service Studies. No.20)

- Statistics, Vital

    RICHARDS (I.D. GERALD) Infant mortality in Scotland.
        [Edinburgh], 1971. pp. 52. bibliog. (Scottish
        Health Service Studies. No. 16.)

SCOTT (KATHERINE GRACE HEPBURNE)

BARBOUR (G.F.) Katherine Scott: a memoir and other
    records. Edinburgh, 1929. pp. 135.

SCOTTISH NATIONAL PARTY

SCOTTISH NATIONAL PARTY. [Policy leaflets]. [Glasgow, 193-?-196-?]. 11 parts (in 1 vol).

SCRAP METAL INDUSTRY
- Europe

ERZER (WILLY) Der Schrottausgleich der Montanunion. Basel, 1964. pp. 120. bibliog.

SEA BED
See OCEAN BOTTOM

SEA BIRDS

U.K. Natural Environment Research Council. 1970. The seabird wreck of 1969 in the Irish Sea; a report...; edited by M.W. Holdgate; (with Supplement: analytical and other data). [London, 1970]. 2 pts. bibliog.

U.K. Natural Environment Research Council. 1971. The sea bird wreck in the Irish Sea, Autumn 1969. [London], 1971. pp. 17. (Publications Series C. No. 4)

SEA-POWER

ELLER (ERNEST McNEILL) The Soviet sea challenge. [Chicago, 1971]. pp. 315. bibliog.

SEALING

PEREIRA SALAS (EUGENIO) Los primeros contactos entre Chile y los Estados Unidos, 1778-1809. Santiago de Chile, [1971]. pp. 353.

SEAMEN

WEIBUST (KNUT) The crew as a social system. Oslo, 1958. pp. 66. (Norsk Sjöfartsmuseum. Skrifter. Nr. 40)

- Laws and regulations

FILIPE (EUSEBIO) O direito do trabalho maritimo. Lisboa, 1972. pp. 134. bibliog. (Portugal. Direcção de Serviços do Trabalho. Estudos Laborais. 1) With abstracts in English, French and German.

NORWAY. Komitéen for Internasjonale Sosial-politiske Saker. 1959. Norway and her sailors: a survey of social legislation. Oslo, 1959. pp. 159.

- United Kingdom

COMMISSION ON INDUSTRIAL RELATIONS [U.K.]. Approved closed shop agreement: British Shipping Federation/National Union of Seamen. London, H.M.S.O., 1972. pp. 31. (Reports. No. 30)

HILL (JOHN MICHAEL MEATH) The seafaring career: a study of the forces affecting joining, serving and leaving the Merchant Navy. London, 1972. pp. 158.

U.K. Department of Trade and Industry. 1972. Census of seamen, 26 April 1971: vessels registered in the United Kingdom. London, 1972. pp. 14.

SEARCH AND RESCUE OPERATIONS

U.K. Committee to review the Marine Search and Rescue Organisation of the United Kingdom. 1970. Marine search and rescue organisation: report: [E.R. Hargreaves, chairman]. London, 1970. pp. 49. 3 maps and table in end pocket.

SEASONAL LABOUR
- Switzerland

CALVARUSO (CLAUDIO) Sottoproletariato in Svizzera: 152,000 lavoratori stagionali; perché? Roma, 1971. pp. 182. bibliog.

SEASONAL VARIATIONS (ECONOMICS)

SIMS (CHRISTOPHER A.) Seasonality in regression. Minneapolis, 1972. fo 26. (Minnesota University Center for Economic Research. Discussion Papers. No. 23)

SEAWEED
See MARINE ALGAE

SECOND HAND TRADE
- Switzerland

MEIER (PETER) Die wirtschaftliche Bedeutung des Occasionswagens in der Schweiz. Zürich, 1971. pp. 105. bibliog.

SECONDAT (CHARLES LOUIS DE) Baron de Montesquieu

FICKERT (ARTUR) Montesquieus und Rousseaus Einfluss auf den vormärzlichen Liberalismus Badens. Leipzig, 1913. pp. 112. bibliog.

ALTHUSSER (LOUIS) Politics and history: Montesquieu, Rousseau, Hegel and Marx; translated from the French by Ben Brewster. London, 1972. pp. 192. bibliog.

MOLIERE (JEAN JACQUES GRANPRE) La théorie de la constitution anglaise chez Montesquieu. Leyde, 1972. pp. 386. bibliog. (Leiden. Rijks Universiteit. Publications Historiques. tome 16)

SECRET SOCIETIES

HUTIN (SERGE) Les sociétés secrètes. 7th ed. Paris, 1970. pp. 128. bibliog.

ROBERTS (JOHN MORRIS) The mythology of the secret societies. London, 1972. pp. 370.

- China

CHESNEAUX (JEAN) and others, eds. Mouvements populaires et sociétés secrètes en Chine aux XIXe et XXe siècles; [collected conference papers]; textes de L. Bianco [and others]. Paris, 1970. pp. 492. bibliog.

CHESNEAUX (JEAN) Secret societies in China in the nineteenth and twentieth centuries;... translated by Gillian Nettle. Ann Arbor, [1971]. pp. 210. bibliog.

- France

GEYRAUD (PIERRE) Sectes et rites: petites églises, religions nouvelles, sociétés secrètes de Paris. Paris, [1954]. pp. 279.

- Russia

    MEN'SHCHIKOV (LEONID PETROVICH) Okhrana i
revoliutsiia: k istorii tainykh politicheskikh organizatsii v Rossii. ch.1,2, vyp.
1,2. Moskva, 1925-29. 2 vols. Pt.2 has
subtitle:...organizatsii, sushchestvovavshikh vo vremena samoderzhaviia. Xerographic reprint. There is another copy of
pt.2 vyp.1 at R(Coll.) Russ/D/126.

- United Kingdom - Ireland

    WILLIAMS (T. DESMOND) ed. Secret societies in
Ireland. Dublin, 1973. pp. 207. bibliog.

SECTS

    STARK (WERNER) The sociology of religion: a study
of Christendom. London, 1966-1972. 5 vols.

    SCHWARTZ (GARY) Sect ideologies and social status.
Chicago, 1970. pp. 260.

    KOERSCHGEN (WOLFGANG) Revolution als Aufgabe
und Hoffnung: ein soziologischer Beitrag zur
Anpassungsfähigkeit revolutionärer Gruppen.
Köln, 1972. pp. 171. bibliog. (Aachen. Technische
Hochschule. Institut für Soziologie. Soziologische
Studien. Band 3)

- Caribbean area

    SIMPSON (GEORGE EATON) Religious cults of the
Caribbean: Trinidad, Jamaica, and Haiti. rev.
ed. Rio Piedras, 1970. pp. 308. bibliog. (Puerto
Rico University. Institute of Caribbean Studies.
Caribbean Monograph Series. No. 7)

- France

    GEYRAUD (PIERRE) Sectes et rites: petites églises,
religions nouvelles, sociétés secrètes de Paris.
Paris, [1954]. pp. 279.

- Poland

    PAWLUCZUK (WŁODZIMIERZ) Światopogląd jednost-
ki w warunkach rozpadu społeczności tradycyjnej. Warszawa, 1972. pp. 240. With English
summary.

- Russia

    MEL'GUNOV (SERGEI PETROVICH) Moskva i staraia
vera: ocherk iz istorii religiozno-obshchestvennykh dvizhenii na rubezhe XVII-XVIII vv.
Moskva, 1917. pp. 32.

    MEL'GUNOV (SERGEI PETROVICH) Religiozno-obshchest-
vennye dvizheniia XVII-XVIII v.v. v Rossii.
Moskva, 1922. pp. 194.

    MALAKHOVA (IRINA ALEKSANDROVNA) Dukhovnye khri-
stiane. Moskva, 1970. pp. 128.

SECULARISM

    HOLYOAKE (GEORGE JACOB) The principles of
secularism illustrated. 3rd ed. London,
1870. pp. 50.

    BESANT (ANNIE) Catholicism and rationalism: a
review of a two nights' discussion...held...
October 26th and 28th, 1875, between Charles
Watts and "a Catholic"; with an essay on the
relative merits of secularism and catholicism.
London, [1875?]. pp. 16

    FOOTE (GEORGE WILLIAM) Secularism, the true philo-
sophy of life: an exposition and a defence. London,
1879. pp. 32.

    HOLYOAKE (GEORGE JACOB) Plain words about secularism.
[London, 1882]. pp. 4.

    FOOTE (GEORGE WILLIAM) Secularism and theosophy:
a rejoinder to Mrs. Besant's pamphlet. London,
1889. pp. 16.

    THIS-worldism. [London, c. 1900]. pp. 18.

    LEE (W.T.) and McCABE (JOSEPH) Christianity or
secularism: which is the better for mankind?;
verbatim report of two nights' debate,... March
9 and 10, 1911. London, 1911. pp. 63.

- India

    GAJENDRAGADKAR (PRALHAD BALACHARYA) Secularism
and the constitution of India. Bombay, 1971.
pp. 182. bibliog. (Bombay (City). University.
Kashinath Trimbak Telang Lectures. [3])

    KLIMKEIT (HANS JOACHIM) Anti-religiöse Bewegungen
im modernen Südindien: eine religionssoziologische
Untersuchung zur Säkularisierungsfrage. Bonn,
1971. pp. 155. bibliog.

- United Kingdom

    HOLYOAKE (GEORGE JACOB) and WATTS (CHARLES ALBERT)
English secularism; and, The progress of
society:...two papers read at the Brussels International Congress...1880. London, [1880?].
pp. 8.

    GOULD (FREDERICK JAMES) The history of the
Leicester Secular Society. Leicester, 1900.
pp. 48.

- United States

    WHEELER (RICHARD S.) b.1935. The children of
darkness. New Rochelle, N.Y., [1973]. pp.
189.

SECULARIZATION

- Germany

    BUETTNER (RICHARD) Die Säkularisation der Kölner
geistlichen Institutionen: wirtschaftliche und
soziale Bedeutung und Auswirkungen. Köln, 1971.
pp. 454. bibliog. (Cologne. Archiv für Rheinisch-
westfälische Wirtschaftsgeschichte. Schriften
zur Rheinisch-Westfälischen Wirtschaftsgeschichte.
Band 23)

SECULARIZATION (THEOLOGY)

    GLASNER (PETER EGON) A critique of the major
theories of the secularisation process, with
special reference to Great Britain, the United
States of America and Japan; [Ph. D. (London)
thesis]. 1973. fo. 307. bibliog. Typescript:
unpublished. This thesis is the property of
London University and may not be removed from
the Library.

SECURITIES

    GRAHAM (BENJAMIN) and others. Security analysis:
principles and technique;...with the collaboration
of Charles Tatham. 4th ed. New York, [1962].
pp. 778.

- Germany

    LUEDTKE (LOTHAR) Die Struktur und das Verhalten
der Emittenten und Anleger am deutschen Renten-
markt nach dem Zweiten Weltkrieg. [Munich,
imprint], 1972. pp. 322. bibliog.

SECURITIES (Cont'd)

- United Kingdom

LONDON. Stock Exchange. Council. Admission of securities to listing. London, 1973. pp. 179. Loose leaf.

- United States

GROSVENOR (WILLIAM MASON) American securities: the causes influencing investment and speculation and the fluctuations in values, from 1872 to 1885; [reprint of work first published in 1885]. New York, 1969. pp. 270, lxxxiii.

MORGAN GUARANTY TRUST COMPANY OF NEW YORK. The care of securities. New York, 1919. pp. 20.

SECURITY (LAW)

- Indonesia

GAUTAMA (SUDARGO) Credit and security in Indonesia: the legal problems of development finance. St. Lucia, [1973]. pp. 155. bibliog. (Asian Development Bank and Law Association for Asia and the Western Pacific. Law and Development Finance in Asia)

- Japan

TANIKAWA (HISASHI) Credit and security in Japan: the legal problems of development finance. St. Lucia, [1973]. pp. 170. (Asian Development Bank and Law Association for Asia and the Western Pacific. Law and Development Finance in Asia)

- Netherlands

STEIN (P.A.) Zekerheidsrechten: zekerheidsoverdracht, pand en borgtocht. Deventer, 1970. pp. 265.

- Singapore

LIAN (KOH KHENG) and others. Credit and security in Singapore: the legal problems of development finance. St. Lucia, [1973]. pp. 363. (Asian Development Bank and Law Association for Asia and the Western Pacific. Law and Development Finance in Asia)

SECURITY, INTERNATIONAL

RABL (KURT O.) Die Völkerrechtsgrundlagen der modernen Friedensordnung. Hannover, 1967-69. 2 vols. (in 1). (Niedersaechsische Landeszentrale für Politische Bildung. Schriftenreihe. Friedensprobleme. Heft 2-3)

WATERKAMP (RAINER) Die Entwicklungsländer und die Friedenssicherung. Hannover, 1967. pp. 63. bibliog. (Niedersächsische Landeszentrale für Politische Bildung. Schriftenreihe. Friedensprobleme. Heft 4)

GERMANY (BUNDESREPUBLIK). Deutscher Bundestag. Wissenschaftliche Dienste. 1968. Gewaltverzicht und Nichtangriffsverpflichtungen, 1919-1968; [edited by Günter Hindrichs]. Bonn, 1968. pp. 7. (Materialien.8)

BAUMANN (GERHARD) Sicherheit: deutsche Friedenspolitik im Bündnis. Darmstadt, [1970]. pp. 560. bibliog.

DENMARK. Regeringsudvalget vedrørende Danmarks Sikkerhedspolitik. 1970. Problemer omkring dansk sikkerhedspolitik: en redegørelse fra det sagkyndige udvalg; (Gunnar Seidenfaden, chairman). København, 1970. 2 vols.

DOMDEY (KARL HEINZ) and SCHMIDT (J.L.) eds. Europäische Sicherheit und internationale Wirtschaftsbeziehungen. Frankfurt/M., 1970. pp. 134.

GARNETT (JOHN C.) ed. Theories of peace and security: a reader in contemporary strategic thought. London, 1970. pp. 272. bibliog.

INTERVENTION och avskräckning: supermakternas agerande i några internationella konflikter efter 1945; (ett urval av studier...vilka författats på Utrikespolitiska institutet). Stockholm, [1970]. pp. 179. bibliogs.

SCHWARZ (HANS PETER) and HAFTENDORN (HELGA) eds. Europäische Sicherheitskonferenz. Opladen, 1970. pp. 157. (Deutsche Gesellschaft für Auswärtige Politik. Forschungsinstitut. Aktuelle Aussenpolitik)

CHAI (F.Y.) Consultation and consensus in the Security Council. New York, United Nations Institute for Training and Research, 1971. pp. 55. ([Peaceful Settlement Series] No.4)

KINTNER (WILLIAM ROSCOE) and KLAIBER (WOLFGANG) Eastern Europe and European security. New York, [1971]. pp. 393. bibliog.

ANDRÉN (NILS) Den totala säkerhetspolitiken. Stockholm, 1972. pp. 126

BEATON (LEONARD) The reform of power: a proposal for an international security system. London, 1972. pp. 240.

GDR COMMITTEE FOR EUROPEAN SECURITY. Information Bulletins. No.2.[Papers of a conference on European security, Brussels, 1972]. Berlin, 1972. pp. 28.

HUNTER (ROBERT EDWARDS) Security in Europe. rev. ed. London, 1972. pp. 281. bibliog.

BRITISH COUNCIL OF CHURCHES. Department of International Affairs, and CONFERENCE OF BRITISH MISSIONARY SOCIETIES. Working Party on Defence and Disarmament. The search for security: a Christian appraisal. London, 1973. pp. 144. bibliog.

JACOBSEN (HANS ADOLF) and others, eds. Sicherheit und Zusammenarbeit in Europa: K[onferenz für] S[icherheit und] Z[usammenarbeit in] E[uropa]; Analyse und Dokumentation. Köln, [1973]. pp. 472.

RADICE (ELISABETH ANNE) Negotiations for an eastern security pact, 1933-1936; [Ph.D. (London) thesis]. [1973]. fo. 309. bibliog. Typescript: unpublished. This thesis is the property of London University and may not be removed from the Library.

- Bibliography

GERMANY (BUNDESREPUBLIK). Deutscher Bundestag. Wissenschaftliche Dienste. 1971. Mutual and balanced force reductions, MBFR; beiderseitige ausgewogene Truppenreduzierungen, Sommer 1968-1971: Auswahlbibliographie; [compiled by Wolfram Georg Riggert]. Bonn, 1971. pp. 19. (Bibliographien. 27)

SECURITY CLASSIFICATION (GOVERNMENT DOCUMENTS)

- United States

BARKER (CAROL M.) and FOX (MATTHEW H.) Classified files: the yellowing pages: a report on scholars' access to government documents. New York, 1972. pp. 115. bibliog.

SHAPIRO (MARTIN) ed. The Pentagon papers and the courts: a study in foreign policy-making and freedom of the press. San Francisco, [1972]. pp. 131.

SEDAR SENGHOR (LEOPOLD)

HYMANS (JACQUES LOUIS) Léopold Sédar Senghor: an intellectual biography. Edinburgh, [1971]. pp. 312. bibliog.

SEDIMENTATION AND DEPOSITION

ALLEN (JOHN R.L.) Physical processes of sedimentation: an introduction. London, 1970. pp. 248. bibliogs.

SEDIN (MITROFAN KARPOVICH)

SEDINA (ANASTASIIA MITROFANOVNA) Mitrofan Sedin. Krasnodar, 1965. pp. 124.

SEDITION

- United Kingdom

GLOUCESTER. [Minutes of a meeting of the Mayor, citizens and other inhabitants to appoint a committee for the preservation of the constitution and the suppression of sedition; with minutes of meetings of the committee]. 1792-94. pp. (63). Manuscript.

SEDLABANKI ISLANDS

RUEHL (HARALD) Das währungspolitische Instrumentarium der nordischen Zentralbanken. Bern, 1972. pp. 250, xxxviii. bibliog.

SEDOVA (NATAL'IA IVANOVNA)

NATALIA Trotsky and the Fourth International. London, [1972]. pp. 15.

SEEDS

- Grading

ORGANISATION FOR ECONOMIC CO-OPERATION AND DEVELOPMENT. Documentation in Food and Agriculture. [1966-1967 Series] 88. OECD scheme for the varietal certification of cereal seed moving in international trade. Paris, 1967. pp 35.

SEGREGATION

- United States - New York.

KANTROWITZ (NATHAN) Ethnic and racial segregation in the New York metropolis: residential patterns among white ethnic groups, blacks, and Puerto Ricans. New York, 1973. pp. 104.

SEGREGATION IN EDUCATION

- United States

McMILLEN (NEIL R.) The Citizens' Council: organized resistance to the Second Reconstruction, 1954-64. Urbana, Ill., [1971]. pp. 397. bibliog.

RUBIN (LILLIAN B.) Busing and backlash: white against white in a California school district. Berkeley, [1972]. pp. 248. bibliog.

SALTZMAN (HAROLD) Race war in high school: the ten-year destruction of Franklin K. Lane High School in Brooklyn. New Rochelle, N.Y., [1972]. pp. 237.

SEGREGATION IN HIGHER EDUCATION

- United States - New York

WILLIE (CHARLES V.) and McCORD (ARLINE SAKUMA) Black students at white colleges. New York, 1972. pp. 110.

SEIPEL (IGNAZ)

KLEMPERER (KLEMENS VON) Ignaz Seipel: Christian statesman in a time of crisis. Princeton, 1972. pp. 468. bibliog.

SELECTIVE EMPLOYMENT TAX

ECONOMIC DEVELOPMENT COMMITTEE FOR THE DISTRIBUTIVE TRADES. Selective employment tax in the distributive trades. [London], National Economic Development Office, [1971]. pp. 4.

PELLEGRINI (JULIAN GAVAN) The effects of the selective employment tax on British manufacturing industries; [Ph.D. (London) thesis]. 1972. fo.148. bibliog. Typescript: unpublished. This thesis is the property of London University and may not be removed from the Library.

REDDAWAY (WILLIAM BRIAN) and others. Effects of selective employment tax: final report. Cambridge, 1973. pp. 275. (Cambridge. University. Department of Applied Economics. Occasional Papers. 32)

SELEME VARGAS (ANTONIO)

SELEME VARGAS (ANTONIO) Memorias...: mi actuacion en la Junta Militar de Gobierno con el Pronunciamiento Revolucionario del 9 de abril de 1952. La Paz, 1969. pp. 111.

SELEZNEV (ARKHIP ANDREEVICH)

KOZLOV (ALEKSANDR DMITRIEVICH) Rabochie-revoliutsionery Altaia. Barnaul, 1963. pp. 71.

SELF

WILLIAMS (BERNARD ARTHUR OWEN) Problems of the self: philosophical papers, 1956-1972. Cambridge, 1973. pp. 267. bibliog.

SELF-DEFENCE (INTERNATIONAL LAW)

DERPA (ROLF M.) Das Gewaltverbot der Satzung der Vereinten Nationen und die Anwendung nichtmilitärischer Gewalt. Bad Homburg, [1970]. pp. 149. bibliog.

SCHAUMANN (WILFRIED) ed. Völkerrechtliches Gewaltverbot und Friedenssicherung: Berichte, Referate, Diskussionen einer Studientagung der Deutschen Gesellschaft für Völkerrecht; mit Beiträgen von Michael Bothe [and others]. Baden-Baden, 1971. pp. 352. bibliog. With English summaries.

SELF-DETERMINATION, NATIONAL

GHISLERI (ARCANGELO) Le razze umane e il diritto nella questione coloniale; [reprint of second edition originally published 1896] a cura di Romain Rainero. Milano, 1972. pp. 155. bibliog.

INHALT, Wesen und gegenwärtige praktische Bedeutung des Selbstbestimmungsrechts der Völker: 1. Fachtagung, veranstaltet vom 12.-14. März 1963...; Vorträge und Aussprachen; herausgegeben im Auftrag der Evangelischen Akademie in Hessen und Nassau [and others] von Kurt Rabl. München, 1964. pp. 264. With English summary.

SELF-DETERMINATION, NATIONAL
(Cont'd)

CHOWDHURY (SUBRATA ROY) The genesis of Bangladesh: a study in international legal norms and permissive conscience. London, [1972]. pp. 345. bibliog.

RIGO SUREDA (A.) The evolution of the right of self-determination: a study of United Nations practice. Leiden, 1973. pp. 397. bibliog.

SELF EMPLOYED
- France

NICOUD (GERARD) Les dernières libertés...menottes aux mains. Paris, [1972 in progress].

SELF RELIANCE

GOSLING (ROBERT) ed. Support, innovation, and autonomy: Tavistock Clinic Golden Jubilee papers. London, 1973. pp. 299. bibliogs.

SEMANTICS, COMPARATIVE

BERLIN (BRENT) and KAY (PAUL) Basic color terms: their universality and evolution. Berkeley, 1969. pp. 178. bibliog. Chart in end pocket.

SEMICONDUCTORS

TILTON (JOHN E.) International diffusion of technology: the case of semiconductors. Washington, [1971]. pp. 183. (Brookings Institution. Studies in the Regulation of Economic Activity)

SEMINOLE INDIANS

GARBARINO (MERWYN STEPHENS) Big Cypress: a changing Seminole community. New York, [1972]. pp. 132. bibliogs.

SENEGAL
- Foreign relations

SKURNIK (W.A.E.) The foreign policy of Senegal. Evanston, 1972. pp. 308 bibliog.

- Foreign relations - France

N'DIAYE (JEAN PIERRE) La jeunesse africaine face à l'impérialisme. Paris, 1971. pp. 190.

- History

JOHNSON (G. WESLEY) The emergence of black politics in Senegal: the struggle for power in the four communes, 1900-1920. Stanford, 1971. pp. 260. bibliog. (Stanford University. Hoover Institution on War, Revolution and Peace. Hoover Institution Publications. 107)

- Kings and rulers

GIRARD (JEAN) Genèse du pouvoir charismatique en basse Casamance, Sénégal. Dakar, 1969. pp. 372. bibliog. (Institut Fondamental d'Afrique Noire. Initiations et Etudes Africaines. No. 27)

- Politics and government

HYMANS (JACQUES LOUIS) Léopold Sédar Senghor: an intellectual biography. Edinburgh, [1971]. pp. 312. bibliog.

JOHNSON (G. WESLEY) The emergence of black politics in Senegal: the struggle for power in the four communes, 1900-1920. Stanford, 1971. pp. 260. bibliog. (Stanford University. Hoover Institution on War, Revolution and Peace. Hoover Institution Publications. 107)

N'DIAYE (JEAN PIERRE) La jeunesse africaine face à l'impérialisme. Paris, 1971. pp. 190.

- Religion

GIRARD (JEAN) Genèse du pouvoir charismatique en basse Casamance, Sénégal. Dakar, 1969. pp. 372. bibliog. (Institut Fondamental d'Afrique Noire. Initiations et Etudes Africaines. No. 27)

- Social conditions

FOUGEYROLLAS (PIERRE) Television and the social education of women...a first report on the Unesco-Senegal pilot project at Dakar. [Paris], United Nations Educational, Scientific and Cultural Organization, [1967]. pp. 40. (Department of Mass Communication. Reports and Papers on Mass Communication. No. 50)

MAINTENANCE sociale et changement économique au Sénégal. 1. Doctrine économique et pratique du travail chez les Mourides; [by] J. Copans [and others]. Paris, 1972. pp. 274. bibliogs. (France. Office de la Recherche Scientifique et Technique Outre-Mer. Travaux et Documents. 15)

SENIOR (THOMAS GEORGE)

FOOTE (GEORGE WILLIAM) Peculiar people: an open letter to Mr. Justice Wills, on his sentencing Thomas George Senior to four months' imprisonment with hard labor for obeying the Bible. London, [1899]. pp. 14. (Reprinted from the 'Freethinker')

SENSES AND SENSATION

CORNMAN (JAMES W.) Materialism and sensations. New Haven, 1971. pp. 352. bibliog.

SENTENCES (CRIMINAL PROCEDURE)

PARIS. Université. Institut de Droit Comparé. Section de Science Criminelle. Suspended sentence: a report presented by the Department of Criminal Science of the Institute of Comparative Law, University of Paris, under the direction of Marc Ancel...to the Cambridge Institute of Criminology. London, 1971. pp. 102. (Cambridge. University. Institute of Criminology. Cambridge Studies in Criminology. vol. 27[bis])

- Canada

HOGARTH (JOHN) Sentencing as a human process. Toronto, 1971. pp. 434. bibliog. (Toronto. University. Centre of Criminology. Canadian Studies in Criminology. 1)

- Finland

ANTTILA (INKERI) and others. Elinkautinen kuritushuonerangaistus, etc.: [A study of the frequency of life imprisonment sentences in Finland]. Helsinki, 1964. pp. 23. bibliog. (Kriminologinen Tutkimuslaitos. Sarja A. 1) With English summary.

- Netherlands

SHARPLES (KENNETH STRANG) The legal framework of judicial sentencing policy: (a study based on the Dutch and English systems). Amsterdam, 1972. pp. 373. bibliog.

- Nigeria

    MILNER (ALAN) The Nigerian penal system. London, 1972. pp. 446. bibliog.

- United Kingdom

    HOOD (ROGER GRAHAME) Sentencing the motoring offender: a study of magistrates' views and practices. London, 1972. pp. 244. bibliog. (Cambridge. University. Institute of Criminology. Cambridge Studies in Criminology. 31)

    SHARPLES (KENNETH STRANG) The legal framework of judicial sentencing policy: (a study based on the Dutch and English systems). Amsterdam, 1972. pp. 373. bibliog.

    WALKER (NIGEL) Sentencing in a rational society. Harmondsworth, 1972. pp. 286. bibliog.

    WILLETT (TERENCE CHARLES) Drivers after sentence. London, 1973. pp. 182. bibliog. (Cambridge. University. Institute of Criminology. Cambridge Studies in Criminology. vol. 23)

SEPARATION (LAW)

- Italy

    CIPRIANI (FRANCO) Dalla separazione al divorzio. Camerino, 1971. pp. 200. (Camerino. Università. Scuola di Perfezionamento in Diritto Civile. Pubblicazioni. 2)

SEPARATION OF POWERS

WAGNER (JOHANN JAKOB) Ueber die Trennung der legislativen und executiven Staatsgewalt: ein Beitrag zu Beurtheilung des Werthes landständischer Verfassungen. München, 1804; Leipzig, 1971. pp. 99.

ABASHMADZE (V.V.) Uchenie o razdelenii gosudarstvennoi vlasti i ego kritika. Tbilisi, 1972. pp. 51.

- Germany

    WEISS (SIEGFRIED) Dr. Auswärtige Gewalt und Gewaltenteilung. Berlin, [1971]. pp. 253. bibliog.

- United Kingdom

    FOSTER (WILLIAM PETER) The separatism of the British executive; [essay for the Diploma in Public Administration, London University]. 1971. fo. 14. bibliog. Typescript: unpublished. This essay is the property of London University and may not be removed from the Library.

- Social history

    SAINT MOULIN (LEON DE) La construction et la propriété des maisons: expressions des structures sociales; Seraing depuis le début du XIX siècle. [Brussels, 1969]. pp. 306. bibliog. (Credit Communal de Belgique. Pro Civitate. Collection Histoire. Série in-8°. No.21)

SERBIA

- Constitutional history

    GRACHEV (VIKTOR PETROVICH) Serbskaia gosudarstvennost' v X-XIV vv.: kritika teorii "zhupnoi organizatsii". Moskva, 1972. pp. 332. bibliog.

- Economic conditions

    LOTIĆ (LJUBOMIR) Prilozi o ekonomskom stanju u Ugarskoj i u našem narodu. Novi Sad, 1908. pp. 154. (Matica Srpska. Knjige. br.23). In Cyrillic.

- Foreign relations

    MARKOVIĆ (SVETOZAR) Srbija na Istoku. [rev. ed.] Beograd, 1946. pp. 183. In Cyrillic. First published 1892.

- Rural conditions

    HALPERN (JOEL MARTIN) and HALPERN (BARBARA KEREWSKY) A Serbian village in historical perspective. New York, [1972]. pp. 152. bibliog.

SERBO-BULGARIAN WAR, 1885

BULGARIA. Ministerstvo na Narodnata Otbrana. Generalen Shtab. Voennoistoricheski Otdel. 1971. Istoriia na Srŭbsko-bŭlgarskata voina, 1885. Sofiia, 1971. pp. 491. bibliog.

SERFDOM

- Germany

    CONZE (WERNER) ed. Quellen zur Geschichte der deutschen Bauernbefreiung. Göttingen, [1957]. pp. 219. bibliog.

    SPIES (KLAUS) Gutsherr und Untertan in der Mittelmark Brandenburg zu Beginn der Bauernbefreiung. Berlin, 1972. pp. 398. bibliog. (Munich. Universität. Juristische Fakultät. Abhandlungen zur Rechtswissenschaftlichen Grundlagenforschung. Band 2)

- Russia

    SHCHEPETOV (KONSTANTIN NIKANOROVICH) Iz zhizni krepostnykh krest'ian Rossii XVIII-XIX vekov: po materialam Sheremetevskikh votchin. Moskva, 1963. pp. 100. bibliog.

    HELLIE (RICHARD) Enserfment and military change in Muscovy. Chicago, 1971. pp. 432. bibliog.

    LITVAK (BORIS GRIGOR'EVICH) Russkaia derevnia v reforme 1861 goda: chernozemnyi tsentr 1861-1895 gg. Moskva, 1972. pp. 423.

SERGEEV (FEDOR ANDREEVICH)

TUVAIEV (VOLODYMYR ILLICH) Artem-publitsyst: dzhereloznavchyi ta istoriohrafichnyi analiz spadshchyny revoliutsionera-bil'shovyka. Kyïv, 1965. pp. 142.

SERGENT (PIERRE)

SERGENT (PIERRE) Je ne regrette rien: la poignante histoire des légionnaires-parachutistes du 1er R.E.P. Paris, [1972]. pp. 406.

SERGIPE

- Statistics

    BRAZIL. Instituto Brasileiro de Estatistica. Grupo Executivo de Pesquisas Domiciliares. População, mão-de-obra, salario. Região 5: Maranhão, Piaui, Ceara, Rio Grande do Norte, Paraiba, Pernambuco, Alagoas, Sergipe, Bahia. q., 4.° trimestre de 1968. Rio de Janeiro.

SERMON ON THE MOUNT

DEIST, A, pseud. Is the sermon on the mount impracticable?: an open letter to the Revd. William Clarke Leeper, etc. London, [1894?]. pp. 7.

SERVAN-SCHREIBER (JEAN JACQUES)

DRON (PIERRE) J.J.-S.S.: attention, danger. Paris, [1971]. pp. 125.

SERVANTS
- Norway

NORWAY. Kommunal- og Arbeidsdepartementet. Hushjelplovkomitéen. 1960. Innstilling til lov om arbeidsvilkår for hushjelp m. fl. Oslo, 1960. pp. 170.

SERVICE, COMPULSORY NON-MILITARY
- Germany

EWALD (KLAUS) Ersatzdienstverweigerung und Bekenntnisfreiheit: ein Beitrag zur Auslegung von Art. 4 GG. Frankfurt am Main, [1970]. pp. 77.

SERVICE INDUSTRIES

LEWIS (W. RUSSELL) The new service society. London, 1973. pp. 179.

- Australia

AUSTRALIA. Commonwealth Bureau of Census and Statistics. 1971. Economic censuses: 1968-69: retail establishments and selected service establishments: preliminary statement. Canberra, [1971]. pp. 17.

- France

FRANCE. Institut National de la Statistique et des Etudes Economiques. 1971. Recensement de la distribution année 1966: résultats généraux définitifs: tableaux détaillés. [Paris], 1971. pp. 517.

- Kenya

KENYA. Ministry of Finance and Economic Planning. Statistics Division. 1971. Survey of services, 1966. [Nairobi, 1971]. pp. 11,37.

- Rhodesia

RHODESIA. Central Statistical Office. 1972. The census of distribution in 1969/70: retail and wholesale trade, hotels and restaurants. Salisbury, 1972. pp. 44,(8).

- Russia

KATANIAN (NINA GRIGOR'EVNA) Dogovor podriada s organizatsiiami bytovogo obsluzhivaniia. Moskva, 1964. pp. 76.

BYTOVOE obsluzhivanie naseleniia: pravovye voprosy. Moskva, 1968. pp. 174.

KORCHAGIN (VIKTOR PAVLOVICH) and SBYTOVA (LIDIIA SERGEEVNA) Sfera uslug i zaniatost' naseleniia. Moskva, 1970. pp. 172.

BOBROV (LEV ALEKSANDROVICH) and others. Ekonomika bytovogo obsluzhivaniia naseleniia, etc. Moskva, 1971. pp. 373.

GRIBOV (VLADIMIR DMITRIEVICH) Analiz i prognozirovanie sprosa na bytovye uslugi. Moskva, 1971. pp. 129.

MASLENNIKOV (VIACHESLAV NIKITICH) and KHEIFETS (SARRA BORISOVNA) Vzaimootnosheniia s biudzhetom predpriiatii mestnoi promyshlennosti i bytovogo obsluzhivaniia. Moskva, 1971. pp. 128.

EKONOMICHESKIE voprosy razvitiia byta na sele. Moskva, 1972. pp. 145.

KABALKIN (ALEKSANDR IUR'EVICH) Sfera obsluzhivaniia: grazhdanskopravovoe regulirovanie. Moskva, 1972. pp. 199.

SOLODKOV (MIKHAIL VASIL'EVICH) and others. Teoreticheskie problemy uslug i neproizvodstvennoi sfery pri sotsializme. Moskva, 1972. pp. 348.

OFER (GUR) The service sector in Soviet economic growth: a comparative study. Cambridge, Mass., 1973. pp. 202. bibliog. (Harvard University. Harvard Economic Studies. vol. 141)

PRAVDIN (DMITRII IVANOVICH) Neproizvodstvennaia sfera: effektivnost' i stimulirovanie. Moskva, 1973. pp. 301.

SINITSKAIA (MAIIA EFIMOVNA) Zashchita interesov grazhdan po dogovoru bytovogo podriada. Moskva, 1973. pp. 48.

- Thailand

THAILAND. National Statistical Office. 1969. Census of business trade or services, 1966: Bangkok and Thon Buri municipalities. [Bangkok], 1969. pp. xiii,100,(4). In English and Thai.

THAILAND. National Statistical Office. 1969. Census of business trade or services, 1966: central region. [Bangkok], 1969. pp. 65. In English and Thai.

- United Kingdom

SMITH (ANTHONY D.) The measurement and interpretation of service output changes...; a report carried out on behalf of the National Economic Development Office. London, National Economic Development Office, 1972. pp. 181.

YORKSHIRE AND HUMBERSIDE ECONOMIC PLANNING BOARD. Research Group. The service industries: prospects in Yorkshire and Humberside. Leeds, 1972. pp. 133.

- United States

SSHA: sfera uslug v ekonomike. Moskva, 1971. pp. 414.

SERVITUDES
- France

BERGEL (JEAN LOUIS) Les servitudes de lotissement à usage d'habitation. Paris, 1973. pp. 427.

- United Kingdom

GALE (CHARLES JAMES) On easements; fourteenth edition by Spencer G. Maurice, assisted by Robert Wakefield. London, 1972. pp. 410.

SET-OFF AND COUNTERCLAIM
- Russia

KLEIN (NINA ISAEVNA) Vstrechnyi isk v sude i arbitrazhe. Moskva, 1964. pp. 132.

SET THEORY, AXIOMATIC
See AXIOMATIC SET THEORY

SETALVAD (MOTILAL CHIMANLAL)

SETALVAD (MOTILAL CHIMANLAL) My life: law and other things. London, 1971. pp. 636.

SETTLEMENTS (LAW)

- United Kingdom

HARVEY (BRIAN W.) Settlements of land. London, 1973. pp. 148.

SEVENTH-DAY ADVENTISTS

- United States

SCHWARTZ (GARY) Sect ideologies and social status. Chicago, 1970. pp. 260.

SEVERN

SHAW (T.L.) and MORGAN (R.G.) The Severn estuary: the key to the future of a region. Bristol, [1967]. pp. 15.

- Bridges

CLEARY (ESMOND JOHN) and THOMAS (RAYMOND ELLIOTT) The economic consequences of the Severn Bridge and its associated motorways. Bath, 1973. pp. 177.

SEVILLE

- Social history

PIKE (RUTH) Aristocrats and traders: Sevillian society in the sixteenth century. Ithaca, [1972]. pp. 243. bibliog.

SEWAGE DISPOSAL

- Denmark

DENMARK. Forureningsrådet. Sekretariatet. 1970. Kommuneundersøgelsen 1970: en redegørelse for spildevandsforhold og affaldsbehandling i Danmark. København, 1970. pp. 64. (Rapporter. 1)

- United Kingdom

[SOUTHGATE (BERNARD ALFRED)] South Hampshire Plan: main drainage and sewage disposal: [a study undertaken on behalf of The Counties Public Health Laboratories for the South Hampshire Plan Advisory Committee]. [London, 1971?]. fo. 18. bibliog.

U.K. Department of the Environment. 1973. Report of a survey of the discharges of foul sewage to the coastal waters of England and Wales. London, 1973. pp. 20.

SEWAGE SLUDGE

U.K. Working Party on the Disposal of Sludge in Liverpool Bay. 1972- . Out of sight, out of mind; report; [R. Best, chairman]. London, 1972 in progress. Vol. 1 bound separately and filed at R(O) 42(f1697). Vol.2 containing technical appendices not held by Library.

SEWERAGE - Underdeveloped areas
See UNDERDEVELOPED AREAS - Sewerage

SEWERAGE

- United Kingdom

SOUTH HAMPSHIRE PLAN ADVISORY COMMITTEE. Study Reports. Group B. Urban Services. No. 2. Drainage. Winchester, 1969. pp. (22).

SEX

KENEALY (ARABELLA) Feminism and sex-extinction. London, 1920. pp. 313.

HUGHES (VIOLET MARJORIE) Women in bondage. London, [1958]. pp. 158.

GRONSETH (ERIK) Familie, seksualitet og samfunn. 2nd ed. Oslo, [1972]. pp. 198. bibliog.

- Statistics

SCHWARZENBACH (HANSRUEDI) Das Geschlechtsverhältnis der Geborenen: seine Schwankungen und Besonderheiten;... im Lichte der schweizerischen Geburtenstatistik. [Zürich, imprint], 1972. pp. 217. bibliog.

SEX (PSYCHOLOGY)

ROBINSON (PAUL A.) The sexual radicals. London, 1972. pp. 192.

RYCROFT (CHARLES) Wilhelm Reich. New York, 1972. pp. 115. bibliog.

JUHASZ (ANNE McCREARY) ed. Sexual development and behavior: selected readings. Homewood, Ill., 1973. pp. 380. bibliogs.

SEX AND LAW

LEE (LUKE TSUNG-CHOU) and LARSON (ARTHUR) eds. Population and law: a study of the relations between population problems and law. Leiden, 1971. pp. 452.

- United States

DIENES (C. THOMAS) Law, politics and birth control. Urbana, [1972]. pp. 374. bibliog.

SEX CRIMES

- Germany

KUHN (GERHARD) Das Phänomen der Strichjungen in Hamburg. Wiesbaden, 1957. pp. 120. bibliog. (Germany (Bundesrepublik). Bundeskriminalamt. Schriftenreihe. 1957. 2)

- United Kingdom

TENNENT (GAVIN) and others. The control of deviant sexual behaviour by drugs: a double-blind controlled study of benperidol, chlorpromazine and placebo. [Crowthorne, Special Hospitals Research Unit], 1972. pp. 11, 3. (Special Hospitals Research Reports. No. 5)

SEX CUSTOMS

HUMAN sexual behaviour: variations in the ethnographic spectrum; [including papers presented at a symposium organized by the Central States Anthropological Society, held at Lexington in 1965]; edited by Donald S. Marshall and Robert C. Suggs. New York, [1971]. pp. 302. bibliogs. (Indiana University. Institute for Sex Research. Studies in Sex and Society)

- United Kingdom

NATIONAL OPINION POLLS LIMITED. Report on attitudes towards crime, violence and permissiveness in society; prepared for The Daily Mail. London, 1970. 1 vol. (various foliations).

GORER (GEOFFREY) Sex and marriage in England today: a study of the views and experience of the under-45s. London, 1971. pp. 319. bibliog.

SEX CUSTOMS - United Kingdom (Cont'd)

MORTON (ROBERT STEEL) Sexual freedom and venereal disease. London, 1971. pp. 141. bibliog.

- United States

POLAND (JEFFERSON F.) and ALISON (VALERIE) The records of the San Francisco Sexual Freedom League. London, [1971]. pp. 184. bibliog.

SEX INSTRUCTION

RESPONSIBLE parenthood and sex education; proceedings of a working group ([of the] International Planned Parenthood Federation) held in Tunisia, November 1969; edited by Susan Burke. London, 1970. pp. 136.

SOMERVILLE (ROSE M.) Introduction to family life and sex education. Englewood Cliffs, [1972]. pp. 393. bibliogs.

SEX RESEARCH

POMEROY (WARDELL B.) Dr. Kinsey and the Institute for Sex Research. London, [1972]. pp. 479.

SEX ROLE

OAKLEY (ANN) Sex, gender and society. London, 1972. pp. 225. bibliog.

SCANZONI (JOHN H.) Sexual bargaining: power politics in the American marriage. Englewood Cliffs, N.J., [1972]. pp. 180. bibliog.

STOLL (CLARICE STASZ) ed. Sexism: scientific debates. Reading, Mass., [1973]. pp. 137. bibliogs.

SEXUAL ETHICS

The LIBERAL ethic. Dublin, 1950. pp. 89. (Reprinted from The Irish Times)

RASMUSSEN (AGNETE) Dansk Kvindesamfund og saedelighedsfejden 1887. Grenå, 1972. pp. 89. bibliog.

SEYCHELLES

- Social life and customs

BENEDICT (BURTON) People of the Seychelles. 3rd ed. London, 1970. pp. 74, 1 map. bibliog. (U.K. Ministry of Overseas Development. Overseas Research Publications. No. 14)

SEYSS-INQUART (ARTHUR)

ROSAR (WOLFGANG) Deutsche Gemeinschaft: Seyss-Inquart und der Anschluss. Wien, [1971]. pp. 441. bibliog.

SEYSSEL (CLAUDE DE) Successively Bishop of Marseilles and Archbishop of Turin

HEXTER (JACK H.) The vision of politics on the eve of the Reformation: More, Machiavelli, and Seyssel. London, 1973. pp. 243. bibliog.

SHABA

- Foreign relations

SALMON (JEAN J.A.) La reconnaissance d'état: quatre cas; Mandchoukouo, Katanga, Biafra, Rhodésie du Sud. Paris, [1971]. pp. 287. bibliogs.

- Religion

FABIAN (JOHANNES) Jamaa: a charismatic movement in Katanga. Evanston, Ill., 1971. pp. 284. bibliog.

SHAKERS

DESROCHES (HENRI CHARLES) The American Shakers: from neo-Christianity to presocialism;...translated...and edited by John K. Savacool. Amherst, 1971. pp. 357.

SHAKHOVSKOI (VSEVOLOD NIKOLAEVICH) Prince

SHAKHOVSKOI (VSEVOLOD NIKOLAEVICH) Prince. "Sic transit gloria mundi", tak prokhodit mirskaia slava, 1893-1917 g.g. Parizh, 1952. pp. 218.

SHAMANISM

LEWIS (IOAN MYRDDIN) Ecstatic religion: an anthropological study of spirit possession and shamanism. Harmondsworth, 1971. pp. 221. bibliog.

SHAME

MORRIS (HERBERT) ed. Guilt and shame: [readings]. Belmont, Calif., [1971]. pp. 208. bibliog.

SHANGHAI

- Politics and government

CHEN (JOSEPH T.) The May Fourth Movement in Shanghai: the making of a social movement in modern China. Leiden, 1971. pp. 219. bibliog.

SHAUMIAN (STEPAN GEORGIEVICH)

GARIBDZHANIAN (GEVORG BAGRATOVICH) Revoliutsionnaia deiatel'nost' S.G. Shaumiana za granitsei, 1902-1907 gg. Erevan, 1971. pp. 141.

SHAW (GEORGE BERNARD)

McCABE (JOSEPH) George Bernard Shaw: a critical study. London, 1914. pp. 261.

SKIMPOLE (HERBERT) Bernard Shaw: the man and his work. London, 1918. pp. 192.

ALBERT (SIDNEY P.) Reflections on Shaw and psychoanalysis. [Lawrence, Kansas, 1971]. pp. 169-194. (Reprinted from Modern Drama, vol. 14, no. 2, Sept. 1971)

SHEA NUTS

- Ghana

GHANA. 1929. Despatches relating to the shea nut industry of the Northern Territories. Sessional paper No. 11 of 1929-30. in GHANA. Legislative Council. Minutes (formerly Minutes...and sessional papers).

SHEEP

- Australia

AUSTRALIA. Bureau of Agricultural Economics. 1969. The Australian sheep industry survey, 1964-65 to 1966-67; (with Supplement). Canberra, 1969. 2 pts.

- Bolivia

   CARDOZO (ARMANDO) El altiplano de Bolivia y la cria de ovejas. Cochabamba, 1970. pp. 165. bibliog.

- Italy

   MUSTO (DORA) La Regia Dogana della mena delle pecore di Puglia. Roma, 1964. pp. 115. bibliog. (Rassegna degli Archivi di Stato. Quaderni. 28)

- Russia - Kazakstan

   OVTSEVODSTVO Kazakhstana. Alma-Ata, 1968. pp. 438.

- United Kingdom

   JOCE (E.H.B.) and WALSH (W.A.) Yorks/Lancs hill farming survey: a report on a fact finding investigation into physical and financial factors affecting hill sheep and hill cows in Lancashire and the West Riding of Yorkshire. Leeds, Ministry of Agriculture, Fisheries and Food, 1971. pp. 149.

- United Kingdom - Scotland

   HIGHLANDS AND ISLANDS DEVELOPMENT BOARD. Hill and upland farming in the highlands and islands: a provisional assessment of implications of entry into the EEC. [Inverness, 1971]. pp. 16. (Special Reports. 6)

SHELEST (PETR EFIMOVICH)

SHELEST (PETR EFIMOVICH) Idei Lenina pobezhdaiut. Kiev, 1971. pp. 395.

SHELL-FISH FISHERIES

- Australia

   AUSTRALIA. Commonwealth Fisheries Office. 1946. Pearl shell, beche-de-mer and trochus industry of northern Australia; prepared for the Northern Australia Development Committee. Sydney, 1946. pp. 136. bibliog. (Economic Reports. No. 1)

- Canada

   MORSE (N.H.) An economic study of the oyster fishery of the Maritime provinces. Ottawa, 1971. pp. 81. bibliog. (Canada. Fisheries Research Board. Bulletins. No. 175)

SHERRY

SANDEMAN (GEORGE G.) SONS AND COMPANY. Port and sherry: the story of two fine wines. London, [1955]. pp. 63.

SHIFT SYSTEMS

NATIONAL ECONOMIC DEVELOPMENT OFFICE. Multiple shiftwork: a problem for decision by management and labour; based on a paper prepared by R.L. Marris. London, H.M.S.O., 1970. pp. 28. (NEDO Monographs. 1)

SHINWELL (EMANUEL) BARON SHINWELL

SHINWELL (EMANUEL) Baron Shinwell. I've lived through it all. London, 1973. pp. 280. bibliog.

SHIPBUILDING

MOECKELMANN (KLAUS) Kalkulation und Preisbildung bei langfristiger Fertigung, insbesondere im Schiffbau. Berlin, [1970]. pp. 195. bibliog. (Berlin. Technische Universität Berlin-Charlottenburg. Fakultät für Wirtschaftswissenschaften. Betriebswirtschaftliche Forschungen. Band 18)

- America, Latin

   ASOCIACION LATINOAMERICANA DE LIBRE COMERCIO. 1970. La industria naval en los paises de la ALALC. [Montevideo], 1970. 2 vols. (in 1). bibliog.

   INSTITUTE FOR LATIN AMERICAN INTEGRATION. 1971. La industria naval en la ALALC. Buenos Aires, 1971. pp. 635. bibliog.

- Brazil

   FRANCE. French Embassy, Rio de Janeiro. Conseiller Commercial. 1972. La construction navale et la flotte marchande brésiliennes. [Rio de Janeiro], 1972. fo. 94.

- European Economic Community countries

   EUROPEAN COMMUNITIES. Commission. 1972. Rapport sur l'évolution à moyen et à long terme du marché de la construction navale. [Luxembourg], 1972. pp. 177.

   EUROPEAN COMMUNITIES. Commission. 1972. Report on the long and medium term development of the shipbuilding market. [Luxembourg], 1972. pp. 166.

- France

   FRANCE. Comité de la Construction Navale. 1971. Préparation du VIe Plan...: rapport. Paris, 1971. pp. 171.

- Russia - Mari Republic

   TERESHKINA (MARIIA IVANOVNA) and SANUKOV (KSENOFONT NIKANOROVICH) Est' na Volge zavod imeni Geroia. Ioshkar-Ola, 1971. pp. 135.

- United Kingdom

   SURTEES SOCIETY. Publications. vols. 181,184. The records of the Company of Shipwrights of Newcastle upon Tyne, 1622-1967;...edited by D.J. Rowe. Gateshead, 1970-71. 2 vols.

   CLARK (T.) A century of shipbuilding: products of Barrow-in-Furness. Lancaster, 1971. pp. 144.

   FARR (GRAHAME E.) Bristol shipbuilding in the nineteenth century. Bristol, 1971. pp. 25. (Historical Association. Bristol Branch. Local History Pamphlets. [No. 27])

   HOLLAND (A.J.) Ships of British oak: the rise and decline of wooden shipbuilding in Hampshire. Newton Abbot, [1971]. pp. 204.

   BOOZ, ALLEN AND HAMILTON INTERNATIONAL BV. British shipbuilding, 1972; a report to the Department of Trade and Industry. London, H.M.S.O., 1973. pp. 262.

- United Kingdom - Production standards

   SHIPBUILDING AND SHIP REPAIRING COUNCIL [U.K.]. Working Party on Statistics of Production and Productivity. Statistics of production and productivity in the shipbuilding industry: a report;...[Richard Hill, chairman]. London, 1968. pp. 34.

SHIPBUILDING (Cont'd)

- United Kingdom - Statistics

SHIPBUILDING AND SHIP REPAIRING COUNCIL [U.K.]. Working Party on Statistics of Production and Productivity. Statistics of production and productivity in the shipbuilding industry: a report;...[Richard Hill, chairman]. London, 1968. pp. 34.

- United Kingdom - Scotland

BUCHAN (ALASDAIR) The right to work: the story of the Upper Clyde confrontation. London, 1972. pp. 160.

MURRAY (ROBIN) UCS: the anatomy of bankruptcy. Nottingham, 1972. pp. 86.

THOMPSON (WILLIE) and HART (FINLAY) The UCS work-in;...foreword by Jimmy Reid. London, 1972. pp. 95.

- United States

FISHBAUGH (CHARLES PRESTON) From paddle wheels to propellers. Indianapolis, 1970. pp. 240.

BEAZER (WILLIAM F.) and others. U.S. shipbuilding in the 1970s. Lexington, [1972]. pp. 180. bibliog.

SHIPBUILDING WORKERS

- Denmark

DUE (JESPER) and MADSEN (JØRGEN STEEN) Tillidsmanden i klassekampen: Ålborgstrejken; en sociologisk analyse. København, [1972]. pp. 200. bibliog.

SHIPPING

COUPER (A.D.) The geography of sea transport. London, 1972. pp. 208.

LAWRENCE (SAMUEL A.) International sea transport: the years ahead. Lexington, Mass., [1972]. pp. 316.

BOYER (ALBERT) Les transports maritimes. Paris, 1973. pp. 128.

KNUDSEN (OLAV) The politics of international shipping: conflict and interaction in a transnational issue-area, 1946-1968. Lexington, Mass., [1973]. pp. 221. bibliog.

- Rates

SHNEORSON (DAN) Price discrimination in liner sea transport; [Ph. D. (London) thesis]. [1972 or rather 1973]. fo. 216. bibliog. Typescript: unpublished. This thesis is the property of London University and may not be removed from the Library.

- America, Latin

ASOCIACION LATINOAMERICANA DE LIBRE COMERCIO. 1970. La industria naval en los paises de la ALALC. [Montevideo], 1970. 2 vols. (in 1). bibliog.

- America, North

SHEPHERD (JAMES F.) and WALTON (GARY M.) Shipping, maritime trade, and the economic development of colonial North America. Cambridge, 1972. pp. 255. bibliog.

- Communist countries

RENTNER (HEINZ) Sozialistische internationale Arbeitsteilung und Kooperation im Seeverkehr. Berlin, 1972. pp. 110.

- European Economic Community countries

FRANCE. Direction de la Documentation. La Documentation Française. Notes et Etudes Documentaires. No.3909-3910. Les activités maritimes de la Communauté Economique Européenne; [by] Albert Boyer. [Paris], 1972. pp. 59.

- France

FRANCE. Comité des Transports Maritimes. 1971. Préparation du VIe Plan...: rapport. Paris, 1971. pp. 187.

- Italy

CAGLIOZZI (ROBERTO) Prospettive del traffico marittimo e problemi portuali del Mezzogiorno. Roma, 1970. pp. 221. (Associazione per lo Sviluppo dell'Industria nel Mezzogiorno. Centro per gli Studi sullo Sviluppo Economico. Collana di Monografie)

- New Hebrides - Statistics

NEW HEBRIDES. Condominium Bureau of Statistics. Statistical bulletin: Overseas shipping and aircraft statistics. a., 1972- Vila. In English and French.

- New Zealand

NEW ZEALAND. Commission of Inquiry into New Zealand Shipping. 1971. New Zealand shipping; report; [R.D. Jamieson, chairman]. Wellington, 1971. pp. 301, 1 map.

- Norway - Mathematical models

NORMAN (VICTOR D.) Norwegian shipping in the national economy. Bergen, 1971. pp. 67. bibliog.

- Rhine - Rates

MUELLER (JOSEF HEINZ) and WILLEKE (RAINER JOSEF) Die Preisbildungsorgane in der Rheinschiffahrt. [Düsseldorf], 1963. fo. iv,236. (North Rhine-Westphalia. Technische und Volkswirtschaftliche Berichte des Ministeriums für Wirtschaft, Mittelstand und Verkehr. Nr. 62)

- United Kingdom

WORKING PARTY ON SHORT SEA SHIPPING. Short sea shipping; (the report...to the Economic Development Committee for the Movement of Exports); [A.R. Glen, chairman]. London, National Economic Development Office, 1970. pp. 134.

PORTS and shipping in the South-West: papers presented at two seminars... held at Dartington Hall... 1968 and... 1969; edited by H.E.S. Fisher. Exeter, 1971. pp. 174. (Exeter. University. Department of Economic History. Exeter Papers in Economic History. No. 4)

SHIPPING: a survey of historical records [conducted by the Business Archives Council and the National Maritime Museum]; edited by P. Mathias and A.W.H. Pearsall. Newton Abbot, [1971]. pp. 162. bibliogs.

- United Kingdom - Scotland - Rates

GASKIN (MAXWELL) Freight rates and prices in the Islands;...report of a study of the impact of freight charges on prices and development...for the Highlands and Islands Development Board; (with Board's comments on...report). [Inverness] 1971. pp. 68; fo. 5.

- Venezuela

VENEZUELA. Dirección General de Estadística. Censos Economicos Nacionales. Primer censo de transporte maritimo, fluvial y lacustre 1952. Caracas, 1958. pp. 63.

SHIPPING CONFERENCES

JUERGENSEN (HARALD) Der Rationalisierungseffekt von Linienkonferenzen in Fahrtgebieten von besonderem Interesse für die kontinentaleuropäische Schiffahrt. Göttingen, [1971]. pp. 234. bibliogs. (Hamburg. Hansische Universität. Institut für Verkehrswissenschaft. Verkehrswissenschaftliche Studien. Heft 18)

DEAKIN (BRIAN MEASURES) Shipping conferences: a study of their origins, development and economic practices;...in collaboration with T. Seward. Cambridge, 1973. pp. 261. (Cambridge. University. Department of Applied Economics. Occasional Papers. 37)

SHIPS

- Cargo

INTERGOVERNMENTAL MARITIME CONSULTATIVE ORGANIZATION. 1965-1971. International Maritime dangerous goods code. London, 1965-71. 9 vols. (loose-leaf).

INTER-GOVERNMENTAL MARITIME CONSULTATIVE ORGANIZATION. 1972. International Maritime Dangerous Goods Code. London, 1972. 4 pts. (in 1 vol.) List of old IMCO Code page numbers with corresponding new IMCO Code page numbers and UN numbers is bound with this set.

- Nationality

NAESS (ERLING D.) The great PanLibHon controversy: the fight over the flags of shipping. Epping, 1972. pp. 175.

SHOEMAKERS

- Austria

MOELLER (HEINRICH) Geschichte der Schuhmacher Österreichs: Erinnerungsgabe zum sechzigjährigen Jubiläum der Schuhmacherorganisation, 1871-1931. Wien, 1931. pp. 555, xx. bibliog.

HUNDERT Jahre Gewerkschaft der Schuharbeiter: (Festschrift zum hundertjährigen Bestand der gewerkschaftlichen Organisation der Schuharbeiter, 1871-1971;...im Auftrage der Gewerkschaft der Textil-, Bekleidungs- und Lederarbeiter verfasst). [Vienna, 1971]. pp. 71.

- United Kingdom

SHOEMAKERS in Northamptonshire, 1762-1911: a statistical survey. Northampton, [1971]. pp. 36.

SHOP ASSISTANTS

- United Kingdom

ECONOMIC DEVELOPMENT COMMITTEE FOR THE DISTRIBUTIVE TRADES. Training for selling: a four-step guide to the training of retail staff. London, H.M.S.O., 1971. pp. 93.

WHITAKER (WILFRED BARNETT) Victorian and Edwardian shopworkers: the struggle to obtain better conditions and a half-holiday. Newton Abbot, [1973]. pp. 222. bibliog.

SHOP STEWARDS

ERICKSON (HERMAN) The steward's role in the union, and a history of American unions. New York, [1971]. pp. 123. bibliog.

- Denmark

MØLLER (IVER HORNEMANN). Arbejdspladsens tillidsmaend. København, 1970. pp. 35. bibliog. (Socialforskningsinstituttet. Publikationer. 45)

DUE (JESPER) and MADSEN (JØRGEN STEEN) Tillidsmanden i klassekampen: Alborgstrejken; en sociologisk analyse. København, [1972]. pp. 200. bibliog.

- United Kingdom

GOODMAN (J.F.B.) and WHITTINGHAM (T.G.) Shop stewards. rev. ed. London, 1973. pp. 286.

HINTON (JAMES) The first shop stewards' movement. London, 1973. pp. 352. bibliog.

SHOPLIFTING

AROMAA (KAUKO) and others. Department store shoplifters. Helsinki, 1970. fo. 47. bibliog. (Kriminologinen Tutkimuslaitos. Sarja M.6)

SHOPPING

- Mathematical models

LEWIS (JOHN PARRY) Profitability in a shopping model. [Manchester, 1971?]. fo. 14. (Manchester. University. Centre for Urban and Regional Research. Occasional Papers. No. 6)

- France

LE ROUX (PIERRE) Les comportements de loisirs des Français; Les vacances d'été en 1969; Données sur l'environnement de l'habitat en France. [Paris, 1970]. pp. 107. bibliog. (France. Institut National de la Statistique et des Etudes Economiques. Collections de l'INSEE. Série M. Ménages. 2) With summaries in English and Spanish.

SHOPPING CENTRES

GROUPE ALPHA. L'aménagement du territoire au service du commerce. Bruxelles, [1958]. pp. 31. (Cahiers d'Urbanisme et d'Aménagement du Territoire. No. 26)

- Germany

GREIPL (ERICH) Einkaufszentren in der Bundesrepublik Deutschland: Bedeutung sowie Grundlagen und Methoden ihrer ökonomischen Planung. Berlin, [1972]. pp. 210. bibliog. (Ifo-Institut für Wirtschaftsforschung. Schriftenreihe. Nr. 79)

- United Kingdom

SOUTH HAMPSHIRE PLAN ADVISORY COMMITTEE. Study Reports. Group D. People, Activities and Housing. No. 3. Shopping. Winchester, 1969. pp. 22.

CHRISTIE (A.W.) and others. Urban freight distribution: a study of operations in High Street Putney. Crowthorne, 1973. pp. 67. (U.K. Transport and Road Research Laboratory. Reports. LR 556)

- United States

COHEN (YEHOSHUA S.) Diffusion of an innovation in an urban system: the spread of planned regional shopping centers in the United States, 1949-1968. Chicago, 1972. pp. 136. bibliog. (Chicago. University. Department of Geography. Research Papers. No. 140)

SHOPPING HOURS
- Germany
REICHERT (KLAUS) Das Ladenschluss Problem in der Bundesrepublik Deutschland. Wien, 1971. pp. 128. bibliog.

- Netherlands
ECONOMISCH INSTITUUT VOOR HET MIDDEN- EN KLEINBEDRIJF. Winkelsluiting en koopavond. 's-Gravenhage, 1968. pp. 18.

- Rhodesia
RHODESIA. Shop Hours Commission. 1972. Report; [John Armstrong, chairman]. [Salisbury], 1972. pp. 18. ([Command Papers]. 1972. Comd. R.R. 26)

- United Kingdom
McDONAGH (THERESA) Redbridge trading survey. [London], 1972. pp. 14. (London. Greater London Council. Department of Planning and Transportation. Research Memoranda. 338)

SHOPPING MALLS
LONDON. Greater London Council. Traffic and Development Branch. Policy group. GLC study tour of Europe and America: pedestrianised streets. [London, 1973]. pp. 245.

SHOREDITCH
- Charities
WARE (JOHN) An account of the several charities and estates, held in trust, for the use of the poor of the parish of Saint Leonard Shoreditch, Middlesex; and of benefactions to the same; compiled in the years 1833, 1834, 1835, etc. London, [imprint], 1836. pp. (v), 175. 24cm.

SHOTMAN (ALEKSANDR VASIL'EVICH)
BONDAREVSKAIA (TAISIIA PAVLOVNA) A.V. Shotman. Moskva, 1963. pp. 48.

SHROPSHIRE
- Economic history
TRINDER (BARRIE STUART) The industrial revolution in Shropshire. London, 1973. pp. 455. bibliog.

- Population
JONES (RICHARD ELLIS) Parish registers and population history: North Shropshire, 1538-1837; [Ph. D. (London) thesis]. [1973]. fo. 341. Typescript: unpublished. This thesis is the property of London University and may not be removed from the Library.

SHUDRAS
AMBEDKAR (BHIMARAO RAMJI) Who were the Shudras?: how they came to be the fourth Varna in the Indo-Aryan society. Bombay, 1946 repr. 1970. pp. 268.

SIAM
See THAILAND

SIBERIA
- Bibliography
MEZHOV (VLADIMIR IZMAILOVICH) compiler. Sibirskaia bibliografiia: ukazatel' knig i statei o Sibiri na russkom iazyke i odnikh tol'ko knig na inostrannykh iazykakh za ves' period knigopechataniia. S.-Peterburg, 1892-1903. 3 vols. (Kraus Slavonic Reference Series. Series II. v.3) Xerographic reprint.

- Commerce
DIBB (PAUL) Siberia and the Pacific: a study of economic development and trade prospects. New York, 1972. pp. 288. bibliog.

- Constitutional history
SANZHIEV (GARMAZHAP LUDUPOVICH) V.I. Lenin i natsional'no-gosudarstvennoe stroitel'stvo v Sibiri, 1917-1937 gg. Ulan-Ude, 1971. pp. 176.

- Economic conditions
AKADEMIIA NAUK SSSR. Sibirskoe Otdelenie. Institut Geografii Sibiri i Dal'nego Vostoka. Srednesibirskaia Iuzhnotaezhnaia Ekspeditsiia, 1960-62. Srednee i Nizhnee Priangar'e: geograficheskie usloviia i problemy khoziaistvennogo osvoeniia; [rezul'taty rabot...ekspeditsii], etc. vyp.2. Irkutsk, 1967. pp. 216. bibliog.

DIBB (PAUL) Siberia and the Pacific: a study of economic development and trade prospects. New York, 1972. pp. 288. bibliog.

LAZHENTSEV (VITALII NIKOLAEVICH) Ekonomiko-geograficheskii analiz spetsializatsii raiona; na primere Vostochnogo Zabaikal'ia; otvetstvennyi redaktor... A.A. Nedeshev. Novosibirsk, 1972. pp. 96. bibliog.

- Economic conditions - Bibliography
VOROB'EV (VLADIMIR VASIL'EVICH) and VERSHINSKAIA (N.I.) compilers. Publikatsii sibirskikh i dal'nevostochnykh organizatsii Geograficheskogo obshchestva SSSR, 1945-1963 gg.: sistematicheskii i avtorskii ukazatel'. Irkutsk, 1966. pp. 166.

- Economic history
IRKUTSK. Universitet. Trudy. tom 30. Seriia Istoricheskaia. vyp.3. Iz istorii partiinykh organizatsii Vostochnoi Sibiri. Irkutsk, 1962. pp. 349.

SIBIR' i Dal'nii Vostok v period vosstanovleniia narodnogo khoziaistva. vyp.1. Tomsk, 1963. pp. 212.

OCHERKI naseleniia i khoziaistva Zapadnoi Sibiri: sbornik statei. Novosibirsk, 1965. pp. 95. bibliog.

IRKUTSK. Universitet. Trudy. t.43. Seriia Istoricheskaia. vyp.7. Deiatel'nost' partiinykh organizatsii Vostochnoi Sibiri po sozdaniiu material'no-tekhnicheskoi bazy kommunizma. Irkutsk, 1967. pp. 211.

SOTSIALISTICHESKOE i kommunisticheskoe stroitel'stvo v Zapadnoi Sibiri. Omsk, 1968. pp. 110.

SIBIR' i Dal'nii Vostok v period vosstanovleniia narodnogo khoziaistva. vyp.5. Tomsk, 1971. pp. 194.

PREOBRAZHENSKII (ALEKSANDR ALEKSANDROVICH) Ural i Zapadnaia Sibir' v kontse XVI - nachale XVIII veka. Moskva, 1972. pp. 392.

GUSHCHIN (NIKOLAI IAKOVLEVICH) Sibirskaia derevnia na puti k sotsializmu: sotsial'no-ekonomicheskoe razvitie sibirskoi derevni v gody sotsialisticheskoi rekonstruktsii narodnogo khoziaistva, 1926-1937 gg.; otvetstvennyi redaktor... A.S. Moskovskii. Novosibirsk, 1973. pp. 518.

- Economic policy

KOLOSOVSKII (NIKOLAI NIKOLAEVICH) Problemy territorial'noi organizatsii proizvoditel'nykh sil Sibiri; pod redaktsiei T.M. Kalashnikovoi, B.P. Orlova, Iu.G. Saushkina. Novosibirsk, 1971. pp. 176.

DIBB (PAUL) Siberia and the Pacific: a study of economic development and trade prospects. New York, 1972. pp. 288. bibliog.

- History

BOGDANOV (MIKHAIL ANDREEVICH) Razgrom zapadno-sibirskogo kulatsko-eserovskogo miatezha 1921 g. Tiumen', 1961. pp. 111.

OCHERKI istorii Sibiri. t.1. Irkutsk, 1970. pp. 207. bibliog.

- History - Historiography

BASHARIN (GEORGII PROKOP'EVICH) Nekotorye voprosy istoriografii vkhozhdeniia Sibiri v sostav Rossii. Iakutsk, 1971. pp. 135.

ISTORICHESKAIA nauka v Sibiri za 50 let: osnovnye problemy istorii Sovetskoi Sibiri. Novosibirsk, 1972. pp. 276.

- History - 1917-1921 Revolution

BOR'BA za vlast' Sovetov v Vostochnom Zabaikal'e. Irkutsk, 1967. pp. 365.

- Industries

IRKUTSK. Universitet. Trudy. t.34. Seriia Istoricheskaia. vyp.5. Bor'ba partiinykh organizatsii Vostochnoi Sibiri za sozdanie moshchnoi industrial'noi bazy. Irkutsk, 1965. pp. 271.

RODIONOV (DMITRII MAKSIMOVICH) and ROGACHEVSKII (ANATOLII MORDUKHOVICH) Zapadno-Sibirskaia partiinaia organizatsiia v bor'be za sotsialisticheskuiu industrializatsiiu, 1926-1937 gg. Novosibirsk. 1965. pp. 100.

KARPENKO (ZINAIDA GENNADIEVNA) and others, eds. Istoriia industrializatsii Zapadnoi Sibiri, 1926-1941 gg. Novosibirsk, 1967. pp. 392.

MOROZOVA (T.G.) Razvitie i razmeshchenie vedushchikh otraslei promyshlennosti Vostochnoi Sibiri. Moskva, 1969. pp. 106.

- Industries - Bibliography

KIRSANOVA (M.I.) and others, compilers. Ekonomika, razmeshchenie i organizatsiia promyshlennogo proizvodstva Sibiri i Dal'nego Vostoka: bibliografiia, 1917-1965. Novosibirsk, 1968-69. 2 vols.

- Intellectual life

SOSKIN (VARLEN L'VOVICH) Kul'turnaia zhizn' Sibiri v pervye gody novoi ekonomicheskoi politiki, 1921-1923 gg.;...redaktor...V.S.Flerov. Novosibirsk, 1971. pp. 350.

- Native races

SANZHIEV (GARMAZHAP LUDUPOVICH) V.I. Lenin i natsional'no-gosudarstvennoe stroitel'stvo v Sibiri, 1917-1937 gg. Ulan-Ude, 1971. pp. 176.

- Politics and government

IRKUTSK. Universitet. Trudy. tom 30. Seriia Istoricheskaia. vyp.3. Iz istorii partiinykh organizatsii Vostochnoi Sibiri. Irkutsk, 1962. pp. 349.

- Population

OCHERKI raseleniia i khoziaistva Zapadnoi Sibiri: sbornik statei. Novosibirsk, 1965. pp. 95. bibliog.

- Social conditions

ELOVIKOV (LEONID ANDREEVICH) Ot rubezha k rubezhu: rost blagosostoianiia sibiriakov; itogi, perspektivy. Novosibirsk, 1972. pp. 126.

SICILY

- Bibliography

BONASERA (FRANCESCO) Fonti per lo studio geografico della Sicilia, 1861-1960. Palermo, [1968?]. pp. 182.

- History

TURCO (NATALE) Storia della nazione siciliana. [Catania, 1971 in progress].

- Industries

TORNEO (FRANCESCO) Gli incentivi per la industrializzazione della Sicilia. 2nd ed. Caltanissetta, [1963]. pp. 396.

- Politics and government

TOCCO (MATTEO G.) Libro nero di Sicilia: dietro le quinte della politica, degli affari e della cronaca della regione siciliana. Milano, [1972]. pp. 396. bibliog.

- Rural conditions

GALTUNG (JOHAN) Members of two worlds: a development study of three villages in western Sicily. New York, 1971. pp. 302.

- Social conditions

WURR (RUEDIGER) Perpetuierung und Wandel von Selbstverständnissen in einer fremden Gesellschaft: Untersuchungen in einer sizilianischen Küstenstadt. [Heidelberg?], 1971. pp. 264. bibliog.

SICK

PUSKA (PEKKA) and SOURANDER (LEIF B.) Pitkäaikaissairaiden selviytyminen sairaalahoidon jälkeen; [with English summary]: A follow-up of long term patients after hospital treatment. Helsinki, 1969. pp. 44. bibliog.

LEWIS (GILBERT AGUILAR) The recognition of sickness and its causes: a medical anthropological study of the Gnau, West Sepik district, New Guinea; [Ph.D. (London) thesis]. 1972. fo. 495. bibliog. Typescript: unpublished. This thesis is the property of London University and may not be removed from the Library.

SICK (Cont'd.)

HAYWARD (JACK CHARLES) Some relationships between pre-operative information and post-operative pain and anxiety in surgical patients: an experimental study; [Ph.D. (London) thesis]. 1973. fo. 444. bibliog. Typescript: unpublished. This thesis is the property of London University and may not be removed from the Library.

SICK LEAVE

- Australia - New South Wales

The COST of sickness and unemployment: (the proceedings of a seminar)... held at Sydney University on Saturday, 3rd May, 1969; [organized by the Council of Social Service of New South Wales]. Sydney, [1969]. pp. 79.

- Denmark

DANSK ARBEJDSGIVERFORENING. Statistisk-Økonomisk Afdeling. Fravaer fra arbejdet: sygefravaer og andet fravaer. [Copenhagen], 1971. pp. 85.

- Germany

HOLZER-THIESER (ALFRED) Der Lohnfortzahlungsanspruch des Arbeiters im Krankheitsfalle bei gleichzeitiger Arbeitsverhinderung aus anderen Gründen. [Erlangen, imprint, 1971]. pp. 194. bibliog.

- Switzerland

LAUTNER (JULIUS GEORG) Der Anspruch des Fabrikarbeiters auf Entgeltzahlung im Krankheitsfalle nach Art. 335 des schweizerischen Obligationenrechts. [Zürich, 1947]. pp. 75.

SIEBELDINGEN

- Politics and government

WALLER-ALBRECHT (ULRIKE) Bestimmungsgründe politischer Orientierungen und Verhaltensweisen in regionalen Subsystemen, dargestellt am Beispiel der rheinland-pfälzischen Landgemeinde Siebeldingen. [Bamberg, imprint], 1971. 1 vol.(various pagings). bibliog.

SIEG-LAHN-DILL

- Economic conditions

DITTRICH (ERICH) and others. Étude sur la structure sociale et économique de la région Sieg-Lahn-Dill. Luxembourg, [European Coal and Steel Community], 1968. pp. 160. bibliog. (Collection d'Économie et Politique Régionale. 2. Programmes de Développement et de Conversion. 10)

- Social conditions

DITTRICH (ERICH) and others. Étude sur la structure sociale et économique de la région Sieg-Lahn-Dill. Luxembourg, [European Coal and Steel Community], 1968. pp. 160. bibliog. (Collection d'Économie et Politique Régionale. 2. Programmes de Développement et de Conversion. 10)

SIEGEN

- Economic history

IRLE (TRUTZHART) Die Wirtschaft der Stadt Siegen in der Vergangenheit. Siegen, 1972. pp. 262. bibliog.

SIEGMUND-SCHULTZE (FRIEDRICH)

WEYER (ADAM) Kirche im Arbeiterviertel. Gütersloh, [1971]. pp. 180. bibliog.

SIERRA LEONE

- Economic conditions

BANK OF SIERRA LEONE. Annual report and statement of accounts. a., 1966 [3rd], 1969 [6th]. Freetown.

SIGN LANGUAGE

STOKOE (WILLIAM C.) Semiotics and human sign languages The Hague, 1972. pp. 177. bibliogs.

SIGNS AND SIGN BOARDS

WILDMAN (SAMUEL GERALD) The black horsemen: English inns and King Arthur. London, 1971. pp. 176. bibliog.

SIGNS AND SYMBOLS

BAUDRILLARD (JEAN) Pour une critique de l'économie politique du signe. [Paris, 1972]. pp. 270.

SIHANOUK (NORODOM)
See NORODOM SIHANOUK VARMAN, Head of State of Cambodia

ŠIK (OTA)

MRACHKOVSKAIA (IRINA MIKHAILOVNA) Ot revizionizma k predatel'stvu: kritika ekonomicheskikh vzgliadov O.Shika. Moskva, 1970. pp. 110.

SIKHS

LEAF (MURRAY J.) Information and behavior in a Sikh village: social organization reconsidered. Berkeley, [1972]. pp. 296. bibliog.

SIKKIM

- Constitutional history

HECKER (HELLMUTH) Sikkim und Bhutan: die verfassungsgeschichtliche und politische Entwicklung der indischen Himalaya-Protektorate. Hamburg, 1970. pp. 73. bibliog.

SILESIA

- Constitutional history

ELVERT (CHRISTIAN D') Die Verfassung und Verwaltung von Oesterreichisch-Schlesien, in ihrer historischen Ausbildung, dann die Rechtsverhältnisse zwischen Mähren, Troppau und Jägerndorf, so wie der mährischen Enklaven zu Schlesien; [reprint of work originally published in 1854]. Wien, 1970. pp. 312.

- History

SCHUMANN (WOLFGANG) Oberschlesien, 1918-19: vom gemeinsamen Kampf deutscher und polnischer Arbeiter. Berlin, 1961. pp. 314. bibliog.

PRZEWŁOCKI (JAN) Międzysojusznicza komisja rządząca i plebiscytowa na Górnym Śląsku w latach 1920-1922; The inter-allied control and plebiscite commission in Upper Silesia, etc. Warszawa, 1970. pp. 193. bibliog. With Russian and English summaries.

DĄBROWSKI (WŁODZIMIERZ) Trzecie powstanie śląskie: rok 1921. Londyn, 1973. pp. 227.

- Intellectual life

GRUND (BERNHARD) Das kulturelle Leben der Deutschen in Niederschlesien unter polnischer Verwaltung, 1947-1958. Bonn, 1967. pp. 147. bibliog. (Germany. (Bundesrepublik). Bundesministerium für Gesamtdeutsche Fragen. Bonner Berichte aus Mittel- und Ostdeutschland)

- Politics and government

RECHOWICZ (HENRYK) Polska Partia Robotnicza w Śląsko-Dąbrowskim Obwodzie. Katowice, 1972 [or rather, 1973]. pp. 478. bibliog.

- Population

SZAROTA (TOMASZ) Osadnictwo miejskie na Dolnym Śląsku w latach, 1945-1948. Wrocław, 1969. pp. 328. bibliog. With French summary.

SILK MANUFACTURE AND TRADE
- France

FRANCE. Direction de la Documentation. La Documentation Française Illustrée. No. 59. Tissus et soieries de Lyon. [Paris], 1951. pp. 36.

SILVA PRADO (EDUARDO DE)
See PRADO (EDUARDO DE SILVA)

SILVER

The SILVER policy of the government and the advice of a Royal Commission, etc. London, 1891. pp. 28.

SILVER MINES AND MINING
- Mexico

BAKEWELL (P. J.) Silver mining and society in colonial Mexico: Zacatecas, 1546-1700. Cambridge, 1971. pp. 294. bibliog.

RANDALL (ROBERT W.) Real del Monte: a British mining venture in Mexico. Austin, Tex., [1972]. pp. 257. bibliog. (Texas University. Institute of Latin American Studies. Latin American Monographs. No. 26)

SIMKHOVITCH (MARY KINGSBURY)

SIMKHOVITCH (MARY KINGSBURY) Neighborhood: my story of Greenwich House. New York, [1938]. pp. 301.

SIMMEL (GEORG)

BECHER (HERIBERT J.) Georg Simmel: die Grundlagen seiner Soziologie. Stuttgart, 1971. pp. 107. bibliog.

SIMON (JOHN ALLSEBROOK) 1st Viscount Simon

EDWARDS (GEOFFREY RICHARD) Sir Austen Chamberlain's and Sir John Simon's conduct of Anglo-Soviet relations: a case study in the relationship between the House of Commons and the Foreign Secretary; [Ph.D.(London) thesis]. 1973. fo.306. bibliog. Typescript: unpublished. This thesis is the property of London University and may not be removed from the Library.

SIMONDE DE SISMONDI (JEAN CHARLES LEONARD)

GUILLAUMONT (PATRICK) La pensée demo-économique de Jean-Baptiste Say et de Sismondi. Paris, [1969]. pp. 144. bibliog.

SIMONDE DE SISMONDI (JEAN CHARLES LEONARD) Statistique du département du Léman; publiée d'après le manuscrit original et présentée par H.O. Pappe. Genève, 1971. pp. 211. (Geneva. Société d'Histoire et d'Archéologie. Mémoires et Documents. tome 44)

SIMPSON (EDWARD) Unitarian

CHARLESWORTH (SAMUEL) Brief memoir of the late Mr. Edward Simpson. [Newcastle-on-Tyne], 1862. pp. 16.

SIMPSON (Sir GEORGE)

HUDSON'S BAY RECORD SOCIETY. Publications. 29. London correspondence inward from Sir George Simpson, 1841-42: edited by Glyndwr Williams. London, 1973. pp. 212.

SIMPSON (RICHARD)

McELRATH (DAMIAN) Richard Simpson, 1820-1876: a study in XIXth century English liberal Catholicism. Louvain, 1972. pp. 163. (Revue d'Histoire Ecclésiastique. Bibliothèque. Fasc. 55)

SIMULATION METHODS

SIKORA (KLAUS) Wirtschaftsplanung und Simulation:... Wirtschaftsplanung industrieller Unternehmungen als Bedingungsrahmen für die gegenwärtige Anwendung der Simulation als Voraussageverfahren. [Berlin, 1969?]. pp. 381, 23. bibliog.

CROSINA (SERGIO) Ein Versuch zur Konstruktion von gesamtwirtschaftlichen Simulationsmodellen auf einzelwirtschaftlicher Grundlage. Zürich, 1971. pp. 161. bibliog.

GUETZKOW (HAROLD) and others, eds. Simulation in social and administrative science: overviews and case examples. Englewood Cliffs, [1972]. pp. 768. bibliogs.

INBAR (MICHAEL) and STOLL (CLARICE STASZ) Simulation and gaming in social science. New York, [1972]. pp. 313. bibliog.

INGRAM (GREGORY K.) and others. The Detroit prototype of the N[ational] B[ureau of] E[conomic] R[esearch] urban simulation model. New York, 1972. pp. 233. bibliog. (National Bureau of Economic Research. Urban and Regional Studies. 1)

NORLÉN (URBAN) Simulation model building: a statistical approach to modelling in the social sciences with the simulation method. Göteborg, 1972. pp. 172. bibliogs. (Göteborgs Universitet. Statistiska Institutionen. Skriftserie. 15)

SHAFFER (WILLIAM R.) Computer simulations of voting behavior. New York, 1972. pp. 164. bibliog.

SINGAPORE
- Commerce

SARDESAI (D.R.) Trade and empire in Malaya and Singapore, 1869-1874. Athens, Ohio, 1970. fo.17. (Ohio University. Center for International Studies. Papers in International Studies. Southeast Asia Series. No. 16)

SINGAPORE (Cont'd.)

- Economic conditions

BUCHANAN (IAIN) Singapore in Southeast Asia: an economic and political appraisal. London, [1972]. pp. 336.

DUPUIS (JACQUES) Singapour et la Malaysia. Paris, 1972. pp. 128. bibliog.

- Economic history

HERRMANN (MICHAEL) Hong Kong versus Singapore: ein Erklärungsversuch divergierender Entwicklungsverläufe. Stuttgart, 1970. pp. 314. bibliog. (Hamburg. Hansische Universität. Institut für Aussenhandel und Überseewirtschaft. Ökonomische Studien. Band 18) With English summary.

- Economic policy

GOH (KENG SWEE) The economics of modernization and other essays. Singapore, 1972. pp. 294.

GEORGE (THAYIL JACOB SONY) Lee Kuan Yew's Singapore. London, 1973. pp. 222. bibliog.

- Foreign relations

WILSON (RICHARD GARRATT) The future role of Singapore. London, 1972. pp. 120. bibliog.

- Foreign relations - Malaysia

SOPIEE (MOHAMED NOORDIN) Political unification in the Malaysia region, 1945-1965; [Ph.D. (London) thesis]. 1972. fo. 401. bibliog. Typescript: unpublished. This thesis is the property of London University and may not be removed from the Library.

- History

CLUTTERBUCK (RICHARD LEWIS) Riot and revolution in Singapore and Malaya, 1945-1963. London, 1973. pp. 321. bibliog.

- Industries

CHIANG (TAO-CHANG) The Jurong industrial estate: present pattern and future prospects. Singapore, 1969. pp. 73. bibliog.

HERRMANN (MICHAEL) Hong Kong versus Singapore: ein Erklärungsversuch divergierender Entwicklungsverläufe. Stuttgart, 1970. pp. 314. bibliog. (Hamburg. Hansische Universität. Institut für Aussenhandel und Überseewirtschaft. Ökonomische Studien. Band 18) With English summary.

- Nationalism

CHAN (HENG CHEE) Nation-building in southeast Asia: the Singapore case. Singapore, [1972]. fo. 19. (Institute of Southeast Asian Studies. Occasional Papers. No. 3)

- Politics and government

BUCHANAN (IAIN) Singapore in Southeast Asia: an economic and political appraisal. London, [1972]. pp. 336.

CHAN (HENG CHEE) Nation-building in southeast Asia: the Singapore case. Singapore, [1972]. fo. 19. (Institute of Southeast Asian Studies. Occasional Papers. No. 3)

SOPIEE (MOHAMED NOORDIN) Political unification in the Malaysia region, 1945-1965; [Ph.D. (London) thesis]. 1972. fo. 401. bibliog. Typescript: unpublished. This thesis is the property of London University and may not be removed from the Library.

GEORGE (THAYIL JACOB SONY) Lee Kuan Yew's Singapore. London, 1973. pp. 222. bibliog.

- Social conditions

KLEEVENS (J.W.L.) Housing and health in a tropical city: a selective study in Singapore, 1964-1967. Assen, 1972. pp. 134. bibliog.

- Social policy

GEORGE (THAYIL JACOB SONY) Lee Kuan Yew's Singapore. London, 1973. pp. 222. bibliog.

SINGLE PARENT FAMILY

FATHERLESS families: report of a conference held on Tuesday 30th June 1964; organised jointly by Council for Children's Welfare [and] National Council for the Unmarried Mother and her Child. London, [1964]. pp. 37.

FATHERLESS families: do we meet their needs?; (report of a day conference), Saturday, 15 June 1968 [held in] Edinburgh; conveners, the Scottish Council for the Unmarried Mother and her Child [and others]. Edinburgh, [1968]. pp. 62.

CONSERVATIVE POLITICAL CENTRE. [Publications]. No. 477. Unhappy families. London, 1971. pp. 47.

A MISCELLANY of current care: proceedings of a conference held on 17th November 1971; [by the] National Council for the Unmarried Mother and her Child. London, [1972]. pp. 22.

NATIONAL COUNCIL FOR THE UNMARRIED MOTHER AND HER CHILD. Committee of Management. (Forward for the fatherless): memorandum of evidence to the Committee on One-Parent Families. London, 1971. pp. 192

GEORGE (VICTOR N.) and WILDING (PAUL) Motherless families. London, 1972. pp. 232. bibliog.

HOLMAN (ROBERT) Unsupported mothers and the care of their children;...(with additional notes by Mothers in Action). 2nd ed. London, 1972. pp. 61.

NATIONAL COUNCIL FOR THE UNMARRIED MOTHER AND HER CHILD. Additional evidence for the committee on one-parent families. London, 1972. pp. 58.

SINGLE PEOPLE

U.K. Department of the Environment. 1971. Housing single people: 1. How they live at present. London, 1971. pp. 59. (Design Bulletins. 23)

SINGLE TAX

DUDDEN (ARTHUR POWER) Joseph Fels and the single tax movement. Philadelphia, 1971. pp. 308.

SINGLE WOMEN

INSTITUUT VOOR TOEGEPASTE SOCIOLOGIE. De ongehuwde vrouw: onderzoek naar de levensomstandigheden van de ongehuwde vrouwen van 40 tot 65 jaar: samenvatting; (in opdracht van het Ministerie van Sociale Zaken en Volksgezondheid). 's-Gravenhage, 1971. pp. 89. (Netherlands. Ministerie van Sociale Zaken. Verslagen en Rapporten: Sociale Zaken. 1971. 1)

SINN FEIN

SINN FEIN. Eire nua: the social and economic programme of Sinn Féin. Eanáir, 1971. pp. 54.

SINO-INDIAN BORDER DISPUTE, 1957-

BHAT (SUDHAKAR) India and China. New Delhi, Popular Book Services, 1967. pp. 260. 21½cm.

SINO-JAPANESE CONFLICT, 1937-1945
See CHINESE-JAPANESE WAR, 1937-1945

SIR GEORGE WILLIAMS UNIVERSITY

LET the niggers burn!..the Sir George Williams University affair and its Caribbean aftermath; (edited by Dennis Forsythe). Montreal, [1971]. pp. 209.

SIRIONO INDIANS

SCHEFFLER (HAROLD WALTER) and LOUNSBURY (FLOYD G.) A study in structural semantics: the Siriono kinship system. Englewood Cliffs, N.J., [1971]. pp. 260. bibliog.

SISAL HEMP

LAWRENCE (PETER R.) The sisal industry of Tanzania: a review of the informal commodity agreement and related questions of strategy. [Dar es Salaam, 1971]. pp. 34. (Dar es Salaam. University. Economic Research Bureau. ERB Papers. 71.9)

SIT DOWN STRIKES
- United Kingdom

METRA CONSULTING GROUP LTD. An analysis of sit-ins. London, 1972. fo. 29.

SITUATIONIST INTERNATIONAL

RASPAUD (JEAN JACQUES) and VOYER (JEAN PIERRE) L'internationale situationniste: chronologie, bibliographie, protagonistes, avec un index des noms insultés. Paris, [1972]. pp. 168.

SKILLED LABOUR

DANILIN (GENNADII DMITRIEVICH) Avtomatizatsiia i ee sotsial'no-ekonomicheskie posledstviia pri kapitalizme: izmeneniia v kvalifikatsii rabochego klassa. Moskva, 1971. pp. 190.

- Russia

PASHKOV (ALEKSEI STEPANOVICH) Pravovoe regulirovanie podgotovki i raspredeleniia kadrov: nekotorye voprosy teorii i praktiki. Leningrad, 1966. pp. 188.

BUTENKO (ANATOLII MIKHAILOVICH) Vosproizvodstvo kvalifitsirovannoi rabochei sily v sel'skom khoziaistve. Moskva, 1970. pp. 157.

IVANOVA (MARINA ALEKSEEVNA) and SAMARINA (IZOL'DA ALEKSANDROVNA) Tekhnicheskii progress i struktura ITR i sluzhashchikh. Moskva, 1970. pp. 128.

PRAVA i obiazannosti molodykh spetsialistov. Moskva, 1970. pp. 144. Cover gives title as: O pravakh i obiazannostiakh, etc.

ROMANKO (FEDIR HORDIIOVYCH) Ekonomichni osnovy i zakonomirnosti zrostannia kul'turno-tekhnichnoho rivnia robitnychoho klasu. Kharkiv, 1971. pp. 135.

ARTEMOVA (VERA NIKOLAEVNA) Povyshenie kvalifikatsii rabochikh i sluzhashchikh: pravovye voprosy. Minsk, 1972. pp. 123.

GOMBERG (IAKOV IZRAILEVICH) Kvalifitsirovannyi trud i metody ego izmereniia. Moskva, 1972. pp. 231.

KOMAROV (VASILII EFIMOVICH) Ekonomicheskie problemy podgotovki i ispol'zovaniia kadrov spetsialistov. Moskva, 1972. pp. 200.

POPOV (GAVRIIL KHARITONOVICH) and DZHAVADOV (GATAM AGALIEVICH) eds. Upravlenie i problema kadrov. Moskva, 1972. pp. 175. bibliog.

SHAFRANOVA (OL'GA IVANOVNA) Professional'nyi sostav rabochikh promyshlennosti SSSR. Moskva, 1972. pp. 71. bibliog.

SKINNER (BURRHUS FREDERIC)

CHOMSKY (NOAM) For reasons of state. [London], 1973. pp. 220.

SKOVORODA (HRYHORII SAVYCH)

FUHRMANN (JOSEPH T.) and others. Essays on Russian intellectual history;...edited by Leon Borden Blair. Austin, [1971]. pp. 123. bibliogs. (Texas University. Walter Prescott Webb Memorial Lectures. 5)

SKVORTSOV-STEPANOV (IVAN IVANOVICH)

SKVORTSOV-STEPANOV (IVAN IVANOVICH) Izbrannoe. Moskva, 1970. pp. 254.

SLÁNSKÝ (RUDOLF)

SLÁNSKÝ (RUDOLF) Za vítězství socialismu: stati a projevy, 1925-(1951). Praha, 1951. 2 vols.

SLASHCHEV-KRYMSKII (IAKOV ALEKSANDROVICH)

SLASHCHEV-KRYMSKII (IAKOV ALEKSANDROVICH) Krym v 1920 g.: otryvki iz vospominanii; s predisloviem Dm. Furmanova. Moskva, [1923]. pp. 148.

SLASHCHOV (IAKOV ALEKSANDROVICH)
See SLASHCHEV-KRYMSKII (IAKOV ALEKSANDROVICH)

SLATINA
- Growth

CONSTANTINESCU (MIRON) and STAHL (HENRI H.) eds. Procesul de urbanizare în R.S. România: zona Slatina-Olt. București, 1970. pp. 398. With French and Russian summaries.

SLAUGHTERING AND SLAUGHTERHOUSES
- France

FRANCE. Ministère de l'Agriculture. Statistique Agricole. Supplément. Série Etudes. No. 96. Etude sur la structure des abattoirs, 1964-1969. [Paris], 1972. pp. 71.

- Netherlands

ECONOMISCH INSTITUUT VOOR HET MIDDEN- EN KLEINBEDRIJF. Bedrijfsgegevens voor het slagersbedrijf over 1965 en de geraamde uitkomsten 1966. 's-Gravenhage, 1967. pp. 50.

SLAVE-TRADE

SMITH (WILLIAM) M.P. for Norwich. A letter to William Wilberforce, Esq., M.P., on the proposed abolition of the slave trade, at present under the consideration of Parliament. London, Longman, 1807. pp. 48.

The JAMAICA movement, for promoting the enforcement of the slave-trade treaties, and the suppression of the slave-trade; with statements of fact, convention, and law; prepared at the request of the Kingston Committee [by D. Turnbull]; [reprint of work originally published in 1850]. New York, [1969]. pp. 430.

- Africa

DOCUMENTOS relativos ao apresamento, julgamento e entrega da barca franceza Charles et Georges e em geral ao engajamento de negros, debaixo da denominação de trabalhadores livres nas possessões da coroa de Portugal na Costa Oriental e Occidental de Africa para as colonias francezas; apresentados ás Cortes na Sessão Legislativa de 1858. Lisboa, 1858. pp. 249, 17.

RENAULT (FRANÇOIS) Lavigerie, l'esclavage africain et l'Europe, 1868-1892. Paris, 1971. 2 vols. bibliog.

- Africa, East

HARRIS (JOSEPH E.) The African presence in Asia: consequences of the East African slave trade. Evanston, 1971. pp. 156. bibliog.

SLAVERY

ROBERT DE LA MENNAIS (HUGUES FELICITE) Modern slavery;... [translated from the French, with appendix and notes; by W.J. Linton]. London, 1840. pp. 32.

PLUMB (JOHN HAROLD) In the light of history. London, 1972. pp. 273.

TEMPERLEY (HOWARD) British antislavery, 1833-1870. London, 1972. pp. 298. bibliog.

- Emancipation

GRATUS (JACK) The great white lie: slavery, emancipation and changing racial attitudes. London, 1973. pp. 324.

SLAVERY IN ANCIENT ROME

WEAVER (PAUL RICHARD CAREY) Familia Caesaris: a social study of the emperor's freedmen and slaves. Cambridge, 1972. pp. 330. bibliog.

SLAVERY IN BRAZIL

IANNI (OCTÁVIO) As metamorfoses do escravo: apogeu e crise da escravatura no Brasil meridional. São Paulo, 1962. pp. 312. bibliog.

DEGLER (CARL N.) Neither black nor white: slavery and race relations in Brazil and the United States. New York, [1971]. pp. 302.

- Emancipation

TOPLIN (ROBERT BRENT) The abolition of slavery in Brazil. New York, 1972. pp. 299. bibliog.

SLAVERY IN CUBA

HALL (GWENDOLYN MIDLO) Social control in slave population societies: a comparison of St. Domingue and Cuba. Baltimore, [1971]. pp. 166. bibliog. (Johns Hopkins University. Studies in Historical and Political Science. Series 89. [No.] 1)

SLAVERY IN PANAMA

DIEZ CASTILLO (LUIS A.) Los cimarrones y la esclavitud en Panama. [Panama, 1968]. pp. 86. bibliog.

SLAVERY IN PUERTO RICO

COLL Y TOSTE (CAYETANO) Historia de la esclavitud en Puerto Rico: informacion y documentos; compilacion de Isabel Cuchi Coll. San Juan, P.R., 1969 reprinted 1972. pp. 272.

SLAVERY IN THE BRITISH EMPIRE

- Emancipation

HURWITZ (EDITH F.) Politics and the public conscience: slave emancipation and the abolitionist movement in Britain. London, 1973. pp. 179.

SLAVERY IN THE DOMINICAN REPUBLIC

LARRAZABAL BLANCO (CARLOS) Los negros y la esclavitud en Santo Domingo. Santo Domingo, 1967. pp. 202.

HALL (GWENDOLYN MIDLO) Social control in slave population societies: a comparison of St. Domingue and Cuba. Baltimore, [1971]. pp. 166. bibliog. (Johns Hopkins University. Studies in Historical and Political Science. Series 89. [No.] 1)

SLAVERY IN THE UNITED KINGDOM

- Antislavery movements

TEMPERLEY (HOWARD) British antislavery, 1833-1870. London, 1972. pp. 298. bibliog.

SLAVERY IN THE UNITED STATES

The LIBERTY bell; by friends of freedom. Boston, Mass., 1846. pp. 268.

NYE (RUSSEL BLAINE) Fettered freedom: civil liberties and the slavery controversy, 1830-1860; [originally published in East Lansing, 1963]. [rev. ed.] Urbana, 1972. pp. 353. bibliog.

DEGLER (CARL N.) Neither black nor white: slavery and race relations in Brazil and the United States. New York, [1971]. pp. 302.

FELDSTEIN (STANLEY) Once a slave: the slaves' view of slavery. New York, 1971. pp. 329. bibliog.

LANE (ANN J.) ed. The debate over slavery: Stanley Elkins and his critics. Urbana, [1971]. pp. 378. Published without index.

ROBINSON (DONALD L.) Slavery in the structure of American politics, 1765-1820. New York, [1971]. pp. 564.

BLASSINGAME (JOHN W.) The slave community: plantation life in the antebellum South. New York, 1972. pp. 262. bibliog.

RUSSEL (ROBERT ROYAL) Critical studies in antebellum sectionalism: essays in American political and economic history. Westport, Conn., [1972]. pp. 223. bibliogs.

WEINSTEIN (ALLEN) and GATELL (FRANK OTTO) eds. American negro slavery: a modern reader. 2nd ed. New York, 1973. pp. 439. bibliog.

- Antislavery movements

PERRY (LEWIS) Radical abolitionism: anarchy and the government of God in antislavery thought. Ithaca, N.Y., 1973. pp. 328. bibliog.

- Emancipation

   BROWN (LETITIA WOODS) Free negroes in the District of Columbia, 1790-1846. New York, 1972. pp. 226. bibliog.

   DAVIS (DANIEL S.) Struggle for freedom: the history of black Americans. New York, [1972]. pp. 256. bibliog.

- Insurrections, etc.

   FONER (ERIC) ed. Nat Turner. Englewood Cliffs, [1971]. pp. 184. bibliog.

SLAVERY IN THE WEST INDIES

GRATUS (JACK) The great white lie: slavery, emancipation and changing racial attitudes. London, 1973. pp. 324.

SLAVERY IN VENEZUELA

TROCONIS DE VERACOECHEA (ERMILA) ed. Documentos para el estudio de los esclavos negros en Venezuela. Caracas, 1969. pp. 348.

- Emancipation

   LOMBARDI (JOHN V.) The decline and abolition of negro slavery in Venezuela, 1820-1854. Westport, Conn., [1971]. pp. 217. bibliog.

SLAVIC STUDIES

- Germany

   ZOTSCHEW (THEODOR) Strukturwandel in Wirtschaft und Gesellschaft Südosteuropas: eine sozial-ökonomische und statistische Analyse anlässlich des 20jährigen Bestehens der Südosteuropa-Gesellschaft. München, 1972. pp. 113. (Südosteuropa-Gesellschaft. Südosteuropa-Studien. 20)

SLAVICH (VALERIAN VECHESLAVOVICH)

SLAVICH (VALERIAN VECHESLAVOVICH) Ispoved' smenovekhovtsa. Sofiia, 1924. pp. 152.

SLAVOPHILISM

GLEASON (ABBOTT) European and Muscovite: Ivan Kireevsky and the origins of slavophilism. Cambridge, Mass., 1972. pp. 376. bibliog. (Harvard University. Russian Research Center. Studies. [No.] 68)

SLAVS

KLASSEN (EGOR') Novye materialy dlia drevneishei istorii slavian voobshche i slaviano-russov do riurikovskogo vremeni v osobennosti, s legkim ocherkom istorii russov do rozhdestva Khristova. Moskva, 1854. pp. various.

- Religion

   MORDVINTSEV (ALEKSANDR ALEKSANDROVICH) Slavianskaia antireligioznaia skazka. Kiev, 1970. pp. 134.

SLEPTSOV (VASILII ALEKSEEVICH)

NEKHAI (MIKHAIL VASIL'EVICH) Russkii demokraticheskii ocherk 60-kh godov XIX stoletiia: N. Uspenskii, V. Sleptsov, A. Levitov. Minsk, 1971. pp. 146. bibliog.

SLOPES (PHYSICAL GEOGRAPHY)

CARSON (MICHAEL ANTHONY) and KIRKBY (M.J.) Hillslope form and process. Cambridge, 1972. pp. 475. bibliog.

SLOVAKIA

- Economic conditions

   IVANIČKA (KOLOMAN) ed. The analysis of economic territorial nuclei of Slovakia: Analyza ekonomických územných jadier slovenska. Bratislava, 1970. pp. 231. (Univerzita Komenského Bratislava. Acta Geographica Universitatis Comenianae. Economico-Geographica. 9) In English and Slovak. Maps in end pocket.

- History

   PRÍSPEVKY k dejinám východného Slovenska: materiály zo IV. sjazdu slovenských historikov v Košiciach dňa 28.-30.VI. 1962. Bratislava, 1964. pp. 449.

   HUSÁK (GUSTÁV) Svidetel'stvo o Slovatskom natsional'nom vosstanii; [translated from the Slovak]. Moskva, 1969. pp. 870. bibliog. Translation of the 2nd Slovak ed., 1969.

   DRESS (HANS) Slowakei und faschistische Neuordnung Europas, 1939-1941. Berlin, 1972. pp. 199. bibliog. (Deutsche Akademie der Wissenschaften zu Berlin. Institut für Geschichte. Schriften. Reihe 1. Band 37)

   HUSÁK (GUSTÁV) Der Slowakische Nationalaufstand; [translated from the Slovak]. Berlin, 1972. pp. 740.

- Nationalism

   ARATÓ (ENDRE) Egykorú demokratikus nézetek az 1848-1849.évi magyarországi forradalomról és ellenforradalomról: az 1848-1849.évi szlovák nemzeti mozgalom értékeléséről folytatott vitához. Budapest, 1971. pp. 140.

   STEINER (EUGEN) The Slovak dilemma. Cambridge, 1973. pp. 229. bibliog. (London. University. London School of Economics and Political Science. Centre for International Studies. International Studies)

SLOVENIA

- Industries

   BEITRÄGE zur Geschichte der Industrialisierung des Südostalpenraumes im 19. Jahrhundert: [four papers read at a symposium in 1968]; herausgegeben von Othmar Pickl. Graz, 1970. pp. 59. (Historische Landeskommission für Steiermark. Forschungen zur Geschichtlichen Landeskunde der Steiermark. Band 24)

SLOW LEARNING CHILDREN

U.K. Department of Education and Science. 1971. Slow learners in secondary schools. London, 1971. pp. 28. (Education Surveys. 15)

SLUMS

- Brazil - Guanabara

   BRAZIL. Census, 1960. Censo demografico de 1960: favelas do Estado da Guanabara. [Rio de Janeiro, 1968]. pp. 97.

SLUMS (Cont'd.)

- Brazil - Rio de Janeiro

LEEDS (ELIZABETH) and LEEDS (ANTHONY) Brazil in the 1960's: favelas and polity, the continuity of the structure of social control. Austin, 1972. pp. 91. bibliog. (American Society for Public Administration. Latin American Development Administration Committee and Texas University. Institute of Latin American Studies. LADAC Occasional Papers. Series 2. No. 5)

- United Kingdom

SHELTER. Condemned: a...report on housing and poverty. London, [1971]. pp. 86.

SHELTER. Reprieve for slums: a...report. London, [1972]. pp. 54.

ROWLAND (JON) Community decay. Harmondsworth, 1973. pp. 159. bibliog.

- United States

FORMAN (ROBERT E.) Black ghettos, white ghettos and slums. Englewood Cliffs, [1971]. pp. 184.

- United States - Baltimore

STEGMAN (MICHAEL A.) Housing investment in the inner city: the dynamics of decline; a study of Baltimore, Maryland, 1968-1970. Cambridge, Mass., [1972]. pp. 289. bibliog.

- United States - New York (City)

DORMAN (MICHAEL) The making of a slum. New York, [1972]. pp. 216.

SMALL BUSINESS

ORGANISATION FOR ECONOMIC CO-OPERATION AND DEVELOPMENT. Industry Committee. 1971. Problems and policies relating to small and medium-sized businesses: analytic report. Paris, 1971. pp. 57.

- Management

ROBINSON (J. GEORGE) Programmed training for managers of small business. Singapore, Asian Productivity Organization, 1971. pp. 129.

- Brazil

PEREIRA (C.J. DA COSTA) Assistência ao artesanato brasileiro. [Recife, 1963]. pp. 15.

- Chile - Mathematical models

ANDERSON (MICHAEL B.) A model of the small Chilean firm. [Ithaca], 1972. pp. 155. bibliog. (Cornell University. Latin American Studies Program. Dissertation Series. No. 38)

- European Economic Community countries

CONFEDERATION OF BRITISH INDUSTRY. Small firms and the Common Market: action that small firms should take. London, 1972. pp. 59.

- Germany

SCHLAGHECKEN (ARNIM) Der ökonomische Differenzierungsprozess im heutigen Handwerk. Berlin, [1969]. pp. 146. bibliog. (Rheinisch-Westfälisches Institut für Wirtschaftsforschung, Essen. Schriftenreihe. Neue Folge. 29)

KEUTMANN (DIETER) and DIECK (MARGRET) Auswirkungen der Konzentrationstendenzen auf das Handwerk. Göttingen, 1971. pp. 338. bibliog. (Cologne. Universität. Seminar für Genossenschaftswesen. Schriften. Band 16)

SCHULTHOFF (HANS JOACHIM) Kooperation und Konzentration im Hamburger Handwerk: ein Vergleich von Entwicklungen und gewerbepolitischen Gestaltungsmöglichkeiten. Hamburg, 1971. 1 vol. (various pagings). bibliog.

WINKLER (HEINRICH AUGUST) Mittelstand, Demokratie und Nationalsozialismus: die politische Entwicklung von Handwerk und Kleinhandel in der Weimarer Republik. Köln, [1972]. pp. 307. bibliog.

- Germany - Finance

PARK (HE KYONG) Die Finanzierung von Mittel- und Kleinbetrieben in Westdeutschland und Südkorea. [Cologne, imprint], 1971. pp. 134. bibliog.

- India

INDIA. Development Commissioner (Small Scale Industries). 1968. Small scale industries: programme of work for the fourth five year plan. New Delhi, 1968. pp. 182.

INDIA. Development Commissioner (Small Scale Industries). 1971. Small scale industries. New Delhi, [1971]. pp. 842.

NATIONAL COUNCIL OF APPLIED ECONOMIC RESEARCH. Study of selected small industrial units. New Delhi, [1973?]. pp. 75.

- India - Bibliography

CHATTERJEE (CHANCHAL KUMAR) and CHAND (RAMESH) compilers. Bibliography of small scale and cottage industries and handicrafts. [Delhi, 1969]. pp. 111. (India. Census, 1961. Vol.1. Part XI(i))

- India - Finance

TARAPOREVALA (RUSSI JAL) Banks and the financing of small scale industries in India;... speech delivered at the second Chief Agents' Conference of Central Bank of India... 1968. [Bombay, 1968]. pp. 8.

- Japan

INDIA. Delegation to Japan to Study Small Scale Industries. 1969. Report; [Bhanu Prakash Singh, leader]. New Delhi, [1969]. pp. 53.

VEPA (RAM K.) Productivity in small industries: some lessons from Japan. [Tokyo], Asian Productivity Organization, 1969. pp. 98.

TOKYO. Bureau of General Affairs. Liaison and Protocol Section. Minor industries and workers in Tokyo. Tokyo, 1972. pp. 190. (Tokyo. Metropolitan Government. Municipal Library. No. 8)

- Korea - Finance

PARK (HE KYONG) Die Finanzierung von Mittel- und Kleinbetrieben in Westdeutschland und Südkorea. [Cologne, imprint], 1971. pp. 134. bibliog.

- Netherlands

RAAD VOOR HET MIDDEN- EN KLEINBEDRIJF. Rapport inkomenspositie en -ontwikkeling van werknemers en zelfstandigen in het midden- en kleinbedrijf. 's-Gravenhage, 1969. pp. 63. (Publikaties. 1969, no. 4)

- Nigeria

ALUKO (SAMUEL ADEPOJU) and others, eds. Small-scale industries: Western State of Nigeria. Ile-Ife, 1972. pp. 380.

- Pakistan

>WEST PAKISTAN SMALL INDUSTRIES CORPORATION. Small Industries Survey Organization. Planning, Survey and Evaluation Wing. Industrial potential of the rural areas of West Pakistan: [district reports]. Lahore, [1967 in progress].

>PAKISTAN. Central Statistical Office. Economic Affairs Division. 1969- . Survey of small and household manufacturing industries. [Karachi, 1969 in progress].

- Russia

>BELIANOV (VLADISLAV ALEKSANDROVICH) Lichnoe podsobnoe khoziaistvo pri sotsializme. Moskva, 1970. pp. 184.

- Spain

>SPAIN. Comisaria del Plan de Desarrollo Economico y Social. 1972. (III Plan de desarrollo economico y social): la pequeña y mediana empresa. [Madrid], 1972. pp. 277.

SMALL BUSINESS : Underdeveloped areas
SeeUNDERDEVELOPED AREAS - Small business

- United Kingdom

>DESIGN AND INDUSTRIES ASSOCIATION. On the encouragement of small industrial centres to assist in the reconstruction of rural life and in the employment of discharged soldiers...: memorandum...to the Rt. Hon. Christopher Addison, etc. London, 1918. pp. 7.

>ECONOMIC DEVELOPMENT COMMITTEE FOR HOTELS AND CATERING. Marketing Working Group. Marketing in a small business. [London, National Economic Development Office, 1971]. pp. 44.

>TODD (DOUGLAS) The relative efficiency of small and large firms. London, 1971. pp. 39. bibliog. (U.K. Committee of Inquiry on Small Firms. Research Reports. No. 18)

>CLARKE (PHILIP) Small businesses: how they survive and succeed. Newton Abbot, [1972]. pp. 395.

>DAVIES (J.R.) and KELLY (M.) Small firms in the manufacturing sector. London, 1972. pp. 85. (U.K. Committee of Inquiry on Small Firms. Research Reports. No. 3)

>U.K. Committee of Inquiry on Small Firms. 1972. A postal questionnaire survey of small firms: non-financial data. London, 1972. pp. 42. (Research Reports. No. 17)

>U.K. Committee of Inquiry on Small Firms. 1972. Summary of recommendations and government action. London, 1972. pp. 13. The main report of the Committee is published as a British Parliamentary Paper, Cmnd. 4811.

>BOSWELL (JONATHAN) The rise and decline of small firms. London, 1973. pp. 272. bibliog.

- Finance

>TAMARI (M.) A postal questionnaire survey of small firms: an analysis of financial data. London, 1972. pp. 58. (U.K. Committee of Inquiry on Small Firms. Research Reports. No. 16)

- Information services

>U.K. Ministry of Technology. 1970. Assistance for industry through the industrial liaison scheme. [London], 1970. pp. 43.

>U.K. Department of Trade and Industry. 1971. Assistance for small firms through the industrial liaison service. [London], 1971. pp. 47.

>U.K. Department of Trade and Industry. 1972. Assistance for small firms through the industrial liaison service. [rev. ed.] [London], 1972. pp. 44.

SMALL BUSINESS INVESTMENT COMPANIES

>JÖNSSON (STEN A.) Om utvecklingsbolagens planeringsproblem: (resurskombinering och organisatorisk strukturering). Göteborg, 1971. pp. 141. bibliog. (Gothenburg. Handelshögskolan. Företagsekonomiska Studier. 11) With English summary.

SMALL GROUPS

>ASCHAUER (ERIKA) Führung: eine soziologische Analyse anhand kleiner Gruppen; ... mit einem Vorwort von G. Eisermann, Bonn. Stuttgart, 1970. pp. 120. bibliog. (Bonn. Universität. Institut für Soziologie. Bonner Beiträge zur Soziologie. Nr.8)

>HARTFORD (MARGARET E.) Groups in social work: application of small group theory and research to social work practice. New York, 1972. pp. 297. bibliog.

SMALL HOLDINGS

- Kenya

>HAUGWITZ (HANS WILHELM VON) Some experiences with smallholder settlement in Kenya. München, [1972]. pp. 94. bibliog. (Ifo-Institut für Wirtschaftsforschung. Afrika-Studien. 72)

- Russia

>BELIANOV (VLADISLAV ALEKSANDROVICH) Lichnoe podsobnoe khoziaistvo pri sotsializme. Moskva, 1970. pp. 184.

SMIRNOV (DMITRII MIKHAILOVICH)

>SMIRNOV (DMITRII MIKHAILOVICH) Zapiski chekista. 2nd ed. Minsk, 1972. pp. 288.

SMIT (ERASMUS)

>SMIT (ERASMUS) The diary of Erasmus Smit; edited by H.F. Schoon; translated by W.G.A. Mears. Cape Town, 1972. pp. 189.

SMITH (ADAM)

>CADET (FELIX) Histoire de l'économie politique: les précurseurs; Adam Smith, Franklin. Reims, 1869. pp. 73. (Société Industrielle de Reims. Conférences. 1869-1870)

>[HORTON (SAMUEL DANA)] The parity of moneys as regarded by Adam Smith, Ricardo, and Mill: an open letter answering a question of a member of the Royal Commission on Gold and Silver; by Amicus Curiae [pseud]. London, 1888. pp. 31.

>FIORITO (RICCARDO) Divisione del lavoro e teoria del valore: l'economia sociologica di Adam Smith. Bari, [1971]. pp. 207.

>HOLLANDER (SAMUEL) The economics of Adam Smith. London, 1973. pp. 351. bibliog.

SMITH (ADAM) (Cont'd.)

MEDICK (HANS) Naturzustand und Naturgeschichte der bürgerlichen Gesellschaft: die Ursprünge der bürgerlichen Sozialtheorie...bei Samuel Pufendorf, John Locke und Adam Smith. Göttingen, 1973. pp. 330. bibliog.

SMOKING

CANADA. Epidemiology Division. 1966. A Canadian study of smoking and health. [Ottawa], 1966. pp. 137.

WHITESIDE (THOMAS) Selling death: cigarette advertising and public health. New York, [1971]. pp. 150.

BEWLEY (BEULAH R.) and others. Smoking by children in Great Britain: a review of the literature. London, Social Science Research Council, [1973]. pp. 21. bibliog.

- Statistics

BEESE (D.H.) ed. Tobacco consumption in various countries. 3rd ed. London, 1972. pp. 66. (Tobacco Research Council. Research Papers. [No.]6)

TODD (GEORGE FREDERICK) ed. Statistics of smoking in the United Kingdom. 6th ed. London, 1972. pp. 132. (Tobacco Research Council. Research Papers. No. 1)

SNOW (CHARLES PERCY) Baron Snow

MEILAKH (BORIS SOLOMONOVICH) Na rubezhe nauki i iskusstva: spor o dvukh sferakh poznaniia i tvorchestva. Leningrad, 1971. pp. 247.

SOCCER

- United Kingdom

SAUNDERS (L.) The characteristics and impact of travel generated by Chelsea football stadium. [London], 1972. pp. 17. (London. Greater London Council. Department of Planning and Transportation. Research Memoranda. 344)

SOCIAL ACTION

CARKHUFF (ROBERT R.) The development of human resources: education psychology, and social change. New York, [1971]. pp. 422. bibliogs.

SOCIAL ADJUSTMENT

MARTINDALE (DON ALBERT) and MARTINDALE (EDITH) The social dimensions of mental illness, alcoholism, and drug dependence. Westport, [1971]. pp. 330. bibliog.

SMITH (COURTLAND L.) The Salt River project: a case study in cultural adaptation to an urbanizing community. Tucson, [1972]. pp. 151. bibliog.

SOCIAL CASE WORK

LE ROUX (P. OWEN) Maatskaplike gevallewerk 'n Christelik-Wetenskaplike benadering. Wellington, N.Z., 1970. pp. 265. bibliog.

BRIAR (SCOTT) and MILLER (HENRY) of the School of Social Welfare, University of California. Problems and issues in social casework. New York, 1971. pp. 274.

PERLMAN (HELEN HARRIS) Perspectives on social casework. Philadelphia, [1971]. pp. 199. bibliog.

ADAMS (MARGARET) and LOVEJOY (HOWARD) eds. The mentally subnormal: social work approaches. 2nd ed. [London], 1972. pp. 296.

BEHAVIOUR modification in social work; [by] Derek Jehu [and others]. London, [1972]. pp. 193. bibliog.

HOLLIS (FLORENCE) Casework: a psychosocial therapy. 2nd ed. New York, [1972]. pp. 393. bibliogs.

MILLER (JOAN B.) The casework ministry. London, 1972. pp. 128. bibliogs.

MONGER (MARK) Casework in probation. 2nd ed. London, 1972. pp. 233.

O'SULLIVAN (MAEVE) Let the client choose: non-directive casework: fact or fallacy? London, [1972]. pp. 45.

TIMMS (NOEL) Recording in social work. London, 1972. pp. 112. bibliog.

- Research

NETHERLANDS. Ministerie van Cultuur, Recreatie en Maatschappelijk Werk. 1970. A brief record of research commissioned by or conducted with the co-operation of the Ministry of Cultural Affairs, Recreation and Social Welfare. The Hague, 1970. pp. 76.

SOCIAL CASE WORK WITH FAMILIES
See FAMILY SOCIAL WORK

SOCIAL CHANGE

CIVARDI (LUIGI) Nuevo orden social. 3rd ed. Madrid, 1960. pp. 168.

BUSLINSKII (VLADIMIR ANDREEVICH) O svoeobrazii skachka pri perekhode ot sotsializma k kommunizmu. Moskva, 1964. pp. 56.

SITUAZIONI e problemi sociali dell'Italia in trasformazione; [by Guido Baglione and others]. Milano, 1965 repr. 1969. pp. 237. bibliogs. (Istituto Sociale Ambrosiano. Quaderni di Formazione Sociale. N.8)

ARON (RAYMOND) Les désillusions du progrès: essai sur la dialectique de la modernité. [Paris 1969]. pp. 377.

DESARROLLO comunitario y cambio social; ([by] Hugo Calello [and others]). [Caracas?, 1969]. pp. 253.

DNEPROPETROVSK. Universitet. Kafedra Filosofii. Dialektika obshchestvennogo razvitiia: sbornik nauchnykh rabot, soobshchennykh na mezhvuzovskoi konferentsii, provedennoi kafedroi filosofii universiteta v chest' 150-letiia so dnia rozhdeniia Karla Marksa. Dnepropetrovsk, 1969. pp. 293. bibliog.

GOTTHEIL (JULIO) El compromiso argentino: presente y futuro de una crisis de cambio en América latina. Buenos Aires, [1969]. pp. 175.

ASPIRATIONS et transformations sociales: [papers of two conferences organized by UNESCO and others];.. publié sous la direction de Paul-Henry Chombart de Lauwe. Paris, [1970]. pp. 387.

BAUDOT (JACQUES) Social prognosis. (UNRISD Reports. No.70.19) (UNRISD /70/C.69). Geneva, United Nations Research Institute for Social Development, 1970. pp. 41. bibliog.

1971

BARBER (BERNARD REUBEN) and INKELES (ALEX) eds. Stability and social change: (a volume in honor of Talcott Parsons). Boston, [1971]. pp. 451.

CARKHUFF (ROBERT R.) The development of human resources: education, psychology, and social change. New York, [1971]. pp. 422. bibliogs.

ERMOLAEV (IVAN DMITRIEVICH) Zakony razvitiia obshchestva i stroitel'stvo kommunizma. Moskva, 1971. pp. 224.

ESSAYS on modernization of underdeveloped societies [published on the fiftieth anniversary of the Department of Sociology, Bombay University]; editor, A.R. Desai. Bombay, 1971. 2 vols.

FILOSOFSKIE problemy obshchestvennogo razvitiia. Moskva, 1971. pp. 300.

GRUSON (CLAUDE) Renaissance du plan. Paris, [1971]. pp. 174.

KONJUNKTURPOLITIK: Zeitschrift für angewandte Konjunkturforschung. Beihefte. Heft 18. Wirtschaftlicher und sozialer Wandel durch technischen Fortschritt: Bericht über den wissenschaftlichen Teil der 34. Mitgliederversammlung der Arbeitsgemeinschaft deutscher wirtschaftswissenschaftlicher Forschungsinstitute...1971. Berlin, [1971]. pp. 194.

MISABISHVILI (SHOTA VLADIMIROVICH) Dialektika obshchego i osobennogo v sotsial'nom razvitii. Sukhumi, 1971. pp. 247

POLITICAL development in changing societies: an analysis of modernization; edited by Monte Palmer [and] Larry Stern. Lexington, [1971]. pp. 179.

PROTAGONISTS of change: subcultures in development and revolution; (Abdul A. Said, editor). Englewood Cliffs, [1971]. pp. 181.

SMITH (DONALD EUGENE) ed. Religion, politics, and social change in the Third World: a sourcebook. New York, [1971]. pp. 286. bibliog.

SOCIAL intervention: a behavioural science approach; (edited and with introductions by Harvey A. Hornstein [and others]. New York, [1971]. pp. 597. bibliogs.

The SOCIOLOGY of the future: theory, cases, and annotated bibliography; edited by Wendell Bell and James A. Mau. New York, [1971]. pp. 464. bibliogs.

SWANSON (GUY EDWIN) Social change. Glenview, Ill., [1971]. pp. 185. bibliog.

TAYLOR (JAMES CHAPMAN) Technology and planned organizational change. Ann Arbor, [1971]. pp. 151. bibliog.

1972

ADISESHIAH (MALCOLM SATHIANATHAN) It is a time to begin: the human role in development; some further reflections for the seventies. Paris, United Nations Educational, Scientific and Cultural Organization, 1972. pp. 182. bibliog.

BARBER (BENJAMIN R.) Superman and common men: freedom, anarchy and the revolution. Harmondsworth, 1972. pp. 127.

BERNARD (H. RUSSELL) and PELTO (PERTTI JUHO) eds. Technology and social change. New York, [1972]. pp. 354. bibliog.

BETEILLE (ANDRE) Inequality and social change. Delhi, 1972. pp. 36. (Kerala University. Ramaswami Mudaliar Lectures. 1971)

BOTCHWAY (FRANCIS A.) Political development and social change in Ghana: Ghana under Nkrumah; a study of the influence of Kwame Nkrumah and the role of ideas in rapid social change. Buffalo, N.Y., [1972]. pp. 174. bibliog.

BREWER (GARRY D.) On innovation, social change and reality: (abstract). [Santa Monica], 1972. pp. 9. (Rand Corporation. [Papers]. 4876)

COCHRAN (THOMAS CHILDS) Social change in industrial society: twentieth-century America. London, 1972. pp. 178. bibliog. (Oxford. University. St. Antony's College. Publications. No. 5)

DORE (RONALD PHILIP) The late development effect. Brighton, 1972. pp. 11. (Brighton. University of Sussex. Institute of Development Studies. Communications. [No.] 103)

GARAUDY (ROGER) L'alternative. Paris, [1972]. pp. 252.

HOCHMAN (JOEL SIMON) Marijuana and social evolution. Englewood Cliffs, N.J., [1972]. pp. 184. bibliog.

HOROWITZ (IRVING LOUIS) Three worlds of development: the theory and practice of international stratification. 2nd ed. New York, 1972. pp. 556.

INSTITUTION building: a model for applied social change (papers presented at a workshop held at Purdue University... 1969... sponsored by the Agency for International Development and the Committee on Institutional Cooperation); edited by D. Woods Thomas [and others]. Cambridge, Mass., [1972]. pp. 291.

JESSOP (ROBERT DOUGLAS) Social order, reform and revolution: a power, exchange and institutionalisation perspective. London, 1972. pp. 189. bibliog.

KAUTSKY (JOHN HANS) The political consequences of modernization. New York, [1972]. pp. 267.

KHARIN (IURII ANDREEVICH) Dialektika sotsial'nogo otritsaniia. Minsk, 1972. pp. 277.

KING (BERT T.) and McGINNIES (ELLIOTT) eds. Attitudes, conflict, and social change;...[based on a symposium held at the University of Maryland]. New York, 1972. pp. 234. bibliogs.

McLUHAN (MARSHALL) and NEVITT (BARRINGTON) Take today: the executive as dropout. New York, [1972] pp. 304. bibliog.

MARCUSE (HERBERT) Counterrevolution and revolt. Boston, [Mass., 1972]. pp. 138. bibliog.

MATTICK (PAUL) Critique of Marcuse: one-dimensional man in class society. London, 1972. pp. 110.

MAYER (ROBERT R.) Social planning and social change. Englewood Cliffs, [1972]. pp. 147. bibliog.

NISBET (ROBERT ALEXANDER) ed. Social change: [a reader]. Oxford, 1972. pp. 270.

PERSPECTIVES on modernization: essays in memory of Ian Weinberg; (edited by Edward B. Harvey). Toronto, [1972]. pp. 197. bibliog.

PIGOTT (FRANCIS) Free fall to -? Boston, Lincs., 1972. pp. 23.

SOCIAL CHANGE (Cont'd.)

POPULATION and social change: [papers of two international conferences jointly sponsored by Harvard Centre for Population Studies and the American Academy of Arts and Sciences]; edited by D.V.Glass and Roger Revelle. London, 1972. pp. 520. bibliogs. An expanded version of the Spring 1968 issue of Daedalus.

SCARRITT (JAMES R.) Political development and cultural change theory: a propositional synthesis with application to Africa. Beverly Hills, [1972]. pp. 62. bibliog.

SOCIAL development: critical perspectives; [papers contributed to a symposium]; edited by Manfred Stanley. New York, [1972]. pp. 335. bibliogs.

SOFRANKO (ANDREW J.) and BEALER (ROBERT C.) Unbalanced modernization and domestic instability: a comparative analysis. Beverly Hills, [1972]. pp. 83. bibliog.

TAYLOR (GORDON RATTRAY) Rethink: a paraprimitive solution. London, 1972. pp. 277. bibliog.

ZALTMAN (GERALD) and others, eds. Creating social change. New York, [1972]. pp. 676 bibliogs.

ZWART (CORNELIS JACOB) Professionele organisatieontwikkeling: een bijdrage tot synthese van organisatiekunde en veranderingskunde. Rotterdam, [1972]. pp. 372. bibliog. With English summary.

1973

BELL (DANIEL) The coming of post-industrial society: a venture in social forecasting. New York, [1973]. pp. 507.

FRIJLING (B.W.) ed. Social change in Europe: some demographic consequences. Leiden, 1973. pp. 146. bibliogs.

GERLACH (LUTHER P.) and HINE (VIRGINIA H.) Lifeway leap: the dynamics of change in America. Minneapolis, [1973]. pp. 332. bibliog.

HUNTER (ROBERT) b. 1942. The enemies of anarchy: a gestalt approach to change. New York, 1973. pp. 254. bibliog.

REEDY (GEORGE EDWARD) The presidency in flux. New York, 1973. pp. 133. (George B. Pegram Lectures. [11?])

SCOTT (ROBERT EDWIN) ed. Latin American modernization problems: case studies in the crisis of change. Urbana, [1973]. pp. 365.

SMITH (ANTHONY D.) The concept of social change: a critique of the functionalist theory of social change. London, 1973. pp. 198. bibliog.

WIATR (JERZY J.) Marksistowska teoria rozwoju społecznego. Warszawa, 1973. pp. 607.

WILKINSON (RICHARD G.) Poverty and progress: an ecological model of economic development. London, 1973. pp. 225.

ZALTMAN (GERALD) ed. Processes and phenomena of social change. New York, [1973]. pp. 463. bibliog.

SOCIAL CLASSES

SCHUMPETER (JOSEPH ALOIS) Imperialism; [and] Social classes; two essays...translated by Heinz Norden. New York, 1955 repr. 1971. pp. 181. bibliog.

FERNANDES (FLORESTAN) Sociedade de classes e subdesenvolvimento. Rio de Janeiro, 1968. pp. 256. bibliog.

JACKSON (JOHN ARCHER) ed. Social stratification. Cambridge, C.U.P., 1968. pp. ix, 238. 22½cm. (Sociological Studies. 1)

LAMATA (PEDRO) Clases sociales y posmarxismo. Buenos Aires, 1969. pp. 319. bibliog.

STAVENHAGEN (RODOLFO) Las clases sociales en las sociedades agrarias. Mexico, 1969 repr. 1970. pp. 292. bibliog.

THOMAS (KONRAD) Schichten in der modernen Gesellschaft. Hannover, 1969. pp. 70. bibliog. (Niedersächsische Landeszentrale für Politische Bildung. Schriftenreihe. Gesellschaft und Politik. 1)

SCHWARTZ (GARY) Sect ideologies and social status. Chicago, 1970. pp. 260.

CARBONARO (ANTONIO) ed. Stratificazione e classi sociali: [readings reprinted from various periodicals]. Bologna, 1971. pp. 284. bibliog.

HALBWACHS (MAURICE) Classes sociales et morphologie. Paris, [1972]. pp. 461. bibliog.

LAROQUE (PIERRE) Les classes sociales. 5th ed. Paris, 1972. pp. 128.

LITTLEJOHN (JAMES) Social stratification. London, 1972. pp. 150.

LOPREATO (JOSEPH) and HAZELRIGG (LAWRENCE E.) Class, conflict, and mobility: theories and studies of class structure. San Francisco, [1972]. pp. 576. bibliog.

NEALE (R.S.) Class and ideology in the nineteenth century. London, 1972. pp. 200.

MOUSNIER (ROLAND) Social hierarchies: 1450 to the present;... translated from the French by Peter Evans; edited by Margaret Clarke. London, 1973. pp. 206. bibliog.

- Bibliography

GLENN (NORVAL D.) and others, compilers. Social stratification: a research bibliography. Berkeley, Calif., 1970. repr. 1972. pp. 466. bibliog.

- Africa, Subsaharan

TUDEN (ARTHUR) and PLOTNICOV (LEONARD) eds. Social stratification in Africa. New York, [1970]. pp. 392. bibliogs.

- Africa, West

DIOP (MAJHEMOUT) Histoire des classes sociales dans l'Afrique de l'Ouest. Paris, 1971 in progress. bibliog.

- America, Latin

MACHADO (CARLOS) ed. Las clases sociales en America Latina: documentos. Montevideo, [1969]. pp. 158.

WILSON (SAMUEL) Occupational mobility and social stratification in Latin American cities. [Ithaca], 1972. pp. 123. bibliog. (Cornell University. Latin American Studies Program. Dissertation Series. No. 43)

- Argentine Republic

SEBRELI (JUAN JOSE) Buenos Aires, vida cotidiana y alienacion. Buenos Aires, 1969. pp. 191.

TELLA (TORCUATO S. DI) and HALPERIN DONGHI (TULIO) eds. Los fragmentos del poder: de la oligarquia a la poliarquia argentina; [collected essays]. Buenos Aires, [1969]. pp. 535.

IMAZ (JOSE LUIS DE) Los que mandan: Those who rule;... translated and with an introduction by Carlos A. Astiz with Mary F. McCarthy. Albany, [1970]. pp. 279.

- Canada

TEEPLE (GARY) ed. Capitalism and the national question in Canada. Toronto, [1972]. pp. 256.

CURTIS (JAMES E.) and SCOTT (WILLIAM G.) eds. Social stratification: Canada. Scarborough, Ont., [1973]. pp. 275. bibliogs.

- Czechoslovakia

KREJČÍ (JAROSLAV) Social change and stratification in postwar Czechoslovakia. London, 1972. pp. 208.

- Europe

ANDERSON (ROBERT THOMAS) Traditional Europe: a study in anthropology and history. Belmont, Calif., [1971]. pp. 195.

- Germany

GRAF (HERBERT) and SEILER (GUENTHER) Wahl und Wahlrecht im Klassenkampf. Frankfurt am Main, [1971]. pp. 441.

TJADEN-STEINHAUER (MARGARETE) and TJADEN (KARL HERMANN) Klassenverhältnisse im Spätkapitalismus: Beitrag zur Analyse der Sozialstruktur unter besonderer Berücksichtigung der BRD. Stuttgart, 1973. pp. 282. bibliog.

- Greece, Ancient

RECHERCHES sur les structures sociales dans l'antiquité classique:... (actes du colloque national... organisé...à la Faculté des Lettres de) Caen, 25-26 avril 1969. Paris, 1970. pp. 287. (Centre National de la Recherche Scientifique. Colloques Nationaux. Sciences Humaines) In various languages.

- India

MADDISON (ANGUS) Class structure and economic growth: India and Pakistan since the Moghuls. London, 1971. pp. 181. bibliog.

- Iran

BILL (JAMES ALBAN) The politics of Iran: groups, classes and modernization. Columbus, Ohio, [1972]. pp. 174. bibliog.

- Ireland (Republic)

HUTCHINSON (BERTRAM A.) Social status in Dublin: marriage, mobility and first employment. Dublin, 1973. pp. 66. (Economic and Social Research Institute. Papers. No. 67)

- Mediterranean

SOCIAL stratification and development in the Mediterranean basin: Stratification sociale et développement dans le Bassin Mediterranéen; [papers presented at the Hamamet meeting of the Mediterranean Social Sciences Research Council]; edited by... Mübeccel B. Kiray. The Hague, 1973. pp. 288. bibliogs. (Hague. Institute of Social Studies. Publications. Paperback Series. 9) In English or French.

- Mexico

POZAS ARCINIEGA (RICARDO) and HORCASITAS DE POZAS (ISABEL) Los indios en las clases sociales de Mexico. Mexico, 1971. pp. 181. bibliog.

- Pakistan

RAZA (MUHAMMAD RAFIQUE) Two Pakistani villages: a study in social stratification. Lahore, 1969. pp. 104. bibliog.

MADDISON (ANGUS) Class structure and economic growth: India and Pakistan since the Moghuls. London, 1971. pp. 181. bibliog.

- Puerto Rico

TUMIN (MELVIN MARVIN) and FELDMAN (ARNOLD S.) Social class and social change in Puerto Rico. 2nd ed. Indianapolis, [1971]. pp. 549.

- Rome, Ancient

GARNSEY (PETER D.A.) Social status and legal privilege in the Roman Empire. Oxford, 1970. pp. 320. bibliog.

RECHERCHES sur les structures sociales dans l'antiquité classique:... (actes du colloque national... organisé...à la Faculté des Lettres de) Caen, 25-26 avril 1969. Paris, 1970. pp. 287. (Centre National de la Recherche Scientifique. Colloques Nationaux. Sciences Humaines) In various languages.

- Russia

EVSEEV (V.P.) ed. Sotsial'no-klassovye problemy razvitiia sotsialisticheskogo obshchestva: sbornik statei. Moskva, 1969. pp. 188.

SOTSIAL'NYE razlichiia i ikh preodolenie: sotsiologicheskie issledovaniia. vyp. 3. Sverdlovsk, 1969. pp. 158.

CHIKHICHIN (I.N.) ed. Sotsial'no-klassovaia struktura i politicheskaia organizatsiia sotsialisticheskogo obshchestva. Saratov, 1971. pp. 143.

AMVROSOV (ANATOLII ALEKSEEVICH) Ot klassovoi differentsiatsii k sotsial'noi odnorodnosti obshchestva. Moskva, 1972. pp. 271.

MATTHEWS (MERVYN) Class and society in Soviet Russia. London, [1972]. pp. 366. bibliog.

- Spain

MARIMON I CAIROL (JOSEP) Les classes socials a Catalunya en el decurs de l'era industrial. Paris, 1971. pp. 319. bibliog.

MORENO NAVARRO (ISIDORO) Propiedad, clases sociales y hermandades en la Baja Andalucia: la estructura social de un pueblo del Aljarafe. Madrid, 1972. pp. 323. bibliog.

PIKE (RUTH) Aristocrats and traders: Sevillian society in the sixteenth century. Ithaca, [1972]. pp. 243. bibliog.

- Turkey

HINDERINK (JAN) and KIRAY (MÜBECCEL B.) Social stratification as an obstacle to development: a study of four Turkish villages. New York, 1970. pp. 248.

SOCIAL CLASSES (Cont'd.)

- United Kingdom

COOK-GUMPERZ (JENNY) Social control and socialization: a study of class differences in the language of maternal control. London, 1973. pp. 290. bibliog. (London. University. Institute of Education. Sociological Research Unit. Primary Socialization, Language and Education. [Series]. 6)

- United States

NEW YORK (STATE). Department of Health. 1958. Social class, maternal health and child care; by Walter E. Boek [and others]; with a foreword by Herman E. Hilleboe. rev. ed. Albany, 1958. pp. 138. bibliog.

DUNCAN (OTIS DUDLEY) and others. Socioeconomic background and achievement. New York, 1972. pp. 284. bibliog.

HAMILTON (RICHARD F.) Class and politics in the United States. New York, [1972]. pp. 589.

KERCKHOFF (ALAN C.) Socialization and social class. Englewood Cliffs, [1972]. pp. 170. bibliog.

MANDELL (BETTY REID) Where are the children?: a class analysis of foster care and adoption. Lexington, Mass., [1973]. pp. 215.

- West Indies

LOWENTHAL (DAVID) and COMITAS (LAMBROS) eds. Consequences of class and color: West Indian perspectives. Garden City, 1973. pp. 334. bibliog.

SOCIAL CONDITIONS

ELGOZY (GEORGES) Les damnés de l'opulence. [Paris, 1970]. pp. 331. bibliog.

BIRD (CAROLINE) The crowding syndrome: learning to live with too much and too many. New York, [1972]. pp. 337.

HOROWITZ (IRVING LOUIS) Three worlds of development: the theory and practice of international stratification. 2nd ed. New York, 1972. pp. 556.

- Bibliography

BRIGHTON. University of Sussex. Institute of Development Studies. Library. Occasional Guides. No.1. Non-official serials holding list, as at 30 March 1972. Brighton, [1972]. 1 pamphlet (unpaged).

- Statistics

BOEHME (MONIKA) Die Moralstatistik: ein Beitrag zur Geschichte der Quantifizierung in der Soziologie, dargestellt an den Werken Adolphe Quetelets und Alexander von Oettingens. Köln, 1971. pp. 185. bibliog.

FELIX (FREMONT) World markets of tomorrow: economic growth; population trends, electricity and energy; quality of life. London, 1972. pp. 364. bibliog.

SOCIAL CONFLICT

HOEVEN (P.J.A. TER) Arbeiders tussen welvaart en onvrede. Alphen aan den Rijn, 1969. pp. 308.

BOR'BA klassov i sovremennyi mir: aktual'nye problemy rabochego dvizheniia stran razvitogo kapitalizma. Moskva, 1970. pp. 251.

LEO (RITA DI) Operai e sistema sovietico. Bari, 1970. pp. 349. bibliog.

KROES (R.) Conflict en radicalisme. Meppel, [1971]. pp. 219. bibliog.

POULANTZAS (NICOS) Pouvoir politique et classes sociales. Paris, 1971. 2 vols.

SMITH (CLAGETT GORDON) ed. Conflict resolution: contributions of the behavioral sciences. Notre Dame, Ind., [1971]. pp. 553. bibliogs.

SPERLICH (PETER W.) Conflict and harmony in human affairs: a study of cross-pressures and political behavior. Chicago, [1971]. pp. 256. bibliog.

GUICHARD (JEAN) Eglise, luttes de classes et stratégies politiques. Paris, 1972. pp. 193.

KING (BERT T.) and McGINNIES (ELLIOTT) eds. Attitudes, conflict, and social change;...[based on a symposium held at the University of Maryland]. New York, 1972. pp. 234. bibliogs.

LEVINE (ROBERT ALAN) and CAMPBELL (DONALD THOMAS) Ethnocentrism: theories of conflict, ethnic attitudes, and group behavior. New York, [1972]. pp. 310. bibliog.

PERGOLA (GIULIANO DELLA) La conflittualità urbana: saggi di sociologia critica. Milano, 1972. pp. 174.

GELFAND (DONALD E.) and LEE (RUSSELL D.) eds. Ethnic conflicts and power: a cross-national perspective. New York, [1973]. pp. 354. bibliogs.

KRIESBERG (LOUIS) The sociology of social conflicts. Englewood Cliffs, 1973. pp. 300. bibliogs.

MANN (J. MICHAEL) Consciousness and action among the Western working class. London, 1973. pp. 80. bibliog.

OBERSCHALL (ANTHONY) Social conflict and social movements. Englewood Cliffs, [1973]. pp. 371. bibliog.

POULANTZAS (NICOS) Political power and social classes; translation editor, Timothy O'Hagan. London, [1973]. pp. 367.

- Arab countries

EL KODSY (AHMAD) and LOBEL (ELI) The Arab world and Israel: two essays...; translated by Brian Pearce and Alfred Ehrenfeld. New York, [1971]. pp. 137.

- Chile

LECHNER (NORBERT) La democracia en Chile. Buenos Aires, 1970. pp. 176. bibliog.

- Cyprus

PATRICK (RICHARD ARTHUR) A general systems theory approach to geopolitical aspects of conflict between communities with particular reference to Cyprus since 1960; [Ph.D. (London) thesis]. [1972]. 1 vol. (various foliations). bibliog. Typescript: unpublished. This thesis is the property of London University and may not be removed from the Library.

- Dutch Guiana

PAËRL (ERIC) Klassenstrijd in Suriname. Nijmegen, 1972. pp. 63.

- Egypt

HUSSEIN (MAHMOUD) La lutte de classes en Egypte; deuxième édition mise à jour, 1945-1970. Paris, 1971. pp. 389.

HUSSEIN (MAHMOUD) Class conflict in Egypt, 1945-1970;...translated by Michel Chirman [and others]. New York, [1973]. pp. 379.

- France

FREMONTIER (JACQUES) La forteresse ouvrière: Renault; une enquête à Boulogne-Billancourt chez les ouvriers de la régie. [Paris, 1971]. pp. 380.

GRATTON (PHILIPPE) Les luttes de classes dans les campagnes. Paris, [1971]. pp. 482. bibliog.

GRATTON (PHILIPPE) Les paysans français contre l'agrarisme. Paris, 1972. pp. 224.

- Germany

KUCZYNSKI (JUERGEN) Klassen und Klassenkämpfe im imperialistischen Deutschland und in der BRD. Frankfurt am Main, 1972. pp. 568.

- Italy

TORO (CLAUDIO DI) and ILLUMINATI (AUGUSTO) Prima e dopo il centrosinistra: capitalismo e lotta di classe in Italia nell'attuale fase dell'imperialismo. Roma, 1970. pp. 319.

CITTÀ e conflitto sociale: inchiesta al Garibaldi-Isola e in altri quartieri periferici di Milano; [by] M. Boffi [and others]. Milano, 1972. pp. 160.

MEA (LUCIANO DELLA) Proletari senza comunismo: lotta di classe e Lotta Continua, etc. Verona, [1972]. pp. 332.

- Nigeria

MELSON (ROBERT FRANK) and WOLPE (HOWARD) eds. Nigeria: modernization and the politics of communalism. [East Lansing, 1971]. pp. 680.

- Russia

POKROVSKII (MIKHAIL NIKOLAEVICH) Bor'ba klassov i russkaia istoricheskaia literatura; lektsii, chitannye v kommunisticheskom universitete imeni tov. Zinov'eva, 3-7 maia 1923 g. 2nd ed. Leningrad, [1926]. pp. 124. Xerographic reprint.

SOTSIAL'NYE razlichiia i ikh preodolenie: sotsiologicheskie issledovaniia. vyp. 3. Sverdlovsk, 1969. pp. 158.

SUTIAGIN (VASILII SERGEEVICH) and SUTIAGIN (ANDREI SERGEEVICH) Osobennosti protivorechii v sotsialisticheskom obshchestve i puti ikh preodoleniia. Moskva, 1972. pp. 207.

- Russia - Kirghizia

CHOKUSHOV (BEIMANALY) Klassovaia bor'ba i uprochenie Sovetskoi vlasti v kirgizskikh ailakh, 1918-1924 gg. Frunze, 1968. pp. 99.

CHOKUSHOV (BEIMANALY) Klassovaia bor'ba v kirgizskikh ailakh v pervye gody sotsialisticheskikh preobrazovanii, 1918-1924 gg. Frunze, 1970. pp. 171.

- Russia - White Russia

CHEPKO (VALENTINA VLADIMIROVNA) Klassovaia bor'ba v belorusskoi derevne v pervoi polovine XIX v. Minsk, 1972. pp. 267.

- Spain

CALAMAI (MARCO) La lotta di classe sotto il franchismo: le Commissioni Operaie. Bari, [1971]. pp. 311.

- United Kingdom

PRITT (DENIS NOWELL) Law, class and society. London, 1970-72. 4 vols.

HOLLIS (PATRICIA) ed. Class and conflict in nineteenth century England, 1815-1850. London, 1973. pp. 372.

- United Kingdom - Ireland, Northern

ELLIOT (R.S.P.) and HICKIE (JOHN) Ulster: a case study in conflict theory. London, 1971. pp. 180.

- United States

DUNNE (WILLIAM F.) Gastonia: citadel of the class struggle in the new South;...for the National Textile Workers Union. New York, 1929. pp. 58.

IULINA (NINA STEPANOVNA) Burzhuaznye ideologicheskie techeniia v SShA: problemy i protivorechiia "amerikanskogo soznaniia". Moskva, 1971. pp. 136.

BOSKIN (JOSEPH) and ROSENSTONE (ROBERT A.) eds. Seasons of rebellion: protest and radicalism in recent America. New York, [1972]. pp. 336.

MILNER (MURRAY) The illusion of equality: (the effect of education on opportunity, inequality and social conflict). San Francisco, 1972. pp. 172. bibliog.

NEWMAN (WILLIAM M.) American pluralism: a study of minority groups and social theory. New York, [1973]. pp. 307. bibliogs.

SOCIAL CONTROL

LEMERT (EDWIN M.) Human deviance, social problems, and social control; [selected papers]. Englewood Cliffs, [1967]. pp. 211.

BASAGLIA (FRANCO) and BASAGLIA ONGARO (FRANCA) La maggioranza deviante. Torino, [1971]. pp. 183.

HUNTFORD (ROLAND) The new totalitarians. London, 1971. pp. 354.

MÉSZÁROS (ISTVÁN) The necessity of social control. London, 1971. pp. 70. (Isaac Deutscher Memorial Lectures. 1971)

PUTNEY (SNELL) The conquest of society...; sociological observations for the autonomous revolt against the autosystems which turn humanity into servomen. Belmont, Calif., [1972]. pp. 237.

SOCIAL COSTS
See EXTERNALITIES (ECONOMICS)

SOCIAL CREDIT

DOUGLAS (CLIFFORD HUGH) Money and the price system; a speech delivered at Oslo on February 14, 1935, to H.M. the King of Norway, H.E. the British Minister, the President, and members of the Oslo Merchants' Club. London, [1935?]. pp. 18.

The NATION'S credit: a précis of Major C.H. Douglas' proposals; by C.G.M. rev. ed. Leeds, 1967. pp. 25.

PINARD (MAURICE) The rise of a third party: a study in crisis politics. Englewood Cliffs, [1971]. pp. 285.

SOCIAL CREDIT (Cont'd.)

FINLAY (JOHN L.) Social credit: the English origins. Montreal, 1972. pp. 272.

SOCIAL DEMOCRATIC PARTY (DENMARK)

HANSEN (SØREN) and STUBTOFT (ERIK) eds. I stedet for klassesamfundet;...udgivet i anledning af Socialdemokratiets og AOFs oplysningskampagne i forbindelse med Socialdemokratiets 100 års jubilaeum 1971. København, 1971. pp. 156. bibliog.

KRAG (JENS OTTO) and ANDERSEN (K.B.) Kamp og fornyelse: Socialdemokratiets indsats i dansk politik, 1955-71. [Copenhagen, 1971]. pp. 403.

SOCIAL DEMOCRATIC PARTY (GERMANY)

AVELING (EDWARD BIBBINS) Wilhelm Liebknecht and the social-democratic movement in Germany;...on behalf of the Zürich Committee for the International Socialist Workers and Trade Union Congress. London, July 26 to August 1, 1896. London, [1896]. pp. 16.

OELSSNER (FRED) Das Kompromiss von Gotha und seine Lehren: überarbeitete Rede anlässlich der 75. Wiederkehr des Vereinigungskongresses der deutschen Arbeiterparteien...1875 in Gotha. Berlin, 1950. pp. 60.

WAGNER (BRUNO) Die Bodenreformpolitik der SPD; mit einem Dokumentenanhang. Berlin, 1959. pp. 155. bibliog.

BAUER (ROLAND) Der wissenschaftliche Sozialismus und das Godesberger Grundsatzprogramm. Berlin, 1960. pp. 112. (Berlin. Parteihochschule Karl Marx. Lektionen)

SOZIALDEMOKRATISCHE PARTEI DEUTSCHLANDS. Kreis Mannheim. 100 Jahre SPD in Mannheim: eine Dokumentation. Mannheim, 1967. pp. 171. bibliog.

MORING (KARL ERNST) Die Sozialdemokratische Partei in Bremen, 1890-1914: Reformismus und Radikalismus in der Sozialdemokratischen Partei Bremens. Hannover, [1968]. pp. 223. bibliog. (Friedrich-Ebert-Stiftung. Forschungsinstitut. Schriftenreihe. B. Historisch-politische Schriften)

LOEWKE (UDO F.) Für den Fall, dass...: die Haltung der SPD zur Wehrfrage, 1949-1955; mit einem dokumentarischen Anhang und dem letzten Interview Fritz Erlers. Hannover, [1969]. pp. 264. bibliog. (Friedrich-Ebert-Stiftung. Forschungsinstitut. Schriftenreihe. B. Historisch-politische Schriften)

SCHNEIDER (DIETER) Zwischen Römer und Revolution: 1869-1969, hundert Jahr Sozialdemokraten in Frankfurt am Main; herausgegeben von der Sozialdemokratischen Partei, Unterbezirk Frankfurt am Main. Frankfurt am Main, [1969]. pp. 143.

BERGMANN (GUENTHER) Das Sozialistengesetz im rechtsrheinischen Industriegebiet: ein Beitrag zur Auseinandersetzung...im Wuppertal und im Bergischen Land, 1878-1890. Hannover, [1970]. pp. 116. bibliog. (Friedrich-Ebert-Stiftung. Forschungsinstitut. Schriftenreihe. Band 77)

KASTNING (ALFRED) Die deutsche Sozialdemokratie zwischen Koalition und Opposition, 1919-1923. Paderborn, [1970]. pp. 195. bibliog.

REISBERG (ARNOLD) Lenins Beziehungen zur deutschen Arbeiterbewegung. Berlin, 1970. pp. 623. bibliog.

WOLTER (HEINZ) Alternative zu Bismarck: die deutsche Sozialdemokratie und die Aussenpolitik des preussisch deutschen Reiches 1878 bis 1890. Berlin, 1970. pp. 288. bibliog. (Deutsche Akademie der Wissenschaften zu Berlin. Institut für Geschichte. Schriften. Reihe 1. Band 35)

BACHMANN (KURT) and MIES (HERBERT) Kommunisten und Sozialdemokraten in der Bundesrepublik; ein Gespräch; [Kurt Schacht, interviewer]. Hamburg, [1971]. pp. 37.

BANDHOLZ (EMIL) Zwischen Godesberg und Grossindustrie; oder, Wo steht die SPD? Reinbek bei Hamburg, 1971. pp. 140.

BROUE (PIERRE) Révolution en Allemagne, 1917-1923. [Paris, 1971]. pp. 988. bibliog.

FOERSTER (ALFRED) Die Gewerkschaftspolitik der deutschen Sozialdemokratie während des Sozialistengesetzes, vom Wydener Parteikongress 1880 bis zum Parteitag von St. Gallen 1887. Berlin, 1971. pp. 384.

JUNGSOZIALISTEN. Kommunalpolitische Konferenz, 1971. Kommunalpolitik, für wen?: Arbeitsprogramm der Jungsozialisten; herausgegeben...von Wolfgang Roth. Frankfurt am Main, 1971. pp. 202.

MAYER (PAUL) Bruno Schoenlank, 1859-1901: Reformer der sozialdemokratischen Tagespresse. Hannover, [1971]. pp. 158. bibliog. (Friedrich-Ebert-Stiftung. Forschungsinstitut. Schriftenreihe. Band 87)

SCHADT (JOERG) Die Sozialdemokratische Partei in Baden von den Anfängen bis zur Jahrhundertwende, 1868-1900. Hannover, [1971]. pp. 214. bibliog. (Friedrich-Ebert-Stiftung. Forschungsinstitut. Schriftenreihe. Band 88)

SCHMITZ (KURT THOMAS) Opposition im Landtag: Merkmale oppositionellen Verhaltens in Länderparlamenten am Beispiel der SPD in Rheinland-Pfalz, 1951-1963. Hannover, [1971]. pp. 163. bibliog. (Friedrich-Ebert-Stiftung. Forschungsinstitut. Schriftenreihe. Band 82)

SEELIGER (ROLF) ed. Quo vadis SPD?: aktuelle Beiträge zur Mobilisierung der Sozialdemokratie. München, 1971. pp. 144.

STRUVE (GUENTER) Kampf um die Mehrheit: (die Wahlkampagne der SPD 1965). Köln, [1971]. pp. 204. bibliog.

WITT (FRIEDRICH WILHELM) Die Hamburger Sozialdemokratie in der Weimarer Republik, unter besonderer Berücksichtigung der Jahre 1929/30-1933. Hannover, [1971]. pp. 219. bibliog. (Friedrich-Ebert-Stiftung. Forschungsinstitut. Schriftenreihe. Band 89)

LUXEMBURG (ROSA) Gesammelte Werke; (Leitung der Redaktion: G. Radczun). Berlin, 1972 in progress.

REUTER (ERNST) Schriften, Reden; herausgegeben von Hans. E. Hirschfeld und Hans J. Reichhardt; mit einem Vorwort von Willy Brandt. Berlin, [1972 in progress].

BRANDT (WILLY) Der Wille zum Frieden: Perspektiven der Politik; [articles, speeches and other writings]; Vorwort [by] Golo Mann. Hamburg, 1972. pp. 380.

EICHLER (WILLI G.) Zur Einführung in den demokratischen Sozialismus. Bonn-Bad Godesberg, [1972]. pp. 156.

HRBEK (RUDOLF) Die SPD: Deutschland und Europa; die Haltung der Sozialdemokratie zum Verhältnis von Deutschland-Politik und West-Integration, 1945-1957. Bonn, [1972]. pp. 384. bibliog.

MUELLER (EMIL PETER) Juso-Sozialismus: Programm und Strategie der Jungsozialisten in der SPD. Köln, [1972]. pp. 115. bibliog.

MUELLER (GUENTHER) Rote Zelle Deutschland; oder, Was wollen die Jungsozialisten wirklich? Stuttgart, [1972]. pp. 143.

SEELIGER (ROLF) ed. SPD 72: neue Beiträge zur Mobilisierung der Sozialdemokratie. München, 1972. pp. 115.

LIEBKNECHT (WILHELM PHILIPP MARTIN CHRISTIAN LUDWIG) and others. Briefwechsel mit deutschen Sozialdemokraten;... herausgegeben und bearbeitet von Georg Eckert. Assen, 1973 in progress. bibliog. (International Institute of Social History. Quellen und Untersuchungen zur Geschichte der Deutschen und Österreichischen Arbeiterbewegung. Neue Folge. 4)

BUCHWITZ (OTTO) 50 Jahre Funktionär der deutschen Arbeiterbewegung. new ed. Berlin, 1973. pp. 179.

GLEISSBERG (GERHARD) SPD und Gesellschaftssystem: Aktualität der Programmdiskussion von 1934 bis 1946; Dokumente und Kommentar; herausgegeben vom Institut für Marxistische Studien und Forschungen, etc. Frankfurt/Main, 1973. pp. 112.

GROH (DIETER) Negative Integration und revolutionärer Attentismus: die deutsche Sozialdemokratie am Vorabend des Ersten Weltkrieges. Frankfurt/Main, [1973]. pp. 783. bibliog.

JAHNKE (KARL HEINZ) and others. Geschichte der deutschen Arbeiterjugendbewegung, 1904-1945. Berlin, [1973]. pp. 632. bibliog.

NOWKA (HARRY) Das Machtverhältnis zwischen Partei und Fraktion in der SPD: eine historisch-empirische Untersuchung. Köln, 1973. pp. 167. bibliog.

SCHMIDT (HELMUT) Dipl.rer.pol. Auf dem Fundament des Godesberger Programms: [collection of speeches, articles, etc.]. Bonn-Bad Godesberg, [1973]. pp. 153.

- Congresses

DITTBERNER (JUERGEN) Die Bundesparteitage der Christlich Demokratischen Union und der Sozialdemokratischen Partei Deutschlands von 1946 bis 1968: eine Untersuchung der Funktionen von Parteitagen. Augsburg, 1969. pp. 291. bibliog.

SOCIAL DEMOCRATIC PARTY (ITALY)

AVERARDI (GIUSEPPE) I socialisti democratici da Palazzo Barberini alla costituente socialista. Roma, [1971]. pp. 455.

SOCIAL DEMOCRATIC PARTY (LATVIA)

DRIZULIS (ALEKSANDR ARVIDOVICH) V.I. Lenin i revoliutsionnaia Latviia. Riga, 1970. pp. 239.

SOCIAL DEMOCRATIC PARTY (RUSSIA)

MAIOROV (M.) Iz istorii revoliutsionnoi bor'by na Ukraine. 1914-1919. Kyïv, 1922. pp. 109.

SHLIAPNIKOV (ALEKSANDR GAVRILOVICH) Kanun semnadtsatogo goda [i] Semnadtsatyi god. Moskva, [1923?]-27. 3 vols (in 1). Vol. 3 has title Semnadtsatyi god. The 1st ed. of vol.1 has title Nakanune 1917 goda. In this volume vol.1 is of the 3rd ed., vol.2 of the 4th.

MATERIALY po istorii Ekaterinoslavskoi sotsial-demokraticheskoi organizatsii bol'shevikov i revoliutsionnykh sobytii 1904 - 1905 - 1906: k 20-ti letnemu iubileiu revoliutsii 1905 g. Ekaterinoslav, 1924. pp. 529.

LIADOV (MARTYN NIKOLAEVICH) pseud. [i.e. Martyn Nikolaevich MANDEL'SHTAM]. Iz zhizni partii nakanune i v gody pervoi revoliutsii: vospominaniia. Moskva, 1926. pp. 208. For 1956 ed. with abridgements see his Iz zhizni partii v 1903-1907 godakh. Xerographic reprint.

POZNER (SELIMA MARKOVNA) compiler. 1905: boevaia gruppa pri TsK RSDRP/b/, 1905-1907 g.g.: stat'i i vospominaniia. Moskva, 1927. pp. 284. Xerographic reprint.

SOTSIAL-demokraticheskie listovki 1894-1917 gg.: bibliograficheskii ukazatel'. t.2, ch.1. Listovki Peterburgskoi bol'shevistskoi organizatsii R.S.-D.R.P.; pod redaktsiei G.I. Kramol'nikova i P.G. Sennikovskogo, etc. Moskva, 1934 pp. 192.

TSENTRAL'NYI ARKHIV REVOLIUTSII. Bol'sheviki v gody imperialisticheskoi voiny, 1914-fevral' 1917: sbornik dokumentov mestnykh bol'shevistskikh organizatsii. [Moskva], 1939. pp. 229. Xerographic reprint.

NALBANDIAN (ERMONIIA ALEKSANDROVNA) V.I. Lenin i Bakinskaia organizatsiia RSDRP, 1901-1904 gg. Baku, 1963. pp. 132.

TRAININ (A.S.) Partiia bol'shevikov - rukovoditel' revoliutsionnogo dvizheniia rabochei molodezhi v 1917 godu. Krasnodar, 1965. pp. 175. (Krasnodarskii Gosudarstvennyi Pedagogicheskii Institut. Nauchnye Trudy. vyp.58)

KOVAL'CHUK (M.A.) and others. V.I. Lenin - sozdatel' marksistskoi partii v Rossii. Leningrad, 1970. pp. 216.

NARYMSKAIA ssylka, 1906-1917 gg.: sbornik dokumentov i materialov o ssyl'nykh bol'shevikakh. Tomsk, 1970. pp. 386.

ONIANI (VASIL SARIIONISOVICH) Bol'shevistskaia partiia i intelligentsiia v pervoi russkoi revoliutsii. Tbilisi, 1970. pp. 447.

ZHUKOV (TIMOFII IVANOVYCH) Bil'shovyky u borot'bi za selianstvo u revoliutsii 1905-1907 rr.: na materialakh ievropeis'koï chastyny Rosiï. L'viv, 1970. pp. 224.

ARSEN'EV (IURII MIKHAILOVICH) Lenin i sotsial-demokraticheskaia emigratsiia, 1900-1904 gg. Moskva, 1971. pp. 366.

DEIATEL'NOST' partiinoi organizatsii Tatarii po osushchestvleniiu leninskikh idei stroitel'stva sotsialisticheskogo obshchestva. Kazan', 1971. pp. 286.

RAKHMANOV (NIKOLAI MIKHAILOVICH) Bor'ba Kommunisticheskoi partii za razvitie sotsialisticheskoi revoliutsii i uprochenie Sovetskoi vlasti, noiabr' 1917 - iiul' 1918 g. Moskva, 1971. pp. 57.

SYCHEVSKII (PETR FOMICH) V bor'be s samoderzhaviem. Blagoveshchensk, 1971. pp. 56.

V.I. Lenin i sovremennost': materialy nauchno-teoreticheskoi konferentsii, posviashchennoi 100-letiiu so dnia rozhdeniia V.I. Lenina. Erevan, 1971. pp. 175.

DEMOCHKIN (NIKOLAI NIKOLAEVICH) Partiia bol'shevikov nakanune i v gody pervoi revoliutsii v Rossii, 1904-1907 gg. Moskva, 1972. pp. 152.

IAKUSHINA (ANTONINA PAVLOVNA) Lenin i zagranichnaia organizatsiia RSDRP, 1905-1917. Moskva, 1972. pp. 399.

SOCIAL DEMOCRATIC PARTY (RUSSIA)
(Cont'd.)

KIRILLOV (VIKTOR SERGEEVICH) Kurs, podtverzhdennyi zhizn'iu: k istorii ekonomicheskoi platformy bol'shevikov, aprel'-oktiabr' 1917 g. Moskva, 1972. pp. 334. bibliog.

LAVRIN (VLADIMIR ALEKSANDROVICH) Bol'shevistskaia partiia v nachale pervoi mirovoi voiny, 1914-1915 gg. Moskva, 1972. pp. 312.

LISOVSKII (NIKOLAI KUZ'MICH) ed. Ocherki istorii bol'shevistskikh organizatsii Iuzhnogo Urala. Cheliabinsk, 1972. pp. 434.

NOSOV (FEDOR VASIL'EVICH) Lenin o voine i mire: iz istorii bor'by bol'shevistskoi partii protiv opportunizma, 1914-1918 gg. Leningrad, 1972. pp. 174.

PANAVAS (CHESLOVAS VLADOVICH) Bor'ba bol'shevikov protiv opportunisticheskoi teorii i politiki Bunda, 1903-oktiabr' 1917 g. Moskva, 1972. pp. 116.

STRATEGIIA i taktika bol'shevistskoi partii v bor'be za diktaturu proletariata, 1903-1917 gg. Moskva, 1972. pp. 328.

ZAPOROZHETS (MARIIA IAKOVLEVNA) Istoki velikikh svershenii: V.I. Lenin i partiinye organizatsii Donbassa. Donetsk, 1972. pp. 240.

SOCIAL DEMOCRATIC PARTY (RUSSIA)
See also COMMUNIST PARTY : RUSSIA

- Russia - Bibliography

BESHKIN (G.) ed. Legal'naia sotsial-demokraticheskaia literatura v Rossii za 1906-14 gody: bibliografiia. Moskva, 1924. pp. 280. Xerographic reprint.

- Congresses

IVANIDZE (KOBA) Pervyi Kraevoi s"ezd bol'shevistskikh organizatsii Kavkaza, 2-7 oktiabria 1917 g. Tbilisi, 1969. pp. 82.

- Periodicals

BONCH-BRUEVICH (VLADIMIR DMITRIEVICH) Bol'shevistskie izdatel'skie dela v 1905-1907 gg.: moi vospominaniia. Leningrad, 1933. pp. 194. Xerographic reprint.

ZHDANOVSKAIA (ZOIA VASIL'EVNA) Bol'shevistskaia periodicheskaia pechat' kak istochnik pri izuchenii istorii KPSS, 1900-1917. Moskva, 1965. pp. 84.

AKBAROV (ADKHAM IBRAGIMOVICH) Rol' gazety "Pravda" v pobede sotsialisticheskoi revoliutsii v Turkestane. Tashkent, 1968. pp. 304. bibliog

LENINSKAIA "Iskra" i mestnye partiinye organizatsii Rossii, 1900-1903 gg. Perm', 1971. pp. 530. bibliog.

LOGINOV (VLADLEN TERENT'EVICH) Leninskaia "Pravda", 1912-1914 gg. Moskva, 1972. pp. 408.

OVSEPIAN (RAFAIL POGOSOVICH) Mnogonatsional'naia pechat' bol'shevikov, 1900-1917 gg. Moskva, 1972. pp. 230.

SALADKAŬ (TSIMAFEI ERAFEEVICH) Bol'shevistskaia gazeta "Pravda" v Belorussii, 1912-1917 gg. 2nd ed. Minsk, 1972. pp. 296. For 1st White Russian ed. see his Bal'shavitskaia hazeta "Pravda" ŭ Belarusi, 1912-1917 hh.

SOCIAL DEMOCRATIC PARTY (RUSSIA) (MENSHEVIKS)

POTRESOV (ALEKSANDR NIKOLAEVICH) V plenu u illiuzii: moi spor s offitsial'nym men'shevizmom. Parizh, 1927. pp. 104.

LISOVSKII (P.) Na sluzhbe kapitala: esero-men'shevistskaia kontr-revoliutsiia. Leningrad, 1928. pp. 142. bibliog.

ARONSON (GREGOR) and others. Spor, vzveshennyi sud'boi. n.p., [1933]. pp. 104. Lacks title page.

ASCHER (ABRAHAM) Pavel Axelrod and the development of menshevism. Cambridge, Mass., 1972. pp. 420. bibliog. (Stanford University. Hoover Institution on War, Revolution and Peace. Hoover Institution Publications. 115.)

SOCIAL DEMOCRATIC PARTY (SWITZERLAND)

Der FALL Oprecht. [Zürich, imprint, 1939]. pp. 52.

BOLLIGER (MARKUS) Die Basler Arbeiterbewegung im Zeitalter des Ersten Weltkrieges und der Spaltung der Sozialdemokratischen Partei: ein Beitrag zur Geschichte der schweizerischen Arbeiterbewegung. Basel, 1970. pp. 379. bibliog.

SOCIAL ETHICS

MARQUIS (FREDERICK JAMES) 1st Earl of Woolton. The inter-relationship of human nature and social progress. London, [1958?]. pp. 14. (London. University. Birkbeck College. Foundation Orations. 1957)

CHILDRESS (JAMES F.) Civil disobedience and political obligation: a study in Christian social ethics. New Haven, 1971. pp. 250.

DOMENACH (JEAN MARIE) Our moral involvement in development. New York, United Nations, 1971. pp. 36. bibliog. (Centre for Economic and Social Information. Executive Briefing Papers. 4)

FINKELSTEIN (LOUIS) ed. Social responsibility in an age of revolution. New York, 1971. pp. 283.

SCOTT (JOHN FINLEY) Internalization of norms: a sociological theory of moral commitment. Englewood Cliffs, [1971]. pp. 237. bibliog.

ALLSOPP (BRUCE) Ecological morality. London, 1972. pp. 117.

BARNSLEY (JOHN H.) The social reality of ethics: the comparative analysis of moral codes. London, 1972. pp. 452.

BRITISH HUMANIST ASSOCIATION. People first: (a humanist manifesto). London, [1972]. pp. (9).

CHAMBERLAIN (NEIL WOLVERTON) The place of business in America's future: a study in social values. New York, [1973]. pp. 338.

SOCIAL GROUP WORK

SULLIVAN (DOROTHEA F.) ed. The practice of group work. New York, 1947. pp. 230.

TRECKER (HARLEIGH BRADLEY) Social group work: principles and practices. rev. ed. New York, [1955]. pp. 442.

TRECKER (HARLEIGH BRADLEY) ed. Group work: foundations and frontiers. New York, 1955. pp. 418.

VINTER (ROBERT D.) ed. Readings in group work practice; contributors: Rosemary C. Sarri [and others]. Ann Arbor, [1967]. pp. 127. bibliog.

DOUGLAS (TOM) A decade of small group theory, 1960-1970. London, 1970. pp. 80. bibliogs.

PARE (SIMONE) Groupes et service social. 2nd ed. Québec, 1971. pp. 337. bibliog.

PARFIT (JESSIE) Spotlight on group work with parents in special circumstances. London, [1971]. pp. 152. (National Children's Bureau. Spotlight. 2)

HARTFORD (MARGARET E.) Groups in social work: application of small group theory and research to social work practice. New York, 1972. pp. 297. bibliog.

KLEIN (ALAN F.) Effective groupwork: an introduction to principle and method. New York, [1972]. pp. 384.

KONOPKA (GISELA) Social group work: a helping process. 2nd ed. Englewood Cliffs, [1972]. pp. 226. bibliog.

LIFTON (WALTER M.) Groups: facilitating individual growth and societal change;...and a...bibliography of references in group work by David G. Zimpfer. New York, [1972]. pp. 356. bibliog.

SOCIAL GROUPS

BERNSTEIN (SAUL) ed. Explorations in group work: essays in theory and practice;...[by] Louise A. Frey [and others; originally published 1965]. London, 1972. pp. 136. bibliogs.

LODGE (MILTON C.) Soviet elite attitudes since Stalin. Columbus, Ohio, [1969]. pp. 135. bibliog.

BERNSTEIN (SAUL) ed. Further explorations in group work; [by] Robert Daniels [and others; originally published 1970]. London, 1972. pp. 179. bibliogs.

MOUREY (JEAN LOUIS) Les équilibres socio-psychologiques de la copropriété. Paris, 1970. pp. 318. bibliog.

DUBOIS (JEAN) Les cadres, enjeu politique. Paris, [1971]. pp. 318. bibliog.

KRAUSE (ELLIOTT A.) The sociology of occupations. Boston, [Mass., 1971]. pp. 398.

ZANDER (ALVIN F.) Motives and goals in groups. New York, 1971. pp. 212. bibliog.

BARRITT (DENIS P.) and CARTER (CHARLES FREDERICK) Professor of political economy, Manchester University. The Northern Ireland problem: a study in group relations. 2nd ed. London, 1972. pp. 176.

JANIS (IRVING LESTER) Victims of groupthink: a psychological study of foreign-policy decisions and fiascoes. Boston, [Mass.], [1972]. pp. 276. bibliog.

BRADFIELD (RICHARD MAITLAND) A natural history of associations. London, 1973. 2 vols. bibliog.

NEWMAN (WILLIAM M.) American pluralism: a study of minority groups and social theory. New York, [1973]. pp. 307. bibliogs.

URRY (JOHN) Reference groups and the theory of revolution. London, 1973. pp. 244. bibliog.

- Mathematical models

COHEN (JOEL E.) Casual groups of monkeys and men: stochastic models of elemental social systems. Cambridge, Mass., 1971. pp. 175. bibliog.

SOCIAL HISTORY

KOELNER ZEITSCHRIFT FÜR SOZIOLOGIE UND SOZIALPSYCHOLOGIE. Sonderhefte. 16. Soziologie und Sozialgeschichte: Aspekte und Probleme; herausgegeben von Peter Christian Ludz. Opladen, 1972. pp. 623. bibliogs.

BRAUDEL (FERNAND) Capitalism and material life, 1400-1800; ...translated by Miriam Kochan. London, [1973 in progress].

- Methodology

CLOUSCARD (MICHEL) L'être et le code; le procès de production d'un ensemble précapitaliste. Paris, [1972]. pp. 623. bibliog.

- Philosophy

CLOUSCARD (MICHEL) L'être et le code; le procès de production d'un ensemble précapitaliste. Paris, [1972]. pp. 623. bibliog.

SOCIAL INDICATORS

TAYLOR (CHARLES LEWIS) and HUDSON (MICHAEL C.) World handbook of political and social indicators. 2nd ed. New Haven, Conn., 1972. pp. 443.

- Bibliography

WILCOX (LESLIE D.) and others, compilers. Social indicators and societal monitoring: an annotated bibliography. Amsterdam, 1972. pp. 464.

- Canada

SEMINAR ON SOCIAL INDICATORS, OTTAWA, 1972. Social indicators: proceedings of a seminar...1972, [convened by the Research and Development Branch of] the Canadian Council on Social Development. Ottawa, 1972. pp. 182.

SOCIAL INTERACTION

SEDA BONILLA (EDUARDO) Interaccion social y personalidad en una comunidad de Puerto Rico. 2nd ed. San Juan, 1969. pp. 190. bibliog.

YEE (ALBERT H.) ed. Social interaction in educational settings: [readings]. Englewood Cliffs, [1971]. pp. 468. bibliogs.

BANNESTER (E. MICHAEL) Relevance and power: the elemental sociodynamics. London, 1972. pp. 236. bibliog.

LAVER (JOHN) and HUTCHESON (SANDY) eds. Communication in face to face interaction. Harmondsworth, 1972. pp. 418. bibliogs.

STUDIES in social interaction; edited by David Sudnow. New York, [1972]. pp. 455. bibliogs.

ARGYLE (MICHAEL) ed. Social encounters: readings in social interaction. Harmondsworth, 1973. pp. 416. bibliog.

CICOUREL (AARON VICTOR) Cognitive sociology: language and meaning in social interaction. Harmondsworth, 1973. pp. 191. bibliog.

EHRLICH (HOWARD J.) The social psychology of prejudice a systematic theoretical review and propositional inventory of the American social psychological study of prejudice. New York, [1973]. pp. 208. bibliog.

NETWORK analysis: studies in human interaction; [papers presented at a conference organized by the Afrika-Studiecentrum at Leiden in 1969]; edited by Jeremy Boissevain and J. Clyde Mitchell. The Hague, [1973]. pp. 271. bibliog. (Afrika-Studiecentrum. Change and Continuity in Africa)

SOCIAL INTERACTION (Cont'd.)

PLUMMER (KENNETH JOHN) Deviance, sexuality and the interactionist perspective: the case of male homosexuality; [Ph.D. (London) thesis]. 1973. fo. 386. bibliog. Typescript: unpublished. This thesis is the property of London University and may not be removed from the Library.

SOCIAL ISOLATION

RAMIAN (KNUD) Kontaktproblemer i alderdommen. København, 1971. pp. 98. bibliog. (Socialpolitisk Forening. Småskrifter. Nr. 42)

SOCIAL LEGISLATION

- Denmark

FURSTNOW-SØRENSEN (BENT) Outlines of the National Assistance Act. 2nd ed. Copenhagen, 1968. pp. 27. (Social Conditions in Denmark. 1)

- European Economic Community countries

TRINE (ANDRE) Les principales obligations des employeurs en matière sociale dans les 6 pays de la C.E.E: (employers' liabilities under social service legislation in the countries of the European Common Market). Bruxelles, 1971-72. Loose leaf. In French and English.

- Germany

ZOELLNER (DETLEV) Social legislation in the Federal Republic of Germany;...translation by F. Kenny. 2nd ed. Bonn, 1970. pp. 61.

- India

CHATTERJEE (BISHWA BANDHU) and others. Impact of social legislation on social change. Calcutta, 1971. pp. 261.

- Italy

ITALY. Statutes, etc. 1950-57. Current legislation on the Cassa per il Mezzogiorno; translation. Rome, Cassa per il Mezzogiorno, 1958. fo. vi, 97.

ITALY. Statutes, etc. 1957-1964. Current legislation on the Cassa per il Mezzogiorno, (1957-1964); translation. Rome, 1964. fo. 172.

LEVI SANDRI (LIONELLO R.) Istituzioni di legislazione sociale. 10th ed. Milano, 1971. pp. 428.

- Norway

NORWAY. Komitéen for Internasjonale Sosialpolitiske Saker. Social and Labour News from Norway. 1959. No. 2. Social developments in Norway, 1957-1959: a short survey. Oslo, 1959. fo. 3.

- United Kingdom

SMITH (N.J.) A guide to social legislation. London, 1972. pp. 190. bibliog.

SOCIAL MEDICINE

SMULEVICH (BOLESLAV IAKOVLEVICH) Narodnoe zdorov'e i sotsiologiia. Moskva, 1965. pp. 232.

HERZLICH (CLAUDINE) Médecine, maladie et société; recueil de textes présentés et commentés. Paris, [1970]. pp. 318. bibliogs. (Paris. Ecole Pratique des Hautes Etudes. Section des Sciences Economiques et Sociales. Les Textes Sociologiques. 4)

FERBER (CHRISTIAN VON) Gesundheit und Gesellschaft: haben wir eine Gesundheitspolitik? Stuttgart, [1971]. pp. 104. bibliog.

HUMAN aspects of biomedical innovation; Everett Mendelsohn [and others], editors. Cambridge, Mass., 1971. pp. 234. (Harvard University. Harvard University Program on Technology and Society. Harvard Studies in Technology and Society)

POLACK (JEAN CLAUDE) La médecine du capital. Paris, 1971. pp. 223. bibliog.

FREEMAN (HOWARD E.) and others, eds. Handbook of medical sociology. 2nd ed. Englewood Cliffs, [1972]. pp. 598. bibliogs.

FREIDSON (ELIOT) and LORBER (JUDITH) eds. Medical men and their work; [a sociological reader]. Chicago, 1972. pp. 482. bibliogs.

JEFCOAT (L. ALLURE) Health and human values: an ecological approach. New York, [1972]. pp. 255. bibliogs.

OFFICE OF HEALTH ECONOMICS. [Studies in Current Health Problems]. No. 43. Medicine and society: the changing demands for medical care. London, [1972]. pp. 29. bibliog.

PATIENT, doctor, society: a symposium of introspections [sponsored by the Nuffield Provincial Hospitals Trust]; contributors, Ferguson Anderson [and others]; edited by Gordon McLachlan. London, 1972. pp. 151.

STEUDLER (FRANÇOIS) Sociologie médicale. Paris, [1972]. pp. 388. bibliog.

MILLER (HENRY) Vice-Chancellor of Newcastle University. Medicine and society. London, 1973. pp. 87. bibliog.

SOCIAL MOBILITY

GIROD (ROGER) Mobilité sociale: faits établis et problèmes ouverts. Genève, 1971. pp. 204.

WESTLEY (WILLIAM A.) and WESTLEY (MARGARET W.) The emerging worker: equality and conflict in the mass consumption society. Montreal, 1971. pp. 155. bibliog.

LOPREATO (JOSEPH) and HAZELRIGG (LAWRENCE E.) Class, conflict, and mobility: theories and studies of class structure. San Francisco, [1972]. pp. 576. bibliog.

- Austria

MADERNER (JOSEF) Die Führungsschichten Klagenfurts: eine Untersuchung über vertikale Mobilität. Graz, 1970. fo.122, 9. bibliog. (Graz. Universität. Institut für Soziologie. Schriftenreihe. Nr. 4)

- Brazil

GREENFIELD (SIDNEY M.) Differentiation, stratification, and mobility in traditional Brazilian society. Milwaukee, 1970. pp. 21. (Wisconsin University. Center for Latin American Studies. Center Reprints. No. 8) (Reprinted from Luso-Brazilian Review, vol. 6:2, winter, 1969)

- France

LEVY-LEBOYER (CLAUDE) L'ambition professionnelle et la mobilité sociale. Paris, 1971. pp. 398. bibliog.

- India - Kerala

ALEXANDER (K.C.) Social mobility in Kerala. Poona, 1968. pp. 258. bibliog. (Deccan College. Deccan College Dissertation Series. 29)

- Mexico

BALAN (JORGE) and others. Man in a developing society: geographic and social mobility in Monterrey, Mexico. Austin, Texas, [1973]. pp. 384. bibliog. (Texas University. Institute of Latin American Studies. Latin American Monographs. No. 30)

- Russia

RUTKEVICH (MIKHAIL NIKOLAEVICH) and FILIPPOV (FRIDRIKH RAFAILOVICH) Sotsial'nye peremeshcheniia. Moskva, 1970. pp. 253.

- United Kingdom

The ANALYSIS of social mobility: methods and approaches; edited by Keith Hope. Oxford, 1972. pp. 254. bibliogs. (Oxford Group for the Study of Social Mobility. Oxford Studies in Social Mobility. 1.)

- United States

HELLER (CELIA STOPNICKA) New converts to the American dream?: mobility aspirations of young Mexican Americans. New Haven, [1971]. pp. 287.

DUNCAN (OTIS DUDLEY) and others. Socioeconomic background and achievement. New York, 1972. pp. 284. bibliog.

SOCIAL MOVEMENTS

PINARD (MAURICE) The rise of a third party: a study in crisis politics. Englewood Cliffs, [1971]. pp. 285.

PLETNIKOV (IURII KONSTANTINOVICH) O prirode sotsial'noi formy dvizheniia. Moskva, 1971. pp. 247.

SALTMAN (JULIET Z.) Open housing as a social movement: challenge, conflict and change. Lexington, [1971]. pp. 213. bibliog.

ASH (ROBERTA) Social movements in America. Chicago, [1972]. pp. 274. bibliogs.

BANKS (JOSEPH AMBROSE) The sociology of social movements. London, 1972. pp. 62. (British Sociological Association. Studies in Sociology)

GERLACH (LUTHER P.) and HINE (VIRGINIA H.) Lifeway leap: the dynamics of change in America. Minneapolis, [1973]. pp. 332. bibliog.

OBERSCHALL (ANTHONY) Social conflict and social movements. Englewood Cliffs, [1973]. pp. 371. bibliog.

SOCIAL PARTICIPATION

BOURASSA (GUY) Study on participation and regional planning;... translation. [Ottawa], Canadian Council on Rural Development, 1969. pp. 101. bibliog.

CAHN (EDGAR S.) and PASSETT (BARRY A.) eds. Citizen participation: effecting community change. New York, 1971. pp. 294.

LUUKA (ULO) Gemeinwesenarbeit: ein Weg zur Lösung gesellschaftlicher Konflikte. Freiburg im Breisgau, [1971]. pp. 56. bibliog.

SPYROPOULOS (G.) and others. Participation by employers' and workers' organisations in economic and social planning: a general introduction. Geneva, International Labour Office, 1971. pp. 247. bibliog.

DENNIS (NORMAN) Public participation and planners' blight. London, 1972. pp. 352.

FERRIS (JOHN) Dip. Soc. Admin. Participation in urban planning: the Barnsbury case; a study of environmental improvement in London. London, 1972. pp. 95. (Social Administration Research Trust. Occasional Papers on Social Administration. No. 48)

JOLLES (HIDDO M.) Sociologie van de participatie: een onderzoek in enkele Amsterdamse verenigingen. Alphen aan den Rijn, 1972. pp. 245. bibliog.

MEYERS (WILLIAM) and RINARD (PARK) Making activism work. New York, [1972]. pp. 102.

SMITH (CONSTANCE ELIZABETH) and FREEDMAN (ANNE) Voluntary associations: perspectives on the literature. Cambridge, Mass., 1972. pp. 250. bibliogs.

FABIAN SOCIETY. Fabian Tracts. [No.] 419. Towards participation in local services; editor, Stephen Hatch. London, 1973. pp. 52.

McKINSEY AND COMPANY INCORPORATED. The Sunderland study. London, H.M.S.O., 1973. 2 pts.

McLEOD (J.T.) and McLEOD (J.T.) RESEARCH ASSOCIATES LIMITED. Consumer participation, regulation of the professions and decentralization of health services; a report submitted to the Minister of Public Health, Saskatchewan. [Regina], 1973. fo. 214.

U.K. Department of the Environment. 1973. Participation in road planning. [London], 1973. pp. (15).

U.K. Department of the Environment. 1973. Participation in road planning: a consultation paper. [London], 1973. fo. 5.

SOCIAL PERCEPTION

HASTORF (ALBERT HERMAN) and others. Person perception. Reading, Mass., [1970]. pp. 113. bibliog.

SOCIAL POLICY

SECRETAN (CHARLES) Professor of Philosophy at Lausanne. La question sociale. Lausanne, 1886. pp. 96.

NEARING (SCOTT) The conscience of a radical. Harborside, Maine, 1965 repr. 1966. pp. 191.

MANNOURY (J.) Kernpunten van de social politiek. Groningen, 1970. pp. 86.

DELEECK (HERMAN) and others. Introduction à la planification sociale;...([commissioned by] la Centrale Chrétienne des Travailleurs du Bois et du Bâtiment); editée à l'occasion de son Congrès d'Anvers des 22 et 23 mai 1971; (traduit du Néerlandais). Bruxelles, 1971. pp. 286. bibliog.

DROR (YEHEZKEL) Design for policy sciences. New York, [1971]. pp. 156. bibliog.

DROR (YEHEZKEL) Ventures in policy sciences: concepts and applications. New York, [1971]. pp. 321.

JEFFERY (CLARENCE RAY) Crime prevention through environmental design. Beverly Hills, [1971]. pp. 290.

WILLIAMS (WALTER) Dr. Social policy research and analysis: the experience in the federal social agencies. New York, 1971. pp. 204. bibliogs.

COHN (ELCHANAN) Public expenditure analysis: with special reference to human resources. Lexington, Mass., [1972]. pp. 157. bibliog.

SOCIAL POLICY (Cont'd.)

CONFERENCE ON SOCIAL SCIENCE POLICY, 1ST, 1970. Social science and government: policies and problems; [papers and discussions] edited by A.B. Cherns [and others]. London, 1972. pp. 269. bibliog.

GRUDULS (ANTON IANOVICH) "Sotsial'naia inzheneriia" na sluzhbe sovremennogo kapitalizma. Moskva, 1972. pp. 72.

JANTSCH (ERICH) Technological planning and social futures. London, 1972. pp. 256. bibliog.

LEES (RAY) Politics and social work. London, 1972. pp. 114. bibliog.

MOURA (JOÃO) Desenvolvimento e produtividade. Lisboa, 1972. pp. 44. (Portugal. Ministerio das Corporações e Previdência Social. Gabinete de Planeamento. Serie Estudos. 6) With abstracts in English, French and German.

PERLMAN (ROBERT) and GURIN (ARNOLD) Community organization and social planning. New York, [1972]. pp. 292.

RESCHER (NICHOLAS) Welfare: the social issues in philosophical perspective. [Pittsburgh, 1972]. pp. 186. bibliogs.

ROSSI (PETER HENRY) and WILLIAMS (WALTER) Dr., eds. Evaluating social programs: theory, practice and politics. New York, 1972. pp. 326.

ZIÓŁKOWSKI (JANUSZ) Socjologia i planowanie społeczne. Warszawa, 1972. pp. 299.

CULYER (ANTHONY J.) The economics of social policy. London, 1973. pp. 268. bibliogs.

GREVE (JOHN) Comparisons, perspectives and values: some observations on the study of social policy; an inaugural lecture delivered...11th December, 1972. Southampton, 1973. pp. 24.

PETERSON (RICHARD A.) The industrial order and social policy. Englewood Cliffs, [1973]. pp. 159. bibliog.

PINKER (ROBERT ARTHUR) The welfare state: a comparative perspective. London, 1973. pp. 30. (James Seth Memorial Lectures. 1972)

ROOS (J.P.) Welfare theory and social policy: a study in policy science. Helsinki, 1973. pp. 251. bibliog. (Societas Scientiarum Fennica. Commentationes Scientiarum Socialium. 4. 1973)

SOCIAL administration: readings in applied social science; edited by W.D. Birrell [and others]. Harmondsworth, 1973. pp. 441.

WEGER (HANS DIETER) Sozialpolitische Analyse der Konjunkturpolitik: ein Beitrag zu einer rationalen Wirtschaftspolitik...unter Berücksichtigung sozialpolitischer Zielsetzungen. Berlin, [1973]. pp. 219. bibliog.

- Bibliography

WILCOX (LESLIE D.) and others, compilers. Social indicators and societal monitoring: an annotated bibliography. Amsterdam, 1972. pp. 464.

SOCIAL PROBLEMS

NEARING (SCOTT) Social adjustment. New York, 1911 repr. 1913. pp. 377.

DICKMANN (ENRIQUE) Ideas e ideales. Valencia, [1920?]. pp. 235.

HORTON (PAUL BURLEIGH) and LESLIE (GERALD RONNELL) The sociology of social problems. 4th ed. New York, [1970]. pp. 668.

ATTESLANDER (PETER M.) Die letzten Tage der Gegenwart; oder, Das Alibi-Syndrom. Bern, [1971]. pp. 308. bibliog.

MERTON (ROBERT KING) and NISBET (ROBERT ALEXANDER) eds. Contemporary social problems. 3rd ed. New York, [1971]. pp. 881.

SMIGEL (ERWIN O.) ed. Handbook on the study of social problems. Chicago, [1971]. pp. 734. bibliogs.

WEINBERG (CARL) Education and social problems. New York, [1971]. pp. 350.

BREDEMEIER (HARRY CHARLES) and TOBY (JACKSON) Social problems in America: costs and casualties in an acquisitive society. 2nd ed. New York, [1972]. pp. 464.

BUTTERWORTH (ERIC) and WEIR (DAVID) eds. Social problems of modern Britain. London, 1972. pp. 447. bibliogs.

DAM (MARCEL VAN) De ombudsman. Amsterdam, 1972. pp. 210.

JEFCOAT (L. ALLURE) Health and human values: an ecological approach. New York [1972]. pp. 255. bibliogs.

KUTSENKO (VLADIMIR IL'ICH) Sotsial'naia zadacha kak kategoriia istoricheskogo materializma. Kiev, 1972. pp. 371.

MOORE (BARRINGTON) Reflections on the causes of human misery and upon certain proposals to eliminate them. London, 1972. pp. 201.

WORSLEY (PETER MAURICE) ed. Problems of modern society: a sociological perspective. Harmondsworth, 1972. pp. 637.

BAILEY (ROY V.) and YOUNG (JOCK) eds. Contemporary social problems in Britain; [readings]. Farnborough, Hants., [1973]. pp. 194.

BREDEMEIER (HARRY CHARLES) and GETIS (JUDITH) eds. Environments, people, and inequalities: some current problems. New York, [1973]. pp. 341. bibliogs.

BUTT (J.) and CLARKE (IGNATIUS FREDERICK) eds. The Victorians and social protest: a symposium. Newton Abbot, 1973. pp. 243.

COHEN (STANLEY) and YOUNG (JOCK) eds. The manufacture of news: social problems, deviance and the mass media. London, 1973. pp. 383. bibliogs.

ETZIONI (AMITAI) and REMP (RICHARD) Technological shortcuts to social change. New York, [1973]. pp. 235.

HENDERSON (IAN) ed. The new poor: anatomy of underprivilege. London. 1973. pp. 182.

KRIESBERG (LOUIS) The sociology of social conflicts. Englewood Cliffs, 1973. pp. 300. bibliogs.

SHEPARD (JON M.) ed. Spectrum on social problems: society, economy, and man; [readings]. Columbus, Oh., [1973]. pp. 260. bibliogs.

TOWNSEND (PETER BRERETON) The social minority. London, [1973]. pp. 319.

WEINBERG (MARTIN S.) and RUBINGTON (EARL) eds. The solution of social problems: five perspectives; [readings]. New York, 1973. pp. 310.

SOCIAL PROBLEMS IN LITERATURE

MAES-JELINEK (HENA) Criticism of society in the English novel between the wars. Paris, 1970. pp. 551. bibliog. (Liège. Université. Faculté de Philosophie et Lettres. Bibliothèque. Fasc. 190)

SOCIAL PSYCHIATRY

SOZIALPSYCHIATRIE in der sozialistischen Gesellschaft; herausgegeben von Bernhard Schwarz [and others]. Leipzig, 1971. pp. 320. bibliogs.

SOCIAL PSYCHOLOGY

TANNENBAUM (ARNOLD SHERWOOD) Social psychology of the work organization. London, 1966. pp. 136.

DEMICHEV (VITALII ANATOL'EVICH) Obshchestvennoe bytie i obshchestvennoe soznanie, mekhanizm ikh vzaimosviazi. Kishinev, 1969. pp. 216.

CHOISELLE (ROLAND) and ESPARRE (PAUL LOUIS) Psychologie sociale des entreprises. Paris, 1970 in progress. bibliog.

ARGYRIS (CHRIS) Intervention theory and method: a behavioral science view. Reading, Mass., [1970]. pp. 374

OBSHCHESTVENNAIA psikhologiia i religioznye predrassudki. Frunze, 1970. pp. 85.

LAMBERT (WILLIAM WILSON) and WEISBROD (RITA) eds. Comparative perspectives on social psychology. Boston, Mass., [1971]. pp. 309. bibliogs.

McGINNIES (ELLIOTT) and FERSTER (C.B.) eds. The reinforcement of social behavior; [readings]. Boston, [1971]. pp. 468. bibliogs.

MANAGEMENT of the urban crisis: government and the behavioral sciences; edited by Stanley E. Seashore and Robert J. McNeill. New York, [1971]. pp. 518. bibliogs.

PLETNIKOV (IURII KONSTANTINOVICH) O prirode sotsial'noi formy dvizheniia. Moskva, 1971. pp. 247.

PROBLEMY sotsial'noi psikhologii i propaganda. Moskva, 1971. pp. 183.

VARELA (JACOBO A.) Psychological solutions to social problems: an introduction to social technology. New York, 1971. pp. 317. bibliog.

ALDERFER (CLAYTON P.) Existence, relatedness, and growth: human needs in organizational settings. New York, [1972]. pp. 198. bibliog.

CURLE (ADAM) Mystics and militants: a study of awareness, identity and social action. London, 1972. pp. 121. bibliog.

EYSENCK (HANS JÜRGEN) Psychology is about people. London, 1972. pp. 331. bibliog.

FISHER (GLEN H.) Public diplomacy and the behavioral sciences. Bloomington, Ind., [1972]. pp. 180.

GRONSETH (ERIK) Familie, seksualitet og samfunn. 2nd ed. Oslo, [1972]. pp. 198. bibliog.

HARRÉ (HORACE ROMANO) and SECORD (PAUL FRANK) The explanation of social behaviour. Oxford, [1972]. pp. 327.

HENDRICK (CLYDE) and JONES (RUSSELL A.) The nature of theory and research in social psychology. New York, [1972]. pp. 364. bibliogs.

HOLBROOK (DAVID) The masks of hate: the problem of false solutions in the culture of an acquisitive society. Oxford, 1972. pp. 275. bibliog.

HOLLANDER (EDWIN PAUL) and HUNT (RAYMOND GEORGE) eds. Classic contributions to social psychology. New York, 1972. pp. 419. bibliog.

ISRAEL (JOACHIM) and TAJFEL (HENRI) eds. The context of social psychology: a critical assessment. London, 1972. pp. 438. bibliogs.

KOVALEV (ALEKSANDR GRIGOR'EVICH) Kurs lektsii po sotsial'noi psikhologii. Moskva, 1972. pp. 176. bibliog.

McCLINTOCK (CHARLES GRAHAM) ed. Experimental social psychology. New York, [1972]. pp. 585. bibliogs.

MILLER (ARTHUR G.) ed. The social psychology of psychological research. New York, [1972]. pp. 454. bibliogs.

PARK (ROBERT EZRA) The crowd and the public, and other essays; edited and with an introduction by Henry Elsner, etc. Chicago, 1972. pp. 146.

PSYCHOLOGIE sociale et religion; par Louis Debarge [and others]; symposium de l'Association Française de Sociologie Religieuse, Orsay, 22 Octobre 1970: communications et débats. Paris, 1972. pp. 123. bibliogs. (Centre National de la Recherche Scientifique. Centre d'Etudes Sociologiques. Travaux et Documents.3)

REICH (WILHELM) The mass psychology of fascism; newly translated from the German [3rd ed.] by Vincent R. Carfagno. London, 1972. pp. 400.

WATERHOUSE (ALAN) Die Reaktion der Bewohner auf die äussere Veränderung der Städte. Berlin, 1972. pp. 181. bibliog. With English and French summaries.

DAVIES (JOHN GUY) Self and action: a study in the social philosophy of George Herbert Mead; [Ph. D. (London) thesis]. [1973]. fo. 552. bibliog. Typescript: unpublished. This thesis is the property of London University and may not be removed from the Library.

- Methodology

GROSS (ALAN E.) and others. An introduction to research in social psychology: exercises and examples. New York, [1972]. pp. 447. bibliogs.

MANASTER (GUY J.) and HAVIGHURST (ROBERT JAMES) Cross-national research: social-psychological methods and problems. Boston, [Mass.], [1972]. pp. 224. bibliog.

MEY (HARALD) Field-theory: a study of its application in the social sciences;...translated by Douglas Scott. London, 1972. pp. 326. bibliog.

CRANO (WILLIAM D.) and BREWER (MARILYNN B.) Principles of research in social psychology. New York, [1973]. pp. 361. bibliog.

- Research

MANASTER (GUY J.) and HAVIGHURST (ROBERT JAMES) Cross-national research: social-psychological methods and problems. Boston, [Mass.], [1972]. pp. 224. bibliog.

SOCIAL REFORMERS

- United States

GILBERT (JAMES BURKHART) Designing the industrial state: the intellectual pursuit of collectivism in America, 1880-1940. Chicago, 1972. pp. 335.

SOCIAL ROLE

ROLE; edited by J.A.Jackson. Cambridge, 1972. pp. 152.

DAHRENDORF (RALF) Homo sociologicus; [first published in English in his Essays in the theory of society, 1968; reprinted with a new preface and minor revisions; translated from the German by the author]. London, 1973. pp. 99. bibliog.

SOCIAL SCIENCE RESEARCH

DIECKMANN (BERNHARD) Zur Strategie des systematischen internationalen Vergleichs: Probleme der Datenbasis und der Entwicklungsbegriffe. Stuttgart, 1970. pp. 188. bibliog. With English summary.

DESROCHES (HENRI CHARLES) Apprentissage en sciences sociales et éducation permanente. Paris, [1971]. pp. 200. bibliog.

The RESEARCH procedures of social scientists; project head; Maurice B. Line, etc. Bath, 1971. fo. 23. (University of Bath. Library. Investigation into Information Requirements of the Social Sciences. Research Reports. No. 5)

CONFERENCE ON SOCIAL SCIENCE POLICY, 1ST, 1970. Social science and government: policies and problems; [papers and discussions] edited by A.B. Cherns [and others]. London, 1972. pp. 269. bibliog.

KARPINSKI (ADAM) and SAMSON (MARCEL) L'interdisciplinarité;...sous la direction de Pierre Lamonde. Montréal, 1972. fo. 72. bibliog. (Quebec. Université Laval. Centre de Recherches Urbaines et Régionales. Cahiers. No. 2)

ROSSI (PETER HENRY) and WILLIAMS (WALTER) Dr., eds. Evaluating social programs: theory, practice and politics. New York, 1972. pp. 326.

COCHRANE (RAYMOND) ed. Advances in social research: a book of readings in research methods. London, 1973. pp. 460. bibliogs.

WARWICK (DONALD P.) and OSHERSON (SAMUEL) eds. Comparative research methods. Englewood Cliffs N.J., [1973]. pp. 312.

SOCIAL SCIENCE RESEARCH
See also ECONOMIC RESEARCH ; POLITICAL SCIENCE RESEARCH ; SOCIOLOGICAL RESEARCH

- Bulgaria

BURDAROV (GEORGI) Sotsiologiia i partiina rabota. Sofiia, 1972. pp. 151. bibliog.

- Cuba

ESTUDIOS y documentos suecos sobre Cuba. Stockholm, 1971. pp. 87. bibliog. (Latinamerika-Institutet. Skrifter. Serie B. Meddelanden 2)

- Japan

FAIRBANK (JOHN KING) and others. Japanese studies of modern China: a bibliographical guide to historical and social-science research on the 19th and 20th centuries; [reprinted from the 1955 edition without correction]. Cambridge, Mass., [1971]. pp. 331. (Harvard-Yenching Institute. Studies. 26)

- Mexico

COVO (MILENA E.) Las instituciones de investigacion social en la ciudad de Mexico. Mexico, 1969. pp. 147.

- Netherlands

NETHERLANDS. Ministerie van Cultuur, Recreatie en Maatschappelijk Werk. 1970. A brief record of research commissioned by or conducted with the co-operation of the Ministry of Cultural Affairs, Recreation and Social Welfare. The Hague, 1970. pp. 76.

- South Africa

HUMAN SCIENCES RESEARCH COUNCIL [SOUTH AFRICA]. Annual report. a., 1969/70 (1st)- Pretoria.

- Sweden

SWEDEN. Statens Råd för Samhällsforskning. 1972. Social science research in Sweden. Stockholm, 1972. pp. 278.

- United Kingdom

MICHAELS (RUTH) and WOOLLEY (PENELOPE) Social science research in colleges in the further education sector. Hatfield, [1971]. pp. 73.

UNIVERSITY OF BATH. Library. Investigation into Information Requirements of the Social Sciences. Research Reports. No. 2. Information requirements of social scientists in government departments; project head, Maurice B. Line, senior research fellow, J. Michael Brittain [and] research fellow, Frank A. Cranmer. [Bath], 1971. 1 vol. (various foliations).

- United States

EVALUATIVE research: strategies and methods; [a seminar arranged by the] American Institutes for Research [in Washington, January 1970]. [Pittsburgh, 1970]. pp. 160. bibliogs.

AMERICAN ACADEMY OF POLITICAL AND SOCIAL SCIENCE. Annals. vol. 394. Social science and the federal government; special editor of this volume, Gene M. Lyons. Philadelphia, 1971. pp. 210. bibliog.

NATIONAL RESEARCH COUNCIL. Division of Behavioral Sciences. Advisory Committee for Assessment of University Based Institutes for Research on Poverty. Policy and program research in a university setting; a case study; (report of the... Committee, etc.). Washington, D.C., 1971. pp. 55.

HYMAN (HERBERT HIRAM) Secondary analysis of sample surveys: principles, procedures, and potentialities. New York, [1972]. pp. 347. bibliog.

SIEBER (SAM D.) Reforming the university: the role of the social research center. New York, 1972. pp. 228.

ORLANS (HAROLD) Contracting for knowledge: (values and limitations of social science research). San Francisco, 1973. pp. 286. bibliog.

SOCIAL SCIENCES

The CONTRIBUTION of social sciences in social work training: report of a United Nations - Unesco meeting of experts, Paris ... 1960. Paris, 1961. pp. 90.

BECKER (ERNEST) The structure of evil: an essay on the unification of the science of man. New York, [1968]. pp. 430. bibliog.

GOULD (WESLEY LARSON) and BARKUN (MICHAEL) International law and the social sciences. Princeton, N.J., 1970. pp. 338.

CALHOUN (DONALD W.) Social science in an age of change. New York, [1971]. pp. 529. bibliogs.

STANKIEWICZ (WLADYSLAW JOZEF) What is behavioralism?; thoughts on the crisis in the social sciences. West Chesterfield, 1971. 1 pamphlet (unpaged).

ANDRESKI (STANISLAV) Social sciences as sorcery. London, 1972. pp. 238.

BLACKBURN (ROBIN) ed. Ideology in social science: readings in critical social theory. [London], 1972. pp. 382. bibliog.

BRUECKNER (PETER) and KROVOZA (ALFRED) Was heisst Politisierung der Wissenschaft und was kann sie für die Sozialwissenschaften heissen? Frankfurt am Main, [1972]. pp. 137. bibliog. (Hanover. Technische Hochschule. Psychologisches Seminar. Veröffentlichungen)

GLUCKSMANN (MIRIAM ANNE) Varieties of the structural analysis of social phenomena with special reference to Claude Levi-Strauss and Louis Althusser: [Ph.D. (London) thesis]. 1971 [or rather 1972]. fo. 326. bibliogs. Typescript: unpublished. This thesis is the property of London University and may not be removed from the Library.

IMAGINATION and precision in the social sciences: (essays in memory of Peter Nettl); edited by T.J. Nossiter [and others]. London, 1972. pp. 464. bibliogs.

MAN and the social sciences; twelve lectures delivered at the London School of Economics and Political Science tracing the development of the social sciences during the present century; edited by William A. Robson. London, [1972]. pp. 284. bibliogs.

SCHNEIDER (LOUIS) and BONJEAN (CHARLES M.) eds. The idea of culture in the social sciences. Cambridge, [1973]. pp. 149.

- Bibliography

KNIZHNIK-VETROV (IVAN SERGEEVICH) compiler. Chto chitat' po obshchestvennym naukam: sistematicheskii ukazatel' kommunisticheskoi i marksistskoi literatury, 1917-1923 g.g., etc. 2nd ed. Leningrad, 1924. pp. 491.

PERU. Junta Nacional de la Vivienda. Oficina de Programacion y Coordinacion. Biblioteca. 1964. Material bibliográfico al 30 de abril de 1964. [Lima?], 1964. pp. 69.

BAKINOVA (R.) Obshchestvenno-politicheskaia kniga v period stanovleniia i razvitiia knigoizdatel'skogo dela v Kirgizii. Frunze, 1969. pp. 46.

INTERNATIONAL LABOUR OFFICE. Library. 1970. International labour documentation: cumulative edition, 1965-1969. Boston, Mass., 1970. 8 vols.

GOULD (WESLEY LARSON) and BARKUN (MICHAEL) Social science literature: a bibliography for international law. Princeton, 1972. pp. 641.

INTERNATIONAL LABOUR OFFICE. Library. 1972. International labour documentation: cumulative edition, 1970-1971. Boston, Mass., 1972. 2 vols.

- Dictionaries and encyclopaedias

BRUNNER (OTTO) and others, eds. Geschichtliche Grundbegriffe: historisches Lexikon zur politisch-sozialen Sprache in Deutschland. Stuttgart, [1972 in progress]. bibliogs.

- Field work

SCHATZMAN (LEONARD) and STRAUSS (ANSELM LEONARD) Field research: strategies for a natural sociology. Englewood Cliffs, [1973]. pp. 149. bibliogs.

- History

MEDICK (HANS) Naturzustand und Naturgeschichte der bürgerlichen Gesellschaft: die Ursprünge der bürgerlichen Sozialtheorie...bei Samuel Pufendorf John Locke und Adam Smith. Göttingen, 1973. pp. 330. bibliog.

- History - Germany

LEWIN (KARL) Die Entwicklung der Sozialwissenschaften in Göttingen im Zeitalter der Aufklärung 1734 bis 1812, etc. Göttingen, 1971. pp. 437, 19. bibliog.

SCHAEFER (ULLA G.) Historische Nationalökonomie und Sozialstatistik als Gesellschaftswissenschaften: Forschungen zur Vorgeschichte der theoretischen Soziologie und der empirischen Sozialforschung in Deutschland in der zweiten Hälfte des 19. Jahrhunderts. Köln, 1971. pp. 398. bibliog.

- Information services

UNIVERSITY OF BATH. Library. Investigation into Information Requirements of the Social Sciences. Research Reports. No. 2. Information requirements of social scientists in government departments; project head, Maurice B. Line, senior research fellow, J. Michael Brittain [and] research fellow, Frank A. Cranmer. [Bath], 1971. 1 vol. (various foliations).

CAMPBELL (HENRY CUMMINGS) A data clearing house for the social sciences in Canada: a feasibility study; un centre d'échange de données en sciences sociales; compte rendu d'une enquête de rentabilité. Ottawa, 1972. pp. 74.

UNIVERSITY OF BATH. Library. Design of Information Systems in the Social Sciences. Working Papers. No.4. Characteristics of citations in social science monographs. [Bath], 1972. pp. 14.

- Mathematical models

MEEK (RONALD LINDLEY) Figuring out society. London, 1971. pp. 236. bibliogs.

BLALOCK (HUBERT M.) ed. Causal models in the social sciences. London, 1972. pp. 515. bibliogs.

ECONOMICS of engineering and social systems; [lectures sponsored in 1969 by University Extension of the University of California]; edited by J. Morley English. New York, [1972]. pp. 321. bibliogs.

MATHEMATICS in the social sciences in Australia: (Australian Unesco seminar), University of Sydney, May 1968. Canberra, Australian Government Publishing Service, 1972. pp. 670. bibliogs.

- Methodology

GREEF (GUILLAUME JOSEPH DE) L'évolution des croyances et des doctrines politiques; [prefaced by two introductory lectures for 1889 and 1890 on methodology in the social sciences]. Bruxelles, 1895. pp. 331.

O metodologicheskikh problemakh obshchestvennykh nauk. Novosibirsk, 1969. pp. 231.

ALBERT (HANS) and TOPITSCH (ERNST) eds. Werturteilsstreit. Darmstadt, 1971. pp. 552. bibliog.

BLACKMAN (SHELDON) and GOLDSTEIN (KENNETH M.) An introduction to data management in the behavioral and social sciences. New York, [1971]. pp. 104. bibliog.

BOUDON (RAYMOND) The uses of structuralism...; translated by Michalina Vaughan; introduced by Donald MacRae. London, 1971. pp. 159. bibliog.

SOCIAL SCIENCES - Methodology (Cont'd.)

DESROCHES (HENRI CHARLES) Apprentissage en sciences sociales et éducation permanente. Paris, [1971]. pp. 200. bibliog.

DIESING (PAUL) Patterns of discovery in the social sciences. Chicago, 1971. pp. 350. bibliog.

GEER (JOHN P. VAN DE) Introduction to multivariate analysis for the social sciences. San Francisco, [1971]. pp. 293. bibliog.

LUPTON (THOMAS) Management and the social sciences. 2nd ed. Harmondsworth, 1971 repr. 1972. pp. 151. bibliog.

METODOLOGICHESKIE voprosy obshchestvennykh nauk. vyp.2. Metodologicheskie aspekty strukturno-funktsional'nogo analiza v obshchestvoznanii. Moskva, 1971. pp. 232.

TUMA (ELIAS H.) Economic history and the social sciences: problems of methodology. Berkeley, 1971. pp. 316. bibliog.

APTER (DAVID ERNEST) and ANDRAIN (CHARLES FRANKLIN) eds. Contemporary analytical theory. Englewood Cliffs, N.J., [1972]. pp. 688. bibliogs.

GUETZKOW (HAROLD) and others, eds. Simulation in social and administrative science: overviews and case examples. Englewood Cliffs, [1972]. pp. 768. bibliogs.

HYMAN (HERBERT HIRAM) Secondary analysis of sample surveys: principles, procedures, and potentialities. New York, [1972]. pp. 347. bibliog.

INBAR (MICHAEL) and STOLL (CLARICE STASZ) Simulation and gaming in social science. New York, [1972]. pp. 313. bibliog.

MATHEMATICS in the social sciences in Australia: (Australian Unesco seminar), University of Sydney, May 1968. Canberra, Australian Government Publishing Service, 1972. pp. 670. bibliogs.

MEY (HARALD) Field-theory: a study of its application in the social sciences;...translated by Douglas Scott. London, 1972. pp. 326. bibliog.

NORLÉN (URBAN) Simulation model building: a statistical approach to modelling in the social sciences with the simulation method. Göteborg, 1972. pp. 172. bibliogs. (Göteborgs Universitet. Statistiska Institutionen. Skriftserie. 15)

PLATONOV (GRIGORII VASIL'EVICH) and PETRUSHEVSKII (S.A.) eds. Marksistsko-leninskaia filosofiia kak metodologiia obshchestvennykh i estestvennykh nauk. Moskva, 1972. pp. 196.

ROSSI (PETER HENRY) and WILLIAMS (WALTER) Dr., eds. Evaluating social programs: theory, practice and politics. New York, 1972. pp. 326

RUNKEL (PHILIP J.) and McGRATH (JOSEPH EDWARD) Research on human behaviour: a systematic guide to method. New York, [1972]. pp. 493. bibliogs.

COCHRANE (RAYMOND) ed. Advances in social research: a book of readings in research methods. London, 1973. pp. 460. bibliogs.

HAYS (WILLIAM LEE) Statistics for the social sciences. 2nd ed. New York, [1973]. pp. 954.

O'NEILL (JOHN) ed. Modes of individualism and collectivism. London, 1973. pp. 358. bibliog.

WILLER (DAVID) and WILLER (JUDITH) Systematic empiricism: critique of a pseudoscience. Englewood Cliffs, [1973]. pp. 145.

- Methodology - Bibliography

WILCOX (LESLIE D.) and others, compilers. Social indicators and societal monitoring: an annotated bibliography. Amsterdam, 1972. pp. 464.

BELSON (WILLIAM A.) and THOMPSON (BERYL ANNE) compilers. Bibliography on methods of social and business research. London, 1973. pp. 300.

- Philosophy

O'NEILL (JOHN) ed. Modes of individualism and collectivism. London, 1973. pp. 358. bibliog.

ROCHE (MAURICE CRAWFORD) Phenomenology, language and the social sciences. London, 1973. pp. 361. bibliog.

- Societies

UNITED NATIONS EDUCATIONAL, SCIENTIFIC AND CULTURAL ORGANIZATION. 1959. List of institutions specialized or interested in the social sciences. [Paris, 1959]. pp. 24.

- Study and teaching

UNESCO INSTITUTE FOR EDUCATION. 1962. L'enseignement des sciences sociales au niveau préuniversitaire: rapport de la réunion des 16-21 janvier, 1961. Hambourg, 1962. pp. 67. (International Studies in Education)

LAWTON (DENIS) and others. Social studies, 8-13: a report on the middle years of schooling. London, 1971. pp. 256. (U.K. Department of Education and Science. Schools Council. Working Papers. 39)

SOCIAL science in the schools: a search for rationale; [proceedings of a conference held at West Lafayette, Indiana, 1967]; Irving Morrissett [and] W. Williams Stevens, editors. New York, [1971]. pp. 204.

- Study and teaching - Directories

GRADUATE studies, 1970-71: vol.4. Social Sciences; ([edited by] Audrey Segal [and others]). London, [1970]. pp. various.

- Study and teaching - Russia.

VASINA (EMILIIA LEONIDOVNA) and others, eds. Osnovy metodiki prepodavaniia obshchestvennykh nauk v vysshei shkole. Moskva, 1971. pp. 388.

PLATONOV (GRIGORII VASIL'EVICH) and PETRUSHEVSKII (S.A.) eds. Marksistsko-leninskaia filosofiia kak metodologiia obshchestvennykh i estestvennykh nauk. Moskva, 1972. pp. 196.

SOCIAL SCIENCES AND STATE

CONFERENCE ON SOCIAL SCIENCE POLICY, 1ST, 1970. Social science and government: policies and problems; [papers and discussions] edited by A.B. Cherns [and others]. London, 1972. pp. 269. bibliog.

- Canada

CANADA. Statistics Canada. Federal government activities in the human sciences. a., 1971/3 [1st issue]- Ottawa. [in English and French]

- Netherlands

NETHERLANDS. Ministerie van Cultuur, Recreatie en Maatschappelijk Werk. 1970. A brief record of research commissioned by or conducted with the co-operation of the Ministry of Cultural Affairs, Recreation and Social Welfare. The Hague, 1970. pp. 76.

- United States

> AMERICAN ACADEMY OF POLITICAL AND SOCIAL SCIENCE. Annals. vol. 394. Social science and the federal government; special editor of this volume, Gene M. Lyons. Philadelphia, 1971. pp. 210. bibliog.
>
> ORLANS (HAROLD) Contracting for knowledge: (values and limitations of social science research). San Francisco, 1973. pp. 286. bibliog.
>
> BRITTAIN (JOHN A.) The payroll tax for social security. Washington, [1972]. pp. 285. (Brookings Institution. National Committee on Government Finance. Studies of Government Finance)

SOCIAL SERVICE

> BARTLETT (HARRIETT M.) The common base of social work practice. New York, [1970]. pp. 224.
>
> KLENK (ROBERT W.) and RYAN (ROBERT M.) eds. The practice of social work. Belmont, Calif., [1970]. pp. 373. bibliogs.
>
> INTERREGIONAL MEETING OF EXPERTS ON THE SOCIAL WELFARE ASPECTS OF FAMILY PLANNING, NEW YORK, 1971. Report of the...meeting...[held at] United Nations Headquarters, 22-30 March 1971. (ST/SOA/111). New York, United Nations, 1971. pp. 48.
>
> DAY (PETER RUSSELL) Communication in social work. Oxford, 1972. pp. 121. bibliog.
>
> The IMPACT of psychology on social work and teaching: the report on an interprofessional conference held at Madeley College of Education on March 24-26, 1972;...directed by F.G.Lennhoff. Shrewsbury, [1972]. pp. 51.
>
> LEES (RAY) Politics and social work. London, 1972. pp. 114. bibliog.
>
> SOCIAL administration: readings in applied social science; edited by W.D. Birrell [and others]. Harmondsworth, 1973. pp. 441.
>
> TOWLE (CHARLOTTE) Common human needs;... new edition prepared by Eileen Younghusband. London, 1973. pp. 149. (National Institute for Social Work Training. National Institute Social Services Library. No. 26)

- Dictionaries and encyclopaedias

> CLEGG (JOAN) Dictionary of social services: policy and practice. London, [1971]. pp. 126. bibliog.
>
> SOUTH AFRICA. Terminology Committee for Social Work. 1971. Defining Afrikaans dictionary of social work, with equivalent terminology in English. [Pretoria, Government Printer], 1971. pp. 83. Terminology in Afrikaans, with English alphabetical index.

- Methodology

> TIMMS (NOEL) Recording in social work. London, 1972. pp. 112. bibliog.

- Study and teaching

> The CONTRIBUTION of social sciences in social work training: report of a United Nations - Unesco meeting of experts, Paris ... 1960. Paris, 1961. pp. 90.

- Canada

> CANADA. 1967. Canada. (ST/SOA/72). New York, United Nations, 1967. pp. 126. (Department of Economic and Social Affairs. Organization and Administration of Social Welfare Programmes: A Series of Country Studies)
>
> SOCIAL SECURITY AND PUBLIC WELFARE SERVICES IN CANADA; pd. by Health and Welfare, Canada. a.. 1972 [1st]- Ottawa.
>
> CANADIAN COUNCIL ON SOCIAL DEVELOPMENT, and COMMUNITY FUNDS AND COUNCILS OF CANADA. Project information exchange; an inventory of studies, briefs and action projects undertaken by social planning councils in Canada during 1971: Relevé des travaux des conseils, etc. 2nd ed. [Ottawa], 1972. pp. 57. In English or French.

- Canada - New Brunswick

> MULTI-DISCIPLINE TEAM ASSOCIATES. Welfare services in New Brunswick; prepared for Department of Health and Welfare, Government of New Brunswick. Fredericton, 1969. 2 vols. (in 1).

- Canada - Nova Scotia

> FITZNER (STAN) The development of social welfare in Nova Scotia; a history written... as a centennial project for the Department of Public Welfare. [Halifax], 1967 [or rather 1968]. fo. 69.
>
> CANADIAN COUNCIL ON SOCIAL DEVELOPMENT. Research and Development Branch. Case Studies in Social Planning. 3. Public social planning in Halifax. Ottawa, 1972. pp. 152. bibliog.

- Denmark

> FURSTNOW-SØRENSEN (BENT) Care of the old and sick. 2nd rev. ed. Copenhagen, 1968. pp. 26. (Social Conditions in Denmark. 2)
>
> DENMARK. Uddannelseskommissionen for det Sociale Område. 1970. Uddannelse til omsorg. [Copenhagen?], 1970. pp. 153. (Denmark. Betaenkninger. Nr. 571)

- Egypt

> UNITED ARAB REPUBLIC. 1967. United Arab Republic. (ST/SOA/74). New York, United Nations, 1967. pp. 25. (Department of Economic and Social Affairs. Organization and Administration of Social Welfare Programmes: A Series of Country Studies)

- Europe

> COCQ (GUSTAVE A. DE) Citizen participation: doomed to extinction or last foothold of democracy?; an exploratory study in... the Netherlands, Denmark, the Federal Republic of Germany, and Great Britain, with some comparisons to North America. Leyden, 1969. pp. 278. bibliog.

- Finland

> FINLAND. Sosiaali- ja Terveysministeriö. 1969. Social welfare. Helsinki, [1969]. pp. 28. (Social Services in Finland. 1)

- France

> FRANCE. Direction de la Documentation. La Documentation Française Illustrée. No. 267-268. Le Ministère de la Santé Publique et de la Sécurité Sociale. [Paris], 1971. pp. 63.
>
> SOTO (JEAN DE) Grands services publics et entreprises nationales. Paris, [1971]. pp. 599. bibliogs.
>
> STEVENS (CINDY) Public assistance in France. London, 1973. pp. 94. (Social Administration Research Trust. Occasional Papers on Social Administration. No. 50)

- Ghana

> BENZIES (DOUGLAS) Report of a tour in India to study social service work done by schools (with Proposals for social service work at Achimota). Sessional paper No. 5 of 1928-29. in GHANA. Legislative Council. Minutes (formerly Minutes...and sessional papers).

SOCIAL SERVICE (Cont'd.)

- India

BENZIES (DOUGLAS) Report of a tour in India to study social service work done by schools (with Proposals for social service work at Achimota). Sessional paper No. 5 of 1928-29. in GHANA. Legislative Council. Minutes (formerly Minutes...and sessional papers).

INDIA. Planning Commission. 1960. Social welfare in India; (editorial committee: Durgabai Deshmukh, chairman; Raj Narain Gupta, editor). rev. and abridged ed. Delhi, 1960. pp. 380. bibliog.

NAGPAUL (HANS) The study of Indian society: a sociological analysis of social welfare and social work education. New Delhi, 1972. pp. 510. bibliog.

- India - Gujarat

GUJARAT. Study Group on Labour Welfare, Social Welfare and Welfare of Backward Classes. 1964-65. Fourth five year plan, 1966-67 to 1970-71; report. [Baroda], 1964-65. 3 pts. (in 1)

- Israel

ISRAEL NATIONAL COMMITTEE FOR SOCIAL SERVICE. Report on new strategies for social development: the role of social welfare; submitted by the...Committee...in co-operation with the Ministry of Social Welfare, Government of Israel, to the Fifteenth International Conference on Social Welfare (Manila, Philippines, 1970). Jerusalem, 1970. fo. 56,5. bibliog.

- Italy

ITALY. 1969. Italy. (ST/SOA/82). New York, United Nations, 1969. pp. 44. (Department of Economic and Social Affairs. Organization and Administration of Social Welfare Programmes A Series of Country Studies)

ASSISTENZA e regioni: [proceedings of a conference organised by the Movimento Femminile della Democrazia Cristiana in November 1971]. [Rome, 1972]. pp. 174. (Programma dc/9)

EMILIA-ROMAGNA. Ufficio Programmazione. 1972. Sanità assistenza e tutela dell'ambiente: linee programmatiche del dipartimento sicurezza sociale; elaborazioni degli assessorati sanità, servizi sociali, igiene e tutela dell'ambiente. Bologna, 1972. pp. 108,(fo. 5). (Problemi della Programmazione in Emilia-Romagna. Ricerche e Ipotesi di Lavoro. 9)

- Jordan

UNITED NATIONS. Economic and Social Office in Beirut. 1968. Jordan. (ST/SOA/78). New York, 1968. pp. 38. (Department of Economic and Social Affairs. Organization and Administration of Social Welfare Programmes: A Series of Country Studies)

- Netherlands

KAMPHUIS (M.) Social actie nu?!; rede uitgesproken op 29 April 1970, etc. Lochem, 1970. pp. 32. bibliog.

ROESSINGH (K.H.) Welzijn, cultuur en vormingswerk. Groningen, 1970. pp. 153.

NETHERLANDS. Werkgroep Gemeentelijke Uitgaven voor Sociale Zorg. 1971. Eindrapport. 's-Gravenhage, 1971. 1 vol. (various pagings).

- Norway

NORWAY. Komitéen for Internasjonale Sosialpolitiske Saker. Social and Labour News from Norway. 1964. No.4. The Social Care Act. Oslo, 1964. fo. 7.

NORWAY. 1967. Norway. (ST/SOA/67). New York, United Nations, 1967. pp. 71. (Department of Economic and Social Affairs. Organization and Administration of Social Welfare Programmes: A Series of Country Studies)

NORWAY. Komitéen for Internasjonale Sosialpolitiske Saker. Social and Labour News from Norway. 1967. No. 2. The humanitarian organizations' place in the modern welfare community; by Ole Martin Larsen. Oslo, 1967. pp. 6.

NORWAY. Komitéen for Internasjonale Sosialpolitiske Saker. Social and Labour News from Norway. 1967. No. 3. Basic trends in our social welfare policy; by Kaare Salvesen. Oslo, 1967. pp. 6.

NORWAY. Komitéen for Internasjonale Sosialpolitiske Saker. Social and Labour News from Norway. 1967. No. 4. Social care - the new approach. Oslo, 1967. pp. 6.

NORWAY. Sosialreformkomitéen. 1970. Innstilling om økonomisk hjelp etter lov om sosial omsorg: innstilling I; (Odd With, chairman). Bergen, 1970. pp. 38.

- Poland - Statistics

POLAND. Główny Urząd Statystyczny. Statystyka Regionalna. Nr.18. Czyny społeczne, 1956-1968. Warszawa, 1969. pp. 121.

- Portugal

FUNDO DE DESENVOLVIMENTO DA MÃO-DE-OBRA. Serviço Nacional de Emprego. Sector Social. 1969. Actividade do Sector Social nas divisões regionais do S.N.E. de setembro a dezembro de 1968. Lisboa, 1969. pp. 19. (Fundo de Desenvolvimento da Mão-de-Obra. Boletim bimestral. Suplementos. N.°30) With abstracts in English and French.

- Roumania

ROUMANIA. 1967. Romania. (ST/SOA/69). New York, United Nations, 1967. pp. 64. (Department of Economic and Social Affairs. Organization and Administration of Social Welfare Programmes: A Series of Country Studies)

- Russia

RUSSIA (U.S.S.R.) 1967. The Union of Soviet Socialist Republics. (ST/SOA/75). New York, United Nations, 1967. pp. 78. (Department of Economic and Social Affairs. Organization and Administration of Social Welfare Programmes: A Series of Country Studies)

- South Africa

SOUTH AFRICA. National Welfare Board. Report...on the operation and administration of the National Welfare Act, 1965. July 1966/Dec. 1968 [1st] to date included in SOUTH AFRICA. Parliament. House of Assembly. Votes and proceedings; (with Printed annexures).

- Spain

SOLIS RUIZ (JOSE) The assistant action of Spanish syndicalism. Madrid, 1966. pp. 30. (Tiempo Nuevo. 1)

SPAIN. Ministerio de la Gobernacion. Secretaria General Tecnica. 1967. Guia de actividades publicas asistenciales; (with) La asistencia social como servicio publico; estudio preliminar de Ramon Martin Mateo. Madrid, 1967. pp. 387. (Coleccion Documentos. 3)

SPAIN. Comisaria del Plan de Desarrollo Economico y Social. 1972. (III Plan de desarrollo economico y social): seguridad social, sanidad y asistencia social. [Madrid], 1972. pp. 101.

- **United Kingdom**

UNITED KINGDOM. 1967. The United Kingdom of Great Britain and Northern Ireland. (ST/SOA/ 68). New York, United Nations, 1967. pp. 48. (Department of Economic and Social Affairs. Organization and Administration of Social Welfare Programmes: A Series of Country Studies)

The ROAD to community care: papers presented at three one-day conferences, 10, 11, 12 December 1969; sponsored by the National Society for Mentally Handicapped Children, etc.; [by] the Baroness Serota [and others]. London, [1969]. pp. 59.

WHITE (EMILY E.) A history of the Manchester and Salford Council of Social Service, 1919-1969. Manchester, 1969. pp. 56.

BROWN (MURIEL) Introduction to social administration in Britain. 2nd ed. London, 1971. pp. 216. bibliog.

EYDEN (JOAN L.M.) ed. The welfare society: a guide for discussion groups. London, [1971]. pp. 44. bibliog.

ROYCE (JOHN CRAVEN) An investigation of some interrelated problems affecting policy and decision making in the social services of a local authority: Leeds C.B.C., 1964-1970; [essay for the Diploma in Public Administration, London University]. 1971. fo. 31. Typescript: unpublished. This essay is the property of London University and may not be removed from the Library.

SOCIAL SERVICES CONFERENCE, EASTBOURNE, 1971. (Papers delivered at the Conference); [organised by] the County Councils Association [and the] Association of Municipal Corporations; (edited by Laurence Welsh). Redhill, [imprint], [1971]. pp. 56.

CHEESEMAN (DAVID) and others. Neighbourhood care and old people: a community development project. London, [1972]. pp. 95.

CHEETHAM (JULIET) Social work with immigrants. London, 1972. pp. 230. bibliog.

INSTITUTE OF MUNICIPAL TREASURERS AND ACCOUNTANTS. Output Measurement Research Working Party. Output Measurement Discussion Papers. 2. Personal social services. London, 1972. pp. 27.

KNEEBONE (ROGER) The development of social services in Reading: a brief history. [Reading, 1972]. pp. 13.

MARTIN (ERNEST WALTER) ed. Comparative development in social welfare. London, 1972. pp. 247. bibliogs.

PRINS (HERSCHEL A.) and WHYTE (MARION B.H.) Social work and medical practice. Oxford, [1972]. pp. 81. bibliogs.

SHELTER. Policy for the homeless. London, [1972]. 1 pamphlet (unpaged).

SOMERSET. Social Services Research Department. The preparation of ten year plans; (by John Crook). [Taunton, 1972?]. pp. (18). (Social Services Research Group. Papers. No.1)

TRISELIOTIS (JOHN P.) ed. Social work with coloured immigrants and their families. London, 1972. pp. 123. bibliog.

BAUGH (W.E.) Introduction to the social services. London, 1973. pp. 176. bibliogs.

BELL (KATHLEEN) Disequilibrium in welfare: an inaugural lecture delivered before the University of Newcastle upon Tyne on Tuesday, 17 October 1972. Newcastle upon Tyne, 1973. pp. 22.

COMMUNITY WORK GROUP. Current issues in community work; a study by the... group; chairman: Lord Boyle of Handsworth, etc. London, 1973. pp. 180. bibliog.

FABIAN SOCIETY. Fabian Tracts. [No.] 419. Towards participation in local services; editor, Stephen Hatch. London, 1973. pp. 52.

LEIGH (ANDREW) ed. Better social services: the Observer papers on a policy for social change. London, 1973. pp. 83. bibliogs.

NATIONAL COUNCIL OF SOCIAL SERVICE. Public social services: handbook of information; editor Phyllis Willmott. [13th ed.] London, [1973]. pp. 201.

RODGERS (BARBARA N.) and STEVENSON (JUNE) A new portrait of social work: a study of the social services in a northern town from Younghusband to Seebohm. London, 1973. pp. 363.

SEED (PHILIP) The expansion of social work in Britain. London, 1973. pp. 116. bibliog.

SLEEMAN (JOHN F.) The welfare state: its aims, benefits and costs. London, 1973. pp. 199. bibliog.

STEVENSON (OLIVE) Claimant or client?: a social worker's view of the Supplementary Benefits Commission. London, 1973. pp. 234. bibliog. (National Institute for Social Work Training. National Institute Social Services Library. No. 25)

WILLMOTT (PHYLLIS) Consumer's guide to the British social services. 3rd ed. Harmondsworth, 1973. pp. 330. bibliog.

- **United Kingdom - Directories**

OXFORDSHIRE. Social Services Department. A guide to welfare benefits and services in Oxfordshire. Oxford, 1970. 1 vol. (looseleaf).

WANDSWORTH. Borough Council. Contact: a guide to social services in Wandsworth. [new ed.] London, [1971?]. pp. 96.

SOCIAL SERVICES YEAR BOOK. a., 1972/3 [1st issue]. London.

KESSLER (JACK) compiler. London community planning directory. London, 1972. pp. 73. (Quest News Service. Quest Action Directories. No.1.)

NATIONAL COUNCIL OF SOCIAL SERVICE. Voluntary social services: directory of organisations and handbook of information. new ed. London, [1973]. pp. 149.

WESTMINSTER COUNCIL OF SOCIAL SERVICE. Directory of voluntary organisations in Westminster, 1973. 3rd ed. London, 1973. pp. 39.

- **United Kingdom - Research**

HAMMOND (ALEC R.) Research and information requirements of social services departments. [London], 1971. pp. 24. (London. Greater London Council. Department of Planning and Transportation. Research Memoranda. 298)

SOCIAL SERVICE (Cont'd.)

- United Kingdom - Ireland, Northern

IRELAND, NORTHERN. Ministry of Health and Social Services. 1972. Summary of a report on An integrated service: the re-organisation of health and personal social services in Northern Ireland. Belfast, 1972. pp. 24.

- United Kingdom - Scotland - Directories

SCOTTISH COUNCIL OF SOCIAL SERVICE. Scotland directory of national services and organisations. Edinburgh, 1972. pp. 76.

- United States

HOPKINS (HARRY LLOYD) Spending to save: the complete story of relief; [reprint of work issued in 1936 with new] introduction by Roger Daniels. Seattle, [1972]. pp. 197.

CAROTHERS (DORIS) Chronology of the Federal Emergency Relief Administration, May 12, 1933, to December 31, 1935: [reprint of the work originally published in Washington, 1937]. New York, 1971. pp. 163. (United States. Work Projects Administration. Division of Social Research. Research Monographs. 6)

GEDDES (ANN ELIZABETH) Trends in relief expenditures, 1910-1935; [reprint of work first published in Washington, 1937]. New York, 1971. pp. 117. (United States. Work Projects Administration. Division of Social Research. Research Monographs. 10)

BURNS (ARTHUR EDWARD) and WILLIAMS (EDWARD AINSWORTH) Federal work, security, and relief programs; [reprint of work first published in Washington, 1941]. New York, 1971. pp. 159. (United States. Work Projects Administration. Division of Social Research. Research Monographs. 24)

CAHN (EDGAR S.) and PASSETT (BARRY A.) eds. Citizen participation: effecting community change. New York, 1971. pp. 294.

ROMANYSHYN (JOHN M.) Social welfare: charity to justice. New York, [1971]. pp. 450. bibliog.

TRECKER (HARLEIGH BRADLEY) Social work administration: principles and practices. New York, [1971]. pp. 287. bibliog.

LEVITAN (SAR A.) and others. Work and welfare go together. Baltimore, 1972. pp. 143.

MARTIN (ERNEST WALTER) ed. Comparative development in social welfare. London, 1972. pp. 247. bibliogs.

[MONK (ABRAHAM) and others.] Social welfare planning: issues, values and policy directions; (with Summary report). Albany, New York State Temporary Commission to Revise the Social Services Law, 1972. 2 pts. (Interim Study Reports. Nos. 3 and 3-S).

SOCIAL, EDUCATIONAL RESEARCH AND DEVELOPMENT, INC. A model social service program for a county jail. New York, 1972. pp. 107.

GOALS for social welfare, 1973-1993: an overview of the next two decades; edited by Harleigh B. Trecker. New York, [1973]. pp. 288. bibliog.

KAHN (ALFRED J.) Social policy and social services. New York, [1973]. pp. 210. bibliog.

- Dictionaries and encyclopaedias

ENCYCLOPEDIA of social work; sixteenth issue;...Robert Morris, editor-in-chief. New York, [1971]. 2 vols. bibliogs.

- United States - Periodicals

CHAMBERS (CLARKE A.) Paul U. Kellogg and the Survey: voices for social welfare and social justice. Minneapolis, [1971]. pp. 283. bibliog.

- United States - California.

PUBLIC WELFARE IN CALIFORNIA; [pd. by] Department of Social Welfare [and] Human Relations Agency. a., 1970/71- Sacramento.

- United States - Illinois

ILLINOIS. Commission on Human Relations. Biennial report. bien., 1969/1970 (14th)- Chicago.

- United States - New York (City)

NEW YORK (CITY). Special Committee to Make an In-Depth Study of Human Resources Administration. Final report. [New York, 1969]. fo. (47). (Reproduced from the City Record, Aug. 5, 1969) Photographic copy.

- United States - New York (State)

NEW YORK (STATE). Temporary Commission to Revise the Social Services Law. 1972. An interim progress report, [including first, second and third interim reports, etc.; William E. Adams and subsequently William T. Smith, chairmen]. Albany, 1972. pp. 195.

SOCIAL SETTLEMENTS

- United States - New York

SIMKHOVITCH (MARY KINGSBURY) Neighborhood: my story of Greenwich House. New York, [1938]. pp. 301.

SOCIAL STABILITY

BARBER (BERNARD REUBEN) and INKELES (ALEX) eds. Stability and social change: (a volume in honor of Talcott Parsons). Boston, [1971]. pp. 451.

SOFRANKO (ANDREW J.) and BEALER (ROBERT C.) Unbalanced modernization and domestic instability: a comparative analysis. Beverly Hills, [1972]. pp. 83. bibliog.

SOCIAL STATUS

TESCH (CHRISTIAN) Die Prestigeordnung der Berufe als Masstab sozialer Wertvorstellungen in der DDR. [Erlangen-Nürnberg, 1970?]. pp. 350. bibliog.

GLASER (BARNEY G.) and STRAUSS (ANSELM LEONARD) Status passage. London, 1971. pp. 205.

SOCIAL SURVEYS

AGE CONCERN (THE NATIONAL OLD PEOPLE'S WELFARE COUNCIL). A short guide to social survey methods; [by Mark Abrams]. rev. ed. London, [1972]. pp. 23. bibliog.

SMITH (JOAN MACFARLANE) Interviewing in market and social research. London, 1972. pp. 169. bibliog.

WEINER (R.S.P.) Community self survey: a do it yourself guide. [Belfast], Northern Ireland Community Relations Commission, 1972. pp. 29.

HOPKINS (HARRY) The numbers game: the bland totalitarianism. London, 1973. pp. 310.

- Bibliography

BELSON (WILLIAM A.) and THOMPSON (BERYL ANNE) compilers. Bibliography on methods of social and business research. London, 1973. pp. 300.

- Costs

MONK (DONALD) The use of survey research organizations, and the costing of survey research. London, Social Science Research Council Survey Unit, [1972]. pp. 51. (Occasional Papers in Survey Research. 1)

- Denmark

SOCIALREFORMUNDERSØGELSERNE;... Studies for social reform, [by Jytte Ussing and others]. København, 1970-72. 4 parts (in 1). (Socialforskningsinstituttet. Publikationer. 43-44, 49, 53)

- Thailand

THOMLINSON (RALPH) and others. The methodology of the longitudinal study of social, economic, and demographic change. Bangkok, 1971. pp. 71. (Chulalongkorn University. Institute of Population Studies. Research Reports. No. 6)

- United Kingdom

MOSS (LOUIS) Survey research and government. [Toronto, 1968 or rather 1969]. fo. 19. (U.K. Social Survey. Papers. General Series. No. C. 67.)

DAVIDSON (JOAN) Outdoor recreation surveys: the design and use of questionnaires for site surveys. London, Countryside Commission, 1970. pp. 78. bibliog.

U.K. Countryside Commission. 1970. Outdoor recreation information: suggested standard classifications for use in questionnaire surveys. [London], 1970. pp. 34. bibliog.

GRAY (SHEILA) The electoral register: practical information for use when drawing samples, both for interview and postal surveys. [London],1971. fo. 18. (U.K. Social Survey. [Papers. Methodological Series.] No. M. 151. New Sampling Series. No. 3)

U.K. Social Survey. [Reports. New Series.] 477. Sample surveys in local authority areas, with particular reference to the handicapped and elderly; by Amelia I. Harris and Elizabeth Head; a guide commissioned by the Department of Health and Social Security. [London], 1971. pp. 69.

PERRY (N.H.) Greater London recreation study: final report on pre-tests. [London], 1972. pp. 41. (London. Greater London Council. Department of Planning and Tranportation. Research Memoranda. 383)

PERRY (N.H.) Greater London recreation study: report on fieldwork and coding. [London], 1973. pp. 60. (London. Greater London Council. Department of Planning and Transportation. Research Memoranda. 411)

PERRY (N.H.) Greater London recreation study: report on sampling procedures. [London], 1973. pp. 18. (London. Greater London Council. Department of Planning and Transportation. Research Memoranda. 407)

- United States

MORGAN (JAMES NEWTON) and SMITH (JAMES D.) A panel study of income dynamics: study design, procedures, and forms...: wave 1 ([and]2): a report on research in process under contract to the Office of Economic Opportunity. Ann Arbor, 1969. 2 vols.

SOCIAL VALUES

DALKEY (NORMAN) and others. Studies in the quality of life: Delphi and decision-making. Lexington, Mass., [1972]. pp. 161. bibliog.

SOCIAL WORK AS A PROFESSION

BRITISH ASSOCIATION OF SOCIAL WORKERS. A code of ethics for social work; [draft prepared by a working party]. London, [1972]. pp. 14. (Discussion Papers. No. 2)

TOREN (NINA) Social work: the case of a semi-profession. Beverly Hills, [1972]. pp. 264. bibliog.

SOCIAL WORK EDUCATION

INTERNATIONAL CONFERENCE ON SOCIAL WORK EDUCATION, POPULATION, AND FAMILY PLANNING, HAWAII, 1970. Population dynamics and family planning: a new responsibility for social work education; [papers of the conference sponsored by the Council on Social Work Education] edited by Katherine A. Kendall. New York, [1971]. pp. 159.

TIMMS (NOEL) '...and Renoir and Matisse and...'; an inaugural lecture delivered at the University of Bradford on 25 November 1971. [Bradford, 1972]. pp. 7.

ASSOCIATION OF BRITISH ADOPTION AGENCIES. Analysis of adoption and in-service training guide. London, [1972?]. pp. (20).

ECKLEIN (JOAN LEVIN) and LAUFFER (ARMAND A.) Community organizers and social planners: a volume of case and illustrative materials. New York, [1972]. pp. 378.

- Canada

CANADA. Statistics Canada. Statistical information on schools of social work in Canada. a., 1971 (1st issue)- Ottawa. In English and French.

- Denmark

DENMARK. Uddannelseskommissionen for det Sociale Område. 1970. Socialpaedagogiske uddannelsers indhold: betaenkning. [Copenhagen?], 1970. pp. 139. (Denmark. Betaenkninger. Nr. 547)

DENMARK. Uddannelseskommissionen for det Sociale Område. 1970. Uddannelse til kommunernes sociale forvaltning: betaenkning; [Henning Friis, chairman]. [Copenhagen?], 1970. pp. 167. (Denmark. Betaenkninger. Nr.548)

- India

NAGPAUL (HANS) The study of Indian society: a sociological analysis of social welfare and social work education. New Delhi, 1972. pp. 510. bibliog.

- Norway

LUND (BERNT H.) Utdanningen av sosialarbeidere i Norge: utredning og forslag. Oslo, 1963. pp. 92.

SOCIAL WORK EDUCATION - Underdeveloped areas
See UNDERDEVELOPED AREAS - Social work education

- United Kingdom

ASHLEY (BRIAN J.) Training for youth and community work in the 1970's. Leicester, 1971. pp. 17. (Youth Service Information Centre. Occasional Papers. 1)

SOCIAL WORK EDUCATION - United Kingdom (Cont'd.)

SOCIAL education: special day conference, 'The common ground', to identify...the ground common to workers in social education and to seek appropriate forms of association and servicing, November 26, 1971,...London; report. Leicester, [1971]. pp. 21. (Youth Service Information Centre. Occasional Papers. 3)

U.K. Advisory Council on Child Care. 1971. Fieldwork training for social work: discussion papers on six aspects of training for social work. London, 1971. pp. 215.

COUNCIL FOR TRAINING IN SOCIAL WORK [U.K.] Sociology Study Group. The teaching of sociology in social work courses; report; [J.H. Smith, chairman]. London, 1972. pp. 32. (Council for Training in Social Work [U.K.]. Discussion Papers. No. 5)

WATKINS (OWEN C.) Professional training for youth work: educational method at the National College for the Training of Youth Leaders, 1961-1970;...with chapters by Jean L. Clark and Joan E. Matthews. Leicester, [1972]. pp. 151. (Youth Service Information Centre. Reports. 4)

SOCIAL WORK WITH CHILDREN

BERRY (JULIET) Social work with children. London, 1972. pp. 180. bibliog.

SOCIAL WORK WITH DELINQUENTS AND CRIMINALS

- United Kingdom

HATTON (S.F.) London's bad boys. London, 1931. pp. 203.

SMITH (CYRIL S.) and others. The Wincroft Youth Project: a social-work programme in a slum area. London, 1972. pp. 283.

SOCIAL WORK WITH YOUTH

PATON (JOHN BROWN) Recreative instruction of young people;...a paper read at the Conference of the National Vigilance Association at Exeter Hall, March 18th, 1886. [London, 1886?]. pp. 7.

INTERREGIONAL SEMINAR ON THE TRAINING OF PROFESSIONAL AND VOLUNTARY YOUTH LEADERS, HOLTE, 1969. Report of the...seminar...[held at] Holte, Denmark, 6-22 October, 1969. (ST/TAO/SER.C/120). New York, United Nations, 1970. pp. 127.

CANADIAN COUNCIL ON SOCIAL DEVELOPMENT. A right to opportunity: a report on youth and social assistance. Ottawa, 1972. pp. 301.

- America, Latin

SEMINAR "JUGENDPFLEGE UND JUGENDFÜRSORGE", 1964. Bericht über das Seminar, etc. Berlin-Tegel, Reiherwerder, 1964. fo. 47,9,5. 29½cm.

- Germany

DIELMANN (KLAUS) Jugendarbeit der Gewerkschaften in der Bundesrepublik Deutschland: eine Untersuchung zur Sozialpolitik und Jugendhilfe. [Erlangen, 1968]. pp. v,289,vii-xxvii. bibliog.

VIERNSTEIN (NIKOLAUS) and GAENSSLEN (HERMANN) Materialien zur Situation der Jugendämter: Teilwiederholung der Erhebung der Deutschen Vereins [für öffentliche und private Fürsorge] ... von 1957/58. München, 1971. pp. 95. (Munich. Deutsches Jugendinstitut. Forschungsberichte. 02-1971)

- India

INDIA. Planning Commission. Programme Evaluation Organisation. 1967. Case studies of selected youth clubs. New Delhi, 1967. pp. 125.

- United Kingdom

HAYCOCKS (NORMAN) The voluntary organisations in the youth service. London, Methodist Youth Department, 1962. pp. 12. 18½cm.

U.K. Central Office of Information. Reference Division. 1963. Youth services in Britain. London, 1963. pp. 36. bibliog. 23½cm.

RINK REPORT, THE: (the experimental project with unattached young people in the West End of London), [pd. by Rink Club]. a., 1967-1969 (nos.[1]-3); ceased pbln. London.

MILSON (FREDERICK W.) Operation Integration Two: the coloured teenager in Birmingham. n.p., [1967?]. pp. 13. bibliog. (Westhill College of Education. Westhill Occasional Papers. No. 13)

STUDY GROUP ON THE YOUTH SERVICE IN LONDON. Report; [H.W. Hinds, chairman]. London, [1967]. pp. 52.

ASSOCIATION OF LONDON HOUSING ESTATES. Youth Advisory Service Project. Report on the ... Project, 1962-67. London, [1968?] fo. 131.

HOGAN (JAMES MARTIN) The relationship between youth service and secondary schools. Leeds, 1968. pp. 16. (Leeds. University. Institute of Education. Papers. No. 7)

NATIONAL ASSOCIATION OF YOUTH CLUBS. The relationships of the youth services with the adult community. London, [1968?]. pp. irreg.

KELLY (N. M.) Clubscape: a youth worker's view. London, [1969]. pp. 50.

LIVERPOOL. Liverpool Youth Organisations Committee. Special but not separate; a report, etc. Liverpool. [1969]. pp. 20.

YOUTH SERVICE DEVELOPMENT COUNCIL. Youth and community work in the 70s: proposals by the...Council. London, H.M.S.O., 1969. pp. 175.

YOUTH SERVICE INFORMATION CENTRE. Reports. 1. The Blenheim project, 1964-1969, etc. Leicester, 1970. pp. 17.

ASHLEY (BRIAN J.) Training for youth and community work in the 1970's. Leicester, 1971. pp. 17. (Youth Service Information Centre. Occasional Papers. 1)

LOVELL (GEORGE) The youth worker as a first-aid counsellor in impromptu situations. London, 1971. pp. 36.

SOCIAL education: special day conference, 'The common ground', to identify...the ground common to workers in social education and to seek appropriate forms of association and servicing, November 26, 1971,...London; report. Leicester, [1971]. pp. 21. (Youth Service Information Centre. Occasional Papers. 3)

STOTT (JOHN) Congregational minister. Development together: a discussion of some of the issues involved in community relations and youth work. London, 1971. pp. 23. bibliog. (Methodist Association of Youth Clubs. King George VI Memorial Lectures. [II])

U.K. Department of Education and Science. Schools Council. 1971. Co-operation between the youth service and schools. London, 1971. pp. 35. (Pamphlets. 8)

VENABLES (ETHEL) Teachers and youth workers: a study of their roles; the report of a research project undertaken for the Schools Council. London, 1971. pp. 128. (U.K. Department of Education and Science. Schools Council. Working Papers. No. 32)

DAVIES (BERNARD D.) and ROGERS (JENNIFER) eds. Working with youth. London, 1972. pp. 64.

HOLDEN (H.M.) Hoxton cafe project: report on seven years' work. Leicester, 1972. pp. 62. (Youth Service Information Centre. Reports. 3)

The ROLE of the professional youth worker: report of a day conference held at St.Anne's College, Oxford, on 30th September 1971, arranged by a joint working party of Western Region of the National Association of Youth Service Officers, and the Community and Youth Service Association. Leicester, 1972. pp. (10). (Youth Service Information Centre. Occasional Papers. 5)

SMITH (CYRIL S.) and others. The Wincroft Youth Project: a social-work programme in a slum area. London, 1972. pp. 283.

U.K. Social Survey. [Reports. New Series.] 437. The youth service and similar provision for young people; by Margaret Bone, assisted by Elizabeth Ross; an enquiry carried out on behalf of the Department of Education and Science. London, 1972. pp. 292. bibliog.

WATKINS (OWEN C.) Professional training for youth work: educational method at the National College for the Training of Youth Leaders, 1961-1970;...with chapters by Jean L. Clark and Joan E. Matthews. Leicester, [1972]. pp. 151. (Youth Service Information Centre. Reports. 4)

YOUTH SERVICE INFORMATION CENTRE. Youth service provision for physically and mentally handicapped young people. Leicester, 1972. pp. 110. (YSIC Surveys. 1)

YOUTH SERVICE INFORMATION CENTRE. Youth service provision for young immigrants. Leicester, 1972. pp. 67. (YSIC Surveys. 2)

- United Kingdom - Scotland

GLASGOW COUNCIL OF JUVENILE ORGANISATIONS. Handbook for the year 1918-19. Glasgow, 1918. pp. 115.

- United States

HERMAN (MELVIN) and MUNK (MICHAEL) Decision-making in poverty programs: case studies from youth-work agencies. New York, Colombia U. P., 1968. pp. xvii, 181. 23½cm.

KLEIN (MALCOLM W.) Street gangs and street workers. Englewood Cliffs, [1971]. pp. 338. bibliogs.

SOCIAL WORKERS

LAMPERT (HERBERT) ed. Social work: challenge and change; highlights of Montreal's 3rd Academic Assembly on Social Work. [Ottawa], 1967. pp. 17. (Canada's Mental Health. Supplements. 55)

- Canada

LAPPIN (BEN) Community workers and the social work tradition: their quest for a role examined in Israel and in Canada. Toronto, [1971]. pp. 191. bibliog.

- Denmark

UDDANNELSE af socionomer; betaenkning afgivet af de sociale højskoler og Uddannelseskommissionen for det Sociale Område; [Henning Friis, chairman]. [Copenhagen?], 1970. pp. 42. (Denmark. Betaenkninger. Nr. 549)

- Germany

EVANGELISCHE KIRCHE IN DEUTSCHLAND. Hauptgeschäftsstelle. Innere Mission und Hilfswerk. Richtlinien für Arbeitsverträge in Anstalten und Einrichtungen, die dem Werk Innere Mission und Hilfswerk...angeschlossen sind; vom 1. Juli 1962; ([with] Überleitungsregelung...[and] Erste Ergänzung...Stand 1. Oktober 1963). Stuttgart, 1962-63. 3 pts. (in 1 vol.).

- Israel

LAPPIN (BEN) Community workers and the social work tradition: their quest for a role examined in Israel and in Canada. Toronto, [1971]. pp. 191. bibliog.

- Netherlands

NETHERLANDS. Centraal Bureau voor de Statistiek. Statistiek van de gezinsverzorging en gezinshulp. a., 1969 [1st issue]- 's-Gravenhage.

- Norway

NORWAY. Komitéen for Internasjonale Sosialpolitiske Saker. Social and Labour News from Norway. 1962. No.1. Social work: an old trade but a new profession; [by] Bernt H. Lund. Oslo, 1962. fo. 6.

- United Kingdom

TOWARDS insight: for the worker with people; papers given at Shotton Hall conferences...by W.H. Allchin and others. Shrewsbury, 1971. pp. 78.

JORDAN (WILLIAM) The social worker in family situations. London, 1972. pp. 151. bibliog.

The ROLE of the professional youth worker: report of a day conference held at St.Anne's College, Oxford, on 30th September 1971, arranged by a joint working party of Western Region of the National Association of Youth Service Officers and the Community and Youth Service Association. Leicester, 1972. pp. (10). (Youth Service Information Centre. Occasional Papers. 5)

STEVENSON (OLIVE) Claimant or client?: a social worker's view of the Supplementary Benefits Commission. London, 1973. pp. 234. bibliog. (National Institute for Social Work Training. National Institute Social Services Library. No. 25)

SOCIALISM

HANSON (JOHN) The dissection of Owenism dissected; or, A socialist's answer to Mr. Frederic R. Lees's pamphlet entitled "A calm examination of the fundamental principles of Robert Owen's misnamed rational system". Leeds, Hobson, 1838. pp. 34.

PROUDHON (PIERRE JOSEPH) Organisation du crédit et de la circulation, et solution du problème social. 2nd ed. Paris, Garnier, 1848. pp. 43.

SOCIALISM (Cont'd.)

[KOL (HENRI HUBERT VAN)] Kapitalisme en socialisme; of, Arbeidsloon, zooals het is, en zooals het worden moet; door Rienzi [pseud.]. Gent, 1888-89. 2 vols. (in 1). (Reprinted from De Toekomst, 1886)

HUBER (JOHANNES) Die Philosophie in der Sozialdemokratie;...zuerst veröffentlicht in der Beilage zur "Allgemeinen Zeitung" 1878. München, [1894]. pp. 40.

EEDEN (FREDERIK VAN) Socialism without political revolution: an address delivered before the Economic Club of New York ... April 1, 1908. New York, 1908. pp. 23.

LANG (OTTO) of Zürich, Oberrichter. Sozialismus oder Kapitalismus? [Bern, 1919]. pp. 128.

MARR (HEINZ) Proletarisches Verlangen: ein Beitrag zur Psychologie der Massen. Jena, 1921. pp. 71. bibliog.

POHLE (LUDWIG) Kapitalismus und Sozialismus: Betrachtungen über die Grundlagen der gegenwärtigen Wirtschaftsordnung, etc. 3rd ed. Leipzig, 1921. pp. 181.

RENNER (KARL) Wege der Verwirklichung;...Betrachtungen über politische Demokratie, Wirtschaftsdemokratie und Sozialismus, etc. Berlin, 1929. pp. 141.

HICKS (GEORGE) The struggle for socialism: the immediate tasks of the working-class movement in the present situation. London, [1932?] pp. 14.

LEICHTER (OTTO) Die Sprengung des Kapitalismus: die Wirtschaftspolitik der Sozialisierung. Wien, 1932. pp. 171.

NEARING (HELEN KOTHE) and NEARING (SCOTT) Socialists around the world. New York, 1958. pp. 160.

HINDELS (JOSEF) Der Sozialismus kommt nicht von selbst. Wien, [1959]. pp. 131.

O nekotorykh sotsial-reformistskikh kontseptsiiakh gosudarstva. Moskva, 1964. pp. 130.

PENFENTENYO (MICHEL DE) Socialisme: débâcle ou replâtrage; à propos du livre de Claude Bruclain, Le Socialisme et l'Europe. Paris, [1967]. pp. 45.

WARD (BENJAMIN N.) The socialist economy: a study of organizational alternatives. New York, [1967]. pp. 272.

TROTSKII (LEV DAVYDOVICH) Writings of Leon Trotsky ...; (edited by George Breitman [and others]). New York, 1969 in progress.

FRANK (PIERRE) and others. Key problems of the transition from capitalism to socialism; three articles. New York, 1969 repr. 1970. pp. 63.

ALBERTINI (JEAN MARIE) Capitalismes et socialismes à l'épreuve. Paris, [1970]. pp. 304. bibliog.

ANSART (PIERRE) Naissance de l'anarchisme: esquisse d'une explication sociologique du proudhonisme. Paris, 1970. pp. 261. bibliog.

GOL'MAN (LEV ISAAKOVICH) Ot Soiuza kommunistov k Pervomu Internatsionalu: deiatel'nost' Karla Marksa v 1852-1864gg. Moskva, 1970. pp. 476.

MIHALIK (ISTVÁN) and SZIGETI (ENDRE) Fejezetek a marxista-leninista közgazdaságtan történetéből. Budapest, 1970. pp. 431. bibliog.

1971

AMBRÉE (KURT) and MANN (HELMUT) eds. Das Preissystem in der sozialistischen Industrie. Berlin, 1971. pp. 247. bibliog.

BASMANOV (M.I.) Antirevoliutsionnaia sushchnost' sovremennogo trotskizma. Moskva, 1971. pp. 230.

BRAVO (GIAN MARIO) ed. Il pensiero socialista, 1797-1848: testi e note biografiche. Roma, 1971. pp. 1289. bibliog.

CANNON (JAMES PATRICK) Speeches for socialism. New York, 1971. pp. 462.

COATES (KEN) Essays on industrial democracy; [reprinted from various periodicals]. Nottingham, 1971. pp. 64.

CORRADO (GIOVANNI BATTISTA) God-made socialism. American ed. New York, [1971]. pp. 126. bibliog.

GROTH (ALEXANDER J.) Major ideologies: an interpretative survey of democracy, socialism, and nationalism. New York, [1971]. pp. 244.

HANEY (GERHARD) Die Demokratie: Wahrheit, Illusionen und Verfälschungen. Frankfurt a. M., 1971. pp. 334.

LAVERGNE (BERNARD) Le socialisme à visage humain: l'ordre coopératif. Paris, 1971. pp. 142. bibliog.

LEFORT (CLAUDE) Eléments d'une critique de la bureaucratie. Genève, 1971. pp. 367.

LESER (NORBERT) Die Odyssee des Marxismus: auf dem Weg zum Sozialismus. Wien, [1971]. pp. 432.

MALLET (SERGE) Le pouvoir ouvrier: bureaucratie ou démocratie ouvrière. Paris, [1971]. pp. 247.

NOVACK (GEORGE) Democracy and revolution. New York, 1971. pp. 286. bibliog.

PETERSEN (JØRN HENRIK) Aspekter af den økonomiske problematik i en centraldirigeret økonomi. Odense, 1971. pp. 311. bibliog. (Odense Universitet. Studies in History and Social Sciences. vol. 2)

POPOV (SERGEI IVANOVICH) Sotsial-reformizm: teoriia i politika. Moskva, 1971. pp. 271.

RUEHLE (OTTO) Baupläne für eine neue Gesellschaft;.. aus dem Nachlass herausgegeben von Henry Jacoby. Reinbek bei Hamburg, 1971. pp. 251. bibliog.

ŠIK (OTA) Demokratische und sozialistische Plan- und Marktwirtschaft. Zürich, [1971]. pp. 47. bibliog.

SUPEK (RUDI) and BOŠNJAK (BRANKO) eds. Jugoslawien denkt anders: Marxismus und Kritik des etatistischen Sozialismus; (ins Deutsche übertragen von Eleonore von Steiner). Wien, [1971]. pp. 280.

SWEEZY (PAUL MARLOR) and BETTELHEIM (CHARLES) On the transition to socialism; [articles from Monthly Review, 1967-1971]. New York, [1971]. pp. 122.

ZINN (KARL GEORG) Sozialistische Planwirtschaftstheorie: Grundlagen und aktuelle Probleme der Arbeitswertlehre. Stuttgart, [1971]. pp. 246. bibliog.

1972

AFANAS'EV (VIKTOR GRIGOR'EVICH) Socialism and communism; (translated from the Russian by J. Gibbons). Moscow, 1972. pp. 182.

ESSAYS on socialist humanism in honour of the centenary of Bertrand Russell, 1872-1970; edited by Ken Coates. Nottingham, 1972. pp. 217.

FOURIER (FRANÇOIS CHARLES MARIE) L'ordre subversif: trois textes sur la civilisation. Paris, [1972]. pp. 251. bibliog.

FOURIER (FRANÇOIS CHARLES MARIE) The Utopian vision of Charles Fourier: selected texts on work, love and passionate attraction; translated, edited and with an introduction by Jonathan Beecher and Richard Bienvenu. London, 1972. pp. 427. bibliog.

GARAUDY (ROGER) L'alternative. Paris, [1972]. pp. 252.

HARRINGTON (MICHAEL) b. 1928. Socialism. New York, [1972]. pp. 436.

HOWE (IRVING) ed. A handbook of socialist thought. London, 1972. pp. 850.

KACHANOV (VALERII ANDREEVICH) and SHUMSKII (VLADISLAV STANISLAVOVICH) Politika klassovogo razoruzheniia: antikommunizm v ideino-politicheskom arsenale pravoi sotsial-demokratii. Moskva, 1972. pp. 104.

MACDONALD (JAMES RAMSAY) Political writings; edited...by Bernard Barker. London, [1972]. pp. 259. bibliog.

MAZZINI (GIUSEPPE) Processo al socialismo; a cura di Adrian Popa. Milano, [1972]. pp. 239.

NOSOV (ALEKSEI VASIL'EVICH) Utopicheskii sotsializm i revoliutsionnyi demokratizm. Khar'kov, 1972. pp. 159. bibliog.

PERTICONE (GIACOMO) Socialismo difficile o anarchismo selvaggio? Milano, [1972]. pp. 164.

POLIANSKII (FEDOR IAKOVLEVICH) Sotsializm i sovremennyi reformizm. Moskva, 1972. pp. 423.

PROTIV burzhuaznykh i melkoburzhuaznykh teorii sotsializma. Moskva, 1972. pp. 295.

ROCARD (MICHEL) Questions à l'état socialiste. [Paris, 1972]. pp. 187.

SALYCHEV (STEPAN STEPANOVICH) "Novye levye": s kem i protiv kogo. Moskva, 1972. pp. 96.

SANAKOEV (SHALVA PARSADANOVICH) The world socialist system: main problems, stages of development. Moscow, 1972. pp. 410.

SHERMAN (HOWARD JAY) Radical political economy: capitalism and socialism from a Marxist-humanist perspective. New York, [1972]. pp. 431. bibliog.

ŠIK (OTA) Der dritte Weg: die marxistisch-leninistische Theorie und die moderne Industriegesellschaft. Hamburg, 1972. pp. 450. bibliog.

SOCIALISM and the environment: essays by Malcolm Caldwell [and others]. Nottingham, 1972. pp. 116.

1973

TROTSKII (LEV DAVYDOVICH) Writings of Leon Trotsky ...; (edited by George Breitman [and others]). 2nd ed. New York, 1973 in progress.

BRUS (WŁODZIMIERZ) The economics and politics of socialism: collected essays. London, 1973. pp. 117.

DUMONT (RENÉ) and MAZOYER (MARCEL) Socialisms and development;...translated [from the French] by Rupert Cunningham. London, 1973. pp. 352. bibliog.

GORZ (ANDRÉ) Socialism and revolution;... translated by Norman Denny. Garden City, N.Y., 1973. pp. 270.

KENDALL (WALTER) State ownership, workers' control and socialism. Nottingham, [1973]. pp. 15. (Institute for Workers' Control. Pamphlet Series. No.35)

MORRIS (WILLIAM) Political writings of William Morris; edited and with an introduction by A.L. Morton. London, 1973. pp. 246.

ROBERTS (ERNIE) Workers' control. London, 1973. pp. 308. bibliog.

STOJANOVIĆ (SVETOZAR) Between ideals and reality: a critique of socialism and its future; translated [from the Serbo-Croat] by Gerson S. Sher. New York, 1973. pp. 222.

- Bibliography

DUTSCHKE (RUDI) compiler. Ausgewählte und kommentierte Bibliographie des revolutionären Sozialismus von K. Marx bis in die Gegenwart. Heidelberg, 1969. pp. 49.

IWK: internationale wissenschaftliche Korrespondenz zur Geschichte der deutschen Arbeiterbewegung. Sonderhefte. 1. Neue Literatur zur Geschichte der deutschen Arbeiterbewegung und angrenzender Gebiete. Berlin, 1969. pp. 69.

- Dictionaries and encyclopaedias

WOERTERBUCH der Ökonomie: Sozialismus; (herausgegeben von Willi Ehlert [and others]). 2nd ed. Berlin, 1969. pp. 940.

- History

NOMAD (MAX) Rebels and renegades; [reprint of work published in 1932]. New York, 1968. pp. 430. bibliog.

LEEUW (A.S. DE) Het socialisme en de natie: van het "Communistisch manifest" tot de strijd tegen het fascisme; [reprint of work originally published in Amsterdam 1939]. Nijmegen, 1971. pp. 376.

KUZNETSOV (KUZ'MA TITOVICH) Utopicheskii sotsializm - odin iz teoreticheskikh istochnikov marksizma. Moskva, 1965. pp. 120.

BRAVO (GIAN MARIO) Storia del socialismo 1789-1848: il pensiero socialista prima di Marx. Roma, 1971. pp. 455. bibliog.

HISTOIRE générale du socialisme; publiée sous la direction de Jacques Droz. Paris, [1972 in progress]. bibliogs.

ISTORIIA obshchestvennoi mysli: sovremennye problemy. Moskva, 1972. pp. 535.

KILROY-SILK (ROBERT M.) Socialism since Marx. London, 1972. pp. 362. bibliog.

LEIST (OLEG ERNESTOVICH) Politicheskaia ideologiia utopicheskikh sotsialistov Frantsii v XVIII veke. Moskva, 1972. pp. 157.

SCHRAEPLER (ERNST) Handwerkerbünde und Arbeitervereine, 1830-1853: die politische Tätigkeit deutscher Sozialisten von Wilhelm Weitling bis Karl Marx. Berlin, 1972. pp. 597. bibliog. (Berlin. Freie Universität. Friedrich-Meinecke-Institut. Historische Kommission zu Berlin. Veröffentlichungen. Band 34)

SOCIALISM, CHRISTIAN

JOHN Groser: East London priest; edited by Kenneth Brill. London, 1971. pp. 246. bibliog.

BREIPOHL (RENATE) ed. Dokumente zum religiösen Sozialismus in Deutschland. München, 1972. pp. 244. bibliog.

SOCIALISM AND AGRICULTURE

SCHWEIZER (HEINRICH) Sozialistische Agrartheorie und Landwirtschaftspolitik in China und der Sowjetunion: ein Modell für Entwicklungsländer? Bern, [1972]. pp. 266. bibliog.

SOCIALISM AND CATHOLIC CHURCH

GOLDSTEIN (DAVID) and AVERY (MARTHA MOORE) Bolshevism: its cure. Boston, Mass., [1919]. pp. 414.

BODART (JEAN) Catholicisme et socialisme: contradictions irréductibles, collaborations nécessaires; (leçon donnée à la XIVe Semaine Sociale Universitaire Catholique le 14 janvier 1937). Marchiennes-au-Pont, [imprint, 1937?]. pp. 15.

CONNOLLY (JAMES) Irish republican leader. Selected political writings; edited and introduced by Owen Dudley Edwards and Bernard Ransom. London, 1973. pp. 382. bibliog.

PELLEGRINI (RINALDO) Socialismo, Chiesa, capitalismo. Padova, 1973. pp. 391.

SOCIALISM AND EDUCATION

KEMSIES (FERDINAND) Socialistische und ethische Erziehung im Jahre 2000. Berlin, 1893. pp. 142

SOCIALISM AND RELIGION

SANDON (LÉON) Les socialistes et la société: (chapitre premier: De la religion). Paris, Garnier, 1849. pp. 50.

CAMARA (HELDER) Archbishop of Olinda and Recife. Revolution through peace;... translated from the Portuguese by Amparo McLean. New York, [1971]. pp. 149.

SOCIALISM AND YOUTH

MUELLER (EMIL PETER) Juso-Sozialismus: Programm und Strategie der Jungsozialisten in der SPD. Köln, [1972]. pp. 115. bibliog.

MUELLER (GUENTHER) Rote Zelle Deutschland; oder, Was wollen die Jungsozialisten wirklich? Stuttgart, [1972]. pp. 143.

JAHNKE (KARL HEINZ) and others. Geschichte der deutschen Arbeiterjugendbewegung, 1904-1945. Berlin, [1973]. pp. 632. bibliog.

SOCIALISM IN AFRICA

NATIONALISMUS und Sozialismus im Befreiungskampf der Völker Asiens und Afrikas: (Protokollband der Sektion I der Tagung des Instituts für Orientforschung der Deutschen Akademie der Wissenschaften zu Berlin...1967; herausgegeben von Horst Krüger). Berlin, 1970. pp. 468. (Deutsche Akademie der Wissenschaften zu Berlin. Institut für Orientforschung. Veröffentlichungen. 74) In various languages.

VEREINIGUNG VON AFRIKANISTEN IN DEUTSCHLAND. Jahrestagung, 2., 1970. Theoretische Probleme des Sozialismus in Afrika: Négritude und Arusha-Deklaration;...herausgegeben von Gerhard Grohs. Hamburg, [1971]. pp. 288. bibliogs. (Vereinigung von Afrikanisten in Deutschland. Schriften. Band 2)

BENOT (YVES) Idéologies des indépendances africaines. 2nd ed. Paris, 1972. pp. 538.

SOCIALISM IN ALGERIA

GUERIN (DANIEL) L'Algérie caporalisée?: suite de L'Algérie qui se cherche. Paris, 1965. pp. 96.

ECKL (JUERGEN) Algerien: Sozialismus in einem islamischen Land. Frankfurt am Main, 1971. pp. 92.

SOCIALISM IN ARAB COUNTRIES

PAJETTA (GIANCARLO) Socialismo e mondo arabo: rapporto presentato alla I. commissione del Comitato Centrale del PCI, febbraio 1970. Roma, [1970]. pp. 113.

SAID (ABDEL MOGHNY) and AHMED (M. SAMIR) Arab socialism; [including an abridged translation of the National Charter submitted by President Nasser to the National Congress of the U.A.R., 21 May 1962]. London, [1972]. pp. 137.

SOCIALISM IN ARMENIA

ARUTIUNIAN (A.M.) Revoliutsionnoe dvizhenie v Armenii, 1905-1907 gg. Erevan, 1970. pp. 312.

- Bibliography

OGANESIAN (DZH.) compiler. [V.I. Lenin i Armenii: bibliograficheskii ukazatel']. Erevan, 1970. pp. 201. In Armenian and Russian.

SOCIALISM IN ASIA

NATIONALISMUS und Sozialismus im Befreiungskampf der Völker Asiens und Afrikas: (Protokollband der Sektion I der Tagung des Instituts für Orientforschung der Deutschen Akademie der Wissenschaften zu Berlin...1967; herausgegeben von Horst Krüger). Berlin, 1970. pp. 468. (Deutsche Akademie der Wissenschaften zu Berlin. Institut für Orientforschung. Veröffentlichungen. 74) In various languages.

SOCIALISM IN AUSTRIA

STRASSER (PETER) Sozialistische Initiative: Reden und Aufsätze. Wien, [1963]. pp. 219.

LEICHTER (KAETHE) Leben und Werk; herausgegeben von Herbert Steiner. Wien, [1973]. pp. 525. bibliog. (Ludwig-Boltzmann-Institut für Geschichte der Arbeiterbewegung. Veröffentlichungen)

SOCIALISM IN AZERBAIJAN

AGAMIROV (MIDKHET) Iz istorii bor'by za marksistsko-leninskoe uchenie v Azerbaidzhane, 1905-1907 gg. Baku, 1971. pp. 190.

SOCIALISM IN BELGIUM

De EERSTE internationale in België: de Belgische afdelingen. Antwerpen, 1964. pp. 49. (Mens en Taak. 1964. Nr. 4)

PIERSON (MARC ANTOINE) Actualiteit van het socialisme. [Ghent, 1972?]. pp. 224.

SOCIALISM IN BULGARIA

KLINCHAROV (IVAN G.) Istoriia na rabotnichesko-to dvizhenie v Bŭlgariia, 1882-1893. Sofiia, 1926. pp. 84.

SOCIALISM IN CANADA

TEEPLE (GARY) ed. Capitalism and the national question in Canada. Toronto, [1972]. pp. 256.

SOCIALISM IN CHILE

ALLENDE (SALVADOR) Nuestro camino al socialismo: la via chilena; seleccion de Joan E. Garces. Buenos Aires, 1971. pp. 175.

CHILE: busqueda de un nuevo socialismo; [by] Alejandro Foxley [and others; papers presented at a seminar organized by the Centro de Estudios de Planificacion Nacional]. Santiago de Chile, [1971]. pp. 266.

DEBRAY (REGIS) Conversations with Allende: socialism in Chile; (translated from the original French and Spanish). London, 1971. pp. 190.

The CHILEAN road to socialism: proceedings of an ODEPLAN-IDS Round Table, March 1972; edited by J. Ann Zammit with co-operation from Gabriel Palma; [a conference sponsored by the Chilean National Planning Office and the Institute of Development Studies, Sussex University]. Brighton, 1973. pp. 465. bibliog.

JOHNSON (DALE L.) ed. The Chilean road to socialism. Garden City, N.Y., 1973. pp. 546.

SOCIALISM IN CUBA

DUMONT (RENÉ) Cuba est-il socialiste? Paris, [1970]. pp. 248. bibliog.

SOCIALISM IN CZECHOSLOVAKIA

KOTEK (MIROSLAV) Česká sociální demokracie za války. Praha, 1920. pp. 62.

PAGE (BENJAMIN B.) The Czechoslovak reform movement, 1963-1968: a study in the theory of socialism. Amsterdam, 1973. pp. 126. bibliog.

SOCIALISM IN DENMARK

SCHMIEDERER (URSULA) Die Sozialistische Volkspartei Dänemarks: eine Partei der Neuen Linken. Frankfurt/M., [1969]. pp. 192. bibliog.

JOHANSSON (MAGNUS) Al den snak om socialisme: samtaler med arbejdere. [Copenhagen, 1972]. pp. 135.

SOCIALISM IN EASTERN EUROPE

RÉVÉSZ (LÁSZLÓ) Die Liquidierung der Sozialdemokratie in Osteuropa. Bern, [1971]. pp. 116.

MATULL (WILHELM) Ostdeutschlands Arbeiterbewegung: Abriss ihrer Geschichte, Leistung und Opfer. Würzburg, 1973. pp. 590. bibliog. (Göttinger Arbeitskreis. Ostdeutsche Beiträge. Band 53)

SOCIALISM IN EASTERN GERMANY

GRAF (HERBERT) and SEILER (GUENTHER) Wahl und Wahlrecht im Klassenkampf. Frankfurt am Main, [1971]. pp. 441.

KELLER (DIETMAR) Lebendige Demokratie: der Übergang von der antifaschistischen zur sozialistischen Demokratie in der volkseigenen Industrie der DDR, 1948 bis 1952. Berlin, 1971. pp. 323.

HAGER (KURT) Socialist cultural policy. Dresden, 1972. pp. 68.

The SENSE of life: the welfare of man. Dresden, [1972]. pp. 46.

SOCIALISM IN EGYPT

EL KOSHERI MAHFOUZ ( ) Socialisme et pouvoir en Egypte. Paris, 1972. pp. 292. bibliog.

SOCIALISM IN EUROPE

[SHIFRIN (ALEKSANDR MIKHAILOVICH)] Sozialismus, Krieg und Europa; ([by] Max Werner [pseud.]). Strasbourg, 1938. pp. 165.

NIEKISCH (ERNST) Europäische Bilanz. Potsdam, 1951. pp. 392.

DERFLER (LESLIE) Socialism since Marx: a century of the European left. London, 1973. pp. 216. bibliogs.

SOCIALISM IN FRANCE

RECLUS (JEAN JACQUES ÉLISÉE) À mon frère le paysan. Paris, 1911. pp. 8. (Temps Nouveaux. Publications. No.11)

PUECH (JULES L.) Les saint-simoniens dans l'Aude, 1833: (contribution à l'étude des idées sociales avant 1848). Carcassonne, [192-?]. pp. 31.

HERVE (PIERRE) La libération trahie. Paris, [1945]. pp. 217.

PAILLET (MARC) Vers une société nouvelle. [Paris, 1966]. pp. 30. (Convention des Institutions Républicaines. Cahiers. 2)(Supplément à "Combat Républicain", no.14, Mars 1966)

FAUCHER (JEAN ANDRE) 13 mai 1958-13 mai 1968: la gauche française sous de Gaulle. Paris, [1969]. pp. 288.

ESTIER (CLAUDE) Journal d'un fédéré: la Fédération de la Gauche au jour le jour, 1965-1969. [Paris, 1970]. pp. 275.

CRAIPEAU (YVAN) Le mouvement trotskyste en France: des origines aux enseignements de mai 68. Paris, [1971]. pp. 285.

LOSCHAK (DANIELE) La Convention des Institutions Républicaines: François Mitterrand et le socialisme. [Paris, 1971]. pp. 96. bibliog.

MAIRE (EDMOND) Pour un socialisme démocratique: contribution de la C[onfédération] F[rançaise] D[émocratique des] T[ravailleurs]. Paris, [1971]. pp. 168.

SEMAINE DE LA PENSEE MARXISTE, 1971. 100 ans après la Commune: problèmes de la révolution socialiste en France;... avec la participation de G. Destanne de Bernis [and others]. Paris, [1971]. pp. 285

BLUM (LEON) Socialisme démocratique. [Paris, 1972]. pp. 215. bibliog.

DEPREUX (EDOUARD) Souvenirs d'un militant: cinquante ans de lutte, de la social-démocratie au socialisme, 1918-1968. [Paris, 1972]. pp. 608.

HERZOG (PHILIPPE) L'union populaire et la maîtrise de l'économie. Paris, 1972. pp. 224.

SOCIALISM IN FRANCE (Cont'd.)

MASSON (EMILE) Les Bretons et le socialisme; texte de présentation et notes par Jean-Yves Guiomar. Paris, 1972. pp. 287. bibliog. (Paris. Université de Paris I (Panthéon-Sorbonne). Centre d'Histoire du Syndicalisme. Collection)

POPEREN (JEAN) La gauche française: le nouvel âge, 1958-1965. Paris, [1972]. pp. 492.

SOCIALISM IN GERMANY

[GEL'FAND (ALEKSANDR LAZAREVICH)] Die Reichstagswahlen und die Arbeiterschaft; von Parvus, [pseud]. Leipzig, 1907. pp. 43.

SUENDEN des Freisinns: Material zur Bekämpfung der fortschrittlichen Volkspartei; [presented by the Parteivorstand of the Sozialdemokratische Partei Deutschlands]. Berlin, 1911. pp. 64.

BRUHNS (JULIUS) "Es klingt im Sturm ein altes Lied!-": aus der Jugendzeit der Sozialdemokratie. Stuttgart, 1921. pp. 109.

KLUEHS (FRANZ) Der Aufstieg: Führer durch die Geschichte der deutschen Arbeiterbewegung. Berlin, 1921. pp. 112. bibliog.

TROTSKII (LEV DAVYDOVICH) Der einzige Weg. Berlin, 1932. pp. 62.

LINDAU (RUDOLF) Probleme der Geschichte der deutschen Arbeiterbewegung. Berlin, [1947]. pp. 63.

WINZER (OTTO) Sozialistische Politik?: eine kritische Stellungnahme zu Reden und Aufsätzen von Dr. Kurt Schumacher. Berlin, [1947]. pp. 112.

LIEBKNECHT (WILHELM PHILIPP MARTIN CHRISTIAN LUDWIG) and others, defendants. Der Leipziger Hochverratsprozess vom Jahre 1872; neu herausgegeben von Karl-Heinz Leidigkeit. Berlin, 1960. pp. 536.

BEBEL (AUGUST) and KAUTSKY (KARL) August Bebels Briefwechsel mit Karl Kautsky; herausgegeben von Karl Kautsky Jr. Assen, 1971. pp. 394. bibliog. (International Institute of Social History. Quellen und Untersuchungen zur Geschichte der Deutschen und Österreichischen Arbeiterbewegung. Neue Folge. 2)

BROUE (PIERRE) Révolution en Allemagne 1917-1923. [Paris, 1971]. pp. 988. bibliog.

HELLER (HERMANN) Constitutional lawyer. Gesammelte Schriften; ...herausgegeben von Martin Drath [and others]. Leiden, 1971. 3 vols. bibliog.

KRAMER (DIETER) Reform und Revolution bei Marx und Engels. Köln, 1971. pp. 201 bibliog.

LUXEMBURG (ROSA) Gesammelte Werke; (Leitung der Redaktion: G. Radczun). Berlin, 1972 in progress.

FUELBERTH (GEORG) Proletarische Partei und bürgerliche Literatur: Auseinandersetzungen in der deutschen Sozialdemokratie... über Möglichkeiten und Grenzen einer sozialistischen Literaturpolitik. Neuwied, 1972. pp. 202. bibliog.

LUXEMBURG (ROSA) Selected political writings; edited and introduced by Robert Looker; translated from the German, etc. London, 1972. pp. 309. bibliog.

MAYER (GUSTAV) Professor at Berlin University. Arbeiterbewegung und Obrigkeitsstaat: [essays originally published 1907-38]; herausgegeben von Hans-Ulrich Wehler. Bonn-Bad Godesberg, [1972]. pp. 192. (Friedrich-Ebert-Stiftung. Forschungsinstitut. Schriftenreihe. Band 92)

SCHRAEPLER (ERNST) Handwerkerbünde und Arbeitervereine 1830-1853: die politische Tätigkeit deutscher Sozialisten von Wilhelm Weitling bis Karl Marx. Berlin, 1972. pp. 597. bibliog. (Berlin. Freie Universität. Friedrich-Meinecke-Institut. Historische Kommission zu Berlin. Veröffentlichungen. Band 34)

MATULL (WILHELM) Ostdeutschlands Arbeiterbewegung: Abriss ihrer Geschichte, Leistung und Opfer. Würzburg, 1973. pp. 590. bibliog. (Göttinger Arbeitskreis. Ostdeutsche Beiträge. Band 53)

- Bibliography

IWK: internationale wissenschaftliche Korrespondenz zur Geschichte der deutschen Arbeiterbewegung. Sonderhefte. 1. Neue Literatur zur Geschichte der deutschen Arbeiterbewegung und angrenzender Gebiete. Berlin, 1969. pp. 69.

- Dictionaries and encyclopaedias

SACHWOERTERBUCH der Geschichte Deutschlands und der deutschen Arbeiterbewegung; (herausgegeben von Horst Bartel [and others]). Berlin, 1969-70. 2 vols.

SOCIALISM IN GUYANA

SINGH (PAUL GAGRAG) Guyana: socialism in a plural society. London, 1972. pp. 24. (Fabian Society. Research Series. [No.] 307)

SOCIALISM IN INDIA

GHOSE (SANKAR) Socialism and communism in India. Bombay, 1971. pp. 468. bibliog.

SOCIALISM in India: [papers of a seminar sponsored by the Nehru Memorial Museum and Library]; edited by B.R. Nanda. Delhi, [1972]. pp. 299. bibliog.

GHOSE (SANKAR) Socialism, democracy and nationalism in India. Bombay, 1973. pp. 503. bibliog.

SOCIALISM IN IRELAND

BEDARIDA (FRANÇOIS) Le socialisme et la nation: James Connolly et l'Irlande. Paris, [1965?]. pp. 31. bibliog. (Extrait de Le Mouvement Social. No. 52, 1965)

EDWARDS (OWEN DUDLEY) The mind of an activist: James Connolly: the centenary lecture delivered on 10 May, 1968, under the auspices of the Irish Congress of Trade Unions, in Liberty Hall. Dublin [1971]. pp. 132.

CONNOLLY (JAMES) Irish republican leader. Selected political writings; edited and introduced by Owen Dudley Edwards and Bernard Ransom. London, 1973. pp. 382. bibliog.

SOCIALISM IN ITALY

FRONTE GIOVANILE EMIGRATI "RISCOSSA COMUNISTA". Lottiamo contro il capitalismo e contro l'imperialismo per un'Italia socialista, etc. Milano, [1969]. pp. 22.

BRAVO (GIAN MARIO) ed. Scritti di socialisti. Napoli, [1972]. pp. 679. bibliogs.

CALOGERO (GUIDO) Difesa del liberalsocialismo ed altri saggi;... a cura di Michele Schiavone e Dino Cofrancesco. 2nd ed. Milano, [1972]. pp. 346.

ROVERI (ALESSANDRO) Dal sindacalismo rivoluzionario al fascismo: capitalismo agrario e socialismo nel Ferrarese, 1870-1920. Firenze, 1972. pp. 397.

SPRIANO (PAOLO) Storia di Torino operaia e socialista, da De Amicis a Gramsci. Torino, [1972]. pp 509.

SOCIALISM IN ISRAEL

LANDMANN (MICHAEL) Das Israelpseudos der Pseudolinken; Antwort an Isaak Deutscher; [and] Schlomo Deregh, Der israelische Sozialismus; [and] S. Barel, Tatsachen zum Nahostkonflikt. Berlin, [1971]. pp. 148.

SOCIALISM IN KAZAKSTAN

BURABAEV (MUKASH SEISEMBAEVICH) Rasprostranenie idei marksizma-leninizma v dooktiabr'skom Kazakhstane; pod redaktsiei... T. Zhangel'dina. Alma-Ata, 1965. pp. 228

SOCIALISM IN KIRGHIZIA

USENBAEV (KUSHBEK USENBAEVICH) Priobshchenie trudiashchikhsia Kirgizii k revoliutsionnoi bor'be v Rossii. Frunze, 1971. pp. 60.

SOCIALISM IN LATIN AMERICA

FLORES OLEA (VICTOR) Marxismo y democracia socialista. Mexico, [1968]. pp. 323. (Mexico City. Universidad Nacional Autonoma de Mexico. Facultad de Ciencias Politicas y Sociales. Serie Estudios. 4)

RAMOS (JORGE ABELARDO) Bolivarismo y marxismo. Buenos Aires, [1969]. pp. 137.

K.Marks i Latinskaia Amerika. Moskva, 1970. pp. 61.

SOCIALISM IN LITERATURE

ALBRECHT (FRIEDRICH) Deutsche Schriftsteller in der Entscheidung: Wege zur Arbeiterklasse, 1918-1933. Berlin, 1970. pp. 699. bibliog. (Deutsche Akademie der Künste. Sektion Literatur und Sprachpflege. Abteilung Geschichte der sozialistischen Literatur. Beiträge zur Geschichte der deutschen sozialistischen Literatur im 20. Jahrhundert. Band 2)

FUELBERTH (GEORG) Proletarische Partei und bürgerliche Literatur: Auseinandersetzungen in der deutschen Sozialdemokratie... über Möglichkeiten und Grenzen einer sozialistischen Literaturpolitik. Neuwied, 1972. pp. 202. bibliog.

SOCIALISM IN MACEDONIA

RABOTNIČKOTO dviženje na Makedonija do 1929 god: materijali od naučnata sredba održana vo Titov Veles na 8, 9 i 10 maj 1969 godina po povod 40-godišninata od smrtta na Vasil Glavinov i 50-godišninata na KPJ. Skopje, 1971. pp. 276. With French table of contents.

SOCIALISM IN NORWAY

LORENZ (EINHART) ed. Norsk sosialisme: en dokumentasjon; utvalg og kommentar. Oslo, [1970]. pp. 158.

SOCIALISM IN POLAND

POLSKA ZJEDNOCZONA PARTIA ROBOTNICZA. Zjazd, 6., 1971. For further development of people's Poland:... basic documents. Warsaw, 1972. pp. 399.

SOCIALISM IN RUSSIA

ISTORIKO-revoliutsionnyi sbornik; pod redaktsiei V.I. Nevskogo. Moskva, 1924-26. 3 vols. Xerographic reprint.

SAVINKOV (BORIS VIKTOROVICH) Vospominaniia terrorista; predislovie Feliksa Kona. 2nd ed. [Khar'kov, 1926?]. pp. 375.

VOLODIN (ALEKSANDR IVANOVICH) V poiskakh revoliutsionnoi teorii: A.I.Gertsen. Moskva, 1962. pp. 112.

BOR'BA V.I. Lenina protiv melkoburzhuaznoi revoliutsionnosti i avantiurizma. Moskva, 1966. pp. 317.

BUKHARIN (NIKOLAI IVANOVICH) Put' k sotsializmu v Rossii: izbrannye proizvedeniia; The path to socialism in Russia: selected works. N'iu Iork, 1967. pp. 415. Introduction and introductory notes in English and Russian.

PROLETARIAT Rossii na puti k Oktiabriu 1917 goda: oblik, bor'ba, gegemoniia; materialy k nauchnoi sessii po istorii proletariata, posviashchennoi 50-letiiu Velikogo Oktiabria, 14-17 noiabria 1967 goda. Odessa, 1967. 2 pts (in 1)

KOTOV (VIKTOR NIKIFOROVICH) K.Marks, F.Enhel's i Rosiia. Kyïv, 1971. pp. 239.

LETUNOVSKII (NIKOLAI IVANOVICH) Leninskaia taktika ispol'zovaniia legal'nykh Vserossiiskikh s"ezdov v bor'be za massy v 1908-1911 gg. Moskva, 1971. pp. 61.

KHOROS (VLADIMIR GEORGIEVICH) Narodnicheskaia ideologiia i marksizm, konets XIX v. Moskva, 1972. pp. 176.

SENCHAKOVA (L.T.) Revoliutsionnoe dvizhenie v russkoi armii i flote v kontse XIX - nachale XX v., 1879-1904 gg. Moskva, 1972. pp. 216.

TIUTIUKIN (STANISLAV VASIL'EVICH) Voina, mir, revoliutsiia: ideinaia bor'ba v rabochem dvizhenii Rossii 1914-1917 gg. Moskva, 1972. pp. 304.

TOBIAS (HENRY J.) The Jewish Bund in Russia: from its origins to 1905. Stanford, 1972. pp. 409. bibliog.

PANTIN (IGOR' KONSTANTINOVICH) Sotsialisticheskaia mysl' v Rossii: perekhod ot utopii k nayke. Moskva, 1973. pp. 358. bibliog.

VOLODIN (ALEKSANDR IVANOVICH) Gegel' i russkaia sotsialisticheskaia mysl' XIX veka. Moskva, 1973. pp. 304. bibliog.

- Bibliography

BESHKIN (G.) ed. Legal'naia sotsial-demokraticheskaia literatura v Rossii za 1906-14 gody: bibliografiia. Moskva, 1924. pp. 280. Xerographic reprint.

SOCIALISM IN SENEGAL

ZUCCARELLI (FRANÇOIS) Un parti politique africain: l'Union Progressiste Sénégalaise. Paris, 1970. pp. 401. bibliog.

SOCIALISM IN SERBIA

PERM'. Universitet. Uchenye zapiski. No.113. Voprosy istorii mezhdunarodnogo rabochego dvizheniia. vyp.2. Perm', 1963. pp. 123.

SOCIALISM IN SPAIN

ELORZA (ANTONIO) Socialismo utopico español. Madrid, 1970. pp. 240. bibliog.

VELARDE FUERTES (JUAN) España ante la socializacion economica: una primera aproximacion. Algorta, Vizcaya, 1970. pp. 167.

CIERVA Y DE HOCES (RICARDO DE LA) La historia perdida del socialismo español. Madrid, [1972]. pp. 294.

GOMEZ LLORENTE (LUIS) Aproximacion a la historia del socialismo español hasta 1921. Madrid, 1972. pp. 573. bibliog.

SOCIALISM IN SUBSAHARAN AFRICA

ARRIGHI (GIOVANNI) and SAUL (JOHN S.) Essays on the political economy of Africa. New York, [1973]. pp. 416.

SOCIALISM IN SWEDEN

HUFFORD (LARRY) Sweden: the myth of socialism. London, 1973. pp. 36. (Young Fabian Group. Young Fabian Pamphlets. 33)

SOCIALISM IN SWITZERLAND

BOLLIGER (MARKUS) Die Basler Arbeiterbewegung im Zeitalter des Ersten Weltkrieges und der Spaltung der Sozialdemokratischen Partei: ein Beitrag zur Geschichte der schweizerischen Arbeiterbewegung. Basel, 1970. pp. 379. bibliog.

SOCIALISM IN THE ARGENTINE REPUBLIC

DICKMANN (ENRIQUE) Pensamiento y accion. Buenos Aires, 1937. pp. 200.

RATZER (JOSE) Los marxistas argentinos del 90. Cordoba, [1970]. pp. 193.

GODIO (JULIO) El movimiento obrero y la cuestion nacional: Argentina; inmigrantes asalariados y lucha de clases, 1880-1910. Buenos Aires, 1972. pp. 242.

SOCIALISM IN THE CAUCASAS

V.I. Lenin i sovremennost': materialy nauchno-teoreticheskoi konferentsii, posviashchennoi 100-letiiu so dnia rozhdeniia V.I. Lenina. Erevan, 1971. pp. 175.

SOCIALISM IN THE NEAR EAST

ELLIS (HOWARD SYLVESTER) Private enterprise and socialism in the Middle East. Washington, 1970. pp. 126. bibliog. (American Enterprise Institute for Public Policy Research. Middle East Research Project. Analyses. No. 17)

SOCIALISM IN THE NETHERLANDS

LEEUW (A.S. DE) Het socialisme en de natie: van het "Communistisch manifest" tot de strijd tegen het fascisme; [reprint of work originally published in Amsterdam 1939]. Nijmegen, 1971. pp. 376.

MOOI rood is niet lelijk; [by] Cor Boef [and others]. Rotterdam, 1969. pp. 172.

SOCIALISM IN THE TATAR REPUBLIC

ISTORIOGRAFIIA fedoseevskikh marksistskikh kruzhkov v Povolzh'e. Kazan', 1972. pp. 167.

SOCIALISM IN THE UKRAINE

MAIOROV (M.) Iz istorii revoliutsionnoi bor'by na Ukraine, 1914-1919. Kyïv, 1922. pp. 109.

OCHERK istorii Khar'kovskogo motorostroitel'nogo zavoda "Serp i molot". ch.1. Revoliutsionnaia bor'ba rabochikh zavoda protiv tsarizma i kapitalizma, 1882-1917 gg. Khar'kov, 1966. pp. 240.

- Bibliography

SHMORHUN (PETRO) and others, compilers. Vydannia tvoriv V.I. Lenina na Ukraïni, 1894-1970: bibliohrafichnyi pokazhchyk. Kharkiv, 1971. pp. 710.

SOCIALISM IN THE UNITED KINGDOM

HADDOW (WILLIAM MARTIN) My seventy years. Glasgow, [1943]. pp. 170.

RYZHIKOV (VLADIMIR ALEKSANDROVICH) "Sotsializm" po-leiboristski: mify i real'nost'. Moskva, 1971. pp. 208.

GARNETT (RONALD GEORGE) Co-operation and the Owenite socialist communities in Britain, 1825-45. Manchester, [1972]. pp. 272. bibliog.

GOLDRING (MAURICE) and others. La Grande-Bretagne en crise. Paris, [1972]. pp. 128.

JARMAN (THOMAS LECKIE) Socialism in Britain: from the industrial revolution to the present day. London, 1972. pp. 224. bibliog.

MACDONALD (JAMES RAMSAY) Political writings; edited...by Bernard Barker. London, [1972]. pp. 259. bibliog.

MURPHY (JOHN THOMAS) Preparing for power: a critical study of the history of the British working-class movement;...with a new introduction by James Hinton. 2nd ed. London, 1972. pp. 296.

VESTER (MICHAEL) Die Entstehung des Proletariats als Lernprozess: die Entstehung antikapitalistischer Theorie und Praxis in England, 1792-1848. Frankfurt am Main, 1972. pp. 454. bibliog.

MILIBAND (RALPH) Parliamentary socialism: a study in the politics of labour. 2nd ed. London, 1973. pp. 384.

PIERSON (STANLEY) Marxism and the origins of British socialism: the struggle for a new consciousness. Ithaca, N.Y., 1973. pp. 290. bibliog.

TROTSKII (LEV DAVYDOVICH) Leon Trotsky on Britain: [selected writings]; introduction by George Novack. New York, 1973. pp. 334. bibliog.

TUPOLEVA (LARISA FEDOROVNA) Sotsialisticheskoe dvizhenie v Anglii v 80-e gody XIX veka. Moskva, 1973. pp. 263. bibliog.

WATKINS (KENNETH WILLIAM) Influencing the political future. London, [1973]. pp. 10. (Aims of Industry. The Future of Capitalism)

SOCIALISM IN THE UNITED STATES

BARITZ (LOREN) ed. The American left: radical political thought in the twentieth century. New York, [1971]. pp. 522.

BREITMAN (GEORGE) The new radicalization compared with those of the past; (report given...at the Socialist Activists and Educational Conference...Ohio...1970). New York, [1971]. pp. 30. (Reprinted from International Socialist Review, October 1970)

CANNON (JAMES PATRICK) Speeches for socialism. New York, 1971. pp. 462.

O'RIORDAN (MANUS) Connolly in America. [Belfast, 1971]. pp. 77. A reprint of the thesis presented to the University of New Hampshire, omitting the epilogue.

TOWARDS an American socialist revolution: a strategy for the 1970s; by Jack Barnes [and others]. New York, 1971. pp. 207.

DICK (WILLIAM MILNER) Labour and socialism in America: the Gompers era. Port Washington, N.Y., 1972. pp. 211. bibliog.

REEVE (CARL) The life and times of Daniel de Leon. New York, 1972. pp. 193.

CANNON (JAMES PATRICK) Notebook of an agitator. 2nd ed. New York, 1973. pp. 369. A reprint of the 1st ed. with the addition of an index and illustrations.

KUTCHER (JAMES) The case of the legless veteran. New York, [1973]. pp. 255.

LYND (ROBERT STAUGHTON) and ALPEROVITZ (GAR) Strategy and program: two essays toward a new American socialism. Boston, [1973]. pp. 109.

SOCIALISM IN TURKESTAN

AKBAROV (ADKHAM IBRAGIMOVICH) Rol' gazety "Pravda" v pobede sotsialisticheskoi revoliutsii v Turkestane. Tashkent, 1968. pp. 304. bibliog.

SOCIALISM IN UNDERDEVELOPED AREAS
See UNDERVELOPED AREAS - Socialism

SOCIALISM IN WHITE RUSSIA

SOLOSHENKO (VLADIMIR IVANOVICH) Ot narodnichestva k marksizmu: rasprostranenie marksizma i obrazovanie sotsial-demokraticheskikh organizatsii v Belorussii. Minsk, 1971. pp. 151.

SALADKAŬ (TSIMAFEI ERAFEEVICH) Bol'shevistskaia gazeta "Pravda" v Belorussii, 1912-1917 gg. 2nd ed. Minsk, 1972. pp. 296. For 1st White Russian ed. see his Bal'shavitskaia hazeta "Pravda" ŭ Belarusi, 1912-1917 hh.

SOCIALIST COMPETITION

LEBEDEVA (NINA BORISOVNA) and SHKARATAN (OVSEI IRMOVICH) Ocherki istorii sotsialisticheskogo sorevnovaniia. Leningrad, 1966. pp. 276.

FEDININ (VASILII KUZ'MICH) Sotsializm i sorevnovanie. Moskva, 1970. pp. 150.

SMOL'KOV (VIACHESLAV GRIGOR'EVICH) Sorevnovanie i kommunizm: metodologicheskie i sotsial'nye problemy. Moskva, 1970. pp. 163.

UTENKOV (ANDREI IAKOVLEVICH) KPSS - organizator i rukovoditel' sotsialisticheskogo sorevnovaniia v promyshlennosti v poslevoennye gody, 1946-1950 gg. Moskva, 1970. pp. 164.

PONOMARENKO (GRIGORII IAKOVLEVICH) Vo glave trudovogo pod"ema: kommunisty Donbassa - organizatory sotsialisticheskogo sorevnovaniia rabochego klassa v gody pervoi piatiletki. Kiev, 1971. pp. 175.

SOCIALIST MEDICAL ASSOCIATION

MURRAY (DAVID STARK) Why a National Health Service?: the part played by the Socialist Medical Association. London, 1971. pp. 136.

SOCIALIST PARTY (ARGENTINE REPUBLIC)

RODRIGUEZ (GERMINAL) La crisis politica del socialismo argentino: partido socialista o partido de vanguardia? [Buenos Aires?], 1930. pp. 184.

SOCIALIST PARTY (AUSTRIA)

SOZIALISTISCHE PARTEI ÖSTERREICHS. Bericht der Parteivertretung der Sozialdemokratischen Arbeiterpartei Deutschösterreichs an den Parteitag in Salzburg, 1924. Wien, 1924. pp. 113.

LETINER (FRANZ) Aus der Arbeiterbewegung im Traisental; ([and] Arbeiterbewegung im Bezirk Lilienfeld). Traisen, [1970]. pp. 211. bibliog.

SOZIALISTISCHE PARTEI ÖSTERREICHS. Die österreichische Sozialdemokratie im Spiegel ihrer Programme; mit einer Einleitung von Ernst Winkler. 2nd ed. Wien, [1971]. pp. 103.

ROTE Markierungen: Beiträge zur Ideologie und Praxis der österreichischen Sozialdemokratie. Wien, [1972]. pp. 180.

SOCIALIST PARTY (CHILE)

JOBET (JULIO CESAR) El Partido Socialista de Chile. Santiago de Chile, [1971]. 2 vols. (in 1). bibliog.

SOCIALIST PARTY (FRANCE)

QUILLIOT (ROGER) Les communistes et nous: deuxième série; preface de Guy Mollet. Paris, [1964]. pp. 25.

PARTI COMMUNISTE FRANÇAIS and PARTI SOCIALISTE. Programme commun de gouvernement. Paris, [1972]. pp. 192.

PARTI SOCIALISTE. Changer la vie: programme de gouvernement du Parti Socialiste. Paris, [1972]. pp. 249.

QUILLIOT (ROGER) La S.F.I.O. et l'exercice du pouvoir, 1944-1958. [Paris, 1972]. pp. 837. bibliog.

MITTERRAND (FRANÇOIS) La rose au poing. Paris, [1973]. pp. 224.

PARTI SOCIALISTE, and others. Programme commun de gouvernement: Parti socialiste, Parti communiste, Mouvement des radicaux de gauche. Paris, [1973]. pp. 96.

SOCIALIST PARTY (ITALY)

ALLEGATO (LUIGI) Socialismo e comunismo in Puglia: ricordi di un militante, 1904-1924. Roma, 1971. pp. 163.

CORTESI (LUIGI) Le origini del Partito comunista italiano: il P[artito] s[ocialista] i[taliano] dalla guerra di Libia alla scissione di Livorno. Bari, 1972. pp. 466. bibliog.

FINETTI (UGO) Libro bianco sulla crisi socialista: tre anni, 1969-1972. Milano, [1972]. pp. 267.

SOCIALIST PARTY (POLAND)

ŁADYKA (TEODOR) Polska Partia Socjalistyczna (Frakcja Rewolucyjna) w latach 1906-1914. Warszawa, 1972. pp. 358. bibliog.

LEINWAND (ARTUR) Pogotowie Bojowe i Milicja Ludowa w Polsce, 1917-1919. Warszawa, 1972. pp. 231. bibliog.

SOCIALIST REALISM
See COMMUNISM AND ART; COMMUNISM AND LITERATURE

SOCIALIST-REVOLUTIONARY PARTY (RUSSIA)

CHERNOVA (OL'GA) Vospominaniia o sovetskikh tiur'makh. [Parizh?, 1921?]. pp. 35.

RUSSIA (R.S.F.S.R.). Verkhovnyi Revoliutsionnyi Tribunal. 1922. Protsess P.S.-R.: rechi gosudarstvennykh obvinitelei: Lunacharskogo [and others]...: pechataetsia po stenogramme. Moskva, 1922. pp. 248. Xerographic reprint.

SAVINKOV (BORIS VIKTOROVICH) Vospominaniia terrorista; predislovie Feliksa Kona. 2nd ed. [Khar'kov, 1926?]. pp. 375.

LISOVSKII (P.) Na sluzhbe kapitala: esero-men'shevistskaia kontr-revoliutsiia. Leningrad, 1928. pp. 142. bibliog.

BOGDANOV (MIKHAIL ANDREEVICH) Razgrom zapadnosibirskogo kulatsko-eserovskogo miatezha 1921 g. Tiumen', 1961. pp. 111.

SAUSHKIN (NIKOLAI MAKSIMOVICH) Kritika V.I. Leninym programmy i taktiki partii eserov. Moskva, 1971. pp. 47.

- Congresses

PARTIIA SOTSIALISTOV-REVOLIUTSIONEROV. Sovet, 9-yi, 1919. Deviatyi Sovet partii i ego rezoliutsii, iiun' 1919, Moskva, etc. Paris, 1920. pp. 31.

SOCIALIST WORKERS PARTY (UNITED STATES)

SOCIALIST WORKERS PARTY (UNITED STATES). A revolutionary strategy for the 70s: documents. New York, 1972. pp. 96.

CANNON (JAMES PATRICK) Speeches to the Party: the revolutionary perspective and the revolutionary party. New York, 1973. pp. 431.

SOCIALISTS

NOMAD (MAX) Rebels and renegades; [reprint of work published in 1932]. New York, 1968. pp. 430. bibliog.

NEARING (HELEN KOTHE) and NEARING (SCOTT) Socialists around the world. New York, 1958. pp. 160.

MAITRON (JEAN) and HAUPT (GEORGES) eds. Dictionnaire biographique du mouvement ouvrier international. Paris, [1971 in progress].

BRAVO (GIAN MARIO) ed. Il pensiero socialista, 1797-1848: testi e note biografiche. Roma, 1971. pp. 1289. bibliog.

EICHLER (WILLI G.) Sozialisten: biographische Aufsätze über Karl Marx, etc. Bonn-Bad Godesberg, [1972]. pp. 145. bibliog.

SOCIALISTS, BRITISH

BELLAMY (JOYCE M.) and SAVILLE (JOHN) Dictionary of labour biography. London, 1972 in progress.

KATANKA (MICHAEL) ed. Radicals, reformers and socialists: from the Fabian biographical series. London, 1973. pp. 270. bibliog.

SOCIALISTS, EUROPEAN

TROTSKII (LEV DAVYDOVICH) Political profiles: [newspaper articles]; translated by R. Chappell. London, [1972]. pp. 171.

SOCIALISTS, GERMAN

ALBRECHT (FRIEDRICH) Deutsche Schriftsteller in der Entscheidung: Wege zur Arbeiterklasse, 1918-1933. Berlin, 1970. pp. 699. bibliog. (Deutsche Akademie der Künste. Sektion Literatur und Sprachpflege. Abteilung Geschichte der sozialistischen Literatur. Beiträge zur Geschichte der deutschen sozialistischen Literatur im 20. Jahrhundert. Band 2)

WETTE (WOLFRAM) Kriegstheorien deutscher Sozialisten: Marx, Engels, Lassalle, Bernstein, Kautsky, Luxemburg ein Beitrag zur Friedensforschung. Stuttgart, [1971]. pp. 255. bibliog.

SCHRAEPLER (ERNST) Handwerkerbünde und Arbeitervereine 1830-1853: die politische Tätigkeit deutscher Sozialisten von Wilhelm Weitling bis Karl Marx. Berlin, 1972. pp. 597. bibliog. (Berlin. Freie Universität. Friedrich-Meinecke-Institut. Historische Kommission zu Berlin. Veröffentlichungen. Band 34)

SOCIALIZATION

VASKOVICS (LASZLO A.) Familie und religiöse Sozialisation. Wien, 1970. pp. 450. bibliog.

BERNSTEIN (BASIL) Class, codes and control. London, 1971-73. 2 vols. bibliogs. (London. University. Institute of Education. Sociological Research Unit. Primary Socialization, Language and Education [Series]. 4)

RIES (HEINZ) Soziale Struktur des Bildungssystems und Sozialisation von Talenten: System- und Prozessanalysen; theoretischer Bezugsrahmen zur Bildungs- und Talentforschung. Stuttgart, 1971. pp. 293. bibliog.

SCHAFFER (H. RUDOLPH) The growth of sociability. Harmondsworth, 1971. pp. 199. bibliog.

STUDY GROUP ON THE ORIGINS OF HUMAN SOCIAL RELATIONS, LONDON, 1969. The origins of human social relations; proceedings of a C.A.S.D.S. study group...held jointly with the Ciba Foundation... being the fifth study group in a... programme on "The origins of human behaviour"; (edited by H.R. Schaffer). London, 1971. pp. 297. bibliogs.

THOMPSON (GEORGE GREENE) and others, eds. Social development and personality. New York, [1971]. pp. 743. bibliog.

HUCH (KURT JUERGEN) Einübung in die Klassengesellschaft: über den Zusammenhang von Sozialstruktur und Sozialisation. Frankfurt am Main, 1972. pp. 126. bibliog.

KERCKHOFF (ALAN C.) Socialization and social class. Englewood Cliffs, [1972]. pp. 170. bibliog.

WILLIAMS (THOMAS RHYS) Introduction to socialization: human culture transmitted. Saint Louis, 1972. pp. 308. bibliogs.

YOUTH SERVICE INFORMATION CENTRE. Occasional Papers. 4. Social education of the under-14's: conference reports and recommendations towards a policy; (stemming from the work of an ad hoc group). Leicester, 1972. pp. (8).

COOK-GUMPERZ (JENNY) Social control and socialization: a study of class differences in the language of maternal control. London, 1973. pp. 290. bibliog. (London. University. Institute of Education. Sociological Research Unit. Primary Socialization, Language and Education. [Series]. 6)

SOCIALLY HANDICAPPED

- Employment - United States - Bibliography

PINTO (PATRICK R.) and BUCHMEIER (JEANNE O.) compilers. Problems and issues in the employment of minority, disadvantaged, and female groups: an annotated bibliography. Minneapolis, 1973. pp. 62. (Minnesota University. Industrial Relations Center. Bulletins. 59)

SOCIALLY HANDICAPPED CHILDREN

- Education - Trinidad and Tobago

SEARLE (CHRIS) The forsaken lover: white words and black people; [first published in 1972]. Harmondsworth, 1973. pp. 128.

- Education - United Kingdom

EDUCATION for the less privileged: report of a conference at Ditchley Park, 20-23 February 1970. Enstone, Oxfordshire, [1970]. pp. 32. (Ditchley Foundation. Ditchley Papers. No. 29)

EDUCATIONAL priority...; edited by A.H. Halsey [and others]...; report of a research project sponsored by the Department of Education and Science and the Social Science Research Council. London, H.M.S.O., 1972 in progress. bibliogs.

U.K. Department of Education and Science. Schools Council. Working Papers. No. 27. 'Cross'd with adversity': the education of socially disadvantaged children in secondary schools; [K. Layboum, chairman of the Working Party]. London, 1970. pp. 157. bibliog.

- Education - United States

EDUCATION for the less privileged: report of a conference at Ditchley Park, 20-23 February 1970. Enstone, Oxfordshire, [1970]. pp. 32. (Ditchley Foundation. Ditchley Papers. No. 29)

BRICKMAN (WILLIAM W.) and LEHRER (STANLEY) eds. Education and the many faces of the disadvantaged: cultural and historical perspectives. New York, [1972]. pp. 435. bibliog.

GINSBURG (HERBERT) The myth of the deprived child: poor children's intellect and education. Englewood Cliffs, [1972]. pp. 252. bibliog.

CORWIN (RONALD G.) Reform and organizational survival: the teacher corps as an instrument of educational change. New York, [1973]. pp. 469. bibliog.

SOCIETY, PRIMITIVE

EVANS-PRITCHARD (Sir EDWARD EVAN) The position of women in primitive societies and other essays in social anthropology. London, 1965 repr. 1966. pp. 260. bibliogs.

DIAWARA (FODE) Le manifeste de l'homme primitif. Paris, [1972]. pp. 229.

ENGELS (FRIEDRICH) The origin of the family, private property and the state in the light of the researches of Lewis H. Morgan;...[new ed.] with an introduction and notes by Eleanor Burke Leacock. London, 1972. pp. 285. bibliog.

OKHOTNIKI, sobirateli, rybolovy: problemy sotsial'no-ekonomicheskikh otnoshenii v dozemledel'cheskom obshchestve. Leningrad, 1972. pp. 288. With English summary.

BRADFIELD (RICHARD MAITLAND) A natural history of associations. London, 1973. 2 vols. bibliog.

SOCIOLINGUISTICS

LABOV (WILLIAM) The social stratification of English in New York City. Washington, D.C., 1966. pp. 655.

SHUY (ROGER W.) and others. A study of social dialects in Detroit; (final report). [Washington], U.S. Department of Health, Education and Welfare, Office of Education, 1968. 2 pts. (in 1 vol.)

HAUGEN (EINAR) The Norwegian language in America: a study in bilingual behavior. [2nd ed.] Bloomington, 1969. pp. 699.

WOLFRAM (WALTER A.) A sociolinguistic description of Detroit negro speech. Washington, D.C., 1969. pp. 237. bibliog.

FISHMAN (JOSHUA AARON) Sociolinguistics: a brief introduction. Rowley, Mass., 1970 repr. 1971. pp. 126. bibliog.

FISHMAN (JOSHUA AARON) ed. Advances in the sociology of language. The Hague, 1971 in progress. bibliogs.

BERNSTEIN (BASIL) Class, codes and control. London, 1971-73. 2 vols. bibliogs. (London. University. Institute of Education. Sociological Research Unit. Primary Socialization, Language and Education [Series]. 4)

CAN language be planned?: sociolinguistic theory and practice for developing nations; [papers presented at a meeting in Hawaii, 1969]; edited by Joan Rubin and Björn H. Jernudd. [Honolulu, 1971]. pp. 343. bibliogs.

CARSWELL (E.A.) and ROMMETVEIT (RAGNAR) eds. Social contexts of messages. London, 1971. pp. 163. bibliogs.

DECONCHY (JEAN PIERRE) L'orthodoxie religieuse: essai de logique psycho-sociale. Paris, [1971]. pp. 373. bibliog.

GUMPERZ (JOHN JOSEPH) Language in social groups: essays; ...selected and introduced by Anwar S. Dil. Stanford, 1971. pp. 350. bibliog. (Linguistic Research Group of Pakistan. Language Science and National Development)

KOELNER ZEITSCHRIFT FÜR SOZIOLOGIE UND SOZIALPSYCHOLOGIE. Sonderhefte. 15. Zur Soziologie der Sprache: ausgewählte Beiträge vom 7. Weltkongress der Soziologie; herausgegeben von Rolf Kjolseth und Fritz Sack. Opladen, [1971]. pp. 396. bibliogs.

O MURCHU (MAIRTIN) Language and community. Dublin, Stationery Office, [1971]. pp. 48, 48. bibliog. (Comhairle na Gaeilge. Occasional Papers. No.1) In English and Irish.

SOCIOLINGUISTICS (Cont'd.)

STUDY GROUP ON MECHANISMS OF LANGUAGE DEVELOPMENT, LONDON, 1968. Language acquisition: models and methods;... proceedings of a C.A.S.D.S. study group...held jointly with the Ciba Foundation... being the third study group in a ... programme on "The origins of human behaviour"; (edited by Renira Huxley and Elisabeth Ingram). London, 1971. pp. 311. bibliog.

ABRAHAMS (ROGER D.) and TROIKE (RUDOLPH C.) eds. Language and cultural diversity in American education: [an anthology]. Englewood Cliffs, [1972]. pp. 339. bibliogs.

CREBER (J.W. PATRICK) Lost for words: language and educational failure. Harmondsworth, 1972. pp. 216. bibliog.

FASOLD (RALPH W.) Tense marking in black English: a linguistic and social analysis;... with a chapter on noun plural absence, by Carolyn Kessler. Arlington, 1972. pp. 254. bibliog.

FISHMAN (JOSHUA AARON) Language in sociocultural change: essays...; selected and introduced by Anwar S. Dil. Stanford, 1972. pp. 375. bibliogs.

GUMPERZ (JOHN JOSEPH) and HYMES (DELL HATHAWAY) eds. Directions in sociolinguistics: the ethnography of communication. New York, [1972]. pp. 598. bibliogs

HAUGEN (EINAR) The ecology of language: essays... selected... by Anwar S. Dil. Stanford, Ca., 1972. pp. 366. bibliogs. (Linguistic Research Group of Pakistan. Language Science and National Development)

LAVER (JOHN) and HUTCHESON (SANDY) eds. Communication in face to face interaction. Harmondsworth, 1972. pp. 418. bibliogs.

MOSCOVICI (SERGE) ed. The psychosociology of language. Chicago, [1972]. pp. 462. bibliogs.

PRIDE (J.B.) and HOLMES (JANET) eds. Sociolinguistics: selected readings. Harmondsworth, 1972. pp. 381. bibliogs.

ROSEN (HAROLD) Language and class: a critical look at the theories of Basil Bernstein. 2nd ed. Bristol, 1972. pp. 23. bibliog.

ANNUAL ROUND TABLE MEETING ON LINGUISTICS AND LANGUAGE STUDIES, 23RD, GEORGETOWN UNIVERSITY. Report...; (sociolinguistics; current trends and prospects); Roger W. Shuy, editor. Washington, [1973]. pp. 351. (Georgetown University. School of Languages and Linguistics. Monograph Series on Languages and Linguistics. No.25)

BAZIEV (AKHIIA TANAEVICH) and ISAEV (MAGOMET IZMAILOVICH) Iazyk i natsiia. Moskva, 1973. pp. 247. bibliog.

CICOUREL (AARON VICTOR) Cognitive sociology: language and meaning in social interaction. Harmondsworth, 1973. pp. 191. bibliog.

UNITED NATIONS EDUCATIONAL, SCIENTIFIC AND CULTURAL ORGANIZATION. Educational Studies and Documents. New Series. No. 11. Anthropology and language science in educational development. Paris, 1973. pp. 58.

SOCIOLOGICAL JURISPRUDENCE

CARLE (GIUSEPPE) La vita del diritto nei suoi rapporti colla vita sociale: studio comparativo di filosofia giuridica. 2nd ed. Torino, 1890. pp. 714.

CAPPELLETTI (MAURO) Processo e ideologie. Bologna, [1969]. pp. 569.

POTOPEIKO (DINA ALEKSANDROVNA) Pravosoznanie kak osoboe obshchestvennoe iavlenie. Kiev, 1970. pp. 111.

RECHTSSOCIOLOGIE en jurimetrie; door J.M.M. Maeijer [and others]. Leventer, 1970. pp. 137 bibliog. In Dutch or English.

IAVICH (LEV SAMOILOVICH) Pravo i obshchestvennye otnosheniia: osnovnye aspekty soderzhaniia i formy sovetskogo prava. Moskva, 1971. pp. 152.

LÉVY-BRUHL (HENRI) Sociologie du droit. 4th ed. Paris, 1971. pp. 128.

RODOTÀ (STEFANO) ed. Il diritto privato nella società moderna: (saggi). Bologna, [1971]. pp. 452. bibliog.

ROSTOW (EUGENE VICTOR) ed. Is law dead?: [proceedings of a Symposium held by the Association of the Bar of the City of New York]. New York, [1971]. pp. 416.

FRIEDMANN (WOLFGANG GASTON) Law in a changing society. 2nd ed. London, 1972. pp. 580. bibliog.

GIORNATE DI SOCIOLOGIA DEL DIRITTO, 2e, VARESE, 1971. La domanda e l'offerta di giustizia in Italia: [papers by G. de Rita and others given at a symposium organized by the Centro Nazionale di Prevenzione e Difesa Sociale di Milano]. Padova, 1972. pp. 121.

SOZIALDEMOKRATISCHE PARTEI DEUTSCHLANDS. Rechtspolitischer Kongress, 3rd, 1972. Gerechtigkeit in der Industriegesellschaft...: Dokumentation; herausgegeben von Konrad Duden [and others]. Karlsruhe, 1972. pp. 290. bibliogs.

TREVES (RENATO) Giustizia e giudici nella società italiana: problemi e ricerche di sociologia del diritto. Bari, 1972. pp. 190. (Centro Nazionale di Prevenzione e Difesa Sociale. Indagine su "L'Amministrazione della Giustizia e la Società Italiana in Trasformazione". 11)

HAYEK (FRIEDRICH AUGUST) Law, legislation and liberty: a new statement of the liberal principles of justice and political economy. London, 1973 in progress.

COLLIER (JANE FISHBURNE) Law and social change in Zinacantan. Stanford, 1973. pp. 281. bibliog.

KNOWLEDGE and opinion about law; [by] Adam Podgorecki [and others]. London, 1973. pp. 138. bibliogs.

MORRIS (PAULINE J.) and others. Social needs and legal action. London, 1973. pp. 97.

TWINING (WILLIAM) Karl Llewellyn and the Realist Movement. London, 1973. pp. 574. bibliog.

- Bibliography

CHAMBLISS (WILLIAM J.) and SEIDMAN (ROBERT B.) Sociology of the law: a research bibliography. Berkeley, 1970. pp. 113.

SOUSA E BRITO (MARIA ELISA PINA DE MORAIS DE) Sociology of law: a selected bibliography; Bibliografia selecta de sociologia do direito. Lisboa, 1972. pp. 173. (Portugal. Junta de Investigações do Ultramar. Centro de Estudos Politicos e Sociais. Estudos de Ciências Politicas e Sociais. No.89)

SOCIOLOGICAL RESEARCH
In earlier volumes of the bibliography similar works have been entered under SOCIAL SCIENCE RESEARCH

The ORGANIZATION, management and tactics of social research: [proceedings of a symposium]; edited by Richard O'Toole. Cambridge, Mass., [1971]. pp. 312. bibliogs.

PHILLIPS (BERNARD S.) Social research: strategy and tactics. 2nd ed. New York, 1971. pp. 398.

PHILLIPS (DEREK L.) Knowledge from what?: theories and methods in social research. Chicago, [1971]. pp. 204. bibliog.

WILLIAMS (WALTER) Dr. Social policy research and analysis: the experience in the federal social agencies. New York, 1971. pp. 204. bibliogs.

OBERSCHALL (ANTHONY) ed. The establishment of empirical sociology: studies in continuity, discontinuity, and institutionalization. New York, [1972]. pp. 256.

SHIPMAN (MARTEN D.) The limitations of social research. London, 1972. pp. 195.

HAGEDORN (ROBERT) 1925- , and LABOVITZ (SANFORD) An introduction into sociological orientations. New York, [1973]. pp. 136.

MACQUEEN (DONALD R.) ed. Understanding sociology through research: [a reader]. Reading, Mass., [1973]. pp. 539. bibliogs.

- Denmark

MØLGAARD (KIKA) and WINDING (ANNETTE) eds. Samfundsforskning: forskning for samfundet?; [interviews with] Agnete Diderichsen [and others]. København, 1973. pp. 112.

- Ethiopia

PAUSEWANG (SIEGFRIED) Methods and concepts of social research in a rural developing society: a critical appraisal based on experience in Ethiopia. München, [1973]. pp. 204. bibliog. (Ifo-Institut für Wirtschaftsforschung. Afrika-Studien. 80)

- Europe, Eastern

WIATR (JERZY J.) ed. The state of sociology in eastern Europe today. Carbondale, Ill., [1971]. pp. 273.

- Netherlands

JOLLES (HIDDO M.) Onderzoek en onderzoekbeleid in de Nederlandse sociologie. Assen, 1965. pp. 30.

- Russia

VASIL'EV (VLADIMIR GRIGOR'EVICH) and others. Vashe mnenie?: prikladnye sotsiologicheskie issledovaniia po problemam molodezhi. Moskva, 1967. pp. 184. bibliog.

VORONOV (IU.P.) ed. Izmerenie i modelirovanie v sotsiologii: voprosy metodiki, organizatsii i tekhniki sotsiologicheskikh issledovanii. Novosibirsk, 1969. pp. 174. With brief English summaries and table of contents.

SOTSIOLOGICHESKIE issledovaniia na Kamchatke. Petropavlovsk-Kamchatskii, 1970. pp. 40.

ANDREEVA (GALINA MIKHAILOVNA) ed. Lektsii po metodike konkretnykh sotsial'nykh issledovanii. Moskva, 1972. pp. 202.

GROMOV (IGOR ALEKSANDROVICH) and others. Sotsiologicheskaia laboratoriia na predpriiatii: iz opyta raboty laboratorii sotsiologicheskikh issledovanii Kirovskogo zavoda. Leningrad, 1972. pp. 74.

IADOV (VLADIMIR ALEKSANDROVICH) Sotsiologicheskoe issledovanie: metodologiia, programma, metody. Moskva, 1972. pp. 239. bibliog.

SOCIOLOGICAL RESEARCH - Underveloped areas
See UNDERDEVELOPED AREAS - Sociological research

- United Kingdom

KEY variables in social research...: [papers of a British Sociological Association working party]; edited by Elizabeth Gittus. London, 1972 in progress.

SOCIOLOGISTS

HERPIN (NICOLAS) Les sociologues américains et le siècle. [Paris], 1973. pp. 187. bibliog.

SOCIOLOGY

LA GRASSERIE (RAOUL DE) Essai d'une sociologie globale et synthétique. Paris, 1904. pp. 555.

FRIESEN (HEINRICH VON) Freiherr. Die Notwendigkeit einer Gesellschaftsordnung. Berlin, 1907. pp. 545.

SAVORGNAN (FRANCO) Soziologische Fragmente. Innsbruck, 1909. pp. 106.

LAMBRECHTS (HECTOR) La leçon d'une crise: considerations sociologiques. Utrecht, [1918]. pp. 344. bibliog.

STEIN (LUDWIG) Professor an der Universität Bern. Einführung in die Soziologie. München, 1921. pp. 454.

BUKHARIN (NIKOLAI IVANOVICH) Teoriia istoricheskogo materializma: populiarnyi uchebnik marksistskoi sotsiologii. Moskva, 1923. pp. 383. Xerographic reprint.

WALTER (EMIL J.) Psychologische Grundlagen der geschichtlichen und sozialen Entwicklung. Zürich, [1947]. pp. 172.

ESTUDIOS SOCIOLOGICOS: [trabajos presentados al] Congreso Nacional de Sociologia. a., 1950 (1er congreso), 1952 (3er)- Mexico.

FRANKFURT AM MAIN. Universität. Institut für Sozialforschung. Soziologische Exkurse: nach Vorträgen und Diskussionen; [edited by Johannes Hirzel]. Frankfurt am Main, [1956]. pp. 181.

FRANKFURT AM MAIN. Universität. Institut für Sozialforschung. Frankfurter Beiträge zur Soziologie. Band 10. Sociologica II: Reden und Vorträge; ([by] Max Horkheimer [and] Theodor W. Adorno). Frankfurt am Main, [1962]. pp. 242.

AUBERT (VILHELM) Elements of sociology. London, 1968 repr. 1970. pp. viii, 247.

MERTON (ROBERT KING) On theoretical sociology; five essays, old and new, including part 1 of Social theory and social structure. New York, Free P., 1967. pp. ix, 180. 21cm.

FILOSOFIIA ta sotsiolohiia: materialy naukovoï konferentsiï aspirantiv ta molodykh naukovtsiv Instytutu filosofiï. Kyïv, 1969. pp. 254.

SOCIOLOGY (Cont'd.)

GONZALEZ CASANOVA (PABLO) Sociologia de la explotacion. Mexico, 1969 repr. 1970. pp. 291.

1970

COULSON (MARGARET A.) and RIDDELL (DAVID S.) Approaching sociology: a critical introduction. London, 1970. pp. 130. bibliog.

DEBORD (GUY) Society of the spectacle; a Black and Red translation unauthorized. Detroit, 1970. 1 pamphlet (unpaged).

DOUGLAS (JACK D.) ed. The relevance of sociology: [readings]. New York, [1970]. pp. 233.

Die "FRANKFURTER Schule" im Lichte des Marxismus: zur Kritik der Philosophie und Soziologie von Horkheimer, Adorno, Marcuse, Habermas; Materialien einer wissenschaftlichen Tagung...veranstaltet vom Institut für Marxistische Studien und Forschungen...1970 in Frankfurt am Main; herausgegeben von Johannes Henrich von Heiseler [and others]. Frankfurt am Main, [1970]. pp. 184. This edition includes the discussion.

GLOBAL systems dynamics: ([proceedings of an] international symposium, Charlottesville, Va., 1969); edited by E.O. Attinger. Basel, 1970. pp. 353.

HARTFIEL (GUENTER) ed. Die autoritäre Gesellschaft. 2nd ed. Köln, 1970. pp. 215.

LASSWELL (THOMAS E.) and others, eds. Life in society: readings in sociology. rev. ed. Glenview, Ill., [1970]. pp. 710. bibliogs.

NOLTE (HELMUT) Psychoanalyse und Soziologie: die Systemtheorien Sigmund Freuds und Talcott Parsons'. Bern, [1970]. pp. 247. bibliog.

SZCZEPAŃSKI (JAN) Elementarne pojęcia socjologii. Warszawa, 1970. pp. 542.

WORLD CONGRESS OF SOCIOLOGY, 7th, 1970. Doklady k VII mezhdunarodnomu sotsiologicheskomu kongressu, Varna, sentiabr' 1970 g. Sverdlovsk, 1970. pp. 150. With English summaries.

1971

ADORNO (THEODOR WIESENGRUND) Gesammelte Schriften. Frankfurt am Main, 1971 in progress.

WOLFF (JACQUES) Sociologie économique. Paris, [1971] in progress. bibliog.

ACQUAVIVA (SABINO SAMELE) Una scommessa sul futuro: sociologia e programmazione globale. Milano, 1971. pp. 193.

ADORNO (THEODOR WIESENGRUND) Kritik: kleine Schriften zur Gesellschaft. Frankfurt am Main, 1971. pp. 152. bibliog.

BALANDIER (GEORGES) Sens et puissance: les dynamiques sociales. Paris, 1971. pp. 336. bibliog.

BAUMGARTEN (EDUARD) Gewissen und Macht: Abhandlungen und Vorlesungen, 1933-1963; ausgewählt und eingeleitet von Michael Sukale. Meisenheim am Glan, 1971. pp. 364.

BENTHEM VAN DEN BERGH (GODFRIED VAN) The structure of development: an invitation to the sociology of Norbert Elias. The Hague, 1971. pp. 29. (Hague. Institute of Social Studies. Occasional Papers)

BIRNBAUM (NORMAN) Toward a critical sociology. New York, 1971. pp. 451.

BOUDON (RAYMOND) La crise de la sociologie: questions d'epistémologie sociologique. Genève, 1971. pp. 326.

BUITEN de grenzen: sociologische opstellen aangeboden aan W.F. Wertheim. Meppel, [1971]. pp. 365. bibliog.

DEFLEUR (MELVIN LAWRENCE) and others. Sociology: man in society. Glenview, Ill., [1971]. pp. 626.

Die "FRANKFURTER Schule" im Lichte des Marxismus: zur Kritik der Philosophie und Soziologie von Horkheimer, Adorno, Marcuse und Habermas; [papers read at a conference held in Frankfurt am Main in 1970 organized by the Institut für Marxistische Studien und Forschungen (IMSF)]. Berlin, 1971. pp. 137. This edition contains the papers only.

GERHARDT (UTA) Rollenanalyse als kritische Soziologie: ein konzeptueller Rahmen zur empirischen und methodologischen Begründung einer Theorie der Vergesellschaftung. Neuwied, [1971]. pp. 408. bibliog.

GORMAN (BENJAMIN L.) Social themes. Englewood Cliffs, [1971]. pp. 274. bibliogs.

HABERMAS (JUERGEN) Theorie und Praxis: sozialphilosophische Studien. new ed. Frankfurt am Main, 1971. pp. 466. bibliog.

HODGES (HAROLD MELLOR) Conflict and consensus: an introduction to sociology. New York, [1971]. pp. 587. bibliog.

HOROWITZ (DAVID) ed. Radical sociology: an introduction. San Francisco, [1971]. pp. 307. bibliogs.

HUFNAGEL (GERHARD) Kritik als Beruf: der kritische Gehalt im Werk Max Webers. [Berlin, 1971]. pp. 439. bibliog.

HUGHES (EVERETT CHERRINGTON) The sociological eye: selected papers. Chicago, 1971. pp. 584.

HUMMELL (HANS J.) and OPP (KARL DIETER) Die Reduzierbarkeit von Soziologie auf Psychologie: eine These, ihr Test und ihre theoretische Bedeutung. Braunschweig, 1971. pp. 102.

JENSEN (ALAN F.) and METCALF (HOMER C.) Sociology: concepts and concerns. Chicago, [1971]. pp. 230. bibliog.

KATZ (FRED E.) ed. Contemporary sociological theory. New York, [1971]. pp. 527. bibliogs.

KUNENE (RAYMOND MAZISI) Die Grossfamilie: eine afrikanische Gesellschaftstheorie; [aus dem Englischen übertragen von Max Kretzschmar und Rose Kessler]. Nürnberg, [1971]. pp. 124.

LENGYEL (PETER) ed. Approaches to the science of socio-economic development; ... with contributions by Raymond Aron [and others]. Paris, Unesco, 1971. pp. 383. bibliogs.

LEY (HERMANN) and MUELLER (THOMAS) Kritische Vernunft und Revolution: zur Kontroverse zwischen Hans Albert und Jürgen Habermas. Köln, [1971]. pp. 267.

MILL (JOHN STUART) A logical critique of sociology; [extracts from the writings of John Stuart Mill]; edited and with an introductory essay by Ronald Fletcher. London, 1971. pp. 431. bibliog.

MOTWANI (KEWAL) Towards Indian sociology. Agra, 1971. pp. 138. bibliog.

NESTERENKO (GEORGII IAKOVLEVICH) Problema soznaniia v marksistskoi sotsiologii. Moskva, 1971. pp. 276.

SERGEANT (GRAHAM) A textbook of sociology. Basingstoke, 1971. pp. 354. bibliog.

SIMMEL (GEORG) On individuality and social forms: selected writings; edited and with an introduction by Donald N. Levine. Chicago, 1971. pp. 395. bibliog.

STEWART (ELBERT W.) and GLYNN (JAMES A.) Introduction to sociology. New York, [1971]. pp. 321.

WELLMER (ALBRECHT) Critical theory of society;...translated by John Cumming. New York, 1971. pp. 139.

1972

ABDEL-MALEK (ANOUAR) La dialectique sociale. Paris, [1972 in progress].

ABRAMS (PHILIP) Being and becoming in sociology. [Durham]; Kendal [imprint], 1972. pp. 21.

AGGRESSION und Anpassung in der Industriegesellschaft; mit Beiträgen von Herbert Marcuse [and others]. Frankfurt am Main, 1972. pp. 163.

BERGER (PETER L.) and BERGER (BRIGITTE) Sociology: a biographical approach. New York, [1972]. pp. 372. bibliogs.

BOSKOFF (ALVIN) The mosaic of sociological theory. New York, [1972]. pp. 276. bibliogs.

COTGROVE (STEPHEN FREDERICK) The science of society: an introduction to sociology. rev. ed. London. 1972. pp. 310. bibliogs.

DAHRENDORF (RALF) Konflikt und Freiheit: auf dem Weg zur Dienstklassengesellschaft. München, [1972]. pp. 336.

DAS (A.C.) An introduction to the study of society. Delhi, 1972. pp. 232.

DORTMUND. Sozialakademie Dortmund. Internationale Tagung, 1971. Der Mensch in der Gesellschaft von morgen; herausgegeben von Helmut Duvernell. Berlin, [1972]. pp. 318. bibliog.

DURKHEIM (EMILE) Selected writings; edited, translated, and with an introduction by Anthony Giddens. Cambridge, 1972. pp. 272.

EMMET (DOROTHY MARY) Function, purpose and powers: some concepts in the study of individuals and societies. 2nd ed. London, 1972. pp. 300.

FERRAROTTI (FRANCO) Una sociologia alternativa: dalla sociologia come tecnica del conformismo alla sociologia critica. Bari, 1972. pp. 320. bibliog.

FOURASTIE (JEAN) Economie et société: chroniques du Figaro. [Paris, 1972]. pp. 368.

FRANKFURT AM MAIN. Universität. Institut für Sozialforschung. Aspects of sociology;...translated by John Viertel. Boston, [1972]. pp. 210.

GINER (SALVADOR) Sociology; (revised and translated by the author). London, 1972. pp. 295.

HORTON (PAUL BURLEIGH) and HUNT (CHESTER L.) Sociology. 3rd ed. New York, [1972]. pp. 568. bibliogs.

JARVIE (IAN CHARLES) Concepts and society. London, 1972. pp. 214. bibliog.

KINLOCH (GRAHAM C.) The sociological study of South Africa: an introduction. Johannesburg, 1972. pp. 180. bibliogs.

KOELNER ZEITSCHRIFT FÜR SOZIOLOGIE UND SOZIALPSYCHOLOGIE Sonderhefte. 16. Soziologie und Sozialgeschichte: Aspekte und Probleme; herausgegeben von Peter Christian Ludz. Opladen, 1972. pp. 623. bibliogs.

LOWRY (RITCHIE PETER) and RANKIN (ROBERT P.) Sociology: social science and social concern. 2nd ed. New York, [1972]. pp. 692. bibliogs. 1st ed. subtitled: the science of society.

MATTICK (PAUL) Critique of Marcuse: one-dimensional man in class society. London, 1972. pp. 110.

NEW directions in sociological theory; [by] Paul Filmer [and others]. London, 1972. pp. 246. bibliogs.

O'NEILL (JOHN) Sociology as a skin trade: essays towards a reflexive sociology. London, 1972. pp. 274.

POGGI (GIANFRANCO) Images of society: essays on the sociological theories of Tocqueville, Marx and Durkheim. Stanford, 1972. pp. 267.

RABOW (JEROME) Sociology, students, and society. Pacific Palisades, [1972]. pp. 689. bibliogs.

ROCHER (GUY) A general introduction to sociology: a theoretical perspective;... translated from the French by Peta Sheriff. London, 1972. pp. 580. bibliog.

ROSEN (PAUL L.) The Supreme Court and social science. Chicago, [1972]. pp. 260. bibliog.

SAHAY (ARUN) Sociological analysis. London, 1972. pp. 212. bibliog.

SEGER (IMOGEN) Sociology for the modern mind;... translated [from the German] by the author. New York, [1972]. pp. 336. bibliog.

A SOCIOLOGICAL portrait: (a series from New Society); edited by Paul Barker. Harmondsworth, 1972. pp. 203. bibliog.

SPENCER (HERBERT) On social evolution: selected writings; edited and with an introduction by J.D.Y. Peel. Chicago, 1972. pp. 270. bibliog.

TURNER (JONATHAN H.) Patterns of social organization: a survey of social institutions. New York, [1972]. pp. 423. bibliog.

ZIJDERVELD (ANTON C.) The abstract society: a cultural analysis of our time. London, 1972. pp. 180. First published in 1970.

1973

BROOM (LEONARD) and SELZNICK (PHILIP) Sociology: a text with adapted readings. 5th ed. New York, [1973]. pp. 650. bibliogs.

CAHNMAN (WERNER JACOB) ed. Ferdinand Tönnies: a new evaluation; essays and documents. Leiden, 1973. pp. 302.

DAHRENDORF (RALF) Homo sociologicus; [first published in English in his Essays in the theory of society, 1968; reprinted with a new preface and minor revisions; translated from the German by the author]. London, 1973. pp. 99. bibliog.

DIXON (KEITH) Sociological theory: pretence and possibility. London, 1973. pp. 131.

FARBERMAN (HARVEY A.) and GOODE (ERICH) eds. Social reality: [readings]. Englewood Cliffs, [1973]. pp. 324. bibliogs.

GELLNER (ERNEST ANDRÉ) Cause and meaning in the social sciences;... edited with a preface by I.C. Jarvie and Joseph Agassi. London, 1973. pp. 228.

GOODE (WILLIAM J.) Explorations in social theory. New York, 1973. pp. 449.

SOCIOLOGY (Cont'd.)

GOULDNER (ALVIN WARD) For sociology: renewal and critique in sociology today; [selected articles]. London, [1973]. pp. 465.

HAGEDORN (ROBERT) 1925- , and LABOVITZ (SANFORD) An introduction into sociological orientations. New York, [1973]. pp. 136.

HURD (GEOFFREY) and others. Human societies: an introduction to sociology. London, 1973. pp. 222. bibliogs.

KLAPP (ORRIN E.) Models of social order: an introduction to sociological theory. Palo Alto, 1973. pp. 334. bibliog.

LESLIE (GERALD RONNELL) and others. Order and change: introductory sociology. New York, 1973. pp. 692. bibliogs.

MACK (RAYMOND W.) and PEASE (JOHN) Sociology and social life. 5th ed. New York, [1973]. pp. 561. bibliogs.

MACQUEEN (DONALD R.) ed. Understanding sociology through research: [a reader]. Reading, Mass., [1973]. pp. 539. bibliogs.

MENDOZA (MANUEL G.) and NAPOLI (VINCE) Systems of man: an introduction to social science. Lexington, Mass., [1973]. pp. 582. bibliogs.

ROSS (HUGH LAURENCE) Perspectives on the social order: readings in sociology. 3rd ed. New York, [1973]. pp. 658. bibliogs.

STORER (NORMAN W.) Focus on society: an introduction to sociology. Reading, Mass., [1973]. pp. 274. bibliogs.

A SZOCIOLÓGIA első magyar műhelye: a Huszadik század köre. Budapest, 1973. 2 vols.

- Bibliography

GAŠPAROVIĆ (ZLATKO) compiler. Bibliografija socioloških radova objavljenih u Jugoslaviji u periodu, 1959-1969; Bibliography of sociological literature published in Yugoslavia in the period, 1959-1969. Beograd, 1970. pp. 76.

LAMMINEN (HILKKA SISKO) Bibliography of Finnish sociology, 1960-1969. in WESTERMARCK SOCIETY. Transactions, vol. 19.

- Dictionaries and encyclopaedias

LEXIKON zur Soziologie; herausgegeben von Werner Fuchs [and others]. Opladen, 1973. pp. 783.

- History

OBERSCHALL (ANTHONY) ed. The establishment of empirical sociology: studies in continuity, discontinuity, and institutionalization. New York, [1972]. pp. 256.

STORIA delle idee politiche economiche e sociali; diretta da Luigi Firpo; vol. 5. L'età della rivoluzione industriale; a cura di Gaetano Arfè [and others]. Torino, 1972. pp. 919. bibliog.

- History - Germany

TYROWICZ (STANISŁAW) Światło wiedzy zdeprawowanej: idee niemieckiej socjologii i filozofii, 1933-1945. Poznan, 1970. pp. 186. bibliog. (Poznan. Instytut Zachodni. Prace. nr.42) With German summary.

SCHAD (SUSANNE PETRA) Empirical social research in Weimar-Germany. Paris, 1972. pp. 155. bibliog. (International Social Science Council. Publications. 15)

- History - Russia

KLUSHIN (VLADIMIR IVANOVICH) Pervye uchenye-marksisty Petrograda. Leningrad, 1971. pp. 340.

- History - United States

QUANDT (JEAN BRIGGS) From the small town to the great community: the social thought of Progressive intellectuals. New Brunswick, N.J., [1970]. pp. 260. bibliog.

HERPIN (NICOLAS) Les sociologues américains et le siècle. [Paris], 1973. pp. 187. bibliog.

LADNER (JOYCE A.) ed. The death of white sociology. New York, [1973]. pp. 476.

- Mathematical models

VORONOV (IU.P.) ed. Izmerenie i modelirovanie v sotsiologii: voprosy metodiki, organizatsii i tekhniki sotsiologicheskikh issledovanii. Novosibirsk, 1969. pp. 174. With brief English summaries and table of contents.

COLEMAN (JAMES SAMUEL) The mathematics of collective action. London, 1973. pp. 191. bibliog.

SOCIOLOGICAL REVIEW, THE; [published by] University of Keele. Monographs. No. 19. Stochastic processes in sociology; [a collection of papers presented at a meeting at the University of Essex in 1971 organized by a sub-group of the British Sociological Association]; edited by... R.E.A. Mapes. Keele, 1973. pp. 139. bibliogs.

- Methodology

LAZARSFELD (PAUL FELIX) and HENRY (NEIL W.) Latent structure analysis. New York, [1968]. pp. 294. bibliog.

PURDUE SYMPOSIUM ON ETHNOMETHODOLOGY. Proceedings... edited by Richard J. Hill [and] Kathleen Stones Crittenden. [West Lafayette, 1968]. fo. 259. (Purdue University. Institute for the Study of Social Change. Institute Monograph Series. No. 1)

VORONOV (IU.P.) ed. Izmerenie i modelirovanie v sotsiologii: voprosy metodiki, organizatsii i tekhniki sotsiologicheskikh issledovanii. Novosibirsk, 1969. pp. 174. With brief English summaries and table of contents.

HOUTEN (B.C. VAN) Tussen aanpassing en kritiek: de derde methodenstrijd in de Duitse sociologie. Deventer, 1970. pp. 362. bibliog. With German summary.

MORRISON (DENTON E.) and HENKEL (RAMON E.) eds. The significance test controversy: a reader. London, 1970. pp. 333. bibliog.

CARROLL (CAROLE MAKEIG) and CARROLL (FREDERIC) Methods of sociological research. Meerut, [1971]. pp. 172. bibliog.

COMPARATIVE methods in sociology: essays on trends and applications; edited by Ivan Vallier. Berkeley, 1971. pp. 474. bibliog.

HANNAN (MICHAEL T.) Aggregation and disaggregation in sociology. Lexington, [1971]. pp. 146. bibliog.

KUPRIIAN (ALEKSANDR PETROVICH) Metodologicheskie problemy sotsial'nogo eksperimenta. Moskva, 1971. pp. 157. bibliog.

LEFÈVRE (WOLFGANG) Zum historischen Charakter und zur historischen Funktion der Methode bürgerlicher Soziologie: Untersuchung am Werk Max Webers. Frankfurt am Main, 1971. pp. 158.

LOFLAND (JOHN) Analyzing social settings: a guide to qualitative observation and analysis. Belmont, Calif., [1971]. pp. 136. bibliogs.

MOKRZYCKI (EDMUND) Założenia socjologii humanistycznej. Warszawa, 1971. pp. 115. With English summary.

PHILLIPS (DEREK L.) Knowledge from what?: theories and methods in social research. Chicago, [1971]. pp. 204. bibliog.

The SOCIOLOGY of the future: theory, cases, and annotated bibliography; edited by Wendell Bell and James A. Mau. New York, [1971]. pp. 464. bibliogs.

A SZOCIOLÓGIAI felvétel módszerei. 2nd ed. Budapest, 1971. pp. 430. bibliog.

WALLACE (WALTER L.) The logic of science in sociology. Chicago, 1971. pp. 139. bibliog.

ARGYRIS (CHRIS) The applicability of organizational sociology. Cambridge, 1972. pp. 138. bibliog.

GIBBS (JACK P.) Sociological theory construction. Hinsdale, Ill., [1972]. pp. 416. bibliog.

HAGE (JERALD) Techniques and problems of theory construction in sociology. New York, [1972]. pp. 239. bibliog.

IADOV (VLADIMIR ALEKSANDROVICH) Sotsiologicheskoe issledovanie: metodologiia, programma, metody. Moskva, 1972. pp. 239. bibliog.

LAZARSFELD (PAUL FELIX) Qualitative analysis: historical and critical essays. Boston, [Mass., 1972]. pp. 457.

LAZARSFELD (PAUL FELIX) and others, eds. Continuities in the language of social research. New York, [1972]. pp. 491.

MAITRE, (JACQUES) Sociologie religieuse et méthodes mathematiques. Paris, 1972. pp. 200.

PITT (DAVID C.) Using historical sources in anthropology and sociology. New York, [1972]. pp. 88. bibliog.

POPLIN (DENNIS E.) Communities: a survey of theories and methods of research. New York, [1972]. pp. 313. bibliogs.

SOCIOLOGICAL REVIEW, THE; [published by] University of Keele. Monographs. No. 17. Hungarian sociological studies; edited by Paul Halmos. Keele, 1972. pp. 332. bibliogs.

BROWN (ROBERT) Philosopher. Rules and laws in sociology. London, 1973. pp. 181.

BURR (WESLEY RAY) Theory construction and the sociology of the family. New York, [1973]. pp. 320. bibliog.

LACHENMEYER (CHARLES W.) The essence of social research: a Copernican revolution. New York, [1973]. pp. 309.

NETWORK analysis: studies in human interaction; [papers presented at a conference organized by the Afrika-Studiecentrum at Leiden in 1969]; edited by Jeremy Boissevain and J. Clyde Mitchell. The Hague, [1973]. pp. 271. bibliog. (Afrika-Studiecentrum. Change and Continuity in Africa)

O'BARR (WILLIAM M.) and others, eds. Survey research in Africa: its applications and limits. Evanston, Ill., 1973. pp. 349. bibliog.

PHILLIPS (DEREK L.) Abandoning method: (sociological studies in methodology). San Francisco, 1973. pp. 202. bibliog.

REX (JOHN ARDERNE) Discovering sociology: studies in sociological theory and method. London, 1973. pp. 278. bibliog.

SCHATZMAN (LEONARD) and STRAUSS (ANSELM LEONARD) Field research: strategies for a natural sociology. Englewood Cliffs, [1973]. pp. 149. bibliogs.

- Philosophy

    MISABISHVILI (SHOTA VLADIMIROVICH) Dialektika obshchego i osobennogo v sotsial'nom razvitii. Sukhumi, 1971. pp. 247.

    LIPIEC (JÓZEF) Podstawy ontologii społeczeństwa. Warszawa, 1972. pp. 356.

    BERSHADY (HAROLD J.) Ideology and social knowledge. Oxford, [1973]. pp. 178.

    CHESNOKOV (D.I.) Istoricheskii materializm kak sotsiologiia marksizma-leninizma. Moskva, 1973. pp. 319.

- Statistics

    ISTORIKO-sotsiologicheskie issledovaniia: na materialakh slavianskikh stran. Moskva, 1970. pp. 313.

    BLALOCK (HUBERT M.) Social statistics. 2nd ed. New York, [1972]. pp. 583.

    SIPOVSKAIA (IRINA VASIL'EVNA) Vyborochnoe statisticheskoe nabliudenie i nekotorye voprosy ego primeneniia v sotsiologicheskikh issledovaniiakh. Tbilisi, 1972. pp. 133.

    HINDESS (BARRY) The use of official statistics in sociology: a critique of positivism and ethnomethodology. London, 1973. pp. 63. bibliog. (British Sociological Association. Studies in Sociology)

- Study and teaching - Africa

    KORNEEV (MIKHAIL IAKOVLEVICH) Problemy sotsial'noi tipologii lichnosti. Leningrad, 1971. pp. 152.

- Study and teaching - America, Latin

    CALELLO (HUGO) Hacia una sociologia del subdesarrollo. Caracas, 1968. pp. 137. bibliog.

- Study and teaching - Australia

    CONFERENCE ON THE TEACHING OF SOCIOLOGY IN AUSTRALIA AND NEW ZEALAND, CANBERRA, 1971. The teaching of sociology in Australia and New Zealand: [selected papers from the SAANZ Conference]; edited by Jerzy Zubrzycki. Melbourne, 1971. pp. 167.

- Study and teaching - France

    KORNEEV (MIKHAIL IAKOVLEVICH) Problemy sotsial'noi tipologii lichnosti. Leningrad, 1971. pp. 152.

- Study and teaching - New Zealand

    CONFERENCE ON THE TEACHING OF SOCIOLOGY IN AUSTRALIA AND NEW ZEALAND, CANBERRA, 1971. The teaching of sociology in Australia and New Zealand: [selected papers from the SAANZ Conference]; edited by Jerzy Zubrzycki. Melbourne, 1971. pp. 167.

- Study and teaching - United Kingdom

    COUNCIL FOR TRAINING IN SOCIAL WORK [U.K.] Sociology Study Group. The teaching of sociology in social work courses; report; [J.H. Smith, chairman]. London, 1972. pp. 32. (Council for Training in Social Work [U.K.]. Discussion Papers. No. 5)

SOCIOLOGY (Cont'd.)

- Terminology

LACHENMEYER (CHARLES W.) The language of sociology. New York, 1971. pp. 129. bibliog.

SOCIOLOGY, CHRISTIAN

FONTAINE (JULIEN) Le modernisme sociologique: décadence ou régénération? Paris, [1909]. pp. 515.

ELLWOOD (CHARLES ABRAM) Christianity and social science: a challenge to the church. New York, 1923. pp. 220.

STARK (WERNER) The sociology of religion: a study of Christendom. London, 1966-1972. 5 vols.

DECONCHY (JEAN PIERRE) L'orthodoxie religieuse: essai de logique psycho-sociale. Paris, [1971]. pp. 373. bibliog.

MITTON (C.L.) ed. The social sciences and the churches. Edinburgh, 1972. pp. 270.

PETULLA (JOSEPH M.) Christian political theology: a marxian guide. Maryknoll, N.Y., [1972]. pp. 256. bibliog.

STACKHOUSE (MAX L.) Ethics and the urban ethos: an essay in social theory and theological reconstruction. Boston, Mass., [1972]. pp. 220.

HILL (MICHAEL) Ph.D. A sociology of religion. London, 1973. pp. 285. bibliogs.

- Catholic

SCHINDLER (FRANZ M.) Die soziale Frage der Gegenwart vom Standpunkte des Christentums. [2nd ed.] Wien, 1908. pp. 236.

SOCIOLOGY, MILITARY

HICKMAN (MARTIN B.) ed. The military and American society. Beverly Hills, [1971]. pp. 167.

SOCIAL SCIENCE CONFERENCE ON THE PERCEIVED ROLE OF THE MILITARY, FRANCE, 1970. The perceived role of the military; edited by M.R. Van Gils. Rotterdam, 1971. pp. 390. bibliogs.

The MILITARY-industrial complex: a reassessment; edited by Sam C. Sarkesian; [including papers prepared for an Institute sponsored by the Center for Policy Study, University of Chicago]. Beverly Hills, [1972]. pp. 340. (Inter-University Seminar on Armed Forces and Society. Sage Research Progress Series on War, Revolution, and Peacekeeping. vol. 2)

TEITLER (GER) Toepassing van geweld: sociologische essays over geweld, verzet en militaire organisatie. Meppel, [1972]. pp. 164. bibliog.

- Bibliography

LANG (KURT) Military institutions and the sociology of war: a review of the literature with annotated bibliography. Beverly Hills, [1972]. pp. 337.

SOCIOLOGY, RURAL

BARBERIS (CORRADO) Sociologia del piano Mansholt. Bologna, [1970]. pp. 250. (Istituto Nazionale di Economia Agraria. Osservatorio di Economia Agraria per l'Europa. Collana di Studi e Ricerche. N.4)

LOUX (FRANÇOISE) and VIRVILLE (MICHEL DE) Le système social d'une région rurale: Le Châtillonnais. [Paris], 1970. pp. 135. (Musée National des Arts et Traditions Populaires. Archives d'Ethnologie Française. 1) (Tiré à part de la revue Etudes Rurales, no. 35)

GAŁESKI (BOGUSŁAW) Basic concepts of rural sociology; translated by H.C. Stevens; edited by Teodor Shanin and Peter Worsley. Manchester, [1972]. pp. 209.

SMITH (THOMAS LYNN) The sociology of agricultural development. Leiden, 1972. pp. 103. bibliog.

SOCIOLOGY, RURAL

See also the subdivision Rural conditions under the names of countries, villages, and other appropriate geographical names

SOCIOLOGY, URBAN

In earlier volumes of the Bibliography similar works have been entered under CITIES AND TOWNS

MANGIN (WILLIAM) ed. Peasants in cities: readings in the anthropology of urbanization. Boston, Mass., [1970]. pp. 207. bibliog.

MICHELSON (WILLIAM) Man and his urban environment: a sociological approach. Reading, Mass., [1970]. pp. 242. bibliog.

SOUCY (CLAUDE) Contribution à une sociologie des centres urbains: la crise des centres: orientation de la recherche. [Paris?], 1970. pp. 141. bibliog. (France. Ministère de l'Equipement et du Logement. Publications de Recherches Urbaines)

DIEDERICH (JUL) Soziographie und Städtebau: mit Ergebnissen soziographischer Untersuchungen in der Stadt Hanau. Berlin, 1971. pp. 138. bibliogs.

HUGUET (MICHELE) Les femmes dans les grands ensembles: de la représentation à la mise en scène. Paris, 1971. pp. 295. bibliog.

ROGGEMANS (MARIE LAURE) La ville est un système social: pour une définition sociologique du phénomène urbain. [Brussels, 1971]. pp. (79). bibliog. (Brussels. Université Libre. Centre de Sociologie Générale et de Méthodologie. L'Agglomération Bruxelloise. 1)

The ANTHROPOLOGY of urban environments; edited by Thomas Weaver and Douglas White. Washington, [1972]. pp. 136. bibliog. (Society for Applied Anthropology. Monographs. No. 11)

BIRNBAUM (MAX) and MOGEY (JOHN M.) eds. Social change in urban America. New York, [1972]. pp. 249. bibliogs.

NOTTRIDGE (HAROLD E.) The sociology of urban living. London, 1972. pp. 115. bibliog.

PERGOLA (GIULIANO DELLA) La conflittualità urbana: saggi di sociologia critica. Milano, 1972. pp. 174.

STACKHOUSE (MAX L.) Ethics and the urban ethos: an essay in social theory and theological reconstruction. Boston, Mass., [1972]. pp. 220.

SZALAI (SANDOR) and others, eds. The use of time: daily activities of urban and suburban populations in twelve countries. The Hague, [1972]. pp. 868. bibliog. (European Coordination Centre for Research and Documentation in the Social Sciences. Publications. 5)

CULLINGWORTH (JOHN BARRY) and others. Problems of an urban society. London, 1973. 3 vols. (Birmingham. University. Centre for Urban and Regional Studies. Urban and Regional Studies. Nos. 4-6)

EAMES (EDWIN) and GOODE (JUDITH GRANICH) Urban poverty in a cross-cultural context. New York, [1973]. pp. 299. bibliog.

LAUMANN (EDWARD O.) Bonds of pluralism: the form and substance of urban social networks. New York, [1973]. pp. 342. bibliog.

NEWMAN (OSCAR) Defensible space: people and design in the violent city. London, 1973. pp. 264. bibliog.

SOUTHALL (AIDAN WILLIAM) ed. Urban anthropology: cross-cultural studies of urbanization. New York, 1973. pp. 489. bibliogs.

WALTON (JOHN) and CARNS (DONALD E.) eds. Cities in change: studies on the urban condition. Boston, [Mass., 1973]. pp. 716.

SOCIOLOGY, URBAN
See also the subdivision Social conditions under the names of cities and towns

SOCIOMETRY

RAINIO (KULLERVO) Group maze: experiments and simulations in problem-solving by groups. Helsinki 1972. pp. 119. bibliog. (Societas Scientiarum Fennica. Commentationes Scientiarum Socialium. 3. 1972)

SODA INDUSTRY

- Japan

SEKI (SHOZABURO) The ammonium chloride and soda ash dual manufacturing process in Japan. (ID/SER.F/4). New York, United Nations Industrial Development Organization, 1969. pp. 33. (Fertilizer Industry Series. Monographs. No.4)

SÖDERALA

- Population

RONDAHL (BJÖRN) Emigration, folkomflyttning och säsongarbete i ett sågverksdistrikt i södra Hälsingland, 1865-1910: Söderala kommun, etc. Stockholm, [1972]. pp. 288. bibliog. (Uppsala. Universitet. Historiska Institutionen. Studia Historica Upsaliensia. 40) With English summary.

SOGAS

COHEN (DAVID WILLIAM) The historical tradition of Busoga: Mukama and Kintu. Oxford, 1972. pp. 218. bibliog.

SOIL CONSERVATION

- Germany

LUETTMER (JACOBUS) Bodenschutz in der Flurbereinigung: Untersuchungen über Notwendigkeit und Möglichkeiten des Bodenschutzes in Flurbereinigungsverfahren, dargestellt am Beispiel der Gemarkung Martinshöhe/Pfalz. Lengerich, 1957. pp. 50. bibliog. (Schriftenreihe für Flurbereinigung. Heft 14) 3 maps in end pocket.

- India

INDIA. Planning Commission. Programme Evaluation Organisation. Publications. No.41. Study of soil conservation programme for agricultural land. [Delhi], 1964 [or rather 1965]. pp. 292.

SOILS

- France

JORRE (GEORGES) Le Terrefort toulousain et lauragais: histoire et géographie agraires; texte revu par D. Faucher. [Toulouse, 1971]. pp. 348. bibliog.

- Nigeria

PULLAN (R. A.) The soils, soil landscapes and geomorphological evolution of a metasedimentary area in northern Nigeria. [Liverpool, 1970]. pp. 144. bibliog. (Liverpool. University. Department of Geography. Research Papers. No.6)

- South Africa

PHILLIPS (JOHN) author of The Tugela basin, etc. The Tugela basin and its influent surrounds: third progress report for the period 1st January to 31st December, 1965. [Pietermaritzburg, 1966]. fo. 216. bibliog.

SOKAGAKKAI

MURATA (KIYOAKI) Japan's new Buddhism: an objective account of Soka Gakkai. New York, 1969 repr. 1971. pp. 192. bibliog.

SOLARI (GIOELE)

GIOELE Solari, 1872-1952: testimonianze e bibliografia nel centenario della nascita. Torino, 1972. pp. 125. bibliog. (Turin. Accademia delle Scienze di Torino. Memorie. Classe di Scienze Morali, Storiche e Filologiche. Serie 4a, n.26)

SOLARI (LUIGI)

BRONSARD (CAMILLE) and SALVAS-BRONSARD (LISE) Notes sur "Théorie des choix et fonctions de consommation semi-agrégées" du professeur Luigi Solari. Montréal, 1972. fo. 28. bibliog. (Montreal. Université. Département des Sciences Economiques. Cahiers. No. 7203)

SOLDIERS

- Education, Non-military - Germany

GRIMM (SIEGFRIED) Der Bundesrepublik treu zu dienen: die geistige Rüstung der Bundeswehr. Düsseldorf, 1970. pp. 352. bibliog.

GENSCHEL (DIETRICH) Wehrreform und Reaktion: die Vorbereitung der Inneren Führung,1951-1956. Hamburg, [1972]. pp. 364. bibliog.

- Poland

KUROPIESKA (JÓZEF) Wspomnienia dowódcy kompanii, 1923-1934. Warszawa, 1971. pp. 331.

- Russia

STEMANN (INGEBORG) Russiske Bønder fortaeller. København, 1932. pp. 126.

- United Kingdom

BAYNES (J.C.M.) The soldier in modern society. London, 1972. pp. 227. bibliog.

SOLDIERS (Cont'd.)

- United Kingdon - Religious life

CAIRNS (DAVID SMITH) The army and religion: an enquiry and its bearing upon the religious life of the nation. London, 1919. pp. 455.

SOLIDARITAT CATALANA

CAMPS I ARBOIX (JOAQUIM DE) Historia de la solidaritat catalana. Barcelona, 1970. pp. 285.

SOLIDARITY

VLADIMIRSKII (D.V.) Solidarnost' i obshchestvennoe razvitie. Parizh, 1948. pp. 46.

SOLOMON (GEORGII ALEKSANDROVICH)

SOLOMON (GEORGII ALEKSANDROVICH) Sredi krasnykh vozhdei: lichno perezhitoe i vidennoe na sovetskoi sluzhbe. Parizh, 1930. 2 vols (in 1).

SOLOMON (SAUL)

SOLOMON (WILLIAM EWART GLADSTONE) Saul Solomon, 'the member for Cape Town'. Cape Town, 1948. pp. 362.

SOLOMON ISLANDS

- Census

BRITISH SOLOMON ISLANDS PROTECTORATE. Census, 1970. Report on the census of the population, 1970; by K. Groenewegen...; with an introduction and administrative report by D.C. Horton. n.p., [1972]. pp. 413.

- Economic policy

BRITISH SOLOMON ISLANDS PROTECTORATE. 1963-65. Draft third development plan, 1963-1966; (with) Draft fourth development plan, 1965-1968. [Honiara, 1963-65]. 2 pts. (Legislative Council. Papers. 1965. No. 62) Microfilm: 1 reel.

- Social policy

BRITISH SOLOMON ISLANDS PROTECTORATE. 1963-65. Draft third development plan, 1963-1966; (with) Draft fourth development plan, 1965-1968. [Honiara, 1963-65]. 2 pts. (Legislative Council. Papers. 1965. No. 62) Microfilm: 1 reel.

- Statistics

BRITISH SOLOMON ISLANDS PROTECTORATE. Statistical Office. Annual abstract of statistics. a., 1970 [1st issue]- Honiara.

SOLOV'EV (VLADIMIR SERGEEVICH)

FUHRMANN (JOSEPH T.) and others. Essays on Russian intellectual history;...edited by Leon Borden Blair. Austin, [1971]. pp. 123. bibliogs. (Texas University. Walter Prescott Webb Memorial Lectures. 5)

SOLZHENITSYN (ALEKSANDR ISAEVICH)

LUKÁCS (GEORG) Marxist. Solzhenitsyn;...translated from the German by William David Graf. London, [1970]. pp. 88.

DELO Solzhenitsyna. 1. 2nd ed. Paris, [1971]. pp. 176. bibliog.

BJORKEGREN (HANS) Aleksandr Solzhenitsyn: a biography;...translated from the Swedish by Kaarina Eneberg. Henley, Oxon, 1973. pp. 205. bibliog.

SOMALILAND

- Foreign relations

HOSKYNS (CATHERINE) ed. Case studies in African diplomacy: number 2: the Ethiopia-Somali-Kenya dispute, 1960-67. Dar es Salaam, 1969. pp. 91. bibliog. (Dar es Salaam. University. Institute of Public Administration. Studies. No.9)

SONCINO FAMILY

MANZONI (GIACOMO) Count. Annali tipografici dei Soncino, contenenti la descrizione e illustrazione delle stampe Ebraiche, Talmudiche, Rabbiniche, Greche, Latine ed Italiane eseguite dai medesimi nel secolo XV, etc. Bologna, 1883-86; Farnborough, 1969. 3 vols. (in 1). Library has vols. 2, 3 pt.1, 4 pt.2; probably no more published.

SONG OF SOLOMON

MACCALL (WILLIAM) Author of "The elements of individualism". The song of songs: a lecture, [etc.]. London, 1862. pp. 22.

SONINKE (AFRICAN PEOPLE)

POLLET (ERIC) and WINTER (GRACE) La société soninke: Dyahunu, Mali. Bruxelles, [1971]. pp. 566. bibliog. (Brussels. Université Libre. Institut de Sociologie. Etudes Ethnologiques)

SOONG FAMILY
See SUNG FAMILY

SORBS
See WENDS

SOREL (GEORGES)

FREUND (MICHAEL) Historian. Georges Sorel: der revolutionäre Konservatismus. 2nd ed. Frankfurt am Main, [1972]. pp. 397. bibliogs.

SØRENSEN (POUL)

TOPSØE (VILHELM) Poul Sørensen og dansk politik, 1960-1970. [Copenhagen, 1972]. pp. 174.

SORGHUM

FOOD AND AGRICULTURE ORGANIZATION. Commodity Bulletin Series. No. 49. Survey of export markets for sorghum. Rome, 1971. pp. 40.

SOSUA

- History

KAETSCH (SIEGFRIED) and others. Sosua: verheissenes Land?; eine Dokumentation zu Adaptionsproblemen deutsch-jüdischer Siedler der Dominikanischen Republik. Dortmund, 1970. pp. 297. bibliog. (Kontaktprogramm zur Sozialwissenschaftlichen Forschung in Lateinamerika. Arbeitsunterlage zur Lateinamerikaforschung. 38/39)

SOUL

A LETTER on the reputed immateriality of the human soul, with strictures on the Rev. T. Rennell's late publication entitled "Remarks on scepticism", etc. London, Hunter, 1821. pp. iv, 64.

WESTERBY (W.M.) and BRADLAUGH (CHARLES) Has, or is, man a soul?: verbatim report of a two nights' public debate at Burnley. London, [1879?]. pp. 67, iii.

SOUTH AFRICA

- Bibliography

CAPE TOWN. University. School of Librarianship. Bibliographical Series. Consolidated list, 1941-1966. Cape Town, University of Cape Town Libraries, 1966. pp. (ii), 38. 22½cm.

MUSIKER (REUBEN) compiler. Guide to South African reference books. 5th ed. Cape Town, 1971. pp. 136.

- Commerce

HART (GILLIAN PATRICIA) Some socio-economic aspects of African entrepreneurship: with particular reference to the Transkei and Ciskei. Grahamstown, 1972. pp. 237. bibliog. (Rhodes University. Institute of Social and Economic Research. Occasional Papers. No. 16)

SOUTH AFRICA. Commission of Inquiry into the Export Trade of the Republic of South Africa. 1972. Report; [H.J.J. Reynders, chairman] (R.P. 69/1972). in SOUTH AFRICA. Parliament. House of Assembly. Votes and proceedings; (with Printed annexures).

- Constitution

SOUTH AFRICA. Parliament. House of Assembly. Select Committee on the Constitution and Elections Amendment Bill. 1973. Report (with Proceedings and Minutes of evidence); [S.F. Kotzé, chairman] (S.C.5-1973). in SOUTH AFRICA. Parliament. House of Assembly. Select Committee reports.

- Constitutional law

MATHEWS (ANTHONY S.) Law, order and liberty in South Africa. Berkeley, 1972. pp. 318. bibliog.

- Defences

SOUTH AFRICA. Parliament. House of Assembly. Select Committee on the Defence Amendment Bill. 1972. Report (with Proceedings); [H.H. Smit, chairman]. (S.C.8-1972). in SOUTH AFRICA. Parliament. House of Assembly. Select Committee reports.

- Description and travel

HOAGLAND (JIM) South Africa: civilizations in conflict. London, 1973. pp. 428. bibliog.

- Economic conditions

HORNER (J.A.) Black pay and productivity in South Africa: an address to the South African Institute of Personnel Management, June 1972. [Johannesburg], 1972. pp. 23. bibliog.

DUGGAN (WILLIAM REDMAN) A socioeconomic profile of South Africa. New York, 1973. pp. 181. bibliog.

- Economic history

STUDIES in economics and economic history: essays in honour of Professor H.M. Robertson; edited by Marcelle Kooy. London, 1972. pp. 313. bibliogs.

- Economic History - Sources

HOUGHTON (D. HOBART) and DAGUT (JENIFER) eds. Source material on the South African economy, 1860-1970. Cape Town, 1972-73. 3 vols. bibliogs.

- Economic policy

STEYN (DANIEL H.) Die instelling van die ekonomiese ontwikkelingsprogram vir Suid-Afrika. [Johannesburg, 196-?]. pp. 35.

SWANEPOEL (J.) Enkele gedagtes in verband met die ekonomiese ontwikkeling van die bantoegebiede in Suid-Afrika. Sovenga, S.A., 1967. pp. 20. (University College of the North. Publications. Series C. No. 3)

CILLIERS (STEPHANUS PETRUS) Appeal to reason. Stellenbosch, [1971]. pp. 81.

HART (GILLIAN PATRICIA) Some socio-economic aspects of African entrepreneurship: with particular reference to the Transkei and Ciskei. Grahamstown, 1972. pp. 237. bibliog. (Rhodes University. Institute of Social and Economic Research. Occasional Papers. No. 16)

PERKINS (JAMES OLIVER NEWTON) and others. Macroeconomic policy: a comparative study: Australia, Canada, New Zealand, South Africa. London, 1972. pp. 211. bibliogs.

BELL (TREVOR) Industrial decentralisation in South Africa. Cape Town, 1973. pp. 304. bibliog.

- Emigration and immigration

SOUTH AFRICA. Bureau of Statistics. Migration statistics. [in Afrikaans and English]. irreg., 1966/1969 [1st]- Pretoria. Supersedes its External migration, which see.

STONE (JOHN) D.Phil. Colonist or uitlander?: a study of the British immigrant in South Africa. Oxford, 1973. pp. 313. bibliog.

- Foreign economic relations - Botswana

DALE (RICHARD) Botswana and its southern neighbor: the patterns of linkage and the options in statecraft. [Athens, Ohio, 1970]. fo. 22. (Ohio University. Center for International Studies. Papers in International Studies. Africa Series. No. 6)

- Foreign relations

VORSTER (BALTHAZAR JOHANNES) South Africa's outward policy. Cape Town, 1970. pp. 11.

BARBER (JAMES P.) South Africa's foreign policy, 1945-1970. London, 1973. pp. 325. bibliog.

- Foreign relations - Botswana

DALE (RICHARD) Botswana and its southern neighbor: the patterns of linkage and the options in statecraft. [Athens, Ohio, 1970]. fo. 22. (Ohio University. Center for International Studies. Papers in International Studies. Africa Series. No. 6)

- History

CARTWRIGHT (ALAN PATRICK) The first South African: the life and times of Sir Percy Fitzpatrick. Cape Town, 1971 repr. 1972. pp. 256.

SELBY (JOHN) Shaka's heirs. London, 1971. pp. 232. bibliog.

SILLERY (ANTHONY) John Mackenzie of Bechuanaland, 1835-1899: a study in humanitarian imperialism. Cape Town, 1971. pp. 236. bibliog.

SELBY (JOHN) A short history of South Africa. London, 1973. pp. 288. bibliog.

SOUTH AFRICA (Cont'd.)

- History - Sources

KARIS (THOMAS) and CARTER (GWENDOLEN MARGARET) eds. From protest to challenge: a documentary history of African politics in South Africa, 1882-1964. Stanford, [1972] in progress. (Stanford University. Hoover Institution on War, Revolution and Peace. Hoover Institution Publications. 89)

SMIT (ERASMUS) The diary of Erasmus Smit; edited by H.F. Schoon; translated by W.G.A. Mears. Cape Town, 1972. pp. 189.

- Industries

SOUTH AFRICA. Bureau of Statistics. Reports. Nos. I.C.1-19,21-70. Industrial censuses; 1950-51 to 1960-61: reports. Pretoria, [1964-67]. 69 pts. (in 5 vols.)

SOUTH AFRICA. Board for the Decentralisation of Industry. Report on activities. a., 1969- Pretoria.

BELL (TREVOR) Industrial decentralisation in South Africa. Cape Town, 1973. pp. 304. bibliog.

- Industries - Directories

PRETORIA. University of South Africa. Bureau of Market Research. BM industrial directory; compiled by F.J.C. Oosthuizen [and others] under the supervision of P.A. Nel. Pretoria, 1969. pp. 1223.

- Native races

HORRELL (MURIEL) compiler. The "pass laws". [Johannesburg], 1960. pp. 78. (South African Institute of Race Relations. Fact Papers. No. 7)

REYBURN (LAWRENCE) The urban African in local government: a study of the advisory board system and its operation. Johannesburg, 1960. pp. 61. (South African Institute of Race Relations. Fact Papers. No.9)

SWANEPOEL (J.) Enkele gedagtes in verband met die ekonomiese ontwikkeling van die bantoegebiede in Suid-Afrika. Sovenga, S.A., 1967. pp. 20. (University College of the North. Publications. Series C. No. 3)

DAVIES (WILLIAM J.) Patterns of non-white population distribution in Port Elizabeth with special reference to the application of the Group Areas Act. Port Elizabeth, 1971. pp. 256. bibliog. (University of Port Elizabeth. Institute for Planning Research. Special Publications. No.1)

DESMOND (COSMAS) The discarded people: an account of African resettlement in South Africa. Harmondsworth, 1971. pp. 265. bibliog.

HORRELL (MURIEL) Action, reaction and counter-action: a brief review of non-white political movements in South Africa. [new ed.] Johannesburg, 1971. pp. 151.

KARIS (THOMAS) and CARTER (GWENDOLEN MARGARET) eds. From protest to challenge: a documentary history of African politics in South Africa, 1882-1964. Stanford, [1972] in progress. (Stanford University. Hoover Institution on War, Revolution and Peace. Hoover Institution Publications. 89)

HORNER (J.A.) Black pay and productivity in South Africa: an address to the South African Institute of Personnel Management, June 1972. [Johannesburg], 1972. pp. 23. bibliog.

ROGERS (BARBARA) South Africa: the "Bantu homelands". London, 1972. pp. 45. (International Defence and Aid Fund [for Southern Africa]. Pamphlets)

- Parliament - Elections

LEVER (HENRY) The South African voter: some aspects of voting behaviour with special reference to the general elections of 1966 and 1970. Cape Town, 1972. pp. 221.

- Parliament - Rules and practice

SOUTH AFRICA. Parliament. House of Assembly. 1972. Standing orders of the House of Assembly. Vol. 1. Public business. [Cape Town], 1972. pp. 353. In English and Afrikaans.

- Politics and government

GRAAFF (Sir DE VILLIERS) Sir De Villiers Graaff opens United Party Bloemfontein Congress 2 October, 1964. Johannesburg, [United Party], Division of Information and Research, 1964. pp. 19. In English and Afrikaans.

LASS (HANS DETLEF) Nationale Integration in Südafrika: die Rolle der Parteien zwischen den Jahren 1922 and 1934. Hamburg, 1969. pp. 274. bibliog. (Hamburger Gesellschaft für Völkerrecht und Auswärtige Politik. Darstellungen zur Auswärtigen Politik. Band 8)

NAUDÉ (J.D.) Generaal J.B.M. Hertzog en die ontstaa van die Nasionale Party, 1913-1914. Johannesburg, 1970. pp. 194. bibliog.

SOUTH Africa: government and politics; edited by Denis Worrall. Pretoria, 1971. pp. 366. bibliogs.

VAN ROOYEN (JAN J.) Ons politiek van naby. Kaapstad, 1971. pp. 186.

KARIS (THOMAS) and CARTER (GWENDOLEN MARGARET) eds. From protest to challenge: a documentary history of African politics in South Africa, 1882-1964. Stanford, [1972] in progress. (Stanford University. Hoover Institution on War, Revolution and Peace. Hoover Institution Publications. 89)

SOUTH AFRICA. Department of the Interior. Annual report. 1972 [1st] to date included in SOUTH AFRICA. Parliament. House of Assembly. Votes and proceedings; (with Printed annexures).

DAVIDSON (APOLLON BORISOVICH) Iuzhnaia Afrika: stanovlenie sil protesta, 1870-1924. Moskva, 1972. pp. 614. bibliog.

MATHEWS (ANTHONY S.) Law, order and liberty in South Africa. Berkeley, 1972. pp. 318. bibliog.

- Population

VAN RENSBURG (NIC J.) Population explosion in southern Africa. Pretoria, 1972. pp. 189.

- Public lands

SOUTH AFRICA. Parliament. Senate. Select Committee on Concessions, Expropriation of Property and Leasing of State Land. 1970. Report...together with the proceedings of the Committee and minutes of evidence; [D.G.J. van Rensburg, chairman] (S.C.5/1970). in SOUTH AFRICA. Parliament. Senate. Reports from the Sessional and Select Committees.

SOUTH AFRICA. Commission of Inquiry into Concessions, Expropriation of Property and Leasing of State Land. 1972. Report; [Daniël Grobler Janse van Rensburg, chairman] (R.P. 54/1972). in SOUTH AFRICA. Parliament. House of Assembly. Votes and proceedings; (with Printed annexures).

SOUTH AFRICA. Parliament. House of Assembly. Select Committee on State-owned Land. 1973. Report; [G. de V. Morrison, chairman] (S.C.11-1973). in SOUTH AFRICA. Parliament. House of Assembly. Select Committee reports.

- Race question

MANDELA (NELSON ROLIHLAHLA) defendant. Nelson Mandela versus the state; [speeches at his trial]. London, [196-?]. pp. 36.

MANDELA (NELSON ROLIHLAHLA) defendant. We accuse: (Nelson Mandela addresses South Africa). London, [1962?]. pp. 37.

PRINS (JAN) De beknelde kleurling: Zuid-Afrika's vierstromenbeleid. Assen, 1967. pp. 191. bibliog.

SWEDEN. Utrikesdepartementet. Aktstycken. Ny Serie II. 18. Apartheidfrågan i Förenta Nationerna: en faktasamling. Stockholm, 1967. pp. 135.

HORRELL (MURIEL) The African reserves of South Africa. Johannesburg, 1969. pp. 142.

FOLKERTS (MARTIN) Das Busch- und Bankenveld West-transvaals: wirtschafts- und bevölkerungsgeographische Konsequenzen der Politik der getrennten Entwicklung. Hamburg, 1970. pp. 391. bibliog. (Hamburg. Hansische Universität. Institut für Geographie und Wirtschaftsgeographie. Hamburger Geographische Studien. Heft 22)

VAN DEN BERGHE (PIERRE LOUIS) South Africa: a study in conflict. Berkeley, [Calif.], 1970. pp. 371. bibliog.

DAVENPORT (THOMAS RODNEY HOPE) The beginnings of urban segregation in South Africa: the Natives (Urban Areas) Act of 1923 and its background. Grahamstown, 1971. pp. 23. (Rhodes University. Institute of Social and Economic Research. Occasional Papers. No. 15)

DESMOND (COSMAS) The discarded people: an account of African resettlement in South Africa. Harmondsworth, 1971. pp. 265. bibliog.

HELLMANN (ELLEN P.) Soweto: Johannesburg's African city; based on an address given to the Natal Region of the S.A. Institute of Race Relations, and revised 1971. Johannesburg, 1971. pp. 31.

HORRELL (MURIEL) Action, reaction and counter-action: a brief review of non-white political movements in South Africa. [new ed.] Johannesburg, 1971. pp. 151.

MATHEWS (ANTHONY S.) Freedom and state security in the South African plural society. Johannesburg, [1971]. pp. 26. (South African Institute of Race Relations. Hoernlé Memorial Lectures. 1971)

VAN DER HORST (SHEILA T.) Progress and retrogression in South Africa: a personal appraisal. Johannesburg, [1971]. pp. 32.

WEST (MARTIN E.) Divided community: a study of social groups and racial attitudes in a South African town. Cape Town, 1971. pp. 125. bibliog.

FIRST (RUTH) and others. The South African connection: western investment in apartheid. London, [1972]. pp. 352.

HORRELL (MURIEL) Legislation and race relations: a summary of the main South African laws which affect race relationships. rev. ed. Johannesburg, 1971. pp. 121.

SOUTH AFRICAN COUNCIL OF CHURCHES and CHRISTIAN INSTITUTE OF SOUTHERN AFRICA. Study Project on Christianity in Apartheid Society. Economics Commission. Power, privilege and poverty; report...; [E.A. Barker, chairman]. Johannesburg, 1972. pp. 127. (South African Council of Churches, and Christian Institute of Southern Africa. Study Project on Christianity in Apartheid Society. Spro-cas Publications. 7)

SOUTH African dialogue: contrasts in South African thinking on basic race issues; edited by N.J. Rhoodie. Johannesburg, [1972]. pp. 622.

STUDENT perspectives on South Africa; [papers of the first research workshop of the Abe Bailey Institute of Interracial Studies, Cape Town University]; edited by Hendrik W. van der Merwe and David Welsh. Cape Town, 1972. pp. 229.

ZULU (ALPHEUS HAMILTON ZULU) The dilemma of the black South African. [Cape Town], 1972. pp. 14. (Cape Town. University. T.B. Davie Memorial Lectures. 12)

HOAGLAND (JIM) South Africa: civilizations in conflict. London, 1973. pp. 428. bibliog.

SACHS (ALBIE) Justice in South Africa. London, 1973. pp. 288. bibliog. (Brighton. University of Sussex. Columbus Centre. Studies in Race Relations)

SOUTH AFRICA. Parliament. House of Assembly. Select Committee on Bantu Affairs. 1973. First and second (and third and fourth) reports; [P.Z.J. van Vuuren, chairman] (A.2 and S.C.12 and 13-1973). in SOUTH AFRICA. Parliament. House of Assembly. Select Committee reports.

- Social conditions

KINLOCH (GRAHAM C.) The sociological study of South Africa: an introduction. Johannesburg, 1972. pp. 180. bibliogs.

DUGGAN (WILLIAM REDMAN) A socioeconomic profile of South Africa. New York, 1973. pp. 181. bibliog.

- Social life and customs

SCHREINER (OLIVE) From man to man; or, Perhaps only-: [a novel]. London, 1926. pp. 483. Lacking title-page.

- Social policy

CILLIERS (STEPHANUS PETRUS) Appeal to reason. Stellenbosch, [1971]. pp. 81.

- Statistics, Vital

SOUTH AFRICA. Bureau of Statistics. Report on deaths: South Africa. a., 1963/1966, 1967- Pretoria. [in English and Afrikaans] Earlier reports included in SOUTH AFRICA. Parliament. House of Assembly. Votes and proceedings; [with Printed annexures], U.G.26/1961, R.P.17/1961, 45/1965, 63/1965, which see.

MOSTERT (W.P.) 'N ontleding van die mortaliteit en oorsake van dood by Blankes, Kleurlinge en Asiate in die republiek van Suid-Afrika gedurende die jaar 1961. [Pretoria], 1967. pp. 106. (South Africa. National Bureau of Educational and Social Research. Research Series. No. 48)

ENGELBRECHT (J.) Die fertiliteit van 'n groep Blanke Afrikaanssprekende vroue in Pretoria. Pretoria, 1968. pp. 84. bibliog. (South Africa. National Bureau of Educational and Social Research. Research Series. No.65)

- Territorial expansion

HYAM (RONALD) The failure of South African expansion, 1908-1948. London, 1972. pp. 219. bibliog.

SOUTH AFRICAN WAR, 1899-1902

NIKITINA (IRINA ARKAD'EVNA) Zakhvat burskikh respublik Angliei, 1899-1902 gg. Moskva, 1970. pp. 213. bibliog.

- Public opinion

PRICE (RICHARD) D.Phil. An imperial war and the British working class: working-class attitudes and reactions to the Boer War, 1899-1902. London, 1972. pp. 279. bibliog.

KROELL (ULRICH) Die internationale Buren-Agitation, 1899-1902: Haltung der Öffentlichkeit und Agitation zugunsten der Buren in Deutschland, Frankreich und den Niederlanden während des Burenkrieges. Münster, [1973]. pp. 478. bibliog.

SOUTH SASKATCHEWAN RIVER

CANADA. Prairie Farm Rehabilitation Administration. 1967. South Saskatchewan river project, 1958-1967. Ottawa, 1967. pp. (30).

SOUTH WEST AFRICA

The CASE for South-West Africa; compiled by Anthony Lejeune. London, 1971. pp. 245. bibliog.

- Census

SOUTH WEST AFRICA. Census, 1960. Population census, 6th September, 1960. [Pretoria, 1965-66.] 3 vols. (in 1). In English and Afrikaans.

- International status

DUGARD (JOHN) ed. The South West Africa/Namibia dispute: documents and scholarly writings on the controversy between South Africa and the United Nations. Berkeley, [1973]. pp. 585. bibliog.

SLONIM (SOLOMON) South West Africa and the United Nations: an international mandate in dispute. Baltimore, [1973]. pp. 409. bibliog.

- Politics and government

SOUTH WEST AFRICA. Administration. White paper on the activities of the different branches. a., 1968- n.p.

LAZAR (LEONARD) Namibia. London, [1972]. pp. 107. bibliog.

MANCHESTER NONVIOLENT ACTION GROUP. Namibia: a call to be answered; the facts about South Africa's illegal occupation of South West Africa. London, [1972]. pp. 26. bibliog.

SOUTHAMPTON
- History

SOUTHAMPTON. City Record Office. Southampton in 1620 and the "Mayflower"; an exhibition of documents...to celebrate the 350th anniversary of the sailing of the "Mayflower" from Southampton in 1620; [with a supplement]. Southampton, 1970. 2 pts. (in 1 vol.)

- History - Sources

SOUTHAMPTON. Civic Record Office. Guide to the records of the Corporation and absorbed authorities in the Civic Record Office. Southampton, 1964. pp. 56. (Southampton. Corporation. Southampton Records. 1)

SOUTHWARK
- Almshouses and workhouses

MORLEY (B.G.) A history of Orchard Lodge from 1849 to 1970. [London, 1970]. pp. 19.

SOVEREIGNTY

NELSON (LEONARD) Die Rechtswissenschaft ohne Recht: kritische Betrachtungen über die Grundlagen des Staats- und Völkerrechts, insbesondere über die Lehre von der Souveranität. 2nd ed. Hamburg, [1949]. pp. 221.

RUMPF (HELMUT) Land ohne Souveränität: Beiträge zur Deutschlandfrage. Karlsruhe, 1969. pp. 148.

BLIX (HANS) Sovereignty, aggression and neutrality: (three lectures). Stockholm, 1970. pp. 63.

CARREAU (DOMINIQUE) Souveraineté et coopération monétaire internationale. Paris, [1970]. pp. 530. bibliog.

MILOSAVLEVSKI (SLAVKO) Socijalizam i suverenitet. Beograd, 1971. pp. 95.

USHAKOV (NIKOLAI ALEKSANDROVICH) Nevmeshatel'stvo vo vnutrennie dela gosudarstv. Moskva, 1971. pp. 166.

JOHNSON (DO) Suveränitet i havet och luftrummet: folkrüttsliga studier kring suveränitetsanspråk i öppna havet samt den nationella jurisdiktionens gränser i havet och luftrummet: Souveraineté sur la mer et dans les airs, etc. Stockholm, [1972]. pp. 413. bibliog. With French summary.

COLLOQUE SUR LE DROIT PETROLIER ET LA SOUVERAINETE DES PAYS PRODUCTEURS, ALGER, 1971. Etudes présentées au Colloque... organisé par l'Association Internationale des Juristes Democrates, etc. Paris, 1973. pp. 176.

SOVEREIGNTY, VIOLATION OF
- United States

RUKSENAS (ALGIS) Day of shame: the truth about the murderous happenings aboard the cutter Vigilant during the Russian-American confrontation off Martha's Vineyard. New York, [1973]. pp. 368.

SOVIET CENTRAL ASIA

LENINIZM i opyt stroitel'stva sotsializma v respublikakh Sovetskogo Vostoka: materialy mezhrespublikanskoi nauchnoi konferentsii, posviashchennoi 100-letiiu so dnia rozhdeniia V.I.Lenina 21-23 oktiabria 1969 g. Frunze, 1970. pp. 167.

- Constitutional history

TASHKENT. Universitet. Trudy. vyp.282. Nekotorye voprosy gosudarstva i prava. Tashkent, 1966. pp. 119.

- Economic conditions

SREDNEAZIATSKII ekonomicheskii raion. Moskva, 1972. pp. 298. bibliog. (Akademiia Nauk SSSR. Sovet po Izucheniiu Proizvoditel'nykh Sil. Razvitie i Razmeshchenie Proizvoditel'nykh Sil SSSR)

- Economic history

KHASANOV (KUCHKAR KH.) TsK VKP/b/ v bor'be za postroenie sotsializma v Srednei Azii, 1924-1937 gg. Tashkent, 1968. pp. 219. bibliog.

ABDUSHUKUROV (RUSTAM KHAKIMOVICH) Torzhestvo leninskoi teorii perekhoda otstalykh stran k sotsializmu i kommunizmu, minuia kapitalizm. Tashkent, 1972. pp. 371. bibliog.

- History

KHODZHAEV (FAIZULLA) Izbrannye trudy. Tashkent, 1970-73. 3 vols.

GAFUROVA (KAPITOLINA ALEKSANDROVNA) Bor'ba za internatsional'noe splochenie trudiashchikhsia Srednei Azii i Kazakhstana v pervye gody Sovetskoi vlasti, 1917-1924. Moskva, 1972. pp. 301. bibliog.

- History - Bibliography

VITKIND (N.IA.) compiler. Bibliografiia po Srednei Azii: ukazatel' literatury po kolonial'noi politike tsarizma v Srednei Azii; pod redaktsiei A.V. Shestakova. Moskva, 1929. pp. 166. (Kommunisticheskii Universitet Trudiashchikhsia Vostoka. Nauchno-Issledovatel'skaia Assotsiatsiia. Trudy. vyp.4)

- Nationalism

KHIDOIATOV (GOGA ABRAROVICH) Leninskaia natsional'naia programma i sovremennaia ideologicheskaia bor'ba. Tashkent, 1972. pp. 296.

- Rural conditions

IUSUPOV (ERKIN) Obshchee i osobennoe v unichtozhenii protivopolozhnosti mezhdu gorodom i derevnei v respublikakh Sovetskogo Vostoka. Tashkent, 1972. pp. 285.

SOVIET FAR EAST
- Constitutional history

GLUSHCHENKO (IDA IOSIFOVNA) Bol'shevistskaia organizatsiia Primor'ia v period uprocheniia Sovetskoi vlasti. Vladivostok, 1960. pp. 30.

NAZIMOK (VASILII NIKITICH) Bor'ba Sovetov protiv burzhuaznykh organov samoupravleniia na Dal'nem Vostoke, 1917-1918 gg. Tomsk, 1968. pp. 111.

- Economic conditions - Bibliography

VOROB'EV (VLADIMIR VASIL'EVICH) and VERSHINSKAIA (N.I.) compilers. Publikatsii sibirskikh i dal'nevostochnykh organizatsii Geograficheskogo obshchestva SSSR, 1945-1963 gg.: sistematicheskii i avtorskii ukazateli. Irkutsk, 1966. pp. 166.

- Economic history

SIBIR' i Dal'nii Vostok v period vosstanovleniia narodnogo khoziaistva. vyp.1. Tomsk, 1963. pp. 212.

- History - 1917-1921, Revolution

NAZIMOK (VASILII NIKITICH) Bor'ba Sovetov protiv burzhuaznykh organov samoupravleniia na Dal'nem Vostoke, 1917-1918 gg. Tomsk, 1968. pp. 111.

- Industries - Bibliography

KIRSANOVA (M.I.) and others, compilers. Ekonomika, razmeshchenie i organizatsiia promyshlennogo proizvodstva Sibiri i Dal'nego Vostoka: bibliografiia, 1917-1965. Novosibirsk, 1968-69. 2 vols.

- Politics and government

LENINSKAIA gvardiia na Dal'nem Vostoke: zamechatel'nye dal'nevostochniki. Khabarovsk, 1970. pp. 510.

SOVIET NORTH

SOVETSKAIA Arktika: moria i ostrova Severnogo Ledovitogo okeana. Moskva, 1970. pp. 256. bibliog. (Akademiia Nauk SSSR. Institut Geografii. Prirodnye Usloviia i Estestvennye Resursy SSSR)

- Economic conditions

DANISHEVSKII (I.I.) Ekonomicheskoe polozhenie nashego Severa, ego vneshniia torgovlia v sviazi s perezhivaemymi sobytiiami; Lesnye promysly, tekhnicheskaia i khimicheskaia obrabotka dereva na Severe i spetsial'noe lesotekhnicheskoe obrazovanie na Severe. Arkhangel'sk, 1918. pp. 26. 2 reports given in 1917

CHERTOV (LEONID GEORGIEVICH) Osnovnye problemy ispol'zovaniia prirodnykh resursov Severo-Zapada. Leningrad, 1964. pp. 224. bibliog.

DOGAEV (IURII MIKHAILOVICH) ed. Ekonomicheskie i geograficheskie problemy severnoi tekhniki. Moskva, 1972. pp. 290. bibliog.

KRIUCHKOV (VASILII VASIL'EVICH) Krainii Sever: problemy ratsional'nogo ispol'zovaniia prirodnykh resursov. Moskva, 1973. pp. 184. bibliog.

- Economic history

UVACHAN (VASILII NIKOLAEVICH) Put' narodov Severa k sotsializmu: opyt sotsialisticheskogo stroitel'stva na Eniseiskom Severe; istoricheskii ocherk; predislovie... A.P. Okladnikova. Moskva, 1971. pp. 391.

- Economic policy

AKADEMIIA NAUK SSSR. Sovet po Izucheniiu Proizvoditel'nykh Sil. Komissiia po Problemam Severa. Problemy Severa. vyp.17. Razvitie proizvoditel'nykh sil Severa i nauchno-tekhnicheskii progress. Moskva, 1972. pp. 203.

- Native races

OSUSHCHESTVLENIE leninskoi natsional'noi politiki u narodov Krainego Severa. Moskva, 1971. pp. 344.

KLESHCHENOK (IVAN PAVLOVICH) Istoricheskii opyt KPSS po osushchestvleniiu leninskoi natsional'noi olitiki sredi malykh narodov Severa, 1917-1935, etc. Moskva, 1972. pp. 239. bibliog.

SOVIETS

HILLMANN (GUENTHER) ed. Die Rätebewegung. Reinbek bei Hamburg, 1971-72. 2 vols. bibliogs.

- Germany

HILLMANN (GUENTHER) ed. Die Rätebewegung. Reinbek bei Hamburg, 1971-72. 2 vols. bibliogs.

- Russia

MOSCOW. Gorodskoi Sovet Deputatov Trudiashchikhsia. Osnovnye voprosy sovetskogo i khoziaistvennogo stroitel'stva: lektsii, chitannye na kursakh vydvizhentsev pri Moskovskom Sovete R., K. i K. D. Moskva, 1926. pp. 139.

SOVIETS - Russia (Cont'd.)

SOKOL'SKII (VLADIMIR DMITRIEVICH) "Novorossii-skaia respublika": Sovet rabochikh deputatov Novorossiiska v 1905 godu. Moskva, 1963. pp. 136.

CHERNOPITSKII (PAVEL GRIGOR'EVICH) Na velikom perelome: sel'skie Sovety Dona v period podgotovki i provedeniia massovoi kollektivizatsii, 1928-1931 gg. Rostov, 1965. pp. 174.

SHABANOV (MIKHAIL RODIONOVICH) Akty sel'skikh i poselkovykh Sovetov. Moskva, 1971. pp. 96.

CHANIIA (VALERIAN KALISTRATOVICH) Sovety v pervoi russkoi revoliutsii. Sukhumi, 1972. pp. 230.

- Russia - Statistics

RUSSIA (U.S.S.R.). Verkhovnyi Sovet. Prezidium. Otdel po Voprosam Raboty Sovetov. 1963. Itogi vyborov i sostav deputatov Verkhovnykh Sovetov soiuznykh, avtonomnykh respublik i mestnykh Sovetov deputatov trudiashchikhsia 1963 g.: statisticheskii sbornik. Moskva, 1963. pp. 223.

RUSSIA (U.S.S.R.). Verkhovnyi Sovet. Prezidium. Otdel po Voprosam Raboty Sovetov. 1965. Sostav deputatov mestnykh Sovetov deputatov trudiashchikhsia, izbrannykh v marte 1965 g.: statisticheskii sbornik. Moskva, 1965. pp. 235.

- Russia - Abkhazia

DZIDZARIIA (G.A.) Rol' Sovetov i "Kiaraza" v istorii revoliutsionnoi bor'by v Abkhazii, 1917-1921 gg. Sukhumi, 1971. pp. 80. Revised versions of periodical articles.

- Russia - Non-Russian territories

SAZHIN (GRIGORII MAKSIMOVICH) Sovet deputatov trudiashchikhsia natsional'nogo okruga. Moskva, 1972. pp. 68.

- Russia - Turkestan

RASHIDOV (GULIAMKADYR) Tashkentskii Sovet v bor'be za uprochenie Sovetskoi vlasti. Tashkent, 1960. pp. 184. Xerographic reprint.

- Russia - White Russia

GOLOVKO (ANATOLII ALEKSANDROVICH) Deiatel'nost' Sovetov Belorussii po osushchestvleniiu ekonomicheskoi politiki v derevne v 1917-1936 godakh. Minsk, 1968. pp. 125.

PETRIKOV (PETR TIKHONOVICH) Sovety deputatov trudiashchikhsia BSSR i ikh rol' v sozdanii material'no-tekhnicheskoi bazy kommunizma, 1959-1965 gg. Minsk, 1972. pp. 307.

SOWETO

- Social conditions

HELLMANN (ELLEN P.) Soweto: Johannesburg's African city; based on an address given to the Natal Region of the S.A. Institute of Race Relations, and revised 1971. Johannesburg, 1971. pp. 31.

SOYA-BEANS

- Paraguay

PARAGUAY. Ministerio de Agricultura y Ganaderia. 1972. Programa nacional de soja. Asuncion, 1972. pp. 119.

- United States

HOUCK (JAMES P.) and others. Soybeans and their products: markets, models, and policy. Minneapolis, [1972]. pp. 284.

SOYINKA (WOLE)

SOYINKA (WOLE) The man died: prison notes. London, 1972. pp. 315.

SPACE AND TIME

FRAASSEN (BAS. C. VAN) An introduction to the philosophy of time and space. New York, [1970]. pp. 224.

SCHRECKER (K.A.) Some problems of space and time. Pretoria, 1972. pp. 35. (Pretoria. University of Pretoria. Publications. New Series. No. 73)

SPACE FLIGHT

PEREL'MAN (ROMAN GRIGOR'EVICH) Tseli i puti pokoreniia kosmosa. Moskva, 1967. pp. 211. bibliog. (Akademiia Nauk SSSR. Nauchno-Populiarnaia Seriia)

SPACE FLIGHT TO THE MOON

ROSENGREN (KARL ERIK) Diffusion of news: the case of Sweden and Apollo 13. Stockholm, 1971. pp. 77. bibliog. (Psykologiskt Försvar. Nr. 51)

SPACE IN ECONOMICS

CAMBRE MARINO (JESUS) El espacio regional en el desarrollo economico de España: reflexiones criticas. Madrid, 1970. pp. 81. bibliog.

DEAN (ROBERT D.) and others, eds. Spatial economic theory: [a reader]. New York, [1970]. pp. 365.

FLESZAR (MIECZYSŁAW) and LESZCZYCKI (STANISŁAW) Spatial structure of Poland's economy. Warszawa, 1970. pp. 162. (Instytut Gospodarki Krajów Rozwijających Się. Teaching Materials: Advanced Course in National Economic Planning. vol. 5)

RICHARDSON (HARRY W.) ed. Regional economics: a reader. London, 1970. pp. 245. bibliog.

SIEBERT (HORST) Regionales Wirtschaftswachstum und interregionale Mobilität. 2nd ed. Tübingen, 1970. pp. 258. bibliog.

BERRY (BRIAN JOE LOBLEY) Géographie des marchés et du commerce de détail;...traduction de Bernard Marchand. Paris, [1971]. pp. 254.

GRZESZCZAK (JERZY) Koncepcje polaryzacyjne w przestrzennym zagospodarowaniu kraju: na przykładzie Francji. Warszawa, 1971. pp. 103. bibliog. (Polska Akademia Nauk. Komitet Przestrzennego Zagospodarowania Kraju. Studia. t.36) With Russian and English summaries.

O'NEILL (HELEN B.) Spatial planning in the small economy: a case study of Ireland. New York, 1971. pp. 221. bibliog.

VANNESTE (OLIVIER) The growth pole concept and the regional economic policy; with an example of application to the Westflemish economy. Brugge, 1971. pp. 274. bibliog. (College of Europe. Cahiers de Bruges. Nouvelle Série. [No.] 24)

KUKLIŃSKI (ANTONI) ed. Growth poles and growth centres in regional planning. Paris, [1972]. pp. 306. bibliogs. (United Nations Research Institute for Social Development. Regional Planning. vol. 5)

PERLMAN (MARK) and others, eds. Spatial, regional and population economics: essays in honor of Edgar M. Hoover. New York, [1972]. pp. 399. bibliogs.

SLATER (DAVID) Spatial aspects of the Peruvian socio-economic system, 1925-1968: [Ph.D. (London) thesis]. [1972]. fo. 372. bibliog. Typescript: unpublished. This thesis is the property of London University and may not be removed from the Library.

FREEMAN (DONALD B.) International trade, migration, and capital flows: a quantitative analysis of spatial economic interaction. Chicago, 1973. pp. 201. bibliog. (Chicago. University. Department of Geography. Research Papers. No. 146)

HAMER (ANDREW MARSHALL) Industrial exodus from central city: public policy and the comparative costs of location. Lexington, Mass., [1973]. pp. 107. bibliog.

- Mathematical models

NUTENKO (L.IA.) Ispol'zovanie problemy Shteinera i ee obobshchenii dlia postanovki i resheniia nekotorykh zadach prostranstvennoi ekonomiki. Moskva, 1968. pp. 81. bibliog. With English introduction.

SPACE LAW

KOSMOS i problema vseobshchego mira. Moskva, 1966. pp. 195.

LACHS (MANFRED) The law of outer space: an experience in contemporary law-making. Leiden, 1972. pp. 196. bibliog.

- Bibliography

WHITE (IRVIN L.) and others, compilers. Law and politics in outer space: a bibliography. Tucson, Arizona, [1972]. pp. 176.

SPACE SCIENCES

EUROPEAN ECONOMIC COMMUNITY. Études: Série Industrie. 4. The aeronautical and space industries of the Community compared with those of the United Kingdom and the United States. Brussels, 1971. 5 pts. (in 1 vol.). bibliog.

- International cooperation

TASSIN (JACQUES) Vers l'Europe spatiale. Paris, [1970]. pp. 255.

SPAIN

SPAIN. Oficina de Informacion Diplomatica. 1953. The Spanish controversy: sixty four questions on Spain. Madrid, 1953. pp. 34.

- Army

SPAIN. Ministerio de Defensa Nacional. 1936. Un ejercito popular y democratico al servicio del pueblo. Barcelona, [1936?]. pp. 15. (Charlas Populares lo que Significa la Guerra)

- Biography

DIRIGENTES: España 1970; repertorio biografico de politicos, alta milicia, alto clero y diversos profesionales españoles; [edited by] Joaquin Bardavio. Bilbao, [1970]. pp. 646.

MORATO CALDEIRO (JUAN JOSE) Lideres del movimiento obrero español, 1868-1921;...seleccion, presentacion y notas [by] Victor Manuel Arbeloa. Madrid, 1972. pp. 398.

- Census

SPAIN. Census, 1970. Censo de la poblacion de España.. 1970. Madrid, [1972? in progress].

- Civilization

MALTBY (WILLIAM S.) The black legend in England: the development of anti-Spanish sentiment, 1558-1660. Durham, N.C., 1971. pp. 180. bibliog.

- Colonies

FRANCO FERRAN (JOSE LUCIANO) La batalla por el dominio del Caribe y el golfo de Mexico. La Habana, 1964 [or rather 1965] in progress.

- Colonies - Administration

BERNARD (GILDAS) Le secrétariat d'état et le conseil espagnol des Indes, 1700-1808. Genève, 1972. pp. 296. bibliog. (Paris. Ecole Pratique des Hautes Etudes. Section des Sciences Historiques et Philologiques. Centre de Recherches d'Histoire et de Philologie. Hautes Etudes Médiévales et Modernes. No. 14)

- Colonies - History

MACHADO RIBAS (LINCOLN) Movimientos revolucionarios en las colonias españolas de America. Montevideo, [1940]. pp. 234.

GIBSON (CHARLES) Spain in America. New York, [1966]. pp. 239. bibliog.

- Commerce

SPAIN. Oficina de Estudios Economicos. Serie Comercio Exterior. No. 19. Comercio exterior, presupuestos y desarrollo económico en España; por Higinio Paris Eguilaz. Madrid, 1956. pp. 63.

DRIESCH (WILHELM VON DEN) Die ausländischen Kaufleute während des 18. Jahrhunderts in Spanien und ihre Beteiligung am Kolonialhandel. Köln, 1972. pp. 698,xv. bibliog. With summaries in English and Spanish.

- Constitutional history

COMELLAS GARCIA-LLERA (JOSE LUIS) El trienio constitucional: [1820-1823]. Madrid, 1963. pp. 446. (Pamplona. Universidad de Navarra. Facultad de Filosofia y Letras. Publicaciones. Coleccion Historica. 7)

ESTUDIOS sobre Cortes de Cadiz; [by] Maria Isabel Arriazu [and others]. Pamplona, 1967. pp. 486. (Pamplona. Universidad de Navarra. Facultad de Filosofia y Letras. Coleccion Historica. 15)

- Constitutional law

SPAIN. Statutes, etc. 1870-1971. Leyes politicas de España; ([by] Fernando Garrido Falla [and others]; [with supplementary] Anexo). Madrid, 1969-71. pp. 1991, 51. Supplementary Anexo in end pocket.

SPAIN. Statutes, etc. 1945-67. Fundamental laws of the state: the Spanish constitution. Madrid, 1972. pp. 209.

- Cortes

ESTUDIOS sobre Cortes de Cadiz; [by] Maria Isabel Arriazu [and others]. Pamplona, 1967. pp. 486. (Pamplona. Universidad de Navarra. Facultad de Filosofia y Letras. Coleccion Historica. 15)

SPAIN — Cortes (Cont'd.)

AGUIRRE BELLVER (JOAQUIN) Por los pasillos de las Cortes. Madrid, [1972]. pp. 263.

DIAZ-NOSTY (BERNARDO) Las Cortes de Franco: 30 años organicos. Barcelona, 1972. pp. 237.

- Cortes - Elections

TUSELL GOMEZ (JAVIER) Las elecciones del Frente Popular en España. Madrid, 1971. 2 vols.

- Description and travel

GLADFELTER (BRUCE G.) Meseta and campiña landforms in central Spain: a geomorphology of the Alto Henares basin. Chicago, 1971. pp. 204. bibliog. (Chicago. University. Department of Geography. Research Papers. No. 130)

- Economic conditions

SPAIN. Oficina de Coordinacion y Programacion Economica. Documentacion Economica. No. 20. Informe sobre España del Fondo Monetario Internacional. Madrid, 1961. pp. 135.

SPAIN. Oficina de Coordinacion y Programacion Economica. Documentacion Economica. No. 24. Evolucion de la economia española en el año 1960; (and Anejos). Madrid, 1961. 2 pts.

ESTRUCTURA y posibilidades de desarrollo economico de la[s] provincia[s]. [Madrid], 1970 in progress. bibliogs. Cover title reads: Estructura y perspectivas, [etc.].

LOPEZ MUÑOZ (ARTURO) pseud. Capitalismo español: una etapa decisiva; notas sobre la economia española, 1965-1970. Madrid, 1970 reprinted 1971. pp. 346.

VELARDE FUERTES (JUAN) España ante la socializacion economica: una primera aproximacion. Algorta, Vizcaya, 1970. pp. 167.

BATTELLE MEMORIAL INSTITUTE. La economia española en 1975: aplicacion de un modelo econometrico; investigacion dirigida por E. Fontela; (prologo y traduccion de Rodrigo Vazquez Candame con la colaboracion de Pedro Tedde). [Madrid], 1971. pp. 155. (Instituto de Desarrollo Economico. Estudios. [9])

ROMAN (MANUEL) The limits of economic growth in Spain. New York, 1971. pp. 186. bibliog.

FRAGA IRIBARNE (MANUEL) and others, eds. La España de los años 70. Madrid, 1972 in progress.

- Economic history

VALDEAVELLANO (LUIS G. DE) Origenes de la burguesia en la España medieval. Madrid, 1969. pp. 220. bibliog.

ENSAYOS sobre la economia española a mediados del siglo XIX; realizados en el Servicio de Estudios del Banco de España por Gabriel Tortella Casares [and others]. Madrid, 1970. pp. 399.

ROMEU (FERNANDA) Las clases trabajadoras en España, 1898-1930. Madrid, [1970]. pp. 221. bibliog.

BENAVIDES (LEANDRO) Politica economica en la II Republica española. Madrid, [1972]. pp. 278. bibliog.

TORTELLA CASARES (GABRIEL) Los origenes del capitalismo en España: banca, industria y ferrocarriles en el siglo XIX. Madrid, [1973]. pp. 407. bibliog.

- Economic history - Mathematical models

SPAIN. Comisaria del Plan de Desarrollo Economico y Social. 1972. (III Plan de desarrollo economico y social): series cronologicas del modelo econometrico. [Madrid], 1972. pp. 327.

- Economic policy

SPAIN. Ministerio de Hacienda y Economia. 1936. Utilizacion de la riqueza nacional en beneficio del pueblo. Barcelona, [1936?]. pp. 15. (Charlas Populares lo que Significa la Guerra)

SPAIN. Oficina de Estudios Economicos. Serie Comercio Exterior. No. 19. Comercio exterior, presupuestos y desarrollo economico en España; por Higinio Paris Eguilaz. Madrid, 1956. pp. 63.

SPAIN. Oficina de Coordinacion y Programacion Economica. Documentacion Economica. No. 14. Informes de la O.E.C.E. sobre el plan español de estabilizacion. Madrid, 1960. pp. 57.

SPAIN. Oficina de Coordinacion y Programacion Economica. Documentacion Economica. No. 15. Programa de ordenación de las inversiones para el año 1960. Madrid, 1960. pp. 57.

SPAIN. Oficina de Coordinacion y Programacion Economica. Documentacion Economica. No. 16. Informe sobre la ejecucion del programa de ordenacion de las inversiones para el año 1959. Madrid, 1960. pp. 41.

DIRECTRICES de politica de desarrollo para el periodo, 1968-1971. [Madrid?], 1967. pp. 15.

ESTRUCTURA y posibilidades de desarrollo economico de la[s] provincia[s]. [Madrid], 1970 in progress. bibliogs. Cover title reads: Estructura y perspectivas, [etc.].

CAMBRE MARIÑO (JESUS) El espacio regional en el desarrollo economico de España: reflexiones criticas. Madrid, 1970. pp. 81. bibliog.

SPAIN. Servicio Central de Planes Provinciales. 1970. Normativa de planes provinciales. Madrid, 1970. pp. 187. (Spain. Presidencia. Secretaria General Tecnica. Colección Compilaciones. 5)

ROMAN (MANUEL) The limits of economic growth in Spain. New York, 1971. pp. 186. bibliog.

SPAIN. Comisaria del Plan de Desarrollo Economico y Social. 1971. III Plan de desarrollo, 1972-1975. [Madrid], 1971. pp. 318, lxviii.

BENAVIDES (LEANDRO) Politica economica en la II Republica española. Madrid, [1972]. pp. 278. bibliog.

SPAIN. Comisaria del Plan de Desarrollo Economico y Social. 1972. (III Plan de desarrollo economico y social): desarrollo regional. [Madrid], 1972. pp. 456.

SPAIN. Comisaria del Plan de Desarrollo Economico y Social. 1972. (III Plan de desarrollo economico y social): Sureste español. [Madrid], 1972. pp. 536.

- Economic policy - Mathematical models

SPAIN. Comisaria del Plan de Desarrollo Economico y Social. 1972. (III Plan de desarrollo economico y social): elaboracion y especificacion del modelo econometrico. [Madrid], 1972. pp. 369.

- Emigration and immigration

    INTERNATIONAL CATHOLIC MIGRATION COMMISSION. Migrations: Série Informative. No. 8. Bilan de six années d'émigration espagnole en Europe. Geneva, 1967. pp. 48.

    SPAIN. Instituto Español de Emigracion. Memoria. a., 1969- Madrid. (Ministerio de Trabajo. Memoria. vol.4)

    SPAIN. Instituto Español de Emigracion. Emigracion. a., 1971- [Madrid].

- Executive departments

    SPAIN. Instituto Nacional de Prevision. 1959. El Instituto Nacional de Prevision y los seguros sociales españoles. Madrid, 1959. pp. 126.

    SPAIN. Presidencia. Secretaria General Tecnica. 1972. Organizacion de la administracion del estado. Madrid, 1972. pp. 652.

- Foreign economic relations

    MURY (GILBERT) Franco contre l'Espagne. Paris, [1950]. pp. 52.

- Foreign economic relations - Gibraltar

    VELARDE FUERTES (JUAN) Gibraltar y su campo: una economia deprimida. Barcelona, 1970. pp. 256.

- Foreign opinion

    MALTBY (WILLIAM S.) The black legend in England: the development of anti-Spanish sentiment, 1558-1660. Durham, N.C., 1971. pp. 180. bibliog.

- Foreign relations - United Kingdom

    [GORDON (THOMAS) of Kirkcudbright]. An appeal to the unprejudiced, concerning the present discontents occasioned by the late convention with Spain. London, Cooper, 1739. pp. 32.

- Government publications

    SPAIN. Instituto Nacional de Estadistica. 1956. Publicaciones estadisticas de España: publicaciones del primer centenario de la estadistica española. Madrid, 1956. pp. 202.

    SPAIN. Ministerio de Informacion y Turismo. Servicio de Documentacion. 1966- . Censo de las publicaciones oficiales españolas, 1939-1964. Madrid, 1966 in progress.

- History

    McCABE (JOSEPH) Spain in revolt, 1814-1931. London, 1931. pp. 246.

    JOHNSON (HAROLD B.) ed. From reconquest to empire: the Iberian background to Latin American history; [readings]. New York, [1970]. pp. 226. bibliog.

    VICENS VIVES (JAIME) Approaches to the history of Spain;... translated and edited by Joan Connelly Ullman. 2nd ed. Berkeley, 1970. pp. 189. bibliog.

- History - Sources

    BATLLORI (MIGUEL) and ARBELOA (VICTOR M.) eds. Esglesia i estat durant la segona republica espanyola, 1931-1936: (arxiu Vidal i Barraquer); textos en la llengua original. Montserrat, 1971 in progress. (Monestir de Montserrat. Scripta et Documenta. 20, etc.) Prologue and introductions to texts in Catalan and Castilian.

    FRASER (RONALD) In hiding: the life of Manuel Cortes. London, 1972. pp. 238.

- History - 711-1516

    HIGHFIELD (JOHN ROGER LOXDALE) ed. Spain in the fifteenth century, 1369-1516: essays and extracts by historians of Spain;...translated by Frances M. López-Morillas. London, 1972. pp. 488. bibliogs.

- History - 1814-1868, Bourbon Restoration

    COMELLAS GARCIA-LLERA (JOSE LUIS) El trienio constitucional: [1820-1823]. Madrid, 1963. pp. 446. (Pamplona. Universidad de Navarra. Facultad de Filosofia y Letras. Publicaciones. Coleccion Historica. 7)

- History - 1833-1840, Carlist War

    GARCIA FIGUERAS (TOMAS) La ocupacion carlista de Melilla, 1838-39. Madrid, 1971. pp. 307. bibliog.

- History - 1900-1999

    WILSON (HUGH ROBERT) the Younger. The man who created Franco: General Emilio Mola. Ilfracombe, 1972. pp. 178. bibliog.

- History - 1931-1939, Republic

    BLANCO MOHENO (ROBERTO) Tlatelolco: historia de una infamia. Mexico, 1969. pp. 286.

    NIN (ANDRES) Los problemas de la revolucion española, 1931-1937; prefacio y compilacion de Juan Andrade. [Paris, 1971]. pp. 230.

    AGUADO SANCHEZ (FRANCISCO) La revolucion de octubre de 1934. Madrid, [1972]. pp. 515. bibliog.

    TROTSKII (LEV DAVYDOVICH) The Spanish revolution, 1931-39; [a collection of letters, articles, pamphlets etc. in translation]; (edition by Naomi Allen and George Breitman). New York, 1973. pp. 446.

- History - 1936-1939, Civil War

    SPAIN. Presidencia. 1937. Defendar la independencia de la patria. Barcelona, [1937?]. pp. 15. (Charlas Populares lo que Significa la Guerra)

    SPAIN. Ejercito. Servicio Historico Militar. 1948. Guerra de minas en España, 1936-1939: contribucion al estudio de esta modalidad de nuestra guerra de liberacion. Madrid, 1948. pp. 134. bibliog. 9 maps in end pocket.

    MARICHAL (JUAN) El nuevo pensamiento politico español. Mexico, [1966?]. pp. 148.

    GIBSON (IAN) La represion nacionalista de Granada en 1936 y la muerte de Federico Garcia Lorca. [Paris, 1971]. pp. 166. bibliog.

    PROBLEMY ispanskoi istorii. Moskva, 1971. pp. 399.

    BROUE (PIERRE) and TEMIME (EMILE) The revolution and the civil war in Spain;...translated by Tony White. London, 1972. pp. 591. bibliog.

    LANDIS (ARTHUR H.) Spain!: the unfinished revolution! Baldwin Park, Cal., 1972. pp. 451. bibliog.

    RICHARDS (VERNON) Lessons of the Spanish revolution 1936-1939. [2nd ed.] London, 1972. pp. 240. bibliog.

    VILA-SAN-JUAN (JOSE LUIS) Asi fue?: enigmas de la guerra civil española. Barcelona, 1972. pp. 527. bibliog.

- History - 1936-1939, Civil War - Art and the war

    SPAIN. State Tourist Department. Information Service. 1937. Nine rescued works of art. [Madrid, 1937?]. pp. (20).

SPACE SCIENCES (Cont'd.)

- History - 1936-1939, Civil War - Bibliography

    MONTES (MARIA JOSE) La guerra española en la creacion literaria: ensayo bibliografico. Madrid, 1970. pp. 191. (Cuadernos bibliograficos de la guerra de España, 1936-1939. Anejos. No.2)

- History - 1936-1939, Civil War - Foreign participation

    SPAIN. Ministerio de Estado. 1936. Luchar por la paz y la solidaridad entre todos los pueblos. Barcelona, [1936?]. pp. 15. (Charlas Populares lo que Significa la Guerra)

    MURY (GILBERT) Franco contre l'Espagne. Paris, [1950]. pp. 52.

    SPAIN. Oficina de Informacion Diplomatica. 1952. The international brigades: foreign assistants of the Spanish Reds. Madrid, 1952. pp. 163.

    MARTINEZ BANDE (JOSE MANUEL) La intervencion comunista en la guerra de España, 1936-1939. Madrid, 1965. pp. 165.

    SCHWARTZ (FERNANDO) La internacionalización de la guerra civil española: julio de 1936-marzo de 1937. Barcelona, [1971]. pp. 266. bibliog.

    ŠPANIJA, 1936-1939: zbornik sećanja jugoslovenskih dobrovoljaca u španskom ratu. Beograd, 1971. 5 vols.

    ALCOFAR NASSAES (JOSE LUIS) C.T.V.: los legionarios italianos en la Guerra Civil Española, 1936-1939. Barcelona, 1972. pp. 238. bibliog.

    LONGO (LUIGI) Le brigate internazionali in Spagna; illustrazioni di Giandante. 2nd ed. Roma, 1972. pp. 337.

    SOLIDARNOST' narodov s Ispanskoi Respublikoi, 1936-1939. Moskva, 1972. pp. 368.

- History - 1936-1939, Civil War - Literature and the war

    HOSKINS (KATHARINE BAIL) Today the struggle: literature and politics in England during the Spanish Civil War. Austin, Texas, [1969]. pp. 294. bibliog.

    MONTES (MARIA JOSE) La guerra española en la creacion literaria: ensayo bibliografico. Madrid, 1970. pp. 191. (Cuadernos bibliograficos de la guerra de España, 1936-1939. Anejos. No.2)

- History - 1936-1919, Civil War - Naval operations

    ALCOFAR NASSAES (JOSE LUIS) Las fuerzas navales en la Guerra Civil Española. Barcelona, 1971. pp. 178. bibliog.

- History - 1936-1919, Civil War - Personal narratives

    CARDONA (MARIA DE) La terreur à Madrid: conférence faite au Cercle Interallié, etc. Paris, 1937. pp. 59.

    KOLTSOV (MIKHAIL) Diario de la guerra de España: traduccion del ruso. [Paris, 1963]. pp. 491.

    MANIERA (ARISTODEMO) Nelle trincee dell'antifascismo: (ricordi di un garibaldino di Spagna). Urbino, 1970. pp. 226. (Istituto Regionale per la Storia del Movimento di Liberazione nelle Marche. Studi sulla Resistenza. 1)

    VINIELLES TREPAT (MAGIN) La sexta columna: diario de un combatiente leridano. Barcelona, [1971]. pp. 311.

    PEREZ LOPEZ (FRANCISCO) Dark and bloody ground: a guerrilla diary of the Spanish Civil War...; edited...by Victor Guerrier; translated by Joseph D. Harris. Boston, [1972]. pp. 275.

- History - 1936-1919, Civil War - Refugees

    PIKE (DAVID WINGEATE) Vae victis!: los republicanos españoles refugiados en Francia, 1939-1944. Paris, [1969]. pp. 139. bibliog.

    FERNANDEZ (ALBERTO) Emigracion republicana española, 1939-1945. Algorta, Vizcaya, 1972. pp. 97.

    FAGEN (PATRICIA W.) Exiles and citizens: Spanish republicans in Mexico. Austin, Texas, [1973]. pp. 250. bibliog. (Texas University. Institute of Latin American Studies. Latin American Monographs. No.29)

- History - 1939-

    GALLO (MAX) Spain under Franco: a history;... translated by Jean Stewart. London, 1973. pp. 390. bibliog.

- History, Military

    PARKER (NOEL GEOFFREY) The army of Flanders and the Spanish Road, 1567-1659: the logistics of Spanish victory and defeat in the Low countries' wars. Cambridge, 1972. pp. 309. bibliog.

- Industries

    SPAIN. Ministerio de Industria. 1959. El desarrollo industrial de España, 1939-1958. Madrid, 1959. pp. 101.

    La PEQUEÑA y media industria en España: [round table conferences sponsored by the Centro de Estudios Sociales del Valle de los Caidos]. Madrid, 1971-72. 2 vols. (Centro de Estudios Sociales del Valle de los Caidos. Anales de Moral Social y Economica. vols. 27,29)

    MIGUEL (AMANDO DE) and SALCEDO (JUAN) Dinamica del desarrollo industrial de las regiones españolas. Madrid, [1972]. pp. 337.

    SPAIN. Comisaria del Plan de Desarrollo Economico y Social. 1972. (III Plan de desarrollo economico y social): industrias manufactureras varias y artesania. [Madrid], 1972. pp. 684.

- Intellectual life

    MARICHAL (JUAN) El nuevo pensamiento politico español. Mexico, [1966?]. pp. 148.

    HERRERO (JAVIER) Los origenes del pensamiento reaccionario español. Madrid, 1971. pp. 409.

- Kings and rulers

    FRANCO y el Principe de España: la monarquia del Movimiento Nacional. Madrid, 1969. pp. 105.

    CALVO SERER (RAFAEL) Franco frente al Rey: el proceso del regimen. [Paris], 1972. pp. 254.

- Kings and rulers - Succession

    CALLEJA (JUAN LUIS) Don Juan Carlos, por que?: y articulos concordantes. Madrid, [1972]. pp. 234.

- Militia

    HELLWEGE (JOHANN) Zur Geschichte der spanischen Reitermilizen: die Caballeria de Cuantia unter Philipp II. und Philipp III., 1562-1619. Wiesbaden, 1972. pp. 183. bibliog. (Vierteljahrschrift für Sozial- und Wirtschaftsgeschichte. Beihefte. Nr. 59)

- Navy

    ALCOFAR NASSAES (JOSE LUIS) Las fuerzas navales en la Guerra Civil Española. Barcelona, 1971. pp. 178. bibliog.

- Politics and government

    SPAIN. Oficina de Informacion Diplomatica. 1952. How Spain is governed; [by] Manuel Fraga Iribarne. 2nd ed. Madrid, 1952. pp. 122.

    PRIMO DE RIVERA Y SAENZ DE HEREDIA (JOSE ANTONIO) Jose Antonio, testimonio; ([edited by] Adriano Gomez Molina). Madrid, 1969. pp. 234.

    GEORGEL (JACQUES) Le franquisme: histoire et bilan, 1939-1969. Paris, [1970]. pp. 399. bibliog.

    PIZAN (MANUEL) El poder y la oposicion: once politicos y tres conflictos. Barcelona, [1970]. pp. 235.

    PRIETO (FERNANDO) España politica, 1969. Bilbao, 1970. pp. 351.

    VILAR (SERGIO) Les oppositions à Franco; traduit de l'espagnol par Elena de la Souchère [and others]. Paris, [1970]. pp. 426.

    CARRILLO (SANTIAGO) Libertad y socialismo: [speeches before the Comite Central del Partido Comunista de España, 1970, and before a meeting of Communist Parties in Brussels]. [Paris, 1971]. pp. 149.

    CLEMENTE BALAGUER (JOSE CARLOS) Conversaciones con las corrientes politicas de España. Barcelona, 1971. pp. 232.

    ARRABAL (FERNANDO) Lettre au général Franco: texte intégral de la lettre envoyée par Arrabal à Franco le 18 mars 1971. [Paris, 1972]. pp. 187. In French and Spanish.

    CALVO SERER (RAFAEL) Franco frente al Rey: el proceso del regimen. [Paris], 1972. pp. 254.

    PRIMO DE RIVERA Y SÁENZ DE HEREDIA (JOSÉ ANTONIO) Selected writings; edited and introduced by Hugh Thomas; translations from the Spanish by Gudie Lawaetz. London, 1972. pp. 271. bibliog.

    GALLO (MAX) Spain under Franco: a history;... translated by Jean Stewart. London, 1973. pp. 390. bibliog.

    MEDHURST (KENNETH N.) Government in Spain: the executive at work. Oxford, 1973. pp. 256. bibliog.

- Population

    BARBANCHO (ALFONSO GARCIA) Las migraciones interiores españolas: estudio cuantitativo desde 1900. Madrid, 1967. pp. 209. (Instituto de Desarrollo Economico. Estudios. [2])

    DIEZ NICOLAS (JUAN) Tamaño, densidad y crecimiento de la poblacion en España, 1900-1960. Madrid, 1971. pp. 108. (Consejo Superior de Investigaciones Cientificas. Instituto "Balmes" de Sociologia. Opusculos sobre Desarrollo Economico-Social. No. 9.)

    NADAL OLLER (JORGE) La poblacion española, siglos XVI a XX. 2nd ed. Barcelona, 1971. pp. 239.

    CAMPO URBANO (SALUSTIANO DEL) Analisis de la poblacion de España. Barcelona, [1972]. pp. 192.

    SPAIN. Comisaria del Plan de Desarrollo Economico y Social. 1972. (III Plan de desarrollo economico y social): estudio sobre la poblacion española. [Madrid], 1972. pp. 558.

- Public works

    SPAIN. Ministerio de Comunicaciones, Transportes y Obras Publicas. 1937. Aprovechamiento maximo de los recursos naturales en beneficio del pueblo. Barcelona, [1937?]. pp. 14. (Charlas Populares lo que Significa la Guerra)

- Relations (general) with Latin America

    PIKE (FREDRICK BRAUN) Hispanismo, 1898-1936: Spanish Conservatives and Liberals and their relations with Spanish America. Notre Dame, [1971]. pp. 486.

- Relations (general) with Russia

    PROBLEMY ispanskoi istorii. Moskva, 1971. pp. 399.

- Relations (general) with the United States

    POWELL (PHILIP WAYNE) Tree of hate: propaganda and prejudices affecting United States relations with the Hispanic world. New York, [1971]. pp. 210. bibliog.

- Rural conditions

    ACEVES (JOSEPH) Social change in a Spanish village. Cambridge, Mass., [1971]. pp. 145. bibliog.

    MIGUEL RODRIGUEZ (JESUS M. DE) Notas sobre la estructura social del campo español. Madrid, 1970 [or rather 1971]. pp. 69.

    FRASER (RONALD) The pueblo: a mountain village on the Costa del Sol. London, 1973. pp. 285.

- Social conditions

    FRAGA IRIBARNE (MANUEL) and others, eds. La España de los años 70. Madrid, 1972 in progress.

    ARRABAL (FERNANDO) Lettre au général Franco: texte intégral de la lettre envoyée par Arrabal à Franco le 18 mars 1971. [Paris, 1972]. pp. 187. In French and Spanish.

    FUNDACION FOESSA. Sintesis del informe sociologico sobre la situacion social de España 1970. Madrid, [1972]. pp. 348. bibliog.

- Social conditions - Statistics

    DATA, S.A. Estructura social basica de la poblacion de España y sus provincias; estudio realizado... [for the] Confederacion Española de Cajas de Ahorros. Madrid, [1973]. pp. 397. (Confederacion Española de Cajas de Ahorros. Fondo para la Investigacion Economica y Social. Publicaciones. 50)

- Social policy

    SPAIN. Servicio Central de Planes Provinciales. 1970. Normativa de planes provinciales. Madrid, 1970. pp. 187. (Spain. Presidencia. Secretaria General Tecnica. Coleccion Compilaciones. 5)

    SPAIN. Comisaria del Plan de Desarrollo Economico y Social. 1971. III Plan de desarrollo, 1972-1975. [Madrid], 1971. pp. 318, lxviii.

    SPAIN. Comisaria del Plan de Desarrollo Economico y Social. 1972. (III Plan de desarrollo economico y social): desarrollo regional. [Madrid], 1972. pp. 456.

    SPAIN. Comisaria del Plan de Desarrollo Economico y Social. 1972. (III Plan de desarrollo economico y social): Sureste español. [Madrid], 1972. pp. 536.

    SPAIN. Ministerio de Trabajo. 1973. 3 años de politica laboral, 1970-1972. [Madrid, 1973]. pp. 85.

SPACE SCIENCES (Cont'd.)

- Statistics

SPAIN. Instituto Nacional de Estadistica. 1956. Indice cronologico de legislacion estadistica años, 1813-1956: publicaciones del primer centenario de la estadistica española. Madrid, 1956. pp. 236.

- Statistics - Bibliography

SPAIN. Instituto Nacional de Estadistica. 1956. Publicaciones estadisticas de España: publicaciones del primer centenario de la estadistica espanola. Madrid, 1956. pp. 202.

SPANIARDS IN AMERICA

GIBSON (CHARLES) Spain in America. New York, [1966]. pp. 239. bibliog.

SPANIARDS IN EUROPE

INTERNATIONAL CATHOLIC MIGRATION COMMISSION. Migrations: Série Informative. No. 8. Bilan de six années d'émigration espagnole en Europe. Geneva, 1967. pp. 48.

SPANIARDS IN FRANCE

PIKE (DAVID WINGEATE) Vae victis!: los republicanos españoles refugiados en Francia, 1939-1944. Paris, [1969]. pp. 139. bibliog.

ANGEL (MIGUEL) Los guerrilleros españoles en Francia, [1940-1945]. La Habana, 1971. pp. 257. bibliog.

MUÑOZ ANATOL (JAIME) La familia española migrante en Francia. Madrid, 1972. pp. 212. bibliog.

SPANIARDS IN MEXICO

FLORES CABALLERO (ROMEO) La contrarrevolucion en la independencia: los españoles en la vida politica, social y economica de Mexico, 1804-1838. Mexico, 1969. pp. 201. bibliog. (Mexico City. Colegio de Mexico. Centro de Estudios Historicos. Nueva Serie. 8.)

FAGEN (PATRICIA W.) Exiles and citizens: Spanish republicans in Mexico. Austin, Texas, [1973]. pp. 250. bibliog. (Texas University. Institute of Latin American Studies. Latin American Monographs. No.29)

SPANIARDS IN THE UNITED STATES

LEONARD (OLEN EARL) The role of the land grant in the social organization and social processes of a Spanish-American village in New Mexico. Albuquerque, [1970]. pp. 198. bibliog.

ALMARÁZ (FÉLIX D.) Tragic cavalier: Governor Manuel Salcedo of Texas, 1808-1813. Austin, Texas, [1971]. pp. 206. bibliog.

GOMEZ GIL (ALFREDO) "Cerebros" españoles en U.S.A. Barcelona, 1971. pp. 299.

SPANISH COMPANY

CROFT (PAULINE) The Spanish Company. London, 1973. pp. 142.

SPANISH LANGUAGE

- Dictionaries

ACADEMIA ESPAÑOLA. Diccionario de la lengua española. 19th ed. Madrid, 1970. pp. 1424.

- Dictionaries - English

CASSELL AND COMPANY. Spanish-English, English-Spanish dictionary; edited by Edgar Allison Peers [and others]. 6th ed. London, 1968 repr. 1970. pp. 1477.

SMITH (COLIN C.) and others, compilers. Collins Spanish-English, English-Spanish dictionary. London, [1971]. pp. 602, 640.

SPANISH NEWSPAPERS

[CALVET PASCUAL (ANTONIO)] Historia de La Vanguardia, 1884-1936; ([by] Gaziel [pseud.]). Paris, 1971. pp. 143.

SPANN (OTHMAR)

RIEBER (ARNULF) Vom Positivismus zum Universalismus: Untersuchungen zur Entwicklung und Kritik des Ganzheitsbegriffs von Othmar Spann. Berlin, [1971]. pp. 236. bibliog.

SPARTA

- Social history

OLIVA (PAVEL) Sparta and her social problems. Prague, 1971. pp. 347. bibliog.

SPAVENTA (SILVIO)

CHIODI (GIULIO M.) La giustizia amministrativa nel pensiero politico di Silvio Spaventa. Bari, 1969. pp. 189. bibliog. (Centro Nazionale di Prevenzione e Difesa Sociale. Indagine su l'Amministrazione della Giudizia e la Società Italiana in Trasformazione. 7)

SPECIAL DRAWING RIGHTS

INTERNATIONAL MONETARY FUND. 1968. Establishment of a facility based on special drawing rights in the International Monetary Fund and modifications in the rules and practices of the Fund: a report by the Executive Directors to the Board of Governors proposing amendment of the articles of agreement. Washington, 1968. pp. 80.

GOLD (JOSEPH) Special drawing rights: the role of language. Washington, International Monetary Fund, 1971. pp. 25. (Pamphlet Series. No. 15)

HAAN (ROELF L.) Special drawing rights and development: an inquiry into the monetary aspects of a link between special drawing rights and development finance. Leiden, 1971. pp. 184. bibliog.

POLAK (JACQUES JACOBUS) Some reflections on the nature of special drawing rights. Washington, International Monetary Fund, 1971. pp. 28. (Pamphlet Series. No. 16)

SCHLAEGER (GERT) Die internationale Buchgeldschöpfung: die Sonderziehungsrechte im Internationalen Währungsfonds. Frankfurt am Main, [1971]. pp. 173. bibliog.

DOLMAN (ROBERT) Het vervolg van Bretton Woods: een voorstel tot inbouw van de ontwikkelingshulp in een SDR-standaard. Leiden, 1972. pp. 411. bibliog. With English summary.

HOWE (JAMES W.) Distributing the benefits of special drawing rights among nations rich and poor. Washington D.C., 1972. pp. 24. (Overseas Development Council. Occasional Papers. No. 4)

SPECTACLES

U.K. National Health Service. General Ophthalmic Services. 1972. Statement specifying the fees and charges for the testing of sight and the supply or repair of glasses...; revised as from the 1st August, 1972. London, 1972. pp. 13.

SPECULATION

CHOURAQUI (JEAN CLAUDE) La spéculation et la politique de défense des monnaies. Paris, 1972. pp. 303. bibliog.

DOMINGUEZ (JOHN R.) Devaluation and futures markets. Lexington, Mass., [1972]. pp. 114. bibliog.

GOSS (BARRY ANDREW) The theory of futures trading. London, 1972. pp. 116. bibliog.

CUTILLI (BRUNO) and GANDOLFO (GIANCARLO) Un contributo alla teoria della speculazione in regime di cambi oscillanti. [Rome, 1973]. pp. 143. (Ente per gli Studi Monetari, Bancari e Finanziari Luigi Einaudi. Quaderni di Ricerche. N. 10)

- Mathematical models

LABYS (WALTER C.) and GRANGER (CLIVE W.J.) Speculation, hedging and commodity price forecasts. Lexington, Mass., [1970]. pp. 321. bibliog.

SPEECH

BRAIN mechanisms underlying speech and language: proceedings of a conference held at Princeton... 1965 ...; Frederic L. Darley, editor. New York, 1967, repr.1968. pp. 261. bibliog.

QUINTING (GERD) Hesitation phenomena in adult aphasic and normal speech. The Hague, 1971. pp. 73. bibliog.

SCHOLES (ROBERT J.) Acoustic cues for constituent structure: a series of experiments on the nature of spoken sentence structures. The Hague, 1971. pp. 80. bibliog.

ROBINSON (W. PETER) and RACKSTRAW (SUSAN J.) A question of answers. London, 1972. 2 vols. bibliogs.

DENES (PETER B.) and PINSON (ELLIOT N.) The speech chain: the physics and biology of spoken language. [rev. ed.] Garden City, N.Y., 1973. pp. 217. bibliog.

SPEECH, DISORDERS OF

SPEECH pathology: an international study of the science; edited by R.W. Rieber and R.S. Brubaker. Amsterdam, 1966. pp. 654. bibliogs.

SPEECH THERAPY

SPEECH pathology: an international study of the science; edited by R.W. Rieber and R.S. Brubaker. Amsterdam, 1966. pp. 654. bibliogs.

SPEECH therapy services; report of the Committee appointed by the Secretaries of State for Education and Science, for the Social Services, for Scotland and for Wales in July 1969; [Randolph Quirk, chairman]. London, H.M.S.O., 1972. pp. 135.

SPENCE (THOMAS) Bookseller

THOMPSON (R.H.) The dies of Thomas Spence, 1750-1814. [Oxford, 1970]. pp. 126. bibliog. (Reprinted from The British Numismatic Journal, vol. 38, 1969)

SPIEKER (JOSEF)

SPIEKER (JOSEF) Mein Kampf gegen Unrecht in Staat und Gesellschaft: Erinnerungen eines Kölner Jesuiten. Köln, 1971. pp. 126.

SPINNING

UNITED NATIONS INDUSTRIAL DEVELOPMENT ORGANIZATION. Training for Industry Series. No. 3. The Łódź Textile Seminars. 2. Spinning. (ID/SER.D/3/2). New York, United Nations, 1970. pp. 60.

SPINOZA (BENEDICTUS DE)

BELAIEF (GAIL) Spinoza's philosophy of law. The Hague, 1971. pp. 151. bibliog.

SPIRITUALISM

BRADLAUGH (CHARLES) and BURNS (JAMES) Human immortality proved by facts: report of a two nights' debate on modern spiritualism...December 16th and 17th, 1872, etc. London, [1872]. pp. 52. bibliog.

LEAF (HORACE) and COHEN (CHAPMAN) Does man survive death?: is the belief reasonable?; a debate... in...Glasgow...February 26, 1920. London, [1920?]. pp. 44.

McCABE (JOSEPH) Is spiritualism based on fraud?: the evidence given by Sir A.C. Doyle and others drastically examined. London, [1920]. pp. 160.

SPORTS

SPORT, culture et répression; [by] Ginette Berthaud [and others]. Paris, 1972. pp. 173. bibliogs.

- Social aspects

MAGGLINGER SYMPOSIUM, 10., 1969. Soziologie des Sports;...: Sociology of sport; theoretical foundations and research methods; Referate... [of an international seminar sponsored by the International Committee for Sociology of Sport]; zusammengestellt und kommentiert von Rolf Albonico und Katharina Pfister-Binz. Basel, 1971. pp. 208. (Eidgenössische Turn- und Sportschule, Magglingen. Forschungsinstitut. Wissenschaftliche Schriftenreihe. 2) In German or English.

- France

FRANCE. Commission des Activités Sportives et Socio-Educatives. 1971. Préparation du VIe Plan: rapport. Paris, 1971. pp. 242.

- Ghana

GHANA. Committee appointed to Review the Organization of Sports in Ghana. 1967. The Tibo Committee report on Ghana sports; [A.A. Tibo, chairman]. [Accra, 1967]. pp. 86. Bound with White Paper on the report.

GHANA. 1968. White Paper on the report of the Committee appointed to review the organization of sports in Ghana. [Accra], 1968. pp. 4. (W[hite] P[apers]. 1968. No. 2) Bound with the report.

SPORTS - Ghana (Cont'd.)

GHANA. 1969. White Paper on the report of the audit investigation into the accounts of the Central Organisation of Sport. [Accra], 1969. pp. 3. (W[hite P[apers]. 1969. No.4) Bound with the Report.

GHANA. Office of the Auditor-General. 1969. Report on the audit investigations into the accounts of the Central Organisation of Sport. [Accra, 1969]. pp. 85. Bound with White Paper on the report.

- United Kingdom

U.K. Central Office of Information. Reference Division. Reference Pamphlets. 107. Sport in Britain. London, 1972. pp. 32. bibliog.

SPRETI (KARL VON) Graf

KAPUŚCIŃSKI (RYSZARD) Dlaczego zginął Karl von Spreti. Warszawa, 1970. pp. 92.

SPRINGER (AXEL)

IMPERIUM Springer: Macht und Manipulation; herausgegeben von Bernd Jansen und Arno Klünne, im Auftrage der Kampagne für Demokratie und Abrüstung. Köln, [1968]. pp. 272. bibliog.

SPRINGFIELD, MASSACHUSETTS

- History

FRISCH (MICHAEL H.) Town into city: Springfield, Massachusetts, and the meaning of community, 1840-1880. Cambridge, Mass., 1972. pp. 301.

SPRUENGLI-AMMANN (RUDOLF)

VEREIN FÜR WIRTSCHAFTSHISTORISCHE STUDIEN. Schweizer Pioniere der Wirtschaft und Technik. 22. Die Pioniere Sprüngli und Lindt: Rudolf Sprüngli-Ammann, 1816-1897; Rudolf Sprüngli-Schifferli, 1847-1926; David Robert Sprüngli-Baud, 1851-1944; Rudolf Lindt, 1855-1909; von Hans Rudolf Schmid. Zürich, 1970. pp. 102. bibliog.

SPRUENGLI-BAUD (DAVID ROBERT)

VEREIN FÜR WIRTSCHAFTSHISTORISCHE STUDIEN. Schweizer Pioniere der Wirtschaft und Technik. 22. Die Pioniere Sprüngli und Lindt: Rudolf Sprüngli-Ammann, 1816-1897; Rudolf Sprüngli-Schifferli, 1847-1926; David Robert Sprüngli-Baud, 1851-1944; Rudolf Lindt, 1855-1909; von Hans Rudolf Schmid. Zürich, 1970. pp. 102. bibliog.

SPRUENGLI-SCHIFFERLI (RUDOLF)

VEREIN FÜR WIRTSCHAFTSHISTORISCHE STUDIEN. Schweizer Pioniere der Wirtschaft und Technik. 22. Die Pioniere Sprüngli und Lindt: Rudolf Sprüngli-Ammann, 1816-1897; Rudolf Sprüngli-Schifferli, 1847-1926; David Robert Sprüngli-Baud, 1851-1944; Rudolf Lindt, 1855-1909; von Hans Rudolf Schmid. Zürich, 1970. pp. 102. bibliog.

SPRÜNGLI
See SPRUENGLI

SQUATTERS

ABRAMS (CHARLES) Squatter settlements: the problem and the opportunity; (prepared for the Agency for International Development). Washington, 1966 repr. 1971. pp. 48. (United States. Department of Housing and Urban Development. Office of International Affairs. Ideas and Methods Exchange. No.63)

- Brazil

CONN (STEPHEN) The squatters' rights of favelados. Cuernavaca, 1969. 1 vol. (various pagination). (Centro Intercultural de Documentacion. Cidoc Cuadernos. No. 32)

- Hong Kong

GOLGER (OTTO J.) Squatters and resettlement: symptons of an urban crisis: environmental conditions of low-standard housing in Hong Kong. Wiesbaden, 1972. pp. 112, 55 plates.

- Mexico

BROWN (JANE COWAN) Patterns of intra-urban settlement in Mexico City: an examination of the Turner theory. [Ithaca], 1972. pp. 203. bibliog. (Cornell University. Latin American Studies Program. Dissertation Series. No. 40)

- United Kingdom

BAILEY (RON) The squatters. Harmondsworth, 1973. pp. 206.

SRAFFA (PIERO)

SCHEFOLD (BERTRAM) Piero Sraffas Theorie der Kuppelproduktion, des Kapitals und der Rente: Mr. Sraffa on joint production. [Basel, imprint], 1971. pp. 104. bibliog. In English, with introduction and postscript in German.

SRI LANKA

- Census

CEYLON. Department of Census and Statistics. Census, 1971. Census of population, 1971: preliminary release[s]. Colombo, 1972 in progress.

- Economic conditions - Statisucs.

CEYLON. Department of Census and Statistics. 1971. Preliminary report on the socio economic survey of Ceylon, 1969-70. [Colombo], 1971. pp. 143.

- Economic policy

KARUNATILAKE (HALWALAGE NEVILLE SEPALA) Economic development in Ceylon. New York, 1971. pp. 378. bibliog.

MÖLLER (BIRGER) Employment approaches to economic planning in developing countries; with special reference to the development planning of Ceylon (Sri Lanka). [Copenhagen, 1972]. pp. 304. bibliog. (Scandinavian Institute of Asian Studies. Monograph Series. No. 9)

- Foreign economic relations - Communist countries

D'IACHENKO (KONSTANTIN PAVLOVICH) Tseilon i sotsialisticheskie strany: tendentsii i perspektivy ekonomicheskogo sotrudnichestva. Moskva, 1972. pp. 168. bibliog.

- Full employment policies

    [SEERS (DUDLEY) and others] Matching employment opportunities and expectations: a programme of action for Ceylon: the report [and technical papers] of an inter-agency team organised by the International Labour Office. Geneva, International Labour Office, 1971. 2 pts.(in 1).

- History

    WINIUS (GEORGE DAVISON) The fatal history of Portuguese Ceylon: transition to Dutch rule. Cambridge, Mass., 1971. pp. 215. bibliog.

    DE SILVA (CHANDRA RICHARD) The Portuguese in Ceylon, 1617-1638. Colombo, [1972]. pp. 267. bibliog.

- Industries

    CEYLON. Ministry of Industries and Fisheries. 1968. Statistics of industrial production, 1965-1967. Colombo, 1968. pp. 38.

- Nationalism

    JAYAWARDENA (VISAKHA KUMARI) The rise of the labor movement in Ceylon. Durham, N.C., 1972. pp. 382. bibliog.

- Parliament - Elections

    CEYLON. Elections Department. 1971. Report on the seventh parliamentary general election in Ceylon, 27th May, 1970. Colombo, 1971. pp. 72. (Ceylon. Parliament. Sessional Papers. 1971. No. 7)

- Politics and government

    KEARNEY (ROBERT N.) Trade unions and politics in Ceylon. Berkeley, Calif., 1971. pp. 195. bibliog.

    CEYLON SOLIDARITY CAMPAIGN. Island behind bars. London, [1972?]. pp. 24,iv.

    SOLIDARITY: [for workers' power]. Pamphlets. [No.] 42. Ceylon: the JVP uprising of April 1971. [London, 1972?]. pp. 50.

- Population

    CEYLON. Department of Census and Statistics. 1971. Preliminary report on the socio economic survey of Ceylon, 1969-70. [Colombo], 1971. pp. 143.

- Social conditions

    EVERS (HANS DIETER) Monks, priests and peasants: a study of Buddhism and social structure in central Ceylon. Leiden, 1972. pp. 136. bibliog.

- Social conditions - Statistics

    CEYLON. Department of Census and Statistics. 1971. Preliminary report on the socio economic survey of Ceylon, 1969-70. [Colombo], 1971. pp. 143.

STAEMPFLI (PAUL)

STAEMPFLI (PAUL) In Deutschland zum Tode verurteilt: Tatsachenbericht eines Schweizers. Zürich, [1945]. pp. 152.

STAFFORDSHIRE

- Economic history

    RAYBOULD (T.J.) The economic emergence of the Black Country: a study of the Dudley estate. Newton Abbot, [1973]. pp. 272.

STAJIĆ (VASA)

MILETIĆ (SVETOZAR) Izabrani članci... s predgovorom Vase Stajića; priredio Miroslav Jerkov... Novi Sad, 1939. pp. 216. In Cyrillic.

STALIN (IOSIF VISSARIONOVICH)

IOSIF Vissarionovich Stalin: kratkaia biografiia. Moskva, 1942. pp. 88. For English translation see INSTITUT MARKSIZMA-LENINIZMA. Joseph Stalin [1940].

LAURAT (LUCIEN) Staline: la linguistique et l'impérialisme russe. Paris. [1951]. pp. 93.

VYSHINSKII (ANDREI IANVAR'EVICH) J.V. Stalin's doctrine of the socialist state. Moscow, 1951. pp. 64.

KHRUSHCHEV (NIKITA SERGEEVICH) Rech' Khrushcheva na zakrytom zasedanii XX s"ezda KPSS, 24-25 fevralia 1956 g. Miunkhen, 1956. pp. 57.

REDLIKH (ROMAN N.) Stalinshchina kak dukhovnyi fenomen: ocherki bol'shevizmovedeniia. kniga 1. [2nd ed.] Frankfurt-am-Main, Posev, [1970]. pp. 251. 1st ed. (of which this is the 2nd ed. of the 1st part) had title: Ocherki bol'shevizmovedeniia.

The FOURTH International, Stalinism and the origins of the international socialists: some documents. London, 1971. pp. 104.

TUCKER (ROBERT CHARLES) The Soviet political mind: Stalinism and post-Stalin change. rev. ed. New York, [1971]. pp. 304.

ARSIĆ (DRAGINJA) Društveno-ekonomski koreni staljinizma. Beograd, 1972. pp. 283. bibliog. With English and Russian summaries.

MEDVEDEV (ROI ALEKSANDROVICH) Let history judge: the origins and consequences of Stalinism. London, 1972. pp. 566, xviii.

TUCKER (ROBERT CHARLES) Stalin as revolutionary, 1879-1929: a study in history and personality. New York, [1973]. pp. 519. bibliog.

STAMFORD

- Economic history

    BIRCH (NEVILLE CHARLES) Stamford: an industrial history. [Boston, Lincs., 1972]. pp. 41.

STANDARDIZATION

- Japan

    JAPAN. Agency of Industrial Science and Technology. Standards Section. 1971. Industrial standardization in Japan: standardization's contribution to industrial and economic growth. [Tokyo], 1971. pp. 115. (Asian Productivity Organization. Technical Publications)

- Russia

    LOMAZOV (MIKHAIL EVSEEVICH) and SUL'POVAR (LEV BORISOVICH) Ekonomicheskaia effektivnost' standartizatsii tovarov narodnogo potrebleniia. Moskva, 1971. pp. 200. bibliog.

STANLEY (Sir HENRY MORTON)

SMITH (IAIN R.) The Emin Pasha relief expedition, 1886-1890. Oxford, 1972. pp. 335. bibliog.

STARČEVIĆ (ANTE)

STARČEVIĆ (ANTE) Politički spisi; izbor i predgovor Tomislav Ladan. Zagreb, 1971. pp. 630. bibliog.

STARHEMBERG (ERNST RUEDIGER) Prince

STARHEMBERG (ERNST RUEDIGER) Prince. Memoiren. Wien, [1971]. pp. 344.

STARSKY (MORRIS)

HOULT (THOMAS FORD) The march to the right: a case study in political repression. Cambridge Mass., [1972]. pp. 287.

STATE, THE

MAURUS (HEINRICH) Der moderne Verfassungsstaat als Rechtsstaat, kritisirt von...; [facsimile reprint of work originally published 1878]. [Frankfurt am Main], 1970. pp. 320.

O nekotorykh sotsial-reformistskikh kontseptsiiakh gosudarstva. Moskva, 1964. pp. 130.

ETZIONI (AMITAI) Political unification: a comparative study of leaders and forces. New York, [1965]. pp. 346.

PETROV (VLADIMIR SERGEEVICH) Tip i formy gosudarstva. Leningrad, 1967. pp. 120.

MUSHKIN (ANDREI EFIMOVICH) Gosudarstvo i pravo - istoricheskie raznovidnosti organov i norm upravleniia obshchestvom. Leningrad, 1969. pp. 78.

KAPLAN (MARCOS) El Estado en el desarrollo y la integracion de America Latina: ensayos. Caracas, [1970]. pp. 237. bibliog.

KRUEGER (HERBERT) Staat, Wirtschaft, Völkergemeinschaft: ausgewählte Schriften aus vierzig Jahren...; herausgegeben von Hellmuth Hecker [and others]. Frankfurt am Main, 1970. pp. 273.

STRAYER (JOSEPH REESE) On the medieval origins of the modern state. Princeton, 1970. pp. 114. (Princeton University. Witherspoon Lectures. 1961)

WOLFF (ROBERT PAUL) In defense of anarchism. New York, 1970. pp. 86.

CONRAD (HERMANN) Staatsgedanke und Staatspraxis des aufgeklärten Absolutismus. Opladen, [1971]. pp. 65. (Rheinisch-Westfälische Akademie der Wissenschaften. Geisteswissenschaften. Heft 173) With summaries in English and French.

CONVEGNO SULLA RIFORMA DELLO STATO, ROMA, 1969. Processo allo stato: atti del convegno... (promossa dal Centro Einaudi). Firenze, 1971. pp. 483.

DRONBERGER (ILSE) The political thought of Max Weber: in quest of statesmanship. New York, [1971]. pp. 436.

ERGANG (ROBERT REINHOLD) Emergence of the national state; [with source material]. New York, [1971]. pp. 249. bibliog.

FORSTHOFF (ERNST) Der Staat der Industriegesellschaft, dargestellt am Beispiel der Bundesrepublik Deutschland. München, [1971]. pp. 169.

HALE (DAVID GEORGE) The body politic: a political metaphor in renaissance English literature. The Hague, 1971. pp. 150. bibliog.

Constitutional lawyer.

HELLER (HERMANN) Gesammelte Schriften; ...herausgegeben von Martin Drath [and others]. Leiden, 1971. 3 vols. bibliog.

IMBODEN (MAX) Staat und Recht: ausgewählte Schriften und Vorträge. Basel, 1971. pp. 551.

KRAUTZBERGER (MICHAEL) Die Erfüllung öffentlicher Aufgaben durch Private: zum Begriff des staatlichen Bereichs. Berlin, [1971]. pp. 141. bibliog.

NARDIN (TERRY) Violence and the state: a critique of empirical political theory. Beverly Hills, [1971]. pp. 72. bibliog.

OSNOVY teorii gosudarstva i prava. 2nd ed. Moskva, 1971. pp. 406.

PETROV (VLADIMIR SERGEEVICH) Sushchnost', soderzhanie i forma gosudarstva. Leningrad, 1971. pp. 163.

POULANTZAS (NICOS) Pouvoir politique et classes sociales. Paris, 1971. 2 vols.

TENENBAUM (VIKTOR OSKAROVICH) Gosudarstvo: sistema kategorii. Saratov, 1971. pp. 211.

AVINERI (SHLOMO) Hegel's theory of the modern state. Cambridge, 1972. pp. 252. bibliog.

ENGELS (FRIEDRICH) The origin of the family, private property and the state in the light of the researches of Lewis H. Morgan;...[new ed.] with an introduction and notes by Eleanor Burke Leacock. London, 1972. pp. 285. bibliog.

HALLE (LOUIS JOSEPH) The ideological imagination: ideological conflict in our time and its roots in Hobbes, Rousseau and Marx. London, 1972. pp. 174. bibliog.

HITCHNER (DELL GILLETTE) and HARBOLD (WILLIAM HENRY) Modern government. 3rd ed. New York, 1972. pp. 522. bibliog.

PISIER-KOUCHNER (EVELYNE) Le service public dans la théorie de l'état de Léon Duguit. Paris, 1972. pp. 316. bibliog.

PORTELLI (HUGUES) Gramsci et le bloc historique. Paris, 1972. pp. 175. bibliog.

ROUSSEAU (JEAN JACQUES) Du contrat social; edited with an introduction and notes by Ronald Grimsley. Oxford, 1972. pp. 250. bibliog.

SYMPOSIUM ON THE MYTH OF THE STATE, ÅBO, 1971. The myth of the state: based on papers read at the Symposium...; edited by Haralds Biezais. Stockholm, [1972]. pp. 188. bibliog. (Institutum Donnerianum Aboense. Scripta. 6) In English or German.

VOGEL (URSULA) Konservative Kritik an der bürgerlichen Revolution: August Wilhelm Rehberg. Darmstadt, [1972]. pp. 400. bibliog.

POULANTZAS (NICOS) Political power and social classes; translation editor, Timothy O'Hagan. London, [1973]. pp. 367.

STATE ENCOURAGEMENT OF SCIENCE LITERATURE AND ART

MOLENDIJK (H.) De overheid en de cultuur. Alphen aan den Rijn, 1971. pp. 321.

BLADEN (VINCENT WHEELER) The financing of the performing arts in Canada: an essay in persuasion. Toronto, 1971. fo. 40.

VERPRAET (JEAN) and LEFEBVRE (ALAIN) L'action culturelle et le budget municipal. Paris, [1972]. pp. 214. bibliog.

GOODMAN (ARNOLD ABRAHAM) Baron Goodman. Not for the record: selected speeches and writings. London, 1972. pp. 173.

STATE FARMS

- Poland - Statistics

POLAND. Główny Urząd Statystyczny. Statystyka Polski: Materiały Statystyczne. zeszyt 16(138). Państwowe gospodarstwa rolne w roku gospodarczym 1965/66. Warszawa, 1967. pp. 75.

- Russia

PAKHOMOV (IURII NIKOLAEVICH) Proizvodstvennye otnosheniia i material'nye interesy v sovkhozakh. Kiev, 1969. pp. 148. bibliog.

GONCHARENKO (V.A.) and others, eds. Polnyi khoziaistvennyi raschet v sovkhozakh. Moskva, 1970. pp. 312.

ZAKLADNOI (V.S.) Nachislenie zarabotnoi platy rabochim i sluzhashchim sovkhozov. Moskva, 1970. pp. 192.

POLINA (VALENTINA IVANOVNA) Material'noe stimulirovanie v sovkhozakh. Moskva, 1971. pp. 200.

BOGDENKO (MARIIA LUKINICHNA) Sovkhozy SSSR, 1951-1958. Moskva, 1972. pp. 376.

BORISENKO (N.P.) Khozraschet i ekonomika sovkhozov. Moskva, 1972. pp. 223.

DEINEKO (GRIGORII FEDOROVICH) and others. Sotsial'no-ekonomicheskoe planirovanie v sovkhoze. Moskva, 1972. pp. 143.

KOCHERGIN (ALEKSEI IVANOVICH) Fond material'nogo pooshchreniia sovkhoza: formirovanie i raspredelenie. Moskva, 1972. pp. 95.

ZAPISNAIA knizhka direktora sovkhoza, 1973. Moskva, 1972. pp. 264.

ZELENIN (IL'IA EVGEN'EVICH) Sovkhozy v pervoe desiatiletie Sovetskoi vlasti, 1917-1927. Moskva, 1972. pp. 392.

TUMANOVA (MARIIA DMITRIEVNA) Rasshirennoe vosproizvodstvo v sovkhozakh pri polnom khozraschete. Moskva, 1973. pp. 119.

- Russia - Accounting

SINEVA (LIUDMILA NIKOLAEVNA) Osnovnye fondy i khozraschet v sovkhozakh. Moskva, 1967. pp. 126.

- Russia - Kirghizia

DZHUNUSALIEV (MALABAI DZHUNUSALIEVICH) Razvitie ekonomiki sovkhozov Kirgizskoi SSR. Frunze, 1968. pp. 49.

STATE GOVERNMENTS

- Germany

BILLERBECK (RUDOLF) Die Abgeordneten der ersten Landtage, 1946-1951 und der Nationalsozialismus. Düsseldorf, [1971]. pp. 305. bibliog. (Germany (Bundesrepublik). Kommission für Geschichte des Parlamentarismus und der Politischen Parteien. Beiträge zur Geschichte des Parlamentarismus und der Politischen Parteien. Band 41)

- Germany - Bibliography

GERMANY (BUNDESREPUBLIK). Deutscher Bundestag. Wissenschaftliche Dienste. 1972. Die Landtage in der Bundesrepublik Deutschland. Bonn, 1972. pp. 117. (Bibliographien. 29)

- United States

GERTZOG (IRWIN N.) ed. Readings on state and local government. Englewood Cliffs, [1970]. pp. 379.

ZIMMERMAN (JOSEPH FRANCIS) ed. Subnational politics: readings in state and local government. 2nd ed. New York, [1970]. pp. 446.

CITIZENS CONFERENCE ON STATE LEGISLATURES. State legislatures: an evaluation of their effectiveness; the complete report. New York, 1971. pp. 480. bibliog.

JACOB (HERBERT) and VINES (KENNETH N.) eds. Politics in the American states: a comparative analysis. 2nd ed. Boston, [Mass.], [1971]. pp. 627. bibliogs.

LEBLANC (HUGH LINUS) and ALLENSWORTH (DON TRUDEAU) The politics of states and urban communities. New York, [1971]. pp. 469.

STRENGTHENING the states: essays on legislative reform; [papers presented at conferences organised by the Eagleton Institute of Politics of Rutgers University, the National Conference of State Legislative Leaders and the Citizens Conference on State Legislatures, 1966-1969]; edited by Donald G. Herzberg [and] Alan Rosenthal. New York, 1971. pp. 271. bibliog.

ADRIAN (CHARLES RAYMOND) State and local governments. 3rd ed. New York, [1972]. pp. 600. bibliogs.

HAVARD (WILLIAM C.) ed. The changing politics of the south. Baton Rouge, [1972]. pp. 755. bibliog.

SHARKANSKY (IRA) The maligned states: policy accomplishments, problems, and opportunities. New York, [1972]. pp. 169.

- United States - Officials and employees

EHRENBERG (RONALD G.) The demand for state and local government employees: an economic analysis. Lexington, Mass., [1972]. pp. 145. bibliog.

STATE RIGHTS

MASON (ALPHEUS THOMAS) ed. The states rights debate: antifederalism and the constitution. 2nd ed. New York, 1972. pp. 210. bibliog.

STATE SUCCESSION

UNITED NATIONS. Office of Legal Affairs. Legislative Series. [14]. Materials on succession of states. (ST/LEG/SER.B/14). New York, 1967. pp. 243. In English or French.

FIEDLER (WILFRIED) Staatskontinuität und Verfassungsrechtsprechung: zum Begriff der Kontinuität des deutschen Staatswesens unter besonderer Berücksichtigung der Rechtsprechung des Bundesverfassungsgerichts. Freiburg [im Breisgau, 1970]. pp. 208. bibliog.

OKOYE (FELIX CHUKS) International law and the new African states. London, 1972. pp. 225. bibliog.

UDOKANG (OKON) Succession of new states to international treaties. Dobbs Ferry, N.Y., 1972. pp. 525. bibliog.

STATES, NEW

GONIDEC (PIERRE FRANÇOIS) L'état africain: évolution, fédéralisme, centralisation et décentralisation, panafricanisme. Paris, 1970. pp. 440.

POZDNIAKOV (EL'GIZ ABDULOVICH) Molodye gosudarstva Azii i Afriki v OON. Moskva, 1971. pp. 149. bibliog.

VEDOVATO (GIUSEPPE) Decolonizzazione e sviluppo. Firenze, 1971. pp. 420. (Rivista di Studi Politici Internazionali. Biblioteca. Serie 2. 16)

OKOYE (FELIX CHUKS) International law and the new African states. London, 1972. pp. 225. bibliog.

SIGMUND (PAUL E.) ed. The ideologies of the developing nations. 2nd rev. ed. [i.e. 3rd ed.] New York, 1972. pp. 483. bibliog.

UDOKANG (OKON) Succession of new states to international treaties. Dobbs Ferry, N.Y., 1972. pp. 525. bibliog.

NWABUEZE (BENJAMIN OBI) Constitutionalism in the emergent states. London, [1973]. pp. 316.

SOUSTELLE (JACQUES) Lettre ouverte aux victimes de la décolonisation. Paris, [1973]. pp. 191.

STATES, SIZE OF

YONDO (MARCEL) Dimension nationale et développement économique: théorie, application dans l'UDEAC. Paris, 1970. pp. 251. bibliog.

RUMMEL (RUDOLPH JOSEPH) The dimensions of nations. Beverly Hills, [1972]. pp. 512. bibliog.

STATES, SMALL

MATHISEN (TRYGVE) The functions of small states in the strategies of the great powers. Oslo, [1971]. pp. 288.

NOBEL SYMPOSIUM, 17TH, OSLO. Small states in international relations; edited by August Schou and Arne Olav Brundtland. Stockholm, [1971]. pp. 250.

RAPOPORT (JACQUES) and others. Small states and territories: status and problems; a UNITAR study. New York, 1971. pp. 216.

BRANNER (HANS) Småstat mellem stormagter: beslutningen om mineudlaegning august 1914. [Copenhagen], 1972. pp. 279. bibliog. (Dansk Udenrigspolitisk Institut. Skrifter. 5)

KOHR (LEOPOLD) Development without aid: the translucent society;... [with] critical reflections by Professors Robert J. Alexander and Alfred P. Thorne. Llandybie, Carmarthenshire, 1973. pp. 227. bibliog.

STATESMEN

SWEARINGEN (RODGER) ed. Leaders of the communist world. New York, [1971]. pp. 632.

MACDONALD (MALCOLM JOHN) Titans and others. London, 1972. pp. 287.

PAIGE (GLENN D.) ed. Political leadership: readings for an emerging field. New York, [1972]. pp. 359.

SPULER (BERTOLD) Regenten und Regierungen der Welt: Sovereigns and governments of the world...; Minister-Ploetz. Teil II, Band 5. Neueste Zeit, 1965-1970. Würzburg, [1972]. pp. 220. Table of contents, preface and explanatory notes in various languages.

STATESMEN
See also DIPLOMATS; LEGISLATORS

STATESMEN, AMERICAN

JOYNER (CONRAD) The American politician. Tucson, [1971]. pp. 231. bibliog.

WHO's who in American politics: (a biographical directory of United States political leaders); 3rd edition 1971-1972; edited by Paul A. Theis and Edmund L. Henshaw. New York, 1971. pp. 1171.

STATESMEN, ARAB

KHADDURI (MAJID) Arab contemporaries: the role of personalities in politics. Baltimore, [1973]. pp. 255.

STATESMEN, AUSTRALIAN

MCLEOD (ALAN LINDSEY) ed. Australia speaks: an anthology of Australian speeches. Sydney, [1969]. pp. 213.

STATESMEN, DANISH

HANSEN (JENS ANDERSEN) Politiske Skildringer af afdøde danske Maend, der have gjort sig bemaerkede i vor politiske Udviklings-Historie fra 1830 til Nutiden...Første Bind. Kjøbenhavn, 1854. pp. 319.

STATESMEN, DOMINICAN

PAYNE (JAMES L.) Incentive theory and political process: motivation and leadership in the Dominican Republic. Lexington, Mass., [1972]. pp. 165.

STATESMEN, GERMAN

FISCHER (HEINZ DIETRICH) ed. Deutsche Publizisten des 15. bis 20. Jahrhunderts. München-Pullach, 1971. pp. 419. bibliogs.

KOZA (INGEBORG) Die erste deutsche Republik im Spiegel des politischen Memoirenschrifttums: Untersuchungen zum Selbstverständnis und zur Selbstkritik bei den politisch Handelnden, etc. Wuppertal, [1971]. pp. 167. bibliog.

STATESMEN, LATIN AMERICAN

WILKIE (JAMES W.) Elitelore. Los Angeles, 1973. pp. 87. bibliog. (California University. Latin American Center. Latin American Studies. vol. 22)

STATESMEN, SPANISH

PIZAN (MANUEL) El poder y la oposicion: once politicos y tres conflictos. Barcelona, [1970]. pp. 235.

CLEMENTE BALAGUER (JOSE CARLOS) Conversaciones con las corrientes politicas de España. Barcelona, 1971. pp. 232.

STATIONERY TRADE
- United Kingdom

LOASBY (B.J.) The Swindon project: a report on the relocation of W.H. Smith & Son Ltd's Lambeth warehouse. London, 1973. pp. 76.

STATISTICAL DECISION

DE GROOT (MORRIS H.) Optimal statistical decisions. New York, [1970]. pp. 489. bibliog.

HAMBURG (MORRIS) Statistical analysis for decision making. New York, [1970]. pp. 817. bibliog.

LANGE (OSKAR) Optimal decisions: principles of programming. Oxford, 1971. pp. 292. bibliog.

STATISTICAL decision theory and related topics: (proceedings of a symposium held at Purdue University...1970); edited by Shanti S. Gupta and James Yackel. New York, 1971. pp. 383.

STATISTICS

PETTY (Sir WILLIAM) M.D., Surveyor-General of Ireland to Charles II. Several essays in political arithmetick;...to which are prefix'd, memoirs of the author's life. 4th ed. London, Browne, 1755. pp. iv,vi,184.

INTERNATIONAL BANK FOR RECONSTRUCTION AND DEVELOPMENT. Economic Program Department. Socio-Economic Data Division. 1971. World tables. [Washington], 1971 in progress. 1 vol. (loose leaf).

GERMANY (BUNDESREPUBLIK). Statistisches Bundesamt. 1972. Gegenwarts- und Zukunftsaufgaben der amtlichen Statistik; herausgegeben anlässlich des 100 jährigen Bestehens der zentralen amtlichen Statistik. Stuttgart, [1972]. pp. 89.

ROUMANIA. Direcţia Centrală de Statistică.Consfătuire Ştiinţifică de Statistică, 7-a, 1969. Studii de statistică: lucrările celei de-a şaptea Consfătuiri ştiinţifice de statistică, 11-14 iunie 1969. Bucureşti, 1972. 3 vols. With separate volume of English summaries.

EVERSLEY (DAVID EDWARD CHARLES) A question of numbers? London, 1973. pp. 32. (Runnymede Trust. Runnymede Lectures. 1972)

HOPKINS (HARRY) The numbers game: the bland totalitarianism. London, 1973. pp. 310.

- Bibliography

RUSSIA (U.S.S.R.). Komitet po Pechati. 1971. Annotirovannyi katalog knig izdatel'stva "Statistika", 1966-1970 gg. Moskva, 1971. pp. 423.

BURRINGTON (GILLIAN A.) How to find out about statistics. Oxford, 1972. pp. 153.

POLAND. Główny Urząd Statystyczny. Centralna Biblioteka Statystyczna. Bibliografia polskiego piśmiennictwa statystycznego 1944-1969, bez wydawnictw Głównego Urzędu Statystycznego. Warszawa, 1972. pp. 588.

- Computer programmes

MORRIS (CARL) and ROLPH (JOHN) Introduction to statistics and data analysis with computer applications. [Santa Monica], 1971. 2 vols. (in 1). bibliogs. (Rand Corporation. [Papers]. 4695-6)

- Dictionaries and encyclopaedias

INTER AMERICAN STATISTICAL INSTITUTE. 1960. Statistical vocabulary. 2nd ed. Washington, 1960. pp. 83. In various languages.

- History - Russia

K 50-letiiu sovetskoi statistiki: sbornik statei. Moskva, 1969. pp. 406.

- Study and teaching

BURRINGTON (GILLIAN A.) How to find out about statistics. Oxford, 1972. pp. 153.

- Study and teaching - Russia

SIPOVSKAIA (IRINA VASIL'EVNA) and SUSLOV (IVAN PETROVICH) eds. Istoriia prepodavaniia i razvitiia statistiki v Peterburgskom - Leningradskom universitete, 1819-1971 gg. Leningrad, 1972. pp. 139.

- Theory, methods, etc.

YULE (GEORGE UDNY) and KENDALL (MAURICE GEORGE) An introduction to the theory of statistics. 14th ed. London, 1950. pp. 701.

SMEKHOV (BORIS MOISEEVICH) Statistika i planirovanie. 2nd ed. Moskva, 1964. pp. 104.

BROWNLEE (KENNETH ALEXANDER) Statistical theory and methodology in science and engineering. 2nd ed. New York, [1965]. pp. 590. bibliogs.

DOWNIE (NORVILLE MORGAN) and HEATH (ROBERT WILLIAM) Basic statistical methods. 2nd ed. New York, 1965. pp. 325. bibliog.

YAMANE (TARO) Statistics: an introductory analysis. 2nd ed. New York, [1967]. pp. 919.

BUSLENKO (NIKOLAI PANTELEIMONOVICH) Metod statisticheskogo modelirovaniia. Moskva, 1970. pp. 112. bibliog.

CHRISTOFFERSSON (ANDERS) The one component model with incomplete data. Uppsala, [1970]. pp. 138. bibliog. (Uppsala. Universitet. Institute of Statistics. Selected publications. vol. 25)

GOLENKO (DMITRII ISAAKOVICH) Statisticheskie metody v ekonomicheskikh sistemakh. Moskva, 1970. pp. 203. bibliog.

HARBISON (FREDERICK HARRIS) and others. Quantitative analyses of modernization and development. Princeton, N.J., 1970. pp. 224. bibliog. (Princeton University. Department of Economics and Sociology. Industrial Relations Section. Research Report Series. No. 115)

MAXWELL (ALBERT ERNEST) Basic statistics in behavioural research. Harmondsworth, 1970. pp. 126. bibliog.

SMITH (GEORGE MILTON) A simplified guide to statistics for psychology and education. 4th ed. New York, [1970]. pp. 244.

UNITED NATIONS. Statistical Office. Statistical Papers. Series M. No. 49. United Nations standard country code.(CST/STAT/SER.M/49) New York, 1970. pp. 46.

BAILEY (DANIEL E.) Probability and statistics: models for research. New York, [1971]. pp. 686. bibliogs.

COCKERHAM (COLUMBUS CLARK) and BURROWS (PETER M.) Populations of interacting autogenous components. Raleigh, [1971]. pp. 13-29. (North Carolina University. Institute of Statistics. Reprint Series. No. 239) (Reprinted from The American Naturalist, vol. 105, no. 941, 1971)

DOLLAR (CHARLES M.) and JENSEN (RICHARD J.) Historian's guide to statistics: quantitative analysis and historical research. New York, [1971]. pp. 332. bibliog.

DRUZHININ (NIKOLAI KAPITONOVICH) Matematicheskaia statistika v ekonomike: vvedenie v matematiko-statisticheskuiu metodologiiu. Moskva, 1971. pp. 264. bibliog.

STATISTICS - Theory, methods, etc. (Cont'd.)

FAN (SHUH CHING) Selected topics in statistics for social scientists. Hong Kong, 1971. pp. 94.

HOEL (PAUL GERHARD) Elementary statistics. 3rd ed. New York, [1971]. pp. 309.

KEMPTHORNE (OSCAR) and FOLKS (LEROY) Probability, statistics, and data analysis. Ames, Iowa, 1971. pp. 555. bibliog.

LASS (HARRY) and GOTTLIEB (PETER) Probability and statistics. Reading, Mass., [1971]. pp. 470. bibliogs.

LESHCHINSKII (M.I.) and RIAUZOV (NIKOLAI NIKOLAEVICH) eds. Ekonomicheskaia statistika. Moskva, 1971. pp. 439.

MARASCUILO (LEONARD A.) Statistical methods for behavioral science research. New York, [1971]. pp. 578. bibliog.

MORRIS (CARL) and ROLPH (JOHN) Introduction to statistics and data analysis with computer applications. [Santa Monica], 1971. 2 vols. (in 1). bibliogs. (Rand Corporation. [Papers]. 4695-6)

RIAUZOV (NIKOLAI NIKOLAEVICH) Obshchaia teoriia statistiki. 2nd ed. Moskva, 1971. pp. 368.

SEARLE (S.R.) Linear models. New York, [1971]. pp. 532. bibliog.

SYMPOSIUM ON THE FOUNDATIONS OF STATISTICAL INFERENCE, UNIVERSITY OF WATERLOO, ONTARIO, 1970. Foundations of statistical inference: proceedings of the symposium...prepared under the auspices of the Rene Descartes Foundation...; edited by V.P. Godambe and D.A. Sprott. Toronto, [1971]. pp. 519. bibliogs.

BEALS (RALPH E.) Statistics for economists: an introduction. Chicago, [1972]. pp. 420.

BLALOCK (HUBERT M.) Social statistics. 2nd ed. New York, [1972]. pp. 583.

BOLDRINI (MARCELLO) Scientific truth and statistical method...; translated...by Ruth Kendall. London, 1972. pp. 264. bibliog.

CHOU (YA-LUN) Probability and statistics for decision making. New York, [1972]. pp. 623. bibliog.

EISENBEIS (ROBERT A.) and AVERY (ROBERT B.) Discriminant analysis and classification procedures: theory and applications. Lexington, [1972]. pp. 254.

KLEVMARKEN (ANDERS) Statistical methods for the analysis of earnings data, with special application to salaries in Swedish industry. Stockholm, 1972. pp. 271. bibliog. (Sweden. Statistiska Centralbyrån. Urval. 6)

QUENOUILLE (MAURICE HENRY) Rapid statistical calculations: a collection of distribution-free and easy methods of estimation and testing. 2nd ed. London, 1972. pp. 37bis, (9). bibliog.

SINHA (SNEHESH KUMAR) Life testing and reliability estimation in the presence of an outlier observation: [Ph. D (London) thesis]. [1972]. fo. 126. bibliog. Typescript: unpublished. This thesis is the property of London University and may not be removed from the Library.

STATISTICS: a guide to the unknown; edited by Judith M. Tanur [and others]. San Francisco, [1972]. pp. 430. bibliogs.

THEIL (HENRI) Statistical decomposition analysis; with applications in the social and administrative sciences. Amsterdam, 1972. pp. 337. bibliog.

WONNACOTT (THOMAS HERBERT) and WONNACOTT (RONALD JOHNSTON) Introductory statistics. 2nd ed. New York, [1972]. pp. 510.

GRANGER (CLIVE W.J.) Statistical forecasting of economic series: a review of techniques. Guildford, 1973. pp. 14. (University of Surrey. Surrey Papers in Economics. No. 8)

HAYS (WILLIAM LEE) Statistics for the social sciences. 2nd ed. New York, [1973]. pp. 954.

ROBSON (COLIN) Experiment, design and statistics in psychology. Harmondsworth, 1973. pp. 174.

- Periodicals - Union lists

LIBRARY ASSOCIATION and ROYAL STATISTICAL SOCIETY. Committee of Librarians and Statisticians. A union list of statistical serials in British libraries. London, 1972. pp. 86. (Resources on Economic Statistics. 3)

LONDON. University. Board of Studies in Statistics. List of holdings [in London libraries] of statistical periodicals, collected papers and collections of papers. London, [1973]. pp. 9.

STAVROPOL' (KRAI)

- Politics and government

OCHERKI istorii Stavropol'skoi organizatsii KPSS. Stavropol', 1970. pp. 632.

STEAD (WILLIAM THOMAS)

BAYLEN (JOSEPH O.) The tsar's "lecturer-general": W.T. Stead and the Russian revolution of 1905; with two unpublished memoranda of audiences with the Dowager Empress Marie Fedorovna and Nicholas II. Atlanta, 1969. pp. 91. bibliog. (Georgia State College. School of Arts and Sciences. Research Papers. No. 23)

STEALING

BELSON (WILLIAM A.) and others. The development of a procedure for eliciting information from boys about the nature and extent of their stealing. London, [1971?] pp. 337.

STEAMBOAT LINES

- United Kingdom

SHIPPING: a survey of historical records [conducted by the Business Archives Council and the National Maritime Museum]; edited by P. Mathias and A.W.H. Pearsall. Newton Abbot, [1971]. pp. 162. bibliogs.

FARRANT (JOHN H.) Mid-Victorian Littlehampton: the railway and the cross-Channel steamers. Littlehampton, [1972]. pp. 27. bibliog. (Littlehampton. Urban District Council. Littlehampton Papers. No.4)

- United States

BAXTER (MAURICE GLEN) The steamboat monopoly: Gibbons v. Ogden, 1824. New York, [1972]. pp. 146. bibliog.

STEEL INDUSTRY AND TRADE

UNITED NATIONS. Economic Commission for Europe. 1968. World trade in steel and steel demand in developing countries. (ST/ECE/STEEL/22). New York, 1968. pp. 201.

PECO (FRANCO) L'acier face aux théories économiques. Milano, [1971]. pp. 317.

- Technological innovations

EUROPEAN COAL AND STEEL COMMUNITY. Nouveaux Procédés Techniques dans la Sidérurgie. vol. 3. Les aciéries: manuel destiné à la formation du personnel sidérurgique. Bruxelles, 1971. pp. 283.

- China

HSIA (RONALD) Steel in China: its output, behavior, productivity and growth pattern. Wiesbaden, [1971]. pp. 220. (Hamburg. Institut für Asienkunde. Schriften. Band 29)

- France

MEYRONNEINC (G.) L'acier en France. Levallois, [1967?]. 1 pamphlet (unpaged).

- India

DESAI (PADMA) The Bokaro steel plant: a study of Soviet economic assistance. Amsterdam, 1972. pp. 108.

NATIONAL COUNCIL OF APPLIED ECONOMIC RESEARCH. Demand for steel: 1975 and 1980; [compiled by Ashok V. Desai and others]. New Delhi, [1971]. pp. 108.

- Japan

KAWAHITO (KIYOSHI) The Japanese steel industry: with an anlysis of the U.S. steel import problem. New York, 1972. pp. 203. bibliog.

SCHEPPACH (WALTER) Die japanische Stahlindustrie. Hamburg, 1972. pp. 143,22. (Hamburg. Institut für Asienkunde. Mitteilungen. No. 48)

- Russia

ROZANOV (MIKHAIL DMITRIEVICH) Obukhovtsy: istoriia zavoda "Bol'shevik", byvshego Obukhovskogo staleliteinogo zavoda. [2nd ed.] Leningrad, 1965. pp. 523. 1st ed. published 1938.

- Sweden - Mathematical models

VINELL (LARS) Business cycles and steel markets: studies in demand variations and firms' short-term behaviour in the Swedish steel market;...translation: Roger Tanner. [Stockholm, 1973]. pp. 376. bibliog.

- United Kingdom

HORSFALL (JOHN HENRY COLDWELL) The iron masters of Penns, 1720-1970. Kineton, 1971. pp. 331.

BAILEY (DAVE) Steel: the coming redundancies and how to fight them, including 'the confidential report' on closures. London, [1972?]. pp. 54.

STEFAN BATORY UNIVERSITY
See VILNA UNIVERSITY

STEINSTUECKEN

CATUDAL (HONORE MARC) Steinstücken: a study in coldwar politics. New York, [1971]. pp. 165. bibliog.

STEPANOV (IVAN IVANOVICH SKVORTSOV-)
See SKVORTSOV-STEPANOV (IVAN IVANOVICH)

STEPNEY

- Social conditions

REALITY. Stepney words, no. 2: (a collection of poetry by Stepney children and friends). London, 1971. pp. 39.

STEPPES

PILATOV (P.N.) Stepi SSSR kak uslovie material'noi zhizni obshchestva: k probleme - priroda i chelovek. Iaroslavl', 1966. pp. 287. bibliog.

STERILIZATION (BIRTH CONTROL)

In earlier volumes of the Bibliography similar works have been entered under CONCEPTION- Prevention, and STERILIZATION, HUMAN

PRESSER (HARRIET B.) Sterilization and fertility decline in Puerto Rico. Berkeley, [1973]. pp. 211. bibliog. (California University. Institute of International Studies. Population Monograph Series. No. 13)

STERILIZATION, HUMAN
See STERILIZATION (BIRTH CONTROL)

STERLING AREA

NELSON (JAMES R.) and PALMER (DONALD K.) United States foreign economic policy and the sterling area. Princeton, 1953. fo. 44. (Princeton University. Center of International Studies. [Policy] Memoranda. No. 4)

GRAVES (KENNETH THOMAS HUXLEY) The pound sterling and the restoration of convertibility, 1946-1958; [M. Phil. (London) thesis]. 1971 [or rather 1973]. fo. 249. bibliog. Typescript: unpublished. This thesis is the property of London University and may not be removed from the Library.

MEYER (FREDERICK VICTOR) The functions of sterling. London, 1973. pp. 172.

STEVENAGE

- Social conditions

STEVENAGE DEVELOPMENT CORPORATION. Stevenage household survey, March 1971. [Stevenage], 1971. fo. 63.

- Transit systems

STEVENAGE DEVELOPMENT CORPORATION. Stevenage household survey, March 1971. [Stevenage], 1971. fo. 63.

STEYN (MARTHINUS THEUNIS).

MEINTJES (JOHANNES) Vader van sy volk: 'n lewenskets van President M.T. Steyn. Kaapstad, 1970. pp. 82. bibliog.

STILL-BIRTH

SCHIRAY (MICHEL) and ELIE (PIERRE) Les migrations entre régions et au niveau catégories de commune de 1954 à 1962: [and] Les causes de mortinatalité dans le département de la Seine; par Maurice Aubenque et Louise Deruffe. [Paris, 1970]. pp. 75. (France. Institut National de la Statistique et des Etudes Economiques. Collections de l'INSEE. Série D. Démographie et Emploi. 4) With summaries in English and Spanish.

STILWELL (JOSEPH WARREN)

TUCHMAN (BARBARA WERTHEIM) Sand against wind: Stilwell and the American experience in China, 1911-45. London, 1971. pp. 621. bibliog.

STOCHASTIC DIFFERENTIAL EQUATIONS

HENDRY (DAVID FORBES) and TREVEDI (P.K.) Maximum likelihood estimation of difference equations with moving average errors: a simulation study. [London], 1970. pp. various. bibliog. (London. University. London School of Economics and Political Science. Department of Economics. Discussion Papers. No. 7)

STOCHASTIC PROCESSES

TRANQUILLI (GIOVANNI BATTISTA) Su un generico test caratteristico di normalità e di omoschedasticità per più variabili casuali. Roma, 1966. pp. 64-96. bibliog. (Rome. Università. Istituto di Calcolo delle Probabilità. Pubblicazioni. 2a Serie. 61) (Estratto dal Giornale dell'Istituto Italiano degli Attuari, anno XXIX, n.1, 1966) With English and French summaries.

TRANQUILLI (GIOVANNI BATTISTA) Sul teorema di Basu-Darmois. Roma, 1966. pp. 135-152. bibliog. (Rome. Università. Istituto di Calcolo delle Probabilità. Pubblicazioni. 2a Serie. 62) (Estratto dal Giornale dell' Istituto Italiano degli Attuari, anno XXIX, n.1, 1966) With English and French summaries.

ÅSTRÖM (KARL J.) Introduction to stochastic control theory. New York, 1970. pp. 299. bibliogs.

BHAT (U. NARAYAN) Elements of applied stochastic processes. New York, [1972]. pp. 414.

CASSON (MARK C.) Generalised errors in variables regression. Reading, 1972. fo. 24. bibliog. (Reading. University. Department of Economics. Discussion Papers in Economics. No. 34)

HILDRETH (CLIFFORD G.) Ventures, bets and initial prospects. Minneapolis, 1972. fo. 50. (Minnesota University. Center for Economic Research. Discussion Papers. No.20)

SIMS (CHRISTOPHER A.) Seasonality in regression. Minneapolis, 1972. fo 26. (Minnesota University Center for Economic Research. Discussion Papers. No. 23)

TINTNER (GERHARD) and SENGUPTA (JATIKUMAR) Stochastic economics: stochastic processes, control, and programming. New York, 1972. pp. 315. bibliog.

ENGWALL (LARS) Models of industrial structure. Lexington, Mass., [1973]. pp. 179. bibliog.

STOCHASTIC PROGRAMMING

SENGUPTA (JATI KUMAR) Stochastic programming: methods and applications. Amsterdam, 1972. pp. 313. bibliog.

STOCK AND STOCK BREEDING

CENTO CONFERENCE ON NATIONAL AND REGIONAL LIVESTOCK DEVELOPMENT POLICY, ISLAMABAD, 1969. [Report of the Conference] held in Islamabad, Pakistan, December 15-21, 1969. Ankara, Central Treaty Organization, 1971. pp. 134.

CENTO workshops on marketing of livestock and their products; April 5-8, 1971, Lahore, Pakistan; April 12-13, 1971, Tehran, Iran; April 19-22, 1971, Ankara, Turkey. [Ankara], Central Treaty Organization, [1972]. pp. 78.

- Europe

SHORT-term forecasting of livestock numbers and livestock production in the Federal Republic of Germany, Denmark, the Netherlands and the United Kingdom; [by] E. Böckenhoff [and others]. Stuttgart, 1970. pp. 332. bibliog.

- Ghana

STEWART (J.L.) Report on the livestock of the coastal area of the Eastern Province of the colony. Sessional paper No. 20 of 1928-29. in GHANA. Legislative Council. Minutes (formerly Minutes...and sessional papers).

- India

INDIA. Ministry of Agriculture. Directorate of Economics and Statistics. 1972- . Indian livestock census, 1966. [Delhi], 1972 in progress.

- India - Rajasthan

NATIONAL COUNCIL OF APPLIED ECONOMIC RESEARCH. Agriculture and livestock in Rajasthan. New Delhi, [1964]. pp. 103.

- Kenya

KENYA. Ministry of Finance and Planning. Statistics Division. 1972. Results of aerial livestock surveys of Kaputei division, Samburu district and North Eastern Province; [by R.M. Watson]. [Nairobi, 1972]. pp. 114, fo. (76). bibliog.

- Rhodesia

RHODESIA. Central Statistical Office. 1967- . Report on the 1967 census of livestock on European farms. Salisbury, 1967 in progress.

- Russia

TIMCHENKO (NATAL'IA GRIGOR'EVNA) K istorii okhoty i zhivotnovodstva v Kievskoi Rusi: Srednee Podneprov'e. Kiev, 1972. pp. 204. bibliog.

ZAMYSLOV (IVAN NIKOLAEVICH) Ekonomicheskaia otsenka otraslei zhivotnovodstva. Moskva, 1973. pp. 158.

- Sardinia

OLLA (DOMENICO) Il vecchio e il nuovo dell'economia agro-pastorale in Sardegna. Milano, [1969]. pp. 134.

- Spain

SPAIN. Ministerio de Agricultura. 1958. Censo de la ganadería española, 1955. Madrid, 1958. pp. 145.

- United Kingdom

HILL FARMING GROUP. Report; [S. Culpin, chairman]. Leeds, National Agricultural Advisory Service, 1967. pp. 51.

HILL FARMING GROUP. Second report; [E.S. Carter, chairman]. Leeds, Agricultural Development and Advisory Service. 1972. pp. 91.

- Uruguay

MEDERO (BENITO) El plan agropecuario: antecedentes, características, realizaciones y significado en el desarrollo ganadero del Uruguay. [Montevideo], Comision Honoraria del Plan Agropecuario, 1972. pp. 130. In Spanish and English.

URUGUAY. [Ministerio de Ganaderia y Agricultura]. 1972. Evolucion del sector agropecuario en el periodo 1970/71. [Montevideo, 1972?]. 1 vol. (various pagings).

STOCK COMPANIES

- Germany

NORTH RHINE-WESTPHALIA. Statistisches Landesamt. 1971. Die Kapitalgesellschaften in Nordrhein-Westfalen, 1966-1970. Düsseldorf, 1971. pp. 151. (Beiträge zur Statistik des Landes Nordrhein-Westfalen. Heft 272)

STOCK-EXCHANGE

FRITSCH (THEODOR) Zwei Grundübel: Boden-Wucher und Börse; eine gemein-verständliche Darstellung der brennendsten Zeitfragen. Leipzig, 1894. pp. 299.

PRISSERT (PIERRE) Le marché des changes. [Paris], 1972. pp. 140.

LORIE (JAMES H.) and HAMILTON (MARY T.) The stock market: theories and evidence. Homewood, Ill., 1973. pp. 304. bibliog.

- France

DEFOSSE (GASTON) La Bourse des Valeurs et les opérations de Bourse. 8th ed. Paris, 1972. pp. 128.

- Italy

FOSSATI (GIORGIO) I fondi comuni di investimento, con nozioni di borsa e ricerche sull'azionariato popolare. Milano, 1971. pp. 322. bibliog.

- United Kingdom

The FINANCIAL house that Jack built. 2nd ed. London, Richardson, 1819. pp. 10.

- United States

WEST (RICHARD R.) and TINIÇ (SEHA M.) The economics of the stock market. New York, 1971. pp. 222.

[GOODMAN (GEORGE JEROME WALDO)] Supermoney; by "Adam Smith", [pseud.]. New York, [1972]. pp. 301.

SOBEL (ROBERT) Amex: a history of the American Stock Exchange, 1921-1971. New York, [1972]. pp. 382. bibliog.

WYCKOFF (PETER) Wall Street and the stock markets: a chronology, 1644-1971. Philadelphia, [1972]. pp. 304. bibliog.

JESSUP (PAUL F.) and UPSON (ROGER B.) Returns in over-the-counter stock markets. Minneapolis, [1973]. pp. 109.

STOCK OWNERSHIP

FOSSATI (GIORGIO) I fondi comuni di investimento, con nozioni di borsa e ricerche sull'azionariato popolare. Milano, 1971. pp. 322. bibliog.

STOCKHOLDERS

- Sweden

SWEDEN. Finansdepartementet. Fondbörsutredningen. 1968. Förenklad aktiehantering: nya regler för aktiebrev och aktiebok. Stockholm, 1968. pp. 129. bibliog. (Sweden. Statens Offentliga Utredningar. 1968. 59) With summary in English.

STOCKHOLM

- Economic history

HAMMARSTRÖM (INGRID) Stockholm i svensk ekonomi, 1850-1914. Stockholm, 1970. pp. 396. bibliog. (Stockholm. Kommunalförvaltningen. Monografier)

- Population

NILSSON (FRED) Emigrationen från Stockholm till Nordamerika, 1880-1893: en studie i urban utvandring. Stockholm, 1970. pp. 391. bibliog. (Stockholm. Kommunalförvaltningen. Monografier. 31) With English summary.

STOCKS

- Denmark

STANCKE (BENT) The Danish stock market, 1750-1840. København, 1971. pp. 118. bibliog. (Københavns Universitet. Institut for Økonomisk Historie. Publikationer. Nr. 4)

- France

FRANCE. Commission Chargée d'Etudier le Marché des Actions. 1971. Le marché des actions: rapport présenté au Ministre de l'Economie et des Finances, etc.; [Wilfrid Baumgartner, chairman]. [Paris], 1971. pp. 104.

- United States

BREALEY (RICHARD A.) Security prices in a competitive market: more about risk and return from common stocks. Cambridge, Mass., [1971]. pp. 234. bibliog.

GOLDSMITH (RAYMOND WILLIAM) ed. Institutional investors and corporate stock: a background study. New York, 1973. pp. 469. (National Bureau of Economic Research. Studies in Capital Formation and Financing. 13)

- United States - Tables, etc.

WYCKOFF (PETER) Wall Street and the stock markets: a chronology, 1644-1971. Philadelphia, [1972]. pp. 304. bibliog.

STOECKER (ADOLF)

KUPISCH (KARL) Adolf Stoecker: Hofprediger und Volkstribun; ein historisches Porträt. Berlin, [1970]. pp. 94.

STOKES (CARL BURTON)

ZANNES (ESTELLE) Checkmate in Cleveland: the rhetoric of confrontation during the Stokes years;...assisted by Mary Jean Thomas. Cleveland, 1972. pp. 271.

STOLYPIN (PETR ARKAD'EVICH)

BAZYLOW (LUDWIK) Ostatnie lata Rosji carskiej: rządy Stołypina. Warszawa, 1972. pp. 507.

STONE CUTTERS

CALWER (RICHARD) Die Berufsgefahren der Steinarbeiter;...im Auftrage des X. Kongresses der Steinarbeiter Deutschlands als Denkschrift an den Bundesrat herausgegeben von der Zentralleitung der Organisation der Steinarbeiter Deutschlands. Rixdorf, 1901. pp. 197. bibliog.

STORAGE AND MOVING TRADE
- United States

HESS (JOHN) The mobile society: a history of the moving and storage industry. New York, [1973]. pp. 208.

STORE LOCATION

BERRY (BRIAN JOE LOBLEY) Géographie des marchés et du commerce de détail;...traduction de Bernard Marchand. Paris, [1971]. pp. 254.

STORES, RETAIL

TAKEBAYASHI (YUKICHI) Voluntary retail chains in Japan. [Tokyo], 1971. pp. 31. (Asian Productivity Organization. Technical Publications)

U.K. Department of Employment. 1971. The Offices, Shops and Railway Premises Act, 1963: a general guide. 2nd ed. [London], 1971. pp. 65.

STORES OR STOCK ROOM KEEPING
See INVENTORY CONTROL

STOURBRIDGE
- Economic conditions

SMITH (BARBARA M.D.) Employment opportunities in the Dudley, Stourbridge and Halesowen parts of the Black Country. Birmingham, 1972. pp. 62 (Birmingham. University. Centre for Urban and Regional Studies. Research Memoranda. 16)

STRACHEY (EVELYN JOHN ST. LOE.)

ZORINA (DORA IUL'EVNA) Kak Dzhon Strechi "obnovil" Marksa: antinauchnost' osnov sovremennogo reformizma. Moskva, 1964. pp. 110.

THOMAS (HUGH) John Strachey. London, 1973. pp. 316.

STRAITS QUESTION

VÁLI (FERENC ALBERT) The Turkish straits and NATO. Stanford, Calif., [1972]. pp. 348. bibliog. (Stanford University. Hoover Institution on War, Revolution and Peace. Hoover Institution Studies. 32)

STRALSUND
- History

LANGER (HERBERT) Stralsund, 1600-1630: eine Hansestadt in der Krise und im europäischen Konflikt. Weimar, 1970. pp. 295. bibliog. (Deutsche Historikergesellschaft. Hansische Arbeitsgemeinschaft. Abhandlungen zur Handels- und Sozialgeschichte. Band 9)

STRASBOURG
- Economic conditions

SCHAR (DOMINIQUE) Strasbourg: ville française ou rhénane? [Paris, 1971]. pp. 221.

- Politics and government

SCHAR (DOMINIQUE) Strasbourg: ville française ou rhénane? [Paris, 1971]. pp. 221.

STRATEGY

GARNETT (JOHN C.) ed. Theories of peace and security: a reader in contemporary strategic thought. London, 1970. pp. 272. bibliog.

ART (ROBERT J.) and WALTZ (KENNETH NEAL) eds. The use of force: international politics and foreign policy. Boston, [1971]. pp. 546. bibliog.

COFFEY (JOSEPH IRVING) Strategic power and national security. Pittsburgh, [1971]. pp. 214.

ROSECRANCE (RICHARD NEWTON) ed. The future of the international strategic system. San Francisco, [1972]. pp. 219. bibliog.

MARTIN (LAURENCE WOODWARD) Arms and strategy: an international survey of modern defence. London, [1973]. pp. 320.

STRAWBERRIES

CANADA. Tariff Board. 1972. Report...relative to the investigation ordered by the Minister of Finance respecting strawberries for processing. Ottawa, 1972. 1 vol. (various pagings).

STREET-RAILWAYS
See TRAMWAYS

STREET SIGNS.

ASHLEY/MYER/SMITH. Signs/Lights/Boston. City signs and lights: a policy study; prepared for the Boston Redevelopment Authority and the U.S. Department of Housing and Urban Development. [Boston], 1971. pp. 272. bibliog.

STREICHER (JULIUS)

WAS soll mit den Juden geschehen?: praktische Vorschläge von Julius Streicher und Adolf Hitler. Paris, 1936. pp. 94.

STRESEMANN (GUSTAV)

WALSDORFF (MARTIN) Westorientierung und Ostpolitik: Stresemanns Russlandpolitik in der Locarno-Ära. Bremen, [1971]. pp. 326. bibliog.

MAXELON (MICHAEL OLAF) Stresemann und Frankreich, 1914-1929: deutsche Politik der Ost-West-Balance. Düsseldorf, [1972]. pp. 309. bibliog.

WEIDENFELD (WERNER) Die Englandpolitik Gustav Stresemanns: theoretische und praktische Aspekte der Aussenpolitik. Mainz, [1972]. pp. 382. bibliog.

- Bibliography

WALSDORFF (MARTIN) compiler. Bibliographie Gustav Stresemann. Düsseldorf, [1972]. pp. 207. (Germany (Bundesrepublik). Bibliographien zur Geschichte des Parlamentarismus und der Politischen Parteien. Heft 5)

STRESS (PHYSIOLOGY)

CARLESTAM (GÖSTA) and LEVI (LENNART) Urban conglomerates as psycho-social human stressors: general aspects, Swedish trends, and psychological and medical implications: a contribution to the United Nations Conference on the Human Environment. [Stockholm], Royal Ministry for Foreign Affairs, [1971 repr. 1972]. pp. 74. bibliog.

GLASS (DAVID C.) and SINGER (JEROME E.) Urban stress: experiments on noise and social stressors. New York, 1972. pp. 182. bibliog.

HAYWARD (JACK CHARLES) Some relationships between pre-operative information and post-operative pain and anxiety in surgical patients: an experimental study; [Ph.D. (London) thesis]. 1973. fo. 444. bibliog. Typescript: unpublished. This thesis is the property of London University and may not be removed from the Library.

STRIKES AND LOCKOUTS

MATEOS (   ) Dr. P. Evangelista. Es la huelga un derecho o constituye un delito?: la huelga ante la moral. Madrid, 1965. pp. 54. bibliog.

AARON (BENJAMIN) and WEDDERBURN (KENNETH WILLIAM) eds. Industrial conflict: a comparative legal survey;...[by] Benjamin Aaron [and others]. London, 1972. pp. 396.

JAMES (BERNARD) Ph.D. The right to strike: a concept to legitimise the disruption of industrial relationships by the concerted withdrawal of labour; [Ph.D. (London) thesis]. 1972. fo. 573. bibliog. Typescript: unpublished. This thesis is the property of London University and may not be removed from the Library.

KAHN-FREUND (OTTO) and HEPPLE (BOB ALEXANDER) Laws against strikes. London, 1972. pp. 60. (Fabian Society. International Comparisons in Social Policy. 1) (Fabian Society. Research Series. [No.] 305)

- Bibliography

INSTITUTE OF SCIENTIFIC BUSINESS. Bibliographical Studies. No. 3. A bibliography on strikes; [compiled by] B.O. Pettman. Bradford, [1971]. fo. 40.

- Argentine Republic

GODIO (JULIO) La semana tragica de enero de 1919. Buenos Aires, 1972. pp. 206.

- Australia

AUSTRALIA. Department of Labour and National Service. 1958. Industrial disputes in Australia. Melbourne, 1958. pp. 26.

IREMONGER (JOHN) and others, eds. Strikes: studies in twentieth century Australian social history. Sydney, 1973. pp. 270.

- China

CHEN (JOSEPH T.) The May Fourth Movement in Shanghai: the making of a social movement in modern China. Leiden, 1971. pp. 219. bibliog.

- Colombia

RUEDA ROSERO (ULPIANO) Los conflictos de trabajo: la huelga; el arbitramento. Bogota, 1969. pp. 92. bibliog.

- Denmark

DUE (JESPER) and MADSEN (JØRGEN STEEN) Tillidsmanden i klassekampen: Ålborgstrejken; en sociologisk analyse. København, [1972]. pp. 200. bibliog.

- Europe

SOCIALISTISK UNGDOMS FORBUND. Kampen mod EEC; strejkebevaegelsen i Vesteuropa. [Århus, 1971 repr. 1972]. pp. 62. bibliog. (Røde Haefter. Nr. 2)

- France

CENTRE NATIONAL D'INFORMATION POUR LA PRODUCTIVITE DES ENTREPRISES. Les évenements de mai-juin 1968 vus à travers cent entreprises; document realisé...à partir de témoignages rassemblés au C.N.I.P.E. [Paris, 1969]. pp. 68.

ABSALOM (ROGER) ed. France: the May events 1968; ...[selected documents with a short commentary]. London, 1971. pp. 96.

GAULT (FRANÇOIS) Trois grèves. [Paris, 1971]. pp. 251.

SEGUY (GEORGES) Le mai de la C[onfédération] G[énérale du] T[ravail]. Paris, [1972]. pp. 224.

- Galicia (Eastern Europe)

KAKOVS'KYI (KOSTIANTYN HEORHIIOVYCH) Na shliakhu do Velykoho Zhovtnia: straikovyi rukh v Halychyni, kintsia XIX-pochatku XX st. L'viv, 1970. pp. 156.

- Germany

IMIG (WERNER) Der Streik der Mansfelder Arbeiter im Jahr 1930. Berlin, 1957. pp. 104. (Institut für Marxismus-Leninismus (Berlin). Beiträge zur Geschichte und Theorie der Arbeiter-Bewegung. Heft 19)

KOELLMANN (WOLFGANG) ed. Der Bergarbeiterstreik von 1889 und die Gründung des Alten Verbandes in ausgewählten Dokumenten der Zeit. Bochum, [1969]. pp. 319. bibliog.

OTTE (JUERGEN) Das subjektiv-private Arbeitskampfrecht als Grundlage einer Neuorientierung im Recht des Streiks und der Aussperrung. Hamburg, 1970. pp. 172,xvii. bibliog. (Europa-Kolleg, Hamburg. Schriften. Band 13)

AM Beispiel der Septemberstreiks: Anfang der Rekonstruktionsperiode der Arbeiterklasse; eine empirische Untersuchung von Michael Schumann [and others]. Frankfurt am Main, [1971]. 1 vol. (various pagings). (Soziologisches Forschungsinstitut Göttingen. Studienreihe)

ESCHENHAGEN (WIELAND) Antigewerkschaftlicher Kampf oder Kampf in den Gewerkschaften?: sozialistische Betriebsarbeit und Gewerkschaftsbürokratie; Erfahrungen in Bremen. München, 1971. pp. 183.

HEISELER (JOHANNES HENRICH VON) and others. Über die Streiks in der chemischen Industrie im Juni/Juli 1971 in einigen Zentren der Tarifbewegung in Hessen und Rheinland. 2nd ed. Frankfurt/M, [1971]. pp. 130. (Institut für Marxistische Studien und Forschungen. Informationsberichte. Nr. 7)

ULE (CARL HERMANN) Streik und Polizei. Köln, 1972. pp. 116.

- Italy

BOSIO (GIANNI) La grande paura, settembre 1920: l'occupazione delle fabbriche nei verbali inediti delle riunioni degli stati generali del movimento operaio. Roma, [1970]. pp. 245.

CARINCI (FRANCO) Il conflitto collettivo nella giurisprudenza costituzionale. Milano, 1971. pp. 150. (Bologna. Università. Seminario Giuridico. Pubblicazioni. 60)

- Russia

KANN (PAVEL IAKOVLEVICH) Podvig rabochikh Krengol'mskoi manufaktury: k stoletiiu stachki; istoricheskii ocherk. Tallin, 1972. pp. 118.

STRIKES AND LOCKOUTS (Cont'd.)

- Spain

BAYOD SERRAT (RAMON) La nueva redaccion del articulo 222 del codigo penal (sobre huelgas y cierres patronales). Madrid, 1966. pp. 70. (Tiempo Nuevo. 2)

- Thailand

THAILAND. Division of Labor. 1959. Conciliation and work stoppages, 1958. [Bangkok, 1959]. pp. 39. (Labor Statistics Bulletins. No.3) In English and Thai.

- United Kingdom

TRANSPORT AND GENERAL WORKERS' UNION. Hull Branch. No bus to-day: the case of the East Yorkshire bus strike. Hull, 1966. pp. 20.

LANE (ANTHONY D.) and ROBERTS (KENNETH) Strike at Pilkingtons. London, 1971. pp. 266.

DOUGLASS (DAVID) Pit life in Co. Durham: rank and file movements and workers' control. [Oxford?, 1972]. pp. 92. (History Workshop. Pamphlets. No. 6)

HYMAN (RICHARD) Strikes. London, 1972. pp. 184. bibliog.

KAHN-FREUND (OTTO) and HEPPLE (BOB ALEXANDER) Laws against strikes. London, 1972. pp. 60. (Fabian Society. International Comparisons in Social Policy. 1) (Fabian Society. Research Series. [No.] 305)

MATHEWS (JOHN) b. 1946. Ford strike: the workers' story. London, 1972. pp. 208.

LEESON (R.A.) ed. Strike: a live history, 1887-1971. London, 1973. pp. 246.

- United Kingdom - Mathematical models

KNIGHT (K.G.) Strikes and wage inflation in British manufacturing industry, 1950-1968. Coventry, 1972. pp. 22. (University of Warwick. Centre for Industrial Economic and Business Research. [Warwick Research in Industrial and Business Studies]. No. 27)

- United States

STEIN (LEON) and TAFT (PHILIP) eds. Massacre at Ludlow: four reports, [published in 1914 and 1915, reprinted]...with an introduction. New York, 1971. pp. 189.

HILLMAN (SIDNEY) Defendant. Supreme Court, Monroe County: Joseph Michaels, Morley A. Stern et al., plaintiffs, against Sidney Hillman, individually and as president of the Amalgamated Clothing Workers of America, et al, defendants: memorandum of law; O'Brien & Powell, attorneys for defendants; Felix Frankfurter [and others] of Counsel. New York, [imprint, c.1920]. pp. 93.

DUNNE (WILLIAM F.) Gastonia: citadel of the class struggle in the new South;...for the National Textile Workers Union. New York, 1929. pp. 58.

DAY (MARK) Forty acres: Cesar Chavez and the farm workers. New York, 1971. pp. 222. bibliog.

BROWN (JERALD BARRY) The United Farm Workers grape strike and boycott, 1965-1970: an evaluation of the culture of poverty theory. [Ithaca], 1972. pp. 348. bibliog. (Cornell University. Latin American Studies Program. Dissertation Series. No. 39)

DOBBS (FARRELL) Teamster rebellion. New York, 1972. pp. 192.

LENS (SIDNEY) The labor wars: from the Molly Maguires to the sitdowns. New York, [1973]. pp. 366. bibliog.

SERRIN (WILLIAM) The Company and the Union: the 'civilized relationship' of the General Motors Corporation and the United Automobile Workers. New York, 1973. pp. 308,xiv.

STRONNICTWO LUDOWE

KOWALCZYK (STANISŁAW) and ŁUCZAK (ALEKSANDER) eds. Pisma ulotne Stronnictw Ludowych w Polsce, 1895-1939. Kraków, 1971. pp. 411.

HEMMERLING (ZYGMUNT) ed. Ruch ludowy na Ziemiach Zachodnich i Północnych w Polsce Ludowej: materiały sesji popularnonaukowej w Koszalinie zorganizowanej przez Zakład historii ruchu ludowego przy NK ZSL, etc. Olsztyn, 1972. pp. 568.

STRUCTURAL ANTHROPOLOGY
See ANTHROPOLOGY; STRUCTURALISM

STRUCTURALISM.

BOUDON (RAYMOND) The uses of structuralism...; translated by Michalina Vaughan; introduced by Donald MacRae. London, 1971. pp. 159. bibliog.

BOON (JAMES A.) From symbolism to structuralism: Lévi-Strauss in a literary tradition. Oxford, [1972]. pp. 250. bibliog.

DE GEORGE (RICHARD T.) and DE GEORGE (FERNANDE M.) eds. The structuralists: from Marx to Lévi-Strauss. Garden City, N.Y., 1972. pp. 330. bibliogs.

GLUCKSMANN (MIRIAM ANNE) Varieties of the structural analysis of social phenomena with special reference to Claude Lévi-Strauss and Louis Althusser; [Ph.D. (London) thesis]. 1971 [or rather 1972]. fo. 326. bibliogs. Typescript: unpublished. This thesis is the property of London University and may not be removed from the Library.

MUNZ (PETER) When the golden bough breaks: structuralis or typology? London, 1973. pp. 143. bibliog.

STRUCTURALISM: an introduction...; edited by David Robey. Oxford, 1973. pp. 153. (Oxford. University. Wolfson College. Wolfson College Lectures. 1972)

STRUCTURE (PHILOSOPHY)

DAIX (PIERRE) Structuralisme et révolution culturelle. [Paris], 1971. pp. 149.

RIJK (M.C.) Structuur, macht en geweld: een analyse in het licht van een beschouwing over de mens in de huidige westerse cultuur. Bloemendaal, [1972]. pp. 109.

STRUMA

ROHWER (JUERGEN) Die Versenkung der jüdischen Flüchtlingstransporter Struma und Mefkure im Schwarzen Meer, Februar 1942, August 1944: historische Untersuchung. Frankfurt/Main, 1965. pp. 153. bibliog. (Bibliothek für Zeitgeschichte. Schriften. Heft 4)

STUBBE (HENRY)

NICASTRO (ONOFRIO) Lettere di Henry Stubbe a Thomas Hobbes, 8 luglio 1656 - 6 maggio 1657. Siena, 1973. pp. 91.

STUDENT ACTIVITIES.

- United Kingdom

SURVEYS of space and activities: Reading University; ([by] Nicholas Bullock [and others]). Cambridge, 1970. pp. 42. bibliog. (Cambridge. University. School of Architecture. Land Use and Built Form Studies. Working Papers. No.40)

TOMLINSON (JANET) and others. A model of daily activity patterns: development and sample results. Cambridge, 1971. pp. 78. (Cambridge. University. School of Architecture. Land Use and Built Form Studies. Working Papers. No.43)

SURVEY of day-to-day activities: tabulations and preliminary analyses; [by] Nicholas Bullock [and others]. Cambridge, 1972. pp. 156. bibliog. (Cambridge. University. School of Architecture. Land Use and Built Form Studies. Working Papers. No.44)

STUDENT EMPLOYMENT

THAILAND. Division of Labor. 1959. Vacation employment for students, 1957-1958. [Bangkok, 1959]. pp. 43. (Labor Statistics Bulletins, No. 1) In English and Thai.

THAILAND. Division of Labor. 1959. Vacation employment for students, 1959. [Bangkok, 1959]. pp. 74. (Labor Statistics Bulletins. No.4). In English and Thai.

The DIRECTORY of summer jobs abroad: 1972 edition; editor: Charles J. James. Oxford, [1972]. pp. 152. bibliog.

The DIRECTORY of summer jobs in Britain: 1972 edition; editor Sally E. Moon. Oxford, [1972]. pp. 152.

STUDENT HOUSING

- Canada

BLAND (JOHN) of McGill University, and SCHOENAUER (NORBERT) University housing in Canada. Montreal, 1966. pp. 137.

- United Kingdom

BROTHERS (JOAN) and HATCH (STEPHEN) Residence and student life: a sociological inquiry into residence in higher education. London, 1971. pp. 419. bibliog.

ACADEMIC CONSULTATIVE CONFERENCE, LONDON, 1971. Student accommodation; report of a conference convened by the Committee of Vice-Chancellors and Principals at the University of London on 9 December 1971; conference chairman Sir Fraser Noble. Watford, [imprint], [1972]. pp. 31.

- United States

AGRIA (JOHN J.) College housing: a critique of the Federal College Housing Loan Program. Washington, [1972]. pp. 105. (American Enterprise Institute for Public Policy Research. Evaluative Studies. 1)

STUDENT PARTICIPATION IN ADMINISTRATION.

- United Kingdom

LONDON. University. London School of Economics and Political Science. Socialist Society. L.S.E.; what it is: and how we fought it. London, 1967. pp. 25.

STUDENTS.

HENTIG (HARTMUT VON) Das erste Studienjahr an der Universität: Bericht über eine Tagung vom 8-10. Januar 1963. Hamburg, [1963]. pp. 72. bibliog. (Unesco Institute for Education. International Studies in Education)

STUDENTS, university and society: a comparative sociological review; [papers presented at a series of seminars held by the Graduate School of Contemporary European Studies of Reading University in 1969-1970]; edited by Margaret Scotford Archer. London, 1972. pp. 280. bibliogs.

- Political activity

COSENTINO (SALVATORE) Il seme della protesta; in appendice: Dizionario della contestazione; a cura di Giuliano Zincone. [Catania], 1969. pp. 135.

MIRO (FIDEL) El anarquismo, los estudiantes y la revolucion. Mexico, 1969. pp. 231.

STERLING (SALTERS) ed. Reflections on student protest. London, 1969. pp. 60. (University Teachers' Group. Higher Education Broadsheets. 6)

HUNTLEY (JAMES) The implications of student unrest: report commissioned by NATO. Leeds, [197-?]. pp. 12. (Independent Labour Party. Square One Pamphlets. 7)

GREIG (IAN) Today's revolutionaries:...a study of some prominent modern revolutionary movements and methods of sedition in Europe and the United States. Richmond, Surrey, 1970. pp. 120.

AMERICAN ACADEMY OF POLITICAL AND SOCIAL SCIENCE. Annals. vol. 395. Students protest; special editors of this volume: Philip G. Altbach and Robert S. Laufer. Philadelphia, 1971. pp. 277. bibliog.

BRYCHKOV (ALEKSANDR RODIONOVICH) Bunt v Al'ma-Mater: bor'ba i problemy studentov v razvitykh kapitalisticheskikh stranakh. Moskva, 1971. pp. 48. Xerographic copy.

LOEBL (EUGEN) Conversations with the bewildered; translated by George Gretton. London, 1972. pp. 192.

RÁCZ (MIKLÓS) Universiteit en klassenstrijd: wetenschap, partijdigheid en samenleving. Amsterdam, 1972. pp. 200.

SALYCHEV (STEPAN STEPANOVICH) "Novye levye": s kem i protiv kogo. Moskva, 1972. pp. 96.

UNIVERSITIES in politics: case studies from the late middle ages and early modern period; edited with an introduction by John W. Baldwin and Richard A. Goldthwaite. Baltimore, [1972]. pp. 137. (Johns Hopkins University. Department of History. Johns Hopkins Symposia in Comparative History.2)

ALTBACH (PHILIP G.) and UPHOFF (NORMAN THOMAS) The student internationals. Metuchen, N. J., 1973. pp. 207. bibliog.

SIDOR (KAZIMIERZ) Rewolta studentów. Warszawa, 1973. pp. 313.

- Religious life

MOTT (JOHN RALEIGH) Strategic points in the world's conquest: the universities and colleges as related to the progress of Christianity. London, 1897. pp. 218.

STUDENTS (Cont'd.)

- Algeria - Political activity

INTERNATIONAL UNION OF STUDENTS. Bureau of Students against Colonialism. Solidarity with Algerian students: series of documents on student problems relating to colonialism. [Prague, 1958]. pp. 68.

- America, Latin

LIEBMAN (ARTHUR) and others. Latin American university students: a six nation study; ...with an introduction by Seymour Martin Lipset. Cambridge, Mass., 1972. pp. 296.

- American, Latin - Political activity

ZAMORANO (MANUEL) La rebelion juvenil. Santiago [de Chile], 1968. pp. 186. bibliog.

- Argentine Republic - Political activity

MAZO (GABRIEL DEL) Reforma universitaria y cultura nacional. Buenos Aires, [1955]. pp. 183.

INGLESE (JUAN OSVALDO) and YEGROS DORIA (CARLOS L.) Universidad y estudiantes; [and] Universidad y peronismo; [by] Léon Berdichevsky. Buenos Aires, 1965. pp. 228.

- Brazil

RIOS (JOSE ARTHUR) The university student and Brazilian society. East Lansing, Mich., 1971. fo. 73. (Michigan State University. Latin American Studies Center. Monograph Series. No. 6)

- Canada - Political activity

LET the niggers burn!.. the Sir George Williams University affair and its Caribbean aftermath; (edited by Dennis Forsythe). Montreal, [1971]. pp. 209.

- China - Political activity

SINGER (MARTIN) Educated youth and the cultural revolution in China. Ann Arbor, 1971. pp. 114. bibliog. (Michigan University. Center for Chinese Studies. Michigan Papers in Chinese Studies. No. 10)

HINTON (WILLIAM) Hundred day war: the cultural revolution at Tsinghua University. New York, [1972]. pp. 288.

- France

FRANCE. Commission Nationale Paritaire de la Vie de l'Etudiant. 1970. Rapport. [Paris, 1969 or rather 1970]. pp. 72.

- France - Political activity

BLOCH-MICHEL (JEAN) Une révolution du XXe siècle: les journées de mai 1968. Paris, [1968]. pp. 127.

CANARD ENCHAÎNÉ, LE. Le canard de mai: (numéro spécial exceptionnel...juin, 1968); [articles, photographs and cartoons from the May 26th and June 6th issues, and from the May 30th issue of Combat]. [Paris], 1968. pp. 16.

Les JOURNEES de mai 68; par les journalistes de R.T.L.; présentation de Jean-Pierre Farkas. Philips B 77.757 L, [1968?]. phonodisc.

MAI 68: [speeches by] Jacques Sauvageot, Alain Geismar, Daniel Cohn-Bendit [and] Manifestations étudiantes et témoignages sur la répression; extraits sonores d'un film réalisé par un collectif de travail animé par Guy Chalon. [Paris?], acousti-Yuri Korolkoff, [1968]. phonodisc.

NOOTEBOOM (CEES) De Parijse beroerte. Amsterdam, 1968. pp. 53.

La CHIENLIT: petit guide de la contestation en politique, à l'université, au théâtre, au cinéma, dans la chanson, dans l'Eglise, etc...; sous la direction de Dominique Venner. Paris, 1969. pp. 82.

WILLENER (ALFRED) b. 1928. L'image-action de la société; ou, La politisation culturelle. Paris, [1970]. pp. 351. bibliog.

ABSALOM (ROGER) ed. France: the May events 1968; ...[selected documents with a short commentary]. London, 1971. pp. 96.

TOURAINE (ALAIN) The May movement: revolt and reform; May, 1968, the student rebellion and workers' strikes, the birth of a social movement; translated by Leonard F.X. Mayhew. New York, 1971. pp. 373.

JOHNSON (RICHARD) Political Scientist. The French Communist Party versus the students: revolutionary politics in May-June 1968. New Haven, 1972. pp. 215. bibliog.

- Germany

ALBERNDT (A.) pseud. [i.e. Erich AMBROCK] Establishment, Karl Marx und die neue Elite. Berlin, [1970]. pp. 116. bibliog.

SCHOLZ (RUPERT) and ISENSEE (JOSEF) Zur Krankenversicherung der Studenten. Köln, 1973. fo. 34. (Verband der Privaten Krankenversicherung. Dokumentationen. 1)

- Germany - Political activity

KUHN (HELMUT) Professor of Philosophy at Munich University. Jugend im Aufbruch: zur revolutionären Bewegung unserer Zeit. München, [1970]. pp. 207.

LOEWENTHAL (RICHARD) Der romantische Rückfall: Wege und Irrwege einer rückwärts gewendeten Revolution. Stuttgart, [1970]. pp. 88.

FUCHS (WERNER) Sociologist. Expressive und instrumentale Aktion: Formen und Wirksamkeit studentischer Politik. Düsseldorf, [1971]. pp. 170. bibliog.

LANGGUTH (GERD) ed. Aspekte zur Reformpolitik: Beiträge engagierter Studenten. Mainz, [1971]. pp. 278.

SOZIALISTISCHER DEUTSCHER STUDENTENBUND. SDS Hochschuldenkschrift; ([reprint of the second edition of 1965, with] Nachwort des Verlages, [1972]). Frankfurt am Main, 1972. pp. 183. bibliog.

- Germany - Political activity - Bibliography

GERMANY (BUNDESREPUBLIK). Deutscher Bundestag. Wissenschaftliche Dienste. 1968. Die studentische Opposition in der Bundesrepublik: Auswahlbibliographie; [compiled by Peter Schindler]. Bonn, 1968. pp. 47. (Bibliographien. 18)

- India - Political activity

VISHWA YUVAK KENDRA. The dynamics of student agitations. Bombay, [1973]. pp. 120. bibliog.

- Indonesia - Political activity

ANWAR (YOZAR) Dagboek van een kami-student; vertaling van Beb Vuyk; inleiding en commentaren van Jacob Vredenbregt. Meppel, 1968. pp. 134.

- Italy

> CENTORRINO (MARIO) and APONTE (TULLIO D') Problemi territoriali ed aspetti economici della condizione studentesca meridionale: il caso della Facoltà di Scienze Politiche dell'Università di Messina. Milano, 1972. pp. 117.

- Japan - Political activity

> BERAUD (BERNARD) La gauche révolutionnaire au Japon. Paris, [1970]. pp. 158. bibliog.
>
> SMITH (HENRY DEWITT) Japan's first student radicals. Cambridge, Mass., 1972. pp. 341. bibliog. (Harvard University. East Asian Research Center. Harvard East Asian Series. 70)

- Mexico

> BLANCO MOHENO (ROBERTO) Tlatelolco: historia de una infamia. Mexico, 1969. pp. 286.
>
> PONIATOWSKA (ELENA) ed. La noche de Tlatelolco: testimonios de historia oral. Mexico, 1971. pp. 282.

- Mexico - Political activity

> CONSEJO NACIONAL DE HUELGA. El mondrigo!: (bitacora del Consejo Nacional de Huelga). Mexico, [1968?]. pp. 184.
>
> UNITED STATES COMMITTEE FOR JUSTICE TO LATIN AMERICAN POLITICAL PRISONERS. Mexico '68: the students speak. New York, [1968?]. pp. 30.
>
> HERNANDEZ (SALVADOR) El PRI y el Movimiento Estudiantil de 1968. Mexico, 1971. pp. 126. bibliog.

- Poland

> KRZYZANOWSKI (WITOLD) ed. Budżety czasu młodzieży akademickiej w wybranych uczelniach Krakowa. Wrocław, 1970. pp. 83. (Polska Akademia Nauk. Oddział w Krakowie. Komisja Socjologiczna. Prace. Nr.19) With Russian and English summaries.

- Russia

> ZHABA (SERGEI P.) Petrogradskoe studenchestvo v bor'be za svobodnuiu Vysshuiu Shkolu: (doklad studenta Petrogradskogo universiteta..., predstavlennyi Vtoromu S"ezdu Rossiiskikh emigrantskikh studencheskikh organizatsii). Paris, [1922?]. pp. 61.
>
> VSESOIUZNYI SLET STUDENTOV, 1971. Vsesoiuznyi slet studentov, 19-20 oktiabria 1971 goda: dokumenty i materialy. Moskva, 1972. pp. 175.

- Russia - Political activity

> MEL'GUNOV (SERGEI PETROVICH) Studencheskie organizatsii 80-90 gg. v Moskovskom universitete, po arkhivnym dannym. Moskva, 1908. pp. 103.
>
> FAKUL'TET, na kotorom uchilsia Lenin: ocherki. Kazan', 1970. pp. 135.

- Russia - Uzbekistan

> KARIEV (MUKHAMADZHAN MURADOVICH) Oblik nashego studenchestva. Tashkent, 1969. pp. 61.

- South Africa - Political activity

> STUDENT perspectives on South Africa; [papers of the first research workshop of the Abe Bailey Institute of Interracial Studies, Cape Town University]; edited by Hendrik W. van der Merwe and David Welsh. Cape Town, 1972. pp. 229.

- Spain - Political activity

> FARGA (MANUEL JUAN) Universidad y democracia en España: 30 años de lucha estudiantil. Mexico, 1969. pp. 177.

- Sweden

> SWEDEN. Statistiska Centralbyrån. 1960. 1957 års studentekonomiska undersökning. [Stockholm, 1960]. fo. 81, [48].

- United Kingdom

> NATIONAL UNION OF STUDENTS and NATIONAL COUNCIL FOR CIVIL LIBERTIES. Academic freedom and the law. London, 1970. pp. 106.
>
> WANKOWSKI (J.A.) G.C.E.'s and degrees: some notes and reflections on studies of the relationship between admission requirements and achievement at university. Birmingham, [1970]. fo. various. bibliog.
>
> WANKOWSKI (J.A.) Personality dimensions of students and some educational implications of Eysenck's theory of extraversion and neuroticism: (research report). Birmingham, [1970]. fo. various. bibliog.
>
> WANKOWSKI (J.A.) Random sample analysis: motives and goals in academic achievement: an epilogue. Birmingham, [1970]. fo. various. bibliog.
>
> WANKOWSKI (J.A.) Random sample analysis: motives and goals in university studies. Birmingham, [1970]. fo. various. bibliog.
>
> [BUTTERWORTH (BRIAN) and POWELL (A.)] Marked for life: a criticism of assessment at universities; composed by certain members of University College, London. London, [1971?]. pp. 32.
>
> BARR (ALAN) Student community action. London, [1972]. pp. 135.
>
> HARRIS (W.J.A.) Home study students: a report of a follow-up study of the students who, three to four years earlier in 1967, had enrolled in correspondence courses. Manchester, [1972]. pp. 178. bibliog. (Manchester. University. Department of Adult Education. Manchester Monographs. 1)
>
> MURRAY (G.A.) The welfare net. [Leicester], 1972. pp. 22. bibliog.
>
> YOUNG (WILLIAM STEWART) The student drugtaker: a study of the use of drugs in a London college; [Ph.D. (London) thesis]. [1972]. fo. 311. bibliog. Typescript: unpublished. This thesis is the property of London University and may not be removed from the Library.
>
> MADGE (CHARLES) and WEINBERGER (BARBARA) Art students observed. London, 1973. pp. 282.

- United Kingdom - Political activity

> COMMUNIST PARTY [OF GREAT BRITAIN]. L.S.E. Branch. Lessons from LSE: a communist perspective. [London, 1972]. pp. 25.
>
> DENT (BOB) LSE: a question of degree; [issued by Solidarity (London) on behalf of the author]. London, [1972]. pp. 29.
>
> DENT (BOB) LSE: a question of degree; [with an article by Maggie Wellings]. [London, 1972]. pp. 26. bibliog.

- United States

> HOOK (SIDNEY) Academic freedom and academic anarchy. New York, [1970]. pp. 269.

STUDENTS - United States (Cont'd.)

    BLOUSTEIN (EDWARD J.) The university and the counterculture: inaugural and other addresses. New Brunswick, [1972]. pp. 117.

    LEVITT (MORTON) and RUBENSTEIN (BEN) eds. Youth and social change. Detroit, 1972. pp. 410. Most of the papers were presented at the 47th annual convention of the American Orthopsychiatric Association.

    WITONSKI (PETER) What went wrong with American education and how to make it right. New York, [1973]. pp. 191.

- United States - Political activity

    CASTAGNINO (RAUL HECTOR) "Cambio", confrontaciones estudiantiles y violencia. Buenos Aires, [1970]. pp. 175.

    LEVINE (MARYL) and NAISBITT (JOHN) Right on!: (a documentary on student protest). New York, [1970]. pp. 256.

    NEW YORK (STATE). Temporary Commission to Study the Causes of Campus Unrest. 1970. The academy in turmoil: first report of the...Commission; [Charles D. Fenderson, chairman]. Albany, 1970. pp. 195.

    KLEEMANN (SUSANNE) Ursachen und Formen der amerikanischen Studentenopposition. Frankfurt am Main, 1971. pp. 229. bibliog.

    LIPSET (SEYMOUR MARTIN) and SCHAFLANDER (GERALD M.) Passion and politics: student activism in America. Boston, [1971]. pp. 440.

    ALTBACH (PHILIP G.) and LAUFER (ROBERT S.) eds. The new pilgrims: youth protest in transition; [mainly essays reprinted from Annals of the American Academy of Political and Social Science, vol. 395]. New York, [1972]. pp. 326. bibliogs.

    APTHEKER (BETTINA) The academic rebellion in the United States. Secaucus, N.J., [1972]. pp. 218.

    LIPSET (SEYMOUR MARTIN) Rebellion in the university: a history of student activism in America. London, 1972. pp. 310.

    SEARLE (JOHN ROGERS) The campus war. Harmondsworth, [1972]. pp. 219.

- United States - Religious life

    RIGHT ON! The street people: selections from Right on!, Berkeley's Christian underground student newspaper. London, 1972. pp. 64.

- Uruguay

    MONTEVIDEO. Universidad. Oficina de Planeamiento. Censo de estudiantes ingresados en 1968: proceso de admision y reclutamiento en la Universidad de la Republica; informe preliminar. [Montevideo, 1968?]. pp. 80.

    MONTEVIDEO. Universidad. Oficina de Planeamiento. Censo general de estudiantes, 1968: informe preliminar. [Montevideo, 1968?]. pp. 56.

- Uruguay - Political activity

    COPELMAYER (ROBERTO) and DÍAZ (DIEGO) Montevideo 68: la lucha estudiantil. Montevideo, 1969. pp. 97.

- Venezuela - Political activity

    ARNOVE (ROBERT F.) Student alienation: a Venezuelan study. New York, 1971. pp. 209. bibliog.

STUDENTS, FOREIGN

- Statistics

    UNITED NATIONS EDUCATIONAL, SCIENTIFIC AND CULTURAL ORGANIZATION. Office of Statistics. 1971. Statistics of students abroad, 1962-1968: where they go, where they come from, what they study. Paris, 1971. pp. 416. (Statistical Reports and Studies. [No. 18]) In English and French.

- Denmark

    ØRTING (PETER) and others. Udenlandske studenter i Danmark: nogle resultater af en undersøgelse foretaget af Studenterrådet ved Københavns Universitet. [Copenhagen], 1972. pp. 206. bibliog.

- United States

    HAWES (GENE R.) Student's guide to study in the U.S.A. London, [1971]. pp. 124.

STUDENTS, INTERCHANGE OF

    EIDE (INGRID) ed. Students as links between cultures: a cross cultural survey based on Unesco studies. Paris, United Nations Educational, Scientific and Cultural Organization, [1970]. pp. 243. bibliog.

STUDENTS' SOCIETIES

- Finland

    KLINGE (MATTI) Studenter och idéer: Studentkåren vid Helsingfors Universitet, 1828-1960...; översättning [from the Finnish] av Bertel Kihlman. Helsingfors, [1969 in progress].

- Russia

    MEL'GUNOV (SERGEI PETROVICH) Studencheskie organizatsii 80-90 gg. v Moskovskom universitete, po arkhivnym dannym. Moskva, 1908. pp. 103.

STUDY, METHOD OF

    DRESSEL (PAUL L.) and THOMPSON (MARY MAGDALA) Independent study. San Francisco, 1973. pp. 162. bibliog.

STUDENTS' SOCIETIES

- Russia

    KAZAKEVICH (ROZA ABRAMOVNA) and MANDEL' (SEMEN ZAKHAROVICH) Nauchnaia i kul'turno-prosvetitel'skaia deiatel'nost' progressivnogo studenchestva 80-kh godov XIX v.: studencheskoe nauchno-literaturnoe obshchestvo Peterburgskogo universiteta. Leningrad, 1967. pp. 75.

STURZO (LUIGI)

    GRAMEGNA (MARIO) Luigi Sturzo: la coscienza morale della funzione politica. Campobasso, [1972]. pp. 131. bibliog.

    PIVA (FRANCESCO) and MALGERI (FRANCESCO) Vita di Luigi Sturzo. Rome, [1972]. pp. 463.

    ROSA (GABRIELE DE) L'utopia politica di Luigi Sturzo; [with an appendix of hitherto unpublished writings by Sturzo]. Brescia, 1972. pp. 237.

STUTTGART

- Economic conditions

KAISER (KLAUS) and SCHAEWEN (MANFRED VON) Stuttgart und die Region Mittlerer Neckar. Stuttgart, [1973]. pp. 228. bibliog.

STYRIA

- Industries

BEITRÄGE zur Geschichte der Industrialisierung des Südostalpenraumes im 19. Jahrhundert: [four papers read at a symposium in 1968]; herausgegeben von Othmar Pickl. Graz, 1970. pp. 59. (Historische Landeskommission für Steiermark. Forschungen zur Geschichtlichen Landeskunde der Steiermark. Band 24)

SUBJECTIVITY

POOLE (ROGER) Towards deep subjectivity. London, 1972. pp. 152.

SUBMARINE GEOLOGY

The GEOLOGY of the East Atlantic Continental Margin: (I[nternational] C[ouncil of] S[cientific] U[nions] / S[cientific] C[ommittee on] O[ceanic] R[esearch] Working Party 31 Symposium, Cambridge 1970); edited by F.M. Delany. London, H.M.S.O., 1970-1971. 4 pts. (in 1). bibliogs. (U.K. Institute of Geological Sciences. Reports. Nos. 70/13 - 70/16.) With summaries in French and German.

DESTOMBES (J.P.) and SHEPHARD-THORN (ERNEST ROY) Geological results of the Channel tunnel site investigation, 1964-65. London, 1971. pp. 12. bibliog. (U.K. Institute of Geological Sciences. Reports. No. 71/11) Map in end pocket.

DINGWALL (RICHARD GEORGE) The structural and stratigraphical geology of a portion of the eastern English Channel. London, 1971. pp. 24. bibliog. (U.K. Institute of Geological Sciences. Reports. No. 71/8). Map in end pocket.

U.K. Natural Environment Research Council. 1971. A review of recent investigations of the sea bed on the continental margin around the British Isles. [London], 1971. pp. 28, 3 maps. (Publications. Series C. No. 5)

SUBMARINE WARFARE

HIRDMAN (SVEN) Prospects for arms control in the ocean. Stockholm, 1972. pp. 25. (Stockholm International Peace Research Institute. Research Reports. No. 7)

WADDINGTON (CONRAD HAL) O.R. in World War 2: operational research against the U-boat. London, 1973. pp. 253.

SUBSIDENCES (EARTH MOVEMENTS)

GEOLOGIC HAZARDS CONFERENCE ON LANDSLIDES AND SUBSIDENCE, LOS ANGELES, 1965. Landslides and subsidence: Geologic Hazards Conference, May 26 and 27, 1965. [Los Angeles?, 1966]. pp. (iv), 190.

SUBSIDIARY CORPORATIONS : Europe

ALSEGG (ROBERT J.) Control relationships between American corporations and their European subsidiaries. [New York, 1971]. pp. 220. (American Management Association. Research Studies [No.] 107)

SUBSIDIES

ORGANISATION FOR ECONOMIC CO-OPERATION AND DEVELOPMENT. Committee for Fisheries. 1965. Subsidies and other financial support to the fishing industries of OECD member countries; adopted by the Committee...and approved by the Council at its meeting on the 21st July 1964. [Paris, 1965]. pp. 252.

- Germany

RICHTER (JUERGEN) Die Zinssubventionen in der Bundesrepublik Deutschland: Formen, Entwicklung und Wirkungen auf den Kapitalmarkt. Frankfurt am Main, [1970]. pp. 280. bibliog. (Frankfurt am Main. Universität. Institut für Kapitalmarktforschung. Monographien. 2)

WEGEHENKEL (PETER) Die Beihilfen zur Bekämpfung der Steinkohlenkrisen in der Bundesrepublik Deutschland für den Zeitraum, 1958-1968: eine Analyse ihrer Wirksamkeit im Hinblick auf die Zielsetzung einer billigen Energie. Hamburg, 1970. pp. 316. bibliog.

GERMANY (BUNDESREPUBLIK). Deutscher Bundestag. Wissenschaftliche Dienste. 1971. Subventionsbericht 1970: rechtliche, wirtschaftliche und fiskalische Würdigung; [edited by Diplomvolkswirt Rösner and Regierungsrat Lehmberg]. Bonn, 1971. pp. 56. (Materialien. 24)

HILDEBRANDT (FRANK) Kommunale Wirtschaftsförderung und Wettbewerb. [Nuremberg, 1971]. pp. 173. bibliog.

KIRCHHOFF (GERD) Subventionen als Instrument der Lenkung und Koordinierung. Berlin, [1973]. pp. 319. bibliog.

- India - Andhra Pradesh

ANDHRA PRADESH. Law Commission. 1967. Laws relating to state aid to industries (April 1964). Hyderabad, 1967. pp. 46. (Reports. 24)

- Italy

Gli INVESTIMENTI industriali agevolati nel Mezzogiorno, 1951-1968. Milano, 1971. pp. 204. (Associazione per lo Sviluppo dell'Industria nel Mezzogiorno. Centro per gli Studi sullo Sviluppo Economico. Collana Francesco Giordani)

- Norway

NORWAY. Lønns- og Prisdepartementet. Subsidiekomitéen. 1958. Innstilling. [Oslo], 1958. pp. 82.

- United Kingdom

U.K. Department of Trade and Industry. 1972. Mineral Exploration and Investment Grants Act, 1972: financial assistance for mineral exploration in Great Britain: a guide for industry. London, 1972. pp. 13.

- United States

REDISTRIBUTION to the rich and the poor: the grants economics of income distribution; [papers given in 1969 and 1970 at meetings held by the Association for the Study of the Grants Economy with other organizations]; edited by Kenneth E. Boulding and Martin Pfaff. Belmont, Calif., [1972]. pp. 390. bibliogs.

SUBSTITUTE PRODUCTS

MINFORD (ANTHONY PATRICK LESLIE) Substitution effects in international trade and payments; [Ph.D. (London) thesis]. 1973. fo. 189. bibliogs. Typescript: unpublished. This thesis is the property of London University and may not be removed from the Library.

SUBSTITUTION (ECONOMICS)

ARELLANO (AQUILES) La elasticidad de sustitucion entre factores: una estimacion de su magnitud en la industria chilena. Santiago de Chile, [1970]. pp. 98. bibliog. (Santiago de Chile. Universidad de Chile. Instituto de Economia. Publicaciones. No. 119)

SUBURBAN LIFE

HOSS (JEAN PIERRE) Communes en banlieue: Argenteuil et Bezons. Paris, 1969. pp. 134. (Fondation Nationale des Sciences Politiques. Travaux et Recherches de Science Politique. 4)

HEIL (KAROLUS HEINZ) Kommunikation und Entfremdung: Menschen am Stadtrand, Legende und Wirklichkeit; eine vergleichende Studie in einem Altbauquartier und in einer neuen Grossiedlung in München. Stuttgart, [1971]. pp. 215.

STERNLIEB (GEORGE S.) and others. The affluent suburb: Princeton. New Brunswick, N.J., [1971]. pp. 259.

VOGEL (EZRA FEIVEL) Japan's new middle class: the salary man and his family in a Tokyo suburb. 2nd ed. Berkeley, Calif., 1971. pp. 313. bibliog.

GRUEN (NINA JAFFE) and GRUEN (CLAUDE) Low and moderate income housing in the suburbs: an analysis for the Dayton, Ohio region. New York, 1972. pp. 234. bibliog.

MILLS (EDWIN S.) Studies in the structure of the urban economy. Baltimore, [1972]. pp. 151. bibliog.

THORNS (DAVID C.) Suburbia. London, [1972]. pp. 175. bibliog.

SUBURBS

- United Kingdom

TAYLOR (NICHOLAS) The village in the city. London, 1973. pp. 239.

- United States

DOWNS (ANTHONY) Opening up the suburbs: an urban strategy for America. New Haven, 1973. pp. 219.

SUBVERSIVE ACTIVITIES

ANNUAL OF POWER AND CONFLICT: a survey of political violence and international influence; [pd. by] Institute for the Study of Conflict, London, [and] National Strategy Information Center, New York. a., 1971 [1st issue]- London.

BEILENSON (LAURENCE W.) Power through subversion. Washington, D.C., [1972]. pp. 299. bibliog.

HUTTON (J. BERNARD) The subverters of liberty. London, 1972. pp. 266.

MUCCHIELLI (ROGER) La subversion. Paris, [1972]. pp. 144. bibliog.

GREIG (IAN) Subversion: propaganda, agitation and the spread of people's war. London, 1973. pp. 202.

- France

MAXE (JEAN) pseud. L'anthologie des défaitistes. Paris, 1925. 2 vols.

- Netherlands

VENEMA (ADRIAAN) Handboek voor de nieuwe illegalen. Den Haag, 1970. pp. 96.

- United States

OGDEN (AUGUST RAYMOND) The Dies Committee: a study of the Special House Committee for the Investigation of the Un-American Activities, 1938-1944. 2nd ed. Washington, 1945. pp. 318. bibliog.

BENTLEY (ERIC RUSSELL) ed. Thirty years of treason: excerpts from hearings before the House Committee on Un-American Activities, 1938-1968. London, 1972. pp. 991.

- Uruguay

URUGUAY. Ministerio del Interior. 1972. 7 meses de lucha antisubversiva: accion del estado frente a la sedicion desde el 1° de marzo al 30 de setiembre de 1972. [Montevideo, 1972]. pp. 387.

SUBWAYS

U.K. Ministry of Transport. 1969. Criteria for the provision of pedestrian subways or bridges; [by R.P. Sleep]. [London, 1969]. pp. 6. (Technical Memoranda. No. 69/H8.)

SUCCESS

GREENE (THEODORE P.) America's heroes: the changing models of success in American magazines. New York, 1970. pp. 387.

GIRARD (ALAIN) La réussite sociale. 2nd ed. Paris, 1971. pp. 128. bibliog.

SUDAN

- Economic conditions

UNIVERSITY PRESS OF AFRICA. Sudan today; (produced for the Ministry of Information and Culture, Sudan). Tavistock, 1971. pp. 234. bibliog.

- History

MORRISON (GODFREY) The southern Sudan and Eritrea: aspects of wider African problems. London, [1971]. pp. 36. (Minority Rights Group. Reports. No. 5)

OLORUNTIMEHIN (B. OLATUNJI) The Segu Tukolor empire. London, 1972. pp. 357. bibliog.

WRIGHT (PATRICIA) Conflict on the Nile: the Fashoda incident of 1898. London, 1972. pp. 229. bibliog.

- Nationalism

WAI (DUNSTAN M.) ed. The Southern Sudan: the problem of national integration. London, 1973. pp. 255.

- Politics and government

UNIVERSITY PRESS OF AFRICA. Sudan today; (produced for the Ministry of Information and Culture, Sudan). Tavistock, 1971. pp. 234. bibliog.

WAI (DUNSTAN M.) ed. The Southern Sudan: the problem of national integration. London, 1973. pp. 255.

- Religion

CONSTANTINIDES (PAMELA MAUREEN) Sickness and the spirits: a study of the zaar spirit-possession cult in the northern Sudan; [Ph.D. (London) thesis]. 1972. fo. 349. bibliog. Typescript: unpublished. This thesis is the property of London University and may not be removed from the Library.

- Social conditions

> UNIVERSITY PRESS OF AFRICA. Sudan today; (produced for the Ministry of Information and Culture, Sudan). Tavistock, 1971. pp. 234. bibliog.

SUFFRAGE

> GRAF (HERBERT) and SEILER (GUENTHER) Wahl und Wahlrecht im Klassenkampf. Frankfurt am Main, [1971]. pp. 441.

- Germany

> POLTE (WALTER) Die Wahlrechtskämpfe 1906/10 in Görlitz; [and] Die Auswirkungen des Kapp-Putsches 1920 auf Görlitz; ([by] Jutta Friedrich). Görlitz, 1968. pp. 168. bibliog. (Görlitz. Ratsarchiv. Beiträge zur Geschichte der Görlitzer Arbeiterbewegung. 3)

> GRAF (HERBERT) and SEILER (GUENTHER) Wahl und Wahlrecht im Klassenkampf. Frankfurt am Main, [1971]. pp. 441.

- Rhodesia

> RHODESIA. Information Service. 1965. Rhodesia democracy: the facts. Salisbury, 1965. pp. 4. (This is Rhodesia. 1)

- United Kingdom

> BERTOLACCI (FRANCIS ROBERT) A voice for all subjects; or, A scheme for the consideration of conflicting theories and principles, and for expanding the minds of the working class, to teach them the value of civil and religious liberty, and the use of acquired power, especially with reference to the extension of the suffrage. London, 1851. pp. 27. Privately printed.

SUGAR

- Manufacture and refining - Brazil

> BRAZIL. Superintendência do Desenvolvimento do Nordeste. Assessoria Tecnica. 1963. Projeto de pesquisa da economia canavieira; redação preliminar. Recife, 1963. pp. 11.

- Manufacture and refining - Canada

> CANADA. Statistics Canada. Productivity Research and Analysis Section. 1971. Productivity trends in industry: indexes of output per person employed and per man-hour: sugar refineries... 1959-1969. Ottawa, 1971. pp. 25. In English and French.

> KNEEN (BREWSTER) The economy of sugar: (a "vertical" analysis of the financial and structural aspects of the sugar industry as it related to Canada). Toronto, 1971. pp. 38.

- Manufacture and refining - Pakistan, West

> ANWAR (ABDUL AZIZ) Production of sugar: policies and problems. Lahore, 1971. pp. 397. bibliog. (West Pakistan. Board of Economic Inquiry. Publications. No. 148)

- Manufacture and refining - United Kingdom

> WATSON (J.A.) A hundred years of sugar refining: the story of Love Lane Refinery, 1872-1972. Liverpool, 1973. pp. 155.

SUGAR GROWING

- Brazil

> CANA e reforma agraria; [by] Gilberto Freyre [and others]. [2nd ed.] Recife, Instituto Joaquim Nabuco de Pesquisas Sociais, 1970. pp. 372.

- Ghana

> O'LOUGHLIN (CARLEEN) and others. Structure and prospects of the sugar industry in Ghana. Legon, 1972 in progress. (Ghana University. Institute of Statistical, Social and Economic Research. Technical Publication Series. No. 21)

- Jamaica

> CRATON (MICHAEL) and WALVIN (JAMES) A Jamaican plantation: the history of Worthy Park, 1670-1970. London, 1970. pp. 344. bibliog.

- Pakistan, West

> ANWAR (ABDUL AZIZ) Production of sugar: policies and problems. Lahore, 1971. pp. 397. bibliog. (West Pakistan. Board of Economic Inquiry. Publications. No. 148)

- Peru

> KLAREN (PETER F.) La formacion de las haciendas azucareras y los origenes del APRA. Lima, 1970. pp. 214. bibliog. (Instituto de Estudios Peruanos. Peru Problema. 5)

- West Indies

> DUNN (RICHARD S.) Sugar and slaves: the rise of the planter class in the English West Indies, 1624-1713. London, 1973. pp. 359.

SUGAR LAWS AND LEGISLATION

- Brazil

> JUNGMANN (FERNANDO) O direito da agro-indústria açucareira. São Paulo, 1971. pp. 479.

SUGAR TRADE

- Congresses

> MOROCCO. [Ministère de l'Information et [du] Tourisme. 1959. Le sucre marocain: histoire, consommation, perspectives; Conference Internationale du Sucre, Tanger 23-28 novembre 1959. [Rabat, 1959?] pp. 39. bibliog.

- Argentine Republic

> REPETTO (NICOLAS) Azucar y carne: dos discursos parlamentarios. [Buenos Aires], 1939. pp. 275.

- Morocco

> MOROCCO. [Ministère de l'Information et [du] Tourisme. 1959. Le sucre marocain: histoire, consommation, perspectives; Conference Internationale du Sucre, Tanger 23-28 novembre 1959. [Rabat, 1959?] pp. 39. bibliog.

- United Kingdom - British Empire

> BUJARD (HELMUT) Zuckerpolitische Konsequenzen aus dem EWG-Beitritt Grossbritanniens: Überlegungen zur voraussichtlichen Entwicklung in Westeuropa sowie zur Situation der überseeischen Zuckererzeuger. Hamburg, 1972. pp. 54. bibliog. (Deutsches Übersee-Institut. Aktuelle Fragen der Weltwirtschaft)

- Brazil

> BRAZIL. Superintendência do Desenvolvimento do Nordeste. Assessoria Tecnica. 1963. Projeto de pesquisa da economia canavieira; redação preliminar. Recife, 1963. pp. 11.

SUGAR WORKERS
- Peru
KLAREN (PETER F.) La formacion de las haciendas azucareras y los origenes del APRA. Lima, 1970. pp. 214. bibliog. (Instituto de Estudios Peruanos. Peru Problema. 5)

SUGATHADASA (V.A.)
CEYLON. Parliament. House of Representatives. Select Committee appointed to Inquire into Certain Transactions of Mr. V.A. Sugathadasa, former Minister of Nationalised Services. 1971. Report ...together with the proceedings of the Committee and minutes of evidence: [P.G.B. Keuneman, chairman]. [Colombo], 1971. pp. 575. (Parliamentary Series. 7th Parliament. No. 12)

SUHBATAAR (DAMDINY)
See SUKHE-BATOR (DAMDINY)

SUICIDE
FOOTE (GEORGE WILLIAM) Atheism and suicide: a reply to Alfred Tennyson, Poet Laureate. London, [1881]. pp. 8.

BONSER (THOMAS OWEN) The right to die; a paper read before the Dialectical Society of London, etc. London, 1885. pp. 8.

GROLLMAN (EARL ALAN) Suicide: prevention, intervention, postvention. Boston, [1971]. pp. 145. bibliog.

VARAH (EDWARD CHAD) ed. The Samaritans in the '70s: to befriend the suicidal and despairing. 2nd ed. London, 1973. pp. 260.

- Canada
CANADA. Statistics Canada. Health and Welfare Division. Vital Statistics Section. 1972. Suicide mortality; Mortalité due au suicide; 1950-1968. Ottawa, 1972. pp. 62. In English and French.

- Russia - Armenia
AVAKIAN (ROBERT ZAVENOVICH) Dovedenie do samoubiistva kak ugolovno nakazuemoe deianie. Erevan, 1971. pp. 131.

- United States
REGIONAL WORKSHOP IN SUICIDOLOGY, 2ND, BUFFALO, 1968. Organizing the community to prevent suicide; [presentations given at the conference]; edited by Jack Zusman... and David L. Davidson. Springfield, [1971]. pp. 97.

SUKARNO, President of Indonesia
LEGGE (JOHN DAVID) Sukarno: a political biography. London, 1972. pp. 431. bibliog.

SUKHE-BATOR (DAMDINY)
BAT-OCHIR (L.) and DASHZHAMTS (D.) Damdiny Sukhe-Bator: biografiia; (perevod s mongol'skogo). Moskva, 1971. pp. 135.

SUKIENNICKI (WIKTOR)
SUKIENNICKI (WIKTOR) Legenda i rzeczywistość: wspomnienia i uwagi o dwudziestu latach Uniwersytetu Stefana Batorego w Wilnie. Paryż, 1967. pp. 134. bibliog.

SULPHUR
PRATT (CHRISTOPHER J.) The reduction of sulphur needs in fertilizer manufacture. (ID/SER.F/3). New York, United Nations Industrial Development Organization, 1969. pp. 61. bibliog. (Fertilizer Industry Series. Monographs. No.3)

AIR pollution across national boundaries: the impact on the environment of sulfur [sic] in air and precipitation: Sweden's case study for the United Nations Conference on the Human Environment; [prepared by a working party, Bert Bolin, chairman]. [Stockholm], Royal Ministry for Foreign Affairs, [1971]. pp. 96.

SULU ISLANDS
- Social conditions
NIMMO (H. ARLO) The sea people of Sulu: a study of social change in the Philippines. London, 1972. pp. 104. bibliog.

SUMATRA
- Economic history
WEISFELT (JACOBUS) De Deli Spoorweg Maatschappij als factor in de economische ontwikkeling van de oostkust van Sumatra. Rotterdam, 1972. pp. 230. bibliog. With English summary. Map in endpocket.

- Politics and government
ABDULLAH (TAUFIK) Schools and politics: the Kaum Muda movement in West Sumatra, 1927-1933. Ithaca, 1971. pp. 257. bibliog. (Cornell University. Department of Asian Studies. Southeast Asia Program. Modern Indonesia Project. Monograph Series)

SUMMER HOMES
- France
BRIER (MAX ANDRE) Les résidences secondaires. [Paris, 1970]. pp. 140. bibliog.

- United Kingdom
DOWNING (PETER) and DOWER (MICHAEL) Second homes in England and Wales; an appraisal prepared for the Countryside Commission. [London, Countryside Commission, 1973]. pp. 47. bibliog. (Dartington Amenity Research Trust. Publications. No. 7)

SUMMERHILL SCHOOL
NEILL (ALEXANDER SUTHERLAND) 'Neill! Neill! Orange Peel!': a personal view of ninety years. London, 1973. pp. 291.

SUMNER (CHARLES)
DONALD (DAVID) Charles Sumner and the rights of man. New York, 1970. pp. 595, xxxix. bibliog.

SUN (CHING-LING)
HAHN (EMILY) The Soong sisters; [reprint of the work originally published in New York, 1941]. Westport, Conn., 1970. pp. 349.

SUNDA ISLANDS (LESSER)
See LESSER SUNDA ISLANDS

SUNDAY

NORTHBROOKE (JOHN) A treatise against dicing, dancing, plays, and interludes, with other idle pastimes...from the earliest edition, about A.D. 1577, with an introduction and notes. London, 1843; New York, 1971. pp. 188. Facsimile reprint.

The WORKMAN'S testimony to the sabbath; or, The temporal advantages of that day of rest considered in relation to the working classes; being the first three...competing essays...by working men. Edinburgh, 1853. pp. 176.

SUNDERLAND

- Civic improvement

DENNIS (NORMAN) Public participation and planners' blight. London, 1972. pp. 352.

McKINSEY AND COMPANY INCORPORATED. The Sunderland study. London, H.M.S.O., 1973. 2 pts.

SUNG (CHIAO-JEN)

LIEW (KIT SIONG) Struggle for democracy: Sung Chiao-jen and the 1911 Chinese revolution. Berkeley, 1971. pp. 260. bibliog.

SUNG FAMILY

HAHN (EMILY) The Soong sisters; [reprint of the work originally published in New York, 1941]. Westport, Conn., 1970. pp. 349.

SUPERMARKETS

CORINA (MAURICE) Pile it high, sell it cheap: the authorised biography of Sir John Cohen, founder of Tesco. London, 1971 repr. 1972. pp. 204.

THORPE (D.) Food prices: a study of some northern discount and super stores. Manchester, 1972. fo. 82. (Manchester Business School. Retail Outlets Research Unit. Research Reports. No. 5)

SUPERSONIC TRANSPORT PLANES

WIGGS (RICHARD) Concorde: the case against supersonic transport. London, 1971. pp. 179. bibliog.

LEVY (ELIZABETH) The people lobby: the SST story. New York, [1973]. pp. 160.

SUPERVISION OF EMPLOYEES

THURLEY (KEITH ERNEST) and WIRDENIUS (HANS) Approaches to supervisory development. London, 1973. pp. 92.

THURLEY (KEITH ERNEST) and WIRDENIUS (HANS) Supervision: a reappraisal. London, 1973. pp. 238.

- Study and teaching

RACKMAN (NEIL) Development and evaluation of supervisory training: a report on research conducted in BOAC under the joint sponsorship of BOAC and the Air Transport and Travel Industry Training Board. [Staines], 1971. pp. 43. (Air Transport and Travel Industry Training Board [U.K.]. Research Reports. 71/1)

U.K. Civil Service Department. Behavioural Sciences Research Division. 1971. Job appraisal review: training manual. [London], 1971. pp. 50. bibliog.

SUPPLEMENTARY EMPLOYMENT

- Russia

NIKIFOROV (VLADIMIR NIKOLAEVICH) and PETROVA (TAT'-IANA VASIL'EVNA) Trudovye prava rabotaiushchikh pensionerov. Moskva, 1965. pp. 91.

GLOZMAN (VIL' ABRAMOVICH) Sovmeshchenie professii i dolzhnostei. Moskva, 1969. pp. 102.

SUPPLY AND DEMAND

PEDRAO (FERNANDO C.) La dinamica de las presiones de demanda. Lima, 1963. fo. 10. (Peru. Instituto Nacional de Planificacion. Cuadernillos de Divulgacion. Serie 3. Ensayos. No. 1)

ZVEZDOV (A.T.) Kon"iunktura: ocherk obshchikh problem sprosa i predlozheniia. Riga, 1969. pp. 107. bibliog.

BURACHAS (ANTANAS IONOVICH) Teorii sprosa: makroanaliz. Moskva, 1970. pp. 247.

NATIONAL COUNCIL OF APPLIED ECONOMIC RESEARCH. Projections of demand and supply of agricultural commodities. New Delhi, [1970]. pp. 92.

CHERNIAVSKII (URIEL' GEORGIEVICH) Potrebnosti, spros, tovarooborot v sotsialisticheskom obshchestve. Moskva, 1971. pp. 215.

PORTSMANN (REINER) Zur Theorie der Nachfrage, unter besonderer Berücksichtigung des Konsumentenüberschusses. Berlin, [1971]. pp. 312. bibliog.

PREFERENCES, utility, and demand: a Minnesota symposium; edited by John S. Chipman [and others]. New York, [1971]. pp. 510. bibliog.

TURVEY (RALPH) Demand and supply. London, 1971. pp. 127.

EKELUND (R.B.) and others, eds. The evolution of modern demand theory: a collection of essays. Lexington, [1972]. pp. 484. bibliog.

SOWELL (THOMAS) Say's Law: an historical analysis. Princeton, [1972]. pp. 247. bibliog.

MORISHIMA (MICHIO) and others. Theory of demand: real and monetary. Oxford, 1973. pp. 330. bibliog.

- Mathematical models

TE'ENI (J. R.) A study of the problem of community indifference curves. [Southampton, 1969]. pp. 22. (Southampton. University. Discussion Papers in Economics and Econometrics. No. 6901).

DESAI (NITIN) The theory of asset choice. [Southampton], 1970. fo. 22. bibliog. (Southampton. University. Discussion Papers in Economics and Econometrics. No. 7004)

JAMISON (DEAN T.) and LAWRENCE (J. LAU) Semiorders, revealed preference, and the theory of consumer demand. Stanford, 1970. fo. 20. bibliog. (Stanford University. Institute for Mathematical Studies in the Social Sciences. Technical Reports. [New Series]. No. 31)

BOLLE (MICHAEL DETLEF) Kurz- und langfristige Analyse ungleichgewichtiger makroökonomischer Angebot-Nachfrage-Systeme. Berlin, [1971]. pp. 148. bibliog. (Institut für Theorie der Wirtschaftspolitik. Schriften. Band 5)

SUPPLY AND DEMAND - Mathematical models (Cont'd.)

McMAAHON (P.C.) and SCHLIEPER (ULRICH) Consumers' surplus and its usefulness as a decision criterion. [Birmingham, 1971?]. pp. 27. bibliog. (Birmingham. University. Faculty of Commerce and Social Science. Discussion Papers. Series A. No. 144)

SUPPORT (DOMESTIC RELATIONS)
- United Kingdom

CHILD POVERTY ACTION GROUP. Poverty Leaflets. 4. The cohabitation rule: a guide for single, separated, divorced or widowed women claiming supplementary benefit or National Insurance benefit. London, 1972. pp. 6.

JACKSON (JOSEPH) Matrimonial finance and taxation. London, 1972. pp. 372.

SURETYSHIP AND GUARANTY
- European Economic Community countries

MAX-PLANCK-INSTITUT FÜR AUSLÄNDISCHES UND INTERNATIONALES PRIVATRECHT, HAMBURG. Le cautionnement dans le droit des états membres des Communautés européennes. Bruxelles, European Economic Community, 1971. pp. 115. bibliog. (Études: Série Concurrence: Rapprochement des Législations. No.14)

- Italy

BARBIERA (LELIO) Garanzia del credito e autonomia privata. Napoli, 1971. pp. 356. (Bari. Università. Facoltà Giuridica. Pubblicazioni. 22)

- South Africa

SOUTH AFRICA. Parliament. House of Assembly. Select Committee on the Suretyship Amendment Bill. 1971. Report (with Proceedings and Minutes of evidence); [L. le Grange, chairman]. (S.C.4-1971). in SOUTH AFRICA. Parliament. House of Assembly. Select Committee reports.

SURGERY

HAYWARD (JACK CHARLES) Some relationships between pre-operative information and post-operative pain and anxiety in surgical patients: an experimental study; [Ph.D. (London) thesis]. 1973. fo. 444. bibliog. Typescript: unpublished. This thesis is the property of London University and may not be removed from the Library.

SURGICAL INSTRUMENTS AND APPARATUS

GANICHEV (LEV SIMONOVICH) Na Aptekarskom ostrove: istoriia Leningradskogo ordena Lenina zavoda i ob"edineniia "Krasnogvardeets". 2nd ed. Leningrad, 1967. pp. 275. bibliog.

SURREALISM

THIRION (ANDRE) Révolutionnaires sans révolution. Paris, [1972]. pp. 580.

SURVEYING

WORLD LAND USE SURVEY. Occasional Papers. No.9. New possibilities and techniques for land use and related surveys with special reference to the developing countries: papers presented at an international symposium, London... 1970...; (edited by Ian H. Cox). Berkhamsted, 1970. pp. 138. Map in end-pocket.

WORLD LAND USE SURVEY. Occasional Papers. No. 10. Contributions to land use survey methods; (edited by Hans Boesch). Berkhamsted, 1971. pp. 19.

SURVEYORS
- South Africa - Fees

SOUTH AFRICA. Commission of Enquiry into Remuneration for Professional Services in the Building Industry. 1972. Report; [W.J. Mckenzie, chairman] (R.P. 39/1972). in SOUTH AFRICA. Parliament. House of Assembly. Votes and proceedings; (with Printed annexures).

- United Kingdom

KNOWLES (C.C.) and PITT (PETER HUBERT) The history of building regulation in London, 1189-1972: with an account of the District Surveyors' Association. London, 1972. pp. 164.

SURVEYS - Underdeveloped areas
See UNDERDEVELOPED AREAS - Surveys

SURVIVORS' BENEFITS
- Jamaica

JAMAICA. Ministry of Labour and National Insurance. 1970. Orphan's benefit. [Kingston, 1970?]. pp. 5. (National Insurance Scheme Leaflets. No. 5)

JAMAICA. Ministry of Labour and National Insurance. 1970. Special child's benefit. [Kingston, 1970?]. pp. 5. (National Insurance Scheme Leaflets. No. 6)

JAMAICA. Ministry of Labour and National Insurance. 1970. Widower's benefit. [Kingston, 1970?]. pp. (8). (National Insurance Scheme Leaflets. No. 8)

JAMAICA. Ministry of Labour and National Insurance. 1970. Widow's benefit. [Kingston, 1970?]. pp. (8). (National Insurance Scheme Leaflets. No. 7)

- Norway

NORWAY. Komitéen for Internasjonale Sosialpolitiske Saker. Social and Labour News from Norway. 1964. No.5. Widows' and mothers' pensions introduced in Norway. Oslo, 1964. fo. 9.

- Switzerland

FRISCHKNECHT (WERNER) Die Alters-, Hinterlassenen- und Invalidenversicherung AHV/IV im Strukturwandel. Bern, 1971. pp. 311. bibliog.

- United Kingdom

U.K. Civil Service Department. 1972. Civil service pension scheme: guide to widows' and dependants' benefits. London, 1972. pp. 34.

SUSSEX
- Description and travel

WEST SUSSEX. County Council. Planning Department. Landscape appraisal of West Sussex. [Chichester], 1972. pamphlet (pagination varies). 3 maps in end pocket.

- History - Sources

MOORE (GILES) The journal of Giles Moore, (1656-1679); edited by Ruth Bird. Lewes, 1971. pp. 356.

SUSSEX UNIVERSITY

BRIGHTON. University of Sussex. Admissions Office. Applicants who decline offers: an analysis of the reasons. Brighton, 1971. pp. 25. (Brighton. University of Sussex. Admissions Office. Special Reports. No. 3)

SUTHERLAND
- Economic conditions

ECONOMIST INTELLIGENCE UNIT. Economic survey of Sutherland and Caithness. London, 1949. fo. 102.

- Economic history

RICHARDS (ERIC) The leviathan of wealth: the Sutherland fortune in the Industrial Revolution. London, 1973. pp. 316. bibliog.

- Economic history - Sources

SCOTTISH HISTORY SOCIETY. [Publications]. 4th Series. vols. 8-9. Papers on Sutherland estate management, 1802-1816; edited by R.J. Adam. Edinburgh, 1972. 2 vols. Map in end pocket of vol. 1.

SUTHERLAND FAMILY
See LEVESON-GOWER FAMILY

SUTTNER (BERTHA FELICIE SOPHIE VON) Freifrau

KEMPF (BEATRIX) Suffragette for peace: the life of Bertha von Suttner [with selections from her writings];...translated from the German by R.W. Last. London, [1972]. pp. 200. bibliog.

SUVORIN (ALEKSEI SERGEEVICH)

AMBLER (EFFIE) Russian journalism and politics, 1861-1881: (the career of Aleksei S. Suvorin). Detroit, 1972. pp. 239. bibliog.

SVENSKA FOLKPARTIET

JANSSON (JAN MAGNUS) Idé och verklighet i politiken: [collected articles and speeches]; (redigerad av Håkan Mattlin). [Ekenäs, imprint, 1972]. pp. 363.

SVERDLOV (IAKOV MIKHAILOVICH)

GORODETSKII (EFIM NAUMOVICH) and SHARAPOV (IURII PAVLOVICH) Sverdlov. Moskva, 1971. pp. 400.

SVOBODA (LUDVÍK)

SVOBODA (LUDVÍK) President of Czechoslovakia. Izbrannye stat'i i rechi, [1968-1970]. Moskva, 1970. pp. 167. bibliog.

SWAZILAND
- Politics and government

POTHOLM (CHRISTIAN P.) Swaziland: the dynamics of political modernization. Berkeley, [1972]. pp. 183. bibliog.

- Statistics

SWAZILAND. Central Statistical Office. Annual statistical bulletin. a., 1966 (v.1)- Mbabane. Not pd. 1969.

SWEDEN
- Civilization

HUNTFORD (ROLAND) The new totalitarians. London, 1971. pp. 354.

- Commerce

HÄGGSTRÖM (NILS) Norrland's direct foreign trade, 1850-1914. Umeå, 1971. pp. 235. bibliog. (Universitetet i Umeå. Department of Geography. Geographical Reports. 2)

LANDELL (HANS) Analyser av partihandelns lokalisering. Uppsala, [1972]. pp. 179. bibliog. (Uppsala. Universitet. Kulturgeografiska Institutionen. Geografiska Regionstudier. Nr. 8)

LANDELL (HANS) Marknad och distrikt: metodstudier med anknytning till företagslokalisering. Uppsala, [1972]. pp. 225. bibliog. (Uppsala. Universitet. Kulturgeografiska Institutionen. Geografiska Regionstudier. Nr. 7)

LINDSTRÖM (BERTIL) Utlandstransaktionerna och konjunkturen: svenska erfarenheter under Bretton Woods-perioden; en studie över sambandet mellan den svenska ekonomin och utlandstransaktionerna, etc. Stockholm, 1972. fo. 190. bibliogs.

SWEDEN. Statistiska Cenralbyrån. Historisk Statistik för Sverige. 3. Utrikeshandel: Foreign trade, 1732-1970. Stockholm, 1972. pp. 346. In Swedish and English.

- Constitutional history

NORDENFLYCHT (FERDINAND OTTO VON) Freiherr. Die schwedische Staats-Verfassung in ihrer geschichtlichen Entwicklung. Berlin, Königliche Geheime Ober-Hofbuchdruckerei, 1861 repr. 1970. pp. 385.

LAGERROTH (FREDRIK) Den svenska monarkin inför rätta: en författningshistorisk exposé. Stockholm, [1972]. pp. 258.

- Defences

ALLMÄNHETEN och civilförsvaret: en undersökning av kunskaper och attityder rörande civilförsvaret hos befolkningen i Göteborg, av Kurt Törnqvist [and others]. Stockholm, 1966. pp. 100. 15. (Psykologiskt Försvar. Nr. 29)

FREDSPOLITIK: civilmotstånd; ([by] Tryggve Hedtjärn [and others]). Stockholm, 1969. pp. 232. bibliog.

TORNQVIST (KURT) Försvarsattityder hos ungdom våren 1971. Stockholm, 1971. fo. 54. (Psykologiskt Försvar. Nr. 56)

TORNQVIST (KURT) Försvarsattityder hos vuxna vintern 1971. Stockholm, 1971. fo. 33. (Psykologiskt Försvar. Nr. 52)

ANDRÉN (NILS) Den totala säkerhetspolitiken. Stockholm, 1972. pp. 126.

DÖRFER (INGEMAR) System 37 Viggen: arms, technology and the domestication of glory. Oslo, [1973] pp. 258. bibliog.

- Economic conditions

HÖGLUND (BENGT) and WERIN (LARS A.) The production system of the Swedish economy: an input-output study. Stockholm, [1964]. pp. 231. bibliog. (Stockholms Universitet. Socialvetenskapliga Institutet. Stockholm Economic Studies. New Series 4)

SWEDEN. Finansdepartementet. 1966. The Swedish economy 1966-1970 and the general outlook for the seventies. Stockholm, 1966. pp. 224.

SWEDEN - Economic conditions (Cont'd.)

NORDSTRÖM (LARS) Rumsliga förandringar och ekonomisk utveckling: (Spatial changes and economic development). Göteborg, 1971. pp. 182. bibliog. (Göteborgs Universitet. Geografiska Institutioner. Meddelanden. Ser. B. Nr. 23) With English summary.

FUNKTIONER och kontakter; samhällsgeografisk analys...i Göteborgsregionen...: Functions and contacts; socio-economic geographical analyses...in the Gothenburg region and western Sweden; [collection of essays based on research at the University]. Göteborg, 1972. pp. 135. bibliogs. (Göteborgs Universitet. Geografiska Institutioner. Meddelanden. Ser. B. Nr. 24) (Fortsättningstryck av Gothia 11 utgiven av Geografiska Föreningen i Göteborg) In Swedish or English, with table of contents and summaries in English.

SVENSKA HANDELSBANKEN. Sweden in the world economy. [Stockholm, 1972]. fo. 14.

- Economic conditions - Mathematical models

JACOBSSON (LARS) An econometric model of Sweden. Stockholm, [1972]. pp. 348. bibliog.

- Economic history

Det KONTINENTALA krigets ekonomi: studier i krigsfinansering under svensk stormaktstid; ([by] Hans Landberg [and others]). Stockholm, [1971]. pp. 506. bibliog. (Uppsala. Universitet. Historiska Institutionen. Studia Historica Upsaliensia. 36) With German summary.

MODIG (HANS) Järnvägarnas efterfrågan och den svenska industrin, 1860-1914. Stockholm, [1971]. pp. 195. bibliog. (Uppsala. Universitet. Ekonomisk-Historiska Institution. Ekonomisk-Historiska Studier. 8) With English summary.

ÖSTERBERG (EVA) Gränsbygd under krig: ekonomiska, demografiska och administrativa förhållanden i sydvästra Sverige under och efter nordiska sjuårskriget. Lund, [1971]. pp. 298. bibliog. With English summary.

ADAMSSON (ROLF) and JÖRBERG (LENNART) eds. Problem i svensk ekonomisk historia: [readings]. [Lund, 1972]. pp. 304.

- Economic policy

SWEDEN. Finansdepartementet. 1966. The Swedish economy 1966-1970 and the general outlook for the seventies. Stockholm, 1966. pp. 224.

SWEDEN. Finansdepartementet. Sekretariatet för Ekonomisk Planering. 1970. Svensk ekonomi 1971-1975 med utblick mot 1990: 1970 års långtidsutredning: huvudrapport. Stockholm, 1970. pp. 339. (Sweden. Statens Offentliga Utredningar. 1970. 71)

RUDBERG (KARIN) and ÖHMAN (CHRISTER) Investment funds: the release of 1967. Stockholm, 1971. pp. 213. bibliog. (Stockholm. Konjunkturinstitut Occasional Papers. 5)

SWEDEN. Statskontoret. 1971. Att införa långsiktsplanering. [Stockholm, 1971]. pp. 124.

SOCIAL goals in national planning: a critique of Sweden's long-term economic survey; [by] Åke Burstedt [and others]. Stockholm, [1972]. pp. 105.

MATTHIESSEN (LARS) A study in fiscal theory and policy. [Stockholm, 1973]. 2 vols. (in 1). bibliogs. In English or Swedish.

- Emigration and immigration

NILSSON (FRED) Emigrationen från Stockholm till Nordamerika, 1880-1893: en studie i urban utvandring. Stockholm, 1970. pp. 391. bibliog. (Stockholm. Kommunalförvaltningen. Monografier. 31) With English summary.

KÄLVEMARK (ANN-SOFIE) Reaktionen mot utvandringen: emigrationsfrågan i svensk debatt och politik, 1901-1904. Stockholm, [1972]. pp. 252. bibliog. (Uppsala. Universitet. Historiska Institutionen. Studia Historica Upsaliensia. 41) With English summary.

RONDAHL (BJÖRN) Emigration, folkomflyttning och säsongarbete i ett sågverksdistrikt i södra Hälsingland, 1865-1910: Söderala kommun, etc. Stockholm, [1972]. pp. 288. bibliog. (Uppsala. Universitet. Historiska Institutionen. Studia Historica Upsaliensia. 40) With English summary.

SWEDEN. Forskningsekonomiska Kommittén. 1972. Brain drain and brain gain of Sweden: the findings of four studies by the Committee on Research Economics (FEK); (by G. Friborg and J. Annerstedt). [Stockholm, 1972]. pp. 113. bibliog. (Sweden. Forskningsekonomiska Kommittén. Rapporter. 1)

TEDERBRAND (LARS-GORAN) Västernorrland och Nordamerika, 1875-1913: utvandring och återinvandring. Stockholm, [1972]. pp. 341. bibliog. (Uppsala. Universitet. Historiska Institutionen. Studia Historica Upsaliensia. 42) With English summary.

WADENSJÖ (ESKIL) Immigration och samhällsekonomi: immigrationens ekonomiska orsaker och effekter. Lund, 1972. 2 vols. bibliog. With English summary.

- Executive departments

SWEDEN. Arbetsmarknadsstyrelsen. 1962. Organization of the Labour Market Board and the employment service, personnel, etc. Stockholm, 1962. pp. 12. (Reprinted from the Board's Annual Report for 1961.)

IVARSSON (SVEN IVAR) Program budgeting in Sweden: experiments, experiencies [sic], effects. Stockholm, 1970. pp. 23.

· Foreign relations

HOLM (PETER EDVARD) Danmarks politiske Stilling under den franske Revolution 1791-1797, saerlig med Hensyn til Sverige...; (Indbydelsesskrift til Kjøbenhavns Universitets Fest...den 28de Juli 1869). Kjøbenhavn, 1869. pp. 173.

HÄGGLÖF (GUNNAR) Diplomat: memoirs of a Swedish envoy in London, Paris, Berlin, Moscow, Washington. London, 1972. pp. 221.

HOLMSTRÖM (BARRY) Koreakriget i svensk debatt. Stockholm, 1972. pp. 353. bibliog. (Uppsala. Statsvetenskapliga Föreningen. Skrifter. 61) With English summary.

CARLGREN (WILHELM M.) Svensk utrikespolitik 1939-1945. Stockholm, 1973. pp. 612. (Sweden. Utrikesdepartementet. Aktstycken. Ny Serie II.26)

- Foreign relations - Denmark

HOLM (PETER EDVARD) Danmarks politiske Stilling under den franske Revolution 1791-1797, saerlig med Hensyn til Sverige...; (Indbydelsesskrift til Kjøbenhavns Universitets Fest...den 28de Juli 1869). Kjøbenhavn, 1869. pp. 173.

- Foreign relations - Nigeria

SWEDEN. Utrikesdepartementet. Aktstycken. Ny Serie. II. 22. Sverige och konflikten i Nigeria, 1967-1970: en dokumentsamling. Stockholm, 1970. pp. 270.

- Foreign relations - Vietnam

SWEDEN. Utrikesdepartementet. Aktstycken. Ny Serie. II. 19. Sverige och Vietnamfrågan: anföranden och uttalanden. Stockholm, 1968. pp. 123.

- Full employment policies

STROM (NILS) Manpower: organisation, education, mobility: Sweden's active manpower policy programme. Stockholm, Arbetsmarknadsstyrelsen, 1969. fo. 97. Xerox copy.

- Historical geography

SPORRONG (ULF) Kolonisation, bebyggelseutveckling och administration: studier i agrar kulturlandskapsutveckling under vikingatid, etc. [Stockholm], 1971. pp. 214. bibliog. (Stockholms Universitet. Kulturgeografiska Institutionen. Meddelanden. Nr. B 23) With German summary.

- History - 1523-1718

ROBERTS (MICHAEL) 1908- , Professor of History, ed. Sweden's age of greatness, 1632-1718. London, 1973. pp. 314. bibliog.

- Industries

HÖGLUND (BENGT) and WERIN (LARS A.) The production system of the Swedish economy: an input-output study. Stockholm, [1964]. pp. 231. bibliog. (Stockholms Universitet. Socialvetenskapliga Institutet. Stockholm Economic Studies. New Series 4)

STATSFÖRETAG AB. Group review. a., 1970- Stockholm. In English.

ENGSTRÖM (MATS-G.) Regional arbetsfördelning: nya drag i förvärvsarbetets geografiska organisation i Sverige. Lund, [1970]. pp. 210. bibliog. (Lund. Universitet. Geografiska Institution. Meddelanden. Avhandlingar. 65) With English summary.

HEDBERG (BJÖRN) Kontaktsystem inom svenskt näringsliv: en studie av organisationers externa personkontakter. Lund, [1970]. pp. 216. bibliog. (Lund. Universitet. Geografiska Institution. Meddelanden. Avhandlingar. 64) With English summary.

STATLIGA FÖRETAG: en redogörelse för statens affärsdrivande verk och het- och delägda statliga aktiebolag; utarbetad inom industridepartementet [Sweden]. a., 1972- Stockholm.

LINDSTRÖM (CHRISTIAN) Företagets storlek och belägenhet som determinanter för dess uppfinningsaktivitet. Umeå, 1972. pp. 116. bibliog. (Umeå. Universitet. Ekonomiska Institutionen. Studier i Företagsekonomi. 6) With English summary.

OTTERBECK (LARS) Location and strategic planning: towards a contingency theory of industrial location. Stockholm, 1973. pp. 67. bibliog.

- Officials and employees

SWEDEN. Finansdepartementet. Förarskyddsutredningen. 1968. Statligt förarskydd. Stockholm, 1968. pp. 119. (Sweden. Statens Offentliga Utredningar. 1968.52)

JÄGERSKIÖLD (STIG) Collective bargaining rights of state officials in Sweden. Ann Arbor, 1971. pp. 143. (Michigan University and Wayne State University. Institute of Labor and Industrial Relations. Comparative Studies in Public Employment Labor Relations)

SWEDEN. Finansdepartementet. Testutredningen. 1971. Psykologiska urvalsmetoder inom statsförvaltningen. Stockholm, 1971. pp. 62. (Sweden. Statens Offentliga Utredningar. 1971. 47)

LEVINSON (HAROLD MYER) Collective bargaining by public employees in Sweden. Ann Arbor, 1972. pp. 98.

- Politics and government

HUNTFORD (ROLAND) The new totalitarians. London, 1971. pp. 354.

HANCOCK (M. DONALD) Sweden: the politics of post-industrial change. Hinsdale, Ill., [1972]. pp. 298. bibliog.

JANSSON (JAN MAGNUS) Idé och verklighet i politiken: [collected articles and speeches]; (redigerad av Håkan Mattlin). [Ekenäs, imprint, 1972]. pp. 363.

SWEDEN. Justitiedepartementet. Grundlagberedningen 1972. Ny regeringsform: ny riksdagsordning: betänkande; [and] Följdförfattningar. Stockholm, 1972. 2 vols. (Sweden. Statens Offentliga Utredningar. 1972. 15-16)

- Population

SUNDBÄRG (GUSTAV) Bevölkerungsstatistik Schwedens, 1750-1900; with preface and vocabulary in English. Stockholm, 1907 repr. 1970. pp. 170. (Sweden. Statistiska Centralbyrån. Urval. No. 3)

SWEDEN. Bostadsstyrelsen. Planeringsbyrån. 1969. Uppgifter om bostäder, hushåll och boendeförhållanden åren 1960 och 1965 i länen och storstadsområdena. [Stockholm], 1968 [or rather 1969]. pp. 56. (Statistik/Utredningar/Information. 1968. 18). With tables in English.

SWEDEN. Statistiska Centralbyrån. Historisk Statistik för Sverige. 1. Befolkning: Population, 1720-1967. 2nd ed. Stockholm, 1969. pp. 141. With English summary and translation of tables.

BERNHARDT (EVA M.) Trends and variations in Swedish fertility: a cohort study. [Stockholm], 1971. pp. 227. bibliog. (Sweden. Statistiska Centralbyrån. Urval. 5)

LARSSON (LARS-OLAF) Kolonisation och befolkningsutveckling i det svenska agrarsamhället, 1500-1640. Lund, [1972]. pp. 200. bibliog. With English summary.

- Riksdag - Committees

SWEDEN. Justitiedepartementet. Grundlagberedningen. 1969. Ny utskottsorganisation: betänkande. Stockholm, 1969. pp. 135. (Sweden. Statens Offentliga Utredningar. 1969.62)

- Social conditions

BULTENA (LOUIS) Deviant behavior in Sweden. New York, [1971]. pp. 182.

SVERIGES SOCIALDEMOKRATISKA ARBETAREPARTI and LANDSORGANISATIONEN I SVERIGE. Joint Working Group on Equality. Towards equality; first report of the...group [submitted to the Swedish Social Democratic Party Congress, 1969; Alva Myrdal, chairman; an abridged translation by Roger Ling]. Stockholm, 1971. pp. 134.

SWEDEN (Cont'd.)

- Social history

HELLSPONG (MATS) and LÖFGREN (ORVAR) Land och stad: svenska samhällstyper och livsformer från medeltid till nutid. Lund, [1972]. pp. 350. bibliogs.

- Social policy

SOCIAL goals in national planning: a critique of Sweden's long-term economic survey; [by] Åke Burstedt [and others]. Stockholm, [1972]. pp. 105.

- Statistics, Vital

SWEDEN. Statistiska Centralbyrån. 1964. Dödligheten i länen, 1959-1962. Stockholm, 1964. pp. 13, (29). (Folkmängden och dess Förändringar) With English summary.

SWEDEN. Statistiska Centralbyrån. 1964. Livslängdstabeller för årtiondet, 1951-1960. Stockholm, 1964. pp. 34. (Folkmängden och dess Förändringar) With English summary.

SWEDEN. Statistiska Centralbyrån. 1967. Dödsorsakmönstret i Sverige, 1961-1963: tabeller och diagram med kommentarer över den orsaksspecifika dödligheten; Mortality patterns by cause in Sweden in 1961-1963: tables and diagrams with comments on cause-specific mortality. Stockholm, 1967. pp. 158. (Statistiska Meddelanden. Be/1967/2) Text in Swedish and English.

SWEDES IN THE UNITED STATES

FJELLSTRÖM (PHEBE) Swedish-American colonization in the San Joaquin valley in California: a study of the acculturation and assimilation of an immigrant group. [Uppsala], 1970. pp. 157. (Uppsala. Universitet. Institutionen för Allmän och Jämförande Etnografi. Studia Ethnographica Upsaliensia. No.23)

NILSSON (FRED) Emigrationen från Stockholm till Nordamerika, 1880-1893: en studie i urban utvandring. Stockholm, 1970. pp. 391. bibliog. (Stockholm. Kommunalförvaltningen. Monografier. 31) With English summary.

TEDERBRAND (LARS-GÖRAN) Västernorrland och Nordamerika, 1875-1913: utvandring och återinvandring. Stockholm, [1972]. pp. 341. bibliog. (Uppsala. Universitet. Historiska Institutionen. Studia Historica Upsaliensia. 42) With English summary.

SWEDISH NEWSPAPERS

THOREN (STIG) An American election campaign in Swedish dailies: how ten daily metropolitan newspapers in Sweden covered the 1968 presidential election campaign in the United States. Stockholm, 1970. pp. 76. bibliog. (Psykologiskt Försvar. Nr.50)

SWEENY (CHARLES)

FAHEY (JOHN) The ballyhoo bonanza: Charles Sweeny and the Idaho mines. Seattle, [1971]. pp. 288. bibliog.

SWINDLERS AND SWINDLING

BORZENKOV (GENNADII NIKOLAEVICH) Otvetstvennost' za moshennichestvo: voprosy kvalifikatsii. Moskva, 1971. pp. 168.

SWINDON

- Civic improvement

SWINDON EXPANSION PROJECT JOINT STEERING COMMITTEE. Swindon: a study for further expansion. Swindon, 1968. pp. 158.

SWINE

- Belgium

FERRIN (L.) Analyse des résultats comptables d'une exploitation se livrant à la fois à l'elevage et à l'engraissement intensifs des porcs. Bruxelles, 1972. pp. 45. (Belgium. Institut Economique Agricole. Cahiers. No. 147)

- Costa Rica

COSTA RICA. Direccion General de Estadistica y Censos. Encuesta pecuaria por muestreo: ganado vacuno, ganado porcino, aves de corral. irreg., 1968, 1970- San Jose.

- European Economic Community countries

ECONOMIC DEVELOPMENT COMMITTEE FOR THE AGRICULTURAL INDUSTRY. Common Market Sub-Committee. Livestock Group. UK farming and the Common Market: pigs and pig meat; a report. London, National Economic Development Office, 1972. pp. 34.

- Germany - Marketing

BOYENS (CHRISTIAN) Die Kosten der Schlachtschweinevermarktung in der Bundesrepublik Deutschland. Bonn, 1970. pp. 198. bibliog. (Forschungsgesellschaft für Agrarpolitik und Agrarsoziologie. [Publications]. 213)

- United Kingdom

ECONOMIC DEVELOPMENT COMMITTEE FOR THE AGRICULTURAL INDUSTRY. Common Market Sub-Committee. Livestock Group. UK farming and the Common Market: pigs and pig meat; a report. London, National Economic Development Office, 1972. pp. 34.

THOMAS (W.J.K.) and BURNSIDE (ESTELLE) Pig production: an economic study of 70 herds in South West England, 1970-71. Exeter, 1972. pp. 67. (Exeter. University. Agricultural Economics Unit. Reports. No.186)

SWING (PHILIP DAVID)

MOELLER (BEVERLEY BOWEN) Phil Swing and Boulder Dam. Berkeley, 1971. pp. 199. bibliog.

ŚWINIARY STARE

ŁAPIŃSKA (KRYSTYNA) Wieś uprzemysłowiona a problem czasu wolnego. Wrocław, 1972. pp. 240. With English and Russian summaries.

SWITCHING THEORY

PERRIN (J.P.) and others. Switching machines. Dordrecht, [1972]. 2 vols. bibliogs.

SWITZERLAND

FLUEELER (NIKLAUS) and SCHWERTFEGER (RICHARD) Die Schweiz von morgen: Gespräche über die Zukunft der Schweiz. Zürich, [1971]. pp. 270. bibliog.

- Army - Recruiting, enlistment, etc.

SWITZERLAND. Bureau Fédéral de Statistique. Statistiques de la Suisse. 454e fasc. Turnprüfung bei der Rekrutierung: Examen de gymnastique lors du recrutement, 1967; ([edited by] Rudolf Balsiger). Bern, 1970. pp. 61. In German and French.

- Biography

WHO'S who in Switzerland, including the Principality of Liechtenstein, 1972-1973. [9th ed.] Geneva, [1972]. pp. 778.

- Census

SWITZERLAND. Bureau Fédéral de Statistique. Recensement, 1970. Eidgenössische Volkszählung, 1. Dezember 1970...: Wohnbevölkerung der Gemeinden...: definitive Ergebnisse, etc. Bern, 1971. pp. 53. In German and French.

- Commerce - Communist countries

NAEF (HANS) Die Handelsbeziehungen der Schweiz zu den Zentralplanwirtschaften von 1945-1968. Zürich, 1971. pp. 173. bibliog.

- Constitution

SWITZERLAND. Groupe de Travail pour la Préparation d'une Revision Totale de la Constitution Fédérale, 1970. ...Réponses aux questions du Groupe de Travail...1969/1970. [Bern], 1970. 4 vols. (in 2) Variously in French, German and Italian.

HELVETISCHE Alternativen: eine Kritik am Unternehmen der Totalretuschierung unserer Verfassung, nebst einem neuen Fragebogen; von Beat Bürcher [and others]. Zürich, 1971. pp. 129.

EGGENBERGER (PETER) Bundesrat Emil Welti: sein Einfluss auf die Bundesverfassungsrevision von 1874. Bern, 1972. pp. 208. bibliog.

- Defences

Der FALL Oprecht. [Zürich, imprint, 1939]. pp. 52.

SWITZERLAND. Administration Fédérale des Contributions. Eidg[enössische] Wehrsteuer. a., 1967/8 (14.)- Bern. [in German and French] Earlier issues are to be found in the series SWITZERLAND. Bureau Federale de Statistique. Statistiques de la Suisse, which see.

SWITZERLAND. Bureau Fédéral de Statistique. Statistiques de la Suisse. 408e fasc. Eidg. Wehrsteuer: Statistik der 12. Periode, 1963-64; Impôt fédéral pour la défense nationale: statistique de la 12e période, 1963-64. Berne, 1967. pp. 38.

BACHMANN (ALBERT) and GROSJEAN (GEORGES) Défense civile; publié par le Département Fédéral de Justice et Police à la demande du Conseil Fédéral. Aarau, 1969. pp. 320.

SWITZERLAND. Bureau Fédéral de Statistique. Statistiques de la Suisse. 443e fasc. Eidg. Wehrsteuer: Statistik der 13. Periode (1965-66); Impôt fédéral pour la défense nationale: statistique de la 13e période (1965-66). Bern, 1969. pp. 38.

ERNST (ALFRED) Die Konzeption der schweizerischen Landesverteidigung 1815 bis 1966. Frauenfeld, [1971]. pp. 480.

- Economic history

VEREIN FÜR WIRTSCHAFTSHISTORISCHE STUDIEN. Schweizer Pioniere der Wirtschaft und Technik. 23. Alfred Kern, 1850-1893; Georges Heberlein-Staehelin, 1874-1944; Otto Keller, Gibswil, 1882-1967. Zürich, 1970. pp. 114. bibliog.

- Economic policy

RITTER (ERNST) Eine schweizerische Lösung: Neuordnung des Kapitaleinsatzes unter Berücksichtigung der wirtschaftlich insularen Lage der Schweiz. Zürich, [1941]. pp. 56. bibliog.

HARTMANN (WILLY) Die Gründe des geringen Erfolges der Inflationsbekämpfung des Bundes in den Jahren, 1960-1966. Zürich, 1970. pp. 312. bibliog. (St. Gall. Handelshochschule. Veröffentlichungen. Volkswirtschaftlich-wirtschaftsgeographische Reihe. Band 23)

RUTZ (WILFRIED) Die schweizerische Volkswirtschaft zwischen Währungs- und Beschäftigungspolitik in der Weltwirtschaftskrise: wirtschaftspolitische Analyse der Bewältigung eines Zielkonflikts. Zürich, [1970]. pp. 235. bibliog. (St. Gall. Handelhochschule. Schweizerisches Institut für Aussenwirtschafts- und Marktforschung. Veröffentlichungen. Band 22)

WEBER (LUC) Pour une politique conjoncturelle en Suisse. Lausanne, 1971. pp. 256. bibliog.

- Economic policy - Mathematical models

TSCHOPP (HUBERTUS G.) Entwicklungstendenzen der Inlandsnachfrage nach Industriegütern in der Schweiz. Winterthur, 1973. pp. 170. bibliog.

- Foreign economic relations - America, Latin

ENDERLIN (HANSPETER HERMANN) Strukturelle Wandlungen in den Wirtschaftsbeziehungen der Schweiz mit Lateinamerika. Zürich, 1973. pp. 180. bibliog.

- Foreign relations

RAPPARD (WILLIAM EMMANUEL) Die Politik der Schweiz im Völkerbund, 1920-1925: eine erste Bilanz; (übersetzt [from the French] von S. Zurlinden). Chur, 1925. pp. 109.

[FREY (KARL)] Was geht vor in der Welt? ([by] Konrad Falke [pseud.]). Zürich, [1938]. pp. 47.

SCHEURER (KARL) Bundesrat Karl Scheurer: Tagebücher, 1914-1929; herausgegeben und eingeleitet von Hermann Böschenstein. Bern, 1971. pp. 390.

SWITZERLAND - Foreign relations
See also UNITED NATIONS - Switzerland

- Foreign relations - Austria

KOENIG (FRITZ) Die Verhandlungen über die internationale Rheinregulierung im st. gallisch-vorarlbergischen Rheintal von den Anfängen bis zum schweizerisch-österreichischen Staatsvertrag von 1892. Bern, 1971. pp. 237. bibliog.

- Foreign relations - Europe

SALIS (JEAN R. DE) Switzerland and Europe: essays and reflections; translated from the German by Alexander and Elizabeth Henderson; edited and with an introduction by Christopher Hughes. London, [1971]. pp. 319. bibliog.

- Foreign relations - Germany

RENK (HANSJOERG) Bismarcks Konflikt mit der Schweiz: der Wohlgemuth-Handel von 1889; Vorgeschichte, Hintergründe und Folgen. Basel, 1972. pp. 425. bibliog.

WILLI (JOST NIKOLAUS) Der Fall Jacob-Wesemann, 1935/1936: ein Beitrag zur Geschichte der Schweiz in der Zwischenkriegszeit. Bern, 1972. pp. 434. bibliog.

SWITZERLAND (Cont'd.)

- History

NEUCHÂTEL et la Suisse; ouvrage publié... à l'occasion du cent cinquantième anniversaire de l'entrée de Neuchâtel dans la Confédération. Neuchâtel, Conseil d'Etat de la République et Canton de Neuchâtel, 1969. pp. 442.

Die SCHWEIZ seit 1945: Beiträge zur Zeitgeschichte; (La Suisse depuis 1945...Vorträge, gehalten an den Volkshochschulen Bern und Zürich); herausgegeben von Erich Gruner. Bern, [1971]. pp. 403. (Bern. Universität. Forschungszentrum für Geschichte und Soziologie der Schweizerischen Politik. Helvetia Politica. Series B. vol.6) In German or French.

- Intellectual life

SALIS (JEAN R. DE) Switzerland and Europe: essays and reflections; translated from the German by Alexander and Elizabeth Henderson; edited and with an introduction by Christopher Hughes. London, [1971]. pp. 319. bibliog.

- Military policy

URIO (PAOLO) L'affaire des Mirages: décision administrative et contrôle parlementaire. Genève, 1972. pp. 311.

- Neutrality

[FREY (KARL)] Was geht vor in der Welt? ([by] Konrad Falke [pseud.]). Zürich, [1938]. pp. 47.

DUTTWYLER (HERBERT E.) Der Seekrieg und die Wirtschaftspolitik des neutralen Staates:... mit besonderer Berücksichtigung der Lage der Schweiz, etc. Zürich, 1945. pp. 243.

WAEGER (GERHART) Die Sündenböcke der Schweiz: die Zweihundert im Urteil der geschichtlichen Dokumente, 1940-1946. Olten, [1971]. pp. 288. bibliog.

- Officials and employees - Salaries, allowances, etc.

SAUTER (OTTO) Die Besoldungspolitik der öffentlichen Gemeinwesen auf dem Platze Bern, 1951-1965. Bern, 1970. pp. 142. bibliog.

- Politics and government

LOOSLI (CARL ALBERT) Demokratie und Charakter. Zürich, [1936]. pp. 95.

SCHEURER (KARL) Bundesrat Karl Scheurer: Tagebücher 1914-1929; herausgegeben und eingeleitet von Hermann Böschenstein. Bern, 1971. pp. 390.

TOBLER (JUERG) Dossier Schweiz; betrifft: Demokratie; Testfall: 7. Juni 1970. Zürich, [1971]. pp. 62.

CELIO (NELLO) Demokratie im Wandel: Démocratie en marche: Democrazia dinamica; Reden: Discours: Discorsi, 1967-1971; herausgegeben von Alphons Matt. Frauenfeld, 1972. pp. 200. In various languages.

ROHR (JEAN) La Suisse contemporaine: société et vie politique. Paris, [1972]. pp. 349. bibliogs.

URIO (PAOLO) L'affaire des Mirages: décision administrative et contrôle parlementaire. Genève, 1972. pp. 311.

- Social conditions

ROHR (JEAN) La Suisse contemporaine: société et vie politique. Paris, [1972]. pp. 349. bibliogs.

GRETLER (ARMIN) and MANDL (PIERRE EMERIC) Values, trends and alternatives in Swiss society: a prospective analysis. New York, 1973. pp. 240.

- Social policy

DEGEN (ERNST) Stefan Gschwind als Genossenschafts- und Sozialpolitiker. Basel, 1938. pp. 82. (Verband Schweizerischer Konsumvereine. Genossenschaftliche Volksbibliothek. Nr.40)

- Statistics

SWITZERLAND. Bureau Fédéral de Statistique. 1968. La Suisse en graphiques. Berne, 1968. pp. 82.

- Statistics, Vital

SWITZERLAND. Bureau Fédéral de Statistique. Heiraten, Lebendgeborene und Gestorbene in den Gemeinden: Mariages, naissances et décès dans les communes. a., 1971 [1st]- Bern. In German and French.

BUCHER (ANTON) Die Übersterblichkeit des männlichen Geschlechts. [Zurich, 1972?]. pp. 139. bibliog.

SCHWARZENBACH (HANSRUEDI) Das Geschlechtsverhältnis der Geborenen: seine Schwankungen und Besonderheiten;... im Lichte der schweizerischen Geburtenstatistik. [Zürich, imprint], 1972. pp. 217. bibliog.

SYDNEY

- Civic improvement

SYDNEY. City Council. City of Sydney strategic plan. rev. ed. Sydney, 1971. 1 vol. (pagination varies).

- Growth

PARKER (ROBERT S.) and TROY (P.N.) eds. The politics of urban growth. Canberra, 1972. pp. 160. bibliog.

SYMBOLISM

EDELMAN (MURRAY JACOB) Politics as symbolic action: mass arousal and quiescence. Chicago, [1971]. pp. 188. (Wisconsin University. Institute for Research on Poverty. Monograph Series)

FIRTH (Sir RAYMOND WILLIAM) Symbols: public and private. London, 1973. pp. 469. bibliog.

SYMBOLISM IN ART

BUTTERWORTH (EDRIC ALLAN SCHOFIELD) The tree at the navel of the earth. Berlin, 1970. pp. 239.

SYMBOLISM IN LITERATURE

BOON (JAMES A.) From symbolism to structuralism: Lévi-Strauss in a literary tradition. Oxford, [1972]. pp. 250. bibliog.

SYMPATHY

MERCER (PHILIP C.) Sympathy and ethics: a study of the relationship between sympathy and morality with special reference to Hume's Treatise. Oxford, 1972. pp. 138. bibliog.

SYNDICALISM

LAMATA (PEDRO) Clases sociales y posmarxismo. Buenos Aires, 1969. pp. 319. bibliog.

- Yearbooks

ALMANACH de La Guerre Sociale. [Paris], 1910.

- Bolivia

> BARCELLI S. (AGUSTIN) Medio siglo de luchas sindicales revolucionarias en Bolivia, 1905-1955. La Paz, [1956 or rather 1957]. pp. 336, (24). bibliog.

- Denmark

> PETERSEN (CARL HEINRICH) Danske revolutionaere: ideer, bevaegelser og personligheder. [Copenhagen, 1970]. pp. 388. bibliog.

- Spain

> SOLIS RUIZ (JOSE) The assistant action of Spanish syndicalism. Madrid, 1966. pp. 30. (Tiempo Nuevo. 1)

> GIRALT Y RAVENTOS (EMILIO) and others. Los movimientos sociales en Cataluña, Valencia y Baleares. Barcelona, 1970. pp. 141. bibliog.

> IZARD (MIQUEL) Revolució industrial i obrerisme: les "tres classes de vapor" a Catalunya, 1869-1913. Barcelona, [1970]. pp. 157. bibliog.

> BALCELLS (ALBERT) Crisis economica y agitacion social en Cataluña de 1930 a 1936. Barcelona, [1971]. pp. 295. bibliog.

> CASTIÑEIRAS MUÑOZ (JAIME) and DOMINGUEZ MARTIN-SANCHEZ (JAVIER) Un siglo de lucha obrera en España. Bilbao, 1971. pp. 271. bibliog.

> PAZ (ABEL) Durruti: le peuple en armes; traduit de l'espagnol. [Paris, 1972]. pp. 551. bibliog.

> SANZ OLLER (JULIO) Entre el fraude y la esperanza: las Comisiones obreras de Barcelona. [Paris, 1972]. pp. 364.

> TERMES (JOSEP) Anarquismo y sindicalismo en España: la Primera Internacional, 1864-1881. Barcelona, [1972]. pp. 670. bibliog.

- United Kingdom - Ireland

> CONNOLLY (JAMES) Irish republican leader. Selected political writings; edited and introduced by Owen Dudley Edwards and Bernard Ransom. London, 1973. pp. 382. bibliog.

SYNTHETIC FABRICS

CANADA. Tariff Board. 1970. Report...relative to the investigation ordered by the Minister of Finance respecting woven fabrics of man-made fibres used in the manufacture of garments. Ottawa, 1970. pp. 102.

SYRACUSE (UNITED STATES)

- Politics and government

> FREDERICKSON (H. GEORGE) and O'LEARY (LINDA SCHLUTER) Power, public opinion, and policy in a metropolitan community: a case study of Syracuse, New York. New York, 1973. pp. 184. bibliog.

SYRIA

- Economic conditions

> OFFICE ARABE DE PRESSE ET DE DOCUMENTATION. Etude sur la Fédération des Républiques Arabes: Egypte, Syrie, Libye; rédaction dirigée par Antoine Guine. Damas, [1972?]. fo.233.

- Economic history

> VAVILOV (VIACHESLAV VIKTOROVICH) Sotsial'no-ekonomicheskie preobrazovaniia v Sirii, 1946-1970 gg. Moskva, 1971. pp. 240. bibliog.

- Politics and government

> RABINOVICH (ITAMAR) Syria under the Ba'th, 1963-66: the army-party symbiosis. Jerusalem, [1972]. pp. 276. bibliog. (Tel-Aviv. University. Shiloah Center for Middle Eastern and African Studies. Monograph Series)

- Social history

> VAVILOV (VIACHESLAV VIKTOROVICH) Sotsial'no-ekonomicheskie preobrazovaniia v Sirii, 1946-1970 gg. Moskva, 1971. pp. 240. bibliog.

SYRENIANS
See KOMIS

SYSTEM ANALYSIS

BAREL (YVES) Prospective et analyse de systèmes. [Paris], 1971. pp. 173. bibliog. (France. Délégation à l'Amenagement du Territoire et à l'Action Régionale. Travaux et Recherches de Prospective. 14)

BRYEN (STEPHEN DAVID) The application of cybernetic analysis to the study of international politics. The Hague, 1971. pp. 135. bibliog.

BUCKLEY (WALTER) and SANDKULL (BENGT) A systems study in regional inequality: Norrbotten, a fourth of Sweden. [Stockholm, 1971]. fo. 87. bibliog. (Lund. Universitet. Företagsekonomiska Institutionen. Series SIAR. 22)

FIERING (MYRON B.) and others. Water resources systems analysis. Ottawa, Information Canada, 1971. pp. 47. (Resource Papers. No. 3)

FOUNDOS (S.) Cybernetics and tax law: prediction of courts tax cases. Margate, [imprint], 1971. 1 pamphlet (unpaged). bibliog.

NAGEL (ALBRECHT) Leistungsfähige Entscheidungen in Politik und Verwaltung durch Systemanalyse: ein generell anwendbares Verfahren zur systematischen Erarbeitung vertretbarer Tagesentscheidungen. Berlin, [1971]. pp. 158. bibliog.

NORMANN (RICHARD) Bostadskvotering: effektiv samhällsplanering eller kontrollerad slump? [Stockholm, 1971]. fo. 157. bibliog. (Lund. Universitet. Företagsekonomiska Institutionen. Serie SIAR-S. 42)

SOCIETY FOR GENERAL SYSTEMS RESEARCH. Annual Meeting, 1968. Man in systems: (papers delivered at the annual meeting); edited by Milton D. Rubin. New York, [1971]. pp. 496.

ACKOFF (RUSSELL LINCOLN) and EMERY (FREDERICK E.) On purposeful systems. Chicago, 1972. pp. 288. bibliogs.

ECONOMICS of engineering and social systems; [lectures sponsored in 1969 by University Extension of the University of California]; edited by J. Morley English. New York, [1972]. pp. 321. bibliogs.

HOOS (IDA RUSSAKOFF) Systems analysis in public policy. Berkeley, Calif., 1972. pp. 259.

SYSTEMS SYMPOSIUM, 5TH, CASE WESTERN RESERVE UNIVERSITY, 1970. Systems approach and the city; edited by Mihajlo D. Mesarovic and Arnold Reisman. Amsterdam, 1972. pp. 481.

WRIGHT (CHESTER WHITNEY) and TATE (MICHAEL D.) Economics and systems analysis: introduction for public managers. Reading, Mass., [1973]. pp. 250.

SYSTEM ANALYSIS (Cont'd.)

YEAR-round employment in the construction industry: a systems analysis; report prepared for the Joint Study Group on Construction Seasonality of the U.S. Departments of Labor and Commerce; [by] Jerome B. Gordon [and others]. New York, 1973. pp. 148.

SYSTEM THEORY

VICKERS (JILL McCALLA) An examination of the scientific mode of enquiry in politics with special reference to systems theory in the works of Easton, Almond, Kaplan and Deutsch; [Ph.D. (London) thesis]. 1971. 3 vols. bibliog. Typescript: unpublished. This thesis is the property of London University and may not be removed from the Library. Includes supplementary published material.

BERTALANFFY (LUDWIG VON) General system theory: foundations, development, applications. London, 1971 [or rather 1972]. pp. 311. bibliog. First published in the United States in 1969.

PATRICK (RICHARD ARTHUR) A general systems theory approach to geopolitical aspects of conflict between communities with particular reference to Cyprus since 1960; [Ph.D. (London) thesis]. [1972]. 1 vol. (various foliations). bibliog. Typescript: unpublished. This thesis is the property of London University and may not be removed from the Library.

T-GROUPS
See GROUP RELATIONS TRAINING

TABASCO
- History - Sources

MESTRE GHIGLIAZZA (MANUEL) ed. Invasion norteamericana en Tabasco, 1846-1847: documentos. Mexico, 1948. pp. 369. (Mexico City. Universidad Nacional Autónoma de Mexico. Instituto de Historia. Publicaciones. la Serie. num. 8)

TABLE-CLOTHS

ENCISO RECIO (LUIS MIGUEL) Los establecimientos industriales españoles en el siglo XVIII: la mantelería de la Coruña. Madrid, 1963. pp. 265. bibliog. (Pamplona. Universidad de Navarra. Facultad de Filosofia y Letras. [Publicaciones] Coleccion Historica. 6)

TAGANROG
- Industries

GORDON (LEONID ABRAMOVICH) and RIMASHEVSKAIA (NATAL'IA MIKHAILOVNA) Piatidnevnaia rabochaia nedelia i svobodnoe vremia trudiashchikhsia: taganrogskie issledovaniia. Moskva, 1972. pp. 126.

TAGANTSEV (NIKOLAI STEPANOVICH)

TAGANTSEV (NIKOLAI STEPANOVICH) Perezhitoe. Petrograd, 1919. 2 vols. Xerographic reprint.

TAGORE (Sir RABINDRANATH)

CHAKRAVARTY (AMIYA) Modern humanism: an Indian perspective. Madras, [1968?]. pp. 182. (Madras (City). University. Madras University Lectures. 1963-1964)

TAHITI
- Social life and customs

MARAU TAAROA, Queen of Tahiti. Mémoires...traduits par sa fille la Princesse Ariimanihinihi Takau Pomare. Paris, 1971. pp. 294. (Societé des Océanistes. Publications. No. 27)

T'AI-CHUNG
- Civic improvement

PANNELL (CLIFTON W.) T'ai-chung, T'ai-wan: structure and function. Chicago, 1973. pp. 200. bibliog. (Chicago. University. Department of Geography. Research Papers. No. 144)

- Politics and government

PANNELL (CLIFTON W.) T'ai-chung, T'ai-wan: structure and function. Chicago, 1973. pp. 200. bibliog. (Chicago. University. Department of Geography. Research Papers. No. 144)

TAIMYR NATIONAL OKRUG
- Politics and government

EREMINA (T.S.) Organizatsionnoe oformlenie i deiatel'nost' Taimyrskoi okruzhnoi partiinoi organizatsii, 1930 1941 gg. in Voprosy partiinogo stroitel'stva. Moskva. 1971. pp. 318.

TAIWAN
- Economic conditions

TSUI (T.K.) Taiwan's industrial growth and structure. n.p., [1968]. pp. 21-33. (Reprinted from Industry of Free China, October, 1968)

WU (FONG-I) The strategy of economic development: a case study of Taiwan. Louvain, 1971. pp. 217. bibliog. (Louvain. Universite. Faculte des Sciences Economiques, Sociales et Politiques. [Publications]. Nouvelle Serie. No.90)

ECONOMIC organization in Chinese society; [papers of a conference sponsored by the Subcommittee on Research on Chinese Society, Saint-Adèle-enhaut, Quebec, 1969]; edited by W.E. Willmott. Stanford, 1972. pp. 461. bibliog. (American Council of Learned Societies and Social Science Research Council. Joint Committee on Contemporary China. Subcommittee on Research on Chinese Society. Studies in Chinese Society)

- Economic history

KOCH (WILFRIED) Funktionale Strukturwandlungen in Taiwan: das Beispiel Luchou im Umland der Millionenstadt Taipei. Köln, 1971. pp. 261. bibliog. (Cologne. Universität. Geographisches Institut. Kölner Geographische Arbeiten. Heft 26) With English summary.

LEE (TENG-HUI) Intersectoral capital flows in the economic development of Taiwan, 1895-1960. Ithaca, 1971. pp. 197. bibliog.

HESSE (KURT) and ISCHINGER (WOLFGANG) Die Entwicklungsschwelle: der Übergang vom Entwicklungsland zum entwickelten Land unter Einbeziehung von drei Testfällen. Berlin, [1973]. pp. 252. bibliogs.

- Economic policy

NEGANDHI (ANANT R.) Management and economic development: the case of Taiwan. The Hague, 1973. pp. 176.

- Foreign relations

> TUNG (CHIA-PI) Bitter lessons from diplomatic relations with the Maoists. Taipei, 1972. 2 pts. (in 1 vol.) (Asian Peoples' Anti-Communist League. Pamphlets. Nos. 160-161)

> CHIU (HUNGDAH) ed. China and the question of Taiwan: documents and analysis. New York, 1973. pp. 395. bibliog.

- Foreign relations - United States

> TAIWAN and American policy: the dilemma in U.S.-China relations; [by] Jerome Alan Cohen [and others]: papers of a conference sponsored by] the League of Women Voters Education Fund and the National Committee on United States-China Relations. New York, 1971. pp. 191.

- Politics and government

> CHIU (HUNGDAH) ed. China and the question of Taiwan: documents and analysis. New York, 1973. pp. 395. bibliog.

- Population

> SCHULTZ (T. PAUL) Disequilibrium and variation in birth rates over space and time: a study of Taiwan. Santa Monica, 1972. pp. 65. bibliog. (Rand Corporation. [Rand Reports]. 1079)

- Religion

> JORDAN (DAVID K.) God, ghosts, and ancestors: the folk religion of a Taiwanese village. Berkeley, Calif., [1972]. pp. 197. bibliog.

- Rural conditions

> ECONOMIC organization in Chinese society; [papers of a conference sponsored by the Subcommittee on Research on Chinese Society, Saint-Adèle-en-haut, Quebec, 1969]; edited by W.E. Willmott. Stanford, 1972. pp. 461. bibliog. (American Council of Learned Societies and Social Science Research Council. Joint Committee on Contemporary China. Subcommittee on Research on Chinese Society. Studies in Chinese Society)

TAJIKISTAN

- Appropriations and expenditures

> FAZYLOV (NIGMAT FAZYLOVICH) Formirovanie i razvitie gosudarstvennykh finansov Tadzhikskoi SSR. Dushanbe, 1968. pp. 215.

- Description and travel

> TADJIK Soviet Socialist Republic. Moscow, 1972. pp. 72.

- Economic conditions

> AKADEMIIA NAUK TADZHIKSKOI SSR. Otdel Ekonomiki. Trudy. t.11. Voprosy ekonomiki narodnogo khoziaistva Tadzhikistana. Dushanbe, 1963. pp. 152.

> NEKOTORYE zakonomernosti perekhoda ot sotsializma k kommunizmu. Dushanbe, 1964. pp. 220.

> TADZHIKISTAN: ekonomicheskii rost i effektivnost'. Dushanbe, 1972. pp. 143.

- Economic history

> 50 let bor'by za narodnoe schast'e. Dushanbe, 1967. pp. 219.

- Economic policy

> NEKOTORYE zakonomernosti perekhoda ot sotsializma k kommunizmu. Dushanbe, 1964. pp. 220.

- History

> GAFUROV (BOBODZHAN GAFUROVICH) Tadzhiki: drevneishaia, drevniaia i srednevekovaia istoriia. Moskva, 1972. pp. 664. bibliog.

- History - 1917-1921, Revolution

> IONOVA (V.M.) Kommunisty Severnogo Tadzhikistana v bor'be za vlast' Sovetov, 1917-1923 gg. Dushanbe, 1968. pp. 128.

- Industries

> KLETSEL'MAN (UL'IAN KHAIMOVICH) Kompleksnoe razvitie promyshlennosti Tadzhikskoi SSR; pod redaktsiei... Itina, L.I. Dushanbe, 1969. pp. 177.

- Social life and customs

> MONOGAROVA (LIDIIA FEDOROVNA) Preobrazovaniia v bytu i kul'ture pripamirskikh narodnostei. Moskva, 1972. pp. 174.

TALLEYRAND-PERIGORD (CHARLES MAURICE DE) Prince

> ORIEUX (JEAN) Talleyrand; ou, Le sphinx incompris. Paris, [1972]. pp. 858. bibliog.

TAMBOPATA VALLEY, PERU

> MARTINEZ (HECTOR) Las migraciones altiplanicas y la colonizacion del Tambopata. Lima, 1969. pp. 278. bibliog.

TAMBOV (OBLAST')

- Bibliography

> BRUN (E.IA.) and others, compilers. V.I. Lenin i Chernozemnyi Tsentr Rossii: bibliograficheskii ukazatel'; pod redaktsiei E.G. Shuliakovskogo. Voronezh, 1970. pp. 223.

- Economic conditions

> DOLGOPOLOV (KONSTANTIN VASIL'EVICH) and FEDOROVA (EVGENIIA FEDOROVNA) Tsentral'no-Chernozemnyi raion: ekonomiko-geograficheskii ocherk; posobie dlia uchitelei. Moskva, 1971. pp. 167. bibliog.

TAMMANY HALL

> MOSCOW (WARREN) The last of the big-time bosses: the life and times of Carmine de Sapio and the rise and fall of Tammany Hall. New York, 1971. pp. 227.

TANDON (PRAKASH)

> TANDON (PRAKASH) Beyond Punjab, 1937-1960. Berkeley, [1971]. pp. 222.

TANNING

> WEST BENGAL. State Statistical Bureau. 1964. A short note on tanning industry. [Alipore], 1964. pp. 48.

> INTERNATIONAL LABOUR OFFICE. Development Programme: Technical Assistance Sector. [Afghanistan] R.13. Report to the government of Afghanistan on small-scale leather industries, the leather project at Charikar and training in leather technology. (ILO/TAP/Afghanistan/R.13). Geneva, 1971. pp. 51.

TANZANIA

- Census

UNITED REPUBLIC OF TANZANIA. Census, 1967. 1967 population census: [volume series]. Dar es Salaam, 1969 in progress.

- Commerce

NATIONAL BANK OF COMMERCE [TANZANIA]. Annual report and accounts. a., 1967/8- Dar es Salaam.

- Economic conditions

UNIVERSITY PRESS OF AFRICA. Tanzania today: a portrait of the United Republic; (produced for the Ministry of Information and Tourism, United Republic of Tanzania). Nairobi, 1968. pp. 316, 1 map. bibliog.

HOFMEIER (ROLF) Transport and economic development in Tanzania, with particular reference to roads and road transport. München, [1973]. pp. 353. bibliog. (Ifo-Institut für Wirtschaftsforschung. Afrika-Studien. 78)

- Economic conditions - Bibliography

UNITED REPUBLIC OF TANZANIA. Central Statistical Bureau. 1967. A bibliography of economic and statistical publications on Tanzania. Dar es Salaam, 1967. fo. 23.

- Economic policy

FINUCANE (JAMES ROBERT) Bureaucracy and development in rural Tanzania: the case of Mwanza region; [Ph. D. (London) thesis]. 1972. fo. 350. bibliog. Typescript: unpublished. This thesis is the property of London University and may not be removed from the Library.

INGLE (CLYDE REID) From village to state in Tanzania: the politics of rural development. Ithaca, N.Y., 1972. pp. 279. bibliog.

- History

BATES (Sir JULIAN DARRELL) A gust of plumes: a biography of Lord Twining of Godalming and Tanganyika. London, [1972]. pp. 319.

HATCH (JOHN CHARLES) Tanzania: a profile. London, 1972. pp. 214. bibliog.

- History - Sources

HEUSSLER (ROBERT) British Tanganyika: an essay and documents on district administration. Durham, N.C., 1971. pp. 154. bibliog.

- Industries

EAST AFRICA HIGH COMMISSION. East African Statistical Department. Tanganyika Unit. 1960. Survey of industrial production, 1958. Dar es Salaam, 1960. pp. 49.

- Kings and rulers

SHORTER (AYLWARD) Chiefship in Western Tanzania: a political history of the Kimbu. Oxford, 1972. pp. 439. bibliog.

- Officials and employees

TANGANYIKA. Africanisation Commission. 1963. Report of the... Commission, 1962; [S.A. Maswanya, chairman]. Dar es Salaam, 1963. pp.iv,37.

- Politics and government

FINUCANE (JAMES ROBERT) Bureaucracy and development in rural Tanzania: the case of Mwanza region; [Ph. D. (London) thesis]. 1972. fo. 350. bibliog. Typescript: unpublished. This thesis is the property of London University and may not be removed from the Library.

HATCH (JOHN CHARLES) Tanzania: a profile. London, 1972. pp. 214. bibliog.

INGLE (CLYDE REID) From village to state in Tanzania: the politics of rural development. Ithaca, N.Y., 1972. pp. 279. bibliog.

NELLIS (JOHN R.) A theory of ideology: the Tanzanian example. Nairobi, [1972]. pp. 217. bibliog.

SINITSYNA (IRINA EVGEN'EVNA) Tanzaniia: partiia i gosudarstvo. Moskva, 1972. pp. 281. bibliog

- Population

UNITED REPUBLIC OF TANZANIA. Central Statistical Bureau. 1968. Provisional estimates of fertility, mortality and population growth for Tanzania. Dar es Salaam, 1968. fo. 22.

- Race question

TANGANYIKA. Africanisation Commission. 1963. Report of the... Commission, 1962; [S.A. Maswanya, chairman]. Dar es Salaam, 1963. pp.iv,37.

- Rural conditions

COLLINS (PAUL) The working of Tanzania's rural development fund: a problem in decentralisation. Brighton, 1971. pp. 48. (Brighton. University of Sussex. Institute of Development Studies. Communications. No. 62)

ZANOLLI (NOA VERA) Education toward development in Tanzania: a study of the educative process in a rural area (Ulanga District). Basel, 1971. pp. 386. bibliog. (Geographisch-Ethnologische Gesellschaft and Basel. Museum für Völkerkunde und Schweizerisches Museum für Volkskunde. Basler Beiträge zur Ethnologie. Band 8)

HEKKEN (P.M. VAN) and VELZEN (H.U.E. THODEN VAN) Land scarcity and rural inequality in Tanzania: some case studies from Rungwe District. The Hague, [1972]. pp. 127. bibliog. (Afrika-Studiecentrum. Communications. 3)

INGLE (CLYDE REID) From village to state in Tanzania: the politics of rural development. Ithaca, N.Y., 1972. pp. 279. bibliog.

- Social conditions

UNIVERSITY PRESS OF AFRICA. Tanzania today: a portrait of the United Republic; (produced for the Ministry of Information and Tourism, United Republic of Tanzania). Nairobi, 1968. pp. 316, 1 map. bibliog.

EGGERT (JOHANNA) Missionsschule und sozialer Wandel in Ostafrika: der Beitrag der deutschen evangelischen Missionsgesellschaften zur Entwicklung des Schulwesens in Tanganyika, 1891-1939. Bielefeld, [1970]. pp. 334. bibliog. (Arnold-Bergstraesser-Institut für Kulturwissenschaftliche Forschung. Freiburger Studien zu Politik und Gesellschaft Überseeischer Länder. Band 10) With English summary.

- Social policy

FINUCANE (JAMES ROBERT) Bureaucracy and development in rural Tanzania: the case of Mwanza region; [Ph. D. (London) thesis]. 1972. fo. 350. bibliog. Typescript: unpublished. This thesis is the property of London University and may not be removed from the Library.

- Statistics

TANGANYIKA. Central Statistical Bureau. 1963. Village economic surveys, 1961/62. [Dar es Salaam], 1963. pp. 9,(xiv), viii.

UNITED REPUBLIC OF TANZANIA. Central Statistical Bureau. 1968. A guide to Tanzania statistics. Dar es Salaam, 1968. fo. 51.

- Statistics, Vital

UNITED REPUBLIC OF TANZANIA. Central Statistical Bureau. 1968. Provisional estimates of fertility, mortality and population growth for Tanzania. Dar es Salaam, 1968. fo. 22.

TARIFFS

CURTISS (GEORGE B.) The industrial development of nations and a history of the tariff policies of the United States, and of Great Britain, Germany, France, Russia and other European countries. Binghampton, N.Y., 1912. 3 vols.

GENERAL AGREEMENT ON TARIFFS AND TRADE. 1959. The removal of obstacles to international trade: the role of the General Agreement on Tariffs and Trade: note...submitted to the Inter-Parliamentary Union. [Geneva], 1959. pp. 5.

ROYER (JEAN) L'enjeu de la conférence tarifaire du GATT, 1960-1961: conférence donnée...Paris, le 22 mars 1960. [Geneva, 1960]. pp. 24.

BALASSA (BELA A.) and others. The structure of protection in developing countries. Baltimore, International Bank for Reconstruction and Development, [1971]. pp. 375.

CURTIS (THOMAS B.) and VASTINE (JOHN ROBERT) The Kennedy Round and the future of American trade. New York, 1971. pp. 239.

EVANS (JOHN WALKER) The Kennedy round in American trade policy: the twilight of the GATT? Cambridge, Mass., 1971. pp. 383. bibliog.

- Law

GENERAL AGREEMENT ON TARIFFS AND TRADE. 1971. Status of legal instruments. (GATT/LEG/1). Geneva, 1971. 1 vol. (looseleaf).

- America, Latin

BELL (HARRY H.) Tariff profiles in Latin America: implications for pricing structures and economic integration. New York, 1971. pp. 168.

- Brazil

GENERAL AGREEMENT ON TARIFFS AND TRADE. 1958. Protocol relating to negotiations for the establishment of new schedule III, Brazil, to the General Agreement on Tariffs and Trade. Geneva, 1958. pp. 49.

- Canada

CANADA. Tariff Board. 1969. Report...relative to the investigation ordered by the Minister of Finance respecting binder twine and twine for baling farm produce. Ottawa, 1969. pp. 98.

CANADA. Tariff Board. 1969. Report...relative to the investigation ordered by the Minister of Finance respecting fractions of petroleum for use as feedstocks in the manufacture of organic chemicals. Ottawa, 1969. pp. 100.

CANADA. Tariff Board. 1969. Report...relative to the investigation ordered by the Minister of Finance respecting polyethylene. Ottawa, 1969. pp. 63.

CANADA. Tariff Board. 1970. Report...relative to the investigation ordered by the Minister of Finance respecting knitted outer garments. Ottawa, 1970. 1 vol. (various pagings).

CANADA. Tariff Board. 1970. Report...relative to the investigation ordered by the Minister of Finance respecting woven fabrics of man-made fibres used in the manufacture of garments. Ottawa, 1970. pp. 102.

CANADA. Tariff Board. 1972. Report...relative to the investigation ordered by the Minister of Finance respecting strawberries for processing. Ottawa, 1972. 1 vol. (various pagings).

- Denmark

ENEMARK (POUL) Studier i toldregnskabsmateriale i begyndelsen af 16. århundrede...: Studien über Zollrechnungsunterlagen zu Beginn des 16. Jahrhunderts, etc. Århus, 1971. 2 vols.bibliog. In Danish, with German summary.

- European Economic Community countries

[EUROPEAN COMMUNITIES]. 1961. Tarif douanier des Communautés Européennes. [Brussels], 1961. pp. 298.

CASADIO (GIAN PAOLO) Transatlantic trade: USA-EEC confrontation in the GATT negotiations;... translated from the Italian by John Cuthbert-Brown. Farnborough, [1973]. pp. 260. bibliog.

- European Economic Community countries - Law

DAILLIER (PATRICK) L'harmonisation des législations douanières des Etats membres de la Communauté Economique Européenne. Paris, 1972. pp. 345. bibliog.

- Finland

KORPELA (ASKO) Effect of tariffs on imports to Finland. Helsinki, 1971. pp. 191. (Helsinki. Kauppakorkeakoulu. Julkaisuja. Sarja C.II: 11)

- India

CURRENT economic problems of India; [reprinted articles]; with a foreword by Sir J.C. Coyajee. [Alipore, 1933]. pp. 161.

BANERJEE (TARASANKAR) History of internal trade barriers in British India: a study of transit and town duties. Calcutta, [1972 in progress]. bibliog. (Asiatic Society of Bengal. Monograph Series. vol. 21)

- New Zealand

ELKAN (PETER GABRIEL) Industrial protection in New Zealand, 1952 to 1967. [Wellington, N.Z.], 1972. pp. 90. (New Zealand Institute of Economic Research. Technical Memoranda. No. 15)

- Switzerland

GENERAL AGREEMENT ON TARIFFS AND TRADE. 1958. Declaration on the provisional accession of the Swiss Confederation to the General Agreement on Tariffs and Trade, etc. Geneva, 1958. pp. 294. In English and French.

TARIFFS - Underdeveloped areas
See UNDERDEVELOPED AREAS - Tariffs

- United Kingdom

[ELLIOT (JOHN LETTSOM)] A letter to the electors of Westminster; from an aristocrat. [London], Hearne, 1850. pp. 100.

JONAS (ERICH) Chamberlains handelspolitische Reformprojekte: ihre Grundlagen und ihre Grenzen. [Sagan, imprint], 1906. pp. 126. bibliog.

DUTT (RAJANI PALME) Crisis, tariffs, war. London, [1932]. pp. 19.

OULTON (NICHOLAS) Tariffs, taxes and trade in the UK: the effective protection approach. London, H.M.S.O., 1973. pp. 20. bibliog. (Government Economic Service Occasional Papers. 6)

TARIFFS (Cont'd.)

- United States

CASADIO (GIAN PAOLO) Transatlantic trade: USA-EEC confrontation in the GATT negotiations;... translated from the Italian by John Cuthbert-Brown. Farnborough, [1973]. pp. 260. bibliog.

TARLE (EVGENII VIKTOROVICH)

PROBLEMY istorii mezhdunarodnykh otnoshenii: sbornik statei pamiati akademika E.V. Tarle. Leningrad, 1972. pp. 427.

TARRY (ELLEN)

TARRY (ELLEN) The third door: the autobiography of an American negro woman; [reprint of the work published in New York in 1955]. Westport, Conn., 1971. pp. 304.

TASHKENT

- Earthquake, 1966

LIKVIDATSIIA posledstvii Tashkentskogo zemletriaseniia. Tashkent, 1972. pp. 246.

- History - 1917-1921, Revolution

RASHIDOV (GULIAMKADYR) Tashkentskii Sovet v bor'be za uprochenie Sovetskoi vlasti. Tashkent, 1960. pp. 184. Xerographic reprint.

PULATOV (GULIAM) and RASHIDOV (GULIAMKADYR) Tashkent v pervye gody Sovetskoi vlasti, noiabr' 1917-1920 gg. Tashkent, 1972. pp. 190.

TASMANIA

- Commerce - Asia, South-East

TASMANIA. Trade Survey Mission to Japan and South-East Asia. 1971. Report; [D.F. Clark, leader]. in TASMANIA. Parliament. Journals and Printed Papers, 1971, no. 33.

- Commerce - Japan

TASMANIA. Trade Survey Mission to Japan and South-East Asia. 1971. Report; [D.F. Clark, leader]. in TASMANIA. Parliament. Journals and Printed Papers, 1971, no. 33.

- Rural conditions

TASMANIA. Rural Reconstruction Board. Annual report. 1971/2 [1st] to date included in TASMANIA. Parliament. Journals and printed papers.

TATAR REPUBLIC

- Economic conditions

OSOBENNOSTI sovremennoi narodnokhoziaistvennoi struktury Tatarii. Kazan', 1971. pp. 82.

- History

PLODY velikogo bratstva. Kazan', 1972. pp. 239.

- Nationalism

KHAIRUTDINOV (RIF GALIAUTDINOVICH) Na putiakh k sovetsko avtonomii: provedenie leninskoi natsional'noi politiki Tsentral'nym Tataro-Bashkirskim komissariatom v 1918-1919 gg. Kazan', 1972. pp. 160. bibliog.

- Politics and government

VAKHITOV (MULLANUR MULLAZIANOVICH) Izbrannoe: stat'i, rechi, pis'ma, dokumenty. Kazan', 1967. pp. 121.

DEIATEL'NOST' partiinoi organizatsii Tatarii po osushchestvleniiu leninskikh idei stroitel'stva sotsialisticheskogo obshchestva. Kazan', 1971. pp. 286.

- Population

STRUKTURA naseleniia i gorodov Tatarii. Kazan', 1971. pp. 90. bibliog.

- Verkhovnyi Sovet

KARIMOV (AZAL' MIRGALIMOVICH) Vysshie organy gosudarstvennoi vlasti avtonomnoi respubliki: po materialam Tatarskoi ASSR. Kazan', 1970. pp. 150. In colophon author's forename is spelled Azel'.

TATARBUNARY UPRISING, 1924
See BESSARABIA - History

TATARS

SHEEHY (ANN) The Crimean Tatars and Volga Germans: Soviet treatment of two national minorities. London, [1971]. pp. 31. bibliog. (Minority Rights Group. Reports. No. 6)

TAWNEY (RICHARD HENRY)

TAWNEY (RICHARD HENRY) R.H. Tawney's commonplace book; edited and with an introduction by J.M. Winter and D.M. Joslin. Cambridge, 1972. pp. 88. (Economic History Review, The. Supplements. No.5)

TAX ADMINISTRATION

- Canada

McDONALD (JOHN GRAHAM) Canadian Royal Commission on Taxation: tax administration. Toronto, 1968. pp. 24.

- Colombia

MATIZ SANTOS (NOHRA) Comentarios sobre la descentralizacion fiscal en Colombia. Bogota, 1969. pp. 120. bibliog.

TAX EVASION

- India

INDIA. Direct Taxes Enquiry Committee. 1972. Final report; [K.N. Wanchoo, chairman]. [Delhi], 1971 [or rather 1972]. pp. 315.

- United Kingdom

STAPLES (RONALD) On back duty: being a consideration of the law and practice relating to the settlement of liability to income tax, surtax... where income and capital gains have escaped assessment at the proper time; ninth edition by Percy F. Hughes. London, 1971. pp. 306.

TAX PLANNING

GRUNDY (JAMES MILTON) ed. Tax havens: a world survey. 2nd ed. London, 1972. pp. 173.

HUISKAMP (JOHAN CHRISTIAAN LODEWIJK) Internationale belastingvlucht, etc. Deventer, [1972]. pp. 16.

KUPER SPITZ (BARRY) International tax planning. London, 1972. pp. 159.

- United States

FREEMAN (ROGER A.) Tax loopholes: the legend and the reality. Washington, D.C., 1973. pp. 91. (American Enterprise Institute for Public Policy Research, and Stanford University. Hoover Institution on War, Revolution and Peace. AEI-Hoover Policy Studies. 5)

TAXATION

RICARDO (DAVID) On the principles of political economy, and taxation; [reprint of the 3rd ed. of 1821] edited with an introduction by R.M. Hartwell. Harmondsworth, 1971. pp. 427. bibliog.

FRANTZ (GUSTAV ADOLF CONSTANTIN) Die soziale Steuerreform als die conditio sine qua non, wenn der sozialen Revolution vorgebeugt werden soll; Neudruck der Ausgabe Mainz 1881. Aalen, 1972. pp. 206.

VOCKE (WILHELM) Geheimer Oberrechnungsrat. Die Abgaben, Auflagen und die Steuer vom Standpunkte der Geschichte und der Sittlichkeit; [reprint of edition originally published in 1887]. [Frankfurt am Main], 1970. pp. 625.

BEITRAEGE zur Finanzwissenschaft und zur Geldtheorie: Festschrift für Rudolf Stucken; herausgegeben von Fritz Voigt. Göttingen, 1953. pp. 312. bibliog.

LOECKX (FR.) and others. Eléments de la science des impôts. 3rd ed. [Brussels?], 1970-71. 2 vols. (in 1). bibliogs. (Belgium. Administration des Contributions Directes. Cours Administratifs)

HALLER (HEINZ) Besteuerung und Wirtschaftswachstum. Tübingen, 1970. pp. 70. With summaries in English and French.

ARDANT (GABRIEL) Economist. Histoire de l'impôt. [Paris, 1971-72]. 2 vols. bibliogs.

Der WIRTSCHAFTENDE Staat: Theorie und Praxis; Festschrift zum 70. Geburtstag von Prof. Dr. Theo Keller; ([edited by] Willi Geiger [and others]). Bern, [1971]. pp. 335. bibliog.

PUBLIC expenditures and taxation; fiftieth anniversary [of the National Bureau of Economic Research] colloquium IV. New York, 1972. pp. 74. (National Bureau of Economic Research. [Publications]. No. 96)

SINGER (NEIL M.) Public microeconomics. Boston, [1972]. pp. 329. bibliogs.

VEREIN FÜR SOZIALPOLITIK. Schriften. Neue Folge. Band 68. Besteuerung und Zahlungsbilanz; von Karl Häuser [and others]; herausgegeben von Willi Albers. Berlin, [1972]. pp. 84. In German, with English summaries.

- Law

BERGMANN (ARTHUR) Developing countries and international fiscal law. Hannover, [1968]. pp. 102. (Friedrich-Ebert-Stiftung. Forschungsinstitut. Schriftenreihe A. Sozialwissenschaftliche Schriften)

BURG (F.H. VAN DER) Toezeggingen en pseudo-wetgeving in het administratieve recht; [with] De rechtswaarde van niet op de wet steunende bestuurshandelingen van de belastingadministratie, door Ch. P.A. Geppaart. Deventer, 1969. pp. 103. (Nederlandse Vereniging voor Rechtsvergelijking. Preadviezen. No. 3)

EUROPEAN SEMINAR ON FISCAL LAW, 1969. Problèmes fiscaux de la coopération entre entreprises indépendantes de pays différents: (Fiscal problems of co-operation between independant enterprises of different countries, etc.). Bruxelles, 1970. pp. 395. (Ecole Supérieure des Sciences Fiscales. Bibliothèque. 6) In English, French, or German.

NEEMAN (YAAKOV) The tax consequences upon conversion of property's use. Tel-Aviv, 1970. pp. 241. bibliog.

FOUNDOS (S.) Cybernetics and tax law: prediction of courts tax cases. Margate, [imprint], 1971. 1 pamphlet (unpaged). bibliog.

INTERNATIONAL TAX CONFERENCE, 1972. Conference papers;...conference director, G.S.A. Wheatcroft. London, [1972]. 1 vol. (pagination varies).

- Mathematical models

SPOERNDLI (ERICH) Steuerinzidenz und Wirtschaftswachstum: eine wachstumstheoretische Modellstudie zum Problem der langfristigen Wirkungen von Gewinn- und Umsatzsteuern auf die Einkommensverteilung. Zürich, 1971. pp. 125, 35. bibliog.

- Argentine Republic

JORNADAS DE FINANZAS PUBLICAS, 1AS, CORDOBA. La tributacion en la Argentina: (trabajos presentados en las Primeras Jornadas...) [organized by the Facultad de Ciencias Economicas of the Universidad Nacional de Cordoba]. Cordoba, Arg., 1969. pp. 596.

- Australia

GLAU (THOMAS E.) The impact of tax policy on agricultural investment in Australia. Sydney, 1971. fo. 253. bibliog. (Sydney. University. Department of Agricultural Economics. Mimeographed Reports. No. 5)

- Austria

BALTZAREK (FRANZ) Das Steueramt der Stadt Wien, 1526-1760. Wien, 1971. pp. 403. bibliog. (Vienna. Universität. Dissertationen. 58)

- Brazil - Law

BRAZIL. Statutes, etc. 1930-1971. A legislação tributaria no Brasil: a partir de 1930. Rio de Janeiro, 1971. pp. 275.

- Canada

McDONALD (JOHN GRAHAM) Canadian Royal Commission on Taxation: foreign investment and international transactions. Toronto, 1967. pp. 32.

CANADA. Tax Review Board. Annual report. a., 1972 (2nd)- Ottawa. D 15/31 1971 (1st) not pd.

MASLOVE (ALLAN M.) The pattern of taxation in Canada...; prepared for the Economic Council of Canada. Ottawa, Information Canada, 1973. pp. 189. bibliog.

- Canada - Quebec

DESPRES (ROBERT) Tax aspects of Quebec pension plan legislation; address given by Deputy-Minister of Revenue...on Thursday, September 30, 1965, etc. [Quebec], 1965. fo. 14.

QUEBEC (PROVINCE). Royal Commission on Taxation, 1963. Report: [Marcel Bélanger, chairman]. Quebec, 1965. pp. 512.

- Colombia

CENTRO DE INVESTIGACION Y ACCION SOCIAL [BOGOTA]. Coleccion. 3. Impuestos y desarrollo economico de Colombia. Bogota, 1968. pp. 236.

COLOMBIA. Commission on Tax Reform. 1971. Fiscal reform for Colombia: final report and staff papers...; Richard A. Musgrave, President; edited by Malcolm Gillis. Cambridge, Mass., Law School of Harvard University, 1971. pp. 853.

MENDEZ ALZAMORA (ALVARO) El situado fiscal. Bogato, 1971. pp. 85. bibliog.

TAXATION (Cont'd.)

- Colombia - Law

COLOMBIA. Statutes, etc. 1970-1972. [Selection of laws etc. on finance and taxation in Colombia, 1970-72]. Bogota, 1971-72. 16 pts.(in 1 vol.).

- Ethiopia

PATTERNS OF PROGRESS IN ETHIOPIA. Book. 10. Financial and fiscal policy of Ethiopia. Addis Ababa, Ministry of Information, Publications and Foreign Languages Press Department, 1968. pp. 56.

- European Economic Community countries

EUROPEAN ECONOMIC COMMUNITY. Commission. 1965. Inventaire des impôts perçus dans les États membres de la Communauté économique européenne au profit de l'État de des collectivités locales...avec tableaux des recettes pour les années 1961 et 1962. [Brussels], 1965. pp. (199).

EUROPEAN ECONOMIC COMMUNITY. Commission. 1967. Inventaire des impôts perçus dans les Etats membres des Communautés européennes au profit de l'Etat et des collectivités locales...; avec tableaux des recettes pour les années 1964 et 1965. Bruxelles, 1967. pp. 203.

EUROPEAN ECONOMIC COMMUNITY. Commission. 1967. Taxes in the European communities: a comprehensive inventory of taxes levied by central government and local authorities...; with tables showing tax revenue for the years 1964 and 1965. [Brussels], 1967. pp. 203.

GROEBEN (HANS VON DER) Harmonizing taxes - a step to European integration. [London], European Communities, 1968. pp. 8. ([Press and] Information Service, London Office. Community Topics. 30)

VOGELAAR (T.W.) De stand der belastingharmonisatie. Deventer, 1970. pp. 45. (Vereniging voor Belastingwetenschap. Geschriften. Nr.126)

DOSSER (DOUGLAS G.M.) and others. British taxation and the Common Market: a volume of essays. London, 1973. pp. 180.

STEINAECKER (MICHAEL VON) Freiherr. Domestic taxation and foreign trade: the United States-European border tax dispute. New York, 1973. pp. 169. bibliog.

- Finland

SUVIRANTA (ANTTI) Direct taxation in Finland: an outline; based on a mimeographed outline originally written by Aarne Rekola, etc. Helsinki, Ministry of Finance, 1972. pp. 34. bibliog.

- France

[GAUDET ( ) Directeur Général des Vingtièmes]. Lettres de M**** a différentes personnes sur les finances, les subsistances, les corvées, les communautés religieuses, etc. Amsterdam, M.M. Rey, 1778. pp. (vi), 374.

PROBLEMES budgétaires contemporains: la prévision des recettes et les budgets de programme; [two theses], par Philippe Dunand et Xavier Greffe. Paris, 1970. pp. 293. bibliogs. (Paris. Université. Faculté de Droit et des Sciences Economiques. Travaux et Recherches. Série "Sciences Economiques". No. 8)

HENNEMAN (JOHN BELL) Royal taxation in fourteenth century France: the development of war financing, 1322-1356. Princeton, 1971. pp. 388. bibliog.

RAMALHO (MARIA MADALENA) Redistribuição e fiscalidade: o caso francês. Lisboa, 1971. pp. 67. (Portugal. Ministerio das Corporações e Previdência Social. Gabinete de Planeamento. Serie Estudos. 4) With abstracts in English, French and German.

FRANCE. Direction Générale des Impôts. Code général des impôts. a., Je 1 1973- Paris. 1965-1971 and provisional figures for 1972 (in looseleaf form) catalogued separately and filed at R(O) 44(1264).

- France - Law

TOURNIE (GERARD) Les agréments fiscaux: la fiscalité au service du plan. [Toulouse, imprint, 1970]. pp. 340. bibliog.

BERN (PHILIPPE) La nature juridique du contentieux de l'imposition. Paris, 1972. pp. 197. bibliog.

- Germany

BERNSTEIN (EDUARD) Die Steuerpolitik der Sozialdemokratie: auf Grund des Programms und der Kongressbeschlüsse der Partei gemeinverständlich dargestellt. Berlin, 1914. pp. 48.

MJESSENER (INGO) Der Stand der Reformdiskussion um die Einkommensbesteuerung im Rahmen des Steuersystems der Bundesrepublik Deutschland. Bonn, 1972. pp. 311. bibliog.

- Germany - Lower Saxony

ACHILLES (WALTER) Die steuerliche Belastung der braunschweigischen Landwirtschaft und ihr Beitrag zu den Staatseinnahmen im 17. und 18. Jahrhundert. Hildesheim, 1972. pp. 248. bibliog. (Historischer Verein für Niedersachsen. Quellen und Darstellungen zur Geschichte Niedersachsens. Band 82)

- Germany - Prussia

DIETERICI (CARL FRIEDRICH WILHELM) Zur Geschichte der Steuer-Reform in Preussen (von 1810 bis 1820: Archiv-Studien); [facsimile reprint of work originally published in 1875]. Glashütten im Taunus, 1972. pp. 442.

- Germany - Saarland

SAARGEBIET. Statistisches Amt. Handbuch: Steuern und Finanzen. a., 1970- Saarbrücken.

- Germany - Schleswig-Holstein

EHLERS (FRANZ) ed. Zoll- und Steuergeschichte Schleswig-Holsteins;... mit Beiträgen von Fritz Brinckmann [and others]. [Kiel, 1968]. pp. 549. bibliog.

- India

INDIA. Direct Taxes Enquiry Committee. 1972. Final report; [K.N. Wanchoo, chairman]. [Delhi], 1971 [or rather 1972]. pp. 315.

LAKDAWALA (DANSUKHLAL TULSIDAS) and NAMBIAR (K.V.) Commodity taxation in India. Ahmedabad, 1972. pp. 189.

- India - Andhra Pradesh

MUTHAYYA (B.C.) Panchayat taxes: factors influencing their mobilisation; a study in three panchayats in East Godavari, Andhra Pradesh. Hyderabad 1972. pp. 146.

- India - Mysore

NATIONAL COUNCIL OF APPLIED ECONOMIC RESEARCH. Incidence of taxation in Mysore State. New Delhi, [1972]. pp. 57.

- Israel

WILKENFELD (HAROLD C.) Taxes and people in Israel. Cambridge, Mass., 1973. pp. 307. bibliog.

- Italy

   FLORENCE (PROVINCE). Consiglio Provinciale.
   Riforma tributaria e finanza locale: problemi e
   prospettive; [proceedings of meetings, 4-12
   December 1967]. [Florence, 1968]. pp. 84.

   MOLHO (ANTHONY) Florentine public finances in
   the early Renaissance, 1400-1433. Cambridge,
   Mass., 1971. pp. 230. (Harvard University.
   Harvard Historical Monographs. 65)

   AMATO (ANGELO) Il nostro sistema tributario dopo
   la riforma. Padova, 1973. pp. 277. bibliog.

- Netherlands

   WIJLE (F.C.) Belastingen en gezinseenheid: een
   kritische beschouwing inzake verbanden tussen
   gezinsconnecties en subjectieve-belastingheffing.
   [Deventer, 1972]. pp. 200. bibliog. (Nederlandsche
   Economische Hoogeschool. Fiscaal-Economisch Instituut
   Geschriften. No. 3) With English summary.

- Netherlands - Law

   GRAPPERHAUS (F.H.M.) De aanvaardbaarheid van
   nevendoeleinden in de belastingwetgeving;
   voordracht gehouden op 24 Maart 1969, etc.
   Alphen aan den Rijn, 1969. pp. 11.

- Netherlands Antilles

   WALBOOM (K.F.) Belastingen in de Nederlandse Antillen:
   belastingheffen en fiscale faciliteiten meer
   in het bijzonder ten aanzien van Antilliaanse
   Naamloze Vennootschappen. Deventer, 1970. pp.
   120.

- Norway

   NORWAY. Finans- og Tolldepartementet. Skattelovutvalget. 1948-56. Innstilling fra
   Skattelovutvalget 1947 I-(III; and Uttalelser
   om innstilling III). Oslo, 1948-56. 4 pts.

   NORWAY. Finans- og Tolldepartementet. 1961. The
   general lines of Norwegian tax policy; (translation of chapter 11: summary and recommendations,
   of a Parliamentary report, St. meld. nr.54,
   1960-61). [Oslo, 1961]. fo. 26.

   NORWAY. Finans-og Tollepartementet. Tax Law
   Department. 1970. Taxes in Norway. [Oslo,
   1970]. pp. 142.

- Poland

   GINTOWT-JANKOWICZ (MARIA) Odpowiedzialność po-
   datkowa członków rodziny podatnika i innych
   osób trzecich. Warszawa, 1973. pp. 162. bibliog.
   With Russian and French summaries.

- Rome, Ancient

   BADIAN (ERNST) Publicans and sinners: private
   enterprise in the service of the Roman republic.
   Oxford, 1972. pp. 170. bibliog. (Dunedin. University
   of Otago. De Carle Lectures. 1969)

- Russia

   SCHMIDT (WOLF DIETER) Zielkonformität der sowjetischen
   Betriebssteuern. Berlin, [1973]. pp. 153.
   bibliog. (Osteuropa-Institut, München. Veröffentlichungen. Reihe: Wirtschaft und Gesellschaft.
   Heft 13)

- Sweden

   SWEDEN. Finansdepartementet. Punktskatteutredning. 1970. Översyn av vissa punktskatter: de
   materiella reglerna; betänkande avgivet av
   1969 års punktskatteutredning. Stockholm,
   1970. pp. 96. (Sweden. Statens Offentliga
   Utredningar. 1970. 37)

   ELVANDER (NILS) Svensk skattepolitik, 1945-1970:
   en studie i partiers och organisationers funktioner
   [Stockholm, 1972]. pp. 406.

- Sweden - Law

   LINDENCRONA (GUSTAF) Skatter och kapitalflykt,
   etc. Stockholm, 1972. pp. 470. bibliog. With
   English summary.

- Switzerland

   SWITZERLAND. Administration Fédérale des Contributions.
   Eidg[enössische] Wehrsteuer. a., 1967/8 (14.)-
   Bern. [in German and French] Earlier issues are
   to be found in the series SWITZERLAND. Bureau
   Fédéral de Statistique. Statistiques de la Suisse
   which see.

   SWITZERLAND. Bureau Fédéral de Statistique. Statistiques de la Suisse. 408e fasc. Eidg. Wehrsteuer:
   Statistik der 12. Periode, 1963-64; Impôt
   fédéral pour la défense nationale: statistique
   de la 12e période, 1963-64. Berne, 1967.
   pp. 38.

   SWITZERLAND. Bureau Fédéral de Statistique. Statistiques de la Suisse. 443e fasc. Eidg. Wehrsteuer:
   Statistik der 13. Periode (1965-66); Impôt fédéral
   pour la défense nationale:statistique de la 13e
   période (1965-66). Bern, 1969. pp. 38.

- Switzerland - Aargau (Canton)

   BIERI (MARKUS) Geschichte der aargauischen Steuern
   von 1803-1968, insbesondere der direkten Staats-
   steuer. [Aarau, imprint, 1972]. pp. 387. bibliog.

- Uganda

   UGANDA. Ministry of Finance. 1968. Government
   White Paper on the Tax Inquiry report, 1964/65.
   Entebbe, 1968. pp. 12. (Sessional Papers.
   1968. No. 1)

TAXATION - Underdeveloped areas
   See UNDERDEVELOPED AREAS - Taxation

- United Kingdom

   U.K. Central Office of Information. Reference
   Division. Reference Pamphlets. 10. The British
   system of taxation. 7th ed. London, 1971.
   pp. 68. bibliog.

   CRICK (BERNARD ROWLAND) and ROBSON (WILLIAM
   ALEXANDER) eds. Taxation policy. Harmondsworth,
   1973. pp. 200.

   DOSSER (DOUGLAS G.M.) and others. British taxation
   and the Common Market: a volume of essays. London, 1973. pp. 180.

   KINCAID (J.C.) Poverty and equality in Britain:
   a study of social security and taxation. Harmondsworth, 1973. pp. 278.

   OULTON (NICHOLAS) Tariffs, taxes and trade in
   the UK: the effective protection approach.
   London, H.M.S.O., 1973. pp. 20. bibliog.
   (Government Economic Service Occasional Papers.
   6)

   U.K. Central Office of Information. Reference
   Division. Reference Pamphlets. 112. The new
   British system of taxation. London, 1973. pp.
   57. bibliog.

- United Kingdom - Law

   WILLIAMS (R. GLYNNE) Comprehensive aspects of
   taxation; revised by B. Mendes. 30th ed. London,
   [1971]. pp. 530.

   MELLOWS (ANTHONY ROGER) Taxation for executors
   and trustees. 3rd ed. London, 1972. pp. 140.

TAXATION - United Kingdom - Law (Cont'd.)

   PINSON (BARRY) Revenue law; comprising income tax, capital gains tax, corporation tax, estate duty, stamp duties, tax and estate planning; and including a section on value added tax by John Gardiner. London, 1972. pp. 690.

   SILKE (AUBREY SAMUEL) and SINCLAIR (W.I.) The Hambro tax guide, 1972/73; consulting editor G.S.A. Wheatcroft. London, 1972. pp. 205.

   STANLEY (OLIVER) Taxology: the perpetual battle of wits between the Inland Revenue and the taxpayer. London, [1972]. pp. 189.

   EASSON (A.J.) Cases and materials in revenue law. London, 1973. pp. 544.

- United States

   TAX INSTITUTE OF AMERICA. Symposium, 1969. Tax incentives;... [by] Stanley S. Surrey [and others]. Lexington, [1971]. pp. 303.

   THUROW (LESTER C.) The impact of taxes on the American economy. New York, 1971. pp. 171.

   FEDERAL taxation as an instrument of social and economic policy: a symposium; [by] Irving J. Goffman [and others]. New York, 1972. pp. 97. (Reprinted from the University of Florida Law Review, vol. 20, no.4)

   SINGER (NEIL M.) Public microeconomics. Boston, [1972]. pp. 329. bibliogs.

   MUSGRAVE (RICHARD ABEL) ed. Broad-based taxes: new options and sources;...[by] Harvey E. Brazer [and others]. Baltimore, 1973. pp. 302. (Committee for Economic Development. Supplementary Papers. No.38)

   PHARES (DONALD) State-local tax equity: an empirical analysis of the fifty states. Lexington, Mass., [1973]. pp. 185. bibliog.

- United States - New Jersey.

   NEW YORK (STATE). Bureau of Business Research. 1961. Tax structure of New Jersey. Albany, 1961. fo. 4.

- United States - New York

   NEW YORK (STATE). Department of Audit and Control. 1961. 1959 tax atlas of New York State. [Albany], 1961. pp. 156. (Comptroller's Studies in Local Finance. No. 2)

TAXATION, EXEMPTION FROM

- France

   TOURNIE (GERARD) Les agréments fiscaux: la fiscalité au service du plan. [Toulouse, imprint, 1970]. pp. 340. bibliog.

TAXATION OF BONDS, SECURITIES, ETC.

   INTERNATIONAL CONFERENCE ON CORPORATE AND SHAREHOLDER TAXATION, AMSTERDAM, 1972. Corporate and shareholder taxation: [papers of] conference organised jointly by Associated Business Programmes Limited and International Bureau of Fiscal Documentation. London, [1972]. 1 vol. (various pagings).

TAXES, FARMING OF

- France

   DURAND (YVES) Les fermiers généraux au XVIIIe siècle. Paris, 1971. pp. 664. bibliog. (Paris. Université. Faculté des Lettres et Sciences Humaines. Publications. Série "Recherches". Tome 70)

TAXICABS

   PAILHOUS (JEAN) La représentation de l'espace urbain: l'exemple du chauffeur de taxi. Paris, 1970. pp. 102. bibliog. Summaries in French and English.

TAYLER (WILLIAM)

   TAYLER (WILLIAM) 1807-1892. Diary of William Tayler, footman, 1837; edited by Dorothy Wise, with notes by Ann Cox-Johnson. London, [1962]. pp. 63.

TAYLOR (BERNARD) Baron Taylor of Mansfield
See TAYLOR (HARRY BERNARD) Baron Taylor of Mansfield

TAYLOR (HARRY BERNARD) Baron Taylor of Mansfield

   TAYLOR (HARRY BERNARD) Baron Taylor of Mansfield. Uphill all the way: a miner's struggle. London, 1972. pp. 200.

TAYLOR (JOHN) Publisher

   CHILCOTT (TIM) A publisher and his circle: the life and work of John Taylor, Keats's publisher. London, 1972. pp. 247. bibliog.

TBILISI

- Economic conditions

   DZHAOSHVILI (VAKHTANG SHALVOVICH) Tbilisi: ekonomiko-geograficheskii ocherk. Tbilisi, 1971. pp. 89.

TEA

- Kenya

   STERN (N.H.) An appraisal of tea production on small holdings in Kenya: an experiment with the Little-Mirrlees method. Paris, Organisation for Economic Co-operation and Development, 1972. pp. 134. bibliog. (Development Centre. Studies: Series on Cost-Benefit Analysis. Case Studies. No. 2).

- Russia - Georgia

   KARCHAVA (GRIGORII ZASIMOVICH) K istorii chainoi kul'tury v Gruzii. Tbilisi, 1972. pp. 119.

TEA TRADE

   SARKAR (GOUTAM K.) The world tea economy. Delhi, 1972. pp. 237. bibliog.

- Tanzania

   TANZANIA TEA AUTHORITY. Statistical report. a., 1970- Dar es Salaam.

TEACHER-STUDENT RELATIONSHIPS

   SCHMID (J.P.) Le maître-camarade et la pédagogie libertaire. Paris, 1971. pp. 212. bibliog.

SCHONFELD (WILLIAM R.) Youth and authority in France: a study of secondary schools. Beverly Hills, [1971]. pp. 77. bibliog.

TEACHERS

KENWORTHY (LEONARD S.) The teacher and the post-war child. Paris, [1946]. pp. 47.

UNITED NATIONS EDUCATIONAL, SCIENTIFIC AND CULTURAL ORGANIZATION. Educational Studies and Documents. New Series. No. 3. Teachers and educational policy. [Paris, 1971]. pp. 37.

- Recruiting - Canada

ROBSON (REGINALD ARTHUR HENRY) Sociological factors affecting recruitment into the academic profession. [Ottawa, Association of Universities and Colleges of Canada, 1966]. pp. (ii), 46. 25½cm. (Staffing the Universities and Colleges of Canada. No. 3) In English and French.

- Supply and demand - United Kingdom

NATIONAL ECONOMIC DEVELOPMENT COUNCIL. Management Education, Training and Development Committee. Second report on the supply of teachers for management education. London, National Economic Development Office, 1972. pp. 32.

- Botswana - Salaries, pensions, etc.

BOTSWANA. 1970. Botswana government's memorandum on the report of the Commission on the Salaries and Conditions of Service of the Public Service and the Teaching Service. Gaborone, 1970. pp. 43.

BOTSWANA. Commission on the Salaries and Conditions of Service of the Public Services and the Teaching Service. 1970. Report: [E.K. Okoh, commissioner]. Gaborone, 1970. 1 vol. (unpaged).

- Canada - Salaries, pensions, etc.

CANADA. Statistics Canada. Salaries of teachers in degree-granting institutions. a., 1971/2 [1st issue]- Ottawa. In English and French.

ROBSON (REGINALD ARTHUR HENRY) and LAPOINTE (MIREILLE) A comparison of men's and women's salaries and employment fringe benefits in the academic profession; prepared for the Canadian Association of University Teachers. Ottawa, 1971. pp. 39. (Canada. Royal Commission on the Status of Women in Canada. 1967. Studies. 1)

- France

ECOLE EMANCIPEE, L'. La répression dans l'enseignement. Paris, 1972. pp. 199.

DELANOUE (PAUL) Les enseignants: la lutte syndicale du Front populaire à la libération. Paris [1973]. pp. 414. bibliog.

- France - Legal status, laws, etc.

GUILLEMOTEAU (RENE) and MAYEUR (PIERRE) Traité de législation scolaire et universitaire. Tome 2. Le personnel de l'éducation nationale. Paris, [1970]. pp. 382.

- Germany

SEELIGER (ROLF) ed. Braune Universität: deutsche Hochschullehrer gestern und heute; Dokumentation mit Stellungnahmen. Heft 4. Westberlin. München, [1966]. pp. 123.

BLEUEL (HANS PETER) Deutschlands Bekenner: Professoren zwischen Kaiserreich und Diktatur. Bern, Scherz, [1968]. pp. 256. bibliog.

SEELIGER (ROLF) ed. Braune Universität: deutsche Hochschullehrer gestern und heute; Dokumentation mit Stellungnahmen. Heft 6. München, 1968. pp. 115.

- Kenya - Salaries, pensions, etc.

KENYA. 1962. Consideration of the recommendations contained in the report of the Kenya Teachers' Salaries Commission, Lawrence report, 1961. [Nairobi, 1962?]. pp. 8. (Sessional Papers. 1962/63. No. 1)

- Norway - Salaries, pensions, etc.

NORWAY. Kirke- og Undervisningsdepartementet. Laererlønnskomitéen. 1956. Innstilling fra...Laererlønnskomitéen av 1954. Oslo, 1956. pp. 182.

- Poland

FISZMAN (JOSEPH R.) Revolution and tradition in people's Poland: education and socialization. Princeton, N.J., [1972]. pp. 382. bibliog.

- Russia - Kazakstan - Legal status, laws, etc.

ZHANABILOV (ERKIN) Trudovye prava rabotnikov prosveshcheniia. Alma-Ata, 1964. pp. 112.

- Russia - Kazakstan - Salaries, pensions, etc.

ZHANABILOV (ERKIN) Trudovye prava rabotnikov prosveshcheniia. Alma-Ata, 1964. pp. 112.

- Russia - Latvia - Legal status, laws, etc.

LATVIA. Statutes, etc. 1960-70. Sbornik rukovodiashchikh i metodicheskikh materialov po voprosam okhrany truda v uchrezhdeniiakh sistemy Ministerstva prosveshcheniia Latv. SSR; sostavitel' Vasil'ev, I.E. 2nd ed. Riga, 1971. pp. 257.

- Sweden

SWEDEN. Utbildningsdepartementet. Utredningen rörande Lärarnas Arbetsförhållanden. 1971. Lärarnas arbete: en statistisk arbetstidsstudie. betänkande. Stockholm, 1971. 3 vols. (Sweden. Statens Offentliga Utredningar. 1971. 53-55)

- Uganda - Salaries, pensions, etc.

UGANDA. Teachers' Salaries Commission. 1961. Report; [B.E. Lawrence, chairman]. Entebbe, [1961]. pp. 64.

- United Kingdom

CALDER (ISLA) Our children's teachers. London, 1971. pp. 28. (Young Fabian Group. Young Fabian Pamphlets. 27)

TOWARDS insight: for the worker with people; papers given at Shotton Hall conferences...by W.H. Allchin and others. Shrewsbury, 1971. pp. 78.

VENABLES (ETHEL) Teachers and youth workers: a study of their roles; the report of a research project undertaken for the Schools Council. London, 1971. pp. 128. (U.K. Department of Education and Science. Schools Council. Working Papers. No. 32)

COMMITTEE OF VICE-CHANCELLORS AND PRINCIPALS OF THE UNIVERSITIES OF THE UNITED KINGDOM. Report of an enquiry into the use of academic staff time. London, [1972]. pp. 36.

TEACHERS - United Kingdom (Cont'd.)

U.K. Committee of Inquiry into the Disputes involving Teachers in the area of the Teesside Local Education Authority. 1973. Report; [John C. Wood, chairman]. London, 1973. pp. 38.

- United Kingdom - Salaries, pensions, etc.

U.K. Arbitral Body on Salaries for Teachers in Establishments for Further Education. 1971. Report. London, 1971. pp. 47.

U.K. Arbitral Body on Salaries of Teachers in Primary and Secondary Schools, England and Wales. 1971. Report. London, 1971. pp. 58.

U.K. Department of Education and Science. 1971. Scales of salaries for teachers in primary and secondary schools, England and Wales, 1971; being the document prepared...under sections 2 and 4 of the Remuneration of Teachers Act, 1965, setting out the scales of salaries and other provisions for determining the remuneration of teachers in primary and secondary schools maintained by local education authorities. London, 1971. pp. 65.

U.K. Arbitral Body on Salaries of Teachers in Primary and Secondary Schools, England and Wales. 1972. Report. London, 1972. pp. 29.

U.K. Department of Education and Science, 1972. Scales of salaries for teachers in establishments for further education, England and Wales, 1971... (other than farm institutes). London, 1972. pp. 60.

U.K. Department of Education and Science, 1972. Scales of salaries for teachers in establishments for further education, England and Wales, 1972... (other than farm institutes). London, 1972. pp. 42.

U.K. Department of Education and Science. 1972. Scales of salaries for teachers in primary and secondary schools, England and Wales, 1972; being the document...setting out the scales of salaries and other provisions for determining the remuneration of teachers in primary and secondary schools maintained by local education authorities. London, 1972. pp. 51.

U.K. Department of Education and Science. 1972. Scales of salaries for the teaching staff of farm institutes and for teachers of agricultural (including horticultural) subjects, England and Wales, 1971. London, 1972. pp. 25.

U.K. Department of Education and Science. 1972. Scales of salaries for the teaching staff of farm institutes and for teachers of agricultural (including horticultural) subjects, England and Wales, 1972. London, 1972. pp. 25.

U.K. Department of Education and Science. Committee on Sales of Salaries for the Teaching Staff of Colleges of Education, England and Wales. 1972. Report. London, 1972. pp. 15.

U.K. Department of Education and Science. 1973. Scales of salaries for teachers in establishments for further education, England and Wales, 1973... (other than farm institutes). London, 1973. pp. 42.

U.K. Department of Education and Science. 1973. Scales of salaries for teachers in primary and secondary schools, England and Wales, 1973; being the document...setting out the scales of salaries and other provisions for determining the remuneration of teachers in primary and secondary schools maintained by local education authorities. London, 1973. pp. 53.

- United Kingdom - Scotland

SCOTLAND. Scottish Education Department. 1971. The structure of promoted posts in secondary schools in Scotland: a document for discussion memorandum. Edinburgh, 1971. pp. 60.

SCOTLAND. Scottish Education Department. 1972. Secondary schools staffing survey, 1970. [Edinburgh] 1972 in progress.

- United Kingdom - Scotland - Salaries, pensions, etc.

SCOTLAND. Scottish Education Department. 1973. Scottish teachers salaries memorandum, 1973... setting out the scales and other provisions required for determining the remuneration of teachers employed by education authorities in Scotland. Edinburgh, 1973. pp. 62.

- United Kingdom - Scotland - Selection and appointment

U.K. Privy Council. Scottish Universities Committee. 1968. Education (Scotland) Act, 1962: the Montague Burton Chair of International Relations (Amendment) Scheme, 1968. London, 1968. pp. 3.

- United States

UNITED STATES. Education Office. Staffing American colleges and universities: the demand for...staff in higher education, Nov. 1963 through Oct. 1969. Washington, 1967. pp. x, 220.

EBLE (KENNETH E.) Professors as teachers. San Francisco, 1972. pp. 202. bibliog.

FACULTY power: collective bargaining on campus; [based papers of the national conference held in 1971 by the Institute of Continuing Legal Education]; editor, Terrence N. Tice. Ann Arbor, [1972]. pp. 368. bibliog.

HOULT (THOMAS FORD) The march to the right: a case study in political repression. Cambridge, Mass., [1972]. pp. 287.

MYERS (DONALD A.) Teacher power: professionalization and collective bargaining. Lexington, Mass., [1973]. pp. 197. bibliog.

- United States - Tenure

COMMISSION ON ACADEMIC TENURE IN HIGHER EDUCATION. Faculty tenure: (a report and recommendations). San Francisco, 1973. pp. 276. bibliog.

SMITH (BARDWELL L.) ed. The tenure debate. San Francisco, 1973. pp. 254.

TEACHERS, TRAINING OF

- France

ELIADE (BERNARD) L'école ouverte: témoignages et propositions pour aider à la mise en place d'une éducation permanente et populaire. Paris, [1970]. pp. 253. bibliog.

- Ireland (Republic)

EIRE. Higher Education Authority. 1970. Report to the Minister for Education on teacher education. Dublin, 1970. pp. 41.

- Kenya

LINNÉ (OLGA) An evaluation of the Kenya Science Teachers College. Uppsala, 1972. pp. 67. bibliog. (Nordiska Afrikainstitutet. Research Reports. No. 10)

- United Kingdom

RICH (ROWLAND WILLIAM) The training of teachers in England and Wales during the nineteenth century; [first published in Cambridge, 1933]. Bath, 1972. pp. 286. bibliog.

COMMUNITY RELATIONS COMMISSION. Advisory Committee on Education. Education for a multi-cultural society. 1. Syllabuses. [London, 1970]. fo. 50.

U.K. Central Office of Information. Reference Division. 1971. Teacher training in Britain. rev. ed. London, 1971. pp. 34. bibliog.

WILLEY (FREDERICK THOMAS) and MADDISON (R.E.) An enquiry into teacher training. London, [1971]. pp. 112. bibliogs.

COMMUNITY RELATIONS COMMISSION. Advisory Committee on Education. Education for a multi-cultural society. 2. Language; by Christopher Candlin and June Derrick. [London, 1972]. pp. 67. bibliog.

LONDON. University. Institute of Education. Council. The education and training of teachers: a statement...on the James report. [London], 1972. pp. 14.

N.O.P. MARKET RESEARCH. Attitudes to the James report: a report prepared for The Times Educational Supplement and The Times Higher Education Supplement. [London, 1972]. fo. 18,4.

PARRY (J.P.) The Lord James tricycle: some notes on teacher education and training. London, 1972. pp. 115.

U.K. Teacher Training Inquiry. 1972. Teacher education and training; report...; under the chairmanship of Lord James of Rusholme. London, 1972. pp. 128.

LOMAX (DONALD ERNEST) ed. The education of teachers in Britain. London, [1973]. pp. 467. bibliog.

- United Kingdom - Scotland

GENERAL TEACHING COUNCIL FOR SCOTLAND. Working Party on the Training of Graduates for Secondary Education. The training of graduates for secondary education; a report submitted...to the Secretary of State for Scotland; [J.S. Brunton, chairman]. Edinburgh, H.M.S.O., 1972. pp. 67.

- United Kingdom - British Empire

DODD (WILLIAM ATHERTON) Teacher education in the developing countries of the Commonwealth: a survey of recent trends. [London, Commonwealth Secretariat, 1970]. pp. 77. bibliog.

- United States

CORWIN (RONALD G.) Reform and organizational survival: the teacher corps as an instrument of educational change. New York, [1973]. pp. 469. bibliog.

TEACHERS' COLLEGES

- Ghana

GHANA. Committee appointed...to consider the Problem created by the Closure of Inefficient Schools. 1929. Report and recommendations; [W.J.A. Jones, chairman]. Sessional paper No. 21 of 1928-29. in GHANA. Legislative Council. Minutes (formerly Minutes...and sessional papers).

- United Kingdom - Bibliography

BERRY (MICHAEL) Teacher training institutions in England and Wales: a bibliographical guide to their history. London, 1973. pp. 146. (Society for Research into Higher Education. Research into Higher Education Monographs. 18)

TEACHERS' UNIONS

- United Kingdom

BOURNE (RICHARD) and MACARTHUR (BRIAN) The struggle for education, 1870-1970: a pictorial history of popular education and the National Union of Teachers. London, [1970]. pp. 128.

COATES (R.D.) Teachers' unions and interest group politics: a study in the behaviour of organised teachers in England and Wales. Cambridge, 1972. pp. 138. bibliog.

GOSDEN (PETER HENRY JOHN HEATHER) The evolution of a profession: a study of the contribution of teachers' associations to the development of school teaching as a professional occupation. Oxford, [1972]. pp. 372. bibliog.

- United States

BRAUN (ROBERT J.) Teachers and power: the story of the American Federation of Teachers. New York, [1972]. pp. 287.

TEACHING

CORY (WILLIAM) On the education of the reasoning faculties; [reprint of work first published in 1867]. New York, 1964. pp. 59.

MAGER (ROBERT F.) Developing attitude toward learning. Belmont, [1968]. pp. 104. bibliog.

HENDERSON (NORMAN K.) University teaching. Hong Kong, 1969. pp. 170. bibliog.

DAVIES (IVOR K.) The management of learning. London, [1971]. pp. 256. bibliogs.

FALK (BARBARA) and LEE DOW (KWONG) The assessment of university teaching. London, 1971. pp. 47. bibliog. (Society for Research into Higher Education. Research into Higher Education Monographs. 16)

ROE (ERNEST) Some dilemmas of teaching. Melbourne, 1971. pp. 183. bibliog.

ROSE (BRIAN) ed. Modern trends in education. London, 1971. pp. 295. bibliog.

- Aids and devices

CANADA. Statistics Canada. Instructional media in universities of the Atlantic provinces. a., current issues only kept. Ottawa.

- Research

BEARD (RUTH M.) and BLIGH (DONALD A.) Research into teaching methods in higher education, mainly in British universities. 3rd ed. London, 1971. pp. 104. bibliog. (Society for Research into Higher Education. Research into Higher Education Monographs. 2)

TEACHING, FREEDOM OF

ANASTAPLO (GEORGE) The constitutionalist: notes on the first amendment. Dallas, [1971]. pp. 826.

- United Kingdom

COUNCIL FOR ACADEMIC FREEDOM AND DEMOCRACY. The Bolton dismissals: the findings of a commission of inquiry...in January 1971. London, [1971]. pp. 16.

- United States

HOOK (SIDNEY) Academic freedom and academic anarchy. New York, [1970]. pp. 269.

HOOK (SIDNEY) ed. In defense of academic freedom. New York, [1971]. pp. 266.

TEACHING AS A PROFESSION

MYERS (DONALD A.) Teacher power: professionalization and collective bargaining. Lexington, Mass., [1973]. pp. 197. bibliog.

TEACHING MACHINES

LUMSDAINE (ARTHUR A.) and GLASER (ROBERT) eds. Teaching machines and programmed learning: a source book. Washington, 1960 repr. 1962. pp. 724. bibliog.

SMALLWOOD (RICHARD D.) A decision structure for teaching machines. Cambridge, Mass., 1962. pp. 122. bibliog.

TECHNICAL ASSISTANCE

CHUDSON (WALTER A.) The international transfer of commercial technology to developing countries. New York, United Nations Institute for Training and Research, 1971. pp. 58, 3. (Research Reports. No. 13.)

EPPLER (ERHARD) Not much time for the Third World; translated from the German by Gerard Finan. London, [1972]. pp. 143. bibliog.

RICHMAN (BARRY M.) and COPEN (MELVYN R.) International management and economic development; with particular reference to India and other developing countries. New York, [1972]. pp. 681.

TECHNICAL ASSISTANCE, AMERICAN

CHANG (Y.S.) The transfer of technology: economics of offshore assembly; the case of semiconductor industry. New York, United Nations Institute for Training and Research, 1971. pp. 59. (Research Reports. No. 11)

POATS (RUTHERFORD M.) Technology for developing nations: new directions for U.S. technical assistance. Washington, [1972]. pp. 255.

PADDOCK (WILLIAM) and PADDOCK (ELIZABETH) We don't know how: an independent audit of what they call success in foreign assistance. Ames, 1973. pp. 331.

TECHNICAL ASSISTANCE, BRITISH

U.K. Overseas Development Administration. 1971. An account of the British aid programme: text of United Kingdom memorandum to the Development Assistance Committee of the Organisation for Economic Co-operation and Development. London, 1971. pp. 31.

U.K. Central Office of Information. Reference Division. Reference Pamphlets. 103. Britain and the developing countries: research institutions. London, 1972. pp. 44.

- Colombia

COLOMBIA. Departamento Nacional de Planeacion, 1970. Asistencia tecnica bilateral a Colombia proveniente del gobierno de Gran Bretaña e Irlanda del Norte. [Bogota], 1970. fo. 21.

TECHNICAL ASSISTANCE, DANISH

BETAENKNING om Danmarks samarbejde med udviklingslandene, afgivet af det af regeringen den 2. april 1969 nedsatte udvalg; [Jens Christensen, chairman]. København, 1970. pp. 248. (Denmark. Betaenkninger. Nr. 565)

TECHNICAL ASSISTANCE, DUTCH

NETHERLANDS. Centraal Planbureau. 1969. Varianten voor de ontwikkelingshulp door de overheid: een macro-economische analyse. 's-Gravenhage, 1969. pp. 27. (Monografieën. No. 11)

TECHNICAL ASSISTANCE, FRENCH

- Africa

FRANCE. Direction de la Documentation. La Documentation Française. Notes et Etudes Documentaires. No.3,330. La coopération entre la France, l'Afrique Noire d'expression française et Madagascar. Paris, 1966. pp. 47. bibliog.

FRANCE. French Embassy, London. Service de Presse et d'Information. 1971. French cooperation in Africa and in the Indian Ocean. London, [1971]. pp. 29.

FRANCE. Secrétariat d'Etat aux Affaires Etrangères. Service d'Information et de Presse. 1972. La coopération entre la France et les états francophones d'Afrique Noire et de l'Océan Indien. [Paris], 1972. pp. 66.

- Algeria

FRANCE. Direction de la Documentation. La Documentation Française. Notes et Etudes Documentaires. No.3,252. La coopération culturelle et technique entre la France et l'Algérie, juillet 1962 - juin 1965. Paris, 1966. pp. 55.

- Madagascar

FRANCE. Direction de la Documentation. La Documentation Française. Notes et Etudes Documentaires. No.3,330. La coopération entre la France, l'Afrique Noire d'expression française et Madagascar. Paris, 1966. pp. 47. bibliog.

TECHNICAL ASSISTANCE, JAPANESE

OZAWA (TERUTOMO) Transfer of technology from Japan to developing countries. New York, United Nations Institute for Training and Research, 1971. pp. 50. (Research Reports. No. 7)

TECHNICAL ASSISTANCE, RUSSIAN

- India

DESAI (PADMA) The Bokaro steel plant: a study of Soviet economic assistance. Amsterdam, 1972. pp. 108.

TECHNICAL ASSISTANCE IN AFRICA

BARTOLUCCI (ENRICO) Africa: seconda independenza. Bologna, 1970. pp. 144. bibliog.

EXPERIENCES de développement rural en Afrique tropicale: documents de la conférence régionale européenne de l'Association pour le Développement International...tenue à Paris en Octobre 1968. Paris, [1970?]. 2 vols. (in 1).

TECHNICAL ASSISTANCE IN COMMUNIST COUNTRIES

BYKOV (ALEKSANDR NAUMOVICH) Nauchno-tekhnicheskie sviazi stran sotsializma: etapy, formy, metody i tendentsii razvitiia. Moskva, 1970. pp. 222.

TECHNICAL ASSISTANCE IN INDIA

BALASUBRAMANYAM (V.N.) International transfer of technology to India. New York, 1973. pp. 143.

TECHNICAL ASSISTANCE IN IRAN

CENTRAL TREATY ORGANIZATION. Public Relations Division. 1960. One approach to a better life: CENTO technical assistance. Ankara, [1960]. 1 pamphlet (unpaged).

TECHNICAL ASSISTANCE IN LATIN AMERICA

INSTITUTO LATINOAMERICANO DE INVESTIGACIONES SOCIALES. Seminario Internacional, 3°, 1971. Inversiones extranjeras y transferencia de tecnologia en America Latina: sesiones del seminario realizado en Santiago de Chile del 24 al 30 de octubre de 1971; [organized jointly with the Escuela Latinoamericana de Ciencia Politica y Administracion Publica]; Karl-Heinz Stanzick y Horacio H. Godoy, editores. Santiago de Chile, 1972. pp. 560.

TECHNICAL ASSISTANCE IN MEXICO

MASON (R. HAL) The transfer of technology and the factor proportions problem: the Philippines and Mexico. New York, United Nations Institute for Training and Research, [1971]. pp. 101. (Research Reports. No. 10)

TECHNICAL ASSISTANCE IN PAKISTAN

CENTRAL TREATY ORGANIZATION. Public Relations Division. 1960. One approach to a better life: CENTO technical assistance. Ankara, [1960]. 1 pamphlet (unpaged).

TECHNICAL ASSISTANCE IN SPAIN

ORGANISATION FOR ECONOMIC CO-OPERATION AND DEVELOPMENT. 1971. OECD technical assistance to the Centre for Agricultural Research and Development of the Ebro region. (Spain). Paris, 1971. pp. 103. (Technical Assistance Evaluation Studies)

TECHNICAL ASSISTANCE IN THE PHILIPPINE ISLANDS

MASON (R. HAL) The transfer of technology and the factor proportions problem: the Philippines and Mexico. New York, United Nations Institute for Training and Research, [1971]. pp. 101. (Research Reports. No. 10)

TECHNICAL ASSISTANCE IN TURKEY

CENTRAL TREATY ORGANIZATION. Public Relations Division. 1960. One approach to a better life: CENTO technical assistance. Ankara, [1960]. 1 pamphlet (unpaged).

TECHNICAL EDUCATION

UNITED NATIONS EDUCATIONAL, SCIENTIFIC AND CULTURAL ORGANIZATION. 1964. Technical and vocational education and training: recommendations by Unesco and the International Labour Organisation. Paris, 1964. pp. 36.

- Bibliography

UNITED NATIONS EDUCATIONAL, SCIENTIFIC AND CULTURAL ORGANIZATION. 1959. An international bibliography of technical and vocational education. [Paris, 1959]. pp. 72. (Educational Studies and Documents. No. 31)

- America, Latin

CONGRESO IBEROAMERICANO DE PROMOCION PROFESIONAL DE LA MANO DE OBRA, 1°, MADRID, 1967. I Congreso Iberoamericano de Promocion Profesional de la Mano de Obra: [proceedings]. [Madrid, 1967]. 2 vols.

- Argentine Republic

MATON (JEF) Le enseñanza tecnica industrial en la Argentina: oferta y demanda, 1960-1980; version castellana de Pedro Daniel Weinberg. Buenos Aires, 1967 repr. 1969. pp. 68. (Instituto Torcuato Di Tella. Centro de Investigaciones Economicas. Documentos de Trabajo. 33)

- Australia

MORTENSEN (K.G.) Planning for technological change in Australia. East St. Kilda, Australia, 1971. pp. 151. bibliog.

- Brazil

ECONOMIST INTELLIGENCE UNIT. Secondary technical and vocational education in underdeveloped countries. [Paris, 1959]. pp. 34. (United Nations Educational, Scientific and Cultural Organization. Educational Studies and Documents. No. 33)

BRAZIL. Superintendência do Desenvolvimento do Nordeste. Departamento de Assistência Tecnica e Formação de Pessoal. 1962. Programa de treinamento industrial. Recife, 1962. pp. 31.

- Europe

ORGANISATION FOR ECONOMIC CO-OPERATION AND DEVELOPMENT. 1965. Inventory of training possibilities in Europe. Paris, [1965]. pp. 896. bibliog.

- Ghana

ECONOMIST INTELLIGENCE UNIT. Secondary technical and vocational education in underdeveloped countries. [Paris, 1959]. pp. 34. (United Nations Educational, Scientific and Cultural Organization. Educational Studies and Documents. No. 33)

- Ireland (Republic)

EIRE. Higher Education Authority. 1972. Report on the Ballymun project. Dublin, 1972. pp. 101.

- Norway

NORWAY. Kirke- og Undervisningsdepartementet. 1957. Om tilgangen på og behovet for akademisk utdannet arbeidskraft. [Oslo], 1957. pp. 5. (Norway. Stortinget. Stortingsmeldinger. 1957, nr. 72)

- Philippine Islands

ECONOMIST INTELLIGENCE UNIT. Secondary technical and vocational education in underdeveloped countries. [Paris, 1959]. pp. 34. (United Nations Educational, Scientific and Cultural Organization. Educational Studies and Documents. No. 33)

- Poland

UNITED NATIONS EDUCATIONAL, SCIENTIFIC AND CULTURAL ORGANIZATION. Department of Mass Communication. Reports and Papers on Mass Communication. No.67. Television for higher technical education of workers: final report on a pilot project in Poland. Paris, 1973. pp. 73.

- Russia

SHAPOVALENKO (SERGEI GRIGOR'EVICH) ed. Polytechnical education in the U.S.S.R. Paris, 1963. pp. 433. bibliog. (United Nations Educational, Scientific and Cultural Organization. Monographs on Education. 3)

TECHNICAL EDUCATION - Russia (Cont'd.)

INTERNATIONAL LABOUR OFFICE. Development Programme: Technical Assistance Sector. [International]. R.15. Informe del viaje de estudio interregional sobre la formacion profesional en la U.R.S.S., 26 de mayo- 21 de junio de 1968. (OIT/TAP/INT/R.15) Ginebra, 1968. pp. 72.

- Russia - Bibliography

MOVSHOVICH (M.I.) Technical and vocational education in the U.S.S.R: a bibliographical survey. [Paris, 1959]. pp. 53. (United Nations Educational, Scientific and Cultural Organization. Educational Studies and Documents. No. 30)

- Russia - Moldavian Republic

GRU (VLADIMIR MIKHAILOVICH) Professional'no-tekhnicheskoe obrazovanie v Moldavskoi SSR, 1941-1965 gg.; pod redaktsiei... A.M.Lazareva. Kishinev, 1972. pp. 199.

- Russia - White Russia

MAKSIMOV (L.G.) ed. Ocherki razvitiia professional'no-tekhnicheskogo obrazovaniia v BSSR. Minsk, 1973. pp. 334.

- Spain

CONGRESO IBEROAMERICANO DE PROMOCION PROFESIONAL DE LA MANO DE OBRA, 1°, MADRID, 1967. I Congreso Iberoamericano de Promocion Profesional de la Mano de Obra: [proceedings]. [Madrid, 1967]. 2 vols.

ORGANISATION FOR ECONOMIC CO-OPERATION AND DEVELOPMENT. Directorate for Scientific Affairs. 1968. Design for technological education: the Escuela Tecnica Superior de Ingenieros Industriales of Seville. Paris, 1968. pp. 313. bibliogs.

- Turkey

INTERNATIONAL LABOUR OFFICE. Development Programme. Technical Assistance Sector. [Turkey]. R.30. Rapport au gouvernement de la Turquie sur le développement du programme de la formation dans l'entreprise. (OIT/TAP/Turquie/R.30). Genève, 1970. pp. 22.

- United Kingdom

CARDWELL (DONALD STEPHEN LOWELL) The organisation of science in England. rev. ed. London, 1972. pp. 268. bibliogs.

DAY (NORMAN L.) Further education and employment: a case study of technical education and industrial employment. London, 1972. pp. 91. (Society for Research into Higher Education. Research into Higher Education Monographs. 17)

RODERICK (GORDON W.) and STEPHENS (MICHAEL D.) Scientific and technical education in nineteenth-century England. Newton Abbot, [1972]. pp. 173.

U.K. Department of Employment. 1972. Training for the future: a plan for discussion. [London, 1972]. pp. 80.

TIPTON (BERYL FRANCES A.) Conflict and change in a technical college. London, 1973. pp. 131. bibliog. (Brunel University. Brunel Further Education Monographs. 6)

- United Kingdom - Directories

FREEMAN (RICHARD) Writer on education, compiler. Industrial scholarships and training schemes. 2nd ed. Cambridge, 1971. pp. 47. (Advisory Centre for Education. ACE Educational Booklets. No. 3)

- United States

HEDGES (ANNA CHARLOTTE) Wage worth of school training: an analytical study of six hundred women workers in textile factories. New York, 1914. pp. 174. bibliog.

- United States - Bibliography

UNITED STATES. Office of Education. 1959. Technical and vocational education in the U.S.A.: a bibliographical survey. [Paris, 1959]. pp. 24. (United Nations Educational, Scientific and Cultural Organization. Educational Studies and Documents. No. 36)

- Venezuela

ROTHER (KLAUS) Wirtschaft und Berufserziehung in Venezuela. Berlin, 1972. pp. 118. bibliog. (Ibero-Amerikanisches Institut. Veröffentlichungen. Bibliotheca Ibero-Americana. Band 16)

TECHNICIANS IN INDUSTRY

- United Kingdom

ENGINEERING INDUSTRY TRAINING BOARD [U.K.] The technician in engineering: report of a survey of the employment, recruitment and qualifications of technicians in the engineering industry, 1969. [London], 1970. pp. 88. (Research Reports. No.1)

COMMISSION ON INDUSTRIAL RELATIONS [U.K.]. C.A. Parsons and Co. Limited and associated companies. London, H.M.S.O., 1972. pp. 31. (Reports. No. 32)

ROBERTS (BENJAMIN CHARLES) and others. Reluctant militants: a study of industrial technicians. London, 1972. pp. 342. bibliog. (London. University. London School of Economics and Political Science. Industrial Relations Series)

TECHNOCRACY

NADEL' (S.N.) Nauchno-tekhnicheskaia intelligentsiia v sovremennom burzhuaznom obshchestve. Moskva, 1971. pp. 193.

TECHNOLOGICAL FORECASTING

NAUKOVEDENIE, prognozirovanie, informatika. Kiev, 1970. pp. 348.

CETRON (MARVIN J.) and RALPH (CHRISTINE A.) Industrial applications of technological forecasting: its utilization in R and D management. New York, [1971]. pp. 563. bibliog.

COUNCIL FOR MUTUAL ECONOMIC ASSISTANCE. Permanent Commission for the Coordination of Scientific and Technical Research. Teoriia i praktika prognozirovaniia razvitiia nauki i tekhniki v stranakh-chlenakh SEV. Moskva, 1971. pp. 407.

GUSTAVUS ADOLPHUS COLLEGE. Nobel Conference, 7th, 1971. Shaping the future: a discussion at the Nobel Conference;...edited by John D. Roslansky. Amsterdam, 1972. pp. 101.

JANTSCH (ERICH) Technological planning and social futures. London, 1972. pp. 256. bibliog.

ROBINSON (COLIN) The technology of forecasting and the forecasting of technology. Guildford, [1972]. pp. 26. (University of Surrey. Surrey Papers in Economics. No. 7)

MUELLER (JAN) Bedarf der Unternehmen an technologischen Vorausschätzungen. Berlin, [1973]. pp. 174. bibliog. (Ifo-Institut für Wirtschaftsforschung. Schriftenreihe. Nr.80)

TECHNOLOGICAL INNOVATIONS

IVANOV (K.) and BATSANOV (B.) Vzgliad v zavtra. Moskva, 1964. pp. 203.

TOVMASIAN (STEPAN SURENOVICH) Trud i tekhnika: ocherk filosofskikh problem. Erevan, 1965. pp. 237.

SVILUPPO tecnologico ed occupazione; [proceedings of a conference organised by the](Unione Italiana delle Camere di Commercio, Industria, Artigianato e Agricoltura), Roma, 14-15 novembre 1968. [Rome, 1968?]. pp. 222.

FERRARO (PIETRO) Progresso tecnico, ventagli di produttività e sviluppo: un'economia alle soglie del futuro. Milano, [1970]. pp. 512.

GOMULKA (STANISLAW) Inventive activity, diffusion, and the stages of economic growth. Aarhus, 1971. pp. 82. bibliog. (Aarhus. Universitet. Økonomiske Institut. Skrifter. Nr. 24)

KATZENSTEIN (ROBERT) Technischer Fortschritt: Kapitalbewegung, Kapitalfixierung, etc. Berlin, 1971. pp. 222.

KONJUNKTURPOLITIK: Zeitschrift für angewandte Konjunkturforschung. Beihefte. Heft 18. Wirtschaftlicher und sozialer Wandel durch technischen Fortschritt: Bericht über den wissenschaftlichen Teil der 34. Mitgliederversammlung der Arbeitsgemeinschaft deutscher wirtschaftswissenschaftlicher Forschungsinstitute...1971. Berlin, [1971]. pp. 194.

MESARIĆ (MILAN) Suvremena znanstveno-tehnička revolucija. Zagreb, 1971. pp. 169. bibliog. With English and Russian summaries.

PAVITT (KEITH) and WALD (SALOMON) The conditions for success in technological innovation. Paris, 1971. pp. 169. bibliogs.

BREWER (GARRY D.) On innovation, social change and reality: (abstract). [Santa Monica], 1972. pp. 9. (Rand Corporation. [Papers]. 4876)

FUNK (LEBERECHT FRANZ THEODOR) Die technologische Entwicklung und ihre risikopolitischen Konsequenzen für die Industrie-Versicherung. Hamburg, 1972. pp. 163. bibliog.

JANTSCH (ERICH) Technological planning and social futures. London, 1972. pp. 256. bibliog.

POPULATION growth: anthropological implications; proceedings of a colloquium... entitled "Population resources, and technology" held at the University of Pennsylvania... 1970, under the... auspices of the Near East Center [and others]; edited by Brian Spooner. Cambridge, Mass., [1972]. pp. 425. bibliog.

SKOLNIKOFF (EUGENE B.) The international imperatives of technology: technological development and the international political system. Berkeley, [1972]. pp. 194. bibliog. (California University. Institute of International Studies. Research Series. No.16)

SOLO (ROBERT A.) and ROGERS (EVERETT MITCHELL) eds. Inducing technological change for economic growth and development: [papers of a graduate seminar held at Michigan State University in 1968]. [East Lansing, Mich.], 1972. pp. 237.

UNITED NATIONS. Advisory Committee on the Application of Science and Technology to Development. 1972. Appropriate technology and research for industrial development; report of the Advisory Committee...on two aspects of industrial growth. (ST/ECA/152). New York, 1972. pp. 51.

HETZLER (STANLEY A.) Applied measures for promoting technological growth. London, 1973. pp. 337. bibliogs.

NORRIS (KEITH) and VAIZEY (JOHN ERNEST) The economics of research and technology. London, 1973. pp. 172.

TECHNOLOGICAL INNOVATIONS
See also the subheading - Technological innovations under the names of particular industries

- Mathematical models

BOSWORTH (DEREK L.) Changes in the quality of inventive output and patent based indices of technological change. Coventry, 1972. fo. 13, 2. (University of Warwick. Centre for Industrial Economic and Business Research. Warwick Research in Industrial and Business Studies. No.17)

- Social aspects

INTERNATIONAL LABOUR ORGANISATION. Committee on Work on Plantations. 6th Session. Reports. 2. Social consequences of technological development on plantations: second item on the agenda. Geneva, International Labour Office, 1970. pp. 74.

MALKOV (L.N.) Sotsial'nye problemy sovremennoi nauchno-tekhnicheskoi revoliutsii: material k seminarskim zaniatiiam. Novokuznetsk, 1970. pp. 51.

SEMINAR ON THE EFFECTS OF SCIENTIFIC AND TECHNOLOGICAL DEVELOPMENTS ON THE STATUS OF WOMEN, IASI, 1969. Seminar...[held in] Iasi, Romania, 5-18 August 1969; organized by the United Nations, Division of Human Rights, in co-operation with the government of Romania. (ST/TAO/HR/37). New York, United Nations, 1970. pp. 43.

BERNARD (H. RUSSELL) and PELTO (PERTTI JUHO) eds. Technology and social change. New York, [1972]. pp. 354. bibliog.

MAIZEL' (ISAAK ALEKSANDROVICH) Nauka, avtomatizatsiia, obshchestvo. Leningrad, 1972. pp. 280.

TOVMASIAN (STEPAN SURENOVICH) Filosofskie problemy truda i tekhniki. Moskva, 1972. pp. 279.

- Canada

CANADA. Science Council of Canada. Reports. No. 15 Innovation in a cold climate: the dilemma of Canadian manufacturing; [P.R. Gendron, chairman]. Ottawa, 1971. pp. 47.

CORDELL (ARTHUR J.) The multinational firm, foreign direct investment, and Canadian science policy. Ottawa, 1971. pp. 91. (Canada. Science Council of Canada. Special Studies. No. 22)

BOURGAULT (PIERRE L.) Innovation and the structure of Canadian industry. Ottawa, 1972. pp. 132. (Canada. Science Council of Canada. Special Studies. No.23)

- Communist countries

LUCHKINA (LIUDMILA SEMENOVNA) Sovershenstvovanie struktury promyshlennosti zarubezhnykh stran-chlenov SEV v usloviiakh nauchno-tekhnicheskogo progressa. Moskva, 1972. pp. 151.

TECHNOLOGICAL INNOVATIONS (Cont'd.)

- Germany - Mathematical models

ANDRE (DORIS) Indikatoren des technischen Fortschritts: eine Analyse der Wirtschaftsentwicklung in Deutschland von 1850 bis 1913. Göttingen, [1971]. pp. 156. bibliog. (Hamburg. Hansische Universität. Institut für Europäische Wirtschaftspolitik. Weltwirtschaftliche Studien. Heft 16)

MAJER (HELGE) Die "technologische Lücke" zwischen der Bundesrepublik Deutschland und den Vereinigten Staaten von Amerika: eine empirische Analyse. Tübingen, 1973. pp. 438. bibliog. (Tübingen. Institut für Angewandte Wirtschaftsforschung. Schriftenreihe. Band 22)

- Germany, Eastern

ZECHLIN (PAUL) and SCHNASE (WOLFGANG) Neuererräte: Aufgaben und Arbeitsweise; herausgegeben vom Amt für Erfindungs- und Patentwesen der Deutschen Demokratischen Republik. 2nd ed. Berlin, 1970. pp. 126. bibliog.

- India

SCHOENHERR (SIEGFRIED) Probleme der Modernisierung von Führung in ländlichen Gesellschaften Indiens: untersucht am Beispiel ausgewählter indischer Dörfer und Landkreise. [Erlangen, imprint, 1972?]. pp. 343. bibliog.

- Italy

PRODI (ROMANO) La diffusione delle innovazioni nell'industria italiana. Bologna, 1971. pp. 128. (Bologna. Università. Centro di Economia e Politica Industriale. Pubblicazioni)

SOCIETÀ RICERCHE E STUDI, and others. Innovazione e strategia dello sviluppo industriale...; a cura della SORIS e di Adriano De Maio e Giorgio Giargia. Milano, 1971. 3 vols. (in 1).

- Norway - Mathematical models

RINGSTAD (VIDAR) Estimating production functions and technical change from micro data: an exploratory study of individual establishment time-series from Norwegian mining and manufacturing, 1959-1967; Estimering av produktfunksjoner og tekniske endringer fra mikro data, etc. Oslo, 1971. pp. 224. bibliog. (Norway. Statistiske Centralbyrå. Samfunnsøkonomiske Studier. 21) In English with Norwegian summary.

- Russia

BREEV (BORIS DMITRIEVICH) Tekhnicheskii progress i struktura rabochikh kadrov. Moskva, 1963. pp. 88.

EGIAZARIAN (GEVORK ASHOTOVICH) Material'noe stimulirovanie za novuiu tekhniku. Moskva, 1964. pp. 183.

GOLUBKOV (ALEKSANDR IVANOVICH) Otsenka tekhniko-ekonomicheskoi effektivnosti vnedreniia novoi tekhniki: metodicheskoe rukovodstvo. Moskva, 1964. pp. 143.

LEBEDINSKII (IGOR' LEONIDOVICH) Tekhnicheskii progress i sroki sluzhby oborudovaniia. Leningrad, 1968. pp. 112. bibliog.

IVANOVA (MARINA ALEKSEEVNA) and SAMARINA (IZOL'DA ALEKSANDROVNA) Tekhnicheskii progress i struktura ITR i sluzhashchikh. Moskva, 1970. pp. 128.

KLIMENKO (K.I.) ed. Ekonomicheskie problemy nauchno-tekhnicheskogo progressa, etc. Moskva, 1970. pp. 167.

MALKOV (L.N.) Sotsial'nye problemy sovremennoi nauchno-tekhnicheskoi revoliutsii: material k seminarskim zaniatiiam. Novokuznetsk, 1970. pp. 51.

KLIMENKO (KONSTANTIN IVANOVICH) and PETROVA (ELIZAVETA VASIL'EVNA) Ekonomicheskaia effektivnost' tekhnicheskogo progressa v tiazheloi promyshlennosti SSSR. Moskva, 1971. pp. 240.

KORIAGIN (ALEKSANDR GEORGIEVICH) Nauchno-tekhnicheskaia revoliutsiia i proportsii sotsialisticheskogo vosproizvodstva. Moskva, 1971. pp. 303.

SOIFER (VLADIMIR GRIGOR'EVICH) Stimulirovanie rabotnikov za razvitie novoi tekhniki: pravovye voprosy. Moskva, 1971. pp. 175.

AFANAS'EV (VIKTOR GRIGOR'EVICH) Nauchno-tekhnicheskaia revoliutsiia, upravlenie, obrazovanie. Moskva, 1972. pp. 431.

AITOV (NARIMAN ABDRAKHMANOVICH) Tekhnicheskii progress i dvizhenie rabochikh kadrov. Moskva, 1972. pp. 112.

IL'IN (SERGEI SERGEEVICH) ed. V.I.Lenin ob ekonomicheskikh problemakh nauchno-tekhnicheskogo progressa v SSSR. Moskva, 1972. pp. 295.

KAMAEV (VLADIMIR DOROFEEVICH) Sovremennaia nauchno-tekhnicheskaia revoliutsiia: ekonomicheskie formy i zakonomernosti. Moskva, 1972. pp. 261.

KOZLOV (IURII KONSTANTINOVICH) Organizatsionnye problemy nauchno-tekhnicheskogo progressa. Moskva, 1972. pp. 436.

LEBEDEV (V.G.) and others, eds. Effektivnost' tekhniki: rezervy, novye tendentsii rosta. Moskva, 1972. pp. 288.

MARGULIS (IURII IAKOVLEVICH) Analiz effektivnosti zatrat na novuiu tekhniku. Moskva, 1972. pp. 78.

NAUCHNO-tekhnicheskii progress i effektivnost' obshchestvennogo proizvodstva. Moskva, 1972. pp. 391.

NAUCHNO-tekhnicheskii progress i proizvoditel'nost' truda, etc. Moskva, 1972. pp. 255.

SAVICHEV (GRIGORII PAVLOVICH) Tekhnicheskii progress i voprosy izobretatel'skogo prava. Moskva, 1972. pp. 132.

TORKANOVSKII (EVGENII PETROVICH) Sozdanie i vnedrenie novoi tekhniki na predpriiatii: pravovye voprosy. Moskva, 1972. pp 126.

ZAKHAROV (VASILII GEORGIEVICH) Osobennosti vosproizvodstva osnovnykh fondov v usloviiakh nauchno-tekhnicheskoi revoliutsii. Moskva, 1972. pp. 199.

KHOZRASCHETNYE faktory uskoreniia tekhnicheskogo progressa v promyshlennosti. Kiev, 1973. pp. 255.

PROSTIAKOV (IGOR' IGNAT'EVICH) Uskorenie tekhnicheskogo progressa v usloviiakh khoziaistvennoi reformy. Moskva, 1973. pp. 158.

- Russia - Bibliography

GRISHINA (G.I.) compiler. Sovremennaia nauchno-tekhnicheskaia revoliutsiia i sozdanie fundamenta kommunizma: rekomendatel'nyi ukazatel' literatury. Moskva, 1972. pp. 177. bibliog.

- Russia - Latvia

   VALESKALN (PETR IVANOVICH) and RAMAN (M.) Puti nauchno-tekhnicheskogo progressa. Riga, 1965. pp. 77.

- Russia - Soviet North

   AKADEMIIA NAUK SSSR. Sovet po Izucheniiu Proizvoditel'nykh Sil. Komissiia po Problemam Severa. Problemy Severa. vyp.17. Razvitie proizvoditel'nykh sil Severa i nauchno-tekhnicheskii progress. Moskva, 1972. pp. 203.

- Russia - White Russia

   DRONOV (FEDOR AMOSOVICH) ed. Problemy effektivnosti novoi tekhniki. Minsk, 1972. pp. 287.

TECHNOLOGICAL INNOVATIONS: Underdeveloped areas
   See UNDERDEVELOPED AREAS - Technological innovations

- United Kingdom

   TRIST (ERIC LANSDOWNE) and MURRAY (H.) Work organization at the coal face: a comparative study of mining systems. London, 1958. pp. various.

   PROGRAMMES ANALYSIS UNIT. A report... on the role of machinery in the garment industry which has been made available by the Clothing E[conomic D[evelopment] C[ommittee]; [by A.G. Hamlin and G.I.W. Llewelyn]. London, H.M.S.O., 1971. pp. 187.

   LAYTON (CHRISTOPHER) Ten innovations: an international study on technological development and the use of qualified scientists and engineers in ten industries. London, 1972. pp. 199.

   ECONOMIC DEVELOPMENT COMMITTEE FOR CHEMICALS. Pharmaceuticals Working Party. Innovative activity in the pharmaceutical industry; a report; [C.J.M. Bennett, chairman]. London, National Economic Development Office, 1973. pp. 38. bibliog.

- United States

   NELKIN (DOROTHY) The politics of housing innovation: the fate of the civilian industrial technology program. Ithaca, 1971. pp. 124. (Cornell University. Program on Science, Technology, and Society. Science, Technology and Society Series)

   RESEARCH and innovation in the modern corporation; [by] Edwin Mansfield [and others]. London, 1972. pp. 239.

   ROSENBERG (NATHAN) Technology and American economic growth. New York, [1972]. pp. 211.

- United States - Mathematical models

   MAJER (HELGE) Die "technologische Lücke" zwischen der Bundesrepublik Deutschland und den Vereinigte Staaten von Amerika: eine empirische Analyse. Tübingen, 1973. pp. 438. bibliog. (Tübingen. Institut für Angewandte Wirtschaftsforschung. Schriftenreihe. Band 22)

TECHNOLOGISTS

   UNITED NATIONS EDUCATIONAL, SCIENTIFIC AND CULTURAL ORGANIZATION. Statistical Reports and Studies. [No.17]. World summary of statistics on science and technology: results of experimental surveys of scientific and technical manpower and expenditures for research and experimental development. Paris, 1970. pp. 66. In English and French.

   BIDDLE (WILLIAM FRANCIS) Military technology and arms control; [Ph.D. (London) thesis]. 1971 [or rather 1972]. fo. 581. bibliog. Typescript: unpublished. This thesis is the property of London University and may not be removed from the Library.

- India

   INDIA. Census. Papers. 1966. No. 1. 1961 census: scientific and technical personnel tables. [Delhi, 1966]. pp. 223.

- New Zealand

   NEW ZEALAND. National Research Advisory Council. 1967. Some aspects of technical manpower in New Zealand: an interim report to the ... Council. Wellington, 1967. pp. 73. (Publications. No. 2)

TECHNOLOGISTS: Underdeveloped areas
   See UNDERDEVELOPED AREAS - Technologists

TECHNOLOGISTS, GERMAN

   HERGENROEDER (UDO) Männer, die Erfolg erfinden: Techniker und Wissenschaftler als Motoren der Wirtschaft. Düsseldorf, 1970. pp. 310. bibliog.

TECHNOLOGY

   MEISSNER (MARTIN) Technology and the worker: technical demands and social processes in industry. San Francisco, [1969]. pp. 264.

   GRIES (WERNER) Ausbildung, Forschung und Wirtschaftswachstum. Meisenheim, 1971. pp. 148. bibliog.

   TAYLOR (JAMES CHAPMAN) Technology and planned organizational change. Ann Arbor, [1971]. pp. 151. bibliog.

   GABOR (DENNIS) The proper priorities of science and technology. Southampton, 1972. pp. 16. (Southampton. University. Fawley Foundation. Lectures. 18)

   INTERNATIONAL ECONOMIC ASSOCIATION. Conference, [1972?], St. Anton. Science and technology in economic growth: proceedings of a conference...; edited by B.R. Williams. London, 1973. pp. 446.

- Bibliography

   BLACKWELL'S. Catalogues. 865. Rare and interesting books on science mainly related to transport and technology. Oxford, 1969. pp. 203.

- History

   PISCITELLI (DOMENICO) Per uno studio sui problemi della localizzazione, distribuzione ed utilizzazione delle fonti di energia nel basso medioevo: con alcuni aspetti geografico-economici pugliesi. Bari, [1969]. pp. 104.

   INTERNATIONAL CONGRESS OF THE HISTORY OF SCIENCE AND TECHNOLOGY, 1931. Science at the cross roads: papers presented to the... Congress... by the delegates of the U.S.S.R.; with a new foreword by Joseph Needham, etc. London, 1971. pp. 235.

   PERSPECTIVES in the history of science and technology: [papers and commentaries presented at a symposium at the University of Oklahoma, April 8-12, 1969, sponsored by the University, the Midwest Junto, and the Society for the History of Technology]; edited by Duane H.D. Roller. Norman, Oklahoma, [1971]. pp. 307.

TECHNOLOGY (Cont'd.)

- History - Baltic States

IZ istorii estestvoznaniia i tekhniki Pribaltiki. t.4. Riga, 1972. pp. 412. With English table of contents.

- History - France

HARRIS (J.R.) M.A., Ph.D. Industry and technology in the eighteenth century: Britain and France. Birmingham, 1972. pp. 18.

- History - Germany

TROITZSCH (ULRICH) Ansätze technologischen Denkens bei den Kameralisten des 17. und 18. Jahrhunderts. Berlin, [1966]. pp. 193. bibliog.

KROKER (WERNER) Wege zur Verbreitung technologischer Kenntnisse zwischen England und Deutschland in der zweiten Hälfte des 18. Jahrhunderts. Berlin, [1971]. pp. 203. bibliog.

- History - United Kingdom

HARRIS (J.R.) M.A., Ph.D. Industry and technology in the eighteenth century: Britain and France. Birmingham, 1972. pp. 18.

KROKER (WERNER) Wege zur Verbreitung technologischer Kenntnisse zwischen England und Deutschland in der zweiten Hälfte des 18. Jahrhunderts. Berlin, [1971]. pp. 203. bibliog.

MUSSON (ALBERT EDWARD) ed. Science, technology, and economic growth in the eighteenth century. London, 1972. pp. 211. bibliog.

- Information services

ORGANISATION FOR ECONOMIC CO-OPERATION AND DEVELOPMENT. Information Policy Group. 1971. Canada. Paris, 1971. pp. 161. bibliog. (Reviews of National Scientific and Technical Information Policy. [No.1.])

- Philosophy

LEY (HERMANN) Technik und Weltanschauung: einige philosophische Konsequenzen der wissenschaftlich-technischen Revolution. Schwerte/Ruhr, 1971. pp. 132.

- Social aspects

FRIEDMANN (GEORGES) Le progrès technique: liberté ou servitude? Paris, 1966. pp. 157-172. bibliog. (From Cahiers Laïques, No. 96, 1966)

BOLTZ (C. L.) Technology and economic development; [a summary of the papers and discussion at an international seminar held in 1969 at Istanbul under the auspices of the Economic Research Foundation]. Istanbul, 1970. pp. 167. (Economic Research Foundation. Series in International Seminars)

FULLER (RICHARD BUCKMINSTER) and others. Approaching the benign environment. [New York], 1970. pp. 160. (Auburn University. Franklin Lectures in the Sciences and Humanities. 1st Series)

CHERMAYEFF (SERGE) and TZONIS (ALEXANDER) Shape of community: realization of human potential. Harmondsworth, 1971. pp. 247.

DOUGLAS (JACK D.) ed. The technological threat: [readings]. Englewood Cliffs, [1971]. pp. 185.

FABUN (DON) Dimensions of change. Beverly Hills, [1971]. pp. 230. bibliog.

LEY (HERMANN) Technik und Weltanschauung: einige philosophische Konsequenzen der wissenschaftlich-technischen Revolution. Schwerte/Ruhr, 1971. pp. 132.

ORGANISATION FOR ECONOMIC CO-OPERATION AND DEVELOPMENT. Ad Hoc Group on New Concepts of Science Policy. 1971. Science, growth and society: a new perspective. Paris, 1971. pp. 113.

SCHWARTZ (EUGENE S.) Overskill: (the decline of technology in modern civilization). Chicago, 1971. pp. 339. bibliog.

WILLIAMS (ROGER) b. 1942. Politics and technology. London, 1971. pp. 80. bibliog.

CAN we survive our future?: a symposium; (versions of interviews originally broadcast, in 1970-71, over Radio Free Europe) edited... by G.R. Urban in collaboration with Michael Glenny. London, 1972. pp. 400.

DE NEVERS (NOEL) ed. Technology and society: [readings] Reading, Mass., [1972]. pp. 307.

GABOR (DENNIS) The mature society. London, 1972. pp. 208.

HARVARD UNIVERSITY. Harvard University program on technology and society, 1964-1972: a final review. Cambridge, Mass., 1972. pp. 285. bibliog.

JANTSCH (ERICH) Technological planning and social futures. London, 1972. pp. 256. bibliog.

KING (ALEXANDER) Another kind of growth: industrial society and the quality of life. [London, 1972]. pp. 22. (David Davies Memorial Institute of International Studies. Annual Memorial Lectures. 1972)

TECHNOLOGY, power, and social change; [proceedings of a conference organized in 1971 by the International Affairs Association of the University of Pennsylvania]; edited by Charles A. Thrall and Jerold M. Starr. Lexington, Mass., [1972]. pp. 166.

ETZIONI (AMITAI) and REMP (RICHARD) Technological shortcuts to social change. New York, [1973]. pp. 235.

HAMILTON (DAVID) Technology, man and the environment. London, 1973. pp. 357. bibliog.

HETZLER (STANLEY A.) Applied measures for promoting technological growth. London, 1973. pp. 337. bibliogs.

HIGGIN (GURTH WEDDERBURN) Symptoms of tomorrow: letters from a sociologist on the present state of society. London, 1973. pp. 158. bibliog.

MAN, science, technology: a marxist analysis of the scientific-technological revolution. Moscow, 1973. pp. 387. bibliog.

MISHAN (EDWARD JOSHUA) Making the world safe for pornography, and other intellectual fashions. London, 1973. pp. 262.

PETERSON (RICHARD A.) The industrial order and social policy. Englewood Cliffs, [1973]. pp. 159. bibliog.

SALZBURG ASSEMBLY: IMPACT OF THE NEW TECHNOLOGY. General Conference, 4th, 1972. Technology assessment and quality of life: proceedings ...; edited by Gerhard J. Stöber and Dieter Schumacher. Amsterdam, 1973. pp. 300.

SCHUMACHER (E.F.) Small is beautiful: a study of economics as if people mattered. London, 1973. pp. 288.

SEMINAR ON SOCIAL ASPECTS OF SCIENCE AND TECHNOLOGY, UNIVERSITY OF EDINBURGH, 1970. Meaning and control: essays in social aspects of science and technology. edited by D.O. Edge and J.N. Wolfe. London, 1973. pp. 274. bibliogs.

SKLAIR (LESLIE ALLAN) Organized knowledge: a sociological view of science and technology. London, 1973. pp. 284. bibliog.

- Social aspects - France

LAFFAY (JEAN) La civilisation industrielle contre la démocratie parlementaire. Paris, [1971]. pp. 183.

- Social aspects - Russia - White Russia

NAUCHNO-tekhnicheskii progress i sotsial'nye izmeneniia na sele: na materialakh Belorusskoi SSR. Minsk, 1972. pp. 271.

- Social aspects - Sweden

HUNTFORD (ROLAND) The new totalitarians. London, 1971. pp. 354.

- Social aspects - United Kingdom

WEDDERBURN (DOROTHY) and CROMPTON (ROSEMARY) Workers' attitudes and technology. Cambridge, 1972. pp. 176. bibliog.

- Social aspects - United States

RASMUSSEN (JOHN P.) ed. The new American revolution: the dawning of the technetronic era. New York, [1972]. pp. 250. bibliog.

- Statistics

FREEMAN (CHRISTOPHER) The measurement of scientific and technological activities: proposals for the collection of statistics on science and technology on an internationally uniform basis. Paris, United Nations Educational, Scientific and Cultural Organization, 1969. pp. 63. (Statistical Reports and Studies. [No. 15])

- Austria

KOSTA (H.G.JIŘÍ) and others. Der technologische Fortschritt in Österreich und in der Tschechoslowakei. Wien, 1971. pp. 102. (Österreichisches Institut für Wirtschaftsforschung. Abteilung Internationale Wirtschaftsvergleiche. Studien über Wirtschafts- und Systemvergleiche. Band 2) With English summary.

- Canada

CANADA. Ministry of State for Science and Technology. Annual report. a., 1971/72 [1st]- Ottawa. [In English and French]

- Czechoslovakia

KOSTA (H.G.JIŘÍ) and others. Der technologische Fortschritt in Österreich und in der Tschechoslowakei. Wien, 1971. pp. 102. (Österreichisches Institut für Wirtschaftsforschung. Abteilung Internationale Wirtschaftsvergleiche. Studien über Wirtschafts- und Systemvergleiche. Band 2) With English summary.

- Europe

WILLIAMS (ROGER) b. 1942. European technology: the politics of collaboration. London, 1973. pp. 214.

- Germany, Eastern

GERMANY (DEUTSCHE DEMOKRATISCHE REPUBLIK). Staatssekretariat für Westdeutsche Fragen. 1970. Meeting the challenge of the year 2000: problems of the scientific and technological revolution in the GDR. Dresden, [1970?]. pp. 67.

- India

BALASUBRAMANYAM (V.N.) International transfer of technology to India. New York, 1973. pp. 143.

- Israel

ZAHLAN (ANTOINE B.) Science and higher education in Israel. Beirut, [1970]. pp. 153. (Institute for Palestine Studies. Monograph Series. No. 22.)

- Russia

AL'PEROVICH (IURII IZRAILEVICH) Na poliakh budushchego. Moskva, 1964. pp. 175.

CHEMODANOV (MARK PETROVICH) Prevrashchenie nauki v neposredstvennuiu proizvoditel'nuiu silu v protsesse stroitel'stva kommunizma. Moskva, 1966. pp. 92. Colophon gives author's name as Marki.

- Spain

SPAIN. Comisaria del Plan de Desarrollo Economico y Social. 1972. (III Plan de desarrollo economico y social): investigacion cientifica y desarrollo tecnologico. [Madrid], 1972. pp. 241.

TECHNOLOGY AND CIVILIZATION

STOSKOVA (NINA NIKOLAEVNA) F. Engel's o roli tekhniki v razvitii obshchestva. Moskva, 1970. pp. 80. bibliog.

DRIAKHLOV (NIKOLAI IVANOVICH) Sotsial'nye problemy nauchno-tekhnicheskoi revoliutsii. Moskva, 1972. pp. 191. bibliog.

- Abstracts

WEISS (JOHN H.) Technology and social history. Cambridge, Mass., 1971. pp. 93. (Harvard University Harvard University Program on Technology and Society. Research Reviews. No.8)

TECHNOLOGY AND STATE

JEWKES (JOHN) Government and high technology; third Wincott Memorial Lecture...1972. London, 1972. pp. 24. (Institute of Economic Affairs. Occasional Papers. 37)

TECHNOLOGY ASSESSMENT

CETRON (MARVIN J.) and BARTOCHA (BODA) eds. The methodology of technology assessment. New York, [1972]. pp. 235.

KASPER (RAPHAEL G.) ed. Technology assessment: understanding the social consequences of technological applications. New York, 1972. pp. 291.

MEDFORD (DEREK) Environmental harassment or technology assessment? Amsterdam, 1973. pp. 358. bibliogs.

TECHNOLOGY TRANSFER

BARANSON (JACK) International transfer of automotive technology to developing countries. New York, United Nations Institute for Training and Research, 1971. pp. 95. (Research Reports. No. 8)

CHANG (Y.S.) The transfer of technology: economics of offshore assembly; the case of semiconductor industry. New York, United Nations Institute for Training and Research, 1971. pp. 59. (Research Reports. No. 11)

TECHNOLOGY TRANSFER (Cont'd.)

CHUDSON (WALTER A.) The international transfer of commercial technology to developing countries. New York, United Nations Institute for Training and Research, 1971. pp. 58, 3. (Research Reports. No. 13.)

HAWTHORNE (EDWARD P.) The transfer of technology; [based upon the discussions and recommendations of the seminar held in] Istanbul, 5th-9th October, 1970. Paris, Organisation for Economic Co-operation and Development, 1971. pp. 148. bibliog.

MASON (R. HAL) The transfer of technology and the factor proportions problem: the Philippines and Mexico. New York, United Nations Institute for Training and Research, [1971]. pp. 101. (Research Reports. No. 10)

OZAWA (TERUTOMO) Transfer of technology from Japan to developing countries. New York, United Nations Institute for Training and Research, 1971. pp. 50. (Research Reports. No. 7)

STOBAUGH (ROBERT B.) The international transfer of technology in the establishment of the petrochemical industry in developing countries. New York, United Nations Institute for Training and Research, 1971. pp. 67. (Research Reports. No. 12)

TILTON (JOHN E.) International diffusion of technology: the case of semiconductors. Washington, [1971]. pp. 183. (Brookings Institution. Studies in the Regulation of Economic Activity)

WORTZEL (LAWRENCE H.) Technology transfer in the pharmaceutical industry. New York, United Nations Institute for Training and Research, 1971. pp. 53. (Research Reports. No. 14)

BHATTASALI (B.N.) Transfer of technology among the developing countries. Tokyo, Asian Productivity Organization, [1972]. pp. 94. (Economic and Industrial Development and Productivity).

INTERREGIONAL EXPERT GROUP ON TRANSFER OF OPERATIVE TECHNOLOGY AT THE ENTERPRISE LEVEL, NEW YORK, 1971. Transfer of operative technology at the enterprise level; report of...Group on its Meeting held in New York from 21 to 26 June 1971. (ST/ECA/151). New York, United Nations, 1972. pp. 42.

PANEL ON FOREIGN INVESTMENT IN DEVELOPING COUNTRIES, 3RD, TOKYO, 1971. Report on a meeting held in Tokyo from 29 November to 2 December 1971. (ST/ECA/158). New York, United Nations, 1972. pp. 31.

BALASUBRAMANYAM (V.N.) International transfer of technology to India. New York, 1973. pp. 143.

SCHULZ (CHRISTA) Möglichkeiten der Übertragung von Wirtschaftswachstum durch internationalen Kapitaltransfer. Hamburg, 1973. pp. 165,xxxiv. bibliog.

TELECOMMUNICATION

NGUYEN TIEN PHUC and DENNERY (GILBERT) L'économie des télécommunications. Paris, 1972. pp. 231. bibliog.

- Laws and legislation - Canada

CANADA. Telecommission. 1971. An analysis of the constitutional and legal basis for the regulation of telecommunications in Canada. Ottawa, 1971. pp. 158. (Studies. 1(a))

- Africa, East - Employees

EAST AFRICA HIGH COMMISSION. East African Posts and Telecommunications Administration. Report by H.A. Whitson on the industrial relations machinery within the E.A.P. & T. administration. [Nairobi, 1961]. pp. 11.

- Canada

CANADA. Telecommission. 1971. Analysis of relationship between the functions of the common carriers and those engaged in broadcasting. Ottawa, 1971. pp. 127. (Studies. 1(d))

CANADA. Telecommission. 1971. Northern Communications study. Ottawa, 1971. pp. 123. (Studies. 8(c))

SMYTHE (DALLAS WALKER) The relevance of United States legislative-regulatory experience to the Canadian telecommunications situation. Ottawa, 1971. pp. 225. bibliog. (Canada. Telecommission. Studies. 1(e))

CANADA. Computer/Communications Task Force. 1972. Branching out; report; [H.J. von Baeyer, chairman]. Ottawa, 1972. 2 vols. bibliogs.

CANADA. Telecommission. 1972. Regulatory bodies: structures and roles. Ottawa, 1972. pp. 129. (Studies. 7(a)(b))

- France

FRANCE. Délégation à l'Aménagement du Territoire et à l'Action Régionale. 1969. Eléments pour un schéma directeur des télécommunications. [Paris], 1969. pp. 149. bibliog. (Travaux et Recherches de Prospective. 2)

FRANCE. Commissariat Général du Plan. 1970. Postes et télécommunications. [Paris, 1970]. pp. 258. (Plan et prospectives. 5)

- Luxembourg

LUXEMBOURG. Administration des Postes et Télécommunications. Rapport de gestion. a., 1969- Luxembourg.

- Spain

SPAIN. Comisaria del Plan de Desarrollo Economico y Social. 1972. (III Plan de desarrollo economico y social): telecomunicaciones y correos. [Madrid], 1972. pp. 178.

TELECOMMUNICATION: Underdeveloped areas
See UNDERDEVELOPED AREAS - Telecommunication

- United Kingdom

SCOTT (J.M.) Extel 100: the centenary history of the Exchange Telegraph Company. London, 1972. pp. 239.

- United States

IRWIN (MANLEY R.) The telecommunications industry: integration vs. competition. New York, 1971. pp. 223. bibliog.

SMYTHE (DALLAS WALKER) The relevance of United States legislative-regulatory experience to the Canadian telecommunications situation. Ottawa, 1971. pp. 225. bibliog. (Canada. Telecommission. Studies. 1(e))

TELEGRAPH

- Argentine Republic

CASTRO ESTEVES (RAMON DE) Historia de correos y telegrafos de la Republica Argentina, etc. Buenos Aires, 1934-38. 2 vols. (in 1). bibliogs.

TELEPHONE

- United Kingdom

GREGORY (PETER G.) Telephones for the elderly. London, 1973. pp. 128. (Social Administration Research Trust. Occasional Papers on Social Administration. No.53)

TELEVISION

- Law and legislation - Italy

FRAGOLA (AUGUSTO) La radiotelevisione nella giurisprudenza. Padova, [1971]. pp. 262.

LIBERTÀ di espressione e organizzazione radiotelevisiva: la riorganizzazione legislativa della Radiotelevisione italiana; dibattiti e progetti di riforma. vol. 2. Milano, [1971]. pp. 209. (Istituto per la Documentazione Legislativa. Pubblicazioni. 32)

- Law and legislation - United States

EMERY (WALTER BYRON) Broadcasting and government: responsibilities and regulations. [2nd ed.] [East Lansing, 1971]. pp. 569. bibliog.

RIVKIN (STEVEN R.) Cable television: a guide to federal regulations prepared for the National Science Foundation. Santa Monica, Ca., 1973. pp. 343. (Rand Corporation. [Rand Reports]. 1138)

- Production and direction

ELLIOTT (PHILIP) The making of a television series: a case study in the sociology of culture. London, 1972. pp. 180.

- Study and teaching

GEORGIN (B.) L'enseignement de l'art cinématographique aux différents niveaux scolaires et perspectives d'un enseignement visuel en dehors du cinéma: rapport...à la table ronde de La Mendola...17, 18 et 19 août 1962. Paris, 1962. pp. 47.

TELEVISION AND CHILDREN

MELODY (WILLIAM H.) Children's television: the economics of exploitation. New Haven, 1973. pp. 164. bibliogs.

TELEVISION AUDIENCES

GERMANY (BUNDESREPUBLIK). Deutscher Bundestag. Wissenschaftliche Dienste. 1971. Wirkungen von Gewaltdarstellungen auf dem Bildschirm: Zusammenhänge zwischen dargestellter Gewalt und aggressiven Verhaltensweisen; [edited by Claus-Peter Gerber]. Bonn, 1971. pp. 76. bibliog. (Materialien. 28)

TELEVISION BROADCASTING

PARISH (ROSS M.) The political economy of broadcasting. [Armidale, N.S.W., 1968]. pp. 23. bibliog.

PROBLEMY televideniia i radio: issledovaniia, kritika, materialy. Moskva, 1971. pp. 247.

GREEN (TIMOTHY) The universal eye: world television in the seventies. London, 1972. pp. 327. bibliog.

- Social aspects

SHULMAN (MILTON) The ravenous eye: the impact of the fifth factor. London, 1973. pp. 334.

- Australia

PARISH (ROSS M.) The political economy of broadcasting. [Armidale, N.S.W., 1968]. pp. 23. bibliog.

- France

FRANCE. Commission d'Etude du Statut de l'O[ffice de] R[adiodiffusion]-T[élévision] F[rançaise]. 1970. Rapport; [Lucien Paye, chairman]. [Paris], 1970. pp. 297.

- Russia

OCHERKI istorii sovetskogo radioveshchaniia i televideniia: uchebnoe posobie. Moskva, 1972 in progress.

- United Kingdom

RAYNOR (HENRY) Radio and television. London, 1971. pp. 57. bibliog.

ELLIOTT (PHILIP) The making of a television series: a case study in the sociology of culture. London, 1972. pp. 180.

GREENE (Sir HUGH CARLETON) The future of broadcasting in Britain;...with an afterword by... Lord Aylestone. London, 1972. pp. 45. (British Association for the Advancement of Science. Granada Lectures. 1972)

TRIBE (DAVID) Broadcasting, brainwashing, conditioning. London, 1972. pp. 33.

U.K. Television Advisory Committee. 1972. Report; [Sir Robert Cockburn, chairman]. London, 1972. repr. 1973. pp. 21.

SHULMAN (MILTON) The ravenous eye: the impact of the fifth factor. London, 1973. pp. 334.

U.K. Central Office of Information. Reference Division. Reference Pamphlets. 111. Broadcasting in Britain. London, 1973. pp. 44. bibliog.

U.K. Television Advisory Committee. Technical Sub-Committee. 1973. Papers; [C.W. Sowton, chairman]. London, 1973. pp. 87.

- United Kingdom - Bibliography

BRITISH BROADCASTING CORPORATION. British broadcasting, 1922-1972: a select bibliography. London, 1972. pp. 49.

- United States

NEW YORK (CITY). Commission on Human Rights. Report: affirmative action follow-up to advertising and broadcasting hearing. [New York], 1968. pp. 27.

NEW YORK (CITY). Commission on Human Rights. Report of the public hearing on the employment practices of the broadcasting and advertising industries: the image projection of members of minority groups in television and radio; held...March 11-22, 1968, [chairman, William H. Booth]. New York, [1968]. pp. 141, A 24.

KOENIG (ALLEN E.) ed. Broadcasting and bargaining: labor relations in radio and television. Madison, Wisc., 1970. pp. 344.

HEAD (SYDNEY W.) Broadcasting in America:...a survey of television and radio. 2nd ed. Boston, [1972]. pp. 563. bibliog.

NOLL (ROGER G.) and others. Economic aspects of television regulation. Washington, D.C., [1973]. pp. 342. (Brookings Institution. Studies in the Regulation of Economic Activity)

TELEVISION BROADCASTING - United States (Cont'd.)

SHULMAN (MILTON) The ravenous eye: the impact of the fifth factor. London, 1973. pp. 334.

TELEVISION IN ADULT EDUCATION

MADDISON (JOHN) Radio and television in literacy: a survey of the use of the broadcasting media in combating illiteracy among adults. [Paris], United Nations Educational, Scientific and Cultural Organization, 1971. pp. 82. bibliog. (Department of Mass Communication. Reports and Papers on Mass Communication. No. 62)

TELEVISION IN EDUCATION

- Asia

MEETING ON RADIO AND TELEVISION IN THE SERVICE OF EDUCATION AND DEVELOPMENT, BANGKOK, 1966. Radio and television in the service of education and development in Asia. Paris, United Nations Educational, Scientific and Cultural Organization, [1967]. pp. 58. (Department of Mass Communication. Reports and Papers on Mass Communication. No. 49)

- Senegal

FOUGEYROLLAS (PIERRE) Television and the social education of women...a first report on the Unesco-Senegal pilot project at Dakar. [Paris], United Nations Educational, Scientific and Cultural Organization, [1967]. pp. 40. (Department of Mass Communication. Reports and Papers on Mass Communication. No. 50)

TELEVISION IN POLITICS

ARNIM (GABRIELE VON) Der Einfluss von Massenmedien auf politisches Verhalten: der Stand der politischen Wirkungsforschung in der Massenkommunikationssoziologie. Hamburg, 1971. pp. 279. bibliog.

- United States

GILBERT (ROBERT E.) Television and presidential politics. North Quincy, Mass., [1972]. pp. 335. bibliog.

BARRETT (MARVIN) The politics of broadcasting. New York, [1973]. pp. 247. (Alfred I. duPont-Columbia University survey of broadcast journalism, 1971-1972)

TELEVISION IN TECHNICAL EDUCATION

UNITED NATIONS EDUCATIONAL, SCIENTIFIC AND CULTURAL ORGANIZATION. Department of Mass Communication. Reports and Papers on Mass Communication. No.67. Television for higher technical education of workers: final report on a pilot project in Poland. Paris, 1973. pp. 73.

TELEVISION PROGRAMMES

- Germany

GERHARDT (ULF DIETMAR) Der Kriminalfilm im Fernsehen: eine systematische Inhaltsanalyse von 50 Kriminalfernsehfilmen im Zweiten Deutschen Fernsehen... 1968. [Clausthal-Zellerfeld, imprint], 1971. pp. 208. bibliog.

- Venezuela

PASQUALI (ANTONIO) El aparato singular: analisis de un dia de TV en Caracas. Caracas, 1967. pp. 121.

TEMPERANCE

HARRISON (BRIAN HOWARD) Dictionary of British temperance biography. Coventry, 1973. pp. 139. (Society for the Study of Labour History. Aids to Research. No. 1)

- Study and teaching

U.K. Social Survey. [Reports. New Series.] 463. Vol. 1. Children and alcohol: a developmental study in Glasgow; by Gustav Jahoda, assisted by Joyce Cramond; an enquiry conducted...by the Department of Psychology, University of Strathclyde for the Health Education Unit of the Scottish Home and Health Department. London, 1972. pp. 57. bibliog.

U.K. Social Survey. [Reports. New Series.] 463. Vol. 2. Teenagers and alcohol: a developmental study in Glasgow; by John Davies and Barrie Stacey; an inquiry conducted...by the Department of Psychology, University of Strathclyde for the Health Education Unit of the Scottish Home and Health Department. London, 1972. pp. 178. bibliog.

TEMPLE (HENRY JOHN) 3rd Viscount Palmerston

BULLEN (ROGER JOHN) Lord Palmerston and Anglo-French relations, 1841-1848; [Ph. D. (London) thesis]. 1971. fo. 372. bibliog. Typescript: unpublished. This thesis is the property of London University and may not be removed from the Library.

TENNERY (THOMAS DOUTHIT)

TENNERY (THOMAS DOUTHIT) The Mexican War diary of Thomas D. Tennery; edited and with an introduction by D.E. Livingston-Little. Norman, Okla., [1970]. pp. 117. bibliog.

TENNESSEE

- Economic conditions

LEE (TONG HUN) and others. Regional and interregional intersectoral flow analysis: the method and an application to the Tennessee economy. Knoxville, [1973]. pp. 164. bibliog.

TENNESSEE VALLEY AUTHORITY

McCRAW (THOMAS K.) TVA and the power fight, 1933-1939. Philadelphia, [1971]. pp. 201. bibliog.

OWEN (MARGUERITE) The Tennessee Valley Authority. New York, 1973. pp. 275. bibliog.

TENNYSON (ALFRED) 1st Baron Tennyson

FOOTE (GEORGE WILLIAM) Atheism and suicide: a reply to Alfred Tennyson, Poet Laureate. London, [1881]. pp. 8.

TEREK

- Economic history

GRITSENKO (NIKOLAI PAVLOVICH) Gorskii aul i kazach'ia stanitsa Tereka nakanune Velikoi Oktiabr'skoi sotsialisticheskoi revoliutsii. Groznyi, 1972. pp. 278. bibliog.

TER-PETROSIAN (SIMON ARSHAKOVICH) called KAMO

BAYNAC (JACQUES) Kamo: l'homme de main de Lénine. [Paris, 1972]. pp. 269. bibliog.

TERRITORIAL WATERS
- Portugal

BRANDÃO (EDUARDO HENRIQUE SERRA) Aguas jurisdicionais portuguesas. Lisboa, 1971. pp. 166. (Portugal. Junta de Investigações do Ultramar. Centro de Estudos Politicos e Sociais. Estudos de Ciências Politicas e Sociais. No. 86)

TERRITORY, NATIONAL

WEBER (HERMANN) Writer on international law. Die Bukowina im Zweiten Weltkrieg: völkerrechtliche Aspekte der Lage der Bukowina im Spannungsfeld zwischen Rumänien, der Sowjetunion und Deutschland. Hamburg, 1972. pp. 86. bibliog. (Hamburg. Institut für Auswärtige Politik. Darstellungen zur Auswärtigen Politik. Band 11)

TERRORISM

COMITÉ FRANCO-ESPAGNOL. Attentats et terreur: instruments de conquête politique: preface de Albert Bayet. Paris, [1937?]. pp. 23.

BAUMANN (CAROL EDLER) The diplomatic kidnappings: a revolutionary tactic of urban terrorism. The Hague, 1973. pp. 182.

- America, Latin

BARREIRO (JULIO) Violencia y politica en America Latina. Mexico, 1971. pp. 205.

- Canada - Quebec

SAYWELL (JOHN T.) Quebec 70: a documentary narrative. Toronto, [1971]. pp. 152.

- East (Near East)

HADAWI (SAMI) Crime and no punishment: Zionist Israeli terrorism, 1939-1972. Beirut, 1972. pp. 99.

- Germany

La BANDE à Baader; ou, La violence révolutionnaire. Paris, [1972]. pp. 218.

RAUBALL (REINHARD) ed. Die Baader-Meinhof-Gruppe. Berlin, 1973. pp. 265.

- Guatemala

AGUILERA PERALTA (GABRIEL EDGARDO) La violencia en Guatemala como fenomeno politico. Cuernavaca, 1971. 1 vol. (various pagings). bibliog. (Centro Intercultural de Documentacion. Cidoc Cuadernos. No. 61)

- Italy

Le BOMBE di Milano; testimonianze di Giampaolo Pansa [and others]. Parma, 1970. pp. 254.

La STRAGE di stato: controinchiesta. [Rome, 1970]. pp. 160.

COLETTI (ALESSANDRO) Anarchici e questori. Padova, 1971 repr. 1972. pp. 134.

SASSANO (MARCO) Pinelli: un suicidio di stato. Padova, 1971 repr. 1972. pp. 233.

- United States

NOVACK (GEORGE) Marxism versus neo-anarchist terrorism. New York, [1970]. pp. 15. (Reprinted from International Socialist Review, June 1970)

TEXAS
- Economic conditions

CLARK (CHARLES TALLIFERO) and HOLZ (ROBERT K.) Economic and population growth in the Guadalupe-Blanco River area. Austin, 1971. pp. 65. (Texas University. Bureau of Business Research. Area Economic Surveys. No. 32)

- History

ALMARÁZ (FÉLIX D.) Tragic cavalier: Governor Manuel Salcedo of Texas, 1808-1813. Austin, Texas, [1971]. pp. 206. bibliog.

BARR (ALWYN) Reconstruction to reform: Texas politics, 1876-1906. Austin, Texas, [1971]. pp. 315. bibliog.

- Politics and government

BARR (ALWYN) Reconstruction to reform: Texas politics, 1876-1906. Austin, Texas, [1971]. pp. 315. bibliog.

- Population

CLARK (CHARLES TALLIFERO) and HOLZ (ROBERT K.) Economic and population growth in the Guadalupe-Blanco River area. Austin, 1971. pp. 65. (Texas University. Bureau of Business Research. Area Economic Surveys. No. 32)

TEXTBOOKS
- Germany

SIEBERT (HORST) Der andere Teil Deutschlands in Schulbüchern der DDR und der BRD: ein Beitrag zur politischen Bildung in Deutschland. Hamburg, 1970. pp. 125. bibliog.

- Germany, Eastern

SIEBERT (HORST) Der andere Teil Deutschlands in Schulbüchern der DDR und der BRD: ein Beitrag zur politischen Bildung in Deutschland. Hamburg, 1970. pp. 125. bibliog.

- Italy

LIBRI di testo e Resistenza: atti del convegno nazionale tenuto a Ferrara il 14-15 novembre 1970; ([paper by] Borghi [and others]). Roma, 1971. pp. 125.

TEXTILE FIBRES

UNITED NATIONS INDUSTRIAL DEVELOPMENT ORGANIZATION. Training for Industry Series. No. 3. The Łódź Textile Seminars. 1. Textile fibres. (ID/SER.D/3/1) New York, United Nations, 1970. pp. 52.

TEXTILE FIBRES, SYNTHETIC

UNITED NATIONS INDUSTRIAL DEVELOPMENT ORGANIZATION. Training for Industry Series. No. 3. The Łódź Textile Seminars. 2. Spinning. (ID/SER.D/3/2). New York, United Nations, 1970. pp. 60.

- Germany, Eastern

MARTEN (IRMA) Grundlagen und Formen der Entlohnung nach Arbeitsleistung, untersucht in Kunstfaserbetrieben der DDR. Berlin, 1957. pp. 156. bibliog.

- United Kingdom

U.K. Department of Industry. Business monitor: Production series. P 117. Production of man-made fibres. q. 1971- . London.

TEXTILE FINISHING

UNITED NATIONS INDUSTRIAL DEVELOPMENT ORGANIZATION. Training for Industry Series. No. 3. The Łódź Textile Seminars. 6. Textile finishing. (ID/SER.D/3/6). New York, United Nations, 1970. pp. 59. bibliog.

TEXTILE INDUSTRY AND FABRICS

BANDT (JACQUES DE) Les fonctions de production: discussion du schéma théorique à partir du cas des productions textiles. [Paris], 1970. pp. 98. (Institut de Recherches en Economie de la Production. Cahiers I.R.E.P. No. 2) With English summary.

UNITED NATIONS INDUSTRIAL DEVELOPMENT ORGANIZATION. Training for Industry Series. No. 3. The Łódź Textile Seminars. 1-8. New York, United Nations, 1970.

FERREIRA (MARIA MARGARIDA PONTE) Emprego e salarios na industria têxtil: tendências internacionais. Lisboa, 1971. pp. 109. (Fundo de Desenvolvimento da Mão-de-Obra. Cadernos. 37) With abstracts in French, English and German.

- Quality control

UNITED NATIONS INDUSTRIAL DEVELOPMENT ORGANIZATION. Training for Industry Series. No. 3. The Łódź Textile Seminars. 7. Testing and quality control. (ID/SER.D/3/7). New York, United Nations, 1970. pp. 81. bibliog.

- Technological innovations

UNITED NATIONS INDUSTRIAL DEVELOPMENT ORGANIZATION. Training for Industry Series. No. 3. The Łódź Textile Seminars. 5. Non-conventional methods of fabric production. (ID/SER.D/3/5). New York, United Nations, 1970. pp. 44. bibliogs.

- Testing

UNITED NATIONS INDUSTRIAL DEVELOPMENT ORGANIZATION. Training for Industry Series. No. 3. The Łódź Textile Seminars. 7. Testing and quality control. (ID/SER.D/3/7). New York, United Nations, 1970. pp. 81. bibliog.

- Austria

GREINER (WOLFGANG) Der Textileinzelhandel in Vorarlberg. Innsbruck, 1971. pp. 105. bibliog.

- France

GOSSART (MICHEL) Une industrie féodale et dynastique: le textile à Avesnelles au XIXème siècle. Avesnes-sur-Helpe, 1966. pp. 63.

FRANCE. Comité sectoriel de l'Industrie Textile. 1971. Préparation du 6e Plan...: rapport. [Paris], 1971. pp. 104.

- Germany

SCHMIDT (FRITZ) Stadtarchivar. Die Entwicklung der Cottbuser Tuchindustrie. Cottbus, 1928. pp. 255.

BREITENACHER (MICHAEL) Textilindustrie. 2nd ed. Berlin, [1971]. pp. 156. (Ifo-Institut für Wirtschaftsforschung. Struktur und Wachstum. Reihe Industrie. Heft 1)

- India

CHITALE (V.P.) and RAM (V.SRI) The exporting mills: a review of the investment, technology and export performance of the textile industry. New Delhi, 1970. pp. 112.

- India - Uttar Pradesh

UTTAR PRADESH. Kanpur Textile Mills Rationalization Enquiry Committee. 1961. Report...relating to (i) New Victoria Mills Co.Ltd., (ii) The Lakshmi Ratan Cotton Mills Co.Ltd., (iii) J.K. Cotton Manufacturers Ltd.; [Bind Basni Prasad, sole member]. Allahabad, 1961. pp. 106.

- Italy

SPECHT (KLAUS) Der Textileinzelhandel in Südtirol. Innsbruck, 1972. pp. 95. bibliog.

- Netherlands

MANDT (THOMAS) Stellung und Struktur der Textilveredlungsindustrie in den Niederlanden. Köln, 1965. pp. 73. bibliog. (North Rhine-Westphalia. Forschungsberichte des Landes Nordrhein-Westfalen. Nr.1559)

- Poland

HEIKE (OTTO) Aufbau und Entwicklung der Lodzer Textilindustrie: eine Arbeit deutscher Einwanderer in Polen für Europa. Mönchengladbach, 1971. pp. 326. bibliog.

- Russia

FOMIN (IVAN ALEKSEEVICH) Molodost' v sto piat'-desiat: k 150-letiiu Aleksandrovskoi tkatskoi fabriki imeni rabochego F.I. Kalinina. Vladimir, 1968. pp. 96.

IUSUPOV (ABDULLA IBRAGIMOVICH) Daleko i blizkoe: [istoricheskii ocherk]. Ul'ianovsk, 1969. pp. 163.

D'IACHENKO (A.A.) and others. Vyplaty i vozmeshcheniia khozorganam sredstv iz biudzheta. Moskva, 1970. pp. 95.

IOFFE (IOSIF GRIGOR'EVICH) and others. Ekonomika tekstil'noi promyshlennosti. Moskva, 1972. pp. 368.

- Russia - Bibliography

GRUZDEVA (I.V.) and others, compilers. Tekstil'naia promyshlennost': bibliograficheskii ukazatel', 1917-1965 gg. Moskva, 1968-70. 3 pts. (in 1).

- Russia - Tajikistan

UMAROV (ZAFAR) Rezervy ekonomii v tekstil'noi promyshlennosti Tadzhikistana. Dushanbe, 1968. pp. 52.

- Russia - Ukraine

DEREV'IANKIN (TYMOFII IVANOVYCH) Manufaktura na Ukraïni v kintsi XVIII - pershii polovyni XIX st.: tekstyl'ne vyrobnytstvo. Kyïv, 1960. pp. 127. bibliog.

- Russia - White Russia

MUKHINA (VALENTINA ALEKSANDROVNA) Ekonomika tekstil'noi promyshlennosti BSSR. Minsk, 1971. pp. 214.

- Spain

ENCISO RECIO (LUIS MIGUEL) Los establecimientos industriales españoles en el siglo XVIII: la manteleria de la Coruña. Madrid, 1963. pp. 265. bibliog. (Pamplona. Universidad de Navarra Facultad de Filosofia y Letras. [Publicaciones] Coleccion Historica. 6)

- United Kingdom

U.K. Department of Industry. Business monitor: Production series. P 131. Canvas goods and sacks and other made-up textiles. q. 1971- . London.

MORTON (JOCELYN) Three generations in a family textile firm. London, 1971. pp. 481.

EWING (A.F.) Planning and policies in the textile finishing industry. Bradford, 1972. pp. 114.

LOWE (NORMAN) The Lancashire textile industry in the sixteenth century. Manchester, 1972. pp. 122. bibliog. (Chetham Society. Remains, Historical and Literary, connected with the Palatine Counties of Lancaster and Chester. 3rd Series. vol. 20)

- United States

SIEGENTHALER (HANSJOERG) Das Gewicht monopolistischer Elemente in der amerikanischen Textilindustrie, 1840-1880: modische Produktvariation unter Führung des Kommissionshauses. Berlin, [1972]. pp. 127. bibliog.

TEXTILE MACHINERY

ANSTIE (JOHN) Observations on the importance and necessity of introducing improved machinery into the woollen manufactory; most particularly as it respects the interests of... Wilts, Gloucester and Somerset;... [reprint of work published in 1803]. Shannon, [1971]. pp. 99.

UNITED NATIONS INDUSTRIAL DEVELOPMENT ORGANIZATION. Training for Industry Series. No. 3. The Łódź Textile Seminars. 8. Plant and power engineering. (ID/SER.D/3/8). New York, United Nations, 1970. pp. 84.

TEXTILE WORKERS

FERREIRA (MARIA MARGARIDA PONTE) Emprego e salarios na industria têxtil: tendências internacionais. Lisboa, 1971. pp. 109. (Fundo de Desenvolvimento da Mão-de-Obra. Cadernos. 37) With abstracts in French, English and German.

- Austria

RAUTER (FRANZ) Das Fremdarbeiterproblem in Innsbrucker Textil- und Bekleidungsbetrieben. Innsbruck, 1972. pp. 68. bibliog.

- European Economic Community countries

ECONOMIC DEVELOPMENT COMMITTEE FOR THE WOOL TEXTILE INDUSTRY. Manpower Working Party. Employment practices in EEC textile industries; a report on the visit by members of the... Working Party to textile employers' organisations and trade unions in France, West Germany and Italy. London, National Economic Development Office, 1973. pp. 76.

- United Kingdom

HUNTER (LAURENCE C.) Report ... of an inquiry into a difference between members of the Association of Scientific, Technical and Managerial Staffs and Courtaulds Limited over the termination of employment at Spennymoor of certain members of the Association. London, H.M.S.O., [1971]. pp. 33.

REPORT of a Committee of Inquiry into a dispute between employees of the Mansfield Hosiery Mills Limited, Loughborough, and their employer; [Kenneth Robinson, chairman]. London, H.M.S.O., [1972]. pp. 23.

- United States

DUNNE (WILLIAM F.) **Gastonia: citadel of the class struggle in the new South;...for the National Textile Workers Union.** New York, 1929. pp. 58.

THAELMANN (ERNST)

Dem KAEMPFER für Frieden und Freiheit, Ernst Thälmann; [edited by H. Most and E. Walter]. Moskau, [1936]. pp. 139.

THAILAND

BABIĆ (BLAGOJE S.) Laos, Kambodža, Tajland. Beograd, 1971. pp. 331. bibliog. (Institut Za Medjunarodnu Politiku i Privredu. Priručnici o Stranim Zemljama).

- Bibliography

THROMBLEY (WOODWORTH G.) and SIFFIN (WILLIAM JOSEPH) Thailand: politics, economy and socio-cultural setting; a selective guide to the literature. Bloomington, [1972]. pp. 148.

- Census

THAILAND. Census, 1970. 1970 population and housing census; changwat [series]. [Bangkok], 1972 in progress.

THAILAND. Census, 1970. Selected tables from 1°/° sample, 1970 population and housing census. [Bangkok], 1973. pp. 14.

- Commerce

SITTON (GORDON R.) and others. The growing importance of upland crops in the foreign trade of Thailand. Bangkok, 1962. pp. 115. (Bangkok. Kasetsart University. Department of Agricultural Economics. Kasetsart Economic Reports. No. 16) In Thai and English.

- Description and travel

KALMYKOV (ANDREI DMITRIEVICH) Memoirs of a Russian diplomat: outposts of the empire, 1893-1917;... edited by Alexandra Kalmykow. New Haven, 1971. pp. 290.

- Economic conditions

MARZOUK (GIRGIS ABDO) Economic development and policies: case study of Thailand. Rotterdam, 1972. pp. 472.

THAILAND. Ministry of National Development. Information Bureau. 1972. Ministry of National Development handbook, (1972). [3rd ed.] [Bangkok], 1972. pp. 198.

- Economic conditions - Mathematical models

ENOS (JOHN LAWRENCE) Modeling the economic development of a poorly endowed region: the northeast of Thailand. Santa Monica, Calif., 1970. pp. 328. bibliog. (Rand Corporation. Research Memoranda. 6185)

- Economic history

INGRAM (JAMES CARLTON) Economic change in Thailand, 1850-1970. new ed. Stanford, 1971. pp. 352. bibliog.

HESSE (KURT) and ISCHINGER (WOLFGANG) Die Entwicklungsschwelle: der Übergang vom Entwicklungsland zum entwickelten Land unter Einbeziehung von drei Testfällen. Berlin, [1973]. pp. 252. bibliogs.

- Economic policy

THAILAND. National Economic Development Board, 1967. Evaluation of the first six-year plan, 1961-1966. Bangkok, 1967. pp. 107.

MARZOUK (GIRGIS ABDO) Economic development and policies: case study of Thailand. Rotterdam, 1972. pp. 472.

THAILAND - Economic policy (Cont'd.)

PAKKASEM (PHISIT) Thailand's northeast economic development planning: a case study in regional planning; a thesis...for the degree of Doctor of Philosophy, University of Pittsburgh. [Bangkok, National Economic and Social Development Board, 1973]. fo. 220. bibliog. (Studies in the Regional Economic Development Planning in Thailand. No. 1)

- Economic policy - Mathematical models

ENOS (JOHN LAWRENCE) Modeling the economic development of a poorly endowed region: the northeast of Thailand. Santa Monica, Calif., 1970. pp. 328. bibliog. (Rand Corporation. Research Memoranda. 6185)

- Executive departments

THAILAND. Ministry of National Development. Information Bureau. 1972. Ministry of National Development handbook, (1972). [3rd ed.] [Bangkok], 1972. pp. 198.

- Foreign relations - China

LOVELACE (DANIEL D.) China and "People's War" in Thailand, 1964-1969. Berkeley, Calif., [1971]. pp. 99. (California University. Center for Chinese Studies. China Research Monographs. No.8)

- Politics and government

LOVELACE (DANIEL D.) China and "People's War" in Thailand, 1964-1969. Berkeley, Calif., [1971]. pp. 99. (California University. Center for Chinese Studies. China Research Monographs. No.8)

- Population

THOMLINSON (RALPH) and others. The methodology of the longitudinal study of social, economic, and demographic change. Bangkok, 1971. pp. 71. (Chulalongkorn University. Institute of Population Studies. Research Reports. No. 6)

- Rural conditions

HANKS (LUCIEN MASON) Rice and man: agricultural ecology in southeast Asia. Chicago, 1972. pp. 174. bibliog.

- Social conditions

THOMLINSON (RALPH) and others. The methodology of the longitudinal study of social, economic, and demographic change. Bangkok, 1971. pp. 71. (Chulalongkorn University. Institute of Population Studies. Research Reports. No. 6)

- Social policy

THAILAND. National Economic Development Board, 1967. Evaluation of the first six-year plan, 1961-1966. Bangkok, 1967. pp. 107.

- Statistics, Vital

THAILAND. National Statistical Office. 1970. Report: the survey of population change, 1964-67. [Bangkok, 1970]. pp. 42. bibliog. In English and Thai.

THALIDOMIDE

PRINGLE (MIA LILLY KELLMER) and FIDDES (D.O.) The challenge of thalidomide: a pilot study of the educational needs of children in Scotland affected by the drug. London, 1970. pp. 102. bibliog.

ROSKIES (ETHEL) Abnormality and normality: the mothering of thalidomide children. Ithaca, 1972. pp. 347. bibliog.

SJÖSTRÖM (HENNING) and NILSSON (ROBERT) Thalidomide and the power of the drug companies. Harmondsworth, 1972. pp. 281.

THAMES, RIVER

LONDON. Greater London Council. Department of Architecture and Civic Design. Thames-side environmental assessment: a study of environmental quality on Thames-side within Greater London. London, [1968]. pp. 91.

THEATRE

COPFERMANN (EMILE) La mise en crise théâtrale. Paris, 1972. pp. 251.

- Moral and religious aspects

NORTHBROOKE (JOHN) A treatise against dicing, dancing, plays, and interludes, with other idle pastimes...from the earliest edition, about A.D. 1577, with an introduction and notes. London, 1843; New York, 1971. pp. 188. Facsimile reprint.

FOOTE (GEORGE WILLIAM) The sign of the cross: a candid criticism of Mr. Wilson Barrett's play. London, 1896. pp. 47.

- United Kingdom

WILKIE (ROY) and BRADLEY (DAVID A.) The subsidised theatre: its organisation and audience. Glasgow, 1970. pp. 65.

THEATRE AUDIENCES

WILKIE (ROY) and BRADLEY (DAVID A.) The subsidised theatre: its organisation and audience. Glasgow, 1970. pp. 65.

THEODŌRAKIS (MIKES)

THEODŌRAKIS (MIKES) Journal de résistance; traduit du grec par Jean Criticos et Pierre Comberousse. Paris, [1971]. pp. 323.

THEODŌRAKIS (MIKES) Journals of resistance; translated from the French by Graham Webb. London, 1973. pp. 334.

THEOLOGY, Dutch Reformed Church

HEYNS (J. A.) Die huidige stand van die gereformeerde teologie in Nederland en ons verantwoordelikheid. Pretoria, 1971. pp. 35. (Pretoria. University of Pretoria. Publications. New Series. No. 57)

THEOSOPHY

BLAVATSKAYA (ELENA PETROVNA) The Thersites of freethought: being a reply to certain attacks. London, [1889?]. pp. 15.

FOOTE (GEORGE WILLIAM) The new Cagliostro: an open letter to Madame Blavatsky. London, 1889. pp. 16.

FOOTE (GEORGE WILLIAM) Secularism and theosophy: a rejoinder to Mrs. Besant's pamphlet. London, 1889. pp. 16.

BESTERMAN (THEODORE) The Annie Besant calendar. London, 1927. 1 vol. (unpaged).

THESAURI

AITCHISON (JEAN) and GILCHRIST (ALAN) Thesaurus construction: a practical manual. London, [1972]. pp. 95. bibliog.

THIRION (ANDRE)

THIRION (ANDRE) Révolutionnaires sans révolution. Paris, [1972]. pp. 580.

THIRTY YEARS' WAR, 1618-1648

POLIŠENSKÝ (J.V.) The Thirty Years War;...translated by Robert Evans. London, [1971]. pp. 305. bibliog.

- Economic aspects

Det KONTINENTALA krigets ekonomi: studier i krigsfinansering under svensk stormaktstid; ([by] Hans Landberg [and others]). Stockholm, [1971]. pp. 506. bibliog. (Uppsala. Universitet. Historiska Institutionen. Studia Historica Upsaliensia. 36) With German summary.

THOMAS, Aquinas, Saint

DOIG (JAMES C.) Aquinas on metaphysics: a historico-doctrinal study of the Commentary on the Metaphysics. The Hague, 1972. pp. 417. bibliog.

THONGA TRIBE

COLSON (ELIZABETH) The social consequences of resettlement: the impact of the Kariba resettlement upon the Gwembe Tonga. Manchester, [1971]. pp. 277. bibliog. (Zambia University. Institute for African Studies. Kariba Studies. 4).

THOREZ (MAURICE)

THOREZ (MAURICE) Fils du peuple. rev. ed. Paris, [1970]. pp. 369.

THOUGHT AND THINKING

AYER (Sir ALFRED JULES) Thinking and meaning: [inaugural lecture]. London, 1947. pp. 28.

The CULTURAL context of learning and thinking: an exploration in experimental anthropology; by Michael Cole [and others]. London, 1971. pp. 304. bibliog.

PRIOR (ARTHUR NORMAN) Objects of thought; edited [from incomplete manuscripts left by the author] by P.T. Geach and A.J.P. Kenny. Oxford, 1971. pp. 175. bibliog.

ADAMS (PARVEEN) ed. Language in thinking: selected readings. Harmondsworth, 1972. pp. 391. bibliogs.

BOLTON (NEIL) The psychology of thinking. London, 1972. pp. 291. bibliog.

ROBINSON (W. PETER) and RACKSTRAW (SUSAN J.) A question of answers. London, 1972. 2 vols. bibliogs.

RUBINSHTEIN (S.L.) Das Denken und die Wege seiner Erforschung; (übersetzt aus dem Russischen von Peter G. Klemm). Berlin, 1972. pp. 141.

MODES of thought: essays on thinking in western and non-western societies; [dedicated to Sir Edward Evans-Pritchard]; edited by Robin Horton and Ruth Finnegan. London, 1973. pp. 399. bibliog.

THURGAU

- Constitution

THURGAU (CANTON). Grosser Rat. 1969. Hundert Jahre Thurgauische Kantonsverfassung, 1869-1969; Gedenkfeier des Grossen Rates am 28. Februar 1969 in Frauenfeld. [Frauenfeld, 1969]. pp. 24.

THURNEYSEN (JOHANN JAKOB)

GERMANN (MARTIN) Johann Jakob Thurneysen der Jüngere 1754-1803, Verleger, Buchdrucker und Buchhändler in Basel: ein Beitrag zur Geschichte der Spätaufklärung in Basel, etc. Basel, 1973. pp. 141. bibliog.

TIBET

Die LEIDEN eines Volkes: die Tragödie Tibets und der tibetischen Flüchtlinge; mit...Beiträgen verschiedener Autoren;... herausgegeben von der Schweizer Tibethilfe, Solothurn. 2nd ed. Solothurn, [1961]. pp. 320. bibliog.

- Economic conditions

GREAT changes in Tibet; [by] Pasang [and others]. Peking, 1972. pp. 53.

- Foreign relations

MULLIK (B.N.) The Chinese betrayal: (my years with Nehru). Bombay, 1971. pp. 650.

- Foreign relations - China

PETECH (LUCIANO) China and Tibet in the early XVIIIth century: history of the establishment of Chinese protectorate in Tibet. 2nd ed. Leiden, 1972. pp. 309. bibliog.

TIJERINA (REIES)

BLAWIS (PATRICIA BELL) Tijerina and the land grants: Mexican Americans in struggle for their heritage. New York, 1971. pp. 191.

TIJUANA

- Social conditions

PRICE (JOHN A.) Tijuana: urbanization in a border culture. Notre Dame, [1973]. pp. 195. bibliog.

TILLICH (PAUL JOHANNES OSKAR)

REITZ (RUEDIGER) Paul Tillich und New Harmony. Stuttgart, 1970. pp. 128. bibliog.

TILLON (CHARLES)

TILLON (CHARLES) Un "procès de Moscou" à Paris; précédé de L'interrogation; par Raymond Jean. Paris, [1971]. pp. 201.

TIMBER

- Russia

IARMOLA (IVAN SEMENOVICH) Voprosy lesosnabzheniia v SSSR. 2nd ed. Moskva, 1972. pp. 248. bibliog.

- United States

OLSON (SHERRY H.) The depletion myth: a history of railroad use of timber. Cambridge, Mass., 1971. pp. 228.

TIME

BASIC issues in the philosophy of time; edited by Eugene Freeman and Wilfrid Sellars. La Salle, Ill., [1971]. pp. 241.

RESCHER (NICHOLAS) and URQUHART (ALASDAIR) Temporal logic. New York, 1971. pp. 273. bibliog.

TIME in science and philosophy: an international study of some current problems; edited by Jiří Zeman. Amsterdam. 1971. pp. 305. bibliogs.

POCOCK (JOHN GREVILLE AGARD) Politics, language and time: essays on political thought and history. London, 1972. pp. 291.

- Systems and standards

U.K. Ministry of Public Building and Works. 1970. Survey on the effect of B[ritish] S[tandard] T[ime], winter 1969/70. [London,] 1970. fo.4,(15).

TIME (LAW)

- Scandinavia

NORWAY. Justis- og Politidepartementet. Norske Delegerte til å Revidere Foreldelsesloven i Nordisk Samarbeid. 1957. Innstilling. Oslo, 1957. pp. 80.

TIME ALLOCATION

LEWIS (JOHN PARRY) The values of time: an approach to a new theory and its use in cost-benefit studies. [Manchester, 1970?]. fo. 49. (Manchester. University. Centre for Urban and Regional Research. Occasional Papers. No. 5)

Das ZEITBUDGET der Bevölkerung; [by] Gerhard Lippold [and others]. Berlin, 1971. pp. 189.

SZALAI (SANDOR) and others, eds. The use of time: daily activities of urban and suburban populations in twelve countries. The Hague, [1972]. pp. 868. bibliog. (European Coordination Centre for Research and Documentation in the Social Sciences. Publications. 5)

- Mathematical models

LEWIS (HAROLD GREGG) Income and substitution effects in labor force participation and hours of work. Minneapolis, 1972. fo. 20. (Minnesota University. Center for Economic Research. Discussion Papers. No. 18)

TIME ALLOCATION SURVEYS

- Belgium

JAVEAU (CLAUDE) Les vingt-quatre heures du Belge; l'enquête belge du Projet International Budgets-Temps; recherche comparative multi-nationale réalisée sous les auspices du Centre Européen de Coordination de Recherche et de Documentation en Sciences Sociales, à Vienne. Bruxelles, [1970]. pp. 146. bibliog. (Centre National de Sociologie du Travail. Section "Loisir et Culture Modernes". Etudes)

TIME AND ECONOMIC REACTIONS

POTEMKIN (PETR IVANOVICH) Natsional'noe bogatstvo i faktor vremeni. Novosibirsk, 1965. pp. 41.

TEMPORAL dimensions of development administration: [essays deriving from a seminar sponsored by the Comparative Administration Group of the American Society for Public Administration, 1965]; edited by Dwight Waldo. Durham, N.C., 1970. pp. 312. (American Society for Public Administration. Comparative Administration Group. Comparative Administration Group Series)

VREMIA: ego ekonomiia i ispol'zovanie. Moskva, 1970. pp. 190.

DHRYMES (PHOEBUS J.) Distributed lags: problems of estimation and formulation. San Francisco, 1971. pp. 414. bibliog.

KOLPAKOV (B.T.) and PATRUSHEV (VASILII DMITRIEVICH) eds. Biudzhet vremeni gorodskogo naseleniia. Moskva, 1971. pp. 248. bibliog.

WINTER (TILMANN) Handlungs- und Wirkungsverzögerungen in der Wirtschaftspolitik: Versuch einer ökonomisch-politischen Analyse. Berlin, [1971]. pp. 154. bibliog.

SUPRUN (PETR IVANOVICH) Biudzhet vremeni trudiashchikhsia. Moskva, 1972. pp. 175. bibliog.

TIME AND MOTION STUDY

SHAW (ANNE GILLESPIE) An introduction to the theory and application of motion study. London, Ministry of Aircraft Production, 1944. pp. 42. bibliog.

ANSELL (D. J.) and GILES (A. K.) The farmer and his time: an agricultural exercise in activity sampling'. Reading, 1969. pp. 16, 17 tables. (Reading. University. Faculty of Agriculture and Horticulture. Agricultural Economics Department. Miscellaneous Studies. No.46)

U.K. Department of Employment and Productivity. Manpower and Productivity Service. Central Information Service. 1969. Predetermined motion time systems. London, 1969. fo.10. (Information Papers. New Series. No.1)

LOCAL AUTHORITIES MANAGEMENT SERVICES AND COMPUTER COMMITTEE. National Conference, 4th, 1971. The effective use of resources in the seventies: report of Eastbourne Conference, etc. London, 1971. pp. 483. bibliogs.

SUPRUN (PETR IVANOVICH) Biudzhet vremeni trudiashchikhsia. Moskva, 1972. pp. 175. bibliog.

TIME PERCEPTION

LYNCH (KEVIN) What time is this place? Cambridge, Mass., [1972]. pp. 277. bibliog.

TIME SERIES ANALYSIS

CANADA. Dominion Bureau of Statistics. General Time Series Section. 1969- . CANSIM [Canadian Socio-Economic Information Management System]: users' manual for data retrieval and manipulation. Ottawa, 1969 in progress. Loose-leaf binder.

HANNAN (EDWARD JAMES) Multiple time series. New York, [1970]. pp. 536. bibliog.

COOPER (RICHARD V.L.) The use of spectral analytic techniques in economics. [Santa Monica], 1972. pp. 26. bibliog. (Rand Corporation. [Papers]. 4882)

TIN

LA SPADA (A.) Patterns of world tin consumption, 1957-1968. London, International Tin Council, [1970]. pp. 99.

LA SPADA (A.) Prospects for world tin consumption up to 1975. London, International Tin Council, 1971. pp. 47.

TIN INDUSTRY
- Malaya

TREGONNING (KENNEDY GORDON) Straits tin: a brief account of the first seventy-five years of the Straits Trading Company, Limited, 1887-1962. Singapore, [1962?]. pp. 84.

TIN MINES AND MINING
- United Kingdom

PENNINGTON (ROBERT ROLAND) Stannary law: a history of the mining law of Cornwall and Devon. Newton Abbot, [1973]. pp. 229.

- United Kingdom - Cornwall

NOALL (CYRIL) Levant: the mine beneath the sea. Truro, 1970. pp. 142.

TIOS

VANSINA (JAN) The Tio kingdom of the Middle Congo, 1880-1892. London, 1973. pp. 586. bibliog.

TIRPITZ (ALFRED VON)

BERGHAHN (VOLKER R.) Der Tirpitz-Plan: Genesis und Verfall einer innenpolitischen Krisenstrategie unter Wilhelm II. Düsseldorf, [1971]. pp. 640. bibliog.

TITO (JOSIP BROZ)

MOLLET (GUY) Le socialisme selon Tito. [Paris, 1971]. pp. 160.

BEGOVIĆ (VLAJKO) Tito: biografske beleške. Beograd, 1972. pp. 91. With illustrations.

ROBERTS (WALTER R.) Tito, Mihailović and the Allies, 1941-1945. New Brunswick, N.J., [1973]. pp. 406. bibliog.

TIUMEN'
See TYUMEN'

TOBACCO
- United States

WAGNER (SUSAN) Cigarette country: tobacco in American history and politics. New York, 1971. pp. 248.

TOBACCO HABIT

ZACUNE (JIM) and HENSMAN (CELIA) Drugs, alcohol and tobacco in Britain. London, 1971. pp. 239. bibliogs.

TOBACCO MANUFACTURE AND TRADE
- Canada - Quebec

QUEBEC (PROVINCE). Commission Royale d'Enquête sur l'Agriculture au Québec, 1965. La culture et la mise en marché du tabac au Québec; rapport. [Québec], 1967 [or rather 1968]. pp. 21.

- Europe

MAURER (WERNER CARL) Probleme der Tabakwirtschaft im Hinblick auf den wirtschaftlichen Zusammenschluss Europas. Mainz, 1964. pp. 65. bibliog.

- Germany

GERMANY. Taback-Enquête-Kommission. 1880. Tabackbau, Tabackfabrikation und Tabackhandel im Deutschen Reich und in Luxemburg, etc. In Band 42 of

GERMANY. Statistisches Reichsamt. Statistik des Deutschen Reichs. [Alte Folge]. Band 1-63; (with Alphabetisches Inhalts-Verzeichniss). [Berlin, 1873-83, repr. 1969]. 96 pts. (in 76).

- India - Andhra Pradesh

NATIONAL COUNCIL OF APPLIED ECONOMIC RESEARCH. Cotton and tobacco in Andhra Pradesh: production and marketing. New Delhi, 1971. pp. 158.

- Russia - Ukraine

HALYCH (HRYHORII VASYL'OVYCH) and NAKONECHNYI (DMYTRO PETROVYCH) L'vivs'ka tiutiunova fabryka. L'viv, 1968. pp. 76.

- United Kingdom

ALFORD (BERNARD WILLIAM ERNEST) W.D. and H.O. Wills and the development of the U.K. tobacco industry, 1786-1965. London, 1973. pp. 500.

TODD (JUDITH)

TODD (JUDITH) The right to say no. London, 1972. pp. 200.

TOENNIES (FERDINAND)

CAHNMAN (WERNER JACOB) ed. Ferdinand Tönnies: a new evaluation; essays and documents. Leiden, 1973. pp. 302.

TOGLIATTI (PALMIRO)

CHERCHI (GIOVANNI MARIA) Togliatti a Sassari, 1908-1911: una provincia sarda nell'età giolittiana. Roma, 1972. pp. 140.

BOCCA (GIORGIO) Palmiro Togliatti. Bari, 1973. pp. 753.

TOGO
- Economic conditions

BANQUE TOGOLAISE DE DEVELOPPEMENT. Rapport annuel. a., 1969/70- Lomé.

TOKENS
- United Kingdom

THOMPSON (R.H.) The dies of Thomas Spence, 1750-1814. [Oxford, 1970]. pp. 126. bibliog. (Reprinted from The British Numismatic Journal, vol. 38, 1969)

TOKYO

TOKYO METROPOLITAN RESEARCH INSTITUTE FOR ENVIRONMENTAL PROTECTION. Environmental protection in Tokyo. Tokyo, 1970. pp. 88.

TOKYO. Bureau of General Affairs. Liaison and Protocol Section. Tokyo fights pollution: an urgent appeal for reform. Tokyo, 1971. pp. 267. (Tokyo. Metropolitan Government. Municipal Library. No. 4)

TOKYO. Metropolitan Government. Outline of plan to protect citizens of Tokyo from environmental pollution, 1972. Tokyo, 1972. pp. 122.

TOKYO (Cont'd.)

- Civic improvement

TOKYO. Bureau of General Affairs. Liaison and Protocol Section. Tokyo for the people: concepts for urban renewal. Tokyo, 1972. pp. 144. (Tokyo. Metropolitan Government. Municipal Library. No. 6)

TOLERATION

Die FREIHEIT des Glaubens: Untersuchungen zu Artikel 4 des Grundgesetzes für die Bundesrepublik Deutschland. 1. [Hannover, 1967]. pp. 264. bibliog. (Niedersaechsische Landeszentrale für Politische Bildung. Schriftenreihe. Verfassungsrecht und Verfassungswirklichkeit. Heft 6)

SEMINAR ON THE DANGERS OF A RECRUDESCENCE OF INTOLERANCE IN ALL ITS FORMS AND THE SEARCH FOR WAYS OF PREVENTING AND COMBATING IT, NICE, 1971. Seminar...; (organized by the United Nations Division of Human Rights, in co-operation with the government of France) [held at] Nice, France, 24 August - 6 September, 1971. (ST/TAO/HR/44). New York, United Nations, 1971. pp. 31.

GRAY (TONY) Psalms and slaughter: a study in bigotry. London, 1972. pp. 248. bibliog.

TOLL ROADS

WIGAN (M. RAMSAY) and BAMFORD (T.J.G.) A comparative network simulation of different methods of traffic restraint. Crowthorne, 1973. pp. 40. (U.K. Transport and Road Research Laboratory. Reports. LR 566)

- Mathematical models

WIGAN (M. RAMSAY) Benefit assessment for network traffic models and application to road pricing. Crowthorne, 1971. pp. 22. (U.K. Road Research Laboratory. Reports. LR 417)

- United Kingdom

TEMPLE (JOHN) Darlington and the turnpike roads. Darlington, 1971. pp. 33. bibliog. (Darlington. Public Library. Local History Publications. No.1)

ALBERT (WILLIAM ISADORE) The turnpike road system in England, 1663-1840. Cambridge, 1972. pp. 300. bibliog.

TOLLS

- Argentine Republic

CINCUNEGUI (JUAN BAUTISTA) El peaje en la legislacion argentina: la concesion de obra publica y peaje como sistema de financiacion de obras de infraestructura. Rosario, 1968. pp. 121. bibliog.

TOLMER (ALEXANDER)

BLAKE (L.J.) Gold escort. Melbourne, 1971. pp. 228. bibliog.

TOLSTOI (LEV NIKOLAEVICH) Graf

POLNER (TIKHON IVANOVICH) Lev Tolstoi i ego zhena: istoriia odnoi liubvi. Parizh, 1928. pp. 237.

ROZANOVA (SUSANNA ABRAMOVNA) Tolstoi i Gertsen. Moskva, 1972. pp. 303.

TOMATO PRODUCTS

FOOD AND AGRICULTURE ORGANIZATION. Commodity Bulletin Series. No. 47. Processed fruit and vegetables: trends in world production and trade of citrus products, canned peaches and apricots, and tomato products. Rome, 1970. pp. 76.

TOMILIN (SERGEI ARKAD'EVICH)

TOMILIN (SERGEI ARKAD'EVICH) Demografiia i sotsial'naia gigiena: [sbornik statei]. Moskva, 1973. pp. 311. bibliog.

TONGA

- History

RUTHERFORD (NOEL) Shirley Baker and the King of Tonga. Melbourne, 1971. pp. 202. bibliog.

TONNAGE

- Tables, etc.

INTER-GOVERNMENTAL MARITIME CONSULTATIVE ORGANIZATION. 1959. International regulations for tonnage measurement of ships; (with Figures). London, 1959. 2 pts.

TOOKE (THOMAS)

RIETER (HEINZ) Die gegenwärtige Inflationstheorie und ihre Ansätze im Werk von Thomas Tooke. Berlin, 1971. pp. 383. bibliog.

TOPOLOGY

JOHNSON (DALE MARTIN) The role of axiomatisation in the logic of mathematical discovery with special reference to the axiomatisation of general topology; [Ph.D. (London) thesis]. 1972. fo. 317. bibliog. Typescript: unpublished. This thesis is the property of London University and may not be removed from the Library.

TORBAY

- Transit systems

TORBAY. County Borough Council. Torbay development plan: transportation strategies: (final report); director of technical services, M.R. Hawkins. [Torquay, 1972]. 1 vol. (various pagings).

TORO

- Politics and government

UGANDA. Commission of Inquiry into the Recent Disturbances amongst the Baamba and Bakonjo People of Toro. 1962. Report; [F.C. Ssembeguya, chairman]. Entebbe, [1962]. pp. 29.

TORONTO

- Growth

GOHEEN (PETER G.) Victorian Toronto, 1850 to 1900: pattern and process of growth. Chicago, 1970. pp. 278. bibliog. (Chicago. University. Department of Geography. Research Papers. No. 127)

- History

GOHEEN (PETER G.) Victorian Toronto, 1850 to 1900: pattern and process of growth. Chicago, 1970. pp. 278. bibliog. (Chicago. University. Department of Geography. Research Papers. No. 127)

- Police

> ONTARIO. Royal Commission of Inquiry in relation to the Conduct of the Public and the Metropolitan Toronto Police, 1971. Report...; by I.A. Vannini. [Toronto, 1972.] fo. 181.

- Politics and government

> ROSE (ALBERT) Governing metropolitan Toronto: a social and political analysis, 1953-1971. Berkeley, Calif., [1972]. pp. 201.

- Social conditions

> WOODSWORTH (JAMES S.) My neighbor: a study of city conditions; a plea for social service; [reprint of work first published in 1911]; with an introduction by Richard Allen. Toronto, [1972]. pp. 216. bibliogs.

- Social policy

> ROSE (ALBERT) Governing metropolitan Toronto: a social and political analysis, 1953-1971. Berkeley, Calif., [1972]. pp. 201.

TORONTO UNIVERSITY

> TORONTO. University. Commission on the Government of the University of Toronto. Toward community in university government: report of the Commission, etc. Toronto, [1970]. pp. 240.

TORRE (LISANDRO DE LA)

> MONTEAGUDO (PIO ISAAC) Migraciones internas en la Argentina y las utopias revolucionarias de L. de la Torre: problemas agrarios. Buenos Aires, 1956. pp. 187.

TORRE (VICTOR RAUL HAYA DE LA)
See HAYA DE LA TORRE (VICTOR RAUL)

TORRES BODET (JAIME)

> TORRES BODET (JAIME) Memorias. vols. 2-3. Mexico, 1970-71. 2 vols.

TORRES RESTREPO (CAMILO)

> TORRES RESTREPO (CAMILO) Camilo, el cura revolucionario: sus obras; [edited by Juan Garcia Elorrio]. [Buenos Aires, 1968]. pp. 317. bibliog.

> TORRES RESTREPO (CAMILO) Cristianismo y revolucion; prologo, seleccion y notas de Oscar Maldonado, Guitemie Olivieri y German Zabala. Mexico, 1970. pp. 612. bibliogs.

TORRIENTE Y BRAU (PABLO FELIX ALEJANDRO SALVADOR DE LA)

> TORRIENTE (LOLO DE LA) Torriente-Brau: retrato de un hombre. La Habana, 1968. pp. 235.

TORTS

- United Kingdom

> BAKER (C.D.) Tort. London, 1972. pp. 295.

> STREET (HARRY) The law of torts. 5th ed. London, 1972. pp. 524.

> HEYDON (JOHN DYSON) Economic torts. London, 1973. pp. 99.

- United States

> KEETON (PAGE) and KEETON (ROBERT E.) Cases and materials on the law of torts. St. Paul, Minn., 1971. pp. 1193.

TORTS (INTERNATIONAL LAW)

> GRISOLI (ANGELO) L'illecito e la responsabilità delle Comunita Europee. Padova, 1970. pp. 150. bibliog. (Estratto dal vol.38 degli St di nelle Scienze Giuridiche e Sociali dell'universita di Pavia)

TORTURE

> [WINDISCH-GRAETZ (JOSEPH NIKOLAS VON) Graf.] Mémoire sur la difficulté et la possibilite d'elever la morale et la législation au rang des sciences exactes. 2de partie. De la peine de morte et de la torture. [Vienna], 1801. pp. 236. 24cm. Lacking final pages. No more published?

- Algeria

> KERAMANE (HAFID) La pacification: livre noir de six années de guerre en Algérie. Lausanne, [1960]. pp. 272.

> BOLLARDIERE (JACQUES PARIS DE) Bataille d'Alger, bataille de l'homme. 2nd ed. [Paris, 1972]. pp. 167.

> DEMERON (PIERRE) Les 400 coups de Massu. [Paris, 1972]. pp. 41. (Extrait du mensuel Lui de mars 1972, no. 98)

> ROY (JULES) J'accuse le général Massu. Paris, [1972]. pp. 119.

- Brazil

> ALARCON (RODRIGO) Tortures au Brésil; (traduit et adapté par Christine Royer). Montreal, [1971]. pp. 187.

> BRUNE (JOHANNES MARIA) ed. Die Papageienschaukel: Diktatur und Folter in Brasilien; eine Dokumentation; übersetzt und in Zusammenarbeit mit der Brasiliengruppe von Amnesty international herausgegeben, etc. Düsseldorf, 1971. pp. 160.

> "PAU de Arara": la violence militaire au Brésil; avec en annexe un dossier de tortures; traduit du portugais. Paris, 1971. pp. 175.

- Israel

> ISRAELI LEAGUE FOR HUMAN AND CIVIL RIGHTS. Israelis versus Israel: (memorandum to the U.N. Commission on the Israeli Practices in the Occupied Territories...and the International League for the Rights of Man; drafted by...Israel Shahak and...Uriel Davis). [London], 1970. pp. 20.

- South Africa

> CARLSON (JOEL) No neutral ground. London, 1973. pp. 382.

- Spain

> BATASUNA: la répression au pays basque; traduit du basque. Paris, 1970. pp. 132.

- United Kingdom - Ireland, Northern

> JOHNS (STEPHEN) Tory torture in Ulster. London, 1971. pp. 29. (Socialist Labour League. Pocket Library. No. 2)

> NORTHERN AID and ASSOCIATION FOR LEGAL JUSTICE. Torture: the record of British brutality in Ireland. Dublin, [1971?]. pp. 39.

TORTURE - United Kingdom - Ireland, Northern (Cont'd.)

AMNESTY INTERNATIONAL. Report of an enquiry into allegations of ill-treatment in Northern Ireland. London, [1972]. pp. 46.

McGUFFIN (JOHN) Internment. Tralee, [1973]. pp. 228.

- Venezuela

LABANA CORDERO (EFRAIN) T03-campo antiguerrillero;... epilogo de Freddy Balzan. Caracas, 1969 repr. 1970. pp. 115.

TOTALITARIANISM

ARENDT (HANNAH) The origins of totalitarianism. 3rd ed. New York, [1966]. pp. 526. bibliog.

SCHAPIRO (LEONARD BERTRAM) Totalitarianism. London, 1972. pp. 144. bibliog.

SZAMUELY (TIBOR) Unique Conservative: three extracts from the works of Tibor Szamuely. London, 1973. pp. 28. (Conservative Political Centre. [Publications]. No. 531)

TOUCOULEURS

WANE (YAYA) Les Toucouleur du Fouta Tooro, Sénégal: stratification sociale et structure familiale. Dakar, 1969. pp. 250. bibliog. (Institut Fondamental d'Afrique Noire. Initiations Africaines. 25)

SAINT-MARTIN (YVES) L'Empire toucouleur, 1848-1897. Paris, [1970]. pp. 192. bibliog.

TOULOUSE

- Growth

BERINGUIER (CHRISTIAN) and others. Toulouse, Midi-Pyrénées: la transition. [Paris, 1972]. pp. 381.

- History

HIGGS (DAVID) Ultraroyalism in Toulouse: from its origins to the revolution of 1830. Baltimore, [1973]. pp. 223. bibliog. (Johns Hopkins University. Studies in Historical and Political Science. Series 90. No. 2)

- Industries

FRANCE. French Embassy, London. Service de Presse et d'Information. 1971. The city of Toulouse. London, [1971]. pp. 48.

- Social conditions

BERINGUIER (CHRISTIAN) and others. Toulouse, Midi-Pyrénées: la transition. [Paris, 1972]. pp. 381.

TOURIST CAMPS, HOSTELS, ETC

- Poland

POLAND. Główny Urząd Statystyczny. Statystyka Polski: Materiały Statystyczne. Nr.109(231). Hotele robotnicze, 1971. Warszawa, 1972. pp. 78.

TOURISTS

ITALY. Ente Nazionale Italiano per il Turismo. Centro di Documentazione. 1969. Indagine sulla efficacia della pubblicità turistica. Roma, 1969. pp. 259. (Collana di Monografie Turistiche. 24)

Der TOURISMUS und seine Perspektiven für Südosteuropa: [papers of an international conference convened by the Südosteuropa-Gesellschaft in Munich in 1970]; Beiträge zusammengestellt von Karl Ruppert [and] Jörg Maier. München, 1971. pp. 185. bibliog. (Munich. Universität. Wirtschaftsgeographisches Institut. WGI-Berichte zur Regionalforschung. Heft 6)

BARETJE (RENÉ) and DEFERT (PIERRE P.) Aspects économiques du tourisme. Paris, 1972. pp. 355. bibliog.

- Bibliography

COMMONWEALTH BUREAU OF AGRICULTURAL ECONOMICS. Tourism and recreation in rural areas: aspects of land use planning and structural change (1965-1971); (with Supplements); edited by K.P. Broadbent. [Oxford], 1972 in progress. (Annotated Bibliographies. No. 11)

- Law and legislation - France

LEONNET (JEAN) and FONTAINE (PIERRE) Le droit du tourisme et des voyages. Paris, [1971]. pp. 315. bibliog.

- Africa, East

POPOVIC (VOJISLAV) Tourism in Eastern Africa. München, [1972]. pp. 198. bibliog. (Ifo-Institut für Wirtschaftsforschung. Afrika-Studien. 73)

- Bahamas

CHECCHI AND COMPANY. A plan for managing the growth of tourism in the commonwealth of the Bahama Islands; a feasibility study prepared for the Bahamas Ministry of Tourism. [Washington?, 1969]. 1 vol. (various pagings).

- Dutch Guiana

DUTCH GUIANA. Algemeen Bureau voor de Statistiek. Maandstatistiek scheepvaart en reizigersverkeer. m., Ja 1972 [no.1]- Paramaribo.

- Europe, Eastern

Der TOURISMUS und seine Perspektiven für Südosteuropa: [papers of an international conference convened by the Südosteuropa-Gesellschaft in Munich in 1970]; Beiträge zusammengestellt von Karl Ruppert [and] Jörg Maier. München, 1971. pp. 185. bibliog. (Munich. Universität. Wirtschaftsgeographisches Institut. WGI-Berichte zur Regionalforschung. Heft 6)

- France

ARRAS (MARC) Le tourisme en Dordogne: (L'économie de la Dordogne, Tome 2). Bordeaux, 1969. pp. 252. bibliog. (Bordeaux. Université. Faculté de Droit. Institut d'Economie Régionale du Sud-Ouest. Collection. 16. Tome 2)

FRANCE. Commission du Tourisme. 1971. Préparation du 6e Plan: rapport. [Paris], 1971. pp. 69.

CASTEX (FRANÇOIS) L'équipement touristique de la France. Paris, [1972]. pp. 604.

- Ireland (Republic)

NATIONAL INSTITUTE FOR PHYSICAL PLANNING AND CONSTRUCTION RESEARCH. Nature and Amenity Conservation Committee. Specimen development plan manual. 2-3. Planning for amenity and tourism: illustrated by excerpts from the model amenity tourism study of County Donegal. Dublin, the Institute, 1966 [repr.1969]. pp. 110.

- Israel

  ISRAEL. Central Bureau of Statistics. Technical Publications. No.30. Seasonality and trends in Israel tourism; by R.R.V. Baron. Jerusalem, 1968. pp. 121. bibliog. In English and Hebrew.

- Italy

  CHITI (MARIO) and MOCCIA (ROCCO) Turismo e regioni. Roma, 1972. pp. 213.

  REGIONI e turismo: relazioni e dibattito [of a conference organised by the Istituto per la Documentazione e gli Studi Legislativi]. Milano, 1972. pp. 161. (Istituto per la Documentazione Legislativa. Pubblicazioni. 33)

- Malta - Mathematical models

  MENGES (GUENTER) and LEINER (BERND) Ökonometrische Untersuchungen über die Wirtschaft Maltas unter besonderer Berücksichtigung des Tourismus. Meisenheim am Glan, 1971. pp. 82.

- Poland

  STALSKI (MICHAŁ) Przestrzenne aspekty zagospodarowania turystycznego. Warszawa, 1973. pp. 88. bibliog. (Polska Akademia Nauk. Komitet Przestrzennego Zagospodarowania Kraju. Studia. t.41) With Russian and English summaries.

- Russia

  AZAR (VIL'IAM IL'ICH) Ekonomika i organizatsiia turizma: metodologicheskie voprosy. Moskva, 1972. pp. 184.

- Spain

  DOMINGO (XAVIER) La paella des gogos; traduit de l'espagnol par Elisabeth Chopard-Lallier. Paris, [1971]. pp. 191.

  SPAIN. Instituto Nacional de Estadistica. 1971. Encuesta de turismo receptivo, 1970. Madrid, 1971. pp. 156.

  MOSER (CARSTEN R.) Tourismus und Entwicklungspolitik, dargestellt am Beispiel Spaniens. Hamburg, 1972. pp. 277. bibliog. (Hamburg. Hamburgisches Welt-Wirtschafts-Archiv. Veröffentlichungen) With English summary.

  SPAIN. Comisaria del Plan de Desarrollo Economico y Social. 1972. (III Plan de desarrollo economico y social): turismo e informacion y actividades culturales. [Madrid], 1972. pp. 334.

- Switzerland

  MAEDER (BRUNO) Strukturwandlungen im Fremdenverkehr der schweizerischen Hotellerie in den Jahren, 1948-1968. Bern, 1971. pp. 231. bibliog.

TOURISTS : Underdeveloped areas
   See UNDERDEVELOPED AREAS - Tourists

- United Kingdom

  ENGLISH TOURIST BOARD. Annual report. a., 1970/71 [2nd]- London.

  ENGLISH TOURIST BOARD. Towards a national tourism marketing and development strategy. [London, 1972?]. fo. 11.

  U.K. Central Office of Information. Reference Division. Reference Pamphlets. 102. Britain and international tourism. London, 1972. pp. 42. bibliog.

  WESTMINSTER. Department of Architecture and Planning. Tourism and hotel development. London, [1972]. pp. 92. (Westminster Development Plan Publications. Topic Papers. T1)

  TOURISM in London: towards a short term plan: a consultation text; [prepared by a steering group composed of officers appointed by the GLC, the English and London Tourist Boards and the London Boroughs Association; B.T. Buckle, chairman]. London, Greater London Council, 1973. pp. 55.

  YOUNG TOURISM STUDY GROUP. Young tourists in England; a report to the English Tourist Board. London, English Tourist Board, [1973]. pp. 53.

- United Kingdom - Ireland, Northern

  NORTHERN IRELAND TOURIST BOARD. Annual report. a., 1968/9 (22nd)- [Belfast]. 1948/9-1967/8 (1st - 21st) included in IRELAND, NORTHERN. Parliament. [Command Papers], which see.

- United Kingdom - Scotland

  SCOTTISH TOURIST BOARD. Report. a., 1970/1 (2nd)- Edinburgh.

- United Kingdom - Wales

  WALES TOURIST BOARD. Annual report. a., 1971/2 [2nd]- Cardiff. In English and Welsh.

- United Kingdom - British Empire

  COMMONWEALTH SECRETARIAT. Organisation of the tourist industry in Commonwealth countries as at December, 1969. London, 1970. pp. 191.

- West Indies

  BRYDEN (JOHN M.) Tourism and development: a case study of the Commonwealth Caribbean. Cambridge, 1973. pp. 236. bibliog.

TOYNBEE (ARNOLD JOSEPH)

ZLATKIN (I. Ia.) Kontseptsii istorii kochevykh narodov A. Toinbi i istoricheskaia deistvitel'nost'. in Akademiia Nauk SSSR. Institut Vostokovedeniia. Sovremennaia Istoriografiia Stran Zarubezhnogo Vostoka. [vyp. 4]. Problemy sotsial'no-politicheskogo razvitiia. Moskva, 1971. pp. 256.

TRACTOR INDUSTRY

- Russia

  TRAKTOROSTROENIE v tsentre Rossii: k 25-letiiu so dnia organizatsii Lipetskogo traktornogo zavoda. Voronezh, 1968. pp. 60..

  KOMAROV (L. S.) and others. Letopis' Cheliabinskogo traktornogo, 1929-1945 gg. Moskva, 1972. pp. 375.

TRACTORS

FRANCE. Ministère de l'Agriculture. Statistique Agricole. Supplément. Série Etudes. No.82. L'équipement des exploitations agricoles en tracteurs et autres moyens de traction en 1967: projections du parc de tracteurs en 1975: 1ère partie; [étude...réalisée par M. Loyat]. [Paris], 1971. pp. 364.

TRADE AND PROFESSIONAL ASSOCIATIONS

- Belgium

  PAULUS (DANIEL) Les milieux dirigeants belges et les demandes d'adhésion du Royaume-Uni à la Communauté Economique Européenne. Bruxelles, 1971. pp. 325. bibliog. (Brussels. Université Libre. Institut d'Etudes Européennes. Thèses et Travaux Politiques)

TRADE AND PROFESSIONAL ASSOCIATIONS
(Cont'd.)

- Denmark

HASSØ (ARTHUR G.) Et bidrag til københavnsk Haandvaerks Historie i det sidste Hundredaar: Haandvaerkerforeningen i København, 1840-1940. København, 1940. pp. 583.

- European Economic Community countries

Le REGIME juridique des organisations professionnelles dans les pays membres de la C.E.C.A.; par G. Boldt [and others]. Luxembourg, Communauté Européenne du Charbon et de l'Acier, 1966. pp. 666. (European Coal and Steel Community. Collection du Droit du Travail)

- Germany

DEUTSCHER WIRTSCHAFTSVERBAND FÜR SÜD- UND MITTELAMERIKA. Satzungen. Berlin, [192-?]. pp. 7.

HUENGER (HEINZ) 50 Jahre Gesamtverband der deutschen Maschen-Industrie, 1916-1966. Stuttgart, [1966]. pp. 116.

BOERSENVEREIN DES DEUTSCHEN BUCHHANDELS. Der Börsenverein des Deutschen Buchhandels: Organisation, Aufgaben, Tätigkeit. Frankfurt am Main, [1968]. pp. 60. (Abteilung für Information und Öffentlichkeitsarbeit. Schriftenreihe. Band 1)

BLECKER (GUSTAV WERNER) Die Besteuerung der Berufsverbände ohne öffentlich-rechtlichen Charakter. [Mannheim?, 1971?]. pp. 187. bibliog.

BORKENHAGEN (ERICH) 100 Jahre Deutscher Brauer-Bund e.V. 1871-1971: zur Geschichte des Bieres im 19. und 20. Jahrhundert. Bonn, 1971. pp. 298. bibliog.

- United Kingdom

KNOWLES (C.C.) and PITT (PETER HUBERT) The history of building regulation in London, 1189-1972: with an account of the District Surveyors' Association. London, 1972. pp. 164.

PRIESTLEY (BARBARA) compiler. British qualifications: a comprehensive guide to educational, technical, professional and academic qualifications in Britain. 3rd ed. London, 1972. pp. 1243.

- Venezuela - Directories

VENEZUELA. Direccion de Comercio. Division del Costo de Vida e Informacion General. 1964. Directorio de asociaciones de caracter economico que operan en el pais. Caracas, 1964. fo. 142.

VENEZUELA. Direccion de Comercio. Division del Costo de Vida e Informacion General. 1964. Directorio de organizaciones diversas de caracter economico que operan en el pais. Caracas, 1964. fo. 64.

TRADE-MARKS

- European Economic Community countries

LAUMER (HELMUT) Der Markenartikelvertrieb in den Ländern der Europäischen Wirtschaftsgemeinschaft und seine Auswirkungen auf den Wettbewerb. Berlin, [1970]. pp. 148. bibliog. (Ifo-Institut für Wirtschaftsforschung. Schriftenreihe. Nr. 72)

EUROPEAN ECONOMIC COMMUNITY. Working Party on Trade Marks. 1973. Proposed European trade mark: unofficial translation of a preliminary draft of a Convention for a European trade mark. London, H.M.S.O., 1973. pp. 62.

- Germany, Eastern

HIERSE (KLAUS) Wesen, Funktion und Gegenstand des Warenzeichenrechts der DDR; (herausgegeben vom Amt für Erfindungs- und Patentwesen der Deutschen Demokratischen Republik). Berlin, 1967. pp. 95. ([Schriftenreihe] Warenzeichenrecht. Heft 1)

HIERSE (KLAUS) and others. Kennzeichnungspflicht für industrielle Erzeugnisse und die Anmeldung, Eintragung und Löschung von Warenzeichen in der DDR; (herausgegeben vom Amt für Erfindungs- und Patentwesen). Berlin, 1967. pp. 171. (Schriftenreihe Warenzeichenrecht. Heft 2)

- Russia

ADUEV (AL'FRED NIKOLAEVICH) and BELOGORSKAIA (EKATERINA MIKHAILOVNA) Tovarnyi znak i ego pravovoe znachenie. Moskva, 1972. pp. 72. bibliog.

- United Kingdom

MEINHARDT (PETER) Inventions, patents and trade marks. London, 1971. pp. 397. bibliog.

KERLY (Sir DUNCAN MACKENZIE) Law of trade marks and trade names; tenth edition by T.A. Blanco White and Robin Jacob. London, 1972. pp. 807.

TRADE-MARKS (INTERNATIONAL LAW)

BECHER (KARL) and HIERSE (KLAUS) Die Bedeutung der Pariser Verbandsübereinkunft für das Warenkennzeichnungswesen und die internationale Registrierung von Warenzeichen. Berlin, 1967. pp. 132. (Schriftenreihe Warenzeichenrecht. Heft 5)

TRADE REGULATION

BODDEWYN (JEAN J.) and HOLLANDER (STANLEY C.) eds. Public policy toward retailing: an international symposium. Lexington, Mass., [1972]. pp. 482. bibliogs.

TRADE SECRETS

CONGRES INTERNATIONAL DE DROIT COMPARE, 1970. 8e Congrès. The protection of know-how in 13 countries: reports to the 8th... congress...; editor Herman Cohen Jehoram. Deventer, 1972. pp. 164.

TRADE UNIONS EMBLEMS

- United Kingdom

LEESON (R.A.) United we stand: an illustrated account of trade union emblems. Bath, 1971. pp. 72. bibliog.

TRADE-UNIONS

INTERNATIONAL FEDERATION OF TRADE UNIONS. Bericht für die Jahre 1913 bis 1919. Berlin, 1919. pp. 66.

RENNER (KARL) Wege der Verwirklichung;...Betrachtungen über politische Demokratie, Wirtschaftsdemokratie und Sozialismus, etc. Berlin, 1929. pp. 141.

SOUTO VILAS (MANUEL) Teoria de los sindicatos nacionales. Madrid, 1941. pp. 211.

UNITED KINGDOM. 1963. Ministry of Labour. The World Federation of Trade Unions. (Overseas Information Papers. No. 11) Rev. ed. [London, 1963]. pp. 8, (10).

LIESS (OTTO RUDOLF) Weltgewerkschaftsbund: Internationaler Bund Freier Gewerkschaften: gewerkschaftspolitische Konfrontation und Ost-West-Gespräche. Wien, 1966. pp. 131. bibliog.

WORLD FEDERATION OF TRADE UNIONS. General Council, 16th Session, Sofia, 1966. The W.F.T.U.: outlines for the future. [Berlin, Verlag Tribuene, 1967]. pp. 127. 20cm.

CRUSIUS (REINHARD) and WILKE (MANFRED) Elemente einer Theorie der Gewerkschaften im Spätkapitalismus. Berlin, [1971]. pp. 126. bibliog.

CARTTER (ALLAN MURRAY) and MARSHALL (F. RAY) Labor economics: wages, employment, and trade unionism. rev. ed. Homewood, Ill., 1972. pp. 594. bibliogs.

FELD (WERNER J.) Nongovernmental forces and world politics: a study of business, labor, and political groups. New York, 1972. pp. 284. bibliog.

JACKSON (DUDLEY A.S.) and others. Do trade unions cause inflation?: two studies, with a theoretical introduction and policy conclusion. Cambridge, 1972. pp. 126. (Cambridge. University. Department of Applied Economics. Occasional Papers. 36)

LEVINSON (CHARLES) International trade unionism. London, 1972. pp. 402.

STURMTHAL (ADOLF FOX) Comparative labor movements: ideological roots and institutional development. Belmont, Calif., [1972]. pp. 176. bibliog.

JUNGNICKEL (ROLF) and MATTHIES (KLAUS) Multinationale Unternehmen und Gewerkschaften. Hamburg, 1973. pp. 83. bibliog. (Hamburg. Hamburgisches Welt-Wirtschafts-Archiv. Studien zur Aussenwirtschaft und Entwicklungspolitik)

WORLD FEDERATION OF TRADE UNIONS. The trade unions and the United Nations. Prag, 1973. pp. 35.

- Political activity

WORLD FEDERATION OF TRADE UNIONS. A fighting record: the World Federation of Trade Unions against apartheid. [Prague, 1964]. pp. 33.

- Africa

MOROCCO. Ambassade (U.K.). Press Department. 1961. Charter of the first Pan-African Labour Federation as adopted on May 30, 1961, at the first Pan-African Labour Congress held at Casablanca, Morocco: French text. London, [1961]. pp. 4. (Statements and Documents)

- Argentine Republic

SENEN GONZALEZ (SANTIAGO) EL sindicalismo despues de Peron. Buenos Aires, [1971]. pp. 166.

- Armed forces - Political activity

ABAD DE SANTILLAN (DIEGO) La F.O.R.A.: ideologia y trayectoria del movimiento obrero revolucionario en la Argentina. 2nd ed. Buenos Aires, 1971. pp. 298.

- Australia

BUCKLEY (KENNETH D.) The Amalgamated Engineers in Australia, 1852-1920. Canberra, 1970. pp. 318.

RAWSON (DONALD WILLIAM) A handbook of Australian trade unions and employees' associations. 2nd ed. Canberra, 1973. pp. 100. (Australian National University. Research School of Social Sciences. Department of Political Science. Occasional Papers. No. 8)

- Australia - New South Wales

NAIRN (BEDE) Civilising capitalism: the labor movement in New South Wales, 1870-1900. Canberra, 1973. pp. 260. bibliog.

- Austria

HUNDERT Jahre Gewerkschaft der Schuharbeiter: (Festschrift zum hundertjährigen Bestand der gewerkschaftlichen Organisation der Schuharbeiter, 1871-1971;...im Auftrage der Gewerkschaft der Textil-, Bekleidungs- und Lederarbeiter verfasst). [Vienna, 1971]. pp. 71.

80 Jahre Gewerkschaft der Eisenbahner. [Vienna, 1972]. pp. 543.

- Belgium

THIJS (VIC) Twintig jaar syndicale kroniek. Antwerpen, 1967. pp. 312.

BLANPAIN (ROGER) Public employee unionism in Belgium. Ann Arbor, 1971. pp. 99. (Michigan University and Wayne State University. Institute of Labor and Industrial Relations. Comparative Studies in Public Employment Labor Relations)

- Bolivia - Law

VILLALPANDO RETAMOZO (ABELARDO) El derecho de sindicalizacion en Bolivia: breves apuntaciones y comentarios. Potosi, [1969]. pp. 131.

- Brazil

FUECHTNER (HANS) Die brasilianischen Arbeitergewerkschaften, ihre Organisation und ihre politische Funktion. Frankfurt am Main, 1972. pp. 278. bibliog.

- Canada

CANADA. Department of Labour. Economics and Research Branch. 1970. Union growth in Canada, 1921-1967. Ottawa, 1970. pp. 106.

CHARPENTIER (ALFRED) Cinquante ans d'action ouvrière: les mémoires d'Alfred Charpentier; présentés par Gérard Dion. Québec, 1971. pp. 540.

- Canada - Political activity

KWAVNICK (DAVID) Organised labour and pressure politics: the Canadian Labour Congress, 1956-1968. Montreal, 1972. pp. 287.

- Canada - New Brunswick

DIRECTORY OF LABOUR ORGANIZATIONS IN NEW BRUNSWICK; [pd. by] Research and Planning Branch, Department of Labour, Province of New Brunswick. a., current issue only kept. New Brunswick.

- Canada - Quebec

QUEBEC labour: the Confederation of National Trade Unions yesterday and today; edited by a Black Rose Books editorial collective. Montreal, 1972. pp. 215.

- Chile - Political activity

ANGELL (ALAN) Politics and the labour movement in Chile. London, 1972. pp. 290. bibliog.

TRADE UNIONS (Cont'd.)

- China - Law

CHEN (KANG-SHEN) Die Gewerkschaften als Körperschaften des öffentlichen Rechts: eine Untersuchung über die Rechtsstellung der Gewerkschaften in der Republik China und in den Entwicklungsländern. [Mannheim, 1973]. pp. 182. bibliog.

- Colombia - Political activity

MUSTAFA BARBOSA (FEISAL) Los grupos de presion y el sindicalismo contemporaneo. Bogota, 1970. pp. 138. bibliog.

- Communist countries

BLIT (LUCJAN) Trade unions in communist countries. Birmingham, 1951. pp. 19.

- Cuba

ORGANIZACION REGIONAL INTERAMERICANA DE TRABAJADORES and INTERNATIONAL CONFEDERATION OF FREE TRADE UNIONS. Publicaciones Especiales. Trade unions and people of Cuba against despotism. new ed. Mexico City, 1961. pp. 64.

RIERA HERNANDEZ (MARIO) Historial obrero cubano, 1574-1965: sindicalismo, huelgas, economia, agrarismo, etc. Miami, 1965. pp. 305. bibliog.

- Czechoslovakia

INTERNATIONAL CONFEDERATION OF FREE TRADE UNIONS. Československé odbory, 1870-1970: pražské jaro okupace a "normalisace". [Brussels, 1970]. pp. 56.

- Denmark

MØLGAARD (JOHN) and others, eds. LO: magt eller afmagt? København, [1972]. pp. 223.

MØLLER (TORGNY) Arbejderopposition: magt og magtmisbrug i dansk fagbevaegelse; en rapport. København, [1972]. pp. 233.

KOCH-OLSEN (IB) ed. Kampens gang: LO gennem 75 år, 1898-1973; af Ernst Christiansen [and others]. København, 1973. pp. 527.

- Europe

FORD (CHARLES) B. Sc. (Econ.) The role of trade unions in the economic development of Europe: free trade unions and the Organisation for Economic Cooperation and Development. Brussels, 1966. pp. 83.

BARBASH (JACK) and BARBASH (KATE) Trade unions and national economic policy. Baltimore, [1972]. pp. 206. bibliogs.

- Europe, Eastern

LOWIT (THOMAS) Le syndicalisme de type soviétique: l'U.R.S.S. et les pays de l'Est européen. Paris, 1971. pp. 430. bibliog. (Paris. Université de Paris XI (Sud). Centre de Recherches en Sciences Sociales du Travail. Enquêtes et Etudes. Collection "Sciences Sociales du Travail". 5)

MATULL (WILHELM) Ostdeutschlands Arbeiterbewegung: Abriss ihrer Geschichte, Leistung und Opfer. Würzburg, 1973. pp. 590. bibliog. (Göttinger Arbeitskreis. Ostdeutsche Beiträge. Band 53)

- European Economic Community countries

L'AZIONE sindacale nella Europa comunitaria: incontro unitario CGIL, CISL, UIL. Roma, 1971. pp. 80.

BERGSTRØM (VILLY) and SVENNING (OLLE) Fackföreningsrörelsen och EEC. [Stockholm, 1971]. pp. 240. bibliog.

SEEGER (HEINZ) EWG Monopole: gewerkschaftliche Gegenmacht. Frankfurt am Main, [1971]. pp. 112.

BOUVARD (MARGUERITE) Labor movements in the Common Market countries: the growth of a European pressure group. New York, 1972. pp. 272. bibliog.

INDUSTRIAL RESEARCH AND INFORMATION SERVICES. Trade unions and the E.E.C. London, 1973. pp. 35.

- France

FEDERATION NATIONALE DES CHEMINOTS. Les cheminots dans l'histoire sociale de la France; rédigé sous la direction de Joseph Jacquet. Paris, [1967]. pp. 318. bibliog.

TAVERNIER (YVES) Le syndicalisme paysan: F.N.S.E.A., C.N.J.A.; [a one-volume and updated edition of two works originally published in 1965 and 1967]. Paris, 1969. pp. 227. bibliog. (Fondation Nationale des Sciences Politiques. Travaux et Recherches de Science Politique. Etudes Syndicales. 5)

OUVRIERS face aux appareils: une expérience militante chez Hispano-Suiza. Paris, 1970. pp. 275.

BERGERON (ANDRE) Confédération Force ouvrière. Paris, [1971]. pp. 109.

ERBES-SEGUIN (SABINE) Démocratie dans les syndicats. Paris, [1971]. pp. 189. bibliog. (Paris. Ecole Pratique des Hautes Etudes. Section des Sciences Economiques et Sociales. Société, Mouvements Sociaux et Idéologies. 1e Série. Etudes. 11)

LAUGA (LOUIS) Centre National des Jeunes Agriculteurs. Paris, [1971]. pp. 142.

MEYERS (FREDERIC) The state and government employee unions in France. Ann Arbor, 1971. pp. 59. bibliogs. (Michigan University and Wayne State University. Institute of Labor and Industrial Relations. Comparative Studies in Public Employment Labor Relations)

GANI (LEON) Syndicats et travailleurs immigrés. Paris, [1972]. pp. 254.

- France - Law

DRAVET (HENRI) Le droit syndical. Paris, [1972]. pp. 189.

- France - Political activity

BAUCHARD (PHILIPPE) Les syndicats en quête d'une révolution. Paris, [1972]. pp. 359.

- Germany

SILBERMANN (JOSEF) Vierzig Jahre VWA, 1889-1929: Jubiläumsschrift über vier Jahrzehnte Geschichte des Verbandes der weiblichen Handels- und Büroangestellten E.V. Berlin, 1929. pp. 94.

LINDAU (RUDOLF) Probleme der Geschichte der deutschen Arbeiterbewegung. Berlin, [1947]. pp. 63.

FUGGER (KARL) Geschichte der deutschen Gewerkschaftsbewegung: (eine kurzgefasste Darstellung); [reprint of work originally published in 1949, with critical introduction and biographical notes]. Berlin, 1971. pp. 301. bibliog.

INDUSTRIEGEWERKSCHAFT METALL FÜR DIE BUNDESREPUBLIK DEUTSCHLAND. 2. Weissbuch zur Unternehmermoral. Frankfurt am Main, [1967]. pp. 64.

Die WESTDEUTSCHEN Gewerkschaften und das staatsmonopolistische Herrschaftssystem, 1945-1966; ([edited by] Albert Behrendt [and others]). Berlin, 1968. pp. 687.

AGARTZ (VIKTOR) Gewerkschaft und Arbeiterklasse: die ideologischen und soziologischen Wandlungen in der westdeutschen Arbeiterbewegung. München, 1971. pp. 144.

ESCHENHAGEN (WIELAND) Antigewerkschaftlicher Kampf oder Kampf in den Gewerkschaften?: sozialistische Betriebsarbeit und Gewerkschaftsbürokratie; Erfahrungen in Bremen. München, 1971. pp. 183.

FOERSTER (ALFRED) Die Gewerkschaftspolitik der deutschen Sozialdemokratie während des Sozialistengesetzes, vom Wydener Parteikongress 1880 bis zum Parteitag von St. Gallen 1887. Berlin, 1971. pp. 384.

HEER (HANNES) Burgfrieden oder Klassenkampf: zur Politik der sozialdemokratischen Gewerkschaften, 1930-1933. Neuwied, 1971. pp. 240. bibliog.

WILLEY (RICHARD J.) Democracy in the West German trade unions: a reappraisal of the "iron law". Beverly Hills, [1971]. pp. 53. bibliog.

GREUTER (DIETER) Der Schweizerische Metall- und Uhrenarbeiter-Verband und die Industriegewerkschaft Metall für die Bundesrepublik Deutschland: ein Vergleich. Berlin, [1972]. pp. 209. bibliog. (St. Gall. Handelshochschule. Schweizerisches Institut für Gewerbliche Wirtschaft. Schriftenreihe. 7)

HERDING (RICHARD) Job control and union structure: a study on plant-level industrial conflict in the United States with a comparative perspective on West Germany. Rotterdam, 1972. pp. 401. bibliog.

KLEIN (JUERGEN) Vereint sind sie alles?: Untersuchungen zur Entstehung von Einheitsgewerkschaften in Deutschland von der Weimarer Republik bis 1946/47. Hamburg, 1972. pp. 436. bibliog. (Europa-Kolleg, Hamburg. Schriften. Band 23)

NICKEL (WALTER) Zum Verhältnis von Arbeiterschaft und Gewerkschaft: eine soziologische Untersuchung...in der Bundesrepublik Deutschland. Köln, [1972]. pp. 499. bibliog. (Stiftung Mitbestimmung, and Hans-Böckler-Gesellschaft. Schriftenreihe)

Die REVOLUTIONAERE Gewerkschaftsopposition: (Dokumente... aus den Jahren 1924 bis 1932; [collection of reprints compiled by the] Gewerkschaftsabteilung des ZK der Kommunistischen Partei Deutschlands). Berlin, 1972. 2 vols. (Dokumente und Analysen zur Kommunistischen Arbeiterbewegung. Bände 4-5)

MATULL (WILHELM) Ostdeutschlands Arbeiterbewegung: Abriss ihrer Geschichte, Leistung und Opfer. Würzburg, 1973. pp. 590. bibliog. (Göttinger Arbeitskreis. Ostdeutsche Beiträge. Band 53)

- Germany - Finance

HIRCHE (KURT) Die Finanzen der Gewerkschaften. Düsseldorf, 1972. pp. 495.

- Germany - Berlin

DEUTSCHER GEWERKSCHAFTSBUND. Landesbezirk Berlin. Berliner Gewerkschaftsgeschichte von 1945 bis 1950: FDGB, UGO, DGB. Berlin, 1971. pp. 319. bibliog.

- Germany - Ruhr

NEUMANN (WALTER) Die Gewerkschaften im Ruhrgebiet: Voraussetzungen, Entwicklung und Wirksamkeit. Köln, [1951]. pp. 228. bibliog.

- Germany - Saxony

WAECHTLER (EBERHARD) Zur Geschichte des Kampfes des Bergarbeiterverbandes in Sachsen: evangelische Arbeitervereine und gelbe Gewerkschaften als Instrumente der Zechenherren. Berlin, 1959. pp. 74. (Deutsche Akademie der Wissenschaften zu Berlin. Institut für Geschichte. Schriften. Reihe 3. Band 3)

- Germany, Eastern

SIEBERT (GERD) Mitbestimmung drüben: aus der überbetrieblichen Arbeit der Gewerkschaften der DDR. Frankfurt a. M., [1971]. pp. 159.

- Ghana - Finance

GHANA. Commission of Enquiry into the Funds of the Ghana Trades Union Congress. 1968. Report; [A.A. Munufie, chairman]. [Accra, 1968]. pp. 161. Bound with White Paper on the report.

GHANA. 1969. White Paper on the report of the Commission of Enquiry into the Ghana Trades Union Congress funds. [Accra], 1969. pp. 4. (W[hite] P[apers]. 1969. No. 7) Bound with the Report.

- India

DHYANI (S.N.) Trade unions and the right to strike: a comparative socio-legal study in labour-management relations. Delhi, [1970]. pp. 424. bibliog.

JHA (SHIVA CHANDRA) The Indian trade union movement: an account and an interpretation. Calcutta, 1970. pp. 341.

MUNSON (FRED CALEB) Indian trade unions: structure and function. Ann Arbor, Mich., [1970]. pp. 132. bibliog.

CHOUDHARY (SUKHBIR) Peasants' and workers' movement in India, 1905-1929. New Delhi, 1971. pp. 328. bibliog.

SHARMA (G.K.) Labour movement in India: its past and present. [2nd ed.] New Delhi, 1971. pp. 296. bibliog.

- Israel

LEFKOWITZ (JEROME) Public employee unionism in Israel. Ann Arbor, 1971. pp. 91. bibliog. (Michigan University and Wayne State University. Institute of Labor and Industrial Relations. Comparative Studies in Public Employment Labor Relations)

- Italy

CAMERA CONFEDERALE DEL LAVORO DI NAPOLI E PROVINCIA. Segretaria. Un anno di lotta per i salari e l'occupazione, per lo sviluppo di Napoli e del Mezzogiorno. [Naples, 1968]. pp. 263.

I BRACCIANTI: 20 anni di lotte. Roma, 1969. pp. 382.

VALLI (VITTORIO) Programmazione e sindacati in Italia. Milano, [1970]. pp. 303. bibliogs. (Istituto per lo Sviluppo Culturale dei Lavoratori. Collana I.S.C.LA. N.4)

Il SINDACATO in Italia, 1960-1970. Roma, 1971. pp. 237. bibliog. (Rassegna Sindacale. Quaderni N. 31-32)

INSTITUT FÜR MARXISTISCHE STUDIEN UND FORSCHUNGEN. Probleme des Klassenkampfes und des Kampfes um gewerkschaftliche Einheit in Italien: Dokumente, Statistiken, Analysen. Frankfurt/Main, 1972. pp. 391. bibliog. (Arbeitsmaterialen. 3)

SCHWARZENBERG (CLAUDIO) Il sindacalismo fascista. Milano, [1972]. pp. 142. bibliog.

TRADE UNIONS (Cont'd.)

- Italy - Law

GIORNATE DI STUDIO "LA RAPPRESENTANZA PROFESSIONALE E LO STATUTO DEI LAVORATORI", PERUGIA, 1970. La rappresentanza professionale e lo statuto dei lavoratori: atti. Milano, 1971. pp. 222. (Associazione Italiana di Diritto del Lavoro e della Sicurezza Sociale. Annuario di Diritto del Lavoro. N. 4)

- Italy - Political activity

LIZZADRI (ORESTE) Il potere ai sindacati? Roma, 1972. pp. 167.

- Jamaica

HARROD (JEFFREY) Trade union foreign policy: a study of British and American trade union activities in Jamaica. London, 1972. pp. 485. bibliog.

- Japan

LARGE (STEPHEN S.) The rise of labor in Japan: the Yuaikai, 1912-19. Tokyo, [1972]. pp. 218. bibliog.

- Mexico

LEVENSTEIN (HARVEY A.) Labor organizations in the United States and Mexico: a history of their relations. Westport, Conn., 1971. pp. 258. bibliog.

- Mongolia

IADAMSUREN (D.) Profsoiuzy Mongol'skoi Narodnoi Respubliki; perevod s mongol'skogo. Moskva, 1967. pp. 48.

- Netherlands

ALBEDA (W.) Vakbeweging en maatschappijstruktuur. Rotterdam, 1972. pp. 114.

WAL (T. VAN DER) Op zoek naar een nieuwe vrijheid: een kwart eeuw arbeidersbeweging in Friesland, 1870-1895. Leiden, 1972. pp. 435. bibliog. With English summary.

- New Zealand - Bibliography

ROTH (H.O.) compiler. New Zealand trade unions: a bibliography. Auckland, 1970. pp. 71.

- Norway

SEIM (JARDAR) Hvordan Hovedavtalen av 1935 ble til: staten, organisasjonene og arbeidsfreden, 1930-35. [Oslo, 1972]. pp. 278. bibliog.

- Poland

BARTON (PAUL) pseud. Misère et révolte de l'ouvrier polonais:...25 ans du syndicalisme d'état, les 74 jours du prolétariat. Paris, 1971. pp. 159.

GILEJKO (LESZEK) Związki zawodowe w procesie przemian społecznych w PRL. Warszawa, 1972. pp. 167. bibliog.

KIESZCZYŃSKI (LUCJAN) Kronika ruchu zawodowego w Polsce, 1808-1939: ważniejsze wydarzenia. Warszawa, 1972. pp. 435.

SASIN (WACŁAW) Funkcje kontrolne związków zawodowych. Warszawa, 1972. pp. 118.

- Russia

KISELEVSKII (IU.N.) Zadachi professional'nykh soiuzov. Peterburg, 1917. pp. 15. Xerographic reprint.

PANKRATOVA (ANNA MIKHAILOVNA) Fabzavkomy Rossii v bor'be za sotsialisticheskuiu fabriku; pod redaktsiei M.N. Pokrovskogo. [Moskva], 1923. pp. 426. bibliog. Xerographic reprint.

AINZAFT (S.) Pervyi etap professional'nogo dvizheniia v Rossii, 1905-1907 gg.; pod redaktsiei i s predisloviem V. Iarotskogo. vyp.1. Gomel', 1924. pp. 284.

KOSTIN (LEONID ALEKSEEVICH) Profsoiuzy i proizvoditel'nost' truda v period postroeniia kommunizma. Moskva, 1964. pp. 171.

MUKHTASIPOV (MEDEKHAT) Sovetskie profsoiuzy v bor'be za mezhdunarodnoe edinstvo rabochego klassa, 1918-1939 gg. Moskva, 1966. pp. 110.

VSESOIUZNYI TSENTRAL'NYI SOVET PROFESSIONAL'NYKH SOIUZOV. Ustav professional'nykh soiuzov SSSR; utverzhden XIII s"ezdom profsoiuzov SSSR; chastichnye izmeneniia vneseny XIV s"ezdom profsoiuzov SSSR 4 marta 1968 goda. Moskva, 1968. pp. 48.

LOWIT (THOMAS) Le syndicalisme de type soviétique: l'U.R.S.S. et les pays de l'Est européen. Paris, 1971. pp. 430. bibliog. (Paris. Université de Paris XI (Sud). Centre de Recherches en Sciences Sociales du Travail. Enquêtes et Etudes. Collection "Sciences Sociales du Travail". 5)

BRUEGMANN (UWE) Die russischen Gewerkschaften in Revolution und Bürgerkrieg, 1917-1919. Frankfurt am Main, [1972]. pp. 285. bibliog.

POTICHNYJ (PETER J.) Soviet agricultural trade unions, 1917-70. Toronto, [1972]. pp. 258. bibliog.

VLADIMIRSKII (BORIS DAVIDOVICH) Ekonomicheskie zadachi promyshlennykh predpriiatii i pervichnykh proforganizatsii v novykh usloviiakh. Erevan, 1972. pp. 127.

- Russia - Bibliography

RAPOPORT (S.) and IAKUB (R.) compilers. Sistematicheskii ukazatel' literatury po professional'nomu dvizheniiu v Rossii. vyp.1. Professional'noe dvizhenie do revoliutsii 1917 goda. Moskva, 1923. pp. 64.

- Russia - Latvia

KIRSNE (Z.) Rukovodstvo KP Latvii profsoiuznymi organizatsiiami respubliki v dele uluchsheniia organizatsionno-massovoi raboty, 1956-1962 gg. in Latviiskii Gosudarstvennyi Universitet. Uchenye Zapiski Aspirantov. t.2. Sbornik nauchnykh rabot aspirantov kafedr obshchestvennykh nauk. vyp.1. Riga, 1963. pp. 117.

- Russia - Uzbekistan

GENTSHKE (L.V.) Organizatsionnoe oformlenie profsoiuzov Uzbekistana, 1924-1925; pod redaktsii...M.M. Musaeva. Tashkent, 1960. pp. 218. (Tashkent. Universitet. [Nauchnye] Trudy. vyp.171 [being also] Istoricheskie Nauki. kn. 36)

AIUPOV (MIRZA TELIAPOVICH) Nekotorye voprosy istorii profsoiuznogo dvizheniia v Uzbekistane. Tashkent, 1969. pp. 269.

- Spain

GIRALT Y RAVENTOS (EMILIO) and others. Los movimientos sociales en Cataluña, Valencia y Baleares. Barcelona, 1970. pp. 141. bibliog.

IZARD (MIQUEL) Revolució industrial i obrerisme: les "tres classes de vapor" a Catalunya, 1869-1913. Barcelona, [1970]. pp. 157. bibliog.

TUÑON DE LARA (MANUEL) El movimiento obrero en la historia de España. Madrid, [1972]. pp. 963. bibliog.

- Spain - Law

ALBIOL MONTESINOS (IGNACIO) Representacion sindical en España: un estudio sobre la normativa electoral sindical. Madrid, 1972. pp. 429.

- Sri Lanka

JAYAWARDENA (VISAKHA KUMARI) The rise of the labor movement in Ceylon. Durham, N.C., 1972. pp. 382. bibliog.

- Sri Lanka - Political activity

KEARNEY (ROBERT N.) Trade unions and politics in Ceylon. Berkeley, Calif., 1971. pp. 195. bibliog.

- Sweden

CARLSON (BO) Trade unions in Sweden. Stockholm, [1969]. pp. 176.

JOHANSON (JÖRN) LO som organisation. Stockholm, [1971]. pp. 57. bibliog.

LANDSORGANISATIONEN I SVERIGE. Kommitté för Ökad Företagsdemokrati. Demokrati i företagen: rapport till LO-kongressen 1971. Stockholm, [1971]. pp. 156.

MYRMAN (YNGVE) Maktkampen på arbetsmarknaden, 1905-1907: en studie av de icke-socialistiska arbetarna som faktor i arbetsgivarpolitiken. [Stockholm, 1973]. pp. 251. bibliog. (Stockholms Universitet. Statsvetenskapliga Institutionen. Stockholm Studies in Politics. 4) With English summary.

- Switzerland

KOMMUNISTISCHE PARTEI DER SCHWEIZ. Zentralkomitee. Quo vadis?: wohin geht der Weg?; ein Mahnwort, gerichtet an alle klassenbewussten Arbeiter der Schweiz. Zürich, [imprint, 1928?]. pp. 88.

BOLLIGER (MARKUS) Die Basler Arbeiterbewegung im Zeitalter des Ersten Weltkrieges und der Spaltung der Sozialdemokratischen Partei: ein Beitrag zur Geschichte der schweizerischen Arbeiterbewegung. Basel, 1970. pp. 379. bibliog.

BOLZ (ROBERT) (Schweizerischer Bau- und Holzarbeiterverband): 50 Jahr Einheitsgewerkschaft. Zürich, 1972. pp. 53.

GREUTER (DIETER) Der Schweizerische Metall- und Uhrenarbeiter-Verband und die Industriegewerkschaft Metall für die Bundesrepublik Deutschland: ein Vergleich. Berlin, [1972]. pp. 209. bibliog. (St. Gall. Handelshochschule. Schweizerisches Institut für Gewerbliche Wirtschaft. Schriftenreihe. 7)

- United Kingdom

[TRADE union broadsheets and other documents: various trades]. v.p., [1854-97]. 1 vol. (unpaged).

HOWELL (GEORGE) Trade unionism, new and old; [reprint of the fourth revised edition of 1907]; edited...by F.M. Leventhal. Brighton, 1973. pp. 282, 1v. bibliog.

INSTITUTE FOR WORKERS' CONTROL. Archives in Trade Union History and Theory. Series 2. No. 7. Democracy or disruption; [by] Tom Mann; [originally published in 1927]. Nottingham, [1971?]. fo. 2.

MANCHESTER AND SALFORD TRADES COUNCIL. Working class unity in Manchester and Salford: statement of the executive committee, etc. [Manchester, 1933]. pp. (4).

NATIONAL UNION OF VEHICLE BUILDERS. General rules...: adopted by delegate meeting at Manchester, October 1936. Watford, [imprint], [1936]. pp. 153.

NATIONAL UNION OF VEHICLE BUILDERS. General rules...: adopted by delegate meeting at Dublin, June, 1947; [with] Partial alteration of rules,...1952. Manchester, [imprint], 1947-52. pp. 65,3.

SHANE (T.N.) pseud. [i.e. H.A. HEALEY] Passed for press: a centenary history of the Association of Correctors of the Press. London, [1954]. pp. 63.

BAIN (GEORGE SAYERS) and PRICE (ROBERT) Writer on labour. Union growth and employment trends in the United Kingdom, 1964-1970. Coventry, 1972. pp. 24. (U.K. Social Science Research Council. Industrial Relations Research Unit. Discussion Papers)

BAUMAN (ZYGMUNT) Between class and elite: the evolution of the British labour movement; a sociological study; translated by Sheila Patterson. Manchester, [1972]. pp. 334.

CHALLINOR (RAYMOND) The Lancashire and Cheshire miners. Newcastle upon Tyne, 1972. pp. 320. bibliog.

COATES (KEN) and TOPHAM (ANTHONY) The new unionism: the case for workers' control. London, 1972. pp. 250. bibliog.

DICKENS (LINDA) U[nited] K[ingdom] A[ssociation of] P[rofessional] E[ngineers]: what future for the professional union? Coventry, 1972. pp. 32. (U.K. Social Science Research Council. Industrial Relations Research Unit. Discussion Papers)

FERRIS (PAUL) The new militants: crisis in the trade unions. Harmondsworth, 1972. pp. 112.

HABERLER (GOTTFRIED VON) and others. Inflation and the unions: three studies in the effects of labour monopoly power on inflation in Britain and the U.S.A. London, 1972. pp. 88. bibliogs. (Institute of Economic Affairs. Readings in Political Economy. 6)

HARROD (JEFFREY) Trade union foreign policy: a study of British and American trade union activities in Jamaica. London, 1972. pp. 485. bibliog.

HOWARD (CAROL) White collar unions: a review. London, 1972. pp. 118. (Institute of Personnel Management. Information Reports. New Series. 11)

MARLOW (JOYCE) The Tolpuddle martyrs. London, 1972. pp. 320.

MURPHY (JOHN THOMAS) Preparing for power: a critical study of the history of the British working-class movement;...with a new introduction by James Hinton. 2nd ed. London, 1972. pp. 296.

MUSSON (ALBERT EDWARD) British trade unions, 1800-1875. London, 1972. pp. 80. bibliog. (Economic History Society. Studies in Economic History)

PAYNTER (WILL) My generation. London, 1972. pp. 172.

PELLING (HENRY MATHISON) A history of British trade unionism. 2nd ed. London, 1972. pp. 310. bibliog.

TRADE UNIONS - United Kingdom (Cont'd.)

ROBERTS (BENJAMIN CHARLES) and others. Reluctant militants: a study of industrial technicians. London, 1972. pp. 342. bibliog. (London. University. London School of Economics and Political Science. Industrial Relations Series)

ROBERTSON (NORMAN) and SAMS (K.I.) eds. British trade unionism: select documents. Oxford, [1972]. 2 vols.

TRADE unions and training for the future: report of a conference of trade union members of Industrial Training Boards, (Trades Union Congress),...April 5, 1972; chairman, G.H. Lowthian. [London, 1972]. pp. 51.

MORTIMER (J.E.) History of the Boilermakers' Society. London, 1973 in progress.

DORFMAN (GERALD ALLEN) Wage politics in Britain, 1945-1967: government vs. the TUC. Ames, 1973. pp. 180. bibliog.

HIKINS (HAROLD R.) ed. Building the union: studies in the growth of the workers' movement, Merseyside, 1756-1967...to celebrate the 125th anniversary of the Liverpool Trades Council. Liverpool, 1973. pp. 198.

HUGHES (JOHN DENNIS) and POLLINS (HAROLD) eds. Trade unions in Great Britain: [selected documents]. Newton Abbot, [1973]. pp. 264. bibliog.

LUMLEY (ROGER) White collar unionism in Britain: a survey of the present position. London, 1973. pp. 160. bibliog.

TRADES UNION CONGRESS. The TUC and the non-manual worker, 1972-73. London, [1973]. pp. 30.

WIGHAM (ERIC LEONARD) Participation in the trade unions. London, [1973?]. pp. 12. (Working Together Campaign. Working Together Studies)

- United Kingdom - Flags, insignia, etc.

GORMAN (JOHN) Banner bright: an illustrated history of the banners of the British trade union movement. London, [1973]. pp. 184.

- United Kingdom - Law

HEPPLE (BOB ALEXANDER) and O'HIGGINS (PAUL) Public employee trade unionism in the United Kingdom: the legal framework. Ann Arbor, 1971. pp. 221. bibliog. (Michigan University and Wayne State University. Institute of Labor and Industrial Relations. Comparative Studies in Public Employment Labor Relations)

BALFOUR (CAMPBELL) Unions and the law. Farnborough, [1973]. pp. 141. bibliog.

HANSON (CHARLES GORING) Trade unions: a century of privilege?; an historical explanation of the 1971 Industrial Relations Act and the perennial issues of trade union power and law. [London], 1973. pp. 34. bibliog. (Institute of Economic Affairs. Occasional Papers. 38)

RIDEOUT (ROGER W.) Trade unions and the law. London, 1973. pp. 276. bibliog.

- United Kingdom - Officials and employees

BROWN (WILLIAM) Economist and LAWSON (MARGARET) The training of trade union officers: the training experience and requirements of full-time trade union officers. Coventry, 1972. pp. 51, 10. (U.K. Social Science Research Council. Industrial Relations Research Unit. Discussion Papers. No. 7)

- United Kingdom - Political activity

RICHTER (IRVING) Political purpose in trade unions. London, 1973. pp. 258.

SIMPSON (BILL) Labour: the unions and the Party: a study of the trade unions and the British labour movement. London, 1973. pp. 256. bibliog.

- United Kingdom - Ireland

BOYD (ANDREW) The rise of the Irish trade unions, 1729-1970. Tralee, [1972]. pp. 155. bibliog.

- United States

PERLMAN (SELIG) A history of trade unionism in the United States; [reprint of the work first published in 1923]. New York, Kelley, 1950. pp. viii, 313. bibliog. $16\frac{1}{2}$cm. (Reprints of Economic Classics)

KEIR (MALCOLM) Labor's search for more. New York, [1937] repr. 1940. pp. 527. bibliog.

BONOSKY (PHILLIP) Brother Bill McKie: building the union at Ford. New York, [1953]. pp. 192.

The PUBLIC stake in union power; [lectures given at University of Virginia, 1958]; edited by Philip D. Bradley. Charlottesville, Va., 1959. pp. 382.

NEW YORK (STATE). Commission of Inquiry concerning Employer Employee Relations in that Segment of the Thoroughbred Racing Industry Affecting Grooms, Exercise Boys and Hot Walkers. 1962. Report. [Albany], 1962. fo. 134.

INTERNATIONAL UNION, UNITED AUTOMOBILE, AEROSPACE AND AGRICULTURAL IMPLEMENT WORKERS OF AMERICA. [Leaflets and publications]. [Detroit, 1964-67]. pp. various.

HUTCHINSON (JOHN) of the Institute of Industrial Relations, California University. George Meany and the wayward. Los Angeles, 1972. pp. 51-60. (California University. Institute of Industrial Relations. [Northern Division]. Reprints. No. 224) (Reprinted from California Management Review, 1969)

LIVEN' (VALENTINA ANDREEVNA) Amerykans'ki profspilky i zovnishnia polityka SShA, 1960-1968 rr. Kyïv, 1969. pp. 180. bibliog. With Russian and English summaries.

KEREMETSKII (IAKOV NIKOLAEVICH) SShA: profsoiuzy v bor'be s kapitalom. Moskva, 1970. pp. 266.

KOENIG (ALLEN E.) ed. Broadcasting and bargaining: labor relations in radio and television. Madison, Wisc., 1970. pp. 344.

AURAND (HAROLD W.) From the Molly Maguires to the United Mine Workers: the social ecology of an industrial union, 1869-1897. Philadelphia, 1971. pp. 221. bibliog.

BURPO (JOHN H.) The police labor movement: problems and perspectives. Springfield, Ill., [1971]. pp. 203.

CLAGUE (EWAN) and others. The aging worker and the union: employment and retirement of middle-aged and older workers. New York, 1971. pp. 144.

ERICKSON (HERMAN) The steward's role in the union, and a history of American unions. New York, [1971]. pp. 123. bibliog.

LEVENSTEIN (HARVEY A.) Labor organizations in the United States and Mexico: a history of their relations. Westport, Conn., 1971. pp. 258. bibliog.

MORRIS (GEORGE) Rebellion in the unions: a handbook for rank and file action. New York, 1971. pp. 159.

PFLUG (WARNER W.) The UAW in pictures. Detroit, 1971. pp. 194.

WELLINGTON (HARRY H.) and WINTER (RALPH K.) The unions and the cities. Washington, [1971]. pp. 226. (Brookings Institution. Studies of Unionism in Government)

DICK (WILLIAM MILNER) Labour and socialism in America: the Gompers era. Port Washington, N.Y., 1972. pp. 211. bibliog.

GARNEL (DONALD) The rise of Teamster power in the West. Berkeley, 1972. pp. 363. bibliog.

GOULD (JEAN) and HICKOK (LORENA) Walter Reuther: labor's rugged individualist. New York, [1972]. pp. 399. bibliog.

HABERLER (GOTTFRIED VON) and others. Inflation and the unions: three studies in the effects of labour monopoly power on inflation in Britain and the U.S.A. London, 1972. pp. 88. bibliogs. (Institute of Economic Affairs. Readings in Political Economy. 6)

HARROD (JEFFREY) Trade union foreign policy: a study of British and American trade union activities in Jamaica. London, 1972. pp. 485. bibliog.

HERDING (RICHARD) Job control and union structure: a study on plant-level industrial conflict in the United States with a comparative perspective on West Germany. Rotterdam, 1972. pp. 401. bibliog.

HERLING (JOHN) Right to challenge: people and power in the Steelworkers Union. New York, [1972]. pp. 415.

LARROWE (CHARLES P.) Harry Bridges: the rise and fall of radical labor in the United States. New York, 1972. pp. 404.

SHERIDAN (WALTER) The fall and rise of Jimmy Hoffa. New York, [1972]. pp. 554.

STANLEY (DAVID T.) Managing local government under union pressure. Washington, D.C., [1972]. pp. 177. bibliog. (Brookings Institution. Studies of Unionism in Government)

TAX FOUNDATION. Research Publications. New Series. No. 27. Unions and government employment. New York, 1972. pp. 45.

DOBBS (FARRELL) Teamster power. New York, 1973. pp. 255.

GERSUNY (CARL) Punishment and redress in a modern factory. Lexington, Mass., [1973]. pp. 96. bibliog.

JURIS (HERVEY A.) and FEUILLE (PETER) Police unionism: power and impact in public-sector bargaining. Lexington, Mass., [1973]. pp. 228.

LYND (ROBERT STAUGHTON) ed. American labor radicalism: testimonies and interpretations. New York, [1973]. pp. 217. bibliog.

SERRIN (WILLIAM) The Company and the Union: the 'civilized relationship' of the General Motors Corporation and the United Automobile Workers. New York, 1973. pp. 308,xiv.

SNYDER (CARL DEAN) b. 1921. White-collar workers and the UAW. Urbana, Ill., [1973]. pp. 197. bibliog.

STIEBER (JACK W.) Public employee unionism: structure, growth, policy. Washington, D.C., [1973]. pp. 256. (Brookings Institution. Studies of Unionism in Government)

- United States - Negro membership

WOLKINSON (BENJAMIN W.) Blacks, unions, and the EEOC: a study of administrative futility. Lexington, Mass., [1973]. pp. 175. bibliog.

- United States - California.

BROWN (JERALD BARRY) The United Farm Workers grape strike and boycott, 1965-1970: an evaluation of the culture of poverty theory. [Ithaca], 1972. pp. 348. bibliog. (Cornell University. Latin American Studies Program. Dissertation Series. No. 39)

- United States - Michigan

McLAUGHLIN (DORIS B.) Michigan labor: a brief history from 1818 to the present. Ann Arbor, 1970. pp. 179. bibliog.

- United States - Minnesota

FLAGLER (JOHN J.) Profile of the Minnesota labor movement. Minneapolis, 1972. pp. 45. bibliog. (Minnesota University. Industrial Relations Center. Bulletins. 56)

- Venezuela

CHEN (CHI-YI) Economia social del trabajo: caso de Venezuela; (con la colaboracion de Enrique Brücker). Caracas, [1969]. pp. 449. bibliog.

- Yugoslavia

TOPALOVIĆ (ŽIVKO) Slom demokratije. London, 1961. pp. 75.

TRADE-UNIONS, CATHOLIC

- Austria

PELINKA (ANTON) Stand oder Klasse?: die Christliche Arbeiterbewegung Österreichs, 1933 bis 1938. Wien, [1972]. pp. 334. (Ludwig-Boltzmann-Institut für Geschichte der Arbeiterbewegung. Veröffentlichungen)

- France

MAIRE (EDMOND) Pour un socialisme démocratique: contribution de la C[onfédération] F[rançaise] D[émocratique des] T[ravailleurs]. Paris, [1971]. pp. 168.

- Germany

REXHAEUSER (LUDWIG) Die christlichen Gewerkschaften: zur Geschichte der Arbeiterzersplitterung in Deutschland. Leipzig, [1909]. pp. 96. (Sonderabdruck aus dem Korrespondent für Deutschlands Buchdrucker und Schriftgiesser)

- Germany - Saarland

KIEFER (PETER) 25 Jahre Gewerkverein christlicher Bergarbeiter im Saarrevier. Saarbrücken, 1929. pp. 130. bibliog.

- Italy

[ASSOCIAZIONI CRISTIANE DEI LAVORATORI ITALIANI]. Le ACLI per lo sviluppo della società italiana, 1966-1969. Roma, [1969?]. pp. 326.

LABOR (LIVIO) In campo aperto. Firenze, 1969. pp. 193.

TRADE-UNIONS AND COMMUNISM

HAZARD (JOHN NEWBOLD) Labor law and revolutionary socialism. [Stockholm, 1972]. pp. 102-117. (Reprinted from Mélanges de Droit Comparé en l'Honneur du Doyen Ake Malmström, 1972)

TRADE UNIONS AND COMMUNISM (Cont'd.)

- Canada

ABELLA (IRVING MARTIN) Nationalism, communism, and Canadian labour: the CIO, the Communist Party, and the Canadian Congress of Labour, 1935-1956. Toronto, [1973]. pp. 256. bibliog.

- France

KRASUCKI (HENRI) Syndicats et socialisme. Paris, [1972]. pp. 126.

- Germany

Die REVOLUTIONAERE Gewerkschaftsopposition: (Dokumente... aus den Jahren 1924 bis 1932; [collection of reprints compiled by the] Gewerkschaftsabteilung des ZK der Kommunistischen Partei Deutschlands). Berlin, 1972. 2 vols. (Dokumente und Analysen zur Kommunistischen Arbeiterbewegung. Bände 4-5)

- Italy

PILLON (CESARE) I comunisti e il Sindacato. Milano, [1972]. pp. 482.

TRADE UNIONS AND FOREIGN POLICY

- United States

HERO (ALFRED OLIVIER) and STARR (EMIL) The Reuther-Meany foreign policy dispute: union leaders and members view world affairs. Dobbs Ferry, 1970. 1 vol. (various pagings).

FONER (PHILIP SHELDON) American labor and the Indochina War. New York, 1971. pp. 126.

TRAFFIC ASSIGNMENT

- Mathematical models

WIGAN (M. RAMSAY) Benefit assessment for network traffic models and application to road pricing. Crowthorne, 1971. pp. 22. (U.K. Road Research Laboratory. Reports. LR 417)

WIGAN (M. RAMSAY) and BAMFORD (T.J.G.) A perturbation model for congested and overloaded transportation networks. Crowthorne, 1971. pp. 22. (U.K. Road Research Laboratory. Reports. LR 411.)

TRAFFIC ENGINEERING

The URBAN transportation planning process. Paris, Organisation for Economic Co-operation and Development, 1971. pp. 351. bibliog. In English and French.

- Mathematical models

POMPILJ (GIUSEPPE) Uno strumento operativo per la valutazione degli interventi sul traffico "Il SOST". Roma, 1966. pp. 6. (Rome. Università. Istituto di Calcolo delle Probabilità. Pubblicazioni Omaggio. 17) (Estratto dagli Atti della XXIII Conferenza del Traffico e della Circolazione...Stresa...1965)

POMPILJ (GIUSEPPE) Valutazione degli interventi sul traffico urbano. Roma, 1967. pp. 15. (Rome. Università. Istituto di Calcolo delle Probabilità. Pubblicazioni Omaggio. 18) (Estratto del Periodico di Matematiche, serie IV, vol. XLIV, 1966)

VENTKER (RUEDIGER) Die ökonomischen Grundlagen der Verkehrsnetzplanung. Göttingen, [1970]. pp. 174. bibliog. (Hamburg. Hansische Universität. Institut für Verkehrswissenschaft. Verkehrswissenschaftliche Studien. 11)

GERHARDT (HEINZ) Verkehrserzeugung und Verkehrsprognose des Personenverkehrs in Ballungsgebieten. Göttingen, [1971]. pp. 125. bibliog. (Hamburg. Hansische Universität. Institut für Verkehrswissenschaft. Verkehrswissenschaftliche Studien. 19)

INTERNATIONAL SYMPOSIUM ON THE THEORY OF TRAFFIC FLOW AND TRANSPORTATION, 5TH, 1971. Traffic flow and transportation: proceedings of the...Symposium...held at Berkeley, California...1971. New York [1972]. pp. 453.

- Germany

TAMMS (FRIEDRICH) Über die untersuchungen für einen Generalverkehrsplan der Stadt Düsseldorf:... Bericht vor dem Rat der Stadt Düsseldorf am 19. Mai 1961. Düsseldorf, [1961]. pp. 68.

- Italy

PROBLEMI del traffico nel territorio della Bazzanese: [proceedings of a conference convened by the provincial administration of Bologna], Casalecchio di Reno, 13 novembre 1971. [Bologna, 1971?]. fo. 96. With tables in end pocket.

- New Zealand

HAMILTON, NEW ZEALAND. City Council. Hamilton transportation study. Hamilton, 1969. 2 vols. (in 1).

- United Kingdom

FREEMAN FOX AND ASSOCIATES. Kingston upon Hull and nearby areas: land use/transportation study. London, 1969-72. 2 vols. (in 1).

ANTONIOU (JIM) Environmental management: planning for traffic. London, [1971]. pp. 171.

BUCHANAN (COLIN) AND PARTNERS and FREEMAN FOX AND ASSOCIATES. Analysis of the problem: city of Edinburgh planning and transport study. Edinburgh, 1971. pp. 77.

HOLROYD (JOYCE) and OWENS (D.) Measuring the effectiveness of area traffic control systems. Crowthorne, 1971. pp. 20. (U.K. Road Research Laboratory. Reports. LR 420)

BRITISH ASSOCIATION FOR THE ADVANCEMENT OF SCIENCE. Section F. Meeting, 1971. Uses of economics; papers...; [with the Presidential Address of Sir Alec Cairncross, and the papers of a Symposium on Traffic and Towns organized jointly by Section F and Section G]; edited by G.D.N. Worswick. Oxford, 1972. pp. 227.

BUCHANAN (COLIN) AND PARTNERS and FREEMAN FOX AND ASSOCIATES. Edinburgh: the recommended plan; city of Edinburgh planning and transport study...final report. [Edinburgh], 1972. pp. 183.

HOLROYD (JOYCE) The practical implementation of combination method and TRANSYT programs. Crowthorne, 1972. pp. 14. (U.K. Transport and Road Research Laboratory. Reports. LR 518)

MORGAN (R. TRAVERS) AND PARTNERS. Cambridge transportation plan: the final report of the Cambridge transportation study, carried out for Cambridgeshire and Isle of Ely County Council, Cambridge City Council [and] University of Cambridge. London, 1972. pp. 117.

PLOWDEN (STEPHEN) Towns against traffic. London, 1972. pp. 183.

- United States

CARNEGIE-MELLON CONFERENCE ON ADVANCED URBAN TRANSPORTATION SYSTEMS, PITTSBURGH, 1970. Advanced urban transportation systems: (proceedings of the... conference). [Pittsburgh, 1970]. pp. 148. bibliog. (Carnegie-Mellon University. Transportation Research Institute. Research Report Series. 5)

TRAFFIC ESTIMATION

- United Kingdom

LEWIS (JOHN PARRY) Mis-used techniques in planning. 4: The forecasts of Roskill, part 1. [Manchester, 1971]. fo. 57. (Manchester, University. Centre for Urban and Regional Research. Occasional Papers. No. 11)

VOORHEES (ALAN M.) AND ASSOCIATES, LTD., and BUCHANAN (COLIN) AND PARTNERS. Tyne-Wear plan: technical report. [London], 1973. pp. 112.

- United Kingdom - London

LONDON. Greater London Council. Transportation Branch. Test 7: report; [by] G. Lamb [and others]. [London], 1968. pp. 55, 3. (London. Greater London Council. Department of Highways and Transportation. Research Memoranda. 91)

SHORTREED (J.) and MAY (A.D.) Test 6 report. [London], 1969. 1 vol. (various pagings). (London. Greater London Council. Department of Highways and Transportation. Research Memoranda. 90)

TRAFFIC FLOW

- United Kingdom

CAPLAN (RUTH) and DUNCAN (N.C.) Traffic flows on M4 motorway, 1961-70. Crowthorne, 1972. pp. 53. bibliog. (U.K. Transport and Road Research Laboratory. Reports. LR 452)

GYENES (L.) The distribution of hourly volumes of traffic at fifty sites in 1970. Crowthorne, 1973. pp. 27. (U.K. Transport and Road Research Laboratory. Reports. LR 549)

TRAFFIC NOISE

ORGANISATION FOR ECONOMIC CO-OPERATION AND DEVELOPMENT. Consultative Group on Transportation Research. 1971. Urban traffic noise: strategy for an improved environment. Paris, 1971. pp. 166. bibliog.

- United Kingdom

NOISE ADVISORY COUNCIL [U.K.]. Traffic noise: the vehicle regulations and their enforcement; report by a working group of the Council; [D.B. Harrison, chairman]. London, H.M.S.O., 1972. pp. 67.

TRAFFIC OFFENCES

- Russia

KICHIGINA (EKATERINA VASIL'EVNA) Otvetstvennost' za narushenie bezopasnosti dvizheniia gorodskogo transporta. Moskva, 1966. pp. 124.

KURINOV (BORIS ALEKSANDROVICH) Avtotransportnye prestupleniia: kvalifikatsiia i nakazanie. Moskva, 1970. pp. 223.

- Russia - Armenia

AVAKIAN (LIPARIT AVAKOVICH) Nekotorye problemy preduprezhdeniia dorozhno-transportnykh proisshestvii v Armianskoi SSR. Erevan, 1972. pp. 144.

- United Kingdom

HOOD (ROGER GRAHAME) Sentencing the motoring offender: a study of magistrates' views and practices. London, 1972. pp. 244. bibliog. (Cambridge. University. Institute of Criminology. Cambridge Studies in Criminology. 31)

TRAFFIC POLICE

- United Kingdom

RIVERS (K.) History of the Traffic Department of the metropolitan police. [London, Metropolitan Police, 1972?]. pp. 63.

TRAFFIC REGULATIONS

- Sweden

BJÖRKMAN (JOHAN) Kortsiktiga effekter av trafikinformation: en studie av förekomsten och effekten av informationen via massmedia i samband med högertrafikomläggningen 1967. Stockholm, [1971]. pp. 398. bibliog. With English summary.

TRAFFIC SIGNS AND SIGNALS

HOLROYD (JOYCE) The practical implementation of combination method and TRANSYT programs. Crowthorne, 1972. pp. 14. (U.K. Transport and Road Research Laboratory. Reports. LR 518)

HOLROYD (JOYCE) and ROBERTSON (D.I.) Strategies for area traffic control systems: present and future. Crowthorne, 1973. pp. 14. (U.K. Transport and Road Research Laboratory. Reports. LR 569)

TRAFFIC SURVEYS

- Denmark

KOFOED (JENS) Beboernes faerden i byen. København, 1972. pp. 191. bibliog. (Denmark. Statens Byggeforskningsinstitut. SBI-Byplanlaegninger. 15) With English summary.

- Switzerland

SWITZERLAND. Bureau Fédéral de Statistique. 1971. Die schweizerischen Strassenverkehrszählungen: Recensement suisse de la circulation routière, 1970. Berne, 1971. pp. 65. (Statistique de la Suisse. 472e fasc.) 3 maps in end pocket.

TRAFFIC SURVEYS ; Underdeveloped areas
See UNDERDEVELOPED AREAS -
Traffic surveys

- United Kingdom

STEVENAGE DEVELOPMENT CORPORATION. Stevenage household survey, March 1971. [Stevenage], 1971. fo. 63.

- United Kingdom - London

CRAWFORD (K.A.J.) and others. Greater London transportation survey (GLTS): internal zone coding. [London], 1971. pp. 24. (London. Greater London Council. Department of Planning and Transportation. Research Memoranda. 300)

TRAFFIC SURVEYS - United Kingdom - London (Cont'd.)

HAVERS (G.E.) An outline of the transportation model used in tests 14-18. [London], 1971. pp. 15, 4. (London. Greater London Council. Department of Planning and Transportation. Research Memoranda. 263)

MINT (P.W.) Speed studies in Greater London: the primary routes, 1967-68. [London], 1971. pp. 12, ii. (London. Greater London Council. Department of Planning and Transportation. Research Memoranda. 285)

REDDING (B.G.) A study of industrial traffic generation in London. [London], 1971. pp. 133. (London. Greater London Council. Department of Planning and Transportation. Research Memoranda. 292)

STROUD (A.A.) Greater London transportation survey (GLTS): external district coding. [London], 1971. pp. 19. (London. Greater London Council. Department of Planning and Transportation. Research Memoranda. 301)

TOWNSLEY (C.H.) Traffic generation of suburban London offices. [London], 1973. pp. 46. (London. Greater London Council. Department of Planning and Transportation. Research Memoranda. 398)

TOWNSLEY (C.H.) and HOLLOWAY (JAN L.) Surveys for office traffic generation studies. [London], 1973. pp. 34. (London. Greater London Council. Department of Planning and Transportation. Research Memoranda. 385)

TRAILER CAMPS

URBAN LAND INSTITUTE. Technical Bulletins. [Nos.] 66, 68. Mobile home parks; by Robinson Newcomb ([and] Max S. Wehrly). Washington, D.C., [1971-72]. 2 pts. bibliog.

ANGLESEY. Planning Department. Touring caravans, 1971. [Llangefni], 1971. pp. 12.

- Laws and legislation - United Kingdom

JOINT WORKING PARTY OF THE LOCAL AUTHORITY ASSOCIATIONS AND THE GYPSY COUNCIL. Caravan Sites Act, 1968, Part II. London, [1971?]. pp. 4,iii.

TRAMPS

- United States

SOLENBERGER (ALICE WILLARD) One thousand homeless men: a study of original records. New York, 1911 repr. 1914. pp. 374.

TRAMWAYS

- India - Employees

INDIA. Labour Investigation Committee. 1946. Report on labour conditions in tram and bus services; by Ahmad Mukhtar. Delhi, 1946. pp. 124.

- Netherlands

DIJKERS (A.) De Rotterdamsche Tramweg-Maatschappÿ op de Zuid-Hollandse en Zeeuwse eilanden. Leiden, 1971. pp. 262. bibliog. (Nederlandsche Vereeniging van Belangstellenden in het Spoor- en Tramwegwezen. Uitgaven. Deel 7) 5 maps in end pocket.

- United Kingdom

DUNCAN (WILLIAM WALLACE) Stockbroker. Manual of tramway companies in the United Kingdom, together with traffic tables of the principal companies, and map of those in London. London, 1877. pp. 73. Cover title: Duncan's tramway manual, etc.

- United States

CHICAGO. Street Railway Commission. Report...to the City Council of the City of Chicago. Chicago, 1900. pp. 136.

TRANSCAUCASIA
See CAUCASUS

TRANSFER PRICING

ARPAN (JEFFREY S.) International intracorporate pricing: non-American systems and views. New York, 1972. pp. 126.

ARVIDSSON (GÖRAN) Internal transfer negotiations: eight experiments. Stockholm, 1973. pp. 191. bibliog.

TRANSFORMATIONS (MATHEMATICS)

ANGEL (SHLOMO) and HYMAN (GEOFFREY M.) Transformations and geographic theory. London, 1971. pp. 34. bibliog. (Centre for Environmental Studies. Working Papers. 72)

TRANSIT, INTERNATIONAL

ROHWEDER (GERD) Der Transithandelsbetrieb als spezieller Aussenhandelsbetrieb: eine Untersuchung seiner strukturpolitischen Handlungsmöglichkeiten. Hamburg, 1971. pp. 187. bibliog.

- Germany

TREATY between the German Democratic Republic and the Federal Republic of Germany on questions relating to traffic. Dresden, [1972]. pp. 29.

TRANSKEIAN TERRITORIES

- Appropriations and expenditures

TRANSKEI. Estimate of the expenditure to be defrayed from the Transkeian Revenue Fund. a., 1964/5- Umtata. 1970/71- in English, Afrikaans and Xhosa.

TRANSPORT LIBRARIES

LONDON AND HOME COUNTIES REGIONAL ADVISORY COUNCIL FOR TECHNOLOGICAL EDUCATION. Libraries in the region which specialise in transport and kindred subjects, 1972. London, [1972]. pp. 6.

TRANSPORT WORKERS

INTERNATIONAL LABOUR ORGANISATION. Inland Transport Committee. 9th Session. Reports. 1. General report: first item on the agenda. Geneva, International Labour Office, 1972. pp. 264.

- Russia

PERETRUTOV (VALENTIN NIKOLAEVICH) and EZERIN (ARNOL'D ERNESTOVICH) Trud i zarabotnaia plata na promyshlennom transporte. Moskva, 1972. pp. 240.

- United States

DOBBS (FARRELL) Teamster power. New York, 1973. pp. 255.

TRANSPORTATION

MILNE (ALASTAIR MURRAY) The economics of inland transport. London, 1955. pp. 292. bibliog.

TROXEL (EMERY) Economics of transport. New York, [1955]. pp. 837.

Der VERKEHR in der wirtschaftlichen Entwicklung des Industriezeitalters: (Festschrift zum 40-jährigen Jubiläum des Instituts für Verkehrswissenschaft an der Universität Köln); herausgegeben von Paul Berkenkopf. Düsseldorf, 1961. pp. 203.

HAMILTON (FREDERICK EDWARD IAN) ed. Festschrift: Arthur E. Moodie. Evanston, Ill., 1971. pp. 110. bibliog. (Northwestern University. Studies in Geography. No. 18)

KRAFT (GERALD) and others. The role of transportation in regional economic development: a Charles River Associates research study. Lexington, Mass., [1971]. pp. 129. bibliog.

HEGGIE (IAN G.) Transport engineering economics. London, [1972]. pp. 265. bibliog.

HIBBS (JOHN ALFRED BLYTH) People and transport. London, [1972]. pp. 14. (Unservile State Group. Unservile State Papers. No. 19)

RIVERS (PATRICK) The restless generation: a crisis in mobility. London, 1972. pp. 208. bibliog.

SCHNEIDER (WILHELM LUDWIG) Bestimmungsgründe für Verkehrsnachfrage und Verkehrswegeplanung: zwei Beiträge, etc. Berlin, [1972]. pp. 84. bibliog. (Ifo-Institut für Wirtschaftsforschung. Schriftenreihe. Nr. 78)

BETRIEBSWIRTSCHAFTLICHE Logistik: Systeme, Entscheidungen, Methoden; ([by] Werner Kirsch [and others]). Weisbaden, [1973]. pp. 816. bibliog.

MURRAY (JAMES J.) ed. Urban and regional ground transportation: surveys and readings. Durham, N.C., [1973]. pp. 472. bibliogs.

TAAFFE (EDWARD JAMES) and GAUTHIER (HOWARD L.) Geography of transportation. Englewood Cliffs, N.J., [1973]. pp. 226. bibliog.

- Bibliography

BLACKWELL'S. Catalogues. 865. Rare and interesting books on science mainly related to transport and technology. Oxford, 1969. pp. 203.

CLERC-PECHINE (NICOLE) compiler. Bibliographie d'économie des transports 1960-1971. Paris, [1972?]. pp. 224. (Centre National de la Recherche Scientifique. Centre de Documentation Sciences Humaines. Collection Documentation)

- Directories

LONDON AND HOME COUNTIES REGIONAL ADVISORY COUNCIL FOR TECHNOLOGICAL EDUCATION. Libraries in the region which specialise in transport and kindred subjects, 1972. London, [1972]. pp. 6.

- Finance

PREST (ALAN RICHMOND) Financing transport in developing countries. Washington, 1967. 1 vol. (various fo.).

- Mathematical models

LONDON GRADUATE SCHOOL OF BUSINESS STUDIES. Transport Network Theory Unit. Reports. London, 1964-69. 48 pts. (in 2 vols.).

INTERNATIONAL SYMPOSIUM ON THE THEORY OF TRAFFIC FLOW AND TRANSPORTATION, 5TH, 1971. Traffic flow and transportation: proceedings of the...Symposium...held at Berkeley, California...1971. New York, [1972]. pp. 453.

DRAKE (JOHN W.) The administration of transportation modeling projects. Lexington, Mass., [1973]. pp. 246. bibliog.

- Passenger traffic

CANADAIR LIMITED. Guided ground transportation: a review and bibliography of advanced systems; [by] William S. McLaren [and others]...; prepared for Transportation Development Agency, Ministry of Transport. Ottawa, Information Canada, 1972. pp. 515.

- Passenger traffic - Mathematical models

WIGAN (M. RAMSAY) and WALMSLEY (D. A.) A modal split model for long distance travel. Crowthorne, 1972. pp. 16. (U.K. Transport and Road Research Laboratory. Reports. LR 501)

- Research - Canada

LEWIS (C. BEAUMONT) A survey of Canadian activity in transportation R & D. Ottawa, 1971. pp. 27. (Canada. Science Council of Canada. Special Studies. No.17)

- Research - United Kingdom

U.K. Science Research Council. Transport Panel. 1971. Transport Panel report; [D.J. Lyons, chairman]. [London], 1971. pp. 41.

- America, Latin

OBERLAENDER (DIETER) Verkehrssystem und Integrationsbestrebungen als Determinanten der wirtschaftlichen Entwicklung Lateinamerikas. Bonn, 1971. pp. 330. bibliog.

- Asia, Southeast

ASIAN DEVELOPMENT BANK. 1972. Southeast Asian regional transport survey. [Pasay City, 1972]. 5 vols. bibliog.

- Austria

AUSTRIA. Bundesministerium für Verkehr und verstaatlichte Unternehmungen. 1968. Gesamtverkehrskonzept der österreichischen Bundesregierung. Wien, 1968. pp. 111.

- Belgium - Statistics

BELGIUM. Service de Promotion et de Coordination des Communications. 1965. Recueil des statistiques concernant les transports en Belgique, période 1950-1964. 4th ed. [Brussels, 1965?]. pp. 172.

- Canada - Passenger traffic

CULLEY (ERIC K.) Forecasting intercity travel...; paper presented to the sixth annual meeting of the Canadian Transportation Research Forum, Winnipeg, May 1970. [Ottawa, Canadian Transport Commission, 1970]. fo. 33. bibliog.

CLARK (GEORGE A.) Comparison of strategies for development of intercity transport...; paper presented to the seventh annual meeting of the Canadian Transportation Research Forum, Ottawa, April 1971. [Ottawa, Canadian Transport Commission, 1971]. fo. 27. bibliog.

CANADAIR LIMITED. Guided ground transportation: a review and bibliography of advanced systems; [by] William S. McLaren [and others]...; prepared for Transportation Development Agency, Ministry of Transport. Ottawa, Information Canada, 1972. pp. 515.

- Europe

LEIGHTON (ALBERT C.) Transport and communication in early medieval Europe, AD 500-1100. Newton Abbot, 1972. pp. 257. bibliog.

TRANSPORTATION (Cont'd.)

- European Economic Community countries

EUROPEAN COMMUNITIES. Commission. 1971. Development of the common transport policy: Commission memorandum to the Council: submitted on 8 November 1971. Brussels, 1971. pp. 21. (Bulletin of the European Communities. Supplements. [1971/8])

STAND und Möglichkeiten einer gemeinsamen EWG-Verkehrspolitik: ([four reports by members of the] Institut für Verkehrswissenschaft an der Universität Münster). Göttingen, 1971. pp. 405. bibliog.

STIESCH (HORST) Die Bedeutung der gemeinsamen Verkehrspolitik der Europäischen Wirtschaftsgemeinschaft für die Entwicklung der Raumstruktur der Bundesrepublik Deutschland. Berlin, [1971] pp. 176. bibliog. (Bonn. Universität. Institut für Industrie- und Verkehrspolitik. Verkehrswissenschaftliche Forschungen. Band 22). With English and French summaries.

- European Economic Community countries - Laws and regulations

SAUPE (GERD) Technische Vereinbarungen und Unternehmensgemeinschaften im Verkehrskartellrecht der EWG: Eisenbahn-, Strassen- und Binnenschiffsverkehr. Köln, 1972. pp. 184. bibliog. (Cologne. Universität. Institut für das Recht der Europäischen Gemeinschaften. Kölner Schriten zum Europarecht. Band 16)

WISSENSCHAFTLICHE GESELLSCHAFT FÜR EUROPARECHT. Wissenschaftliches Kolloquium, Bad Ems, 1971. Verkehr und Gemeinschaftsrecht. Köln, 1972. pp. 109. (Cologne. Universität. Institut für das Recht der Europäischen Gemeinschaften. Kölner Schriften zum Europarecht. Band 18)

- France

FRANCE. Comité des Transports Intérieurs. 1971. Préparation du VIe Plan...: rapport. Paris, 1971. 2 pts. (in 1).

FRANCE. Commission des Transports. 1971. Préparation du VIe Plan: rapport. Paris, 1971. 2 pts.

PARIS. Préfecture. Le dossier des transports de la région parisienne. [Paris], 1971. pp. 55.

FRANCE. Commissariat Général du Plan. 1972. Les transports. Paris, 1972. pp. 352. (Plan et Prospectives. 7)

- Germany

JOHN (GUENTHER) Ermittlung und Analyse der Investitionen und des Anlagevermögens im Verkehr in der Bundesrepublik Deutschland. Berlin, 1971. pp. 86. (Deutsches Institut für Wirtschaftsforschung. DIW-Beiträge zur Strukturforschung. Heft 17) With English summary.

STIESCH (HORST) Die Bedeutung der gemeinsamen Verkehrspolitik der Europäischen Wirtschaftsgemeinschaft für die Entwicklung der Raumstruktur der Bundesrepublik Deutschland. Berlin, [1971] pp. 176. bibliog. (Bonn. Universität. Institut für Industrie- und Verkehrspolitik. Verkehrswissenschaftliche Forschungen. Band 22). With English and French summaries.

BARTHOLMAI (BERND) Analyse des Angebotspotentials und Projektion des Investitionsbedarfs im Verkehr der Bundesrepublik Deutschland. Berlin, 1972. pp. 176. bibliog. (Deutsches Institut für Wirtschaftsforschung. DIW-Beiträge zur Strukturforschung. Heft 20) With English summary.

VERKEHRSENTWICKLUNG Nürnbergs im 19. und 20. Jahrhundert. Nürnberg, 1972. pp. 349. bibliogs. (Nuremberg. Verein für Geschichte der Stadt Nürnberg. Nürnberger Forschungen. 17. Band)

- Germany - Laws and regulations

BRAUNTHAL (GERARD) The West German legislative process: a case study of two transportation bills. Ithaca, 1972. pp. 290.

- Germany - Statistics

GERMANY (BUNDESREPUBLIK). Statistisches Bundesamt. Grenzüberschreitender Reiseverkehr. m. and a., Ja 1973 [1st issue]- Wiesbaden. Formerly pd. as the Bundesamt's Verkehr. Reihe 7 and filed at R(O) 43(R165).

- India

INDIA. Planning Commission. Programme Evaluation Organisation. Publications. No. 42. Role of bullock carts and trucks in rural transport: case studies; undertaken at the instance of Committee on Transport Policy and Coordination. [Delhi], 1963[or rather 1964]. pp. 160.

- India - Mysore

REGIONAL transport survey of Mysore State; [prepared in the Transport Division of the National Council of Applied Economic Research]. New Delhi, [1970]. pp. 570.

- Ireland (Republic)

McKINSEY AND COMPANY INCORPORATED. Defining the role of public transport in a changing environment; a report prepared for Department of Transport and Power, Department of Finance, Coras Iompair Eireann. Dublin, Stationery Office, 1971. pp. 122.

- Ireland (Republic) - Rates

EIRE. National Prices Commission. 1972. C.I.E. rates and fares. Dublin, 1972. pp. 46. (Occasional Papers. No. 4)

ECONOMISTS ADVISORY GROUP. The pricing policy of Coras Iompair Eireann. Dublin, 1973. pp. 128. (Eire. National Prices Commission. Occasional Papers. No.10)

- Italy

PALA (GIANFRANCO) Investimenti sociali ed economia dei trasporti: [collected papers]. Milano, [1968]. pp. 259. bibliog. (Centro di Studi e Piani Economici. Quaderni. Studi di Pianificazione dei Trasporti. N.1)

CONVEGNO PROVINCIALE SULLA PRIMA IPOTESI DI SCHEMA DELLA VIABILITÀ E DEI TRASPORTI PER L'EMILIA-ROMAGNA, BOLOGNA, 1970. (Prima ipotesi di schema della viabilità e dei trasporti per l'Emilia-Romagna): convegno provinciale...; (atti editi dall'Assessorato ai Lavori Pubblici e Trasporti). Bologna, [1971]. pp. 170.

ITALY. Camera dei Deputati. Commissioni Permanenti. X. Trasporti e Aviazione Civile, Poste e Telecomunicazioni, Marina Mercantile. 1972. Trasporti pubblici e privati nelle aree metropolitane e nel Mezzogiorno: indagine conoscitiva, etc. [Rome], 1972. pp. 418. (Italy. Servizio Commissioni Parlamentari. Indagini Conoscitive e Documentazioni Legislative. 10)

VISCOVO (MARIO DEL) I trasporti terrestri. Milano, 1972. pp. 408. (Società Italiana di Economia dei Trasporti. Ricerca CNR sulla Struttura dei Trasporti Italiani. vol. 1)

- Italy - Costs

TANCI (MARIO) L'idrovia Torino-Milano-Adriatico e diramazioni: i costi comparati dei trasporti e le zone d'influenza. 2. Le relazioni fra gli scali interni ed i servizi combinati coi centri dell'entroterra; Le zone d'influenza degli scali di Marghera, etc. Cremona, 1971. pp. 265. (Comunità Padana delle Camere di Commercio, Industria, Artigianato e Agricoltura. Pubblicazioni)

- Mexico - Statistics

MEXICO. Direccion General de Estadistica. Censo de Transportes, 1966. VI censo de transportes, 1966; datos de 1965. Mexico, 1969. pp. 176.

- Netherlands

NEDERLANDS ECONOMISCH INSTITUUT. Integrale verkeers- en vervoerstudie; uitgevoerd door het Nederlands Economisch Instituut in opdracht van de Minister van Verkeer en Waterstaat. 's-Gravenhage, 1972. 9 vols. (in 2).

WAAR moet't heen... [Utrecht, 1972]. pp. 64,(16).

- New Guinea

HALCROW (Sir WILLIAM THOMSON) AND PARTNERS. Transport survey of the territories of Papua and New Guinea: draft final report on part 1; [comissioned by the International Bank for Reconstruction and Development for the United Nations Development Programme]. London, 1969. 5 vols.

- Nigeria

SMITH (FREDERICK) Writer on transportation. Transport in Nigeria. n.p., 1939. 1 vol. (various pagings).

- Norway - Bibliography

PARKER (MARJORIE) and RØED (ANNE) compilers. Planning in Norway: literature in English. Oslo, 1971. fo. 18. (Norsk Institutt for By- og Regionforskning. Biblioteket. Publications. 1971. 1)

- Poland - Laws and regulations

GÓRSKI (WŁADYSŁAW) Umowa przewozu. Warszawa, 1972. pp 358. With French and Russian summaries.

- Russia

EKONOMIKA transporta. Moskva, 1968. pp. 205. (Institut Kompleksnykh Transportnykh Problem. Trudy. vyp.10)

VOPROSY razvitiia transportnoi seti SSSR. Moskva, 1968. pp. 219. (Institut Kompleksnykh Transportnykh Problem. Trudy. vyp.9)

- Russia - Costs

POPOVA (ELENA IVANOVNA) Transportnye zatraty v obshchestvennom proizvodstve: na primere zapadnykh i vostochnykh raionov SSSR. Moskva, 1973. pp. 173.

- Russia - Caucasus

KHURSHUDIAN (KORIUN NIKOLAEVICH) Problemy razvitiia transporta Zakavkazskogo ekonomicheskogo raiona. Erevan, 1972. pp. 238. bibliog.

- Spain

SPAIN. Comisaria del Plan de Desarrollo Economico y Social. 1972. (III Plan de desarrollo economico y social): transportes. [Madrid], 1972. pp. 319.

- Sweden

WESTERBERG (STEN) Den ofärdiga trafikpolitiken: en studie i offentlig prissättning. Stockholm, 1970 repr. 1971. pp. 121. (Studieförbundet Näringsliv och Samhälle. Studier och Debatt. 1970. Nr. 4)

- Sweden - Costs

SWEDEN. Kommunikationsdepartementet. Gotlandstrafikutredning. 1967. Transportkostnaderna i Gotlandstrafiken: betänkande avgivet av 1964 års Gotlandstrafikutredning. Stockholm, 1967. pp. 74. (Sweden. Statens Offentliga Utredningar. 1967.29)

- Switzerland

BAUER (KARL) Die Gleichbehandlung der Verkehrsträger durch den Staat: ein Beitrag zur Diskussion um die schweizerische Gesamtverkehrskonzeption. Bern, [1972]. pp. 158. bibliog. (St. Gall. Handelshochschule. Seminar für Fremdenverkehr und Verkehrswirtschaft. St. Galler Beiträge zum Fremdenverkehr und zur Verkehrswirtschaft. Reihe Verkehrswirtschaft. 4)

- Tanzania

HOFMEIER (ROLF) Transport and economic development in Tanzania, with particular reference to roads and road transport. München, [1973]. pp. 353. bibliog. (Ifo-Institut für Wirtschaftsforschung. Afrika-Studien. 78)

- United Kingdom

SOUTH EAST LANCASHIRE AND NORTH EAST CHESHIRE TRANSPORTATION STUDY. Technical Control Team. Technical Working Papers. Manchester, 1968 in progress.

DEAKIN (BRIAN MEASURES) and SEWARD (THELMA) Productivity in transport: a study of employment, capital, output, productivity and technical change. Cambridge, 1969. pp. 248. (Cambridge. University. Department of Applied Economics. Occasional Papers. 17)

SOUTH HAMPSHIRE PLAN ADVISORY COMMITTEE. Study Reports. Group E. Transportation. Nos. 1 and 2. Public and private transport. Winchester, 1970. pp. 53, fo.17.

MINCHINTON (WALTER EDWARD) ed. Farming and transport in the South-West. Exeter, 1972. pp. 69. (Exeter. University. Department of Economic History. Exeter Papers in Economic History. No. 5)

SOUTH EAST LANCASHIRE AND NORTH EAST CHESHIRE TRANSPORTATION STUDY. Technical Control Team. A broad transportation plan for 1984; report of the...Team to the Steering Committee; report presented 23rd March 1971. Manchester, 1972. pp. 154. Plan in end pocket.

WOODWARD (FRANK HARRIS) Managing the transport services function. London, 1972. pp. 306. bibliog.

BROMHEAD (PETER ALEXANDER) The great white elephant of Maplin Sands: the neglect of comprehensive transport planning in Government decision-making. London, 1973. pp. 296. bibliog.

RICHARDS (ERIC) The leviathan of wealth: the Sutherland fortune in the Industrial Revolution. London, 1973. pp. 316. bibliog.

- United Kingdom - Bibliography

DERBY. Borough Libraries. Derby borough libraries centenary, 1871-1971: by rail, road and canal; a select list of books and manuscripts relating to travel in Derby and Derbyshire. [Derby], 1971. pp. 17. (Derby. Borough Libraries. Guides to the Resources of the Local History Collection)

TRANSPORTATION (Cont'd.)

- **United Kingdom - Costs**

COOPERS AND LYBRAND ASSOCIATES LIMITED. The Channel tunnel: a United Kingdom transport cost benefit study; report presented to the Secretary of State for the Environment. London, H.M.S.O., 1973. pp. 48.

- **United Kingdom - Government ownership**

POLANYI (GEORGE) Contrasts in nationalised transport since 1947. London, 1968. pp. 54. (Institute of Economic Affairs. Background Memoranda. 2)

THOMSON (ANDREW W.J.) and HUNTER (LAURENCE C.) The nationalized transport industries. London, 1973. pp. 356.

- **United Kingdom - Passenger traffic**

LEEDS. University. Centre for Transport Studies. Inter-city modal split in Great Britain: air v. rail...; final report; prepared for the Department of Trade and Industry; [by G.R. Leake under the direction of C.A. O'Flaherty]. [London?], 1971. pp. 181, (26). bibliog.

STUDY of rural transport in Devon; report by the Steering Group; [T.L. Beagley, chairman]. [London], Department of the Environment, [1971?]. pp. 25.

STUDY of rural transport in West Suffolk; report by the Steering Group; [C.N. Tebay, chairman]. [London], Department of the Environment, [1971]. pp. 36.

FREEMAN FOX AND ASSOCIATES. Screen line study of inter urban travel. Phase 1. London, Department of the Environment, 1972. 2 pts.

FREEMAN FOX AND ASSOCIATES. Screen line study of inter urban travel. Phase 2. London, Department of the Environment, 1972. 2 pts.

- **United Kingdom - Ireland, Northern - Rates**

IRELAND, NORTHERN. Transport Tribunal. 1962. Maximum charges attaching to the services and facilities provided by the Ulster Transport Authority, confirmed by order of the Tribunal dated the 27th day of October, 1961. Belfast, [1962]. pp. 32.

- **United States**

AMERICAN ASSEMBLY. 39th Assembly, April, 1971. The future of American transportation; [edited by Ernest W. Williams]. Englewood Cliffs, [1971]. pp. 215.

CONFERENCE ON REGIONAL TRANSPORTATION PLANNING, SANTA MONICA, CALIFORNIA, 1971. Proceedings...; edited by Joseph S. DeSalvo; a report prepared [by the Rand Corporation] for U.S. Department of Transportation, etc. Santa Monica, 1971. pp. 509. bibliogs. (Rand Corporation. Rand Reports. R.706)

STONE (TABOR R.) Beyond the automobile: reshaping the transportation environment. Englewood Cliffs, [1971]. pp. 148.

MERTINS (HERMAN) National transportation policy in transition. Lexington, [1972]. pp. 224. bibliog.

CONFERENCE ON REGIONAL TRANSPORTATION PLANNING, SANTA MONICA, 1971 Perspectives on regional transportation planning; [revised versions of papers presented at the conference]; edited by Joseph S De Salvo. Lexington, Mass, [1973] pp. 441. bibliogs

- **United States - Finance**

GOVERNORS' SPECIAL COMMISSION ON THE FINANCING OF MASS TRANSPORTATION. Financing mass transportation: a positive approach; final report of the... Commission; [David Yunich, chairman]. [New York], 1972. pp. 90.

- **United States - Connecticut**

CONNECTICUT. Department of Transportation. 1971. Connecticut master transportation plan, 1971; prepared...with the assistance of Charles A. Maguire and Associates Inc. [Hartford, 1971]. pp. 86.

- **United States - Massachusetts**

STEERING GROUP ON THE BOSTON TRANSPORTATION PLANNING REVIEW. Study design for a balanced transportation development program for the Boston metropolitan region; prepared for Governor Francis W. Sargent...; consultant: System Design Concepts, Inc.; [Alan A. Altshuler, chairman]; (with Summary). [Boston], 1970. 2 pts. bibliog.

- **United States - New York**

NEW YORK (STATE). Office of Planning Coordination. 1970. New York State Appalachian resource studies: transportation. Phase 1: inventory. Albany, 1970. pp. 43. 9 Maps in end pocket.

NEW YORK (STATE). Department of Transportation. Planning Division. 1971. Goals for transportation in New York State. Albany, 1971. pp. 47.

- **Venezuela - Laws and regulations**

BREWER-CARIAS (ALLAN RANDOLPH) Aspectos institucionales del transporte y transito en el area metropolitana de Caracas. Caracas, 1971. pp. 146.

- **Zaire**

LEDERER (ANDRE) L'exploitation des transports au Congo pendant la décennie 1959-1969. Bruxelles, 1970. pp. 147. bibliog. (Academie Royale des Sciences d'Outre-Mer. Classe des Sciences Techniques. Mémoires in-8°. Nouvelle Serie. tome 16, fasc. 8)

TRANSPORTATION, AUTOMOTIVE

ADAMASCHEK (BERND) Verkehrssteuerung und Gemeingebrauch: Möglichkeiten der Bekämpfung des Engpassproblems im Strassenverkehr. Göttingen, 1972. pp. 139. bibliog. (Münster in Westfalen. Westfälische Wilhelms-Universität. Institut für Verkehrswissenschaft. Beiträge. Heft 66)

- **Freight**

KELLER (HEINZ E.) Die Funktionsfähigkeit des Wettbewerbs zwischen Schiene und Strasse im Güterverkehr. [Zuerich, 1970?]. pp. 242. bibliog.

- **Statistics**

ROSTOCKI (A.) and WIENIAWSKI (W.) Motoryzacja w liczbach, 1969. Warszawa, 1970. pp. 312.

- **Afghanistan**

FITTER (JOERN C.) Der Einfluss der Verkehrsinvestitionen auf die wirtschaftliche Entwicklung Afghanistans. Meisenheim am Glan, 1973. pp. 131. bibliog. With table of contents in English.

- **Europe**

BOYER (ALBERT) Les transports routiers. Paris, 1973. pp. 127.

- European Economic Community countries - Freight

> BAYLISS (BRIAN T.) The transport of freight in the United Kingdom and the countries comprising the European Economic Community, with special reference to road haulage; [Ph.D (Birmingham) thesis]. 1964. fo.233. bibliog.

- France

> SERMAGE (ROBERT) and GLACET (MARIE FRANCE) Les transports routiers de marchandises en 1966 et 1967; [with three other transportation studies]. [Paris, 1969]. pp. 80. (France. Institut National de la Statistique et des Etudes Economiques. Collections de l'INSEE. Série E. Entreprises. 3) With summaries in English. Cover title: Quatre études sur les transports routiers.

- France - Freight

> FRANCE. Commission d'Etude des Coûts d'Infrastructure [de Transport]. 1970. Rapport sur l'imputation des charges d'infrastructure aux véhicules routiers de marchandises; ([and] Premier rapport...janvier 1968). [Paris], 1970. pp. 189.

- Germany

> RIEKE (HEILWIG) Die künftige Entwicklung des Strassenverkehrs in der Bundesrepublik Deutschland: Fahrleistungen, Kraftstoffverbrauch und Mineralölsteueraufkommen. Berlin, 1972. pp. 87. (Deutsches Institut für Wirtschaftsforschung. DIW-Beiträge zur Strukturforschung. Heft 22) With English summary.

- Germany - Freight

> LUENSDORF (PETER) Güternahverkehr und Strassenbelastung in der Bundesrepublik Deutschland, insbesondere in Ballungsgebieten. Berlin, 1972. pp. 98. (Deutsches Institut für Wirtschaftsforschung. DIW-Beiträge zur Strukturforschung. Heft 24) With English summary.

- Ireland (Republic) - Freight

> EIRE. Central Statistics Office. 1966. Sample survey of road freight transport, 1964: preliminary results. Dublin, 1966. pp. 17.

- New Guinea - Statistics

> PAPUA AND NEW GUINEA, TERRITORY OF. Bureau of Statistics. 1968. Census of motor vehicles registered as at 31 December 1967. Konedobu, [1968]. pp. 15. (Statistical Bulletins. No. 12)

- New Zealand

> NEW ZEALAND. Committee of Inquiry into Overseas Interests in New Zealand Road Transport. 1971. Overseas interests in New Zealand road transport; report to the Transport Advisory Council by the Committee of Inquiry: [R.J. Polaschek, chairman]. Wellington, 1971. pp. 80.

- Russia

> GORSKII (MIKHAIL IGNAT'EVICH) Planirovanie ispol'zovaniia avtomobil'nogo transporta. Minsk, 1972. pp. 232. bibliog.

- Russia - Kirghizia

> ZAGULOV (ZHAKEN) Voprosy ekonomiki avtotransporta v Kirgizskoi SSR. Frunze, 1969. pp. 163. bibliog.

- Russia - Latvia

> KLESAREV (ANATOLII DMITRIEVICH) and PUSTOVOITOV (BORIS NIKOLAEVICH) Avtomobil'nyi transport Latvii. Riga, 1972. pp. 96.

- Sweden - Freight

> KRANTZ (OLLE) Studier i svensk godstransportutveckling med särskild hänsyn till lastbilismens expansion efter 1920. Lund, 1972. pp. 235. bibliog. (Lund. Ekonomisk-Historiska Föreningen. Skrifter. vol. 12) With English summary.

- United Kingdom

> BADDELEY (GEOFFREY E.) The economies and diseconomies of large and small scale operation in road passenger transport...: report to the Trustees of the Rees Jeffreys Studentship. 1956. fo. 236. Typescript (carbon copy).

> WEST MIDLANDS PASSENGER TRANSPORT. Report. a., 1970 (1st)- [Birmingham].

> ROAD TRANSPORT INDUSTRY TRAINING BOARD [U.K.] A progress report, 1966-1970. [Wembley, 1970]. pp. 16.

> BURT (M.E.) Roads and the environment...; text of a paper given to the Conference on Urban Environment, Development and Pollution at the University of Surrey, Guildford, 16-18 September 1970. Crowthorne, 1972. pp. 38. bibliog. (U.K. Transport and Road Research Laboratory. Reports. LR 441)

- United Kingdom - Freight

> BAYLISS (BRIAN T.) The transport of freight in the United Kingdom and the countries comprising the European Economic Community, with special reference to road haulage; [Ph.D (Birmingham) thesis]. 1964. fo.233. bibliog.

> U.K. Department of the Environment. 1971. Survey of the transport of goods by road, 1967-1968: report and tables: Great Britain. [London], 1971. pp. 47.

> U.K. Road Freight Division. 1971. Conditions of entry into Great Britain for vehicles used for the transport of goods by road. London, 1971. 1 pamphlet (various pagings).

> TULPULE (A.H.) Trends in transport of freight in Great Britain. Crowthorne, 1972. pp. 20. (U.K. Road Research Laboratory. Reports. LR 429)

> WEBB (MICHAEL H. J.) Transporting goods by road. London, [1972]. pp. 435. (London. University. London School of Economics and Political Science. Research Monographs. 10)

> BAYLISS (BRIAN T.) The road haulage industry since 1968. London, H.M.S.O., 1973. pp. 38.

- United States

> NATIONAL RESEARCH COUNCIL. Highway Research Board. Highway Research Records. No. 348. Planning and evaluation of transportation systems: 17 reports. Washington, D.C., 1971. pp. 210. bibliogs.

- Venezuela - Statistics

> VENEZUELA. Dirección General de Estadistica. Censos Economicos Nacionales. Primer censo da vehiculos automotores para el transporte terrestre comercial, 1° de Noviembre de 1951- 31 de Octubre de 1952. Caracas, 1957. pp. 111.

TRANSPORTATION, PRIMITIVE

> INDIA. Planning Commission. Programme Evaluation Organisation. Publications. No. 42. Role of bullock carts and trucks in rural transport: case studies; undertaken at the instance of Committee on Transport Policy and Coordination. [Delhi], 1963[or rather 1964]. pp. 160.

TRANSPORTATION, URBAN
See URBAN TRANSPORTATION

TRANSVAAL

- Economic conditions

FOLKERTS (MARTIN) Das Busch- und Bankenveld West-transvaals: wirtschafts- und bevölkerungsgeographische Konsequenzen der Politik der getrennten Entwicklung. Hamburg, 1970. pp. 391. bibliog. (Hamburg. Hansische Universität. Institut für Geographie und Wirtschaftsgeographie. Hamburger Geographische Studien. Heft 22)

- History

SCHUTTE (G.J.) De Hollanders in Krugers republiek, 1884-1899. Pretoria. 1968. pp. 123. bibliog. (Pretoria. University of South Africa. Communications. Series C.63) With English summary.

- Politics and government

TRANSVAAL. Provincial Administration. 1971. Transvaal, 1961-71: the growth and progress of the Transvaal Provincial Administration,...published to commemorate the tenth anniversary of the Republic of South Africa. [Johannesburg], 1971. pp. 200. In Afrikaans and English.

- Population

FOLKERTS (MARTIN) Das Busch- und Bankenveld West-transvaals: wirtschafts- und bevölkerungsgeographische Konsequenzen der Politik der getrennten Entwicklung. Hamburg, 1970. pp. 391. bibliog. (Hamburg. Hansische Universität. Institut für Geographie und Wirtschaftsgeographie. Hamburger Geographische Studien. Heft 22)

- Race question

FOLKERTS (MARTIN) Das Busch- und Bankenveld West-transvaals: wirtschafts- und bevölkerungsgeographische Konsequenzen der Politik der getrennten Entwicklung. Hamburg, 1970. pp. 391. bibliog. (Hamburg. Hansische Universität. Institut für Geographie und Wirtschaftsgeographie. Hamburger Geographische Studien. Heft 22)

TRANSYLVANIA

- Annexation to Roumania - Bibliography

CONTRIBUȚII bibliografice privind unirea Transil-vaniei cu România, etc . București, 1969. pp. 648. With Russian, French, English and German tables of contents.

- Economic conditions

KLAUBE (MANFRED) Das sächsische Minderheitensied-lungsgebiet in Südsiebenbürgen. München, 1971. pp. 136. bibliog.

- Nationalism

BERNATH (MATHIAS) Habsburg und die Anfänge der rumänischen Nationsbildung. Leiden, 1972. pp. 249. bibliog.

TRAVEL

GRAY (H. PETER) International travel-international trade. Lexington, [1970]. pp. 264.

BURYN (ED) Vagabonding in Europe and North Africa. New York, 1971. pp. 214.

TRAVEL AGENTS

- United Kingdom

COMMISSION ON INDUSTRIAL RELATIONS [U.K.]. Horizon Holidays Limited and associated companies. London, H.M.S.O., 1973. pp. 28. (Reports. No.43)

TRAVEL TIME (TRAFFIC ENGINEERING)

CONFERENCE ON RESEARCH INTO THE VALUE OF TIME, LONDON, 1970. Papers and proceedings...;editor of the proceedings: N.W. Mansfield. [London], Department of the Environment, 1970 [or rather 1971]. pp. 131. (Time Research Notes. No. 16)

DAWSON (R.F.F.) and EVERALL (P.F.) The value of motorists' time: a study in Italy. Crowthorne, 1972. pp. 34. (U.K.Transport and Road Research Laboratory. Reports. LR 426)

TREASON

- Germany

SCHRAMM (WILHELM VON) Verrat im Zweiten Weltkrieg: vom Kampf der Geheimdienste in Europa; Berichte und Dokumentation. 2nd ed. Düsseldorf, 1969. pp. 407. bibliog.

TREATIES

LUKASHUK (IGOR' IVANOVICH) Storony v mezhduna-rodnykh dogovorakh. Moskva, 1966. pp. 151. bibliog.

UNITED NATIONS. Conference on the Law of Treaties, Vienna, 1968-69. Official records: (summary records and documents). (A/CONF.39/11 and 11/Adds. 1 and 2). New York, 1969-71. 3 vols. (in 1).

AGREEMENTS of international organizations and the Vienna Convention on the Law of Treaties; edited by K. Zemanek. Wien, 1971. pp. 268. (Österreichische Zeitschrift für Öffentliches Recht. Supplementa. 1)

KOLLER (ARNOLD) Die unmittelbare Anwendbarkeit völkerrechtlicher Verträge und des EWG-Vertrages im innerstaatlichen Bereich. Bern, 1971. pp. 216. bibliog. (St. Gall. Handelshochschule. Institut für Europaisches und Internationales Wirtschafts- und Sozialrecht, and Geneva. Université. Faculté de Droit. Centre d'Etudes Juridiques Européennes. Schweizerische Beiträge zum Europarecht. Band 8)

MATARADZE (LEVAN NIKOLAEVICH) Forma mezhdunarod-nogo dogovora. Tbilisi, 1971. pp. 59.

CHIU (HUNGDAH) The people's republic of China and the law of treaties. Cambridge, Mass., 1972. pp. 178. bibliog. (Harvard University. Harvard Studies in East Asian Law. 5)

HURST (MICHAEL) ed. Key treaties for the great powers, 1814-1914. Newton Abbot, [1972]. 2 vols.

CRAISON (ANDRE) L'erreur dans les traités. Paris, 1972. pp. 251. bibliog.

SIMMA (BRUNO) Das Reziprozitätselement im Zustande-kommen völkerrechtlicher Verträge: Gedanken zu einem Bauprinzip der internationalen Rechtsbezie-hungen. Berlin, [1972]. pp. 347. bibliog.

UDOKANG (OKON) Succession of new states to international treaties. Dobbs Ferry, N.Y., 1972. pp. 525. bibliog.

ALEXANDROWICZ (CHARLES HENRY) The European-African confrontation: a study in treaty making. Leiden, 1973. pp. 176.

SINCLAIR (IAN McTAGGART) The Vienna Convention on the Law of Treaties. Manchester, [1973]. pp. 150. (Manchester. University. Melland Schill Lectures.[1972])

TALALAEV (ANATOLII NIKOLAEVICH) Mezhdunarodnye dogovory v sovremennom mire: voprosy prava mezhdunarodnykh dogovorov v svete raboty Venskoi konferentsii OON, 1968-1969 gg. Moskva, 1973. pp. 247. bibliog.

- Bibliography

SPRUDZS (ADOLF) Treaty sources in legal and political research: tools, techniques and problems; the conventional and the new. Tucson, [1971]. pp. 63. (Arizona University. Institute of Government Research. International Studies. No. 3)

- Interpretation and construction

MATHIJSEN (PIERRE S.R.F.) Teleologische interpretatie der Europese verdragen. Nijmegen, [1970]. pp. 27.

- Ratification

ORGANIZATION OF AMERICAN STATES. Inter-American Council of Jurists. Inter-American Juridical Committee. 1960. Reserva de adhesion teorica a los tratados multilaterales: informe preparado de conformidad con la resolucion XI de la cuarta Reunion del Consejo Interamericano de Jurisconsultos. Washington, 1960. pp. 6. (Organization of American States. Official Records. Series I/VI. 2. CIJ.57)

SCHACHTER (OSCAR) and others. Towards wider acceptance of UN treaties. New York, 1971. pp. 190. (United Nations Institute for Training and Research. UNITAR Studies)

- Reservations

ORGANIZATION OF AMERICAN STATES. Inter-American Council of Jurists. Inter-American Juridical Committee. 1957. Study to serve as the basis for the preparation of a second draft text of rules on reservations to multilateral treaties. Washington, 1957. pp. 58.

- Revision

GUARINO (GIANCARLO) La revisione dei trattati: spunti critico ricostruttivi. Napoli, 1971. pp. 237.

TREATY-MAKING POWER

- Germany

DOEHRING (KARL) and RESS (GEORG) Die parlamentarische Zustimmungsbedürftigkeit von Verträgen zwischen der Bundesrepublik Deutschland und der Deutschen Demokratischen Republik. Frankfurt am Main, [1971]. pp. 66.

TREE OF LIFE

BUTTERWORTH (EDRIC ALLAN SCHOFIELD) The tree at the navel of the earth. Berlin, 1970. pp. 239.

TREES

- United Kingdom

U.K. Natural Environment Research Council. 1971. Tree, forest and woodland research. [London], 1971. 1 pamphlet (unpaged). (Publications. Series B. No.2)

TRENT, COUNCIL OF, 1545-1563

ROME. Archivio di Stato. 1964. Aspetti della riforma cattolica e del Concilio di Trento: mostra documentaria: catalogo a cura di Edvige Aleandri Barletta. Roma, 1964. pp. 278. bibliog. (Italy. Ufficio centrale degli Archivi di Stato. Pubblicazioni degli Archivi di Stato. 55.)

TRENT RIVER

The TRENT research programme. London, 1972 in progress. (U.K. Water Resources Board. Publications. No. 18)

TRENTINO-ALTO ADIGE

- Economic conditions

ITALY. Presidenza del Consiglio dei Ministri. Servizio delle Informazioni. 1964. La regione Trentino-Alto Adige. Roma, 1964. pp. 64. (Italy. Vita Italiana: documenti e informazioni. Supplementi.)

- Politics and government

ITALY. Presidenza del Consiglio dei Ministri. Servizio delle Informazioni. 1964. La regione Trentino-Alto Adige. Roma, 1964. pp. 64. (Italy. Vita Italiana: documenti e informazioni. Supplementi.)

TRES MARIAS

PIÑA Y PALACIOS (JAVIER) La colonia penal de las Islas Marias: su historia, organizacion y regimen. Mexico, 1970. pp. 241. bibliog.

TRESPASS

- United Kingdom

U.K. Law Commission. Working Papers. No. 52. Liability for damage or injury to trespassers and related questions of occupiers' liability. London, 1973. pp. 87.

TREUTLER (KARL GEORG VON)

TREUTLER (KARL GEORG VON) Die graue Exzellenz: zwischen Staatsräson und Vasallentreue; aus den Papieren des kaiserlichen Gesandten...; herausgegeben und eingeleitet von Karl-Heinz Janssen. Frankfurt/Main, [1971]. pp. 277.

TREVELYAN (Sir CHARLES EDWARD)

TREVELYAN (HUMPHREY) Baron Trevelyan. The India we left: Charles Trevelyan, 1826-65, Humphrey Trevelyan, 1929-47. London, 1972. pp. 255.

TREVELYAN (HUMPHREY) Baron Trevelyan

TREVELYAN (HUMPHREY) Baron Trevelyan. The India we left: Charles Trevelyan, 1826-65, Humphrey Trevelyan, 1929-47. London, 1972. pp. 255.

TRIAL PRACTICE

- Russia

VOPROSY primeneniia osnov grazhdanskogo zakonodatel'stva v sudebnoi praktike. Moskva, 1964. pp. 166.

TRIALS

- Russia

ROSSEL'S (VLADIMIR L'VOVICH) Sudebnye zashchititel'nye rechi. Moskva, 1966. pp. 115.

TRIALS - Russia (Cont'd.)

KISELEV (IAKOV SEMENOVICH) Sudebnye rechi. Leningrad, 1967. pp. 222.

- United Kingdom

MACDONELL (Sir JOHN) and WALLIS (Sir JOHN EDWARD POWER) eds. Reports of state trials: new series... 1820-(1858); published under the direction of the State Trials Committee. London, 1888-1898 repr. 1970. 8 vols.

- United States

HAYS (ARTHUR GARFIELD) Trial by prejudice; [facsimile reprint of the work originally published in New York, 1933]. Westport, Conn., 1970. pp. 369.

FIRESTONE (ROSS) ed. Getting busted: personal experiences of arrest, trial and prison; [reprint of work published in 1970]. Harmondsworth, 1972. pp. 426.

TRIALS (BLASPHEMY)

- United Kingdom

HOLYOAKE (GEORGE JACOB) The case of Thomas Pooley, the Cornish well-sinker, [etc.]. London, [1857]. pp. 32. (Reprinted from the Reasoner of September 23rd and 30th, 1857)

CALDER-MARSHALL (ARTHUR) Lewd, blasphemous and obscene: being the trials and tribulations of sundry founding fathers of today's alternative societies, etc. London, 1972. pp. 248. bibliog.

TRIALS (CONSPIRACY)

- Japan

JOHNSON (CHALMERS) Conspiracy at Matsukawa. Berkeley, Calif., 1972. pp. 460. bibliog.

- United States

DELLINGER (DAVID T.) and others, defendants. On trial: U.S.A. versus David T. Dellinger and others; condensed verbatim from the transcript of the five-month trial...by Christopher Burstall (and) Stuart Hood; [B.B.C. television script]. [London, 1971]. 1 vol. (various foliations).

HAYDEN (THOMAS) Trial. London, 1971. pp. 168.

TRIALS (ESPIONAGE)

- United States

SERVICE (JOHN S.) The Amerasia papers: some problems in the history of US-China relations. Berkeley, [1971]. pp. 218. bibliog. (California University. Center for Chinese Studies. China Research Monographs. No. 7)

TRIALS (HERESY)

- United Kingdom

LOADES (D.M.) The Oxford martyrs. London, 1970. pp. 296. bibliog.

TRIALS (IMPEACHMENT)

- United States

BENEDICT (MICHAEL LES) The impeachment and trial of Andrew Johnson. New York, [1973]. pp. 212. bibliog.

TRIALS (MILITARY OFFENCES)

- United States

McCARTHY (MARY THERESE) Medina; [her report of the trial of Captain Ernest L. Medina, U.S. Army]. London, 1973. pp. 92.

TRIALS (MURDER)

- Spain

HALIMI (GISELE) Le procès de Burgos. Paris, 1971. pp. 321.

- United States

WEISBERG (HAROLD) Frame-up: the Martin Luther King/James Earl Ray case, containing suppressed evidence;...with a postscript by James Earl Ray. New York, 1971. pp. 530.

TRIALS (OBSCENITY)

- United Kingdom

CALDER-MARSHALL (ARTHUR) Lewd, blasphemous and obscene: being the trials and tribulations of sundry founding fathers of today's alternative societies, etc. London, 1972. pp. 248. bibliog.

TRIALS (POLITICAL CRIMES AND OFFENCES)

- Cameroun

UNION DES POPULATIONS DU CAMEROUN. L'U.P.C. parle. Paris, 1971. pp. 116.

- Communist countries

KRIEGEL (ANNIE) Les grands procès dans les systèmes communistes: la pédagogie infernale. Paris, [1972]. pp. 189.

- Czechoslovakia

LONDON (ARTUR) L'aveu: dans l'engrenage du Procès de Prague; version française d'Artur et Lise London. [Paris, 1970]. pp. 457.

- Germany

WALDECK (BENEDIKT FRANZ LEO) defendant. Der Waldeck'sche Prozess; authentischer Bericht über die öffentlichen Verhandlungen des Berliner Schwurgerichts in der Waldeck'schen Untersuchungssache; nach den...stenographischen Aufzeichnungen und Mittheilungen betheiligter Personen. 2nd ed. Berlin, Hempel, 1849. pp. 311.

TRIALS (POLITICAL CRIMES AND OFFENCES)
Germany
See also TRIALS (TREASON) : Germany

- Poland

SĄD orzekł... Paryż, 1972. pp. 319.

- Rhodesia

NIESEWAND (PETER) In camera: secret justice in Rhodesia. London, [1973]. pp. 209.

- Russia

SAVINKOV (BORIS VIKTOROVICH) defendant. Delo Borisa Savinkova, so stat'ei B. Savinkova "Pochemu ia priznal Sovetskuiu vlast'"; s predisloviem Em. Iaroslavskogo, etc. Moskva, [1924?]. pp. 161.

SMITH (IRVING H.) ed. Trotsky. Englewood Cliffs, [1973]. pp. 181. bibliog.

TROUT

MILLS (DEREK) Salmon and trout: a resource, its ecology, conservation and management. Edinburgh, 1971. pp. 351.

TRUCK SYSTEM

- United Kingdom

REDGRAVE (ALEXANDER) Factories Acts; twenty second edition by Ian Fife and E. Anthony Machin. London, 1972. pp. 1537.

TRUDEAU (PIERRE ELLIOTT)

THORDARSON (BRUCE) Trudeau and foreign policy: a study in decision-making. Toronto, 1972. pp. 231. bibliog.

TRUJILLO MOLINA (RAFAEL LEONIDAS)

GALLEGOS (GERARDO) Trujillo: cara y cruz de su dictadura. Madrid, 1968. pp. 395.

ENZENSBERGER (HANS MAGNUS) Las Casas y Trujillo. La Habana, 1969. pp. 82. bibliog.

GALINDEZ SUAREZ (JESUS DE) The era of Trujillo, Dominican dictator;...edited by Russell H. Fitzgibbon. Tucson, [1973]. pp. 298. bibliogs.

TRUMAN (HARRY SHIPPE) President of the United States

HARTMANN (SUSAN MECKFESSEL) Truman and the 80th Congress. Columbia, Mo., 1971. pp. 241. bibliog.

FREELAND (RICHARD M.) The Truman doctrine and the origins of McCarthyism: foreign policy, domestic politics, and internal security, 1946-1948. New York, 1972. pp. 419,xii. bibliog.

TRUMAN (MARGARET) Harry S. Truman. London, 1973. pp. 602.

TRUST TERRITORIES

VEICOPOULOS (NICOLAS) Traité des territoires dépendants. Athènes, 1960 in progress.

- Pacific, The

NATIONAL security and international trusteeship in the Pacific: [essays by officers of the United States Naval War College]; edited by Wm. Roger Louis. Annapolis, Md., [1972]. pp. 182. bibliog.

- South West Africa

SLONIM (SOLOMON) South West Africa and the United Nations: an international mandate in dispute. Baltimore, [1973]. pp. 409. bibliog.

TRUSTS, INDUSTRIAL

WRUCK (HORST) Internationale Marktvereinbarungen: Wesen und volkswirtschaftliche Bedeutung. Berlin, [1970]. pp. 244. bibliog. With English and French summaries.

ROWLEY (CHARLES KERSHAW) Antitrust and economic efficiency. London, 1973. pp. 96. bibliog.

- Law

EDWARDS (CORWIN D.) Trade regulations overseas: the national laws; a study in comparative law. Dobbs Ferry, N.Y., 1966. pp. 752.

GUNDERSEN (FRIDTJOF FRANK) Kontrollen med karteller og storbedrifter: internasjonal handel og EEC. Oslo, 1972. pp. 330.

KRONSTEIN (HEINRICH) The law of international cartels. Ithaca, N.Y., 1973. pp. 489.

SCHMIDT (INGO) US-amerikanische und deutsche Wettbewerbspolitik gegenüber Marktmacht: eine vergleichende Untersuchung und kritische Analyse der Rechtsprechung, etc. Berlin, [1973]. pp. 482. bibliog.

- Mathematical models

BIABAUT (JEAN) Les liaisons financières dans les groupes de sociétés: The financial liaisons in groups of companies, etc. Paris, [1969]. pp. 164. bibliog. (Metra. Série Spéciale. No. 13) With summaries in various languages.

- European Economic Community countries - Law

DEUTSCHE GESELLSCHAFT FÜR AGRARRECHT. Ausschuss für Agrarkartellrecht. Die kartellrechtliche Sonderregelung für die Landwirtschaft im EWG-Recht unter besonderer Berücksichtigung der nationalen Regelungen: Schlussbericht, etc. Bonn, 1970. pp. 99. In German and French.

WILLEMSEN (ADRIAAN) Wettbewerbstheorie, Wettbewerbspolitik, und die kartellrechtlichen Bestimmungen des EWG-Vertrages und des EFTA-Vertrages. Bern, 1971. pp. 313. bibliog. (St. Gall. Handelshochschule. Institut für Europäisches und Internationales Wirtschafts- und Sozialrecht, and Geneva. Université. Faculté de Droit. Centre d'Etudes Juridiques Européennes. Schweizerische Beiträge zum Europarecht. Band 6)

GUNDERSEN (FRIDTJOF FRANK) Kontrollen med karteller og storbedrifter: internasjonal handel og EEC. Oslo, 1972. pp. 330.

SAUPE (GERD) Technische Vereinbarungen und Unternehmensgemeinschaften im Verkehrskartellrecht der EWG: Eisenbahn-, Strassen- und Binnenschiffsverkehr. Köln, 1972. pp. 184. bibliog. (Cologne. Universität. Institut für das Recht der Europäischen Gemeinschaften. Kölner Schriften zum Europarecht. Band 16)

ALEXANDER (WILLY) The EEC rules of competition. London, 1973. pp. 187.

BELLAMY (CHRISTOPHER) and CHILD (GRAHAM D.) Common Market law of competition. London, 1973. pp. 361.

CUNNINGHAM (JAMES PATRICK) The competition law of the E.E.C.: a practical guide. London, 1973. pp. 315.

CUNNINGHAM (JAMES PATRICK) Restrictive practices and monopolies in E.E.C. law. London, 1973. pp. 94.

- France - Law

BRACHVOGEL (GERRIT) Aktiengesellschaft und Gesellschaftsgruppe im französischen Recht. Stuttgart, 1971. pp. 215. bibliog. (Zeitschrift für das Gesamte Handelsrecht und Wirtschaftsrecht. Beihefte: Abhandlungen aus dem Gesamten Bürgerlichen Recht, Handelsrecht und Wirtschaftsrecht. 41. Heft)

OHR (PETER FRIEDRICH) Die Konzeption der französischen Kartellkontrolle in der "Rechtsprechung" der Technischen Kartellkommission. Mannheim, 1972. 1 vol. (various pagings). bibliog.

TRUSTS, INDUSTRIAL (Cont'd.)

- Germany

GLAMANN (HANS FRIEDRICH) Die Analytische Kommission der I.G. Farbenindustrie Aktiengesellschaft (Anako) als Beispiel einer Arbeitsgemeinschaft innerhalb des Farbenkonzerns in der Zwischenkriegszeit. Marburg/Lahn, 1969. pp. 237. bibliog.

VEREIN FÜR SOZIALPOLITIK. Schriften. Neue Folge. Band 62. Rationalisierung durch Kartelle?; herausgegeben von Erich Hoppmann. Berlin, 1971. pp. 460.

- Germany - Law

HUEBNER (KLAUS) Ausserkartellrechtliche Einschränkungen des Kartellverbotes. Köln, 1971. pp. 83. bibliog. (Forschungsinstitut für Wirtschaftsverfassung und Wettbewerb. FIW-Schriftenreihe. Heft 59)

KARST (PETER) Die kartellrechtliche Sonderstellung der Energieversorgungsunternehmen und ihre Vereinbarkeit mit dem Grundgesetz. München, 1971. pp. 123. bibliog.

MARTIN (URSULA) Die volkswirtschaftliche Bedeutung und rechtliche Zulässigkeit von Verkaufssyndikaten. Berlin, [1971]. pp. 158. bibliog.

SCHOLZ (RUPERT) Konzentrationskontrolle und Grundgesetz. Stuttgart, 1971. pp. 152. (Zeitschrift für das Gesamte Handelsrecht und Wirtschaftsrecht. Beihefte. Abhandlungen aus dem Gesamten Bürgerlichen Recht, Handelsrecht und Wirtschaftsrecht. 43. Heft)

BAUR (JUERGEN F.) Der Missbrauch im deutschen Kartellrecht. Tübingen, 1972. pp. 262. bibliog.

- Netherlands - Law

WESTBROEK (W.) Zijn wettelijke bepalingen gewenst in verband met concern-verhoudingen? Zwolle, 1969. pp. 85.

- United States

SAMPSON (ANTHONY) Sovereign state: the secret history of ITT. London, 1973. pp. 288.

- United States - Law

ZWARENSTEYN (HENDRIK) Some aspects of the extraterritorial reach of the American antitrust laws. Deventer, 1970. pp. 174. bibliog.

SCHWARTZ (LOUIS BROWN) Free enterprise and economic organization: antitrust and regulatory controls. 4th ed. Mineola, N.Y., 1972. pp. 1380.

BOWMAN (WARD S.) Patent and antitrust law: a legal and economic appraisal. Chicago, [1973]. pp. 272.

TRUSTS AND TRUSTEES

- Taxation - United Kingdom

MELLOWS (ANTHONY ROGER) Taxation for executors and trustees. 3rd ed. London, 1972. pp. 140.

- United Kingdom

KEETON (GEORGE WILLIAMS) Modern developments in the law of trusts. Belfast, 1971. pp. 342. bibliog.

TRUTH

SLEIGH (R.C.) ed. Necessary truth. Englewood Cliffs, N.J., [1972]. pp. 202. bibliog.

RESCHER (NICHOLAS) The coherence theory of truth. Oxford, 1973. pp. 374. bibliog.

TSELINOGRAD (OBLAST')

- Statistics

RUSSIA (EMPIRE). Pereselencheskoe Upravlenie. 1909. Kirgizskoe khoziaistvo v Akmolinskoi oblasti. t.1. Kokchetavskii uezd; povtornoe issledovanie 1907 goda. S.-Peterburg, 1909. pp. 329, 69.

TSENG (KUO-FAN)

PORTER (JONATHAN) Tseng Kuo-fan's private bureaucracy. Berkeley, [1972]. pp. 149. bibliog. (California University. Center for Chinese Studies. China Research Monographs. No. 9)

TSING HUA UNIVERSITY

HINTON (WILLIAM) Hundred day war: the cultural revolution at Tsinghua University. New York, [1972]. pp. 288.

TSR 2 (TURBOJET FIGHTER PLANES)
See BAC TSR 2 (TURBOJET FIGHTER PLANES)

TUBERCULOSIS

- Hospitals and sanatoriums - Belgium

PHILIPS (J.F.R.) Vijftig jaar Hornerheide: historische beschouwingen over de medische zorg in Limburg. Assen, 1971. pp. 135. (Extract from Studies over de sociaal-economische geschiedenis van Limburg, deel 16)

TUBMAN (WILLIAM VACANARAT SHADRACH)

HENRIES (ARTISTE DORIS BANKS) A biography of President William V.S. Tubman. London, 1967. pp. 180.

TUGBOATS

ZEEVENHOOVEN (E.C.H.N.) Onderzoek naar de toekomstige mogelijkheden van duwvaart in Nederland: een economische evaluatie. Rotterdam, 1969. pp. 258.

TUGELA BASIN

PHILLIPS (JOHN) author of The Tugela basin, etc. The Tugela basin and its influent surrounds: third progress report for the period 1st January to 31st December, 1965. [Pietermaritzburg, 1966]. fo. 216. bibliog.

TULA (OBLAST')

- Constitutional history

SOVETY - vlast' narodnaia. Tula, 1971. pp. 222.

- Industries

BURTSEV (DMITRII IVANOVICH) Tul'skaia khimiia za 50 let. Tula, 1969. pp. 160. bibliog.

- Politics and government

KRUTIKOV (VSEVOLOD IVANOVICH) Revoliutsionnoe dvizhenie v Tul'skoi gubernii v gody pervoi mirovoi voiny, iiul' 1914-fevral' 1917. Tula, 1964. pp. 60.

TUNGSTEN

BARBIER (CLAUDE) The economics of tungsten. London, 1971. pp. 191. bibliog.

BURROWS (JAMES C.) Tungsten: an industry analysis: a Charles River Associates research study. Lexington, Mass., [1971]. pp. 287. bibliog.

SLATER (D.) Tungsten. London, H.M.S.O., 1973. pp. 43. bibliog. (Mineral Dossiers. No. 5)

TUNIS UNIVERSITY

ABDEL MOULA (MAHMOUD) L'Université Zaytounienne et la société tunisienne. Tunis, 1971. pp. 240. bibliog.

TUNISIA

- Economic conditions

PONCET (JEAN) Le sous-développement vaincu?: la lutte pour le développement en Italie méridionale, en Tunisie et en Roumanie. Paris, [1970]. pp. 286.

PONCET (JEAN) and RAYMOND (ANDRÉ) La Tunisie. 2nd ed. Paris, 1971. pp. 127.

- Economic policy

PONCET (JEAN) Le sous-développement vaincu?: la lutte pour le développement en Italie méridionale, en Tunisie et en Roumanie. Paris, [1970]. pp. 286.

- Executive departments

ECOLE NATIONALE D'ADMINISTRATION [TUNIS]. Centre de Recherches et d'Etudes Administratives. 1972. Organisation de l'administration tunisienne; édité avec le concours de l'Institut International d'Administration Publique. [Tunis, 1972]. pp. 619.

- Foreign relations - France

Le NEO-DESTOUR et le front populaire en France...1936-38; (documents). [Tunis, 1969]. 2 vols.

- Foreign relations - United Kingdom

MARSDEN (ARTHUR) British diplomacy and Tunis, 1875-1902: a case study in Mediterranean policy. Edinburgh, 1971. pp. 276. bibliog.

- Manufactures

FERCHIOU (SOPHIE) Techniques et sociétés: exemple de la fabrication des chéchias en Tunisie. Paris, 1971. pp. 239. bibliog. (Paris. Université. Institut d'Ethnologie. Mémoires. 7)

- Nationalism

BOURGUIBA (HABIB) Articles de presse, 1929-1934. [Tunis, 1967]. pp. 388.

Le NEO-DESTOUR et le front populaire en France...1936-38; (documents). [Tunis, 1969]. 2 vols.

Le NEO-DESTOUR face à la première épreuve, 1934-36: (documents). [Tunis, 1969]. pp. 274.

PONCET (JEAN) and RAYMOND (ANDRÉ) La Tunisie. 2nd ed. Paris, 1971. pp. 127.

- Politics and government

BOURGUIBA (HABIB) Articles de presse, 1929-1934. [Tunis, 1967]. pp. 388.

Le NEO-DESTOUR et le front populaire en France...1936-38; (documents). [Tunis, 1969]. 2 vols.

Le NEO-DESTOUR face à la première épreuve, 1934-36: (documents). [Tunis, 1969]. pp. 274.

MOORE (CLEMENT HENRY) Politics in North Africa: Algeria, Morocco and Tunisia. Boston, [1970]. pp. 360.

- Social conditions

PONCET (JEAN) and RAYMOND (ANDRÉ) La Tunisie. 2nd ed. Paris, 1971. pp. 127.

- Social history

ABDEL MOULA (MAHMOUD) L'Université Zaytounienne et la société tunisienne. Tunis, 1971. pp. 240. bibliog.

- Statistics, Vital

TUNIS. Institut National de la Statistique. 1971. Mouvement naturel de la population, 1961-1969. Tunis, 1971. fo. 96. (Statistiques de l'I.N.S. Série Démographie. No.1)

TURCIOS LIMA (LUIS AUGUSTO)

TURCIOS Lima. [Havana, 1970]. pp. 191.

TURGENEV (NIKOLAI IVANOVICH)

LANDA (S. S.) Neizvestnyi politicheskii traktat dekabrista N.I. Turgeneva. in Problemy istorii obshchestvennogo dvizheniia i istoriografii. Moskva, 1971. pp. 471. bibliog.

TARASOVA (V. M.) Iz istorii izdaniia knigi N.I. Turgeneva "Rossiia i Russkie." in Problemy istorii obshchestvennogo dvizheniia i istoriografii. Moskva, 1971. pp. 471. bibliog.

TURIN

- History

SPRIANO (PAOLO) Storia di Torino operaia e socialista, da De Amicis a Gramsci. Torino, [1972]. pp. 509.

- Schools

TORINO: sindacati e piano della scuola; convegno provinciale unitario, comitati di quartiere ACLI-CGIL-CISL-UIL, Torino, 20 maggio 1971. Roma, 1971. pp. 156.

TURKESTAN

- Constitutional history

MANELIS (BORIS LIPOVICH) Iz istorii gosudarstvenno-pravovykh vzaimootnoshenii Turkestanskoi ASSR i RSFSR. Tashkent, 1966. pp. 88.

- Economic history

SAFAROV (GEORGII IVANOVICH) Kolonial'naia revoliutsiia: opyt Turkestana. [Moskva], 1921. pp. 148. Xerographic reprint.

DAVLET-IUSUPOV (M.KH.) Soiuz "Koshchi" i ego rol' v ukreplenii Sovetskoi vlasti i vosstanovlenii sel'skogo khoziaistva v Turkestanskoi ASSR, 1919-1924 gg. Tashkent, 1956. pp. 67.

IUNUSKHODZHAEVA (M.IU.) Iz istorii zemlevladeniia v dorevoliutsionnom Turkestane: na materialakh khoziaistva kniazia N.K. Romanova. Tashkent, 1970. pp. 111. bibliog.

TURKESTAN (Cont'd.)

- History

SOTSIAL'NO-ekonomicheskoe i politicheskoe polozhenie Uzbekistana nakanune Oktiabria. Tashkent, 1973. pp. 235.

- History - 1917-1921, Revolution

AKBAROV (ADKHAM IBRAGIMOVICH) Rol' gazety "Pravda" v pobede sotsialisticheskoi revoliutsii v Turkestane. Tashkent, 1968. pp. 304. bibliog.

KOMPARTIIA Uzbekistana v bor'be za pobedu Sovetskoi vlasti i postroenie sotsializma. Tashkent, 1968. pp. 162.

- Industries

VIATKIN (MIKHAIL PORFIR'EVICH) Monopolisticheskii kapital v Srednei Azii. Frunze, 1962. pp. 163.

- Nationalism

TURSUNOV (KHABIB TURSUNOVICH) Natsional'naia politika Kommunisticheskoi partii v Turkestane, 1917-1924 gg. Tashkent, 1971. pp. 367.

TURKEY

HOTHAM (DAVID) The Turks. London, [1972]. pp. 220. bibliog.

- Commerce - Bulgaria

ZLATAROV (IVAN) and others, compilers. Iztochnite pazari: Turtsiia, Gŭrtsiia, Egipet; anketni svedeniia i belezhki, etc. Sofiia, 1911. pp. 480.

- Economic conditions

HINDERINK (JAN) and KIRAY (MÜBECCEL B.) Social stratification as an obstacle to development: a study of four Turkish villages. New York, 1970. pp. 248.

ŞENEL (ŞENGÜN) Aufstellung einer Input-Output-Tabelle und Input-Output-Analyse für die Türkei. Bonn, 1971. pp. 168. bibliog.

- Economic policy

CENTRAL TREATY ORGANIZATION. Economic Division. 1965. Economic data and development plans of the CENTO region countries: Iran, Pakistan and Turkey. Ankara, 1965. pp. 48.

HERSHLAG (ZVI YEHUDA) Economic planning in Turkey; [summary of an international seminar on economic planning in Turkey, held in 1966, under the auspices of the Economic Research Foundation]. Istanbul, 1968. pp. 75.

AKSU (YUSUF ZIYA) Die Entwicklungsmöglichkeiten der türkischen Finanzmärkte. [Bamberg, imprint, 1971?]. pp. 240, xxxii. bibliog.

FRY (MAXWELL JOHN) Finance and development planning in Turkey. Leiden, 1972. pp. 231. bibliogs.

TURKEY. Devlet Plânlama Teşkilâti. Kalkinma plani üçüncü beş yil, 1973-1977: programi [and] icra plani. a., 1973 [1st]- Ankara.

DURDAĞ (METE) Some problems of development financing: a case study of the Turkish first five-year plan, 1963-1967. Dordrecht, [1973]. pp. 297. bibliog.

TURKEY. Devlet Plânlama Teşkilâti, 1973. Yeni strateji ve kalkinma plani üçüncü beş yil, 1973-1977. [Ankara, 1973]. pp. 1048.

- Foreign relations

WEISBAND (EDWARD) Turkish foreign policy, 1943-1945: small state diplomacy and great power politics. [Princeton, 1973]. pp. 377. bibliog. (New York (City). University. Center for International Studies. Studies in Peaceful Change)

- Foreign relations - United States

TRASK (ROGER R.) The United States response to Turkish nationalism and reform, 1914-1939. Minneapolis, [1971]. pp. 280. bibliog.

HARRIS (GEORGE S.) Troubled alliance: Turkish-American problems in historical perspective, 1945-1971. Washington, D.C., [1972]. pp. 263. bibliog. (American Enterprise Institute for Public Policy Research and Stanford University. Hoover Institution on War, Revolution and Peace. AEI-Hoover Policy Studies)

- History

MANSFIELD (PETER) The Ottoman empire and its successors. London, 1973. pp. 210. bibliog.

- History - Historiography

BULGARU (MARIA MATILDA ALEXANDRESCU-DERSCA) Nicolae Iorga: a Romanian historian of the Ottoman Empire; (translated by Mary Lăzărescu). Bucharest, 1972. pp. 190. bibliog. (Academia de Ştiinţe Sociale şi Politice a Republicii Socialiste România. Bibliotheca Historica Romaniae. Studies. 40)

- History - 1453-1683

INTERNATIONALES GRAZER SYMPOSION ZUR WIRTSCHAFTS- UND SOZIALGESCHICHTE SÜDOSTEUROPAS, 1., 1970. Die wirtschaftlichen Auswirkungen der Türkenkriege: die Vorträge...; herausgegeben von Othmar Pickl. Graz, 1971. pp. 366.

- Politics and government

IDEI Lenina i razvitie progressivnoi mysli narodov Vostoka: Iran, Turtsiia, Irak. Baku, 1970. pp. 193. Some articles in Azerbaijani.

ROOS (LESLIE L.) and ROOS (NORALOU P.) Managers of modernization: organizations and elites in Turkey, 1950-1969. Cambridge, Mass., 1971. pp. 292. bibliog.

- Rural conditions

INTERNATIONAL LABOUR OFFICE. Regular Programme of Technical Assistance. [Turkey] R.29. Report to the government of Turkey on the development of forest villages. (ILO/OTA/Turkey/R.29). Geneva, 1969. pp. 96.

- Social conditions

ROOS (LESLIE L.) and ROOS (NORALOU P.) Managers of modernization: organizations and elites in Turkey, 1950-1969. Cambridge, Mass., 1971. pp. 292. bibliog.

- Social life and customs

HINDERINK (JAN) and KIRAY (MÜBECCEL B.) Social stratification as an obstacle to development: a study of four Turkish villages. New York, 1970. pp. 248.

- Social policy

TURKEY. Devlet Plânlama Teşkilâti. Kalkinma plani üçüncü beş yil, 1973-1977: programi [and] icra plani. a., 1973 [1st]- Ankara.

TURKEY. Devlet Plânlama Teşkilâti, 1973. Yeni strateji ve kalkinma plani üçüncü beş yil, 1973-1977. [Ankara, 1973]. pp. 1048.

- Description and travel

> TURKMEN Soviet Socialist Republic. Moscow, 1972. pp. 80.

- Economic history

> OVEZOV (BALYSH) Po leninskomu puti: sorokaletie Turkmenskoi SSR i Kommunisticheskoi partii Turkmenistana. Ashkhabad, 1964. pp. 208.

- History

> ANNANEPESOV (M.) Uchastie soldatskikh mass v revoliutsii 1905-1907 godov v Turkmenistane. Ashkhabad, 1966. pp. 171.

- History - 1917-1921, Revolution - Bibliography

> VELIKAIA Oktiabr'skaia sotsialisticheskaia revoliutsiia i grazhdanskaia voina v Turkmenistane: bibliograficheskii ukazatel'. Ashkhabad, 1968. pp. 187. In Turkmen and Russian.

TURNER (NAT)

> FONER (ERIC) ed. Nat Turner. Englewood Cliffs, [1971]. pp. 184. bibliog.

TUSCANY

- Foreign relations - Austria

> FILIPUZZI (ANGELO) ed. Le relazioni diplomatiche fra l'Austria e il Granducato di Toscana. Serie 3: 1848-1860. Roma, 1966 in progress. (Istituto Storico Italiano per l'Età Moderna e Contemporanea. Fonti per la Storia d'Italia)

- History - Sources

> LEOPOLD II., Emperor of Germany. Relazioni sul governo della Toscana; a cura di Arnaldo Salvestrini. Firenze, 1969 in progress. (Unione Regionale delle Provincie Toscane. Biblioteca di Storia Toscana Moderna e Contemporanea. Studi e Documenti. 5)

TUVA

- Politics and government

> SHIRSHIN (GRIGORII CHOODUEVICH) Pod znamia Lenina: iz opyta ideino-politicheskoi raboty Tuvinskoi narodno-revoliutsionnoi partii po vospitaniiu trudovogo aratstva na ideiakh leninizma v 1922-1944 gg. Kyzyl, 1972. pp. 147.

TUVANS

> VAINSHTEIN (SEV'IAN IZRAILEVICH) Istoricheskaia etnografiia tuvintsev: problemy kochevogo khoziaistva. Moskva, 1972. pp. 314. bibliog.

TWENTIETH CENTURY

> ATTESLANDER (PETER M.) Die letzten Tage der Gegenwart; oder, Das Alibi-Syndrom. Bern, [1971]. pp. 308. bibliog

- Forecasts

> YOUNG (NORWOOD) England conquers the world. London, 1937. pp. 239.

> DORTMUND. Sozialakademie Dortmund. Internationale Tagung, 1971. Der Mensch in der Gesellschaft von morgen; herausgegeben von Helmut Duvernell. Berlin, [1972]. pp. 318. bibliog.

> KAHN (HERMAN) and BRUCE-BRIGGS (B.) Things to come: thinking about the seventies and eighties. New York, [1972]. pp. 262.

> AMERICAN ACADEMY OF POLITICAL AND SOCIAL SCIENCE. Annals. vol.408. The future society: aspects of America in the year 2000; special editor of this volume Martin E. Wolfgang. Philadelphia, 1973. pp. 205.

> GEIGER (THEODORE) The fortunes of the West: the future of the Atlantic nations. Bloomington, Ind., [1973]. pp. 304.

> CITIZEN and city in the year 2000: [proceedings of a conference held in Rotterdam, sponsored by the] European Cultural Foundation. Deventer, 1971. pp. 254.

> OMNIUM TECHNIQUE D'AMENAGEMENT. Une image de la France en l'an 2000; scénario de l'inacceptable. [Paris], 1971. pp. 173. (France. Délégation à l'Aménagement du Territoire et à l'Action Régionale. Travaux et Recherches de Prospective. 20)

> ANGELOPOULOS (ANGELOS) The Third World and the rich countries: prospects for the year 2000; translated by N. Constantinidis [and] C.R. Corner. New York, 1972. pp. 248.

> EUROPEAN CULTURAL FOUNDATION. Plan Europe 2000. General Prospective Studies. The future is tomorrow: 17 prospective studies. The Hague, 1972. 2 vols. (in 1).

> SCHMACKE (ERNST) ed. Hessen auf dem Weg in das Jahr 2000: Prognosen. Düsseldorf, [1972]. pp. 352.

TWINE

> CANADA. Tariff Board. 1969. Report...relative to the investigation ordered by the Minister of Finance respecting binder twine and twine for baling farm produce. Ottawa, 1969. pp. 98.

TWINING (EDWARD FRANCIS) Baron Twining

> BATES (Sir JULIAN DARRELL) A gust of plumes: a biography of Lord Twining of Godalming and Tanganyika. London, [1972]. pp. 319.

TWINS

> MITTLER (PETER J.) The study of twins. Harmondsworth, 1971. pp. 192. bibliog.

TYLER (JOHN) President of the United States

> MERK (FREDERICK) Fruits of propaganda in the Tyler administration. Cambridge, Mass., 1971. pp. 259.

TYLER'S INSURRECTION, 1381

> SOKOLOVA (A. M.) Nekotorye voprosy, otnosiashchiesia k issledovaniiu M.D. Petrushevskim vosstaniia angliiskogo naroda v 1381 godu. in Irkutsk. Universitet. [Trudy]. tom 39. Seriia Istoricheskaia. vyp.7. Voprosy sovetskogo gosudarstva i prava. Irkutsk, 1962. 2 vols (in 1).

> HILTON (RODNEY HOWARD) Bond men made free: medieval peasant movements and the English rising of 1381. London, 1973. pp. 240.

TYNESIDE

- History

> BEAN (DAVID) Tyneside: a biography. London, 1971. pp. 242. bibliog.

TYNESIDE (Cont'd.)

- Transit systems

VOORHEES (ALAN M.) AND ASSOCIATES, LTD., and BUCHANAN (COLIN) AND PARTNERS. Tyne-Wear plan: transport plan for the 1980's. [London], 1972. pp. 172.

VOORHEES (ALAN M.) AND ASSOCIATES, LTD., and BUCHANAN (COLIN) AND PARTNERS. Tyne-Wear plan: technical report. [London], 1973. pp. 112.

VOORHEES (ALAN M.) AND ASSOCIATES, LTD. and BUCHANAN (COLIN) AND PARTNERS. Tyne-Wear plan: urban strategy. [London], 1973. pp. 250.

TYPE AND TYPE-FOUNDING

HEIDERHOFF (HORST) Antiqua oder Fraktur?: zur Problemgeschichte eines Streits. [Frankfurt am Main, 1971]. pp. 66. bibliog. (Burgverein Eltville am Rhein. Eltviller Drucke. 20)

TYPOLOGY (PSYCHOLOGY)

KORNEEV (MIKHAIL IAKOVLEVICH) Problemy sotsial'noi tipologii lichnosti. Leningrad, 1971. pp. 152.

MUNZ (PETER) When the golden bough breaks: structuralism or typology? London, 1973. pp. 143. bibliog.

TYROL

- Economic conditions

WIRTSCHAFTS- und Sozialforschung in Tirol und Vorarlberg: Festschrift für Univ.-Prof. DDr. Ferdinand Ulmer...; herausgegeben und bearbeitet von Christoph Pan und Gerhard Marinell. Wien, [1972]. pp. 587. bibliog.

- Population

TYROL. Landesstelle für Statistik und Landeskunde. 1948. Die Bevölkerung Tirols von 1910 bis 1948. Innsbruck, 1948. pp. 53. (Veröffentlichungen. Nr. 5) Chart in end pocket.

TYRONE

- Economic policy

WEST Tyrone area plan; [the Duke of Abercorn, chairman of the Steering Committee]. Belfast, H.M.S.O., 1972. pp. 122.

TYUMEN' (OBLAST')

- Social history

RAZVITIE zdravookhraneniia v Tiumenskoi oblasti za gody Sovetskoi vlasti. Tiumen', 1968. pp. 136.

U. V. F.
See ULSTER VOLUNTEER FORCE

UDMURT REPUBLIC

- Constitutional history

TRONIN (ARKADII ANDREEVICH) and others. V sem'e narodov; formirovanie udmurtskoi sotsialisticheskoi natsii. Izhevsk, 1969. pp. 139.

- Constitutional history - Sources

K istorii obrazovaniia Udmurtskoi avtonomii: sbornik dokumentov. Izhevsk, 1960. pp. 128.

- History - Chronology

UDMURTIIA: fakty, sversheniia, sobytiia, 1920-1970. Izhevsk, 1970. pp. 40.

- Rural conditions

TIUREV (KONSTANTIN IVANOVICH) Edinstvenno vernyi put': ekonomicheskoe razvitie udmurtskoi derevni. Izhevsk, 1970. pp. 64.

UGANDA

- Constitutional history

IBINGIRA (GRACE STUART K.) The forging of an African nation: the political and constitutional evolution of Uganda from colonial rule to independence, 1894-1962. New York, 1973. pp. 332. bibliog.

- Economic policy

UGANDA. 1972. Third five-year development plan, 1971/2-1975/6. [Entebbe, 1972]. pp. 428.

- History

KARUGIRE (SAMWIRI RUBARAZA) A history of the kingdom of Nkore in Western Uganda to 1896. Oxford, 1971. pp. 291. bibliog.

- Industries

STOUTJESDIJK (E.J.) Uganda's manufacturing sector: a contribution to the analysis of industrialisation in East Africa. Nairobi, 1967. pp. 101. (Makerere Institute of Social Research. East African Studies. No. 28)

GERKEN (EGBERT) Die Industriestadt als Faktor sozialen Wandels: Untersuchungen zur gesellschaftlichen Urbanisierung und Industrialisierung in Jinja und Busoga, Uganda. Berlin, 1970. pp. 335. bibliog.

- Legislative Council - Elections

UGANDA. 1956. Report by representatives of the Protectorate and Kabaka's governments on discussions on the introduction of direct elections to the Legislative Council in Buganda in 1957. [Entebbe, 1956]. pp. 6.

UGANDA. Supervisor of Elections. 1959. Uganda Legislative Council elections, 1958: a report on the first direct elections to the Legislative Council of the Uganda Protectorate; by C.P.S. Allen. [Entebbe, 1959]. pp. 118.

- Officials and employees

UGANDA. Housing Policy Committee. 1962. Report; [A.R.G. Prosser, chairman]. Entebbe, [1962]. pp. 24.

- Officials and employees - Salaries, allowances, etc.

UGANDA. Grading Committee on the Uganda Civil Service. 1961. Report; [F.J. Lattin chairman]. Entebbe, 1961. pp. 159.

UGANDA. Committee on Wages and Conditions of Service of Government Unestablished Employees. 1962. Report; [T.A. Kennedy, chairman]. Entebbe, 1962. pp. 22.

UGANDA. 1963. Proposals for the implementation of the recommendations contained in the report of the Uganda Civil Service Salaries Commission, 1963, and other matters arising out of the report. Entebbe, 1963. pp. 25. (Uganda. Sessional Papers. 1963. No. 6)

- Politics and government

  UGANDA. Uganda Relationships Commission. 1961. Report; under the chairmanship of the Earl of Munster. [Entebbe, 1961]. pp. 232.

  GUKIINA (PETER M.) Uganda: a case study in African political development. Notre Dame, Ind., [1972]. pp. 190. bibliog.

  LISTOWEL (JUDITH) Amin. Dublin, 1973. pp. 188.

- Race question

  UGANDA. 1969. Government memorandum on the report of the Committee on Africanisation of commerce and industry in Uganda. Entebbe, 1969. pp. 5. (Sessional Papers. 1969. No.1)

- Social conditions

  GERKEN (EGBERT) Die Industriestadt als Faktor sozialen Wandels: Untersuchungen zur gesellschaftlichen Urbanisierung und Industrialisierung in Jinja und Busoga, Uganda. Berlin, 1970. pp. 335. bibliog.

- Social policy

  UGANDA. 1972. Third five-year development plan, 1971/2-1975/6. [Entebbe, 1972]. pp. 428.

UIGURS

NIKOL'SKAIA (G.B.) Iz istorii obshchestvenno-politicheskoi zhizni uigurov i dungan v Turkestane v 1920-1921 gg. in Tashmukhamedov (A.M.) ed. Istoricheskoe znachenie pobedy Oktiabr'skoi sotsialisticheskoi revoliutsii v Uzbekistane. Tashkent, 1967. pp. 167.

UKRAINE

- Constitution

  UKRAINE. Constitution. 1969. Konstitutsiia (Osnovnoi Zakon) Ukrainskoi S... S... R...; s izmeneniiami i dopolneniiami, priniatymi na chetvertoi sessii Verkhovnogo Soveta Ukrainskoi SSR sed'mogo sozyva. Kiev, 1969. pp. 30.

- Constitutional history

  BABII (BORYS MOISEIOVYCH) Soiuz RSR i rol' Ukraïny v ioho utvorenni. Kyïv, 1972. pp. 254. With Russian summary and table of contents.

- Description and travel

  UKRAINIAN Soviet Socialist Republic. Moscow, 1972. pp. 100.

- Economic conditions

  UKRAINA i Moldaviia. Moskva, 1972. pp. 440. bibliog. (Akademiia Nauk SSSR. Institut Geografii. Prirodnye Usloviia i Estestvennye Resursy SSSR)

- Economic conditions - Statistics.

  DESIAT' rokiv spozhivchoï kooperatsiï USRR, 1920-1930. Kharkiv, 1930. 2 pts. (in 1). Pt. 2 is a statistical supplement.

- Economic history

  BAHALII (DMYTRO IVANOVYCH) Narys istoriï Ukraïny na sotsiial'no-ekonomichnomu grunti. t.1. Istoriohrafichnyi vstup i doba natural'noho hospodarstva. Kyïv, 1928. pp. 392. bibliog. Xerographic reprint.

  BAKUMENKO (PETRO IVANOVYCH) Ukraïns'ka RSR v period vidbudovy narodnoho hospodarstva, 1921-1925 rr. Kyïv, 1960. pp. 107.

  DEREV'IANKIN (TYMOFII IVANOVYCH) and KUL'CHYTS'KYI (STANYSLAV VLADYSLAVOVYCH) Ekonomichnyi rozvytok Radians'koï Ukraïny, 1917-1970. Kyïv, 1970. pp. 115.

  BESSARABOV (MYKOLA ANTONOVYCH) Komunistychna partiia Ukraïny v borot'bi za zmitsnennia i rozvytok sotsialistychnoho suspil'stva, 1937 - cherven' 1941 rr. Kyïv, 1971. pp. 176.

  MEL'NYK (LEONID HARASYMOVYCH) Tekhnichnyi perevorot na Ukraïni u XIX st. Kyïv, 1972. pp. 240.

  RADIANS'KA Ukraïna v bratnii sim"ï narodiv SRSR. Kyïv, 1972. pp. 275.

- Economic history - Sources

  V bratskoi sem'e: dokumenty i materialy o bor'be trudiashchikhsia ukrainskikh pridunaiskikh zemel' za vosstanovlenie i dal'neishee razvitie narodnogo khoziaistva, 1946-1953 gg. Odessa, 1972. pp. 247.

- Economic policy

  FORMIROVANIE osnovnykh fondov promyshlennosti v usloviiakh khoziaistvennoi reformy. Kiev, 1971. pp. 151.

  POHORILKO (VIKTOR FEDOROVYCH) Hospodars'ko-orhanizators'ka diial'nist' mistsevykh Rad deputativ trudiashchykh Ukraïns'koï RSR. Kyïv, 1972. pp. 147. With Russian summary and table of contents.

  UKRAÏNS'KA RSR u radians'ko-uhors'komu spivrobitnytstvi, 1945-1970 rr. Kyïv, 1972. pp. 292.

  VOLOBOI (PETRO VASYL'OVYCH) and POPOVKIN (VALERII ARKADIIOVYCH) Problemy terytorial'noï spetsializatsiï i kompleksnoho rozvytku narodnoho hospodarstva Ukraïns'koï RSR. Kyïv, 1972. pp. 251. bibliog. With Russian summary and table of contents.

- Foreign economic relations - Communist Countries

  EKONOMICHNI osnovy spivrobitnytstva URSR z kraïnamy-chlenamy REV. Kyïv, 1971. pp. 128. With Russian summary.

- History

  PORTAL (ROGER) Russes et Ukrainiens. [Paris, 1970]. pp. 140. bibliog.

  IZ istorii ukrainsko-gruzinskikh sviazei. Kiev, 1971. pp. 195.

  KUCHER (OLEKSANDR OMELIANOVYCH) Rozhrom zbroïnoï vnutrishn'oï kontrrevoliutsiï na Ukraïni u 1921-1923 rr. Kharkiv, 1971. pp. 171. bibliog.

  SERCZYK (WŁADYSŁAW A.) Hajdamacy. Kraków, 1972. pp. 461. bibliog.

- History - Bibliography

  PIDHAINY (OLEH SEMENOVYCH) and PIDHAINY (OLEXANDRA IVANIVNA) compilers. The Ukrainian Republic in the great East-European revolution: a bibliography. Toronto, 1971 in progress. (The Ukrainian Republic in the great East-European revolution. vol.5)

UKRAINE - History - Bibliography (Cont'd.)

LIPOVCHENKO (NIKOLAI NIKOLAEVICH) K vyrabotke vzgliadov V.I. Lenina na istoriiu Ukrainy: bibliograficheskii obzor. Khar'kov, 1971. pp. 114.

- History - Historiography

SARBEI (VITALII GRIGOR'EVICH) V.I. Lenin i dozhovtneva spadshchyna istoriohrafiï Ukraïny. Kyïv, 1972. pp. 287.

- History - Sources

SANTSEVYCH (ANATOLII VASYL'OVYCH) Dzhereloznavstvo z istoriï Ukraïns'koï RSR pisliavoennoho periodu, 1945-1970. Kyïv, 1972. pp. 203. bibliog. With Russian summary and table of contents.

- History - 1917-1921, Revolution

MAIOROV (M.) Iz istorii revoliutsionnoi bor'by na Ukraine, 1914-1919. Kyïv, 1922. pp. 109.

SHTIF (N.I.) Pogromy na Ukraine: period Dobrovol'cheskoi Armii. Berlin, 1922. pp. 96.

RUDNEV (V.V.) Makhnovshchina. [Khar'kov, 1928]. pp. 103.

- History - 1917-1921, Revolution - Historiography

NAHORNA (LARYSA PANASIVNA) Proty suchasnoï burzhuaznoï i burzhuazno-natsionalistychnoï fal'syfikatsiï istoriï Zhovtnia na Ukraïni. Kyïv, 1971. pp. 251.

- History - 1917-1921, Revolution - Personal narratives

MARGOLIN (ARNOLD DAVIDOVICH) Ukraina i politika Antanty: zapiski evreia i grazhdanina. Berlin, [1921?]. pp. 397.

BAUMGART (WINFRIED) ed. Von Brest-Litovsk zur deutschen Novemberrevolution: aus den Tagebüchern... von Alfons Paquet, Wilhelm Groener und Albert Hopman, März bis November 1918. Göttingen, [1971]. pp. 750. bibliog. (Bayerische Akademie der Wissenschaften. Historische Kommission. Deutsche Geschichtsquellen des 19. und 20. Jahrhunderts. Band 47)

- History - 1918-1920, Allied intervention

SHLIKHTER (OLEKSANDR HRYHOROVYCH) ed. Chernaia kniga: sbornik statei i materialov ob interventsii antanty na Ukraine v 1918-1919 gg. [Ekaterinoslav], 1925. pp. 432.

- History - 1941-1944, German occupation

TORZECKI (RYSZARD) Kwestia ukraińska w polityce III Rzeszy, 1933-1945. Warszawa, 1972. pp. 378. bibliog.

- Industries

BOHAIENKO (VSEVOLOD OLEKSANDROVYCH) Rezervy zbil'shennia vyrobnytstva tovariv narodnoho spozhyvannia v mistsevii promyslovosti. Kyïv, 1960. pp. 75.

FORMIROVANIE osnovnykh fondov promyshlennosti v usloviiakh khoziaistvennoi reformy. Kiev, 1971. pp. 151.

KOROPECKYJ (I.S.) Location problems in Soviet industry before World War II: the case of the Ukraine. Chapel Hill, [1971]. pp. 219. bibliog.

PALAMARCHUK (MAKSIM MARTYNOVICH) and GORLENKO (INGA ALEKSANDROVNA) Mineral'ni resursy i struktura raionnoho promyslovoho kompleksu. Kyïv, 1972. pp. 215. With Russian summary and table of contents.

- Manufactures

DEREV'IANKIN (TYMOFII IVANOVYCH) Manufaktura na Ukraïni v kintsi XVIII - pershii polovyni XIX st.: tekstyl'ne vyrobnytstvo. Kyïv, 1960. pp. 127. bibliog.

- Nationalism

ROMANOVSKII (IU.D.) Ukrainskii separatizm i Germaniia. Tokio, 1920. pp. 15.

MARGOLIN (ARNOLD DAVIDOVICH) Ukraina i politika Antanty: zapiski evreia i grazhdanina. Berlin, [1921?]. pp. 397.

PORTAL (ROGER) Russes et Ukrainiens. [Paris, 1970]. pp. 140. bibliog.

KULICHENKO (MIKHAIL IVANOVICH) and MALANCHUK (VALENTYN IUKHYMOVYCH) V.I.Lenin i rozv"iazannia natsional'noho pitannia na Ukraïni. Kyïv, 1971. pp. 318.

KOZIK (JAN) Ukraiński ruch narodowy w Galicji w latach 1830-1848. Kraków, 1973. pp. 308.

SZELĄGOWSKI (WŁADYSŁAW) Wzburzony San. Warszawa, 1973. pp. 425.

- Politics and government

MARGOLIN (ARNOLD DAVIDOVICH) Ukraina i politika Antanty: zapiski evreia i grazhdanina. Berlin, [1921?]. pp. 397.

IVANOVA (RAÏSA PETRIVNA) Mykhailo Drahomanov u suspil'no-politychnomu rusi Rosiï ta Ukraïny: II polovyna XIX st. Kyïv, 1971. pp. 235.

SHELEST (PETR EFIMOVICH) Idei Lenina pobezhdaiut. Kiev, 1971. pp. 395.

- Relations (general) with France

FROLKIN (MYKOLA MYKOLAIOVYCH) Paryz'ka Komuna i Ukraïna. Kyïv, 1971. pp. 68.

- Relations (general) with Germany

ROMANOVSKII (IU.D.) Ukrainskii separatizm i Germaniia. Tokio, 1920. pp. 15.

TORZECKI (RYSZARD) Kwestia ukraińska w polityce III Rzeszy, 1933-1945. Warszawa, 1972. pp. 378. bibliog.

- Religion

RELIHIINE prystosovnytstvo ta ateïstychne vykhovannia. Kyïv, 1965. pp. 172. With Russian summary and table of contents.

MYKULA (WOLODYMYR) La religion et l'église en Ukraine sous la régime communiste russe. Paris, [1971]. pp. 80.

UKRAINE, WESTERN

- Politics and government

DIIAL'NIST' partiinykh orhanizatsii zakhidnykh oblastei URSR po komunistychnomu vykhovanniu trudiashchykh, 1953-1963 rr. L'viv, 1964. pp. 130.

- Relations (general) with Poland

> SHVYDAK (OLEH MYKHAILOVYCH) Internatsional'na iednist' trudiashchykh Zakhidnoï Ukraïny i Pol'shchi u revoliutsiino-vyzvol'nii borot'bi, 1929-1939 rr. Kyïv, 1972. pp. 228.

UL'IANOV (ALEKSANDR IL'ICH)

> ITENBERG (BORIS SAMUILOVICH) and CHERNIAK (ARON IAKOVLEVICH) Zhizn' Aleksandra Ul'ianova. Moskva, 1966. pp. 160.

> KAZAKEVICH (ROZA ABRAMOVNA) and MANDEL' (SEMEN ZAKHAROVICH) Nauchnaia i kul'turno-prosvetitel'skaia deiatel'nost' progressivnogo studenchestva 80-kh godov XIX v.: studencheskoe nauchno-literaturnoe obshchestvo Peterburgskogo universiteta. Leningrad, 1967. pp. 75.

UL'IANOV (IL'IA NIKOLAEVICH)

> KUZNETSOV (PETR PETROVICH) and LASHKO (VLAS TROFIMOVICH) I.N. Ul'ianov i prosveshchenie mordovskogo naroda. Saransk, 1970. pp. 174.

UL'IANOVA (MARIIA IL'INICHNA)

> KARAVASHKOVA (SVETLANA VASIL'EVNA) M.I. Ul'ianova - zhurnalist. Moskva, 1972. pp. 153.

ULSTER (NORTHERN IRELAND)
See IRELAND, NORTHERN

ULSTER VOLUNTEER FORCE

> BOULTON (DAVID) The UVF, 1966-73: an anatomy of loyalist rebellion. Dublin, 1973. pp. 188.

UMBRIA

- Economic conditions

> ITALY. Comitato Regionale per la Programmazione Economica dell'Umbria. 1969. Atti della discussione alla Camera dei Deputati sulla situazione economica dell'Umbria. Perugia, 1969. pp. 283.

- Economic policy

> ITALY. Comitato Regionale per la Programmazione Economica dell'Umbria. 1968. L'insediamento e l'avvio dell'attività del Comitato Regionale per la Programmazione Economica dell'Umbria. Roma, 1968. pp. 150.

> ITALY. Comitato Regionale per la Programmazione Economica dell'Umbria. 1968. Schema regionale di sviluppo economico dell'Umbria. Capitolo IV. Gli obiettivi dello schema e gli interventi. Foligno, 1968. pp. 86. Reprinted from 'Bollettino d'informazioni del Centro Regionale per il Piano di Sviluppo Economico dell'Umbria', 1/2, 1968.

UMEDAS (NEW GUINEA PEOPLE)

> GELL (ANTONY FRANCIS) Society, ritual and symbolism in Umeda village, West Sepik district, New Guinea; [Ph.D.(London) thesis]. 1973. fo.637. bibliog. Typescript: unpublished. This thesis is the property of London University and may not be removed from the Library.

UNBORN CHILDREN (LAW)

- United Kingdom

> U.K. Law Commission. Published Working Papers. No. 47. Injuries to unborn children. London, 1973. pp. 20,viii.

UNCERTAINTY

> COHEN (JOHN) Psychological probability; or, The art of doubt. London, 1972. pp. 141.

UNDERDEVELOPED AREAS

> IVANOV (K.) and BATSANOV (B.) Vzgliad v zavtra. Moskva, 1964. pp. 203.

> WATERKAMP (RAINER) Die Entwicklungsländer und die Friedenssicherung. Hannover, 1967. pp. 63. bibliog. (Niedersächsische Landeszentrale für Politische Bildung. Schriftenreihe. Friedensprobleme. Heft 4)

> La COMMUNAUTE et le problème du développement. Bruxelles, 1969-70. 3 pts. (Brussels. Université Libre. Institut d'Etudes Européennes. Enseignement Complémentaire. Nouvelle Série. 4)

> AMIN (SAMIR) L'accumulation à l'échelle mondiale: critique de la théorie du sous-développement. Dakar, [1970]. pp. 591.

> BOSERUP (ESTER) Evolution agraire et pression démographique; traduit de l'anglais par le docteur Métadier. Paris, [1970]. pp. 221.

> DUNCAN (W. RAYMOND) ed. Soviet policy in developing countries: (case studies in conflict-management). Waltham, Mass., [1970]. pp. 350. bibliogs

> HOPE (ROBERT) Impact '69: a survey of United Kingdom examination questions related to world poverty and development. London, 1970. pp. 139.

> RHODES (ROBERT I.) ed. Imperialism and underdevelopment: a reader. New York, [1970]. pp. 416. bibliog.

> SMITH (DONALD EUGENE) Religion and political development: (an analytic study). Boston, [1970]. pp. 298.

> THOLE (GUENTHER) and WUENSCHE (RENATE) Leninismus und antiimperialistische Befreiungsbewegung heute. Berlin, 1970. pp. 91.

> UTTING (JOHN EDWARD GEORGE) Economics in underdeveloped countries. Blantyre, 1970. pp. 20.

> AMIN (SAMIR) L'accumulation à l'échelle mondiale critique de la théorie du sous-développement. 2nd ed. Paris, 1971. pp. 619.

> ANTIRASSISMUS, Antiimperialismus: der Beitrag der Christen zum Kampf gegen rassistische und kolonialistische Unterdrückung; [proceedings of a conference organized by the Christlich-Demokratische Union [D.D.R.] in 1971]. Berlin, [1971]. pp. 135.

> BUGNICOURT (JACQUES) Disparités régionales et aménagement du territoire en Afrique. Paris, [1971]. pp. 349. bibliog.

> CAMARA (HELDER) Archbishop of Olinda and Recife. Race against time;...translated by Della Couling. London, 1971. pp. 136.

> CASTEL (HELENE) ed. World development: an introductory reader. New York, 1971. pp. 296.

> DONALDSON (PETER) Worlds apart: the economic gulf between nations. London, 1971. pp. 160. bibliog.

UNDERDEVELOPED AREAS (Cont'd.)

DUVE (FREIMUT) Der Rassenkrieg findet nicht statt: Entwicklungspolitik zwischen Angst und Armut. Düsseldorf, 1971. pp. 224.

ESSAYS on modernization of underdeveloped societies [published on the fiftieth anniversary of the Department of Sociology, Bombay University]; editor, A.R. Desai. Bombay, 1971. 2 vols.

EUROPEAN COMMUNITIES. Commission. 1971. Commission memorandum on a Community policy for development co-operation: summary, 27 July 1971. Brussels, 1971. pp. 37. (Bulletin of the European Communities. Supplements. [1971/5])

The GDR: a staunch ally of the emergent countries. Dresden, [1971?]. pp 83.

HIRSCHMAN (ALBERT O.) A bias for hope: essays on development and Latin America. New Haven, 1971. pp. 374.

The POOR and the superpoor: contributions serving to rectify the opinion of the public concerning the revolution in underdeveloped countries; [originally published in French in Internationale Situationniste, no.11, October 1967]. New York, [1971]. pp. 46.

REVOLUTION und Tradition: zur Rolle der Tradition im antiimperialistischen Kampf der Völker Afrikas und Asiens; [papers presented at a symposium in 1969]. Leipzig, 1971. pp. 222. Table of contents in various languages.

SANTOS (MILTON) Le métier de géographe en pays sous-développé: un essai méthodologique. [Paris], 1971. pp. 119.

SMITH (DONALD EUGENE) ed. Religion, politics, and social change in the Third World: a sourcebook. New York, [1971]. pp. 286. bibliog.

BLARDONE (GILBERT) Progrès économique dans le tiers-monde: environnement socio-politique, croissance démographique et urbanisation. Paris, [1972]. pp. 233. bibliogs.

INTERNATIONAL ECONOMIC ASSOCIATION. Conference, [1970], Bled. The gap between rich and poor nations: proceedings of a conference... edited by Gustav Ranis. London, 1972. pp. 439.

NICHTKAPITALISTISCHER Entwicklungsweg: aktuelle Probleme in Theorie und Praxis; Protokoll einer Konferenz des Zentralen Rates für Asien-, Afrika- und Lateinamerikawissenschaften in der DDR, die...1971 in Leipzig veranstaltet wurde. Berlin, 1972. pp. 439. (Studien über Asien, Afrika und Lateinamerika. Band 1)

SIGMUND (PAUL E.) ed. The ideologies of the developing nations. 2nd rev. ed. [i.e. 3rd ed.] New York, 1972. pp. 483. bibliog.

SOCIAL development: critical perspectives; [papers contributed to a symposium]; edited by Manfred Stanley. New York, [1972]. pp. 335. bibliogs.

BERNSTEIN (HENRY) ed. Underdevelopment and development: the third world today; selected readings. Harmondsworth, 1973. pp. 384. bibliogs.

IAROSHEVSKII (BORIS EFIMOVICH) Teoriia periferiinoi ekonomiki. Moskva, 1973. pp. 214.

- Administration

BHATTACHARYYA (JNANABROTA) Organisation administrative pour le développement. Bruxelles, 1971. pp. 152.

SEMINAR ON SPATIAL ASPECTS OF DEVELOPMENT ADMINISTRATION, UNIVERSITY OF PITTSBURGH, 1965. Spatial dimensions of development administration; ...paper edited by James J. Heaphey. Durham, N.C., 1971. pp. 276. (American Society for Public Administration. Comparative Administration Group. Comparative Administration Group Series)

PACKARD (PHILIP C.) Critical path analysis for development administration. The Hague, 1972. pp. 84. bibliog. (Hague. Institute of Social Studies. Publications. Paperback Series. 7)

- Agricultural credit

UNITED STATES. Agency for International Development. 1973. A.I.D. spring review of small farmer credit. Washington, 1973. 20 vols.(in 7). bibliogs

- Agriculture

FOOD AND AGRICULTURE ORGANIZATION. Agricultural Planning Studies No. 8. Incentives and disincentives for farmers in developing countries. Rome, 1967. pp. 43.

RASK (NORMAN) Analysis of capital formation and utilization in less developed countries. Columbus, Ohio, 1969. fo. 126. bibliog. (Ohio State University Department of Agricultural Economics and Rural Sociology. Economics and Sociology Occasional Papers. No. 4)

SZCZEPANIK (EDWARD FRANCISZEK) Agricultural capital formation in selected developing countries. Rome, Food and Agriculture Organization, 1970 pp. 43. (Agricultural Planning Studies. No. 11)

BEHAVIORAL change in agriculture: concepts and strategies for influencing transition; edited by J. Paul Leagans and Charles P. Loomis. Ithaca, 1971. pp. 507. bibliog.

BRENNER (Y.S.) Agriculture and the economic development of low income countries. The Hague, 1971. pp. 254. (Hague. Institute of Social Studies. Publications. Paperback Series. 2)

CRAWFORD (Sir JOHN GRENFELL) Agriculture in development: the Australian case and some contrasts with developing countries. Cairo, 1971. pp. 48,7. (National Bank of Egypt. Fiftieth Anniversary Commemoration Lectures)

FOOD AND AGRICULTURE ORGANIZATION. Agricultural Planning Studies. No. 15. Regional training course in agricultural project analysis; held at New Delhi, India, 2-28 November 1970. Rome, 1971. pp. 74. bibliog.

MALINSCHI (VASILE) Studii de reformă agrară. Bucureşti, 1971. pp. 314. With English summary.

YUDELMAN (MONTAGUE) and others. Technological change in agriculture and employment in developing countries. Paris, Organisation for Economic Co-operation and Development, 1971. pp. 204. (Development Centre. Studies: Employment Series. No. 4)

GITTINGER (JAMES PRICE) Economic analysis of agricultural projects. Baltimore, [1972]. pp. 221. bibliog.

INTERNATIONAL BANK FOR RECONSTRUCTION AND DEVELOPMENT. Sector Working Papers. Agriculture. [Washington], 1972. pp. 83.

SCHWEIZER (HEINRICH) Sozialistische Agrartheorie und Landwirtschaftspolitik in China und der Sowjetunion: ein Modell für Entwicklungsländer? Bern, [1972]. pp. 266. bibliog.

WINKELMAN (DON) The traditional farmer: maximization and mechanization. Paris, Organisation for Economic Co-operation and Development, 1972. pp. 94. bibliog. (Development Centre. Studies: Employment Series. No. 7)

- Agriculture, Cooperative

DRACHOUSSOFF (VLADIMIR) Les moissons et les hommes: la coopération au développement rural dans les pays non industrialisés. Bruxelles, 1971. pp. 295. bibliog. (Brussels. Université Libre. Institut de Sociologie. Collection d'Écologie Humaine)

- Automobile industry and trade

BARANSON (JACK) International transfer of automotive technology to developing countries. New York, United Nations Institute for Training and Research, 1971. pp. 95. (Research Reports. No. 8)

- Bibliography

BRIGHTON. University of Sussex. Institute of Development Studies. Library. Occasional Guides. No. 2. A guide to information on developing countries in U.S. government publications, 1962-1971. Brighton, [1972]. pp. 82.

- Birth control

BAADE (FRITZ) and KARTSAKLIS (RENATA) Probleme der Familienplanung in Entwicklungsländern, unter besonderer Berücksichtigung der Länder Indien, Pakistan und der Türkei. Hannover, 1970. pp. 56. (Friedrich-Ebert-Stiftung. Forschungsinstitut. Vierteljahresberichte. Sonderhefte. 6)

- Capital

STEVENS (WILLY J.) Capital absorptive capacity in developing countries. Leiden, 1971. pp. 215. bibliog.

SALAMA (PIERRE) Le procès de "sous-développement": essai sur les limites de l'accumulation nationale du capital dans les économies semi-industrialisées. Paris, 1972. pp. 183.

- Chemical industries

STOBAUGH (ROBERT B.) The international transfer of technology in the establishment of the petrochemical industry in developing countries. New York, United Nations Institute for Training and Research, 1971. pp. 67. (Research Reports. No. 12)

- Child welfare

REUBENS (EDWIN PIERCE) Planning for children and youth within national development planning. Geneva, United Nations Research Institute for Social Development, 1967. pp. 131.

MANDL (PIERRE EMERIC) Preparation of the child for modernization: skills and intellectual requirements; a review of the literature. (UNRISD Reports No.70.16) (UNRISD/70/C/55). Geneva, United Nations Research Institute for Social Development, 1969. pp. 88. bibliog.

SINGER (HANS WOLFGANG) Children in the strategy of development, etc. New York, United Nations, 1972. pp. 64. bibliog. (Centre for Economic and Social Information. Executive Briefing Papers. 6)

- Cities and towns

INTERNATIONAL BANK FOR RECONSTRUCTION AND DEVELOPMENT. Sector Working Papers. Urbanization. [Washington], 1972. pp. 111.

REHOVOT CONFERENCE, 6TH, 1971. Rehovot Conference on Urbanization and Development in Developing Countries: conference papers. [Rehovot?, 1972?] 1 vol. (various pagings). bibliogs.

RITTER (ULRICH PETER) Siedlungsstruktur und wirtschaftliche Entwicklung: der Verstädterungsprozess ...in den Ländern der Dritten Welt, vorwiegend exemplifiziert an Lateinamerika. Berlin, [1972]. pp. 177. bibliog.

SANTOS (MILTON) Les villes du tiers monde. Paris, [1972]. pp. 428.

- Cities and towns - Bibliography

BRUNN (STANLEY D.) Urbanization in developing countries: an international bibliography. East Lansing, 1971. pp. 693. (Michigan State University. Latin American Studies Center. Research Reports. No. 8)

UNDERDEVELOPED AREAS - City planning
See UNDERDEVELOPED AREAS -
Cities and towns

- Civil rights

SEMINAR ON HUMAN RIGHTS IN DEVELOPING COUNTRIES, KABUL, AFGHANISTAN, 1964. Seminar...[held at] Kabul, Afghanistan, 12-25 May 1964; organized by the United Nations in co-operation with the government of Afghanistan. (ST/TAO/HR/21). New York, United Nations, 1964. pp. 49.

SEMINAR ON SPECIAL PROBLEMS RELATING TO HUMAN RIGHTS IN DEVELOPING COUNTRIES, NICOSIA, 1969. Seminar...[held at] Nicosia, Cyprus, 26 June - 9 July 1969; organized by the United Nations, Division of Human Rights, in co-operation with the government of Cyprus. (ST/TAO/HR/36). New York, United Nations, 1970. pp. 49.

- Civil service

CHAPEL (YVES) compiler. The central organs of the civil service in the developing countries. (ST/TAO/M/41). New York, United Nations, 1969. pp. 229. bibliog.

UNITED NATIONS. Interregional Seminar on the Employment, Development and Role of Scientists and Technical Personnel in the Public Service of Developing Countries, Tashkent, 1969. Report of the...Seminar...[held in] Tashkent, Union of Soviet Socialist Republics, 1-14 October 1969. (ST/TAO/M/48 and Adds. 1 and 2). New York, 1970-71. 3 vols.(in 1).

LONDON. University. Institute of Commonwealth Studies. Collected seminar papers on bureaucratic change in new states, October 1969 - March 1970. London, [1970]. pp. 56. (London. University. Institute of Commonwealth Studies. Collected Seminar Papers. No. 9)

- Commerce

ROYER (JEAN) Le commerce des pays sous-développés: conférence prononcée...au Centre de Recherches des Pays Sous-Développés de l'Université de Toulouse. [Geneva], 1959. pp. 13.

GENERAL AGREEMENT ON TARIFFS AND TRADE. 1962. GATT programme for expansion of international trade: trade of less-developed countries: development plans: study of the second five-year plan of Pakistan. Geneva, 1962. pp. 45.

UNDERDEVELOPED AREAS - Commerce
(Cont'd.)

GENERAL AGREEMENT ON TARIFFS AND TRADE. 1962. GATT programme for expansion of international trade: trade of less-developed countries: special report of Committee III; development plans; study of the third five-year plan of India. Geneva, 1962. pp. 60.

ECONOMIC AND SCIENTIFIC RESEARCH FOUNDATION. Papers. 3. Perspectives for India's trade with developing countries. New Delhi, [1966]. pp. 70.

MEASURES for trade expansion of developing countries: report of a JERC International Conference. Tokyo, 1966. pp. 315. (Japan Economic Research Center. Center Papers. No. 5.)

CROSLAND (CHARLES ANTHONY RAVEN) Speech by the Rt. Hon. Anthony Crosland M.P., President of the Board of Trade, on Tuesday, 6th February, 1968, at the UNCTAD II meeting in New Delhi. [London, 1968]. pp. 7.

HASELBECK (FRITZ) Die Terms of Trade zwischen Rohstoffländern und Industrieländern. [Zurich, 1969]. pp. 214. bibliog.

WRUCK (HORST) Internationale Marktvereinbarungen: Wesen und volkswirtschaftliche Bedeutung. Berlin, [1970]. pp. 244. bibliog. With English and French summaries.

BALASSA (BELA A.) and others. The structure of protection in developing countries. Baltimore, International Bank for Reconstruction and Development, [1971]. pp. 375.

BATZER (ERICH) and others. Der deutsche Ein- und Ausfuhrhandel im Entwicklungsländergeschäft: Aktivitäten, entwicklungsfördernde Leistungen, Schwierigkeiten. Berlin, [1971]. pp. 93. bibliog. (Ifo-Institut für Wirtschaftsforschung. Schriftenreihe. Nr. 76) With summaries in English and French.

BRITAIN, the EEC and the third world: report of an international conference; jointly sponsored by the Society for International Development and the Overseas Development Institute, at the Royal Society, 26-27 April 1971. London, [1971] pp. 91.

FRIEDMANN (WOLFGANG GASTON) and BEGUIN (JEAN PIERRE) Joint international business ventures in developing countries: case studies and analysis of recent trends. New York, 1971. pp. 448. bibliog.

KHAN (KISHWAR SHABBIR) Gains from international trade: their distribution between investing and borrowing countries. Bombay, [1971]. pp. 306. bibliog. (Aligarh (City). Muslim University. Faculty of Social Sciences. Publications Series)

MORDI (OBI) Entwicklungshilfe und Terms-of-trade-Effekt: eine statistisch-theoretische Untersuchung. Freiburg i. Br., 1971. pp. 160. bibliog. (Heidelberg. Universität. Institut für International Vergleichend Wirtschafts- und Sozialstatistik. Schriftenreihe. Band 11)

BEGUIN (JEAN PIERRE) Les entreprises conjointes internationales dans les pays en voie de développement: le régime des participations. Genève, 1972. pp. 271. bibliog. (Geneva. Graduate Institute of International Studies. Publications. No.50)

BOURRINET (JACQUES) Les échanges internationaux: pays en voie de développement. [Paris, 1972]. pp. 96.

CONSTANTOPOULOS (MARIA) The theory of commercial policy in a developing world economy; [Ph.D. (London) thesis]. 1972. fo. 170. bibliog. Typescript: unpublished. This thesis is the property of London University and may not be removed from the Library.

LABOUR PARTY. UNCTAD III: (a statement of proposals on the third session...to be held in Santiago, Chile in April, 1972). [London, 1972]. pp. 8.

SMALL (ALBERT H.) The American market for manufactured exports from the developing countries. New York, 1972. pp. 189. bibliog.

VERMARKTUNG und Verteilung von Rohstoffen; [by] Dietrich Kebschull [and others]. Hamburg, 1973. pp. 227,36. bibliog. (Hamburg. Hamburgisches Welt-Wirtschafts-Archiv. Studien zur Aussenwirtschaft und Entwicklungspolitik) With English summary.

- Commerce - Mathematical models

HORESH (E.) and LAWSON (C.W.) The measurement of economic instability: an empirical and theoretical analysis with particular reference to trade and planning in less developed countries. [Bath], 1972. fo. 16. bibliog. (University of Bath. Occasional Papers in Economics)

- Communism

KIERNAN (BERNARD P.) The United States, communism, and the emergent world. Bloomington, [Ind., 1972]. pp. 248. bibliog.

UL'IANOVSKII (ROSTISLAV ALEKSANDROVICH) Sotsializm i osvobodivshiesia strany. Moskva, 1972. pp. 557. Collected articles

Construction industry

INTERNATIONAL LABOUR ORGANISATION. Building, Civil Engineering and Public Works Committee. 8th Session Reports. 3. Social problems in the construction industry arising out of the industrialisation of developing countries: third item on the agenda. Geneva, International Labour Office, 1968. pp. 67.

- Copyright

SCHULZE (ERICH) Förderung des Welturheberrechts durch Entwicklungshilfe...Advancement of world copyright through aid to developing countries, etc. Berlin, [1970]. pp. 107. bibliog. (Internationale Gesellschaft für Urheberrecht. Schriftenreihe. Band 44) In various languages.

- Cost and standard of living

BASTER (NANCY) and SCOTT (WOLF) Levels of living and economic growth: a comparative study of six countries 1950-1965; report on an Institute study. Geneva, United Nations Research Institute for Social Development, 1969. pp. 153. bibliog.

- Debts, External

ÅKESSON (ROLF) The transfer mechanism and the foreign debts of low-income countries. [Lund, 1972]. pp. 223. bibliog.

- Defences

BENOIT (EMILE) Defense and economic growth in developing countries. Lexington, Mass., [1973]. pp. 326.

- Deficit financing

MONGIA (J.N.) Impact of deficit financing on economic growth in underdeveloped countries: with a special reference to India. New Delhi, [1971] pp 40.

- Drug trade (pharmaceutical)

WORTZEL (LAWRENCE H.) Technology transfer in the pharmaceutical industry. New York, United Nations Institute for Training and Research, 1971. pp. 53. (Research Reports. No. 14)

UNDERDEVELOPED AREAS - Economic assistance
See ECONOMIC ASSISTANCE

- Economic conditions

SKOROV (GEORGII EFIMOVICH) Razvivaiushchiesia strany: obrazovanie, zaniatost', ekonomicheskii rost. Moskva, 1971. pp. 368.

PETER (HANS BALZ) Sozialökonomische Grundprobleme der Entwicklungsländer. Zürich, [1972]. pp. 187. bibliog.

STEIN (LESLIE) Economic realities in poor countries. Sydney, 1972. pp. 199. bibliog.

- Economic conditions - Mathematical models

ROBINSON (SHERMAN) Sources of growth in less developed countries: a cross-section study. [London], 1970. fo. 31. (London. University. London School of Economics and Political Science. Department of Economics. Discussion Papers. No. 5)

- Economic history

BAIROCH (PAUL) Diagnostic de l'évolution économique du tiers-monde, 1900-1968. 4th ed. Paris, 1970. pp. 259.

BAIROCH (PAUL) Le Tiers-Monde dans l'impasse: le démarrage économique du XVIIIe au XXe siècle. [Paris, 1971]. pp. 372. bibliog.

KHALATBARI (PARVIZ) Ökonomische Unterentwicklung: Mechanismus, Probleme, Ausweg; Einführung in die Probleme des wirtschaftlichen Wachstums der Entwicklungsländer. Frankfurt/M, 1972. pp. 337.

HESSE (KURT) and ISCHINGER (WOLFGANG) Die Entwicklungsschwelle: der Übergang vom Entwicklungsland zum entwickelten Land unter Einbeziehung von drei Testfällen. Berlin, [1973]. pp. 252. bibliogs.

- Economic integration

MENNES (LUDOVICUS BERNARDUS MARIE) Planning economic integration among developing countries. Rotterdam, 1972. pp. 155. bibliog.

- Economic policy

RAYNAUD (EDGAR) Investissements humains: illusions et réalités; essai de problématique sur le sous-emploi rural et les conditions objectives de son utilisation à des fins d'accumulation du capital. Paris, 1969. pp. 318. bibliog.

LEWIS (Sir WILLIAM ARTHUR) The development process, etc. New York, United Nations, 1970. pp. 34. bibliog. (Centre for Economic and Social Information. Executive Briefing Papers. 2)

MILLIKAN (MAX F.) A strategy of development, etc. New York, United Nations, 1970. pp. 50. bibliog. (Centre for Economic and Social Information. Executive Briefing Papers. 1)

PAAUW (DOUGLAS S.) Development strategies in open dualistic economies. [Washington, D.C., 1970]. pp. 53. (National Planning Association. Center for Development Planning. Planning Experience Series. No. 3)

SEMINAR ON THE REALIZATION OF ECONOMIC AND SOCIAL RIGHTS WITH PARTICULAR REFERENCE TO DEVELOPING COUNTRIES, LUSAKA, 1970. Seminar...; organized by the United Nations, Division of Human Rights, in co-operation with the government of Zambia [held at] Lusaka, Zambia, 23 June - 4 July 1970. (ST/TAO/HR/40). New York, United Nations, 1970. pp. 23.

YAYKIRAN (IBRAHIM) Untersuchung zu den Problemen wirtschaftlicher Entwicklung unter besonderer Berücksichtigung der Bedeutung der modernen Wachstumstheorie für die Situation unterentwickelter Länder. [Bamberg, imprint], 1970. pp. 151. bibliog.

BAIROCH (PAUL) Le Tiers-Monde dans l'impasse: le démarrage économique du XVIIIe au XXe siècle. [Paris, 1971]. pp. 372. bibliog.

MUJUNI (FELICIAN) Das Auftreten inländischer Unternehmer in den Entwicklungsländern und ihre Beeinflussung durch die staatliche Wirtschaftspolitik. [Erlangen, imprint, 1971?]. pp. 249,xlvi. bibliog.

"TRETII mir": strategiia razvitiia i upravlenie ekonomikoi. Moskva, 1971. pp. 399.

ANGELOPOULOS (ANGELOS) Le tiers-monde face aux pays riches: perspectives pour l'an 2000. Paris, 1972. pp. 222.

EPPLER (ERHARD) Not much time for the Third World; translated from the German by Gerard Finan. London, [1972]. pp. 143. bibliog.

INTERNATIONAL ECONOMIC ASSOCIATION. Conference, [1970], Bled. The gap between rich and poor nations: proceedings of a conference... edited by Gustav Ranis. London, 1972. pp. 439.

KHALATBARI (PARVIZ) Ökonomische Unterentwicklung: Mechanismus, Probleme, Ausweg; Einführung in die Probleme des wirtschaftlichen Wachstums der Entwicklungsländer. Frankfurt/M, 1972. pp. 337.

KONJUNKTURPOLITIK: Zeitschrift für angewandte Konjunkturforschung. Beihefte. Heft 19. Probleme der Arbeitsteilung zwischen Industrie- und Entwicklungsländern: Bericht über den wissenschaftlichen Teil der 35. Mitgliederversammlung der Arbeitsgemeinschaft deutscher wirtschaftswissenschaftlicher Forschungsinstitute...1972. Berlin, [1972]. pp. 197.

KONRAD (ANTON) Investitionskriterien und Preismechanismus in Entwicklungsländern. Berlin, [1972]. pp. 133. bibliog.

MARCO (LUIS EUGENIO DI) ed. International economics and development: essays in honor of Raúl Prebisch. New York, 1972. pp. 515.

MÖLLER (BIRGER) Employment approaches to economic planning in developing countries; with special reference to the development planning of Ceylon (Sri Lanka). [Copenhagen, 1972]. pp. 304. bibliog. (Scandinavian Institute of Asian Studies. Monograph Series. No. 9)

NAINI (AHMAD) and others. Analyse der Themen und Ergebnisse der dritten Welthandelskonferenz: Probleme der Entwicklungsländer nach der dritten UN-Konferenz für Handel und Entwicklung, UNCTAD III. Hamburg, 1972. pp. 211. bibliog. (Hamburg. Hamburgisches Welt-Wirtschafts-Archiv. Studien zur Aussenwirtschaft und Entwicklungspolitik)

TIUL'PANOV (S.I.) Politische Ökonomie und ihre Anwendung in den Entwicklungsländern; Übersetzung aus dem Russischen ([by] Hermann Mertens [and others]). Frankfurt/Main, [1972]. pp. 463. With summaries in various languages.

UNDERDEVELOPED AREAS - Economic policy (Cont'd.)

VEREIN FÜR SOZIALPOLITIK. Schriften. Neue Folge. Band 69. Das Eigenpotential im Entwicklungsprozess; von Winfried Böll [and others]; herausgegeben von Hermann Priebe. Berlin, [1972]. pp. 100.

BENOIT (EMILE) Defense and economic growth in developing countries. Lexington, Mass., [1973]. pp. 326.

BRATENSTEIN (ROGER) Konjunkturschwankungen in Entwicklungsländern: Erklärungsansätze und theoretische Grundlagen einer Konjunkturpolitik. [Erlangen, imprint, 1973]. pp. 156, xxvii. bibliog.

CORNELISSE (PETRUS AUGUSTUS) Price consistency in development planning. Rotterdam, 1973. pp. 159. bibliog.

RANIS (GUSTAV) ed. The United States and the developing economies. rev. ed. New York, [1973]. pp. 350. bibliog.

SCHULZ (CHRISTA) Möglichkeiten der Übertragung von Wirtschaftswachstum durch internationalen Kapitaltransfer. Hamburg, 1973. pp. 165, xxxiv. bibliog.

- Education

MANDL (PIERRE EMERIC) Preparation of the child for modernization: skills and intellectual requirements; a review of the literature. (UNRISD Reports No.70.16) (UNRISD/70/C/55). Geneva, United Nations Research Institute for Social Development, 1969. pp. 88. bibliog.

SOCIETY FOR INTERNATIONAL DEVELOPMENT. Section Française. Problèmes de l'aide à l'éducation dans les pays du tiers monde: études adressées par la section...à la conference europeenne...a Cologne, en Mai 1970. Paris, [1970?]. pp. 202.

EL-RASHIDI (FATHI) Human aspects of development. Brussels, 1971. pp. 277. bibliog.

HOPKINSON (PETER) The role of film in development. [Paris], United Nations Educational, Scientific and Cultural Organization, [1971]. pp. 51. (Department of Mass Communication. Reports and Papers on Mass Communication. No. 64)

INTERNATIONAL BANK FOR RECONSTRUCTION AND DEVELOPMENT. Sector Working Papers. Education. [Washington], 1971. pp. 35.

ROWLEY (CHARLES DUNFORD) The politics of educational planning in developing countries. Paris, Unesco, 1971. pp. 57. (International Institute for Educational Planning. Fundamentals of Educational Planning. 15)

CASTLE (EDGAR BRADSHAW) Education for self-help: new strategies for developing countries. London, 1972. pp. 163. bibliog.

HAWES (HUGH W.R.) Planning the primary school curriculum in developing countries. Paris, Unesco, 1972. pp. 50. bibliog. (International Institute for Educational Planning. Fundamentals of Educational Planning. 17)

CURLE (ADAM) Educational problems of developing societies with case studies of Ghana, Pakistan, and Nigeria. 2nd ed. New York 1973. pp. 200.

- Education - Bibliography

ALTBACH (PHILIP G.) and NYSTROM (BRADLEY) compilers. Higher education in developing countries: a select bibliography. Cambridge, Mass., 1970. pp. 113. (Harvard University. Center for International Affairs. Occasional Papers in International Affairs. No.24)

- Education - Finance

CHÂU (TA NGOC) and others. Population growth and costs of education in developing countries. Paris, International Institute for Educational Planning, 1972. pp. 313.

- Education - Statistics

KENDALL (W.L.) Statistics of education in developing countries: an introduction to their collection and presentation. Paris, United Nations Educational, Scientific and Cultural Organization, 1968. pp. 88. bibliog. (Statistical Studies and Reports. [No. 13])

- Electricity supply

INTERNATIONAL BANK FOR RECONSTRUCTION AND DEVELOPMENT. Sector Working Papers. Electric power. [Washington], 1971. pp. 23.

- Electronic industries

CHANG (Y.S.) The transfer of technology: economics of offshore assembly; the case of semiconductor industry. New York, United Nations Institute for Training and Research, 1971. pp. 59. (Research Reports. No. 11)

- Emigration and immigration

MARSHALL (ADRIANA) The import of labour: the case of the Netherlands. Rotterdam, 1973. pp. 177. bibliog.

- Fertilizer industry

PRATT (CHRISTOPHER J.) Chemical fertilizer projects: their creation, evaluation and establishment. (ID/SER.F/1). New York, United Nations Industrial Development Organization, 1968. pp. 52. bibliog. (Fertilizer Industry Series. Monographs. No.1)

FINNERAN (J. A.) and MASUR (P. J.) Guide to building an ammonia fertilizer complex. (ID/SER.F/2). New York, United Nations Industrial Development Organization, 1969. pp. 24. (Fertilizer Industry Series. Monographs. No.2)

- Finance

SHAHIN (AMIN MOUSTAFA) Rolle und Bedeutung von Geld und Banken in unterentwickelten Ländern, mit besonderer Berücksichtigung der wirtschaftlichen Entwicklung, dargestellt am Beispiel Aegyptens. Riehen, 1970. pp. 145. bibliog.

HAAN (ROELF L.) Special drawing rights and development: an inquiry into the monetary aspects of a link between special drawing rights and development finance. Leiden, 1971. pp. 184. bibliog.

JAŠIĆ (ZORAN) Fiskalna politika u zemljama u razvoju. Zagreb, 1971. pp. 42. bibliog.

PEACOCK (ALAN TURNER) and SHAW (GRAHAM KEITH) Fiscal policy and the employment problem in less developed countries. Paris, Organisation for Economic Co-operation and Development, 1971. pp. 133. bibliog. (Development Centre. Studies: Employment Series. No. 5).

PIDGEON (G.W.F.) Financial control in developing countries: with particular reference to state corporations. London, 1971. pp. 102.

STOLPER (WOLFGANG FRIEDRICH) Budget, economic policy, and economic performance in underdeveloped countries. Tübingen, 1971. pp. 33. (Kiel. Universität. Institut für Weltwirtschaft. Kieler Vorträge. Neue Folge. 69)

WAGNER (ANTONIN) Steuerprobleme der Entwicklungsländer: die stufenweise Rationalisierung von Steuersystemen als Methode der Entwicklungsfinanzierung. Zürich, [1971]. pp. 272. bibliogs (Zürich. Universität. Wirtschaftswissenschaftliches Institut. [Publications]. Reihe B. Nr.1)

WHITE (JOHN) 1933- . Regional development banks: a study of institutional style. London, [1971]. pp. 204.

GRAIVER (BORIS ZINOV'EVICH) Mezhdunarodnyi bank i razvivaiushchiesia strany. Moskva, 1972. pp. 200.

PREST (ALAN RICHMOND) Public finance in underdeveloped countries. 2nd ed. London, 1972. pp. 208. bibliog.

- Food storage

LIPTON (MICHAEL) Research into the economics of food storage in less developed countries: prospects for a contribution from U.K. technical assistance. Brighton, 1971. pp. 18,2. (Brighton. University of Sussex. Institute of Development Studies. Communications. No. 61)

- Food supply

SANTOS (MILTON) Croissance démographique et consommation alimentaire dans les pays sous-développés. Paris, [1967 in progress]. bibliog. (Centre de Documentation Universitaire. Les Cours de Géographie)

ORR (ELIZABETH) The use of protein-rich foods for the relief of malnutrition in developing countries: an analysis of experience; [published on behalf of the Protein Advisory Group of the United Nations System]. London, Tropical Products Institute, 1972. pp. 71. ([Reports]. G 73)

- Foreign economic relations

KODACHENKO (ALEKSANDR SERGEEVICH) Ekonomicheskoe sotrudnichestvo razvivaiushchikhsia stran: problemy i perspektivy. Moskva, 1968. pp. 326.

DVOŘÁK (LADISLAV) Ekonomicheskie osnovy neokolonializma. Moskva, 1969. pp. 278.

WIGHTMAN (DAVID) The economic interest of industrial countries in the development of the third world, etc. New York, United Nations, 1971. pp. 93. (Centre for Economic and Social Information. Executive Briefing Papers. 5)

ANGELOPOULOS (ANGELOS) The Third World and the rich countries: prospects for the year 2000; translated by N. Constantinidis [and] C.R. Corner. New York, 1972. pp. 248.

HUNTER (ROBERT EDWARDS) and RIELLY (JOHN E.) eds. Development today: a new look at U.S. relations with the poor countries. New York, 1972. pp. 286. bibliog.

ALPERT (PAUL) Partnership or confrontation?: poor lands and rich. New York, [1973]. pp. 269.

- Full employment policies

CAMBRIDGE. University. Overseas Studies Committee. [Summer Conference, 1970]. Prospects for employment opportunities in the nineteen seventies; papers and impressions of the seventh Cambridge Conference on Development Problems, 13th to 24th September 1970 at Jesus College, Cambridge; edited by Ronald Robinson and Peter Johnston. London, H.M.S.O., 1971. pp. 246.

- Handicapped children - Education

COMMONWEALTH SECRETARIAT. Special education in the developing countries of the Commonwealth. London, 1972. pp. 201. bibliog. (Education in the Commonwealth. No. 5)

- Housing

UNITED NATIONS. Committee on Housing, Building and Planning. 1968. Financing for housing and community facilities in developing countries. (ST/SOA/79). New York, 1968. pp. 67.

- Industrial management

ROSS (HAROLD) and others. Management in the developing countries: a field survey. (UNRISD Reports. No. 72.2) Geneva, United Nations Research Institute for Social Development, 1972. pp. 144.

- Industries

UNITED NATIONS INDUSTRIAL DEVELOPMENT ORGANIZATION. 1970- . Summaries of industrial development plans. New York, 1970 in progress. bibliogs. vol. 1. is entitled Summaries of the industrial development plans of thirty countries.

PROBLEMY industrializatsii razvivaiushchikhsia stran. Moskva, 1971. pp. 406.

The ROLE of group action in the industrialization of rural areas: [proceedings of a symposium held in Tel Aviv, 1969]; edited by Joseph Klatzmann [and others]. New York, 1971. pp. 599.

VEREIN FÜR SOZIALPOLITIK. Schriften. Neue Folge. Band 60. Investitions- und Industrialisierungsprobleme in Entwicklungsländern; herausgegeben von Bernhard Pfister. Berlin, 1971. pp. 172.

INTERNATIONAL BANK FOR RECONSTRUCTION AND DEVELOPMENT. Sector Working Papers. Industry. [Washington], 1972. pp. 59.

KAYNOR (RICHARD S.) and SCHULTZ (KONRAD F.) Industrial development: a practical handbook for planning and implementing development programs. New York, 1973. pp. 185. bibliog.

- Information services

U.K. Ministry of Overseas Development. Library. 1970. Guide to sources of information on developing countries: the resources of the Institute of Development Studies, Overseas Development Institute, Voluntary Committee on Overseas Aid and Development and the Ministry of Overseas Development. [London], 1970. pp. 13.

DEUTSCHE STIFTUNG FÜR ENTWICKLUNGSLÄNDER. Central Documentation Branch. Task, working method and information services of the Documentation Branch of the German Foundation for Developing Countries. Bonn, [1971]. pp. 23.

- Investment of public funds

U.K. Overseas Development Administration. 1972. A guide to project appraisal in developing countries. London, 1972. pp. 126. bibliog.

UNDERDEVELOPED AREAS (Cont'd.)

- Investments

INTERNATIONAL CENTRE FOR SETTLEMENT OF INVESTMENT DISPUTES. 1972- . Investment laws of the world: the developing nations. Dobbs Ferry, [1972] in progress. Loose leaf. In English and French.

HALBACH (AXEL J.) Theorie und Praxis der Evaluierung von Projekten in Entwicklungsländern: eine Bestandsaufnahme. München, 1972. pp. 178. bibliog.

- Investments, Foreign

DURAND-REVILLE (LUC) Les investissements privés au service du tiers-monde. Paris, [1970]. pp. 368. bibliog.

PRIVATE foreign investment and the developing world: [papers of a conference]; (edited by Peter Ady). New York, 1971. pp. 275.

VEREIN FÜR SOZIALPOLITIK. Schriften. Neue Folge. Band 60. Investitions- und Industrialisierungsprobleme in Entwicklungsländern; herausgegeben von Bernhard Pfister. Berlin, 1971. pp. 172.

INTERNATIONAL CENTRE FOR SETTLEMENT OF INVESTMENT DISPUTES. 1972- . Investment laws of the world: the developing nations. Dobbs Ferry, [1972] in progress. Loose leaf. In English and French.

CHRISTIAN AID and CATHOLIC FUND FOR OVERSEAS DEVELOPMENT. A third force for the third world: a study of the channels for investment of church trust funds in economic development: report of a working party. London, [1972]. pp. 19.

PANEL ON FOREIGN INVESTMENT IN DEVELOPING COUNTRIES, 3RD, TOKYO, 1971. Report on a meeting held in Tokyo from 29 November to 2 December 1971. (ST/ECA/158). New York, United Nations, 1972. pp. 31.

DOIMI DI DELUPIS (INGRID) Finance and protection of investments in developing countries. Epping, 1973. pp. 183.

- Investments, Foreign (International law)

INTERNATIONAL CENTRE FOR SETTLEMENT OF INVESTMENT DISPUTES. 1972- . Investment laws of the world: the developing nations. Dobbs Ferry, N.Y., [1972] in progress. Loose leaf. In English and French.

- Investments, German

JACOBI (INGO VON) Direktinvestitionen und Export: deutsche Produktions- und Beteiligungsgesellschaften in Entwicklungsländern. Hamburg, 1972. pp. 213. bibliog. (Hamburg. Hamburgisches Welt-Wirtschafts-Archiv. Studien zur Aussenwirtschaft und Entwicklungspolitik) With English summary.

- Investments, Swiss

Les INVESTISSEMENTS privés suisses dans le tiers monde: colloqueséminaire, 2 et 3 juillet 1971; ([organised by the] Institut Universitaire de Hautes Etudes Internationales). 2nd ed. Genève, 1971. pp. 229.

- Labour supply

HOEK (F.J. VAN) The migration of high level manpower from developing to developed countries. The Hague, 1970. pp. 52. bibliog. (Hague. Institute of Social Studies. Publications. Paperback Series. 1)

CAMBRIDGE. University. Overseas Studies Committee. [Summer Conference, 1970]. Prospects for employment opportunities in the nineteen seventies; papers and impressions of the seventh Cambridge Conference on Development Problems, 13th to 24th September 1970 at Jesus College, Cambridge; edited by Ronald Robinson and Peter Johnston. London, H.M.S.O., 1971. pp. 246.

TOWARDS a system of human resources indicators for less developed countries: papers prepared for a UNESCO research project; edited by Zygmunt Gostkowski. Wrocław, 1972. pp. 257. bibliog.

- Libraries

INTERNATIONAL FEDERATION OF LIBRARY ASSOCIATIONS. Pre-Session Seminar for Developing Countries, 1971. International librarianship: surveys of recent developments in developing countries and in advanced librarianship...; edited by George Chandler. London, 1972. pp. 208.

- Medical auxiliaries

FENDALL (N.R.E.) Auxiliaries in health care: programs in developing countries. Baltimore, [1972]. pp. 200. bibliogs.

- Medical care

OFFICE OF HEALTH ECONOMICS. [Studies in Current Health Problems]. No.44. Medical care in developing countries. London, [1972]. pp. 38. bibliog.

- Municipal government

EINFUEHRUNGSSEMINAR UBER FRAGEN DER KOMMUNALEN SELBSTVERWALTUNG, 1962. Bericht über ein Gespräch, etc. Berlin-Charlottenburg, 1962. fo. (iii), pp. 47, fo. 4.

- Munitions

STOCKHOLM INTERNATIONAL PEACE RESEARCH INSTITUTE. The arms trade with the third world. Stockholm, [1971]. pp. 910. bibliog.

- Nutrition

BERG (ALAN) The nutrition factor: its role in national development. Washington, D.C.. [1973]. pp. 290.

INTERNATIONAL CONFERENCE ON NUTRITION, NATIONAL DEVELOPMENT AND PLANNING, MASSACHUSETTS INSTITUTE OF TECHNOLOGY, 1971. Nutrition, national development, and planning: proceedings...; edited by Alan Berg [and others]. Cambridge, Mass., [1973]. pp. 401. bibliogs.

- Physicians

GISH (OSCAR) Doctor migration and world health: the impact of the international demand for doctors on health services in developing countries. London, 1971. pp. 151. bibliog. (Social Administration Research Trust. Occasional Papers on Social Administration. No.43)

- Plantations

BECKFORD (GEORGE L.) Persistent poverty: underdevelopment in plantation economies of the third world. New York, 1972. pp. 303. bibliog.

- Politics

EMERSON (RUPERT) Political modernization: the single-party system. Denver, [1963?]. pp. 30. (Denver. University. Social Science Foundation and Graduate School of International Studies. Monograph Series in World Affairs. [vol. 1]. no. 1)

TIAGUNENKO (VIKTOR LEONIDOVICH) Problemy sovremennykh natsional'no-osvoboditel'nykh revoliutsii. 2nd ed. Moskva, 1969. pp. 352.

NEF, LA. Nouvelle série. 29e année. Nos. 44-45. Mouvements révolutionnaires du tiers-monde. Paris, 1971-72. pp. 255.

POLITICAL development in changing societies: an analysis of modernization; edited by Monte Palmer [and] Larry Stern. Lexington, [1971]. pp. 179.

DODD (C.H.) Political development. London, 1972. pp. 64. bibliog.

PALMER (MONTE) The dilemmas of political development: an introduction to the politics of the developing areas. Itasca, [1973]. pp. 213.

TSURUTANI (TAKETSUGU) The politics of national development: political leadership in transitional societies. New York, [1973]. pp. 193. bibliog.

TULLIS (F. LAMOND) Politics and social change in third world countries. New York, [1973]. pp. 372. bibliog.

- Population

SANTOS (MILTON) Croissance démographique et consommation alimentaire dans les pays sous-développés. Paris, [1967 in progress]. bibliog. (Centre de Documentation Universitaire. Les Cours de Géographie)

CHÂU (TA NGOC) and others. Population growth and costs of education in developing countries. Paris, International Institute for Educational Planning, 1972. pp. 313.

INTERNATIONAL BANK FOR RECONSTRUCTION AND DEVELOPMENT. Sector Working Papers. Population planning. [Washington], 1972. pp. 83.

PETER (HANS BALZ) Sozialökonomische Grundprobleme der Entwicklungsländer. Zürich, [1972]. pp. 187. bibliog.

TREWARTHA (GLENN THOMAS) The less developed realm: a geography of its population. New York, [1972]. pp. 449. bibliogs.

- Religion

WILSON (BRYAN RONALD) Magic and the millennium: a sociological study of religious movements of protest among tribal and third-world peoples. London, 1973. pp. 547. bibliog.

- Research - United Kingdom.

U.K. Central Office of Information. Reference Division. Reference Pamphlets. 103. Britain and the developing countries: research institutions. London, 1972. pp. 44.

BRIGHTON. University of Sussex. Institute of Development Studies. Development studies:...register of UK-based ongoing research. 3rd ed. [Brighton], 1973. 1 vol (unpaged).

- Road accidents

JACOBS (G.D.) and HUTCHINSON (P.) A study of accident rates in developing countries. Crowthorne, 1973. pp. 33. (U.K. Transport and Road Research Laboratory. Reports. LR 546)

- Rural conditions

The ROLE of group action in the industrialization of rural areas: [proceedings of a symposium held in Tel Aviv, 1969]; edited by Joseph Klatzmann [and others]. New York, 1971. pp. 599.

- Saving and investment

RASK (NORMAN) Analysis of capital formation and utilization in less developed countries. Columbus, Ohio, 1969. fo. 126. bibliog. (Ohio State University Department of Agricultural Economics and Rural Sociology. Economics and Sociology Occasional Papers. No. 4)

KRUL (NICLAUS G.) Epargne financière et développement économique: problèmes et politiques d'encouragement à l'épargne des particuliers dans les pays en voie de développement. Paris, [1970]. pp. 177. bibliog.

TUN WAI, U. Financial intermediaries and national savings in developing countries. New York, 1972. pp. 240.

- School sports

SCRIVEN (F.B.) Sports facilities for schools in developing countries: an inventory of experience and proposals for future projects. Paris, United Nations Educational, Scientific and Cultural Organization, 1973. pp. 39. bibliog. (Educational Studies and Documents. New Series. No. 8)

- Scientists

UNITED NATIONS. Interregional Seminar on the Employment, Development and Role of Scientists and Technical Personnel in the Public Service of Developing Countries, Tashkent, 1969. Report of the...Seminar...[held in] Tashkent, Union of Soviet Socialist Republics, 1-14 October 1969. (ST/TAO/M/48 and Adds. 1 and 2). New York, 1970-71. 3 vols.(in 1).

- Sewerage

INTERNATIONAL BANK FOR RECONSTRUCTION AND DEVELOPMENT. Sector Working Papers. Water supply and sewerage. [Washington], 1971. pp. 15.

- Small business

VEPA (RAM K.) Small industry in the seventies. London, [1971]. pp. 307. bibliog.

- Small holdings

UNITED STATES. Agency for International Development. 1973. A.I.D. spring review of small farmer credit. Washington, 1973. 20 vols.(in 7). bibliogs.

- Social conditions

HYMAN (HERBERT HIRAM) and others. Inducing social change in developing communities: an international survey of expert advice. [Geneva], United Nations, Research Institute for Social Development, [1967]. pp. 224.

STAVENHAGEN (RODOLFO) Las clases sociales en las sociedades agrarias. Mexico, 1969 repr. 1970. pp. 292. bibliog.

LLOYD (PETER CUTT) Classes, crises and coups: themes in the sociology of developing countries. London, 1971. pp. 224. bibliog.

TULLIS (F. LAMOND) Politics and social change in third world countries. New York, [1973]. pp. 372. bibliog.

- Social policy

SEMINAR ON THE REALIZATION OF ECONOMIC AND SOCIAL RIGHTS WITH PARTICULAR REFERENCE TO DEVELOPING COUNTRIES, LUSAKA, 1970. Seminar...; organized by the United Nations, Division of Human Rights, in co-operation with the government of Zambia [held at] Lusaka, Zambia, 23 June - 4 July 1970. (ST/TAO/HR/40). New York, United Nations, 1970. pp. 23.

UNDERDEVELOPED AREAS (Cont'd.)

- Social work education

UNITED NATIONS. Department of Economic and Social Affairs. 1969. A handbook of training for family and child welfare. (ST/SOA/85) New York, 1969. pp. 110. bibliog.

- Socialism

DUMONT (RENÉ) and MAZOYER (MARCEL) Socialisms and development;...translated [from the French] by Rupert Cunningham. London, 1973. pp. 352. bibliog.

- Sociological research

AMERICAN ACADEMY OF POLITICAL AND SOCIAL SCIENCE. Annals. vol. 393. Social information for developing countries; special editor of this volume Itzhak Galnoor. Philadelphia, 1971. pp. 205.

PAUSEWANG (SIEGFRIED) Methods and concepts of social research in a rural developing society: a critical appraisal based on experience in Ethiopia. München, [1973]. pp. 204. bibliog. (Ifo-Institut für Wirtschaftsforschung. Afrikastudien. 80)

- Surveys

WORLD LAND USE SURVEY. Occasional Papers. No.9. New possibilities and techniques for land use and related surveys with special reference to the developing countries: papers presented at an international symposium, London... 1970...; (edited by Ian H. Cox). Berkhamsted, 1970. pp. 138. Map in end-pocket.

- Tariffs

JOHANN (HERMANN) Zollpräferenzen zugunsten von unterentwickelten Ländern: ein Beitrag zur aktuellen Diskussion. Hamburg, 1969. pp. 94. (Deutsches Übersee-Institut. Aktuelle Fragen der Weltwirtschaft)

- Taxation

BERGMANN (ARTHUR) Developing countries and international fiscal law. Hannover, [1968]. pp. 102. (Friedrich-Ebert-Stiftung. Forschungsinstitut. Schriftenreihe A. Sozialwissenschaftliche Schriften)

WAGNER (ANTONIN) Steuerprobleme der Entwicklungsländer: die stufenweise Rationalisierung von Steuersystemen als Methode der Entwicklungsfinanzierung. Zürich, [1971]. pp. 272. bibliogs (Zürich. Universität. Wirtschaftswissenschaftliches Institut. [Publications]. Reihe B. Nr.1)

UNDERDEVELOPED AREAS - Technical assistance
See TECHNICAL ASSISTANCE

- Technological innovations

COOPER (CHARLES A.) ed. Science, technology and development: the political economy of technical advance in underdeveloped countries. London, 1973. pp. 199. bibliogs.

- Technologists

UNITED NATIONS. Interregional Seminar on the Employment, Development and Role of Scientists and Technical Personnel in the Public Service of Developing Countries, Tashkent, 1969. Report of the...Seminar...[held in] Tashkent, Union of Soviet Socialist Republics, 1-14 October 1969. (ST/TAO/M/48 and Adds. 1 and 2). New York, 1970-71. 3 vols.(in 1).

- Technology transfer

INTERREGIONAL EXPERT GROUP ON TRANSFER OF OPERATIVE TECHNOLOGY AT THE ENTERPRISE LEVEL, NEW YORK, 1971. Transfer of operative technology at the enterprise level; report of...Group on its Meeting held in New York from 21 to 26 June 1971. (ST/ECA/151). New York, United Nations, 1972. pp. 42.

- Telecommunication

INTERNATIONAL BANK FOR RECONSTRUCTION AND DEVELOPMENT. Sector Working Papers. Telecommunication. [Washington], 1971. pp. 23.

- Tourists

INTERNATIONAL BANK FOR RECONSTRUCTION AND DEVELOPMENT. Sector Working Papers. Tourism. [Washington], 1972. pp. 33.

- Traffic surveys

HOWE (J.D.G.F.) A review of rural traffic-counting methods in developing countries. Crowthorne, 1972. pp. 23. (U.K. Road Research Laboratory. Reports. LR 427)

- Transportation

PREST (ALAN RICHMOND) Financing transport in developing countries. Washington, 1967. 1 vol. (various fo.).

ATTAR (H.) and others. Verkehrsprobleme in Entwicklungsländern. Bern, [1972]. pp. 156.

INTERNATIONAL BANK FOR RECONSTRUCTION AND DEVELOPMENT. Sector Working Papers. Transportation. [Washington], 1972. pp. 56.

HOYLE (B.S.) ed. Transport and development: [readings]. London, 1973. pp. 230. bibliogs.

- Unemployed

The CHALLENGE of unemployment to development and the role of training and research institutes in development; meeting of Directors of Development, Training and Research Institutes Montebello (Quebec)... 13th-17th July, 1970. Paris, Organisation for Economic Co-operation and Development, 1971. pp. 337.

PEACOCK (ALAN TURNER) and SHAW (GRAHAM KEITH) Fiscal policy and the employment problem in less developed countries. Paris, Organisation for Economic Co-operation and Development, 1971. pp. 133. bibliog. (Development Centre. Studies: Employment Series. No. 5).

TURNHAM (DAVID) and JAEGER (INGELIES) The employment problem in less developed countries: a review of evidence. Paris, Organisation for Economic Co-operation and Development, 1971. pp. 154. bibliog. (Development Centre. Studies: Employment Series. No. 1).

- Vocational education

INTERNATIONAL LABOUR ORGANISATION. Metal Trades Committee. 9th Session. Reports. 3. Problems of training at different levels in the metal trades, with particular reference to developing countries: third item on the agenda. Geneva, International Labour Office, 1970. pp. 51.

- Wages - Mathematical models

MODIGLIANI (FRANCO) and TARANTELLI (EZIO) Curva di Phillips, sottosviluppo e disoccupazione strutturali...: tre saggi. [Rome, 1972]. pp. 93. (Ente per gli Studi Monetari, Bancari, e Finanziari Luigi Einaudi. Quaderni di Ricerche. N. 9)

- Water supply

    INTERNATIONAL BANK FOR RECONSTRUCTION AND DEVELOPMENT. Sector Working Papers. Water supply and sewerage. [Washington], 1971. pp. 15.

- Youth

    REUBENS (EDWIN PIERCE) Planning for children and youth within national development planning. Geneva, United Nations Research Institute for Social Development, 1967. pp. 131.

UNDERGROUND LITERATURE

NUTTALL (JEFF) Bomb culture. London, 1970. pp. 252. Originally published in 1968.

FORCADE (THOMAS KING) ed. Underground press anthology. New York, [1972]. pp. 191.

- Canada - Bibliography

    WOODSWORTH (ANNE) compiler. The 'alternative' press in Canada: a checklist of underground, revolutionary, radical, and other alternative serials from 1960. Toronto, [1972]. pp. 74. bibliog.

- Russia

    GERSTENMAIER (CORNELIA) Die Stimme der Stummen: die demokratische Bewegung in der Sowjetunion. 3rd ed. Stuttgart, 1972. pp. 395. bibliog.

    KHRONIKA TEKUSHCHIKH SOBYTII. Uncensored Russia: the human rights movement in the Soviet Union: the annotated text of the unofficial Moscow journal A Chronicle of Current Events, nos. 1-11; edited, introduced and translated by Peter Reddaway. London, 1972. pp. 499.

- United Kingdom - Directories

    NOYCE (JOHN) ed. Directory of alternative media periodicals. Worthing, 1970. pp. 74.

    NOYCE (JOHN) ed. Directory of alternative media periodicals;...with an index compiled by Stephen Watts. 2nd ed. Brighton, 1972. pp. 101, index and suppl. no.1.

- United States

    LEWIS (ROGER) Outlaws of America: the underground press and its context. Harmondsworth, 1972. pp. 204. bibliog.

UNDERGROUND RAILWAYS

- Germany

    JAHNKE (JENS) Beziehungen zwischen Effizienzkriterien unterschiedlich weit gefasster Nutzen-Kosten-Analysen:...dargestellt am Beispiel der Hamburger U-Bahn-Linie Billstedt-Innenstadt. Hamburg, 1972. pp. 257. bibliog.

- United Kingdom - London

    BRUCE (JAMES GRAEME) Steam to silver: an illustrated history of London Transport railway surface rolling stock. London, London Transport Executive, 1970. pp. 166.

    COLLINS (P.H.) and FISHER (R.M.) Victoria Line land use/activity study. [London], London Transport Executive, 1971. pp. 25. (Department of Operational Research. Operational Research Reports. 179)

    NESS (M.P.) Victoria Line study: household data analysis manual. [London], 1971. pp. 9. (London. Greater London Council. Department of Planning and Transportation. Research Memoranda. 278)

    BATES (J.J.) Land redevelopment potential and utilisation of capacity on the Victoria Line. [London], London Transport Executive, 1972. 1 pamphlet (various pagings). (Department of Operational Research. Operational Research Reports. 183)

    BRUCE (JAMES GRAEME) Tube trains under London: a short illustrated history of London Transport tube rolling stock. rev. ed. London, London Transport Executive, 1972. pp. 116.

    BATES (J.J.) Fleet Line land-use redevelopment study: methodology and modelling assumptions. [London], London Transport Executive, 1973. 1 pamphlet (various pagings). (Department of Operational Research. Operational Research Reports. 196)

    LONDON TRANSPORT EXECUTIVE. Victoria Line traffic study: a report on the traffic implications of the Victoria Line north of Victoria. London, 1973. pp. 44, 2 maps.

UNEMPLOYED

[RED INTERNATIONAL OF LABOUR UNIONS]. The world economic situation during recent years; [and] The position of the working class during 1924-1927; [and] Unemployment. n.p., [192-?]. fo. various. Mimeographed copy, unpublished.

PUEL (HUGUES) Chômage et capitalismes contemporains. Paris, [1971]. pp. 287. bibliog.

PHELPS (EDMUND S.) Inflation policy and unemployment theory: the cost-benefit approach to monetary planning. London, 1972. pp. 322.

- Mathematical models

    SABOLO (Y.) La croissance sectorielle de l'emploi. Genève, Bureau International du Travail, 1969. pp. 46.

    GAGLIANI (GIORGIO) Disoccupazione involuntaria e curva di Phillips. Milano, 1971. pp. 47. bibliog. (Rome. Università. Istituto di Politica Economica e Finanziaria. Pubblicazioni)

- Africa

    RAYNAUD (EDGAR) Investissements humains: illusions et réalités; essai de problématique sur le sous-emploi rural et les conditions objectives de son utilisation à des fins d'accumulation du capital. Paris, 1969. pp. 318. bibliog.

- Argentine Republic

    ARGENTINE REPUBLIC. Instituto Nacional de Estadistica y Censos. Encuesta de empleo y desempleo. a., 1970- n.p. 1966/1969 catalogued separately and filed at R(0) 82(315)

- Australia - New South Wales

    The COST of sickness and unemployment: (the proceedings of a seminar)... held at Sydney University on Saturday, 3rd May, 1969; [organized by the Council of Social Service of New South Wales]. Sydney, [1969]. pp. 79.

- Austria

    JAHODA (MARIE) and others. Marienthal: the sociography of an unemployed community. Chicago, 1971. pp. 128.

- Canada

    CANADA. Statistics Canada. Labour Division. 1971. Facts about the unemployed; Données sur le chômage, 1960-1971. Ottawa, 1971. pp. 48. In English and French.

UNEMPLOYED - Canada (Cont'd.)

CANADA. Prices and Incomes Commission. 1972. Final report: inflation, unemployment and incomes policy; Rapport final: l'inflation le chômage et la politique des revenus; (with Summary report). Ottawa, 1972. pp. 135,56; 139,67. In English and French.

KALISKI (S.F.) The trade-off between inflation and unemployment: some explorations of the recent evidence for Canada. Ottawa, 1972. pp. 114. (Canada. Economic Council. Special Studies. No. 22)

THIRSK (WAYNE R.) Regional dimensions of inflation and unemployment; Les aspects régionaux des problèmes de l'inflation et du chômage; a research report prepared for the Prices and Incomes Commission. Ottawa, Information Canada, 1973. pp. 155,165. bibliog.

- Columbia

UNIVERSIDAD DE LOS ANDES [BOGOTA]. Centro de Estudios sobre Desarrollo Economico. Empleo y desempleo en Colombia. Bogota, 1968. pp. 315.

- Europe

DELAMOTTE (YVES) The social partners face the problems of productivity and employment: a study in comparative industrial relations. Paris, Organisation for Economic Co-operation and Development, 1971. pp. 202.

KAYSER (BERNARD) Manpower movements and labour markets: report on the findings of the surveys conducted under the programme initiated by the Working Party on Migration, etc. Paris, Organisation for Economic Co-operation and Development, 1971. pp. 210.

- India

INDIA. Committee of Experts on Unemployment Estimates. 1970. Report; [M.L. Dantwala, chairman] [Delhi], 1970. pp. 203.

- Guatemala

THORBECKE (ERIK) and STOUTJESDIJK (E.) Employment and output: a methodology applied to Peru and Guatemala. Paris, Organisation for Economic Co-operation and Development, 1971. pp. 213. bibliog. (Development Centre. Studies: Employment Series. No. 2)

- Iran

BARTSCH (WILLIAM HENRY) Problems of employment creation in Iran. Geneva, International Labour Office, 1970. pp. 86. bibliog. (Employment Research Papers)

- Italy

FERRI (PIERO) La disoccupazione in un processo di sviluppo economico: alcuni aspetti dell'esperienza italiana 1951-1968. Milano, 1971. pp. 160.

MELDOLESI (LUCA) Disoccupazione ed esercito industriale di riserva in Italia. Bari, 1972. pp. 204.

- Kenya

KENYA. National Assembly. Select Committee on Unemployment. 1970. Report. Nairobi, 1970. pp. 59.

EMPLOYMENT, incomes and equality: a strategy for increasing productive employment in Kenya; report of an inter-agency team financed by the United Nations Development Programme and organised by the International Labour Office. Geneva, International Labour Office, 1972. pp. 600.

- Malaysia

CHOUDHRY (N.S.) Socio-economic sample survey of households, Malaysia, 1967-68: employment and unemployment (west Malaysia). [Kuala Lumpur, Department of Statistics, 1970]. 1 vol. (various pagings).

- Morocco

MOROCCO. Service Central des Statistiques. 1958. Une enquête par sondage sur l'emploi à Casablanca, mars, 1958; (réalisée par P. Dubois). Rabat, [1958?]. pp. (24).

- Netherlands

HAGUE. Bureau voor Statistiek. Tweede onderzoek naar de levensomstandigheten van ondersteunde gezinnen te 's-Gravenhage, Maart t./m. Mei 1935, etc. s'-Gravenhage, 1937. pp. 106. Title page, contents and some tables in Dutch and French, with French summary.

- Pakistan

KUHNEN (FRITHJOF) Problems of employment promotion in Pakistan. Geneva, International Labour Office, [1971]. pp. 55. bibliog. (Employment Research Papers)

- Peru

THORBECKE (ERIK) and STOUTJESDIJK (E.) Employment and output: a methodology applied to Peru and Guatemala. Paris, Organisation for Economic Co-operation and Development, 1971. pp. 213. bibliog. (Development Centre. Studies: Employment Series. No. 2)

- Philippine Islands

HSIEH (C.) Employment problems and policies in the Philippines. Geneva, International Labour Office, 1969. pp. 135. (Employment Research Papers)

- Russia

ROGACHEVSKAIA (LIUDMILA SOLOMONOVNA) Likvidatsiia bezrabotitsy v SSSR, 1917-1930 gg. Moskva, 1973. pp. 382. bibliog.

- Sri Lanka

RICHARDS (P.J.) Employment and unemployment in Ceylon. Paris, Organisation for Economic Co-operation and Development, 1971. pp. 211. bibliog. (Development Centre. Studies: Employment Series. No. 3)

[SEERS (DUDLEY) and others] Matching employment opportunities and expectations: a programme of action for Ceylon: the report [and technical papers] of an inter-agency team organised by the International Labour Office. Geneva, International Labour Office, 1971. 2 pts.(in 1).

- United Kingdom

MANUFACTURERS' RELIEF COMMITTEE. Report of the committee appointed at a public meeting, held at the City of London Tavern...on the 2nd of May, 1826, for considering the best means to afford relief to the "working manufacturers" suffering distress through want of employment; with an appendix. London, 1829. pp. 119.

LABOUR PARTY. Job's talks: unemployment. London, [1924]. pp. (4).

FREEMAN (C.R. BOYD) A million jobs for our unemployed. Ripley, [c.1930]. pp. 8.

MANCHESTER AND SALFORD TRADES COUNCIL. What the Trades Council wants to know: the slow murder of the unemployed. [Manchester, 1932]. pp. (4).

WARBURTON (EDWARD) and BUTLER (CARL) 'Disallowed' the tragedy of the means test. London, 1935. pp. 160.

GOLDTHORPE (HARRY) Room at the bottom. Leeds, 1959 repr. 1972. pp. 48. (Independent Labour Party. Square One Pamphlets. 4)

FOOT (PAUL) Unemployment: (the socialist answer). Glasgow, 1963. pp. 24. (Labour Worker, The. Pamphlets)

GOULD (TONY) and KENYON (JOE) Stories from the dole queue. London, 1972. pp. 191.

HARMAN (CHRIS) and PEERS (DAVE) Unemployment and how to fight it. London, 1971. pp. 27.

HARRIS (JOSÉ) Unemployment and politics: a study in English social policy, 1886-1914. Oxford, 1972. pp. 411. bibliog.

PROSPECTS for employment: a Tory view; [by] Adam Butler [and others]; edited by Timothy Raison. London, 1972. pp. 118. (Conservative Political Centre. [Publications]. No. 504)

ROBERTS (ERNIE) The fight against unemployment. Nottingham, [1972]. pp. 17. (Institute for Workers' Control. Pamphlet Series. No. 30)

SMITH (BARBARA M.D.) Employment opportunities in Bilston. Birmingham, 1972. fo.31,5. (Birmingham. University. Centre for Urban and Regional Studies. Research Memoranda. 15)

WE demand the right to work; [by Stephen Johns and others]. London, [1972]. pp. 64. (Young Socialists (Trotskyite). Pamphlets)

MEN out of work: a study of unemployment in three English towns; [by] M.J. Hill [and others]. Cambridge, 1973. pp. 194. bibliog.

- United Kingdom - Wales

JONES (MERVYN) Life on the dole. London, [1972]. pp. 142.

WELSH COUNCIL. Wales: employment and the economy; a report submitted by the Welsh Council to the Secretary of State for Wales. [Cardiff?], 1972. fo. 23.

- United States

HOPKINS (HARRY LLOYD) Spending to save: the complete story of relief; [reprint of work issued in 1936 with new] introduction by Roger Daniels. Seattle, [1972]. pp. 197.

PALMER (GLADYS LOUISE) and WOOD (KATHERINE D.) Urban workers on relief...; [reprint in one volume of the two-volume first edition published in 1936]. New York, 1971. 2 vols.(in 1). (United States. Work Projects Administration. Division of Social Research. Research Monographs. 4)

GEDDES (ANN ELIZABETH) Trends in relief expenditures 1910-1935; [reprint of work first published in Washington, 1937]. New York, 1971. pp. 117. (United States. Work Projects Administration. Division of Social Research. Research Monographs. 10)

KOMAROVSKY (MIRRA) The unemployed man and his family: the effect of unemployment upon the status of the man in fifty-nine families. New York, [1940] repr. 1971. pp. 163. bibliog.

SALMOND (JOHN A.) The Civilian Conservation Corps, 1933-1942: a New Deal case study. Durham, N.C., 1967. pp. vii, 240. bibliog.

HARD-CORE UNEMPLOYMENT CONFERENCE, WEST VIRGINIA UNIVERSITY, 1968. The poor and the hard-core unemployed: recommendations for new approaches; edited by Wil J. Smith. Morgantown, 1970 repr 1971. pp. 111. bibliog.

CONGRESSIONAL SEMINAR ON PUBLIC SERVICE EMPLOYMENT, 1971. The political economy of public service employment; [papers and discussions of the...seminar... conducted by the W.E. Upjohn Institute for Employment Research]; edited by Harold L. Sheppard [and others]. Lexington, Mass., [1972]. pp. 463. bibliogs.

FRIEDLANDER (STANLEY) Unemployment in the urban core: an analysis of thirty cities with policy recommendations. New York, 1972. pp. 255. (Columbia University. Graduate School of Business. Conservation of Human Resources Project. Conservation of Human Resources Studies)

- United States - Mathematical models

ROSTKER (BERNARD) Performance rewards for services to the employable poor: a theoretical framework. [Santa Monica?], 1972. pp. 27 (Rand Corporation. [Papers]. 4885)

- United States - New York (City)

NATIONAL COMMITTEE AGAINST DISCRIMINATION IN HOUSING. Jobs and housing: a study of employment and housing opportunities for racial minorities in the suburban areas of the New York Metropolitan Region: an interim report, etc. New York, 1970. pp. 250.

- Uruguay - Statistics

URUGUAY. Direccion General de Estadistica y Censos. 1969. Encuesta de hogares: ocupacion y desocupacion, Montevideo, octubre-diciembre, 1968. Montevideo, [1969?]. fo. 31.

UNEMPLOYMENT, TECHNOLOGICAL

YUDELMAN (MONTAGUE) and others. Technological change in agriculture and employment in developing countries. Paris, Organisation for Economic Co-operation and Development, 1971. pp. 204. (Development Centre. Studies: Employment Series. No. 4)

- Mathematical models

MODIGLIANI (FRANCO) and TARANTELLI (EZIO) Curva di Phillips, sottosviluppo e disoccupazione strutturali...: tre saggi. [Rome, 1972]. pp. 93. (Ente per gli Studi Monetari, Bancari, e Finanziari Luigi Einaudi. Quaderni di Ricerche. N. 9)

UNIDAD POPULAR

CLARK (KATE) Chile: reality and prospects of Popular Unity. London, 1972. pp. 142. bibliog.

NORTH AMERICAN CONGRESS ON LATIN AMERICA. New Chile. [New York, 1972]. pp. 175.

UNINCORPORATED SOCIETIES

- United Kingdom

DALY (D.) Club law; sixth edition by J.N.Martin. London, 1970. pp. 308

UNION CIVICA RADICAL

El RADICALISMO; [by] Luis Alberto Romero [and others]. Buenos Aires 1968. pp. 319.

UNION DES DEMOCRATES POUR LA REPUBLIQUE

AVRIL (PIERRE) U.D.R. et gaullistes. [Paris, 1971]. pp. 96. bibliog.

UNION POUR LA NOUVELLE REPUBLIQUE

DEBRE (MICHEL) Sur le gaullisme. [Paris, 1967]. pp. 24.

UNION POUR LA NOUVELLE REPUBLIQUE
See also UNION DES DEMOCRATES POUR LA REPUBLIQUE

UNION PROGRESSISTE SENEGALAISE

ZUCCARELLI (FRANÇOIS) Un parti politique africain: l'Union Progressiste Sénégalaise. Paris, 1970. pp. 401. bibliog.

UNITARIAN CHURCHES IN THE UNITED KINGDOM

CARLTON (ERIC JAMES) The Unitarian movement in England; [Ph. D. (London) thesis]. 1972. fo. 258. bibliog. Typescript: unpublished. This thesis is the property of London University and may not be removed from the Library.

UNITARIANISM

CARLTON (ERIC JAMES) The Unitarian movement in England; [Ph. D. (London) thesis]. 1972. fo. 258. bibliog. Typescript: unpublished. This thesis is the property of London University and may not be removed from the Library.

UNITARIAN ARAB EMIRATES

- Economic conditions

FENELON (KEVIN GERARD) The United Arab Emirates: an economic and social survey. London, 1973. pp. 145. bibliog

- Social conditions

FENELON (KEVIN GERARD) The United Arab Emirates: an economic and social survey. London, 1973. pp. 145. bibliog.

UNITED KINGDOM

- Air force

BALFOUR (HAROLD HARINGTON) 1st Baron Balfour of Inchrye. Wings over Westminster. London, 1973. pp. 224.

- Antiquities

ALCOCK (LESLIE) Arthur's Britain: history and archaeology, A.D. 367-634. Harmondsworth, 1973. pp. 415. bibliog. First published 1971.

SPARROW (CHARLES) and PEACE (DAVID) Public inquiries: presenting the conservation case; notes from a C[ouncil for] B[ritish A[rchaeology] conference. London, 1971. pp. 23.

WILDMAN (SAMUEL GERALD) The black horsemen: English inns and King Arthur. London, 1971. pp. 176. bibliog.

BRUCE-MITFORD (RUPERT LEO SCOTT) The Sutton Hoo ship-burial: a handbook. 2nd ed. London, 1972. pp. 103. bibliog.

- Appropriations and expenditures

FEINSTEIN (CHARLES HILLIARD) National income, expenditure and output of the United Kingdom, 1855-1965. Cambridge, 1972. 1 vol. (various pagings). bibliog. (National Institute of Economic and Social Research and Cambridge. University. Department of Applied Economics. Studies in the National Income and Expenditure of the United Kingdom. 6)

U.K. Treasury. 1972. Public expenditure white papers: handbook on methodology. London, 1972. pp. 57.

U.K. Treasury. 1972. Supply and other financial procedure of the House of Commons. [London, 1972]. pp. 114. Loose-leaf binder.

GOLDMAN (Sir SAMUEL) The developing system of public expenditure management and control. London, H.M.S.O., 1973. pp. 89. (Civil Service College [U.K.]. Studies. 2)

- Armed forces

D'OMBRAIN (NICHOLAS) War machinery and high policy: defence administration in peacetime Britain, 1902-1914. London, 1973. pp. 302. bibliog.

- Armed forces - Finance

STOCKHOLM INTERNATIONAL PEACE RESEARCH INSTITUTE. Research Reports. No. 10. The meaning and measurement of military expenditure. Stockholm, [1973]. pp. 34.

- Armed forces - Religious life

RATIONALIST PRESS ASSOCIATION. Compulsory church-going in the Army and Navy. London, 1918. pp. 6.

- Army

DASH (SAMUEL) Justice denied: a challenge to Lord Widgery's report on "Bloody Sunday". New York, [1972]. pp. 48.

- Army - Accounting

CLINTON (Sir HENRY) A letter...to the commissioners of public accounts relative to some observations in their seventh report which may be judged to imply censure on the late commanders in chief of His Majesty's army in North America. London, Debrett, 1784. pp. 31.

- Army - History

BOND (BRIAN JAMES) The Victorian army and the Staff College, 1854-1914. London, 1972. pp. 350.

- Army - History - Sources

POWNALL (Sir HENRY ROYDS) Chief of staff: the diaries of Lieutenant-General Sir Henry Pownall;... edited by Brian Bond. London, 1972 in progress.

- Biography

The DICTIONARY of national biography: (corrections and additions...) cumulated from the Bulletin of the Institute of Historical Research, University of London, covering the years 1923-1963. Boston, Mass., 1966. pp. 212.

BELLAMY (JOYCE M.) and SAVILLE (JOHN) Dictionary of labour biography. London, 1972 in progress.

WHO'S who in finance. Epping, [1972]. pp. 615.

HARRISON (BRIAN HOWARD) Dictionary of British temperance biography. Coventry, 1973. pp. 139. (Society for the Study of Labour History. Aids to Research. No. 1)

- Census

    GLASS (DAVID VICTOR) Numbering the people: the eighteenth-century population controversy and the development of census and vital statistics in Britain. Farnborough, 1973. pp. 205.

- Census - 1966

    THRASHER (P.A.) General Register Office sample census, 1966: extracts from workplace and transport tables, Part 2. [London], 1968. pp. 8. (London. Greater London Council. Department of Highways and Transportation. Research Memoranda. 122)

    U.K. Census, 1966. Sample census, 1966: availability of data. London, 1969. fo. (46).

    U.K. Department of Employment and Productivity. Statistics Division. 1969. 1966 census of population: Department of Employment and Productivity Paper No. 2: the economically inactive. [London, 1969]. fo. 4; various.

    U.K. Department of Employment and Productivity. Statistics Division. 1970. 1966 sample census of population: Department of Employment and Productivity paper no. 3: part-time workers. [London, 1970?]. fo. 7; various.

    U.K. Department of Employment and Productivity. Statistics Division. 1970. 1966 sample census of population: Department of Employment and Productivity paper no. 4: [Activity rates for regions and sub-regions]. London, [1970]. fo. (4).

    U.K. Department of Employment and Productivity. Statistics Division. 1970. 1966 sample census of population: Department of Employment and Productivity paper no. 5: [General notes]. [London, 1970]. fo. 8.

    U.K. Department of Employment. [Statistics Division]. 1971. 1966 sample census of population: Department of Employment paper no. 6: females at work. [London, 1971]. fo. (14).

    U.K. Department of Employment. [Statistics Division]. 1971. 1966 sample census of population: Department of Employment paper no. 7: females not at work. [London, 1971]. pp. 2; fo. (10).

    U.K. Department of Employment. [Statistics Division]. 1971. 1966 sample census of population: Department of Employment paper no. 8: sub-divisional information. [London, 1971]. fo. (14).

    U.K. Social Survey. [Reports. New Series.] 391. A quality check on the 1966 ten per cent sample census of England and Wales; by Percy Gray and Frances A. Gee. London, 1972. pp. 226.

- Census - 1971

    U.K. Census, 1971. Census, 1971: Great Britain: advance analysis. London, 1972. pp. 281.

    U.K. Census, 1971. Information papers. 5. Statistics for grid squares. [Titchfield, 1972]. pp. 6.

    U.K. Census, 1971. Census, 1971: Great Britain: tabulation prospectus. No. 5. Migration. [Titchfield], 1973. 1 vol. (unpaged).

    U.K. Census, 1971. Census, 1971: Great Britain: tabulation prospectus. No.6. Workplace. [Titchfield], 1973. 1 pamphlet (unpaged).

    U.K. Census, 1971. Census, 1971: England and Wales: tabulation prospectus. No. 7. Fertility. Titchfield, 1973. 1 vol. (unpaged).

    U.K. Census, 1971. Census, 1971: Great Britain: tabulation prospectus. No.8. Welsh language in Wales. [Titchfield], 1973. 1 pamphlet (unpaged).

    U.K. Census, 1971. Census, 1971: Great Britain: tabulation prospectus. No.9. Qualified manpower. [Titchfield], 1973. 1 vol. (unpaged).

    U.K. Census, 1971. Census, 1971: Great Britain: tabulation prospectus. No. 10. Economic activity. [Titchfield], 1973. 1 vol. (unpaged).

    U.K. Census, 1971. Census, 1971: Great Britain: tabulation prospects. No. 11. H[ousehold] c[omposition] a[nalysis]. [Titchfield], 1973. 1 vol. (unpaged).

- Charters, grants, privileges, etc.

    FINBERG (HERBERT PATRICK REGINALD) The early charters of the West Midlands. 2nd ed. Leicester, 1972. pp. 263.

- Church history

    BELLAIRS (KENNETH FFARINGTON) Is Christianity a forgery?: is English history a fraud? London, [1895]. pp. 36.

    MACKINTOSH (WILLIAM HORATIUS) Disestablishment and liberation: the movement for the separation of the Anglican Church from state control. London, 1972. pp. 344.

- Church history - Sources

    PORTER (HARRY CULVERWELL) ed. Puritanism in Tudor England. London, 1970. pp. 311. bibliog.

- Civilization

    COX (CHARLES BRIAN) and DYSON (ANTHONY EDWARD) eds. The twentieth-century mind: history, ideas, and literature in Britain. London, 1972 in progress. bibliogs.

    JOHNSON (PAUL) The offshore islanders. London, [1972]. pp. 466.

    McMILLAN (JAMES) The roots of corruption: the erosion of traditional values in Britain from 1960 to the present day. London, 1972. pp. 210.

- Climate

    LAMB (HUBERT HORACE) British Isles weather types and a register of the daily sequence of circulation patterns, 1861-1971. London, 1972. pp. 85. bibliog. (U.K. Meteorological Office. Geophysical Memoirs. No. 116)

- Clubs

    COMMISSION ON INDUSTRIAL RELATIONS [U.K.]. The hotel and catering industry. Part 3. Public houses, clubs and other sectors. London, H.M.S.O., 1973. pp. 70. (Reports. No.36) Part 1 issued as British Parliamentary Paper, Cmnd. 4789, session 1970/71.

- Commerce

    MISSELDEN (EDWARD) Free trade; or, The meanes to make trade florish, etc: [facsimile reprint of the work originally published in London, 1622]. 2nd ed. New York, 1971. pp. 135.

    MERCHANT (THOMAS) Esq., pseud. Peace and trade, war and taxes; or, The irreparable damage of our trade in case of a war, etc. London, Brindley, 1729. pp. 32.

    HOW to capture German trade; compiled and edited from articles published in The Standard and The Evening Standard and St. James's Gazette. London, 1914. pp. 96.

UNITED KINGDOM - Commerce (Cont'd.)

ECONOMIC DEVELOPMENT COMMITTEE FOR PRINTING AND PUBLISHING. Imports and exports of print. [London, 1969]. pp. 8.

U.K. Board of Trade. 1969. An introduction to the Board of Trade. London, 1969. pp. 53.

HAN (S.S.) and LIESNER (HANS HUBERTUS KARL KURT OTTO) Britain and the Common Market: the effect of entry on the pattern of manufacturing production. Cambridge, 1971. pp. 116. (Cambridge. University. Department of Applied Economics. Occasional Papers. 27)

FRANCIS (ALAN DAVID) The wine trade. London, 1972. pp. 353. bibliog.

HORSMAN (MALCOLM) The case for the international trading companies. London, [1972]. pp. 7.

KREDIETBANK. Le marché britannique à votre portée. [Brussels], 1972. pp. 72

NATIONAL PORTS COUNCIL. Economics Division. United Kingdom international trade, 1975. London, 1972. pp. 38. bibliog.

OHL (INGO) Die Levante und Indien in der Verkehrspolitik Venedigs, der Engländer und der Holländer 1580-1623. Kiel, 1972. pp. 145. bibliog. With English summary.

SOROKINA (VALENTINA FEDOROVNA) Vnutrenniaia torgovlia Anglii. Moskva, 1972. pp. 188. bibliog.

U.K. Central Office of Information. Reference Division. 1972. Britain's external trade and payments. rev. ed. London, 1972. pp. 25. bibliog.

WILLIAMS (JUDITH BLOW) British commercial policy and trade expansion 1750-1850; with a bibliographical chapter by David M. Williams. Oxford, 1972. pp. 514. bibliog.

DAVIS (RALPH) Professor of Economic History, Leiceste University. English overseas trade 1500-1700. London, 1973. pp. 64. bibliog. (Economic History Society. Studies in Economic History)

POSTAN (MICHAEL MOISSEY) Medieval trade and finance. Cambridge, 1973. pp. 382.

TOOKEY (DOUGLAS) ed. Harmonization of business practice in the Common Market: a guide to essential changes in UK procedures and training. Epping, 1973. pp. 204. bibliogs.

- Commerce - Bibliography

QUARITCH (BERNARD). Catalogues. No. 888. A catalogue of books illustrating the growth of English trade, 1700-1750, offered for sale by Bernard Quaritch Ltd. London, 1968. pp. 140.

- Commerce - Directories

STUBBS' directory, 1972: manufacturers, merchant shippers, and professional. London, 1972. 1 vol. (various pagings).

- Commerce - Mathematical models

REES (R.D.) and LAYARD (PETER RICHARD GRENVILLE) The determinants of UK imports. London, H.M.S.O., 1971. pp. 25. bibliog. (Government Economic Service Occasional Papers. 3)

HEATHFIELD (DAVID F.) and PEARCE (I.F.) A view of the Southampton econometric model of the U.K. and its trading partners. Southampton, 1972. fo. 89. (Southampton. University. Department of Economics and Department of Econometrics. An Econometric Model of the U.K. Economy and its Trading Partners. Progress Papers. T.7)

- Commerce - America, Latin

NARANJO (JOHN) and PORTER (RICHARD C.) The impact of the Commonwealth preference system on the exports of Latin America to the United Kingdom. Ann Arbor, 1972. pp. 37. bibliog. (Michigan University. Center for Research on Economic Development. Discussion Papers. No. 18)

PLATT (DESMOND CHRISTOPHER ST MARTIN) Latin America and British trade, 1806-1914. London, 1972. pp. 352.

MARETT (Sir ROBERT HUGH KIRK) Latin America: British trade and investment. London, 1973. pp. 248.

- Commerce - Austria

PISTOR (ERICH) Die Wiederbelebung der Handelsbeziehungen zu England und die kaufmännische Gesellschaftsreise der Wiener Handelskammer nach London. Wien, 1920. pp. 39. (Niederösterreichische Handels- und Gewerbekammer. Exportberichte. Nr. 21)

- Commerce - Baltic States

ZINS (HENRYK) England and the Baltic in the Elizabethan era; translated by H.C. Stevens. Totowa, N.J., [1972]. pp. 347. bibliog.

- Commerce - Belgium

WERKGROEP INTERNATIONALE ECONOMIE. Het Verenigd Koninkrijk in de E.E.G.?: voor- en nadelen voor de Belgische economie. Antwerpen, 1970. pp. 327. (Katholieke Universiteit te Leuven. Instituut voor Economisch, Sociaal en Politiek Onderzoek. Centrum voor Economische Studiën. [Publications]. 27)

- Commerce - France

NALLY (MARGARET) Selling consumer goods to France; [written for the British National Export Council] London, H.M.S.O., 1971. pp. 83.

- Commerce - Germany

LUNTOWSKI (GUSTAV) Dortmunder Kaufleute in England im 13. und 14. Jahrhundert: ein Quellennachweis. Dortmund, 1970. pp. 114. (Dortmund. Stadtarchiv. Veröffentlichungen. Heft 4)

P.A. MANAGEMENT CONSULTANTS LTD. South Germany report; [originally prepared on behalf of British National Export Council]. London, Department of Trade and Industry, 1971. 2 pts.

- Commerce - India

INDIA. Office of the Economic Adviser. 1947. A memorandum on the imperial preference and India's export trade with the United Kingdom. [Delhi], 1947. pp. 31.

- Commerce - Ireland (Republic)

McALEESE (DERMOT) and MARTIN (JOHN PAUL) Irish manufactured imports from the UK in the sixties: the effects of AIFTA. Dublin, 1973. pp. 88. bibliog. (Economic and Social Research Institute. Papers. No. 70)

- Commerce - Roumania

CERNOVODEANU (PAUL) England's trade policy in the Levant and her exchange of goods with the Romanian countries under the latter Stuarts, 1660-1714; (translated by Mary Lăzărescu). Bucharest, 1972. pp. 157. bibliog. (Academia de Ştiinte Sociale şi Politice a Republicii Socialiste România. Bibliotheca Historica Romaniae Studies. 41(2))

- **Commercial policy**

    [BRIGHT (HENRY ARTHUR)] Our free trade policy examined with respect to its real bearing upon native industry, our colonial system and the institutions and ultimate destinies of the nation: by a Liverpool merchant. London, Whittaker, 1846. pp. 46.

    YOUNG (GEORGE FREDERICK) Free-trade fallacies refuted; in a series of letters to the editor of the Morning Herald. London, Madden, 1852. pp. 47.

    JONAS (ERICH) Chamberlains handelspolitische Reformprojekte: ihre Grundlagen und ihre Grenzen. [Sagan, imprint], 1906. pp. 126. bibliog.

    BURN (DUNCAN LYALL) Chemicals under free trade: European and global options. London, 1971. pp. 141. (Atlantic Trade Study. Papers)

    TURNER (BARRY HORACE PAGE) Free trade and protection. London, 1971. pp. 147. bibliog.

    WENDT (BERND JUERGEN) Economic Appeasement: Handel und Finanz in der britischen Deutschland-Politik 1933-1939. Düsseldorf, [1971]. pp. 695. bibliog. (Hamburg. Hansische Universität. Studien zur Modernen Geschichte. Band 3)

    CERNOVODEANU (PAUL) England's trade policy in the Levant and her exchange of goods with the Romanian countries under the latter Stuarts, 1660-1714; (translated by Mary Lăzărescu). Bucharest, 1972. pp. 157. bibliog. (Academia de Ştiinţe Sociale şi Politice a Republicii Socialiste România. Bibliotheca Historica Romaniae. Studies. 41(2))

    REMPEL (RICHARD A.) Unionists divided: Arthur Balfour, Joseph Chamberlain and the Unionist Free Traders. Newton Abbot, 1972. pp. 236. bibliog.

    WILLIAMS (JUDITH BLOW) British commercial policy and trade expansion 1750-1850; with a bibliographical chapter by David M. Williams. Oxford, 1972. pp. 514. bibliog.

- **Commercial treaties - Ireland (Republic)**

    McALEESE (DERMOT) and MARTIN (JOHN PAUL) Irish manufactured imports from the UK in the sixties: the effects of AIFTA. Dublin, 1973. pp. 88. bibliog. (Economic and Social Research Institute. Papers. No. 70)

- **Constitution**

    MARSHALL (GEOFFREY) and MOODIE (GRAEME COCHRANE) Some problems of the constitution. 5th ed. London, 1971. pp. 160. bibliog.

    U.K. Central Office of Information. Reference Division. Reference Pamphlets. 40. The central government of Britain. 7th ed. London, 1971. pp. 34. bibliog.

    BRENNAN (T.) Politics and government in Britain: an introductory survey. Cambridge, [1972]. pp. 332. bibliog

    CROSS (JOHN ARTHUR) Modern British government. London, 1972. pp. 214. bibliogs.

    CROSSMAN (RICHARD HOWARD STAFFORD) Inside view: three lectures on prime ministerial government. London, 1972. pp. 117. (Harvard University. Godkin Lectures. 1970)

    MOLIERE (JEAN JACQUES GRANPRE) La théorie de la constitution anglaise chez Montesquieu. Leyde, 1972. pp. 386. bibliog. (Leiden. Rijks Universiteit. Publications Historiques. tome 16)

- **Constitutional history**

    BLEWETT (NEAL) The peers, the parties and the people: the general elections of 1910. London, 1972. pp. 548. bibliog.

    CANNON (JOHN) Parliamentary reform, 1640-1832. Cambridge, 1973. pp. 333. bibliog.

- **Constitutional law**

    DICEY (ALBERT VENN) Introduction to the study of the law of the constitution. 7th ed. London, 1908. pp. 571.

    DE SMITH (STANLEY ALEXANDER) Constitutional and administrative law. Harmondsworth, 1971. pp. 712.

    CLARKE (H.W.) Cases and statutes on constitutional and administrative law. London, 1973. pp. 216.

    PHILLIPS (OWEN HOOD) Constitutional and administrative law. 5th ed. London, 1973. pp. 669.

- **Defences**

    BARTLETT (CHRISTOPHER JOHN) The long retreat: a short history of British defence policy, 1945-70. London, 1972 [or rather 1971]. pp. 306.

    HOWARD (MICHAEL ELIOT) The continental commitment: the dilemma of British defence in the era of the two world wars. London, 1972. pp. 176. (Oxford. University. Ford Lectures. 1971)

    OWEN (DAVID) The politics of defence. London, 1972. pp. 249.

    PIERRE (ANDREW J.) Nuclear politics: the British experience with an independent strategic force, 1939-1970. London, 1972. pp. 378. bibliog.

    D'OMBRAIN (NICHOLAS) War machinery and high policy: defence administration in peacetime Britain, 1902-1914. London, 1973. pp. 302. bibliog.

    FABIAN SOCIETY. Fabian Tracts. [No.] 423. Still no disarmament; [by] Wayland Kennet. London, 1973. pp. 24.

    IN defence of peace: defence planning in the seventies; [by] Sir John Peel [and others]. London, 1973. pp. 36. (Conservative Political Centre. [Publications]. No. 519)

    U.K. Defence Lands Committee. 1973. Report... 1971-73; chairman: Lord Nugent of Guildford. London, 1973. pp. 432.

- **Description and travel**

    [SERE-DEPOIN (ERNEST)?] La XIme Légion à Londres: par un caporal des radis de la banlieue: détails, curieux, historiques, inédits sur le voyage des Gardes Nationaux Français en Angleterre pendant l'année 1848; avec des notes de M. de Bilboquet, Sergent-Major socialiste et de Sir Mackintosh de l'Université de Greenwich, etc. Paris, Maulde et Renou, 1849. pp. 200.

    SIMMONS (JACK) ed. Journeys in England: an anthology. London, 1951. pp. 288.

    GUSAROV (VLADIMIR NIKOLAEVICH) Po dorogam Anglii. Cheliabinsk, 1968. pp. 73.

- **Diplomatic and consular service**

    CUTTINO (GEORGE PEDDY) English diplomatic administration, 1259-1339. 2nd ed. Oxford, 1971. pp. 280. bibliog.

    PLATT (DESMOND CHRISTOPHER ST. MARTIN) The Cinderella service: British consuls since 1825. London, 1971. pp. 272. bibliog.

UNITED KINGDOM (Cont'd.)

- Directories

CIVIC TRUST. An environmental directory: national and regional organisations concerned with amenity and the environment. London, [1971]. pp. 20.

- Economic conditions

KNICKERBOCKER (HUBERT RENFRO) Die Schwarzhemden in England und Englands wirtschaftlicher Aufstieg; (deutsch von Franz Fein). Berlin, 1934. pp. 107.

GENDEL' (G.M.) Angliia v 1960-1968 gg.: uchebnoe posobie dlia studentov. Gor'kii, 1969. pp. 36.

CAMBRIDGE. University. Department of Applied Economics. A Programme for Growth. 9. Exploring 1972; with special reference to the balance of payments. Cambridge, 1970. pp. 137. bibliog.

CAMBRIDGE. University. Department of Applied Economics. A Programme for Growth. No. 11. The financial interdependence of the economy, 1957-1966. [London], 1971. pp. 147. bibliog.

MONKHOUSE (FRANCIS JOHN) The material resources of Britain: an economic geography of the United Kingdom. London, 1971. pp. 241. bibliogs.

[NORTHERN ECONOMIC DEVELOPMENT COUNCIL] The North in the sixties: a survey on the Northern region and regional policy, 1960-1969. [Newcastle-upon-Tyne, 1971] fo. 95.

PARTISANS. No. 58. Quelle Grande-Bretagne? Paris, 1971. pp. 171.

SANT (MORGAN EUGENE CYRIL) The geography of business cycles: a case study of short-term fluctuations in East Anglia, 1951-1968; [Ph. D. (London) thesis]. 1971. fo. 266. Typescript: unpublished. This thesis is the property of London University and may not be removed from the Library.

U.K. Department of Trade and Industry. 1971 Room to expand: the assisted areas. [London, 1971]. pp. 32. Map in end pocket.

WEST MIDLAND REGIONAL STUDY. A developing strategy for the West Midlands: report; [with] Technical appendices 1, 3(in 3 parts), 4,5). Birmingham, 1971. 7 vols.

BELOUS (IOSIF DAVYDOVICH) and LARIUSHIN (IURII DMITRIEVICH) Novye iavleniia v ekonomike sovremennogo kapitalizma: na primere SShA i Anglii. Kishinev, 1972. pp. 148.

BROWN (ARTHUR JOSEPH), Professor of Economics in the University of Leeds. The framework of regional economics in the United Kingdom. Cambridge, 1972. pp. 352. bibliog. (National Institute of Economic and Social Research. Economic and Social Studies. 27)

BYATT (I.C.R.) and JONES (I.S.) Economic and political factors affecting economic growth; with special reference to the effects of economic growth on regions and urban areas; paper presented to the 31st World Congress of the International Federation for Housing and Planning, Liverpool, June 1972. [London], Department of the Environment, 1972. fo. 5,25.

CHALINE (CLAUDE) L'économie britannique. 4th ed. Paris, 1972. pp. 128. bibliog.

GLYN (ANDREW) and SUTCLIFFE (ROBERT B.) British capitalism, workers and the profits squeeze. Harmondsworth, 1972. pp. 286.

GOLDRING (MAURICE) and others. La Grande-Bretagne en crise. Paris, [1972]. pp. 128.

KREDIETBANK. Le marché britannique à votre portée [Brussels], 1972. pp. 72.

LEICESTER (COLIN S.) Britain 2001 AD: An analysis of economic activity, work and leisure time at the turn of the century. London, H.M.S.O., 1972. pp. 46. bibliog.

MEASURING development: the role and adequacy of development indicators; edited by Nancy Baster. London, 1972. pp. 182. bibliogs. (Reprint of special issue of Journal of Development Studies. vol. 8 no.3)

PREST (ALAN RICHMOND) and COPPOCK (D.J.) eds. The UK economy: a manual of applied economics. 4th ed. London, [1972]. pp. 279.

The REMOTER rural areas of Britain; [papers presented at a symposium organized by the Agricultural Adjustment Unit of the University of Newcastle-upon-Tyne]; edited by J. Ashton and W.H. Long. Edinburgh, 1972. pp. 246. bibliogs.

RESOURCES for Britain's future: a series from the Geographical Magazine; edited... by Michael Chisholm. Harmondsworth, 1972. pp. 182. bibliogs.

U.K. Central Office of Information. Reference Division. 1972. The British economy. rev. ed. London, 1972. pp. 14. bibliog.

POLANYI (GEORGE) Short-term forecasting: a case study. London, 1973. pp. 39. (Institute of Economic Affairs. Background Memoranda. 4)

SALOMON (WALTER HANS) One man's view: an account of an individualist's crusade over twenty years on inflation, taxation, capitalism and liberty in the speeches and writing of Walter Salomon. Enfield, 1973. pp. 129.

URRY (JOHN) and WAKEFORD (JOHN) Lecturer in Sociology at Brunel University, eds. Power in Britain: sociological readings. London, 1973. pp. 330. bibliog.

- Economic conditions - Mathematical models

SURREY (M.J.C.) The analysis and forecasting of the British economy. Cambridge, 1971. pp. 107. (National Institute of Economic and Social Research. Occasional Papers. 25)

- Economic conditions - Statistics

U.K. Department of Trade and Industry. 1971. The Business Statistics Office. London, 1971. pp. 10.

EDWARDS (BERNARD) Sources of economic and business statistics. London, 1972. pp. 272.

LONDON AND CAMBRIDGE ECONOMIC SERVICE. The British economy: key statistics, 1900-1970. [London], [1973]. pp. 28.

- Economic history

TUCKETT (JOHN DEBELL) A history of the past and present state of the labouring population including the progress of agriculture, manufactures and commerce [originally published London 1846]. Shannon, 1971. 2 vols.

BURNLEY (JAMES) Author of "The history of wool and wool-combing". The romance of modern industry. London, 1889. pp. 372.

FLINN (MICHAEL W.) Origins of the industrial revolution. London, 1966 repr. 1972. pp. 114. bibliog.

HOBSBAWM (ERIC JOHN ERNEST) Industry and empire: an economic history of Britain since 1750. London, 1968 repr. 1969. pp. 336. bibliog.

ALDCROFT (DEREK H.) and FEARON (PETER) eds. British economic fluctuations, 1790-1939;...[a selection of writings with introductions]. London, 1972. pp. 300. bibliog.

ALFORD (BERNARD WILLIAM ERNEST) Depression and recovery?: British economic growth, 1918-1939. London, 1972. pp. 96. bibliog. (Economic History Society. Studies in Economic History)

CROUZET (FRANÇOIS) ed. Capital formation in the Industrial Revolution; edited with an introduction. London, 1972. pp. 261. bibliog.

JENKINS (GERAINT) The craft industries. London, 1972. pp. 128. bibliog.

The LONG debate on poverty: eight essays on industrialisation and 'the condition of England'; [by] R.M. Hartwell [and others]. [London], 1972. pp. 243. bibliogs. (Institute of Economic Affairs. Readings, 9)

MARX (ROLAND) Le déclin de l'économie britannique, 1870-1929. Paris, 1972. pp. 96. bibliog.

MINCHINTON (WALTER EDWARD) ed. Wage regulation in pre-industrial England; (comprising works by R.H. Tawney and R. Keith Kelsall). Newton Abbot, [1972]. pp. 263. bibliog.

MUSSON (ALBERT EDWARD) ed. Science, technology, and economic growth in the eighteenth century. London, 1972. pp. 211. bibliog.

POSTAN (MICHAEL MOISSEY) The medieval economy and society: an economic history of Britain in the middle ages. London, 1972. pp. 261. bibliog.

TAMES (RICHARD LAWRENCE AMOS) Economy and society in nineteenth-century Britain. London, 1972. pp. 156. bibliogs.

CHANNON (DEREK F.) The strategy and structure of British enterprise. London, 1973. pp. 257.

MARSHALL (DOROTHY) Industrial England, 1776-1851. London, 1973. pp. 242. bibliog.

MURPHY (BRIAN) A history of the British economy, 1086-1970. London, 1973. pp. 817, xlii. bibliog.

PHILLIPS (G.A.) and MADDOCK (R.T.) The growth of the British economy, 1918-1968. London, 1973. pp. 188. bibliogs.

POSTAN (MICHAEL MOISSEY) Essays on medieval agriculture and general problems of the medieval economy. Cambridge, 1973. pp. 302.

RUNDLE (RAYMOND NORMAN) Britain's economic and social development from 1700 to the present day. London, 1973. pp. 240.

THOMPSON (ALLAN) The dynamics of the industrial revolution. London, 1973. pp. 174. bibliogs.

TRANTER (N.L.) ed. Population and industrialization: the evolution of a concept and its practical application; [a reader]. London, 1973. pp. 296.

- Economic history - Bibliography

KASHNOR (LEON) The Kashnor collection: the catalogue of a collection relating chiefly to the political economy of Great Britain and Ireland from the 17th to the 19th centuries. Canberra, National Library of Australia, 1969. 2 vols.

- Economic History - Sources

BATTLE ABBEY. Accounts of the cellarers of Battle Abbey, 1275-1513; edited by Eleanor Searle and Barbara Ross. Sydney, 1967. pp. 199. bibliog.

TITOW (J.Z.) English rural society, 1200-1350; [with documents]. London, 1969. pp. 208.

SHIPPING: a survey of historical records [conducted by the Business Archives Council and the National Maritime Museum]; edited by P. Mathias and A.W.H. Pearsall. Newton Abbot, [1971]. pp. 162. bibliogs.

AULT (WARREN ORTMAN) Open-field farming in medieval England: a study of village by-laws; [with documents]. London, 1972. pp. 183.

BREACH (R.W.) and HARTWELL (R. MAX) compilers. British economy and society, 1870-1970: documents; descriptions; statistics. London, 1972. pp. 406.

HEAL AND SONS. Heal's catalogue, 1853-1934: middle class furnishing; pages reproduced [in facsimile]. Newton Abbot, 1972. 1 vol. various pagings.

THIRSK (JOAN) and COOPER (JOHN PHILLIPS) eds. Seventeenth-century economic documents. Oxford, 1972. pp. 849.

LONDON AND CAMBRIDGE ECONOMIC SERVICE. The British economy: key statistics, 1900-1970. [London], [1973]. pp. 28.

- Economic policy

CHAPMAN (Sir SYDNEY JOHN) [Unpublished autobiography of Sir Sydney John Chapman]. [194-?]. fo. 315. Xerographic copy of typescript.

BENTE (HERMANN) England und Deutschland im Kampf um die Neuordnung der Weltwirtschaft. Berlin, 1940. pp. 54. (Deutsches Institut für Aussenpolitische Forschung and Hamburg. Institut für Auswärtige Politik. Schriften. Heft 53)

BAKKER (JAN NICO FRANS) Het economisch beleid op middellange termijn in West-Europa: een terreinverkenning. Leiden, 1970. pp. 319. bibliog. With English summary.

NORTH WEST INDUSTRIAL DEVELOPMENT ASSOCIATION. General Council. Annual report. a., 1971/2 (26th)- Manchester.

KOENKE (JOERN) Die institutionelle Koordination von Geld- und Finanzpolitik in Grossbritannien. Berlin, [1971]. pp. 155. bibliog.

NORTH EAST DEVELOPMENT COUNCIL. Regional policies in Britain and in Europe. [Newcastle-upon-Tyne, 1971]. pp. 16.

[NORTHERN ECONOMIC DEVELOPMENT COUNCIL] The North in the sixties: a survey on the Northern region and regional policy, 1960-1969. [Newcastle-upon-Tyne, 1971]. fo. 95.

U.K. Department of the Environment. 1971. Department of Employment local office areas; Assisted areas as defined by the Department of Trade and Industry at 5.8.1971; Ordnance Survey administration areas. [London], 1971. 2 maps.

BROWN (ARTHUR JOSEPH), Professor of Economics in the University of Leeds. The framework of regional economics in the United Kingdom. Cambridge, 1972. pp. 352. bibliog. (National Institute of Economic and Social Research. Economic and Social Studies. 27)

BROWN (MICHAEL BARRATT) From labourism to socialism: the political economy of Labour in the 1970's. Nottingham, 1972. pp. 252.

CHALINE (CLAUDE) L'économie britannique. 4th ed. Paris, 1972. pp. 128. bibliog.

CHERKASOVA (L.A.) ed. Formy gosudarstvennogo regulirovaniia ekonomiki pri kapitalizme: aktual'nye voprosy. Moskva, 1972. pp. 124.

UNITED KINGDOM - Economic policy
(Cont'd.)

CREASEY (JOHN) Evolution to democracy. rev. ed. London, 1972. pp. 152.

FABIAN SOCIETY. Fabian Tracts. [No.] 413. Labour and the economy: a socialist strategy; [by] Michael Stewart. London, 1972. pp. 35.

FABIAN SOCIETY. Fabian Tracts. [No.] 417. Regional development; [by] Trevor Fisk [and] Ken Jones. London, 1972. pp. 36.

FELS (ALLAN) The British Prices and Incomes Board. Cambridge, 1972. pp. 298. (Cambridge. University. Department of Applied Economics. Occasional Papers. 29)

GLUSHKOV (VASILII PROKHOROVICH) Korporatsii, gosudarstvo, ekonomika: angliiskii gosudarstvenno-monopolisticheskii kapitalizm na poroge 70-kh godov. Moskva, 1972. pp. 415. bibliog.

GLYN (ANDREW) and SUTCLIFFE (ROBERT B.) British capitalism, workers and the profits squeeze. Harmondsworth, 1972. pp. 286.

GRONDONA (L. ST. CLARE) A built-in basic-economy stabilizer. London, [1972]. pp. 68.

INDUSTRIAL RESEARCH AND INFORMATION SERVICES. Incomes policy. London, 1972. pp. 33.

KRYLOVA (NINEL' SERGEEVNA) Gosudarstvennyi apparat ekonomicheskogo regulirovaniia v Velikobritanii. Moskva, 1972. pp. 214.

The LABOUR government's economic record: 1964-1970; edited by Wilfred Beckerman. London, 1972. pp. 343.

LERUEZ (JACQUES) Planification et politique en Grande-Bretagne, 1945-1971. Paris, 1972. pp. 315. bibliog. (Fondation Nationale des Sciences Politiques. Cahiers. 186)

MILLS (JOHN) Labour Councillor. Growth and welfare: a new policy for Britain. London, 1972. pp. 206.

MORGAN (EDWARD VICTOR) and MORGAN (ANN D.) The economics of public policy. Edinburgh, [1972]. pp. 321. bibliogs.

NEWBOULD (GERALD D.) and JACKSON (ANDREW S.) The receding ideal. Liverpool, [1972]. pp. 282.

PARKIN (MICHAEL) and SUMNER (MICHAEL T.) eds. Incomes policy and inflation. Manchester, [1972]. pp. 283.

PREST (ALAN RICHMOND) and COPPOCK (D.J.) eds. The UK economy: a manual of applied economics. 4th ed. London, [1972]. pp. 279.

The REMOTER rural areas of Britain; [papers presented at a symposium organized by the Agricultural Adjustment Unit of the University of Newcastle-upon-Tyne]; edited by J. Ashton and W.H. Long. Edinburgh, 1972. pp. 246. bibliogs.

REVELL (JACK) Financial structure and government regulation in the United Kingdom, 1952-1980. London, 1972. pp. 64. (Inter-Bank Research Organisation. Occasional Papers. No. 1)

ROBERTS (ERNIE) The fight against unemployment. Nottingham, [1972]. pp. 17. (Institute for Workers' Control. Pamphlet Series. No. 30)

SANDFORD (CEDRIC T.) National economic planning. London, 1972. pp. 88. bibliog.

The SHORT-term regulation of the national economy: a symposium [organised by the Foundation for Business Responsibilities; papers by] Sir Donald MacDougall [and others]. London, 1972. pp. 56. (Foundation for Business Responsibilities. Discussion Papers)

TAYLOR (ARTHUR JOHN) Laissez-faire and state intervention in nineteenth-century Britain. London, 1972. pp. 80. bibliog. (Economic History Society. Studies in Economic History)

BRITTAN (SAMUEL) Capitalism and the permissive society. London, 1973. pp. 397. bibliog.

BRITTAN (SAMUEL) Is there an economic consensus?: an attitude survey. London, 1973. pp. 118.

CARTER (ANTHONY J.) Wrong diagnosis, wrong remedies. London, 1973. pp. 23. (Economic and Social Science Research Association. Discussion Papers. No. 1)

DORFMAN (GERALD ALLEN) Wage politics in Britain 1945-1967: government vs. the TUC. Ames, 1973. pp. 180. bibliog.

HALLETT (GRAHAM) and others. Regional policy for ever?: essays on the history, theory and political economy of forty years of 'regionalism'. London, 1973. pp. 152. bibliogs. (Institute of Economic Affairs. Readings. 11)

REES (MERLYN) The public sector in the mixed economy. London, 1973. pp. 240. bibliogs.

SALOMON (WALTER HANS) One man's view: an account of an individualist's crusade over twenty years on inflation, taxation, capitalism and liberty in the speeches and writing of Walter Salomon. Enfield, 1973. pp. 129.

TRADES UNION CONGRESS. The Chequers and Downing Street talks, July to November 1972: report. London, [1973]. pp. 27.

TRADES UNION CONGRESS. Prices and incomes: the case for the unions. London, 1973. pp. 25.

TRADES UNION CONGRESS. Special Congress, 1973. Economic policy and collective bargaining in 1973 and report of Special Trades Union Congress. London, 1973. pp. 109.

- Emigration and immigration

DOMNITZ (MYER) Immigration and integration: experiences of the Anglo-Jewish community. London, [1956?]. pp. 29. bibliog. (Council of Christians and Jews. Shilling Series. No. 27)

PATTERSON (SHEILA) Immigration and race relations in Britain, 1960-1967. London, O.U.P., 1969. pp. xviii, 460. bibliog. 21½cm.

LABOUR PARTY. Opposition Green Papers. Citizenship, immigration and integration: a Labour Party report, published for debate and decision within the movement. London, [1971]. pp. 47. bibliog.

STEPHEN (DAVID) and others, compilers. Race and Jobs: 71 questions answered on immigration, race relations and the Race Relations Act. 2nd ed. London, 1971. 1 pamphlet (unpaged).

CHEETHAM (JULIET) Social work with immigrants. London, 1972. pp. 230. bibliog.

COLEMAN (TERRY) Passage to America: a history of emigrants from Great Britain and Ireland to America in the mid-nineteenth century. London, 1972. pp. 317. bibliog.

ERICKSON (CHARLOTTE JOANNE) Invisible immigrants: the adaptation of English and Scottish immigrants in nineteenth century America. London, [1972]. pp. 531.

GAINER (BERNARD) The alien invasion: the origins of the Aliens Act of 1905. London, 1972. pp. 305. bibliog.

JOHNSTON (H.J.M.) British emigration policy, 1815-1830: 'shovelling out paupers'. Oxford, 1972. pp. 197. bibliog.

THOMAS (BRINLEY) Migration and urban development: a reappraisal of British and American long cycles London, 1972. pp. 259. bibliog.

TRISELIOTIS (JOHN P.) ed. Social work with coloured immigrants and their families. London, 1972. pp. 123. bibliog.

DOHERTY (JOSEPH MICHAEL) Immigrants in London: a study of the relationship between spatial structure and social structure; [Ph.D.(London) thesis]. [1973]. fo. 368. bibliog. Typescript: unpublished. This thesis is the property of London University and may not be removed from the Library.

MISHAN (EDWARD JOSHUA) Making the world safe for pornography, and other intellectual fashions. London, 1973. pp. 262.

MULLARD (CHRIS) Black Britain;...with an account of recent events at the Institute of Race Relations by Alexander Kirby. London, 1973. pp. 194. bibliog.

RUNNYMEDE TRUST. Questions and answers on race relations and immigration. London, 1973. pp. 26.

THOMAS (BRINLEY) Migration and economic growth: a study of Great Britain and the Atlantic economy. 2nd ed. Cambridge, 1973. pp. 498. bibliog.

- Emigration and immigration - Bibliography

HILL (JANET) Books for children: the homelands of immigrants in Britain, etc. London, [1971]. pp. 85. (Institute of Race Relations. Special Series)

- Executive departments

An INQUIRY into the conduct of Mr. Serjeant Praed as chairman of the Audit Board; dedicated to George Harrison, Esq., assistant secretary to the Treasury. Paris, Volland, 1819. pp. vii, 74.

U.K. Committee on the Administration of Trade Boards. 1921. Report to the Minister of Labour of the Committee appointed to make recommendations with respect to the work of the Trade Boards and the administration of the Trade Boards Acts: [Humbert Wolfe, chairman]. London, 1921. pp. 18.

U.K. Board of Trade. 1969. An introduction to the Board of Trade. London, 1969. pp. 53.

HONIGSBAUM (FRANK) The struggle for the Ministry of Health, 1914-1919. London, 1970. pp. 80. bibliog. (Social Administration Research Trust. Occasional Papers on Social Administration. No. 37)

U.K. Department of Employment and Productivity. 1970. Commission for Industry and Manpower: consultative document. [London, 1970]. fo. 12.

U.K. Department of Trade and Industry. 1971. The Business Statistics Office. London, 1971. pp. 10.

BLAKELEY (BRIAN L.) The Colonial Office, 1868-1892. Durham, N.C., 1972. pp. 195. bibliog.

KRYLOVA (NINEL' SERGEEVNA) Gosudarstvennyi apparat ekonomicheskogo regulirovaniia v Velikobritanii. Moskva, 1972. pp. 214.

MASEFIELD (GEOFFREY BUSSELL) A history of the Colonial Agricultural Service. Oxford, 1972. pp. 184. bibliog.

STUDIES in the growth of nineteenth-century government: [a collection of papers based on a colloquium on the reform of the English civil service, 1780-1914, held under the auspices of Past and Present at Birkbeck College, London, on 8th July 1969]; edited by Gillian Sutherland. London, 1972. pp. 295.

U.K. Department of Employment. Information Branch. 1972. Work of the Department. 2nd ed. London, 1972. pp. 28. (Background Briefings. No.1)

U.K. Public Record Office. 1972. The second world war: a guide to documents in the Public Record Office; [by L. Bell and others]. London, 1972. pp. 303. (Handbooks. No. 15)

D'OMBRAIN (NICHOLAS) War machinery and high policy: defence administration in peacetime Britain, 1902-1914. London, 1973. pp. 302. bibliog.

ROSEVEARE (HENRY) The Treasury, 1660-1870: the foundations of control; [with selected documents]. London, 1973. pp. 219. bibliog.

U.K. Treasury. 1973. Her Majesty's Treasury. [London, 1973]. pp. 39. bibliog.

- Executive departments - Bibliography

U.K. Department of the Environment. Library. 1972. Literature about DOE. London, [1972]. pp. (5). (Bibliographies. No.158)

- Foreign economic relations

CHAPMAN (Sir SYDNEY JOHN) [Unpublished autobiography of Sir Sydney John Chapman]. [194-?]. fo. 315. Xerographic copy of typescript.

BOARDMAN (ROBERT) and GROOM (A.J.R.) eds. The management of Britain's external relations. London, 1973. pp. 362. bibliogs.

- Foreign economic relations - Argentine Republic

ORTEGA PEÑA (RODOLFO) and DUHALDE (EDUARDO LUIS) Felipe Varela contra el imperio britanico: las masas de la union americana enfrentan a las potencias europeas. Buenos Aires, 1966. pp. 363.

- Foreign economic relations - Balkan States

VAN KESSEL (GERARD JOSEPH) The British reaction to German economic penetration in Southeastern Europe, 1936-1939; [Ph. D. (London) thesis]. [1972]. fo. 394. bibliog. Typescript: unpublished. This thesis is the property of London University and may not be removed from the Library.

- Foreign economic relations - China

BASU (DILIP) and MURPHEY (RHOADS) eds. Nineteenth century China: five imperialist perspectives. Ann Arbor, 1972. pp. 82. (Michigan University. Center for Chinese Studies. Michigan Papers in Chinese Studies. No. 13)

- Foreign economic relations - Germany

WENDT (BERND JUERGEN) Economic Appeasement: Handel und Finanz in der britischen Deutschland-Politik 1933-1939. Düsseldorf, [1971]. pp. 695. bibliog. (Hamburg. Hansische Universität. Studien zur Modernen Geschichte. Band 3)

- Foreign economic relations - Russia - Latvia

VARSLAVAN (AL'BERT IANOVICH) Angliiskii kapital v burzhuaznoi Latvii, 1920-1929 gg. Riga, 1972. pp. 2??. bibliog.

UNITED KINGDOM (Cont'd.)

- Foreign economic relations - Scandinavia

KENT (HEINZ SIGFRID KOPLOWITZ) War and trade in Northern seas: Anglo-Scandinavian economic relations in the mid-eighteenth century. Cambridge, 1973. pp. 240. bibliog.

- Foreign relations

A SECOND letter from Wiltshire to the Monitor, on the vindication of his constitutional principles. London, Hooper, 1759. pp. 32. 21 cm.

DISRAELI (BENJAMIN) 1st Earl of Beaconsfield. The Hughenden papers: [selections from the papers relating to Benjamin Disraeli, Earl of Beaconsfield, preserved at Hughenden Manor, near High Wycombe, Buckinghamshire]; Group A, sections I,V,X-XII; Group B; Group R ["Rose papers"]. [1820-1918]. Microfilm: 73 reels. For details of Library holdings readers should consult the Handlist of the Hughenden papers, kept in Room Z.

KIRWAN (A.V.) A letter from Munich to the right honourable the Lord Palmerston, his Britanic [sic] Majesty's minister of state for foreign affairs on the late happy change of ministry in England. Munich, Wolf, 1830. pp. 72.

ESCOTT (THOMAS HAY SWEET) National and international links. London, 1922. pp. 333.

YOUNG (NORWOOD) England conquers the world. London, 1937. pp. 239.

ALBRECHT-CARRIÉ (RENÉ) Britain and France: adaptation to a changing context of power. New York, 1970. pp. 652. bibliog.

U.K. Foreign and Commonwealth Office. 1970. Speech by the Secretary of State for Foreign and Commonwealth Affairs in the General Assembly of the United Nations, New York, September 24, 1970. [London, 1970]. pp. 10.

U.K. Prime Minister. 1970. Speech by...Edward Heath at the commemorative session for the twenty-fifth anniversary of the United Nations, New York, October 23, 1970. [London, 1970.] pp. 10.

BUTLER (RICHARD AUSTEN) Baron Butler of Saffron Walden. Problems of diplomacy, past and present. [Canberra], 1971. pp. 23. (Australian National University. Arthur F. Yencken Memorial Lectures. 1970)

PARKINSON (ROGER) Peace for our time: Munich to Dunkirk: the inside story. London, 1971. pp. 412. bibliog.

U.K. Foreign and Commonwealth Office. 1971. Speech by the Secretary of State for Foreign and Commonwealth Affairs in the General Assembly of the United Nations, New York, September 29, 1971. [London, 1971.] pp. 11.

1972

BARNETT (CORRELLI) The collapse of British power. London, 1972. pp. 643. bibliog.

COLLIER (BASIL) The lion and the eagle: British and Anglo-American strategy, 1900-1950. London, [1972]. pp. 499. bibliog.

CONSTRAINTS and adjustments in British foreign policy; edited by Michael Leifer. London, 1972. pp. 210. (Acton Society. Studies. No. 2)

FERGUSON (JOHN) of the University of Texas. English diplomacy, 1422-1461. Oxford, 1972. pp. 289. bibliog.

FRY (MICHAEL GRAHAM) Illusions of security: North Atlantic diplomacy, 1918-1922. Toronto, [1972]. pp. 221. bibliog.

GREGG (GARY EDWARD) The Protestant succession in international politics, 1710-1716; [Ph. D. (London) thesis]. [1972]. fo. 457. bibliog. Supplementary article in end pocket. Typescript: unpublished. This thesis is the property of London University and may not be removed from the Library.

IRONSIDE (WILLIAM EDMUND) 1st Baron Ironside. High road to command: the diaries of Major-General Sir Edmund Ironside, 1920-1922; edited by Lord Ironside. London, 1972. pp. 251.

JEBB (HUBERT MILES GLADWYN) 1st Baron Gladwyn. The memoirs of Lord Gladwyn. London, [1972]. pp. 422.

JENKINS (ROY HARRIS) Afternoon on the Potomac?: a British view of America's changing position in the world. New Haven, Conn., 1972. pp. 59. (Yale University. Henry L. Stimson Lectures. 1971)

LOWE (CEDRIC JAMES) and DOCKRILL (MICHAEL LAWRENCE) The mirage of power...: British foreign policy 1902-(1922). London, 1972. 3 vols. bibliog.

MACMILLAN (HAROLD) Pointing the way, 1959-1961. London, 1972. pp. 504.

MORRIS (A.J. ANTHONY) Radicalism against war, 1906-1914: the advocacy of peace and retrenchment. London, 1972. pp. 448. bibliog.

NORTHEDGE (FREDERICK SAMUEL) Freedom and necessity in British foreign policy; an inaugural lecture delivered on 14 October 1971. London, [1972]. pp. 28.

PIRNIE (BRUCE R.) Das britische Parlament in der Aussenpolitik, 1892-1902. [Heidelberg?], 1972. pp. 260. bibliog.

PROBLEMY britanskoi istorii. 1972; Stadies [sic] on British history. Moskva, 1972. pp. 335. bibliog.

THORNE (CHRISTOPHER) The limits of foreign policy: the West, the League, and the Far Eastern crisis of 1931-1933. London, 1972. pp. 442. bibliog.

1973

BELOFF (NORA) Transit of Britain: a report on Britain's changing role in the post-war world. London, 1973. pp. 287.

BRUEGEL (JOHANN WOLFGANG) Czechoslovakia before Munich: the German minority problem and British appeasement policy. Cambridge, 1973. pp. 334. bibliog.

CROWSON (PAUL S.) Tudor foreign policy. London, 1973. pp. 288. bibliog.

CROZIER (WILLIAM PERCIVAL) Off the record: political interviews, 1933-1943; edited with an introduction by A.J.P. Taylor. London, 1973. pp. 397.

FABIAN SOCIETY. Fabian Tracts. [No.] 423. Still no disarmament; [by] Wayland Kennet. London, 1973. pp. 24.

MACMILLAN (HAROLD) At the end of the day, 1961-1963. London, 1973. pp. 572.

PARKINSON (ROGER) Blood, toil, tears and sweat: the war history from Dunkirk to Alamein, based on the War Cabinet papers of 1940 to 1942. London, 1973. pp. 539. bibliog.

RAMM (AGATHA) Sir Robert Morier: envoy and ambassador in the age of imperialism, 1876-1893. Oxford, 1973. pp. 386. bibliog.

- Foreign relations - Africa, East

  GALBRAITH (JOHN S.) Mackinnon and East Africa, 1878-1895: a study in the 'new imperialism'. Cambridge, 1972. pp. 253. bibliog.

- Foreign relations - America, Latin

  OSEGUEDA (RAUL) Operacion Centroamerica: £$ OK £$. Mexico, 1957. pp. 238. bibliog.

- Foreign relations - Arab countries

  BUSCH (BRITON COOPER) Britain, India, and the Arabs, 1914-1921. Berkeley, Calif., 1971. pp. 522. bibliog.

- Foreign relations - Austria-Hungary

  BRIDGE (F.R.) Great Britain and Austria-Hungary 1906-1914: a diplomatic history. London, [1972]. pp. 320. bibliog. (London. University. London School of Economics and Political Science. Research Monongraphs)

- Foreign relations - Brunei

  TARLING (NICHOLAS) Britain, the Brookes and Brunei. Kuala Lumpur, 1971. pp. 578. bibliog.

- Foreign relations - Canada

  BEATON (LEONARD) The strategic and political issues facing America, Britain and Canada. London, 1971. pp. 21. (British-North American Committee. Publications. 5)

  BURROUGHS (PETER) British attitudes towards Canada, 1822-1849. Scarborough, Ont., [1971]. pp. 152.

- Foreign relations - Catholic church

  U.K. Legation (Holy See). 1922-39. Anglo-Vatican relations, 1914-1939: confidential annual reports of the British Ministers to the Holy See;... edited by Thomas E. Hachey. Boston (Mass.), 1972. pp. 403. Photographic reprint from the Foreign Office General Correspondence (Political) held in the Public Record Office.

- Foreign relations - China

  ZARINA (LILIA LEONIDOVNA) and LIVSHITS (SOLOMON GRIGOR'EVICH) Britanskii imperializm v Kitae, 1896-1901. Moskva, 1970. pp. 248. bibliog.

- Foreign relations - Denmark

  HJELHOLT (HOLGER) Great Britain, the Danish-German conflict and the Danish succession, 1850-1852, etc. København, 1971. pp. 323. (Danske Videnskabernes Selskab. Historisk-filosofiske Meddelelser. Bind 45, Nr.1)

  ESMANN JENSEN (FRANK) Da fornuften sejrede: det britiske udenrigsministeriums politik over for Danmark under 2. verdenskrig. [Copenhagen, 1972]. pp. 240.

- Foreign relations - East (Far East)

  LEE (BRADFORD A.) Britain and the Sino-Japanese war, 1937-1939: a study in the dilemmas of British decline. Stanford, 1973. pp. 319. bibliog.

- Foreign relations - East (Near East)

  FRIEDMAN (ISAIAH) The question of Palestine, 1914-1918: British-Jewish-Arab relations. London, 1973. pp. 433. bibliog.

- Foreign relations - Egypt.

  LAMPSON (MILES WEDDERBURN) 1st Baron Killearn. The Killearn diaries, 1934-1946: the diplomatic and personal record of Lord Killearn (Sir Miles Lampson), High Commissioner and Ambassador, Egypt; edited and introduced by Trefor E. Evans. London, 1972. pp. 400.

- Foreign relations - France

  WILLIAM III., King of Great Britain and Ireland, and others. Letters of William III and Louis XIV and of their ministers, illustrative of the domestic and foreign politics of England...1697 to 1700; edited by Paul Grimblot. London, 1848. 2 vols.

  BULLEN (ROGER JOHN) Lord Palmerston and Anglo-French relations, 1841-1848; [Ph. D. (London) thesis]. 1971. fo. 372. bibliog. Typescript: unpublished. This thesis is the property of London University and may not be removed from the Library.

  CHANDRAN (J.) The Burma-Yunnan railway: Anglo-French rivalry in mainland Southeast Asia and South China, 1895-1902. Athens, Ohio, 1971. pp. 112. (Ohio University. Center for International Studies. Papers in International Studies. Southeast Asia Series. No. 21)

  CUTTINO (GEORGE PEDDY) English diplomatic administration, 1259-1339. 2nd ed. Oxford, 1971. pp. 280. bibliog.

  GIFFORD (PROSSER) and LOUIS (WILLIAM ROGER) eds. France and Britain in Africa: imperial rivalry and colonial rule. New Haven, 1971. pp. 989. bibliog.

  LEE (H.I.) Mediterranean strategy and Anglo-French relations, 1908-1912. [New York, 1971]. pp. 267-286. (Reprinted from The Mariner's Mirror, vol. 57, no.3, 1971)

  SEN (S.P.) The French in India, 1763-1816. 2nd ed. New Delhi, 1971. pp. 621. bibliog.

  ALLMAND (C.T.) ed. Documents relating to the Anglo-French negotiations of 1439. in Camden Society. [Publications]. 4th Series. vol. 9. Camden miscellany. vol. 24. London, 1972.

  NARINSKII (MIKHAIL MATVEEVICH) Angliia i Frantsiia v poslevoennoi Evrope, 1945-1949 gg. Moskva, 1972. pp. 277. bibliog.

  WRIGHT (PATRICIA) Conflict on the Nile: the Fashoda incident of 1898. London, 1972. pp. 229. bibliog.

- Foreign relations - Germany

  DECKART (GERALD) Deutsch-englische Verständigung: eine Darstellung der nichtoffiziellen Bemühungen um eine Wiederannäherung der beiden Länder zwischen 1905 und 1914. [Munich, 1967?]. pp. 263. bibliog.

  LADEWIG (WILHELM) Zur Frage der Einkreisung Deutschlands: Rückblick auf die politische Betätigung König Eduards VII. von England. Pähl, 1967. pp. 64.

  AZZOLA (AXEL CHRISTIAN) Die Diskussion um die Aufrüstung der BRD im Unterhaus und in der Presse Grossbritanniens November 1949-Juli 1952. Meisenheim, 1971. pp. 393. bibliog.

  HAUSER (OSWALD) England und das Dritte Reich. Stuttgart, [1972 in progress]. bibliog.

  BERTRAM-LIBAL (GISELA) Aspekte der britischen Deutschlandpolitik 1919-1922. Göppingen, 1972. pp. 196. bibliog. With English summary.

  MIDDLEMAS (ROBERT KEITH) Diplomacy of illusion: the British government and Germany, 1937-39. London, [1972]. pp. 510. bibliog.

UNITED KINGDOM - Foreign relations - Germany (Cont'd.)

VAN KESSEL (GERARD JOSEPH) The British reaction to German economic penetration in Southeastern Europe, 1936-1939; [Ph.D. (London) thesis]. [1972]. fo. 394. bibliog. Typescript: unpublished. This thesis is the property of London University and may not be removed from the Library.

WEIDENFELD (WERNER) Die Englandpolitik Gustav Stresemanns: theoretische und praktische Aspekte der Aussenpolitik. Mainz, [1972]. pp. 382. bibliog.

HENKE (JOSEF) England in Hitlers politischem Kalkül 1935-1939. Boppard am Rhein, 1973. pp. 346. bibliog. (Germany (Bundesrepublik). Bundesarchiv. Schriften. 20)

- Foreign relations - Germany - Prussia

HJELHOLT (HOLGER) Great Britain, the Danish-German conflict and the Danish succession, 1850-1852, etc. København, 1971. pp. 323. (Danske Videnskabernes Selskab. Historisk-filosofiske Meddelelser. Bind 45, Nr.1)

- Foreign relations - Ghana

AGBODEKA (FRANCIS) African politics and British policy in the Gold Coast, 1868-1900: a study in the forms and force of protest. Evanston, Ill., 1971. pp. 206. bibliog.

- Foreign relations - Greece

KOLIOPOULOS (JOHN) Britain and Greece, 1935-1941: some aspects of Anglo-Greek relations; [Ph.D. (London) thesis]. [1972]. fo. 337. bibliog. Typescript: unpublished. This thesis is the property of London University and may not be removed from the Library.

- Foreign relations - India

BANERJI (ARUN KUMAR) Ph.D. Some aspects of the strains and stresses in Indo-British relations, 1947-65: an analysis of the causes and course of the gradual decline in Britain's importance to India; [Ph.D. (London) thesis]. 1972. fo. 368, xxvi. bibliog. Typescript: unpublished. This thesis is the property of London University and may not be removed from the Library.

- Foreign relations - Iran

ABDULLAEV (FATKHULLA) Iz istorii russko-iranskikh otnoshenii i angliiskoi politiki v Irane v nachale XIX v. Tashkent, 1971. pp. 135. bibliog.

- Foreign relations - Ireland (Republic)

LYNCH (JOHN) Prime Minister of the Irish Republic. Speeches and statements [on] Irish unity; Northern Ireland; Anglo-Irish relations; August 1969 - October 1971. [Dublin], Government Information Bureau, [1971]. pp. 106.

- Foreign relations - Italy

ROTUNDA (DONALD THEODORE) The Rome embassy of Sir Eric Drummond, 16th Earl of Perth, 1933-939; [Ph.D. (London) thesis]. 1972. fo. 423. bibliog. Typescript: unpublished. This thesis is the property of London University and may not be removed from the Library.

- Foreign relations - Japan

PEKING AND TIENTSIN TIMES. The Anglo-Japanese alliance. [Peking, 1920]. pp. 11.

NISH (IAN HILL) Alliance in decline: a study in Anglo-Japanese relations, 1908-23. London, 1972. pp. 424. bibliog. (London. University. Historical Studies. 33)

- Foreign relations - Jordan

JOHNSTON (Sir CHARLES HEPBURN) The brink of Jordan. London, 1972. pp. 179.

- Foreign relations - Nigeria

CRONJE (SUZANNE) The world and Nigeria: the diplomatic history of the Biafran war 1967-1970. London, 1972. pp. 409.

- Foreign relations - Palestine

COHEN (MICHAEL JOSEPH) Policies and politics in Palestine, 1936-1939: an analysis of British, Zionist and Arab aspirations in Palestine and in the Middle East; [Ph.D. (London) thesis]. 1971. fo. 340. bibliog. Typescript: unpublished. This thesis is the property of London University and may not be removed from the Library.

INGRAMS (DOREEN) compiler. Palestine papers, 1917-1922: seeds of conflict. London, [1972]. pp. 198.

ROSE (NORMAN ANTHONY) The gentle Zionists: a study in Anglo-Zionist diplomacy, 1929-1939. London, 1973. pp. 242. bibliog.

- Foreign relations - Rhodesia

RHODESIA. Prime Minister's Office. 1969. Statement on Anglo-Rhodesian relations, December 1966 to May 1969. Salisbury, 1969. pp. 19. ([Sessional Papers]. 1969. C.S.R. 36.)

- Foreign relations - Russia

BABAKHODZHAEV (ABDUSAMAD KHANTURAEVICH) Proval angliiskoi antisovetskoi politiki v Srednei Azii i na Srednem Vostoke v period priznaniia Sovetskogo gosudarstva de-fakto i de-iure, 1921-1924 gg. Tashkent, 1957. pp. 214. bibliog. For 2nd ed. see his Proval angliiskoi politiki v Srednei Azii i na Srednem Vostoke.

PANKRASHOVA (M.) and SIPOLS (VILNIS IANOVICH) Pochemu ne udalos' predotvratit' voinu: moskovskie peregovory SSSR, Anglii i Frantsii 1939 goda; dokumental'nyi obzor. Moskva, 1970. pp. 122.

IBRAGIMBEILI (KHADZHI MURAT) Kavkaz v Krymskoi voine 1853-1856 gg. i mezhdunarodnye otnosheniia. Moskva, 1971. pp. 404.

NIEDHART (GOTTFRIED) Grossbritannien und die Sowjetunion 1934-1939: Studien zur britischen Politik der Friedenssicherung zwischen den beiden Weltkriegen. München, 1972. pp. 497. bibliog. (Mannheim. Universität. Historisches Institut. Veröffentlichungen. Band 2)

EDWARDS (GEOFFREY RICHARD) Sir Austen Chamberlain's and Sir John Simon's conduct of Anglo-Soviet relations: a case study in the relationship between the House of Commons and the Foreign Secretary; [Ph.D.(London) thesis]. 1973. fo.306. bibliog. Typescript: unpublished. This thesis is the property of London University and may not be removed from the Library.

- Foreign relations - Spain

[GORDON (THOMAS) of Kirkcudbright] An appeal to the unprejudiced, concerning the present discontents occasioned by the late convention with Spain. London, Cooper, 1739. pp. 32.

- Foreign relations - Tunisia

> MARSDEN (ARTHUR) British diplomacy and Tunis, 1875-1902: a case study in Mediterranean policy. Edinburgh, 1971. pp. 276. bibliog.

- Foreign relations - United States

> BICKEL (WOLF HEINRICH) Die anglo-amerikanischen Beziehungen 1927-1930 im Licht der Flottenfrage: das Problem des Machtausgleichs zwischen Grossbritannien und den Vereinigten Staaten in der Zwischenkriegszeit und seine Lösung. Zürich, 1970. pp. 227. bibliog.
>
> BEATON (LEONARD) The strategic and political issues facing America, Britain and Canada. London, 1971. pp. 21. (British-North American Committee. Publications. 5)
>
> COLLIER (BASIL) The lion and the eagle: British and Anglo-American strategy, 1900-1950. London, [1972]. pp. 499. bibliog.
>
> MANDERSON-JONES (RONALD BRANDIS) The special relationship: Anglo-American relations and western European unity, 1947-56. London, [1972]. pp. 168. bibliog.
>
> NUNNERLEY (DAVID) President Kennedy and Britain. London, 1972. pp. 242.
>
> WILLERT (Sir ARTHUR) Washington and other memories. Boston, 1972. pp. 248.

- Foreign relations - Venezuela

> PEDRO FERNANDEZ (ANTONIO DE) La historia y el derecho en la reclamacion venezolana de la guayana Esequiba. Caracas, 1969. pp. 333.

- Foreign relations administration

> CUTTINO (GEORGE PEDDY) English diplomatic administration, 1259-1339. 2nd ed. Oxford, 1971. pp. 280. bibliog.
>
> BOARDMAN (ROBERT) and GROOM (A.J.R.) eds. The management of Britain's external relations. London, 1973. pp. 362. bibliogs.
>
> EDWARDS (GEOFFREY RICHARD) Sir Austen Chamberlain's and Sir John Simon's conduct of Anglo-Soviet relations: a case study in the relationship between the House of Commons and the Foreign Secretary; [Ph.D.(London) thesis]. 1973. fo.306. bibliog. Typescript: unpublished. This thesis is the property of London University and may not be removed from the Library.

- Gazetteers

> MASON (OLIVER) The gazetteer of England: England's cities, towns, villages and hamlets: a comprehensive list with basic details on each. Newton Abbot, [1972]. 2 vols.

- Government publications

> ARGLES (MICHAEL) British government publications in education during the 19th century. [Lancaster, 1971]. pp. 20. (History of Education Society. Guides to Sources in the History of Education. No. 1)
>
> RODGERS (FRANK) F.L.A., compiler. Serial publications in the British Parliamentary Papers, 1900-1968: a bibliography. London, 1971. pp. 146.
>
> FORD (PERCY) and FORD (GRACE) A guide to parliamentary papers: what they are, how to find them, how to use them. 3rd ed. Shannon, 1972. pp. 87. bibliog.
>
> OLLÉ (JAMES GORDON) An introduction to British government publications. 2nd ed. London, 1973. pp. 175. bibliog.

- Historical geography

> DARBY (HENRY CLIFFORD) and TERRETT (IAN BREMNER) eds. The Domesday geography of midland England. 2nd ed. Cambridge, 1971. pp. 490. bibliogs.

- History

> ANGLO-DUTCH HISTORICAL CONFERENCE, 4TH, 1969. Britain and the Netherlands...: metropolis, dominion and province; papers delivered to the... conference; edited by J.S. Bromley and E.H. Kossmann. The Hague, 1971. pp. 233.
>
> CLARK (Sir GEORGE NORMAN) English history: a survey. Oxford, 1971. pp. 567.
>
> JOHNSON (PAUL) The offshore islanders. London, [1972]. pp. 466.
>
> PROBLEMY britanskoi istorii. 1972; Stadies [sic] on British history. Moskva, 1972. pp. 335. bibliog.

- History - Caricatures and cartoons

> JONES (MICHAEL WYNN) The cartoon history of Britain. London, 1971. pp. 287.

- History - Historiography

> McKISACK (MAY) Medieval history in the Tudor age. Oxford, 1971. pp. 180.
>
> TREVOR-ROPER (HUGH REDWALD) Queen Elizabeth's first historian: William Camden and the beginnings of English 'civil history'. London, [1971]. pp. 38. (London. University. University College. Neale Lectures in English History. 1971)
>
> STONE (LAWRENCE) The causes of the English Revolution, 1529-1642. London, 1972. pp. 168.

- History - Sources

> WILLIAM III., King of Great Britain and Ireland, and others. Letters of William III and Louis XIV and of their ministers, illustrative of the domestic and foreign politics of England...1697 to 1700; edited by Paul Grimblot. London, 1848. 2 vols.
>
> ASHTON (ROBERT) ed. James I by his contemporaries: an account of his career and character as seen by some of his contemporaries. London, 1969. pp. 290.
>
> [GARRETT (K.I.) compiler.] A handlist of poll books and registers of electors in Guildhall Library. [London], 1970. pp. 87,4.
>
> PORTER (HARRY CULVERWELL) ed. Puritanism in Tudor England. London, 1970. pp. 311. bibliog.
>
> U.K. Ministry of Health. Poor Law Union papers. Parts 2 and 3. London, 1971-72. 2 vols. (List and Index Society. [Publications]. Vols. 64, 77) Part 1 out of print.
>
> CUTTINO (GEORGE PEDDY) English diplomatic administration, 1259-1339. 2nd ed. Oxford, 1971. pp. 280. bibliog.
>
> ENGLAND before the Conquest: studies in primary sources presented to Dorothy Whitelock; edited by Peter Clemoes and Kathleen Hughes. Cambridge, 1971. pp. 418.
>
> GUERNSEY BOOKS. Century of change, 1815-1914: a collection of original pamphlets, tracts, posters, holograph letters, manuscripts, etc. St. Peter Port, [c.1971]. pp. 40.
>
> JONES (W.J.) Politics and the bench: the judges and the origins of the English Civil War. London, 1971. pp. 228.

UNITED KINGDOM - History - Sources
(Cont'd.)

BAGLEY (JOHN JOSEPH) Historical interpretations. Newton Abbot, 1972. 2 vols. bibliogs.

BENET (JOHN) Chronicle for the years 1400 to 1462; edited by G.L.Harriss and M.A.Harriss. in Camden Society. [Publications]. 4th Series. vol. 9. Camden miscellany. vol. 24. London, 1972.

PIPE ROLL SOCIETY. Publications. New Series. vol. 39. The great roll of the pipe for the second year of the reign of King Henry III, Michaelmas 1218, Pipe Roll 62...; edited by E. Pauline Ebden. London, 1972. pp. 137.

U.K. Cabinet Office. 1922. Subject index (A-Z) of Cabinet conclusions, 1922 Jan. - Oct. London, 1973-4. 2 vols. (List and Index Society. [Publications]. Vols. 92, 100)

CAMDEN SOCIETY. [Publications]. 4th Series. vol. 12. Wentworth papers, 1597-1628; edited... by J.P. Cooper. London, 1973. pp. 337.

FLETCHER (ANTHONY) Tudor rebellions; [with selected documents]. 2nd ed. London, 1973. pp. 168. bibliog.

- History - Sources - Bibliography

KELLY (PAUL) compiler. Modern historical manuscripts in the University of London library: a subject guide. London, 1972. fo. 35. Typescript.

- History - to 1066

ALCOCK (LESLIE) Arthur's Britain: history and archaeology, A.D. 367-634. Harmondsworth, 1973. pp. 415. bibliog. First published 1971.

MORRIS (JOHN) Historian. The age of Arthur: a history of the British Isles from 350 to 650. London, [1973]. pp. 665.

- History - 449-1066, Anglo-Saxon period

ENGLAND before the Conquest: studies in primary sources presented to Dorothy Whitelock; edited by Peter Clemoes and Kathleen Hughes. Cambridge, 1971. pp. 418.

- History - 1066-1485, Mediaeval period

McFARLANE (KENNETH BRUCE) The nobility of later medieval England: the Ford Lectures for 1953 and related studies. Oxford, 1973. pp. 315.

- History - 1154-1216, Angevin period

WARREN (WILFRED LEWIS) Henry II. London, 1973. pp. 693. bibliog.

- History - 1200-1299

PRESTWICH (MICHAEL) War, politics and finance under Edward I. London, [1972]. pp. 317. bibliog.

- History - 1300-1399

The REIGN of Richard II: essays in honour of May McKisack; edited by F.R.H. Du Boulay and Caroline M. Barron. London, 1971. pp. 335.

- History - 1399-1485, Lancaster and York

BENET (JOHN) Chronicle for the years 1400 to 1462; edited by G.L.Harriss and M.A.Harriss. in Camden Society. [Publications]. 4th Series. vol. 9. Camden miscellany. vol. 24. London, 1972.

FIFTEENTH-century England, 1399-1509: studies in politics and society; [papers read at a colloquium held in Cardiff in 1970]; edited by S.B. Chrimes [and others]. Manchester, [1972]. pp. 192.

- History - 1485-1603, Tudors

SCARISBRICK (J.J.) Henry VIII; [reprint of work first published in 1968]. Harmondsworth, 1971. pp. 715. bibliog.

STOREY (ROBIN LINDSAY) The reign of Henry VII. London, 1968. pp. 243. bibliog.

ELTON (GEOFFREY RUDOLPH) Policy and police: the enforcement of the reformation in the age of Thomas Cromwell. Cambridge, 1972. pp. 447.

FIFTEENTH-century England, 1399-1509: studies in politics and sociey; [papers read at a colloquium held in Cardiff in 1970]; edited by S.B. Chrimes [and others]. Manchester, [1972]. pp. 192.

WALDMAN (MILTON) The lady Mary: a biography of Mary Tudor, 1516-1558. London, 1972. pp. 224.

ELTON (GEOFFREY RUDOLPH) Reform and renewal: Thomas Cromwell and the common weal. Cambridge, 1973. pp. 175. (Belfast. Queen's University. Wiles Lectures. 1972)

FLETCHER (ANTHONY) Tudor rebellions; [with selected documents]. 2nd ed. London, 1973. pp. 168. bibliog.

HURSTFIELD (JOEL) Freedom, corruption and government in Elizabethan England. London, 1973. pp. 368.

- History - 1603-1714, Stuarts

AYLMER (GERALD EDWARD) The struggle for the constitution: England in the seventeenth century, (1603-1689). 3rd ed. London, 1968 repr. 1971. pp. 263. bibliog.

IVES (E.W.) ed. The English revolution 1600-1660; essays [originating in a series of talks broadcast by the BBC in 1966]. London, 1968, repr. 1971. pp. 164. bibliogs.

History - 1603-1649, Early Stuarts

LEVACK (BRIAN P.) The civil lawyers in England, 1603-1641: a political study. Oxford, 1973. pp. 311. bibliog.

- History - 1642-1660, Puritan Revolution

ROOTS (I.A.) The great rebellion, 1642-1660. London, 1966 repr. 1972. pp. 326. bibliog.

HILL (JOHN EDWARD CHRISTOPHER) The world turned upside down: radical ideas during the English Revolution. London, 1972. pp. 353.

STONE (LAWRENCE) The causes of the English Revolution, 1529-1642. London, 1972. pp. 168.

FRASER (Lady ANTONIA) Cromwell: our chief of men. London, [1973]. pp. 774. bibliog.

- History - 1642-1649, Civil War

JONES (W.J.) Politics and the bench: the judges and the origins of the English Civil War. London, 1971. pp. 228.

- History - 1660-1688, Restoration

KORTHALS (ECKEHARD) Die antipapistische Bewegung in England während der Restaurationszeit von 1660 bis 1673 unter besonderer Berücksichtigung der antimonarchischen Strömungen in den Anfängen der Whig-Partei. Hamburg, 1970. pp. 152. bibliog.

WESTERN (JOHN RANDLE) Monarchy and revolution: the English state in the 1680s. London, 1972. pp. 421. bibliog.

- History - 1688, Revolution of

JONES (JAMES REES) The revolution of 1688 in England. London, [1972]. pp. 345. bibliog.

WESTERN (JOHN RANDLE) Monarchy and revolution: the English state in the 1680s. London, 1972. pp. 421. bibliog.

- History - 1689-1714

WILLIAM III., King of Great Britain and Ireland, and others. Letters of William III and Louis XIV and of their ministers, illustrative of the domestic and foreign politics of England...1697 to 1700; edited by Paul Grimblot. London, 1848. 2 vols.

CARSWELL (JOHN) From revolution to revolution: England 1688-1776. London, 1973. pp. 204. bibliog.

- History - 1700-1799

GREGG (GARY EDWARD) The Protestant succession in international politics, 1710-1716; [Ph. D. (London) thesis]. [1972]. fo. 457. bibliog. Supplementary article in end pocket. Typescript: unpublished. This thesis is the property of London University and may not be removed from the Library.

PLUMB (JOHN HAROLD) In the light of history. London, 1972. pp. 273.

CARSWELL (JOHN) From revolution to revolution: England 1688-1776. London, 1973. pp. 204. bibliog.

STATESMEN, scholars and merchants: essays in eighteenth century history presented to Dame Lucy Sutherland; edited by Anne Whiteman [and others]. Oxford, 1973. pp. 375. bibliog.

- History - 1714-1837

PETRIE (Sir CHARLES ALEXANDER) The four Georges: a revaluation of the period from 1714-1830; [facsimile reprint of work originally published in 1935]. Bath, 1973. pp. 321.

- History - 1760-1789

JARRETT (JOHN DEREK) The begetters of revolution: England's involvement with France, 1759-1789. London, 1973. pp. 320. bibliog.

- History - 1800-1899

BRIGGS (ASA) 1851;...reprinted with illustrations. London, 1951 repr. 1972. pp. 32. (Historical Association. General Series. G. 18)

LLEWELLYN (ALEXANDER) The decade of reform: the 1830s. Newton Abbot, [1972]. pp. 221. bibliog.

- History - 1837-

JARMAN (THOMAS LECKIE) Democracy and world conflict: a history of modern Britain (1868-1970). 3rd ed. London, 1970. pp. 214. bibliog.

- History - 1900-1999

PELLING (HENRY MATHISON) Britain and the Second World War. [London, 1970]. pp. 352. bibliog.

READ (DONALD) Edwardian England, 1901-15: society and politics. London. 1972. pp. 288.

COCKBURN (CLAUD) The devil's decade. London, 1973. pp. 256.

- History, Local

EVERITT (ALAN MILNER) Ways and means in local history. London, [1971]. pp. 50.

HEDGES and local history; [papers of a conference held jointly by the Standing Conference for Local History and the Botanical Society of the British Isles. London, [1971]. pp. 36.

CRISIS and order in English towns, 1500-1700: essays in urban history; edited by Peter Clark and Paul Slack. London, 1972. pp. 364.

HOSKINS (WILLIAM GEORGE) Local history in England. 2nd ed. London, 1972. pp. 268. bibliog.

ROGERS (ALAN) This was their world: approaches to local history. London, 1972. pp. 284.

- History, Local - Bibliography

MARTIN (GEOFFREY HAWARD) and McINTYRE (SYLVIA) A bibliography of British and Irish municipal history. Leicester, 1972 in progress.

- History, Local - Sources

STEPHENS (W.B.) Sources for English local history. Manchester, [1973]. pp. 260

- History, Military - Sources

HIGHAM (ROBIN) ed. A guide to the sources of British military history. London, 1972. pp. 630. bibliogs.

- History, Naval

BICKEL (WOLF HEINRICH) Die anglo-amerikanischen Beziehungen 1927-1930 im Licht der Flottenfrage: das Problem des Machtausgleichs zwischen Grossbritannien und den Vereinigten Staaten in der Zwischenkriegszeit und seine Lösung. Zürich, 1970. pp. 227. bibliog.

- Industries

U.K. Business Statistics Office. Census of Production. Report on the census of production. a., 1970- London. Previous censuses catalogued separately; 1907-1958 shelved at R(O) : 42(f431), 1959-1968 at S : 42[HA 251].

U.K. Board of Trade. 1970. Get ahead in Britain: the facts. 7th ed. [London, 1970]. pp. 25.

NORTH WEST INDUSTRIAL DEVELOPMENT ASSOCIATION. General Council. Annual report. a., 1971/2 (26th)- Manchester.

NATIONAL ECONOMIC DEVELOPMENT OFFICE. Process Plant Working Party. Process industries investment forecasts: the sixth report by the...Working Party, including industrial forecasts made in th period January to March 1971. [London], 1971. pp. 41.

U.K. Department of Trade and Industry. 1971. The Business Statistics Office. London, 1971. pp. 10.

FLORENCE (PHILIP SARGANT) The logic of British and American industry: a realistic analysis of economic structure and government. 3rd ed. London, 1972. pp. 413.

MUSSON (ALBERT EDWARD) ed. Science, technology, and economic growth in the eighteenth century. London, 1972. pp. 211. bibliog.

NOTTINGHAMSHIRE AND DERBYSHIRE SUB-REGIONAL MANAGEMENT COMMITTEE. Mobility of firms. Loughborough, 1972. 1 vol. (various pagings).

PELLEGRINI (JULIAN GAVAN) The effects of the selective employment tax on British manufacturing industries; [Ph.D. (London) thesis]. 1972. fo.148. bibliog. Typescript: unpublished. This thesis is the property of London University and may not be removed from the Library.

UNITED KINGDOM - Industries (Cont'd.)

>REGIONAL development in Britain; [by] Gerald Manners [and others]. London, [1972]. pp. 448. bibliogs.
>
>CHANNON (DEREK F.) The strategy and structure of British enterprise. London, 1973. pp. 257.

UNITED KINGDOM - Industries
See also INDUSTRIAL PROMOTION - United Kingdom

- Industries - Information services

>U.K. Ministry of Technology. 1970. Assistance for industry through the industrial liaison scheme. [London], 1970. pp. 43.
>
>U.K. Department of Trade and Industry. 1971. Assistance for small firms through the industrial liaison service. [London], 1971. pp. 47.
>
>U.K. Department of Trade and Industry. 1972. Assistance for small firms through the industrial liaison service. [rev. ed.] [London], 1972. pp. 44.

- Industries - Mathematical models

>BUXTON (A. J.) Calculation of labour services in U.K. manufacturing, 1948-67. Coventry, 1972. fo. 16. (University of Warwick. Centre for Industrial Economic and Business Research. Warwick Research in Industrial and Business Studies. No.18)
>
>BUXTON (A.J.) An examination of the residual factor in U.K. manufacturing. Coventry, 1972. fo. 12. bibliog. (University of Warwick. Centre for Industrial Economic and Business Research. Warwick Research in Industrial and Business Studies. No. 19)

- Intellectual life

>KOJECKY (ROGER) T.S. Eliot's social criticism. London, 1971. pp. 255.
>
>NELSON (JAMES GRAHAM) The early nineties: a view from the Bodley Head. Cambridge, Mass., 1971. pp. 387.
>
>COX (CHARLES BRIAN) and DYSON (ANTHONY EDWARD) eds. The twentieth-century mind: history, ideas, and literature in Britain. London, 1972 in progress. bibliogs.
>
>PLUMB (JOHN HAROLD) In the light of history. London, 1972. pp. 273.
>
>SZAMUELY (TIBOR) Unique Conservative: three extracts from the works of Tibor Szamuely. London, 1973. pp. 28. (Conservative Political Centre. [Publications]. No. 531)

- Kings and rulers

>BRADLAUGH (CHARLES) George, Prince of Wales; with recent contrasts and coincidences. London, [1870?]. pp. 16.
>
>U.K. Central Office of Information. Reference Division. 1971. The monarchy in Britain. rev. ed. London, 1971. pp. 31. bibliog.

- Manufactures

>DAVIES (J.R.) and KELLY (M.) Small firms in the manufacturing sector. London, 1972. pp. 85. (U.K. Committee of Inquiry on Small Firms. Research Reports. No. 3)

- Maps

>U.K. Department of the Environment. 1971. Department of Employment local office areas; Assisted areas as defined by the Department of Trade and Industry at 5.8.1971; Ordnance Survey administration areas. [London], 1971. 2 maps.

- Military policy

>ANGELL (NORMAN) pseud. [i.e. Sir Ralph Norman Angell LANE] The menace to our national defence. London, 1934. pp. 170.
>
>TUNSTALL (WILLIAM CUTHBERT BRIAN) The Commonwealth and regional defence. London, 1959. pp. 68. (London. University. Institute of Commonwealth Studies. Commonwealth Papers. No. 6)
>
>BARNETT (CORRELLI) The collapse of British power. London, 1972. pp. 643. bibliog.
>
>DENNIS (PETER) Decision by default: peacetime conscription and British defence 1919-39. London, 1972. pp. 243. bibliog.
>
>OXFORD UNIVERSITY CONSERVATIVE ASSOCIATION. Research Committees on Defence. In defence of Europe. [Oxford, 1972]. pp. (24).
>
>DARBY (PHILLIP) British defence policy east of Suez, 1947-1968. London, 1973. pp. 366. bibliog.
>
>PRATT (LAWRENCE R.) The strategic element in Britain's policy in the east Mediterranean, 1936-1939; [Ph. D. (London) thesis]. 1972 [or rather 1973]. fo. 315. bibliog. Typescript: unpublished. This thesis is the property of London University and may not be removed from the Library.

- Militia

>CAMDEN SOCIETY. [Publications]. 4th Series. vol. 10. Herefordshire militia assessments of 1663; edited...by M.A. Faraday. London, 1972. pp. 242.
>
>NORTHAMPTONSHIRE RECORD SOCIETY. Publications. vol. 25. Northamptonshire militia lists, 1777; edited by Victor A. Hatley. [Northampton], 1973. pp. 260.

- Moral conditions

>NATIONAL OPINION POLLS LIMITED. Report on attitudes towards crime, violence and permissiveness in society; prepared for The Daily Mail. London, 1970. 1 vol. (various foliations).
>
>McMILLAN (JAMES) The roots of corruption: the erosion of traditional values in Britain from 1960 to the present day. London, 1972. pp. 210.

- Navy - History

>GOUGH (BARRY M.) The Royal Navy and the northwest coast of North America, 1810-1914: a study of British maritime ascendancy. Vancouver, [1971]. pp. 294. bibliog.

- Nobility

>ROSENTHAL (JOEL T.) The purchase of paradise: gift giving and the aristocracy, 1307-1485. London, 1972. pp. 169.
>
>McFARLANE (KENNETH BRUCE) The nobility of later medieval England: the Ford Lectures for 1953 and related studies. Oxford, 1973. pp. 315.
>
>STONE (LAWRENCE) Family and fortune: studies in aristocratic finance in the sixteenth and seventeenth centuries. Oxford, 1973. pp. 315.

- Occupations

U.K. Department of Employment. 1972. Classification of occupations and directory of occupational titles. London, 1972. 3 vols.

- Officials and employees

U.K. Civil Service Commission. 1970. Economists in government service. London, 1970. pp. 27.

HEPPLE (BOB ALEXANDER) and O'HIGGINS (PAUL) Public employee trade unionism in the United Kingdom: the legal framework. Ann Arbor, 1971. pp. 221. bibliog. (Michigan University and Wayne State University. Institute of Labor and Industrial Relations. Comparative Studies in Public Employment Labor Relations)

SAINTY (JOHN CHRISTOPHER) Treasury officials, 1660-1870. London, 1972. pp. 161. bibliog. (London. University. Institute of Historical Research. Office-holders in Modern Britain. 1)

U.K. Civil Service Commission. 1972. Scientists in government service. Basingstoke, 1972. pp. 103.

MELVILLE (Sir RONALD) and BURNEY (Sir ANTHONY GEORGE BERNARD) The use of accountants in the civil service; report of an enquiry. [London], Civil Service Department, 1973. pp. 47.

SAINTY (JOHN CHRISTOPHER) Officials of the Secretaries of State, 1660-1782. London, 1973. pp. 119. (London. University. Institute of Historical Research. Office-Holders in Modern Britain. 2)

U.K. Supplementary Benefits Commission. 1973. Training of staff. London, 1973. pp. 40. (Supplementary Benefits Administration Papers. 3)

- Parliament

LENNOX (CHARLES) 3rd Duke of Richmond. A letter ...to Lieutenant Colonel Sharman, chairman to the committee of correspondence appointed by the delegates of forty-five corps of volunteers, assembled at Lisburn in Ireland; with notes, etc. London, 1792. pp. 16.

YATE (WALTER HONYWOOD) Political and historical arguments proving the necessity of a parliamentary reform, etc. London, 1812. 2 vols. (in 1).

U.K. Central Office of Information. Reference Division. Reference Pamphlets. 33. The British Parliament. [7th ed.] London, 1971. pp. 54. bibliog.

BRADSHAW (KENNETH) and PRING (DAVID) Parliament and Congress. London, 1972. pp. 426.

CREASEY (JOHN) Evolution to democracy. rev. ed. London, 1972. pp. 152.

PETERSMANN (HANS G.) Die Souveränität des britischen Parlaments in den Europäischen Gemeinschaften. Baden-Baden, [1972]. pp. 338. bibliog.

WILDING (NORMAN W.) and LAUNDY (PHILIP A.C.) An encyclopaedia of Parliament. 4th ed. London, 1972. pp. 931. bibliog.

HOLLIS (MAURICE CHRISTOPHER) Parliament and its sovereignty. London, 1973. pp. 189. bibliog.

PUNNETT (ROBERT MALCOLM) Front-bench opposition: the role of the Leader of the Opposition, the Shadow Cabinet and shadow government in British politics. London, 1973. pp. 500. bibliog.

U.K. Central Office of Information. Reference Division. Reference Pamphlets. 33. The British parliament. 8th ed. London, 1973. pp. 56. bibliog.

- Parliament - Dissolution

MARKESINIS (B.S.) The theory and practice of dissolution of parliament: a comparative study with special reference to the United Kingdom and Greek experience. Cambridge, 1972. pp. 283. bibliog.

- Parliament - Elections

LAWS concerning the election of Members of Parliament; with the determinations of the House of Commons thereon, and all their incidents continued down to the present time...; by a gentleman of the Inner Temple [J.R.]. 6th ed. London, W. Owen, 1780. pp. xxxvix, 383,(20).

[NORTHUMBERLAND and Durham election broadsides]. Newcastle on Tyne, etc., 1820-32. 69 items (in 1 vol.).

[NORTHUMBERLAND elections, 1826: a collection of cartoons, newspaper cuttings and election literature, with one autograph letter]. v.p., 1826. 1 vol. (unpaged).

MEREWETHER (HENRY ALWORTH) the Elder. Speech of Mr. Sergeant Merewether, counsel for the Hon. J.E. Elliot, M.P., before the select committee of the House of Commons upon the Roxburgh election petition, 16th February 1838; from Mr. Gurney's notes. Edinburgh, Black, 1838. pp. 63.

SMITH (HENRY STOOKS) The parliaments of England from 1715 to 1847; [reprint of work first published in 3 volumes in 1844-1850];... edited by F.W.S. Craig. Chichester, 1973. pp. 772.

HALES (HAROLD KEATES) The road to Westminster, and my impressions of Parliament. London, [1936]. pp. 96.

LABOUR PARTY. Labour's election who's who: main list...parliamentary candidates, general election, 1950; [with supplementary list]. London, [1950]. pp. 113, 12.

LABOUR PARTY. Labour's election who's who: main list...parliamentary candidates, general election, 1951; [with 3 supplementary lists]. London, [1951]. pp. 115,6,4, fo. 4.

LABOUR PARTY. [Labour's election who's who: main list...parliamentary candidates, general election, 1955]; ([with] Supplementary list). London, [1955]. pp. 113,12. Wanting title-page.

LABOUR PARTY. Labour's election who's who: main list...parliamentary candidates, general election, 1959; [with final supplement]. London, [1959]. pp. 116, 6.

LABOUR PARTY. Labour's election who's who: main list...parliamentary candidates, general election 1966. London, [1966]. pp. 134.

CRAIG (FRED W.S.) compiler. British parliamentary election results, 1950-1970. Chichester, 1971. pp. 780.

McCALMONT (FREDERICK HAYNES) Parliamentary poll book: British election results 1832-1918; eighth edition [i.e. 7th ed. reprinted] with introduction and additional material [to 1918] by J. Vincent and M. Stenton. Brighton, 1971. 1 vol. (various pagings). Facsimile text of 7th ed. of 1910.

BLEWETT (NEAL) The peers, the parties and the people: the general elections of 1910. London, 1972. pp. 548. bibliog.

CHARLOT (MONICA) La democratie à l'Anglaise: les campagnes électorales en Grande-Bretagne depuis 1931. Paris, 1972. pp. 446. (Fondation Nationale des Sciences Politiques. Cahiers. 185)

UNITED KINGDOM - Parliament
Elections (Cont'd.)

DOD (CHARLES ROGER) Electoral facts from 1832 to 1853 impartially stated, constituting a complete political gazetteer; [reprint of rev. 1853 ed.] edited with an introduction and bibliographical guide to electoral sources, 1832-1885, by H.J. Hanham. Brighton, 1972. pp. 388. bibliog.

PULZER (PETER GEORGE JULIUS) Political representation and elections in Britain. 2nd ed. London, 1972. pp. 176. bibliog.

RICHARDS (JAMES O.) Party propaganda under Queen Anne: the general elections of 1702-1713. Athens, Ga., [1972]. pp. 191. bibliog.

CANNON (JOHN) Parliamentary reform, 1640-1832. Cambridge, 1973. pp. 333. bibliog.

COOK (CHRISTOPHER PIERS) and RAMSDEN (JOHN) b. 1947, eds. By-elections in British politics. London, 1973. pp. 406. bibliog.

RUSSELL (ALAN K.) Liberal landslide: the general election of 1906. Newton Abbot, 1973. pp. 260. bibliog.

- Parliament - History

JONES (ANDREW) The politics of reform, 1884. Cambridge, 1972. pp. 281. bibliog.

JONES (WILBUR DEVEREUX) and ERICKSON (ARVEL BENJAMIN) The Peelites, 1846-1857. [Columbus, 1972]. pp. 259. bibliog.

PIRNIE (BRUCE R.) Das britische Parlament in der Aussenpolitik, 1892-1902. [Heidelberg?], 1972. pp. 260. bibliog.

CANNON (JOHN) Parliamentary reform, 1640-1832. Cambridge, 1973. pp. 333. bibliog.

MacCORMACK (JOHN R.) Revolutionary politics in the Long Parliament. Cambridge, Mass., 1973. pp. 365.

- Parliament - History - Bibliography

COBB (HENRY STEPHEN) compiler. A handlist of articles in periodicals and other serial publications relating to the history of Parliament. [London], 1973. fo. 82. (U.K. Parliament. House of Lords. Record Office. Supplementary Memoranda)

- Parliament - History - Sources

BOND (MAURICE F.) A short guide to the records of parliament. 2nd ed. [London], House of Lords Record Office, 1973. pp. 23.

- Parliament - Privileges and immunities

PACHAURI (P.S.) The law of parliamentary privileges in U.K. and in India. Bombay, 1971. pp. 507.

- Parliament - Reporters and reporting

KEMP (BETTY) Votes and standing orders of the House of Commons: the beginning. London, 1971. pp. 50. (U.K. Parliament. House of Commons. Library. Documents. No. 8)

MENHENNET (DAVID) The Journal of the House of Commons: a bibliographical and historical guide. London, 1971. pp. 96. bibliog. (U.K. Parliament. House of Commons. Library. Documents. No. 7)

- Parliament - Rules and practice

The GROWTH of parliamentary scrutiny by committee: a symposium by Alfred Morris... with essays by seven other M.P.s of the 1966-70 Parliament. Oxford, [1970]. pp. 141.

KEMP (BETTY) Votes and standing orders of the House of Commons: the beginning. London, 1971. pp. 50. (U.K. Parliament. House of Commons. Library. Documents. No. 8)

LAMBERT (SHEILA) Bills and acts: legislative procedure in eighteenth-century England. Cambridge, 1971. pp. 246. bibliog.

THORNE (PETER F.) The mace in the House of Commons. rev. ed. London, 1971. pp. 11. (U.K. Parliament. House of Commons. Library. Documents. No. 3)

U.K. Treasury. 1972. Supply and other financial procedure of the House of Commons. [London, 1972]. pp. 114. Loose-leaf binder.

- Parliament - Salaries, allowances, etc.

PALMER (HERBERT JOHN) Ministerial salaries. [London, 1971]. fo. 8. bibliog. (U.K. Parliament. House of Commons. Library. Research Division. Background Papers. No. 19)

- Parliament - House of Commons

LAWS concerning the election of Members of Parliament; with the determinations of the House of Commons thereon, and all their incidents continued down to the present time...; by a gentleman of the Inner Temple [J.R.]. 6th ed. London, W. Owen, 1780. pp. xxxvix, 383,(20).

GAVAN-DUFFY (THOMAS) Capitalism in Parliament: the crimes of a session. London, 1905. pp. 16. (Independent Labour Party. Tracts for the Times. No.6)

HALES (HAROLD KEATES) The road to Westminster, and my impressions of Parliament. London, [1936]. pp. 96.

JOHNSON (DONALD McINTOSH) Ted Heath, a latter day Charlemagne: Europe, slave or free? London, 1971. pp. 64.

LEONARD (RICHARD LAWRENCE) and HERMAN (VALENTINE) eds. The backbencher and Parliament: a reader. London, 1972. pp. 268. bibliog.

LUTTRELL (NARCISSUS) The parliamentary diary of Narcissus Luttrell, 1691-1693; edited by Henry Horwitz. Oxford, 1972. pp. 538. bibliog.

RICHARDS (PETER GODFREY) The backbenchers. London, 1972. pp. 248. bibliog

KING (ANTHONY) and SLOMAN (ANNE) Westminster and beyond: based on the B.B.C. radio series 'Talking Politics'. London, 1973. pp. 175.

MEDAWAR (THERESE) and PALMER (HERBERT JOHN) The financial interests of Ministers and Members of Parliament. [London, 1973]. pp. 32. (U.K. Parliament. House of Commons. Library. Research Division. Background Papers. No. 28)

The PARLIAMENTARY lists of the early eighteenth century: their compilation and use: the proceedings of a colloquium held at Leicester... 1970; edited... by Aubrey Newman. Leicester, 1973. pp. 95. bibliog.

UNITED KINGDOM - Parliament - House of Commons
See also LEGISLATORS - United Kingdom

- Parliament - House of Lords

U.K. Parliament. House of Lords. 1641-1805. House of Lords sessional papers, 1641-1805; edited by F. William Torrington. Dobbs Ferry, 1972 in progress.

BLOM-COOPER (LOUIS JACQUES) and DREWRY (GAVIN) Final appeal: a study of the House of Lords in its judicial capacity. Oxford, 1972. pp. 584. bibliog.

- Peerage

ROTH (ANDREW) Lord on the board: 1972 edition. London, 1972. pp. 824. (Parliamentary Profile Services. Parliamentary Profiles)

- Politics and government

TROTSKII (LEV DAVYDOVICH) Europe et Amérique; [and] Où va l'Angleterre?; [reprints of the works originally published in 1926 with] préface de Pierre Naville. Paris, 1970. 2 vols. (in 1).

MAXTON (JAMES) If I were dictator. London, 1935. pp. 110.

CLARKE (Sir RICHARD WILLIAM BARNES) New trends in government; lectures delivered...at the Civil Service College between March 1 and April 5, 1971. London, H.M.S.O., 1971. pp. 130. (Civil Service College [U.K.]. Studies. 1)

U.K. Parliament. House of Lords. 1641-1805. House of Lords sessional papers, 1641-1805; edited by F. William Torrington. Dobbs Ferry, 1972 in progress.

GLADDEN (EDGAR NORMAN) A student's guide to public administration. London, 1972. 2 vols. bibliogs. vol. 1. Central government administration. vol. 2. Local, corporational and international administration.

CANNON (JOHN) Parliamentary reform, 1640-1832. Cambridge, 1973. pp. 333. bibliog.

- Politics and government - To 1603

PRESTWICH (MICHAEL) War, politics and finance under Edward I. London, [1972]. pp. 317. bibliog.

- Politics and government - 1485-1603

PULMAN (MICHAEL BARRACLOUGH) The Elizabethan Privy Council in the fifteen-seventies. Berkeley, Calif., 1971. pp. 279. bibliog.

HURSTFIELD (JOEL) Freedom, corruption and government in Elizabethan England. London, 1973. pp. 368

- Politics and government - 1603-1714

JONES (W.J.) Politics and the bench: the judges and the origins of the English Civil War. London, 1971. pp. 228.

LUTTRELL (NARCISSUS) The parliamentary diary of Narcissus Luttrell, 1691-1693; edited by Henry Horwitz. Oxford, 1972. pp. 538. bibliog.

AYLMER (GERALD EDWARD) The state's servants: the civil service of the English republic, 1649-1660. London, 1973. pp. 484.

MacCORMACK (JOHN R.) Revolutionary politics in the Long Parliament. Cambridge, Mass., 1973. pp. 365.

The PARLIAMENTARY lists of the early eighteenth century: their compilation and use: the proceedings of a colloquium held at Leicester... 1970; edited... by Aubrey Newman. Leicester, 1973. pp. 95. bibliog.

- Politics and government - 1700-1799

SMITH (ROBERT ARTHUR) Eighteenth-century English politics: patrons and place-hunters. New York, [1972]. pp. 214. bibliog.

The PARLIAMENTARY lists of the early eighteenth century: their compilation and use: the proceedings of a colloquium held at Leicester... 1970; edited... by Aubrey Newman. Leicester, 1973. pp. 95. bibliog.

- Politics and government - 1714-1756

[GORDON (THOMAS) of Kirkcudbright] An appeal to the unprejudiced, concerning the present discontents occasioned by the late convention with Spain. London, Cooper, 1739. pp. 32.

- Politics and government - 1756-1837

A SECOND letter from Wiltshire to the Monitor, on the vindication of his constitutional principles. London, Hooper, 1759. pp. 32. 21 cm.

- Politics and government - 1756-1837

The LEGITIMATE consequences of reform, and an exposure of the abuses in church and state, with a detailed account of the chief acts of the Grey administration. Edinburgh, Tait, 1834. pp 433.

VESTER (MICHAEL) Die Entstehung des Proletariats als Lernprozess: die Entstehung antikapitalistischer Theorie und Praxis in England 1792-1848. Frankfurt am Main, 1972. pp. 454. bibliog.

LANGFORD (PAUL) The first Rockingham administration, 1765-1766. London, 1973. pp. 318. bibliog.

- Politics and government - 1800-1899

REID (STUART J.) Lord John Russell. rev. ed. London, 1895. pp. 380.

GLADSTONE (WILLIAM EWART) Autobiographica; edited by John Brooke and Mary Sorensen. London, 1971. pp. 263. (U.K. Historical Manuscripts Commission. The Prime Ministers' Papers. W.E. Gladstone. 1)

GASH (NORMAN) Sir Robert Peel: the life of Sir Robert Peel after 1830. London, 1972. pp. 743. bibliog.

GLADSTONE (WILLIAM EWART) Autobiographical memoranda, 1832-1845; edited by John Brooke and Mary Sorensen. London, 1972. pp. 294. (U.K. Historical Manuscripts Commission. The Prime Ministers' Papers. W.E. Gladstone. 2)

LLEWELLYN (ALEXANDER) The decade of reform: the 1830s. Newton Abbot, [1972]. pp. 221. bibliog.

- Politics and government - 1800-1837

KIRWAN (A.V.) A letter from Munich to the right honourable the Lord Palmerston, his Britanic [sic] Majesty's minister of state for foreign affairs on the late happy change of ministry in England. Munich, Wolf, 1830. pp. 72.

- Politics and government - 1837-1901

DISRAELI (BENJAMIN) 1st Earl of Beaconsfield. The Hughenden papers: [selections from the papers relating to Benjamin Disraeli, Earl of Beaconsfield, preserved at Hughenden Manor, near High Wycombe, Buckinghamshire]; Group A, sections I,V,X-XII; Group B; Group R ["Rose papers"]. [1820-1918]. Microfilm: 73 reels. For details of Library holdings readers should consult the Handlist of the Hughenden papers, kept in Room Z.

CECIL (ROBERT ARTHUR TALBOT GASCOYNE) 3rd Marquis of Salisbury. Lord Salisbury on politics: a selection from his articles in the Quarterly Review, 1860-1883; edited with an introduction and notes by Paul Smith. Cambridge, 1972. pp. 386. bibliog.

UNITED KINGDOM - Politics and government - 1837-1901 (Cont'd.)

HAMILTON (Sir EDWARD WALTER) The diary of Sir Edward Walter Hamilton, 1880-1885; edited by Dudley W.R. Bahlman. Oxford, 1972. 2 vols.

JONES (ANDREW) The politics of reform, 1884. Cambridge, 1972. pp. 281. bibliog.

JONES (WILBUR DEVEREUX) and ERICKSON (ARVEL BENJAMIN) The Peelites, 1846-1857. [Columbus, 1972]. pp. 259. bibliog.

PREST (JOHN) Lord John Russell. London, 1972. pp. 558. bibliog.

VESTER (MICHAEL) Die Entstehung des Proletariats als Lernprozess: die Entstehung antikapitalistischer Theorie und Praxis in England 1792-1848. Frankfurt am Main, 1972. pp. 454. bibliog.

EMY (HUGH VINCENT) Liberals, radicals and social politics, 1892-1914. Cambridge, 1973. pp. 318. bibliog.

MATTHEW (HENRY COLIN GRAY) The Liberal imperialists: the ideas and politics of a post-Gladstonian élite. London, 1973. pp. 331. bibliog.

WATSON (GEORGE) The English ideology: studies in the language of Victorian politics. London, 1973. pp. 276.

WILSON (JOHN) b. 1924. CB: a life of Sir Henry Campbell-Bannerman. London, 1973. pp. 718. bibliog.

ZEBEL (SYDNEY H.) Balfour: a political biography. Cambridge, 1973. pp. 312. bibliog.

- **Politics and government - 1900-1999**

CHAPMAN (Sir SYDNEY JOHN) [Unpublished autobiography of Sir Sydney John Chapman]. [194-?]. fo. 315. Xerographic copy of typescript.

RYZHIKOV (VLADIMIR ALEKSANDROVICH) "Sotsializm" po-leiboristski: mify i real'nost'. Moskva, 1971. pp. 208.

MACDONALD (JAMES RAMSAY) Political writings; edited...by Bernard Barker. London, [1972]. pp. 259. bibliog.

TARIQ ALI. The coming British revolution. London, 1972. pp. 259.

TAYLOR (ALAN JOHN PERCIVALE) Beaverbrook. London, 1972. pp. 712. bibliog.

BIRCH (ANTHONY HAROLD) The British system of government. 3rd ed. London, 1973. pp. 306.

COOK (CHRISTOPHER PIERS) and RAMSDEN (JOHN) b. 1947, eds. By-elections in British politics. London, 1973. pp. 406. bibliog.

DONOUGHUE (BERNARD) and JONES (GEORGE WILLIAM) D.Phil.(Oxon.). Herbert Morrison: portrait of a politician. London, [1973]. pp. 696.

SHINWELL (EMANUEL) Baron Shinwell. I've lived through it all. London, 1973. pp. 280. bibliog.

ZEBEL (SYDNEY H.) Balfour: a political biography. Cambridge, 1973. pp. 312. bibliog.

- **Politics and government - 1901-1945**

HAMILTON (MARY AGNES) Margaret Bondfield. London, 1924. pp. 191.

TAYLOR (HENRY ARCHIBALD) The strange case of Andrew Bonar Law. London, [1932]. pp. 284.

MARRIOTT (Sir JOHN ARTHUR RANSOME) Memories of four score years: the autobiography of the late Sir John Marriott. London, 1946. pp. 252.

- **Politics and government - 1901-1918**

ROWLAND (PETER) The last Liberal governments: unfinished business, 1911-1914. London, 1971. pp. 405. bibliog.

BLEWETT (NEAL) The peers, the parties and the people: the general elections of 1910. London, 1972. pp. 548. bibliog.

REMPEL (RICHARD A.) Unionists divided: Arthur Balfour, Joseph Chamberlain and the Unionist Free Traders. Newton Abbot, 1972. pp. 236. bibliog.

EMY (HUGH VINCENT) Liberals, radicals and social politics, 1892-1914. Cambridge, 1973. pp. 318. bibliog.

WILSON (JOHN) b. 1924. CB: a life of Sir Henry Campbell-Bannerman. London, 1973. pp. 718. bibliog.

- **Politics and government - 1918-1945**

DUTT (RAJANI PALME) The coming war. London, 1929. pp. 24.

SCANLON (JOHN) Pillars of cloud. London, 1936. pp. 320.

BENEWICK (ROBERT) The fascist movement in Britain rev. ed. London, 1972. pp. 340. bibliog.

BOYCE (DAVID GEORGE) Englishmen and Irish troubles: British public opinion and the making of Irish policy 1918-22. London, 1972. pp. 253. bibliog.

BALFOUR (HAROLD HARINGTON) 1st Baron Balfour of Inchrye. Wings over Westminster. London, 1973. pp. 224.

KINNEAR (MICHAEL) The fall of Lloyd George: the political crisis of 1922. London, 1973. pp. 317. bibliog.

THOMAS (HUGH) John Strachey. London, 1973. pp. 316.

TROTSKII (LEV DAVYDOVICH) Leon Trotsky on Britain: [selected writings]; introduction by George Novack. New York, 1973. pp. 334. bibliog.

- **Politics and government - 1945-**

POLLITT (HARRY) For Britain free and independent: the report made by Harry Pollitt to the 20th National Congress of the Communist Party, together with his reply to discussion. London, 1948. pp. 51.

CONSERVATIVE CENTRAL OFFICE. The campaign guide 1966 the unique political reference book; [edited by Oliver Stebbings]. London, 1966. pp. 375.

CATO pseud. Pride, prejudice and persuasion:...how the establishment got hooked on Europe; (a study in the manipulation of public opinion in Britain). London, [1971]. pp. 33.

MONAHAN (BRYAN WILLIS) The survival of Britain: contemporaneous commentaries on linked events of 1968-1970; [articles from The Social Crediter, pamphlets, unpublished material]; edited and arranged by T.N. Morris. London, 1971. pp. 124.

PARTISANS. No. 58. Quelle Grande-Bretagne? Paris, 1971. pp. 171.

PUNNETT (ROBERT MALCOLM) British government and politics. 2nd ed. London, 1971 repr. 1973. pp. 512. bibliog.

SALYCHEV (S.S.) ed. Politicheskie bitvy v stranakh kapitala. Moskva, 1971. pp. 344.

[SHORE (PETER)] The case against entry: the United Kingdom and the European Communities;... the answer to the white paper. [London, 1971]. pp. 32.

1972

BENEWICK (ROBERT) and SMITH (TREVOR) Liberal, eds. Direct action and democratic politics. London, 1972. pp. 324. (Acton Society. Studies. 1)

BERKELEY (HUMPHRY) Crossing the floor. London, 1972. pp. 170.

BRENNAN (T.) Politics and government in Britain: an introductry survey. Cambridge, [1972]. pp. 332. bibliog.

The DECADE of disillusion: British politics in the sixties; edited by David McKie and Chris Cook. London, 1972. pp. 250.

FABIAN SOCIETY. Fabian Tracts. [No.] 414. Towards a radical agenda: comments on Labour's programme. London, 1972. pp. 60.

GILISON (JEROME MARTIN) British and Soviet politics: legitimacy and convergence. Baltimore, [1972]. pp. 186.

GOLDRING (MAURICE) and others. La Grande-Bretagne en crise. Paris, [1972]. pp. 128.

GOODMAN (ARNOLD ABRAHAM) Baron Goodman. Not for the record: selected speeches and writings. London, 1972. pp. 173.

HARGROVE (ERWIN C.) Professional roles in society and government: the English case. Beverly Hills [1972]. pp. 84. bibliog.

HEATH (EDWARD RICHARD GEORGE) My style of government; by the Rt. Hon. Edward Heath, in an exclusive interview with Charles Wintour...and Robert Carvel, etc. [London, 1972]. pp. 11.

JAMES (ROBERT RHODES) Ambitions and realities: British politics, 1964-70. London, [1972]. pp. 311. bibliog

JENKINS (ROY HARRIS) What matters now. [London], 1972. pp. 122.

KING (CECIL HARMSWORTH) The Cecil King diary. 1965-1970. London, 1972. pp. 353.

LABOUR PARTY. Conference, 1972. Labour's programme for Britain. London, [1972]. pp. 80.

LAING (MARGARET) Edward Heath, Prime Minister. London, 1972. pp. 258.

MACMILLAN (HAROLD) Pointing the way, 1959-1961. London 1972. pp. 504.

POWELL (JOHN ENOCH) Still to decide; edited by John Wood. London, 1972. pp. 246.

ROTH (ANDREW) Heath and the Heathmen. London, 1972. pp. 253.

SMITH (TREVOR) Liberal. Anti-politics: consensus, reform and protest in Britain...assisted by Alison Thomson. London, 1972. pp. 200. bibliog.

WIGG (GEORGE EDWARD CECIL) Baron Wigg. George Wigg. London, 1972. pp. 384. bibliog.

WILLIAMS (MARCIA) Inside Number 10. London, [1972]. pp. 385.

1973

CHAPMAN (RICHARD A.) ed. The role of commissions in policy-making. London, 1973. pp. 206.

FABIAN SOCIETY. Fabian Tracts. [No.] 426. Administrative reform: the next step; [by] John Garrett [and] Robert Sheldon. London, 1973. pp. 18.

FISHER (Sir NIGEL THOMAS LOVERIDGE) Iain Macleod. London, 1973. pp. 352.

HEFFER (ERIC SAMUEL) The class struggle in Parliament: a socialist view of industrial relations. London, 1973. pp. 350. bibliog.

LABOUR PARTY. National Executive Committee. Labour's programme for Britain: annual conference, 1973. London. [1973]. pp. 122.

MACMILLAN (HAROLD) At the end of the day, 1961-1963. London, 1973. pp. 572.

PUNNETT (ROBERT MALCOLM) Front-bench opposition: the role of the Leader of the Opposition, the Shadow Cabinet and shadow government in British politics. London, 1973. pp. 500. bibliog.

PUTNAM (ROBERT D.) The beliefs of politicians: ideology, conflict and democracy in Britain and Italy. New Haven, 1973. pp. 309.

The RED paper: a response to the Labour Party's Green Paper, "Labour's programme for Britain"; [produced by a group under the chairmanship of Ernie Roberts]. n.p., [1973?]. pp. 20.

THOMAS (HUGH) John Strachey. London, 1973. pp. 316.

URRY (JOHN) and WAKEFORD (JOHN) Lecturer in Sociology at Brunel University, eds. Power in Britain: sociological readings. London, 1973. pp. 330. bibliog.

WATKINS (KENNETH WILLIAM) Influencing the political future. London, [1973]. pp. 10. (Aims of Industry. The Future of Capitalism)

- Population

MASS-OBSERVATION. Britain and her birth-rate: a report prepared... for the Advertising Service Guild, etc. London, 1945. pp. 245. bibliog.

FLINN (MICHAEL W.) British population growth, 1700-1850. London, 1970, repr. 1972. pp. 66. bibliog. (Economic History Society. Studies in Economic History)

OGILVY (AUDREY ANNE) Employment expansion and the development of new town hinterlands, 1961-1966. Garston, [1971]. pp. (13). (U.K. Building Research Station. Current Papers. 10/71)

CHAMBERS (JONATHAN DAVID) Population, economy, and society in pre-industrial England; edited with a preface and introduction by W.A. Armstrong. London, 1972. pp. 162. bibliog. (University of Kent at Canterbury. Kent Co-operative Lectures. 1967)

CONSERVATION SOCIETY. A population policy for Britain. Walton-on-Thames, [1972]. pp. 23.

JOHNSON (STANLEY P.) A population policy for Britain. [London], 1972. pp. 15. (Conservative Research Department. Old Queen Street Papers. No. 18)

KELSALL (ROGER KEITH) Population. 2nd ed. London, 1972. pp. 127. bibliog.

NINETEENTH century society: essays in the use of quantitative methods for the study of social data; edited by E.A. Wrigley. Cambridge, 1972. pp. 448. bibliog. (Cambridge Group for the History of Population and Social Structure. Publications. [No. 3?])

UNITED KINGDOM - Population (Cont'd.)

OGILVY (AUDREY ANNE) Migration and the growth of population of Bracknell New Town, 1951-1968; [Ph.D. (London) thesis]. 1972. fo. 327. bibliog. Typescript: unpublished. This thesis is the property of London University and may not be removed from the Library.

THOMAS (BRINLEY) Migration and urban development: a reappraisal of British and American long cycles. London, 1972. pp. 259. bibliog.

U.K. Parliament. House of Commons. Library. Research Division. Background Papers. No. 23. A background note on population in the United Kingdom. [London, 1972]. fo. 11.

BROOKS (EDWIN) This crowded kingdom: an essay on population pressure in Great Britain. London, 1973. pp. 176. bibliog.

EVERSLEY (DAVID EDWARD CHARLES) A question of numbers? London, 1973. pp. 32. (Runnymede Trust. Runnymede Lectures. 1972)

GLASS (DAVID VICTOR) Numbering the people: the eighteenth-century population controversy and the development of census and vital statistics in Britain. Farnborough, 1973. pp. 205.

TRANTER (N.L.) ed. Population and industrialization: the evolution of a concept and its practical application; [a reader]. London, 1973. pp. 296.

U.K. Office of Population Censuses and Surveys. 1973. Cohort studies: new developments. London, 1973. pp. 14. (Studies on Medical and Population Subjects. No. 25)

- Public lands

WISDOM (ALLEN SIDNEY) Appropriation of land by local authorities. 2nd ed. Chichester, 1971. 1 pamphlet (unpaged).

- Public works

COLVIN (HOWARD MONTAGU) ed. The history of the King's works. London, H.M.S.O., 1963 in progress.

- Race question

LONDON. London Committee of Deputies of the British Jews. Working Party on Race Relations. Improving race relations: a Jewish contribution; a report and recommendations. London, 1969. pp. 37. bibliog.

PATTERSON (SHEILA) Immigration and race relations in Britain, 1960-1967. London, O.U.P., 1969. pp. xviii, 460. bibliog. 21½cm.

WAINWRIGHT (DAVID) Race and employment: managing a multi-racial labour force. London, 1970. pp. 88.

ALLEN (SHEILA) New minorities, old conflicts: Asian and West Indian migrants in Britain. New York, [1971]. pp. 223. bibliog.

The MULTI-racial school: a professional perspective; edited by Julia McNeal and Margaret Rogers. Harmondsworth, 1971. pp. 154. bibliogs.

STEPHEN (DAVID) and others, compilers. Race and jobs: 71 questions answered on immigration, race relations and the Race Relations Act. 2nd ed. London, 1971. 1 pamphlet (unpaged).

U.K. Race Relations Board. East Midlands Conciliation Committee. Annual report. a., 1972- London.

U.K. Race Relations Board. North West Conciliation Committee. Annual report. a., 1972- London.

U.K. Race Relations Board. Wales and South West Conciliation Committee. Annual report. a., 1972 [1st]- [Birmingham].

U.K. Race Relations Board. West Metropolitan Conciliation Committee. Annual report. a., 1972- London.

U.K. Race Relations Board. West Midlands Conciliation Committee. Annual report. a., 1972- [London].

U.K. Race Relations Board. Yorkshire and North East Conciliation Committee. Annual report. a., 1972- London.

BANTON (MICHAEL PARKER) Racial minorities. London, 1972. pp. 192. bibliog.

BOLTON (FELICITY) and LAISHLEY (JENNIE) Education for a multi-racial Britain. London, 1972. pp. 20. (Fabian Society. Research Series. [No.] 303)

CHARLOT (MONICA) Naissance d'un problème racial: minorités de couleur en Grande-Bretagne. Paris, [1972]. pp. 344. bibliog. In French and English.

CHEETHAM (JULIET) Social work with immigrants. London, 1972. pp. 230. bibliog.

RIMMER (MALCOLM) Race and industrial conflict: a study in a group of Midland foundries. London, 1972. pp. 74. (Warwick Studies in Industrial Relations)

SCOBIE (EDWARD) Black Britannia: a history of blacks in Britain. Chicago, 1972. pp. 316. bibliogs.

U.K. Central Office of Information. Reference Division. Reference Pamphlets. 108. Race relations in Britain. London, 1972. pp. 29. bibliog.

U.K. Department of Employment. 1972. Take 7: the report on a survey undertaken by the Department of Employment into immigrant labour relations at seven English firms. London, 1972. pp. 118.

BANTON (MICHAEL PARKER) Police-community relations. London, 1973. pp. 176. bibliog.

DUMMETT (ANN) A portrait of English racism. Harmondsworth, 1973. pp. 300. bibliog.

KATZNELSON (IRA) Black men, white cities: race, politics, and migration in the United States, 1900-30, and Britain, 1948-68. London, 1973. pp. 219.

MULLARD (CHRIS) Black Britain;...with an account of recent events at the Institute of Race Relations by Alexander Kirby. London, 1973. pp. 194. bibliog.

RUNNYMEDE TRUST. Questions and answers on race relations and immigration. London, 1973. pp. 26.

U.K. Race Relations Board. 1973. A project on race relations; (...produced...for use in schools and other educational establishments). [London, 1973]. pp. 14. bibliog.

- Race question - Bibliography

COMMUNITY RELATIONS COMMISSION. Race relations in Britain: selected bibliography with emphasis on Commonwealth immigrants. 2nd ed. London, [1971]. pp. 12.

- Relations (general) with France

JARRETT (JOHN DEREK) The begetters of revolution: England's involvement with France, 1759-1789. London, 1973. pp. 320. bibliog.

- Relations (general) with Latin America

   U.K. Central Office of Information. Reference Division. Reference Pamphlets. 86. Britain and Latin America. 2nd ed. London, 1973. pp. 63. bibliog.

   WALNE (PETER) ed. A guide to manuscript sources for the history of Latin America and the Caribbean in the British Isles. London, 1973. pp. 580.

- Relations (general) with Malta

   U.K. Central Office of Information. Reference Division. 1971. Anglo-Maltese relations. London, 1971. pp. 8.

- Relations (general) with the United States

   OLSON (ALISON GILBERT) Anglo-American politics, 1660-1775: the relationship between parties in England and colonial America. Oxford, 1973. pp. 192.

- Relations (military) with the Mediterranean

   PRATT (LAWRENCE R.) The strategic element in Britain's policy in the east Mediterranean, 1936-1939; [Ph. D. (London) thesis]. 1972 [or rather 1973]. fo. 315. bibliog. Typescript: unpublished. This thesis is the property of London University and may not be removed from the Library.

- Relations (military) with the United States

   TRASK (DAVID F.) Captains and cabinets: Anglo-American naval relations, 1917-1918. Columbia, Mo., [1972]. pp. 396. bibliog.

- Religion

   KORTHALS (ECKEHARD) Die antipapistische Bewegung in England während der Restaurationszeit von 1660 bis 1673 unter besonderer Berücksichtigung der antimonarchischen Strömungen in den Anfängen der Whig-Partei. Hamburg, 1970. pp. 152. bibliog.

   THOMAS (KEITH) Religion and the decline of magic: studies in popular beliefs in sixteenth and seventeenth century England. London, 1971. pp. 716.

   KEY variables in social research...: [papers of a British Sociological Association working party]; edited by Elizabeth Gittus. London, 1972 in progress.

- Rural conditions

   POLSKA AKADEMIA NAUK. Instytut Geografii. Geographia Polonica. 24. (Geographical aspects of rural-urban interaction: proceedings of the Anglo-Polish Geographical Seminar, Nottingham, September 1970; edited by Kazimierz Dziewoński [and others]). Warszawa, 1972. pp. 254. bibliogs. 5 maps, 2 diagrams in end pocket.

   The REMOTER rural areas of Britain; [papers presented at a symposium organized by the Agricultural Adjustment Unit of the University of Newcastle-upon-Tyne]; edited by J. Ashton and W.H. Long. Edinburgh, 1972. pp. 246. bibliogs.

- Social conditions

   GODWIN (GEORGE) F.R.S. Town swamps and social bridges; [facsimile reproduction of the 1859 edition] with an introduction by Anthony D. King. Leicester, 1972. pp. 102.

   BROWN (MURIEL) Introduction to social administration in Britain. 2nd ed. London, 1971. pp. 216. bibliog.

   HOLE (WINIFRED VERE) The effects of current and future changes on house design. Garston, [1971]. pp. (8). (U.K. Building Research Station. Current Papers. 8/71)

   PARTISANS. No. 58. Quelle Grande-Bretagne? Paris, 1971. pp. 171.

   BUTTERWORTH (ERIC) and WEIR (DAVID) eds. Social problems of modern Britain. London, 1972. pp. 447. bibliogs.

   ONE for sorrow, two for joy: ten years of New Society; edited by Paul Barker. London, 1972. pp. 367.

   RESOURCES for Britain's future: a series from the Geographical Magazine; edited... by Michael Chisholm. Harmondsworth, 1972. pp. 182. bibliogs.

   BAILEY (ROY V.) and YOUNG (JOCK) eds. Contemporary social problems in Britain; [readings]. Farnborough, Hants., [1973]. pp. 194.

   HENDERSON (IAN) ed. The new poor: anatomy of underprivilege. London, 1973. pp. 182.

   TOWNSEND (PETER BRERETON) The social minority. London, [1973]. pp. 319.

   URRY (JOHN) and WAKEFORD (JOHN) Lecturer in Sociology at Brunel University, eds. Power in Britain: sociological readings. London, 1973. pp. 330. bibliog.

- Social conditions - Statistics

   HALSEY (ALBERT HENRY) ed. Trends in British society since 1900: a guide to the changing social structure of Britain. London, 1972. pp. 578. bibliogs.

- Social history

   TAWNEY (RICHARD HENRY) The agrarian problem in the sixteenth century: [reprint of work first published in 1912; with a new] introduction by Lawrence Stone. New York, 1967. pp. 464. bibliog.

   KIRILLOVA (A.A.) and others. Voprosy sotsial'noi i klassovoi bor'by v angliiskikh gorodakh XIV-XVII vv. Moskva, 1969. pp. 319. (Moscow. Moskovskii Gosudarstvennyi Pedagogicheskii Institut. Uchenye Zapiski. no.321)

   FOSS (MICHAEL) The age of patronage: the arts in England, 1660-1750. Ithaca, N.Y., 1972. pp. 234.

   NEALE (R.S.) Class and ideology in the nineteenth century. London, 1972. pp. 200.

   NINETEENTH century society: essays in the use of quantitative methods for the study of social data; edited by E.A. Wrigley. Cambridge, 1972. pp. 448. bibliog. (Cambridge Group for the History of Population and Social Structure. Publications. [No. 3?])

   READ (DONALD) Edwardian England, 1901-15: society and politics. London, 1972. pp. 288.

   TAMES (RICHARD LAWRENCE AMOS) Economy and society in nineteenth-century Britain. London, 1972. pp. 156. bibliogs.

   BUTT (J.) and CLARKE (IGNATIUS FREDERICK) eds. The Victorians and social protest: a symposium. Newton Abbot, 1973. pp. 243.

   CARSWELL (JOHN) From revolution to revolution: England, 1688-1776. London, 1973. pp. 204. bibliog.

   DYOS (HAROLD JAMES) and WOLFF (MICHAEL) eds. The Victorian city: images and realities. London, 1973. 2 vols.

UNITED KINGDOM - Social history
(Cont'd.)

EMMISON (FREDERICK GEORGE) Elizabethan life: morals and the church courts, mainly from Essex archidiaconal records. Chelmsford, 1973. pp. 348. (Essex. Records Committee. Essex Record Office Publications. No. 63)

FLETCHER (ANTHONY) Tudor rebellions; [with selected documents]. 2nd ed. London, 1973. pp. 168. bibliog.

FRASER (DEREK) The evolution of the British welfare state: a history of social policy since the industrial revolution. London, 1973. pp. 299. bibliog.

MALCOLMSON (ROBERT W.) Popular recreations in English society, 1700-1850. Cambridge, 1973. pp. 188. bibliog.

ROEBUCK (JANET) The making of modern English society from 1850. London, 1973. pp. 205. bibliog.

RUNDLE (RAYMOND NORMAN) Britain's economic and social development from 1700 to the present day. London, 1973. pp. 240.

SHELTON (WALTER JAMES) English hunger and industrial disorders: a study of social conflict during the first decade of George III's reign. London, 1973. pp. 226. bibliog.

STONE (LAWRENCE) Family and fortune: studies in aristocratic finance in the sixteenth and seventeenth centuries. Oxford, 1973. pp. 315.

TROTSKII (LEV DAVYDOVICH) Leon Trotsky on Britain: [selected writings]; introduction by George Novack. New York, 1973. pp. 334. bibliog.

- Social history - Dictionaries and encyclopaedias

COWIE (LEONARD WALLACE) A dictionary of British social history. London, 1973. pp. 326.

- Social history - Sources

TAYLER (WILLIAM) 1807-1892. Diary of William Tayler, footman, 1837; edited by Dorothy Wise, with notes by Ann Cox-Johnson. London, [1962]. pp. 63.

FOCAL aspects of the Industrial Revolution, 1825-1842: five pamphlets. Shannon, [1971]. pp. 198.

GUERNSEY BOOKS. Century of change, 1815-1914: a collection of original pamphlets, tracts, posters, holograph letters, manuscripts, etc. St. Peter Port, [c.1971]. pp. 40.

PIKE (EDGAR ROYSTON) ed. Human documents of the Lloyd George era. London, 1972. pp. 270.

TOBIAS (JOHN JACOB) ed. Nineteenth-century crime in England: prevention and punishment. New York, 1972. pp. 183.

BRUCE (MAURICE) ed. The rise of the welfare state: English social policy, 1601-1971: [contemporary documents and sources]. London, [1973]. pp. 299.

HOLLIS (PATRICIA) ed. Class and conflict in nineteenth century England, 1815-1850. London, 1973. pp. 372.

- Social life and customs

[SERE-DEPOIN (ERNEST)?] La XIme Légion à Londres: par un caporal des radis de la banlieue: détails, curieux, historiques, inédits sur le voyage des Gardes Nationaux Français en Angleterre pendant l'année 1848; avec des notes de M. de Bilboquet, Sergent-Major socialiste et de Sir Mackintosh de l'Université de Greenwich, etc. Paris, Maulde et Renou, 1849. pp. 200.

ESCOTT (THOMAS HAY SWEET) National and international links. London, 1922. pp. 333.

HOPKINSON (JAMES) Victorian cabinet maker: the memoirs of James Hopkinson, 1819-1894; edited by Jocelyne Baty Goodman. London, 1968. pp. 138.

CAREY (LYNNETTE) and MAPES (ROY) The sociology of planning: a study of social activity on new housing estates. London, 1972. pp. 161.

PALMER (GEOFFREY) and LLOYD (NOEL) A year of festivals: a guide to British calendar customs. London, 1972. pp. 192.

PLUMB (JOHN HAROLD) In the light of history. London, 1972. pp. 273.

- Social policy

UNITED KINGDOM. 1967. The United Kingdom of Great Britain and Northern Ireland. (ST/SOA/68). New York, United Nations, 1967. pp. 48. (Department of Economic and Social Affairs. Organization and Administration of Social Welfare Programmes: A Series of Country Studies)

BROWN (MURIEL) Introduction to social administration in Britain. 2nd ed. London, 1971. pp. 216. bibliog.

EYDEN (JOAN L.M.) ed. The welfare society: a guide for discussion groups. London, [1971]. pp. 44. bibliog.

FAMILY poverty: (programme for the seventies); [based on talks given to meetings of the Child Poverty Action Group's Manchester and District Branch]; edited by David Bull. 2nd ed. London, 1972. pp. 216.

LABOUR and inequality; [sixteen Fabian essays; edited by Peter Townsend and Nicholas Bosanquet]. London, 1972. pp. 301.

BRUCE (MAURICE) ed. The rise of the welfare state: English social policy, 1601-1971: [contemporary documents and sources]. London, [1973]. pp. 299.

CULYER (ANTHONY J.) The economics of social policy. London, 1973. pp. 268. bibliogs.

EMY (HUGH VINCENT) Liberals, radicals and social politics, 1892-1914. Cambridge, 1973. pp. 318. bibliog.

FRASER (DEREK) The evolution of the British welfare state: a history of social policy since the industrial revolution. London, 1973. pp. 299. bibliog.

LABOUR PARTY. Research Department. The deprived child: a discussion document on policies for socially deprived children (prepared...for presentation to the 50th National Conference of Labour Women...1973). London, [1973]. pp. 33.

TRADES UNION CONGRESS. Prices and incomes: the case for the unions. London, 1973. pp. 25.

- Statistics

HALSEY (ALBERT HENRY) ed. Trends in British society since 1900: a guide to the changing social structure of Britain. London, 1972. pp. 578. bibliogs.

U.K. Central Statistical Office. 1972. Facts in focus. Harmondsworth, 1972. pp. 222.

- Statistics - Bibliography

UNIVERSITY OF ESSEX. Library. Reference Leaflets. No. 3. British statistics: a select list of sources. [Colchester], 1972. pp. 60.

- Statistics, Vital

    U.K. Social Survey. [Reports. New Series.] 408.
    Family intentions; by Myra Woolf; an enquiry
    undertaken for the General Register Office.
    London, 1971. pp. 153. bibliog.

    TROWBRIDGE (BARRY) and WEBSTER (MARTIN) Birth
    registrations in England and Wales, 1965-1971.
    [London], 1972. pp. 26. (London. Greater London
    Council. Department of Planning and Transportation.
    Research Memoranda. 343)

    U.K. Office of Population Censuses and Surveys.
    1972. Vital statistics in England and Wales.
    London, 1972. pp. 67.

- Voting registers

    GRAY (SHEILA) The electoral register: practical
    information for use when drawing samples, both
    for interview and postal surveys. [London],1971.
    fo. 18. (U.K. Social Survey. [Papers. Metho-
    dological Series.] No. M. 151. New Sampling
    Series. No. 3)

- British Empire

    BALL (MARY MARGARET) The "open" commonwealth
    Durham, N.C., 1971. pp. 286. bibliog. (Duke
    University. Commonwealth-Studies Center. Publications.
    No. 39)

    BUTLER (RICHARD AUSTEN) Baron Butler of Saffron
    Walden. Problems of diplomacy, past and present.
    [Canberra], 1971. pp. 23. (Australian National
    University. Arthur F. Yencken Memorial Lectures.
    1970)

    GIFFORD (PROSSER) and LOUIS (WILLIAM ROGER) eds.
    France and Britain in Africa: imperial rivalry
    and colonial rule. New Haven, 1971. pp. 989.
    bibliog.

    HIND (ROBERT JAMES) Henry Labouchere and the
    Empire, 1880-1905. London, 1972. pp. 271.
    bibliog. (London. University. Historical Studies.
    31)

    U.K. Central Office of Information. Reference
    Division. 1972. Britain's associated states and
    dependencies. 2nd ed. London, 1972. pp. 41.

    BRETT (E.A.) Colonialism and underdevelopment
    in East Africa: the politics of economic change,
    1919-1939. London, 1973. pp. 330. bibliog.

    FLINT (JOHN E.) and WILLIAMS (GLYNDWR) eds. Perspective
    of empire: essays presented to Gerald S. Graham.
    London, 1973. pp. 200. bibliog.

    U.K. Central Office of Information. Reference
    Division. 1973. Britain and the Commonwealth.
    London, 1973. pp. 42.

- British Empire - Bibliography

    LONDON. University. Institute of Commonwealth Studies.
    Theses in progress in Commonwealth studies: a
    cumulative list. [London], 1972. pp. 26, 3.

- British Empire - Constitutional law

    O'CONNELL (DANIEL PATRICK) and RIORDAN (ANN) eds.
    Opinions [of the Law Officers of the Crown] on
    imperial constitutional law. Sydney, 1971.
    pp. 436.

    WILSON (ROBERT RENBERT) International law and
    contemporary Commonwealth issues. Durham, N.C.,
    1971. pp. 245. bibliog. (Duke University. Common-
    wealth Studies Center. Publications. 38)

- British Empire - Defences

    TUNSTALL (WILLIAM CUTHBERT BRIAN) The Common-
    wealth and regional defence. London, 1959.
    pp. 68. (London. University. Institute of Commonwealth
    Studies. Commonwealth Papers. No. 6)

- British Empire - Economic conditions

    LONDON. University. Institute of Commonwealth Studies.
    Collected seminar papers on the changing role
    of Commonwealth economic connections, October
    1967 - March 1968. London, [1970]. pp. 110.
    (London. University. Institute of Commonwealth
    Studies. Collected Seminar Papers. No. 8)

    LONDON. University. Institute of Commonwealth Studies.
    Collected seminar papers on changing economic
    links in the Commonwealth in the 1970's. London,
    [1971]. pp. 105. (London. University. Institute
    of Commonwealth Studies. Collected Seminar Papers.
    No. 14)

- British Empire - Economic history

    ROBINSON (EDWARD AUSTIN GOSSAGE) Fifty years of
    Commonwealth economic development. Cambridge,
    1972. pp. 31. (Cambridge. University. Smuts
    Memorial Lectures. 1971)

- British Empire - Economic policy

    COMMONWEALTH CONFERENCE ON DEVELOPMENT AND HUMAN
    ECOLOGY, 1ST, MALTA, 1970. Human ecology in the
    Commonwealth: proceedings of the...Conference...;
    sponsored by the Government of Malta [and others;
    edited by H. Bowen-Jones]. London, 1972.
    pp. 192.

    DRUMMOND (IAN MACDONALD) British economic policy
    and the Empire, 1919-1939. London, 1972. pp.
    241.

- British Empire - History

    CÉSAR (JAROSLAV) Britská říše v období imperia-
    lismu, 1870-1945. Praha, 1970. pp. 226. bibliog.
    With English summary.

    COLLECTED seminar papers on the Dominions between
    the wars; by Max Beloff [and others]. London,
    [1972]. pp. 82. (London. University. Institute
    of Commonwealth Studies. Collected Seminar
    Papers. No.13)

    BOLTON (GEOFFREY CURGENVEN) Britain's legacy overseas.
    London, 1973. pp. 168. bibliog.

    ELDRIDGE (C.C.) England's mission: the imperial
    idea in the age of Gladstone and Disraeli, 1868-1880.
    London, 1973. pp. 288. bibliog.

    LOW (D.A.) Lion rampant: essays in the study
    of British imperialism. London, 1973. pp.
    230.

    MORRIS (JAMES) Heaven's command: an imperial
    progress. London, 1973. pp. 554.

- British Empire - Periodicals - Bibliography

    LONDON. University. Institute of Commonwealth Studies.
    Library. Current periodicals: a select list. 2nd
    ed. [London], 1972. pp. 19.

- British Empire - Politics and government

    PERHAM (Dame MARGERY FREDA) Colonial sequence,
    1949 to 1969: a chronological commentary upon
    British colonial policy in Africa; [articles,
    letters and writings]. London, 1970. pp. 377.

    BLAKELEY (BRIAN L.) The Colonial Office, 1868-
    1892. Durham, N.C., 1972. pp. 195. bibliog.

    BURROUGHS (PETER) The Canadian crisis and British
    colonial policy, 1828-1841. London, 1972. pp.
    120. bibliog.

    HENRETTA (JAMES A.) "Salutary neglect": colonial
    administration under the Duke of Newcastle.
    Princeton, 1972. pp. 381. bibliog.

    MARTIN (GED) The Durham Report and British policy:
    a critical essay. Cambridge, 1972. pp. 120.
    bibliog.

UNITED NATIONS

BROWDER (EARL RUSSELL) Victory - and after. New York, [1942]. pp. 256.

VENEZUELA. Direccion de Comercio Exterior y Consulados. 1962. XVII periodo de las Naciones Unidas: temas economicos. [Caracas], 1962. fo. (53). (Estudios sobre Comercio Exterior. 11)

DMITRIEV (BOR.) and PAVLOV (BOR.) OON - 20 let. Moskva, 1965. pp. 60.

MIKHEEV (IURII IAKOVLEVICH) Primenenie prinuditel'nykh mer po Ustavu OON. Moskva, 1967. pp. 207.

SWEDEN. Utrikesdepartementet. Aktstycken. Ny Serie II. 18. Apartheidfrågan i Förenta Nationerna: en faktasamling. Stockholm, 1967. pp. 135.

WATERS (MAURICE) The United Nations: international organization and administration. London, [1967] repr. 1970. pp. 583.

UNITED NATIONS. Office of Public Information. 1968-71. Everyman's United Nations: a complete handbook of the activities and evolution of the United Nations during its first twenty years 1945-1965; (with Supplement [covering] the five-year period 1966-1970). 8th ed. New York, 1968-71. 2 vols. (in 1).

KAHNG (TAE JIN) Law, politics and the Security Council: an inquiry into the handling of legal questions involved in international disputes and situations. 2nd ed. The Hague, 1969. pp. 268. bibliog.

COSGROVE (CAROL ANN) and TWITCHETT (KENNETH J.) eds. The new international actors: the United Nations and the European Economic Community. London, 1970. pp. 272. bibliog.

LALL (ARTHUR S.) The UN and the Middle East crisis, 1967. rev. ed. New York. 1970. pp. 350.

MANIN (PHILIPPE) L'Organisation des Nations Unies et le maintien de la paix: le respect du consentement de l'état. Paris, [1970]. pp. 343. bibliog.

SCHUEMPERLI (WALTER) Die Vereinten Nationen und die Dekolonisation. Bern, 1970. pp. 158. bibliog.

SWEDEN. Utrikesdepartementet. Aktstycken. Ny Serie II. 23. Förenta Nationerna och problemen i Södra Afrika. Stockholm, 1970. pp. 92.

U.K. Foreign and Commonwealth Office. 1970. Speech by the Secretary of State for Foreign and Commonwealth Affairs in the General Assembly of the United Nations, New York, September 24, 1970. [London, 1970]. pp. 10.

U.K. Prime Minister. 1970. Speech by...Edward Heath at the commemorative session for the twenty-fifth anniversary of the United Nations, New York, October 23, 1970. [London, 1970.] pp. 10.

YOUNGER (KENNETH) The United Nations Charter and the challenge of the 70's;...a special lecture sponsored by UNITAR and given at U.N. Headquarters, New York on 2 November, 1970, etc. New York, United Nations Institute for Training and Research, 1970. pp. 26. (Lecture Series. No. 1)

1971

The CASE for South-West Africa; compiled by Anthony Lejeune. London. 1971. pp. 245. bibliog.

CHAI (F.Y.) Consultation and consensus in the Security Council. New York, United Nations Institute for Training and Research, 1971. pp. 55. ([Peaceful Settlement Series] No.4)

COPAKEN (ROBERT RANDOLPH) The political role of the United Nations Secretariat in the Congo peacekeeping operation, 1960-1963; [Ph. D. (London) thesis]. 1971. fo. 421. bibliog. Typescript: unpublished. This thesis is the property of London University and may not be removed from the Library.

EL-AYOUTY (YASSIN) The United Nations and decolonization: the role of Afro-Asia. The Hague, 1971. pp. 286. bibliog.

ERMACORA (FELIX) Diskriminierungsschutz und Diskriminierungsverbot in der Arbeit der Vereinten Nationen. Wien, 1971. pp. 265. bibliog. (Forschungsstelle für Nationalitäten- und Sprachenfragen. Ethnos. Band 11)

FOMIN (VALENTIN VASIL'EVICH) OON i mezhdunarodnaia torgovlia: pravovye voprosy. Moskva, 1971 pp. 168.

IANOVSKII (MIKHAIL VLADIMIROVICH) General'naia assambleia OON: mezhdunarodnopravovye voprosy. Kishinev, 1971. pp. 301.

NICHOLAS (HERBERT GEORGE) The United Nations as a political institution. 4th ed. London, 1971. pp. 254. bibliog.

PAWELKA (PETER) Die UNO und das Deutschlandproblem: das Deutschlandproblem im Spannungsfeld zwischen der Bundesrepublik Deutschland und den Vereinten Nationen, unter besonderer Berücksichtigung der Aussenpolitik der Bundesrepublik Deutschland, 1949 bis 1967. Tübingen, 1971. pp. 232. bibliog.

POZDNIAKOV (EL'GIZ ABDULOVICH) Molodye gosudarstva Azii i Afriki v OON. Moskva, 1971. pp. 149. bibliog.

U.K. Foreign and Commonwealth Office. 1971. Speech by the Secretary of State for Foreign and Commonwealth Affairs in the General Assembly of the United Nations, New York, September 29, 1971. [London, 1971.] pp. 11.

The UNITED Nations in international politics; edited by Leon Gordenker. Princeton, 1971. pp. 241.

1972

BARROS (JAMES) ed. The United Nations: past, present, and future; edited by James Barros. New York, [1972]. pp. 279.

BARYSHEV (ALEKSANDR PETROVICH) Strategiia Belogo doma i OON; pod redaktsiei...Anat.A. Gromyko. Moskva, 1972. pp. 312.

BRIGHTON. University of Sussex. Institute for the Study of International Organisation. ISIO Monographs. 1st Series. No. 6. The United Nations and East-West relations; by Roderick Ogley. Brighton, [1972]. pp. 58. bibliog.

CHIAO (KUAN-HUA) Speech by...chairman of the delegation of the People's Republic of China at the plenary meeting of the 27th session of the U.N. General Assembly, October 3. 1972. Peking, 1972. pp. 24.

CLARK (ROGER STENSON) A United Nations high commissioner for human rights. The Hague, 1972. pp. 186. bibliog.

FABIAN SOCIETY. Fabian Tracts. [No.] 415. The United Nations in a new era; [by] Evan Luard. London, 1972. pp. 24.

KIM (JUNG-GUN) and HOWELL (JOHN M.) Conflict of international obligations and state interests. The Hague, 1972. pp. 135.

KUZNETSOV (VALERII IVANOVICH) and others. Ot Dekreta o mire k Deklaratsii mira, etc. Moskva, 1972. pp. 144.

LANCASTER (CAROL JANE) The politics of the powerless: pressures in the United Nations for economic development; [Ph.D. (London) thesis]. [1972]. fo. 313. bibliog. Typescript: unpublished. This thesis is the property of London University and may not be removed from the Library.

The UNITED Nations in perspective; edited by E. Berkeley Tompkins; [a Hoover Institution conference]. Stanford, [1972]. pp. 155. (Stanford University. Hoover Institution on War, Revolution and Peace. Hoover Institution Publications. 110)

1973

DUGARD (JOHN) ed. The South West Africa/Namibia dispute: documents and scholarly writings on the controversy between South Africa and the United Nations. Berkeley, [1973]. pp. 585. bibliog.

ELMANDJRA (MAHDI SAADI) The United Nations system: an analysis. London, 1973. pp. 368. bibliog.

HAZZARD (SHIRLEY) Defeat of an ideal: a study of the self-destruction of the United Nations. London, 1973. pp. 286.

PARTAN (DANIEL G.) Population in the United Nations system: developing the legal capacity and programs of UN agencies. Leiden, 1973. pp. 219. (Tufts University. Fletcher School of Law and Diplomacy. Law and Population Book Series. No. 3)

RIGO SUREDA (A.) The evolution of the right of self-determination: a study of United Nations practice. Leiden, 1973. pp. 397. bibliog.

SLONIM (SOLOMON) South West Africa and the United Nations: an international mandate in dispute. Baltimore, [1973]. pp. 409. bibliog.

STOESSINGER (JOHN GEORGE) The might of nations: world politics in our time. 4th ed. New York, 1973. pp. 461. bibliogs.

SYMONDS (RICHARD) 1918-   , and CARDER (MICHAEL) The United Nations and the population question 1945-1970. London, 1973. pp. 236.

URQUHART (BRIAN) Hammarskjold. London, 1973. pp. 630,xxv.

WORLD FEDERATION OF TRADE UNIONS. The trade unions and the United Nations. Prag, 1973. pp. 35.

- Armed forces

HILL (R.J.) Command and control problems of UN and similar peace keeping forces. Ottawa, 1968. fo. 39,12. bibliog. (Canada. Department of National Defence. Operational Research Division. ORD Reports. No. 68/R5)

KARAOSMANOĞLU (ALI L.) Les actions militaires coercitives et non coercitives des Nations Unies. Genève, 1970. pp. 320. bibliog.

KRISTIANSEN (ROLF) Norsk militaer innsats for de Forente Nasjoner, 1949-1970. [Oslo?], Forsvarets Krigshistoriske Avdeling, [1972?]. pp. 248. bibliog.

LUARD (DAVID EVAN TRANT) ed. The international regulation of civil wars. London, [1972]. pp. 240.

- Bibliography

ROTHMAN (MARIE H.) Citation rules and forms for United Nations documents and publications. Brooklyn, N.Y., 1971. pp. 64.

- Charter

DERPA (ROLF M.) Das Gewaltverbot der Satzung der Vereinten Nationen und die Anwendung nichtmilitärischer Gewalt. Bad Homburg, [1970]. pp. 149. bibliog.

- Commissions

FORSYTHE (DAVID P.) United Nations peacemaking: the Conciliation Commission for Palestine. Baltimore, [1972]. pp. 201. bibliog.

- Economic assistance

MICHANEK (ERNST) The world development plan: a Swedish perspective. Stockholm, 1971. pp. 71.

UNITED NATIONS. Development Programme. Compendium of approved projects. s-a., current issues only kept. New York.

- Membership

SPEECHES welcoming the delegation of the People's Republic of China; by the U.N. General Assembly President and representatives of various countries; at the plenary meeting of the 26th session of the U.N. General Assembly, November 15, 1971. Peking. 1971. pp. 158.

MUNTIAN (MIKHAIL ALEKSEEVICH) Bor'ba Sovetskogo Soiuza za priem v OON Bolgarii, Vengrii i Rumynii. Kishinev, 1972. pp. 191. bibliog.

- Officials and employees

UNITED NATIONS. Administrative Tribunal. 1958- Judgements of the United Nations Administrative Tribunal. (AT/DEC/1-   ). New York, 1958 in progress.

SMOUTS (MARIE CLAUDE) Le Secrétaire général des Nations Unies: son rôle dans la solution des conflits internationaux. Paris, 1971. pp. 298. bibliog. (Fondation Nationale des Sciences Politiques. Travaux et Recherches de Science Politique. 16)

PECHOTA (VRATISLAV) The quiet approach: a study of the good offices exercised by the United Nations Secretary-General in the cause of peace. New York, United Nations Institute for Training and Research, 1972. pp. 92. bibliog. ([Peaceful Settlement Series] No.6)

- Sanctions

KAPUNGU (LEONARD TAWAYENA) The United Nations and economic sanctions against Rhodesia. Lexington, Mass., [1973]. pp. 155.

- Technical assistance

LEONARD (WILLIAM RAMSDELL) and others. UN development aid: criteria and methods of evaluation. New York, 1971. pp. 135. (United Nations Institute for Training and Research. UNITAR Studies)

VAS-ZOLTÁN (PÉTER) United Nations technical assistance. Budapest, 1972. pp. 404. bibliog.

UNITED NATIONS. Development Programme. Compendium of approved projects. s-a., current issues only kept. New York.

- Treaty-making power

SCHACHTER (OSCAR) and others. Towards wider acceptance of UN treaties. New York, 1971. pp. 190. (United Nations Institute for Training and Research. UNITAR Studies)

- America, Latin

PRAT GAY (GASTON DE) Politica internacional del grupo latinoamericano. Buenos Aires, 1967. pp. 140. bibliog.

UNITED NATIONS (Cont'd.)

- China

WENG (BYRON S.J.) Peking's UN policy: continuity and change. New York, 1972. pp. 337. bibliog.

- Germany

CZEMPIEL (ERNST OTTO) Macht und Kompromiss: die Beziehungen der Bundesrepublik Deutschland zu den Vereinten Nationen, 1956-1970. Düsseldorf, [1971]. pp. 189.

- Germany, Eastern

The GDR and UNO. n.p., [1972]. pp. 20.

WORLD PEACE COUNCIL. For the admission of the GDR to the UN and its special agencies: for the universality of international organizations. Helsinki, [1972]. pp. 31.

- Israel

FEINBERG (NATHAN) On an Arab jurist's approach to Zionism and the State of Israel. Jerusalem, 1971. pp. 139.

- Mexico

GARCIA ROBLES (ALFONSO) Mexico en las Naciones Unidas. Mexico, 1970. 2 vols. (in 1).

- Switzerland

SWITZERLAND. Conseil Fédéral. 1969. Report... to the Federal Assembly concerning Switzerland's relations with the United Nations. [Bern], 1969. pp. 174.

HAUG (HANS) Das Verhältnis der Schweiz zu den Vereinten Nationen. Bern, [1972]. pp. 224. bibliog. (Schweizerische Gesellschaft für Aussenpolitik. Schriftenreihe. Band 1)

UNITED NATIONS CONFERENCE ON TRADE AND DEVELOPMENT

CHILE. Oficina de Planificacion Nacional. 1972. Chile ante los problemas monetarios y financieros internacionales: [documents relating to the third United Nations Conference on Trade and Development]. Santiago de Chile, 1972. pp. 506.

GOSOVIC (BRANISLAV) UNCTAD: conflict and compromise; the third world's quest for an equitable world economic order through the United Nations. Leiden, 1972. pp. 349. bibliog.

NAINI (AHMAD) Grundfragen der dritten Welthandelskonferenz. Hamburg, 1972. pp. 163. bibliog. (Hamburg. Hamburgisches Welt-Wirtschafts-Archiv. Studien zur Aussenwirtschaft und Entwicklungspolitik)

NAINI (AHMAD) and others. Analyse der Themen und Ergebnisse der dritten Welthandelskonferenz: Probleme der Entwicklungsländer nach der dritten UN-Konferenz für Handel und Entwicklung, UNCTAD III. Hamburg, 1972. pp. 211. bibliog. (Hamburg. Hamburgisches Welt-Wirtschafts-Archiv. Studien zur Aussenwirtschaft und Entwicklungspolitik)

VEL'IAMINOV (GEORGII MIKHAILOVICH) Pravovoe uregulirovanie mezhdunarodnoi torgovli: opyt IuNKTAD. Moskva, 1972. pp. 240.

UNITED NATIONS ECONOMIC COMMISSION FOR EUROPE

UNITED NATIONS. Economic Commission for Europe. 1972. The work of the Economic Commission for Europe, 1947-1972. (E/ECE/831). New York, 1972. pp. 200.

UNITED NATIONS EDUCATIONAL, SCIENTIFIC AND CULTURAL ORGANIZATION

UNITED NATIONS EDUCATIONAL, SCIENTIFIC AND CULTURAL ORGANIZATION. 1962. What is Unesco? 3rd ed. Paris, 1962. pp. 62. (Unesco Information Manuals. 1)

POMPEI (GIAN FRANCO) and others. In the minds of men: Unesco 1946 to 1971. Paris, United Nations Educational, Scientific and Cultural Organization, 1972. pp. 319.

- Bibliography

GERMANY (BUNDESREPUBLIK). UNESCO-Kommission. 1968. Bibliographie der deutschsprachigen UNESCO-Literatur, 1946-1966; (Redaktion: Horst Richter und Hans Wieczorek). Köln, 1968. pp. 62.

- Russia

OSAKWE (CHRIS O.) The participation of the Soviet Union in universal international organizations: a political and legal analysis of Soviet strategies and aspirations inside ILO, UNESCO and WHO. Leiden, 1972. pp. 194. bibliog.

UNITED NATIONS INDUSTRIAL DEVELOPMENT ORGANIZATION

- Directories

UNITED NATIONS INDUSTRIAL DEVELOPMENT ORGANIZATION. Permanent missions. Current issue only kept. Vienna.

UNITED NATIONS RELIEF AND WORKS AGENCY FOR PALESTINE REFUGEES IN THE NEAR EAST

BUEHRIG (EDWARD HENRY) The UN and the Palestinian refugees: a study in nonterritorial administration. Bloomington, Ind., [1971]. pp. 215.

UNITED SOUTH AFRICAN NATIONAL PARTY

GRAAFF (Sir DE VILLIERS) Sir De Villiers Graaff opens United Party Bloemfontein Congress 2 October 1964. Johannesburg, [United Party], Division of Information and Research, 1964. pp. 19. In English and Afrikaans.

UNITED STATES

- Appropriations and expenditures

GEDDES (ANN ELIZABETH) Trends in relief expenditures, 1910-1935; [reprint of work first published in Washington, 1937]. New York, 1971. pp. 117. (United States. Work Projects Administration. Division of Social Research. Research Monographs. 10)

PELNY (STEFAN E.) Die legislative Finanzkontrolle in der Bundesrepublik Deutschland und in den Vereinigten Staaten von Amerika. Berlin, [1972]. pp. 162. bibliog.

SINGER (NEIL M.) Public microeconomics. Boston, [1972]. pp. 329. bibliogs.

- **Armed forces**

    HICKMAN (MARTIN B.) ed. The military and American society. Beverly Hills, [1971]. pp. 167.

    ACKLEY (CHARLES WALTON) The modern military in American society: a study in the nature of military power. Philadelphia, [1972]. pp. 400. bibliog.

    CHODES (JOHN J.) The myth of America's military power. Boston, [Mass.], [1972]. pp. 224.

    AMERICAN ACADEMY OF POLITICAL AND SOCIAL SCIENCE. Annals. vol. 406. The military and American society; special editor of this volume, Adam Yarmolinsky. Philadelphia, 1973. pp. 268.

    INTERNATIONAL INSTITUTE FOR STRATEGIC STUDIES. Adelphi Papers. No.94. The U.S. forces and the zero draft; by Morris Janowitz. London, 1973. pp. 30.

- **Armed forces - Negroes**

    GATEWOOD (WILLARD BADGETTE) ed. "Smoked Yankees" and the struggle for empire: letters from negro soldiers, 1898-1902. Urbana, Ill., [1971]. pp. 328. bibliog.

- **Armed forces - Political activity**

    CLOTFELTER (JAMES) The military in American politics. New York, [1973]. pp. 244. bibliogs.

- **Armed forces - Europe**

    NEWHOUSE (JOHN) and others. U.S. troops in Europe: issues, costs, and choices. Washington, [1971]. pp. 177.

- **Army**

    HAMPTON (H. DUANE) How the U.S. cavalry saved our national parks. Bloomington, [1972]. pp. 246. bibliog.

    KOPKIND (ANDREW DAVID) and RIDGEWAY (JAMES) eds. Decade of crisis: America in the '60s. New York, [1972]. pp. 293.

- **Army - Officers**

    BLETZ (DONALD F.) The role of the military professional in U.S. foreign policy. New York, [1972]. pp. 320. bibliog.

- **Army - Prisons**

    SHERRILL (ROBERT) Military justice is to justice as military music is to music. New York, [1970]. pp. 235.

- **Army - Recruiting, enlistment, etc.**

    INTERNATIONAL INSTITUTE FOR STRATEGIC STUDIES. Adelphi Papers. No.94. The U.S. forces and the zero draft; by Morris Janowitz. London, 1973. pp. 30.

- **Biography**

    WHO's who in American politics: (a biographical directory of United States political leaders); 3rd edition 1971-1972; edited by Paul A. Theis and Edmund L. Henshaw. New York, 1971. pp. 1171.

    STEINBERG (ALFRED) The bosses. New York, [1972]. pp. 379. bibliog.

- **Census**

    ECKLER (A. ROSS) The Bureau of the Census. New York, 1972. pp. 268. bibliog.

    NATIONAL RESEARCH COUNCIL. Division of Behavioral Sciences. Advisory Committee on Problems of Census Enumeration. America's uncounted people; report...; Carole W. Parsons, editor. Washington, D.C., 1972. pp. 159. bibliog.

- **Civilization**

    CAMPBELL (ALEXANDER) Journalist. The trouble with Americans. London, 1971. pp. 215.

    MULLER (HERBERT JOSEPH) In pursuit of relevance. Bloomington, [1971]. pp. 306.

    McGIFFERT (MICHAEL) and SKOTHEIM (ROBERT ALLEN) eds. American social thought: sources and interpretations. Reading, Mass., [1972 in progress]. bibliogs.

    ACHESON (DEAN GOODERHAM) Grapes from thorns; [extracts from articles, books, lectures, letters, etc.]. New York, [1972]. pp. 253.

    ADLER (NATHAN) The underground stream: new life styles and the antinomian personality. New York, [1972]. pp. 135

    BEICHMAN (ARNOLD) Nine lies about America. London, 1972. pp. 314. bibliog.

    CRUNDEN (ROBERT M.) From self to society, 1919-1941. Englewood Cliffs, [1972]. pp. 212. bibliog.

    FLEMING (DENNA FRANK) The issues of survival. London, 1972. pp. 124.

    KATZMAN (ALLEN) ed. Our time: an anthology of interviews from the East Village Other. New York, 1972. pp. 407.

    KING (RICHARD) Professor of History and Philosophy. The party of Eros: radical social thought and the realm of freedom. Chapel Hill, [1972]. pp. 227. bibliog.

    KOPKIND (ANDREW DAVID) and RIDGEWAY (JAMES) eds. Decade of crisis: America in the '60s. New York, [1972]. pp. 293.

    [MONK (ABRAHAM) and others.] Social welfare planning: issues, values and policy directions; (with Summary report). Albany, New York State Temporary Commission to Revise the Social Services Law, 1972. 2 pts. (Interim Study Reports. Nos. 3 and 3-S).

    PUTNEY (SNELL) The conquest of society...; sociological observations for the autonomous revolt against the autosystems which turn humanity into servomen. Belmont, Calif., [1972]. pp. 237.

    ROCHE (GEORGE CHARLES) The bewildered society. New Rochelle, N.Y., [1972]. pp. 346.

    SCHRAG (PETER) The vanishing American: the decline and fall of the White Anglo-Saxon Protestant. London, 1972. pp. 255.

    AMERICAN ACADEMY OF POLITICAL AND SOCIAL SCIENCE. Annals. vol.408. The future society: aspects of America in the year 2000; special editor of this volume Martin E. Wolfgang. Philadelphia, 1973. pp. 205.

    HENRY (JULES) On sham, vulnerability and other forms of self-destruction: [collected essays]. London, 1973. pp. 234.

    WHEELER (RICHARD S.) b.1935. The children of darkness. New Rochelle, N.Y., [1973]. pp. 189.

UNITED STATES (Cont'd.)

- Claims vs. Mexico

DOS reclamaciones internacionales fraudulentas contra Mexico: los casos de Weil y de La Abra, 1868-1902; con un estudio preliminar de Cesar Sepulveda. Mexico, 1965. pp. 263. bibliog. (Archivo Historico Diplomatico Mexicano. Serie 2. No. 17)

- Commerce

PRICE (KARL F.) and WALKER (JAMES W.) Issues in business: an introduction to American enterprise. New York, [1972 in progress]. 1 vol. (looseleaf).

COCHRAN (THOMAS CHILDS) Business in American life: a history. New York, [1972]. pp. 402. bibliog.

KNIGHT (RICHARD VICTOR) Employment expansion and metropolitan trade: an analysis of 368 metropolitan labor markets in the United States over the period 1940-1960; [with addendum]; [Ph.D. (London) thesis]. 1971 [or rather 1972]. fo. 249, 12. bibliog. Typescript: unpublished. This thesis is the property of London University and may not be removed from the Library.

KROOSS (HERMAN EDWARD) and GILBERT (CHARLES) American business history. Englewood Cliffs, [1972]. pp. 358. bibliog.

LIGHT (IVAN H.) Ethnic enterprise in America: business and welfare among Chinese, Japanese, and blacks. Berkeley, Calif., 1972. pp. 209. bibliog.

SMALL (ALBERT H.) The American market for manufactured exports from the developing countries. New York, 1972. pp. 189. bibliog.

- Commerce - Africa, West

BROOKS (GEORGE E.) Yankee traders, old coasters and African middlemen: a history of American legitimate trade with west Africa in the nineteenth century. Boston, 1970. pp. 370. bibliog. (Boston, Massachusetts. University. African Studies Center. African Research Studies. No. 11)

- Commerce - Chile

PEREIRA SALAS (EUGENIO) Los primeros contactos entre Chile y los Estados Unidos, 1778-1809. Santiago de Chile, [1971]. pp. 353.

- Commerce - European Economic Community countries

CASADIO (GIAN PAOLO) Transatlantic trade: USA-EEC confrontation in the GATT negotiations;... translated from the Italian by John Cuthbert-Brown. Farnborough, [1973]. pp. 260. bibliog.

- Commerce - Japan

COHEN (JEROME BERNARD) ed. Pacific partnership: United States-Japan trade: prospects and recommendations for the seventies; [papers and policy recommendations drawn up by the Committee on Economic Policy Studies and the Businessmen's Advisory Committee of the Japan Society]. Lexington, Mass., [1972]. pp. 265.

- Commercial policy

MITCHELL (DANIEL J.B.) Essays on labor and international trade. Los Angeles, [1970]. pp. 109. (California University. Institute of Industrial Relations. Industrial Relations Monographs. No. 15)

CANADIAN-AMERICAN COMMITTEE. The U.S. import surcharge and Canada. [Washington, D.C., 1971]. pp. 7.

CURTIS (THOMAS B.) and VASTINE (JOHN ROBERT) The Kennedy Round and the future of American trade. New York, 1971. pp. 239.

EVANS (JOHN WALKER) The Kennedy round in American trade policy: the twilight of the GATT? Cambridge Mass., 1971. pp. 383. bibliog.

HAWKINS (ROBERT G.) and WALTER (INGO) eds. The United States and international markets: commercial policy options in an age of controls. Lexington, [1972]. pp. 419. (New York (City). University. Center for International Studies. Studies in Peaceful Change)

STEINAECKER (MICHAEL VON) Freiherr. Domestic taxation and foreign trade: the United States-European border tax dispute. New York, 1973. pp. 169. bibliog.

WALTER (INGO) U.S. trade policy in a changing world economy. Tübingen, 1973. pp. 14. (Kiel. Universität. Institut für Weltwirtschaft. Kieler Vorträge. Neue Folge. 76)

WOLF (THOMAS A.) U.S. East-West trade policy: economic warfare versus economic welfare. Lexington, Mass., [1973]. pp. 208.

- Congress

CONGRESSIONAL QUARTERLY INC. The Washington lobby. Washington, [1971]. pp. 123.

HARTMANN (SUSAN MECKFESSEL) Truman and the 80th Congress. Columbia, Mo., 1971. pp. 241. bibliog.

KRAUS (HANNELORE) Vorstellungen von Senatoren und Repräsentanten des amerikanischen Kongresses zur Deutschlandpolitik nach dem Zweiten Weltkriege: Kriegsprogramme, Nachkriegspolitik und ihre heutigen Aspekte. [Frankfurt am Main, imprint], 1971. pp. 224. bibliog.

POLSBY (NELSON WOOLF) Congress and the Presidency. 2nd ed. Englewood Cliffs, [1971]. pp. 162. bibliog.

STENNIS (JOHN C.) and FULBRIGHT (JAMES WILLIAM) The role of Congress in foreign policy. Washington, [1971]. pp. 139. (American Enterprise Institute for Public Policy Research. Rational Debate Seminars. 5th Series. 2)

WILCOX (FRANCIS ORLANDO) Congress, the executive, and foreign policy. New York, [1971]. pp. 176.

BARONE (MICHAEL) and others. The almanac of American politics: the Senators, the Representatives; their records, states and districts, 1972. London, 1972. pp. 1030.

BRADSHAW (KENNETH) and PRING (DAVID) Parliament and Congress. London, 1972. pp. 426.

FISHER (LOUIS) President and Congress: power and policy. New York, [1972]. pp. 347. bibliog.

GREEN (MARK J.) and others. Who runs Congress?: (Ralph Nader Congress project). Toronto, 1972. pp. 307.

TO enact a law: Congress and campaign financing; [by] Robert L. Peabody [and others]. New York, 1972. pp. 225. bibliogs.

TOINET (MARIE FRANCE) Le Congrès des Etats-Unis. [Paris], 1972. pp. 230. bibliog.

WEAVER (WARREN) the Younger. Both your Houses: the truth about Congress. New York, 1972. pp. 307. bibliog.

ABRAMS (MATTHEW JOHN) The Canada-United States interparliamentary group. Ottawa, 1973. pp. 148.

JAVITS (JACOB KOPPEL) Who makes war: the President versus Congress;... with Don Kellermann. New York, 1973. pp. 300. bibliog.

JOHNSTON (BRIAN LESLIE) The United States Defence Department and Congressional control; [M.Sc.(Econ.) (London) thesis]. [1973]. fo. 154. bibliog. Typescript: unpublished. This thesis is the property of London University and may not be removed from the Library.

RIESELBACH (LEROY N.) Congressional politics. New York, [1973]. pp. 426. bibliog.

UNITED STATES - Congress
See also LEGISLATORS - United States

- Congress - Committees

OGDEN (AUGUST RAYMOND) The Dies Committee: a study of the Special House Committee for the Investigation of the Un-American Activities, 1938-1944. 2nd ed. Washington. 1945. pp. 318. bibliog.

LEIBBRANDT (GOTTFRIED JOHANN) Economen in dienst van politici: enige ervaringen met de "Council of Economic Advisers to the President" en het "Joint Economic Committee of the United States Congress". Haarlem, 1968. pp. 160. bibliog. With English summary.

VOGLER (DAVID J.) The third house: conference committees in the United States Congress. Evanston, 1971. pp. 133. bibliog.

- Congress - Elections

UNITED STATES. Congress. House of Representatives. Statistics of the Presidential and Congressional elections. irreg., 1920-1970. Washington, D.C. Microfilm : 2 reels.

MOVEMENT FOR A NEW CONGRESS. Vote power: the official activist campaigner's handbook Englewood Cliffs, [1970]. pp. 85.

TWENTIETH CENTURY FUND. Task force. Electing Congress: the financial dilemma: report...on financing congressional campaigns; background paper by David L. Rosenbloom. New York, 1970. pp. 91.

- Congress - House of Representatives

WEEKS (KENT M.) Adam Clayton Powell and the Supreme Court. New York, [1971]. pp. 311. bibliog.

- Constitution

SPOONER (LYSANDER) Let's abolish government: [An essay on the trial by jury, and other works, originally published 1852-86]. New York, 1972. 1 vol.(various pagings).

AMERICAN ACADEMY OF ARTS AND SCIENCES. Commission on the Year 2000. The future of the United States government toward the year 2000; edited by Harvey S. Perloff. New York, [1971]. pp. 388.

GARVEY (GERALD) Constitutional bricolage. Princeton, 1971. pp. 160.

BALDWIN (LELAND DEWITT) Reframing the constitution: an imperative for modern America. Santa Barbara Calif., 1972. pp. 145.

FISHER (LOUIS) President and Congress: power and policy. New York, [1972]. pp. 347. bibliog.

SCHECHTER (ALAN H.) Contemporary constitutional issues. New York, [1972]. pp. 293. bibliog.

WARREN (EARL) A republic, if you can keep it. New York, [1972]. pp. 203. bibliog.

WATSON (RICHARD A.) Promise and performance of American democracy. New York, [1972]. pp. 619. bibliogs.

WIECEK (WILLIAM M.) The guarantee clause of the U.S. constitution. Ithaca, N.Y., 1972. pp. 324. bibliog.

BERGER (RAOUL) Impeachment: the constitutional problems. Cambridge, Mass., 1973. pp. 345. bibliog. (American Society for Legal History. Studies in Legal History)

CORWIN (EDWARD SAMUEL) The constitution and what it means today; revised by Harold W. Chase and Craig R. Ducat. 13th ed. Princeton, 1973. pp. 601.

MAGRATH (C. PETER) and others. The American democracy. 2nd ed. New York, [1973]. pp. 717. bibliogs.

MONSMA (STEPHEN V.) American politics: a systems approach. 2nd ed. Hinsdale, Ill., [1973]. pp. 430. bibliogs.

NIMMO (DAN D.) and UNGS (THOMAS D.) American political patterns: conflict and consensus. 3rd ed. Boston, [1973]. pp. 575. bibliogs.

- Constitution - 1st-10th Amendments

EMERSON (THOMAS IRWIN) The system of freedom of expression. New York, [1970]. pp. 754.

ANASTAPLO (GEORGE) The constitutionalist: notes on the first amendment. Dallas, [1971]. pp. 826.

- Constitution - 11th Amendment

JACOBS (CLYDE EDWARD) The eleventh amendment and sovereign immunity. Westport, 1972. pp. 216. bibliog.

- Constitutional history

STEAMER (ROBERT J.) The Supreme Court in crisis: a history of conflict. [Amherst], 1971. pp. 333.

MASON (ALPHEUS THOMAS) ed. The states rights debate: antifederalism and the constitution. 2nd ed. New York, 1972. pp. 210. bibliog.

MURPHY (PAUL L.) The constitution in crisis times, 1918-1969. New York, [1972]. pp. 570. bibliog.

POMPER (GERALD M.) and others. The performance of American government: checks and minuses. New York, [1972]. pp. 372. bibliog.

VOSE (CLEMENT ELLERY) Constitutional change: amendment politics and Supreme Court litigation since 1900. Lexington, Mass., [1972]. pp. 446. bibliog

- Constitutional history - Sources

KURTZ (STEPHEN GUILD) ed. The Federalists: creators and critics of the Union, 1780-1801; [selected readings]. New York, [1972]. pp. 212. bibliog.

- Constitutional law

GUNTHER (GERALD) and DOWLING (NOEL THOMAS) Cases and materials on constitutional law; (with Supplement). 8th ed. Mineola, N.Y., 1970. pp. 1468.

GROSSMAN (JOEL B.) and WELLS (RICHARD S.) Constitutional law and judicial policy making. New York, 1972. pp. 869.

LANE (PATRICK HARDING) The Australian federal system with United States analogues. Sydney, 1972. pp. 1075.

UNITED STATES - Constitutional law (Cont'd.)

SCHUG (WILLIS E.) ed. United States law and the armed forces: cases and materials on constitutional law, courts-martial, and the rights of servicemen. New York, 1972. pp. 546.

ROSENBLUM (VICTOR G.) and CASTBERG (A. DIDRICK) Cases on constitutional law: political roles of the Supreme Court. Homewood, Ill., 1973. pp. 662.

- Defences

STROMBERG (JOHN L.) The internal mechanisms of the defense budget process, fiscal 1953-1968. Santa Monica, Ca., 1970. pp. 285. bibliog. (Rand Corporation. Research Memoranda. 6243)

ADAMS (BENSON D.) Ballistic missile defense. New York, 1971. pp. 274. bibliog.

COFFEY (JOSEPH IRVING) Strategic power and national security. Pittsburgh, [1971]. pp. 214.

LASBY (CLARENCE G.) Project paperclip: German scientists and the cold war. New York, 1971. pp. 338. bibliog.

MEMBERS OF CONGRESS FOR PEACE THROUGH LAW. Military Spending Committee. The economics of defense: a bipartisan review of military spending. New York, 1971. pp. 256. bibliog.

TREWHITT (HENRY L.) McNamara. New York, 1971. pp. 307.

VANSANT (CARL) Strategic energy supply and national security. New York, 1971. pp. 135. bibliog.

BUCKLEY (JAMES LANE) and WARNKE (PAUL C.) Strategic sufficiency: fact or fiction? Washington, [1972]. pp. 87. (American Enterprise Institute for Public Policy Research. Rational Debate Seminars. 6th Series. 1)

The DEFENSE budget: (a town hall meeting on national security policy sponsored by the American Enterprise Institute...Washington, October 17, 1972); [paper by] Caspar W. Weinberger; [commentaries by] Murray L. Weidenbaum [and] Gene R. La Rocque]. Washington, [1972]. pp. 62.

The MILITARY-industrial complex: a reassessment; edited by Sam C. Sarkesian; [including papers prepared for an Institute sponsored by the Center for Policy Study, University of Chicago]. Beverly Hills, [1972]. pp. 340. (Inter-University Seminar on Armed Forces and Society. Sage Research Progress Series on War, Revolution, and Peacekeeping. vol. 2)

NATIONAL security and international trusteeship in the Pacific: [essays by officers of the United States Naval War College]; edited by Wm. Roger Louis. Annapolis, Md., [1972]. pp. 182. bibliog.

OWEN (DAVID) The politics of defence. London, 1972. pp. 249.

PURSELL (CARROLL W.) ed. The military-industrial complex: [readings]. New York, [1972]. pp. 342. bibliog.

SMITH (ROBERT) pseud. The economics of the cold war. New York, [1972]. pp. 126.

JOHNSTON (BRIAN LESLIE) The United States Defence Department and Congressional control; [M.Sc.(Econ.) (London) thesis]. [1973]. fo. 154. bibliog. Typescript: unpublished. This thesis is the property of London University and may not be removed from the Library.

QUANBECK (ALTON H.) and BLECHMAN (BARRY M.) Strategic forces: issues for the mid-seventies. Washington, D.C., [1973]. pp. 94. (Brookings Institution. Studies in Defense Policy)

ROSEN (STEVEN) ed. Testing the theory of the military-industrial complex. Lexington, Mass., [1973]. pp. 311. bibliogs.

- Description and travel

THWAITES (REUBEN GOLD) ed. Early western travels, 1748-1846... vol. 18. Pattie's Personal narrative, 1824-1830, etc.; [reprint of the volume originally published in Cleveland, Ohio, 1905]. New York, 1966. pp. 379.

- Diplomatic and consular service

BURKE (LEE H.) Ambassador at Large: diplomat extraordinary. The Hague, 1972. pp. 176. bibliog.

- Economic conditions

SELDES (GILBERT) The years of the locust: America, 1929-1932; (reprint of work originally published in 1933). New York, 1973. pp. 355.

WOYTINSKY (WLADIMIR SAVELEVICH) Fluctuations in employment covered by the federal old-age insurance program. Washington, D.C., 1939. pp. 77. (United States. Social Security Board. Bureau of Research and Statistics. Memoranda. No. 40)

GAUMENT (ERIC) Le mythe américain. Paris, [1970]. pp. 272.

CHAMBERLAIN (NEIL WOLVERTON) and CULLEN (DONALD EUGENE) The labor sector. 2nd ed. New York, [1971]. pp. 676. bibliogs.

GUERIN (DANIEL) and MANDEL (ERNEST) La concentration économique aux Etats-Unis. Paris, [1971]. pp. 230.

HOOVER (EDGAR MALONE) the Younger. An introduction to regional economics. New York, [1971]. pp. 395. bibliogs.

LAMPMAN (ROBERT J.) Ends and means of reducing income poverty. Chicago, [1971]. pp. 178. bibliog. (Wisconsin University, Madison. Institute for Research on Poverty. Monograph Series)

MORRILL (RICHARD L.) and WOHLENBERG (ERNEST H.) The geography of poverty in the United States. New York, [1971]. pp. 148. bibliogs.

BELOUS (IOSIF DAVYDOVICH) and LARIUSHIN (IURII DMITRIEVICH) Novye iavleniia v ekonomike sovremennogo kapitalizma: na primere SShA i Anglii. Kishinev, 1972. pp. 148.

BRANDIS (ROYALL) Principles of economics. rev. ed. Homewood, Ill., 1972. pp. 878.

EDWARDS (RICHARD C.) and others, eds. The capitalist system: a radical analysis of American society. Englewood Cliffs, [1972]. pp. 543. bibliogs.

ESTALL (ROBERT CHARLES) A modern geography of the United States: aspects of life and economy. Harmondsworth, 1972. pp. 401. bibliog.

HARING (JOSEPH E.) ed. Urban and regional economics: perspectives for publication. Boston, [Mass., 1972]. pp. 307. bibliog.

IAKOVLEVA (STELLA IVANOVNA) Osobennosti metodov kapitalisticheskoi ekspluatatsii v sovremennuiu epokhu: na materialakh SShA. Leningrad, 1972. pp. 120.

JANEWAY (ELIOT) You and your money: a survival guide to the controlled economy. New York, [1972]. pp. 284.

MANKOFF (MILTON) ed. The poverty of progress: the political economy of American social problems. New York, [1972]. pp. 524. bibliog.

MILLER (ROGER LEROY) and WILLIAMS (RABURN M.) The economics of national issues. San Francisco, [1972]. pp. 177.

PARKER (WILLIAM HENRY) The superpowers: the United States and the Soviet Union compared. London, 1972. pp. 347.

POLSKA AKADEMIA NAUK. Instytut Geografii. Geographia Polonica. 20. [Collected papers on aspects of physical and economic geography]. Warsaw, 1972. pp. 186. bibliogs.

PERLO (VICTOR) The unstable economy: booms and recessions in the United States since 1945. London, 1973. pp. 238.

PETERS (HARVEY W.) America's coming bankruptcy: how the government is wrecking your dollar. New Rochelle, [1973]. pp. 222.

STANFIELD (RON) The economic surplus and neo-Marxism. Lexington, Mass., [1973]. pp. 125. bibliog.

- Economic conditions - Mathematical models

FAIR (RAY C.) A short-run forecasting model of the United States economy. Lexington, [1971] repr. 1972. pp. 264. bibliog.

- Economic conditions - Statistics

NATIONAL PLANNING ASSOCIATION. Center for Economic Projections. Regional Economic Projections Series. Report No. 70-R-1. State economic and demographic projections to 1975 and 1980. Washington, D.C., 1970. pp. 49, 129.

- Economic history

ANDREANO (RALPH) ed. The economic impact of the American Civil War. 2nd ed. Cambridge, Mass., 1967. pp. 244. bibliog.

HOAR (VICTOR) ed. The great depression: essays and memoirs from Canada and the United States; ([by] James T. Patterson [and others]). Vancouver, [1969]. pp. 232.

SCHEIBER (HARRY N.) ed. The old Northwest: studies in regional history, 1787-1910. Lincoln, Neb., [1969]. pp. 395.

APPROACHES to American economic history; edited by George Rogers Taylor and Lucius F. Ellsworth. Charlottesville, 1971. pp. 135. bibliog.

DOUGLASS (ELISHA P.) The coming of age of American business: three centuries of enterprise, 1600-1900. Chapel Hill. N.C., [1971]. pp. 606. bibliog.

HIGGS (ROBERT) The transformation of the American economy, 1865-1914: an essay in interpretation. New York, [1971]. pp. 143. bibliog.

AMERICAN economic growth: an economist's history of the United States; by Lance E. Davis [and others]. New York, [1972]. pp. 683. bibliogs.

COCHRAN (THOMAS CHILDS) American business in the twentieth century. Cambridge, Mass., 1972. pp. 259.

ROSENBERG (NATHAN) Technology and American economic growth. New York, [1972]. pp. 211.

SINGER-KEREL (JEANNE) La New Economics et l'expansion américaine, 1961-1966. Paris, 1972. pp. 302. (Fondation Nationale des Sciences Politiques. Travaux et Recherches de Sciences Economiques. Politiques Economiques. 1)

CRAMER (CLARENCE HENLEY) American enterprise: the rise of U.S. commerce. London, 1973. pp. 728. bibliog.

HUGHES (JONATHAN ROBERTS TYSON) The vital few: American economic progress and its protagonists. London, [1973]. pp. 504. bibliog.

ROBERTSON (ROSS M.) History of the American economy. 3rd ed. New York, [1973]. pp. 788. bibliog.

- Economic history - Bibliography

LOVETT (ROBERT W.) compiler. American economic and business history: information sources:...an annotated bibliography of recent works, etc. Detroit, [1971]. pp. 323.

- Economic history - Sources

LOVETT (ROBERT W.) and BISHOP (ELEANOR C.) compilers. List of business manuscripts in Baker Library. 3rd ed. Boston. Mass., 1969. pp. 334.

ERICKSON (CHARLOTTE JOANNE) Invisible immigrants: the adaptation of English and Scottish immigrants in nineteenth century America. London, [1972]. pp. 531.

LETWIN (WILLIAM) ed. A documentary history of American economic policy since 1789. rev. ed. New York, [1972]. pp. 480.

- Economic policy

COMMITTEE FOR ECONOMIC DEVELOPMENT. Research and Policy Committee. Statements on National Policy. Further weapons against inflation: measures to supplement general fiscal and monetary policies. New York, 1970 repr. 1971. pp. 90.

EICHNER (ALFRED S.) State development agencies and employment expansion. Ann Arbor, 1970. pp. 76. bibliog. (Michigan University and Wayne State University. Institute of Labor and Industrial Relations. Policy Papers in Human Resources and Industrial Relations. No. 18)

CLAYTON (WILLIAM LOCKHART) Selected papers of Will Clayton; edited by Fredrick J. Dobney. Baltimore, [1971]. pp. 298.

CUMBERLAND (JOHN HAMMETT) Regional development: experiences and prospects in the United States of America. The Hague, [1971]. pp. 170. bibliog. (United Nations Research Institute for Social Development. Regional Planning. vol. 2)

ECONOMIC policies in the 1970s: six lectures on current economic issues given at Western Michigan University under the sponsorship of the Department of Economics, winter 1971: Alfred K. Ho, editor. Ann Arbor, [1971]. pp. 95. (Michigan University. Bureau of Business Research. Michigan Business Papers. No. 57)

ESSAYS in regional economics; edited by John F. Kain and John R. Meyer. Cambridge, Mass., 1971. pp. 412.

LAMPMAN (ROBERT J.) Ends and means of reducing income poverty. Chicago, [1971]. pp. 178. bibliog. (Wisconsin University, Madison. Institute for Research on Poverty. Monograph Series)

THUROW (LESTER C.) The impact of taxes on the American economy. New York, 1971. pp. 171.

AMERICAN ACADEMY OF POLITICAL AND SOCIAL SCIENCE. Annals. vol. 400. The government as regulator; special editor of this volume Marver H. Bernstein. Philadelphia, 1972. pp. 237.

UNITED STATES - Economic policy (Cont'd.)

CARTTER (ALLAN MURRAY) and MARSHALL (F. RAY) Labor economics: wages, employment, and trade unionism. rev. ed. Homewood, Ill., 1972. pp. 594. bibliogs.

CHERKASOVA (L.A.) ed. Formy gosudarstvennogo regulirovaniia ekonomiki pri kapitalizme: aktual'nye voprosy. Moskva, 1972. pp. 124.

CONVERSION from war to peace: social, economic and political problems; [abstracted from two conferences organized by the Fund for New Priorities in America at Boston in 1969 and at Hempstead, Long Island in 1971]; editor William Meyers; assistant editor M. Vincent Haves. New York, [1972]. pp. 121

DYE (THOMAS R.) Understanding public policy. Englewood Cliffs, [1972]. pp. 305. bibliogs.

ECONOMIC policy and inflation in the sixties; [by] Phillip Cagan [and others]. Washington, D.C., [1972]. pp. 267. (American Enterprise Institute for Public Policy Research. Domestic Affairs Studies.4)

FRIEDMAN (MILTON) An economist's protest: columns in political economy; [originally published in Newsweek Magazine and the New York Times, 1966-72]. Glen Ridge, N.J., [1972]. pp. 219.

LETWIN (WILLIAM) ed. A documentary history of American economic policy since 1789. rev. ed. New York, [1972]. pp. 480.

MANKOFF (MILTON) ed. The poverty of progress: the political economy of American social problems. New York, [1972]. pp. 524. bibliog.

MILKMAN (RAYMOND H.) and others. Alleviating economic distress: evaluating a federal effort. Lexington, Mass., [1972]. pp. 412. bibliog.

PETERS (FRANK R.) b. 1943. An economics for survival: a plea for the attainment of prosperity without waste. Philadelphia, [1972]. pp. 62.

SILK (LEONARD SOLOMON) Nixonomics: how the dismal science of free enterprise became the black art of controls. New York, 1972. pp. 212.

SINGER-KEREL (JEANNE) La New Economics et l'expansion américaine, 1961-1966. Paris, 1972. pp. 302. (Fondation Nationale des Sciences Politiques. Travaux et Recherches de Sciences Economiques. Politiques Economiques. 1)

BACH (GEORGE LELAND) The new inflation: causes, effects, cures. Providence, 1973. pp. 103.

MILLER (ROGER LEROY) Economics today. San Francisco, [1973]. pp. 750. bibliogs.

REYNOLDS (LLOYD GEORGE) and others, eds. Current issues of economic policy. Homewood, Ill., 1973. pp. 543.

- Economic policy - Mathematical models

FISHER (GORDON R.) and SHEPPARD (DAVID K.) Effects on monetary policy on the United States economy: a survey of econometric evidence. Paris, Organisation for Economic Co-operation and Development, 1972. pp. 128. bibliog. (OECD Economic Outlook. Occasional Studies)

- Emigration and immigration

BANNICK (CHRISTIAN JOHN) Portuguese immigration to the United States: its distribution and status: [reprint of the thesis originally presented in 1917]. San Francisco, 1971. pp. 87. bibliog.

LEINENWEBER (CHARLES ROBERT) Immigration and the decline of internationalism in the American working class movement, 1864-1919. 1968. fo. 251. bibliog. Xerox copy of Ph. D. (California) dissertation.

APPEL (JOHN J.) ed. The new immigration. New York, [1971]. pp. 215. bibliog.

BRANDES (JOSEPH) and DOUGLAS (MARTIN) Immigrants to freedom: Jewish communities in rural New Jersey since 1882. Philadelphia, [1971]. pp. 424. bibliog. (Jewish Theological Seminary of America. American Jewish History Center. Regional History Series)

PRPIC (GEORGE J.) The Croatian immigrants in America. New York, [1971]. pp. 519. bibliog.

RESEARCH INSTITUTE OF THE SOCIAL WELFARE CONSEQUENCES OF MIGRATION AND RESIDENTIAL MOVEMENT, SAN JUAN, PUERTO RICO, 1969. Migration and social welfare: report of the Research Institute [convened by the Council on Social Work Research of the National Association of Social Workers] ...; edited by Joseph W. Eaton. New York, [1971] pp. 240. bibliog.

COLEMAN (TERRY) Passage to America: a history of emigrants from Great Britain and Ireland to America in the mid-nineteenth century. London, 1972. pp. 317. bibliog.

ERICKSON (CHARLOTTE JOANNE) Invisible immigrants: the adaptation of English and Scottish immigrants in nineteenth century America. London, [1972]. pp. 531.

THOMAS (BRINLEY) Migration and urban development: a reappraisal of British and American long cycles. London, 1972. pp. 259. bibliog.

TROPER (HAROLD MARTIN) Only farmers need apply: official Canadian government encouragement of immigration from the United States, 1896-1911. Toronto, 1972. pp. 192.

THOMAS (BRINLEY) Migration and economic growth: a study of Great Britain and the Atlantic economy. 2nd ed. Cambridge, 1973. pp. 498. bibliog.

- Emigration and immigration - Bibliography

BROOKS (THOMAS R.) Labor and migration: an annotated bibliography. Brooklyn, N.Y., [1970]. 1 vol. (unpaged).

- Executive departments

CAROTHERS (DORIS) Chronology of the Federal Emergency Relief Administration, May 12, 1933, to December 31, 1935: [reprint of the work originally published in Washington, 1937]. New York, 1971. pp. 163. (United States. Work Projects Administration. Division of Social Research. Research Monographs. 6)

SALMOND (JOHN A.) The Civilian Conservation Corps, 1933-1942: A New Deal case study. Durham, N.C., Duke U.P., 1967. pp. vii, 240. bibliog. 21½cm.

FROME (MICHAEL) The forest service. New York, 1971. pp. 241. bibliog.

ROTHBLATT (DONALD N.) Regional planning: the Appalachian experience. Lexington, Mass., [1971]. pp. 281. bibliog.

ECKLER (A. ROSS) The Bureau of the Census. New York, 1972. pp. 268. bibliog.

EVERHART (WILLIAM C.) The National Park Service. New York, 1972. pp. 275. bibliog.

CORWIN (RONALD G.) Reform and organizational survival: the teacher corps as an instrument of educational change. New York, [1973]. pp. 469. bibliog.

JOHNSTON (BRIAN LESLIE) The United States Defence Department and Congressional control; [M.Sc.(Econ.) (London) thesis]. [1973]. fo. 154. bibliog. Typescript: unpublished. This thesis is the property of London University and may not be removed from the Library.

- Foreign economic relations

KNORR (KLAUS EUGEN) Strengthening the free world economy: a report... of a conference held at Princeton on December 16-17, 1952. Princeton, 1953. fo. 45. (Princeton University. Center of International Studies. [Policy] Memoranda. No. 3)

NELSON (JAMES R.) and PALMER (DONALD K.) United States foreign economic policy and the sterling area. Princeton, 1953. fo. 44. (Princeton University. Center of International Studies. [Policy] Memoranda. No. 4)

BACKLUND (LEIF) Dollarn och Västeuropa: den internationella valutafrågans politiska aspekt. Stockholm, 1971. pp. 191.

CLAYTON (WILLIAM LOCKHART) Selected papers of Will Clayton; edited by Fredrick J. Dobney. Baltimore, [1971]. pp. 298.

BUCHANAN (KEITH McPHERSON) The geography of empire; [articles reprinted from The Spokesman, 1971]. Nottingham, 1972. pp. 64.

DAVIS (JOSEPH STANCLIFFE) America and the world, 1946-71, in the perspective of 1914-39. Stanford, Calif., [1972]. pp. 24. (Stanford University. Food Research Institute. Studies in Agricultural Economics, Trade and Development. vol. 11, 1972. Supplement)

HUDSON (MICHAEL) Ph.D. Super imperialism: the economic strategy of American empire. New York, [1972]. pp. 304.

HUNTER (ROBERT EDWARDS) and RIELLY (JOHN E.) eds. Development today: a new look at U.S. relations with the poor countries. New York, 1972. pp. 286. bibliog.

SHCHETININ (VALENTIN DMITRIEVICH) Evoliutsiia amerikanskogo neokolonializma: kritika teorii i praktiki neokolonialistskogo "partnerstva". Moskva, 1972. pp. 272.

CALLEO (DAVID PATRICK) and ROWLAND (BENJAMIN M.) America and the world political economy: Atlantic dreams and national realities. Bloomington, Ind., [1973]. pp. 371. bibliog.

Foreign economic relations - America, Latin

ORCAJO ACUNA (FEDERICO) Pan-America?: la politica internacional americana, union economica, etc. Montevideo, 1933. pp. 117.

ARISMENDI (RODNEY) Para un prontuario del dolar: al margen del plan Truman. Montevideo; [1947]. pp. 292.

MELAZZI (GUSTAVO) ed. Industrializacion y dependencia en America Latina: textos de CEPAL, Jalée, Romanova, Frank, Guevara, Franco y Testa. [Montevideo, 1969]. pp. 133.

DOUGLAS (WILLIAM ORVILLE) Holocaust or hemispheric co-op: cross currents in Latin America. New York, [1971]. pp. 215

GRUNWALD (JOSEPH) and others. Latin American economic integration and U.S. policy. Washington, D.C., [1972]. pp. 216. bibliog.

TARASOV (KONSTANTIN SERGEEVICH) SShA i Latinskaia Amerika: voenno-politicheskie i voenno-ekonomicheskie otnosheniia. Moskva, 1972. pp. 359.

- Foreign economic relations - Canada

MILLER (JOHN THOMAS) Foreign trade in gas and electricity in North America. New York, [1970]. pp. 316.

CANADIAN-AMERICAN COMMITTEE. The U.S. import surcharge and Canada. [Washington, D.C., 1971]. pp. 7.

CANADIAN-AMERICAN COMMITTEE. The new environment for Canadian-American relations. Washington, D.C., 1972. pp. 61.

- Foreign economic relations - East (Near East)

ROBERTS (DICK) Mideast oil & U.S. imperialism. New York, 1971. pp. 23. (Reprinted from International Socialist Review, 1971)

- Foreign economic relations - Germany

OBERMANN (KARL) Die Beziehungen des amerikanischen Imperialismus zum deutschen Imperialismus in der Zeit der Weimarer Republik, 1918-1925. Berlin, 1952. pp. 167. bibliog.

- Foreign economic relations - Japan

SHARKOV (ALEKSANDR MIKHAILOVICH) Iaponiia i SShA: analiz sovremennykh ekonomicheskikh otnoshenii. Moskva, 1971. pp. 408.

- Foreign economic relations - Mexico

BAERRESEN (DONALD W.) The border industrialization program of Mexico. Lexington, Mass., [1971]. pp. 133.

- Foreign economic relations - Pacific, The

PACIFIC Basin development: the American interests: [papers covering topics discussed at seminar meetings sponsored by the Overseas Development Council];... edited by Harald B. Malmgren. Lexington, [1972]. pp. 148.

- Foreign economic relations - Vietnam

TRUONG-TRUNG-THU and NGUYEN-MANH-DE. Ekonomicheskaia politika amerikanskikh neokolonizatorov v Iuzhnom V'etname; perevod s v'etnamskogo, etc. Moskva, 1965. pp. 239.

- Foreign opinion.

STEARN (GERALD EMANUEL) ed. Broken image: foreign critiques of America; selected and edited with notes and introduction. New York, [1972]. pp. 298.

WHITE (JO ANN) ed. African views of the West. New York, [1972]. pp. 206.

- Foreign relations

ROOSEVELT (THEODORE) President of the United States. Colonial policies of the United States; [reprint of the 1937 ed.]. New York, 1970. pp. 204. bibliog.

ROSENAU (JAMES N.) Public opinion and foreign policy: an operational formulation. New York. [1961]. pp. 118. bibliog.

The REVOLUTION in world politics; [papers presented at a conference at Princeton in 1961 in preparation for the international relations panels of the 1961 meeting of the American Political Science Association at St. Louis]; Morton A. Kaplan, editor. New York, [1962] repr. 1966. pp. 477.

UNITED STATES - Foreign relations (Cont'd.)

SELSER (GREGORIO) El rapto de Panama: de como los Estados Unidos inventaron un pais y se apropiaron de un canal. Buenos Aires, [1964]. pp. 189.

SCOTT (ANDREW McKAY) The revolution in statecraft: informal penetration. New York, [1965]. pp. 194. bibliog.

DRAPER (HAL) ed. Independent socialism and war;... articles [selected from Labor Action, The New International and Anvil]. Berkeley, Calif., [1966]. pp. 194. (Independent Socialist Committee. Independent Socialist Clippingbooks. No. 2)

SAPIN (BURTON MALCOLM) The making of United States foreign policy. Washington, 1966 repr. 1969. pp. 415.

DE RIVERA (JOSEPH H.) The psychological dimension of foreign policy. Columbus, Ohio, [1968]. pp. 441.

STRUGGLE against history: U.S. foreign policy in an age of revolution: [papers of a seminar held in Estes Park, Colorado in 1967]; edited by Neal D. Houghton. New York, [1968]. pp. 375.

BENTHEM VAN DEN BERGH (G. VAN) De ideologie van het Westen. Amsterdam, 1969. pp. 215.

HERO (ALFRED OLIVIER) and STARR (EMIL) The Reuther-Meany foreign policy dispute: union leaders and members view world affairs. Dobbs Ferry, 1970. 1 vol. (various pagings).

HOYT (EDWIN PALMER) The American attitude: the story of the making of foreign policy in the United States. London, [1970]. pp. 254. bibliog.

1971

CAMPBELL (JOHN FRANKLIN) The foreign affairs fudge factory. New York, [1971]. pp. 292.

CONFERENCE ON PEACE RESEARCH IN HISTORY, 1968. Power and law: American dilemma in world affairs; papers...edited by Charles A. Barker. Baltimore, [1971]. pp. 205.

FERRELL (ROBERT H.) ed. America as a world power, 1872-1945: [documents]. [2nd ed.] Columbia, S.C., 1971. pp. 306. bibliog.

HANCOCK (M. DONALD) and RUSTOW (DANKWART ALEXANDER) eds. American foreign policy in international perspective. Englewood Cliffs, [1971]. pp. 375.

HAYES (LOUIS D.) The impact of U.S. policy on the Kashmir conflict. Tucson, [1971]. pp. 59. (Arizona University. Institute of Government Research. International Studies. No. 2)

JOHNSON (EDGAR AUGUSTUS JEROME) American imperialism in the image of Peer Gynt: memoirs of a professor-bureaucrat. Minneapolis, [1971]. pp. 352. bibliog.

LEPPER (MARY MILLING) Foreign policy formulation: a case study of the Nuclear Test Ban Treaty of 1963. Columbus, Ohio, [1971]. pp. 191. bibliog.

MERK (FREDERICK) Fruits of propaganda in the Tyler administration. Cambridge, Mass., 1971. pp. 259.

STENNIS (JOHN C.) and FULBRIGHT (JAMES WILLIAM) The role of Congress in foreign policy. Washington, [1971]. pp. 139. (American Enterprise Institute for Public Policy Research. Rational Debate Seminars. 5th Series. 2)

STONE (ISIDOR F.) Polemics and prophecies, 1967-1970; [articles and essays from his Weekly and the New York Review of Books]. New York, [1971]. pp. 497.

VORONTSOV (VLADILEN BORISOVICH) Senator ot Arkanzasa. Moskva, 1971. pp. 271.

WILCOX (FRANCIS ORLANDO) Congress, the executive, and foreign policy. New York, [1971]. pp. 176.

WILSON (JOAN HOFF) American business and foreign policy, 1920-1933. Lexington, Ky., [1971]. pp. 339. bibliog.

1972

ARKES (HADLEY) Bureaucracy, the Marshall plan, and the national interest. Princeton, [1972]. pp. 395. bibliog.

BARNDS (WILLIAM J.) India, Pakistan, and the great powers. New York, 1972. pp. 386. bibliog.

BARYSHEV (ALEKSANDR PETROVICH) Strategiia Belogo doma i OON; pod redaktsiei...Anat.A. Gromyko. Moskva, 1972. pp. 312.

BELL (SIDNEY) Righteous conquest: Woodrow Wilson and the evolution of the new diplomacy. Port Washington, N.Y., 1972. pp. 209. bibliog.

BLETZ (DONALD F.) The role of the military professional in U.S. foreign policy. New York, [1972]. pp. 320. bibliog.

BRUTENTS (K.) A historical view of neo-colonialism. Moscow, 1972. pp. 307.

BUCHANAN (KEITH McPHERSON) The geography of empire; [articles reprinted from The Spokesman, 1971]. Nottingham, 1972. pp. 64.

BURKE (LEE H.) Ambassador at Large: diplomat extraordinary. The Hague, 1972. pp. 176. bibliog.

COLLIER (BASIL) The lion and the eagle: British and Anglo-American strategy, 1900-1950. London. [1972]. pp. 499. bibliog.

COMBS (JERALD A.) ed. Nationalist, realist, and radical: three views of American diplomacy. New York, [1972]. pp. 526.

CRABB (CECIL VAN METER) American foreign policy in the nuclear age. 3rd ed. New York, [1972]. pp. 528. bibliog.

DAVIS (DAVID HOWARD) How the bureaucracy makes foreign policy: an exchange analysis. Lexington, Mass., [1972]. pp. 164. bibliog.

DESTLER (I.M.) Presidents, bureaucrats and foreign policy: the politics of organizational reform. Princeton, 1972. pp. 329. bibliog.

DOKTRINA Niksona. Moskva. 1972. pp. 232.

DULLES (ELEANOR LANSING) The wall: a tragedy in three acts. Columbia, S.C., 1972. pp. 105. (South Carolina University. Institute of International Studies. Studies in International Affairs. No. 9)

FLEMING (DENNA FRANK) The issues of survival. London, 1972. pp. 124.

FREELAND (RICHARD M.) The Truman doctrine and the origins of McCarthyism: foreign policy, domestic politics, and internal security, 1946-1948. New York, 1972. pp. 419,xii. bibliog.

FROM colony to empire: essays in the history of American foreign relations; edited by William Appleman Williams. New York, [1972]. pp. 506.

FRY (MICHAEL GRAHAM) Illusions of security: North Atlantic diplomacy, 1918-1922. Toronto, [1972]. pp. 221. bibliog.

FULBRIGHT (JAMES WILLIAM) The crippled giant: American foreign policy and its domestic consequences. New York, [1972]. pp. 292.

GUHIN (MICHAEL ALAN) John Foster Dulles: a statesman and his times. New York, 1972. pp. 404. bibliog.

IMLAY (ROBERT) The cool war. London, [1972]. pp. 90. bibliog.

JANIS (IRVING LESTER) Victims of groupthink: a psychological study of foreign-policy decisions and fiascoes. Boston, [Mass.], [1972]. pp. 276. bibliog.

JENKINS (ROY HARRIS) Afternoon on the Potomac?: a British view of America's changing position in the world. New Haven, Conn., 1972. pp. 59. (Yale University. Henry L. Stimson Lectures. 1971)

KAPLAN (LAWRENCE SAMUEL) Colonies into nation: American diplomacy, 1763-1801. New York, [1972]. pp. 331. bibliog.

KIERNAN (BERNARD P.) The United States, communism, and the emergent world. Bloomington, [Ind., 1972]. pp. 248. bibliog.

KOLKO (JOYCE) and KOLKO (GABRIEL) The limits of power: the world and United States foreign policy, 1945-1954. New York, [1972]. pp. 820.

KOPKIND (ANDREW DAVID) and RIDGEWAY (JAMES) eds. Decade of crisis: America in the '60s. New York, [1972]. pp. 293.

PELL (CLAIBORNE) Power and policy: America's role in world affairs. New York, [1972]. pp. 173.

PILISUK (MARC) International conflict and social policy. Englewood Cliffs, [1972]. pp. 199. bibliogs.

PRANGER (ROBERT JOHN) Defense implications of international indeterminacy. Washington, 1972. pp. 31. (American Enterprise Institute for Public Policy Research. Foreign Affairs Studies. 4)

ROSTOW (EUGENE VICTOR) Peace in the balance: the future of American foreign policy. New York, [1972]. pp. 352.

ROSTOW (WALT WHITMAN) The diffusion of power: an essay in recent history. New York, [1972]. pp. 739.

ROTHSTEIN (ROBERT L.) Planning, prediction, and policymaking in foreign affairs: theory and practice. Boston, [Mass., 1972]. pp. 214.

ROURKE (FRANCIS EDWARD) Bureaucracy and foreign policy. Baltimore, 1972. pp. 80. (Johns Hopkins University. Washington Center of Foreign Policy Research. Studies in International Affairs. No. 17)

SHAPIRO (MARTIN) ed. The Pentagon papers and the courts: a study in foreign policy-making and freedom of the press. San Francisco, [1972]. pp. 131.

SMITH (ROBERT) pseud. The economics of the cold war. New York, [1972]. pp. 126.

THORNE (CHRISTOPHER) The limits of foreign policy: the West, the League, and the Far Eastern crisis of 1931-1933. London, 1972. pp. 442. bibliog.

TOWARD a wiser colossus; reviewing and recasting United States foreign policy;...edited by James A. Stegenga. Lafayette, Ind., 1972. pp. 147. (Purdue University. Louis Martin Sears Lectures. 1970-71)

VAN DER LINDEN (FRANK) Nixon's quest for peace. Washington, [1972]. pp. 248.

VOENNAIA sila i mezhdunarodnye otnosheniia: voennye aspekty vneshnepoliticheskikh kontseptsii SShA. Moskva, 1972. pp. 239.

WESTON (RUBIN FRANCIS) Racism in U.S. imperialism: the influence of racial assumptions on American foreign policy, 1893-1946. Columbia, S.C., 1972. pp. 291. bibliog.

1973

ARON (RAYMOND) République impériale: les Etats-Unis dans le monde, 1945-1972. [Paris, 1973]. pp. 340.

BOHLEN (CHARLES EUSTIS) Witness to history, 1929-1969. London, 1973. pp. 562.

BRANDON (HENRY) The retreat of American power. New York, 1973. pp. 368.

BUHITE (RUSSELL D.) Patrick J. Hurley and American foreign policy. Ithaca, 1973. pp. 342. bibliog.

CHALLENER (RICHARD D.) Admirals, generals and American foreign policy, 1898-1914. Princeton, 1973. pp. 433. bibliog.

FLOTO (INGA) Colonel House in Paris: a study of American policy at the Paris Peace Conference, 1919. Aarhus, 1973. pp. 374. bibliog.

KILDOW (JUDITH TEGGER) INTELSAT: policy-maker's dilemma. Lexington, Mass., [1973]. pp 118. bibliog.

LODGE (HENRY CABOT) 1902- . The storm has many eyes: a personal narrative. New York, [1973]. pp. 272.

MADDOX (ROBERT JAMES) The New Left and the origins of the Cold War. Princeton, [1973]. pp. 169.

NASH (HENRY T.) American foreign policy: response to a sense of threat. Homewood, Ill., 1973. pp. 247.

OWEN (HENRY) 1920- , ed. The next phase in foreign policy;... essays by Morton H. Halperin [and others]. Washington, D.C., [1973]. pp. 345.

PACKENHAM (ROBERT A.) Liberal America and the third world: political development ideas in foreign aid and social science. Princeton, [1973]. pp. 395. bibliog.

PAUL (ROLAND A.) American military commitments abroad. New Brunswick, [1973]. pp. 237. bibliog.

SHEPPARD (BARRY) and ROBERTS (DICK) The meaning of the Vietnam accords: Nixon's world strategy, the role of Moscow and Peking, prospects for the Vietnamese revolution. New York, [1973]. pp. 15.

STONE (ISIDOR F.) The best of I.F. Stone's Weekly: pages from a radical newspaper; edited and introduced by Neil Middleton. Harmondsworth, 1973. pp. 321.

STONE (RALPH A.) The irreconcilables: the fight against the League of Nations. New York, 1973. pp. 208. bibliog.

- Foreign relations - Treaties

CUE CANOVAS (AGUSTIN) Juarez, los EE.UU. y Europa: el tratado McLane-Ocampo. 4th ed. Mexico, 1970. pp. 254. bibliog.

UNITED STATES (Cont'd.)

- Foreign relations - America, Latin

  CRICHFIELD (GEORGE WASHINGTON) American supremacy: the rise and progress of the Latin American republics and their relations to the United States under the Monroe doctrine. New York 1908. 2 vols.

  OSEGUEDA (RAUL) Operacion Centroamerica: £8 OK £8. Mexico, 1957. pp. 238. bibliog.

  FABELA (ISIDRO) Buena y mala vecindad. Mexico, 1958. pp. 333.

  MEDINA CASTRO (MANUEL) Estados Unidos y America Latina, siglo XIX. La Habana, 1968. pp. 774. bibliog.

  NORTH AMERICAN CONGRESS ON LATIN AMERICA. Subliminal warfare: the role of Latin American studies. New York, [1970?]. pp. 63.

  GIL (FEDERICO GUILLERMO) Latin American-United States relations. New York, [1971]. pp. 339.

  GRAY (RICHARD BUTLER) ed. Latin America and the United States in the 1970's: [a reader]. Itasca, Ill., [1971]. pp. 369. bibliog.

  GREEN (DAVID) 1942-   . The containment of Latin America: a history of the myths and realities of the Good Neighbor Policy. Chicago, 1971. pp. 368. bibliog.

  HAVERSTOCK (NATHAN A.) and SCHROEDER (RICHARD C.) Dateline Latin America: a review of trends and events of 1970. [Washington, D.C., 1971]. pp. 106. bibliog.

  MATLINA (ANNA ALEKSANDROVNA) Kritika kontseptsii "mirnoi reguliruemoi revoliutsii" dlia Latinskoi Ameriki. Moskva, 1971.. pp. 319.

  PETRAS (JAMES) and LAPORTE (ROBERT) Cultivating revolution: the United States and agrarian reform in Latin America. New York, [1971]. pp. 469.

  WILLIAMS (EDWARD J.) The political themes of inter-American relations. Belmont, [1971]. pp. 178. bibliog.

  KANE (WILLIAM EVERETT) Civil strife in Latin America: a legal history of U.S. involvement. Baltimore, [1972]. pp. 240.

  NEEDLER (MARTIN CYRIL) The United States and the Latin American revolution. Boston. [Mass., 1972]. pp. 167. bibliog.

  PETRAS (JAMES) ed. Latin America: from dependence to revolution. New York, [1973]. pp. 274. bibliog.

- Foreign relations - America, Latin - Bibliography

  WOLPIN (MILES D.) compiler. United States intervention in Latin America: a selected and annotated bibliography. New York, 1971. pp. 56. (American Institute for Marxist Studies. Bibliographical Series. No. 8)

- Foreign relations - Argentine Republic

  GARCIA LUPO (ROGELIO) Historia de unas malas relacione [Buenos Aires], 1964. pp. 112.

  SCENNA (MIGUEL ANGEL) Como fueron las relaciones argentino-norteamericanas. Buenos Aires, [1970]. pp. 270. bibliog.

- Foreign relations - Asia

  WILCOX (WAYNE AYRES) Asia and United States policy. Englewood Cliffs, [1967]. pp. 116. bibliog.

  GREENE (FRED) U.S. policy and the security of Asia. New York, [1968]. pp. 423. (Council on Foreign Relations. United States and China in World Affairs)

  AMERICAN ACADEMY OF POLITICAL AND SOCIAL SCIENCE. Annals. vol. 390. A new American posture toward Asia: special editor of this volume James C. Charlesworth. Philadelphia, 1970. pp. 204.

  CHO (M.Y.) Die Volksdiplomatie in Ostasien...; die Asienpolitik der Vereinigten Staaten und die Beziehungen zwischen der Volksrepublik China und Japan. Wiesbaden, [1971]. pp. 240. bibliog. (Hamburg. Institut für Asienkunde. Schriften. Band 30) With English summary.

  LI (VLADIMIR FEDOROVICH) Strategiia i politika neokolonializma SShA: diplomatiia "novykh rubezhei" i strany Iuzhnoi i Iugo-Vostochnoi Azii. Moskva, 1971. pp. 400.

  BRODINE (VIRGINIA) and SELDEN (MARK) eds. Open secret: the Kissinger-Nixon doctrine in Asia. New York, 1972. pp. 218.

  SCALAPINO (ROBERT A.) Asia and the major powers. Washington, 1972. pp. 117. (American Enterprise Institute for Public Policy Research and Stanford University. Hoover Institution on War, Revolution and Peace. AEI-Hoover Policy Studies. 3)

- Foreign relations - Asia, Southeast

  FIFIELD (RUSSELL HUNT) Americans in Southeast Asia: the roots of commitment. New York, [1973]. pp. 417. bibliog.

- Foreign relations - Australia

  HARPER (NORMAN DENHOLM) ed. Australia and the United States: (documents and readings in Australian history). Melbourne, [1971]. pp. 274. bibliog.

- Foreign relations - Bolivia

  SELSER (GREGORIO) La CIA en Bolivia. Buenos Aires, [1970]. pp. 398.

- Foreign relations - Brazil

  LUZ (NICIA VILELA) A Amazônia para os negros americanos: as origens de uma controversia internacional. Rio de Janeiro, 1968. pp. 188. bibliog.

- Foreign relations - Cambodia

  POOLE (PETER A.) The expansion of the Vietnam war into Cambodia: action and response by the governments of North Vietnam, South Vietnam, Cambodia, and the United States. Athens, Ohio, 1970. fo. 59. (Ohio University. Center for International Studies. Papers in International Studies. Southeast Asia Series. No. 17)

  CAMBODIA: the widening war in Indochina; edited by Jonathan S. Grant [and others]. New York, 1971. pp. 355. bibliog.

  HAMMARSKJÖLD FORUM, 15TH, 1970. The Cambodian incursion: legal issues: proceedings...Donald T. Fox, editor. Dobbs Ferry, N.Y., 1971. pp. 89. bibliog.

- Foreign relations - Canada

  BEATON (LEONARD) The strategic and political issues facing America, Britain and Canada. London, 1971. pp. 21. (British-North American Committee. Publications. 5)

- Foreign relations - Caribbean area

  JONES (CHESTER LLOYD) Caribbean interests of the United States;... [reprint of the work originally published in 1916]. New York, 1970. pp. 379. bibliog.

CRASSWELLER (ROBERT D.) The Caribbean community: changing societies and U.S. policy. New York, 1972. pp. 468. bibliog.

- Foreign relations - China

FAIRBANK (JOHN KING) The United States and China. 3rd ed. Cambridge, Mass., 1971. pp. 500. bibliog.

GRIFFITH (WILLIAM E.) Cold war and coexistence: Russia, China, and the United States. Englewood Cliffs, [1971]. pp. 115.

MOORSTEEN (RICHARD) and ABRAMOWITZ (MORTON) Remaking China policy: U.S.-China relations and governmental decisionmaking. Cambridge, Mass., 1971. pp. 136.

PEACE with China?: U.S. decisions for Asia; edited by Earl C. Ravenal. New York, [1971]. pp. 248.

SERVICE (JOHN S.) The Amerasia papers: some problems in the history of US-China relations. Berkeley, [1971]. pp. 218. bibliog. (California University. Center for Chinese Studies. China Research Monographs. No. 7)

TAIWAN and American policy: the dilemma in U.S.-China relations; [by] Jerome Alan Cohen [and others: papers of a conference sponsored by] the League of Women Voters Education Fund and the National Committee on United States-China Relations. New York, 1971. pp. 191.

TUCHMAN (BARBARA WERTHEIM) Sand against wind: Stilwell and the American experience in China, 1911-45. London, 1971. pp. 621. bibliog.

MACFARQUHAR (RODERICK L.) ed. Sino-American relations, 1949-71. Newton Abbot, 1972. pp. 265. bibliog.

SINO-U.S. joint communique, February 28, 1972. Peking, 1972. pp. 7.

YEH (HSIANG-CHIH) Maoist new internal power struggle and Nixon's visit. [Taipei], 1972. pp. 25. (Asian Peoples' Anti-Communist League. Pamphlets. No. 162)

- Foreign relations - Cuba

GUGGENHEIM (HARRY FRANK) The United States and Cuba: a study in international relations. New York, 1934; St. Clair Shores, 1970. pp. 268. bibliog. Facsimile reprint.

ALLISON (GRAHAM T.) Essence of decision: explaining the Cuban missile crisis. Boston, [Mass.], 1971. pp. 338.

BONSAL (PHILIP WILSON) Cuba, Castro, and the United States. Pittsburgh, [1971]. pp. 318. bibliog.

HITCHMAN (JAMES H.) Leonard Wood and Cuban independence 1898-1902. The Hague, 1971. pp. 238. bibliog.

FONER (PHILIP SHELDON) The Spanish-Cuban-American War and the birth of American imperialism, 1895-1902. New York, [1972]. 2 vols.

- Foreign relations - Dominican Republic

ODENA (ISIDRO J.) La intervención ilegal en Santo Domingo. Buenos Aires, [1965]. pp. 79.

ORTEGA (GREGORIO) Santo Domingo, 1965. La Habana, 1965. pp. 269.

MANSBACH (RICHARD W.) ed. Dominican crisis 1965. New York, [1971]. pp. 133.

ATKINS (G. POPE) and WILSON (LARMAN C.) The United States and the Trujillo regime. New Brunswick, [1972]. pp. 245. bibliog.

LOWENTHAL (ABRAHAM F.) The Dominican intervention. Cambridge, Massachusetts, 1972. pp. 246. bibliog.

- Foreign relations - East (Far East)

MAY (ERNEST RICHARD) and THOMSON (JAMES C.) eds. American-East Asian relations: a survey. Cambridge, Mass., 1972. pp. 425. (Harvard University. Harvard Studies in American-East Asian Relations. 1)

VAN ALSTYNE (RICHARD WARNER) The United States and east Asia. London, [1973]. pp. 180. bibliog.

- Foreign relations - East (Near East)

GRABILL (JOSEPH L.) Protestant diplomacy and the Near East: missionary influence on American policy, 1810-1927. Minneapolis, [1971]. pp. 395. bibliog.

PRANGER (ROBERT JOHN) American policy for peace in the Middle East, 1969-1971: problems of principle, maneuver and time. Washington, D.C., 1971. pp. 69. (American Enterprise Institute for Public Policy Research. Foreign Affairs Studies. 1)

AMERICAN ACADEMY OF POLITICAL AND SOCIAL SCIENCE. Annals. vol. 401. America and the Middle East; special editor of this volume, Parker T. Hart. Philadelphia, 1972. pp. 239.

BOSE (TARUN CHANDRA) The superpowers and the Middle East. London, [1972]. pp. 208.

TAYLOR (TREVOR) The supply of arms to the Middle East and the United States' foreign policy, 1950-68; [Ph.D. (London) thesis]. 1972. 1 vol. (various foliations). bibliog. Typescript: unpublished. This thesis is the property of London University and may not be removed from the Library.

- Foreign relations - Europe

McGEEHAN (ROBERT) The German rearmament question: American diplomacy and European defense after World War II. Urbana, Ill., [1971]. pp. 280. bibliog.

NALIN (IU.) and NIKOLAEV (A.) Sovetskii Soiuz i evropeiskaia bezopasnost'. Moskva, 1971. pp. 104.

CATALANO (FRANCO) Europa e Stati Uniti negli anni della guerra fredda: economia e politica, 1944-1956. Milano, 1972. pp. 446

SILBERSCHMIDT (MAX) The United States and Europe: rivals and partners. London, [1972]. pp. 216. bibliog.

ROOSEVELT (FRANKLIN DELANO) President of the United States, and BULLITT (WILLIAM CHRISTIAN) For the President: personal and secret; correspondence between Franklin D. Roosevelt and William C. Bullitt; Orville H. Bullitt, editor. London, 1973. pp. 655. bibliog.

- Foreign relations - Europe, Eastern

KOVRIG (BENNETT) The myth of liberation: east-central Europe in U.S. diplomacy and politics since 1941. Baltimore, [1973]. pp. 360. bibliog.

- Foreign relations - European Economic Community countries

GEIGER (THEODORE) Transatlantic relations in the prospect of an enlarged European Community. London, 1970. pp. 61. (British-North American Committee. Publications. 2)

UNITED STATES (Cont'd.)

- Foreign relations - France

SALYCHEVA (LEONORA ALEKSANDROVNA) SShA i Frantsii: problemy imperialisticheskogo soiuza v 1945-1958 gg. Moskva, 1970. pp. 252.

HENRY-HAYE (GASTON) La grande éclipse franco-américaine. [Paris, 1972]. pp. 393.

- Foreign relations - Germany

KRAUS (HANNELORE) Vorstellungen von Senatoren und Repräsentanten des amerikanischen Kongresses zur Deutschlandpolitik nach dem Zweiten Weltkriege: Kriegsprogramme, Nachkriegspolitik und ihre heutigen Aspekte. [Frankfurt am Main, imprint], 1971. pp. 224. bibliog.

STUETZLE (WALTHER) Kennedy und Adenauer in der Berlin-Krise, 1961-1962. Bonn-Bad Godesberg, [1973]. pp. 253. bibliog. (Friedrich-Ebert-Stiftung. Forschungsinstitut. Schriftenreihe. Band 96)

- Foreign relations - Hungary

RADVÁNYI (JÁNOS) Hungary and the superpowers: the 1956 revolution and Realpolitik. Stanford, [1972]. pp. 197. bibliog. (Stanford University. Hoover Institution on War, Revolution and Peace. Hoover Institution Publications. 111)

- Foreign relations - India

HESS (GARY R.) America encounters India, 1941-1947. Baltimore, [1971]. pp. 211. bibliog.

- Foreign relations - Indochina

MIKHEEV (IURII IAKOVLEVICH) Amerikantsy v Indokitae: kritika protivopravnoi doktriny i politiki SShA. Moskva, 1972. pp. 248.

SCOTT (PETER DALE) The war conspiracy: the secret road to the second Indochina war. Indianapolis, [1972]. pp. 238.

- Foreign relations - Israel

ARAKIE (MARGARET) The broken sword of justice: America, Israel and the Palestine tragedy. London, 1973. pp. 195. bibliog.

- Foreign relations - Italy

ŽIVOJINOVIĆ (DRAGAN R.) America, Italy and the birth of Yugoslavia, 1917-1919. Boulder, Col., 1972. pp. 338. bibliog. (East European Quarterly East European Monographs. 2)

- Foreign relations - Japan

JAPANESE-American relations in the 1970s: [originally prepared as background reading for participants in the second Japanese-American Assembly, sponsored by the Japan Council for International Understanding and the American Assembly... in Shimoda, Japan, 1969; edited by Gerald L. Curtis]. Washington, D.C., 1970. pp. 204.

LIBAL (MICHAEL) Japans Weg in den Krieg: die Aussenpolitik der Kabinette Konoye 1940/1941. Düsseldorf, [1971]. pp. 261. bibliog.

ASAHI SHIMBUN. The Pacific rivals: a Japanese view of Japanese-American relations; by the staff of the Asahi Shimbun; translated from the Japanese by Ken'ichi Otsuka; [edited by] Peter Grilli and Yoshio Murakami. New York, 1972. pp. 431.

IRIYE (AKIRA) Pacific estrangement: Japanese and American expansion, 1897-1911. Cambridge, Mass., 1972. pp. 290. bibliog. (Harvard University. Committee on American-Far Eastern Policy Studies. Harvard Studies in American-East Asian Relations. 2)

MICHAEL (FRANZ HENRY) and SIGUR (GASTON J.) The Asian alliance: Japan and United States policy. [New York, 1972]. pp. 92. bibliog. (National Strategy Information Center. Strategy Papers No.15)

OSGOOD (ROBERT ENDICOTT) The weary and the wary: U.S. and Japanese security policies in transition. Baltimore, 1972. pp. 95. (Johns Hopkins University. Washington Center of Foreign Policy Research. Studies in International Affairs. No. 16)

VERBITSKII (SEMEN IL'ICH) Iapono-amerikanskii voenno-politicheskii soiuz, 1951-1970 gg. Moskva, 1972. pp. 285.

- Foreign relations - Korea

KIM (IL-SUNG) Progressive journalists of the five continents, wield your powerful revolutionary pen and sternly condemn U.S. imperialism. Pyongyang, 1969. pp. 19.

- Foreign relations - Mexico

BOSCH GARCIA (CARLOS) Material para la historia diplomatica de Mexico: Mexico y los Estados Unidos, 1820-1848. Mexico, 1957. pp. 655. bibliog.

CRAIG (RICHARD B.) The bracero program: interest groups and foreign policy. Austin, [1971]. pp. 233. bibliog.

ULLOA (BERTA) La revolucion intervenida: relaciones diplomaticas entre Mexico y Estados Unidos, 1910-1914. Mexico, [1971]. pp. 394. (Mexico City. Colegio de Mexico. Centro de Estudios Historicos. Nueva Serie. 12)

SMITH (ROBERT FREEMAN) The United States and revolutionary nationalism in Mexico, 1916-1932. Chicago, 1972. pp. 288. bibliog.

PRICE (JOHN A.) Tijuana: urbanization in a border culture. Notre Dame, [1973]. pp. 195. bibliog.

- Foreign relations - Nicaragua

STIMSON (HENRY LEWIS) American policy in Nicaragua. New York, 1927 repr. 1971. pp. 129.

RODRIGUEZ SERRANO (FELIPE) El canal por Nicaragua: estudio de la negociacion canalera y su proyeccion en la historia de Nicaragua. [Managua, 1968?]. pp. 292.

MACAULAY (NEILL) The Sandino affair. Chicago, 1971. pp. 319. bibliog.

- Foreign relations - Pacific, The

HOHENBERG (JOHN) New era in the Pacific: an adventure in public diplomacy. New York, [1972]. pp. 539.

NATIONAL security and international trusteeship in the Pacific: [essays by officers of the United States Naval War College]; edited by Wm. Roger Louis. Annapolis, Md., [1972]. pp. 182. bibliog.

- Foreign relations - Palestine

JANSEN (MICHAEL E.) The United States and the Palestinian people. Beirut, [1970]. pp. 215. bibliog. (Institute for Palestine Studies. Monograph Series. No. 23)

- Foreign relations - Peru

U.S. foreign policy and Peru; [papers presented at a conference of the Peru Policy Seminar at Racine, Wisconsin, May 24-26, 1970]; edited by Daniel A. Sharp. Austin, [1972]. pp. 485. (Texas University. Institute of Latin American Studies. Special Publications)

- Foreign relations - Portugal

CAETANO (MARCELLO) Welcome to the Azores: speech delivered... in honour of the President of the United States of America, Richard Nixon, and the President of the French Republic, Georges Pompidou, at Angra do Heroísmo, Azores Islands, on 13 December 1971. [Lisbon?], Secretaria de Estado da Informação e Turismo, 1971. pp. 8.

MINTER (WILLIAM) Portuguese Africa and the West. Harmondsworth, 1972. pp. 176. bibliog.

- Foreign relations - Puerto Rico

MALDONADO DENIS (MANUEL) Puerto Rico: una interpretacion historico-social. Mexico, 1969 repr. 1970. pp. 255. bibliog.

- Foreign relations - Russia

ZERI I POPULLIT. Soviet-U.S. alliance at work against the Czechoslovak people. Tirana, 1969. pp. 16.

ALLISON (GRAHAM T.) Essence of decision: explaining the Cuban missile crisis. Boston, [Mass.], 1971. pp. 338.

GRIFFITH (WILLIAM E.) Cold war and coexistence: Russia, China, and the United States. Englewood Cliffs, [1971]. pp. 115.

ULAM (ADAM BRUNO) The rivals: America and Russia since World War II. New York, 1971. pp. 405.

GADDIS (JOHN LEWIS) The United States and the origins of the cold war, 1941-1947. New York, 1972. pp. 396. bibliog.

HOLSTI (OLE R.) Crisis, escalation, war. Montreal, 1972. pp. 290.

LAFEBER (WALTER) America, Russia, and the cold war, 1945-1971. 2nd ed. New York, [1972]. pp. 339. bibliog.

BOHLEN (CHARLES EUSTIS) Witness to history, 1929-1969. London, 1973. pp. 562.

HERRING (GEORGE C.) Aid to Russia, 1941-1946: strategy, diplomacy, the origins of the Cold War. New York, 1973. pp. 365. bibliog.

JOXE (ALAIN) Socialisme et crise nucléaire. Paris, [1973]. pp. 561.

ROSE (LISLE A.) After Yalta. New York, [1973]. pp. 216. bibliog.

SLUSSER (ROBERT M.) The Berlin crisis of 1961: Soviet-American relations and the struggle for power in the Kremlin, June-November 1961. Baltimore, [1973]. pp. 509. bibliog.

TSVETKOV (GLEB NIKOLAEVICH) Politika SShA v otnoshenii SSSR nakanune voiny. Kiev, 1973. pp. 192.

- Foreign relations - Taiwan

TAIWAN and American policy: the dilemma in U.S.-China relations; [by] Jerome Alan Cohen [and others: papers of a conference sponsored by] the League of Women Voters Education Fund and the National Committee on United States-China Relations. New York, 1971. pp. 191.

- Foreign relations - Turkey

TRASK (ROGER R.) The United States response to Turkish nationalism and reform, 1914-1939. Minneapolis, [1971]. pp. 280. bibliog.

HARRIS (GEORGE S.) Troubled alliance: Turkish-American problems in historical perspective, 1945-1971. Washington, D.C., [1972]. pp. 263. bibliog. (American Enterprise Institute for Public Policy Research and Stanford University. Hoover Institution on War, Revolution and Peace. AEI-Hoover Policy Studies)

- Foreign relations - United Kingdom

BICKEL (WOLF HEINRICH) Die anglo-amerikanischen Beziehungen 1927-1930 im Licht der Flottenfrage: das Problem des Machtausgleichs zwischen Grossbritannien und den Vereinigten Staaten in der Zwischenkriegszeit und seine Lösung. Zürich, 1970. pp. 227. bibliog.

BEATON (LEONARD) The strategic and political issues facing America, Britain and Canada. London, 1971. pp. 21. (British-North American Committee. Publications. 5)

COLLIER (BASIL) The lion and the eagle: British and Anglo-American strategy, 1900-1950. London, [1972]. pp. 499. bibliog.

MANDERSON-JONES (RONALD BRANDIS) The special relationship: Anglo-American relations and western European unity, 1947-56. London, [1972]. pp. 168. bibliog.

NUNNERLEY (DAVID) President Kennedy and Britain. London, 1972. pp. 242.

WILLERT (Sir ARTHUR) Washington and other memories. Boston, 1972. pp. 248.

- Foreign relations - Vietnam

STANDARD (WILLIAM L.) Aggression: our Asian disaster. New York, [1971]. pp. 227. bibliog.

FITZGERALD (FRANCES) Fire in the lake: the Vietnamese and the Americans in Vietnam. Boston, 1972]. pp. 491. bibliog.

STAVINS (RALPH) and others. Washington plans an aggressive war: (a documented account of the United States adventure in Indochina). London, 1972. pp. 374.

UNGAR (SANFORD J.) The Papers and the papers: an account of the legal and political battle over the Pentagon Papers. New York, 1972. pp. 319.

CHOMSKY (NOAM) The backroom boys. [London], 1973. pp. 222.

- Foreign relations administration

CAMPBELL (JOHN FRANKLIN) The foreign affairs fudge factory. New York, [1971]. pp. 292.

ARKES (HADLEY) Bureaucracy, the Marshall plan, and the national interest. Princeton, [1972]. pp. 395. bibliog.

- Government publications - Bibliography

BRIGHTON. University of Sussex. Institute of Development Studies. Library. Occasional Guides. No. 2. A guide to information on developing countries in U.S. government publications, 1962-1971. Brighton, [1972]. pp. 82.

- Government publications - Indexes

PRZEBIENDA (EDWARD) ed. United States government publications: monthly catalog: decennial cumulative personal author index, 1941-(1960). Ann Arbor, 1971. 2 vols.

UNITED STATES - Government publications - Indexes (Cont'd.)

PRZEBIENDA (EDWARD) ed. United States government publications: monthly catalog: quinquennial cumulative personal author index, 1961-1965. Ann Arbor, 1971. pp. 293.

CHECKLIST of United States public documents, 1789-1970: (a dual media edition of the U.S. Superintendent of Documents' Public Documents Library shelf lists): indexes; compiled by Daniel W. Lester and Marilyn A. Lester ([and] the United States Historical Documents Institute). Washington, 1972. 4 vols. Library has index vols. 2-5 (vol. 1 not purchased).

- Historical geography

MEINIG (DONALD WILLIAM) Southwest: three peoples in geographical change, 1600-1970. New York, 1971. pp. 151.

ROSENKRANTZ (BARBARA GUTMANN) and KOELSCH (WILLIAM A.) eds. American habitat: a historical perspective. New York, [1973]. pp. 372.

- History

CARLETON (MARK T.) Study guide to The democratic experience; to accompany The democratic experience by Louis B. Wright [and others]. Glenview, Ill., [1966]. pp. 124.

SCHEIBER (HARRY N.) ed. The old Northwest: studies in regional history, 1787-1910. Lincoln, Neb., [1969]. pp. 395.

RIEGEL (ROBERT EDGAR) and ATHEARN (ROBERT GREENLEAF) America moves west. 5th ed. New York, [1971]. pp. 599. bibliogs.

- History - Bibliography

NEW YORK (STATE). Education Department. Bureau of Secondary Curriculum Development. 1956. American history: bibliography. Albany, [1956]. pp. 112.

- History - Historiography

MORTON (MARIAN J.) The terrors of ideological politics: liberal historians in a conservative mood. Cleveland. 1972. pp. 192. bibliog.

- History - Philosophy

NORLIN (GEORGE) The quest of American life. Boulder, Colorado, 1945. pp. 280. (Colorado University. Studies. Series B. Studies in the Humanities. vol. 2, no. 3)

- History - Sources

VAUGHAN (ALDEN T.) ed. The Puritan tradition in America, 1620-1730; [sources]. New York, [1972]. pp. 348.

- History - 1607-1783, Colonial period

MAIER (PAULINE) From resistance to revolution: colonial radicals and the development of American opposition to Britain, 1765-1776. London, 1973. pp. 344. bibliog.

- History - 1775-1783, Revolution

WRIGHT (ESMOND) Washington and the American revolution; [reprint of the work originally published in London, 1957]. Harmondsworth, 1973. pp. 206. bibliog.

HAWKE (DAVID) Benjamin Rush: revolutionary gadfly. Indianapolis, [1971]. pp. 490. bibliog.

ESSAYS on the American revolution; [papers originally presented at a symposium held at the Institute of Early American History and Culture, Williamsburg, 1971]; edited by Stephen G. Kurtz and James H. Hutson. Williamsburg, Va., [1973]. pp. 318.

- History - 1800-1899

GATELL (FRANK OTTO) and GOODMAN (PAUL) b. 1934. Democracy and union: the United States, 1815-1877. New York, [1972]. pp. 198. bibliogs.

- History - 1845-1848, War with Mexico

MESTRE GHIGLIAZZA (MANUEL) ed. Invasion norteamericana en Tabasco, 1846-1847: documentos. Mexico, 1948. pp. 369. (Mexico City. Universidad Nacional Autonoma de Mexico. Instituto de Historia. Publicaciones. la Serie. num. 8)

CONNOR (SEYMOUR V.) and FAULK (ODIE B.) North America divided: the Mexican War, 1846-1848. New York, 1971. pp. 300. bibliog.

- History - 1845-1848, War with Mexico - Personal narratives

TENNERY (THOMAS DOUTHIT) The Mexican War diary of Thomas D. Tennery; edited and with an introduction by D.E. Livingston-Little. Norman, Okla., [1970]. pp. 117. bibliog.

- History - 1861-1865, Civil War

DICEY (Sir EDWARD) Spectator of America; [reprint of Six Months in the Federal States, published in 1863]; edited with an introduction by Herbert Mitgang. London, 1972. pp. 318.

THOMAS (EMORY M.) The Confederacy as a revolutionary experience. Englewood Cliffs, [1971]. pp. 150. bibliog.

MYERS (ROBERT MANSON) ed. The children of pride: a true story of Georgia and the Civil War. New Haven, 1972. pp. 1845.

- History - 1861-1865, Civil War - Causes

RUSSEL (ROBERT ROYAL) Critical studies in antebellum sectionalism: essays in American political and economic history. Westport, Conn., [1972]. pp. 223. bibliogs.

- History - 1861-1865, Civil War - Economic aspects

ANDREANO (RALPH) ed. The economic impact of the American Civil War. 2nd ed. Cambridge, Mass., 1967. pp. 244. bibliog.

- History - 1861-1865, Civil War - Foreign public opinion

WEINBERG (ADELAIDE) John Elliot Cairnes and the American civil war: a study in Anglo-American relations. London, [1970]. pp. 224.

ELLISON (MARY L.A.) Support for secession: Lancashire and the American Civil War;... epilogue by Peter d'A. Jones. Chicago, 1972. pp. 259. bibliog.

- History - 1898, War of

CHIDSEY (DONALD BARR) The Spanish-American war: a behind-the-scenes account of the war in Cuba. New York, [1971]. pp. 191. bibliog.

GATEWOOD (WILLARD BADGETTE) ed. "Smoked Yankees" and the struggle for empire: letters from negro soldiers, 1898-1902. Urbana, Ill., [1971]. pp. 328. bibliog.

FONER (PHILIP SHELDON) The Spanish-Cuban-American War and the birth of American imperialism, 1895-1902. New York, [1972]. 2 vols.

- History - 1919-1933

    GOODMAN (PAUL) b. 1934, and GATELL (FRANK OTTO) America in the twenties: the beginnings of contemporary America. New York, [1972]. pp. 247. bibliogs.

- History - 1933-1945

    POLENBERG (RICHARD) War and society: the United States, 1941-1945. Philadelphia, [1972]. pp. 298. bibliog.

- History, Military

    CHODES (JOHN J.) The myth of America's military power. Boston, [Mass.], [1972]. pp. 224.

    WEIGLEY (RUSSELL F.) The American way of war: a history of United States military strategy and policy. New York, 1973. pp. 584. bibliog.

- History, Naval

    BICKEL (WOLF HEINRICH) Die anglo-amerikanischen Beziehungen 1927-1930 im Licht der Flottenfrage: das Problem des Machtausgleichs zwischen Grossbritannien und den Vereinigten Staaten in der Zwischenkriegszeit und seine Lösung. Zürich, 1970. pp. 227. bibliog.

- Industries

    VASIL'EV (IURII PETROVICH) Vnutrifirmennoe upravlenie v SShA: sovremennye formy i metody upravleniia v promyshlennykh kompaniiakh. Moskva, 1970. pp. 404.

    BURROWS (JAMES C.) and others. Industrial location in the United States: a Charles River Associates research study; an econometric analysis. Lexington, Mass., [1971]. pp. 123.

    WEST (E.C.) Canada-United States price and productivity differences in manufacturing industries, 1963. Ottawa, 1971. pp. 81. (Canada. Economic Council. Staff Studies. No. 32)

    CAVES (RICHARD E.) American industry: structure, conduct, performance. 3rd ed. Englewood Cliffs, N.J., [1972]. pp. 117. bibliog.

    FLORENCE (PHILIP SARGANT) The logic of British and American industry: a realistic analysis of economic structure and government. 3rd ed. London, 1972. pp. 413.

    GORGOL (JOHN FRANCIS) The military-industrial firm: a practical theory and model; prepared for publication by Ira Kleinfeld. New York, 1972. pp. 143. bibliog.

    HARRIS (CURTIS C.) and HOPKINS (FRANK E.) Locational analysis: an interregional econometric model of agriculture, mining, manufacturing and services. Lexington, [1972]. pp. 303.

    MORONEY (J.R.) The structure of production in American manufacturing. Chapel Hill, N.C.. [1972]. pp. 174. bibliog.

    RODGERS (JOHN M.) State estimates of outputs, employment and payrolls, 1947, 1958, 1963. Lexington, Mass., [1972]. pp. 252. bibliog.

- Intellectual life

    TOMSICH (JOHN) A genteel endeavor: American culture and politics in the Gilded Age. Stanford, 1971. pp. 236. bibliog.

    BEICHMAN (ARNOLD) Nine lies about America. London, 1972. pp. 314. bibliog.

    CLAYTON (BRUCE) The savage ideal: intolerance and intellectual leadership in the South, 1890-1914. Baltimore, [1972]. pp. 231. bibliog. (Johns Hopkins University. Studies in Historical and Political Science. Series 90. No. 1)

    CRUNDEN (ROBERT M.) From self to society, 1919-1941. Englewood Cliffs, [1972]. pp. 212. bibliog.

    KING (RICHARD) Professor of History and Philosophy. The party of Eros: radical social thought and the realm of freedom. Chapel Hill, [1972]. pp. 227. bibliog.

    McWILLIAMS (WILSON CAREY) The idea of fraternity in America. Berkeley, 1973. pp. 695. bibliog.

    WHITE (MORTON GABRIEL) Pragmatism and the American mind: essays and reviews in philosophy and intellectual history. New York, 1973. pp. 265.

- Marine Corps - Prisons

    SHERRILL (ROBERT) Military justice is to justice as military music is to music. New York, [1970]. pp. 235.

- Military policy

    ACKLEY (CHARLES WALTON) The modern military in American society: a study in the nature of military power. Philadelphia, [1972]. pp. 400. bibliog.

    BLETZ (DONALD F.) The role of the military professional in U.S. foreign policy. New York, [1972]. pp. 320. bibliog.

    CONVERSION from war to peace: social, economic and political problems; [abstracted from two conferences organized by the Fund for New Priorities in America at Boston in 1969 and at Hempstead, Long Island in 1971]; editor William Meyers; assistant editor M. Vincent Hayes. New York, [1972]. pp. 121.

    EFREMOV (ALEKSANDR EFREMOVICH) Evropa i iadernoe oruzhie. Moskva, 1972. pp. 390.

    LIVEN' (VALENTINA ANDREEVNA) Voina vo V'etname i vnutripoliticheskaia bor'ba v SShA. Kiev 1972. pp. 112.

    PURSELL (CARROLL W.) ed. The military-industrial complex: [readings]. New York, [1972]. pp. 342. bibliog.

    STANLEY (JOHN) American troops in Europe: an anachronism or a necessity? London, 1972. pp. 22. (Conservative Political Centre. [Publications]. No. 502)

    VOENNAIA sila i mezhdunarodnye otnosheniia: voennye aspekty vneshnepoliticheskikh kontseptsii SShA. Moskva, 1972. pp. 239.

    MIDDLETON (DREW) Retreat from victory: a critical appraisal of American foreign and military policy from 1920 to the 1970s. New York, [1973]. pp. 250. bibliog.

    MITIAEV (VLADIMIR GRIGOR'EVICH) Iadernaia politika SShA v NATO. Moskva, 1973. pp. 208. bibliog.

    PAUL (ROLAND A.) American military commitments abroad. New Brunswick, [1973]. pp. 237. bibliog.

    RUSSETT (BRUCE MARTIN) and STEPAN (ALFRED C.) eds. Military force and American society. New York, [1973]. pp. 371. bibliog.

    TILLEMA (HERBERT K.) Appeal to force: American military intervention in the era of containment. New York, [1973]. pp. 260. bibliog.

    WEIGLEY (RUSSELL F.) The American way of war: a history of United States military strategy and policy. New York, 1973. pp. 584. bibliog.

UNITED STATES (Cont'd.)

- Moral conditions

BLUMENTHAL (MONICA D.) and others. Justifying violence: attitudes of American men. Ann Arbor, [1972]. pp. 367. bibliog.

- Nationalism

NAGEL (PAUL CHESTER) This sacred trust: American nationality, 1798-1898. New York, 1971. pp. 376.

- Navy

ELLER (ERNEST McNEILL) The Soviet sea challenge. [Chicago, 1971]. pp. 315. bibliog.

- Navy - Negroes

PURDON (ERIC) Black company: the story of Subchaser 1264. Washington, [1972]. pp. 255.

- Occupations

CAMPBELL (DAVID P.) Handbook for the Strong Vocational Interest Blank. Stanford, 1971. pp. 516. bibliog.

- Officials and employees

CONGRESSIONAL SEMINAR ON PUBLIC SERVICE EMPLOYMENT, 1971. The political economy of public service employment; [papers and discussions of the...seminar.. conducted by the W.E. Upjohn Institute for Employment Research]; edited by Harold L. Sheppard [and others]. Lexington, Mass., [1972]. pp. 463. bibliogs.

TAX FOUNDATION. Research Publications. New Series. No. 27. Unions and government employment. New York, 1972. pp. 45.

KAUFMAN (HERBERT) and COUZENS (MICHAEL) Administrative feedback: monitoring subordinates' behavior. Washington, D.C., [1973]. pp. 83. bibliog.

STIEBER (JACK W.) Public employee unionism: structure, growth, policy. Washington, D.C., [1973]. pp. 256. (Brookings Institution. Studies of Unionism in Government)

- Peace Corps

NIGERIAN YOUTH CONGRESS. Revolutionary Council. Peace corps: agents of neo-colonialism; facts about the "peace corps" and the U.S.A. information agency. [1964?]. pp. 37.

- Politics and government

GARRETTE (EVE) A political handbook for women. Garden City, N.Y., 1944. pp. 219.

KRINSKY (FRED) ed. Democracy and complexity: who governs the governors?; [an anthology compiled with introductory remarks]. Beverly Hills, 1968 repr. 1969. pp. 147.

BLACKMORE (CHARLES P.) and YESELSON (ABRAHAM) eds. The fabric of democracy: readings in American government. 2nd ed. New York, [1969]. pp. 420.

EPSTEIN (EDWIN M.) The corporation in American politics. Englewood Cliffs, N.J., [1969]. pp. 365. bibliog.

TAYLOR (JOHN) Political writer and agriculturalist. An inquiry into the principles and policy of the government of the United States;...[text of the first edition] edited by Loren Baritz [with an introduction and additional footnotes]. Indianapolis, [1969]. pp. 560.

DYE (THOMAS R.) and ZEIGLER (LUTHER HARMON) The irony of democracy: an uncommon introduction to American politics. Belmont, Calif., [1970]. pp. 348. bibliogs.

GAUMENT (ERIC) Le mythe américain. Paris, [1970]. pp. 272.

SHARKANSKY (IRA) The routines of politics. New York, [1970]. pp. 192.

EMMERICH (HERBERT) Federal organization and administrative management. University, Alabama, [1971]. pp. 304.

NISKANEN (WILLIAM A.) Bureaucracy and representative government. Chicago, 1971. pp. 241.

RICCI (DAVID M.) Community power and democratic theory: the logic of political analysis. New York, [1971]. pp. 244. bibliog.

ROBINSON (DONALD L.) Slavery in the structure of American politics, 1765-1820. New York, [1971]. pp. 564.

SAIPA (AXEL) Politischer Prozess und Lobbyismus in der Bundesrepublik und in den USA: eine rechtsvergleichende und verfassungspolitische Untersuchung. Göttingen, 1971. pp. 233, vi. bibliog.

SEXTON (PATRICIA CAYO) and SEXTON (BRENDAN) Blue collars and hard-hats: the working class and the future of American politics. New York, [1971]. pp. 327.

VERBA (SIDNEY) and others. Caste, race, and politics: a comparative study of India and the United States. Beverly Hills, Calif., [1971]. pp. 279. bibliog.

WEBER (CHRISTIAN EGBERT) Die Integration eines Kontinents als Problem: Amerika, Europa. Berlin, [1971]. pp. 96. bibliog.

WHEELER (JOHN HARVEY) The politics of revolution. Berkeley, [1971]. pp. 308.

DEVINE (DONALD J.) The political culture of the United States: the influence of member values on regime maintenance. Boston, [Mass., 1972]. pp. 383.

GATELL (FRANK OTTO) and others, eds. The growth of American politics;...a modern reader. New York, 1972. 2 vols. bibliogs.

OTTENSOSER (MILTON D.) and SIGALL (MICHAEL W.) eds. The American political reality. New York, [1972]. pp. 278.

PARKER (WILLIAM HENRY) The superpowers: the United States and the Soviet Union compared. London, 1972. pp. 347.

POMPER (GERALD M.) and others. The performance of American government: checks and minuses. New York, [1972]. pp. 372. bibliog.

SIGLER (JAY A.) and GETZ (ROBERT S.) Contemporary American government: problems and prospects. New York, [1972]. pp. 846. bibliog.

WATSON (RICHARD A.) Promise and performance of American democracy. New York, [1972]. pp. 619. bibliogs.

EBENSTEIN (WILLIAM) and others. American democracy in world perspective. 3rd ed. New York, [1973]. pp. 528. bibliog.

FERGUSON (JOHN HENRY) and McHENRY (DEAN EUGENE) The American federal government. 12th ed. New York, [1973]. 1 vol. (various pagings). bibliogs.

McWILLIAMS (WILSON CAREY) The idea of fraternity in America. Berkeley, 1973. pp. 695. bibliog.

MAGRATH (C. PETER) and others. The American democracy. 2nd ed. New York, [1973]. pp. 717. bibliogs.

MONSMA (STEPHEN V.) American politics: a systems approach. 2nd ed. Hinsdale, Ill., [1973]. pp. 430. bibliogs.

NIMMO (DAN D.) and UNGS (THOMAS D.) American political patterns: conflict and consensus. 3rd ed. Boston, [1973]. pp. 575. bibliogs.

- Politics and government - Public opinion

ROLL (CHARLES W.) and CANTRIL (ALBERT HADLEY) 1940- . Polls: their use and misuse in politics. New York, [1972]. pp. 177.

- Politics and government - 1607-1783, Colonial period

LEONARD (DANIEL) and ADAMS (JOHN) President of the United States. The American colonial crisis: the Daniel Leonard-John Adams letters to the press, 1774-1775; edited by Bernard Mason. New York, [1972]. pp. 266.

OLSON (ALISON GILBERT) Anglo-American politics 1660-1775: the relationship between parties in England and colonial America. Oxford, 1973. pp. 192.

- Politics and government - 1783-1865

MERK (FREDERICK) Fruits of propaganda in the Tyler administration. Cambridge, Mass., 1971. pp. 259.

BUEL (RICHARD) Securing the revolution: ideology in American politics, 1789-1815. Ithaca, 1972. pp. 391.

CHAMBERS (WILLIAM NISBET) ed. The first party system: Federalists and Republicans; [selected readings]. New York, [1972]. pp. 201. bibliog.

- Politics and government - 1800-1899

JOHNSON (ANDREW) President of the United States. The papers of Andrew Johnson...; editors, Leroy P. Graf and Ralph W. Haskins. Knoxville, Tenn., 1967 in progress.

DONALD (DAVID) Charles Sumner and the rights of man. New York, 1970. pp. 595, xxxix. bibliog.

WELCH (RICHARD E.) George Frisbie Hoar and the Half-Breed Republicans. Cambridge, Mass., 1971. pp. 364. bibliog.

- Politics and government - 1815-1861

McFAUL (JOHN M.) The politics of Jacksonian finance. Ithaca, 1972. pp. 230.

MILLER (DOUGLAS T.) ed. The nature of Jacksonian America. New York, [1972]. pp. 152. bibliog.

BLUE (FREDERICK J.) The free soilers: third party politics, 1848-54. Urbana, [1973]. pp. 350. bibliogs.

JOHANNSEN (ROBERT WALTER) Stephen A. Douglas. New York, 1973. pp. 993.

- Politics and government - 1865-

DOWNES (RANDOLPH C.) The rise of Warren Gamaliel Harding, 1865-1920. Columbus, Ohio, [1970]. pp. 734. bibliog.

TOMSICH (JOHN) A genteel endeavor: American culture and politics in the Gilded Age. Stanford, 1971. pp. 236. bibliog.

- Politics and government - 1865-1898

JENSEN (RICHARD) The winning of the Midwest: social and political conflict, 1888-1896. Chicago, 1971. pp. 357. bibliog.

McSEVENEY (SAMUEL T.) The politics of depression: political behavior in the northeast, 1893-1896. New York 1972. pp. 333. bibliog.

- Politics and government - 1898-1945

SELDES (GILBERT) The years of the locust: America, 1929-1932; (reprint of work originally published in 1933). New York, 1973. pp. 355.

BROWDER (EARL RUSSELL) Unity for peace and democracy. New York, 1939. pp. 95.

FEIS (HERBERT) 1933: characters in crisis. Boston, [Mass.], [1966]. pp. 366.

LOWITT (RICHARD) George W. Norris: the persistence of a progressive, 1913-1933. Urbana, [1971]. pp. 590. bibliog.

McCRAW (THOMAS K.) TVA and the power fight, 1933-1939. Philadelphia, [1971]. pp. 201. bibliog.

MOELLER (BEVERLEY BOWEN) Phil Swing and Boulder Dam. Berkeley, 1971. pp. 199. bibliog.

GILBERT (JAMES BURKHART) Designing the industrial state: the intellectual pursuit of collectivism in America, 1880-1940. Chicago, 1972. pp. 335.

LLOYD (CRAIG M.) Aggressive introvert: a study of Herbert Hoover and public relations management 1912-1932. Columbus, 1972. pp. 206. bibliog.

STEINBERG (ALFRED) The bosses. New York, [1972]. pp. 379. bibliog.

- Politics and government - 1900-1999

AMERICAN ACADEMY OF ARTS AND SCIENCES. Commission on the Year 2000. The future of the United States government: toward the year 2000; edited by Harvey S. Perloff. New York, [1971]. pp. 388.

DRUCKER (PETER FERDINAND) Men, ideas and politics: essays. New York, [1971]. pp. 278.

JOYNER (CONRAD) The American politician. Tucson, [1971]. pp. 231. bibliog.

KROCK (ARTHUR) The consent of the governed and other deceits. Boston, [1971]. pp. 309.

ACHESON (DEAN GOODERHAM) Grapes from thorns; [extracts from articles, books, lectures, letters, etc.]. New York, [1972]. pp. 253.

JAMES (DOROTHY BUCKTON) ed. Outside, looking in: critiques of American policies and institutions, left and right. New York, [1972]. pp. 439.

MARKEL (LESTER) What you don't know can't hurt you: a study of public opinion and public emotion. Washington, [1972]. pp. 288. bibliog.

CANNON (JAMES PATRICK) Notebook of an agitator. 2nd ed. New York, 1973. pp. 369. A reprint of the 1st ed. with the addition of an index and illustrations.

POLSBY (NELSON WOOLF) ed. The modern presidency New York, [1973]. pp. 236.

TRUMAN (MARGARET) Harry S. Truman. London, 1973. pp. 602.

- Politics and government - 1945-

ELLSWORTH (RALPH EUGENE) and HARRIS (SARAH M.) The American right wing: a report to the Fund for the Republic, Inc. Urbana, 1960. pp. 50. (Illinois University. Library School. Occasional Papers. No. 59)

UNITED STATES - Politics and government - 1945- (Cont'd.)

REPUBLICAN NATIONAL COMMITTEE. House Republican Policy Committee. Meeting the challenges of the sixties: [digests of seven speeches by members of the...Committee]. [Washington, D.C., 1960]. pp. 35.

ETZIONI (AMITAI) Demonstration democracy...: a policy-paper prepared for the Task Force on Demonstrations, Protests and Group Violence of the President's National Commission on the Causes and Prevention of Violence. New York, [1970]. pp. 108.

GOLEMBIEWSKI (ROBERT T.) and others, eds. The new politics: polarization or utopia?; [readings with introductory matter]. New York, [1970]. pp. 387.

1971

BURKHART (JAMES AUSTIN) and KENDRICK (FRANK J.) eds. The new politics: mood or movement? Englewood Cliffs, [1971]. pp. 236.

EVANS (ROWLAND) and NOVAK (ROBERT D.) Nixon in the White House: the frustration of power. New York, [1971]. pp. 431.

HARTMANN (SUSAN MECKFESSEL) Truman and the 80th Congress. Columbia, Mo., 1971. pp. 241. bibliog.

HENDEL (SAMUEL) ed. The politics of confrontation. New York, [1971]. pp. 352.

IULINA (NINA STEPANOVNA) Burzhuaznye ideologicheskie techeniia v SShA: problemy i protivorechiia "amerikanskogo soznaniia". Moskva, 1971. pp. 136.

LEVIN (MURRAY BURTON) Political hysteria in America: the democratic capacity for repression. New York, [1971]. pp. 312. bibliog.

MILTON S. EISENHOWER SYMPOSIUM, BALTIMORE, 1970. Violence: the crisis of American confidence; [papers presented at the symposium: The United States in the 1970s: perspectives on violence]; edited by Hugh Davis Graham [and others]. Baltimore, [1971]. pp. 180. bibliogs.

REVEL (JEAN FRANÇOIS) Without Marx or Jesus: the new American revolution has begun;... translated by J.F. Bernard. New York, [1971]. pp. 269.

ROSS (ROBERT S.) ed. Public choice and public policy: seven cases in American government; [readings]. Chicago, [1971]. pp. 190.

SALYCHEV (S.S.) ed. Politicheskie bitvy v stranakh kapitala. Moskva, 1971. pp. 344.

STONE (ISIDOR F.) Polemics and prophecies, 1967-1970; [articles and essays from his Weekly and the New York Review of Books]. New York, [1971]. pp. 497.

1972

ALBRIGHT (JOSEPH) What makes Spiro run: the life and times of Spiro Agnew. New York, [1972]. pp. 295.

ALEXANDER (HERBERT E.) Money in politics. Washington, [1972]. pp. 353.

AMERICAN ACADEMY OF POLITICAL AND SOCIAL SCIENCE. Annals. vol. 400. The government as regulator; special editor of this volume Marver H. Bernstein. Philadelphia, 1972. pp. 237.

ANSON (ROBERT SAM) McGovern: a biography. New York, [1972]. pp. 303.

BOSKIN (JOSEPH) and ROSENSTONE (ROBERT A.) eds. Seasons of rebellion: protest and radicalism in recent America. New York, [1972]. pp. 336.

BRODER (DAVID S.) The party's over: the failure of politics in America. New York, [1972]. pp. 280.

BROWN (STUART GERRY) The Presidency on trial: Robert Kennedy's 1968 campaign and afterwards. Honolulu, 1972. pp. 155.

CHOMSKY (NOAM) Problems of knowledge and freedom. London, 1972. pp. 95. (Cambridge. University. Trinity College. Bertrand Russell Memorial Lectures. 1971)

DAVIDSON (CHANDLER) Biracial politics: conflict and coalition in the metropolitan south. Baton Rouge, [1972]. pp. 301.

DOUGLAS (PAUL HOWARD) In the fullness of time: the memoirs of Paul H. Douglas. New York, [1972]. pp. 642.

DRURY (ALLEN) Courage and hesitation: inside the Nixon administration. London, 1972. pp. 317.

FREELAND (RICHARD M.) The Truman doctrine and the origins of McCarthyism: foreign policy, domestic politics, and internal security, 1946-1948. New York, 1972. pp. 419.xii. bibliog.

FULBRIGHT (JAMES WILLIAM) The crippled giant: American foreign policy and its domestic consequences. New York, [1972]. pp. 292.

GOGGIN (TERENCE P.) and SEIDL (JOHN M.) eds. Politics American style: race, environment and central cities. Englewood Cliffs, [1972]. pp. 404.

HALBERSTAM (DAVID) The best and the brightest. London, [1972]. pp. 688. bibliog.

HAMILTON (RICHARD F.) Class and politics in the United States. New York, [1972]. pp. 589.

HAVARD (WILLIAM C.) ed. The changing politics of the south. Baton Rouge, [1972]. pp. 755. bibliog.

HOWE (IRVING) b. 1928, and HARRINGTON (MICHAEL) eds. The seventies: problems and proposals; [essays originally appearing in Dissent magazine]. New York, [1972]. pp. 519.

JOHNSON (LYNDON BAINES) President of the United States. The vantage point: perspectives of the Presidency, 1963-1969. London, 1972. pp. 630.

KOPKIND (ANDREW DAVID) and RIDGEWAY (JAMES) eds. Decade of crisis: America in the '60s. New York, [1972]. pp. 293.

KRIVITSKII (ALEKSANDR IU.) Koe-chto o Pentagone: pamflety. Moskva, 1972. pp. 112.

LADD (EVERETT CARLL) and LIPSET (SEYMOUR MARTIN) Contours of academic politics, 1972. Washington, D.C., [1972]. pp. (8). (Reprinted from New York Magazine, October 16, 1972)

LIVEN' (VALENTINA ANDREEVNA) Voina vo V'etname i vnutripoliticheskaia bor'ba v SShA. Kiev, 1972. pp. 112.

McPHERSON (HARRY) A political education. Boston, [Mass.], [1972]. pp. 467.

MOLLENHOFF (CLARK R.) Strike force: organized crime and the government. Englewood Cliffs, N.J., [1972]. pp. 274.

NIXON (RICHARD MILHOUS) President of the United States. A new road for America: major policy statements, March 1970 to October 1971;... preface and commentaries by Richard Wilson. Garden City, N.Y., 1972. pp. 720.

NOVAK (MICHAEL) The rise of the unmeltable ethnics: politics and culture in the seventies. New York, [1972]. pp. 321. bibliog.

PARMET (HERBERT S.) Eisenhower and the American crusades. New York, [1972]. pp. 660. bibliog.

PETERS (CHARLES) and BRANCH (TAYLOR) eds. Blowing the whistle: dissent in the public interest. New York, 1972. pp. 305.

POLITICAL brokers: money, organizations, power and people; by the editors and reporters of National Journal; edited by Judith G. Smith. New York, [1972]. pp. 363.

ROCHE (GEORGE CHARLES) The bewildered society. New Rochelle, N.Y., [1972]. pp. 346.

ROSTOW (WALT WHITMAN) The diffusion of power: an essay in recent history. New York, [1972]. pp. 739.

SAPOLSKY (HARVEY M.) The Polaris system development: bureaucratic and programmatic success in government. Cambridge, Mass., 1972. pp. 261.

SMITH (ROBERT) pseud. The economics of the cold war. New York, [1972]. pp. 126.

VAILLAND (ELISABETH) Voyage dans l'Amérique de gauche. [Paris, 1972]. pp. 188.

WEISSBERG (ROBERT) and NADEL (MARK V.) eds. American democracy: theory and reality. New York, 1972. pp. 560. bibliog.

WITCOVER (JULES) White knight: the rise of Spiro Agnew. New York, [1972]. pp. 465.

WOLFF (ROBERT PAUL) ed. Styles of political action in America: [an anthology]. New York, [1972]. pp. 248.

1973

ARENDT (HANNAH) Crises of the Republic. Harmondsworth, 1973. pp. 200.

BENVENISTE (GUY) The politics of expertise. Berkeley, 1973. pp. 232. bibliog.

FAIRLIE (HENRY) The Kennedy promise: the politics of expectation. London, 1973. pp. 376.

HAVEMAN (ROBERT H.) and HAMRIN (ROBERT D.) eds. The political economy of federal policy. New York, [1973]. pp. 302.

LODGE (HENRY CABOT) 1902- . The storm has many eyes: a personal narrative. New York, [1973]. pp. 272.

OSBORNE (JOHN) 1907- . The fourth year of the Nixon watch. New York, [1973]. pp. 218.

REEDY (GEORGE EDWARD) The presidency in flux. New York, 1973. pp. 133. (George B. Pegram Lectures. [11?])

STONE (ISIDOR F.) The best of I.F. Stone's Weekly: pages from a radical newspaper; edited and introduced by Neil Middleton. Harmondsworth, 1973. pp. 321.

WEED (PERRY L.) The white ethnic movement and ethnic politics. New York, 1973. pp. 243. bibliog.

Population

WOOFTER (THOMAS JACKSON) the Younger. Negro migration: changes in rural organization and population of the cotton belt; (reprinted from the edition of 1920). New York, 1971. pp. 195. bibliog.

FERRISS (ABBOTT L.) Indicators of change in the American family. New York, 1970. pp. 145. bibliog.

NATIONAL PLANNING ASSOCIATION. Center for Economic Projections. Regional Economic Projections Series. Report No. 70-R-1. State economic and demographic projections to 1975 and 1980. Washington, D.C., 1970. pp. 49, 129.

BEAN (LEE L.) and others. Population and family planning manpower and training. New York, [1971]. pp. 118. (Population Council. Occasional Papers)

CALLAHAN (DANIEL) ed. The American population debate. New York, [1971]. pp. 380.

RESEARCH INSTITUTE OF THE SOCIAL WELFARE CONSEQUENCES OF MIGRATION AND RESIDENTIAL MOVEMENT, SAN JUAN, PUERTO RICO, 1969. Migration and social welfare: report of the Research Institute [convened by the Council on Social Work Research of the National Association of Social Workers] ...; edited by Joseph W. Eaton. New York, [1971]. pp. 240. bibliog.

DRIVER (EDWIN D.) Essays on population policy. Lexington, Mass., [1972]. pp. 202.

FORSTER (COLIN) and TUCKER (GRAHAM SHARDALOW LEE) Economic opportunity and white American fertility ratios, 1800-1860. New Haven, 1972. pp. 121.

MORRISON (PETER A.) Population movements and the shape of urban growth: implications for public policy; prepared for the Commission on Population Growth and the American Future. Santa Monica, 1972. pp. 71.

PACKARD (VANCE OAKLEY) A nation of strangers. New York, [1972]. pp. 368.

THOMAS (BRINLEY) Migration and urban development: a reappraisal of British and American long cycles. London, 1972. pp. 259. bibliog.

CANADA CENTRE FOR INLAND WATERS. Population estimates for the Great Lakes basins and their major tributaries. Ottawa, 1973. pp. 52. (Canada. Department of the Environment. Social Science Series. No. 1) Map in end pocket.

HANSEN (NILES M.) Location preferences, migration and regional growth: a study of the south and southwest United States. New York, 1973. pp. 186.

PIOTROW (PHYLLIS TILSON) World population crisis: the United States response. New York, 1973. pp. 276. bibliog.

- Population - Bibliography

BROOKS (THOMAS R.) Labor and migration: an annotated bibliography. Brooklyn, N.Y., [1970]. 1 vol. (unpaged).

- Presidents

LEIBBRANDT (GOTTFRIED JOHANN) Economen in dienst van politici: enige ervaringen met de "Council of Economic Advisers to the President" en het "Joint Economic Committee of the United States Congress". Haarlem, 1968. pp. 160. bibliog. With English summary.

POLSBY (NELSON WOOLF) Congress and the Presidency. 2nd ed. Englewood Cliffs, [1971]. pp. 162. bibliog.

UNITED STATES - Presidents (Cont'd.)

TUGWELL (REXFORD GUY) Off course: from Truman to Nixon. New York, 1971. pp. 326.

BARBER (JAMES DAVID) The presidential character: predicting performance in the White House. Englewood Cliffs, N.J., 1972. pp. 479.

ROSTOW (WALT WHITMAN) The diffusion of power: an essay in recent history. New York, [1972]. pp. 739.

POLSBY (NELSON WOOLF) ed. The modern presidency. New York, [1973]. pp. 236.

- Presidents - Election

THOREN (STIG) An American election campaign in Swedish dailies: how ten daily metropolitan newspapers in Sweden covered the 1968 presidential election campaign in the United States. Stockholm, 1970. pp. 76. bibliog. (Psykologiskt Försvar. Nr.50)

ALEXANDER (HERBERT E.) Financing the 1968 election. Lexington, Mass., [1971]. pp. 355.

POLSBY (NELSON WOOLF) and WILDAVSKY (AARON BERNARD) Strategies of American electoral politics: presidential elections. 3rd ed. New York, [1971]. pp. 332. bibliog.

RUNYON (JOHN H.) and others, compilers. Source book of American presidential campaign and election statistics, 1948-1968. New York, [1971]. pp. 380. bibliog.

SILBER (IRWIN) compiler. Songs America voted by: with the words and music that won and lost elections and influenced the democratic process. Harrisburg, [1971]. pp. 320. bibliog.

DUNN (DELMER D.) Financing presidential campaigns. Washington, [1972]. pp. 168. (Brookings Institution. Studies in Presidential Selection).

GILBERT (ROBERT E.) Television and presidential politics. North Quincy, Mass., [1972]. pp. 335. bibliog.

LONGLEY (LAWRENCE D.) and BRAUN (ALAN G.) The politics of electoral college reform. New Haven, 1972. pp. 222.

PARRIS (JUDITH H.) The convention problem: issues in reform of presidential nominating procedures. Washington, [1972]. pp. 194. bibliog. (Brookings Institution. Studies in Presidential Selection)

CAMPAIGN '72: the managers speak; [proceedings of a conference held in Cambridge, Mass., in 1973, sponsored jointly by the Institute of Politics in the John Fitzgerald Kennedy School of Government, Harvard University and the Niemar Foundation for Journalism, Harvard University]; edited by Ernest R. May and Janet Fraser. Cambridge, Mass., 1973. pp. 318.

LUBELL (SAMUEL) The future while it happened. New York, [1973]. pp. 162.

MATTHEWS (DONALD ROWE) ed. Perspectives on presidential selection. Washington, D.C., [1973]. pp. 246. (Brookings Institution. Studies in Presidential Selection)

SCHLESINGER (ARTHUR MEIER) the Younger, and ISRAEL (FRED L.) eds. The coming to power: critical presidential elections of American history: (a selection of essays from... History of American presidential elections). London, 1973. pp. 550.

WHITE (THEODORE HAROLD) The making of the President 1972. New York, 1973. pp. 391.

ZEIDENSTEIN (HARVEY G.) Direct election of the president. Lexington, Mass., [1973]. pp. 118.

- Presidents - Messages

NIXON (RICHARD MILHOUS) President of the United States. A new road for America: major policy statements, March 1970 to October 1971;... preface and commentaries by Richard Wilson. Garden City, N.Y., 1972. pp. 720.

- Presidents - Powers and duties

STENNIS (JOHN C.) and FULBRIGHT (JAMES WILLIAM) The role of Congress in foreign policy. Washington, [1971]. pp. 139. (American Enterprise Institute for Public Policy Research. Rational Debate Seminars. 5th Series. 2)

BROWN (STUART GERRY) The Presidency on trial: Robert Kennedy's 1968 campaign and afterwards. Honolulu, 1972. pp. 155.

FISHER (LOUIS) President and Congress: power and policy. New York, [1972]. pp. 347. bibliog.

LATHAM (EARL GANSON) ed. J.F. Kennedy and presidential power. Lexington, [1972]. pp. 296.

JAVITS (JACOB KOPPEL) Who makes war: the President versus Congress;... with Don Kellermann. New York, 1973. pp. 300. bibliog.

REEDY (GEORGE EDWARD) The presidency in flux. New York 1973. pp. 133. (George B. Pegram Lectures. [11?])

- Presidents - Public opinion

MUELLER (JOHN E.) War, presidents and public opinion. New York, [1973]. pp. 300. bibliog.

- Public lands

GATES (PAUL WALLACE) Landlords and tenants on the prairie frontier: studies in American land policy. Ithaca, 1973. pp. 333.

- Public works

BURNS (ARTHUR EDWARD) and WILLIAMS (EDWARD AINSWORTH) Federal work, security, and relief programs; [reprint of work first published in Washington, 1941]. New York 1971. pp. 159. (United States. Work Projects Administration. Division of Social Research. Research Monographs. 24)

- Race question

ROHRER (WAYNE C.) Black profiles of white Americans. Philadelphia, [1970]. pp. 207.

ANDERSON (DAVID C.) Children of special value: interracial adoption in America. New York, [1971]. pp. 184. bibliog.

BOESEL (DAVID) and ROSSI (PETER HENRY) eds. Cities under siege: an anatomy of the ghetto riots, 1964-1968. New York, [1971]. pp. 436.

BURKEY (RICHARD M.) Racial discrimination and public policy in the United States. Lexington, Mass., [1971]. pp. 144. bibliog.

CAMPBELL (ALBERT ANGUS) White attitudes toward black people. Ann Arbor, [1971]. pp. 177. bibliog.

DAVIS (ANGELA YVONNE) and others. If they come in the morning: voices of resistance. London [1971]. pp. 266.

DEGLER (CARL N.) Neither black nor white: slavery and race relations in Brazil and the United States. New York, [1971]. pp. 302.

DYE (THOMAS R.) The politics of equality. Indianapolis [1971]. pp. 241.

FREDERICKSON (GEORGE M.) The black image in the white mind: the debate on Afro-American character and destiny, 1817-1914. New York, [1971]. pp. 343.

GINGER (ANN FAGAN) What can be done to minimize racism in jury trials? [Atlanta, 1971]. pp. 427-441. Photostat copy.

HAYDEN (THOMAS) Trial. London, 1971. pp. 168.

SMITH (DREW L.) The legacy of the melting pot: a sociological - historical study. North Quincy, Mass., [1971]. pp. 225. bibliog.

BALDWIN (JAMES) No name in the street. London, 1972. pp. 168.

BLAUNER (ROBERT) Racial oppression in America; [selected essays]. New York, [1972]. pp. 309.

CLAYTON (BRUCE) The savage ideal: intolerance and intellectual leadership in the South, 1890-1914. Baltimore, [1972]. pp. 231. bibliog. (Johns Hopkins University. Studies in Historical and Political Science. Series 90. No. 1)

DAY (BETH) Sexual life between blacks and whites: the roots of racism. New York, 1972. pp. 376. bibliog.

FELDSTEIN (STANLEY) ed. The poisoned tongue: a documentary history of American racism and prejudice. New York, 1972. pp. 330.

GOGGIN (TERENCE P.) and SEIDL (JOHN M.) eds. Politics American style: race, environment and central cities. Englewood Cliffs, [1972]. pp. 404.

JACKSON (GEORGE LESTER) Blood in my eye. London, 1972. pp. 217.

JONES (JAMES M.) Prejudice and racism. Reading, Mass., [1972]. pp. 196. bibliog.

PASCAL (ANTHONY H.) ed. Racial discrimination in economic life. Lexington, Mass., [1972]. pp. 228. bibliogs.

PURCELL (THEODORE VINCENT) and CAVANAGH (GERALD F.) Blacks in the industrial world: issues for the manager. New York, [1972]. pp. 358.

ROSE (PETER ISAAC) ed. Nation of nations: the ethnic experience and the racial crisis; [an anthology]. New York, [1972]. pp. 351.

FEAGIN (JOE R.) and HAHN (HARLAN) Ghetto revolts: the politics of violence in American cities. New York, 1973. pp. 338.

KATZNELSON (IRA) Black men, white cities: race, politics, and migration in the United States, 1900-30, and Britain, 1948-68. London, 1973. pp. 219.

MILLER (KENT S.) and DREGER (RALPH MASON) Comparative studies of blacks and whites in the United States. New York, 1973. pp. 572. bibliogs.

PARKER (J.A.) Angela Davis: the making of a revolutionary. New Rochelle, N.Y., [1973]. pp. 272.

- Relations (general) with Asia

BUCK (PEARL SYDENSTRICKER) American unity and Asia. New York, [1942]. pp. 140.

- Relations (general) with Burma

KOTLIAROV (VLADIMIR SERGEEVICH) SShA i Birma: amerikanskaia strategia i politika. Moskva. 1970. pp. 248.

Relations (general) with Canada

MOFFETT (SAMUEL E.) The Americanization of Canada;... [reprint of the work originally published in 1907] with an introduction by Allan Smith. Toronto, [1972]. pp. 124. bibliog.

UNITED STATES. United States Information Service, Ottawa. 1967. Canadian-American relations, 1867-1967: a compilation of selected documents concerning the relations between Canada and the United States during the first centruy of Canada's confederation. [Ottawa, 1967]. 3 vols. bibliogs.

PRESTON (RICHARD ARTHUR) ed. The influence of the United States on Canadian development: eleven case studies; by Irving M. Abella [and others] Durham, N.C., 1972. pp. 269.

ABRAMS (MATTHEW JOHN) The Canada-United States interparliamentary group. Ottawa, 1973. pp. 148.

- Relations (general) with Canada - Bibliography

UNITED STATES. United States Information Service, Ottawa. 1966. A list of selected publications and sources of information on Canadian-American relations. [Ottawa, 1966]. pp. 75.

- Relations (general) with Europe

TROTSKII (LEV DAVYDOVICH) Europe et Amérique; [and] Où va l'Angleterre?; [reprints of the works originally published in 1926 with] préface de Pierre Naville. Paris, 1970. 2 vols. (in 1).

SILBERSCHMIDT (MAX) The United States and Europe: rivals and partners. London, [1972]. pp. 216. bibliog.

- Relations (general) with Japan

KITAMURA (HIROSHI) Psychological dimensions of U.S.-Japanese relations. Cambridge, Mass., 1971. pp. 42. (Harvard University. Center for International Affairs. Occasional Papers in International Affairs. No. 28)

EXPOSE the U.S. and Japanese reactionaries' plot to resurrect the dead past: three reactionary Japanese films in review; [by] Chi Ping-Chih [and] Tao Ti-Wen. Peking, 1972. pp. 65.

- Relations (general) with Latin America

KHACHATUROV (KAREN ARMENOVICH) Ideologicheskaia diversiia pod vidom informatsii: kontrol' SShA nad sredstvami massovoi informatsii Latinskoi Ameriki. Moskva, 1970. pp. 206. bibliog.

POWELL (PHILIP WAYNE) Tree of hate: propaganda and prejudices affecting United States relations with the Hispanic world. New York, [1971]. pp. 210. bibliog.

- Relations (general) with Russia

VEL'TOV (NIKOLAI) Uspekhi sotsializma v SSSR i ikh vliianie na SShA; pod redaktsiei N.N. Iakovleva. Moskva, 1971. pp. 215. bibliog.

TSVETKOV (GLEB NIKOLAEVICH) Politika SShA v otnoshenii SSSR nakanune voiny. Kiev, 1973. pp. 192.

- Relations (general) with Spain

POWELL (PHILIP WAYNE) Tree of hate: propaganda and prejudices affecting United States relations with the Hispanic world. New York, [1971]. pp. 210. bibliog.

UNITED STATES (Cont'd.)

– Relations (general) with the United Kingdom

OLSON (ALISON GILBERT) Anglo-American politics 1660-1775: the relationship between parties in England and colonial America. Oxford, 1973. pp. 192.

– Relations (military) with Japan

VERBITSKII (SEMEN IL'ICH) Iapono-amerikanskii voenno-politicheskii soiuz, 1951-1970 gg. Moskva, 1972. pp. 285

INTERNATIONAL INSTITUTE FOR STRATEGIC STUDIES. Adelphi Papers. No. 95. Japanese security and the United States; by Kunio Muraoka. London, 1973. pp. 39.

– Relations (military) with Latin America

TARASOV (KONSTANTIN SERGEEVICH) SShA i Latinskaia Amerika: voenno-politicheskie i voenno-ekonomicheskie otnosheniia. Moskva, 1972. pp. 359.

– Relations (military) with the United Kingdom

TRASK (DAVID F.) Captains and cabinets: Anglo-American naval relations, 1917-1918. Columbia, Mo., [1972]. pp. 396. bibliog.

– Religion

AHLSTROM (SYDNEY E.) A religious history of the American people. New Haven, [1972 repr. 1973]. pp. 1158. bibliog.

WHEELER (RICHARD S.) b.1935. The children of darkness. New Rochelle, N.Y., [1973]. pp. 189.

– Rural conditions

WOOFTER (THOMAS JACKSON) the Younger. Negro migration: changes in rural organization and population of the cotton belt; (reprinted from the edition of 1920). New York, 1971. pp. 195. bibliog.

NATIONAL FARM INSTITUTE, 1970. The 70's: challeng and opportunity: [papers]. etc. Ames, Iowa, [1970]. pp. 91.

BRIGGS (VERNON M.) Chicanos and rural poverty. Baltimore, [1973]. pp. 81.

– Social conditions

NEARING (SCOTT) Social adjustment. New York, 1911 repr. 1913. pp. 377.

AMERICAN bureaucracy: [essays which originally appeared in Trans-action Magazine]; edited by Warren G. Bennis. [Chicago, 1970]. pp. 187. (Trans-Action – Social Science and Modern Society. Trans-action Books. 14)

HORTON (PAUL BURLEIGH) and LESLIE (GERALD RONNELL) The sociology of social problems. 4th ed. New York, [1970]. pp. 668.

BERKLEY (GEORGE E.) The administrative revolution: notes on the passing of organization man Englewood Cliffs, [1971]. pp. 181. bibliog.

FRIEDMAN (MURRAY) ed. Overcoming middle class rage. Philadelphia, [1971]. pp. 383.

IULINA (NINA STEPANOVNA) Burzhuaznye ideologicheskie techeniia v SShA: problemy i protivorechiia "amerikanskogo soznaniia". Moskva, 1971. pp. 136.

MILTON S. EISENHOWER SYMPOSIUM, BALTIMORE, 1970. Violence: the crisis of American confidence; [papers presented at the symposium: The United States in the 1970s: perspectives on violence]; edited by Hugh Davis Graham [and others]. Baltimore, [1971]. pp. 180. bibliogs.

SYKES (GRESHAM M'CREADY) Social problems in America. Glenview, Ill., [1971]. pp. 334.

WEINBERG (CARL) Education and social problems. New York, [1971]. pp. 350.

BEICHMAN (ARNOLD) Nine lies about America. London, 1972. pp. 314. bibliog.

BOSKIN (JOSEPH) and ROSENSTONE (ROBERT A.) eds. Seasons of rebellion: protest and radicalism in recent America. New York, [1972]. pp. 336.

BREDEMEIER (HARRY CHARLES) and TOBY (JACKSON) Social problems in America: costs and casualties in an acquisitive society. 2nd ed. New York, [1972]. pp. 464.

COCHRAN (THOMAS CHILDS) Social change in industrial society: twentieth-century America. London, 1972. pp. 178. bibliog. (Oxford. University. St. Antony's College. Publications. No. 5)

EDWARDS (RICHARD C.) and others, eds. The capitalist system: a radical analysis of American society. Englewood Cliffs, [1972]. pp. 543. bibliogs.

HARING (JOSEPH E.) ed. Urban and regional economics: perspectives for publication. Boston, [Mass., 1972]. pp. 307. bibliog.

HOWE (IRVING) b. 1928, and HARRINGTON (MICHAEL) eds. The seventies: problems and proposals; [essays originally appearing in Dissent magazine]. New York, [1972]. pp. 519.

JEFCOAT (L. ALLURE) Health and human values: an ecological approach. New York [1972]. pp. 255. bibliogs.

LUBOVE (ROY) ed. Poverty and social welfare in the United States. New York, [1972]. pp. 122. bibliog.

LUTHANS (FRED) and HODGETTS (RICHARD M.) Social issues in business: poverty, civil rights, ecology and consumerism. New York, [1972]. pp. 282. bibliogs.

MANKOFF (MILTON) ed. The poverty of progress: the political economy of American social problems. New York [1972]. pp. 524. bibliog.

MOORE (BARRINGTON) Reflections on the causes of human misery and upon certain proposals to eliminate them. London, 1972. pp. 201.

PACKARD (VANCE OAKLEY) A nation of strangers. New York, [1972]. pp. 368.

PARKER (WILLIAM HENRY) The superpowers: the United States and the Soviet Union compared. London, 1972. pp. 347.

RASMUSSEN (JOHN P.) ed. The new American revolution: the dawning of the technetronic era. New York, [1972]. pp. 250. bibliog.

TURNER (JONATHAN H.) American society: problems of structure. New York, [1972]. pp. 299. bibliog.

WARREN (ROLAND LESLIE) The community in America. 2nd ed. Chicago, [1972]. pp. 418.

CHAMBERLAIN (NEIL WOLVERTON) The place of business in America's future: a study in social values. New York, [1973]. pp. 338.

FARBERMAN (HARVEY A.) and GOODE (ERICH) eds. Social reality: [readings]. Englewood Cliffs, [1973]. pp. 324. bibliogs.

HOLLANDER (PAUL) Soviet and American society: a comparison. New York, 1973. pp. 476. bibliog.

KLEINBERG (BENJAMIN S.) American society in the postindustrial age: technocracy, power, and the end of ideology. Columbus, Ohio, [1973]. pp. 279. bibliog.

MILLER (KENT S.) and DREGER (RALPH MASON) Comparative studies of blacks and whites in the United States. New York, 1973. pp. 572. bibliogs.

SHEPARD (JON M.) ed. Spectrum on social problems: society, economy, and man; [readings]. Columbus, Oh., [1973]. pp. 260. bibliogs

STONE (ISIDOR F.) The best of I.F. Stone's Weekly: pages from a radical newspaper; edited and introduced by Neil Middleton. Harmondsworth, 1973. pp. 321.

- Social history

ANONYMOUS Americans: explorations in nineteenth-century social history; edited by Tamara K. Hareven. Englewood Cliffs, [1971]. pp. 314.

BERTHOFF (ROWLAND TAPPAN) An unsettled people: social order abd disorder in American history. New York, [1971]. pp. 528. bibliog.

DANIELS (GEORGE H.) Science in American society: a social history. New York, 1971. pp. 390,x. bibliog.

WEBER (CHRISTIAN EGBERT) Die Integration eines Kontinents als Problem: Amerika, Europa. Berlin, [1971]. pp. 96. bibliog.

ASH (ROBERTA) Social movements in America. Chicago, [1972]. pp. 274. bibliogs.

HOFSTADTER (RICHARD) America at 1750: a social portrait. London, 1972. pp. 304.

ISRAEL (JERRY MICHAEL) ed. Building the organizational society: essays on associational activities in modern America. New York, [1972]. pp. 341.

LUDMERER (KENNETH M.) Genetics and American society: a historical appraisal. Baltimore, [1972]. pp. 222. bibliog.

ROCHE (GEORGE CHARLES) The bewildered society. New Rochelle, N.Y., [1972]. pp. 346.

- Social history - Sources

PLATT (ANTHONY M.) ed. The politics of riot commissions, 1917-1970: a collection of official reports and critical essays. New York, [1971]. pp. 534.

ERICKSON (CHARLOTTE JOANNE) Invisible immigrants: the adaptation of English and Scottish immigrants in nineteenth century America. London, [1972]. pp. 531.

- Social life and customs

WOLFE (TOM) Radical chic; and, Mau-mauing the flak catchers. London, 1971. pp. 153.

- Social policy

DONOVAN (JOHN C.) The politics of poverty. New York, [1967 repr. 1969]. pp. 157. bibliog.

CAHN (EDGAR S.) and PASSETT (BARRY A.) eds. Citizen participation: effecting community change. New York, 1971. pp. 294.

DEVELOPING improved social programs; [the second of a series of seminars sponsored by American Institutes for Research, held in Washington, 1971]. Pittsburgh, Pa., [1971]. pp. 128. bibliogs.

GOLDSTON (ELI) The quantification of concern: some aspects of social accounting. [Pittsburgh], 1971. pp. 76. (Carnegie-Mellon University. Benjamin F. Fairless Memorial Lectures. 1971)

KNAPP (DANIEL) and POLK (KENNETH) Scouting the war on poverty: social reform politics in the Kennedy administration. Lexington, Mass., [1971]. pp. 227. bibliog.

MARMOR (THEODORE R.) ed. Poverty policy: a compendium of cash transfer proposals. Chicago, 1971. pp. 241.

WILLIAMS (WALTER) Dr. Social policy research and analysis: the experience in the federal social agencies. New York, 1971. pp. 204. bibliogs.

McGIFFERT (MICHAEL) and SKOTHEIM (ROBERT ALLEN) eds. American social thought: sources and interpretations. Reading, Mass., [1972 in progress]. bibliogs.

CONVERSION from war to peace: social, economic and political problems; [abstracted from two conferences organized by the Fund for New Priorities in America at Boston in 1969 and at Hempstead, Long Island in 1971]; editor William Meyers; assistant editor M. Vincent Hayes. New York, [1972]. pp. 121

DYE (THOMAS R.) Understanding public policy. Englewood Cliffs, [1972]. pp. 305. bibliogs.

ESTERLY (STANLEY) and ESTERLY (GLENN) Freedom from dependence: welfare reform as a solution to poverty. Washington, [1972]. pp. 178.

HANDLER (JOEL F.) Reforming the poor: welfare policy, federalism, and morality. New York, [1972]. pp. 168. bibliog.

HOWE (IRVING) and HARRINGTON (MICHAEL) b. 1928, eds. The seventies: problems and proposals; [essays originally appearing in Dissent magazine]. New York, [1972]. pp. 519.

LUBOVE (ROY) ed. Poverty and social welfare in the United States. New York, [1972]. pp. 122. bibliog.

MANKOFF (MILTON) ed. The poverty of progress: the political economy of American social problems. New York, [1972]. pp. 524. bibliog.

MAYER (ROBERT R.) Social planning and social change. Englewood Cliffs, [1972]. pp. 147. bibliog.

TURNER (JONATHAN H.) American society: problems of structure. New York, [1972]. pp. 299. bibliog.

WORCESTER (DEAN A.) Beyond welfare and full employment: the economics of optimal employment without inflation. Lexington, Mass., [1972]. pp. 155.

GOALS for social welfare, 1973-1993: an overview of the next two decades; edited by Harleigh B. Trecker. New York, [1973]. pp. 288. bibliog.

KAHN (ALFRED J.) Social policy and social services. New York, [1973]. pp. 210. bibliog.

MOYNIHAN (DANIEL PATRICK) The politics of a guaranteed income: the Nixon administration and the family assistance plan. New York, [1973]. pp. 579.

UNITED STATES (Cont'd.)

- Statistics

DOUTY (H.M.) The development of wage statistics in the United States. Ithaca, N.Y., 1972. pp. 45. bibliog. (Cornell University. New York State School of Industrial and Labor Relations. Bulletins. 64)

- Statistics - Vital

CHO (LEE-JAY) and others. Differential current fertility in the United States. Chicago, [1970]. pp. 426. (Chicago. University. Community and Family Study Center. Books and Monographs)

KITAGAWA (EVELYN MAE) and HAUSER (PHILIP MORRIS) Differential mortality in the United States: a study in socioeconomic epidemiology. Cambridge, Mass., 1973. pp. 255. bibliog. (American Public Health Association. Vital and Health Statistics Monographs)

- Territorial expansion

WINKS (ROBIN WILLIAM) The myth of the American frontier: its relevance to America, Canada and Australia. [Leicester], 1971. pp. 39. (Sir George Watson Lectures. 1971)

ACUNA (RODOLFO) Occupied America: the Chicano's struggle toward liberation. San Francisco, [1972]. pp. 282.

- Territories and possessions

DE SMITH (STANLEY ALEXANDER) Options for Micronesia: a potential crisis for America's Pacific trust territory. New York, [1969]. pp. 29. (New York (City). University. Center for International Studies. Policy Papers. vol. 3, no. 1)

UNITIZED CARGO SYSTEMS

NORTHLAND HARBOUR BOARD. The farmer and the container age: will the farmer gain anything?; if so, how? Whangarei, [1969]. pp. 32.

NORTHLAND HARBOUR BOARD. New Zealand national container port: report on the siting and operation. Whangarei, 1969. pp. 76.

NORTHLAND HARBOUR BOARD. A coastal container transport service: is such a service feasible?: is it important in the national interest? Whangarei, 1970. pp. 37.

BREMEN. Bremer Ausschuss für Wirtschaftsforschung. Container facilities and traffic in 71 ports of the world, midyear 1970. Bremen, 1971. fo. 190. bibliog.

SCHUH (GERHARD) Die Aufgabenteilung im binnenländischen Seehafenverkehr mit Containern: ein Leistungs- und Kostenvergleich. Düsseldorf, 1971. pp. 221. bibliog. (Cologne. Universität. Institut für Verkehrswissenschaft. Buchreihe. Nr.26)

UNIVERSAL DECLARATION OF HUMAN RIGHTS, 1948

SEMINAR ON THE REALIZATION OF ECONOMIC AND SOCIAL RIGHTS CONTAINED IN THE UNIVERSAL DECLARATION OF HUMAN RIGHTS, WARSAW, 1967. Seminar...[held at] Warsaw, Poland, 15-28 August 1967; organized by the United Nations, Division of Human Rights, in co-operation with the government of Poland. (ST/TAO/HR/31). New York, United Nations, 1967. pp. 49.

UNIVERSALS (PHILOSOPHY)

LANDESMAN (CHARLES) ed. The problem of universals: [an anthology]. New York, [1971]. pp. 314. bibliog.

UNIVERSITIES AND COLLEGES

UNITED NATIONS EDUCATIONAL, SCIENTIFIC AND CULTURAL ORGANIZATION. 1948. Universities in need. [Paris, 1948]. pp. 32. (Publications. No.217)

VACHON (LOUIS ALBERT) Excellence et loyauté des universitaires. Québec, 1969. pp. 103.

BUEDINGER TAGUNG, 1966. Universität und Gelehrtenstand. 1400-1800: Büdinger Vorträge 1966; herausgegeben von Hellmuth Rössler und Günther Franz. Limburg, 1970. pp. 288. bibliogs. (Ranke Gesellschaft. Deutsche Führungsschichten in der Neuzeit. Gesamtreihe. Band 4)

ONUSHKIN (VICTOR GRIGOR'EVICH) ed. An IIEP Seminar, Paris 7-11 July, 1969. Paris, International Institute for Educational Planning, 1971. pp. 318. (Planning the Development of Universities. 1)

FOURASTIE (JEAN) Faillité de l'université? [Paris, 1972]. pp. 186. bibliog.

KOURGANOFF (VLADIMIR) La face cachée de l'université. Paris, 1972. pp. 316. bibliog.

LAWRENCE (CLIFFORD HUGH) The medieval idea of a university. [London], 1972. pp. 16.

STUDENTS, university and society: a comparative sociological review; [papers presented at a series of seminars held by the Graduate School of Contemporary European Studies of Reading University in 1969-1970]; edited by Margaret Scotford Archer. London, 1972. pp. 280. bibliogs.

CHOMSKY (NOAM) For reasons of state. [London], 1973. pp. 220.

UNIVERSITIES AND COLLEGES
See also CATHOLIC UNIVERSITIES AND COLLEGES

- Administration

WALKER (W.G.) and others, eds. Explorations in educational administration: [articles selected from the Journal of Educational Administration, 1963-1969]. St. Lucia, Queensland, [1973]. pp. 433. bibliog.

- Bibliography

POWELL (JOHN P.) compiler. Universities and university education: a select bibliography. vol. 2. 1965-70 and supplement to vol. 1. Windsor, 1971. pp. 158.

- Buildings

LONDON. University. University College. Environmental Research Group. Use of space and facilities in universities: report. London, 1968. fo. 69,(45).

- Curricula

HENTIG (HARTMUT VON) Das erste Studienjahr an der Universität: Bericht über eine Tagung vom 8-10. Januar 1963. Hamburg,[1963]. pp. 72. bibliog. (Unesco Institute for Education. International Studies in Education)

CLAUSSE (ROGER) L'enseignement universitaire du journalisme et de la communication sociale. Bruxelles, [1971?]. pp. 135. (Brussels. Université Libre. College de la Diffusion Culturelle. Cahiers d'Etude de Sociologie Culturelle. 1)

COUNTER course: a handbook for course criticism; edited by Trevor Pateman. Harmondsworth, 1972. pp. 393. bibliogs.

- History

UNIVERSITIES in politics: case studies from the late middle ages and early modern period; edited with an introduction by John W. Baldwin and Richard A. Goldthwaite. Baltimore, [1972]. pp. 137. (Johns Hopkins University. Department of History. Johns Hopkins Symposia in Comparative History.2)

BAYEN (MAURICE) Histoire des universités. Paris, 1973. pp. 128. bibliog.

- Law and legislation - Italy

DEMOCRAZIA CRISTIANA. Ufficio del Programma. La legge universitaria: la discussione generale ed il testo approvato al Senato, etc. [Rome, 1971]. pp. 738. (Programma dc/5)

DEMOCRAZIA CRISTIANA. Ufficio del Programma. La riforma universitaria: l'incontro della DC con i docenti, etc. Roma, 1971. pp. 774. (Programma dc/4)

- Law and legislation - United Kingdom

NATIONAL UNION OF STUDENTS and NATIONAL COUNCIL FOR CIVIL LIBERTIES. Academic freedom and the law. London, 1970. pp. 106.

UNIVERSITIES AND COLLEGES - Teachers
See TEACHERS

- Africa

DUMONT (RENÉ) University autonomy and rural development in Africa. Cape Town, 1973. pp. 11. bibliog. (Cape Town. University. T.B. Davie Memorial Lectures. 14)

- America, Latin

ORGANIZATION OF AMERICAN STATES. 1961. Latin American higher education and inter-American cooperation: report and recommendations. Washington, 1961. pp. 20.

CAMARA (HELDER) Archbishop of Olinda and Recife. Helder Camara, universidad y revolucion: textos seleccionados por Fernando Reyes Matta [with a short study of Camara by Jesus Manuel Martinez]. [Santiago de Chile], 1969. pp. 108.

SUNKEL (OSVALDO) Reforma universitaria, subdesarrollo y dependencia. Santiago, Chile, [1969]. pp. 47.

- Argentine Republic

MAZO (GABRIEL DEL) Reforma universitaria y cultura nacional. Buenos Aires, [1955]. pp. 183.

INGLESE (JUAN OSVALDO) and YEGROS DORIA (CARLOS L.) Universidad y estudiantes; [and] Universidad y peronismo; [by] Léon Berdichevsky. Buenos Aires, 1965. p. 228.

- Asia, Southeast

ROLE of universities in national development planning in Southeast Asia; proceedings of the workshop held in Singapore [and sponsored by the Regional Institute of Higher Education and Development]; edited by Yip Yat Hoong. Singapore, 1971. pp. 198.

ROLE of universities in management education for national development in Southeast Asia; proceedings of the workshop held [by the] (Regional Institute of Higher Education and Development) in Singapore...1972; edited by Yip Yat Hoong. Singapore, 1972. pp. 346.

- Australia - Administration

SCHOOL, college, and university: the administration of education in Australia; [papers delivered at a conference at Armidale, January 1968]; edited by W.G. Walker. St. Lucia, [1972]. pp. 250.

- Belgium

DEJEAN (CHRISTIAN) and BINNEMANS (CHARLES LOUIS) L'université belge: du pari au défi. Bruxelles, [1971]. pp. 579. (Brussels. Université Libre. Institut de Sociologie. Etudes des Problèmes de l'Enseignement Supérieur)

- Canada

CANADA. Statistics Canada. Instructional media in universities of the Atlantic provinces. a., current issues only kept. Ottawa.

- Canada - Buildings

BLAND (JOHN) of McGill University, and SCHOENAUER (NORBERT) University housing in Canada. Montreal, 1966. pp. 137.

- Canada - Graduate work - Directories

POPULATION ASSOCIATION OF AMERICA. Directory of population study centers: United States and Canada. Washington, 1971. pp. 78.

- China

LUTZ (JESSIE GREGORY) China and the Christian colleges, 1850-1950. Ithaca, 1971. pp. 575. bibliog.

- Colombia

GUZMAN MORA (IGNACIO DE) and LLOREDA LONDOÑO (JOSE ANTONIO) Cual sociedad? cual universidad? Bogota, 1971. pp. 126. bibliog.

- Denmark - Examinations

DANSKE STUDERENDES FAELLESRÅD. Eksamen: klassekamp, social skaevhed, alternativer, magtmiddel, elendig undervisning, nåleøje. [Copenhagen, 1971]. pp. 54. bibliog.

- France

CENTRE DE REGROUPEMENT DES INFORMATIONS UNIVERSITAIRES. Quelle université? Quelle société? Paris, Éditions du Seuil, [1968]. pp. 223. 20½cm. (Combats)

ROBERT (FERNAND) Un mandarin prend la parole. Paris, [1970]. pp. 269.

GRAPPIN (PIERRE) Réflexions sur les universités françaises. London, 1971. pp. 23. (London. University. Cassal Bequest Lectures. 1970)

DUCHÊNE (ROGER) A la recherche de l'université. Paris, [1972]. pp. 160.

- Germany

BUEDINGER TAGUNG, 1966. Universität und Gelehrtenstand, 1400-1800: Büdinger Vorträge 1966; herausgegeben von Hellmuth Rössler und Günther Franz. Limburg, 1970. pp. 288. bibliogs. (Ranke Gesellschaft. Deutsche Führungsschichten in der Neuzeit. Gesamtreihe. Band 4)

THROLL (MANFRED) Soziologie und Hochschulraumplanung: soziologische Überlegungen zum Raumkonzept einer praktisch-experimentellen Hochschule. Göttingen, 1971. pp. 366. bibliog.

ELM (LUDWIG) Hochschule und Neofaschismus: zeitgeschichtliche Studien zur Hochschulpolitik in der BRD. Berlin, 1972. pp. 299. bibliog.

UNIVERSITIES AND COLLEGES - Germany (Cont'd.)

SOZIALISTISCHER DEUTSCHER STUDENTENBUND. SDS Hochschuldenkschrift; ([reprint of the second edition of 1965, with] Nachwort des Verlages, [1972]). Frankfurt am Main, 1972. pp. 183. bibliog.

GERMANY (BUNDESREPUBLIK). Wissenschaftsrat. 1973. Empfehlungen zum dritten Rahmenplan nach dem Hochschulbauförderungsgesetz; [with 2 appendixes]. [Cologne?] 1973. 3 pts. (in 1 vol.).

- Germany, Eastern

GERMANY (DEUTSCHE DEMOKRATISCHE REPUBLIK). Staatssekretariat für Westdeutsche Fragen. 1970. How does the GDR solve the problems of higher education? Dresden, [1970?]. pp. 84.

- Ireland (Republic)

EIRE. Higher Education Authority. 1972. Report on the Ballymun project. Dublin, 1972. pp. 101.

EIRE. Higher Education Authority. 1972. Report to the Minister for education on university reorganisation with special reference to the projected formation of a single university in Dublin and to the alternative solution put forward jointly by the National University of Ireland and Trinity College, Dublin. Dublin, 1972. pp. 124.

- Italy

CECCHI (OTTAVIO) La laurea di proletario. [Rome, 1971]. pp. 135.

- Italy - Religion

MARCUCCI FANELLO (GABRIELLA) Storia della F[ederazione] U[niversitaria] C[attolica] I[taliana]. Roma, [1971]. pp. 335.

- Mexico

KING (RICHARD G.) and others. The provincial universities of Mexico: on analysis of growth and development. New York, 1971. pp. 234. bibliog.

- Netherlands

POSTHUMUS (K.) Universitair onderwijs, structuren: tweede voortgangsnota, etc. 's-Gravenhage, Staatsuitgeverij, 1970. pp. 43.

- Netherlands - Administration

BRAAM (ARIS VAN) Universitaire organisatie en bestuur. Rotterdam, 1970. pp. 64.

- Nigeria

VAN DEN BERGHE (PIERRE LOUIS) Power and privilege at an African university;... with the assistance of Paul Alabi [and others]. London, 1973. pp. 278. bibliog.

- Spain

ORGANISATION FOR ECONOMIC CO-OPERATION AND DEVELOPMENT. Directorate for Scientific Affairs. 1968. Design for technological education: the Escuela Tecnica Superior de Ingenieros Industriales of Seville. Paris, 1968. pp. 313. bibliogs.

FARGA (MANUEL JUAN) Universidad y democracia en España: 30 años de lucha estudiantil. Mexico, 1969. pp. 177.

- Sweden

HÖGRE utbildning: regional rekrytering och samhällsekonomiska kalkyler:...rapporter från undersökningar genomförda av 1968 års utbildningsutredning 4; (with English summary: Higher education: regional recruitment and calculations relating to the national economy). Stockholm, 1972. pp. 208. (Sweden. Statens Offentliga Utredningar. 1972. 23)

- United Kingdom

UNIVERSITY independence: the main questions; [by] Sydney Caine [and others]...; edited by John H. MacCallum Scott. London, 1971. pp. 162.

CROUCH (COLIN) and MENNELL (STEPHEN) The universities: pressures and prospects. London, 1972. pp. 47. (Young Fabian Group. Young Fabian Pamphlets. 28)

SANDERSON (MICHAEL) The universities and British industry, 1850-1970. London, 1972. pp. 436. bibliog.

LONDON. Greater London Council. Inner London Education Authority. Review of vocational further and higher education; report by the Education Officer, May 1973, (to the governors of area colleges (including specialist colleges), colleges for further education and general and commercial colleges). [London], 1973. pp. 19.

- United Kingdom - Accounting

OWEN (GWILYM BEYNON) University accounts and financial control; [M.Phil.(London) thesis]. [1972]. fo. 251. bibliog. Typescript: unpublished. This thesis is the property of London University and may not be removed from the Library.

- United Kingdom - Administration

WILLIAMS (KEITH ALFRED) Internal organisation of colleges of further education; [essay for the Diploma in Public Administration, London University]. 1971. fo. 38. Typescript: unpublished. This essay is the property of London University and may not be removed from the Library.

FIELDEN (JOHN) Management consultant, and LOCKWOOD (GEOFFREY) Planning and management in universities: a study of British universities. London, 1973. pp. 352. bibliog.

- United Kingdom - Admission

BRIGHTON. University of Sussex. Admissions Office. Applicants who decline offers: an analysis of the reasons. Brighton, 1971. pp. 25. (Brighton. University of Sussex. Admissions Office. Special Reports. No. 3)

SQUIBB (GEORGE DREWRY) Founders' kin: privilege and pedigree. Oxford, 1972. pp. 245. bibliog.

- United Kingdom - Admission - Bibliography

CHOPPIN (BRUCE) and FARA (PATRICIA) compilers. Admission to higher education: a select annotated bibliography. Windsor, 1972. pp. 38.

- United Kingdom - Buildings

BIRKS (TONY) Building the new universities;...photographs by Michael Holford. Newton Abbot, [1972]. pp. 128. bibliog.

- United Kingdom - Curricula

FOGELMAN (K.R.) Leaving the sixth form: a selection of opinions. Windsor, 1972. pp. 48.

HAJNAL (JOHN) The student trap: a critique of university and sixth-form curricula. Harmondsworth, 1972. pp. 288.

WHAT kinds of graduates do we need?; edited by F.R. Jevons and H.D. Turner. London, 1972. pp. 120. bibliogs.

- United Kingdom - Directories

WHICH university?: 1973; (editor Audrey Segal). London, [1972]. pp. 847.

- United Kingdom - Entrance requirements

WANKOWSKI (J.A.) G.C.E.'s and degrees: some notes and reflections on studies of the relationship between admission requirements and achievement at university. Birmingham, [1970]. fo. various. bibliog.

- United Kingdom - Finance

OWEN (GWILYM BEYNON) University accounts and financial control; [M.Phil.(London) thesis]. [1972]. fo. 251. bibliog. Typescript: unpublished. This thesis is the property of London University and may not be removed from the Library.

MISHAN (EDWARD JOSHUA) Making the world safe for pornography, and other intellectual fashions. London, 1973. pp. 262.

- United Kingdom - Graduate work

SCHEDULE OF POSTGRADUATE COURSES IN UNITED KINGDOM UNIVERSITIES; [pd. by] the Association of Commonwealth Universities for the Committee of Vice-Chancellors and Principals of the Universities of the United Kingdom. a., current issue only kept. London.

- United Kingdom - Scotland - Entrance requirements

POWELL (JOHN L.) Selection for university in Scotland: a first report on the Assessment for Higher Education Project. London, [1973]. pp. 100. bibliog. (Scottish Council for Research in Education. Publications. 64)

- United States

HARLACHER (ERVIN L.) The community dimension of the community college. Englewood Cliffs, [1969]. pp. 140. bibliog.

CLARK (BURTON R.) The distinctive college: Antioch, Reed and Swarthmore. Chicago, 1970. pp. 280. bibliog.

BOWLES (FRANK) and DECOSTA (FRANK A.) Between two worlds: a profile of negro higher education; ...with a commentary by Kenneth S. Tollett. New York, [1971]. pp. 326. bibliogs.

COLLEGE AND UNIVERSITY SELF-STUDY INSTITUTE, 13TH, BERKELEY, 1971. The public challenge and the campus response; edited by Robert A. Altman and Carolyn M. Byerly. Boulder, Col., 1971. pp. 124.

JOHNSON (ELDON L.) From riot to reason. Urbana, Ill., [1971]. pp. 127.

THACKREY (RUSSELL I.) The future of the state university. Urbana, [1971]. pp. 137. bibliog.

APTHEKER (BETTINA) The academic rebellion in the United States. Secaucus, N.J., [1972]. pp. 218.

BLOUSTEIN (EDWARD J.) The university and the counterculture: inaugural and other addresses. New Brunswick, [1972]. pp. 117.

LAUB (JULIAN MARTIN) The college and community development: a socioeconomic analysis for urban and regional growth. New York, 1972. pp. 304. bibliog.

LIPSET (SEYMOUR MARTIN) Rebellion in the university: a history of student activism in America. London, 1972. pp. 310.

SEARLE (JOHN ROGERS) The campus war. Harmondsworth, [1972]. pp. 219.

SIEBER (SAM D.) Reforming the university: the role of the social research center. New York, 1972. pp. 228.

ULAM (ADAM BRUNO) The fall of the American university. London, 1972. pp. 217.

- United States - Administration

DRESSEL (PAUL L.) and others. Institutional research in the university. San Francisco, 1971. pp. 347. bibliogs.

LEE (EUGENE C.) and BOWEN (FRANK M.) The multicampus university: a study of academic governance;... with a commentary by William Friday; a report prepared for the Carnegie Commission on Higher Education. New York, [1971]. pp. 481. bibliog.

CARNEGIE COMMISSION ON HIGHER EDUCATION. The more effective use of resources: an imperative for higher education; a report and recommendations... 1972. New York, [1972]. pp. 201. bibliog.

BENNIS (WARREN G.) The leaning ivory tower;...with the assistance of Patricia Ward Biederman. San Francisco, 1973. pp. 154.

DURYEA (E.D.) and FISK (ROBERT S.) eds. Faculty unions and collective bargaining; [by] E.D. Duryea, Robert S. Fisk, and associates. San Francisco, 1973. pp. 236. bibliog.

CROSS (K. PATRICIA) Beyond the open door. San Francisco, 1971. pp. 200. bibliogs.

- United States - Curricula

BLASSINGAME (JOHN W.) ed. New perspective on black studies. Urbana, Ill., [1971]. pp. 243. bibliog.

SNELLING (W. RODMAN) and BORUCH (ROBERT F.) Science in liberal arts colleges: a longitudinal study of 49 selective colleges. New York, 1972. pp. 285. bibliog.

- United States - Finance

GELLHORN (WALTER) and GREENAWALT (R. KENT) The sectarian college and the public purse: Fordham- a case study. Dobbs Ferry, 1970. pp. 211.

- United States - Graduate work

NATIONAL RESEARCH COUNCIL. Office of Scientific Personnel. Research Division. Careers of PhD's: academic versus nonacademic; a second report on follow-up of doctorate cohorts, 1935-1960. Washington, D.C., 1968. pp. 106. (National Research Council. Publications. [No.] 1577)

SCIENTIFIC manpower: a dilemma for graduate education: [report of a symposium held at the Massachusetts Institute of Technology, 1970]; edited by Sanborn C. Brown and Brian B. Schwartz. Cambridge, Mass., [1971]. pp. 180. bibliog. (Massachusetts Institute of Technology. M.I.T. Reports. No. 22)

- United States - Graduate work - Directories

POPULATION ASSOCIATION OF AMERICA. Directory of population study centers: United States and Canada. Washington, 1971. pp. 78.

- United States - New York

NEW YORK (STATE). Education Department. Committee on Higher Education. 1960. Meeting the increasing demand for higher education in New York State: a report. Albany, 1960. pp. 74.

UNIVERSITIES AND COLLEGES - United States - New York (Cont'd.)

NEW YORK (STATE). Temporary Commission to Study the Causes of Campus Unrest. 1970. The academy in turmoil: first report of the...Commission; [Charles D. Henderson, chairman]. Albany, 1970. pp. 195.

UNIVERSITY COOPERATION

INTERNATIONAL ASSOCIATION OF UNIVERSITIES. International Committee of Experts. Formal programmes of international co-operation between university institutions: report. [Paris, 1960]. pp. 39. (United Nations Educational, Scientific and Cultural Organization. Educational Studies and Documents. No. 37)

La COOPERATION inter-universitaire dans la promotion du développement: compte rendu du colloque [of the Association des Universités Partiellement ou Entièrement de Langue Française] tenu à Tunis sous les auspices de l'Université de Tunis... 10-21 décembre 1968. [Montréal, 1969]. pp. 176.

UNIVERSITY INVESTMENTS

SIMON (JOHN G.) and others. The ethical investor: universities and corporate responsibility. New Haven, Conn., 1972. pp. 208.

UNIVERSITY OF THE SOUTH PACIFIC

UNIVERSITY OF THE SOUTH PACIFIC. First development plan. [Suva, Fiji], 1970. pp. 68.

UNIVERSITY PRESSES

- United Kingdom

CAMBRIDGE UNIVERSITY PRESS. Cambridge University Press: a short history. [Cambridge, 1969]. pp. 24.

- United States

ADDRESSES in honor of the fiftieth anniversary of Oxford University Press, New York, 27 September 1946. New York, 1947. pp. 39.

UNIVERSITY TEACHING
See TEACHING

UNMARRIED FATHERS

- United States

PANNOR (REUBEN) and others. The unmarried father: new approaches for helping unmarried young parents. New York, [1971]. pp. 196.

UNMARRIED MOTHERS

UNITED NATIONS. Commission on the Status of Women. 1971. The status of the unmarried mother: law and practice; report of the Secretary-General. (E/CN.6/540/Rev.1). New York, 1971. pp. 104. bibliog.

- United Kingdom

FRENCH (EILEEN) and BEER (JEAN) Voluntary welfare associations and unmarried mothers in Greater London. [London], 1972. pp. 56. (London. Greater London Council. Department of Planning and Transportation. Research Memoranda. 345)

- United Kingdom - Scotland

WEIR (SYLVIA) A study of unmarried mothers and their children in Scotland, with special references to the factors affecting the placement decision. [Edinburgh], 1970. pp. 121. bibliog. (Scottish Health Service Studies. No. 13.)

- United States

NEW YORK (STATE). Department of Social Welfare. 1961. Deterrents to early prenatal care and social services among women pregnant out-of-wedlock; by Blanche Bernstein and Mignon Sauber. Albany, [1961]. pp. 179.

UNTOUCHABLES

AMBEDKAR (BHIMARAO RAMJI) Thus spoke Ambedkar: selected speeches, vol. 2; [edited and with an introduction by] Bhagwan Das. Jullundur, 1969. pp. 208.

AMBEDKAR (BHIMARAO RAMJI) The untouchables. 2nd ed. Gonda, 1969. pp. 203.

KEER (DHANANJAY) Dr. Ambedkar: life and mission. 3rd ed. Bombay, 1971. pp. 532.

VERBA (SIDNEY) and others. Caste, race, and politics: a comparative study of India and the United States. Beverly Hills, Calif., [1971]. pp. 279. bibliog.

UNTOUCHABLES
See also SHUDRAS

UNWIN (THOMAS FISHER)

WEST SUSSEX. County Record Office. The Cobden and Unwin papers: a catalogue; edited by Patricia Gill. Chichester, 1967. pp. 50.

UNWIN FAMILY

UNWIN (PHILIP) The publishing Unwins. London, 1972. pp. 182. bibliog.

UPPER ADIGE

- Economic conditions

WIRTSCHAFTS- und Sozialforschung in Tirol und Vorarlberg: Festschrift für Univ.-Prof. DDr. Ferdinand Ulmer...; herausgegeben und bearbeitet von Christoph Pan und Gerhard Marinell. Wien, [1972]. pp. 587. bibliog.

- Nationalism

VEDOVATO (GIUSEPPE) Il problema dell'autonomia per la minoranza di lingua tedesca dell'Alto Adige. Firenze, 1971. pp. 350. (Rivista di Studi Politici Internazionali. Biblioteca. Serie 2. 15)

WOLF (WERNER) Political scientist. Südtirol in Österreich: die Südtirolfrage in der österreichischen Diskussion von 1945 bis 1969. Würzburg, [1972]. pp. 282. bibliog.

- Social conditions

WIRTSCHAFTS- und Sozialforschung in Tirol und Vorarlberg: Festschrift für Univ.-Prof. DDr. Ferdinand Ulmer...; herausgegeben und bearbeitet von Christoph Pan und Gerhard Marinell. Wien, [1972]. pp. 587. bibliog.

UPPER SILESIAN QUESTION

ZIELIŃSKI (WŁADYSŁAW) Polska i niemiecka propaganda plebiscytowa na Górnym Śląsku. Wrocław, 1972. pp. 256. bibliog. With Russian and English summaries.

UPPER VOLTA

- Population

MAFFIOLI (DIONISIA) La fecondità delle popolazioni Guen dell'Alto Volta. Roma, 1971. pp. 117. bibliog. (Rome. Università. Istituto di Demografia. Pubblicazioni. 21) With summaries in various languages.

URAL REGION

- Economic conditions

URAL'SKII POLITEKHNICHESKII INSTITUT. Trudy. sbornik no.164. Nekotorye voprosy stroitel'stva sotsializma i kommunizma. Sverdlovsk, 1968. pp. 226.

- Economic history

PREOBRAZHENSKII (ALEKSANDR ALEKSANDROVICH) Ural i Zapadnaia Sibir' v kontse XVI - nachale XVIII veka. Moskva, 1972. pp. 392.

- History - 1917-1921 Revolution

LISOVSKII (NIKOLAI KUZ'MICH) Razgrom dutovshchiny, 1917-1919. Moskva, 1964. pp. 148.

- Industries

BOL'SHAIA khimiia Srednego Urala. Sverdlovsk, 1964. pp. 71.

PERM'. Universitet. Uchenye zapiski. No.161. Voprosy ekonomiki promyshlennosti Zapadnogo Urala. Perm', 1967. pp. 180.

KORSAKOV (ALEKSANDR IAKOVLEVICH) Razvitie i razmeshchenie promyshlennosti na Srednem Urale. Sverdlovsk, 1972. pp. 96.

- Politics and government

OCHERKI istorii kommunisticheskikh organizatsii Urala. Sverdlovsk, 1971 in progress.

LISOVSKII (NIKOLAI KUZ'MICH) ed. Ocherki istorii bol'shevistskikh organizatsii Iuzhnogo Urala. Cheliabinsk, 1972. pp. 434.

OBSHCHESTVENNO-politicheskoe dvizhenie i klassovaia bor'ba na Srednei Volge, konets XIX - nachalo XX veka. Kazan', 1972. pp. 166.

URANIUM MINES AND MINING

- Russia - Safety measures

PARKHOMENKO (G.M.) and others, eds. Voprosy gigieny truda na uranovykh rudnikakh i obogatitel'nykh predpriiatiiakh: sbornik statei. Moskva, 1971. pp. 117. bibliog.

URBAN ECONOMICS

AMERICA'S cities: five lectures on economic policy, given at Western Michigan University under the sponsorship of the Department of Economics... 1969; Wayland D. Gardner, editor. Ann Arbor, [1970]. pp. 56. (Michigan University. Bureau of Business Research. Michigan Business Papers. No. 54)

DERYCKE (PIERRE HENRI) L'économie urbaine. Paris, 1970. pp. 261. bibliog.

DURR (FRED) The urban economy. Scranton, Penn., [1971]. pp. 201. bibliog.

GORDON (DAVID M.) ed. Problems in political economy: an urban perspective; [readings]. Lexington, [1971]. pp. 478. bibliogs.

MUELLER-HILLEBRAND (VEIT) Die Weltstädte als Absatz- und Verbrauchszentren. Opladen, 1971. pp. 296, xxxiii. bibliogs. (Erlangen. Universität. Wirtschafts- und Sozialwissenschaftliche Fakultät. Institut für Exportforschung. Berichte)

RICHARDSON (HARRY W.) Urban economics. Harmondsworth, 1971. pp. 208. bibliog.

ULLMAN (EDWARD L.) and others. The economic base of American cities: profiles for the 101 metropolitan areas over 250,000 population based on minimum requirements for 1960. rev. ed. Seattle, 1971. pp. 118. bibliog. (Seattle. University of Washington. Center for Urban and Regional Research. Monograph Series. No. 1)

GOODALL (BRIAN) The economics of urban areas. Oxford, [1972]. pp. 379. bibliog.

HANSEN (NILES M.) ed. Growth centers in regional economic development. New York, [1972]. pp. 298.

HENDERSON (WILLIAM L.) and LEDEBUR (LARRY C.) Urban economics: processes and problems. New York, [1972]. pp. 216.

McLENNAN (KENNETH) and SEIDENSTAT (PAUL) New businesses and urban employment opportunities. Lexington, [1972]. pp. 251. bibliog.

PERLMAN (MARK) and others, eds. Spatial, regional and population economics: essays in honor of Edgar M. Hoover. New York, [1972]. pp. 399. bibliogs.

CITIES, regions and public policy; [papers presented at a conference in Glasgow in 1971 jointly organized by Resources for the Future, Inc., and Glasgow University]; edited by Gordon C. Cameron and Lowdon Wingo. Edinburgh, [1973]. pp. 337.

CULLINGWORTH (JOHN BARRY) and others. Problems of an urban society. London, 1973. 3 vols. (Birmingham. University. Centre for Urban and Regional Studies. Urban and Regional Studies. Nos. 4-6)

HIRSCH (WERNER ZVI) Urban economic analysis. New York, [1973]. pp. 450.

RASMUSSEN (DAVID W.) Urban economics. New York, [1973]. pp. 196. bibliogs.

RASMUSSEN (DAVID W.) and HAWORTH (CHARLES T.) eds. The modern city: readings in urban economics. New York, [1973]. pp. 302.

SACKREY (CHARLES) The political economy of urban poverty. New York, [1973]. pp. 172. bibliog.

- Mathematical models

HARTWICK (JOHN M.) and CROWLEY (RONALD W.) Urban economic growth: the Canadian case. Ottawa, 1973. pp. 401. bibliog. (Canada. Ministry of State for Urban Affairs. Working Papers. A-73-5)

URBAN SOCIOLOGY
See SOCIOLOGY, URBAN

URBAN TRANSPORTATION

HUTCHINSON (B.G.) The economic evaluation of urban transportation investments. London, 1969. pp. 40. bibliog. (Centre for Environmental Studies. Working Papers. 39)

SYMPOSIUM ON THE FUTURE OF CONURBATION TRANSPORT, 4TH, MANCHESTER, 1970. Fourth Symposium on the future of conurbation transport, October 20th-22nd, 1970: [proceedings of Symposium sponsored by The Department of Extra Mural Studies, University of Manchester]. Manchester, 1970. fo. 83.

The URBAN transportation planning process. Paris, Organisation for Economic Co-operation and Development, 1971. pp. 351. bibliog. In English and French.

KENDALL (SARITA) Comparative planning data and transportation characteristics of major cities. [London], 1972. pp. 70. bibliog. (London. Greater London Council. Department of Planning and Transportation. Research Memoranda. 370)

- Cost of operation

ANGEL (SHLOMO) and HYMAN (GEOFFREY M.) Urban transport expenditures. London, 1971. pp. 34. bibliog. (Centre for Environmental Studies. Working Papers. 70)

- Research

CATANESE (ANTHONY JAMES) ed. New perspectives in urban transportation research. Lexington, Mass., [1972]. pp. 272. bibliogs.

- Canada

CANADIAN URBAN TRANSPORTATION CONFERENCE, 1ST, TORONTO. Proceedings...; edited by John Steel. Ottawa, [1969?]. pp. 377.

PARKINSON (TOM E.) Passenger transport in Canadian urban areas. 3rd ed. [Ottawa], 1971. pp. 92. (Canada. Transport Commission. Research [Branch]. [Reports].9)

STEGER (WILBUR A.) Reflections on citizen involvement in urban transportation planning: towards a positive approach. Toronto, 1972. fo. 36. (Toronto. University, and York University (Toronto). Joint Program in Transportation. Research Reports. No. 4)

- France

Les TRANSPORTS collectifs urbains: colloque de Tours, 25-26 mai, 1970. Paris, 1970. pp. 176. (Equipement, Logement, Transports, no. 48-49, mars-avril 1970)

- India

INDIA. Metropolitan Transport Team. 1967. Traffic and transportation problems in metropolitan cities: interim report. New Delhi, 1967. pp. 109.

- Netherlands

DONNEA (FRANÇOIS XAVIER DE) The determinants of transport mode choice in Dutch cities. Rotterdam, 1971. pp. 233. bibliog. With summary in Dutch.

- Russia

KOGANOV (BORIS SAMOILOVICH) and LIVSHITS (DAVID MIKHAILOVICH) Ekonomika gorodskogo passazhirskogo transporta. Moskva. 1972. pp. 49.

- Spain

JANE SOLA (JOSE) ed. El transporte colectivo urbano en España. Barcelona. [1972]. pp. 342.

- United Kingdom

U.K. Ministry of Transport. 1968. The preparation of traffic and transport plans. London, 1968. fo. 42. (Technical Memoranda. 68/T7)

DE LEUW, HENNESSEY, CHADWICK, OhEOCHA. Project report: study of intermediate capacity rapid transit systems; prepared for the Ministry of Transport. [London, Ministry of Transport], 1970. fo. 23.

BAXTER (J.H.H.) Issues of urban traffic policy. London, 1971. pp. 6. (Seminar on Urban Traffic Control, Crowthorne, 1971. Papers. 6)

BLOWS (J.W.) Traffic and transport planning. London, 1971. pp. 6. (Seminar on Urban Traffic Control, Crowthorne, 1971. Papers. 1)

JAMIESON AND MACKAY. Blackpool transportation study: summary ([and] supplementary report[s]). London, 1972-73. 5 vols. (in 1).

WATKINS (L.H.) Urban transport and environmental pollution...; text of a paper presented to the 5th Symposium on the Future of Conurbation Transport held at the University of Manchester on 19-21 October 1971. Crowthorne, 1972. pp. 19 bibliog. (U.K. Transport and Road Research Laboratory. Reports. LR 455)

HASELL (B.B.) and others. A summary of the results of traffic generation studies. [London], 1973. pp. 111. (London. Greater London Council. Department of Planning and Transportation. Research Memoranda. 379)

- United States

SEBURN (THOMAS J.) and MARSH (BERNARD L.) Urban transportation administration. New Haven, 1959. pp. 134.

CARNEGIE-MELLON CONFERENCE ON ADVANCED URBAN TRANSPORTATION SYSTEMS, PITTSBURGH, 1970. Advanced urban transportation systems: (proceedings of the... conference). [Pittsburgh, 1970]. pp. 148. bibliog. (Carnegie-Mellon University. Transportation Research Institute. Research Report Series. 5)

MURIN (WILLIAM J.) Mass transit policy planning: an incremental approach. Lexington, Mass., [1971]. pp. 123. bibliog.

INDUSTRIAL approaches to urban problems: discussions of housing, transportation, education, and solid waste management issues; (based on papers presented at a symposium sponsored by the American Association for the Advancement of Science... 1970); edited by Jordan D. Lewis [and] Lynn Lewis. New York, 1972. pp. 185.

OWEN (WILFRED) The accessible city. Washington, [1972]. pp. 150. bibliog.

URBAN TRANSPORTATION POLICY SEMINAR, SYRACUSE UNIVERSITY, 1970. Urban transportation policy: new perspectives; [essays prepared for the seminar]; David R. Miller, editor. Lexington, [1972]. pp. 209. bibliog.

URUGUAY

- Biography

PARKER (WILLIAM BELMONT) ed. Uruguayans of today; [reprint of the original published in London in 1921]. New York, 1967. pp. 575. (Hispanic Society of America. Hispanic Notes and Monographs. 7)

- Civilization

BENEDETTI (MARIO) El pais de la cole de paja. [2nd ed.] Montevideo, 1963 repr. 1970. pp. 194.

- Constitutional law

PRAT (JULIO A.) Los entes autonomos en la descentralizacion funcional uruguaya. Montevideo, 1971. pp. 195. bibliog.

- Economic conditions - Statistics

MONTEVIDEO. Universidad. Instituto de Economia. Uruguay: estadisticas basicas. [Montevideo, 1969]. pp. 175.

- Economic history

BERAZA (AGUSTIN) La economia en la Banda Oriental, 1811-1820. Montevideo, 1964. pp. 107.

El PROCESO economico del Uruguay: contribucion al estudio de su evolucion y perspectivas. [Montevideo, 1969]. pp. 423.

ASTORI (DANILO) Latifundio y crisis agraria en el Uruguay. Montevideo, 1971. pp. 101.

VAZQUEZ VARINI (FELIPE S.) Formacion economica del Uruguay. Montevideo, [1971]. pp. 215. With English summary.

- Economic policy

URUGUAY. Comision de Inversiones y Desarrollo Economico. 1966. Plan nacional de desarrollo economico y social, 1965-1974: elaborado por la CIDE; compendio. Montevideo, 1966. 2 vols. (in 1).

TRIAS (VIVIAN) Economia y politica en el Uruguay contemporaneo. Montevideo, [1968]. pp. 178.

LOUIS (JULIO A.) Batlle y Ordóñez: apogeo y muerte de la democracia burguesa. Montevideo, 1969. pp. 208. bibliog.

El PROCESO economico del Uruguay: contribucion al estudio de su evolucion y perspectivas. [Montevideo, 1969]. pp. 423.

- Emigration and immigration

APOLANT (JUAN ALEJANDRO) Operativo Patagonia: historia de la mayor aportacion demografica masiva a la Banda Oriental con la nomina completa, filiaciones y destino de las familias pobladoras. Montevideo, 1970. pp. 429. bibliog.

- Gazetteers

URUGUAY. Direccion General de Estadistica y Censos. 1972. Indice toponimico de los lugares poblados. Montevideo, 1972. pp. 528.

- History

PINTOS (FRANCISCO R.) Ubicacion de Artigas. Montevideo, [1965]. pp. 165.

FERNANDEZ CABRELLI (ALFONSO) De Batlle a Pacheco Areco: etapas de la lucha entre oligarquia y pueblo. [Montevideo?, 1969]. pp. 275.

- History - Sources

ARTIGAS (JOSE GERVASIO) Artigas; ([edited with an introduction by] Oscar H. Bruschera). Montevideo, [1969]. pp. 252. bibliog.

- Intellectual life

LOCKHART (WASHINGTON) El Uruguay de veras: ensayo. Montevideo, [1969]. pp. 183.

- Officials and employees

URUGUAY. Oficina Nacional del Servicio Civil. 1970. Datos preliminares: 1er censo nacional de funcionarios publicos, 27 agosto 1969. [Montevideo], 1970. 1 vol. (unpaged).

- Politics and government

TRIAS (VIVIAN) Economia y politica en el Uruguay contemporaneo. Montevideo [1968]. pp. 178.

NUÑEZ (CARLOS) Los Tupamaros: vanguardia armada en el Uruguay; y antologia documental seleccionada por Hugo Alonso Bula. 2nd ed. Montevideo, [1969]. pp. 149.

CAMPIGLIA (NESTOR) El Uruguay movilizado. Montevideo, 1971. pp. 177.

- Population

URUGUAY. Direccion General de Estadistica y Censos. 1972. Indice toponimico de los lugares poblados. Montevideo, 1972. pp. 528.

- Social conditions

GILIO (MARIA ESTER) The Tupamaros;...translated from the Spanish by Anne Edmondson. London, 1972. pp. 198.

- Social policy

URUGUAY. Comision de Inversiones y Desarrollo Economico. 1966. Plan nacional de desarrollo economico y social, 1965-1974: elaborado por la CIDE; compendio. Montevideo, 1966. 2 vols. (in 1).

- Statistics

SEMINARIO NACIONAL DE ESTADISTICA [URUGUAY], 1ST, MONTEVIDEO, 1970. Primer Seminario Nacional de Estadistica: recomendaciones finales. Montevideo, 1970. pp. 157.

USPENSKII (NIKOLAI VASIL'EVICH)

NEKHAI (MIKHAIL VASIL'EVICH) Russkii demokraticheskii ocherk 60-kh godov XIX stoletiia: N. Uspenskii, V. Sleptsov, A. Levitov. Minsk, 1971. pp. 146. bibliog.

USTINOV (S. M.)

USTINOV (S.M.) Zapiski Nachal'nika kontr-razvedki, 1915-1920g. Berlin, 1923. pp. 144.

UTILITARIANISM

LOEWENHAUPT (WILFRIED) Politischer Utilitarismus und bürgerliches Rechtsdenken: John Austin, 1790-1859, und die "Philosophie des positiven Rechts". Berlin, [1972]. pp. 386. bibliog. With English summary.

BENTHAM (JEREMY) Bentham's political thought: (selections... from Bentham's manuscripts held by University College, London); edited by Bhikhu Parekh. London, 1973. pp. 340.

LYONS (DAVID) In the interest of the governed: a study in Bentham's philosophy of utility and law. Oxford, 1973. pp. 150. bibliog.

UTOPIAS

LA MARMOTTE (DE) Chevalier, pseud. Les songes du Chevalier de la Marmotte. Au Palais de Morphée, 1745; [Paris, 1970]. pp. 108. Facsimile reprint.

OWEN (ROBERT) A new view of society; or, Essays on the formation of the human character...; [facsimile reprint of the second edition, 1816] with an introduction by John Saville. London, 1972. pp. 184.

UTOPIAS (Cont'd.)

KEMSIES (FERDINAND) Socialistische und ethische Erziehung im Jahre 2000. Berlin, 1893. pp. 142.

POLAK (FRED L.) The image of the future: enlightening the past, orientating the present, forecasting the future; (translated from the Dutch by Elise Boulding). Leyden, 1961. 2 vols. (Council of Europe. European Aspects. Series A: Culture. No. 1)

WALSH (CHAD) From utopia to nightmare. London, 1962. pp. 191. bibliog.

ELORZA (ANTONIO) Socialismo utopico español. Madrid, 1970. pp. 240. bibliog.

AWARE of utopia; [essays based on a Conference on utopia in comparative focus, held at Urbana, 1968]; edited by David W. Plath. Urbana, Ill., [1971]. pp. 150. bibliogs.

RUEHLE (OTTO) Baupläne für eine neue Gesellschaft;... aus dem Nachlass herausgegeben von Henry Jacoby. Reinbek bei Hamburg, 1971. pp. 251. bibliog.

MEIER (PAUL) La pensée utopique de William Morris. Paris, [1972]. pp. 862. bibliog.

POLLETTA (NICHOLAS VICTOR) Platonic utopia and the ideal state in the Italian renaissance of the sixteenth century; [Ph.D. (London) thesis]. [1972]. fo. 316. bibliog. Typescript: unpublished. This thesis is the property of London University and may not be removed from the Library.

SAUNDERS (TREVOR J.) Notes on the Laws of Plato. London, 1972. pp. 148. (London. University. Institute of Classical Studies. Bulletin Supplements. No. 28)

- Bibliography

SVIATLOVSKII (VLADIMIR VLADIMIROVICH) compiler. Katalog utopii. Moskva, 1923. pp. 100. Bibliography of titles in Russian, English, French and German. Xerographic reprint.

UTTAR PRADESH

- Economic conditions

CROOKE (WILLIAM) The North-Western Provinces of India: their history, ethnology and administration; [reprint of work originally published in 1897]... with a new introduction by Philip Mason. Karachi, 1972. pp. 361.

- Economic policy

UNITED PROVINCES OF AGRA AND OUDH. Board of Economic Inquiry. Committee on Economic Planning. 1937. Report on economic planning in the United Provinces; [Muhammad Obaidur Rahman, chairman]. Allahabad, 1937. pp. 151.

- History

CROOKE (WILLIAM) The North-Western Provinces of India: their history, ethnology and administration; [reprint of work originally published in 1897]... with a new introduction by Philip Mason. Karachi, 1972. pp. 361.

- Nationalism

LUETT (JUERGEN) Hindu-Nationalismus in Uttar Prades, 1867-1900. Stuttgart, [1970]. pp. 171. bibliog.

- Politics and government

ZAHEER (M.) and GUPTA (JAGDEO) The organization of the government of Uttar Pradesh: a study of state administration. Delhi, [1970]. pp. 770.

- Rural conditions

KANTOWSKY (DETLEF) Dorfentwicklung und Dorfdemokratie in Indien: Formen und Wirkungen von Community Development und Panchayati Raj...im östlichen Uttar Pradesh. Bielefeld, [1970]. pp. 170. bibliog. (Arnold-Bergstraesser-Institut für Kulturwissenschaftliche Forschung. Freiburger Studien zu Politik und Gesellschaft Überseeischer Länder. Band 9) With English summary.

- Social conditions

CROOKE (WILLIAM) The North-Western Provinces of India: their history, ethnology and administration; [reprint of work originally published in 1897]... with a new introduction by Philip Mason. Karachi, 1972. pp. 361.

UVF.
See ULSTER VOLUNTEER FORCE

UZBEKISTAN

UZBEK Soviet Socialist Republic. Moscow, 1972. pp. 88.

UZBEKISTAN
See also TURKESTAN

- Constitutional history

ISHANOV (ATABAI I.) and others. Istoriia gosudarstva i prava Uzbekistana. Tashkent, 1969 in progress.

- Constitution history - Sources

KPSS i Sovetskoe pravitel'stvo ob Uzbekistane: sbornik dokumentov, 1925-1970. Tashkent, 1972. pp. 557.

- Economic conditions

ZOLOTAREV (EDUARD LEONIDOVICH) Problemy vosproizvodstva i okhrany prirodnykh resursov Uzbekistana v protsesse ikh ispol'zovaniia. Tashkent, 1972. pp. 211. bibliog. Cover and colophon have title: Prirodnye resursy Uzbekistana.

- Economic history

MUSAEV (MAKHMUD MUSAEVICH) Uzbekskaia SSR: kratkii istoriko-ekonomicheskii ocherk. Moskva, 1959. pp. 182.

TASHKENTSKII INSTITUT NARODNOGO KHOZIAISTVA. Nauchnye Zapiski. vyp.19. Voprosy istorii narodnogo khoziaistva Uzbekistana, etc. Tashkent, 1962. pp. 254.

VOPROSY ekonomiki sotsializma. Tashkent, 1966. pp. 139. (Tashkent. Universitet. Trudy. vyp.274)

TASHKENTSKII INSTITUT NARODNOGO KHOZIAISTVA. Nauchnye Zapiski. vyp.53. Voprosy istorii narodnogo khoziaistva Uzbekistana. Tashkent, 1969. pp. 222.

- Economic policy

SHARIFKHODZHAEV (M.) Kapital'noe stroitel'stvo v Uzbekistane i ego material'no-tekhnicheskaia baza. Tashkent, 1971. pp. 228.

TASHKENTSKII INSTITUT NARODNOGO KHOZIAISTVA. Nauchnye Zapiski. vyp. 51. Voprosy sovershenstvovaniia planirovaniia narodnogo khoziaistva. Tashkent, 1971. pp. 253.

ZIIADULLAEV (SAID-KARIM) Planirovanie i razvitie ekonomiki Uzbekskoi SSR. Tashkent, 1972. pp. 229.

ZOLOTAREV (EDUARD LEONIDOVICH) Problemy vosproizvodstva i okhrany prirodnykh resursov Uzbekistana v protsesse ikh ispol'zovaniia. Tashkent, 1972. pp. 211. bibliog. Cover and colophon have title: Prirodnye resursy Uzbekistana.

- Executive departments.

SOVETY deputatov trudiashchikhsia Uzbekskoi SSR v sovremennykh usloviiakh. Tashkent, 1971. pp. 327.

- History

KASTEL'SKAIA (ZINAIDA DMITRIEVNA) Osnovnye predposylki vosstaniia 1916 goda v Uzbekistane. 2nd ed. Moskva, 1972. pp. 146. bibliog.

- History - Sources

KPSS i Sovetskoe pravitel'stvo ob Uzbekistane: sbornik dokumentov, 1925-1970. Tashkent, 1972. pp. 557.

- History - 1917-1921, Revolution

TASHMUKHAMEDOV (A.M.) ed. Istoricheskoe znachenie pobedy Oktiabr'skoi sotsialisticheskoi revoliutsii v Uzbekistane. Tashkent, 1967. pp. 167. (Tashkent. Universitet. Nauchnye Trudy. vyp.314)

- History - 1917-1921, Revolution - Sources

POBEDA Oktiabr'skoi revoliutsii v Uzbekistane: sbornik dokumentov. Tashkent, 1963-72. 2 vols.

- Industries

ERGASHEV (TASHTURGUN) and TURSUNKHODZHAEV (MARAT LUTFULLAEVICH) Ekonomicheskaia reforma v legkoi promyshlennosti Uzbekistana. Tashkent, 1969. pp. 52.

FONDY ekonomicheskogo stimulirovaniia v promyshlennosti Uzbekistana. Tashkent, 1971. pp. 187.

DZHAMALOV (OMER BAIMBETOVICH) ed. Vosproizvodstvo valovogo produkta v promyshlennosti Uzbekskoi SSR. Tashkent, 1972. pp. 184.

ZAKIROV (SH. N.) Problemy ratsional'nogo razmeshcheniia promyshlennosti Uzbekistana. Tashkent, 1972. pp. 171. bibliog.

- Intellectual life

NASYRKHODZHAEV (SABITKHAN KHASHIMOVICH) Intelligentsiia Uzbekistana i ee rol' v stroitel'stve kommunizma. Tashkent. 1972. pp. 239.

- Politics and government

KARIEV (MAKSUD) Soiuz rabochikh i krest'ian — osnova Sovetskogo obshchenarodnogo gosudarstva: na materialakh Uzbekskoi SSR. Tashkent, 1965. pp. 133.

KOMPARTIIA Uzbekistana v bor'be za pobedu Sovetskoi vlasti i postroenie sotsializma. Tashkent, 1968. pp. 162.

- Rural conditions

TASHKENT. Universitet. Trudy. vyp. 278. Kommunisticheskaia partiia - organizator soiuza rabochego klassa s krest'ianstvom: po materialam Uzbekistana. Tashkent, 1966. pp. 126.

UZBEKS

ETNOGRAFICHESKOE izuchenie byta i kul'tury uzbekov. Tashkent, 1972. pp. 160.

VACCINATION

RIGBY (EDWARD) M.D., the Elder. Further facts relating to the care of the poor, and the management of the workhouse in the city of Norwich, etc.; ([with] Report of the Norwich pauper vaccination from August 10, 1812, to August 10, 1813). Norwich, 1812-13. pp. 103, 15, 14.

VAKHITOV (MULLANUR MULLAZIANOVICH)

VAKHITOV (MULLANUR MULLAZIANOVICH) Izbrannoe: stat'i, rechi, pis'ma, dokumenty. Kazan', 1967. pp. 121.

VAL D'ARDA

- Economic policy

PROBLEMI economici e sociali del comprensorio della Val d'Arda: [reports of conferences held during 1969 and 1970 under the sponsorship of the provincial administration of Piacenza]. [Piacenza], 1970. pp. 126. (Piacenza (Province). Ufficio Studi. Documenti e Notizie)

- Social policy

PROBLEMI economici e sociali del comprensorio della Val d'Arda: [reports of conferences held during 1969 and 1970 under the sponsorship of the provincial administration of Piacenza]. [Piacenza], 1970. pp. 126. (Piacenza (Province). Ufficio Studi. Documenti e Notizie)

VAL-DE-MARNE

FRANCE. Direction de la Documentation. La Documentation Française. Notes et Etudes Documentaires. No.3,409. Les nouveaux départements de la région parisienne: le département du Val-de-Marne. Paris, 1967. pp. 67. bibliog.

VAL TIDONE

- Economic policy

PROBLEMI economici e sociali del comprensorio della Val Tidone: [reports of conferences held during 1969 and 1970 under the sponsorship of the provincial administration of Piacenza]. [Piacenza], 1970. pp. 127. (Piacenza (Province). Ufficio Studi. Documenti e Notizie)

- Social policy

PROBLEMI economici e sociali del comprensorio della Val Tidone: [reports of conferences held during 1969 and 1970 under the sponsorship of the provincial administration of Piacenza]. [Piacenza], 1970. pp. 127. (Piacenza (Province). Ufficio Studi. Documenti e Notizie)

VALAIS

- Rural conditions

LOUP (JEAN) Pasteurs et agriculteurs Valaisans: contributions à l'étude des problèmes montagnards. Grenoble, [imprint], 1965. pp. 679. bibliog.

VALENZUELA PALOS (ROSALIO MOISÉS)
See MOISÉS (ROSALIO)

VALGAUDEMAR
- Economic policy

HAUTES-ALPES. Direction Départementale de l'Agriculture, and ATELIER CENTRAL D'ETUDES D'AMENAGEMENT RURAL. Champsaur-Valgaudemar: la mutation d'une région. [Gap?, 1971]. pp. 72.

VALIKHANOV (CHOKAN CHINGISOVICH)

KAZAKHSKII GOSUDARSTVENNYI UNIVERSITET. Uchenye zapiski. Seriia Istoricheskaia. t.54. vyp.12. Voprosy istorii Kazakhstana. Alma-Ata, 1963. pp. 228. bibliog.

VALLESE (FELIPE)

ORTEGA PEÑA (RODOLFO) and DUHALDE (EDUARDO LUIS) Felipe Vallese: proceso al sistema. Buenos Aires, 1965 rep. 1967. pp. 135.

VALLIERES (PIERRE)

VALLIERES (PIERRE) White niggers of America: the precocious autobiography of a Quebec "terrorist";... translated by Joan Pinkham. New York, [1971]. pp. 288.

VALUE

BUKHARIN (NIKOLAI IVANOVICH) Ataka: sbornik teoreticheskikh statei. 2nd ed. Moskva, [1924]. pp. 303. Xerographic reprint.

AGEEV (VALENTIN MIKHAILOVICH) Proizvodstvo vnov' sozdannoi stoimosti pri sotsializme. Moskva, 1970. pp. 97.

AMILIBIA (MIGUEL DE) Los dos robinsones: un ensayo sobre el valor de cambio. Buenos Aires, [1970]. pp. 156.

KRONROD (IAKOV ABRAMOVICH) Zakon stoimosti i sotsialisticheskaia ekonomika: nekotorye aktual'nye problemy. Moskva. 1970. pp. 159.

NIKITIN (SERGEI MIKHAILOVICH) Teorii stoimosti i ikh evoliutsiia. Moskva, 1970. pp. 196.

WAGNER (THOMAS) Arbeitswährung: das Ende der Lohn-Preisspirale. 4th ed. Wien, [1970]. pp. 205. bibliog.

FIORITO (RICCARDO) Divisione del lavoro e teoria del valore: l'economia sociologica di Adam Smith. Bari, [1971]. pp. 207.

KOLM (SERGE CHRISTOPHE) La valeur publique. Paris, 1971. pp. 221.

MARKSISTSKO-leninskaia teoriia stoimosti. Moskva, 1971. pp. 211.

STOIMOST' v usloviiakh sotsializma. Minsk, 1971. pp. 435. bibliog.

NEILL (ROBIN) A new theory of value: the Canadian economics of H.A. Innis. Toronto, [1972]. pp. 159. bibliog.

MEEK (RONALD LINDLEY) Studies in the labour theory of value. 2nd ed. London, 1973. pp. 332.

- Mathematical models

KOLM (SERGE CHRISTOPHE) La théorie des contraintes de valeur et ses applications. Paris, 1971. pp. 577.

VALUE-ADDED TAX
- Bibliography

BUCHANAN (D.S.) compiler. Value added: the tax and the concept. London, [1972]. pp. 28.

- Belgium

BELGIUM. Administration de la T.V.A., de l'Enregistrement et des Domaines. 1972. Manuel de la T.V.A; nouvelle édition. [Brussels], 1972. 1 vol. (looseleaf).

- Europe

HOORN (JACOBUS VAN) and others, eds. Value added taxation in Europe. Amsterdam, 1971. Loose leaf. (International Bureau of Fiscal Documentation. Guides to European Taxation. vol.4)

- European Economic Community countries

[JANSEN (JOHANNES)] The value-added tax in the European Community. rev. ed. [London], European Communities, 1970. pp. 12. bibliog. Press and Information [Service]. London Office. Community Topics. 36)

TORCASIO (SAVERIO) L'imposta sul valore aggiunto in agricoltura. Roma, 1970. pp. 247. bibliog.

TAIT (ALAN A.) Value added tax. London, [1972]. pp. 184. bibliog.

WHEATCROFT (GEORGE SHORROCK ASHCOMBE) ed. Value added tax in the enlarged Common Market. London, 1973. pp. 140. bibliog.

- France

COZIAN (MAURICE) Les dessous de la T.V.A. Paris, [1971]. pp. 147. bibliog.

GALAVIELLE (JEAN PIERRE) La T.V.A.: impôt moderne. [Paris, 1972]. pp. 96. bibliog.

- Ireland (Republic)

EIRE. Dail Eireann. Special Committee on the Value-added Tax Bill, 1971. 1972. Official report, unrevised; [Augustine A. Healy, chairman]. Dublin, 1972. 6 pts.

EIRE. Dail Eireann. Special Committee on the Value-added Tax Bill, 1971. 1972. Report...together with the proceedings of the...Committee; [Augustine A. Healy, chairman]. Dublin, 1972. pp. 24.

- Italy

TORCASIO (SAVERIO) L'imposta sul valore aggiunto in agricoltura. Roma, 1970. pp. 247. bibliog.

- Netherlands

BEEKMAN (E.) De invloed van de BTW op de administratie. 3rd ed. Deventer, 1968. pp. 111.

VERENIGING VOOR BELASTINGWETENSCHAP. Geschriften. Nr. 123. Belasting over de toegevoegde waarde; (lezingen gehouden...op 27 april 1968). Deventer, 1969. pp. 37.

- Rhodesia

RHODESIA. Committee on Value Added Turnover Taxation, 1967. Report; [J.E. Baker, chairman]. [Salisbury], 1967. pp. (iii), 27. ([Sessional Papers]. 1967. C.S.R. 34)

- United Kingdom

U.K. Parliament. House of Commons. Library. Research Division. Background Papers. No. 16. A value-added tax; [by E.C. Thompson]. [London, 1971]. fo. 10.

CBI SEMINAR ON VALUE ADDED TAX, LONDON, 1972.
Transcript of proceedings. London, 1972. pp. 127.

CHOWN (JOHN F.) VAT explained: the business man's and manager's guide to value added tax. London, 1972. pp. 224.

DE VOIL (PAUL W.) Value added tax. London, 1972. Loose-leaf.

U.K. Customs and Excise Department. 1972. VAT: 1. Partial exemption. 2. Self-supply (stationery). [London], 1972. pp. 16. (Notices. No. 706)

U.K. Customs and Excise Department. 1972. VAT: construction industry. [London], 1972. pp. 20. (Notices. No. 708)

U.K. Customs and Excise Department. 1972. VAT: exports. [London], 1972. pp. 13. (Notices. No. 703)

U.K. Customs and Excise Department. 1972. VAT: general guide. [London], 1972. pp. 76. (Notices. No. 700).

U.K. Customs and Excise Department. 1972. VAT: hotels and catering. [London], 1972. pp. 14. (Notices. No. 709)

U.K. Customs and Excise Department. 1972. VAT: imports. [London], 1972. pp. 14. (Notices. No. 702)

U.K. Customs and Excise Department. 1972. VAT: retail export schemes. [London], 1972. pp. 10. (Notices. No. 704)

U.K. Customs and Excise Department. 1972. VAT: scope and coverage. [London], 1972. pp. 75. (Notices. No. 701).

U.K. Customs and Excise Department. 1972. VAT: special schemes for retailers. [London], 1972. pp. 24. (Notices. No. 707)

U.K. Customs and Excise Department. 1972. VAT: supplies by or through agents. [London], 1972. pp. 10. (Notices. No. 710)

U.K. Customs and Excise Department. 1972. VAT and car tax: tax-free sales of motor vehicles to tourists, etc. [London], 1972. pp. 6. (Notices. No. 705)

U.K. Customs and Excise Department. 1972. VAT trade classification. [London], 1972. pp. 14.

ENCYCLOPEDIA of value added tax; [edited by] G.S.A. Wheatcroft [and] J.F. Avery Jones. London, 1973. Loose-leaf.

U.K. Customs and Excise Department. 1973. VAT: construction industry. rev. ed. [London], 1973. pp. 28. (Notices. No. 708)

U.K. Customs and Excise Department. 1973. VAT: construction industry: alterations and repairs and maintenance. [London], 1973. pp. 9. (Notices. No.715)

U.K. Customs and Excise Department. 1973. VAT: guidance on transitional problems. [London], 1973. pp. 7. (Notices. No. 700. Supplement No. 1)

U.K. Customs and Excise Department. 1973. VAT: second-hand caravans and motor cycles. [London], 1973. pp. 15. (Notices. No. 713)

U.K. Customs and Excise Department. 1973. VAT: second-hand cars. [London], 1973. pp. 13. (Notices. No. 711)

U.K. Customs and Excise Department. 1973. VAT: second-hand works of art, antiques and scientific collections. [London], 1973. pp. 19. (Notices. No. 712)

U.K. Customs and Excise Department. 1973. VAT: special schemes for retailers. rev. ed. [London], 1973. pp. 30. (Notices. No.707)

U.K. Customs and Excise Department. 1973. VAT Notices: Amendment Leaflet No. 1. [London], 1973. fo. 29.

WHEATCROFT (GEORGE SHORROCK ASHCOMBE) and others. Value added tax in Great Britain for businesses and professions. London, 1973. pp. 364.

- United States

McLURE (CHARLES E.) and TURE (NORMAN B.) Value added tax: two views. Washington, D.C., 1972. pp. 97. (American Enterprise Institute for Public Policy Research. Domestic Affairs Studies. 7)

VALUE ANALYSIS (COST CONTROL)

GILCHRIST (R.R.) Managing for profit: the added value concept. London, 1971. pp. 165. bibliog.

VANCOUVER

- Harbour

KHAN (EMAMUDDEEN) Industrial relations in the Canadian longshoring industry: a case study of collective bargaining in the ports of Montreal and Vancouver; [Ph.D. (London) thesis]. 1972. fo. 341. bibliog. Typescript: unpublished. This thesis is the property of London University and may not be removed from the Library.

VANDERVELDE (ÉMILE)

EMILE Vandervelde: l'homme et son oeuvre; ([by] Louis de Brouckère [and others]). Bruxelles, 1928. pp. 285. bibliog.

VANZETTI (BARTOLOMEO)

CANNON (JAMES PATRICK) Notebook of an agitator. 2nd ed. New York, 1973. pp. 369. A reprint of the 1st ed. with the addition of an index and illustrations.

VARELA (FELIPE)

ORTEGA PEÑA (RODOLFO) and DUHALDE (EDUARDO LUIS) Felipe Varela contra el imperio britanico: las masas de la union americana enfrentan a las potencias europeas. Buenos Aires, 1966. pp. 363.

VARGAS (GETÚLIO)

FRISCHAUER (PAUL) Presidente Vargas; traduccion por Javier Gonzalez Pombo. Buenos Aires, 1943. pp. 386.

MALTA (OCTAVIO) Os tenentes na revolução brasileira. Rio de Janeiro, 1969. pp. 136.

VARSHER (TATIANA S.)

VARSHER (TATIANA S.) Vidennoe i perezhitoe v Sovetskoi Rossii. Berlin, 1923. pp. 155.

VASIL'CHIKOV (ALEKSANDR ILLARIONOVICH) Prince

GOLUBEV (A.) Kniaz' Aleksandr Illarionovich Vasil'chikov: biograficheskii ocherk; [with an appendix entitled] Stat'i gazet i zhurnalov, posviashchennye pamiati Kniazia A.I. Vasil'chikova. S.-Peterburg, 1882. pp. 156,(46).

VASKIN (VASIL KHRISTOV-)
See KHRISTOV-VASKIN (VASIL)

VÄSTERNORRLAND

- Population

TEDERBRAND (LARS-GÖRAN) Västernorrland och Nordamerika, 1875-1913: utvandring och återinvandring. Stockholm, [1972]. pp. 341. bibliog. (Uppsala. Universitet. Historiska Institutionen. Studia Historica Upsaliensia. 42) With English summary.

VASTO (LANZA DEL)

VASTO (LANZA DEL) Return to the source: a translation of Le pèlerinage aux sources by Jean Sidgwick. London, 1971. pp. 319.

VATICAN
See CATHOLIC CHURCH

VATICAN COUNCIL, 1962-1965

SCHAMBECK (HERBERT) Kirche, Staat, Gesellschaft: Probleme von heute und morgen. Wien, [1967]. pp. 115.

CARLI (LUIGI MARIA) Nova et vetera: tradizione e progresso nella chiesa dopo il Vaticano II. Roma, [1969]. pp. 212.

SPINELLI (LORENZO) La chiesa e gli stati alla luce del Concilio Vaticano II: riflessioni sui principi conciliari sotto il profilo giuridico. Modena, 1969. pp. 148. bibliog.

ROOS (LOTHAR) Ordnung und Gestaltung der Wirtschaft: Grundlagen und Grundsätze der Wirtschaftsethik nach dem II. Vatikanischen Konzil. Köln, 1971. pp. 190. bibliog. (Katholische Sozialwissenschaftliche Zentralstelle. Veröffentlichungen)

GISMONDI (PIETRO) Il diritto della Chiesa dopo il Concilio. Milano, 1972. pp. 194.

WELLS (DAVID F.) Revolution in Rome. London, 1973. pp. 128. bibliog.

VAUD (CANTON)

- Economic conditions

BARBIER (JACQUES) Le Nord vaudois: étude socio-économique;...rapport executé à la demande de l'Office de l'urbanisme et en collaboration avec l'équipe de l'aménagement du territoire de la région d'Yverdon. [Yverdon], 1963. pp. 124. (Vaud (Canton). Office Cantonal Vaudois de l'Urbanisme. Cahiers de l'Aménagement Régional. No.1)

- Population

BARBIER (JACQUES) Le Nord vaudois: étude socio-économique;...rapport executé à la demande de l'Office de l'urbanisme et en collaboration avec l'équipe de l'aménagement du territoire de la région d'Yverdon. [Yverdon], 1963. pp. 124. (Vaud (Canton). Office Cantonal Vaudois de l'Urbanisme. Cahiers de l'Aménagement Régional. No.1)

VAUGHAN (HENRY HALFORD)

BILL (E.G.W.) University reform in nineteenth-century Oxford: a study of Henry Halford Vaughan, 1811-1885. Oxford, 1973. pp. 274.

VAZQUEZ COBO CARRIZOSA (CAMILO)

VAZQUEZ COBO CARRIZOSA (CAMILO) El frente nacional, su origen y desarrollo: memorias...;[edited by Sylvia Wills de Vazquez]. [Cali, imprint, 196-]. pp. 436.

VECKINCHUSEN (HILDEBRAND)

VECKINCHUSEN (HILDEBRAND) Die Handelsbücher des hansischen Kaufmannes Veckinchusen; ([edited by] Michail P. Lesnikov). Berlin, 1973. pp. 560.

VEGETABLE TRADE

- Ireland (Republic)

The MARKETING of fruit and vegetables; [by T.O'Dwyer and others]. Dublin, 1973. pp. 107. (Eire. National Prices Commission. Occasional Papers. No. 7)

- Italy

VENZI (LORENZO) Il mercato delle produzioni sericole. Portici, 1970. pp. 144. bibliog. (Naples. Università. Centro di Specializzazione e Ricerche Economico-Agrarie per il Mezzogiorno. Saggi e Ricerche. 6) With English summary.

VEGETABLES

- Grading

ORGANISATION FOR ECONOMIC CO-OPERATION AND DEVELOPMENT. Documentation in Food and Agriculture. [1968 Series] 89. International standardisation of fruit and vegetables: artichokes, cherries, cabbages, cucumbers, asparagus. Paris, 1969. pp. 349-513.

- Marketing

ABBOTT (J.C.) ed. Marketing fruit and vegetables...; prepared on the basis of an original text by a Netherlands team led by M. Mathot, etc. 2nd ed. Rome, Food and Agriculture Organization, 1970. pp. 181. bibliog. (Marketing Guides. No.2)

- Packaging

ORGANISATION FOR ECONOMIC CO-OPERATION AND DEVELOPMENT. Documentation in Food and Agriculture. 1966-1967 Series. 85. Recommendations on the international standardisation of packaging for fruit and vegetables. Paris, 1967. pp. 123. In English and French.

- Canada - Quebec - Marketing

QUEBEC (PROVINCE). Commission Royale d'Enquête sur l'Agriculture au Québec, 1965. La mise en marché des fruits et légumes au Québec; rapport; (with annexes). [Québec], 1967 [or rather 1968]. 2 pts.

- East (Near East) - Marketing

FOOD AND AGRICULTURE ORGANIZATION. Marketing Center with Special Reference to Fresh Fruit and Vegetables, Near East Region. 1960. Report. Rome, 1960. pp. 54.

- France

FRANCE. Ministère de l'Agriculture. Statistique Agricole. Supplément. Série Etudes. No. 76. Etude méthodologique sur les superficies et les productions annuelles d'exploitations produisant des légumes: développement des résultats de l'enquête expérimentale pour le Département du Loiret en 1968; [étude rédigée par G. Vandewalle]. [Paris], 1971. pp. 131.

VEGETARIANISM

FORWARD (CHARLES WALTER) Fifty years of food reform: a history of the vegetarian movement in England; from its inception in 1847, down to the close of 1897, etc. London, 1898. pp. 192.

VEHICLES

- Taxation - Sweden

SWEDEN. Finansdepartementet. Bilskatteutredningen. Kilometerbeskattning. Stockholm, 1970. pp. 55. (Sweden. Statens Offentliga Utredningar, 1970. 36)

VELICHKINA (VERA MIKHAILOVNA)

GRODZENSKII (IAKOV D.) and PODLIASHUK (PAVEL I.) Stoikost': rasskaz o zhizni Very Mikhailovny Velichkinoi (Bonch-Bruevich). Voronezh, 1970. pp. 150. bibliog.

VENDETTA

PIGLIARU (ANTONIO) Il banditismo in Sardegna: la vendetta barbaricina come ordinamento giuridico. [Milan, 1970]. pp. 489.

VENDORS AND PURCHASERS

- Russia

IAZEV (VASILII AFRIKANOVICH) Otvetstvennost' prodavtsa za nenadlezhashchee kachestvo prodannykh tovarov. Moskva. 1964. pp. 48.

VENEREAL DISEASES

ROSEBURY (THEODOR) Microbes and morals: the strange story of venereal disease. London, 1972. pp. 361. bibliog.

- United Kingdom

U.K. Central Health Services Council. Standing Medical Advisory Committee. 1969. The venereal diseases. London, 1969. pp. 16.

MORTON (ROBERT STEEL) Sexual freedom and venereal disease. London, 1971. pp. 141. bibliog.

VENEZUELA

- Armed Forces - Political activity

BURGGRAAFF (WINFIELD J.) The Venezuelan armed forces in politics, 1935-1959. Columbia, Miss., 1972. pp. 241. bibliog.

- Bibliography

WATSON (GAYLE HUDGENS) Colombia, Ecuador and Venezuela: an annotated guide to reference materials in the humanities and social sciences. Metuchen, N.J., 1971. pp. 279. bibliog.

- Boundaries - Guyana

HUBBARD (H.J.M.) Venezuelan border issue and occupation of Ankoko: a sell-out by the coalition Government. [Georgetown?, 1967]. pp. 64.

PEDRO FERNANDEZ (ANTONIO DE) La historia y el derecho en la reclamacion venezolana de la guayana Esequiba. Caracas, 1969. pp. 333.

- Commerce - Statistics

VENEZUELA. Direccion General de Estadistica. Comercio exterior: segun pais y articulo. q., with annual cumulation, 1971- Caracas.

- Commerce - America, Latin

VENEZUELA. Direccion de Comercio Exterior y Consulados. 1963. Intercambio comercial entre Venezuela y los paises suramericanos. Caracas, 1963. fo. 59. (Estudios sobre Comercio Exterior. 14)

- Commercial treaties

VENEZUELA. Direccion de Comercio Exterior y Consulados. 1962. Convenios comerciales vigentes. tomo 1. Convenios bilaterales. [Caracas], 1962. pp. 112. (Estudios sobre Comercio Exterior. 10)

- Congress

ANDUEZA (JOSE GUILLERMO) El congreso: estudio juridico. Caracas, Ediciones del Congreso de la Republica, 1971. pp. 94.

- Constitution

VENEZUELA. Constitution. 1961. Constitucion promulgada el 23 de enero de 1961. Caracas, 1971. pp. 88.

- Defences

VENEZUELA. Ministerio de la Defensa. Memoria y cuenta...presenta al Congreso Nacional. a., 1971 [covering 1970]- Caracas.

- Economic conditions

NUÑEZ TENORIO (J.R.) Venezuela, modelo neocolonial: justicia social para ser realmente libres. Caracas, [1969]. pp. 143.

ROTHER (KLAUS) Wirtschaft und Berufserziehung in Venezuela. Berlin, 1972. pp. 118. bibliog. (Ibero-Amerikanisches Institut. Veröffentlichungen. Bibliotheca Ibero-Americana. Band 16)

- Economic conditions - Statistics.

BANCO CENTRAL DE VENEZUELA. La economia venezolana en los ultimos treinta años. Caracas, 1971. pp. 318. (Coleccion XXX Aniversario)

- Economic history - Sources

CARRILLO BATALLA (TOMAS ENRIQUE) ed. Historia de las finanzas publicas en Venezuela...1830-(1846): (materiales para su estudio); con la cooperacion de un grupo de investigacion coordinado por el profesor Pedro Grases. Caracas, 1969. 6 vols.

- Economic policy

VENEZUELA. Corporacion Venezolana de Fomento. Departamento de Relaciones Publicas 1958. Sentido y orientación de la politica economica de la Corporación Venezolana de Fomento: exposición del Rafael Alfonzo Ravard ante la XIV asamblea de la Federación Venezolana de Camaras y Asociaciones de Comercio y Producción. [Caracas, 1958?]. pp. (12). (Coleccion Documentos. 1)

VENEZUELA - Economic policy (Cont'd.)

VENEZUELA. President, 1959-1964 (Betancourt). 1960. Eficacia de la coalición: balance de un año de gobierno; por el Presidente Betancourt, 1959, 13 de febrero, 1960. Caracas, 1960. pp. 27.

VENEZUELA. President, 1959-1964 (Betancourt). 1960. Por buen camino hacia la recuperacion economica del pais: alocucion del Presidente Betancourt el 13 de septiembre de 1960. Caracas, 1960. pp. 19. (Venezuela. Secretaria de la Presidencia de la Republica. Publicaciones)

SUCRE FIGARELLA (LEOPOLDO) Las obras publicas y el desarrollo integral. [Caracas, Oficina Central de Informacion, 1965]. pp. 42. (Temas del Desarrollo Economico de Venezuela. 2)

GABALDON MARQUEZ (EDGAR) Venezuela, su imagen desvelada...: ensayo sobre el coloniaje, la forma societaria peculiar de nuestro pais y de la America Latina. Paris, 1968. pp. 194. bibliog.

INTERNATIONAL LABOUR OFFICE. Development Programme: Technical Assistance Sector. [Venezuela] R.9. Informe al gobierno de Venezuela sobre el proyecto para la integracion de las poblaciones indigenas. (OIT/TAP/Venezuela/R.9). Geneva, 1970. pp. 31.

ZWIEFELHOFER (HANS) Integration von Bildungs- und Wirtschaftsplanung in Venezuela; allgemeine und regionale Probleme. Berlin, [1972]. pp. 246. bibliog.

- Foreign relations - United Kingdom

PEDRO FERNANDEZ (ANTONIO DE) La historia y el derecho en la reclamacion venezolana de la guayana Esequiba. Caracas, 1969. pp. 333.

- History

LEVEL DE GODA (LUIS) Historia contemporanea de Venezuela politica y militar, 1858-1886. Tomo primero. Caracas, 1954. pp. 791,xx. No more published. Vol. 1 covers the period 1858-1868.

ROJAS (JOSE MARIA DE) Marquis. Recuerdos de la patria; prologo de Pedro Grases. Caracas, 1963. pp. 199. (Coleccion Venezuela Peregrina. 5)

LOMBARDI (JOHN V.) The decline and abolition of negro slavery in Venezuela, 1820-1854. Westport, Conn., [1971]. pp. 217. bibliog.

- History - Dictionaries

RUDOLPH (DONNA KEYSE) and RUDOLPH (G.A.) Historical dictionary of Venezuela. Metuchen, N.J., 1971. pp. 142. bibliog.

- History - Sources

CATALA (JOSE AGUSTIN) ed. Documentos para la historia de la resistencia. Caracas, 1969 in progress.

TROCONIS DE VERACOECHEA (ERMILA) ed. Documentos para el estudio de los esclavos negros en Venezuela. Caracas, 1969. pp. 348.

- Industries

VENEZUELA. Ministerio de Obras Públicas. Dirección de Planeamiento. 1966. Analisis de la Region Central. 3. Economia. 5. Industria manufacturera. [Caracas], 1965 [or rather 1966]. pp. 208.

ARAUJO (ORLANDO) Situacion industrial de Venezuela. Caracas, [1969]. pp. 119. bibliog.

VENEZUELA. Direccion General de Estadistica. Censos Economicos, 1963. [Terceros] censos economicos: resultados definitivos: manufactura. Vols. 2-4. Caracas, 1970. 3 vols. Vol. 1 out of print.

- Manufactures

VENEZUELA. Direccion General de Estadistica. Censos Economicos, 1963. [Terceros] censos economicos: resultados definitivos: manufactura. Vols. 2-4. Caracas, 1970. 3 vols. Vol. 1 out of print.

- Native races

INTERNATIONAL LABOUR OFFICE. Development Programme: Technical Assistance Sector. [Venezuela] R.9. Informe al gobierno de Venezuela sobre el proyecto para la integracion de las poblaciones indigenas. (OIT/TAP/Venezuela/R.9). Geneva, 1970. pp. 31.

- Politics and government

DUPRAY (NORMAND H.) Aves de rapiña sobre Venezuela: analisis de la situacion politica contemporanea de Venezuela y de las causas por las cuales fue asesinado el coronel Carlos Delgado Chalbaud. Buenos Aires, [1958]. pp. 159.

VENEZUELA. President, 1959-1964 (Betancourt). 1960. Eficacia de la coalición: balance de un año de gobierno; por el Presidente Betancourt, 1959, 13 de febrero, 1960. Caracas, 1960. pp. 27.

CASTILLO (DOMINGO B.) Memorias de Mano Lobo; [and] La cuestion monetaria en Venezuela. Caracas, 1962. pp. 429. (Coleccion Venezuela Peregrina. 1)

LOPEZ CONTRERAS (ELEAZAR) Gobierno y administracion, 1936-1941. Caracas, [1966]. pp. 159.

ROJAS (PEDRO JOSE) Pedro José Rojas o una pasion al servicio de la politica. Caracas, 1966. pp. 113. (Venezuela. Presidencia de la Republica. Publicaciones. Coleccion Nuestro Siglo XIX.7)

FUENMAYOR (JUAN BAUTISTA) 1928-1948: veinte años de politica. Caracas, [1968]. pp. 358.

CATALA (JOSE AGUSTIN) ed. Documentos para la historia de la resistencia. Caracas, 1969 in progress.

PETKOFF (TEODORO) Socialismo para Venezuela? Caracas, 1970. pp. 141.

RIVERA OVIEDO (JOSE ELIAS) Historia e ideologia de los democratas cristianos venezolanos. Caracas, [1970]. 1 vol. (unpaged). bibliog.

BURGGRAAFF (WINFIELD J.) The Venezuelan armed forces in politics, 1935-1959. Columbia, Miss., 1972. pp. 241. bibliog.

LOTT (LEO B.) Venezuela and Paraguay: political modernity and tradition in conflict. New York, [1972]. pp. 395. bibliog.

LEVINE (DANIEL H.) Conflict and political change in Venezuela. [Princeton, 1973]. pp. 285. bibliog.

- Population

LOPEZ (JOSE ELISEO) La expansion demografica de Venezuela. Merida, Ven., 1963. pp. 111. bibliog. (Merida. Universidad de los Andes. Instituto de Geografia y de Conservacion de Recursos Naturales. Cuadernos Geograficos. No. 2)

- Public works

  VENEZUELA. Ministerio de Obras Publicas. 1959. Plan nacional de obras publicas: exposicion del ministro de obras publicas Santiago Hernandez Ron a la Camara Venezolana de la Construccion. Caracas, 1959. pp. 21.

  SUCRE FIGARELLA (LEOPOLDO) Las obras publicas y el desarrollo integral. [Caracas, Oficina Central de Informacion, 1965]. pp. 42. (Temas del Desarrollo Economico de Venezuela. 2)

- Social conditions

  QUINTERO (RODOLFO) La cultura del petroleo. Caracas, 1968. pp. 117. bibliog.

  NUÑEZ TENORIO (J.R.) Venezuela, modelo neocolonial: justicia social para ser realmente libres. Caracas, [1969]. pp. 143.

  ABOUHAMAD (JEANNETTE) Los hombres de Venezuela: sus necesidades, sus aspiraciones. Caracas, 1970. pp. 338. bibliog.

VENICE

- Commerce

  OHL (INGO) Die Levante und Indien in der Verkehrspolitik Venedigs, der Engländer und der Holländer, 1580-1623. Kiel, 1972. pp. 145. bibliog. With English summary.

- Commerce - India

  BRULEZ (WILFRID) Venetiaanse handelsbetrekkingen met Perzië en Indië omstreeks 1600. Gent, 1965. pp. 27. (Ghent. Université. Seminaries voor Geschiedenis. Studia Historica Gandensia. 33) (Overdruk uit Orientalia Gandensia, Jaarboek 1, 1964) With French summary.

- Commerce - Iran

  BRULEZ (WILFRID) Venetiaanse handelsbetrekkingen met Perzië en Indië omstreeks 1600. Gent, 1965. pp. 27. (Ghent. Université. Seminaries voor Geschiedenis. Studia Historica Gandensia. 33) (Overdruk uit Orientalia Gandensia, Jaarboek 1, 1964) With French summary.

- Social history

  SOKOLOV (N. P.) Iz istorii sotsial'nykh dvizhenii v Venetsii v pervoi polovine XIV veka. in Issledovaniia po istorii narodnykh dvizhenii v stranakh Zapadnoi Evropy, XIII-XV vv. Gor'kii, 1971. pp. 291.

VERCELLI (PROVINCE)

- History

  VERCELLI (PROVINCE). Amministrazione Provinciale. Ventennale della Resistenza, 1945-1965. [Vercelli, 1968]. pp. 70.

VERNE (JULES)

CHESNEAUX (JEAN) Une lecture politique de Jules Verne. Paris, 1971. pp. 195. bibliog.

CHESNEAUX (JEAN) The political and social ideas of Jules Verne;...translated by Thomas Wikeley. London, [1972]. pp. 224. bibliog.

VERSAILLES, TREATY OF, JUNE 28, 1919 (GERMANY)

GODART (JUSTIN) Les clauses du travail dans le Traité de Versailles, 28 Juin 1919: les décisions de la Conférence de Washington, Novembre 1919. Paris, 1920. pp. 229.

"ŁAD wersalski" w Europie Środkowej: konferencja naukowa w Instytucie Historii Polskiej Akademii Nauk w Warszawie 2-3 grudnia 1969 r. Wrocław, 1971. pp. 167.

ELCOCK (HOWARD JAMES) Portrait of a decision: the Council of Four and the Treaty of Versailles. London, 1972. pp. 386. bibliog.

MIQUEL (PIERRE) La paix de Versailles et l'opinion publique française. Paris, [1972]. pp. 610. bibliog.

VERTICALLY RISING AEROPLANES

SOUTHAMPTON. University. Department of Civil Engineering. Transportation Research Group. V[ertical] T[ake-] O[ff and] L[anding aircraft]: a European study: potential sites and business traffic;...prepared for the Department of Trade and Industry [under the direction of T.E.H. Williams]; final report. London, 1971. 3 vols.(in 1).

VETERINARIANS

- India

  INDIA. Department of Agriculture. Manpower Planning Unit. 1970. Technical manpower for Indian agriculture: an enquiry into demand, supply and organization. [Delhi], 1969 [or rather 1970]. pp. 33.

VETERINARY MEDICINE

- Diagnosis

  CENTO SEMINAR ON VETERINARY INVESTIGATIONAL AND DIAGNOSTIC METHODS, ISTANBUL, 1970. Cento seminar...[held] September 14-18, 1970 [in] Istanbul, Turkey. [Ankara], Central Treaty Organization, 1971. pp. 108.

- Canada - Quebec

  QUEBEC (PROVINCE). Commission Royale d'Enquête sur l'Agriculture au Québec, 1965. La médecine vétérinaire et les produits de médecine vétérinaire au Québec; rapport. [Québec], 1967. pp. 75.

VETLUGIN (A.) ps.

VETLUGIN (A.) pseud. [i.e. Vladimir Il'ich RYNDZIUN] Geroi i voobrazhaemye portrety. Berlin, 1922. pp. 247.

VETO

MURHARD (FRIEDRICH) Das königliche Veto: eine wichtige Aufgabe in der Staatslehre der konstitutionellen Monarchie; Neudruck der Ausgabe Kassel 1832. Aalen, 1970. pp. 344.

VICO (GIAMBATTISTA)

PASINI (DINO) Diritto, società e stato in Vico. Napoli, 1970. pp. 251. (Bari. Università. Facoltà Giuridica. Pubblicazioni. 28)

VAUGHAN (FREDERICK) The political philosophy of Giambattista Vico: an introduction to La scienza nuova. The Hague, 1972. pp. 67. bibliog.

VICOS, (PERU)

DOBYNS (HENRY F.) and others, eds. Peasants, power, and applied social change: Vicos as a model. Beverly Hills, [1971]. pp. 234. bibliog.

VICTIMS OF CRIMES

FATTAH (EZZAT ABDEL) La victime, est-elle coupable?: le rôle de la victime dans le meutre en vue de vol. Montréal, 1971. pp. 259. bibliog.

- Bulgaria

KOCHEV (KOSTADIN V.) Postradaliiat kato obvinitel v nakazatelniia protses. Sofiia, 1971. pp. 111. With French summary.

VICTORIA, Queen of Great Britain and Ireland

WOODHAM-SMITH (CECIL) Queen Victoria: her life and times. London, 1972 in progress.

VICTORIA, AUSTRALIA

- Biography

THOMSON (KATHLEEN) and SERLE (GEOFFREY) compilers. A biographical register of the Victorian parliament, 1859-1900. Canberra, 1972. pp. 238.

- Economic conditions

ROBINSON (ARTHUR) The real calumniator: a reply to Mr. B. Hoare's "Slaying a slander". Melbourne, 1897. pp. 15.

- History

SERLE (GEOFFREY) The rush to be rich: a history of the colony of Victoria, 1883-1889. Carlton, Victoria, 1971. pp. 392. bibliog.

VIENNA

- Executive departments

CZEIKE (FELIX) and CSENDES (PETER) Die Geschichte der Magistratsabteilungen der Stadt Wien, 1902-1970. München, 1971-72. 2 vols. (in 1). bibliog. (Vienna. Amt für Kultur, Schulverwaltung und Sport. Wiener Schriften. Hefte 33-34)

BALTZAREK (FRANZ) Das Steueramt der Stadt Wien, 1526-1760. Wien, 1971. pp. 403. bibliog. (Vienna. Universität. Dissertationen. 58)

- Politics and government

DANNEBERG (ROBERT) The new Vienna. 4th ed. London, 1931. pp. 92.

- Population

SALOMONSON (ANNA FRANCIS ELIZABETH) Enige sociaalpsychologische aspecten van het lage geboortecijfer in Wenen, etc. Dordrecht, [1956]. pp. 162. With German summary.

KAUFMANN (ALBERT) Demographische Struktur und Haushalts- und Familienformen der Wiener Bevölkerung. Wien, 1971. pp. 356. bibliog. (Vienna. Universität. Dissertationen. 51)

VIENNA CONVENTION ON THE LAW OF TREATIES

AGREEMENTS of international organizations and the Vienna Convention on the Law of Treaties; edited by K. Zemanek. Wien, 1971. pp. 268. (Österreichische Zeitschrift für Öffentliches Recht. Supplementa. 1)

SINCLAIR (IAN McTAGGART) The Vienna Convention on the Law of Treaties. Manchester, [1973]. pp. 150. (Manchester. University. Melland Schill Lectures [1972])

VIERECK (GEORGE SYLVESTER)

JOHNSON (NIEL M.) George Sylvester Viereck: German-American propagandist. Urbana, [1972]. pp. 282. bibliog.

VIETNAM

- Bibliography

CHEN (JOHN HSÜEH-MING) compiler. Vietnam: a comprehensive bibliography. Metuchen, 1973. pp. 314. bibliog.

- Civilization

MUS (PAUL) Hô Chi Minh, le Vietnam, l'Asie: textes rassemblés et mis au point par Annie Nguyen Nguyet Hô. Paris, [1971]. pp. 253.

- Description and travel

VYSOTSKII (S.A.) and GLAZUNOV (I.S.) Zemlia nepokorennykh: v'etnamskii reportazh. Moskva, 1970. pp. 112.

- Economic conditions

KOLB (ALBERT) East Asia: China, Japan, Korea, Vietnam: geography of a cultural region;... translated by C.A.M. Sym. London, 1971. pp. 591. bibliog. Map in end pocket.

LAVALLEE (LEON) Problèmes économiques de la République Démocratique du Viet Nam. Paris, 1971. 2 vols. (in 1). bibliog. (Centre d'Etudes et de Recherches Marxistes. Cahiers. No. 94)

- Economic history

KHATUNTSEV (VASILII MIKHAILOVICH) Ekonomika i finansy Demokraticheskoi Respubliki V'etnam. Leningrad, 1972. pp. 160. bibliog.

- Economic policy

LAVALLEE (LEON) Problèmes économiques de la République Démocratique du Viet Nam. Paris, 1971. 2 vols. (in 1). bibliog. (Centre d'Etudes et de Recherches Marxistes. Cahiers. No. 94)

VAN DYKE (JON M.) North Vietnam's strategy for survival. Palo Alto, [1972]. pp. 336.

- Foreign relations

CAIRNS (JAMES FORD) The eagle and the lotus: Western intervention in Vietnam, 1847-1971. rev. ed. Melbourne, 1971. pp. 252.

HUYEN (N. KHAC) Vision accomplished?: the enigma of Ho Chi Minh. New York, 1971. pp. 377. bibliog.

LAMB (HELEN B.) Vietnam's will to live: resistance to foreign aggression from early times through the nineteenth century. New York, [1972]. pp. 344.

SHEPPARD (BARRY) and ROBERTS (DICK) The meaning of the Vietnam accords: Nixon's world strategy, the role of Moscow and Peking, prospects for the Vietnamese revolution. New York, [1973]. pp. 15.

- Foreign relations - China

O'NEILL (ROBERT J.) Peking-Hanoi relations in 1970. Canberra, 1971. pp. 30. (Australian National University. Contemporary China Centre. Contemporary China Papers. No.2)

- Foreign relations - France

> FRANCE. Ministère des Affaires Etrangères. Services d'Information et de Presse. 1971. La France et le Vietnam: recueil des principales déclarations françaises, août 1963- novembre 1971. [Paris?, 1971]. pp. 123.

- Foreign relations - Germany

> AFRO-ASIAN SOLIDARITY COMMITTEE IN THE GERMAN DEMOCRATIC REPUBLIC. Vietnam Committee. West Germany and the US war in Vietnam: a current documentation. n.p., [1965]. pp. 14.

- Foreign relations - Germany, Eastern

> FOR closer ties of solidarity with Vietnam. Dresden, [1972]. pp. 15.

- Foreign relations - Russia

> USSR-Vietnam: a lasting solidarity. Moscow, 1972. pp. 100.

- Foreign relations - Sweden

> SWEDEN. Utrikesdepartementet. Aktstycken. Ny Serie. II. 19. Sverige och Vietnamfrågan: anföranden och uttalanden. Stockholm, 1968. pp. 123.

- Foreign relations - United States

> FITZGERALD (FRANCES) Fire in the lake: the Vietnamese and the Americans in Vietnam. Boston, [1972]. pp. 491. bibliog.

> STAVINS (RALPH) and others. Washington plans an aggressive war: (a documented account of the United States adventure in Indochina). London, 1972. pp. 374.

> UNGAR (SANFORD J.) The Papers and the papers: an account of the legal and political battle over the Pentagon Papers. New York, 1972. pp. 319.

> CHOMSKY (NOAM) The backroom boys. [London], 1973. pp. 222.

- History

> BROETEL (DIETER) Französischer Imperialismus in Vietnam: die koloniale Expansion und die Errichtung des Protektorates Annam-Tongking, 1880-1885. Zürich, [1971]. pp. 525. bibliog.

> LAMB (HELEN B.) Vietnam's will to live: resistance to foreign aggression from early times through the nineteenth century. New York, [1972]. pp. 344.

> BUTTINGER (JOSEPH) A dragon defiant: a short history of Vietnam. Newton Abbot, [1973]. pp. 147. bibliog.

- Military policy

> VAN DYKE (JON M.) North Vietnam's strategy for survival. Palo Alto, [1972]. pp. 336.

- Politics and government

> HEALY (ALLAN MICHAEL) Why Vietnam? [Wollongong, 1970]. fo. 10.

> NGUYEN-KHAC-VIEN. Expériences vietnamiennes. Paris, [1970]. pp. 270.

> HUYEN (N. KHAC) Vision accomplished?: the enigma of Ho Chi Minh. New York, 1971. pp. 377. bibliog.

> WOODSIDE (ALEXANDER BARTON) Vietnam and the Chinese model: a comparative study of Nguyễn and Ch'ing civil government in the first half of the nineteenth century. Cambridge, Mass., 1971. pp. 358. bibliog. (Harvard University. East Asian Research Center. Harvard East Asian Series. 52)

> FITZGERALD (FRANCES) Fire in the lake: the Vietnamese and the Americans in Vietnam. Boston, [1972]. pp. 491. bibliog.

> FOR closer ties of solidarity with Vietnam. Dresden, [1972]. pp. 15.

> WARBEY (WILLIAM NOBLE) Ho Chi Minh and the struggle for an independent Vietnam. London, [1972]. pp. 274.

> GOODMAN (ALLAN E.) Politics in war: the bases of political community in South Vietnam. Cambridge, Mass., 1973. pp. 313.

> SHEPPARD (BARRY) and ROBERTS (DICK) The meaning of the Vietnam accords: Nixon's world strategy, the role of Moscow and Peking, prospects for the Vietnamese revolution. New York, [1973]. pp. 15.

VIETNAMESE IN THAILAND

> POOLE (PETER A.) The Vietnamese in Thailand: a historical perspective. Ithaca, N.Y., 1970. pp. 180. bibliog.

VIETNAMESE WARS, 1945-

> The VIETNAM war and international law: [a collection of articles and documents reprinted from various sources]...; edited by Richard A. Falk. Princeton, N.J., 1968-72. 3 vols.

> BOURNE (PETER G.) ed. The psychology and physiology of stress: with reference to special studies of the Viet Nam war. New York, 1969. pp. 242. bibliogs.

> WEILER (HEINRICH) Vietnam: eine völkerrechtliche Analyse des amerikanischen Krieges und seiner Vorgeschichte. Frankenthal, 1969. pp. 362. bibliog.

> CAIRNS (JAMES FORD) The eagle and the lotus: Western intervention in Vietnam, 1847-1971. rev. ed. Melbourne, 1971. pp. 252.

> CAMBODIA: the widening war in Indochina; edited by Jonathan S. Grant [and others]. New York, 1971. pp. 355. bibliog.

> CHOMSKY (NOAM) The backroom boys. [London], 1973. pp. 222.

> FONER (PHILIP SHELDON) American labor and the Indochina War. New York, 1971. pp. 126.

> FRANKLIN (BRUCE) From the movement toward revolution. New York, [1971]. pp. 170.

> MANELI (MIECZYSŁAW) War of the vanquished;...translated from the Polish by Maria de Gorgey. New York, [1971]. pp. 228.

> POLNER (MURRAY) No victory parades: the return of the Vietnam veteran. London, 1971. pp. 169. bibliog.

> STANDARD (WILLIAM L.) Aggression: our Asian disaster. New York, [1971]. pp. 227. bibliog.

> STONE (ISIDOR F.) Polemics and prophecies, 1967-1970; [articles and essays from his Weekly and the New York Review of Books]. New York, [1971]. pp. 497.

> CHOMSKY (NOAM) Problems of knowledge and freedom. London, 1972. pp. 95. (Cambridge. University. Trinity College. Bertrand Russell Memorial Lectures. 1971)

VIETNAMESE WARS, 1945- (Cont'd.)

ETHICS and world politics: four perspectives; Ernest W. Lefever, editor. Baltimore, [1972]. pp. 99. bibliog. (Johns Hopkins University. School of Advanced International Studies. Christian A. Herter Lecture Series. 1971)

FRIEDMAN (LEON) and NEUBORNE (BURT) Unquestioning obedience to the president: the ACLU case against the illegal war in Vietnam. New York, [1972]. pp. 284.

HARVEST of death: chemical warfare in Vietnam and Cambodia; [by] J.B. Neilands [and others]. New York, [1972]. pp. 304. bibliog.

INDOCHINA in conflict: a political assessment; [papers of a seminar held by the Vietnam, Laos and Cambodia panel of the Southeast Asia Development Advisory Group in May 1971; edited by] Joseph J. Zasloff and Allan E. Goodman. Lexington, Mass., [1972]. pp. 227.

LIVEN' (VALENTINA ANDREEVNA) Voina vo V'etname i vnutripoliticheskaia bor'ba v SShA. Kiev, 1972. pp. 112.

MIKHEEV (IURII IAKOVLEVICH) Amerikantsy v Indokitae: kritika protivopravnoi doktriny i politiki SShA. Moskva, 1972. pp. 248.

MOORE (JOHN NORTON) Law and the Indo-China war. Princeton, 1972. pp. 794. bibliog.

MUS (PAUL) and McALISTER (JOHN T.) Les Viêtnamiens et leur révolution; l'établissement de l'édition ainsi que les traductions sont dûs à Serge Thion. Paris, [1972]. pp. 318.

RACE (JEFFREY) War comes to Long An: revolutionary conflict in a Vietnamese province. Berkeley, Calif., 1972. pp. 299.

SHAPIRO (MARTIN) ed. The Pentagon papers and the courts: a study in foreign policy-making and freedom of the press. San Francisco, [1972]. pp. 131.

SHCHEDROV (IVAN MIKHAILOVICH) The Vietnam story; V'etnamskii reportazh. Moscow, 1972. pp. 238. In Russian and English.

STAVINS (RALPH) and others. Washington plans an aggressive war: (a documented account of the United States adventure in Indochina). London, 1972. pp. 374.

UNGAR (SANFORD J.) The Papers and the papers: an account of the legal and political battle over the Pentagon Papers. New York, 1972. pp. 319.

VAN DYKE (JON M.) North Vietnam's strategy for survival. Palo Alto, [1972]. pp. 336.

WARBEY (WILLIAM NOBLE) Ho Chi Minh and the struggle for an independent Vietnam. London, [1972]. pp. 274.

ZHUKOV (GEORGII ALEKSANDROVICH) and SHARAPOV (VIKTOR VASIL'EVICH) Narod na voine: v'etnamskie dnevniki. Moskva, 1972. pp. 359.

CALDWELL (MALCOLM) and TAN (LEK) Cambodia in the Southeast Asia war. New York, [1973]. pp. 450.

CHOMSKY (NOAM) For reasons of state. [London], 1973. pp. 220.

FIFIELD (RUSSELL HUNT) Americans in Southeast Asia: the roots of commitment. New York, [1973]. pp. 417. bibliog.

NORODOM SIHANOUK VARMAN, Head of State of Cambodia. My war with the CIA: Cambodia's fight for survival; (as related to Wilfred Burchett). Harmondsworth, 1973. pp. 272.

SHEPPARD (BARRY) and ROBERTS (DICK) The meaning of the Vietnam accords: Nixon's world strategy, the role of Moscow and Peking, prospects for the Vietnamese revolution. New York, [1973]. pp. 15.

- Atrocities

CALLEY (WILLIAM L.) Body count: Lieutenant Calley's story as told to John Sack. London, 1971. pp. 181.

HERSH (SEYMOUR M.) Cover-up: (the Army's secret investigation of the massacre at My Lai 4). New York, [1972]. pp. 305.

SARTRE (JEAN PAUL) Situations, VIII: autour de 68. [Paris, 1972]. pp. 478.

VIETNAM VETERANS AGAINST THE WAR. The winter soldier investigation: an enquiry into American war crimes. [Boston, 1972]. pp. 188.

McCARTHY (MARY THERESE) Medina; [her report of the trial of Captain Ernest L. Medina, U.S. Army]. London, 1973. pp. 92.

- Bibliography

CHEN (JOHN HSÜEH-MING) compiler. Vietnam: a comprehensive bibliography. Metuchen, 1973. pp. 314. bibliog.

- Conscientious objectors

EMERICK (KENNETH FRED) War resisters, Canada, the world of the American military-political refugees. Knox, Pa., [1972]. pp. 320. bibliog.

- Destruction and pillage

WEISBERG (BARRY) Ecocide in Indochina: the ecology of war. San Francisco, [1970]. pp. 241. bibliog.

- Diplomatic history

POOLE (PETER A.) The expansion of the Vietnam war into Cambodia: action and response by the governments of North Vietnam, South Vietnam, Cambodia, and the United States. Athens, Ohio, 1970. fo. 59. (Ohio University. Center for International Studies. Papers in International Studies. Southeast Asia Series. No. 17)

- Personal narratives, American

HAMILTON-PATERSON (JAMES) A very personal war: the story of Cornelius Hawkridge. London, [1971]. pp. 284.

VIETNAM VETERANS AGAINST THE WAR. The winter soldier investigation: an enquiry into American war crimes. [Boston, 1972]. pp. 188.

- Pictorial works

The PEOPLE of Vietnam will triumph! the U.S. aggressors will be defeated!: a collection of Chinese art works in support of the Vietnamese people's struggle. Peking, 1966. pp. 95.

GRIFFITHS (PHILIP JONES) Vietnam Inc.: [photographs]. New York, 1971. pp. 223.

- Public opinion

MUELLER (JOHN E.) War, presidents and public opinion. New York, [1973]. pp. 300. bibliog.

VILLA (FRANCISCO)

CASASOLA (GUSTAVO) Biografia ilustrada del general Francisco Villa, 1878-1966. Mexico, 1969 [or rather 1970]. pp. 146.

VILLAGE COMMUNITIES

MAINE (Sir HENRY SUMNER) Village communities in the East and West: six lectures delivered at Oxford;...third edition to which are added other lectures, addresses and essays. London, 1876. pp. 413.

COLLOQUES D'ALBIEZ-LE-VIEUX, 1e-2e, 1969-1970. Villages en développement; contribution à une sociologie villageoise; actes...publiés sous la direction de Henri Desroche et Placide Rambaud. Paris, 1971. pp. 411. bibliogs. (Paris. Ecole Pratique des Hautes Etudes. Section des Sciences Economiques et Sociales. Recherches Coopératives. [New Series?] 5.)

LAPTIN (PETR FROLOVICH) Obshchina v russkoi istoriografii poslednei treti XIX - nachala XX v. Kiev, 1971. pp. 299.

- China

PASTERNAK (BURTON) Kinship and community in two Chinese villages. Stanford, [1972]. pp. 174. bibliog.

- Germany

PEESCH (REINHARD) Die Fischerkommünen auf Rügen und Hiddensee, etc. Berlin, 1961. pp. 367. (Deutsche Akademie der Wissenschaften zu Berlin. Institut für Deutsche Volkskunde. Band 28)

- India

PRASAD (DEVI) ed. Gramdan; the land revolution of India. London, [1970?]. pp. 49. bibliog.

OOMMEN (T.K.) Charisma, stability and change: an analysis of Bhoodan-Gramdan movement in India. New Delhi, 1972. pp. 186.

- India - Bombay

GODWIN (CLEMENT J.) Change and continuity: a study of two Christian village communities in suburban Bombay. Bombay, [1972]. pp. 248. bibliog.

- Israel

GOLDBERG (HARVEY E.) Cave dwellers and citrus growers: a Jewish community in Libya and Israel. Cambridge, 1972. pp. 208. bibliog.

- Jordan

ANTOUN (RICHARD T.) Arab village: a social structural study of a trans-Jordanian peasant community. Bloomington, 1972. pp. 182. bibliog.

- Korea

BRANDT (VINCENT S.R.) A Korean village between farm and sea. Cambridge, Mass., 1971. pp. 252. bibliog. (Harvard University. East Asian Research Center. Harvard East Asian Series. 65)

- Libya

GOLDBERG (HARVEY E.) Cave dwellers and citrus growers: a Jewish community in Libya and Israel. Cambridge, 1972. pp. 208. bibliog.

- Nigeria

OTTENBERG (SIMON) Leadership and authority in an African society: the Afikpo village-group. Seattle, [1971]. pp. 336. bibliog. (American Ethnological Society. Monographs. 52)

- Tanzania

LUTTRELL (WILLIAM L.) Villagization, co-operative production, and rural cadres: strategies and tactics in Tanzanian socialist rural development. [Dar es Salaam, 1971]. pp. 81. bibliog. (Dar es Salaam. University. Economic Research Bureau. ERB Papers. 71.11)

- Turkey

INTERNATIONAL LABOUR OFFICE. Regular Programme of Technical Assistance. [Turkey] R.29. Report to the government of Turkey on the development of forest villages. (ILO/OTA/Turkey/R.29). Geneva, 1969. pp. 96.

- United States

LEONARD (OLEN EARL) The role of the land grant in the social organization and social processes of a Spanish-American village in New Mexico. Albuquerque, [1970]. pp. 198. bibliog.

- Yugoslavia

HALPERN (JOEL MARTIN) and HALPERN (BARBARA KEREWSKY) A Serbian village in historical perspective. New York, [1972]. pp. 152. bibliog.

VILLAGES

NADEL' (SEMEN NAUMOVICH) Sotsial'naia struktura sovremennoi kapitalisticheskoi derevni. Moskva, 1970. pp. 192.

- Austria

WIRTSCHAFTS- und Sozialforschung in Tirol und Vorarlberg: Festschrift für Univ.-Prof. DDr. Ferdinand Ulmer...; herausgegeben und bearbeitet von Christoph Pan und Gerhard Marinell. Wien, [1972]. pp. 587. bibliog.

- China

McKNIGHT (BRIAN E.) Village and bureaucracy in southern Sung China. Chicago, 1971. pp. 219. bibliog.

- Cyprus

LOIZOS (PETER) Social organizations and political change in a Cypriot village; [Ph.D. (London) thesis]. 1972. 1 vol. (various foliations) bibliog. Typescript: unpublished. This thesis is the property of London University and may not be removed from the Library.

- Dahomey

PETERLI (RITA) Die Kultur eines Bariba-Dorfes im Norden von Dahome. Basel, 1971. pp. 101. (Geographische-Ethnologische Gesellschaft and Basel. Museum für Völkerkunde und Schweizerisches Museum für Volkskunde. Basler Beiträge zur Ethnologie. Band 11)

- France

DION-SALITOT (MICHELE) and DION (MICHEL) La crise d'une société villageoise: "les survivanciers": les paysans de Jura français, 1800-1970. Paris, [1973]. pp. 399. bibliog.

- Germany

DYRENFURTH (GERTRUD) Ein schlesisches Dorf und Rittergut: Geschichte und soziale Verfassung. Leipzig, 1906. pp. 178.

JAENICHEN (HANS) Beiträge zur Wirtschaftsgeschichte des schwäbischen Dorfes. Stuttgart, 1970. pp. 222. bibliog. (Kommission für Geschichtliche Landeskunde in Baden-Württemberg. Veröffentlichungen. Reihe B: Forschungen. 60. Band)

- Greece

MENDRAS (HENRI) and others. Six villages d'Epire: problèmes de développement socio-économique. [Paris], 1961. pp. 92. (United Nations Educational Scientific and Cultural Organization. Mission Reports. 11) With summaries in English and Spanish.

VILLAGES (Cont'd.)

- India

VARSHNEYA (J.K.) and MATHUR (O.N.) compilers. Handbook of rural housing and village planning. Delhi, Manager of Publications, 1968. pp. 110.

SOMJEE (ABDULKARIM HUSSEINBHOY) Democracy and political change in village India: a case study. New Delhi, 1971. pp. 189. bibliog.

BERREMAN (GERALD D.) Hindus of the Himalayas: ethnography and change. 2nd ed. Berkeley, 1972. pp. 440.

LEAF (MURRAY J.) Information and behavior in a Sikh village: social organization reconsidered. Berkeley, [1972]. pp. 296. bibliog.

- India - Delhi

BISWAS (P.C.) Socio-economic survey of Budhpur, a Delhi village. [Delhi, 1967]. pp. 59. (India. Census, 1961. Vol. 1. Part VI. Monograph Series. No. 6)

- India - Mysore

PARVATHAMMA (C.) Politics and religion: a study of historical interaction between socio-political relationships in a Mysore village). New Delhi, 1971. pp. 276. bibliog.

EPSTEIN (TRUDE SCARLETT) South India: yesterday, today and tomorrow; Mysore villages revisited. London, 1973. pp. 273. bibliog.

- Ireland (Republic)

BRODY (HUGH) Inishkillane: change and decline in the west of Ireland. London, 1973. pp. 226. bibliog.

- Israel

BALDWIN (ELAINE) Differentiation and co-operation in an Israeli veteran moshav. Manchester, [1972]. pp. 240. bibliog.

- Italy

BRØGGER (JAN) Montevarese: a study of peasant society and culture in southern Italy. Bergen, [1971]. pp. 160. bibliog. (Oslo. Universitet. Etnografiske Museum. Bulletins. No. 13)

- Mexico

STEININGER (GEORGE RUSSELL) and VAN DE VELDE (PAUL) Three dollars a year:...being the story of San Pablo Cuatro Venados, a typical Zapotecan Indian village, etc. New York, 1935; Detroit, 1971. pp. 121.

- Nepal

CAPLAN (A. PATRICIA) Priests and cobblers: a study of social change in a Hindu village in western Nepal. London, 1972. pp. 103. bibliog.

- Pakistan

RAZA (MUHAMMAD RAFIQUE) Two Pakistani villages: a study in social stratification. Lahore, 1969. pp. 104. bibliog.

- Russia

KONCHUKOV (NIKOLAI PAVLOVICH) Planirovka sel'skikh naselennykh mest. Moskva, 1972. pp. 222. bibliog.

VYDYBORETS (ANATOLII VIKTOROVICH) and ROGOZHIN (GEORGII NIKOLAEVICH) Perspektivy razvitiia sel'skikh naselennykh punktov. Moskva, 1973. pp. 152.

- Russia - Baltic States

SEL'SKIE poseleniia Pribaltiki, XIII-XX vv. Moskva, 1971. pp. 251.

- Samoa

LOCKWOOD (BRIAN) Economic statistics of Samoan village households;...a supplement to Samoan village economy, etc. Canberra, 1970. fo. 46. bibliog.

LOCKWOOD (BRIAN) Samoan village economy. Melbourne, 1971. pp. 232. bibliog.

- Spain

FRASER (RONALD) The pueblo: a mountain village on the Costa del Sol. London, 1973. pp. 285.

- Turkey

HINDERINK (JAN) and KIRAY (MÜBECCEL B.) Social stratification as an obstacle to development: a study of four Turkish villages. New York, 1970. pp. 248.

KANDIYOTI (DENISE) A social psychological study of a Turkish village; [Ph. D. (London) thesis]. 1971. fo. 302. bibliog. Typescript: unpublished. This thesis is the property of London University and may not be removed from the Library.

PLANCK (ULRICH) Die ländliche Türkei: Soziologie und Entwicklungstendenzen. Frankfurt/Main, [1972]. pp. 309. bibliog. (Zeitschrift für Ausländische Landwirtschaft. Materialsammlungen. Heft 19)

- United Kingdom

AULT (WARREN ORTMAN) Open-field farming in medieval England: a study of village by-laws; [with documents] London, 1972. pp. 183.

- United States

BAILEY (ANTHONY) In the village. London, 1972. pp. 226.

- Yugoslavia

WINNER (IRENE) A Slovenian village: Žerovnica. Providence, R.I., 1971. pp. 267. bibliog.

VILNA UNIVERSITY

SUKIENNICKI (WIKTOR) Legenda i rzeczywistość: wspomnienia i uwagi o dwudziestu latach Uniwersytetu Stefana Batorego w Wilnie. Paryż, 1967. pp. 134. bibliog.

VINOGRADOFF (Sir PAUL)

LAPTIN (PETR FROLOVICH) Obshchina v russkoi istoriografii poslednei treti XIX - nachala XX v. Kiev, 1971. pp. 299.

VINOGRADOV (PAVEL GAVRILOVICH)
See VINOGRADOFF (Sir PAUL)

VIOLENCE

CASTAGNINO (RAUL HECTOR) "Cambio", confrontaciones estudiantiles y violencia. Buenos Aires, [1970]. pp. 175.

NATIONAL OPINION POLLS LIMITED. Report on attitudes towards crime, violence and permissiveness in society; prepared for The Daily Mail. London, 1970. 1 vol. (various foliations).

GERMANY (BUNDESREPUBLIK). Deutscher Bundestag. Wissenschaftliche Dienste. 1971. Wirkungen von Gewaltdarstellungen auf dem Bildschirm: Zusammenhänge zwischen dargestellter Gewalt und aggressiven Verhaltensweisen; [edited by Claus-Peter Gerber]. Bonn, 1971. pp. 76. bibliog. (Materialien. 28)

GREENBERG (EDWARD S.) and others, eds. Black politics: the inevitability of conflict; readings. New York, [1971]. pp. 374.

INTERNATIONAL INSTITUTE FOR STRATEGIC STUDIES. Adelphi Papers. Nos. 82-83. Civil violence and the international system; [by] François Duchêne [and others]. London, 1971. 2 pts.

MILTON S. EISENHOWER SYMPOSIUM, BALTIMORE, 1970. Violence: the crisis of American confidence; [papers presented at the symposium: The United States in the 1970s: perspectives on violence]; edited by Hugh Davis Graham [and others]. Baltimore, [1971]. pp. 180. bibliogs.

NARDIN (TERRY) Violence and the state: a critique of empirical political theory. Beverly Hills, [1971]. pp. 72. bibliog.

BLUMENTHAL (MONICA D.) and others. Justifying violence: attitudes of American men. Ann Arbor, [1972]. pp. 367. bibliog.

FEIERABEND (IVO K.) and others, eds. Anger, violence, and politics: theories and research. Englewood Cliffs, [1972]. pp. 423. bibliogs.

INTERNATIONAL INSTITUTE FOR STRATEGIC STUDIES. Adelphi Papers. No. 85. Political violence in Latin America; by Jack Davis. London, 1972. pp. 35.

PERSPECTIVES on violence; [papers of a symposium on the occasion of the annual meeting of the American College of Psychiatrists in 1971]; edited by Gene Usdin. New York, [1972]. pp. 161. bibliog.

SHORT (JAMES F.) and WOLFGANG (MARVIN EUGENE) eds. Collective violence. Chicago, [1972]. pp. 387.

SWOMLEY (JOHN M.) Liberation ethics. New York, [1972]. pp. 243.

TEITLER (GER) Toepassing van geweld: sociologische essays over geweld, verzet en militaire organisatie. Meppel, [1972]. pp. 164. bibliog.

VAN DEN HAAG (ERNEST) Political violence and civil disobedience. New York, [1972]. pp. 123.

ARENDT (HANNAH) Crises of the Republic. Harmondsworth, 1973. pp. 200.

BANDURA (ALBERT) Aggression: a social learning analysis. Englewood Cliffs, [1973]. pp. 390. bibliog.

CLUTTERBUCK (RICHARD LEWIS) Protest and the urban guerrilla. London, [1973]. pp. 277.

FEAGIN (JOE R.) and HAHN (HARLAN) Ghetto revolts: the politics of violence in American cities. New York, 1973. pp. 338.

GUILLÉN (ABRAHAM) Philosophy of the urban guerrilla: the revolutionary writings of Abraham Guillén; translated and edited with an introduction by Donald C. Hodges. New York, 1973. pp. 305. bibliog.

GUNN (JOHN) Psychiatrist. Violence in human society. Newton Abbot, [1973]. pp. 200.

HIBBS (DOUGLAS A.) Mass political violence: a cross-national causal analysis. New York, [1973]. pp. 253.

- Moral and religious aspects

PINTHUS (EVA I.) Violence: where do we stand?; Quaker testimony against oppression; the faith out of which we speak and act. London, [1971]. pp. 5.

GIRARD (RENE) La violence et le sacré. Paris, [1972]. pp. 453. bibliog.

VIOLENCE IN LITERATURE

DORFMAN (ARIEL) Imaginacion y violencia en America. Santiago de Chile, 1970. pp. 224.

VIOLENCE IN MASS MEDIA

BURNET (MARY) The mass media in a violent world; [based on a symposium on the impact of the representation of violence in the mass media held in Paris, 29 June-7 July 1970]. [Paris], United Nations Educational, Scientific and Cultural Organization, 1971. pp. 44. (Department of Mass Communication. Reports and Papers on Mass Communication. No. 63)

VIOLENCE IN TELEVISION

GERHARDT (ULF DIETMAR) Der Kriminalfilm im Fernsehen: eine systematische Inhaltsanalyse von 50 Kriminalfernsehfilmen im Zweiten Deutschen Fernsehen... 1968. [Clausthal-Zellerfeld, imprint], 1971. pp. 208. bibliog.

SHAW (IRENE S.) and NEWELL (DAVID S.) Violence on television: programme content and viewer perception; (a BBC Audience Research Department report). London, 1972. pp. 220.

VIRGIN ISLANDS

LEWIS (GORDON K.) The Virgin Islands: a Caribbean Lilliput. Evanston, 1972. pp. 382.

VIRGIN ISLANDS
See also BRITISH VIRGIN ISLANDS

- Description and travel

TAYLOR (CHARLES EDWIN) Leaflets from the Danish West Indies: descriptive of the social, political, and commercial conditions of these islands;...with a portrait of the author and a biographical sketch written by Ph. Linet. London, 1888; Westport, Conn., 1970. pp. 208.

- History

TAYLOR (CHARLES EDWIN) Leaflets from the Danish West Indies: descriptive of the social, political, and commercial conditions of these islands;...with a portrait of the author and a biographical sketch written by Ph. Linet. London, 1888; Westport, Conn., 1970. pp. 208.

VIRGINIA

- Constitution

VIRGINIA. Commission on Constitutional Revision. 1969. The constitution of Virginia; report, etc.; [Albertis S. Harrison, chairman]. [Richmond], 1969. pp. 542. bibliog.

- Politics and government

MADDEX (JACK P.) The Virginia Conservatives, 1867-1879: a study in Reconstruction politics. Chapel Hill, N.C., [1970]. pp. 328. bibliog.

VISHNIAKOVA-AKIMOVA (VERA VLADIMIROVNA)

VISHNIAKOVA-AKIMOVA (VERA VLADIMIROVNA) Two years in revolutionary China, 1925-1927;... translated by Stephen I. Levine. Cambridge, Mass., 1971. pp. 352. (Harvard University. East Asian Research Center. Harvard East Asian Monographs. 40)

VISIGOTHS

KING (PAUL DAVID) Law and society in the Visigothic kingdom. Cambridge, 1972. pp. 318. bibliog.

VISITING HOUSEKEEPERS
See HOME HELPS

VISION

BESANT (ANNIE) Eyes and ears: six chats on seeing and hearing. London, 1882. pp. 24.

VISUAL EDUCATION

GEORGIN (B.) L'enseignement de l'art cinématographique aux différents niveaux scolaires et perspectives d'un enseignement visuel en dehors du cinéma: rapport...à la table ronde de La Mendola...17, 18 et 19 août 1962. Paris, 1962. pp. 47.

VISUAL PERCEPTION

KOEHLER (WOLFGANG) and WALLACH (HANS) Figural after-effects: an investigation of visual processes. [Philadelphia], 1959. pp. 357. bibliog. (Reprinted from Proceedings of the American Philosophical Society, vol. 88, no. 4, 1944).

VITAL STATISTICS

CENTO SYMPOSIUM ON DEMOGRAPHIC STATISTICS, KARACHI, 1968. Proceedings of a symposium held in Karachi, West Pakistan, November 5-12, 1968. [Ankara], Central Treaty Organization, 1970. pp. 331.

PRESSAT (ROLAND) Démographie statistique. [Paris], 1972. pp. 194.

VITICULTURE

- France

NAPO (FELIX) 1907: la révolte des vignerons. Toulouse, [1971]. pp. 279. bibliog.

VITTE (SERGEI IUL'EVICH) Graf

MEHLINGER (HOWARD D.) and THOMPSON (JOHN M.) Count Witte and the Tsarist government in the 1905 revolution. Bloomington, Ind., [1972]. pp. 434. bibliog.

VIVEKANANDA, Swami, pseud.

ARORA (V.K.) The social and political philosophy of Swami Vivekananda. Calcutta, 1968. pp. 134. bibliog.

VIVIEN DE GOUBERT (ALEXANDRE FRANÇOIS AUGUSTE)

PIROTTE (OLIVIER) Alexandre-François-Auguste Vivien de Goubert, 1799-1854: contribution à l'étude d'un libéral autoritaire. Paris, 1972. pp. 505. bibliog.

VIVISECTION

NETHERLANDS. Centrale Raad voor de Volksgezondheid. 1968. Advies inzake het voorontwerp van een wet op de dierproeven. 's-Gravenhage, 1968. pp. 43. (Netherlands. Ministerie van Sociale Zaken. Verslagen en Mededelingen betreffende de Volksgezondheid. 1968. 25)

VLADIMIR I., Saint, Grand Duke of Kiev

KARTASHEV (A.V.) Sv. Velikii Kniaz' Vladimir: otets russkoi kul'tury. Paris, [1938?]. pp. 24.

VLADIMIR (OBLAST')

- Social life and customs

TRADITSIONNYI fol'klor Vladimirskoi derevni: v zapisiakh, 1963-1969 gg. Moskva, 1972. pp. 215.

VLASOV (ANDREI ANDREEVICH)

ARONSON (GREGOR) Pravda o vlasovtsakh: problemy novoi emigratsii. N'iu Iork, 1949. pp. 95. Collected articles.

SHATOV (MIKHAIL VASIL'EVICH) compiler. Materialy i dokumenty Osvoboditel'nogo Dvizheniia Narodov Rossii v gody Vtoroi mirovoi voiny, 1941-1965; Materials and documents of the Liberation Movement of the Peoples of Russia in World War II. N'iu Iork, 1966. pp. 176. (Russkaia Osvoboditel'naia Armiia. Arkhiv v N'iu Iorke. Trudy. t.2). Introduction and 2 documents in English.

VO NGUYEN GIAP

O'NEILL (ROBERT J.) General Giap: politician and strategist. Melbourne, 1969. pp. 219. bibliog.

VOCATIONAL EDUCATION

UNITED NATIONS EDUCATIONAL, SCIENTIFIC AND CULTURAL ORGANIZATION. 1964. Technical and vocational education and training: recommendations by Unesco and the International Labour Organisation. Paris, 1964. pp. 36.

MAGER (ROBERT F.) and BEACH (KENNETH M.) Developing vocational instruction. Palo Alto, [1967]. pp. 83. bibliog.

- Bibliography

UNITED NATIONS EDUCATIONAL, SCIENTIFIC AND CULTURAL ORGANIZATION. 1959. An international bibliography of technical and vocational education. [Paris, 1959]. pp. 72. (Educational Studies and Documents. No. 31)

- Arab countries

ARAB STATES SEMINAR ON THE ORGANISATION OF VOCATIONAL TRAINING, CAIRO, 1970. Report on the...seminar...[held in] Cairo, 23-29 March 1970. (ILO/INT/R.22). Cairo, League of Arab States, 1970. pp. 44.

- Asia

ASIAN REGIONAL EXPERT MEETING ON VOCATIONAL TRAINING PLANNING, SYDNEY, 1968. Report on the...Meeting...Sydney, 2-20 December 1968. (ILO/TAP/AFE/R.16). Geneva, International Labour Office, 1969. pp. 43.

ONE WORLD ONLY, TOKYO, 1971. Employment and vocational training in an expanding society. Tokyo, [1972?]. pp. 210. (Friedrich-Ebert-Stiftung. Asian Labour Institute. Reports. 6)

- Botswana

MARTIN (ANTHONY) Report on the brigades in Botswana. [Gaborone, 1970?]. pp. 98.

- Canada - Ontario

FORSYTH (G. R.) and NININGER (J. R.) Expanding employability in Ontario: an assessment of the federal-provincial program for training and upgrading the skills of the unemployed and its implications for governments, business, and labour. Toronto, Ontario Economic Council, 1966. pp. 68.

- Denmark

KIIL (PER) Adult vocational training. Copenhagen, 1969. pp. 22. (Social Conditions in Denmark. 8)

- European Economic Community countries

COLLOQUE SUR LA FORMATION PROFESSIONNELLE, BRUXELLES, 1964. Documents du colloque sur la formation professionnelle, Bruxelles, 16-20 novembre 1964. [Brussels, 1966]. pp. 436.

- Germany

GERMANY (BUNDESREPUBLIK). Statistisches Bundesamt. 1970. Ausbildung und berufliche Fortbildung: Ergebnisse des Mikrozensus. Stuttgart, 1970. pp. 45. (Bevölkerung und Kultur. Reihe 6. Erwerbstätigkeit. Sonderbeiträge)

GERMANY (BUNDESREPUBLIK). Statistisches Bundesamt. Bevölkerung und Kultur. Reihe 10. Bildungswesen. 2. Berufsbildende Schulen, 1957 bis 1962. Wiesbaden, [1970]. pp. 238.

SCHULTE (HANS) Der Jugendliche ohne Ausbildungsvertrag in der Berufsschule: bisherige Konzeptionen in der beruflichen Teilzeitschule, etc. Hamburg, 1972. 1 vol. (various pagings). bibliog.

- Greece

INTERNATIONAL LABOUR OFFICE. Development Programme: Technical Assistance Sector. [Greece]. R.22. Rapport au gouvernement de la Grèce sur la formation professionnelle des adultes. (OIT/TAP/Grèce/R.22). Genève, 1971. pp. 31.

- Ivory Coast

INTERNATIONAL LABOUR OFFICE. Development Programme: Technical Assistance Sector [Côte-d'Ivoire].R.4. Rapport au gouvernement de la République de la Côte-d'Ivoire sur la planification et l'organisation de la formation professionnelle. (OIT/TAP/Côte-d'Ivoire/R.4). Genève, 1969. pp. 145.

- Japan

JAPAN. Vocational Training Bureau. 1961. Present situation of vocational training in Japan. [Tokyo], 1961. pp. 20.

JAPAN. Vocational Training Bureau. 1965. Vocational training in Japan. rev. ed. [Tokyo, 1965]. pp. 36.

- Norway

NORWAY. Komitéen for Internasjonale Sosialpolitiske Saker. 1956. Vocational training in Norway: a survey; by Gunnar Mortensen and Sven Persson. Oslo, 1956. pp. 106.

- Portugal

FUNDO DE DESENVOLVIMENTO DA MÃO-DE-OBRA. Gabinete de Estudos de Politica de Emprego. Programação das acções de formação profissional para o ano de 1970. [Lisboa, 1970]. pp. 21. (Fundo de Desenvolvimento da Mão-de-Obra. Boletim bimestral. Suplementos. N.° 33) With abstracts in French and English.

- Russia - Bibliography

MOVSHOVICH (M.I.) Technical and vocational education in the U.S.S.R: a bibliographical survey. [Paris, 1959]. pp. 53. (United Nations Educational, Scientific and Cultural Organization. Educational Studies and Documents. No. 30)

- Sierra Leone

INTERNATIONAL LABOUR OFFICE. T[rust] F[unds]. [Sierra Leone] R.9. Report to the government of Sierra Leone on the development of vocational training programmes at the YWCA Vocational Institute, Freetown. (ILO/TF/Sierra Leone/R.9). Geneva, 1970. pp. 40.

VOCATIONAL EDUCATION - Underdeveloped areas
See UNDERDEVELOPED AREAS - Vocational education

- United Kingdom

U.K. Department of Employment. 1972. Training for the future: a plan for discussion. [London, 1972]. pp. 80.

LONDON. Greater London Council. Inner London Education Authority. Review of vocational further and higher education; report by the Education Officer, May 1973, (to the governors of area colleges (including specialist colleges), colleges for further education and general and commercial colleges). [London], 1973. pp. 19.

- United States

HAMERMESH (DANIEL S.) Economic aspects of manpower training programs: theory and policy. Lexington, [1971]. pp. 145.

BARSBY (STEVE L.) Cost-benefit analysis and manpower programs. Lexington, Mass., [1972]. pp. 180. bibliog.

- United States - Bibliography

UNITED STATES. Office of Education. 1959. Technical and vocational education in the U.S.A.: a bibliographical survey. [Paris, 1959]. pp. 24. (United Nations Educational, Scientific and Cultural Organization. Educational Studies and Documents. No. 36)

VOCATIONAL GUIDANCE

GINZBERG (ELI) Career guidance: who needs it, who provides it, who can improve it. New York. [1971]. pp. 356. bibliog.

HAYES (JOHN) Occupational perceptions and occupational information: an analysis of the way in which work is perceived before and after employment and its implications for occupational choice. Bromsgrove, [1971]. pp. 65. bibliog.

MOREA (PETER C.) Guidance, selection, and training: ideas and applications. London, 1972. pp. 362. bibliogs.

VOCATIONAL GUIDANCE (Cont'd.)

- Barbados

INTERNATIONAL LABOUR OFFICE. Development Programme: Technical Assistance Sector. [Barbados]. R.6. Report to the government of Barbados on the development of a vocational guidance programme. (ILO/TAP/Barbados/R.6) Geneva, 1968. pp. 16.

- Belgium

BELGIUM. Office National de l'Emploi. 1966. Le guide du jeune travailleur. Bruxelles, 1966. pp. 32.

- Canada

CANADA. Department of Manpower and Immigration. Career outlook: university and community college: administration, social sciences and services. a., 1972/73- Ottawa. [in English and French]

CANADA. Department of Manpower and Immigration. Career outlook: university and community college: health and social services. a., 1972/73- Ottawa. [in English and French]

BRETON (RAYMOND) Social and academic factors in the career decisions of Canadian youth: a study of secondary school students; with the collaboration of John McDonald and Stephen Richer. Ottawa, Information Canada, 1972. pp. 612. bibliog.

- Germany

RUPRECHT (HORST) Arbeitslehre im 9. Schuljahr. [Hannover, 1971]. pp. 100. bibliog. (Niedersaechsische Landeszentrale für Politische Bildung. Schriftenreihe. Beiträge zur politischen Bildung an Volksschulen. 1)

- Hong Kong

HONG KONG. Chinese University. Appointments Service. Career prospects in Hong Kong. Hong Kong, 1971. pp. 213.

- India

INTERNATIONAL LABOUR OFFICE. Development Programme: Technical Assistance Sector. [India] R.31. Report to the government of India on the development of a vocational guidance programme. (ILO/TAP/India/R.31). Geneva, 1970. pp. 56.

- Ireland, (Republic)

DUBLIN. University College. Academic Staff Association. Contemporary developments in university education, VII: [a record of a seminar held in Dun Laoghaire, 18-19 February 1972; edited by Philip Pettit]. [Dublin, 1972]. pp. 66.

- Russia

NAZIMOV (IGOR' NIKOLAEVICH) Proforientatsiia i profotbor v sotsialisticheskom obshchestve. Moskva, 1972. pp. 254.

- Switzerland

[THURGAU (CANTON). Zentralstelle für Weibliche Berufsberatung]. 1952. 30 Jahre Thurgauische Zentralstelle für Weibliche Berufsberatung, 1922-1952. [Frauenfeld], 1952. pp. 26.

- United Kingdom

LONDON. University. Careers Advisory Service. Careers for Graduate Series. Main areas of graduate employment. London, 1971. pp. 45.

ROBERTS (KENNETH) From school to work: a study of the Youth Employment Service. Newton Abbot, [1971]. pp. 168. bibliog.

U.K. Central Youth Employment Executive. 1971. Choosing your career. [London, 1971]. 1 pamphlet (unpaged). (Choice of Careers.1)

FOGELMAN (K.R.) Leaving the sixth form: a selection of opinions. Windsor, 1972. pp. 48.

GRADUATE opportunities, 1974: a guide to opportunities for students at universities and other institutes of higher education; [compiled by University of London Careers Advisory Service]. London, [1973]. pp. 705.

- United Kingdom - Scotland

SCOTLAND. Scottish Education Department. 1968. Guidance in Scottish secondary schools. [Edinburgh], 1968. pp. 24. bibliog.

VOCATIONAL INTERESTS

CAMPBELL (DAVID P.) Handbook for the Strong Vocational Interest Blank. Stanford, 1971. pp. 516. bibliog.

WARD (LEWIS B.) and ATHOS (ANTHONY G.) Student expectations of corporate life: implications for management recruiting. Boston, 1972. pp. 211. bibliog.

- South Africa

GEBER (BERYL ANNE) Occupational aspirations and expectations of South African high school children; [Ph.D. (London) thesis]. 1972. fo. 433. bibliog. Typescript: unpublished. This thesis is the property of London University and may not be removed from the Library.

VOCATIONAL REHABILITATION

TAGGART (ROBERT) The prison of unemployment: manpower programs for offenders. Baltimore, [1972]. pp. 116.

- Africa

REGIONAL SEMINAR AND TRAINING COURSE IN VOCATIONAL REHABILITATION OF THE DISABLED, DENMARK, 1969. Report to participating governments on the ILO Regional Seminar held in Denmark, 14 July to 2 August 1969. (ILO/TAP/AFR/R.11) Geneva, International Labour Office, 1969. pp. 190.

- Denmark

REGIONAL SEMINAR AND TRAINING COURSE IN VOCATIONAL REHABILITATION OF THE DISABLED, DENMARK, 1969. Report to participating governments on the ILO Regional Seminar held in Denmark, 14 July to 2 August 1969. (ILO/TAP/AFR/R.11) Geneva, International Labour Office, 1969. pp. 190.

- Guatemala

INTERNATIONAL LABOUR OFFICE. Regular Programme of Technical Assistance. [Guatemala]. R.15. Informe al gobierno de Guatemala sobre la readaptación profesional. (OIT/OTA/Guatemala/R.15). Ginebra, 1966. pp. iv, 79.

- Iraq

INTERNATIONAL LABOUR OFFICE. Regular Programme of Technical Assistance. [Iraq]. R.12. Report to the government of Iraq on the vocational rehabilitation and employment of the disabled. (ILO/OTA/Iraq/R.12). Geneva, 1966. pp. ii,43. A previous report is shelved at R(O) ILO.IV.Iraq/R.8.

- Malaysia

> INTERNATIONAL LABOUR OFFICE. Development Programme: Technical Assistance Sector. [Malaysia]. R.24. Report to the government of Malaysia on the development of vocational rehabilitation services for the handicapped. (ILO/OTA/Malaysia/R.24). Geneva, 1970. pp. 114.

- Portugal

> NASCIMENTO (FERNANDO DO) A reabilitação profissional e as garantias sociais do trabalhador sinistrado. Lisboa, 1968. pp. 28. (Fundo de Desenvolvimento da Mão-de-Obra. Cadernos. 25) With abstracts in French, English and German.

- Syria

> INTERNATIONAL LABOUR OFFICE. Regular Programme of Technical Assistance. [Syria] R.17. Report to the government of the Syrian Arab Republic on the vocational rehabilitation of the disabled. (ILO/OTA/Syria/R.17). Geneva, 1971. pp. 117.

- United States

> COMMITTEE FOR ECONOMIC DEVELOPMENT. Research and Policy Committee. Statements on National Policy. Training and jobs for the urban poor. New York, 1970 repr. 1971. pp. 78.

> CRADDOCK (GEORGE W.) and others. Social disadvantagement and dependency: a community approach for the reduction of dependency through vocational rehabilitation. Lexington, Mass., [1970]. pp. 138. (Northeastern University. Studies in Rehabilitation. No. 8)

> NELSON (NATHAN) Workshops for the handicapped in the United States: an historical and developmental perspective. Springfield, Ill., [1971]. pp. 466.

VOLGA BASIN

- History - 1917-1921, Revolution

> ZAKHAROV (NIKOLAI STEPANOVICH) Oktiabr'skaia revoliutsiia i sovetskoe stroitel'stvo v Srednem Povolzh'e, oktiabr' 1917 - mart 1918 gg. Kazan', 1970. pp. 115.

- Politics and government

> OBSHCHESTVENNO-politicheskoe dvizhenie i klassovaia bor'ba na Srednei Volge, konets XIX - nachalo XX veka. Kazan', 1972. pp. 166.

VOLTA RIVER

> LAWSON (ROWENA M.) The changing economy of the Lower Volta, 1954-67: a study in the dynamics of rural economic growth. London, 1972. pp. 127. bibliog.

VOLTAIRE (FRANÇOIS MARIE AROUET DE)

> ENLIGHTENMENT historiography: three German studies; [by Günther Pflug and others]. Middletown, Conn., [1971]. pp. 86. (History and Theory: studies in the philosophy of history. Beihefte. 11)

VOLUNTEER WORKERS IN CONSERVATION

> U.K. Countryside Commission. Research Branch. 1972. The use of voluntary labour in the countryside of England and Wales. London, 1972. pp. 37.

VOLUNTEER WORKERS IN HOSPITALS

> VOLUNTEERS in hospitals: a guide for organisers; edited by Jean Finzi [and others]. London, 1971. pp. 123.

VON NEUMANN (JOHN)

> MORISHIMA (MICHIO) Consumption-investment frontier, wage-profit frontier and the Von Neumann growth equilibrium. [London], 1970. fo. 12. (London. University. London School of Economics and Political Science. Department of Economics. Discussion Papers. No. 10)

VORARLBERG

- Economic conditions

> WIRTSCHAFTS- und Sozialforschung in Tirol und Vorarlberg: Festschrift für Univ.-Prof. DDr. Ferdinand Ulmer...; herausgegeben und bearbeitet von Christoph Pan und Gerhard Marinell. Wien, [1972]. pp. 587. bibliog.

VORONEZH (OBLAST')

- Bibliography

> BRUN (E.IA.) and others, compilers. V.I. Lenin i Chernozemnyi Tsentr Rossii: bibliograficheskii ukazatel'; pod redaktsiei E.G. Shuliakovskogo. Voronezh, 1970. pp. 223.

- Economic conditions

> DOLGOPOLOV (KONSTANTIN VASIL'EVICH) and FEDOROVA (EVGENIIA FEDOROVNA) Tsentral'no-Chernozemnyi raion: ekonomiko-geograficheskii ocherk; posobie dlia uchitelei. Moskva, 1971. pp. 167. bibliog.

- Economic history

> GRISHIN (GRIGORII TERENT'EVICH) Ekonomika Voronezhskoi gubernii i ee analiz v trudakh V.I.Lenina. Voronezh, 1971. pp. 207.

VOTERS, REGISTRATION OF

> CANADA. Representation Commissioner. 1968. Report of the Representation Commissioner on methods of registration of electors and absentee voting: made pursuant to section 9 of the Representation Commissioner Act (12 Elizabeth II, Chapter 40). Ottawa, 1968. pp. vi,114.

VOTING

- Belgium

> DELRUELLE-VOSSWINKEL (NICOLE) and others. Le comportement politique des électeurs belges: enquête de sociologie électorale, la rupture de 1965, ses prolongements en 1968. Bruxelles, [1970]. pp. 265. (Brussels. Université Libre. Institut de Sociologie. Etudes de Science Politique)

- Chile

> PETRAS (JAMES) and ZEITLIN (MAURICE) El radicalismo politico de la clase trabajadora chilena. Buenos Aires, [1970]. pp. 103.

- Denmark

> HØGH (ERIK) Vaelgeradfaerd i Danmark, 1849-1901. København, 1972. pp. 660. bibliog. With English summary.

> LOKALSAMFUND og landspolitisering: vaelgeradfaerd og politisk rekruttering i danske kommuner; [by] Lars Bugge Andersen [and others]. København, 1972. 5 vols. bibliog.

VOTING (Cont'd.)

- France

BON (FREDERIC) and MICHELAT (GUY) Attitudes et comportement politiques à Boulogne-Billancourt: enquête par panel, 1965-1967. Paris, 1970. pp. 139. (Fondation Nationale des Sciences Politiques. Travaux et Recherches de Science Politique.12)

- Germany

SCHULTE (WOLFGANG) Struktur und Entwicklung des Parteisystems im Königreich Württemberg: Versuche zu einer quantitativen Analyse der Wahlergebnisse. [Mannheim?], 1970. pp. 170, 63. bibliog.

NASCHOLD (FRIEDER) Wahlprognosen und Wählerverhalten in der BRD. Stuttgart, [1971]. pp. 104. bibliog.

WALLER-ALBRECHT (ULRIKE) Bestimmungsgründe politischer Orientierungen und Verhaltungsweisen in regionalen Subsystemen, dargestellt am Beispiel der rheinland-pfälzischen Landgemeinde Siebeldingen. [Bamberg, imprint], 1971. 1 vol.(various pagings). bibliog.

CONRADT (DAVID P.) The West German party system: an ecological analysis of social structure and voting behavior, 1961-1969. Beverly Hills, [1972]. pp. 55. bibliog.

NEUSUESS-HUNKEL (ERMENHILD) Parteien und Wahlen in Marburg nach 1945. Meisenheim am Glan, 1973. pp. 351. bibliog.

- Greece, Ancient

STAVELEY (EASTLAND STUART) Greek and Roman voting and elections. London, [1972]. pp. 271.

- India

REDDY (G. RAM) and SESHADRI (K.) The voter and panchayati raj: a study of the electoral behaviour during panchayat elections in Warangal district, Andhra Pradesh. Hyderabad, 1972. pp. 113.

- Israel

ARIAN (ALAN) The choosing people: voting behavior in Israel. Cleveland, 1973. pp. 259. bibliog.

- Norway

VALEN (HENRY) and MARTINUSSEN (WILLY) Velgere og politiske frontlinier: stemmegivning og stridsspørsmål, 1957-1969. Oslo, 1972. pp. 366.

- Rome, Ancient

STAVELEY (EASTLAND STUART) Greek and Roman voting and elections. London, [1972]. pp. 271.

- South Africa

LEVER (HENRY) The South African voter: some aspects of voting behaviour with special reference to the general elections of 1966 and 1970. Cape Town, 1972. pp. 221.

- Sweden

LEWIN (LEIF) and others. The Swedish electorate, 1887-1968. Stockholm, [1972]. pp. 293. (Uppsala. Statsvetenskapliga Föreningen. Skrifter. 60)

- United Kingdom

McKENZIE (ROBERT TRELFORD) and SILVER (ALLAN) Angels in marble: working class Conservatives in urban England. London, Heinemann, 1968. pp. xi, 295.

- United States

ALEXANDER (THOMAS B.) and BERINGER (RICHARD E.) The anatomy of the Confederate Congress: a study of the influences of member characteristics on legislative voting behavior, 1861-1865. Nashville, Tenn., 1972. pp. 435. bibliog.

DE VRIES (WALTER) and TARRANCE (V. LANCE) The ticket-splitter: a new force in American politics Grand Rapids, [1972]. pp. 149.

KIMBALL (PENN) The disconnected. New York, 1972. pp. 317.

LEVY (MARK R.) and KRAMER (MICHAEL S.) The ethnic factor: how America's minorities decide elections. New York, [1972]. pp. 255. bibliog.

SHAFFER (WILLIAM R.) Computer simulations of voting behavior. New York, 1972. pp. 164. bibliog.

- Venezuela

ORTIZ C. (LUIS B.) Bases electorales para las elecciones de 1968: compendio estadistico de los principales partidos politicos por municipios. Caracas, 1968. pp. 101. bibliog.

VOTING, ABSENT

CANADA. Representation Commissioner. 1968. Report of the Representation Commissioner on methods of registration of electors and absentee voting: made pursuant to section 9 of the Representation Commissioner Act (12 Elizabeth II, Chapter 40). Ottawa, 1968. pp. vi,114.

VOTING, COMPULSORY

VUTKOVICH (SÁNDOR) Wahlpflicht: politische Studie...; autorisierte Übersetzung aus dem Ungarischen von Emil Kumlik; [reprint of work published in 1906]. [Frankfurt am Main], 1970. pp. 127. bibliog.

VOYAGES AND TRAVELS

FOUGERET DE MONBRON (LOUIS CHARLES) Le cosmopolite; ou, Le citoyen du monde; suivi de La capitale des Gaules; ou, La nouvelle Babylone; introduction et notes par Raymond Trousson. [Bordeaux], 1970. pp. 207. bibliog.

KEELING (WILLIAM) and BONNER (THOMAS) The East India Company journals of Captain William Keeling and Master Thomas Bonner, 1615-1617; edited by Michael Strachan and Boies Penrose. Minneapolis, [1971]. pp. 237. bibliog. Map in end pocket.

VOZNESENSKII (NIKOLAI ALEKSEEVICH)

KOLOTOV (VASILII VASIL'EVICH) and PETROVICHEV (GENNADII ALEKSEEVICH) N.A. Voznesenskii: biograficheskii ocherk. Moskva, 1963. pp. 48.

VRANGEL' (LIUDMILA S) Baronessa

VRANGEL' (LIUDMILA S.) Baronessa. Dalekoe proshloe: otryvki iz rasskazov moei materi; s predisloviem... B. Vysheslavtseva. Parizh, 1934. pp. 125.

VRANGEL' (PETR NIKOLAEVICH) Baron

ANTANTA i Vrangel': sbornik statei. vyp.1. Moskva, 1923. pp. 260,11.

KALININ (IVAN MIKHAILOVICH) Pod znamenem Vrangelia: zametki byvshego voennogo prokurora. Leningrad, 1925. pp. 273.

VRIES

- Economic conditions

DRENTHE (PROVINCE). Drents Economisch Technologisch Instituut. De economische ontwikkeling van de gemeente Vries: een social-economisch bevolkingsonderzoek. Assen, [1961]. pp. 62.

VSEOBSHCHII EVREISKII RABOCHII SOIUZ V LITVE, POL'SHE I ROSSII (BUND)
See BUND

WABASH VALLEY

BARTON (B.K.) The need for land stabilization in the Wabash Valley; [with] Socioeconomic changes in Northeast Baluchistan (Pakistan); [by] Akhtar Husain Siddiqi. Terre Haute, 1972. pp. 56. (Indiana State University. Department of Geography and Geology. Professional Papers. No. 3) Includes dissertation abstracts.

WAGE PAYMENT SYSTEMS

ALMEIDA (MARIA HENRIQUETA DE) Sistemas de remuneração. Lisboa, 1972. pp. 71. (Portugal. Ministerio das Corporações e Previdência Social. Gabinete de Planeamento. Serie Estudos. 9) With abstracts in English, French and German.

- United Kingdom

GREENWOOD (JOHN A.) Wage payment systems in the clothing industry. London, National Economic Development Office, 1972. pp. 39. bibliog.

OFFICE OF MANPOWER ECONOMICS. Incremental payment systems; report. London, H.M.S.O., 1973. pp. 108.

OFFICE OF MANPOWER ECONOMICS. Measured daywork; report. London, H.M.S.O., 1973. pp. 126.

WAGE-PRICE POLICY

JONES (AUBREY) The new inflation: the politics of prices and incomes. London, 1973. pp. 228.

- Canada

CANADA. Prices and Incomes Commission. 1971. Submission to the Standing Senate Committee on National Finance hearings on growth, employment and price stability... May 25, 1971. Ottawa, [1971]. fo.27.

CANADA. Prices and Incomes Commission. 1972. Final report: inflation, unemployment and incomes policy; Rapport final: l'inflation, le chômage et la politique des revenus; (with Summary report). Ottawa, 1972. pp. 135, 56; 139, 67. In English and French.

BERGER (G.A.) Canada's experience with incomes policy, 1969-70; La politique des revenus au Canada, 1969-70; (report prepared for the Prices and Incomes Commission). Ottawa, Information Canada, 1973. pp. 86,91. In English and French.

- United Kingdom

DORFMAN (GERALD ALLEN) Wage politics in Britain, 1945-1967: government vs. the TUC. Ames, 1973. pp. 180. bibliog.

TRADES UNION CONGRESS. The Chequers and Downing Street talks, July to November 1972: report. London, [1973]. pp. 27.

TRADES UNION CONGRESS. Prices and incomes: the case for the unions. London, 1973. pp. 25.

U.K. Parliament. House of Commons. Library. Research Division. Background Papers. No.24. Inflation and incomes policy. rev. ed. [London, 1973]. fo. 23. bibliogs.

- United States

SHALIT (SOL S.) and BEN-ZION (URI) The impact of the wage-price freeze on relative shares: a test of short-run market expectations. Minneapolis, 1972. fo. 27. (Minnesota University. Center for Economic Research. Discussion Papers. No. 24)

WEBER (ARNOLD R.) In pursuit of price stability: the wage-price freeze of 1971. Washington, D.C., [1973]. pp. 137. (Brookings Institution. Studies in Wage-Price Policy)

- Zambia

INTERNATIONAL LABOUR OFFICE. Development Programme: Technical Assistance Sector. [Zambia]. R.5. Report to the government of Zambia on income, wages and prices in Zambia: policy and machinery. (ILO/TAP/Zambia/R.5). Geneva, 1969. pp. 60.

WAGES

ORGANISATION FOR ECONOMIC CO-OPERATION AND DEVELOPMENT. 1965. Wages and labour mobility: a report by a group of independent experts on the relation between changes in wage differentials and the pattern of employment, etc.; [P. de Wolff, chairman]. Paris, 1965. pp. 258. (Economic Studies)

GUPTA (R.D.) b. 1927. Wage flexibility and full employment. Delhi, [1971]. pp. 104.

HIMMELMANN (GERHARD) Lohnbildung durch Kollektivverhandlungen: eine politologische Analyse unter besonderer Berücksichtigung der Strategie und Taktik der Gewerkschaften. Berlin, [1971]. pp. 240. bibliog.

SINHA (PANDAY RAJENDRA NARAIN) Wage determination. London, [1971]. pp. 362. bibliog.

BURTON (JOHN) Economist. Wage inflation. London, 1972. pp. 94. bibliog.

CARTTER (ALLAN MURRAY) and MARSHALL (F. RAY) Labor economics: wages, employment and trade unionism. rev. ed. Homewood, Ill., 1972. pp. 594. bibliogs.

HAHN (FRANK HORACE) The share of wages in the national income: an enquiry into the theory of distribution. London, [1972]. pp. 183. (London. University. London School of Economics and Political Science. Research Monographs)

REILLY (NOEL MARCUS PROWSE) The relation of real wages to the employment of labour and resources in an industrially developed economy; [Ph. D. (London) thesis]. [1972]. fo. 169. bibliog. Typescript: unpublished. This thesis is the property of London University and may not be removed from the Library.

POHL (KLAUS PETER) Lohnpolitik und internationale wirtschaftliche Integration. [Erlangen, imprint, 1973?]. pp. 179,xliv. bibliog.

WAGES (Cont'd.)

WAGES
See WAGE-PRICE POLICY

- Mathematical models

MUECKL (WOLFGANG) Langfristige Probleme der Lohnpolitik und der Vermögensbildung in Arbeitnehmerhand. Tübingen, 1971. pp. 71. bibliog. (Tübingen. Institut für Angewandte Wirtschaftsforschung. Schriftenreihe. Band 19)

A NEOCLASSICAL approach to the determination of prices and wages; [by] R. Agarwala [and others]. [Ottawa], 1971. pp. 27. bibliog. (Canada. Dominion Bureau of Statistics. Econometric Research Staff. Working Papers. 71-01) (Economic Council. Macromodel Group. Discussion Papers. No. 14)

- Minimum wage

RIBEIRO (MARIA EDUARDA) Síntese de algumas experiências de fixação pelos poderes publicos de salarios minimos legais interprofissionais. [Lisboa, 1969]. pp. 17. (Fundo de Desenvolvimento da Mão-de-Obra. Boletim bimestral. Suplementos. N.º29) With abstracts in English and French.

RIBEIRO (MARIA EDUARDA) Fixação e actualização do salario minimo e problemas conexos. Lisboa, 1971. pp. 69. (Portugal. Ministerio das Corporações e Previdência Social. Gabinete de Planeamento. Serie Estudos. 2) With abstracts in English, French and German.

- Minimum wage - Canada - Ontario

WHITTINGHAM (FRANK J.) Minimum wages in Ontario: analysis and measurement problems. Kingston, Ontario, 1970. pp.55. (Kingston, Ontario. Queen's University. Industrial Relations Centre. Research Series. No. 11)

- Minimum wage - Ethiopia

INTERNATIONAL LABOUR OFFICE. Development Programme: Technical Assistance Sector. [Ethiopia] R.10. Report to the government of Ethiopia on minimum wage fixing. (ILO/TAP/Ethiopia/R.10). Geneva, 1970. pp. 63.

- Minimum wage - French West Africa

FRENCH WEST AFRICA. Service des Études et Coordination Statistiques et Mécanographiques. 1958. Les salaires en A.O.F.: salaires minima hiérarchisés au 28 février 1958. Dakar, 1958. pp. 96.

- Minimum wage - Guatemala

GUATEMALA. Comision Nacional del Salario. 1965. Estudio economico para la determinacion del salario minimo en la industria de productos plasticos. Guatemala, 1965. fo. (34).

GUATEMALA. Comision Nacional del Salario. 1966. Estudio economico para la determinacion del salario minimo en la actividad hotelera. Guatemala, 1966. fo. (40).

GUATEMALA. Comision Nacional del Salario. 1966. Estudio economico para la determinacion del salario minimo en la fabricacion de muebles. Guatemala, 1966. fo. (37).

GUATEMALA. Comision Nacional del Salario. 1966. Estudio economico para la determinacion del salario minimo en la industria de confeccion de ropa. Guatemala, 1966. fo. (34).

GUATEMALA. Comision Nacional del Salario. 1966. Estudio economico para la determinacion del salario minimo en la industria de imprentas, editoriales y actividades conexas. Guatemala, 1966. fo. (39).

GUATEMALA. Comision Nacional del Salario. 1966. Estudio economico para la determinacion del salario minimo en la industria de productos alimenticios. Guatemala, 1966. fo. (38).

GUATEMALA. Comision Nacional del Salario. 1966. Estudio economico para la determinacion del salario minimo en la industria de productos metalicos. Guatemala, 1966. fo. (37).

GUATEMALA. Comision Nacional del Salario. 1966. Estudio economico para la determinacion del salario minimo en la industria del cuero, calzado y productos relacionados. Guatemala, 1966. fo. (40).

GUATEMALA. Comision Nacional del Salario. 1966. Estudio economico para la determinacion del salario minimo en los servicios medicos y sanitarios. Guatemala, 1966. fo. (40).

GUATEMALA. Comision Nacional del Salario. 1967. Estudio economico para la determinacion del salario minimo en la industria de la construccion y reparacion de material de transporte, maquinaria industrial y agricola y de aparatos electricos. Guatemala, 1967. fo. (35).

GUATEMALA. Comision Nacional del Salario. 1967. Estudio economico para la determinacion del salario minimo en la industria de productos de caucho. Guatemala, 1967. fo. (38).

GUATEMALA. Comision Nacional del Salario. 1967. Estudio economico para la determinacion del salario minimo en la industria del pan, galletas y reposteria. Guatemala, 1967. fo. (40).

GUATEMALA. Comision Nacional del Salario. 1967. Estudio para la determinacion del salario minimo en la industria de arcilla, arena, piedra, cemento, vidrio y otras minerales no metalicos. Guatemala, 1967. fo. (39).

- Minimum wage - Puerto Rico

PUERTO RICO. Minimum Wage Board. Economics Division. 1962. La industria de banca, seguros y finanzas. [San Juan], 1962. pp. 65.

- Minimum wage - Switzerland

FREUDIGER (HANS) Das soziale Existenzminimum in ländlichen Bezirken der Schweiz und in der Stadt Bern: eine sozial-statistische Studie, etc. Burgdorf, 1926. pp. 63.

- Minimum wage - United Kingdom

U.K. Committee on the Administration of Trade Boards. 1921. Report to the Minister of Labour of the Committee appointed to make recommendations with respect to the work of the Trade Boards and the administration of the Trade Boards Acts: [Humbert Wolfe, chairman]. London, 1921. pp. 18.

- Austria

NOWOTNY (EWALD) and others. Bestimmungsgründe der Lohnbewegung. Wien, 1972. pp. 280. bibliog. (Linz. Hochschule für Sozial- und Wirtschaftswissenschaften. Linzer Hochschulschriften. Band 5)

- Canada

EARNINGS AND HOURS OF WORK IN CANADA: retail trade industry; [pd. by] Statistics Canada]. a., 1970 [1st issue]- Ottawa. [in English and French]

CANADA. Public Service Staff Relations Board. Pay Research Bureau. 1970. Trends in rates of pay in the public service of Canada, October 1, 1958 to 1968: a research study. Ottawa, [1970]. pp. 86,25.

- Chile

    KOOT (RONALD S.) Wage determination and the role of wages in the inflationary process: a study of Chile and Mexico. [University Park, Pa.], 1969. pp. 77. bibliog.

    SETON (FRANCIS) Shadow wages in the Chilean economy; based on the OECD Development Centre's Manual of Industrial Project Analysis in Developing Countries (vol. II). Paris, Organisation for Economic Co-operation and Development, 1972. pp. 104. (Development Centre. Studies: Series on Cost-Benefit Analysis. Case Studies. No. 4)

- China

    CHEN (CHIEN-JEN) Die Lohnstruktur in der Volksrepublik China. Bern, [1972]. pp. 198. bibliog.

    HOWE (CHRISTOPHER) Wage patterns and wage policy in modern China, 1919-1972. Cambridge, 1973. pp. 171. bibliog.

- European Economic Community countries

    STEWART (MARGARET) Employment conditions in Europe. Epping, Essex, 1972. pp. 206. bibliog.

- Germany

    STEINEBACH (NIKOLAUS) Die Gehaltsstruktur der Angestellten in der Bundesrepublik Deutschland. Berlin, [1973]. pp. 314. bibliog.

- Germany - Mathematical models

    BOMSDORF (ECKART) Bestimmungsfaktoren der Lohndrift: eine Analyse für den Bereich der Industrie in der Bundesrepublik Deutschland. Meisenheim am Glan, 1972. pp. 102. bibliog.

    SCHLOENBACH (KNUT) Ökonometrische Analyse der Lohn- und Arbeitsentwicklung in der Bundesrepublik Deutschland, 1957-1968: eine Erweiterung des "Bonner Prognosemodells". Meisenheim am Glan, 1972. pp. 392. bibliog.

- Germany, Eastern

    MARTEN (IRMA) Grundlagen und Formen der Entlohnung nach Arbeitsleistung, untersucht in Kunstfaserbetrieben der DDR. Berlin, 1957. pp. 156. bibliog.

- Ghana

    ROURKE (B.E.) Wages and incomes of agricultural workers in Ghana. Legon, 1971. pp. 137. (Ghana University. Institute of Statistical, Social and Economic Research. Technical Publication Series. No. 13)

- Guatemala

    MADDOX (ROBERT CASEY) Wage differences between United States and Guatemalan industrial firms in Guatemala. Austin, 1971. pp. 57. (Texas University. Bureau of Business Research. Studies in Latin-American Business. No.10)

- India

    INDIA. Central Wage Board for Port and Dock Workers at Major Ports. 1970. Report... 1969. Delhi, 1970. pp. 371.

    INDIA. Central Wage Board for Road Transport Industry. 1970. Report... 1969. [Delhi, 1970]. pp. 114.

    PAPOLA (TRILOK SINGH) Principles of wage determination: an empirical study. Bombay, [1970]. pp. 243. bibliog.

- India - Bengal, West

    WEST BENGAL. Pay Committee. 1961. Report; [B.B. Dasgupta, chairman]. [Alipore, 1961]. pp. 502.

- Ireland (Republic)

    BEHREND (HILDE) Incomes policy, equity and pay increase differentials: an analysis of employee attitudes towards pay-increases in Ireland and the implications for incomes policy in Britain. Edinburgh, [1973]. pp. 79.

- Italy

    VEZZA (LUIGI DI) and SEPPI (VALENTINO) Contrattazione e dinamica dei salari nell'industria italiana. Roma, [1970]. 2 vols. (in 1). (Centro di Ricerche e Studi Economici. Studi sulla Dinamica Economica. 3)

    PREDETTI (ADALBERTO) Occupazione, retribuzione e reddito di lavoro in Italia. Milano, [1972]. pp. 193.

- Mexico

    KOOT (RONALD S.) Wage determination and the role of wages in the inflationary process: a study of Chile and Mexico. [University Park, Pa.], 1969. pp. 77. bibliog.

- Norway

    BRUNSTAD (ROLF) and AARRESTAD (JOSTEIN) Lønns- og prisutviklinga i Norge, 1950-1969: ein empirisk studie på årsdata. [Bergen], 1972. pp. 12. bibliog. (Norges Handelshøyskole. Saertrykk-Serie. Nr.98)(Saertrykk av Sosialøkonomen nr.7, 1972)

- Poland

    KRENCIK (WIESŁAW) Podstawy i kierunki polityki płac w PRL. Warszawa, 1972. pp. 207. bibliog.

- Portugal

    FUNDO DE DESENVOLVIMENTO DA MAO-DE-OBRA. Divisão de Salarios. Remuneracões medias, segundo a profiassão durante o primeiro semestre de 1969, obtidas a partir do movimento de pedidos e ofertas de emprego da Divisão Regional de Lisboa do Serviço Nacional de Emprego. Lisboa, 1969. pp. 57. (Fundo de Desenvolvimento da Mão-de-Obra. Boletin bimestral. Suplementos. N.° 28) With abstracts in English and French.

    CARVALHO (ODETE ESTEVES DE) Influência da evolução dos salarios sobre o custo de vida: analise do periodo, 1965-68. Lisboa, 1970. pp. 56. (Fundo de Desenvolvimento da Mão-de-Obra. Cadernos. 34) With abstracts in French, English and German.

- Russia

    RIMASHEVSKAIA (NATAL'IA MIKHAILOVNA) Ekonomicheskii analiz dokhodov rabochikh i sluzhashchikh. Moskva, 1965. pp. 128.

    KALINOVSKII (NIKOLAI PETROVICH) Raionnye razlichiia real'noi zarabotnoi platy rabochikh i sluzhashchikh. Moskva, 1966. pp. 112.

    TRONEV (KONSTANTIN PETROVICH) Ekonomicheskie osnovy dinamiki real'nykh dokhodov trudiashchikhsia pri sotsializme. Moskva, 1966. pp. 83.

    HUMENIUK (PETRO DANYLOVYCH) Oplata pratsi v umovakh hospodars'koi reformy: pytannia teorii i praktyky vidnosyn rozpodilu. L'viv, 1969. pp. 178.

WAGES - Russia (Cont'd.)

KARINSKII (SERGEI SERGEEVICH) Oplata truda v promyshlennosti: pravovye voprosy. Moskva, 1971. pp. 200.

KIRSCH (LEONARD JOEL) Soviet wages: changes in structure and administration since 1956. Cambridge, Mass., [1972]. pp. 237. bibliog.

KUNEL'SKII (LEONID EMMANUILOVICH) Sotsial'no-ekonomicheskie problemy zarabotnoi platy. Moskva, 1972. pp. 240.

LIVSHITS (ROMAN ZINOV'EVICH) Zarabotnaia plata v SSSR: pravovoe issledovanie. Moskva, 1972. pp. 271.

OSIPENKOV (PETR SAVEL'EVICH) Problemy sotsialisticheskogo raspredeleniia: zakon raspredeleniia po trudu i mekhanizm ego ispol'zovaniia. Moskva, 1972. pp. 159.

PERETRUTOV (VALENTIN NIKOLAEVICH) and EZERIN (ARNOL'D ERNESTOVICH) Trud i zarabotnaia plata na promyshlennom transporte. Moskva, 1972. pp. 240.

RUSSIA (U.S.S.R.). Statutes, etc. 1929-72. Raschety s rabochimi i sluzhashchimi: sbornik ofitsial'nykh materialov pod red. ... Karinskogo S.S. Moskva, 1973. pp. 407.

- Russia - Dictionaries and encyclopaedias

POPOV-CHERKASOV (IGOR' NIKOLAEVICH) ed. Kratkii slovar'-spravochnik po voprosam truda i zarabotnoi platy. 2nd ed. Moskva, 1972. pp. 415.

- Russia - Mathematical models

RABKINA (NINEL' EFIMOVNA) and RIMASHEVSKAIA (NATAL'IA MIKHAILOVNA) Osnovy differentsiatsii zarabotnoi platy i dokhodov naseleniia: metody ekonomiko-matematicheskogo modelirovaniia. Moskva, 1972. pp. 288.

- Senegal

FRENCH WEST AFRICA. Service des Etudes et Coordination Statistiques et Mécanographiques. 1958. Étude statistique sur les établissements et les salaires réels pratiqués au Sénégal en 1956 et 1957. Dakar, 1958. pp. 91.

- Spain

SPAIN. Consejo Economico Nacional (Organizacion Sindical). Vicesecretaria Nacional de Ordenacion Social. 1964. La tendencia salarial en los convenios colectivos de industria y servicios durante el año 1963. [Madrid?], 1964. fo. 31.

CARRASCO CANALS (FERNANDO) Los salarios en España en el contexto de la politica de rentas. Madrid, 1972. pp. 318. bibliog.

- Sri Lanka

SEGAL (MARTIN) Government pay policies in Ceylon. Geneva, International Labour Office, 1971, pp. 106.

- Sweden

EDGREN (GÖSTA) and others. Lönebildning och samhällsekonomi. Stockholm, [1970]. pp. 267. bibliog

LANDSORGANISATIONEN I SVERIGE. Låglön och välfärd: rapport till LO:s lönepolitiska kommitté inför LO-kongressen 1971. Stockholm, [1971]. pp. 202.

LANDSORGANISATIONEN I SVERIGE. Lönepolitiska Kommittée. Lönepolitik: rapport till LO-kongressen 1971. Stockholm, [1971]. pp. 179.

KLEVMARKEN (ANDERS) Statistical methods for the analysis of earnings data, with special application to salaries in Swedish industry. Stockholm, 1972. pp. 271. bibliog. (Sweden. Statistiska Centralbyrån. Urval. 6)

MEIDNER (RUDOLF) and ÖHMAN (BERNDT) Solidarisk lönepolitik: erfarenheter, problem, framtidsutsikter. Stockholm, [1972]. pp. 57.

STRENDER (BÖRJE) What is a just wage?: a debate brief on wage issues at the workplace. Stockholm, [1972]. pp. 27.

EDGREN (GÖSTA) and others. Wage formation and the economy; [translated by Margareta Eklöf]. London, 1973. pp. 239. bibliog.

- Syria

INTERNATIONAL LABOUR OFFICE. Regular Programme of Technical Assistance. [Syria]. R.18. Rapport au gouvernement de la République Arabe Syrienne sur la réglementation des salaires dans l'industrie. (OIT/OTA/Syrie/R.18). Geneva, 1971. pp. 122.

- Trinidad and Tobago

BREWSTER (HAVELOCK) Wage-policy issues in an underdeveloped economy: Trinidad and Tobago. [Mona], 1969. pp. 101.

WAGES - Underdeveloped areas
See UNDERDEVELOPED AREAS - Wages

- United Kingdom

U.K. Department of Employment and Productivity. 1970. Commission for Industry and Manpower: consultative document. [London, 1970]. fo. 12.

LITTLE (F.M.) and others. The effect of alternative employment and population levels on total and per capita earnings in London in 1981. [London], 1971. pp. 20. (London. Greater London Council. Department of Planning and Transportation. Research Memoranda. 299)

BALFOUR (CAMPBELL) Incomes policy and the public sector. London, 1972. pp. 276.

INDUSTRIAL RESEARCH AND INFORMATION SERVICES. Incomes policy. London, 1972. pp. 33.

MINCHINTON (WALTER EDWARD) ed. Wage regulation in pre-industrial England; (comprising works by R.H. Tawney and R. Keith Kelsall). Newton Abbot, [1972]. pp. 263. bibliog.

U.K. National Joint Advisory Council. 1972. Methods of payment of wages: report of a committee of the...Council; [J.M.Woolf, chairman]. London, 1972. pp. 86.

BEHREND (HILDE) Incomes policy, equity and pay increase differentials: an analysis of employee attitudes towards pay-increases in Ireland and the implications for incomes policy in Britain. Edinburgh, [1973]. pp. 79.

BROWN (WILFRED BANKS DUNCAN) Baron Brown. The earnings conflict: proposals for tackling the emerging crisis of industrial relations, unemployment, and wage inflation. London, 1973. pp. 128. bibliog.

COMMISSION ON INDUSTRIAL RELATIONS [U.K.]. Hollowware Wages Council. London, H.M.S.O., 1973. pp. 41. (Reports. No.47)

COMMISSION ON INDUSTRIAL RELATIONS [U.K.]. Pin, Hook and Eye and Snap Fastener Wages Council. London, H.M.S.O., 1973. pp. 44. (Reports. No. 49)

COMMISSION ON INDUSTRIAL RELATIONS [U.K.]. Stamped or Pressed Metal-Wares Wages Council. London, H.M.S.O., 1973. pp. 42. (Reports. No.50)

FORD NATIONAL JOINT NEGOTIATING COMMITTEE. Trade Union Side. The Ford claim, 1973, submitted on behalf of all UK hourly paid workers; (statement by Moss Evans, chairman). London, 1973. pp. 32.

HUNT (EDWARD HERBERT) Regional wage variations in Britain, 1850-1914. Oxford, 1973. pp. 388. bibliog.

OFFICE OF MANPOWER ECONOMICS. Wage drift: review of literature and research. London, H.M.S.O., 1973. pp. 68. bibliog.

SKINNER (JIM) Fair wages and public sector contracts. London, 1973. pp. 20. (Fabian Society. Research Series. [No.] 310)

U.K. Pay Board. 1973. Pay Board: a guide to its work. [London], 1973. pp. 28.

- United Kingdom - Mathematical models

PRICES and earnings in 1951-69: an econometric assessment: [report of the Working Party: A.R Thatcher, chairman]. London, H.M.S.O., 1971. pp. 42.

KNIGHT (K.G.) Strikes and wage inflation in British manufacturing industry, 1950-1968. Coventry, 1972. pp. 22. (University of Warwick. Centre for Industrial Economic and Business Research. [Warwick Research in Industrial and Business Studies]. No. 27)

- United States - Statistics

DOUTY (H.M.) The development of wage statistics in the United States. Ithaca, N.Y., 1972. pp. 45. bibliog. (Cornell University. New York State School of Industrial and Labor Relations. Bulletins. 64)

- United States - California

CALIFORNIA. Department of Employment. 1967. Employment and payrolls: San Francisco-Oakland labor market area, 1958-1964. [Sacramento?], 1967. pp. 52. (Reports. [No.] 127E #1.)

CALIFORNIA. Department of Industrial Relations. Division of Labor Statistics and Research. Earnings and hours: California and metropolitan areas. a., 1970- San Francisco.

- United States - New York

NEW YORK (STATE). Department of Labor. Division of Research and Statistics. Publications. No. B.124. Wages and hours in the restaurant industry in New York State, 1960. [New York], 1961. pp. 44.

NEW YORK (STATE). Division of Employment. Research and Statistics Office. 1966. Employment statistics. Vol. 1. Monthly nonfarm employment, 1939-1949; hours and earnings of production workers in manufacturing, New York State, 1947-1949, including annual averages. Albany, 1966. pp. 14.

NEW YORK (STATE). Division of Employment. Research and Statistics Office. 1967-68. Employment statistics. Vol. 3. Monthly nonfarm employment, New York State and New York City, 1950-1960, industrial areas, 1951-1960; hours and earnings of production workers in manufacturing, New York State and New York City, 1950-1960; (with Supplement). Albany, 1967-68. 2 pts.

NEW YORK (STATE). Division of Employment. Research and Statistics Office. 1970. Employment statistics. Vol. 6. Civilian work force, New York State, 1957-1965, major areas and counties, 1958-1965; employees in nonagricultural establishments, by industry New York State and major areas, annual averages, 1958-1965... [and] by month, 1958-1965; earnings and hours in nonagricultural establishments, New York State and major areas, 1958-1965. Albany, 1970. pp. 219.

NEW YORK (STATE). Division of Employment. Research and Statistics Office. 1971. Employment statistics. Vol. 8. Data on wage and salary workers in employment covered by old-age, survivors, disability and health insurance, New York State, 1959-1965: employment, industry, age and earnings by sex and color. Albany, 1971. pp. 148.

- Venezuela

CHEN (CHI-YI) Economia social del trabajo: caso de Venezuela; (con la colaboracion de Enrique Brücker). Caracas, [1969]. pp. 449. bibliog.

- Yugoslavia

HORVAT (VLADIMIR) Minuli rad u ekonomskom i pravnom sistemu. Zagreb, 1971. pp. 36.

HORVAT (VLADIMIR) Društveno vlasništvo i minuli rad. Zagreb, 1972. pp. 109. bibliog.

WACHTEL (HOWARD M.) Workers' management and workers' wages in Yugoslavia: the theory and practice of participatory socialism. Ithaca, 1973. pp. 229. bibliog.

- Zaire

KAZADI WA DILE (JACQUES S.) Politiques salariales et développement en République Démocratique du Congo. Paris, [1970]. pp. 478. bibliog. (Kinshasa. Université Lovanium. Institut de Recherches Economiques et Sociales. Recherches Africaines. 15)

WAGES AND PRODUCTIVITY

[RED INTERNATIONAL OF LABOUR UNIONS]. The world economic situation during recent years; [and] The position of the working class during 1924-1927; [and] Unemployment. n.p., [192-?]. fo. various. Mimeographed copy, unpublished.

WILLENER (ALFRED) b. 1928, and others. Travail, salaire, production. Paris, 1972 in progress. (Paris. Ecole Pratique des Hautes Etudes. Section des Sciences Economiques et Sociales. Société, Mouvements Sociaux et Idéologies. 1e Série. Etudes. 12)

McKERSIE (ROBERT B.) and HUNTER (LAURENCE C.) Pay, productivity and collective bargaining. London, 1973. pp. 389.

- Canada

ANTON (FRANK ROBERT) Wages and productivity: the new equation. Toronto, [1969]. pp. 152. bibliog.

WAGES AND PRODUCTIVITY (Cont'd.)

- Europe

DELAMOTTE (YVES) The social partners face the problems of productivity and employment: a study in comparative industrial relations. Paris, Organisation for Economic Co-operation and Development, 1971. pp. 202.

- European Economic Community countries

LUTZ (BURKART) and WILLENER (ALFRED) b. 1928. Niveau de mécanisation et mode de rémunération:.. rapport de synthèse d'une recherche effectuée dans la sidérurgie par des instituts des six pays de la Communauté. Luxembourg, European Coal and Steel Community. 1960. pp. 149.

- Italy

TARANTELLI (EZIO) Produttività del lavoro, salari e inflazione: schema teorico e verifica empirica per l'industria italiana. [Rome, 1970]. pp. 128. (Ente per gli Studi Monetari, Bancari e Finanziari Luigi Einaudi. Quaderni di Ricerche. N.5)

- Russia

EGIAZARIAN (GEVORK ASHOTOVICH) Material'noe stimulirovanie za novuiu tekhniku. Moskva, 1964. pp. 183.

VOPROSY proizvoditel'nosti i oplaty truda v period stroitel'stva kommunizma: sbornik statei. Leningrad, 1964. pp. 176.

KOGAN (KIVA IZRAILEVICH) and KUZIAKOV (NIKITA VASIL'EVICH) Khoziaistvennyi raschet i ekonomicheskoe stimulirovanie na predpriiatii. Moskva, 1966. pp. 78.

OPYT i problemy stimulirovaniia v novykh usloviiakh. Moskva, 1966. pp. 112.

FEDININ (VASILII KUZ'MICH) Vzaimosviaz' material'nykh i moral'nykh stimulov k trudu. Moskva, 1970. pp. 44.

NAIDENOV (VIKTOR SERGEEVICH) and others. Tekushchii plan i ekonomicheskie stimuly. Moskva, 1971. pp. 141.

ARTEMOV (IURII MIKHAILOVICH) and PARASOCHKA (VALENTIN TIMOFEEVICH) Fond material'nogo pooshchreniia i rost proizvoditel'nosti truda. Moskva, 1972. pp. 64.

GARETOVSKII (NIKOLAI VIKTOROVICH) Finansovye metody stimulirovaniia intensifikatsii proizvodstva: problemy teorii, metodologii i praktiki. Moskva, 1972. pp. 319.

MANZA (ANNA PETROVNA) Proizvoditel'nost' truda i stimuly ee rosta: voprosy teorii i metodiki. Kishinev, 1972. pp. 99. bibliog.

MASEVICH (MARGARITA GENRIKHOVNA) and others. Pravovye voprosy material'nogo stimulirovaniia predpriiatii. Alma-Ata, 1972. pp. 229.

OBLOMSKAIA (INGA IAKOVLEVNA) Sistema lichnykh material'nykh stimulov pri sotsializme. Moskva, 1972. pp. 230.

TISHCHENKOV (IL'IA ANDREEVICH) and FATUEV (ANATOLII ANDREEVICH) Pravovye voprosy material'nogo stimulirovaniia rabotnikov promyshlennosti. Moskva, 1972. pp. 216.

VASIL'EV (EVGENII KAPITONOVICH) and CHISTIAKOVA (LIDIIA MIKHAILOVNA) Effektivnost' oplaty upravlencheskogo truda v promyshlennosti. Moskva, 1972. pp. 143.

- Russia - Latvia

MATERIAL'NOE stimulirovanie v promyshlennosti. Riga, 1972. pp. 120.

- South Africa

HORNER (J.A.) Black pay and productivity in South Africa: an address to the South African Institute of Personnel Management, June 1972. [Johannesburg], 1972. pp. 23. bibliog.

- United Kingdom

EDWARDS (Sir RONALD STANLEY) and ROBERTS (ROBERT DAVID VALPO) Status, productivity and pay: a major experiment: a study of the electricity supply industry's agreements and their outcome, 1961-1971. London, 1971. pp. 456.

TOWERS (BRIAN) and others, eds. Bargaining for change. London, 1972. pp. 279. bibliog.

WAGGA WAGGA

- Economic conditions

WAGGA WAGGA. City Council. Selective decentralisation: a case for the selection of the city of Wagga Wagga as one of the growth centres for selective decentralisation in New South Wales. Wagga Wagga, 1971. pp. 112.

- Growth

WAGGA WAGGA. City Council. Selective decentralisation: a case for the selection of the city of Wagga Wagga as one of the growth centres for selective decentralisation in New South Wales. Wagga Wagga, 1971. pp. 112.

WALDECK (BENEDIKT FRANZ LEO)

WALDECK (BENEDIKT FRANZ LEO) defendant. Der Waldeck'sche Prozess; authentischer Bericht über die öffentlichen Verhandlungen des Berliner Schwurgerichts in der Waldeck'schen Untersuchungssache; nach den...stenographischen Aufzeichnungen und Mittheilungen betheiligter Personen. 2nd ed. Berlin, Hempel, 1849. pp. 311.

WALES

- Appropriations and expenditures

U.K. Treasury. 1971. Estimates of central government revenue and expenditure attributable to Wales for the financial year 1968-69: a Welsh budget. London, 1971. pp. 17.

- Economic conditions

HUMPHRYS (GRAHAM) South Wales. Newton Abbot, [1972]. pp. 253. bibliog.

LAW (DAVID) and HOWES (ROGER) Mid-Wales: an assessment of the impact of the Development Commission factory programme. London, H.M.S.O., 1972. pp. 92.

- Economic policy

WELSH COUNCIL. Industrial development policy: an analysis of the measures introduced in March, 1972. [Cardiff?], 1972. fo. 30.

WELSH COUNCIL. Wales: employment and the economy; a report submitted by the Welsh Council to the Secretary of State for Wales. [Cardiff?], 1972. fo. 23.

- History - Sources

    RUTHIN (LORDSHIP). Court. The Court Rolls of the Lordship of Ruthin or Dyffryn-Clwydd of the reign of King Edward the First...; edited, with translation, notes, etc. by Richard Arthur Roberts. London, 1893. pp. xxv, 37 [bis], 38-61. (Honourable Society of Cymmrodorion. Record Series. No. 2)

- Industries

    HUMPHRYS (GRAHAM) South Wales. Newton Abbot, [1972]. pp. 253. bibliog.

WALES - Industries
    See also INDUSTRIAL PROMOTION - United Kingdom - Wales

- Politics and government

    WELSH COUNCIL. Welsh Council, 1968-71. Cardiff, H.M.S.O., 1971. pp. 22.

    GRIFFITHS (RALPH A.) The principality of Wales in the later middle ages: the structure and personnel of government; ...with the assistance of Roger S. Thomas. Cardiff, 1972 in progress. (Wales. University of Wales. Board of Celtic Studies. History and Law Series. No. 26)

- Population

    LAW (DAVID) and HOWES (ROGER) Mid-Wales: an assessment of the impact of the Development Commission factory programme. London, H.M.S.O., 1972. pp. 92.

- Social history

    JONES (DAVID J.V.) Before Rebecca: popular protests in Wales, 1793-1835. London, 1973. pp. 282. bibliogs.

- Social life and customs

    PEATE (IORWERTH CYFEILIOG) Tradition and folk life: a Welsh view. London, 1972. pp. 147. bibliog.

WALL STREET

    WYCKOFF (PETER) Wall Street and the stock markets: a chronology, 1644-1971. Philadelphia, [1972]. pp. 304. bibliog.

WALLACE (HENRY AGARD)

    MARKOWITZ (NORMAN D.) The rise and fall of the people's century: Henry A. Wallace and American liberalism, 1941-1948. New York, [1973]. pp. 369. bibliog.

WALLACHIA

- History

    STAN (APOSTOL) Le problème agraire pendant la révolution de 1848 en Valachie. Bucarest, 1971. pp. 154. bibliog. (Academia de Stiinte Sociale si Politice a Republicii Socialiste România. Bibliotheca Historica Romaniae. Studies. 34)

WALLENBERG (RAOUL)

    SWEDEN. Utrikesdepartementet. Aktstycken. Ny Serie. II. 16. Raoul Wallenberg: dokumentsamling rörande efterforskningarna efter år 1957. Stockholm, 1965. pp. 44.

WALLENSTEIN (ALBRECHT WENZEL EUSEBIUS VON) Herzog von Friedland

WALLER (JAMES MUIR)

    MANN (GOLO) Wallenstein: sein Leben erzählt. Frankfurt am Main, 1971. pp. 1368. bibliog.

WALLISCH (KOLOMAN)

    WALLISCH (PAULA) Ein Held stirbt;...Herausgeber und Verleger: Deutsche Sozialdemokratische Arbeiterpartei in der Tschechoslowakischen Republik. [Prague, 1935?]. pp. 246.

WALLONIA

    ROMUS (PAUL) La Wallonie dans la Communauté européenne. Bruxelles, [1967]. pp. 41. (Brussels. Université Libre. Institut d'Etudes Européennes. Thèses et Travaux Economiques. 2)

- Economic conditions

    NOVA (WALTER) pseud. Dossier pour un gouvernement wallon: fédéralisme et perspectives économiques. Liège, 1970. pp. 279.

- History

    BOLOGNE (MAURICE) Notre passé wallon: esquisse d'une histoire des événements politiques des origines à 1940. [Nalinnes], 1972. pp. 115. bibliogs.

- Population

    ANDRE (ROBERT) and others. Aspects de la démographie de Belgique: population et logement en Wallonie. [Brussels, 1969]. pp. 66.

WALRAS (LEON)

    DIEWERT (W.E.) Walras' theory of capital formation and the existence of a temporary equilibrium. Stanford, 1972. pp. 79. bibliog. (Stanford University. Institute for Mathematical Studies in the Social Sciences. Technical Reports. [New Series]. No. 63)

WALSALL

- History

    DEAN (KENNETH J.) Town and Westminster: a political history of Walsall. Walsall, 1972. pp. 301.

WANDSWORTH

- Social policy

    WANDSWORTH. Borough Council. Contact: a guide to social services in Wandsworth. [new ed.] London, [1971?]. pp. 96.

WANG (CHIEH)

    WANG (CHIEH) The diary of Wang Chieh. Peking, 1967. pp. 96.

WANG (CHING-WEI)

    BUNKER (GERALD E.) The peace conspiracy: Wang Ching-wei and the China War, 1937-1941. Cambridge, 1972. pp. 327. bibliog. (Harvard University. East Asian Research Center. Harvard East Asian Series. 67)

WAR

INTERNATIONAL FEDERATION OF TRADE UNIONS. Nie wieder Krieg!: No more war!... [collection of photographs illustrating the horrors of war]. Amsterdam, 1929. pp. 63.

BAUER (HANS) Warum Krieg? Zürich, [1938]. pp. 78.

GOERGEN (JOSEF MATTHIAS) Mensch, Staat und Krieg. New York, [1940]. pp. 215.

HOGLUND (BENGT) Concepts of conflict, etc. Uppsala, 1970. pp. 44. bibliog. (Uppsala. Universitet. Department of Peace and Conflict Research. Reports. No. 2)

THANT, U. Basic problems of disarmament: reports of the Secretary-General. New York, United Nations, 1970. pp. 264. bibliog.

GOLDMANN (KJELL) International norms and war between states: three studies in international politics. Stockholm, 1971. pp. 368. bibliog. (Utrikespolitiska Institutet. Swedish Studies in International Relations. 1)

NIELSEN (JOHANNES) Historian. Demokratiet og krigen: en undersøgelse af samspillet mellem demokrati, nationalisme og krigsførelse. [Copenhagen, 1971]. pp. 189.

WEIZSAECKER (CARL FRIEDRICH VON) Freiherr, ed. Kriegsfolgen und Kriegsverhütung;...von H. Afheldt [and others]. 3rd ed. München, 1971. pp. 703. bibliogs.

ÅKERMAN (NORDAL) On the doctrine of limited war; (translation Keith Bradfield). [Lund, 1972]. pp. 287. bibliog.

BARRINGER (RICHARD E.) War: patterns of conflict; with the collaboration of Robert K. Ramers. Cambridge, Mass., [1972]. pp. 293. bibliog.

CROSSER (PAUL K.) War is obsolete: the dialectics of military technology and its consequences. Amsterdam, 1972. pp. 244.

GANTZEL (KLAUS JUERGEN) System und Akteur: Beiträge zur vergleichenden Kriegsursachenforschung. Düsseldorf, [1972]. pp. 374. bibliog.

MARXISM-Leninism on war and army; [translated from the 6th Russian ed. by Donald Danemanis] Moscow, [1972]. pp. 431.

MEZHDUNARODNYE konflikty. Moskva, 1972. pp. 238.

RAKOVE (MILTON L.) ed. Arms and foreign policy in the nuclear age. New York, 1972. pp. 485.

RUSSETT (BRUCE MARTIN) ed. Peace, war, and numbers. Beverly Hills, [1972]. pp. 352. bibliog.

TZABAR (SHIMON) The white flag principle: how to lose a war and why. London, 1972. pp. 150. bibliog.

BIDWELL (SHELFORD) Modern warfare: a study of men, weapons and theories. London, 1973. pp. 242. bibliog.

BLAINEY (GEOFFREY) The causes of war. London, 1973. pp. 278. bibliog.

TOLLEY (HOWARD) Children and war: political socialization to international conflict. New York, [1973]. pp. 196. bibliog.

- Casualties (Statistics, etc.)

ÖZERDEN (KEMAL) Le sort des militaires belligérants, victimes de la guerre, débarqués dans un port neutre, d'après la Convention de Genève. Paris, [1971]. pp. 237. bibliog. (Revue Générale de Droit International Public. Publications. Nouvelle Série. No.15)

URLANIS (BORIS TSEZAREVICH) Wars and population. Moscow, 1971. pp. 320.

- Economic aspects

MERCHANT (THOMAS) Esq., pseud. Peace and trade, war and taxes; or, The irreparable damage of our trade in case of a war, etc. London, Brindley, 1729. pp. 32.

ANGELL (NORMAN) pseud. [i.e. Sir Ralph Norman Angell LANE]. Arms and industry: a study of the foundations of international polity;... and The economics of war and conquest: an examination of Mr. Norman Angell's economic doctrines; by John H. Jones: [reprint of two works first published separately in 1914 and 1915] with a new introduction... by Berenice A. Carroll. New York, 1973. 1 vol. (various pagings).

REPNITSKII (VITALII VASIL'EVICH) NATO i voennyi biznes. Moskva, 1970. pp. 184.

BARTENEV (SERGEI ALEKSANDROVICH) Ekonomika - tyl i front sovremennoi voiny. Moskva, 1971. pp. 191.

POTENCJAŁ obronno-gospodarczy państw Układu Warszawskiego. Warszawa, 1971. pp. 339.

- Indexes

U.K. Ministry of Defence. Library (Central and Army). Index of book lists. irreg., current issue only kept. London.

- Medical aspects

GURLT (ERNST) Zur Geschichte der internationalen und freiwilligen Krankenpflege im Kriege;... (unveränderter Neudruck der Ausgabe von 1873). Walluf bei Wiesbaden, 1972. pp. 866.

VERDOORN (J.A.) Arts en oorlog: medische en sociale zorg voor oorlogsslachtoffers in de geschiedenis van Europa; inleiding in de medische polemologie. Amsterdam, 1972. 2 vols.

- Relief of sick and wounded

GURLT (ERNST) Zur Geschichte der internationalen und freiwilligen Krankenpflege im Kriege;... (unveränderter Neudruck der Ausgabe von 1873). Walluf bei Wiesbaden, 1972. pp. 866.

- Statistics

SINGER (J. DAVID) and SMALL (MELVIN) The wages of war, 1816-1965: a statistical handbook. New York, [1972]. pp. 419. bibliog.

WAR (INTERNATIONAL LAW)

The VIETNAM war and international law: [a collection of articles and documents reprinted from various sources]...; edited by Richard A. Falk. Princeton, N.J., 1968-72. 3 vols.

WEILER (HEINRICH) Vietnam: eine völkerrechtliche Analyse des amerikanischen Krieges und seiner Vorgeschichte. Frankenthal, 1969 pp. 362. bibliog.

MEYROWITZ (HENRI) Le principe de l'égalité des belligérants devant le droit de la guerre. Paris, 1970. pp. 418.

THOMAS (ANN VAN WYNEN) and THOMAS (AARON JOSHUA) Legal limits on the use of chemical and biological weapons. Dallas, 1970. pp. 332. (Southern Methodist University. School of Law. Studies)

ÖZERDEN (KEMAL) Le sort des militaires belligérants, victimes de la guerre, débarqués dans un port neutre, d'après la Convention de Genève. Paris, [1971]. pp. 237. bibliog. (Revue Générale de Droit International Public. Publications. Nouvelle Série. No.15)

STANDARD (WILLIAM L.) Aggression: our Asian disaster. New York, [1971]. pp. 227. bibliog.

BAILEY (SYDNEY D.) Prohibitions and restraints in war. London, 1972. pp. 194.

MOORE (JOHN NORTON) Law and the Indo-China war. Princeton, 1972. pp. 794. bibliog.

STOCKHOLM INTERNATIONAL PEACE RESEARCH INSTITUTE. Napalm and incendiary weapons: legal and humanitarian aspects; SIPRI interim report [prepared by Malvern Lumsden from the papers of the SIPRI Symposium on Napalm and Incendiary Weapons held in Stockholm in 1972]. Stockholm, [1972]. fo. 125. bibliog.

MARTIN (PIERRE MARIE) Le conflit israelo-arabe: recherches sur l'emploi de la force en droit international public positif. Paris, 1973. pp. 347. bibliog.

WAR, COST OF

The COST of conflict: lectures given at Western Michigan University under the sponsorship of the Department of Economics, winter semester, 1968; John A. Copps, editor. Ann Arbor, [1969]. pp. 89. (Michigan University. Bureau of Business Research Michigan Business Papers. No. 51)

WAR, DECLARATION OF

JAVITS (JACOB KOPPEL) Who makes war: the President versus Congress;... with Don Kellermann. New York, 1973. pp. 300. bibliog.

WAR, MARITIME (INTERNATIONAL LAW)

DUTTWYLER (HERBERT E.) Der Seekrieg und die Wirtschaftspolitik des neutralen Staates:... mit besonderer Berücksichtigung der Lage der Schweiz, etc. Zürich, 1945. pp. 243.

STEINICKE (DIETRICH) Wirtschaftskrieg und Seekrieg: die allgemeine völkerrechtliche Anerkennung des anglo-amerikanischen Kriegsbegriffes und ihre Rechtsfolgen. Hamburg, 1970. pp. 100. bibliog. (Hamburg. Hansische Universität. Forschungsstelle für Völkerrecht und Ausländisches Öffentliches Recht. Das Geltende Seekriegsrecht in Einzeldarstellungen. Band 1)

HIRDMAN (SVEN) Prospects for arms control in the ocean. Stockholm, 1972. pp. 25. (Stockholm International Peace Research Institute. Research Reports. No. 7)

WAR AND EMERGENCY POWERS

- Germany

NOTSTAND der Demokratie: Referate...vom Kongress am 30. Oktober 1966 in Frankfurt am Main; [[by] Karl Otmar Freiherr von Aretin [and others]]. Frankfurt am Main, [1967]. pp. 213.

- Switzerland

HUBER (ARTHUR) Die Einschränkung der Handels- und Gewerbefreiheit durch das Notverordnungsrecht des Bundes. Bern, 1925. pp. 259.

- United Kingdom - Ireland, Northern

NATIONAL COUNCIL FOR CIVIL LIBERTIES. The Special Powers Acts of Northern Ireland: a review of the NCCL Commission of Inquiry report, 1936, in the light of subsequent events. London, 1972. pp. 20.

- United States

WHITING (WILLIAM) Counsellor at Law. War powers under the constitution of the United States; tenth edition [originally published in 1864]. Glorieta, N.M., 1971. pp. 342.

FRIEDMAN (LEON) and NEUBORNE (BURT) Unquestioning obedience to the president: the ACLU case against the illegal war in Vietnam. New York, [1972]. pp. 284.

JAVITS (JACOB KOPPEL) Who makes war: the President versus Congress;... with Don Kellermann. New York, 1973. pp. 300. bibliog.

WAR AND MORALS

WASSERSTROM (RICHARD ALAN) ed. War and morality. Belmont, California, [1970]. pp. 136. bibliog.

WAR AND RELIGION

Le CHIESE e la guerra: [papers given at a seminar, Rome, 1970; edited by Alceste Santini]. Roma, 1972. pp. 239.

AMERICAN LUTHERAN CHURCH. Conscience and action: social statements...1961-1970; edited by Carl F. Reuss. Minneapolis, [1971]. pp. 184.

CHRISTLICHER Friede und Weltfriede: geschichtliche Entwicklung und Gegenwartsprobleme; [based on contributions to a symposium held in 1969]; herausgegeben von Alexander Hollerbach und Hans Maier; mit Beiträgen von Manfred Abelein [and others]. Paderborn, 1971. pp. 147. bibliog. (Görres-Gesellschaft. Sektion für Rechts- und Staatswissenschaft. Veröffentlichungen. Neue Folge. Heft 8)

BAILEY (SYDNEY D.) Prohibitions and restraints in war. London, 1972. pp. 194.

BRITISH COUNCIL OF CHURCHES. Department of International Affairs, and CONFERENCE OF BRITISH MISSIONARY SOCIETIES. Working Party on Defence and Disarmament. The search for security: a Christian appraisal. London, 1973. pp. 144. bibliog.

WAR AND SOCIALISM

DRAPER (HAL) ed. Independent socialism and war;...articles [selected from Labor Action, The New International and Anvil]. Berkeley, Calif., [1966]. pp. 194. (Independent Socialist Committee. Independent Socialist Clippingbooks. No. 2)

LENIN (VLADIMIR IL'ICH) Lénine et la lutte révolutionnaire contre la guerre mondiale: etude de Paul Jourdan et Renée Roman; textes de Lénine, 1904-1922. Paris, 1971. pp. 128. (Communiste, Le. Numéro Spécial)

WETTE (WOLFRAM) Kriegstheorien deutscher Sozialisten: Marx, Engels, Lassalle, Bernstein, Kautsky, Luxemburg; ein Beitrag zur Friedensforschung. Stuttgart, [1971]. pp. 255. bibliog.

WAR AND SOCIALISM (Cont'd.)

YIN (JOHN) Sino-Soviet dialogue on the problem of war. The Hague, 1971. pp. 247. bibliog.

HAUPT (GEORGES) Socialism and the Great War: the collapse of the Second International. Oxford, 1972. pp. 270.

WAR AND SOCIETY

BOLLARDIERE (JACQUES PARIS DE) Bataille d'Alger, bataille de l'homme. 2nd ed. [Paris, 1972]. pp. 167.

DANIEL (JOSEPH) Guerre et cinéma: grandes illusions et petits soldats, 1895-1971. Paris, 1972. pp. 453. bibliog. (Fondation Nationale des Sciences Politiques. Cahiers. 180)

GENOVES (SANTIAGO) Is peace inevitable?: aggression, evolution, and human destiny. London, 1972. pp. 194. bibliog.

UNIVERSITY OF EAST AFRICA. Annual Social Science Conference, 5th, Nairobi, 1969. War and society in Africa: ten studies; edited by Bethwell A. Ogot. London, 1972. pp. 268.

FOOT (MICHAEL RICHARD DAMELL) ed. War and society: historical essays in honour and memory of J.R. Western, 1928-1971. London, 1973. pp. 349.

WAR CRIMES

ARONEANU (EUGENE) Konzentrationslager: Tatsachenbericht über die an der Menschheit begangenen Verbrechen; Dokument F 321 für den Internationalen Militärgerichtshof in Nürnberg. [Baden-Baden, 1947]. pp. 130.

- Trials - Germany

FEDERATION INTERNATIONALE DES RESISTANTS. Die SS-Henker und ihre Opfer: Auschwitz 1940-1945, Frankfurt/Main 1963-1965; eine notwendige Gegenüberstellung. Wien, 1965. pp. 36. bibliog.

BURG (J.G.) pseud. [i.e. Josef GINSBURG] NS-Verbrechen: Prozesse des schlechten Gewissens; von Deutschen gegen Deutsche, unter Zions Regie geführt. [Munich, 1968]. pp. 192.

- Trials - Japan

MINEAR (RICHARD H.) Victors' justice: the Tokyo war crimes trial. Princeton, N.J., 1971. pp. 229. bibliog.

- Trials - United States

CALLEY (WILLIAM L.) Body count: Lieutenant Calley's story as told to John Sack. London, 1971. pp. 181.

WAR CRIMINALS

- Germany

STEVENSON (WILLIAM) Journalist. The Bormann brotherhood. New York, [1973]. pp. 334. bibliog.

WARBURG (FREDRIC J.)

WARBURG (FREDRIC J.) All authors are equal: the publishing life of Fredric Warburg, 1936-1971. London, 1973. pp. 310.

WAREHOUSES

CUSTOMS CO-OPERATION COUNCIL. 1965. Customs warehousing procedure. Brussels, 1965. pp. 172. (Comparative Studies of Customs Procedures. No. 7)

- United Kingdom

ECONOMIC DEVELOPMENT COMMITTEE FOR THE DISTRIBUTIVE TRADES. Special report: out of stock: report of a study in a wholesale grocer's warehouse. [London], National Economic Development Office, 1971. pp. 12.

WARRINGTON

- Civic improvement

WARRINGTON NEW TOWN DEVELOPMENT CORPORATION. Warrington New Town outline plan. Warrington, [1972]. pp. 94.

WARSAW

- Description

DUNIN-WĄSOWICZ (KRZYSZTOF) ed. Warszawa w pamiętnikach pierwszej wojny światowej. Warszawa, 1971. pp. 593. bibliog.

- History

PIETRZAK-PAWŁOWSKA (IRENA) ed. Wielkomiejski rozwój Warszawy do 1918 r. Warszawa, 1973. pp. 315.

- History - Sources

DUNIN-WĄSOWICZ (KRZYSZTOF) ed. Warszawa w pamiętnikach pierwszej wojny światowej. Warszawa, 1971. pp. 593. bibliog.

KIEPURSKA (HALINA) and PUSTUŁA (ZBIGNIEW) eds. Raporty warszawskich oberpolicmajstrów, 1892-1913. Wrocław, 1971. pp. 139. Editorial matter in Polish, reports in Russian.

- History - 1944, Uprising of

PRZYGOŃSKI (ANTONI) Udział PPR i AL w powstaniu warszawskim. Warszawa, 1970. pp. 265.

CIECHANOWSKI (JAN MIECZYSŁAW) Powstanie Warszawskie: zarys podłoża politycznego i dyplomatycznego. Londyn, 1971. pp. 397.

BRUCE (GEORGE) Military historian. The Warsaw uprising, 1 August - 2 October 1944. London, 1972. pp. 224. bibliog.

- Politics and government

SZCZYGIELSKI (ZBIGNIEW) Walka o jednolity front w Warszawie, 1933-1935. Warszawa, 1972. pp. 414. bibliog.

WARSAW, PACT OF, 1955

POTENCJAŁ obronno-gospodarczy państw Układu Warszawskiego. Warszawa, 1971. pp. 339.

REMINGTON (ROBIN ALISON) The Warsaw Pact: case studies in Communist conflict resolution. Cambridge, Mass., [1971]. pp. 268. bibliog.

WARTENWEILER (FRITZ)

WARTENWEILER (FRITZ) Weckrufe. Zürich, [1969]. pp. 322.

WASHINGTON (BOOKER TALIAFERRO)

HARLAN (LOUIS R.) Booker T. Washington: the making of a black leader, 1856-1901. New York, 1972. pp. 379.

WASHINGTON (GEORGE) President of the United States

BRADLAUGH (CHARLES) Cromwell and Washington: a contrast. London, [1877]. pp. 42.

WRIGHT (ESMOND) Washington and the American revolution; [reprint of the work originally published in London, 1957]. Harmondsworth, 1973. pp. 206. bibliog.

WASHINGTON, D.C.

- Prisons and reformatories

COHEN (HAROLD L.) and FILIPCZAK (JAMES) A new learning environment. San Francisco, 1971. pp. 192. bibliog.

WASTE PRODUCTS

MARX (WESLEY) Man and his environment: waste. New York, [1971]. pp. 179. bibliogs.

WATER

- Fluoridation

DOBBS (C.G.) Fluorine: the favoured pollutant. [Worcester, 1973]. pp. 12. (Reprinted from Protectio Vitae, 3/72)

- Law and legislation - Russia

KOLBASOV (OLEG STEPANOVICH) Zakonodatel'stvo o vodopol'zovanii v SSSR: problemy sovershenstvovaniia sovetskogo zakonodatel'stva ob ispol'zovanii vodnykh resursov. Moskva, 1965. pp. 168.

FOX (IRVING K.) ed. Water resources law and policy in the Soviet Union. Madison, 1971. pp. 256. (Wisconsin University, Madison. Water Resources Center. Water Resources Studies. 1)

- Law and legislation - Russia - Latvia

LATVIA. Statutes, etc. 1973. Vodnyi kodeks Latviiskoi Sovetskoi Sotsialisticheskoi Respubliki. Riga, 1973. pp. 91.

- Pollution

EUTROPHICATION in large lakes and impoundments: report compiled by C.P. Milway [of the] (Uppsala Symposium)... May 1968 [held in] Skokloster, Uppsala, Sweden. Paris, Organisation for Economic Co-operation and Development, 1970. pp. 560. In English and French.

- Pollution - Canada - Ontario

INTERNATIONAL JOINT COMMISSION, CANADA AND UNITED STATES. Pollution of Lake Erie, Lake Ontario and the international section of the St. Lawrence river. [Ottawa, Information Canada, 1970 or rather 1971]. pp. 105.

- Pollution - United Kingdom

U.K. Department of the Environment. 1972. River pollution survey of England and Wales, updated 1972: river quality. London, 1972. pp. 16.

PORTER (ELIZABETH) Pollution in four industrialised estuaries: studies in relation to changes in population and industrial development...; four case studies undertaken for the Royal Commission on Environmental Pollution. London, H.M.S.O., 1973. pp. 98. bibliog.

U.K. Department of the Environment. 1973. Report of a survey of the discharges of foul sewage to the coastal waters of England and Wales. London, 1973. pp. 20.

- Pollution - United Kingdom - Scotland

SCOTLAND. Scottish Development Department. 1972. Towards cleaner water: rivers pollution survey of Scotland. Edinburgh, 1972. pp. 37. 3 maps in end pocket.

- Pollution - United States

INTERNATIONAL JOINT COMMISSION, CANADA AND UNITED STATES. Pollution of Lake Erie, Lake Ontario and the international section of the St. Lawrence river. [Ottawa, Information Canada, 1970 or rather 1971]. pp. 105.

NELKIN (DOROTHY) Nuclear power and its critics: the Cayuga Lake controversy. Ithaca, 1971. pp. 128.

ZWICK (DAVID) and BENSTOCK (MARCY) Water wasteland: (Ralph Nader's study group report on water pollution). New York, 1971. pp. 494.

WATER, UNDERGROUND

COOPER (W.G.G.) Electrical aids in water finding. rev. ed. Zomba, 1965. pp. 25, fo. (22). (Malawi. Geological Survey Department. Bulletins. No. 7)

WATER-POWER ELECTRIC PLANTS

- New Zealand

NEW ZEALAND. [Ministry of Works]. 1967. Power from Manapouri. [Wellington, 1967]. pp. (34).

WATER QUALITY MANAGEMENT

- Canada - British Columbia

McMEIKEN (J. ELIZABETH) Public health professionals and the environment: a study of perceptions and attitudes. Ottawa, 1973. pp. 117. bibliog. (Canada. Department of the Environment. Social Science Series. No. 5) Chart in end pocket.

- United States

KNEESE (ALLEN V.) and BOWER (BLAIR T.) Managing water quality: economics, technology, institutions. Baltimore, [1968]. pp. x, 328.

- United States - Wisconsin

RANNEY (DAVID C.) Water quality management: an analysis of institutional patterns. Madison, Wis., [1972]. pp. 158. (Wisconsin University, Madison. Water Resources Center. Water Resources Studies. 2)

WATER RESOURCES DEVELOPMENT

KUIPER (EDWARD) Water resources project economics. London, 1971. pp. 447. bibliog.

BURAS (NATHAN) Scientific allocation of water resources: water resources development and utilization: a rational approach. New York, [1972]. pp. 208. bibliogs.

WATER RESOURCES DEVELOPMENT
(Cont'd.)

WIENER (AARON) The role of water in development: an analysis of principles of comprehensive planning. New York, [1972]. pp. 483.

PEREIRA (HERBERT CHARLES) Land use and water resources in temperate and tropical climates. Cambridge, 1973. pp. 246. bibliog.

- Mathematical models

BOERLIN (MAX) Econometric model for river basin planning. Paris, Organisation for Economic Cooperation and Development, 1971. pp. 94. bibliog. (Problems of Development)

FIERING (MYRON B.) and others. Water resources systems analysis. Ottawa, Information Canada, 1971. pp. 47. (Resource Papers. No. 3)

- Canada

RICHARDSON (RONALD E.) and others. Developing water resources: the St. Lawrence Seaway and the Columbia/Peace power projects. Toronto, [1969]. pp. 113. bibliog.

- Canada - Manitoba

INTERNATIONAL JOINT COMMISSION CANADA AND UNITED STATES. Report...on the cooperative development of the Pembina river basin. [Ottawa], 1967. pp. 60.

- Canada - Saskatchewan

CANADA. Prairie Farm Rehabilitation Administration. 1967. South Saskatchewan river project, 1958-1967. Ottawa, 1967. pp. (30).

- Mexico

CUMMINGS (RONALD G.) Water resource management in northern Mexico. Washington, [1972]. pp. 68. bibliog.

- Poland

HOFMAN (LUCJAN) and KORTYLEWSKA (ANNA) Ekonomiczne problemy gospodarki wodnej Polski. Warszawa, 1971. pp. 278. bibliog.

- Russia

PROBLEMY ispol'zovaniia i okhrany vodnykh resursov. Minsk, 1972. pp. 276. bibliog.

- Russia - Kalmyk Republic

BOGZYKOV (SERGEI ARTEM'EVICH) Vodnye resursy Kalmykii. Elista, 1970. pp. 86. bibliog.

- Russia - Kazakstan

AKHMEDSAFIN (UFA MENDYBAEVICH) and others. Resursy i ispol'zovanie podzemnykh vod Kazakhstana. Alma-Ata, 1972. pp. 155. bibliog.

- Russia - Latvia - Mathematical models

AKADEMIIA NAUK LATVIISKOI SSR. Institut Ekonomiki. Matematicheskie Metody v Ekonomike. vyp.9. Metodicheskie voprosy razrabotki i vnedreniia avtomatizirovannoi sistemy upravleniia v vodnom khoziaistve. Riga, 1972. pp. 163.

- Russia - Moldavian Republic

ZELENIN (IGOR' VASIL'EVICH) Estestvennye resursy podzemnykh vod Moldavii: usloviia formirovaniia i regional'naia otsenka. Kishinev, 1972. pp. 214. bibliog.

- Russia - Uzbekistan

KUNAKOVA (LIDIIA ZAKHAROVNA) Zemel'no-vodnaia reforma v Uzbekistane, 1925-1929 gg.; otvetstvennyi redaktor... Kh.Sh. Inoiatov. Frunze, 1967. pp. 300.

- Sweden

SWEDEN. Civildepartementet. 1972. Management of land and water resources: information to the United Nations Conference on the Human Environment. Stockholm, 1972. pp. 74.

- United Kingdom

MERSEY AND WEAVER RIVER AUTHORITY. 1971 statement of policy. Great Sankey, 1971. pp. 11.

U.K. Water Resources Board. 1971. Water resources in Wales and the Midlands; report. London, 1971. pp. 61. (Publications. No. 11) 2 maps in end pocket.

The TRENT research programme. London, 1972 in progress. (U.K. Water Resources Board. Publications. No. 18)

SMITH (KEITH) Ph. D. Water in Britain: a study in applied hydrology and resource geography. London, 1972. pp. 241. bibliog.

- United Kingdom - Ireland, Northern

IRELAND, NORTHERN. Lough Neagh Working Group. 1972. Advisory report; [P.D. Bell, leader]. [Belfast], 1971 [or rather 1972]. 2 vols. (in 1) and 7 maps.

- United States

PACIFIC NORTHWEST RIVER BASINS COMMISSION. Columbia - North Pacific region comprehensive framework study [of water and related lands]: main report (and Appendices). Vancouver, Washington, 1969-72. 16 vols. bibliogs. For details of Appendices see following cards.

BURBY (RAYMOND J.) and others. Factors influencing the residential utilization of reservoir shorelands in the southeast: (a preliminary report of the Multipurpose Reservoirs and Urban Development Project). Raleigh, 1970. pp. 50. (North Carolina University. Water Resources Research Institute. Reports. No. 44)

PACIFIC NORTHWEST RIVER BASINS COMMISSION. Annual report. a., 1971/2- Vancouver, Washington.

HAVEMAN (ROBERT H.) The economic performance of public investments: an ex post evaluation of water resources investments. Baltimore, [1972]. pp. 126.

PACIFIC NORTHWEST RIVER BASINS COMMISSION. Columbia-North Pacific region comprehensive framework study of water and related land resources. Vancouver, Washington, [1972?]. pp. 33.

BROWN (CARL) and others. Decision-making in water resource allocation. Lexington, Mass., [1973]. pp. 110. bibliog.

CARSON (JOHN M.) and others. Community growth and water resources policy. New York 1973. pp. 187.

- United States - California

COOPER (ERWIN) Aqueduct empire: a guide to water in California, its turbulent history and its management today. Glendale, Calif., 1968. pp. 439. bibliogs.

CALIFORNIA water: a story in resource management; edited by David Seckler. Berkeley, 1971. pp. 348.

- United States - North Dakota

> INTERNATIONAL JOINT COMMISSION CANADA AND UNITED STATES. Report...on the cooperative development of the Pembina river basin. [Ottawa], 1967. pp. 60.

- Venezuela

> VENEZUELA. Direccion de Obras Hidraulicas. 1966. Plan nacional de obras hidraulicas: programa 1965-1968. [Caracas, 1966]. pp. 194. bibliog.

WATER-STORAGE

- United Kingdom

> MORECAMBE BAY ECONOMIC STUDY GROUP. Morecambe Bay: estuary storage; report; (with Addendum). London, 1972. pp. 213, 12. (U.K. Water Resources Board. Publications. No. 13)

> U.K. Water Resources Board. 1972. Morecambe Bay: estuary storage; report. London, 1972. pp. 45. (Publications. No. 12)

WATER-SUPPLY

> GRIMA (ANGELO P.) Residential water demand: alternative choices for management. Toronto, [1972]. pp. 211. bibliog. (Toronto. University. Department of Geography. Research Publications. 7)

- Africa, East

> CONFERENCE ON RURAL WATER SUPPLY, DAR ES SALAAM, 1971. Water supply; proceedings...; edited by Gerhard Tschannerl. [Dar es Salaam, 1972?]. pp. 274. bibliogs. (Dar es Salaam. University. Bureau of Resource Assessment and Land Use Planning. Research Papers. No. 20)

> WHITE (GILBERT FOWLER) and others. Drawers of water: domestic water use in East Africa. Chicago, 1972. pp. 306. bibliog.

- Canada

> LEE (TERENCE R.) Approaches to water requirement forecasting; a Canadian perspective. [Ottawa], 1972. pp. 9. (Canada. Department of the Environment. Social Science Series. No. 9)

- Canada - Ontario

> GRIMA (ANGELO P.) Residential water demand: alternative choices for management. Toronto, [1972]. pp. 211. bibliog. (Toronto. University. Department of Geography. Research Publications. 7)

- Ghana

> GHANA. Department of Geological Survey. 1931. Reports on the water supply of the coastal area of the Eastern Province of the Gold Coast colony. Sessional paper No. 27 of 1930-31. in GHANA. Legislative Council. Minutes (formerly Minutes...and sessional papers).

- Nigeria

> NIGERIA (EASTERN REGION). [House of Assembly]. Official Documents. 1958. No.5. Rural water supplies in the Eastern Region. Enugu, 1958. pp. 11.

- Rhodesia

> RHODESIA. Commission of Inquiry into Allocations of Water in the Mtilikwe System. 1972. Report; [John Bernard Pittman, chairman]. [Salisbury, 1972]. pp. 23. ([Command Papers]. 1972. Cmd. R.R. 41)

- Tanzania

> GIBB (Sir ALEXANDER) AND PARTNERS. Water resources survey of the Nile basin in Tanganyika; report. [Dar es Salaam, Government Printer], 1956 [or rather 1957]. pp. 86.

WATER SUPPLY - Underdeveloped areas
    See UNDERDEVELOPED AREAS - Water supply

- United Kingdom

> SOUTH HAMPSHIRE PLAN ADVISORY COMMITTEE. Study Reports. Group B. Urban Services. No. 6. Water supply. Winchester, 1969. pp. 15.

> U.K. Water Resources Board. 1971. Water resources in Wales and the Midlands; report. London, 1971. pp. 61. (Publications. No. 11) 2 maps in end pocket.

> SMITH (KEITH) Ph. D. water in Britain: a study in applied hydrology and resource geography. London, 1972. pp. 241. bibliog.

- United Kingdom - Scotland

> SCOTLAND. Scottish Water Advisory Committee. 1972. Local government reform: the water service in Scotland; report; [William L. Taylor, chairman]. Edinburgh, 1972. pp. 28, 1 map.

- United States - Arizona

> SMITH (COURTLAND L.) The Salt River project: a case study in cultural adaptation to an urbanizing community. Tucson, [1972]. pp. 151. bibliog.

WATER SUPPLY, AGRICULTURAL

- East (Near East)

> FRIED (JEROME J.) and EDLUND (MILTON C.) Desalting technology for Middle Eastern agriculture: an economic case. New York, 1971. pp. 113.

- India - Maharashtra

> LAL (DEEPAK) Wells and welfare: an exploratory cost-benefit study of the economics of small-scale irrigation in Maharashtra. Paris, Organisation for Economic Co-operation and Development, 1972. pp. 162. (Development Centre. Studies: Series on Cost-Benefit Analysis. Case Studies. No.1).

WATER-SUPPLY, INDUSTRIAL

> RICHTER (LAVOSLAV) Water-saving techniques in food-processing plants. (ID/SER.I/3). New York, United Nations Industrial Development Organization, 1969. pp. 69. bibliog. (Food Industry Studies. No. 3)

WATERWAYS

- Germany

> GERMANY. Statistisches Reichsamt. 1876. Die deutschen Wasserstrassen: beschreibendes Verzeichniss nach dem Stande des Jahres 1873. in Band 15 of Germany. Statistisches Reichsamt. Statistik des Deutschen Reichs. [Alte Folge]. Berlin, 1876.

WATSON (AARON)

> WATSON (AARON) A newspaper man's memories. [London, 1923?]. pp. 324.

WATSON (DAVID)

WATSON (DAVID) Chords of memory. Edinburgh, 1936. pp. 190.

WATSON (JAMES)

LITERACY and society: [comprising] The rise and dissolution of the infidel societies in this metropolis, by William Hamilton Reid [reprint of the 1800 edition]; together with James Watson: a memoir... by W.J. Linton [reprint of the 1880 edition]; (edited with a new introduction by Victor E. Neuburg). London, 1971. 1 vol. (various pagings).

WATT (Sir ALAN STEWART)

WATT (Sir ALAN STEWART) Australian diplomat: memoirs. Sydney, 1972. pp. 329. bibliog.

WAVELL (ARCHIBALD PERCIVAL) 1st Earl Wavell

WAVELL (ARCHIBALD PERCIVAL) 1st Earl Wavell. The Viceroy's journal; edited by Penderel Moon. London, 1973. pp. 528.

WEALTH

WEYERMANN (MORITZ RUDOLF) Volksvermögen und Staatskredit in Krieg und Frieden. Stuttgart, 1918. pp. 144.

- Bibliography

CHAMBERLAIN (ETHEL L.) Bibliography on the distribution of income and wealth, 1945-1970. [Santa Monica], 1971. pp. 21. (Rand Corporation. [Papers]. 4603)

- Mathematical models

SHORROCKS (ANTHONY FRANK) Aspects of the distribution of personal wealth; [Ph.D. (London) thesis]. 1973. fo. 202. bibliogs. Typescript: unpublished. This thesis is the property of London University and may not be removed from the Library.

- Asia, Southeast

LAMBERT (RICHARD D.) and HOSELITZ (BERTHOLD FRANK) eds. The role of savings and wealth in southern Asia and the West. Paris, [1963]. pp. 432.

- Germany

HOEHNEN (WILFRIED) Die vermögenspolitischen Gesetze und Massnahmen in der Bundesrepublik Deutschland: Entwicklung, Ergebnisse und kritische Beurteilung. Köln, [1968]. pp. 223. bibliog.

EHRENBERG (HERBERT) Vermögenspolitik für die siebziger Jahre. Stuttgart, [1971]. pp. 100.

SAARBRUECKEN. Universität. Annales Universitatis Saraviensis. Rechts- und Wirtschaftswissenschaftliche Abteilung. Band 57. Pläne und Massnahmen zur Vermögensbildung: eine Analyse ihrer Ziele und Funktionselemente; von Michael Bitz. Köln, 1971. pp. 272. bibliog.

WILLGERODT (HANS) and others. Vermögen für alle: Probleme der Bildung, Verteilung und Werterhaltung des Vermögens in der Marktwirtschaft. Düsseldorf, 1971. pp. 452. bibliog. (Ludwig-Erhard-Stiftung. Schriftenreihe. Band 2)

Russia

POTEMKIN (PETR IVANOVICH) Natsional'noe bogatstvo i faktor vremeni. Novosibirsk, 1965. pp. 41.

- United Kingdom

ATKINSON (A.B.) Unequal shares: wealth in Britain. London, 1972. pp. 279. bibliog.

LABOUR PARTY. Study Group on Capital Sharing. Capital and equality: report, etc. London, [1973]. pp. 45. (Labour Party. Opposition Green Papers)

RICHARDS (ERIC) The leviathan of wealth: the Sutherland fortune in the Industrial Revolution. London, 1973. pp. 316. bibliog.

- United States

SMITH (ROBERT) pseud. The economics of the cold war. New York, [1972]. pp. 126.

- United States - Wisconsin

SOLTOW (LEE) Patterns of wealthholding in Wisconsin since 1850. Madison, Wis., 1971. pp. 168.

WEALTH, ETHICS OF

BOWIE (NORMAN E.) Towards a new theory of distributive justice. Amherst, [Mass.], 1971. pp. 148. bibliog.

WEARSIDE

- Transit systems

VOORHEES (ALAN M.) AND ASSOCIATES, LTD., and BUCHANAN (COLIN) AND PARTNERS. Tyne Wear plan: transport plan for the 1980's. [London], 1972. pp. 172.

VOORHEES (ALAN M.) AND ASSOCIATES, LTD., and BUCHANAN (COLIN) AND PARTNERS. Tyne-Wear plan: technical report. [London], 1973. pp. 112.

VOORHEES (ALAN M.) AND ASSOCIATES, LTD. and BUCHANAN (COLIN) AND PARTNERS. Tyne-Wear plan: urban strategy. [London], 1973. pp. 250.

WEATHER

MAUNDER (W. J.) The value of weather. London, 1970. pp. 388. bibliogs.

WEATHERING

OLLIER (CLIFF) Weathering; edited by K.M. Clayton. Edinburgh, 1969. pp. 304. bibliog.

WEAVERS

- Iran

INTERNATIONAL LABOUR OFFICE. Development Programme: Technical Assistance Sector. [Iran] R.26. Report to the government of Iran on hand-weaving training in farm corporation. (ILO/TAP/Iran/R.26). Geneva, 1971. pp. 18.

WEAVING

UNITED NATIONS INDUSTRIAL DEVELOPMENT ORGANIZATION. Training for Industry Series. No. 3. The Łódź Textile Seminars. 4. Weaving and associated processes. (ID/SER.D/3/4). New York, United Nations, 1970. pp. 48.

WEAVING, HAND
See HAND WEAVING

WEBB (BEATRICE)

BRENNAN (EDWARD J.T.) Educational engineering with the Webbs. Newton Abbot, 1972. pp. 173-200. (Offprint from History of Education, vol. 1, no.2)

LONDON. University. London School of Economics and Political Science. British Library of Political and Economic Science. Publications of Sidney and Beatrice Webb: an interim check list; [based on an anonymous list updated by Christine Maddern and revised by Marjorie Plant]. London, 1973. pp. 36.

WEBB (SIDNEY) 1st Baron Passfield

BRENNAN (EDWARD J.T.) Educational engineering with the Webbs. Newton Abbot, 1972. pp. 173-200. (Offprint from History of Education, vol. 1, no.2)

LONDON. University. London School of Economics and Political Science. British Library of Political and Economic Science. Publications of Sidney and Beatrice Webb: an interim check list; [based on an anonymous list updated by Christine Maddern and revised by Marjorie Plant]. London, 1973. pp. 36.

WEBER (MAX)

BESNARD (PHILIPPE) ed. Protestantisme et capitalisme: la controverse post-Weberienne. Paris, [1970]. pp. 427. bibliog.

ALBERT (HANS) and TOPITSCH (ERNST) eds. Werturteilsstreit. Darmstadt, 1971. pp. 552. bibliog.

BRITISH ASSOCIATION FOR THE ADVANCEMENT OF SCIENCE. Section N. Meeting, Durham, 1970. Max Weber and modern sociology; [papers delivered at a special session convened by John Rex]; edited by Arun Sahay. London. 1971. pp. 111.

DRONBERGER (ILSE) The political thought of Max Weber: in quest of statesmanship. New York, [1971]. pp. 436.

HUFNAGEL (GERHARD) Kritik als Beruf: der kritische Gehalt im Werk Max Webers. [Berlin, 1971]. pp. 439. bibliog.

KORF (GERTRAUD) Ausbruch aus dem "Gehäuse der Hörigkeit"?: Kritik der Kulturtheorien Max Webers und Herbert Marcuses. Frankfurt a. M., 1971. pp. 82.

LEFÈVRE (WOLFGANG) Zum historischen Charakter und zur historischen Funktion der Methode bürgerlicher Soziologie: Untersuchung am Werk Max Webers. Frankfurt am Main, 1971. pp. 158.

SCHLUCHTER (WOLFGANG) Wertfreiheit und Verantwortungsethik: zum Verhältnis von Wissenschaft und Politik bei Max Weber. Tübingen, 1971. pp. 60. With summaries in English and French.

GIDDENS (ANTHONY) Politics and sociology in the thought of Max Weber. London, 1972. pp. 64. bibliog. (British Sociological Association. Studies in Sociology)

ZINGERLE (ARNOLD) Max Weber und China: Herrschafts- und religionssoziologische Grundlagen zum Wandel der chinesischen Gesellschaft. Berlin, [1972]. pp. 180. bibliog.

WEBSTER (DANIEL)

NATHANS (SYDNEY) Daniel Webster and Jacksonian democracy. Baltimore, [1973]. pp. 249. bibliog. (Johns Hopkins University. Studies in Historical and Political Science. Series 91. No.1)

WEHBERG (HANS)

WEHBERG (HANS) Als Pazifist im Weltkrieg. Leipzig, [1919?]. pp. 109.

WEIGHTS AND MEASURES

SWEDEN. Finansdepartementet. Utredningen om Metrologiska Enheter. 1971. Mått och vikt: [and] Måttenheter: betänkande avgivet av Utredningen om Metrologiska Enheter. Stockholm, 1971. pp. 47. (Sweden. Statens Offentliga Utredningar. 1971. 18) 'Måttenheter' published as Statens Offentliga Utredningar. 1965. 5.

- Law and legislation - Russia

KOPYLOVSKAIA (MARIIA ABRAMOVNA) Otvetstvennost' za obmerivanie i obveshivanie pokupatelei. Moskva, 1964. pp. 58.

WEISGAL (MEYER WOLFE)

WEISGAL (MEYER WOLFE) Meyer Weisgal...so far: an autobiography. London, [1971]. pp. 404.

WEISS (LOUISE)

WEISS (LOUISE) Le sacrifice du Chevalier, 3 septembre 1939-9 juin 1940; (mémoires d'une Européenne: nouvelle série). Paris, [1971]. pp. 318.

WEISSBERG (ALEX)

WEISSBERG (ALEX) Wielka czystka; przełożył z niemieckiego Adam Ciołkosz, etc. Paryż, 1967. pp. 572.

WEISSBERG-CYBULSKI (ALEKSANDER)
See WEISSBERG (ALEX)

WEIT (ERWIN)

WEIT (ERWIN) Dans l'ombre de Gomulka; traduit de l'allemand par Dorothée Tiocca. Paris, [1971]. pp. 311.

WEIZMANN INSTITUTE OF SCIENCE

WEISGAL (MEYER WOLFE) Meyer Weisgal...so far: an autobiography. London, [1971]. pp. 404.

WELDING

- Hygienic aspects

Le TRAVAIL de la soudure: monographie des aspects technologiques et pathologiques, etc.; par S. Caccuri [and others]. Luxembourg, Communauté Européenne du Charbon et de l'Acier, 1969. pp. 88. bibliog. (European Coal and Steel Community. Collection d'Hygiène et de Médecine du Travail. No. 9)

WELFARE ECONOMICS

MISHAN (EDWARD JOSHUA) Welfare economics: ten introductory essays. 2nd ed. New York, Random House, [1969]. pp. xiv, 333. bibliog. 21cm.

DREWNOWSKI (JAN) Studies in the measurement of levels of living and welfare. (UNRISD Reports. No.70.3) (UNRISD/70/C.20) Geneva, United Nations Research Institute for Social Development, 1970. pp. 103.

WELFARE ECONOMICS (Cont'd.)

GOUDZWAARD (BOB) Ongeprijsde schaarste: expretiale of ongecompenseerde effecten als economisch-theoretisch en economischpolitiek probleem. Den Haag, 1970. pp. 180. bibliog. With English summary.

ZAWADZKI (SYLWESTER) "Państwo dobrobytu": doktryna i praktyka. 2nd ed. Warszawa, 1970. pp. 480.

HARITOS (Z.) A review of marginal cost pricing. Ottawa, 1971. fo. 10. (Canada. Transport Commission. Research Branch. [Reports. 26])

LENGYEL (PETER) ed. Approaches to the science of socio-economic development; ... with contributions by Raymond Aron [and others]. Paris, Unesco, 1971. pp. 383. bibliogs.

NETHERLANDS. Werkgroep Gemeentelijke Uitgaven voor Sociale Zorg. 1971. Eindrapport. 's-Gravenhage, 1971. 1 vol. (various pagings).

PFAFFENBERGER (WOLFGANG) Wohlstandskriterien für die Wirtschaftsplanung in entwickelten kapitalistischen Marktwirtschaften. Berlin, [1971]. pp. 108. bibliog.

RAO (VIJAYANDRA KASTURI RANGA VARADARAJA) Values and economic development: the Indian challenge. London, [1971]. pp. 182.

TINBERGEN (JAN) Towards a better international economic order;...a special lecture sponsored by UNITAR and given at U.N. Headquarters, New York, on 27 May, 1970, etc. New York, United Nations Institute for Training and Research, 1971. pp. 28. bibliog. (Lecture Series. No.2)

BERLINER (JOSEPH SCHOLOM) Economy, society and welfare: a study in social economics. New York, 1972. pp. 196.

COLLARD (DAVID) Prices, markets and welfare. London, 1972. pp. 210. bibliog.

HACKMANN (JOHANNES) Zur wohlfahrtstheoretischen Behandlung von Verteilungsproblemen. Berlin, [1972]. pp. 222. bibliog.

MILLS (JOHN) Labour Councillor. Growth and welfare: a new policy for Britain. London, 1972. pp. 206.

MORGAN (EDWARD VICTOR) and MORGAN (ANN D.) The economics of public policy. Edinburgh, [1972]. pp. 321. bibliogs.

PESTON (MAURICE H.) Public goods and the public sector. London, 1972. pp. 63. bibliog.

PINHEIRO (MARIA MADALENA PACHECO) and SOARES (MARIA CÂNDIDA MEDEIROS) Criterios sociais na orientação e selecção dos investimentos. Lisboa, 1972. pp. 33. (Portugal. Ministerio das Corporações e Previdência Social. Gabinete de Planeamento. Serie Estudos. 8) With abstracts in English, French and German.

TINBERGEN (JAN) An interdisciplinary approach to the measurement of utility or welfare. Dublin, [1972]. pp. 27. bibliog. (Economic and Social Research Institute. Geary Lectures. 1972)

WHITCOMB (DAVID K.) Externalities and welfare. New York, 1972. pp. 158. bibliog.

ROOS (J.P.) Welfare theory and social policy: a study in policy science. Helsinki, 1973. pp. 251. bibliog. (Societas Scientiarum Fennica. Commentationes Scientiarum Socialium. 4. 1973)

SHARP (MARGARET) The state, the enterprise and the individual: an introduction to applied microeconomics. London, [1973]. pp. 296. bibliogs.

SLEEMAN (JOHN F.) The welfare state: its aims, benefits and costs. London, 1973. pp. 199. bibliog.

WELFARE WORK IN INDUSTRY

- Czechoslovakia

DUBREUIL (HYACINTHE) L'exemple de Bat'a: la libération des initiatives individuelles dans une entreprise géante. Paris, [1936]. pp. 374.

- Russia

GROMOV (IGOR' ALEKSANDROVICH) and others. Sotsiologicheskaia laboratoriia na predpriiatii: iz opyta raboty laboratorii sotsiologicheskikh issledovanii Kirovskogo zavoda. Leningrad, 1972. pp. 74.

LUZAN (PETR PAVLOVICH) Planirovanie sotsial'nogo razvitiia proizvodstvennogo kollektiva. Moskva, 1972. pp. 206.

WELLESLEY (ARTHUR) 1st Duke of Wellington

PERCIVAL (VICTOR) The Duke of Wellington: a pictorial survey of his life (1769-1852). London, H.M.S.O., 1969. pp. 86. bibliog.

WELLINGTON, NEW ZEALAND

- Harbour

WELLINGTON. Harbour Board. Annual report and accounts (formerly Statement of accounts with annual reports and other statistics). a., 1890 [7th]-1961/2, 1966/7, 1970/71, 1971/2. Wellington.

WELLS (HERBERT GEORGE)

WELLS (HERBERT GEORGE) Experiment in autobiography: discoveries and conclusions of a very ordinary brain since 1866. London, 1934 repr. 1966. 2 vols.

MACKENZIE (NORMAN IAN) and MACKENZIE (JEANNE) The time traveller: the life of H.G. Wells. London, [1973]. pp. 487.

WELSH IN LONDON

JENKINS (ROBERT THOMAS) and RAMAGE (HELEN MYFANWY) A history of the Honourable Society of Cymmrodorion and of the Gwyneddigion and Cymreigyddion Societies, 1751-1951. London, 1951. pp. 285. (Cymmrodor, Y. vol. 50)

WELTI (EMIL)
See WELTI (FRIEDRICH EMIL)

WELTI (FRIEDRICH EMIL)

EGGENBERGER (PETER) Bundesrat Emil Welti: sein Einfluss auf die Bundesverfassungsrevision von 1874. Bern, 1972. pp. 208. bibliog.

WENDS

SERBSKI biografiski słownik. Budyšin, [1970]. pp. 301.

Die SORBEN: Wissenwertes aus Vergangenheit und Gegenwart der sorbischen nationalen Minderheit. Bautzen, [1970]. pp. 248. bibliog.

STONE (GERALD) The smallest Slavonic nation: the Sorbs of Lusatia. London, 1972. pp. 201. bibliog.

WENTWORTH FAMILY

CAMDEN SOCIETY. [Publications]. 4th Series. vol. 12. Wentworth papers, 1597-1628; edited... by J.P. Cooper. London, 1973. pp. 337.

WERTHEIM

ELLWEIN (THOMAS) and ZIMPEL (GISELA) Wertheim I: Fragen an eine Stadt. München, [1969 in progress].

WESEMANN (HANS)

WILLI (JOST NIKOLAUS) Der Fall Jacob-Wesemann, 1935/1936: ein Beitrag zur Geschichte der Schweiz in der Zwischenkriegszeit. Bern, 1972. pp. 434. bibliog.

WEST FLANDERS

- Economic conditions

WEST-Vlaanderens ekonomische groei (tien jaar WER/WES, 1954/1964). Brugge, 1965. pp. 179. With summaries in French, English and German.

VANNESTE (OLIVIER) The growth pole concept and the regional economic policy; with an example of application to the Westflemish economy. Brugge, 1971. pp. 274. bibliog. (College of Europe. Cahiers de Bruges. Nouvelle Série. [No.] 24)

WEST HAM

- Civic improvement

LONDON. Greater London Council. Development plan of the former county borough of West Ham: written statement: amendment no. 95 (1968). London, [1968]. pp. 64.

WEST INDIAN STUDENTS IN CANADA

LET the niggers burn!..the Sir George Williams University affair and its Caribbean aftermath; (edited by Dennis Forsythe). Montreal, [1971]. pp. 209.

WEST INDIANS IN THE UNITED KINGDOM

ALLEN (SHEILA) New minorities, old conflicts: Asian and West Indian migrants in Britain. New York, [1971]. pp. 223. bibliog.

HILL (CLIFFORD STANLEY) Black churches: West Indian and African sects in Britain. London, 1971. pp. 23. (British Council of Churches. Community and Race Relations Unit. CRRU Booklets.

JACKSON (SONIA) The illegal child-minders: a report on the growth of unregistered childminding and the West Indian community. Cambridge, [1972]. pp. 38.

BRANDON (DAVID) Not proven: some questions about homelessness and young immigrants. London, 1973. pp. 24.

PHILPOTT (STUART BOWMAN) West Indian migration: the Montserrat case. London, 1973. pp. 210. bibliog. (London, University. London School of Economics and Political Science. Monographs on Social Anthropology. No. 47)

WEST INDIES

- Constitutional history

MUNROE (TREVOR) and LEWIS (RUPERT) eds. Readings in government and politics of the West Indies. [rev.ed.]. Mona, 1971. pp. 270. bibliog.

- Economic conditions

HUNTE (K.R.) To work together in unity. [Bridgetown?], 1961. pp. 67.

- Economic policy

BRYDEN (JOHN M.) Tourism and development: a case study of the Commonwealth Caribbean. Cambridge, 1973. pp. 236. bibliog.

- Emigration and immigration

LAURENCE (K.O.) Immigration into the West Indies in the 19th century. St. Lawrence, Barbados, 1971. pp. 85.

- Occupations

LOWENTHAL (DAVID) and COMITAS (LAMBROS) eds. Work and family life: West Indian perspectives. Garden City, 1973. pp. 422. bibliog.

- Politics and government

MUNROE (TREVOR) and LEWIS (RUPERT) eds. Readings in government and politics of the West Indies. [rev.ed.]. Mona, 1971. pp. 270. bibliog.

- Race question

LOWENTHAL (DAVID) and COMITAS (LAMBROS) eds. Consequences of class and color: West Indian perspectives. Garden City, 1973. pp. 334. bibliog.

- Social conditions

LOWENTHAL (DAVID) West Indian societies. London, 1972. pp. 385. bibliog. (American Geographical Society. Research Series. No. 26)

LOWENTHAL (DAVID) and COMITAS (LAMBROS) eds. Consequences of class and color: West Indian perspectives. Garden City, 1973. pp. 334. bibliog.

WILSON (PETER J.) Crab antics: the social anthropology of English-speaking Negro societies of the Caribbean. New Haven, 1973. pp. 258. bibliog.

- Social policy

BRYDEN (JOHN M.) Tourism and development: a case study of the Commonwealth Caribbean. Cambridge, 1973. pp. 236. bibliog.

WEST MALAYSIA
See MALAYSIA

WEST-VLAANDEREN
See WEST FLANDERS

WESTERN AUSTRALIA

- Economic conditions

PROGRESS: a report by the Government of Western Australia. irreg., 1971/1973- Perth.

- Industries

WESTERN AUSTRALIA. Metropolitan Region Planning Authority. 1969. Perth metropolitan region: industrial survey, 1967-68. Perth, 1969. pp. 64, 1 map.

WESTERN AUSTRALIA (Cont'd.)

- Native races

SCHAPPER (HENRY PAUL) Aboriginal advancement to integration: conditions and plans for Western Australia. Canberra, 1970. pp. 195. (Social Science Research Council of Australia. Aborigines in Australian Society. 5)

BISKUP (PETER) Not slaves, not citizens: the aboriginal problem in western Australia, 1898-1954. St. Lucia, Queensland, [1973]. pp. 342. bibliog.

- Social policy

SCHAPPER (HENRY PAUL) Aboriginal advancement to integration: conditions and plans for Western Australia. Canberra, 1970. pp. 195. (Social Science Research Council of Australia. Aborigines in Australian Society. 5)

WESTMINSTER

- Civic improvement

WESTMINSTER. Department of Architecture and Planning. Development Plan Summary Papers. S2. Conservation in Westminster. [Westminster], 1972. pp. 40.

- Growth

WESTMINSTER. Department of Architecture and Planning. Development Plan Summary Papers. S2. Conservation in Westminster. [Westminster], 1972. pp. 40.

- Hotels, taverns, etc.

WESTMINSTER. Department of Architecture and Planning. Tourism and hotel development. London, [1972]. pp. 92. (Westminster Development Plan Publications. Topic Papers. T1)

- Schools

COLQUHOUN (PATRICK) LL.D. A new and appropriate system of education for the labouring people; [facsimile reprint of the first edition originally published in London, 1806]. Shannon, [1971]. pp. 93.

WESTPHALIA

- Economic history

HELMRICH (WILHELM) Die Industrialisierung und wirtschaftliche Verflechtung des Münsterlandes. Münster (Westf.), 1937. pp. 142. bibliog. (Provinzialinstitut für Westfälische Landes- und Volkskunde. Veröffentlichungen. Reihe 1. Heft 1)

WETZ (ALICJA ZAWADZKA-)
See ZAWADZKA-WETZ (ALICJA)

WHALING

PEREIRA SALAS (EUGENIO) Los primeros contactos entre Chile y los Estados Unidos, 1778-1809. Santiago de Chile, [1971]. pp. 353.

WHEAT

AYKROYD (WALLACE RUDDELL) and DOUGHTY (JOYCE) Wheat in human nutrition. Rome, Food and Agriculture Organization, 1970. pp. 163. bibliog. (Nutritional Studies. No.23)

- France

FRANCE. Ministère de l'Agriculture. Statistique Agricole. Supplément. Série Etudes. No. 37. Enquête sur les productions de blé et d'orge en 1967: principaux résultats de 1964 à 1967 par région de programme; [étude...rédigée par Jacqueline Prod'homme.] [Paris], 1968. pp. 149.

- India

INDIA. Ministry of Agriculture. Directorate of Economics and Statistics. 1972. Bulletin on wheat statistics in India (districtwise). [Delhi], 1972. pp. 155.

WHIG PARTY (UNITED KINGDOM)

KORTHALS (ECKEHARD) Die antipapistische Bewegung in England während der Restaurationszeit von 1660 bis 1673 unter besonderer Berücksichtigung der antimonarchischen Strömungen in den Anfängen der Whig-Partei. Hamburg, 1970. pp. 152. bibliog.

WHIG PARTY (UNITED STATES)

HOWE (DANIEL WALKER) compiler. The American Whigs: an anthology. New York, [1973]. pp. 249. bibliog.

WHISKY

McGUIRE (EDWARD B.) Irish whiskey: a history of distilling, the spirit trade and excise controls in Ireland. Dublin, 1973. pp. 462. bibliog.

WHITE (HORACE) 1834-1916

LOGSDON (JOSEPH) Horace White, nineteenth century liberal. Westport, Conn., [1971]. pp. 418. bibliog.

WHITE (JOHN CAMPBELL) Baron Overtoun

LABOUR LEADER. White Slaves' Series. No.5. The Overtoun horror. London, [1899?]. pp. 16.

WHITE FATHERS

PORTUGAL. Secretaria de Estado da Informação e Turismo. 1971. The White Fathers. [Lisbon?], 1971. pp. 23.

WHITE RUSSIA

BYELORUSSIAN Soviet Socialist Republic. Moscow, 1972. pp. 82.

- Constitutional history

SHKLIAR (MIKHAIL EFIMOVICH) Belorusskaia SSR - odna iz uchreditel'nits Soiuza SSR. Minsk, 1972. pp. 159.

- Dictionaries and encyclopaedias

BELARUSKAIA Savetskaia Entsyklapedyia. Minsk, 1969 in progress.

- Economic conditions

LIS (ALEKSEI GEORGIEVICH) Problemy razvitiia i razmeshcheniia proizvoditel'nykh sil Belorussii. Moskva, 1972. pp. 275.

- Economic history

MARTINKEVICH (F.S.) ed. Sotsial'no-ekonomichskie preobrazovaniia v Belorusskoi SSR za gody Sovetskoi vlasti. Minsk, 1970. pp. 527. bibliog.

PETRIKOV (PETR TIKHONOVICH) Sovety deputatov trudiashchikhsia BSSR i ikh rol' v sozdanii material'no-tekhnicheskoi bazy kommunizma, 1959-1965 gg. Minsk, 1972. pp. 307.

- Economic policy

GOLOVKO (ANATOLII ALEKSANDROVICH) Deiatel'nost' Sovetov Belorussii po osushchestvleniiu ekonomicheskoi politiki v derevne v 1917-1936 godakh. Minsk, 1968. pp. 125.

LIS (ALEKSEI GEORGIEVICH) Problemy razvitiia i razmeshcheniia proizvoditel'nykh sil Belorussii. Moskva, 1972. pp. 275.

- Gentry

TAL'VIRSKAIA (Z. IA.) K voprosu o sotsial'nom oblike melkogo dvorianstva v 1860-kh godakh. in Istoriko-sotsiologicheskie issledovaniia: na materialakh slavianskikh stran. Moskva, 1970. pp. 313.

- History

BAIKOVA (S. M.) O dvizhushchikh silakh vosstaniia 1863 g. na territorii Belorussii. in Istoriko-sotsiologicheskie issledovaniia: na materialakh slavianskikh stran. Moskva, 1970. pp. 313.

HISTORYIA Belaruskai SSR. Minsk, 1972 in progress.

BELORUSSIIA v Soiuze Sovetskikh Respublik: k 50-letiiu obrazovaniia SSSR. Minsk, 1972. pp. 271.

- History - 1917-

LUBACHKO (IVAN S.) Belorussia under Soviet rule, 1917-1957. Lexington, Ky., [1972]. pp. 219. bibliog.

- Intellectual life

STRUKTURA sovetskoi intelligentsii: po materialam BSSR. Minsk, 1970. pp. 218. bibliog.

- Politics and government

EFREMOVA (OL'GA IVANOVNA) Iz istorii obshchestvennoi mysli Belorussii kontsa XIX - nachala XX v. Minsk, 1972. pp. 175. bibliog.

MATSKO (ALEKSANDR NIKOLAEVICH) Revoliutsionnaia bor'ba trudiashchikhsia Pol'shi i Zapadnoi Belorussii protiv gneta burzhuazii i pomeshchikov, 1918-1939 gg. Minsk, 1972. pp. 335.

SALADKAŬ (TSIMAFEI ERAFEEVICH) Bol'shevistskaia gazeta "Pravda" v Belorussii, 1912-1917 gg. 2nd ed. Minsk, 1972. pp. 296. For 1st White Russian ed. see his Bal'shavitskaia hazeta "Pravda" ŭ Belarusi, 1912-1917 hh.

- Relations (general) with Poland.

TOLSTOI (VASILII SEMENOVICH) Bratskoe sotrudnichestvo belorusskogo i pol'skogo narodov, 1944-1964. Minsk, 1966. pp. 140.

- Rural conditions

CHEPKO (VALENTINA VLADIMIROVNA) Klassovaia bor'ba v belorusskoi derevne v pervoi polovine XIX v. Minsk, 1972. pp. 267.

- Rural conditions

CHEPKO (VALENTINA VLADIMIROVNA) Klassovaia bor'ba v belorusskoi derevne v pervoi polovine XIX v. Minsk, 1972. pp. 267.

KORZUN (IVAN PAVLOVICH) Preodolenie razlichii mezhdu gorodom i derevnei v bytu i kul'ture: istoriko-etnograficheskoe issledovanie po materialam BSSR. Minsk, 1972. pp. 160.

NAUCHNO-tekhnicheskii progress i sotsial'nye izmeneniia na sele: na materialakh Belorusskoi SSR. Minsk, 1972. pp. 271.

- Social history

IVANOV (VLADIMIR MIKHAILOVICH) Ocherk byta promyshlennykh rabochikh dorevoliutsionnoi Belorussii. Minsk, 1971. pp. 159.

- Social policy

TARATKEVICH (MIKHAIL VASIL'EVICH) Proizvodstvo, trud, chelovek. Minsk, 1969. pp. 128.

DMITRUK (LIUDMILA AL'BINOVNA) Sotsial'naia aktivnost' proizvodstvennogo kollektiva v usloviiakh ekonomicheskoi reformy. Minsk, 1972. pp. 184. bibliog.

- Statistics

WHITE RUSSIA. Tsentral'noe Statisticheskoe Upravlenie. 1969. Narodnoe khoziaistvo Belorusskoi SSR v 1968 godu: statisticheskii sbornik. Minsk, 1969. pp. 531.

WHITE RUSSIANS IN POLAND

PAWLUCZUK (WŁODZIMIERZ) Światopogląd jednostki w warunkach rozpadu społeczności tradycyjnej. Warszawa, 1972. pp. 240. With English summary.

WHITMAN (WALT)

INGERSOLL (ROBERT GREEN) An oration on Walt Whitman. London, 1890. pp. 34.

WHITSON (JOHN)

McGRATH (PATRICK VINCENT) John Whitson and the merchant community of Bristol. Bristol, 1970. pp. 23. (Historical Association. Bristol Branch. Local History Pamphlets. [No. 25]) (Bristol. University. Frederick Creech Jones Memorial Lectures. 1969)

WHOLESALE TRADE

- Australia

AUSTRALIA. Commonwealth Bureau of Census and Statistics. 1971. Economic censuses: 1968-69: wholesale establishments: preliminary statement. Canberra, [1971]. pp. 17.

- Canada

CANADA. Statistics Canada. Merchandising and Services Division. 1972. Wholesale trade; Commerce de gros; 1961-1971. Ottawa, 1972. pp. 29. In English and French.

CANADA. Statistics Canada. Merchandising and Services Division. Wholesale Trade Section. 1972. Wholesale trade: establishments; Commerce de gros: établissements; 1966. Ottawa, 1972. pp. 146,(10). In English and French.

- Cyprus

CYPRUS. Statistics and Research Department. 1971. Census of distribution, 1967: wholesale and retail trade. [Nicosia], 1971. pp. 89,4.

- France

FRANCE. Commission du Commerce. 1971. Préparation du 6e Plan: rapport. [Paris], 1971. pp. 79.

WHOLESALE TRADE - France (Cont'd.)

FRANCE. Institut National de la Statistique et des Etudes Economiques. 1971. Recensement de la distribution année 1966: résultats généraux définitifs: tableaux detaillés. [Paris], 1971. pp. 517.

- Germany - North Rhine-Westphalia

NORTH RHINE-WESTPHALIA. Statistisches Landesamt. 1972. Der Grosshandel in Nordrhein-Westfalen am 30.9.1968: Ergebnisse der Handels- und Gaststättenzählung 1968. Düsseldorf, 1972. pp. 114. (Beiträge zur Statistik des Landes Nordrhein-Westfalen. Heft 285)

- Guatemala

GUATEMALA. Comision Nacional del Salario. 1964. Estudio economico para la determinacion del salario minimo en la industria de comercio. Guatemala, 1964. pp. 116.

- Norway

NORWAY. Statistiske Centralbyrå. Regnskapsstatistikk: engroshandel: Statistics of accounts: wholesale trade. a., 1971 [1st]- Oslo.

- Peru - Directories

PERU. Direccion Nacional de Estadistica y Censos. 1967. Censo economico, 1963: directorio de comercio al por menor: establecimientos con 5 y mas personas ocupadas; directorio de comercio al por mayor: establecimientos con el total de personas ocupadas. Lima, 1967. pp. 185.

- Rhodesia

RHODESIA. Central Statistical Office. 1972. The census of distribution in 1969/70: retail and wholesale trade, hotels and restaurants. Salisbury, 1972. pp. 44,(8).

- Russia

BRODSKII (IOSIF L'VOVICH) and GAL'PERIN (LEV BORISOVICH) Optovye iarmarki v SSSR: pravovye voprosy. Moskva, 1972. pp. 102.

PANKRATOV (FEDOR GRIGOR'EVICH) Povyshenie effektivnosti optovoi torgovli potrebitel'skoi kooperatsii. Moskva, 1972. pp. 143.

- South Africa

SMITH (T.W.F.) Retail and wholesale trade in Zululand. Durban, 1972. pp. 127. bibliog. (Natal University. Natal Regional Survey. Additional Reports. No.7.)

- Spain

SPAIN. Instituto Nacional de Estadistica. 1970. II encuesta nacional de comercio interior: resumen nacional. Madrid, 1970. pp. 301. In Spanish, English and French.

SPAIN. Comisaria del Plan de Desarrollo Economico y Social. 1972. (III Plan de desarrollo economico y social): comercio interior. [Madrid], 1972. pp. 111.

- Sweden

SWEDEN. Statistiska Centralbyrån. Konjunkturbarometern för varuhandeln: Business tendency survey in wholesale and retail trade. (Statistiska Meddelanden: H). q., Mr 1972- Stockholm. With summary and headings of tables in English.

LÄNDELL (HANS) Analyser av partihandelns lokalisering. Uppsala, [1972]. pp. 179. bibliog. (Uppsala. Universitet. Kulturgeografiska Institutionen. Geografiska Regionstudier. Nr. 8)

- Tanzania

UNITED REPUBLIC OF TANZANIA. Bureau of Statistics. 1972. Survey of distributive trade, Dar-es-Salaam, 1970. Dar es Salaam, 1972. fo. 31, 7.

- Thailand

THAILAND. National Statistical Office. 1969. Census of business trade or services, 1966: Bangkok and Thon Buri municipalities. [Bangkok], 1969. pp. xiii, 100, (4). In English and Thai.

THAILAND. National Statistical Office. 1969. Census of business trade or services, 1966: central region. [Bangkok], 1969. pp. 65. In English and Thai.

- United Kingdom

ECONOMIC DEVELOPMENT COMMITTEE FOR THE DISTRIBUTIVE TRADES. Channels and costs of distribution in the NE region. London, H.M.S.O., 1971. pp. 35.

WARD (T.S.) The distribution of consumer goods: structure and performance. London, 1973. pp. 236. (Cambridge. University. Department of Applied Economics. Occasional Papers. 38)

- Venezuela

VENEZUELA. Direccion General de Estadistica. Censos Economicos, 1963. [Terceros] censos economicos: comercio. Caracas, 1968. 2 vols. (in 1).

WICKSELL (JOHAN GUSTAF KNUT)

SIEPER (EDWARD) and SWAN (P.L.) The durability of durable goods: Wicksell revisited. Canberra, 1971. fo. 32. (Australian National University. Working Papers in Economics and Econometrics. No. 6)

WIGG (GEORGE EDWARD CECIL) Baron Wigg

WIGG (GEORGE EDWARD CECIL) Baron Wigg. George Wigg. London, 1972. pp. 384. bibliog.

WIGGINTON

- History - Sources

PRICE (F.D.) ed. The Wigginton constables' book, 1691-1836. London, 1971. pp. 144. (Banbury. Banbury Historical Society. [Publications]. vol.2)

WILBERFORCE (SAMUEL) Successively Bishop of Oxford and of Winchester

MEACHAM (STANDISH) Lord bishop: the life of Samuel Wilberforce, 1805-1873. Cambridge, Mass., 1970. pp. 328.

WILD LIFE, CONSERVATION OF

- Canada

PIMLOTT (DOUGLAS H.) and others. Scientific activities in fisheries and wildlife resources. Ottawa, 1971. pp. 189. (Canada. Science Council of Canada. Special Studies. No.15)

- Rhodesia

RHODESIA. Wild Life Commission. 1970. Report: [G.A. Petrides, chairman]. [Salisbury], 1970. pp. 96. bibliog. (Rhodesia. [Command Papers]. 1970. Cmd. R.R. 16)

- United Kingdom

SOUTH HAMPSHIRE PLAN ADVISORY COMMITTEE. Study Reports. Group A. Rural Conservation. No. 4. Natural history. Winchester, [1969]. pp. (27).

U.K. Working Party on Marine Wildlife Conservation. 1973. Marine wildlife conservation: an assessment of evidence of a threat to marine wildlife and the need for conservation measures; [R.B. Clark, chairman]. [London], 1973. pp. 39. (U.K. Natural Environment Research Council. Publications. Series B. No. 5)

WILL

WILSON (J.R.S.) Emotion and object. Cambridge, 1972. pp. 192. bibliog.

WILLERT (Sir ARTHUR)

WILLERT (Sir ARTHUR) Washington and other memories. Boston, 1972. pp. 248.

WILLIAM II, Emperor of Germany

TREUTLER (KARL GEORG VON) Die graue Exzellenz: zwischen Staatsräson und Vasallentreue; aus den Papieren des kaiserlichen Gesandten...; herausgegeben und eingeleitet von Karl-Heinz Janssen. Frankfurt/Main, [1971]. pp. 277.

WILLIAM IV., King of Great Britain and Ireland

ZIEGLER (PHILIP) King William IV. London, 1971. pp. 335. bibliog.

WILLIAMS (ALBERT RHYS)

PESIKOV (IULII VENIAMINOVICH) Sovetskie druz'ia Vil'iamsa. Moskva, 1972. pp. 96.

WILLIAMS (Sir GEORGE)

BINFIELD (CLYDE) George Williams and the Y.M.C.A.: a study in Victorian social attitudes. London, 1973. pp. 408. bibliog.

WILLIAMS (MARCIA)

WILLIAMS (MARCIA) Inside Number 10. London, [1972]. pp. 385.

WILSON (HAROLD)

WILLIAMS (MARCIA) Inside Number 10. London, [1972]. pp. 385.

WILSON (THOMAS WOODROW) President of the United States

BELL (SIDNEY) Righteous conquest: Woodrow Wilson and the evolution of the new diplomacy. Port Washington, N.Y., 1972. pp. 209. bibliog.

WILTON PARK

KEEZER (DEXTER MERRIAM) A unique contribution to international relations: the story of Wilton Park. London, [1973]. pp. 110.

WINCHESTER (DIOCESE)

TITOW (J.Z.) Winchester yields: a study in medieval agricultural productivity. Cambridge, 1972. pp. 151.

WINDMILLS

- United Kingdom

SHORT (MICHAEL) Windmills in Lambeth: an historical survey. London, 1971. pp. 96. bibliog.

WINDSOR

See NEW WINDSOR

WINE AND WINE MAKING

FRANCIS (ALAN DAVID) The wine trade. London, 1972. pp. 353. bibliog.

- France

SIVERY (GERARD) Les comtes de Hainaut et le commerce du vin au XIVe siècle et au début du XVe siècle. Lille, 1969. pp. 213. bibliog. (Lille. Université. Faculté des Lettres. Centre Regional d'Etudes Historiques. Publications. No.6)

JAMES (MARGERY KIRKBRIDE) Studies in the medieval wine trade;...edited by Elspeth M. Veale. Oxford, 1971. pp. 232. bibliog.

POUPON (PIERRE) and FORGEOT (PIERRE) Les vins de Bourgogne. 6th ed. Paris, 1972. pp. 221. bibliog.

- Germany

WEHLING (HANS GEORG) Die politische Willensbildung auf dem Gebiet der Weinwirtschaft, dargestellt am Beispiel der Weingesetzgebung. Göppingen, 1971. pp. 256,15. bibliog. With English summary.

- United Kingdom

JAMES (MARGERY KIRKBRIDE) Studies in the medieval wine trade;...edited by Elspeth M. Veale. Oxford, 1971. pp. 232. bibliog.

FRANCIS (ALAN DAVID) The wine trade. London, 1972. pp. 353. bibliog.

WINGATE (ORDE CHARLES)

TULLOCH (DEREK) Wingate in peace and war;... edited by... Arthur Swinson. London, 1972. pp. 300.

WINNACKER (KARL)

WINNACKER (KARL) Nie den Mut verlieren: Erinnerungen an Schicksalsjahre der deutschen Chemie. Düsseldorf, 1971. pp. 524. bibliog.

WINNACKER (KARL) Challenging years: my life in chemistry; translated by David Goodman. London, 1972. pp. 440. bibliog.

WINNIPEG

- Politics and government

WINNIPEG. Council. Minutes. a., 1901-1913. Winnipeg.

WIRE INDUSTRY

- United Kingdom

MAIS (STUART PETRE BRODIE) A history of N. Greening and Sons Ltd, Warrington, England, from 1799 to 1949. Warrington, [imprint], [1949?]. pp. 60.

HORSFALL (JOHN HENRY COLDWELL) The iron masters of Penns, 1720-1970. Kineton, 1971. pp. 331.

WISCONSIN
- Politics and government

CHAPPLE (JOHN BOWMAN) LaFollette road to communism - must we go further along that road?: a book of facts, evidence, photographs. [Ashland, Wisc., 1936] pp. 170.

CAINE (STANLEY P.) The myth of a progressive reform: railroad regulation in Wisconsin, 1903-1910. Madison, 1970. pp. 226.

WISCONSIN RIVER

RANNEY (DAVID C.) Water quality management: an analysis of institutional patterns. Madison, Wis., [1972]. pp. 158. (Wisconsin University, Madison. Water Resources Center. Water Resources Studies. 2)

WISCONSIN UNIVERSITY

CHAPPLE (JOHN BOWMAN) LaFollette road to communism - must we go further along that road?: a book of facts, evidence, photographs. [Ashland, Wisc., 1936]. pp. 170.

NATIONAL RESEARCH COUNCIL. Division of Behavioral Sciences. Advisory Committee for Assessment of University Based Institutes for Research on Poverty. Policy and program research in a university setting; a case study; (report of the... Committee, etc.). Washington, D.C., 1971. pp. 55.

WITCHCRAFT

MAIR (LUCY PHILIP) Witchcraft. London, Weidenfeld & Nicolson, [1969]. pp. 256. bibliog. 19cm. (World University Library)

PITHOYS (CLAUDE) A seventeenth century exposure of superstition: select texts of Claude Pithoys, 1587-1676; introduction and notes by P.J.S. Whitmore. The Hague, 1972. pp. 263. bibliog.

- Europe

RUSSELL (JEFFREY BURTON) Witchcraft in the middle ages. Ithaca, N.Y., 1972. pp. 394. bibliog.

WITNESSES
- Bulgaria

KOCHEV (KOSTADIN V.) Postradaliiat kato obvinitel v nakazatelniia protses. Sofiia, 1971. pp. 111. With French summary.

- Russia

TURCHIN (DMITRII AFANAS'EVICH) Esli ty svidetel'. Moskva, 1972. pp. 32.

WITTGENSTEIN (LUDWIG)

ENGEL (S. MORRIS) Wittgenstein's doctrine of the tyranny of language: an historical and critical examination of his Blue Book. The Hague, 1971. pp. 145.

FINCH (HENRY LEROY) Wittgenstein - the early philosophy: an exposition of the "Tractatus". New York, 1971. pp. 291. bibliog.

KLEMKE (ELMER D.) ed. Essays on Wittgenstein. Urbana, [1971]. pp. 552. bibliog.

LANG (MARTIN) Wittgensteins Philosophische Grammatik: Entstehung und Perspektiven der Strategie eines radikalen Aufklärers. Den Haag, 1971. pp. 160.

BOGEN (JAMES) Wittgenstein's philosophy of language: some aspects of its development. London, 1972. pp. 244. bibliog.

HACKER (PETER MICHAEL S.) Insight and illusion: Wittgenstein on philosophy and the metaphysics of experience. Oxford, 1972. pp. 321. bibliog

LUDWIG Wittgenstein: philosophy and language; edited by Alice Ambrose and Morris Lazerowitz. London, 1972. pp. 325. bibliog.

PITKIN (HANNA FENICHEL) Wittgenstein and justice: on the significance of Ludwig Wittgenstein for social and political thought. Berkeley, 1972. pp. 360. bibliog.

BARTLEY (WILLIAM WARREN) Wittgenstein. Philadelphia, [1973]. pp. 192. bibliog.

KENNY (ANTHONY JOHN PATRICK) Wittgenstein. London, 1973. pp. 240. bibliog.

WODZICKI (ROMAN)

WODZICKI (ROMAN) Wspomnienia: Gdańsk, Warszawa, Berlin, 1928-1939. Warszawa, 1972. pp. 686,[xii].

WOHLGEMUTH (AUGUST)

RENK (HANSJOERG) Bismarcks Konflikt mit der Schweiz: der Wohlgemuth-Handel von 1889; Vorgeschichte, Hintergründe und Folgen. Basel, 1972. pp. 425. bibliog.

WOLF CHILDREN

MALSON (LUCIEN) Wolf children; [and] The wild boy of Aveyron [by] Jean Itard. London, 1972. pp. 179.

WOLFSBURG
- Social conditions

HILTERSCHEID (HERMANN) Industrie und Gemeinde: die Beziehungen zwischen der Stadt Wolfsburg und dem Volkswagenwerk und ihre Auswirkungen auf die kommunale Selbstverwaltung. Berlin, [1970]. pp. 348. bibliog.

WOLLSTONECRAFT (MARY)
See GODWIN (MARY)

WOMAN

[COOPER (ANNA JULIA HAYWOOD)] A voice from the South: by a black woman of the South; [reprint of work published in 1892]. New York, 1969. pp. 304.

- Employment

INTERNATIONAL LABOUR ORGANISATION. Committee on Work on Plantations. 6th Session. Reports. 3. Conditions of work of women and young workers on plantations: third item on the agenda. Geneva, International Labour Office, 1970. pp. 95.

SEMINAR ON THE EFFECTS OF SCIENTIFIC AND TECHNOLOGICAL DEVELOPMENTS ON THE STATUS OF WOMEN, IASI, 1969. Seminar...[held in] Iasi, Romania, 5-18 August 1969; organized by the United Nations, Division of Human Rights, in co-operation with the government of Romania. (ST/TAO/HR/37). New York, United Nations, 1970. pp. 43.

SEMINAR ON THE PARTICIPATION OF WOMEN IN THE ECONOMIC LIFE OF THEIR COUNTRIES, MOSCOW, 1970. Seminar...(with reference to the implementation of Article 10 of the Declaration on the Elimination of Discrimination against Women) [held in] Moscow...8-21 September, 1970, etc. (ST/TAO/HR/41). New York, United Nations, 1970. pp. 38.

FAMILY issues of employed women in Europe and America; edited by Andrée Michel. Leiden, 1971. pp. 166. bibliogs.

RAPOPORT (RHONA) and RAPOPORT (ROBERT NORMAN) Dual-career families. Harmondsworth, 1971. pp. 329. bibliog.

- Employment - Africa

MBILINYI (MARJORIE J.) The participation of women in African economies. [Dar es Salaam, 1971]. pp. 32. (Dar es Salaam. University. Economic Research Bureau. ERB Papers. 71.12)

SEMINAR ON THE PARTICIPATION OF WOMEN IN ECONOMIC LIFE, LIBREVILLE (REPUBLIC OF GABON), 1971. Seminar...(with reference to the implementation of Article 10 of the Declaration on the Elimination of Discrimination against Women). [held in] Libreville,...27 July - 9 August 1971. (ST/TAO/HR/43). New York, United Nations, 1971. pp. 48.

- Employment - Austria

SCHEURINGER (BRUNHILDE) Die Berufsmobilität von Frauen. Linz, [1972]. pp. 295. bibliog. (Österreichisches Institut für Arbeitsmarktpolitik. Arbeitsmarktpolitik. Heft 8)

LEICHTER (KAETHE) Leben und Werk; herausgegeben von Herbert Steiner. Wien, [1973]. pp. 525. bibliog. (Ludwig-Boltzmann-Institut für Geschichte der Arbeiterbewegung. Veröffentlichungen)

TRAXLER (GABRIELLE) Zwischen Tradition und Emanzipation: Probleme der Frauenarbeit in Österreich. Wien, [1973]. pp. 195.

- Employment - Brazil

PARTICIPAÇÃO da mulher no mercado de trabalho; [by] Sylvio Rabello [and others]. Recife, Instituto Joaquim Nabuco de Pesquisas Sociais, 1969. pp. 149. bibliog.

- Employment - Canada

ROBSON (REGINALD ARTHUR HENRY) and LAPOINTE (MIREILLE) A comparison of men's and women's salaries and employment fringe benefits in the academic profession; prepared for the Canadian Association of University Teachers. Ottawa, 1971. pp. 39. (Canada. Royal Commission on the Status of Women in Canada. 1967. Studies. 1)

- Employment - Denmark

KVINDER på fabrik; ved Karen Jespersen [and others]. København, 1973. pp. 112.

- Employment - Europe

WERKER-BEAUJON (CORNELIA MATHILDE) Die Mitarbeit der Frau bei der Polizei. 's-Gravenhage, 1912. pp. 136.

- Employment - France

ASSOCIATION NATIONALE POUR LA FORMATION PROFESSIONNELLE DES ADULTES, [FRANCE]. Centre d'Etudes et Recherches Psychotechniques. Le sous-emploi féminin dans quelques zones industrielles et portuaires; [by] Françoise Lantier [and others]. [Paris], 1967-69. 5 parts (in 1 vol.)

CALLET (CHRISTINE) and DU GRANRUT (CLAUDE) Place aux femmes. [Paris, 1973]. pp. 285. bibliog.

- Employment - Germany

LUEDERS (MARIE ELISABETH) Volksdienst der Frau. Berlin, [1937]. pp. 108.

- Employment - India

KAPUR (PROMILLA) Marriage and the working woman in India. Delhi, [1970]. pp. 528. bibliog.

The EDUCATED woman in Indian society today; a study carried out by the YWCA of India. Bombay, [1971]. pp. 287. bibliogs.

- Employment - Ireland (Republic)

WALSH (BRENDAN M.) and O'TOOLE (ANNETTE) Women and employment in Ireland: results of a national survey. Dublin, 1973. pp. 156. bibliog. (Economic and Social Research Institute. Papers. No.69)

- Employment - Russia

MIKHAILIUK (VALENTINA BORISOVNA) Ispol'zovanie zhenskogo truda v narodnom khoziaistve. Moskva, 1970. pp. 151.

ABRAMOVA (ALEKSANDRA AFANAS'EVNA) Okhrana truda zhenshchin: spravochnik po zakonodatel'stvu. Moskva, 1972. pp. 143.

- Employment - Russia - Moldavian Republic

SHISHKAN (N.M.) Sotsial'no-ekonomicheskie problemy zhenskogo truda v gorodakh Moldavii. Kishinev, 1969. pp. 80.

- Employment - South Africa

WESSELS (DINA M.) The employment potential of graduate housewives in the P[retoria-] W[itwatersrand-] V[ereeniging] region. Pretoria, South African Human Sciences Research Council, 1972 in progress. bibliog.

- Employment - Spain

DURAN (MARIA ANGELES) El trabajo de la mujer en España: un estudio sociologico. Madrid, 1972. pp. 252. bibliog.

- Employment - Sweden

SWEDEN.. Arbetsmarknadsstyrelsen. 1971. Kvinnorna och arbetsmarknaden: fördomar, fakta, framtid; (with English summary: Women and the labour market). [Stockholm], 1971. 2 parts. bibliog.

BRADLEY (GUNILLA) Kvinnan och karriären: en studie av kvinnors befordringsintresse i relation till arbetstillfredsställelse, hemmiljö och skolutbildning. [Stockholm, 1972]. pp. 170. bibliog. (Personaladministrativa Rådet. Meddelanden. Nr. 64)

- Employment - United Kingdom

WILD (RAY) and HILL (A.B.) Women in the factory: a study of job satisfaction and labour turnover. London, 1970. pp. 96.

U.K. Department of Employment. [Statistics Division]. 1971. 1966 sample census of population: Department of Employment paper no. 6: females at work. [London, 1971]. fo. (14).

U.K. Department of Employment. [Statistics Division]. 1971. 1966 sample census of population: Department of Employment paper no. 7: females not at work. [London, 1971]. pp. 2; fo. (10).

WOMAN - Employment - United Kingdom
(Cont'd.)

ELLISTON RESEARCH ASSOCIATES. What the girls think! report of the labour turnover attitude survey prepared...for the Clothing E[conomic] D[evelopment] C[ommittee]. London, National Economic Development Office, 1972. pp. 28.

MUSGRAVE (BEATRICE) and WHEELER-BENNETT (JOAN) eds. Women at work: combining family and a career;...including Comeback: a directory to the professions. London, 1972. pp. 156.

ELLISTON RESEARCH ASSOCIATES. Employees' attitudes and their effect on labour turnover in the clothing industry; prepared ...on behalf of the Economic Development Committee for the Clothing Industry. London, National Economic Development Office, 1973. pp. 75.

U.K. Department of Employment. Health and Safety at Work. 23. Hours of employment of women and young persons. 2nd ed. London, 1973. pp. 27.

U.K. National Register of Archives. 1973. Labour Party archives: miscellaneous accessions: Standing Joint Committee of Industrial Women's Organisations: note on first minute book compiled by R.A. Storey. London, 1973. single sheet.

- Employment - United States

HEDGES (ANNA CHARLOTTE) Wage worth of school training: an analytical study of six hundred women workers in textile factories. New York, 1914. pp. 174. bibliog.

OPPENHEIMER (VALERIE KINCADE) The female labor force in the United States: demographic and economic factors governing its growth and changing composition. Berkeley, [1970]. pp. 197. bibliog. (California University. Institute of International Studies. Population Monograph Series. No.5)

LORING (ROSALIND) and WELLS (THEODORA) Breakthrough: women into management. New York, [1972]. pp. 202.

CONFERENCE ON WOMEN'S CHALLENGE TO MANAGEMENT., ARDEN HOUSE, 1971. Corporate lib: women's challenge to management; edited by Eli Ginzberg and Alice M. Yohalem. Baltimore, [1973]. pp. 153. bibliog.

- History and condition of women

FULLER (SARAH MARGARET) afterwards OSSOLI, Marchesa d'. Woman in the nineteenth century: [reprint of the work originally published in 1855]. New York, [1971]. pp. 212.

DIXIE (Lady FLORENCE CAROLINE) Towards freedom: an appeal to thoughtful men and women. London, [c. 1905]. pp. 14. (Reprinted from The Agnostic Annual, 1904)

ERT (KARL) Die Anmassungen der Frauenbewegung...: Studie. Halle a. S., 1911. pp. 110.

FINOT (JEAN) Problems of the sexes;... translated... by Mary J. Safford. London, 1913. pp. 408.

BEARD (MARY RITTER) On understanding women; [facsimile reprint of the work first published in New York, 1931]. New York, 1968. pp. 541. bibliog.

YOUNG (NORWOOD) England conquers the world. London, 1937. pp. 239.

JENSEN (OLIVER) The revolt of American women; [a pictorial history]. New York, [1952 repr. 1971]. pp. 224.

HUGHES (VIOLET MARJORIE) Women in bondage. London, [1958]. pp. 158.

MORGAN (ROBIN) ed. Sisterhood is powerful: an anthology of writings from the women's liberation movement. New York, 1970. pp. 602. bibliog.

SEMINAR ON THE EFFECTS OF SCIENTIFIC AND TECHNOLOGICAL DEVELOPMENTS ON THE STATUS OF WOMEN, IASI, 1969. Semirar...[held in] Iasi, Romania, 5-18 August 1969; organized by the United Nations, Division of Human Rights, in co-operation with the government of Romania. (ST/TAO/HR/37). New York, United Nations, 1970. pp. 43.

SEMINAR ON THE PARTICIPATION OF WOMEN IN THE ECONOMIC LIFE OF THEIR COUNTRIES, MOSCOW, 1970. Seminar...(with reference to the implementation of Article 10 of the Declaration on the Elimination of Discrimination against Women) [held in] Moscow...8-21 September, 1970, etc. (ST/TAO/HR/41) New York, United Nations, 1970. pp. 38.

UNITED NATIONS. Commission on the Status of Women. 1970. Participation of women in the economic and social development of their countries: report of the Secretary-General. (E/CN.6/513/Rev.1). New York. 1970. pp. 104.

BERNARD (JESSIE) Women and the public interest: an essay on policy and protest. Chicago, 1971. pp. 293. bibliogs.

FIRESTONE (SHULAMITH) The dialectic of sex: the case for feminist revolution. London, 1971. pp. 274.

GORNICK (VIVIAN) and MORAN (BARBARA K.) eds. Woman in sexist society: studies in power and powerlessness. New York, [1971]. pp. 515.

GREER (GERMAINE) The female eunuch. London, 1971. pp. 354.

KOMISAR (LUCY) The new feminism. London, [1971]. pp. 166. bibliog.

JANEWAY (ELIZABETH) Man's world, woman's place: a study in social mythology. London, 1972. pp. 319.

REEVES (NANCY) Womankind: beyond the stereotypes; with parallel readings selected and annotated by the author. Chicago, 1971 repr. 1972. pp. 434. bibliog.

O'BRIEN (JO) Women's liberation in labour history: a case study from Nottingham. Nottingham, [1972]. pp. 15. (Spokesman, The. Pamphlets. No.24)

REISCHE (DIANA L.) ed. Women and society. New York, 1972. pp. 234. bibliog.

ROWBOTHAM (SHEILA) Women, resistance and revolution. London, 1972. pp. 288. bibliog.

SALPER (ROBERTA) ed. Female liberation: history and current politics. New York, [1972]. pp. 246. bibliog.

SUFFER and be still: women he Victorian age; edited by Martha Vicinus. Bloomington, Ind., [1972]. pp. 239. bibliog.

TWELLMANN (MARGRIT) ed. Die deutsche Frauenbewegung: ihre Anfänge und erste Entwicklung; Quellen, 1843-1889. Meisenheim am Glan, 1972. pp. 570.

TWELLMANN (MARGRIT) Die deutsche Frauenbewegung im Spiegel repräsentativer Frauenzeitschriften: ihre Anfänge und erste Entwicklung, 1843-1889. Meisenheim am Glan, 1972. pp. 246. bibliog.

WANDOR (MICHELENE) ed. The body politic: writings from the Women's Liberation Movement in Britain, 1969-1972. London, 1972. pp. 262. bibliog.

WORTIS (HELEN) and RABINOWITZ (CLARA) eds. The women's movement: social and psychological perspectives. New York, 1972. pp. 151. bibliog.

ROWBOTHAM (SHEILA) Hidden from history: 300 years of women's oppression and the fight against it. London, 1973. pp. 182. bibliog.

- Legal status, laws, etc. - South Africa

SOUTH AFRICA. Parliament. House of Assembl. Select Committee on the Suretyship Amendment Bill. 1971. Report (with Proceedings and Minutes of evidence); [L. le Grange, chairman]. (S.C.4-1971). in SOUTH AFRICA. Parliament. House of Assembly. Select Committee reports.

- Legal status, laws, etc, United States - California

CALIFORNIA WOMEN; a report of the Advisory Commission on the Status of Women [California]. bien., My 1967 [1st]-   Sacramento.

- Psychology

HUGUET (MICHELE) Les femmes dans les grands ensembles: de la représentation à la mise en scène. Paris, 1971. pp. 295. bibliog.

WORTIS (HELEN) and RABINOWITZ (CLARA) eds. The women's movement: social and psychological perspectives. New York, 1972. pp. 151. bibliog.

- Rights of women

DAVIS (PAULINA W.) A history of the national woman's rights movement, for twenty years, with the proceedings of the decade meeting held at Apollo Hall... 1870, from 1850 to 1870, etc. New York, 1871; New York, 1971. pp. 124.

KENEALY (ARABELLA) Feminism and sex-extinction. London, 1920. pp. 313.

JANSSEN (E.M.) and PUTMAN (TH. M.) De vrouwenemancipatie in Nederland. 's-Hertogenbosch, 1963. pp. 59. bibliog.

SEMINAR ON CIVIC AND POLITICAL EDUCATION OF WOMEN, HELSINKI, 1967. Seminar...[held at] Helsinki, Finland, 1 to 14 August 1967; organized by the United Nations, Division of Human Rights, in co-operation with the government of Finland. (ST/TAO/HR/30). New York, United Nations, 1968. pp. 49.

FRANDSEN (DOROTHEA) and DALDRUP (URSULA) Frauenfragen in internationalen Organisationen. [Hannover, 1970]. pp. 175. bibliog. (Niedersaechsische Landeszentrale für Politische Bildung. Schriftenreihe. Die Rolle der Frau in einer gewandelten Welt. Folge 5)

MORGAN (ROBIN) ed. Sisterhood is powerful: an anthology of writings from the women's liberation movement. New York, 1970. pp. 602. bibliog.

SEMINAR ON THE PARTICIPATION OF WOMEN IN THE ECONOMIC LIFE OF THEIR COUNTRIES, MOSCOW, 1970. Seminar...(with reference to the implementation of Article 10 of the Declaration on the Elimination of Discrimination against Women) [held in] Moscow...8-21 September, 1970, etc. (ST/TAO/HR/41). New York, United Nations, 1970. pp. 38.

UNITED NATIONS. Commission on the Status of Women. 1970. Participation of women in the economic and social development of their countries: report of the Secretary-General. (E/CN.6/513/Rev.1). New York, 1970. pp. 104.

VILLANUEVA Y SAAVEDRA (ETELVINA) Accion socialista de la mujer en Bolivia. La Paz, 1970. pp. 189.

FRANCHINI (SILVIA) La questione femminile nel pensiero di John Stuart Mill. [Milan], 1971-72. pp. 331-374; 243-278. (Estratto dalla rivista Movimento Operaio e Socialista, XVII,n.4; XVIII, n.2)

ANDREAS (CAROL) Sex and caste in America. Englewood Cliffs, [1971]. pp. 146. bibliog.

BERNARD (JESSIE) Women and the public interest: an essay on policy and protest. Chicago, 1971. pp. 293. bibliogs.

FRANKLIN (BRUCE) From the movement toward revolution. New York, [1971]. pp. 170.

GMELIN (OTTO) and SAUSSURE (HELENE) Bankrott der Männerherrschaft: Material zu Problemen der Frauenemanzipation;... Basis, Arbeitsergebnisse. Frankfurt am Main, [1971]. pp. 207.

GORNICK (VIVIAN) and MORAN (BARBARA K.) eds. Woman in sexist society: studies in power and powerlessness. New York, [1971]. pp. 515.

KOMISAR (LUCY) The new feminism. London, [1971]. pp. 166. bibliog.

SCHNETZLER (BARBARA) Die frühe amerikanische Frauenbewegung und ihre Kontakte mit Europa, 1836-1869. Bern, 1971. pp. 146. bibliog.

JENNESS (LINDA) ed. Feminism and socialism. New York, 1972. pp. 160.

MENAPACE (LIDIA) ed. Per un movimento politico di liberazione della donna: saggi e documenti; [translations of Partisans, nos. 54-55, 57, and Casa de las Americas, nos. 65-66]. Verona, [1972]. pp. 438.

SALPER (ROBERTA) ed. Female liberation: history and current politics. New York, [1972]. pp. 246. bibliog.

FLEXNER (ELEANOR) Century of struggle: the woman's rights movement in the United States; [reprint of the edition of 1959 with a new preface and additional bibliography]. New York, 1973. pp. 384. bibliog.

LEMONS (J. STANLEY) The woman citizen: social feminism in the 1920s. Urbana, [1973]. pp. 266. bibliog.

PUERTO RICO. Civil Rights Commission. 1973. La igualdad de derechos y oportunidades de la mujer puertorriqueña. San Juan, 1973. pp. 496. bibliogs.

- Social and moral questions

La DONNA nella fabbrica e nella società...: convegno organizzato dal Movimento Femminile Socialista; (Roma 16-17 dicembre 1961). [Rome, 1962]. pp. 104. (Movimento Femminile Socialista. Quaderni 1) (Mondo Operaio. Supplementi)

BERNARD (JESSIE) Women and the public interest: an essay on policy and protest. Chicago, 1971. pp. 293. bibliogs.

CHABROL (CLAUDE) Le récit féminin: contribution à l'analyse sémiologique du courrier du coeur et des entrevues ou 'enquêtes' sur la femme dans la presse féminine actuelle. The Hague, 1971. pp. 142. bibliog.

FAMILY issues of employed women in Europe and America; edited by Andrée Michel. Leiden, 1971. pp. 166. bibliogs.

GREER (GERMAINE) The female eunuch. London, 1971. pp. 354.

WOMAN - Social and moral questions (Cont'd.)

>REEVES (NANCY) Womankind: beyond the stereotypes; with parallel readings selected and annotated by the author. Chicago, 1971 repr. 1972. pp. 434. bibliog.

>VILAR (ESTHER) The manipulated man; (translated by Eva Borneman). London, 1972. pp. 144.

>JANEWAY (ELIZABETH) Man's world, woman's place: a study in social mythology. London, 1972. pp. 319.

>KOLLONTAI (ALEKSANDRA MIKHAILOVNA) The autobiography of a sexually emancipated woman;...edited with an afterword by Iring Fetscher; translated by Salvator Attanasio. London, 1972. pp. 138. bibliog. A translation is included of The new woman, a chapter from her book Die neue Moral und die Arbeiterklasse.

>PECK (ELLEN) The baby trap; edited by Robert Chartham. London, 1973. pp. 220.

- Societies and clubs

>GESCHICHTE des Badischen Frauenvereins: Festschrift, etc. Karlsruhe, 1881. pp. 652.

>WOOD (MARY I.) The history of the General Federation of Women's Clubs for the first twenty-two years of its organisation. New York, [1912]. pp. 445.

>RASMUSSEN (AGNETE) Dansk Kvindesamfund og saedelighedsfejden 1887. Grenå, 1972. pp. 89. bibliog.

- Suffrage

>GERMANY (BUNDESREPUBLIK). Deutscher Bundestag. Wissenschaftliche Dienste. 1969. Fünfzig Jahre Frauenwahlrecht; [edited by Dagmar Höfig]. Bonn, 1969. pp. 29. (Materialien. 12)

>NEALE (R.S.) Class and ideology in the nineteenth century. London, 1972. pp. 200.

- Suffrage - Netherlands

>JANSSEN (E.M.) and PUTMAN (TH. M.) De vrouwenemancipatie in Nederland. 's-Hertogenbosch, 1963. pp. 59. bibliog.

- Suffrage - New Zealand

>GRIMSHAW (PATRICIA) Women's suffrage in New Zealand. Auckland, 1972. pp. 151. bibliog.

- Suffrage - United Kingdom

>BESANT (ANNIE) The political status of women. 3rd ed. London, [c.1880?]. pp. 14.

>HALE (CICELY B.) A good long time; the autobiography of an octogenarian. London, [1973]. pp. 124.

>RAEBURN (ANTONIA) The militant suffragettes. London, 1973. pp. 269. bibliog.

- Suffrage - United States

>MARTIN (VICTORIA CLAFLIN WOODHULL) A lecture on constitutional equality, delivered at Lincoln Hall, Washington, D.C. ...1871. New York, 1871; [New York, 1971]. pp. 28.

>MORGAN (DAVID) Suffragists and democrats: the politics of woman suffrage in America. [Ann Arbor], 1972. pp. 225. bibliog.

WOMEN, NEGRO

>LERNER (GERDA) ed. Black women in white America: a documentary history. New York, 1973. pp. 630. bibliog.

WOMEN AND PEACE

>KEMPF (BEATRIX) Suffragette for peace: the life of Bertha von Suttner [with selections from her writings];...translated from the German by R.W. Last. London, [1972]. pp. 200. bibliog.

WOMEN AND RELIGION

>DIXIE (Lady FLORENCE CAROLINE) Towards freedom: an appeal to thoughtful men and women. London, [c. 1905]. pp. 14. (Reprinted from The Agnostic Annual, 1904)

>OSIPOV (ALEKSANDR ALEKSANDROVICH) Zhenshchina pod krestom: stat'i, besedy, razmyshleniia. Leningrad, 1966. pp. 214.

WOMEN AND SOCIALISM

>SIEMSEN (ANNA) Frau und Sozialismus. [Zürich, 1953]. pp. 52.

>VILLANUEVA Y SAAVEDRA (ETELVINA) Accion socialista de la mujer en Bolivia. La Paz, 1970. pp. 189.

>KIM (SONG AE) Report on the work of the Central Committee to the Fourth Congress of the Korean Democratic Women's Union. Pyongyang, 1971. pp. 85.

>JENNESS (LINDA) ed. Feminism and socialism. New York, 1972. pp. 160.

>STORA-SANDOR (JUDITH) Alexandra Kollontaï: marxisme et révolution sexuelle. Paris, 1973. pp. 286. bibliog.

>U.K. National Register of Archives. 1973. Labour Party archives: miscellaneous accessions: Standing Joint Committee of Industrial Women's Organisations: note on first minute book compiled by R.A. Storey. London, 1973. single sheet.

WOMEN AS ARTISTS

>GWYN (SANDRA) Women in the arts in Canada; a monograph based on essays by Nathan Cohen [and others]. Ottawa, 1971. pp. 98. bibliog. (Canada. Royal Commission on the Status of Women in Canada, 1967. Studies. 7)

WOMEN AS AUTHORS

>ADBURGHAM (ALISON) Women in print: writing women and women's magazines from the restoration to the accession of Victoria. London, 1972. pp. 302. bibliog.

WOMEN AS BANKERS

>ALEXANDER (RODNEY) and SAPERY (ELISABETH) The shortchanged: women and minorities in banking. New York, [1973]. pp. 186. bibliog.

WOMEN AS FARMERS

>REISEN (LORE) Auswirkungen der Flurbereinigung und Aussiedlung auf die Frauenarbeit im bäuerlichen Familienbetrieb, dargestellt am Beispiel eines Dorfes. Stuttgart, 1959. pp. 99. bibliog. (Schriftenreihe für Flurbereinigung. Heft 23)

>SCHWEITZER (ROSEMARIE VON) Die Frau und ihre Aufgabe in einer modernen Landwirtschaft. [Hannover, 1968]. pp. 80. bibliog. (Niedersaechsische Landeszentrale für Politische Bildung. Schriftenreihe. Die Rolle der Frau in einer gewandelten Welt. Folge 4)

MATERIALIEN zu sozialen Verflechtungen der Landfrauen und Landfamilien in der Bundesrepublik Deutschland: Ergebnisse einer empirischen Untersuchung. Bonn, 1971. pp. 222. bibliog. (Forschungsgesellschaft für Agrarpolitik und Agrarsoziologie. [Publications]. 216)

EVERAET (HUBERT) La situation sociale de la fermière: sa participation au travail de l'exploitation. Bruxelles, 1972. fo. 68. bibliog. (Belgium. Institut Economique Agricole. Cahiers. No. 139)

- Bibliography

COMMONWEALTH BUREAU OF AGRICULTURAL ECONOMICS. Women in rural society; compiled by Jean Kestner. [Oxford], 1972. pp. 6. (Annotated Bibliographies. No. 13)

WOMEN COLLEGE STUDENTS

- India

VREEDE DE STUERS (CORA) Girl students in Jaipur: a study in attitudes towards family life, marriage, and career. Assen, 1970. pp. 141. bibliog.

- United States

LEVER (JANET) and SCHWARTZ (PEPPER) Women at Yale: liberating a college campus. London, 1971. pp. 274.

WOMEN IN AFRICA

SEMINAR ON THE CIVIC AND POLITICAL EDUCATION OF WOMEN, ACCRA, 1968. Seminar...[held at] Accra, Ghana, 19 November to 2 December 1968; organized by the United Nations, Division of Human Rights, in co-operation with the government of Ghana. (ST/TAO/HR/35). New York, United Nations, 1969. pp. 47.

SEMINAR ON THE PARTICIPATION OF WOMEN IN ECONOMIC LIFE, LIBREVILLE (REPUBLIC OF GABON), 1971. Seminar...(with reference to the implementation of Article 10 of the Declaration on the Elimination of Discrimination against Women)...[held in] Libreville,...27 July - 9 August 1971. (ST/TAO/HR/43). New York, United Nations, 1971. pp. 48.

WOMEN IN ASIA

SEMINAR ON MEASURES REQUIRED FOR THE ADVANCEMENT OF WOMEN WITH SPECIAL REFERENCE TO THE ESTABLISHMENT OF A LONG-TERM PROGRAMME, MANILA, 1966. Seminar...[held at] Manila, Philippines 6 to 19 December 1966, organized by the United Nations, Division of Human Rights, in co-operation with the government of the Philippines. (ST/TAO/HR/28). New York, United Nations, 1967. pp. 44.

WOMEN IN BOLIVIA

VILLANUEVA Y SAAVEDRA (ETELVINA) Accion socialista de la mujer en Bolivia. La Paz, 1970. pp. 189.

WOMEN IN BUSINESS

CONFERENCE ON WOMEN'S CHALLENGE TO MANAGEMENT, ARDEN HOUSE, 1971. Corporate lib: women's challenge to management; edited by Eli Ginzberg and Alice M. Yohalem. Baltimore, [1973]. pp. 153. bibliog.

WOMEN IN CANADA

GWYN (SANDRA) Women in the arts in Canada; a monograph based on essays by Nathan Cohen [and others]. Ottawa, 1971. pp. 98. bibliog. (Canada. Royal Commission on the Status of Women in Canada, 1967. Studies. 7)

CANADA. Office of the Co-ordinator, Status of Women. 1972. Status of women in Canada, 1972; report; La situation de la femme au Canada, 1972; rapport; [by] Freda L. Paltiel. Ottawa, 1972. pp. 35,39. In English and French.

WOMEN IN COOPERATIVE SOCIETIES

TOTOMIANTS (VAKHAN FOMICH) Die Frau und das Genossenschaftswesen. Basel, 1924. pp. 96. (Verband Schweizerischer Konsumvereine. Genossenschaftliche Volksbibliothek. Nr. 13)

WOMEN IN DENMARK

RASMUSSEN (AGNETE) Dansk Kvindesamfund og saedelighedsfejden 1887. Grenå, 1972. pp. 89. bibliog.

WOMEN IN FRANCE

MAUDUIT (JEAN) La révolte des femmes: après les Etats généraux de Elle. [Paris, 1971]. pp. 257.

CHARZAT (GISELE) Les françaises sont-elles des citoyennes? Paris, [1972]. pp. 203. bibliog.

WOMEN IN GERMANY

GESCHICHTE des Badischen Frauenvereins: Festschrift, etc. Karlsruhe, 1881. pp. 652.

FUERTH (HENRIETTE) Die deutschen Frauen im Kriege. Tübingen, 1917. pp. 63.

DEUTSCH (REGINE) Parlamentarische Frauenarbeit. 2nd ed. Stuttgart, 1924. pp. 98.

LUEDERS (MARIE ELISABETH) Volksdienst der Frau. Berlin, [1937]. pp. 108.

GERMANY (BUNDESREPUBLIK). Deutscher Bundestag. Wissenschaftliche Dienste. 1971. Frauen im Deutschen Bundestag, I. bis VI. Wahlperiode; [edited by Frau Dalades]. Bonn, 1971. pp. 72. (Materialien. 23)

HEINZ (MARGARETE) Über das politische Bewusstsein von Frauen in der Bundesrepublik. München, [1971]. pp. 151. bibliog.

MABRY (HANNELORE) Unkraut ins Parlament: die Bedeutung weiblicher parlamentarischer Arbeit für die Emanzipation der Frau. München, 1971. pp. 292. bibliog.

TWELLMANN (MARGRIT) ed. Die deutsche Frauenbewegung: ihre Anfänge und erste Entwicklung; Quellen, 1843-1889. Meisenheim am Glan, 1972. pp. 570.

TWELLMANN (MARGRIT) Die deutsche Frauenbewegung im Spiegel repräsentativer Frauenzeitschriften: ihre Anfänge und erste Entwicklung, 1843-1889. Meisenheim am Glan, 1972. pp. 246. bibliog.

WOMEN IN HUNGARY

HOLÁCS (IBOLYA) Sociological survey on the situation of country women in the south western Transdanubian region. Keszthely, 1971. pp. 47. (Keszthelyi Agrartudomanyi Egyetem. Studies. 4)

WOMEN IN INDIA

The EDUCATED woman in Indian society today; a study carried out by the YWCA of India. Bombay, [1971]. pp. 287. bibliogs.

WOMEN IN ITALY

La DONNA nella fabbrica e nella società...: convegno organizzato dal Movimento Femminile Socialista; (Roma 16-17 dicembre 1961). [Rome, 1962]. pp. 104. (Movimento Femminile Socialista. Quaderni 1) (Mondo Operaio. Supplementi)

WOMEN IN JAPAN

KOYAMA (TAKASHI). The changing social position of women in Japan. Paris, 1961. pp. 152.

TSUJI (SEIMEI) ed. Women's movements in postwar Japan: selected articles from Shinyo: sengo nijūnen shi, Source book on twenty postwar years in Japan;...translated by Wake A. Fujioka. Honolulu, 1968. fo.87. (Hawaii University. East-West Center. Institute of Advanced Projects. Occasional Papers of Research Publications and Translations. Translation Series. No. 29)

WOMEN IN KOREA

KOREAN DEMOCRATIC WOMEN'S UNION. Central Committee. Mrs. Kang Ban Sok, mother of the great leader of Korea. [Pyongyang, 1968]. pp. 108.

KIM (SONG AE) Report on the work of the Central Committee to the Fourth Congress of the Korean Democratic Women's Union. Pyongyang, 1971. pp. 85.

WOMEN IN NEW GUINEA

STRATHERN (MARILYN) Women in between: female roles in a male world: Mount Hagen, New Guinea. London, 1972. pp. 372. bibliog.

WOMEN IN NEW ZEALAND

SOCIETY FOR RESEARCH ON WOMEN IN NEW ZEALAND. Urban women. Dunedin, 1972. pp. 104. bibliog.

WOMEN IN NIGER

DIARRA (FATOUMATA AGNES) Femmes africaines en devenir: les femmes zarma du Niger. Paris, [1971]. pp. 318. bibliog.

WOMEN IN NORWAY

NORWAY. Komitéen for Internasjonale Sosialpolitiske Saker. 1960. Facts about women in Norway. Oslo, 1960. pp. 42.

MEANS (INGUNN NORDERVAL) Kvinner i norsk politikk. Oslo, [1973]. pp. 185. bibliog.

WOMEN IN POLITICS

DEUTSCH (REGINE) Parlamentarische Frauenarbeit. 2nd ed. Stuttgart, 1924. pp. 98.

GARRETTE (EVE) A political handbook for women. Garden City, N.Y., 1944. pp. 219.

GERMANY (BUNDESREPUBLIK). Deutscher Bundestag. Wissenschaftliche Dienste. 1971. Frauen im Deutschen Bundestag, I. bis VI. Wahlperiode; [edited by Frau Dalades]. Bonn, 1971. pp. 72. (Materialien. 23)

HEINZ (MARGARETE) Über das politische Bewusstsein von Frauen in der Bundesrepublik. München, [1971]. pp. 151. bibliog.

MABRY (HANNELORE) Unkraut ins Parlament: die Bedeutung weiblicher parlamentarischer Arbeit für die Emanzipation der Frau. München, 1971. pp. 292. bibliog.

CHARZAT (GISELE) Les françaises sont-elles des citoyennes? Paris, [1972]. pp. 203. bibliog.

MEANS (INGUNN NORDERVAL) Kvinner i norsk politikk. Oslo, [1973]. pp. 185. bibliog.

WOMEN IN PUBLIC LIFE

SEMINAR ON CIVIC AND POLITICAL EDUCATION OF WOMEN, HELSINKI, 1967. Seminar...[held at] Helsinki, Finland, 1 to 14 August 1967; organized by the United Nations, Division of Human Rights, in co-operation with the government of Finland. (ST/TAO/HR/30). New York, United Nations, 1968. pp. 49.

UNITED NATIONS. Commission on the Status of Women. 1972. Participation of women in community development; report of the Secretary-General. (E/CN.6/514/Rev.1). New York, 1972. pp. 68.

WOMEN IN PUERTO RICO

PUERTO RICO. Civil Rights Commission. 1973. La igualdad de derechos y oportunidades de la mujer puertorriqueña. San Juan, 1973. pp. 496. bibliogs.

WOMEN IN RUSSIA

- Statistics

RUSSIA (U.S.S.R.). Tsentral'noe Statisticheskoe Upravlenie. 1962. Zhenshchiny i deti v SSSR: statisticheskii sbornik. 2nd ed. Moskva, 1963. pp. 203.

WOMEN IN SWEDEN

SWEDEN. Utrikesdepartementet. Aktstycken. Ny Serie II. 20. Rapport till Förenta Nationerna över kvinnornas status i Sverige. Stockholm, 1968. pp. 81.

BRADLEY (GUNILLA) Kvinnan och karriären: en studie av kvinnors befordringsintresse i relation till arbetstillfredsställelse, hemmiljö och skolutbildning. [Stockholm, 1972]. pp. 170. bibliog. (Personaladministrativa Rådet. Meddelanden. Nr. 64)

WOMEN IN TAIWAN

WOLF (MARGERY) Women and the family in rural Taiwan. Stanford, 1972. pp. 235.

WOMEN IN THE NETHERLANDS

INSTITUUT VOOR TOEGEPASTE SOCIOLOGIE. De ongehuwde vrouw: onderzoek naar de levensomstandigheden van de ongehuwde vrouwen van 40 tot 65 jaar: samenvatting; (in opdracht van het Ministerie van Sociale Zaken en Volksgezondheid). 's-Gravenhage, 1971. pp. 89. (Netherlands. Ministerie van Sociale Zaken. Verslagen en Rapporten: Sociale Zaken. 1971. 1)

WOMEN IN THE UNITED KINGDOM

ADBURGHAM (ALISON) Women in print: writing women and women's magazines from the restoration to the accession of Victoria. London, 1972. pp. 302. bibliog.

LABOUR PARTY. Discrimination against women; report of a Labour Party study group. London, [1972]. pp. 45. (Labour Party. Opposition Green Papers)

O'BRIEN (JO) Women's liberation in labour history: a case study from Nottingham. Nottingham, [1972]. pp. 15. (Spokesman, The. Pamphlets. No.24)

SUFFER and be still: women in the Victorian age; edited by Martha Vicinus. Bloomington, Ind., [1972]. pp. 239. bibliog.

U.K. Central Office of Information. Reference Division. Reference Pamphlets. 67. Women in Britain. [rev. ed.] London, 1972. pp. 50. bibliog.

WANDOR (MICHELENE) ed. The body politic: writings from the Women's Liberation Movement in Britain, 1969-1972. London, 1972. pp. 262. bibliog.

HALE (CICELY B.) A good long time; the autobiography of an octogenarian. London, [1973]. pp. 124.

WOMEN IN THE UNITED STATES

DAVIS (PAULINA W.) A history of the national woman's rights movement, for twenty years, with the proceedings of the decade meeting held at Apollo Hall... 1870, from 1850 to 1870, etc. New York, 1871; New York, 1971. pp. 124.

WOOD (MARY I.) The history of the General Federation of Women's Clubs for the first twenty-two years of its organisation. New York, [1912]. pp. 445.

HAGOOD (MARGARET JARMAN) Mothers of the south: portraiture of the white tenant farm woman; [facsimile reprint of the work first published by the University of North Carolina Press, 1939]. New York, 1969. pp. 252.

JENSEN (OLIVER) The revolt of American women; [a pictorial history]. New York, [1952 repr. 1971]. pp. 224.

FLEXNER (ELEANOR) Century of struggle: the woman's rights movement in the United States; [reprint of the edition of 1959 with a new preface and additional bibliography]. New York, 1973. pp. 384. bibliog.

MORGAN (ROBIN) ed. Sisterhood is powerful: an anthology of writings from the women's liberation movement. New York, 1970. pp. 602. bibliog.

AMUNDSEN (KIRSTEN) The silenced majority: women and American democracy. Englewood Cliffs, [1971]. pp. 184.

ANDREAS (CAROL) Sex and caste in America. Englewood Cliffs, [1971]. pp. 146. bibliog.

SCHNETZLER (BARBARA) Die frühe amerikanische Frauenbewegung und ihre Kontakte mit Europa, 1836-1869. Bern, 1971. pp. 146. bibliog.

CHAFE (WILLIAM HENRY) The American woman: her changing social, economic and political roles, 1920-1970. New York, 1972. pp. 351. bibliog.

REISCHE (DIANA L.) ed. Women and society. New York, 1972. pp. 234. bibliog.

LEMONS (J. STANLEY) The woman citizen: social feminism in the 1920s. Urbana, [1973]. pp. 266. bibliog.

LERNER (GERDA) ed. Black women in white America: a documentary history. New York, 1973. pp. 630. bibliog.

WOMEN IN TRADE UNIONS

- Germany

SILBERMANN (JOSEF) Vierzig Jahre VWA, 1889-1929: Jubiläumsschrift über vier Jahrzehnte Geschichte des Verbandes der weiblichen Handels- und Büroangestellten E.V. Berlin, 1929. pp. 94.

WOMEN IN TURKEY

AFETINAN (A.) The emancipation of the Turkish woman. Paris, 1962. pp. 63.

WOMEN'S COLLEGES

- Russia

NASHA dan' Bestuzhevskim kursam: vospominaniia byvshikh bestuzhevok za rubezhom. Parizh, 1971. pp. 175.

WOMEN'S LIBERATION MOVEMENT

WARE (CELLESTINE) Woman power: the movement for women's liberation. New York, [1970]. pp. 176. bibliog.

FIRESTONE (SHULAMITH) The dialectic of sex: the case for feminist revolution. London, 1971. pp. 274.

LARTEGUY (JEAN) Lettre ouverte aux bonnes femmes. Paris, [1972]. pp. 155.

REISCHE (DIANA L.) ed. Women and society. New York, 1972. pp. 234. bibliog.

ROWBOTHAM (SHEILA) Women, resistance and revolution. London, 1972. pp. 288. bibliog.

WANDOR (MICHELENE) ed. The body politic: writings from the Women's Liberation Movement in Britain, 1969-1972. London, 1972. pp. 262. bibliog.

WORTIS (HELEN) and RABINOWITZ (CLARA) eds. The women's movement: social and psychological perspectives. New York, 1972. pp. 151. bibliog.

WOMEN'S PERIODICALS, ENGLISH

ADBURGHAM (ALISON) Women in print: writing women and women's magazines from the restoration to the accession of Victoria. London, 1972. pp. 302. bibliog.

WOMEN'S PERIODICALS, FRENCH

CHABROL (CLAUDE) Le récit féminin: contribution à l'analyse sémiologique du courrier du coeur et des entrevues ou 'enquêtes' sur la femme dans la presse féminine actuelle. The Hague, 1971. pp. 142. bibliog.

WOMEN'S PERIODICALS, GERMAN

VORMSCHLAG (ELISABETH) Inhalte, Leitbilder und Funktionen politischer Frauenzeitschriften der SPD, der USPD, der KPD in den Jahren 1890-1933 und der NSDAP in den Jahren 1932-1945. Göttingen, 1970. pp. 271. bibliog.

WONG (CHIN-FOO)

A CHINESE missionary. [London, 18--]. s.sh. (Reprinted from the New York Times)

WOOD (LEONARD)

HITCHMAN (JAMES H.) Leonard Wood and Cuban independence, 1898-1902. The Hague, 1971. pp. 238. bibliog.

WOOD
- Preservation

TACK (C.H.) The economics of timber preservation in house-building. Princes Risborough, Forest Products Research Laboratory, 1969. pp. 10. (Timberlab Papers. No. 17.)

WOOD ENGRAVINGS, ENGLISH
- Catalogues

HODNETT (EDWARD) English woodcuts, 1480-1535; ([reprint of the work first published in 1935] with additions and corrections). Oxford, 1973. 2 vols. in 1.

WOOD-PULP INDUSTRY
- Russia

BARR (BRENTON M.) The Soviet wood-processing industry: a linear programming analysis of the role of transportation costs in location and flow patterns. Toronto, 1970. pp. 135. bibliog. (Toronto. University. Department of Geography. Research Publications. 5)

- United States - Waste disposal

COUNCIL ON ECONOMIC PRIORITIES. Paper profits: pollution in the pulp and paper industry;... by Leslie Allan [and others]. New York, [1972]. pp. 504. bibliog.

WOOD-USING INDUSTRIES
- Belgium

CENTRALE CHRETIENNE DES TRAVAILLEURS DU BOIS ET DU BATIMENT. Conditions de travail dans l'industrie debitrice et transformatrice du bois, 1970-1972. Bruxelles, [1971]. pp. 296.

- Canada

BOWLAND (JAMES G.) Economic indicators in forestry and forest-based industries in Canada: 1961/69. Ottawa, Information Canada, 1971. pp. 90.

- Germany

AARON (J.R.) Wood-consuming industries in the Federal German Republic: report on a visit made under the auspices of the Western European Union. London, 1967. pp. 39. bibliog. (U.K. Forestry Commission. Research and Development Papers. No.65)

- Russia

GOROVOI (VIKTOR L'VOVICH) and PRIVALOVSKAIA (GENRIETTA ALEKSEEVNA) Geografiia lesnoi promyshlennosti SSSR. Moskva, 1966. pp. 151. bibliog.

GRIGOR'EV (NIKOLAI GRIGOR'EVICH) Tsenoobrazovanie na lesoproduktsiiu. Moskva, 1970. pp. 64.

BURSIN (EVGENII EGOROVICH) Tsenoobrazovanie v lesopil'no-derevoobrabatyvaiushchei promyshlennosti SSSR. Moskva, 1971. pp. 149.

- Russia - Baltic States

LESOPIL'NO-derevoobrabatyvaiushchaia promyshlennost' Pribaltiiskogo ekonomicheskogo raiona: sostoianie i perspektivy razvitiia. Riga, 1964. pp. 96.

- Russia - White Russia

ZHELEZKO (ALEKSANDR EFIMOVICH) Syr'evye resursy i effektivnost' proizvodstva lesnoi promyshlennosti. Minsk, 1973. pp. 169.

WOOL

BURLET (JEAN ETIENNE) La laine et l'industrie lainière. Paris, 1972. pp. 128.

- Prices

BANCO GANADERO ARGENTINO. Servicio de Investigaciones Economicas. Temas de economia argentina: mercados y precios de la lana; [by Joaquin Padvalskis Simkus and others]. [Buenos Aires, 1969]. pp. 85.

WOOL TRADE AND INDUSTRY
- Algeria

BEL (ALFRED) and RICARD (PROSPER) Les industries indigènes de l'Algérie: le travail de la laine à Tlemcen. Alger, 1913. pp. 359.

- Argentine Republic

BANCO GANADERO ARGENTINO. Servicio de Investigaciones Economicas. Temas de economia argentina: mercados y precios de la lana; [by Joaquin Padvalskis Simkus and others]. [Buenos Aires, 1969]. pp. 85.

- Australia

MANNING (GEOFFREY ARTHUR) The Elder Smith Goldsbrough Mort merger. Canberra, 1970. pp. 59.

- France

BURLET (JEAN ETIENNE) La laine et l'industrie lainière. Paris, 1972. pp. 128.

- United Kingdom

The WOOL textile industry in Great Britain: [including papers delivered to the Anthropology Section of the British Association for the Advancement of Science, Leeds, 1968]; edited by J. Geraint Jenkins. London, 1972. pp. 309. bibliog.

- United Kingdom - Scotland

HIGHLANDS AND ISLANDS DEVELOPMENT BOARD. Planning for progress: Shetland woollen industry. [Inverness, 1971]. pp. 92. (Special Reports. 4)

- United States

CROCKETT (NORMAN L.) The woolen industry of the Midwest. Lexington, Ky., [1970]. pp. 150. bibliog.

WOOLLEN AND WORSTED MANUFACTURE
- European Economic Community countries

ECONOMIC DEVELOPMENT COMMITTEE FOR THE WOOL TEXTILE INDUSTRY. Manpower Working Party. Employment practices in EEC textile industries; a report on the visit by members of the... Working Party to textile employers' organisations and trade unions in France, West Germany and Italy. London, National Economic Development Office, 1973. pp. 76.

- Ireland (Republic)

EIRE. Committee on Industrial Progress. 1972. Report on woollen and worsted industry. Dublin, [1972]. pp. 88.

- United Kingdom

  ANSTIE (JOHN) Observations on the importance and necessity of introducing improved machinery into the woollen manufactory; most particularly as it respects the interests of... Wilts, Gloucester and Somerset;... [reprint of work published in 1803. Shannon, [1971]. pp. 99.

  RANDALL (ADRIAN) The Kettering worsted industry of the eighteenth century. [Northampton?, 1968?]. pp. 20. (Reprinted from Northamptonshire Past and Present, vol IV, nos. 5 and 6)

  WILD (RAY) and GIBB (W.F.) Cost of labour turnover in the wool textile industry; (with Addendum). [London], National Economic Development Office, [1971]. pp. 16,2.

  ATKINS PLANNING. Reclaiming the '70s: the future for the low-cost woollen sector; prepared in association with Berenschot NV for the Economic Development Committee for the Wool Textile Industry. London, National Economic Development Office, 1972. pp. 89.

- United Kingdom - Scotland

  GULVIN (CLIFFORD) The tweedmakers: a history of the Scottish fancy woollen industry, 1600-1914. Newton Abbot, 1973. pp. 240. bibliog.

WORCESTER

- History

  DYER (ALAN D.) The city of Worcester in the sixteenth century. Leicester, 1973. pp. 288. bibliog.

WORCESTERSHIRE

- Economic history

  RAYBOULD (T.J.) The economic emergence of the Black Country: a study of the Dudley estate. Newton Abbot, [1973]. pp. 272.

WORK

SOUTO VILAS (MANUEL) Teoria de los sindicatos nacionales. Madrid, 1941. pp. 211.

MEISSNER (MARTIN) Technology and the worker: technical demands and social processes in industry. San Francisco, [1969]. pp. 264.

BAGOLINI (LUIGI) Filosofia del lavoro. Milano, 1971. pp. 157. (Bologna. Università. Scuola di Perfezionamento in Diritto del Lavoro e della Sicurezza Sociale. Manuali. 1)

HUGHES (EVERETT CHERRINGTON) The sociological eye: selected papers. Chicago, 1971. pp. 584.

KREPS (JUANITA MORRIS) Lifetime allocation of work and income: essays in the economics of aging. Durham, N.C., 1971. pp. 170.

KUENG (EMIL) Arbeit und Freizeit in der nachindustriellen Gesellschaft. Tübingen, 1971. pp. 267. bibliog. (St. Gall. Handelshochschule. St. Galler Wirtschaftswissenschaftliche Forschungen. Band 27)

ROLLE (PIERRE) Introduction à la sociologie du travail. Paris, [1971]. pp. 275. bibliog.

BRYANT (CLIFTON D.) ed. The social dimensions of work. Englewood Cliffs, [1972]. pp. 582.

GOODWIN (LEONARD) Do the poor want to work?: a social-psychological study of work orientations. Washington, D.C., [1972]. pp. 178.

MORRIS (WILLIAM) Political writings of William Morris; edited and with an introduction by A.L. Morton. London, 1973. pp. 246.

WILSON (N.A.B.) On the quality of working life; a report prepared for the Department of Employment. London, 1973. pp. 52. bibliog. (U.K. Department of Employment. Manpower Papers. No. 7)

YOUNG (MICHAEL DUNLOP) and WILLMOTT (PETER) The symmetrical family: a study of work and leisure in the London region. London, 1973. pp. 398. bibliog. (Institute of Community Studies. Reports. [20?])

- Psychological aspects

  HAYES (JOHN) Occupational perceptions and occupational information: an analysis of the way in which work is perceived before and after employment and its implications for occupational choice. Bromsgrove, [1971]. pp. 65. bibliog.

  HOGUE (JEAN PIERRE) Les relations humaines dans l'entreprise. Ottawa, 1971. pp. 187.

  ARGYLE (MICHAEL) The social psychology of work. London, 1972. pp. 291. bibliog.

WORK MEASUREMENT

MIL'NER (BENTSION ZAKHAROVICH) Normirovanie rabot po obsluzhivaniiu proizvodstva. Moskva, 1964. pp. 184.

KERZHENTSEV (PLATON MIKHAILOVICH) Bor'ba za vremia. Moskva, 1965. pp. 111.

NORMIROVANIE truda v sel'skom khoziaistve. Moskva, 1970. pp. 167.

U.K. Department of Employment and Productivity. Manpower and Productivity Service. Central Information Service. 1970. Productivity and work measurement in the white-collar sector. London, 1970. fo.58. (Information Papers. New Series. No.3)

ECONOMIC DEVELOPMENT COMMITTEE FOR THE CLOTHING INDUSTRY. Work study in the clothing industry. London, National Economic Development Office, 1971. pp. 35. bibliog.

PETROCHENKO (PETR FEDOROVICH) and KUZNETSOVA (KIMA EFIMOVNA) Organizatsiia i normirovanie truda v promyshlennosti SSSR: istoriko-ekonomicheskii ocherk. Moskva, 1971. pp. 304.

SOVERSHENSTVOVANIE organizatsii truda v sotsialisticheskom proizvodstve. Kiev, 1971. pp. 243.

TIKHONOV (VLADIMIR ALEKSANDROVICH) ed. Nauchnaia organizatsiia truda v sel'skom khoziaistve. Moskva, 1971. pp. 285.

WORKING-MEN'S CLUBS

HOWELL (GEORGE) A history of the Working Men's Association from 1836 to 1850. Newcastle upon Tyne, [1972]. pp. 99.

TAYLOR (JOHN) of the Ringland Working Men's Club. From self-help to glamour: the working men's club, 1860-1972. Oxford, [1972]. pp. 94. (History Workshop. Pamphlets. No. 7)

WORKMEN'S COMPENSATION

- Jamaica

JAMAICA. Ministry of Labour and National Insurance. 1970. Guide to pharmacists in the dispensing of drugs for national insurance purposes. [Kingston, 1970?]. pp. (3). (National Insurance Scheme Leaflets. No. 11)

JAMAICA. Ministry of Labour and National Insurance. 1970. The National Insurance Act, 1965: employment injury benefits: guide to doctors. [Kingston, 1970?]. pp. 16. (National Insurance Scheme Leaflets. No. 10)

JAMAICA. Ministry of Labour and National Insurance. 1971. Guide to employment injury benefits under the national insurance scheme. [Kingston], 1971. pp. (10). (National Insurance Scheme Leaflets. No. 9)

- Poland

REJMAN (GENOWEFA) Odpowiedzialność karna za niewłaściwe wykonanie nadzoru w zespołowym działaniu. Warszawa, 1972. pp. 306. bibliog. With Russian and French summaries.

- Russia

BATYGIN (KONSTANTIN STEPANOVICH) O vozmeshchenii ushcherba v sviazi s povrezhdeniem zdorov'ia na proizvodstve. Moskva, 1963. pp. 62.

- Scandinavia

RISKA (OLOF) Företagsledningens ansvar för skador på person och sak. Helsingfors, 1971. pp. 96. bibliog. (Svenska Handelshögskolan. Ekonomi och Samhälle. Nr. 20)

- South Africa

SOUTH AFRICA. Office of Census and Statistics. Special Report Series. Workmen's Compensation Act Statistics. Pretoria, 1935 in progress.

- Switzerland

BONER (K.) and HOLZHERR (W.) L'assurance-maladie selon la loi fédérale sur l'assurance en cas de maladie et d'accidents. Berne, [1969]. pp. 122.

SWITZERLAND. Caisse Nationale Suisse d'Assurance en Cas d'Accidents. 1971. Guide de l'assurance obligatoire contre les accidents; à l'usage des chefs d'entreprises et des assurés. 18th ed. [Lucerne], 1971. pp. 184.

- United States

DODD (WALTER FAIRLEIGH) Administration of workmen's compensation. New York, 1936. pp. 845.

DIXON (ROBERT G.) Social security disability and mass justice: a problem in welfare adjudication. New York, 1973. pp. 190.

WORKS COUNCILS

MANDEL (ERNEST) ed. Contrôle ouvrier, conseils ouvriers, autogestion: anthologie. Paris, 1970. pp. 430.

I CONSIGLI operai: (un dibattito tra intellettuali, sindacalisti e quadri operai sull'esperienza consiliare di ieri e di oggi): ([by] G. De Masi [and others]); a cura del Circolo G. Leopardi di Bologna. Roma, [1972]. pp. 202.

- Bibliography

INSTITUTE OF SCIENTIFIC BUSINESS. Bibliographical Studies. No. 5. Industrial democracy: Algeria to Zambia; a selected bibliography. Bradford, [1971]. 1 vol. (unfoliated).

- Algeria

GUERIN (DANIEL) L'Algérie caporalisée?: suite de L'Algérie qui se cherche. Paris, 1965. pp. 96.

- Canada

CANADA. Labour-Management Consultation Branch. 1971. Case histories: labour-management consultation committees. Ottawa, 1971. pp. 12.

- Germany

WIMMER (WALTER) Das Betriebsrätegesetz von 1920 und das Blutbad vor dem Reichstag. Berlin, 1957. pp. 68. (Institut für Marxismus-Leninismus (Berlin). Beiträge zur Geschichte und Theorie der Arbeiter-Bewegung. Heft 11)

- Italy

GRAMSCI (ANTONIO) and BORDIGA (AMADEO) Dibattito sui consigli di fabbrica; introduzione di Alfonso Leonetti. Roma, [1971]. pp. 99.

SALVADORI (MASSIMO L.) Gramsci e l'organizzazione del lavoro nel periodo di transizione dal capitalismo al socialismo. Torino, 1971. pp. 111.

SPRIANO (PAOLO) "L'Ordine Nuovo" e i consigli di fabbrica: (con una scelta di testi dall' "Ordine Nuovo", 1919-1920). Torino, [1971]. pp. 330.

- Netherlands

NETHERLANDS. Statutes, etc. 1971. Wet op de ondernemingsraden: wet van 28 januari 1971, Stb. 54, houdende nieuwe regelen omtrent de medezeggenschap van de werknemers in de onderneming door middel van ondernemingsraden...met aantekeningen... bewerkt door J.G. de Jong. Zwolle, 1971. pp. 160.

- Poland

OWIECZKO (A.) Robotnicy w samorządzie przedsiębiorstwa przemysłowego w Polsce. in Problemy struktury i aktywności społecznej. Warszawa, 1970.

WYRWA (TADEUSZ) La gestion de l'entreprise socialiste: l'expérience polonaise. Paris, 1970. pp. 220. bibliog.

BŁAŻEJCZYK (MARIAN) Prawo samorządu robotniczego... opracowano według stanu prawnego na dzień 1 stycznia 1971 r. 2nd ed. Warszawa, 1971. pp. 297.

STESZENKO (JERZY) Rada zakładowa: z badań w przedsiębiorstwach przemysłu terenowego. Warszawa, 1973. pp. 199. bibliog.

- Russia

PANKRATOVA (ANNA MIKHAILOVNA) Fabzavkomy Rossii v bor'be za sotsialisticheskuiu fabriku; pod redaktsiei M.N. Pokrovskogo. [Moskva], 1923. pp. 426. bibliog. Xerographic reprint.

- Spain

CALAMAI (MARCO) La lotta di classe sotto il franchismo: le Commissioni Operaie. Bari, [1971]. pp. 311.

- Tanzania

MAPOLU (HENRY) The organisation and participation of workers in Tanzania. [Dar es Salaam], 1972. pp. 43. (Dar es Salaam. University. Economic Research Bureau. ERB Papers. 72.1)

- United Kingdom

NICHOLSON (BRIAN) U.C.S.: an open letter. Nottingham, [1971]. pp. 6. (Institute for Workers' Control. Pamphlet Series. No. 27)

SOLIDARITY: [for workers' power]. Pamphlets [No.] 40. Workers' Councils and the economics of a self-managed society. London, 1972. pp. 58.

THOMPSON (WILLIE) and HART (FINLAY) The UCS work-in;...foreword by Jimmy Reid. London, 1972. pp. 95.

PARRIS (HENRY) Staff relations in the civil service: fifty years of Whitleyism. London, 1973. pp. 204.

- Yugoslavia

DANILOVIĆ (RAJKO) Radničko samoupravljanje i osnovi industrijske sociologije: priručnik za obrazovanje odraslih. Beograd, [1970]. pp. 163.

JOVANOVIĆ (VLADIMIR) Statusna pitanja organizacije udruženog rada. Zagreb, 1971. pp. 38.

KALOGJERA (DRAŽEN) Organizaciono-upravljačka struktura i mehanizmi koordinacije udruženog rada u privredi; Samoupravni sporazumi i društveni dogovori. Zagreb, 1971. pp. 89.

LEPOTINEC (SLAVKO) Osnovna organizacija udruženog rada: organizaciono-pravni aspekt. Zagreb, 1971. pp. 48.

SAMOUPRAVNE interesne zajednice. Zagreb, 1971. pp. 64.

STRAHINJIĆ (ČASLAV) Samoupravljanje i rukovodjenje u osnovnoj organizaciji udruženog rada. Zagreb, 1971. pp. 32.

VANEK (JAN) The economics of workers' management: a Yugoslav case study. London, 1972. pp. 315. bibliog.

- Yugoslavia - Bibliography

ANDRIĆ (STANISLAVA) and SEVER-ZEBEC (MARIJA) compilers. Bibliografija o učešću radnika u upravljanju poduzećima u Jugoslaviji: Bibliography on workers' participation in management in Yugoslavia. Zagreb, 1969-1970. 2 pts. Pt. 2 is called Dodatak: Appendix. In Serbo-Croat and English.

WORLD HEALTH ORGANIZATION

SPAIN. Direccion General de Sanidad. Coleccion de Folletos para Medicos sobre Temas de Caracter Sanitario. 49. Sanidad internacional: Organizacion Mundial de la Salud; [by] Manuel Bermudez Pareja. Madrid, 1956. pp. 162.

- Bibliography

WORLD HEALTH ORGANIZATION. Publications: catalogue [title varies]. irreg., 1947/1964- Geneva. 1947/1957 and 1958/1962 catalogued separately and filed at R(0) WHO(25) and WHO(4) respectively.

- Germany, Eastern

The BONN policy of coercion is doomed to failure: government of the FRG again prevents membership of the GDR in the World Health Organization... on a basis of equality. Dresden, [1972]. pp. 24.

- Russia

OSAKWE (CHRIS O.) The participation of the Soviet Union in universal international organizations: a political and legal analysis of Soviet strategies and aspirations inside ILO, UNESCO and WHO. Leiden, 1972. pp. 194. bibliog.

WORLD HISTORY
See HISTORY, UNIVERSAL

WORLD JEWISH CONGRESS

WORLD JEWISH CONGRESS. British Section. National Conference, 1943. Report of the executive officers and proceedings. London, 1943. pp. 28.

WORLD POLITICS

BERDIAEV (NIKOLAI ALEKSANDROVICH) Novoe srednevekov'e: razmyshlenie o sud'be Rossii i Evropy: [tri etiuda]. Berlin, 1924. pp. 143.

YOUNG (NORWOOD) England conquers the world. London, 1937. pp. 239.

ORGANSKI (KATHERINE) and ORGANSKI (A.F.K.) Population and world power. New York, 1961. pp. 263, ix. bibliog.

The REVOLUTION in world politics; [papers presented at a conference at Princeton in 1961 in preparation for the international relations panels of the 1961 meeting of the American Political Science Association at St. Louis]; Morton A. Kaplan, editor. New York, [1962] repr. 1966. pp. 477.

PECHORKIN (VITOL'D KAZIMIROVICH) Mir - glavnoe: problemy voiny i mira v sovremennuiu epokhu. Moskva, 1964. pp. 128. (Akademiia Nauk SSSR. Nauchno-Populiarnaia Seriia)

IAKOVLEV (ALEKSANDR NIKOLAEVICH) Prizyv ubivat': amerikanskie fal'sifikatory problem voiny i mira. Moskva, 1965. pp. 103.

DRAPER (HAL) ed. Independent socialism and war;...articles [selected from Labor Action, The New International and Anvil]. Berkeley, Calif., [1966]. pp. 194. (Independent Socialist Committee. Independent Socialist Clippingbooks. No. 2)

TROTSKII (LEV DAVYDOVICH) Writings of Leon Trotsky...; (edited by George Breitman [and others]). New York, 1969 in progress.

KRAY (BRUNO) Europa gegen, ohne, mit England? Kreuzweingarten/Rhld., 1969. pp. 219.

NUNEZ (CARLOS) Cronicas de este mundo. Montevideo, 1969. pp. 239.

TORNQVIST (KURT) Svenskarna och omvärlden: en opinionsundersökning hösten 1968 om svenska folkets attityder till några internationella problem. Stockholm, 1969. fo. 37. (Psykologiskt Försvar. Nr. 42)

LIBMAN (GEORGII IZRAILEVICH) Sovremennaia epokha i mirovoi revoliutsionnyi protsess. Moskva, 1970. pp. 96.

LIE (TEKTJENG) An Indonesian view: the great proletarian cultural revolution. Djakarta, 1970. pp. 25. (Lembaga Ilmu Pengetahuan Indonesia. Lembaga Research Kebudajaan Nasional. Terbitan Tak Berkala. No. 2/2)

PANKRASHOVA (M.) and SIPOLS (VILNIS IANOVICH) Pochemu ne udalos' predotvratit' voinu: moskovskie peregovory SSSR, Anglii i Frantsii 1939 goda; dokumental'nyi obzor. Moskva, 1970. pp. 122.

SACER (JOZE FRANC) Provokationen in Politik und Wirtschaft. Reinach/Basel, [1970?]. pp. 136.

1971

ANNUAL OF POWER AND CONFLICT: a survey of political violence and international influence; [pd. by] Institute for the Study of Conflict, London, [and] National Strategy Information Center, New York. a., 1971 [1st issue]- London.

WORLD POLITICS (Cont'd.)

ART (ROBERT J.) and WALTZ (KENNETH NEAL) eds. The use of force: international politics and foreign policy. Boston, [1971]. pp. 546. bibliog.

BELL (CORAL) The conventions of crisis: a study in diplomatic management. London, 1971. pp. 131. bibliog.

BRANDT (WILLY) Frieden: Reden und Schriften des Friedensnobelpreisträgers 1971. Bonn-Bad Godesberg, 1971. pp. 176.

CUNLIFFE (MARCUS) ed. The Times history of our times. London, [1971]. pp. 416. bibliog.

EGOROV (VALERII NIKOLAEVICH) Mirnoe sosushchestvovanie i revoliutsionnyi protsess. Moskva, 1971. pp. 224. bibliog.

EICHWEDE (WOLFGANG) Revolution und internationale Politik: zur kommunistischen Interpretation der kapitalistischen Welt, 1921-1925. Köln, 1971. pp. 246. bibliog.

HUTTER (CLEMENS MARIA) Keime künftiger Krisen: Perspektiven der Weltpolitik. Graz, [1971]. pp. 540. bibliog.

ITALIAANDER (ROLF) ed. Diktaturen im Nacken. München, [1971]. pp. 358.

KNUPFFER (GEORGE) The struggle for world power: revolution and counter-revolution. 3rd ed. London, 1971. pp. 240.

LANGSAM (WALTER CONSUELO) and MITCHELL (OTIS C.) The world since 1919; ...eighth edition [of the world since 1914]. New York, [1971]. pp. 743. bibliog.

MONAHAN (BRYAN WILLIS) The survival of Britain: contemporaneous commentaries on linked events of 1968-1970; [articles from The Social Crediter, pamphlets, unpublished material]; edited and arranged by T.N. Morris. London, 1971. pp. 124.

POZDNIAKOV (EL'GIZ ABDULOVICH) Molodye gosudarstva Azii i Afriki v OON. Moskva, 1971. pp. 149. bibliog.

SALIS (JEAN R. DE) Geschichte und Politik: Betrachtungen zur Geschichte und Politik; Beiträge zur Zeitgeschichte. Zürich, [1971]. pp. 400.

SPIEGEL (STEVEN L.) and WALTZ (KENNETH NEAL) eds. Conflict in world politics. Cambridge, Mass., [1971]. pp. 474. bibliogs.

TOLKUNOV (LEV NIKOLAEVICH) Mify i real'nost'. Moskva, 1971. pp. 343. Articles written between 1966 and 1971.

The UNITED Nations in international politics; edited by Leon Gordenker. Princeton, 1971. pp. 241.

1972

The ABERYSTWYTH papers: international politics, 1919-1969; [derived from a conference held at Gregynog Hall, 1969]; edited by Brian Porter. London, 1972. pp. 390. bibliog.

ACHESON (DEAN GOODERHAM) Grapes from thorns; [extracts from articles, books, lectures, letters, etc.]. New York, [1972]. pp. 253.

BRUTENTS (K.) A historical view of neo-colonialism. Moscow, 1972. pp. 307.

CHIAO (KUAN-HUA) Speech by...chairman of the delegation of the People's Republic of China at the plenary meeting of the 27th session of the U.N. General Assembly, October 3. 1972. Peking, 1972. pp. 24.

COUSINS (NORMAN) The improbable triumvirate: John F. Kennedy, Pope John, Nikita Khrushchev. New York, [1972]. pp. 171.

GADDIS (JOHN LEWIS) The United States and the origins of the cold war, 1941-1947. New York, 1972. pp. 396. bibliog.

HOWE (QUINCY) Ashes of victory: World War II and its aftermath. New York, [1972]. pp. 542. bibliog.

KNIAZHINSKII (VSEVOLOD BORISOVICH) Mezhdunarodnaia strategiia antikommunizma. Moskva, 1972. pp. 111.

KOLKO (JOYCE) and KOLKO (GABRIEL) The limits of power: the world and United States foreign policy, 1945-1954. New York, [1972]. pp. 820.

LAFEBER (WALTER) America, Russia, and the cold war, 1945-1971. 2nd ed. New York, [1972]. pp. 339. bibliog.

LENINSKAIA teoriia sotsialisticheskoi revoliutsii i sovremennost'. Moskva, 1972. pp. 526.

MACRIDIS (ROY C.) ed. Foreign policy in world politics. 4th ed. Englewood Cliffs, [1972]. pp. 428. bibliogs.

MEZHDUNARODNYE konflikty. Moskva, 1972. pp. 238.

MILLER (RICHARD H.) ed. The evolution of the Cold War: from confrontation to containment. New York, [1972]. pp. 141. bibliog.

NOVOPASHIN (IURII STEPANOVICH) Strategiia "mirnogo vmeshatel'stva": kritika nekotorykh burzhuaznykh kontseptsii o sovremennom sotsializme. Moskva, 1972. pp. 232.

OWEN (DAVID) The politics of defence. London, 1972. pp. 249.

RACHKOV (BORIS VASIL'EVICH) Neft' i mirovaia politika. Moskva, 1972. pp. 271.

ROSTOW (WALT WHITMAN) The diffusion of power: an essay in recent history. New York, [1972]. pp. 739.

SURIN (VLADIMIR IVANOVICH) Sotsializm i mirovoi sotsial'nyi progress. Leningrad, 1972. pp. 175.

The WORLD socialist system and anti-communism; [edited by A.P. Butenko]; translated from the Russian by A. Bratov. Moscow, 1972. pp. 284.

ZHUKOV (GEORGII ALEKSANDROVICH) 33 vizy: puteshestviia v raznye strany. Moskva, 1972. pp. 463.

1973

TROTSKII (LEV DAVYDOVICH) Writings of Leon Trotsky...; (edited by George Breitman [and others]). 2nd ed. New York, 1973 in progress.

BARSTON (RONALD P.) ed. The other powers: studies in the foreign policies of small states. London, 1973. pp. 341.

BUCHAN (ALASTAIR) Power and equilibrium in the 1970s. New York, 1973. pp. 116. (Council on Foreign Relations. Russell C. Leffingwell Lectures. 1972)

DONELAN (MICHAEL DENIS) and GRIEVE (MURIEL JOY) International disputes: case histories, 1945-1970. London, [1973]. pp. 286. bibliogs.

GEIGER (THEODORE) The fortunes of the West: the future of the Atlantic nations. Bloomington, Ind., [1973]. pp. 304.

HERZFELD (HANS) Historian. Berlin in der Weltpolitik, 1945-1970. Berlin, 1973. pp. 666. bibliog. (Berlin. Freie Universität. Friedrich-Meinecke-Institut. Historische Kommission zu Berlin. Veröffentlichungen. Band 38)

KING (F.P.) The new internationalism: allied policy and the European peace, 1939-1945. Newton Abbot, 1973. pp. 230. bibliog.

MADDOX (ROBERT JAMES) The New Left and the origins of the Cold War. Princeton, [1973]. pp. 169.

STOESSINGER (JOHN GEORGE) The might of nations: world politics in our time. 4th ed. New York, 1973. pp. 461. bibliogs.

- Bibliography

CARNEGIE ENDOWMENT FOR INTERNATIONAL PEACE. Publications of the Carnegie Endowment for International Peace, 1910-1967, including International Conciliation, 1924-1967; compiled by Jane A. Hannigan. New York, 1971. pp. 229.

MISHARINA (V.) and others, compilers. Protiv burzhuaznoi ideologii: rekomendatel'nyi ukazatel' literatury. Moskva, 1971. pp. 96.

U.K. Foreign Office. Library. 1926-68. Catalogue of the Foreign Office Library, 1926-1968. Boston (Mass.), 1972. 8 vols.

- Chronology

THANASSECOS (LUC) Chronologie des relations internationales, 1914-1971; exposés thématiques. Paris, [1972]. pp. 690.

- Indexes

U.K. Ministry of Defence. Library (Central and Army). Index of book lists. irreg., current issue only kept. London.

- Sources

CROZIER (WILLIAM PERCIVAL) Off the record: political interviews, 1933-1943; edited with an introduction by A.J.P. Taylor. London, 1973. pp. 397.

WORLD WAR, 1939-1945

FOSTER (WILLIAM ZEBULON) The war crisis: questions and answers. New York, 1940. pp. 64.

BROWDER (EARL RUSSELL) Victory - and after. New York, [1942]. pp. 256.

DEBORIN (GRIGORII ABRAMOVICH) Secrets of the Second World War; (translated from the Russian by Vic Schneierson). Moscow, 1971. pp. 277.

CALVOCORESSI (PETER) and WINT (GUY) Total war: causes and courses of the Second World War. London, 1972. pp. 959. bibliog.

HOWE (QUINCY) Ashes of victory: World War II and its aftermath. New York, [1972]. pp. 542. bibliog.

VTORAIA mirovaia voina i sovremennost'. Moskva, 1972. pp. 355.

- Aerial operations, American

MARX (JOSEPH LAURANCE) Nagasaki: the necessary bomb? New York, [1971]. pp. 239.

INFIELD (GLENN B.) The Poltava affair: a Russian warning: an American tragedy. New York, [1973]. pp. 265. bibliog.

- Aerial operations, German

SKAWRAN (PAUL ROBERT) Ikaros: Persönlichkeit und Wesen des deutschen Jagdfliegers im Zweiten Weltkrieg. Steinebach am Wörthsee, [1970]. pp. 223. bibliog.

- Aerial operations, Italian

PRICOLO (FRANCESCO) La Regia Aeronautica nella seconda guerra mondiale, novembre 1939-novembre 1941. Milano, [1971]. pp. 490.

- Armistices

PALM (THEDE) ed. The Finnish-Soviet armistice negotiations of 1944. Stockholm, [1971]. pp. 160. (Vetenskapssamhället i Uppsala. Acta Academiae Regiae Scientiarum Upsaliensis. 14)

LAUNAY (MICHEL) L'armistice de 1940. Paris, 1972. pp. 96. bibliog.

- Atrocities

YUGOSLAVIA. Državna Komisija za Utvrdjivanje Zločina Okupatora i Njihovih Pomagača. 1947. Saopštenje o zločinima Austrije i Austrijanaca protiv Jugoslavije i njenih naroda. Beograd, 1947. pp. 154.

RAWICZ (J.) and others, eds. Okupacja i medycyna: wybór artykułów z "Przeglądu Lekarskiego - Oświęcim" z lat 1961-1970. Warszawa, 1971. pp. 451 [xxiii].

- Campaigns

DARCOURT (PIERRE) Armée d'Afrique: la revanche des drapeaux. Paris, [1972]. pp. 285.

NICOLSON (NIGEL) Alex: the life of Field Marshal Earl Alexander of Tunis. London, [1973]. pp. 346. bibliog.

- Campaigns - Balkan States

VAN CREVELD (MARTIN L.) Hitler's strategy 1940-1941: the Balkan clue. Cambridge, [1973]. pp. 248. bibliog. (London. University. London School of Economics and Political Science. Centre for International Studies. International Studies)

- Campaigns - Borneo

HEEKEREN (C. VAN) Rode zon boven Borneo: West-Borneo 1942. Den Haag, 1968. pp. 170. bibliog.

HEEKEREN (C. VAN) Moord en brand: Oost Borneo 1942. Den Haag, 1969. pp. 243. bibliog.

- Campaigns - Burma

TULLOCH (DEREK) Wingate in peace and war;... edited by... Arthur Swinson. London, 1972. pp. 300.

- Campaigns - Eastern

STRANY Tsentral'noi i Iugo-Vostochnoi Evropy vo vtoroi mirovoi voine: voenno-istoricheskii spravochnik. Moskva, 1972. pp. 302. bibliog.

- Campaigns - France

FONVIEILLE-ALQUIER (FRANÇOIS) Les Français dans la drôle de guerre. Paris, [1971]. pp. 471.

KOCH-KENT (HENRI) 10 mai 1940 en Luxembourg: témoignages et documents. Luxembourg, 1971. pp. 336. bibliog.

WORLD WAR, 1939-1945 - Campaigns
- France (Cont'd.)

> FONVIEILLE-ALQUIER (FRANÇOIS) The French and the phoney war, 1939-40; [translated by] Edward Ashcroft. London, 1973. pp. 218.

- Campaign - Greece

> VAN CREVELD (MARTIN L.) Greece and Yugoslavia in Hitler's strategy, 1940-1941; [Ph. D. (London) thesis]. 1971. fo. 299. bibliog. Typescript: unpublished. This thesis is the property of London University and may not be removed from the Library.

- Campaigns - Mediterranean

> La GUERRE en Méditerranée, 1939-1945: actes du colloque international tenu à Paris du 8 au 11 avril 1969. Paris, 1971. pp. 792.

- Campaigns - Pacific

> LENSEN (GEORGE ALEXANDER) The strange neutrality: Soviet-Japanese relations during the Second World War, 1941-1945. Tallahassee, Fla., [1972]. pp. 332. bibliog.

- Campaigns - Poland

> BETHELL (NICHOLAS WILLIAM) 4th Baron Bethell. The war Hitler won: September 1939. London, 1972. pp. 472. bibliog.

- Campaigns - Russia

> ESTEBAN-INFANTES (EMILIO) La Division Azul: donde Asia empieza. Barcelona, 1956. pp. 333. bibliog.
>
> **VOENNO-ISTORICHESKII ZHURNAL. Moskva, monthly, okt.1966 (10). Xerographic reprint.**
>
> CHANEY (OTTO PRESTON) Zhukov. Newton Abbot, 1972. pp. 512. bibliog.
>
> LEACH (BARRY A.) German strategy against Russia, 1939-1941. Oxford, 1973. pp. 308. bibliog.
>
> SOLOV'EV (BORIS GRIGOR'EVICH) Vermakht na puti k gibeli: krushenie planov nemetsko-fashistskogo komandovaniia letom i osen'iu 1943 g. Moskva, 1973. pp. 311. bibliog.

- Campaigns - Russia - Latvia

> RIZHSKIE gvardeiskie: sbornik voenno-istoricheskikh ocherkov. Riga, 1972. pp. 208.

- Campaigns - Western

> **UNDASYNOV (I.N.) Ruzvel't, Cherchill' i vtoroi front. Moskva, 1965. pp. 136.**

- Campaigns - Yugoslavia

> VAN CREVELD (MARTIN L.) Greece and Yugoslavia in Hitler's strategy, 1940-1941; [Ph. D. (London) thesis]. 1971. fo. 299. bibliog. Typescript: unpublished. This thesis is the property of London University and may not be removed from the Library

- Casualties (Statistics, etc)

> MELLOR (W. FRANKLIN) ed. Casualties and medical statistics. London, H.M.S.O., 1972. pp. 893. (U.K. [Ministry of Health]. History of the Second World War. United Kingdom Medical Series)

- Catholic Church

> RHODES (ANTHONY) The Vatican in the age of the dictators, 1922-1945. London, 1973. pp. 383. bibliog.

- Causes

> HELSEY (EDOUARD) Non-resistance; ou, Le chemin de l'abattoir, 1918-1940. [Paris, 1945]. pp. 222.
>
> **SHLEPAKOV (ARNOL'D MYKOLAIOVYCH) V roky zrostannia voiennoï nebezpeky, 1929-1940. Kyïv, 1963. pp. 54.**
>
> GERMANY. Auswärtiges Amt. Akten zur Deutschen Auswärtigen Politik 1918-1945. Akten zur deutschen auswärtigen Politik, 1918-1945. Serie E. 1941-1945. Göttingen, 1969 in progress.
>
> KLEINE-AHLBRANDT (WILLIAM LAIRD) ed. Appeasement of the dictators: crisis diplomacy? New York, [1970]. pp. 138. bibliog.
>
> PANKRASHOVA (M.) and SIPOLS (VILNIS IANOVICH) Pochemu ne udalos' predotvratit' voinu: moskovskie peregovory SSSR, Anglii i Frantsii 1939 goda; dokumental'nyi obzor. Moskva, 1970. pp. 122.
>
> GERMANY. Auswärtiges Amt. Akten zur Deutschen Auswärtigen Politik 1918-1945. Akten zur deutschen auswärtigen Politik, 1918-1945. Serie C. 1933-1937. Göttingen, 1971 in progress.
>
> ANFILOV (VIKTOR ALEKSANDROVICH) Bessmertnyi podvig: issledovanie kanuna i pervogo etapa Velikoi Otechestvennoi voiny. Moskva, 1971. pp. 541.
>
> FABRY (PHILIPP WALTER) Die Sowjetunion und das Dritte Reich: eine dokumentierte Geschichte der deutsch-sowjetischen Beziehungen von 1933 bis 1941. Stuttgart, [1971]. pp. 485. bibliog.
>
> **LIBAL (MICHAEL) Japans Weg in den Krieg: die Aussenpolitik der Kabinette Konoye 1940/1941. Düsseldorf, [1971]. pp. 261. bibliog.**
>
> CARR (WILLIAM) b.1921. Arms, autarky and aggression: a study in German foreign policy, 1933-1939. London, 1972. pp. 136. bibliog.
>
> KUTAKOV (LEONID NIKOLAEVICH) Japanese foreign policy on the eve of the Pacific war: a Soviet view;...edited...by George Alexander Lensen. Tallahassee, Fla, [1972]. pp. 241. bibliog.
>
> RICH (NORMAN) Hitler's war aims: ideology, the Nazi state, and the course of expansion. London, 1973 in progress. bibliog.
>
> ASTER (SIDNEY) 1939: the making of the Second World War. London, 1973. pp. 456. bibliog.

- Censorship - Italy

> POLLORINI (GIUSEPPE) La censura e il censore. Milano, 1971. pp. 203.

- Censorship - Netherlands

> HOFFMAN (GABRIELE) NS-Propaganda in den Niederlanden: Organisation und Lenkung der Publizistik unter deutscher Besatzung, 1940-1945. München-Pullach, 1972. pp. 296. bibliog.

- Children

> SKWARKO (KRYSTYNA) Osiedlenie młodzieży polskiej w Nowej Zelandii w r.1944. Londyn, 1972. pp. 85. (Polskie Towarzystwo Historyczne w Australii. Seria I: Dokumentaryczno-pamiętnikarska. Nr.1)

- Claims

> CANADA. War Claims Commission, World War II. 1970. A consolidation of the reports of the Commission with related documents and including cases to illustrate the principles and procedures of adjudication. Ottawa, 1970. pp. 728.

- Collaborationists

   LITTLEJOHN (DAVID) M.A., A.L.A. The patriotic traitors: a history of collaboration in German-occupied Europe, 1940-45. London, 1972. pp. 391. bibliog.

- Collaborationists - Europe, Eastern

   TRUNK (ISAIAH) Judenrat: the Jewish Councils in Eastern Europe under Nazi occupation. New York, [1972]. pp. 664.

- Collaborationists - France

   AZIZ (PHILIPPE) Au service de l'ennemi: la gestapo française en province. [Paris, 1972]. pp. 187.

   The SORROW and the pity: a film by Marcel Ophuls; [translation of the original filmscript of Le chagrin et la pitié by Mireille Johnston; with] introduction by Stanley Hoffman...[and] biographical and appendix material by Mireille Johnston. New York, 1972. pp. 194. With stills from the film.

- Collaborationists - Netherlands

   ZEE (SYTZE VAN DER) 25,000 landverraders: de SS in Nederland; Nederland in de SS. Den Haag, 1967. pp. 217. bibliog.

- Congresses

   DEUERLEIN (ERNST) Potsdam 1945: Ende und Anfang. Köln, [1970]. pp. 156.

   POTSDAM und die deutsche Frage; mit Beiträgen von Ernst Deuerlein [and others]. Köln, [1970]. pp. 159.

- Conscript labour - Germany

   EVRARD (JACQUES) La déportation des travailleurs français dans le IIIe Reich. [Paris, 1972]. pp. 460. bibliog.

- Conscript labour - Norway

   CHRISTIE (NILS) Fangevoktere i konsentrasjonsleire: en sosiologisk undersøkelse av norske fangevoktere i "serbeleirene" i Nord-Norge i 1942-43. Oslo, [1972]. pp. 191. bibliog.

- Deportaions from France

   WORMSER (OLGA) and MICHEL (HENRI) eds. Tragédie de la déportation, 1940-1945: temoignages de survivants des camps de concentration allemands. [Paris, 1955? repr. 1966]. pp. 512.

   EVRARD (JACQUES) La déportation des travailleurs français dans le IIIe Reich. [Paris, 1972]. pp. 460. bibliog.

- Destruction and pillage - Poland

   NOSKOVA (AL'BINA FEDOROVNA) Razorenie ekonomiki Pol'shi gitlerovskoi Germaniei, 1939-1944: territoriia general-gubernatorstva. Moskva, 1971. pp. 255. bibliog.

- Diplomatic history

   HITLER (ADOLF) Proklamation des Führers an das deutsche Volk und Note des Auswärtigen Amtes an die Sowjet-Regierung nebst Anlagen. [Berlin?, 1941?]. pp. 79. Page 79 imperfect.

   GERMANY. Auswärtiges Amt. Archivkommission. 1943. Roosevelts Weg in den Krieg: Geheimdokumente zur Kriegspolitik des Präsidenten der Vereinigten Staaten. Berlin, 1943. pp. 111. (Entstehung des Krieges von 1939, Die. 1. Schrift)

   UNDASYNOV (I.N.) Ruzvel't, Cherchill' i vtoroi front. Moskva, 1965. pp. 136.

   KLEINE-AHLBRANDT (WILLIAM LAIRD) ed. Appeasement of the dictators: crisis diplomacy? New York, [1970]. pp. 138. bibliog.

   CHAUVEL (JEAN) Commentaire. Paris, [1971 in progress].

   LIBAL (MICHAEL) Japans Weg in den Krieg: die Aussenpolitik der Kabinette Konoye 1940/1941. Düsseldorf, [1971]. pp. 261. bibliog.

   PARKINSON (ROGER) Peace for our time: Munich to Dunkirk: the inside story. London, 1971. pp. 412. bibliog.

   VANLANGENHOVE (FERNAND) La sécurité de la Belgique: contribution à l'histoire de la période, 1940-1950. Bruxelles, [1971]. pp. 263. bibliog. (Brussels. Université Libre. Faculté de Philosophie et Lettres. Travaux. 47)

   BEITZELL (ROBERT) The uneasy alliance: America, Britain, and Russia, 1941-1943. New York, 1972. pp. 404, xvii. bibliog.

   BETHELL (NICHOLAS WILLIAM) 4th Baron Bethell. The war Hitler won: September 1939. London, 1972. pp. 472. bibliog.

   ESMANN JENSEN (FRANK) Da fornuften sejrede: det britiske udenrigsministeriums politik over for Danmark under 2. verdenskrig. [Copenhagen, 1972]. pp. 240.

   FENYO (MARIO D.) Hitler, Horthy and Hungary: German-Hungarian relations, 1941-1944. New Haven, 1972. pp. 279. bibliog.

   FISCHER (LOUIS) The road to Yalta: Soviet foreign relations, 1941-1945. New York, [1972]. pp. 238. bibliog.

   HÄGGLÖF (GUNNAR) Samtida vittne, 1940-1945. 2nd ed. Stockholm, [1972]. pp. 249.

   HENRY-HAYE (GASTON) La grande éclipse franco-américaine. [Paris, 1972]. pp. 393.

   LENSEN (GEORGE ALEXANDER) The strange neutrality: Soviet-Japanese relations during the Second World War, 1941-1945. Tallahassee, Fla., [1972]. pp. 332. bibliog.

   ASTER (SIDNEY) 1939: the making of the Second World War. London, 1973. pp. 456. bibliog.

   INFIELD (GLENN B.) The Poltava affair: a Russian warning: an American tragedy. New York, [1973]. pp. 265. bibliog.

   KING (F.P.) The new internationalism: allied policy and the European peace, 1939-1945. Newton Abbot, 1973. pp. 230. bibliog.

   PARKINSON (ROGER) Blood, toil, tears and sweat: the war history from Dunkirk to Alamein, based on the War Cabinet papers of 1940 to 1942. London, 1973. pp. 539. bibliog.

   ROBERTS (WALTER R.) Tito, Mihailović and the Allies, 1941-1945. New Brunswick, N.J., [1973]. pp. 406. bibliog.

   WEISBAND (EDWARD) Turkish foreign policy, 1943-1945: small state diplomacy and great power politics. [Princeton, 1973]. pp. 377. bibliog. (New York (City). University. Center for International Studies. Studies in Peaceful Change)

- Economic aspects

   MARIOTTE (PIERRE) Le monde cherche son équilibre. Paris, 1943. pp. 124.

WORLD WAR, 1939-1945 - Economic aspects (Cont'd.)

STEINICKE (DIETRICH) Wirtschaftskrieg und Seekrieg: die allgemeine völkerrechtliche Anerkennung des anglo-amerikanischen Kriegsbegriffes und ihre Rechtsfolgen. Hamburg, 1970. pp. 100. bibliog. (Hamburg. Hansische Universität. Forschungsstelle für Völkerrecht und Ausländisches Öffentliches Recht. Das Geltende Seekriegsrecht in Einzeldarstellungen. Band 1)

- Economic aspects - Africa, North

WILMINGTON (MARTIN WIZNITZER) The Middle East Supply Centre. Albany, N.Y., 1971. pp. 248. bibliog.

- Economic aspects - Austria

SCHAUSBERGER (NORBERT) Rüstung in Österreich, 1938-1945: eine Studie über die Wechselwirkung von Wirtschaft, Politik und Kriegsführung. Wien, [1970]. pp. 228. bibliog. (Österreichisches Institut für Zeitgeschichte. Publikationen. Band 8)

- Economic aspects - East (Near East)

WILMINGTON (MARTIN WIZNITZER) The Middle East Supply Centre. Albany, N.Y., 1971. pp. 248. bibliog.

- Economic aspects - Germany

[ROSINSKI (HERBERT)] Deutschlands Kriegsbereitschaft und Kriegsaussichten im Spiegel der deutschen Fachliteratur; ([by] Miles, [pseud.]). Zürich, [1939]. pp. 151.

BENTE (HERMANN) England und Deutschland im Kampf um die Neuordnung der Weltwirtschaft. Berlin, 1940. pp. 54. (Deutsches Institut für Aussenpolitische Forschung and Hamburg. Institut für Auswärtige Politik. Schriften. Heft 53)

SCHAUSBERGER (NORBERT) Rüstung in Österreich, 1938-1945: eine Studie über die Wechselwirkung von Wirtschaft, Politik und Kriegsführung. Wien, [1970]. pp. 228. bibliog. (Österreichisches Institut für Zeitgeschichte. Publikationen. Band 8)

- Economic aspects - India

INDIA. Department of Commerce. Administrative Intelligence Room. 1947. Statistics relating to India's war effort. Delhi, 1947. pp. 46.

- Economic aspects - Norway

NORWAY. Kommunal- og Arbeidsdepartementet. 1957. Om avregning av statens forsyningskjøp under og etter krigen: Prisutjevningsfondet for statens importvarer. [Oslo], 1957. pp. 81. (Norway. Stortinget. Stortingsmeldinger. 1957, nr. 19)

NORWAY. Industridirektoratet. 1958. Industriens drift i krigstid: en orientering om det forberedende arbeid, forutsetninger og lovbestemmelser. Oslo, 1958. pp. 14.

MILWARD (ALAN S.) The fascist economy in Norway. Oxford, 1972. pp. 317. bibliog.

- Economic aspects - Russia

DOKUCHAEV (GEORGII ANTONOVICH) Rabochii klass Sibiri i Dal'nego Vostoka nakanune Velikoi Otechestvennoi voiny, 1937-iiun' 1941 gg, etc. Novosibirsk, 1966. pp. 188.

SOVETSKAIA ekonomika v period Velikoi Otechestvennoi voiny, 1941-1945 gg. Moskva, 1970. pp. 502.

MITROFANOVA (AVGUSTA VASIL'EVNA) Rabochii klass SSSR v gody Velikoi Otechestvennoi voiny. Moskva, 1971. pp. 575.

DZENISKEVICH (ANDREI ROSTISLAVOVICH) Voennaia piatiletka rabochikh Leningrada, 1941-1945. Leningrad, 1972. pp. 215.

- Economic aspects - Russia - Bibliography

MARGOLINA (E.B.) compiler. Narodnoe khoziaistvo SSSR v gody Velikoi Otechestvennoi voiny, iiun' 1941 - mai 1945 gg.: bibliograficheskii ukazatel' knizhnoi i zhurnal'noi literatury na russkom iazyke, 1941-1968 gg. Moskva, 1971. pp. 460.

- Economic aspects - Russia - Azerbaijan

MEKHTIEV (GIAZENFER GIUSEINOVICH) Deiatel'nost' Kommunisticheskoi partii Azerbaidzhana v period Velikoi Otechestvennoi voiny, 1941-1945 gg. Baku, 1967. pp. 292.

- Economic aspects - Russia - Kazakstan

KOZYBAEV (MANASH KABASHEVICH) Kazakhstan - arsenal fronta. Alma-Ata, 1970. pp. 473.

BALAKAEV (TULTAI BALAKAEVICH) Kolkhoznoe krest'ianstvo Kazakhstana v gody Velikoi Otechestvennoi voiny, 1941-1945gg. Alma-Ata, 1971. pp. 350. bibliog.

- Economic aspects - Russia - Uzbekistan

KALYMBETOV (ZH.) Kommunisticheskaia partiia Uzbekistana v bor'be za razvitie promyshlennosti i transporta v gody Velikoi Otechestvennoi voiny. Tashkent, 1966. pp. 174. bibliog.

- Economic aspects - United Kingdom

BENTE (HERMANN) England und Deutschland im Kampf um die Neuordnung der Weltwirtschaft. Berlin, 1940. pp. 54. (Deutsches Institut für Aussenpolitische Forschung and Hamburg. Institut für Auswärtige Politik. Schriften. Heft 53)

U.K. [Cabinet Office]. History of the Second World War: United Kingdom Civil Series. Oil: a study of war-time policy and administration; by D.J. Payton-Smith. London, 1971. pp. 520.

- Education and the war

KENWORTHY (LEONARD S.) The teacher and the post-war child. Paris, [1946]. pp. 47.

UNITED NATIONS EDUCATIONAL, SCIENTIFIC AND CULTURAL ORGANIZATION. 1948. Universities in need. [Paris, 1948]. pp. 32. (Publications. No.217)

- Evacuation of civilians

GIRDNER (AUDRIE) and LOFTIS (ANNE) The great betrayal: the evacuation of the Japanese-Americans during World War II. New York, [1969] repr. 1972. pp. 562. bibliog.

MYER (DILLON S.) Uprooted Americans: the Japanese Americans and the War Relocation Authority during World War II. Tucson, Ariz., 1971 repr. 1972. pp. 360. bibliog.

DANIELS (ROGER) Concentration camps USA: Japanese Americans and World War II. New York, [1972]. pp. 188. bibliog.

- Governments in exile

GIRAUDOUX-MONTAIGNE (JEAN PIERRE) D'exil: quatre discours prononcés à la radio de Londres. Paris, [1945]. pp. 50.

JACOBMEYER (WOLFGANG) Heimat und Exil: die Anfänge der polnischen Untergrundbewegung im Zweiten Weltkrieg. Hamburg, [1973]. pp. 369. bibliog. (Hamburg. Forschungsstelle für die Geschichte des Nationalsozialismus in Hamburg. Hamburger Beiträge zur Zeitgeschichte. Band 9)

- **Historiography**

  BOL'SHAIA lozh' o voine: kritika noveishei burzhuaznoi istoriografii vtoroi mirovoi voiny. Moskva, 1971. pp. 368.

- **Jews**

  LATOUR (ANNY) La résistance juive en France, 1940-1944. [Paris, 1970]. pp. 307. bibliog.

  DIAMANT (DAVID) Les juifs dans la résistance française, 1940-1944; avec armes ou sans armes. Paris, [1971]. pp. 365. bibliog.

  CHARY (FREDERICK B.) The Bulgarian Jews and the final solution, 1940-1944. [Pittsburgh, 1972]. pp. 246. bibliog.

  TRUNK (ISAIAH) Judenrat: the Jewish Councils in Eastern Europe under Nazi occupation. New York, [1972]. pp. 664.

- **Jews - Bibliography**

  ROBINSON (JACOB) and ESH (SHAUL) eds. Guide to unpublished materials of the holocaust period: specimen pages. Jerusalem, 1965. pp. 48,34.

- **Manpower - Russia**

  KIRSANOV (NIKOLAI ANDREEVICH) Partiinye mobilizatsii na front v gody Velikoi Otechestvennoi voiny; pod redaktsiei... N.I. Shatagina. Moskva, 1972. pp. 187.

- **Manpower - Russia - Georgia**

  ASLANISHVILI (A.A.) Trudovye rezervy Gruzii v Velikoi Otechestvennoi voine. Tbilisi, 1972. pp. 152.

- **Naval operations - Submarine**

  WADDINGTON (CONRAD HAL) O.R. in World War 2: operational research against the U-boat. London, 1973. pp. 253.

- **Occupied territories**

  FAŠISMUS a Evropa: Fascism and Europe; mezinárodní symposium: an international symposium...Prague, 28th-29th August 1969. [Prague], 1969-70. 2 vols. (in 1). In German or French.

  GERMAN occupied Great Britain: ordinances of the military authorities; [originally printed in Leipzig in 1941 as a guide to the legislative and administrative power of the intended army of occupation in Great Britain]. London, [1971]. pp. 94. Parallel English and German texts.

  Das JAHR 1941 in der europäischen Politik; unter Mitarbeit von Martin K. Bachstein [and others] herausgegeben von Karl Bosl; Vorträge der Tagung des Collegium Carolinum in Weissach am Tegernsee... 1971. München, 1972. pp. 163.

- **Peace**

  INTERNATIONAL PEACE CAMPAIGN. Schweizer Zweig. Die neue Friedensordnung: ihre politischen, wirtschaftlichen, sozialen und geistigen Grundlagen. [Zürich, 1941]. pp. 55.

  EINZIG (PAUL) Can we win the peace? London, 1942. pp. x, 148.

  DEUERLEIN (ERNST) Potsdam 1945: Ende und Anfang. Köln, [1970]. pp. 196.

  INTERSIMONE (GIUSEPPE) L'Italia e il trattato di pace del 10-2-1947. Roma, [1970]. pp. 153. bibliog.

  KEPPLER (KURT) Tod über Deutschland: der Morgenthauplan; Vorgeschichte, Geschichte, Wesen, Hintergründe. Tübingen, [1971]. pp. 390. (Institut für Deutsche Nachkriegsgeschichte. Veröffentlichungen. Band 6)

  KUKLICK (BRUCE) American policy and the division of Germany: the clash with Russia over reparations. Ithaca, N.Y., 1972. pp. 286. bibliog.

  WHEELER-BENNETT (Sir JOHN WHEELER) and NICHOLLS (ANTHONY JAMES) The semblance of peace: the political settlement after the Second World War. London, 1972. pp. 878. bibliog.

  KING (F.P.) The new internationalism: allied policy and the European peace, 1939-1945. Newton Abbot, 1973. pp. 230. bibliog.

- **Periodicals**

  MATZ (ELISABETH) Die Zeitungen der US-Armee für die deutsche Bevölkerung, 1944-1946. Münster (Westf.), 1969. pp. 174. bibliog.

- **Personal narratives, American**

  LINDBERGH (CHARLES AUGUSTUS) The wartime journals of Charles A. Lindbergh. New York, [1970]. pp. 1038.

  LEE (RAYMOND ELIOT) The London observer: the journal of General Raymond E. Lee, 1940-1941; edited by James Leutze. London, 1972. pp. 489.

- **Personal narratives, British**

  BALFOUR (HAROLD HARINGTON) 1st Baron Balfour of Inchrye. Wings over Westminster. London, 1973. pp. 224.

- **Personal narratives, French**

  CHAUVEL (JEAN) Commentaire. Paris, [1971 in progress].

  JARDIN (PASCAL) La guerre à neuf ans. Paris, [1971]. pp. 198.

  WEISS (LOUISE) Le sacrifice du Chevalier, 3 septembre 1939-9 juin 1940; (mémoires d'une Europeénne: nouvelle série). Paris, [1971]. pp. 318.

- **Personal narratives, German**

  BEZYMENSKII (LEV ALEKSANDROVICH) Konets odnoi legendy. Moskva, 1972. pp. 159.

- **Personal narratives - Italian**

  BONOMI (GIOVANNI) Albania 1943: la tragica marcia dei militari italiani da Tepeleni e Argirocastro a Santi Quaranta. Milano, 1971 repr. 1972. pp. 361.

  PRICOLO (FRANCESCO) La Regia Aeronautica nella seconda guerra mondiale, novembre 1939-novembre 1941. Milano, [1971]. pp. 490.

  RIGONI STERN (MARIO) Quota Albania. Torino, 1971. pp. 151.

- **Personal narratives, Polish**

  ZAWADZKA-WETZ (ALICJA) Refleksje pewnego życia. Paryż, 1967. pp. 238.

  NAŁKOWSKA (ZOFIA) Dzienniki czasu wojny; wstęp, opracowanie i przypisy Hanna Kirchner. Warszawa, 1970. pp. 506.

WORLD WAR, 1939-1945 - Personal narratives - Polish (Cont'd.)

   AUDERSKA (HALINA) and ZIÓŁEK (ZYGMUNT) eds. Akcja N: wspomnienia 1941-1944, etc. Warszawa, 1972. pp. 767.

- Personal narratives, Russian

   FEVR (NIKOLAI) Solntse voskhodit na zapade. [pt.1]. Buenos-Aires, 1950. pp. 287.

   GESSEN (VLADIMIR I.) Geroi i predateli. N'iu-Iork, 1951. pp. 155.

   SAMSONOV (ALEKSANDR MIKHAILOVICH) ed. 9 maia 1945 goda. Moskva, 1970. pp. 758.

- Personal narratives - Spanish

   FERNANDEZ (ALBERTO) Emigracion republicana española, 1939-1945. Algorta, Vizcaya, 1972. pp. 97.

- Personal narratives, Swiss

   SCHINDLER (RENE) Ein Schweizer erlebt das geheime Deutschland: Tatsachenbericht. Zürich, [1945]. pp. 72.

- Prisoners and prisons, American

   JUNG (HERMANN) Die deutschen Kriegsgefangenen in amerikanischer Hand: USA. München, 1972. pp. 380. (Zur Geschichte der deutschen Kriegsgefangenen des zweiten Weltkrieges. Band 10/1)

- Prisoners and prisons, British

   FAULK (HENRY) Die deutschen Kriegsgefangenen in Grossbritannien: Re-education. München, 1970. pp. 783. (Zur Geschichte der deutschen Kriegsgefangenen des Zweiten Weltkrieges. Band 11/2)

- Prisoners and prisons, French

   BOEHME (KURT WILLI) Die deutschen Kriegsgefangenen in französischer Hand;... mit einem Beitrag von Horst Wagenblass. München, 1971. pp. 390. maps. (Zur Geschichte des deutschen Kriegsgefangenen des Zweiten Weltkrieges. Band 13)

- Prisoners and prisons, German

   TROFIMENKO (GRIGORII) Ich war in Deutschland gefangen; (deutsche Übertragung von Th. Granowsky). Zürich, 1945. pp. 85.

- Prisoners and prisons, Russian

   VEYRIER (MARCEL) La Wehrmacht rouge, Moscou 1943-1945. Paris, [1970]. pp. 280. bibliog.

   SAISONS D'ALSACE. Nouvelle Série. No. 39-40. (L'incorporation de force et la captivité des Alsaciens en Russie). Strasbourg, 1971. pp. 518.

- Prisoners and prisons, Spanish

   PRIVES (SERGE) L'an 43:...journal des évadés internés en Espagne. Paris, [1968]. 2 vols.

- Propaganda

   MATZ (ELISABETH) Die Zeitungen der US-Armee für die deutsche Bevölkerung, 1944-1946. Münster (Westf.), 1969. pp. 174. bibliog.

   TOGLIATTI (PALMIRO) Italiani, italiani ascoltate!: discorsi agli italiani [from Radio Mosca, 1941-1943]. Milano, 1972. pp. 471.

- Public opinion - Germany

   STEINERT (MARLIS G.) Hitlers Krieg und die Deutschen: Stimmung und Haltung der deutschen Bevölkerung im Zweiten Weltkrieg. Düsseldorf, 1970. pp. 646. bibliog.

- Public opinion - United States

   BUCK (PEARL SYDENSTRICKER) American unity and Asia. New York, [1942]. pp. 140.

- Refugees

   ROHWER (JUERGEN) Die Versenkung der jüdischen Flüchtlingstransporter Struma und Mefkure im Schwarzen Meer, Februar 1942, August 1944: historische Untersuchung. Frankfurt/Main, 1965. pp. 153. bibliog. (Bibliothek für Zeitgeschichte. Schriften. Heft 4)

   SKWARKO (KRYSTYNA) Osiedlenie młodzieży polskiej w Nowej Zelandii w r.1944. Londyn, 1972. pp. 85. (Polskie Towarzystwo Historyczne w Australii. Seria I: Dokumentaryczno-pamiętnikarska. Nr.1)

- Reparations

   INTER-ALLIED REPARATION AGENCY. 1947. Rules of accounting for German external assets, as approved by the Assembly of I.A.R.A., 21 November 1947. [Brussels?], 1947. pp. 7.

   RINGEL (HERMANN) Die Demontageliste für das Land Nordrhein-Westfalen und ihre wirtschaftlichen und sozialen Auswirkungen: Denkschrift der Vereinigung der Industrie- und Handelskammern des Landes Nordrhein-Westfalen...(zur Demontageliste vom 16. Oktober 1947). [Düsseldorf, 1947]. pp. 71.

   INTER-ALLIED REPARATION AGENCY. 1961. Final report to member governments. [Brussels?], 1961. pp. 84.

   BALABKINS (NICHOLAS) West German reparations to Israel. New Brunswick, N.J., [1971]. pp. 384.

   SEIFERT (HUBERTUS) Die Reparationen Japans: ein Beitrag zum Wandel des Reparationsproblems und zur wirtschaftlichen Entwicklung Japans nach 1945. Opladen, 1971. pp. 208. bibliog. (Aachen. Technische Hochschule. Forschungsinstitut für Internationale Technisch-Wirtschaftliche Zusammenarbeit. Internationale Kooperation. 6) With English summary.

   KUKLICK (BRUCE) American policy and the division of Germany: the clash with Russia over reparations. Ithaca, N.Y., 1972. pp. 286. bibliog.

- Secret service

   SCHRAMM (WILHELM VON) Verrat im Zweiten Weltkrieg: vom Kampf der Geheimdienste in Europa; Berichte und Dokumentation. 2nd ed. Düsseldorf, 1969. pp. 407. bibliog.

   MASTERMAN (Sir JOHN CECIL) The double-cross system in the war of 1939 to 1945. New Haven, 1972. pp. 203.

- Secret service - Germany

   RUMIANTSEV (FRIDRIKH IAKOVLEVICH) Tainaia voina na Blizhnem i Srednem Vostoke. Moskva, 1972. pp. 136.

- Sources

   SEVERO-Osetinskaia partiinaia organizatsiia v gody Velikoi Otechestvennoi voiny: sbornik dokumentov i materialov. Ordzhonikidze, 1968. pp. 628.

GERMANY. Auswärtiges Amt. Akten zur Deutschen Auswärtigen Politik 1918-1945. Akten zur deutschen auswärtigen Politik, 1918-1945. Serie E. 1941-1945. Göttingen, 1969 in progress.

SORSFORDULÓ: iratok magyarország felszabadulásának történetéhez, 1944 szeptember - 1945 április. Budapest, 1970. 2 vols.

GERMANY. Auswärtiges Amt. Akten zur Deutschen Auswärtigen Politik 1918-1945. Akten zur deutschen auswärtigen Politik, 1918-1945. Serie C. 1933-1937. Göttingen, 1971 in progress.

U.K. Public Record Office. 1972. The second world war: a guide to documents in the Public Record Office; [by L. Bell and others]. London, 1972. pp. 303. (Handbooks. No. 15)

U.K. War Cabinet. 1939-45. Subject index of War Cabinet minutes, 1939 Sept. - (1945 July). London, 1972. 2 vols. (List and Index Society. [Publications]. Vols. 73-74)

CROZIER (WILLIAM PERCIVAL) Off the record: political interviews, 1933-1943; edited with an introduction by A.J.P. Taylor. London, 1973. pp. 397.

ROOSEVELT (FRANKLIN DELANO) President of the United States, and BULLITT (WILLIAM CHRISTIAN) For the President: personal and secret; correspondence between Franklin D. Roosevelt and William C. Bullitt; Orville H. Bullitt, editor. London, 1973. pp. 655. bibliog.

- Supplies

TIUMENSKII SEL'SKOKHOZIAISTVENNYI INSTITUT. Trudy. t.2. vyp. 1. Kommunisticheskaia partiia - organizator patrioticheskogo dvizheniia trudiashchikhsia Sibiri po okazaniiu material'noi pomoshchi frontu, 1941-1945 gg. Tiumen', 1963. pp. 132. bibliog.

SCHAUSBERGER (NORBERT) Rüstung in Österreich, 1938-1945: eine Studie über die Wechselwirkung von Wirtschaft, Politik und Kriegsführung. Wien, [1970]. pp. 228. bibliog. (Österreichisches Institut für Zeitgeschichte. Publikationen. Band 8)

WILMINGTON (MARTIN WIZNITZER) The Middle East Supply Centre. Albany, N.Y., 1971. pp. 248. bibliog.

- Territorial questions

WEBER (HERMANN) Writer on international law. Die Bukowina im Zweiten Weltkrieg: völkerrechtliche Aspekte der Lage der Bukowina im Spannungsfeld zwischen Rumänien, der Sowjetunion und Deutschland. Hamburg, 1972. pp. 86. bibliog. (Hamburg. Institut für Auswärtige Politik. Darstellungen zur Auswärtigen Politik. Band 11)

- Territorial questions - Germany

KEPPLER (KURT) Tod über Deutschland: der Morgenthauplan; Vorgeschichte, Geschichte, Wesen, Hintergründe. Tübingen, [1971]. pp. 390. (Institut für Deutsche Nachkriegsgeschichte. Veröffentlichungen. Band 6)

- Transportation

LUTSENKO (VASILII TIKHONOVICH) Deiatel'nost' KPSS po obespecheniiu bespereboinoi raboty zheleznodorozhnogo transporta v period Velikoi Otechestvennoi voiny, 1941-1945 gg., etc. Moskva, 1969. pp. 158. bibliog.

NOCK (OSWALD STEPHENS) Britain's railways at war, 1939-1945. London, 1971. pp. 224.

- Underground literature

DEBU-BRIDEL (JACQUES) ed. La résistance intellectuelle;... textes et témoinages. Paris, [1970]. pp. 267.

GIANNOTTI (PAOLO) Stampa operaia e classi sociali nella lotta clandestina: studi sulla Resistenza. Urbino, [1972]. pp. 229. (Istituto Regionale per la Storia del Movimento di Liberazione nelle Marche. Serie di Documenti, Ricerche e Memorie. 4)

- Underground movements

ASPETTI sociali ed economici della Resistenza in Europa: (atti del convegno organizzato dall' Istituto di Storia medioevale e moderna dell' Università degli Studi e dall'Amministrazione Provinciale, Milano...1966). Milano, 1967. pp. 355. In French or Italian.

DEBU-BRIDEL (JACQUES) ed. La résistance intellectuelle;... textes et témoinages. Paris, [1970]. pp. 267.

JUCHNIEWICZ (MIECZYSŁAW) Poles in the European resistance movement, 1939-1945; (translated by Beryl Arct). Warsaw, 1972. pp. 178.

MICHEL (HENRI) The shadow war: resistance in Europe 1939-1945; translated from the French by Richard Barry. London, 1972. pp. 416. bibliog.

- Underground movements - Austria

HOFER (JOSEF THEODOR) Weggefährten: vom österreichischen Freiheitskampf 1933 bis 1945. Wien, [1946]. pp. 79.

PLIESEIS (SEPP) Partisan der Berge: Lebenskampf eines österreichischen Arbeiters; (herausgegeben von Julius Mader). Wien, [1971]. pp. 319.

- Underground movements - Czechoslovakia

DOLEŽAL (JIŘÍ) and KŘEN (JAN) eds. Die kämpfende Tschechoslowakei: Dokumente über die Widerstandsbewegung...1938-1945; (aus dem Tschechischen übersetzt von Václav Melka). Prag, 1964. pp. 168. bibliog.

HUSÁK (GUSTÁV) Der Slowakische Nationalaufstand; [translated from the Slovak]. Berlin, 1972. pp. 740.

- Underground movements - Denmark

TROMMER (AAGE) Jernbanesabotagen i Danmark under den anden verdenskrig: en krigshistorisk undersøgelse; Railway sabotage in Denmark during the Second World War. Odense, [1971]. pp. 323. bibliog. (Odense Universitet. Studies in History and Social Sciences. vol. 3) With English summary.

TROMMER (AAGE) Modstandsarbejde i naerbillede: det illegale arbejde i Syd- og Sønderjylland under den tyske besaettelse af Danmark, 1940-45. Odense, 1973. pp. 515. bibliog. (Odense Universitet. Studies in History and Social Sciences. vol. 7)

- Underground movements - France

GESSEN (VLADIMIR I.) Geroi i predateli. N'iu-Iork, 1951. pp. 155.

LATOUR (ANNY) La Résistance juive en France, 1940-1944. [Paris, 1970]. pp. 301. bibliog.

WORLD WAR, 1939-1945 - Underground movements - France (Cont'd.)

AGULHON (MAURICE) and BARRAT (FERNAND) C[ompagnies] R[épublicaines de] S[écurité] à Marseille: "la police au service du peuple", 1944-1947. Paris, 1971. pp. 228. bibliog. (Fondation Nationale des Sciences Politiques. Textes et Documents de Sciences Sociales. Archives de Notre Temps. 1)

ANGEL (MIGUEL) Los guerrilleros españoles en Francia, [1940-1945]. La Habana, 1971. pp. 257. bibliog.

DIAMANT (DAVID) Les juifs dans la résistance française, 1940-1944; avec armes ou sans armes. Paris, [1971]. pp. 365. bibliog.

DURAND (ROBERT) ed. La lutte des travailleurs de chez Renault; racontée par eux-mêmes, 1912-1944: la résistance. Paris, [1971]. pp. 190. bibliog.

ZIL'BERFARB (IOGANSON ISAAKOVICH) Idei i traditsii Velikoi Frantsuzskoi revoliutsii v bor'be sil demokratii i fashizma. Moskva, 1971. pp. 231.

FERNANDEZ (ALBERTO) Emigracion republicana española, 1939-1945. Algorta, Vizcaya, 1972. pp. 97.

PAROT'KIN (I.V.) ed. Protiv obshchego vraga: sovetskie liudi vo frantsuzskom dvizhenii Soprotivleniia. Moskva, 1972. pp. 395.

The SORROW and the pity: a film by Marcel Ophuls; [translation of the original filmscript of Le chagrin et la pitié by Mireille Johnston; with] introduction by Stanley Hoffman...[and] biographical and appendix material by Mireille Johnston. New York, 1972. pp. 194. With stills from the film.

DELANOUE (PAUL) Les enseignants: la lutte syndicale du Front populaire à la libération. Paris, [1973]. pp. 414. bibliog.

- Underground movements - Greece

EUDES (DOMINIQUE) The Kapetanios: partisans and civil war in Greece, 1943-1949; translated from the French by John Howe. London, 1972. pp. 381. bibliog.

- Underground movements - Hungary

HARSÁNYI (JÁNOS) ed. Magyar szabadságharcosok a fasizmus ellen: dokumentumok a magyar antifasiszta ellenállási mozgalom történetéből, 1941-1945. 2nd ed. Budapest, 1969. pp. 906. bibliog. With appendix of photographs.

SORSFORDULÓ: iratok magyarország felszabadulásának történetéhez, 1944 szeptember - 1945 április. Budapest, 1970. 2 vols.

- Underground movements - Italy

VERCELLI (PROVINCE). Amministrazione Provinciale. Ventennale della Resistenza, 1945-1965. [Vercelli, 1968]. pp. 70.

MANIERA (ARISTODEMO) Nelle trincee dell'antifascismo: (ricordi di un garibaldino di Spagna). Urbino, 1970. pp. 226. (Istituto Regionale per la Storia del Movimento di Liberazione nelle Marche. Studi sulla Resistenza. 1)

LIBRI di testo e Resistenza: atti del convegno nazionale tenuto a Ferrara il 14-15 novembre 1970; ([paper by] Borghi [and others]). Roma, 1971. pp. 125.

MASERA (DIANA) Langa partigiana, '43-'45. Parma, 1971. pp. 316. (Istituto Storico della Resistenza in Piemonte. Studi e Documenti. 6)

BERGWITZ (HUBERTUS) Die Partisanenrepublik Ossola vom 10. September bis zum 23. Oktober 1944. [Hanover, 1972]. pp. 165. bibliog. (Institut für Sozialgeschichte Braunschweig. Veröffentlichungen)

LAZZARI (PRIMO DE) Storia del Fronte della gioventú nella Resistenza. Roma, 1972. pp. 258. bibliog.

PACOR (MARIO) and CASALI (LUCIANO) Lotte sociali e guerriglia in pianura: la Resistenza a Carpi, Soliera, Novi, Campogalliano. Roma, 1972. pp. 393. bibliog.

SCALPELLI (ADOLFO) Scioperi e guerriglia in Val Padana, 1943-45: studi storici; [a collection of articles from various periodicals]. Urbino, [1972]. pp. 523.

- Underground movements - Norway

RISTE (OLAV) and NÖKLEBY (BERIT) Norway 1940-45: the resistance movement. Oslo, 1970. pp. 93.

- Underground movements - Poland

PRZYGOŃSKI (ANTONI) Udział PPR i AL w powstaniu warszawskim. Warszawa, 1970. pp. 265.

KLESSMANN (CHRISTOPH) Die Selbstbehauptung einer Nation: nationalsozialistische Kulturpolitik und polnische Widerstandsbewegung im Generalgouvernement, 1939-1945. Düsseldorf, [1971]. pp. 277. bibliog. (Hamburg. Hansische Universität. Studien zur Modernen Geschichte. Band 5)

GÓRA (WŁADYSŁAW) Powstanie władzy ludowej w Polsce: z zagadnień kształtowania się zalążków ludowego aparatu władzy w latach 1943-1944. Warszawa, 1972. pp. 162. bibliog.

JACOBMEYER (WOLFGANG) Heimat und Exil: die Anfänge der polnischen Untergrundbewegung im Zweiten Weltkrieg. Hamburg, [1973]. pp. 369. bibliog. (Hamburg. Forschungsstelle für die Geschichte des Nationalsozialismus in Hamburg. Hamburger Beiträge zur Zeitgeschichte. Band 9)

- Underground movements - Russia - Ukraine

SLYN'KO (IVAN IVANOVICH) Pidpillia i partyzans'kyi rukh na Ukraïni: na zavershal'nomy etapi vyzvolennia, 1944 r. Kyïv, 1970. pp. 173.

- Underground movements - Yugoslavia

TOPALOVIĆ (ŽIVKO) Pokreti narodnog otpora u Jugoslaviji, 1941-1945. Paris, 1958. pp. 216.

TITO (JOSIP BROZ) Selected military works; (translated from the Serbo-Croatian by Kordija Kveder). Belgrade, 1966. pp. 336.

- Underground movements - Yugoslavia - Serbia

TOPALOVIĆ (ŽIVKO) Srbija pod Dražom. London, 1968. pp. 147.

AVAKUMOVIĆ (IVAN) Nemački okupator i "DM pokret" u Srbiji januara 1944. Vindzor [i.e. Windsor], Ontario, 1971. pp. 12. In Cyrillic.

- Albania

CERVI (MARIO) The hollow legions: Mussolini's blunder in Greece, 1940-1941;...translated from the Italian by Eric Mosbacher. London, 1972. pp. 336. bibliog.

- Belgium

GERARD-LIBOIS (JULES) and GOTOVITCH (JOSE) L'an 40: la Belgique occupée. Bruxelles, [1971?]. pp. 517. bibliog.

VANLANGENHOVE (FERNAND) La sécurité de la
Belgique: contribution à l'histoire de la
période, 1940-1950. Bruxelles, [1971].
pp. 263. bibliog. (Brussels. Université Libre.
Faculté de Philosophie et Lettres. Travaux. 47)

- Bulgaria

DIMITROV (ILCHO) Burzhoaznata opozitsiia v Bŭlgariia, 1939-1944. Sofiia, 1969. pp. 248.
bibliog.

- Czechoslovakia

DRESS (HANS) Slowakei und faschistische Neuordnung Europas, 1939-1941. Berlin, 1972. pp. 199.
bibliog. (Deutsche Akademie der Wissenschaften
zu Berlin. Institut für Geschichte. Schriften.
Reihe 1. Band 37)

- Denmark

ESMANN JENSEN (FRANK) Da fornuften sejrede: det
britiske udenrigsministeriums politik over for
Danmark under 2. verdenskrig. [Copenhagen, 1972].
pp. 240.

- East (Near East)

RUMIANTSEV (FRIDRIKH IAKOVLEVICH) Tainaia voina na Blizhnem i Srednem Vostoke. Moskva, 1972.
pp. 136.

- Europe

Das JAHR 1941 in der europäischen Politik; unter
Mitarbeit von Martin K. Bachstein [and others]
herausgegeben von Karl Bosl; Vorträge der Tagung
des Collegium Carolinum in Weissach am Tegernsee...
1971. München, 1972. pp. 163.

- Finland

PALM (THEDE) ed. The Finnish-Soviet armistice
negotiations of 1944. Stockholm, [1971]. pp.
160. (Vetenskapssamhället i Uppsala. Acta Academiae
Regiae Scientiarum Upsaliensis. 14)

- France

ALERME (MARIE MARCEL ETIENNE MICHEL) Les causes
militaires de notre défaite. Paris, [1941].
pp. 123.

BONNET (GEORGES ETIENNE) Dans la tourmente, 1938-
1948. [Paris, 1971]. pp. 317.

KASPI (ANDRE) La mission de Jean Monnet à Alger,
mars-octobre 1943. Paris, [1971]. pp. 240.
bibliog. (Paris, Université de Paris I (Panthéon-
Sorbonne) Publications. Série Internationale.
2)

ROSSI-LANDI (GUY) La drôle de guerre: la vie politique
en France 2 septembre 1939 - 10 mai 1940. Paris,
1971. pp. 248. bibliog. (Fondation Nationale
des Sciences Politiques. Travaux et Recherches
de Science Politique. 14)

DARCOURT (PIERRE) Armée d'Afrique: la revanche
des drapeaux. Paris, [1972]. pp. 285.

LAUNAY (MICHEL) L'armistice de 1940. Paris,
1972. pp. 96. bibliog.

- Germany

SCHINDLER (RENE) Ein Schweizer erlebt das geheime
Deutschland: Tatsachenbericht. Zürich, [1945].
pp. 72.

KUKLICK (BRUCE) American policy and the division
of Germany: the clash with Russia over reparations.
Ithaca, N.Y., 1972. pp. 286. bibliog.

- Greece

CERVI (MARIO) The hollow legions: Mussolini's
blunder in Greece, 1940-1941;...translated from
the Italian by Eric Mosbacher. London, 1972.
pp 336. bibliog.

- Hungary

FENYO (MARIO D.) Hitler, Horthy and Hungary:
German-Hungarian relations, 1941-1944. New
Haven, 1972. pp. 279. bibliog.

- India

LEBRA (JOYCE CHAPMAN) Jungle alliance: Japan
and the Indian National Army. Singapore, 1971.
pp. 255. bibliog.

- Italy

BOLLA (NINO) Benedetto Croce fallito in politica:
controdiario. Roma, [1970]. pp. 162.

CERVI (MARIO) The hollow legions: Mussolini's
blunder in Greece, 1940-1941;...translated from
the Italian by Eric Mosbacher. London, 1972.
pp. 336. bibliog.

DAVIS (MELTON S.) Who defends Rome?: the forty-
five days, July 25-September 8, 1943. London,
1972. pp. 560. bibliog.

TOGLIATTI (PALMIRO) Italiani, italiani ascoltate!:
discorsi agli italiani [from Radio Mosca, 1941-
1943]. Milano, 1972. pp. 471.

VENÈ (GIAN FRANCO) La condanna di Mussolini.
Milano, [1973]. pp. 161. bibliog.

- Japan

BERGAMINI (DAVID) Japan's imperial conspiracy.
London, 1971. pp. 1239. bibliog.

LEBRA (JOYCE CHAPMAN) Jungle alliance: Japan
and the Indian National Army. Singapore, 1971.
pp. 255. bibliog.

MARX (JOSEPH LAURANCE) Nagasaki: the necessary
bomb? New York, [1971]. pp. 239.

- Luxembourg

KOCH-KENT (HENRI) 10 mai 1940 en Luxembourg:
témoignages et documents. Luxembourg, 1971.
pp. 336. bibliog.

- Mediterranean

La GUERRE en Méditerranée, 1939-1945: actes du colloque
international tenu à Paris du 8 au 11 avril 1969.
Paris, 1971. pp. 792.

- Norway

FJORD (FRIDTJOF) Norwegens totaler Kriegseinsatz:
vier Jahre Okkupation. Zürich, [1944]. pp.
68. bibliog.

- Russia

OVCHARENKO (PORFYRII MAKAROVYCH) and SAZHENIUK
(STEPAN NYKYFOROVYCH) Pershyi period Velykoï
Vitchyznianoï viiny Radians'koho Soiuzu, 22
chervnia 1941 r. - lystopad 1942r., etc. Kyïv,
1962. pp. 136. bibliog.

ARUTIUNIAN (IURII VARTANOVICH) Sovetskoe krest'ianstvo v gody Velikoi Otechestvennoi voiny.
2nd. ed. Moskva, 1970. pp. 466. bibliog.

ROZANOV (GERMAN LEONT'EVICH) Plan "Barbarossa": zamysly i final. Moskva,
1970. pp. 136.

WORLD WAR, 1939-1945 - Russia (Cont'd.)

ANFILOV (VIKTOR ALEKSANDROVICH) Bessmertnyi podvig: issledovanie kanuna i pervogo etapa Velikoi Otechestvennoi voiny. Moskva, 1971. pp. 541.

- Russia - Bibliography

KIREEVA (M.E.) and others, compilers. Velikaia Otechestvennaia voina Sovetskogo Soiuza, 1941-1945 gg.; rekomendatel'nyi ukazatel' literatury. Moskva, 1965. pp. 250.

VELIKII podvig: rekomendatel'nyi ukazatel' literatury o Velikoi Otechestvennoi voine Sovetskogo Soiuza. Moskva, 1970. pp. 216.

- Russia - Azerbaijan

MEKHTIEV (GIAZENFER GIUSEINOVICH) Deiatel'nost' Kommunisticheskoi partii Azerbaidzhana v period Velikoi Otechestvennoi voiny 1941-1945 gg. Baku, 1967. pp. 292.

- Russia - Bashkir Republic

GIBADULLIN (BARII GIBADULLINOVICH) Sovetskaia Bashkiriia v gody Velikoi Otechestvennoi voiny, 1941-1945 gg.: istoricheskie ocherki. Ufa, 1971. pp. 212.

- Russia - Georgia

BABALASHVILI (IVAN PAVLOVICH) Sovetskaia Gruziia v bitve velikoi, 1941-1945 gg. Tbilisi, 1972. pp. 101.

- Russia - Lithuania

KASLAS (BRONIS J.) ed. The USSR-German aggression against Lithuania. New York, 1973. pp. 543. bibliog.

- Russia - North Ossetian Republic

SEVERO-Osetinskaia partiinaia organizatsiia v gody Velikoi Otechestvennoi voiny: sbornik dokumentov i materialov. Ordzhonikidze, 1968. pp. 628.

TEDTOEV (ASLAMBEK AKHMETOVICH) Severnaia Osetiia v Velikoi Otechestvennoi voine. Ordzhonikidze, 1968. pp. 127.

- Russia - Siberia

TIUMENSKII SEL'SKOKHOZIAISTVENNYI INSTITUT. Trudy. t.2. vyp. 1. Kommunisticheskaia partiia - organizator patrioticheskogo dvizheniia trudiashchikhsia Sibiri po okazaniiu material'noi pomoshchi frontu, 1941-1945 gg. Tiumen', 1963. pp. 132. bibliog.

- Russia - Udmurt Republic

MOSHKIN (NIKOLAI ALEKSEEVICH) Za svobodu i nezavisimost' Rodiny: komsomol'tsy i molodezh' Udmurtii v gody Velikoi Otechestvennoi voiny, 1941-1945 gg. Izhevsk, 1963. pp. 40.

- Spain

ESTEBAN-INFANTES (EMILIO) La Division Azul: donde Asia empieza. Barcelona, 1956. pp. 333. bibliog.

- Switzerland

WAEGER (GERHART) Die Sündenböcke der Schweiz: die Zweihundert im Urteil der geschichtlichen Dokumente, 1940-1946. Olten, [1971]. pp. 288. bibliog.

- United Kingdom

PELLING (HENRY MATHISON) Britain and the Second World War. [London, 1970]. pp. 352. bibliog.

GERMAN occupied Great Britain: ordinances of the military authorities; [originally printed in Leipzig in 1941 as a guide to the legislative and administrative power of the intended army of occupation in Great Britain]. London, [1971]. pp. 94. Parallel English and German texts.

LEE (RAYMOND ELIOT) The London observer: the journal of General Raymond E. Lee, 1940-1941; edited by James Leutze. London, 1972. pp. 489.

PARKINSON (ROGER) Blood, toil, tears and sweat: the war history from Dunkirk to Alamein, based on the War Cabinet papers of 1940 to 1942. London, 1973. pp. 539. bibliog.

- United Kingdom - Alderney

PACKE (MICHAEL ST. JOHN) and DREYFUS (MAURICE) The Alderney story, 1939-1949. Alderney, [1971]. pp. 152.

- United States

GERMANY. Auswärtiges Amt. Archivkommission. 1943. Roosevelts Weg in den Krieg: Geheimdokumente zur Kriegspolitik des Präsidenten der Vereinigten Staaten. Berlin, 1943. pp. 111. (Entstehung des Krieges von 1939, Die. 1. Schrift)

LINDBERGH (CHARLES AUGUSTUS) The wartime journals of Charles A. Lindbergh. New York, [1970]. pp. 1038.

POLENBERG (RICHARD) War and society: the United States, 1941-1945. Philadelphia, [1972]. pp. 298. bibliog.

- Yugoslavia

TITO (JOSIP BROZ) Selected military works; (translated from the Serbo-Croatian by Kordija Kveder). Belgrade, 1966. pp. 336.

FRICKE (GERT) Kroatien, 1941-1944: der "Unabhängige Staat" in der Sicht des Deutschen Bevollmächtigten Generals in Agram, Glaise v. Horstenau. Freiburg, 1972. pp. 206. bibliog. (Militärgeschichtliches Forschungsamt. Einzelschriften zur Militärischen Geschichte des Zweiten Weltkrieges. 8)

ROBERTS (WALTER R.) Tito, Mihailović and the Allies, 1941-1945. New Brunswick, N.J., [1973]. pp. 406. bibliog.

WORLD ZIONIST ORGANIZATION

DULZIN (A. L.) Tasks and challenges facing the World Zionist Organization in the seventies; address on the budget of the...Organization, etc. Jerusalem, 1972. pp. 17.

PINCUS (LOUIS A.) After the Zionist congress: recent developments in the World Zionist Organization and the Jewish Agency. Jerusalem, 1972. pp. 19.

WORTH

AVETISIAN (ARSEN AVETISIANOVICH) Antikommunizm i ego filosofiia dukhovnykh tsennostei: ocherki po istorii religii i ateizma. Kiev, 1967. pp. 120.

ALBERT (HANS) and TOPITSCH (ERNST) eds. Werturteilsstreit. Darmstadt, 1971. pp. 552. bibliog.

ASCHENBRENNER (KARL) The concepts of value: foundations of value theory. Dordrecht, [1971]. pp. 462.

AVETISIAN (ARSEN AVETISIANOVICH) Antikommunizm i ego filosofiia dukhovnykh tsennostei. Kiev, 1972. pp. 233.

CLAESSENS (DIETER) Familie und Wertsystem: eine Studie zur "zweiten, sozio-kulturellen Geburt" des Menschen und der Belastbarkeit der "Kernfamilie". 3rd ed. Berlin, [1972]. pp. 219. bibliog.

RESCHER (NICHOLAS) Welfare: the social issues in philosophical perspective. [Pittsburgh, 1972]. pp. 186. bibliogs.

WRIGHT (FRANCES)

LANE (MARGARET) Frances Wright and the "Great Experiment". Manchester, [1972]. pp. 50. bibliog.

WRITING
- History

JENSEN (HANS) Dr. Phil. of the University of Kiel. Sign, symbol and script: an account of man's efforts to write;...translated from the German [third edition] by George Unwin. London, 1970. pp. 613. bibliog.

WRITS
- United Kingdom

SELDEN SOCIETY. Publications. Vol. 90. The roll and writ file of the Berkshire Eyre of 1248; edited... by M.T. Clanchy. London, 1973. pp. 614. In Latin and English.

WROCŁAW UNIVERSITY

FLORYANA (WŁADYSŁAWA) ed. Uniwersytet Wrocławski w latach 1945-1970; księga jubileuszowa. Wrocław, 1970. pp. 454.

WUERTTEMBERG
- Economic history

BUETTERLIN (RUDOLF) Die merkantilistische Geldpolitik im Herzogtum Württemberg von der Reformation bis Napoleon. [Stuttgart], 1966. pp. 195. bibliog.

- History

LEIBBRANDT (GEORG) Die Auswanderung aus Schwaben nach Russland, 1816-1923: eine schwäbisches Zeit- und Charakterbild. Stuttgart, 1928. pp. 212. bibliog. (Stuttgart. Deutsches Ausland Institut. Schriften. Kulturhistorische Reihe. Band 21)

- Rural conditions

STEINLE (PETER) Die Vermögensverhältnisse der Landbevölkerung in Hohenlohe im 17. und 18. Jahrhundert. Schwäbisch Hall, [1971]. pp. 280. bibliog. (Historischer Verein für Württembergisch Franken. Forschungen aus Württembergisch Franken. Band 5)

WUPPERTAL
- Politics and government

BERGMANN (GUENTHER) Das Sozialistengesetz im rechtsrheinischen Industriegebiet: ein Beitrag zur Auseinandersetzung...im Wuppertal und im Bergischen Land, 1878-1890. Hannover, [1970]. pp. 116. bibliog. (Friedrich-Ebert-Stiftung. Forschungsinstitut. Schriftenreihe. Band 77)

YAKUTIA
- Commerce

BERNVAL'D (ARNOL'D REINGOL'DOVICH) and others. Problemy tovarodvizheniia Iakutskoi ASSR. Iakutsk, 1967. pp. 227.

- Constitutional history

FEDOROV (MIKHAIL MIKHAILOVICH) Razvitie sovetskoi gosudarstvennosti v Iakutii, 1918-1937. Iakutsk, 1968. pp. 339. bibliog.

- Economic history

IVANOVA (ANNA ALEKSEEVNA) Iakutskaia partiinaia organizatsiia v period vosstanovleniia narodnogo khoziaistva, 1923-1925. Iakutsk, 1968. pp. 126. bibliog.

GOGOLEV (ZAKHAR VASIL'EVICH) Iakutiia na rubezhe XIX i XX vekov: sotsial'no-ekonomicheskii ocherk. Novosibirsk, 1970. pp. 235. bibliog.

GOGOLEV (ZAKHAR VASIL'EVICH) Sotsial'no-ekonomicheskoe razvitie Iakutii, 1917 - iiun' 1941 gg. Novosibirsk, 1972. pp. 258.

- History - 1917-1921, Revolution - Personal narratives

VENDRIKH (GERMAN ALEKSANDROVICH) Dekabr'sko-ianvarskie boi 1919-1920 gg. v Irkutske. Irkutsk, 1957. pp. 59.

- Industries

VOPROSY ekonomiki promyshlennosti Iakutii. Iakutsk, 1962. pp. 115.

- Intellectual life

ARGUNOV (IVAN ALEKSANDROVICH) U istokov sotsialisticheskoi kul'tury narodov Iakutii: o partiinom rukovodstve nachal'nym etapom kul'turnoi revoliutsii v IaASSR, 1920-1927 gg.; otvetstvennyi redaktor... I.M. Romanov. Iakutsk, 1971. pp. 231. bibliog.

- Nationalism

MIKHAILOV (IVAN INNOKENT'EVICH) Osushchestvlenie natsional'noi politiki partii v Iakutii v pervye gody Sovetskoi vlasti. Iakutsk, 1968. pp. 56.

- Social life and customs

BIRKENGOF (ANDREI L'VOVICH) Potomki zemleprokhodtsev: vospominaniia-ocherki o russkikh porechanakh nizov'ev i del'ty reki Indigirki. Moskva, 1972. pp. 222. bibliog.

YALE UNIVERSITY

LEVER (JANET) and SCHWARTZ (PEPPER) Women at Yale: liberating a college campus. London, 1971. pp. 274.

YAMAGATA (ARITOMO)

HACKETT (ROGER F.) Yamagata Aritomo in the rise of modern Japan, 1838-1922. Cambridge, Mass., 1971. pp. 377. bibliog. (Harvard University. East Asian Research Center. Harvard East Asian Series. 60)

YAQUI INDIANS

MOISÉS (ROSALIO) and others. The tall candle: the personal chronicle of a Yaqui Indian. Lincoln, Neb., [1971]. pp. 251. bibliog.

YEATS (WILLIAM BUTLER)

O'BRIEN (CONOR CRUISE) The suspecting glance. London, 1972. pp. 91. (University of Kent at Canterbury. T.S. Eliot Memorial Lectures. 1969)

YECUANA INDIANS

ARVELO-JIMENEZ (NELLY) Political relations in a tribal society: a study of the Ye'cuana Indians of Venezuela. [Ithaca], 1971. pp. 383. bibliog. (Cornell University. Latin American Studies Program. Dissertation Series. No. 31)

YENAN

- Politics and government

BISSON (THOMAS ARTHUR) Yenan in June 1937: talks with the communist leaders. Berkeley, [1973]. pp. 72. (California University. Center for Chinese Studies. China Research Monographs. No. 11)

YGLESIAS CASTRO (RAFAEL) President of Costa Rica

PERALTA (HERNAN G.) Don Rafael Yglesias: apuntes para su biografia. San Jose, Costa Rica, 1928 repr. 1968. pp. 171.

YONNE

- Economic history - Sources

FRANCE. Commission de Recherche et de Publication de[s] Documents relatifs à la Vie Economique de la Révolution. Comité de l'Yonne. 1948. Documents relatifs à la vie économique de l'Yonne sur le Consulat et l'Empire; recueillis par Emile Le Gallo. Auxerre, 1948. pp. 105.

YORK

- Economic history - Sources

SURTEES SOCIETY. Publications. vol.186. York memorandum book (1371-1596) [originally lettered B/Y in the Guildhall Muniment Room]; edited by Joyce W. Percy. Gateshead, 1973. pp. 320. bibliog. For earlier volumes see vols. 120 and 125 of the series.

- Social history - Sources

SURTEES SOCIETY. Publications. vol.186. York memorandum book (1371-1596) [originally lettered B/Y in the Guildhall Muniment Room]; edited by Joyce W. Percy. Gateshead, 1973. pp. 320. bibliog. For earlier volumes see vols. 120 and 125 of the series.

YORKSHIRE

- Economic conditions

WORKING PARTY ON THE IMPLICATIONS OF U.K. ENTRY INTO THE COMMON MARKET ON THE YORKSHIRE AND HUMBERSIDE REGION. Implications of U.K. entry into the Common Market for the Yorkshire and Humberside region; report; [W.H. Sales, chairman]. [Leeds?, Yorkshire and Humberside Economic Planning Council], 1972. pp. 73.

- Industries

YORKSHIRE AND HUMBERSIDE ECONOMIC PLANNING COUNCIL. Growth industries in the region: a study by the Council. [Leeds?], 1972. pp. 19.

- Politics and government

SHORE (JOHN) 1st Baron Teignmouth. Remarks on the tendency and results of permissive legislation, especially as exemplified in the County of York. 2nd ed. London, 1865. pp. 85.

YORUBAS

BIOBAKU (SABURI OLADENI) The origin of the Yoruba. Lagos, 1971. pp. 23. (Lagos. University. Humanities Monograph Series. No.1)

ABDUL KARIM (WAZIR JAHAN BEGUM) A study of the varying effects of urbanization and urban growth on the social organization of Yoruba townsmen in Lagos; [M.Phil.(London) thesis]. 1972 [or rather 1973]. fo.352. bibliog. Typescript: unpublished. This thesis is the property of London University and may not be removed from the Library.

YOUNG COMMUNIST INTERNATIONAL

KUULI (OLAF) and TOOM (VELLO) V internatsional'nom stroiu: boevoi put' Estonskoi sektsii Kommunisticheskogo Internatsionala Molodezhi, 1920-1940; (perevod s estonskogo). Tallin, 1971. pp. 88.

MUKHAMEDZHANOV (MANSUR MIKHAILOVICH) Molodezh' i revoliutsiia: u istokov mezhdunarodnogo revoliutsionnogo dvizheniia molodezhi. Moskva, 1972. pp. 357.

YOUNG COMMUNIST LEAGUE

- Russia

VSESOIUZNYI LENINSKII KOMMUNISTICHESKII SOIUZ MOLODEZHI. Tsentral'nyi Komitet. Komsomol - 68: interv'iu, informatsii, stat'i i ocherki. Moskva, 1969. pp. 526.

VSESOIUZNYI LENINSKII KOMMUNISTICHESKII SOIUZ MOLODEZHI. Tsentral'nyi Komitet. Organizatsionno-ustavnye voprosy komsomol'skoi raboty: pamiatka sekretaria pervichnoi komsomol'skoi organizatsii. Moskva, 1970. pp. 128.

KISELEV (VALERII SERGEEVICH) and SUSHCHEVICH (VALENTIN ALEKSANDROVICH) Komsomol'skoe sobranie. Moskva, 1971. pp. 128.

VSESOIUZNYI LENINSKII KOMMUNISTICHESKII SOIUZ MOLODEZHI. Komsomol i podrostki: dokumenty i materialy s"ezdov komsomola, Tsentral'nogo Komiteta VLKSM. Moskva, 1971. pp. 287.

VSESOIUZNYI LENINSKII KOMMUNISTICHESKII SOIUZ MOLODEZHI. Rules of the All-Union Lenin Young Communist League: adopted at the Y.C.L.'s 14th Congress and amended at the 15th Congress. Moscow, 1971. pp. 36.

VSESOIUZNYI LENINSKII KOMMUNISTICHESKII SOIUZ MOLODEZHI. Ustav...; priniat XIV s"ezdom VLKSM, chastichnye izmeneniia vneseny XV s"ezdom VLKSM. Moskva, 1971. pp. 32.

NASH Leninskii komsomol: uchebnoe posobie. Moskva, 1972. pp. 479.

VSESOIUZNYI LENINSKII KOMMUNISTICHESKII SOIUZ MOLODEZHI. Pervichnaia komsomol'skaia organizatsiia. Moskva, 1972. pp. 415.

VSESOIUZNYI LENINSKII KOMMUNISTICHESKII SOIUZ MOLODEZHI. Tsentral'nyi Komitet. Dokumenty TsK VLKSM, 1971. Moskva, 1972. pp. 400.

TRUSHCHENKO (NIKOLAI VLADIMIROVICH) Istochnik sily: partiia - organizator i rukovoditel' komsomola. Moskva, 1973. pp. 288.

- Russia - Bibliography

DUDAREVA (Z.) compiler. Komsomol i iunye pionery: rekomendatel'nyi ukazatel' literatury. Moskva, 1958. pp. 86.

- Russia - Estonia

KUULI (OLAF) and TOOM (VELLO) V internatsional'nom stroiu: boevoi put' Estonskoi sektsii Kommunisticheskogo Internatsionala Molodezhi, 1920-1940; (perevod s estonskogo). Tallin, 1971. pp. 88.

- Russia - Latvia

ANDINIA (DZ.) and others. Trud, zamysli, mechty: opyt raboty komsomol'skoi organizatsii Rizhskogo radiozavoda im. A.S.Popova. Riga, 1969. pp. 92.

ANDRIKSON (A.) Skvoz' gody bespokoinye. Riga, 1970. pp. 101.

RIDZIN' (T. S.) and STOLIAROV (A. I.) Komsomol'skomu propagandistu o metodike. 2nd ed. Riga, 1972. pp. 112.

- Russia - Ukraine

ISTORIIA Lenins'koi Komunistychnoi Spilky Molodi Ukrainy. 2nd ed. Kyïv, 1971. pp. 672.

- Russia - White Russia

ZHUKOVICH (GALINA STEPANOVNA) Uchastie komsomola v gosudarstvennom upravlenii. Minsk, 1969. pp. 116.

YOUNG MEN'S CHRISTIAN ASSOCIATION

BINFIELD (CLYDE) George Williams and the Y.M.C.A.: a study in Victorian social attitudes. London, 1973. pp. 408. bibliog.

YOUNG WOMEN'S CHRISTIAN ASSOCIATION

INTERNATIONAL LABOUR OFFICE. T[rust] F[unds]. [Sierra Leone] R.9. Report to the government of Sierra Leone on the development of vocational training programmes at the YWCA Vocational Institute, Freetown. (ILO/TF/Sierra Leone/R.9). Geneva, 1970. pp. 40.

YOUTH

ISOU (ISIDORE) Le soulèvement de la jeunesse: (traité d'economie nucléaire, 1). Paris, [1958-]71. 3 vols.

UNITED NATIONS EDUCATIONAL, SCIENTIFIC AND CULTURAL ORGANIZATION. 1960. New trends in youth organizations: a comparative survey. Paris, [1960]. pp. 63. (Educational Studies and Documents. No.35)

KRIVOPALOV (ALEKSANDR VLADIMIROVICH) and PONIZOVSKII (VLADIMIR MIRONOVICH) Spor v puti. Moskva, 1970. pp. 159.

SEMINAR ON THE ROLE OF YOUTH IN THE PROMOTION AND PROTECTION OF HUMAN RIGHTS, BELGRADE, 1970. Seminar...[held in] Belgrade, Yugoslavia, 2-12 June, 1970; organized by the United Nations, Division of Human Rights, in co-operation with the government of Yugoslavia. (ST/TAO/HR/39). New York, United Nations, 1970. pp. 38.

UNITED NATIONS. Department of Economic and Social Affairs. 1970. Long-term policies and programmes for youth in national development. (ST/SOA/103). New York, 1970. pp. 56.

ALLABY (MICHAEL) The eco-activists: youth fights for a human environment. London, 1971. pp. 226.

ČOK (VIDA) Pravni položaj omladine u Jugoslaviji i u nekim drugim zemljama. Beograd, 1971. pp. 300. bibliog. With French and English summaries.

ESLER (ANTHONY) Bombs, beards and barricades: 150 years of youth in revolt. New York, 1971. pp. 336.

GUMMER (JOHN SELWYN) The permissive society: fact or fantasy? London, 1971. pp. 181.

JANICKI (JANUSZ) Niepokoje młodzieży Zachodu. Warszawa, 1972. pp. 211.

McMILLAN (JAMES) The roots of corruption: the erosion of traditional values in Britain from 1960 to the present day. London, 1972. pp. 210.

MILSON (FREDERICK W.) Youth in a changing society. London, 1972. pp. 134. bibliogs.

[PATRIKIOS (TITOS)] Rights and responsibilities of youth. [Paris], United Nations Educational, Scientific and Cultural Organization, 1972. pp. 72. bibliog. (Educational Studies and Documents. New Series. No. 6)

YOUTH
See also RURAL YOUTH

- Employment

INTERNATIONAL LABOUR ORGANISATION. Committee on Work on Plantations. 6th Session. Reports. 3. Conditions of work of women and young workers on plantations: third item on the agenda. Geneva, International Labour Office, 1970. pp. 95.

- Employment - France

MAZEAUD (CHANTAL) L'emploi des jeunes en région Poitou-Charentes: étude quantitative et qualitative. [Poitiers?], Echelon Régional de l'Emploi de Bordeaux, Antenne de Poitiers, 1971. fo. 85.

MANGENOT (MARC) and others. Les jeunes face à l'emploi. Paris, [1972]. pp. 300.

- Employment - Russia

ZHELEZNOV (BORIS IVANOVICH) and SHCHUPAKOV (NIKOLAI NIKOLAEVICH) Okhrana truda podrostkov. 2nd ed. Moskva, 1963. pp. 96.

PRAVA i obiazannosti molodykh spetsialistov. Moskva, 1970. pp. 144. Cover gives title as: O pravakh i obiazannostiakh, etc.

ZARIKHTA (TAMARA ROMANOVNA) and NAZIMOV (IGOR' NIKOLAEVICH) Ratsional'noe ispol'zovanie trudovykh resursov molodezhi. Moskva, 1970. pp. 224.

ORLOVSKII (IURII PETROVICH) Spravochnik molodogo rabochego. Moskva, 1972. pp. 175.

- Employment - United Kingdom

HALE (SUSAN) The idle hill: a prospect for young workers in a rural area. London, [1971]. pp. 132.

ROBERTS (KENNETH) From school to work: a study of the Youth Employment Service. Newton Abbot, [1971]. pp. 168. bibliog.

U.K. Department of Employment. Health and Safety at Work. 23. Hours of employment of women and young persons. 2nd ed. London, 1973. pp. 27.

YOUTH (Cont'd.)

- Employment - United States

   WESTEFELD (ALBERT) Getting started: urban youth in the labor market: [reprint of the work first published in Washington, 1943]. New York, 1971. pp. 193. (United States. Work Projects Administration. Division of Social Research. Research Monographs. 26)

   PRINCETON MANPOWER SYMPOSIUM, 1968. The transition from school to work: a report based on the...Symposium, etc. Princeton, [1968]. pp. 282. (Princeton University. Department of Economics and Sociology. Industrial Relations Section. Research Report Series. No.111)

   TWENTIETH CENTURY FUND. Task Force on Employment Problems of Black Youth. The job crisis for black youth: report...with a background paper by Sar A. Levitan and Robert Taggart. New York, 1971. pp. 135.

- Political activity

   ISOU (ISIDORE) La stratégie du soulèvement de la jeunesse, 1949-1968. [Paris, 1968]. pp. 108.

- Political activity - Bibliography

   COUTROT (ALINE) Jeunesse et politique. Paris, 1971. pp. 70. (Fondation Nationale des Sciences Politiques. Bibliographies Françaises de Sciences Sociales. Guides de Recherches. 3)

- Religious life

   MOLODEZH' i ateizm. Moskva, 1971. pp. 148. bibliog.

- America, Latin

   ZAMORANO (MANUEL) La rebelion juvenil. Santiago [de Chile], 1968. pp. 186. bibliog.

   GURRIERI (ADOLFO) and TORRES-RIVAS (EDELBERTO) Estudios sobre la juventud marginal latinoamericana. Mexico, 1971. pp. 287.

- Argentine Republic

   MAFUD (JULIO) Las rebeliones juveniles en la sociedad argentina. Buenos Aires, [1969]. pp. 151. bibliog.

- Australia

   DUNPHY (DEXTER C.) Cliques, crowds and gangs: group life of Sydney adolescents. Melbourne, [1969]. pp. 170. bibliog.

- Canada

   BRETON (RAYMOND) Social and academic factors in the career decisions of Canadian youth: a study of secondary school students; with the collaboration of John McDonald and Stephen Richer. Ottawa, Information Canada, 1972. pp. 612. bibliog.

   CANADA. Dominion Bureau of Statistics. Consumer Finance Research Staff. 1972. Socio-economic characteristics of the population age 14 to 24, 1967. Ottawa, 1972. pp. 67.

   CANADIAN COUNCIL ON SOCIAL DEVELOPMENT. A right to opportunity: a report on youth and social assistance. Ottawa, 1972. pp. 301.

- Canada - Quebec

   LAZURE (JACQUES) La jeunesse du Québec en révolution: essai d'interprétation. Montréal, 1970. pp. 143.

- Cyprus

   COMMONWEALTH YOUTH SEMINAR, CYPRUS, 1972. Youth and development in Cyprus; report of the... Seminar. London, Commonwealth Secretariat, 1972. pp. 126.

- Denmark

   TOFT (ALFRED) Care of children and young people. Copenhagen, 1967. pp. 32. (Social Conditions in Denmark. 5)

- Europe, Eastern

   NEUBURG (PAUL) The hero's children: the postwar generation in eastern Europe. London, 1972. pp. 384. bibliog.

- France

   SAUVY (ALFRED) La révolte des jeunes. [Paris, 1970]. pp. 269.

   SIGUSSE (ALBERT) Salauds de jeunes! Paris, [1970]. pp. 242.

   FRANCE. Comité d'Organisation des Recherches Appliquées sur le Développement Economique et Social. 1972. Indicateurs de changements d'opinions et d'attitudes dans les jeunes générations, 1957-1970: analyse secondaire de données d'enquêtes par sondages. [Paris], 1972. fo. 223.

   MICHAUX (LEON) Les Jeunes et l'autorité. Paris, 1972. pp. 96.

- France - Political activity

   ISOU (ISIDORE) La stratégie du soulèvement de la jeunesse, 1949-1968. [Paris, 1968]. pp. 108.

   JOYEUX (MAURICE) L'anarchie et la révolte de la jeunesse: une hérésie politique dans la société contemporaine. [Tournai, 1970]. pp. 164.

- Germany

   GERMANY (BUNDESREPUBLIK). Statistisches Bundesamt. Öffentliche Jugendhilfe. a., 1970- Wiesbaden.

   JAHNKE (KARL HEINZ) Entscheidungen: Jugend im Widerstand, 1933-1945. Frankfurt/Main, 1970. pp. 252. bibliog.

   WARLOSKI (RONALD) Neudeutschland: German Catholic students, 1919-1939. The Hague, 1970. pp. 220. bibliog.

   NAHOUN (PHILIPPE) Allemagne anti-autoritaire. [Paris, 1971]. pp. 175.

   JAHNKE (KARL HEINZ) and others. Geschichte der deutschen Arbeiterjugendbewegung, 1904-1945. Berlin, [1973]. pp. 632. bibliog.

- Germany - Political activity

   KUHN (HELMUT) Professor of Philosophy at Munich University. Jugend im Aufbruch: zur revolutionären Bewegung unserer Zeit. München, [1970]. pp. 207.

   BILSTEIN (HELMUT) and others. Jungsozialisten, Junge Union, Jungdemokraten: die Nachwuchsorganisationen der Parteien in der Bundesrepublik; herausgegeben von Helmut Bilstein. Opladen, 1971. pp. 108. bibliog. (Hochschule für Wirtschaft und Politik Hamburg. Veröffentlichungen)

   MUELLER (EMIL PETER) Juso-Sozialismus: Programm und Strategie der Jungsozialisten in der SPD. Köln, [1972]. pp. 115. bibliog.

MUELLER (GUENTHER) Rote Zelle Deutschland; oder, Was wollen die Jungsozialisten wirklich? Stuttgart, [1972]. pp. 143.

- India

KAKAR (SUDHIR) and CHOWDHRY (KAMLA) Conflict and choice: Indian youth in a changing society. Bombay, [1970]. pp. 177. bibliog.

- Ireland (Republic)

KELLY (MARY) Young workers in a country town: a social survey report on young workers in Tuam. Dublin, National Institute for Physical Planning and Construction Research, 1971. pp. 136.

- Israel

GROUP care: an Israeli approach: the educational path of Youth Aliyah: [papers of a seminar held in Jerusalem, 1969]; edited by Martin Wolins and Meir Gottesmann. New York, 1971. pp. 437. bibliogs.

- Italy

LAZZARI (PRIMO DE) Storia del Fronte della gioventú nella Resistenza. Roma, 1972. pp. 258. bibliog.

LEDEEN (MICHAEL ARTHUR) Universal fascism: the theory and practice of the Fascist International, 1928-1936. New York, 1972. pp. 200. bibliog.

- Kenya

KENYA. 1962. Transfer of government property, Starehe Boys' Centre, Nairobi. [Nairobi, 1962?]. single sheet. (Sessional Papers. 1962/63. No.2)

- Malta

COMMONWEALTH YOUTH SEMINAR, VALLETTA, 1972. Youth and development in Malta; report of the... Seminar. London, Commonwealth Secretariat, 1972. pp. 179.

- Netherlands

NETHERLANDS. Ministerie van Cultuur, Recreatie en Maatschappelijk Werk. 1969. Nota jeugdbeleid...betreffende standpuntbepaling ten aanzien van het COWER-rapport inzake het jeugdbeleid. 's-Gravenhage, 1969. pp. 96.

- Russia

GARBUZOV (S.) In den Kampf für den Fünfjahrplan; ins Deutsche übertragen von E. Spitz. Moskau, 1931. pp. 63.

TRAININ (A.S.) Partiia bol'shevikov - rukovoditel' revoliutsionnogo dvizheniia rabochei molodezhi v 1917 godu. Krasnodar, 1965. pp. 175. (Krasnodarskii Gosudarstvennyi Pedagogicheskii Institut. Nauchnye Trudy. vyp.58)

VASIL'EV (VLADIMIR GRIGOR'EVICH) and others. Vashe mnenie?: prikladnye sotsiologicheskie issledovaniia po problemam molodezhi. Moskva, 1967. pp. 184. bibliog.

VSESOIUZNYI LENINSKII KOMMUNISTICHESKII SOIUZ MOLODEZHI. Tsentral'nyi Komitet. Dokumenty TsK KPSS i TsK VLKSM o rabote Vsesoiuznoi pionerskoi organizatsii imeni V.I. Lenina. 3rd ed. Moskva, 1970. pp. 238.

MOLODEZH' i ateizm. Moskva, 1971. pp. 148. bibliog.

PUTI formirovaniia sotsial'noi aktivnosti lichnosti pri sotsializme. Moskva, 1972. pp. 141. bibliog.

TROTSKII (LEV DAVYDOVICH) The position of the Republic and the tasks of young workers: report to the 5th All-Russian Congress of the Russian Communist League of Youth, 1922; (translated by R. Chappell). London, 1972. pp. 24.

- Russia - Bibliography

VAISBERG (I.R.) compiler. Vsesoiuznaia pionerskaia organizatsiia imeni V.I. Lenina: rekomendatel'nyi ukazatel' literatury. Moskva, 1969. pp. 304.

- Russia - Udmurt Republic

MOSHKIN (NIKOLAI ALEKSEEVICH) Za svobodu i nezavisimost' Rodiny: komsomol'tsy i molodezh' Udmurtii v gody Velikoi Otechestvennoi voiny, 1941-1945 gg. Izhevsk, 1963. pp. 40.

- Russia - Uzbekistan

BEREZIKOV (EVGENII EFIMOVICH) Komsomol i sotsiologicheskie issledovaniia. Tashkent, 1969. pp. 51. bibliog.

YOUTH : Underdeveloped areas
See UNDERDEVELOPED AREAS - Youth

- United Kingdom

MANDELKAU (JAMIE) ed. Buttons: the making of a president; [comprising autobiographical accounts by Peter Welsh Buttons and others, and newspaper reports]. London, 1971. pp. 157.

50 million volunteers: a report on the role of voluntary organisations and youth in the environment; presented in February 1972 to the Secretary of State for the Environment: a study of public opinion undertaken at his request in connection with the United Nations Conference on the Human Environment, Stockholm, June 1972; [Dennistoun Stevenson, chairman of the Working Party]. London, H.M.S.O., 1972. pp. 103.

COHEN (STANLEY) Folk devils and moral panics: the creation of the mods and rockers. London, 1972. pp. 224.

YOUTH SERVICE INFORMATION CENTRE. Occasional Papers. 4. Social education of the under-14's: conference reports and recommendations towards a policy; (stemming from the work of an ad hoc group). Leicester, 1972. pp. (8).

- United Kingdom - Scotland

CHURCH OF SCOTLAND. Youth Committee. Youth at leisure: a report by a special commission to the Youth Committee, etc. Edinburgh, 1956. pp. 54.

- United States

DEVELOPING improved social programs; [the second of a series of seminars sponsored by American Institutes for Research, held in Washington, 1971]. Pittsburgh, Pa., [1971]. pp. 128. bibliogs.

RAPSON (RICHARD L.) ed. The cult of youth in middle-class America. Lexington, [1971]. pp. 118. bibliog.

VENCEREMOS Brigade: young Americans sharing the life and work of revolutionary Cuba; diaries, letters, interviews, tapes, essays, poetry by the Venceremos Brigade; edited by Sandra Levinson and Carol Brightman. New York, 1971. pp. 412.

KATZMAN (ALLEN) ed. Our time: an anthology of interviews from the East Village Other. New York, 1972. pp. 407.

YOUTH - United States (Cont'd.)

LEVITT (MORTON) and RUBENSTEIN (BEN) eds. Youth and social change. Detroit, 1972. pp. 410. Most of the papers were presented at the 47th annual convention of the American Orthopsychiatric Association.

GOTTLIEB (DAVID) ed. Youth in contemporary society. Beverly Hills, [1973]. pp. 383. bibliogs.

WHEELER (RICHARD S.) b.1935. The children of darkness. New Rochelle, N.Y., [1973]. pp. 189.

- United States - Political activity

[YOUNG REPUBLICAN NATIONAL FEDERATION]. The history of the Young Republicans. [Washington, D.C., 195-?]. pp. 5.

YOUNG REPUBLICAN NATIONAL FEDERATION. Organization manual. [Washington, D.C., 195-]. pp. 17.

YOUNG REPUBLICAN NATIONAL FEDERATION. College Service Committee. Manual for mock conventions. Washington, D.C., [196-?]. pp. 11.

HYMAN (SIDNEY) Youth in politics: expectations and realities. New York, [1972]. pp. 436.

ORUM (ANTHONY M.) ed. The seeds of politics: youth and politics in America. Englewood Cliffs, [1972]. pp. 385.

- Yugoslavia

ČOK (VIDA) Pravni položaj omladine u Jugoslaviji i u nekim drugim zemljama. Beograd, 1971. pp. 300. bibliog. With French and English summaries.

YUGOSLAVIA. Savezni Zavod za Statistiku. Studije, Analize i Prikazi. 58. Smrtnost dece i omladine u Jugoslaviji od 1951-1968; Mortality of children and youth in Yugoslavia, 1951-1968; [by] Nevena Stojkov. Beograd, 1971. pp. 112. bibliog. With English summary.

YOUTH SERVICES
See SOCIAL WORK WITH YOUTH

YOUTH VOLUNTEER WORKERS IN DEVELOPING COUNTRIES

VENCEREMOS Brigade: young Americans sharing the life and work of revolutionary Cuba; diaries, letters, interviews, tapes, essays, poetry by the Venceremos Brigade; edited by Sandra Levinson and Carol Brightman. New York, 1971. pp. 412.

YOUTH VOLUNTEERS IN SOCIAL SERVICE

- United Kingdom

BALL (COLIN) and BALL (MOG) Education for a change: community action and the school. Harmondsworth, 1973. pp. 212.

YUAN (SHIH-K'AI)

CH'EN (JEROME) Yuan Shih-k'ai. 2nd ed. Stanford, 1972. pp. 258. bibliog.

YUGOSLAVIA

MARKERT (WERNER) ed. Jugoslawien; (Osteuropa-Handbuch). Köln, 1954. pp. 400. bibliog.

- Armed forces

RATNIKOV (A.N.) and ZAV'IALOV (V.I.) Vooruzhennye sily Iugoslavii. Moskva, 1971. pp. 165.

- Army

TITO (JOSIP BROZ) Selected military works; (translated from the Serbo-Croatian by Kordija Kveder). Belgrade, 1966. pp. 336.

- Census

YUGOSLAVIA. Census, 1971. Popis stanovništva i stanova 1971. Beograd, 1972 in progress.

- Commerce

SEKULIĆ (MIJO) Utjecaj investicione potrošnje na strukturu proizvodnje i uvoza. Zagreb, 1971. pp. 23. bibliog.

AMACHER (RYAN C.) Yugoslavia's foreign trade: a study of state trade discrimination. New York, 1972. pp. 185. bibliog.

TURČIĆ (IVAN) Regionalni aspekt rezultata poslovanja društvene privrede Jugoslavije od 1964. do 1968. godine: vrijeme pripreme i provodjenja privredne reforme. Zagreb, 1972. pp. 201. bibliog.

- Constitution

USTAVNA reforma: saopćenja sa Kolokvija na Pravnom fakultetu u Zagrebu. Zagreb, 1971. pp. 271.

- Constitutional history

HONDIUS (FRITS W.) The Yugoslav community of nations. The Hague, 1968. pp. 375. bibliog. With Croatian and Dutch summaries.

- Constitutional law

YUGOSLAVIA. Statutes, etc. 1971. Zakon o Saveznom izvršnom veću i Zakon o organizaciji i delokrugu saveznih organa uprave i saveznih organizacija, sa objašnjenjima i napomenama. Beograd, 1971. pp. 87.

- Dictionaries and encyclopaedias

ENCIKLOPEDIJA Jugoslavije. Zagreb, 1955-71. 8 vols.

- Economic conditions

YUGOSLAVIA. 1959. Yougoslavie: étude nationale préparée par le Gouvernement yougoslave pour le Projet de développement méditerranéen. Belgrade, 1959. pp. 165.

HORVAT (BRANKO) Business cycles in Yugoslavia; translated by Helen M. Kramer. White Plains, N.Y., [1971]. pp. 259.

GORUPIĆ (DRAGO) Poduzeće i privredni sistem; The enterprise and the economic system. Zagreb, 1972. pp. 233. With English summaries and table of contents.

MILIĆEVIĆ (DRAGIŠA) Ekonomski položaj regiona Jugoslavije: metodološki ogled. Beograd, 1972. pp. 138. bibliog. In Cyrillic. With English and Russian summaries.

- Economic history

25 years of the Yugoslav economy; [edited by Jože Moravec; translated by Borivoje Ljotić]. Belgrade, [1972?]. pp. 474.

- Economic policy

PROBLEMI daljnjeg razvoja društvenog planiranja u Jugoslaviji. Zagreb, 1970. pp. 169. With English and Russian summaries.

25 years of the Yugoslav economy; [edited by Jože Moravec; translated by Borivoje Ljotić]. Belgrade, [1972?]. pp. 474.

VOJNIĆ (DRAGOMIR) and others, eds. Aktuelni problemi ekonomske politike i privrednih kretanja Jugoslavije. Zagreb, 1972. pp. 206.

BIĆANIĆ (RUDOLF) Economic policy in socialist Yugoslavia. Cambridge, 1973. pp. 254. bibliog. (National Association for Soviet and East European Studies. Soviet and East European Studies.)

CONFEDERAZIONE GENERALE DELL'INDUSTRIA ITALIANA. Servizio Studi e Rilevazioni. Collana di Studi e Documentazione. 30. Aspetti della pianificazione economica in Jugoslavia; [by Giuseppe Schiavone]. Roma, 1973. pp. 85.

- Economic policy - Mathematical models

SEKULIĆ (MIJO) and GJENERO (IVO) Optimalna alokacija zajedničkih resursa u decentraliziranom ekonomskom sistemu: primjena metode dekompozicije linearnog programa. Zagreb, 1971. pp. 134. bibliog.

- Executive departments

YUGOSLAVIA. Statutes, etc. 1971. Zakon o Saveznom izvršnom veću i Zakon o organizaciji i delokrugu saveznih organa uprave i saveznih organizacija, sa objašnjenjima i napomenama. Beograd, 1971. pp. 87.

- Foreign economic relations - Poland

WIECZORKIEWICZ (ANDRZEJ) Polska, Jugosławia: gospodarka współpraca. Warszawa, 1972. pp. 132.

- Foreign relations

YUGOSLAVIA. Yugoslav Information Office, London. 1949. [Information circulars]. London, 1949. 4 parts.

- Foreign relations - China

JOHNSON (A. ROSS) The Sino-Soviet relationship and Yugoslavia, 1949-1971. [Santa Monica], 1971. pp. 13. (Rand Corporation [Papers]. 4591)

- Foreign relations - Germany

FRICKE (GERT) Kroatien, 1941-1944: der "Unabhängige Staat" in der Sicht des Deutschen Bevollmächtigten Generals in Agram, Glaise v. Horstenau. Freiburg, 1972. pp. 206. bibliog. (Militärgeschichtliches Forschungsamt. Einzelschriften zur Militärischen Geschichte des Zweiten Weltkrieges. 8)

- Foreign relations - Russia

JOHNSON (A. ROSS) The Sino-Soviet relationship and Yugoslavia, 1949-1971. [Santa Monica], 1971. pp. 13. (Rand Corporation [Papers]. 4591)

- History

TOPALOVIĆ (ŽIVKO) Kako su komunisti dograbili vlast u Jugoslaviji. London, 1964. pp. 133.

MILJUS (BRANKO) Les Habsbourg, l'église et les Slaves du Sud. Paris, 1970. pp. 252. bibliogs.

- Industries

YUGOSLAVIA. Ministarstvo Trgovine i Industrije. 1941. Statistika industrije Kraljevine Jugoslavije sa adresarom industriskih preduzeća. Beograd, 1941. pp. 189. In Cyrillic.

PADJEN (JURAJ) Industrijska zona u morskoj luci kao faktor racionalnog korištenja prostora i sniženja troškova smještaja. Zagreb, 1970. pp. 19.

BOGDANOVIĆ (MILOŠ) Ekonomika industrije SFRJ. Beograd, 1971. pp. 320.

- Politics and government

YUGOSLAVIA. Yugoslav Information Office, London. 1949. [Information circulars]. London, 1949. 4 parts.

TOPALOVIĆ (ŽIVKO) Slom demokratije. London, 1961. pp. 75.

PIJADE (MOŠA) Izabrani spisi; izbor i redakcija Branislav Ilić [and others]. t.1, knj.5. Beograd, 1966. pp. 1299. bibliog.

BERTSCH (GARY K.) Nation-building in Yugoslavia: a study of political integration and attitudinal consensus. Beverly Hills, [1971]. pp. 48. bibliog.

BIJELIĆ (SREĆKO) Samoupravljačka pozicija. Zagreb, 1971. pp. 319. bibliog. Collected articles and speeches.

ĆETKOVIĆ (VLADAN) Savremena birokratija: rasprava o birokratiji i samoupravljanju. Beograd, 1971. pp. 236. bibliog.

RATKOVIĆ (RADOSLAV) Ideologija i politika. Beograd, 1971. pp. 263.

ŠEFER (BERISLAV) Socijalni razvoj u samoupravnom društvu: socijalni aspekti ekonomskog razvoja u samoupravnom društvu; koncept, praksa, problemi. Beograd, 1971. pp. 187. bibliog.

STARČEVIĆ (ANTE) Politički spisi; izbor i predgovor Tomislav Ladan. Zagreb, 1971. pp. 630. bibliog.

- Social conditions

DANILOVIĆ (RAJKO) Radničko samoupravljanje i osnovi industrijske sociologije: priručnik za obrazovanje odraslih. Beograd, [1970]. pp. 163.

- Social conditions - Bibliography

GAŠPAROVIĆ (ZLATKO) compiler. Bibliografija socioloških radova objavljenih u Jugoslaviji u periodu 1959-1969; Bibliography of sociological literature published in Yugoslavia in the period 1959-1969. Beograd, 1970. pp. 76.

- Statistics, Vital

YUGOSLAVIA. Savezni Zavod za Statistiku. 1971. Fertilitet ženskog stanovništva po popisu 1961. i tekućoj statistici 1950-1967. za SFRJ i SR. Beograd, 1971. pp. 348.

YUGOSLAVIA. Savezni Zavod za Statistiku. Studije, Analize i Prikazi. 58. Uticaj sezonskih i ostalih faktora na mortalitet stanovništva Jugoslavije, 1950-1969; Influence of seasonal and other factors on mortality of population of Yugoslavia; [by] Nevena Stojkov [and] Živojin Jevtić. Beograd, 1971. pp. 75. bibliog. With brief English summary.

YUGOSLAVIA - Statistics, Vital (Cont'd.)

YUGOSLAVIA. Savezni Zavod za Statistiku. Studije, Analize i Prikazi. 59. Smrtnost dece i omladine u Jugoslaviji od 1951-1968; Mortality of children and youth in Yugoslavia, 1951-1968; [by] Nevena Stojkov. Beograd, 1971. pp. 112. bibliog. With English summary.

YUGOSLAVS IN SPAIN

ŠPANIJA, 1936-1939: zbornik sećanja jugoslovenskih dobrovoljaca u španskom ratu. Beograd, 1971. 5 vols.

YUGOSLAVS IN THE UNITED STATES

RESEARCH GROUP FOR EUROPEAN MIGRATION PROBLEMS. Publications. 17. The speech of Yugoslav immigrants in San Pedro, California; by Alexander Albin and Ronelle Alexander. The Hague, 1972. pp. 128.

YUKON

- Economic conditions

CANADA. Parliament. House of Commons. Standing Committee on Indian Affairs and Northern Development. Minutes of proceedings and evidence. [from Jan. 1969 in English and French] Ottawa, irreg., Oct.22 1968 (28th Parl., 1st session, no.1) to date. 25cm.

LOTZ (JIM R.) Northern realities: Canada-U.S. exploitation of the Canadian North. Chicago, 1971. pp. 307. bibliog.

- Economic policy

LOTZ (JIM R.) Northern realities: Canada-U.S. exploitation of the Canadian North. Chicago, 1971. pp. 307. bibliog.

ZADRUGA

HALPERN (JOEL MARTIN) and HALPERN (BARBARA KEREWSKY) A Serbian village in historical perspective. New York, [1972]. pp. 152. bibliog.

ZAIRE

- Constitution

EISELE (HERBERT A.F.) L'affaire Oscar Chinn devant la Cour Permanente de Justice Internationale, 1934: essai d'une appréciation doctrinale. Genève, 1970. pp. 181. bibliog.

- Economic conditions

CONGO: prelude to independence. London, [1961?]. pp. 120.

FRANCE. Direction de l'Aide au Développement des Etats Francophones d'Afrique au Sud du Sahara et de la Republique Malgache. Secteur Information Economique et Conjoncture. 1969. République démocratique du Congo, 1968-69: dossier d'information économique. Paris, 1969. pp. 27, fo. 30.

SAID (SHAFIK G.) De Léopoldville à Kinshasa: la situation économique et financière au Congo ex-belge au jour de l'indépendance. [Bruxelles, 1969]. pp. 262. bibliog.

- Economic history

RYELANDT (BERNARD) L'inflation en pays sous-développé: origines, mécanismes de propagation et effets des pressions inflatoires au Congo, 1960-1969, etc. Paris, [1970]. pp. 432. bibliog. (Kinshasa. Université Lovanium. Institut de Recherches Economique et Sociales. Recherches Africaines. 9)

- Economic policy

DUPRIEZ (PIERRE) Contrôle des changes et structures économiques: Congo, 1960-1967. Paris, [1970]. pp. 334. bibliog. (Kinshasa. Université Lovanium. Institut de Recherches Economiques et Sociales. Recherches Africaines. 11)

INTERNATIONAL LABOUR OFFICE. Regular Programme of Technical Assistance. [Congo(Kin.)].R.14. Rapport au gouvernement de la République Démocratique du Congo sur le projet d'intégration des réfugiés et de développement zonal dans la province du Kivu. (OIT/OTA/Congo(Kin.)/R.14). Genève, 1970. pp. 16.

- Foreign relations - Portugal

PINTO (FRANÇOISE LATOUR DA VEIGA) Le Portugal et le Congo au XIXe siècle: étude d'histoire des relations internationales. Paris, 1972. pp. 343. bibliog. (Calouste Gulbenkian Foundation. Portuguese Cultural Centre. Publications)

- History

HOSKYNS (CATHERINE) ed. Case studies in African diplomacy: number I: the Organization of African Unity and the Congo crisis, 1964-65. Dar es Salaam, 1969. pp. 75. bibliog. (Dar es Salaam. University. Institute of Public Administration. Studies. No. 8.)

PANNEELS (E.) De diplomatieke activiteit van Koning Leopold II: oprichting van de onafhankelijke Kongostaat. Brussel, 1970. pp. 48. bibliog. (Sint Aloysiushandelshogeschool, Brussels. Eclectica. 1) With summaries in various languages.

ARCHER (JULES) Congo: the birth of a new nation. Folkestone, 1971. pp. 190. bibliog.

KAMITATU (CLEOPHAS) La grande mystification du Congo-Kinshasa: les crimes de Mobutu. Paris, 1971. pp. 298.

Les FLEURS du Congo: (Le manifeste de la Fraternité prolétarienne des paysans, ouvriers, intellectuels. et étudiants congolais conscients et révolutionnaires); suivi de commentaires par Gérard Althabe Paris, 1972. pp. 376.

KANZA (THOMAS) former Foreign Minister of Zaire. Conflict in the Congo: the rise and fall of Lumumba; translated from the French. Harmondsworth, 1972. pp. 346.

- Politics and government

CONGO: prelude to independence. London, [1961?]. pp. 120.

ROBERTS (DICK) Revolution in the Congo. [New York, 1965]. pp. 22. (Young Socialist: (voice of American radical youth). Pamphlets)

VERHAEGEN (BENOIT) Notes en marge du tome II de Rébellions au Congo-Maniema. Bruxelles, 1970. 2 vols. (in 1). (Centre de Recherche et d'Information. Socio-Politiques. Etudes Africaines du C.R.I.S.P. [Series] 2)

COPAKEN (ROBERT RANDOLPH) The political role of the United Nations Secretariat in the Congo peace-keeping operation, 1960-1963; [Ph. D. (London) thesis]. 1971. fo. 421. bibliog. Typescript: unpublished. This thesis is the property of London University and may not be removed from the Library.

KAMITATU (CLEOPHAS) La grande mystification du Congo-Kinshasa: les crimes de Mobutu. Paris, 1971. pp. 298.

Les FLEURS du Congo: (Le manifeste de la Fraternité prolétarienne des paysans, ouvriers, intellectuels et étudiants congolais conscients et révolutionnaires); suivi de commentaires par Gérard Althabe. Paris, 1972. pp. 376.

WILLAME (JEAN CLAUDE) Patrimonialism and political change in the Congo. Stanford, 1972. pp. 223. bibliog.

MARKOWITZ (MARVIN D.) Cross and sword: the political role of Christian missions in the Belgian Congo, 1908-1960. Stanford, [1973]. pp. 223. bibliog. (Stanford University. Hoover Institution on War, Revolution and Peace. Hoover Institution Publications. 114)

- Population

PAUWELS (JACQUES) La répartition de la population dans le territoire de Gungu, Congo. [Brussels], 1962. pp. 89-129. (Centre Scientifique et Médical de l'Université Libre de Bruxelles en Afrique Centrale. [Publications]. 60) (From Bulletin de la Société Royale Belge de Géographie, 85e annee, fasc.1-4)

ZALOMOV (PETR ANDREEVICH)

MAKAROV (GERAL'D NIKOLAEVICH) Rabochii-revoliutsioner Petr-Zalomov. Moskva, 1963. pp. 48.

ZAMBIA

- Defences

PETTMAN (JEANETTE) Zambia: the search for security, 1964-1970; [Ph.D. (London) thesis]. 1971. fo. 421. bibliog. Typescript: unpublished. This thesis is the property of London University and may not be removed from the Library.

- Economic conditions

ELLIOTT (CHARLES) Economist, ed. Constraints on the economic development of Zambia. Nairobi, 1971. pp. 413.

SIMONIS (HEIDE) and SIMONIS (UDO ERNST) eds. Socioeconomic development in dual economies: the example of Zambia; Sozialökonomische Entwicklung in dualistischen Wirtschaften: das Beispiel Zambia. München, [1971]. pp. 452. bibliogs. (Ifo-Institut für Wirtschaftsforschung. Afrika-Studien. 71) In English or German, with summaries in German or English.

- Economic policy

ELLIOTT (CHARLES) Economist, ed. Constraints on the economic development of Zambia. Nairobi, 1971. pp. 413.

PETTMAN (JEANETTE) Zambia: the search for security, 1964-1970; [Ph.D. (London) thesis]. 1971. fo. 421. bibliog. Typescript: unpublished. This thesis is the property of London University and may not be removed from the Library.

SIMONIS (HEIDE) and SIMONIS (UDO ERNST) eds. Socioeconomic development in dual economies: the example of Zambia; Sozialökonomische Entwicklung in dualistischen Wirtschaften: das Beispiel Zambia. München, [1971]. pp. 452. bibliogs. (Ifo-Institut für Wirtschaftsforschung. Afrika-Studien. 71) In English or German, with summaries in German or English.

BOSTOCK (MARK) and HARVEY (CHARLES) eds. Economic independence and Zambian copper: a case study of foreign investment. New York, 1972. pp. 276.

MARTIN (ANTONY) Minding their own business: Zambia's struggle against Western control. London, 1972. pp. 272.

- Foreign economic relations

MARTIN (ANTONY) Minding their own business: Zambia's struggle against Western control. London, 1972. pp. 272.

- Foreign relations

HALL (RICHARD) The high price of principles: Kaunda and the white south. rev. ed. Harmondsworth, 1973. pp. 287.

- History

POLLOCK (NORMAN H.) Nyasaland and Northern Rhodesia: corridor to the North. Pittsburgh, 1971. pp. 576. bibliog. (Duquesne University. Duquesne Studies. African Series. 3)

WILLIS (ALFRED JOHN) An introduction to the history of Central Africa. 3rd ed. London, 1973. pp. 458. bibliog.

- Nationalism

SHORT (ROBIN) African sunset. London, 1973. pp. 280.

- Parliament - Elections

ZAMBIA. Elections Office. Annual report of the Electoral Commissions. a., 1970 [1st issue]- Lusaka.

- Politics and government

PETTMAN (JEANETTE) Zambia: the search for security, 1964-1970; [Ph.D. (London) thesis]. 1971. fo. 421. bibliog. Typescript: unpublished. This thesis is the property of London University and may not be removed from the Library.

WRIGHT (MICHAEL A.) Zambia- I changed my mind. London, 1972. pp. 172.

- Race question

BURAWOY (MICHAEL) The colour of class on the copper mines: from African advancement to Zambianization. Manchester, [1972]. pp. 121. bibliog. (Zambia University. Institute for African Studies. Zambian Papers. No. 7)

- Social conditions

SIMONIS (HEIDE) and SIMONIS (UDO ERNST) eds. Socioeconomic development in dual economies: the example of Zambia; Sozialökonomische Entwicklung in dualistischen Wirtschaften: das Beispiel Zambia. München, [1971]. pp. 452. bibliogs. (Ifo-Institut für Wirtschaftsforschung. Afrika-Studien. 71) In English or German, with summaries in German or English.

WRIGHT (MICHAEL A.) Zambia- I changed my mind. London, 1972. pp. 172.

ZANDES

ZANDE themes: essays presented to Sir Edward Evans-Pritchard; edited by Andre Singer and Brian V. Street. Oxford, [1972]. pp. 188. bibliog.

ZAPOROZH'E (OBLAST')

- Economic conditions

KOTSIUBINSKII (TIMOFEI TIMOFEEVICH) Pridneprovskii ekonomicheskii raion: ekonomiko-geograficheskii ocherk. Dnepropetrovsk, 1963. pp. 56. bibliog.

ZAPOTEC INDIANS

STEININGER (GEORGE RUSSELL) and VAN DE VELDE (PAUL) Three dollars a year:...being the story of San Pablo Cuatro Venados, a typical Zapotecan Indian village, etc. New York, 1935; Detroit, 1971. pp. 121.

KEARNEY (MICHAEL) The winds of Ixtepeji: world view and society in a Zapotec town. New York, [1972]. pp. 140. bibliog.

ZARMA (AFRICAN PEOPLE)

DIARRA (FATOUMATA AGNES) Femmes africaines en devenir: les femmes zarma du Niger. Paris, [1971]. pp. 318. bibliog.

ZARNOWIEC

- Economic history

DĄBROWSKI (KAZIMIERZ) Rozwój wielkiej własności ziemskiej klasztoru cysterek w Żarnowcu od XIII do XVI wieku. Gdańsk, 1970. pp. 162. bibliog. (Gdańsk. Gdańskie Towarzystwo Naukowe. Wydział 1 Nauk Społecznych i Humanystycznych. Seria Monografii. Nr.40) With French and Russian summaries.

ZAWADZKA-WETZ (ALICJA)

ZAWADZKA-WETZ (ALICJA) Refleksje pewnego życia. Panyż, 1967. pp. 238.

ZEHRER (HANS)

DEMANT (EBBO) Von Schleicher zu Springer: Hans Zehrer als politischer Publizist. Mainz, [1971]. pp. 263. bibliog.

ZELIKSON-BOBROVSKAIA (TSETSILIIA SAMOILOVNA)

ZELIKSON-BOBROVSKAIA (TSETSILIIA SAMOILOVNA) Zapiski riadovogo podpol'shchika, 1894-1914. ch.1. Moskva, 1922. pp. 83. Xerographic reprint.

ZEMSTVOS

MOLLESON (IVAN IVANOVICH) Der russische Landarzt im 19. Jahrhundert: die Zemstvo-Medizin;...herausgegeben von Heinz Müller-Dietz. Stuttgart, [1970]. pp. 106. (Erstmals in den Heften 4, 5, 6 und 7, 46. Jahrgang (1970) der Zeitschrift für Allgemeinmedizin - Der Landarzt abgedruckt)

GALAI (SHMUEL) The liberation movement in Russia, 1900-1905. Cambridge, 1973. pp. 325. bibliog. (National Association for Soviet and East European Studies. Soviet and East European Studies)

ZERNATTO (GUIDO)

ZERNATTO (GUIDO) Die Wahrheit über Österreich. New York, 1938. pp. 331.

ZEROMSKI (STEFAN)

JANASZEK-IVANIČKOVÁ (HALINA) Świat jako zadanie inteligencji: studium o Stefanie Żeromskim. Warszawa, 1971. pp. 257. (Polska Akademia Nauk. Instytut Badań Literackich. Historia i Teoria Literatury: Studia. 29)

ŽEROVNICA

WINNER (IRENE) A Slovenian village: Žerovnica. Providence, R.I., 1971. pp. 267. bibliog.

ZHENEVSKII (ALEKSANDR FEDOROVICH IL'IN) See IL'IN-ZHENEVSKII (ALEKSANDR FEDOROVICH)

ZHITOMIR (OBLAST')

- Statistics

ZHITOMIR (OBLAST'). Statystychne Upravlinnia. Narodne hospodarstvo Zhytomyrs'koï oblasti: statystychnyi zbirnyk. Kyïv, 1968. pp. 392.

ZHIVKOV (TODOR)

ZHIVKOV (TODOR) Izbrani sŭchineniia. Sofiia, 1971. 8 vols.

ZHLOBA (DMITRII PETROVICH)

SAENKO (IAKOV DMITRIEVICH) Dmitrii Zhloba: istoriko-biograficheskii ocherk. Krasnodar, 1964. pp. 112.

ZHUKEEV (TAVALDY)

SEMENKOV (VASILII NIKOLAEVICH) Borets za narodnoe delo: T. Zhukeev - A.A. Pudovkin. Frunze, 1963. pp. 54.

ZHUKOV (GEORGII KONSTANTINOVICH)

CHANEY (OTTO PRESTON) Zhukov. Newton Abbot, 1972. pp. 512. bibliog.

ZINACANTAN

VOGT (EVON ZARTMAN) The Zinacantecos of Mexico: a modern Maya way of life. New York, [1970]. pp. 113. bibliog.

- Economic conditions

CANCIAN (FRANK) Change and uncertainty in a peasant economy: the Maya corn farmers of Zinacantan. Stanford, 1972. pp. 208. bibliog.

- Social conditions

COLLIER (JANE FISHBURNE) Law and social change in Zinacantan. Stanford, 1973. pp. 281. bibliog.

ZINOV'EV (GRIGORII EVSEEVICH)

TIMONIN (V. I.) Pechat' - oruzhie bor'by leninskoi partii protiv trotskistsko-zinov'evskogo bloka. in Voprosy partiinogo stroitel'stva. Moskva, 1971. pp. 318.

ZIONISM
See JEWS - RESTORATION

ZIONISM AND COMMUNISM
See COMMUNISM AND ZIONISM

ZIONIST CHURCHES (AFRICA)

- Rhodesia

DANEEL (M.L.) Zionism and faith-healing in Rhodesia: aspects of African independent churches; (translated from the Dutch by V.A. February). The Hague, [1970]. pp. 64. bibliog. (Afrika-Studiecentrum. Communications. 2)

ZIPF (GEORGE KINGSLEY)

PETTERSSON (ROLAND) Demographic forecasting models for rural-urban migration and Zipfian distributions. Lisboa, 1970. pp. 35-60. (From Arquivo do Instituto Gulbenkian de Ciência, Secção B, vol. 5, no.2)

ZJEDNOCZONE STRONNICTWO LUDOWE

GRĄDZKI (CZESŁAW) Wspomnienia działacza ludowego, 1909-1945; opracował i wstępem opatrzył Janusz Socha. Warszawa, 1970. pp. 176.

ZLATOVRATSKII (NIKOLAI NIKOLAEVICH)

BUSH (VLADIMIR V.) Ocherki literaturnogo narodnichestva, 70-80 gg. Moskva, 1931. pp. 164. Xerographic reprint.

ZLIN

- Social conditions

DUBREUIL (HYACINTHE) L'exemple de Bat'a: la libération des initiatives individuelles dans une entreprise géante. Paris, [1936]. pp. 374.

ZOLA (ÉMILE ÉDOUARD CHARLES ANTOINE)

SANCTIS (FRANCESCO DE) Il manifesto del realismo: [Studio sopra Emilio Zola, and other writings, originally published 1872-1883]; a cura di Rino Dal Sasso. Roma, 1972. pp. 155.

ZONE FRANC
See FRENCH FRANC AREA

ZONING

- United States

ANDREWS (RICHARD BRUCE) ed. Urban land use policy: the central city; [readings]. New York, [1972]. pp. 285. bibliogs.

SIEGAN (BERNARD H.) Land use without zoning. Lexington, Mass., [1972]. pp. 271.

ZONING LAW

- United Kingdom

HEAP (Sir DESMOND) An outline of planning law. 6th ed. London, 1973. pp. 317.

- United States

NEW YORK (STATE). Department of Commerce. 1960. Local planning and zoning: a manual of powers and procedures for citizens and governmental officials. rev. ed. Albany, 1960. pp. 102.

ZOOLOGY

- Pre-Linnean works

ARISTOTLE. De partibus animalium I; and De generatione animalium I, with passages from II, 1-3; translated with notes by D.M. Balme. Oxford, 1972. pp. 173. bibliog.

ZUERICH (CANTON)

- Constitution

ZUERICH (CANTON). Constitution. 1869-78. Verfassung des eidgenössischen Standes Zürich, vom 18. April 1869; (with [Amendments]). [Zurich, 1878]. pp. 58.

- Politics and government

SIGG (OTTO) Die Entwicklung des Finanzwesens und der Verwaltung Zürichs im ausgehenden 16. und 17. Jahrhundert. Bern, 1971. pp. 209. bibliog. (Zürich. Universität. Historisches Seminar. Geist und Werk der Zeiten. No. 28)

ZUERICH (CITY)

- Civic improvement

ZUERICH. Eidgenössische Technische Hochschule. Institut für Orts- Regional- und Landesplanung. Veränderung der Wohnbevölkerung und der Arbeitsplätze in der Stadt Zürich; (Projektleitung: Jakob Maurer; Bearbeitung: Jürg Lang). [Zurich], 1969. 4 vols. (in 1).

- Population

ZUERICH. Eidgenössische Technische Hochschule. Institut für Orts- Regional- und Landesplanung. Veränderung der Wohnbevölkerung und der Arbeitsplätze in der Stadt Zürich; (Projektleitung: Jakob Maurer; Bearbeitung: Jürg Lang). [Zurich], 1969. 4 vols. (in 1).

- Social conditions

NIGGLI-HUERLIMANN (BERTHA) Anthropologische Untersuchungen in Zürcher Kindergärten mit Berücksichtigung der sozialen Schichtung. Zürich, 1930. pp. 215. bibliog. (Separatabdruck aus dem Archiv der Julius Klaus-Stiftung für Vererbungsforschung, Sozialanthropologie und Rassenhygiene, Zürich, 1930, Band V, Heft 1/2, S. 1-215)

ZULUS

SELBY (JOHN) Shaka's heirs. London, 1971. pp. 232. bibliog.

ZUMAN (FRANTIŠEK)

ZUMAN (FRANTIŠEK) Osvobozenská legenda: vzpomínky a úvahy o československém odboji v Rusku. Praha, 1922. 2 vols (in 1).

List of subject headings used in the Bibliography arranged under topics

TABLE OF SUBJECT SUBDIVISIONS

SUBJECT SUBDIVISIONS UNDER NAMES OF CONTINENTS, COUNTRIES, STATES OR TOWNS

Works on the following subjects, if confined to a particular geographical area, are entered not under subject, but under the name of the country, etc., with the subject subdivision. At the end of the entries under countries are references to the smaller areas comprised therein, e.g. from United Kingdom -- Social conditions to the subdivision Social conditions under Banbury, Cumberland, etc. Such references may serve also in a few cases, such as Municipal Government, where the reference from the subject is made to subject subdivisions 'under the names of towns', without listing the names of towns.

Air force
Annexation
Antiquities
Appropriations and expenditures
Armed forces
Army
Bibliography
Bio-bibliography
Biography
Boundaries
Capital
Census
Centennial celebrations, etc.
Charters, grants, privileges
Church history
Civilization
Claims
Climate
Clubs
Colonies
Colonization
Commerce
Commercial policy
Commercial treaties
Constitution
Constitutional conventions
Constitutional history
Constitutional laws
Courts and courtiers
Defences
Description and travel
Dictionaries and encyclopaedias
Diplomatic and consular service
Directories
Discovery and exploration
Economic conditions
Economic history
Economic integration

Economic policy
Emigration and immigration
Executive departments
Exiles
Fairs
Famines
Foreign economic relations
Foreign opinion
Foreign population
Foreign relations
Foreign relations - Treaties
Foreign relations administration
Gazeteers
Genealogy
Gentry
Government property
Government publications
Government vessels
Governors
Historic houses, etc.
Historical geography
History
History, Local
History, Military
History, Naval
Industries
Intellectual life
International status
Kings and rulers
Languages
Learned institutions and societies
Manufactures
Maps
Military policy
Militia
Minorities
Moral conditions
Nationalism
Native races

Navy
Neutrality
Nobility
Occupations
Officials and employees
Parliament [Congress, Nationalrat, etc.]
Peerage
Politics and government
Population
Presidents
Public buildings
Public lands
Public works
Race question
Registers
Relations (general) with [country]
Relations (military) with [country]
Religion
Religion and mythology
Rural conditions
Sanitary affairs
Seal
Semicentennial celebrations, etc.
Social conditions
Social history
Social life and customs
Social policy
Statistics
Statistics, Medical
Statistics, Vital
Surveys
Territorial expansion
Territories and possessions
Tornadoes
Vice-Presidents
Voting registers
Year-books

SUBJECT SUBDIVISIONS USED ONLY UNDER NAMES OF CITIES OR TOWNS

Works on the following matters, if confined to a particular region or country, are entered under the subject, with local subdivision; if confined to a particular city or town, under the name of the city or town, with subject subdivision. References to particular cities or towns are made under the local subdivision of the subject.

Almshouses and workhouses
Ambulance service
Amusements
Benevolent and moral institutions and societies
Bridges
Buildings
Cemeteries
Charities
Civic improvement
Clubs
Description
Docks
Earthquake
Evening and continuation schools
Exhibitions
Fires and fire prevention

Fortifications
Gilds
Growth
Harbour
Hospitals
Hotels, taverns, etc.
Libraries
Lodging-houses
Markets
Massacre
Music-halls (Variety-theatres, cabarets, etc.)
Office buildings
Parks
Police
Poor
Port

Porters
Prisons and reformatories
Public laundries
Rapid transit
Recreation areas
Recreational activities
Riots
Schools
Sewerage
Stock Exchange [Beurs, Bourse, etc.]
Street cleaning
Streets
Suburbs and environs
Synagogues
Theatres
Transit systems
Water-supply

AGRICULTURE (including ANIMAL AND PLANT INDUSTRIES)

General

AERONAUTICS IN AGRICULTURE
AFFORESTATION
AGRICULTURAL ADMINISTRATION
AGRICULTURAL ASSISTANCE
AGRICULTURAL ASSISTANCE, SWEDISH
AGRICULTURAL COLONIES
AGRICULTURAL COOPERATIVE CREDIT ASSOCIATIONS
AGRICULTURAL CREDIT
AGRICULTURAL EDUCATION
AGRICULTURAL ENGINEERING
AGRICULTURAL ESTIMATING AND REPORTING
AGRICULTURAL EXTENSION WORK
AGRICULTURAL GEOGRAPHY
AGRICULTURAL INNOVATIONS
AGRICULTURAL LAWS AND LEGISLATION
AGRICULTURAL MACHINERY
AGRICULTURAL PRICE SUPPORTS
AGRICULTURAL PRICES
AGRICULTURAL RESEARCH
AGRICULTURAL SOCIETIES
AGRICULTURAL SURPLUS
AGRICULTURAL WAGES
AGRICULTURE
AGRICULTURE, COOPERATIVE
AGRICULTURE, PRIMITIVE
AGRICULTURE AND STATE
AMMONIA AS FERTILIZER
ARTIFICIAL INSEMINATION
BANANA TRADE
BEE CULTURE
BOTANY, ECONOMIC
CASHEW NUT INDUSTRY
CATTLE TRADE
CEREALS AS FOOD
CITRUS FRUIT INDUSTRY
CLEARING OF LAND

CONSOLIDATION OF LAND HOLDINGS
CONTRACTS, AGRICULTURAL
COOPERATIVE MARKETING OF FARM PRODUCE
COTTON GROWING AND MANUFACTURE
CROP YIELDS
CROPS AND CLIMATE
DAIRY PRODUCTS
DAIRYING
DRAINAGE
DRY FARMING
FARM BUILDINGS
FARM CORPORATIONS
FARM EQUIPMENT
FARM INCOME
FARM LIFE
FARM MANAGEMENT
FARM MECHANIZATION
FARM OWNERSHIP
FARM PRODUCE
FARMERS
FARMS
FARMS, COLLECTIVE
FARMS, SIZE OF
FEEDS
FERTILIZER INDUSTRY
FERTILIZERS AND MANURES
FLORICULTURE
FOOD AND AGRICULTURE ORGANIZATION
FOREST CONSERVATION
FOREST PRODUCTS
FOREST SURVEYS
FORESTRY LAW AND LEGISLATION
FORESTRY RESEARCH
FORESTS AND FORESTRY
FRUIT CULTURE
FRUIT TRADE
FUR TRADE
GRAIN AS FEEDING STUFF
GRAIN TRADE
GRAZING DISTRICTS

HEDGES
HILL FARMING
HORSE BREEDING
HORTICULTURE
INCLOSURES
INTER-AMERICAN INSTITUTE OF AGRICULTURAL SCIENCES
INTERNATIONAL AGRICULTURAL COOPERATION
IRRIGATION
LAND SETTLEMENT
MEAT INDUSTRY AND TRADE
MILK TRADE
PART-TIME FARMING
PASTURES
PHOSPHATIC FERTILIZERS
PLANTATIONS
PORK INDUSTRY AND TRADE
PRODUCE TRADE
RADIO IN AGRICULTURE
RANCH LIFE
RANGE MANAGEMENT
RECLAMATION OF LAND
RINDERPEST
ROTATION OF CROPS
SLAUGHTERING AND SLAUGHTERHOUSES
SMALL HOLDINGS
SOCIALISM AND AGRICULTURE
SOIL CONSERVATION
SOILS
STATE FARMS
STOCK AND STOCK BREEDING
SUGAR GROWING
TRACTORS
VETERINARY MEDICINE
VETERINARIANS
VITICULTURE
WATER SUPPLY, AGRICULTURAL
WILD LIFE, CONSERVATION OF
WOMEN AS FARMERS

AGRICULTURE (including ANIMAL AND PLANT INDUSTRIES) (cont'd)

Particular animals and animal products

BEEF
BONE PRODUCTS
CATTLE
EGGS
GORILLAS
HIDES AND SKINS
HONEY
LEMURS
MILK
MONKEYS
POULTRY
SEA BIRDS
SHEEP
SWINE
WOOL

Particular crops and plant products

APPLES
BAGASSE
BARLEY
BEANS
BEETS AND BEET SUGAR
CAULIFLOWER
CHOCOLATE
CITRUS FRUITS

COCOA
COCONUT OIL
COFFEE
COIR
COLA NUT
COPRA
CUCUMBERS
DATE PALM
EUCALYPTUS
FRUIT
GRAIN
GREENHOUSE PLANTS
HASHISH
LETTUCES
MARIHUANA
MATE (TEA)
MUSHROOMS, EDIBLE
NUTS
OIL PALM
PALM OIL
PEANUTS
PEARS
PEAS
PEAT
POTATOES
RAPE (PLANT)
RICE
SEEDS
SHEA NUTS
SISAL HEMP

SORGHUM
SOYA BEANS
STRAWBERRIES
SUGAR
TEA
TIMBER
TOBACCO
TOMATO PRODUCTS
TREES
TROPICAL FRUIT
VEGETABLES
WHEAT
WOOD

Fisheries

FISH TRADE
FISHERIES
FISHERIES, COOPERATIVE
FISHERY LAW AND LEGISLATION
FISHERY PRODUCTS
HERRING FISHERIES
SALMON
SALMON-FISHERIES
SEALING
SHELL FISH FISHERIES
TROUT
WHALING

BIBLIOGRAPHY AND GENERAL WORKS

ABSTRACTING AND INDEXING SERVICES
ACQUISITION OF CUBAN PUBLICATIONS
ACQUISITIONS (LIBRARIES)
ALMANACS, BELGIAN
ANONYMS AND PSEUDONYMS, RUSSIAN
ANONYMS AND PSEUDONYMS, UKRAINIAN
ARCHIVES
BIBLIOGRAPHICAL CENTRES
BIBLIOGRAPHICAL SERVICES

BIBLIOGRAPHY
BIBLIOGRAPHY, NATIONAL
BOOK COLLECTING
BOOK COLLECTORS
BOOK SELECTION
BOOKBINDING
BOOKS
BOOKSELLERS AND BOOKSELLING
CATALOGUES, BOOKSELLERS'

CATALOGUES, COMMERCIAL
CATALOGUES, LIBRARY
CATALOGUES, UNION
CATALOGUING
CLASSIFICATION
CONTENT ANALYSIS (COMMUNICATION)
CYBERNETICS
DICTIONARIES, POLYGLOT
DIRECTORIES

BIBLIOGRAPHY AND GENERAL WORKS (cont'd)

DOCUMENTATION
ENCYCLOPAEDIAS AND DICTIONARIES
EXCHANGES, LITERARY AND SCIENTIFIC
GOVERNMENT PUBLICATIONS
HISTORICAL LIBRARIES
INDEXING
INDUSTRIAL MUSEUMS
INFORMATION SCIENCE
INFORMATION SERVICES
INFORMATION STORAGE AND RETRIEVAL SYSTEMS
INFORMATION THEORY
INTERLIBRARY LOANS
INTERNATIONAL FEDERATION OF LIBRARY ASSOCIATIONS
LAW LIBRARIES
LIBRARIES
LIBRARIES, GOVERNMENTAL, ADMINISTRATIVE, ETC.
LIBRARIES, NATIONAL

LIBRARIES, UNIVERSITY AND COLLEGE
LIBRARIES AND READERS
LIBRARY ADMINISTRATION
LIBRARY ARCHITECTURE
LIBRARY COOPERATION
LIBRARY ORIENTATION
LIBRARY SCHOOLS AND TRAINING
LIBRARY SCIENCE
MANUSCRIPTS
MARC PROJECT
MICROFILMS
MUSEUMS
NEWSPAPER PUBLISHING
NOBEL PRIZES
PAMPHLETS
PAPER
PERIODICALS
PHOTOCOPYING PROCESSES
PHOTOGRAPHY

POPULATION RESEARCH
PRINTING
PRINTING, PRACTICAL
PRINTING INDUSTRY
PROCESSING (LIBRARIES)
PROOF READING
PUBLIC LENDING RIGHTS (OF AUTHORS)
PUBLISHERS AND PUBLISHING
READERSHIP SURVEYS
REFERENCE BOOKS
REPRINTS (PUBLICATIONS)
RESEARCH LIBRARIES
SCHOLARLY PUBLISHING
SIGNS AND SYMBOLS
THESAURI
TRANSPORT LIBRARIES
TYPE AND TYPE-FOUNDING
UNIVERSITY PRESSES

BIOGRAPHY

ABBE (ERNST)
ABRAHAM (PIERRE) pseud.
ACHESON (DEAN GOODERHAM)
ACWORTH (Sir WILLIAM MITCHELL)
ADDAMS (JANE)
ADDISON (JOSEPH)
ADELABU (ADEGOKE)
ADENAUER (KONRAD)
ADORNO (THEODOR WIESENGRUND)
AGABEKOV (GEORGII SERGEEVICH)
AGNELLI (GIOVANNI)
AGNEW (SPIRO THEODORE)
AITKEN (WILLIAM MAXWELL) 1st Baron Beaverbrook
AKPAN (NTIEYONG U.)
AKSEL'ROD (PAVEL BORISOVICH)
ALBERT (HANS)
ALBERTINI (LUIGI)
ALDRED (GUY ALFRED)
ALEM (LEANDRO NICÉFORO)

ALESSANDRI PALMA (ARTURO)
ALEXANDER I., Emperor of Russia
ALEXANDER (HAROLD RUPERT LEOFRIC GEORGE) 1st Earl Alexander of Tunis
ALEXIS, Emperor of Russia
ALFRED, surnamed the Great, King of England
ALGRA (HENDRIK)
AL-HUSRI (SATI')
AL HUSSEINI (HAJ AMIN) Mufti of Jerusalem
ALLEGATO (LUIGI)
ALLEMAND-LAVIGERIE (CHARLES MARTIAL) Cardinal
ALLENDE (SALVADOR)
ALLPORT (GORDON WILLARD)
ALMOND (GABRIEL ABRAHAM)
ALTHUSSER (LOUIS)
ALVAREZ DEL VAYO (JULIO)
ALVES (MARCIO MOREIRA)
AMADI (ELECHI)
AMANULLAH KHAN, Amir of Afghanistan

AMBEDKAR (BHIMARAO RAMJI)
AMIN (IDI)
ANASTAPLO (GEORGE)
ANCHORENA FAMILY
ANDERSON (MARGARET CAROLINE)
ANDREEV (ANDREI ANDREEVICH)
ANDRIEU (JULES)
ANNUNZIO (GABRIELE D')
ANTEQUERA CASTRO (JOSE MIGUEL JESUS DE)
ARISTOTLE
ARMAND (INESSA)
ARNDT (ERNST MORITZ)
ARON (RAYMOND)
ARTIGAS (JOSE GERVASIO)
ARTSYBASHEV (MIKHAIL PETROVICH)
ARZHAKOV (STEPAN MAKSIMOVICH)
ASAN (KUMARAN)
ASTOR (NANCY WITCHER) Viscountess Astor
AUGSTEIN (RUDOLF)
AULIKE (MATTHIAS)

BIOGRAPHY (cont'd)

AUSTIN (JOHN) Barrister-at-Law

AUSTIN (JOHN LANGSHAW)

AZANA Y DIAZ (MANUEL)

AZEF (EVNO FISHELEV)

AZIKIWE (NNAMDI)

BABEL' (ISAAK EMMANUILOVICH)

BABEUF (FRANÇOIS NOËL)

BACH (ALEXANDER VON) Freiherr

BACHELARD (GASTON)

BAECK (LEO)

BAGEHOT (WALTER)

BAJCSY-ZSILINSZKY (ENDRÉ)

BAKER (SHIRLEY WALDEMAR)

BAKUNIN (MIKHAIL ALEKSANDROVICH)

BALBO (PROSPERO) Conte

BALDWIN (JAMES)

BALFOUR (ALEXANDER) of Liverpool

BALFOUR (ARTHUR JAMES) 1st Earl of Balfour

BALFOUR (HAROLD HARINGTON) 1st Baron Balfour of Inchrye

BANDERA (STEPAN)

BANNERMAN (JOHN MACDONALD) Baron Bannerman

BARFORD (EDWARD)

BARKER (JOSEPH)

BARNAVE (ANTOINE PIERRE JOSEPH MARIE)

BARRÈS (AUGUSTE MAURICE)

BARZEL (RAINER)

BASTIDE (GEORGES)

BATA (THOMAS)

BATLLE Y ORDÓÑEZ (JOSÉ)

BAUER (BRUNO)

BAUZE (ROBERTS)

BAYLE (PIERRE)

BEBEL (AUGUST)

BEECHING (RICHARD) Baron Beeching

BEGHELLI (GIUSEPPE)

BELINSKII (VISSARION GRIGOR'EVICH)

BEN BARKA (MEHDI)

BEN-GURION (DAVID)

BENNETT (MARIA) of Plymouth

BENNIS (WARREN G.)

BENTHAM (JEREMY)

BEREZHKOV (VALENTIN MIKHAILOVICH)

BERG (FRIEDRICH VON)

BERGSON (HENRI LOUIS)

BERK (MALCOLM A.)

BERKELEY (GEORGE) Bishop of Cloyne

BERKELEY (HUMPHRY)

BERNSTEIN (BASIL)

BERNSTEIN (EDUARD)

BERRIGAN (DANIEL)

BESANT (ANNIE)

BESEDOVSKII (GRIGORII ZINOV'EVICH)

BETHAM-EDWARDS (MATILDA BARBARA)

BETHLEN (ISTVÁN) Gróf

BETHMANN-HOLLWEG (THEOBALD VON)

BEUTIN (LUDWIG)

BEVERIDGE (WILLIAM HENRY) 1st Baron Beveridge

BIDAULT (SUZANNE)

BISMARCK-SCHOENHAUSEN (OTTO EDUARD LEOPOLD VON) Prince

BITTMAN (LADISLAV)

BLANQUI (LOUIS AUGUSTE)

BLAVATSKAYA (ELENA PETROVNA)

BLISHEN (EDWARD)

BLIUKHER (VASILII KONSTANTINOVICH)

BLOCH (JEAN RICHARD)

BLOCH (MARCEL)

BLONDEL (MAURICE)

BLUM (LÉON)

BODIN (JEAN)

BOEHM-BAWERK (EUGEN VON)

BOEHME (JACOB)

BOGDANOV (PETR ALEKSEEVICH)

BOHLEN (CHARLES EUSTIS)

BOLÍVAR (SIMÓN)

BOLLARDIERE (JACQUES PARIS DE)

BONALD (LOUIS GABRIEL AMBOISE DE) Vicomte

BONAPARTE FAMILY

BONCH-BRUEVICH (VLADIMIR DMITRIEVICH)

BONDFIELD (MARGARET GRACE)

BONHOEFFER (DIETRICH)

BONNER (THOMAS)

BONNET (GEORGES ETIENNE)

BONO (PEDRO FRANCISCO)

BOOT (JOOST JOHANNES GERARDUS)

BOOTH (CHARLES)

BOOTH (MARY CATHERINE)

BORAH (WILLIAM EDGAR)

BORDIGA (AMADEO)

BORMANN (MARTIN)

BOSANQUET (BERNARD)

BOURKE (Sir RICHARD)

BOWLEY (Sir ARTHUR LYON)

BOWLEY (JULIA)

BOYCOTT (CHARLES CUNNINGHAM)

BRAAK (MENNO TER)

BRACTON (HENRICUS DE)

BRADLAUGH (CHARLES)

BRAINE (JOHN)

BRAMSEN (LUDVIG)

BRAND (JOHANNES HENDRICUS)

BRANDEIS (LOUIS DEMBITZ)

BRANDSMA (TITUS)

BRANDT (WILLY)

BRASILLACH (ROBERT)

BRAUER (MAX)

BRAUN (WERNHER VON) Freiherr

BRAZZA (PIERRE PAUL FRANÇOIS CAMILLE SAVORGNAN DE)

BREZHNEV (LEONID IL'ICH)

BRIDGE (ANN) pseud. i.e. [Mary Dolling O'MALLEY, Lady]

BRIDGES (HARRY)

BRIDSON (DOUGLAS GEOFFREY)

BRIEFS (GOETZ A.)

BROMME (MORITZ TH. W.)

BROOKE FAMILY

BROWN (NORMAN OLIVER)

BRUDENELL (GEORGE) 3rd Earl of Cardigan

BRUHNS (JULIUS)

BUBNOV (ANDREI SERGEEVICH)

BUCHHOLZ (PAUL FERDINAND FRIEDRICH)

BUCHWITZ (OTTO)

BUDENNYI (SEMEN MIKHAILOVICH)

BIOGRAPHY (cont'd)

BUKHARIN (NIKOLAI IVANOVICH)

BULLITT (WILLIAM CHRISTIAN)

BULLOCK (JAMES ALLEN)

BUNTING (JABEZ)

BUOL-SCHAUENSTEIN (CARL FERDINAND VON) Graf.

BUONARROTI (PHILIPPE)

BURCKHARDT (CARL JACOB)

BURKE (EDMUND)

BUSCH (JOHANN)

BUSS (FRANCES MARY)

BUSYGIN (ALEKSANDR KHARITONOVICH)

BUTASHEVICH-PETRASHEVSKII (MIKHAIL VASIL'EVICH)

BUTLER (JOSEPHINE ELIZABETH)

CACCIAPUOTI (SALVATORE)

CAESAR (CAIUS JULIUS)

CAILLAUX (JOSEPH MARIE AUGUSTE)

CAINE (WILLIAM SPROSTON)

CAIRNES (JOHN ELLIOT)

CAIRNS (JAMES FORD)

CALLES (PLUTARCO ELIAS)

CALLEY (WILLIAM L.)

CALLIÈRES (FRANÇOIS DE)

CALVO SOTELO (JOSE)

CAMARA (HELDER) Archbishop of Olinda and Recife

CAMDEN (WILLIAM) the Antiquary

CAMPBELL-BANNERMAN (Sir HENRY)

CANNON (Sir LESLIE)

CAPODISTRIA (JOHN) Count

CARABELLESE (PANTALEO)

CARLSON (JOEL)

CARNAP (RUDOLF)

CARNEGIE (ANDREW)

CARNOT (LAZARE NICOLAS MARGUERITE) Comte

CARSON (RACHEL LOUISE)

CARTWRIGHT (JOHN) Major

CASABLANCA

CASAS (BARTOLOME DE LAS) Bishop of Chiapa

CASEMENT (Sir ROGER DAVID)

CASEY (RICHARD GARDINER) Baron Casey

CASSIRER (ERNST)

CASTBERG (FREDE)

CASTILLO (DOMINGO B.)

CASTRO RUZ (FIDEL)

CATHERINE II, Empress of Russia

CATTANEO (CARLO)

CAUWELAERT (FRANS J. VAN)

CAVAIGNAC (GODEFROY)

CAVOUR (CAMILLO BENSO DI) Conte

CEAUSESCU (NICOLAE)

CECIL (ROBERT ARTHUR TALBOT GASCOYNE) 3rd Marquess of Salisbury

CÉLINE (LOUIS FERDINAND)

CHABAN-DELMAS (JACQUES)

CHAIKOVSKII (NIKOLAI VASIL'EVICH)

CHALOULT (RENÉ)

CHAMBERLAIN (ARTHUR NEVILLE)

CHAMBERLAIN (JOSEPH)

CHAMBERLAIN (Sir JOSEPH AUSTEN)

CHANCELLOR (Sir JOHN ROBERT)

CHANG (CHIEN)

CHAPMAN (Sir SYDNEY JOHN)

CHARLES, the Good, Count of Flanders

CHARLES V, Emperor of Germany

CHARPENTIER (ALFRED)

CHARRIERE (HENRI ANTOINE) called Papillon

CHAUVEL (JEAN)

CHAVEZ (CESAR)

CHENIER (LOUIS)

CHERNOV (VIKTOR MIKHAILOVICH)

CHERNOVA (OL'GA)

CHERNYSHEVSKII (NIKOLAI GAVRILOVICH)

CHIANG (KAI-SHEK)

CHIANG (MEI-LING)

CHINN (OSCAR)

CHOMSKY (NOAM)

CHURCHILL (Sir WINSTON LEONARD SPENCER)

CIOŁKOSZ (ADAM)

CLAYTON (WILLIAM LOCKHART)

CLEAVER (ELDRIDGE)

CLÉREL DE TOCQUEVILLE (CHARLES ALEXIS HENRI MAURICE) Comte

CLODD (EDWARD)

CLOUGH (ARTHUR HUGH)

CLUTTON-BROCK (GUY)

COBBETT (WILLIAM)

COBDEN (RICHARD)

CODREANU (CORNELIU ZELEA)

COE FAMILY

COHEN (Sir JOHN EDWARD)

COLIJN (HENDRIKUS)

COLINS (JEAN GUILLAUME CÉSAR ALEXANDRE HIPPOLYTE)

COLLIER (JOHN)

COLLINGWOOD (ROBIN GEORGE)

COLLINS (MICHAEL)

COMTE (ISIDORE AUGUSTE MARIE FRANÇOIS XAVIER)

CONNOLLY (JAMES)

CONSTANT DE REBECQUE (HENRI BENJAMIN DE)

CONTE AGÜERO (LUIS)

COOKWORTHY (WILLIAM)

COPERNICUS (NICOLAUS)

CORMAND FAMILY

CORTES (MANUEL)

COSTIGAN (EDWARD PRENTISS)

COUDENHOVE-KALERGI (RICHARD NICOLAUS) Count

CRAIG (JAMES) 1st Viscount Craigavon

CRANMER (THOMAS) Archbishop of Canterbury

CREMIEUX (GASTON)

CROCE (BENEDETTO)

CROKER (RICHARD)

CROMWELL (OLIVER) Lord Protector

CROMWELL (THOMAS) 1st Earl of Essex

CROSS (JAMES RICHARD)

CURTIN (JOHN)

CUSTINE (ASTOLPHE LOUIS LÉONOR DE) Marquis

DAENS (PIETER)

DANILEVSKII (NIKOLAI IAKOVLEVICH)

DANQUAH (JOSEPH BOAKYE)

DARLING (JAMES)

DARWIN (CHARLES ROBERT)

DAVIES (SAMUEL)

DAVIS (ANGELA YVONNE)

BIOGRAPHY (cont'd)

DEBRAY (RÉGIS)

DEBRÉ (MICHEL)

DEBS (EUGENE VICTOR)

DELANY (MARTIN R.)

DE LEON (DANIEL)

DEMBIŃSKI (HENRYK)

DENIKIN (ANTON IVANOVICH)

DEPREUX (EDOUARD)

DE SAPIO (CARMINE GERARD)

DESCARTES (RENÉ)

DEUTSCH (KARL WOLFGANG)

DEUTSCHER (ISAAC)

DE VALERA (EAMON)

DIAZ (PORFIRIO)

DIBELIUS (FRIEDRICH K. OTTO)

DIDEROT (DENIS)

DIMITROV (GEORGI)

DISRAELI (BENJAMIN) 1st Earl of Beaconsfield

DISRAELI FAMILY

DJILAS (MILOVAN)

DMOWSKI (ROMAN)

DOBROVOL'SKII (ALEKSEI ALEKSANDROVICH)

DOELLINGER (JOHANN JOSEPH IGNAZ VON)

DONATI (GIUSEPPE)

DOOLITTLE (HILDA)

DOSTOEVSKII (FEDOR MIKHAILOVICH)

DOUBLEDAY (FRANK NELSON)

DOUGLAS (CLIFFORD HUGH)

DOUGLAS (PAUL HOWARD)

DOUGLAS (STEPHEN ARNOLD)

DRAGOMANOV (MIKHAIL PETROVICH)

DREES (WILLEM)

DREGGER (ALFRED)

DREYFUS (ALFRED)

DRIEU LA ROCHELLE (PIERRE)

DRUMMOND (JAMES ERIC) 16th Earl of Perth

DUCHARME (LOUIS LEANDRE)

DUGDALE (BLANCHE ELIZABETH CAMPBELL)

DUGUIT (LEON)

DULLES (JOHN FOSTER)

DUMBADZE (EVGENII VASIL'EVICH)

DUNANT (JEAN HENRI)

DUNNER (JOSEPH)

DU PLESSIS (ABRAHAM HERMANUS)

DU PLESSIS (ARMAND JEAN) Cardinal, Duc de Richelieu

DUPLESSIS (MAURICE LENOBLET)

DU PONT (PIERRE SAMUEL) 1870-1954

DU PONT DE NEMOURS FAMILY

DURKHEIM (ÉMILE)

DURRUTI (BUENAVENTURA)

DUVALIER (FRANÇOIS)

DZERZHINSKII (FELIKS EDMUNDOVICH)

EASTON (DAVID)

EATON (DANIEL)

EBERT (FRIEDRICH)

EDWARD VII, King of Great Britain and Ireland

EHINGER (JAKOB)

EINAUDI (LUIGI)

EISENHOWER (DWIGHT DAVID) President of the United States

EL SHEIKH (SHAFIE AHMED)

ELIAS (NORBERT)

ELIOT (THOMAS STEARNS)

ELISEEV (GRIGORII ZAKHAROVICH)

ELKINS (STANLEY M.)

ELLICOTT (JOSEPH)

ELLIOT-MURRAY-KYNYNMOUND (GILBERT) 1st Earl of Minto.

ENDRUPS (RUDOLFS)

ENGELS (FRIEDRICH)

ENKIRI (GABRIEL)

EPICURUS

EPSTEIN (MELECH)

EREMEEV (KONSTANTIN STEPANOVICH)

ERHARD (LUDWIG)

ERIKSON (ERIK HOMBURGER)

ERTEL' (ALEKSANDR IVANOVICH)

EVANS-PRITCHARD (Sir EDWARD EVANS)

FAERBER (WOLFGANG)

FAIRBANK (JOHN KING)

FANON (FRANTZ)

FARADAY (MICHAEL)

FARINACCI (ROBERTO)

FARRAR (FREDERIC WILLIAM)

FAULKNER (ARTHUR BRIAN DEANE)

FEATHER (VICTOR GRAYSON HARDIE)

FEDER (ERNST)

FEDORENKO (NIKOLAI TROFIMOVICH)

FEDOSEEV (NIKOLAI EVGRAFOVICH)

FEHRENBACH (KONSTANTIN)

FEIS (HERBERT)

FELS (JOSEPH)

FELTRINELLI (GIANGIACOMO)

FERRERO (GUGLIELMO)

FEUERBACH (LUDWIG ANDREAS)

FEVR (NIKOLAI)

FICHTE (JOHANN GOTTLIEB)

FIDERKIEWICZ (ALFRED)

FIGL (LEOPOLD)

FIGUEREDO Y DIAZ (FELIX)

FIGUERES (JOSE)

FIGUERES (LEO)

FISCHER (ERNST)

FISHER (Sir NORMAN FENWICK WARREN)

FITZPATRICK (Sir PERCY)

FLEMING (AMALIA) Lady

FLICK (FRIEDRICH)

FOFANOV (TIMOFEI FEDOROVICH)

FORREST (JOHN) 1st Baron Forrest of Forret and Bunbury

FOSTER (WILLIAM ZEBULON)

FOURIER (FRANÇOIS CHARLES MARIE)

FOX (CHARLES JAMES)

FRANCO BAHAMONDE (FRANCISCO)

FRANK FAMILY

FRANKLIN (BENJAMIN)

FRANTSOV (GEORGII PAVLOVICH)

FREDERICA, Queen Consort of Paul I, King of the Hellenes

FREDERICK II, Emperor of Germany

FREGE (GOTTLOB)

FREI (BRUNO)

FREUD (SIGMUND)

FRIEDENSBURG (F.W. FERDINAND)

FRIEDMANN (GEORGES)

FRIGERIO (ROGELIO)

FRONDIZI (ARTURO)

FRUNZE (MIKHAIL VASIL'EVICH)

BIOGRAPHY (cont'd)

FRYE (NORTHROP)

FUGGER FAMILY

FULBRIGHT (JAMES WILLIAM)

FULLER (SARAH MARGARET) afterwards OSSOLI, Marquesa

GAITSKELL (HUGH TODD-NAYLOR)

GALANSKOV (IURII TIMOFEEVICH)

GALBRAITH (JOHN KENNETH)

GALIANI (FERDINANDO)

GAMBETTA (LÉON MICHEL)

GANDHI (MOHANDAS KARAMCHAND)

GANZ (ABRAHAM)

GAPON (GEORGII APOLLONOVICH)

GARAUDY (ROGER)

GARAY (MARTIN DE)

GARCIA (MIGUEL)

GARCIA LORCA (FEDERICO)

GARDINER (ALFRED GEORGE)

GARDNER (OLIVER MAX)

GASPERI (ALCIDE DE)

GAULLE (CHARLES DE)

GEFEN (ABA)

GEHLEN (REINHARD)

GEISMAR (ALAIN)

GENEEN (HAROLD SYDNEY)

GENTILE (GIOVANNI)

GEORGE III, King of Great Britain and Ireland

GEORGE IV., King of Great Britain and Ireland

GEORGE, of Podebrad, King of Bohemia

GEORGE (DAVID LLOYD) 1st Earl Lloyd George

GEORGE (WILLIAM REUBEN)

GEORGE FAMILY

GERHARDSEN (EINAR)

GERSTENMAIER (EUGEN)

GERTSEN (ALEKSANDR IVANOVICH)

GIBBON (EDWARD)

GILL (ARTHUR ERIC ROWTON)

GINI (CORRADO)

GINZBURG (ALEKSANDR IL'ICH)

GINZBURG (EVGENIIA SEMENOVNA)

GIOLITTI (GIOVANNI)

GIPPIUS (ZINAIDA NIKOLAEVNA)

GISCARD D'ESTAING (VALÉRY)

GLADSTONE (WILLIAM EWART)

GLAISE VON HORSTENAU (EDMUND)

GLAVINOV (VASIL)

GODWIN (MARY)

GODWIN (WILLIAM)

GOEBBELS (JOSEPH)

GOLDTHORPE (HARRY)

GOMPERS (SAMUEL)

GOMUŁKA (WŁADYSŁAW)

GOODMAN (PAUL)

GORBANEVSKAIA (NATAL'IA E.)

GOR'KII (MAKSIM) pseud.

GORTON (JOHN GREY)

GRĄDZKI (CZESŁAW)

GRAHAM (GERALD SANFORD)

GRAMSCI (ANTONIO)

GRASS (GUENTER)

GRAUNT (JOHN)

GREGORY FAMILY

GRGURIĆ (HRVOJE)

GRIFFITH (ARTHUR)

GROENER (WILHELM)

GROSER (ST. JOHN BEVERLEY)

GROSZ (GEORGE)

GROULX (LIONEL)

GRUNER (HEINRICH EDUARD)

GRZEDZIŃSKI (JANUARY)

GSCHWIND (STEFAN)

GUBER (ALEKSANDR ANDREEVICH)

GUENTHER (HANS F.K.)

GUEVARA (ERNESTO)

GUILLÉN (ABRAHAM)

GURIAN (WALDEMAR)

GURVICH (GEORGII DAVYDOVICH)

GUSEV (SERGEI IVANOVICH) pseud.

GUTT (CAMILLE)

GUYOTAT (PIERRE)

GUZMAN BLANCO (ANTONIO)

HABERMAS (JUERGEN)

HABSBURG FAMILY

HADDOW (WILLIAM MARTIN)

HAENEL (ALBERT)

HÄGGLÖF (GUNNAR)

HAGUE (FRANK)

HALE (CICELY B)

HALE (Sir MATTHEW)

HALES (HAROLD KEATES)

HAMILTON (ALEXANDER)

HAMILTON (Sir EDWARD WALTER)

HAMMARSKJÖLD (DAG)

HANIFAH (ABU)

HARDING (WARREN GAMALIEL) President of the United States

HARPER (ROBERT)

HARPER (ROBERT GOODLOE)

HARREL (Sir DAVID)

HARRIS (WILLIAM WADE)

HARROD (Sir HENRY ROY FORBES)

HATTA (MOHAMMAD)

HAVEMANN (ROBERT)

HAWKER (CHARLES ALLAN SEYMOUR)

HAWKRIDGE (CORNELIUS)

HAYA DE LA TORRE (VÍCTOR RAÚL)

HAYTER (TERESA)

HEADLAM-MORLEY (Sir JAMES WYCLIFFE)

HEALD (EDWARD T.)

HEATH (EDWARD RICHARD GEORGE)

HEBERLEIN-STAEHELIN (GEORGES)

HEGEL (GEORG WILHELM FRIEDRICH)

HEIDEGGER (MARTIN)

HEINEMANN (GUSTAV W.)

HELD (HEINRICH)

HELFFERICH (KARL)

HELSEY (EDOUARD)

HENDRICKS FAMILY

HENRY II., King of England

HENRY IV., King of England

HENRY V., King of England

HENRY VII., King of England

HENRY VIII, King of England

HENTIG (WERNER OTTO VON)

HERBERT (GEORGE) of Banbury

383

BIOGRAPHY (cont'd)

HERMES (ANDREAS)

HERTZOG (JAMES BARRY MUNNIK)

HEYDRICH (REINHARD)

HICKS (Sir JOHN RICHARD)

HILL (ARTHUR BLUNDELL SANDYS TRUMBULL) 3rd Marquess of Downshire

HIMES (CHESTER)

HIROHITO, Emperor of Japan

HITLER (ADOLF)

HO CHI MINH

HOAR (GEORGE FRISBIE)

HOBBES (THOMAS)

HOBHOUSE (EMILY)

HOBHOUSE (JOHN CAM) Baron Broughton

HOBHOUSE (LEONARD TRELAWNEY)

HOCKING (WILLIAM ERNEST)

HOELDERLIN (FRIEDRICH)

HOFFA (JAMES RIDDLE)

HOFFMANN-LA ROCHE (FRITZ)

HOHENZOLLERN FAMILY

HOMANS (GEORGE CASPAR)

HONECKER (ERICH)

HOOVER (HERBERT CLARK) President of the United States

HOPKINSON (JAMES)

HOPMAN (ALBERT)

HORTON (JAMES AFRICANUS BEALE)

HOSKINS (CHARLES HENRY)

HOSKINS FAMILY

HOUGHTON (HENRY F.)

HOUPHOUËT-BOIGNY (FELIX)

HOUSE (EDWARD MANDELL)

HOWE (JULIA WARD)

HOXHA (ENVER)

HUDSON (LIAM)

HUERTA (VICTORIANO)

HÜGEL (FRIEDRICH VON) Baron

HUGHES (CHARLES EVANS)

HUGHES (HOWARD ROBARD)

HUISH (MARK)

HUMBERT I., King of Italy

HUMBERT-DROZ (JULES)

HUMBOLDT (FRIEDRICH HEINRICH ALEXANDER VON) Baron

HUME (DAVID)

HUMPHREY, Duke of Gloucester

HURLEY (PATRICK JAY)

HUSÁK (GUSTÁV)

HUSSERL (EDMUND)

HUTCHESON (FRANCIS)

HUXLEY (Sir JULIAN SORELL)

HUYGENS (CHRISTIAAN)

IAKOVLEVA (VARVARA N.)

IDENBURG (ALEXANDER WILLEM FREDERIK)

IGNATIUS [LOPEZ DE RECALDE, de Loyola] Saint

IL'IN-ZHENEVSKII (ALEKSANDR FEDOROVICH)

INGENIEROS (JOSÉ)

INNIS (HAROLD ADAMS)

IORGA (NICOLAE)

IRIGOYEN (HIPÓLITO)

IRONSIDE (WILLIAM EDMUND) 1st Baron Ironside

IRVING (CLIFFORD)

ITURBIDE (AGUSTIN DE)

IUDENICH (NIKOLAI NIKOLAEVICH)

IVAN IV, Tsar of Russia

IVANOV (BORIS IVANOVICH)

JACKSON (ANDREW) President of the United States

JACKSON (GEORGE LESTER)

JACOB (BERTHOLD)

JACOBSEN (ERHARD)

JAHN (FRIEDRICH LUDWIG)

JAKOBSON (ROMAN)

JAMES I., King of Great Britain and Ireland

JAMES (ERIC JOHN FRANCIS) Baron James of Rusholme

JAMES (WILLIAM)

JASPERS (KARL)

JAURÈS (JEAN)

JAVOGUES (CLAUDE)

JEANNENEY (JULES)

JEBB (HUBERT MILES GLADWYN) 1st Baron Gladwyn

JEFFERSON (THOMAS) President of the United States

JEŁOWICKI (ALEKSANDER)

JEPSEN (FLORIAN)

JESUS CHRIST

JEVONS (WILLIAM STANLEY)

JOHN XXIII., Pope. (Angelo Giuseppe RONCALLI)

JOHN (OTTO)

JOHNSON (ANDREW) President of the United States

JOHNSON (EDGAR AUGUSTUS JEROME)

JOHNSON (LYNDON BAINES) President of the United States

JOHNSTON (Sir CHARLES HEPBURN)

JONES (CHARLES TENNANT)

JONES FAMILY

JOOS (JOSEPH)

JORDAN (RUDOLPH)

JORDON (EDWARD)

JOSEPH II, Emperor of Germany

JOVELLANOS Y RAMIREZ (GASPAR MELCHOR DE)

JUNG (CHARLES GUSTAVE)

JUSTO (JUAN BAUTISTA)

KALMYKOV (ANDREI DMITRIEVICH)

KANG BAN SOK

KANT (IMMANUEL)

KAPLAN (MORTON A.)

KARABCHEVSKII (NIKOLAI PLATONOVICH)

KARAMANLES (KONSTANTINOS)

KARAMZIN (NIKOLAI MIKHAILOVICH)

KAUNDA (KENNETH DAVID)

KAUTSKY (KARL)

KAZANIN (MARK ISAAKOVICH)

KEATS (JOHN)

KEDROV (MIKHAIL SERGEEVICH)

KEELING (WILLIAM)

KEKKONEN (URHO KALEVA)

KELLER (JOHANN JAKOB)

KELLER (OTTO)

KELLOGG (PAUL UNDERWOOD)

KENNEDY (JOHN FITZGERALD) President of the United States

KENNEDY (ROBERT FRANCIS)

KENNEDY (ROSE ELIZABETH FITZGERALD)

KENNEDY FAMILY

KENYATTA (JOMO)

KERLER FAMILY

KERN (ALFRED)

KEYNES (JOHN MAYNARD) 1st Baron Keynes

BIOGRAPHY (cont'd)

KHADZHIEV (RAZAK BEK)

KHALED (LEILA)

KHAN (KHAN ABDUL GHAFFAR)

KHODZHAEV (FAIZULLA)

KHRISTEV (ASEN)

KHRISTOV-VASKIN (VASIL)

KHRUSHCHEV (NIKITA SERGEEVICH)

KIERKEGAARD (SØREN AABYE)

KIM (IL-SUNG)

KING (CECIL HARMSWORTH)

KING (MARTIN LUTHER)

KINSEY (ALFRED CHARLES)

KIPPING (Sir NORMAN VICTOR)

KIREEVSKII (IVAN VASIL'EVICH)

KIROV (SERGEI MIRONOVICH)

KISELEV (IAKOV SEMENOVICH)

KISSINGER (HENRY ALFRED)

KLAUS (JOSEF)

KLIUCHEVSKII (VASILII OSIPOVICH)

KMIECIK (EDWARD)

KOCHETOV (VSEVOLOD ANISIMOVICH)

KOERBER (ERNEST VON)

KOHOUT (PAVEL)

KOLAKOWSKI (LESZEK)

KOLCHAK (ALEKSANDR VASIL'EVICH)

KOLLONTAI (ALEKSANDRA MIKHAILOVNA)

KOLTSOV (MIKHAIL)

KONOVALETS (IEVHEN)

KOPLENIG (JOHANN)

KORNILOV (LAVR GEORGIEVICH)

KOROLENKO (VLADIMIR GALAKTIONOVICH)

KOSOGOVSKII (VLADIMIR ANDREEVICH)

KOZLOV (NIKOLAI GRIGOR'EVICH)

KOZMIAN (KAJETAN)

KRAFT (OLE BJØRN)

KRAWCZYŃSKA (JADWIGA)

KREIDLER RIVERO (ALFONSO O.)

KREISKY (BRUNO)

KROPOTKIN (PETR ALEKSEEVICH) Prince

KRUGLOV (IVAN SERGEEVICH)

KRUPP FAMILY

KRUPSKAIA (NADEZHDA KONSTANTINOVNA)

KU (CHIEH-KANG)

KUNG (AI-LING)

KUROPIESKA (JÓZEF)

KUTCHER (JAMES)

KUTEPOV (ALEKSANDR PAVLOVICH)

LABADIE (JOSEPH A.)

LABOUCHERE (HENRY DU PRE)

LABRIOLA (ANTONIO)

LAFOLLETTE (PHILIP FOX)

LAING (RONALD DAVID)

LAMBTON (JOHN GEORGE) 1st Earl of Durham

LAMMASCH (HEINRICH)

LAMPSON (MILES WEDDERBURN) 1st Baron Killearn

LANDAUER (GUSTAV)

LANGHOFF (WOLFGANG)

LANUSSE (ALEJANDRO)

LAPORTE (PIERRE)

LASHKOVA (VERA IOSIFOVNA)

LASSALLE (FERDINAND JOHANN GOTTLIEB)

LATIMER (HUGH) Bishop of Worcester

LA TOUR D'AUVERGNE DE TURENNE (HENRI DE) Vicomte

LAVELEYE (EMILE DE) Baron

LAVROV (PETR LAVROVICH)

LAW (ANDREW BONAR)

LAX (WILLIAM HENRY)

LAZO (SERGEI GEORGIEVICH)

LEARY (TIMOTHY)

LEE (JENNIE) Baroness Lee of Asheridge

LEE (KUAN YEW)

LEE (RAYMOND ELIOT)

LEHMANN (THEODOR)

LEIBNIZ (GOTTFRIED WILHELM VON) Baron

LEICHTER (KAETHE)

LEMKE (MIKHAIL KONSTANTINOVICH)

LEMMER (ERNST)

LENIN (VLADIMIR IL'ICH)

LEON (LUIS DE)

LEONHARD (JAKOB)

LEONTIEF (WASSILY W.)

LEOPOLD II, King of the Belgians

LE PESANT (PIERRE) Sieur de Bois-Guillebert

LESOURNE (JACQUES F.)

LEVESON-GOWER FAMILY

LEVINÉ (EUGEN)

LÉVI-STRAUSS (CLAUDE)

LEVITOV (ALEKSANDR IVANOVICH)

LEVUS (IVAN OLEKSIIOVYCH)

LÉVY-BRUHL (LUCIEN)

LEWIS (WYNDHAM)

LIADOV (MARTYN NIKOLAEVICH) pseud.

LIEBKNECHT (KARL)

LIEBKNECHT (SOPHIE)

LIEBKNECHT (WILHELM PHILIPP MARTIN CHRISTIAN LUDWIG)

LILJE (HANNS)

LINCOLN (ABRAHAM) President of the United States

LINDBERGH (CHARLES AUGUSTUS)

LINDSAY (ALEXANDER DUNLOP) 1st Baron Lindsay

LINDT (RUDOLF)

LINNAEUS (CARL)

LINTON (RALPH)

LIPPMANN (WALTER)

LIPSET (SEYMOUR MARTIN)

LIST (GEORG FRIEDRICH)

LIU (SHAO-CHI)

LLEWELLYN (KARL NICKERSON)

LOCH (JAMES)

LOCK FAMILY

LOCKE (JOHN)

LODGE (HENRY CABOT) 1902-

LOMONOSOV (IURII VLADIMIROVICH)

LONDON (ARTUR)

LONDON (JACK) the Novelist

LOPEZ (AARON)

LOPEZ CONTRERAS (ELEAZAR)

LOPEZ MATEOS (ADOLFO)

LORENZ (KONRAD ZACHARIAS)

LORIMER (WILLIAM)

LOUIS XIV, King of France

LOUIS XVI, King of France

BIOGRAPHY (cont'd)

LOUIS XVII., King of France

LOW (DAVID) Bookseller

LOWIE (ROBERT HEINRICH)

LOYD (SAMUEL JONES) Baron Overstone

LUBBOCK (JOHN) 1st Baron Avebury

LUCAS (CHARLES) M.P.

LUETZOW (HEINRICH JOSEPH RUDOLF GOTTFRIED VON) Graf

LUKÁCS (GEORG)

LUMUMBA (PATRICE)

LUNACHARSKII (ANATOLII VASIL'EVICH)

LUNS (JOSEPH MARIE ANTOINE HUBERT)

LUTTRELL (NARCISSUS)

LUXEMBURG (ROSA)

L'VOV (GEORGII EVGEN'EVICH) Prince

LYTTON (EDWARD GEORGE EARLE LYTTON BULWER) Baron Lytton

MACARTNEY (Sir GEORGE)

MACAULAY (THOMAS BABINGTON) Baron Macaulay

MACCHIAVELLI (NICCOLÒ)

MACCURTAIN (TOMAS) Lord Mayor of Cork

MCGARRITY (JOSEPH)

McGOVERN (GEORGE STANLEY)

MACGREGOR (Sir WILLIAM)

MACH (ERNST)

MACHAJSKI (WACŁAW)

MACKENZIE (JOHN)

McKIE (BILL)

MACKINNON (Sir WILLIAM HENRY)

MACLEOD (IAIN NORMAN)

MACMILLAN (HAROLD)

McNAMARA (ROBERT STRANGE)

MACNEILL (EOIN)

McPHERSON (HARRY)

MADERO (FRANCISCO INDALECIO)

MAIAKOVSKII (VLADIMIR VLADIMIROVICH)

MAINE (Sir HENRY SUMNER)

MAISKII (IVAN MIKHAILOVICH)

MAITLAND (FREDERIC WILLIAM)

MAKHNO (NESTOR)

MAKIGUCHI (TSUNESABURO)

MALCOLM X, pseud.

MALKIN (MAURICE L.)

MALKUM KHAN (MIRZA)

MANDELA (NELSON ROLIHLAHLA)

MANLEY (NORMAN WASHINGTON)

MÅNSSON (KARL FABIAN)

MANTEUFFEL (ERNST CHRISTOPH VON) Graf.

MAO (TSE-TUNG)

MARAU TAAROA, Queen of Tahiti

MARCUSE (HERBERT)

MARGOLIN (ARNOLD DAVIDOVICH)

MARIÁTEGUI (JOSÉ CARLOS)

MARMONTEL (JEAN FRANÇOIS)

MARRIOTT (Sir JOHN ARTHUR RANSOME)

MARSHALL (ALFRED)

MARTENS (LIUDVIG KARLOVICH)

MARTÍ (JOSÉ)

MARWICK (Sir JAMES DAVID)

MARX (ELEANOR)

MARX (KARL)

MARX (WILHELM)

MARY I., Queen of England

MARY, Virgin

MASARYK (THOMAS GARRIGUE)

MASLOW (ABRAHAM HAROLD)

MASSU (JACQUES)

MATOVU (MICHAEL)

MATTEI (ENRICO)

MAURICE (JOHN FREDERICK DENISON)

MAURRAS (CHARLES MARIE PHOTIUS)

MAXIMILIAN, Emperor of Mexico

MEAD (GEORGE HERBERT)

MEANY (GEORGE)

MEDINA (ERNEST L.)

MEINECKE (FRIEDRICH)

MEIR (GOLDA)

MENDE (ERICH)

MENGER (CARL)

MERENSKY (HANS)

MERLEAU-PONTY (MAURICE)

MERTON (RICHARD)

MERTON (THOMAS)

MERZLIAKOV (ALEKSANDR FEDOROVICH)

METTERNICH-WINNEBURG (FRANZ GEORG KARL JOSEPH JOHANN NEPOMUCENUS) Graf.

MEWIS (KARL)

MICHELET (EDMOND)

MICHELS (ROBERT)

MIHAILOVIĆ (DRAŽA)

MIHAJLOV (MIHAJLO)

MIKOIAN (ANASTAS IVANOVICH)

MILHAUD (EDGARD)

MILL (JAMES)

MILL (JOHN STUART)

MILNER (ALFRED) 1st Viscount Milner

MILTON (JOHN)

MISÈFARI (BRUNO)

MISIANO (FRANCESCO)

MITTERRAND (FRANÇOIS)

MOELLER VAN DEN BRUCK (ARTUR)

MOHAMMAD (BAKHSHI GHULAM)

MOHAMMED, the Prophet

MOISÉS (ROSALIO)

MOLA Y VIDAL (EMILIO)

MOLTKE (HELMUTH JAMES VON) Graf

MONEY-KYRLE (ROGER ERNIE)

MONNET (JEAN)

MOORE (BARRINGTON)

MOORE (GILES)

MORDVINOV (NIKOLAI ALEKSANDROVICH)

MORE (Sir THOMAS) Saint

MOREAU (EDOUARD)

MORGAN (LEWIS HENRY)

MORIER (Sir ROBERT)

MORISON (STANLEY)

MORRIS (WILLIAM)

MORRISON (GEORGE ERNEST)

MORRISON (HERBERT STANLEY) Baron Morrison of Lambeth

MORTON FAMILY

MOSCA (GAETANO)

MOSS (ARTHUR B.)

MOTTA (GIUSEPPE)

MOUNIER (EMMANUEL)

MUELLER (HERMANN)

MUELLER-ARMACK (ALFRED)

BIOGRAPHY (cont'd)

MUGGERIDGE (MALCOLM)

MUHAMMAD IBN MUHAMMAD, al-Ghazzālī

MUMFORD (LEWIS)

MURRAY (HENRY ALEXANDER)

MURRAY (Sir JOHN HUBERT PLUNKETT)

MURRI (ROMOLO)

MUSSOLINI (BENITO)

MYRDAL (GUNNAR)

NABOKOV (VLADIMIR DMITRIEVICH)

NADEN (CONSTANCE CAROLINE WOODHILL)

NADER (RALPH)

NAŁKOWSKA (ZOFIA)

NAPOLÉON I, Emperor of the French

NAPOLÉON III, Emperor of the French

NASSER (GAMAL ABDEL)

NEARING (HELEN KOTHE)

NEARING (SCOTT)

NECHKINA (MILITSA VASIL'EVNA)

NEILL (ALEXANDER SUTHERLAND)

NENNI (PIETRO)

NERNST (WALTHER HERMANN)

NEWMAN (FRANCIS WILLIAM)

NEWTON (HUEY PIERCE)

NEWTON (Sir ISAAC)

NICHOLAS II., Emperor of Russia

NIEKISCH (ERNST)

NIELSEN (MARTIN)

NIESEWAND (PETER)

NIETZSCHE (FRIEDRICH WILHELM)

NIEUWENHUIS (FERDINAND DOMELA)

NIKITIN (B.V.)

NIN (ANDRÉS)

NIXON (RICHARD MILHOUS) President of the United States

NKRUMAH (KWAME)

NORODOM SIHANOUK VARMAN, Head of State of Cambodia

NORRIS (GEORGE WILLIAM)

NOVOZHILOV (VIKTOR VALENTINOVICH)

NYERERE (JULIUS KAMBARAGE)

OBNORSKII (VIKTOR PAVLOVICH)

OBREGON (ALVARO)

O'BRIEN (JAMES BRONTERRE)

OCCO (POMPEJUS)

OECHELHAUSER (WILHELM)

OETTINGEN (ALEXANDER VON)

OGDEN (PETER SKENE)

OLITSKAIA (EKATERINA L'VOVNA)

O'MALLEY (Sir OWEN ST. CLAIR)

O'NEILL (TERENCE MARNE) Baron O'Neill of the Maine

ONGANIA (JUAN CARLOS)

OPPENHEIMER (JULIUS ROBERT)

OPRECHT (EMIL)

OPRECHT (HANS)

ORLANDO (SALVATORE)

ORTEGA Y GASSET (JOSÉ)

ORWELL (GEORGE) pseud.

OSBORN (Sir FREDERIC JAMES)

OSSIETZKY (CARL VON)

OUANDIE (ERNEST)

OWEN (ROBERT)

OZANAM (ANTOINE FREDERIC)

PAASIKIVI (JUHO KUSTI)

PAINE (THOMAS)

PAISII, Ieromonakh

PALEOLOGUE (MAURICE)

PALLAVICINO TRIVULZIO (GIORGIO GUIDO) Marquis

PANAEV (IVAN IVANOVICH)

PANNEKOEK (ANTON)

PAPIN (DENIS)

PAQUET (ALFONS HERMANN)

PAREDES (ANTONIO)

PARETO (VILFREDO)

PARISH (FRANK)

PARISH (Sir WOODBINE)

PARSONS (TALCOTT)

PATINKIN (DON)

PATRICK, Saint

PAUL, Saint and Apostle

PAVLOV (DMITRII ALEKSANDROVICH)

PAYER (FRIEDRICH)

PAYNTER (WILL)

PEABODY (GEORGE)

PEARSON (DREW)

PEARSON (LESTER BOWLES)

PEÇANHA (NILO)

PECHEL (RUDOLF)

PECHMANN (WILHELM VON) Freiherr

PEEL (Sir ROBERT) 2nd Bart.

PELHAM-HOLLES (THOMAS) 1st Duke of Newcastle

PEREDA (JUAN NEPOMUCENO DE)

PEREDO (INTI)

PÉREZ JIMÉNEZ (MARCOS)

PEREZ LOPEZ (FRANCISCO)

PÉRI (GABRIEL)

PERÓN (JUAN DOMINGO)

PERRIN (JEAN)

PESHEKHONOV (ALEKSEI VASIL'EVICH)

PESTEL' (PAVEL IVANOVICH)

PÉTAIN (HENRI PHILIPPE BÉNONI OMER JOSEPH)

PETERSEN (HANS CHRISTIAN)

PETITOT (EMILE)

PETLIURA (SEMEN)

PETROV (GRIGORII SEMENOVICH)

PETRUSHEVSKII (DMITRII MOISEEVICH)

PETTY (Sir WILLIAM)

PFEIFFER (MAX)

PHEAR (Sir JOHN BUDD)

PIATAKOV (GEORGII LEONIDOVICH)

PIECUCH (KONRAD)

PIJADE (MOŠA)

PINELLI (GIUSEPPE)

PISEMSKII (ALEKSEI FEOFILAKTOVICH)

PITHOYS (CLAUDE)

PLAATJE (SOLOMON TSHEKISHO)

PLACE (FRANCIS)

PLATO

PLATT (ROBERT) Baron Platt

PLEKHANOV (GEORGII VALENTINOVICH)

PLIESEIS (SEPP)

PLUNKETT (Sir HORACE CURZON)

PODVOISKII (NIKOLAI IL'ICH)

POLLITT (HARRY)

POLOVTSOV (PETR A.)

POMPIDOU (GEORGES)

BIOGRAPHY (cont'd)

PONSONBY (ARTHUR AUGUSTUS WILLIAM HARRY) 1st BARON PONSONBY
POOLEY (THOMAS)
POPITZ (HERMANN EDUARD JOHANNES)
POPOV (ALEKSANDR STEPANOVICH)
POPOV (IVAN VASIL'EVICH)
POPPER (Sir KARL RAIMUND)
POSTEL (GUILLAUME)
POTRESOV (ALEKSANDR NIKOLAEVICH)
POUNTNEY (ERNIE)
POUTRE (FELIX)
POWELL (ADAM CLAYTON)
POWER (EILEEN EDNA LE POER)
POWNALL (Sir HENRY ROYDS)
PRADO (EDUARDO DE SILVA)
PRADO UGARTECHE (MANUEL)
PRAED (WILLIAM MACKWORTH)
PRAT DE LA RIBA Y SARRÁ (ENRIQUE)
PREBISCH (RAUL)
PREYSING (KONRAD VON) Graf, Cardinal
PREZZOLINI (GIUSEPPE)
PRICOLO (FRANCESCO)
PRIETO LAURENS (JORGE)
PRONIN (V.M.)
PROUDHON (PIERRE JOSEPH)
PUFENDORF (SAMUEL VON) Baron
PUSTA (KAAREL ROBERT)
PUTIATINA (OL'GA EVGEN'EVNA) Grafinia
PYKHACHEVA (V.D.)
QUARRIER (WILLIAM)
QUESNAY (FRANÇOIS)
QUETELET (LAMBERT ADOLPHE JACQUES)
QUINTANA (MANUEL JOSÉ)
RADCLIFFE-BROWN (ALFRED REGINALD)
RADEK (KARL)
RADIC (STJEPAN)
RAHMAN (MUJIBUR)
RAIFFEISEN (FRIEDRICH WILHELM)
RAIKES (ROBERT)
RAPP (JOHANN GEORG)
RASKOL'NIKOV (FEDOR FEDOROVICH IL'IN-)
RAUSCHNING (HERMANN)

RAY (JAMES EARL)
REED (JOHN)
REEVES (RICHARD AMBROSE) Bishop of Johannesburg
REEVES (WILLIAM PEMBER)
REHBERG (AUGUST WILHELM)
REICH (WILHELM)
REITH (JOHN CHARLES WALSHAM) 1st Baron Reith
RENAUDOT (THÉOPHRASTE)
RENNELL (THOMAS)
RENNER (KARL)
RETINGER (JOSEPH HIERONIM)
REUBELL (JEAN FRANÇOIS)
REUTER (ERNST)
REUTHER (WALTER PHILIP)
RHODES (CECIL JOHN)
RICARDO (DAVID)
RICASOLI (BETTINO) Barone
RICHARD II., King of England
RICHMOND (AL)
RIDLEY (NICHOLAS) successively Bishop of Rochester and of London
RIEZLER (KURT)
ROBENS (ALFRED) Baron Robens of Woldingham
ROBERT DE LA MENNAIS (HUGUES FÉLICITÉ)
ROBESPIERRE (FRANÇOIS MAXIMILIEN JOSEPH ISIDORE)
ROBINSON (JOAN)
RODBERTUS-JAGETZOW (CARL)
RODRIGUEZ DE FRANCIA (JOSE GASPAR)
ROEBLING FAMILY
ROEHM (ERNST)
ROEPKE (WILHELM)
ROGERS (JAMES EDWIN THOROLD)
ROHEIM (GEZA)
ROHRBACH (PAUL)
ROJAS (PEDRO JOSE)
ROLLAND (ROMAIN)
ROMANOV (BORIS ALEKSANDROVICH)
ROOSEVELT (ANNA ELEANOR)
ROOSEVELT (FRANKLIN DELANO) President of the United States
ROSAS (JUAN MANUEL DE)

ROSENBERG (ALFRED)
ROSMER (ALFRED)
ROSMINI SERBATI (ANTONIO)
ROSSI (ALESSANDRO)
ROSTOW (WALT WHITMAN)
ROUSSEAU (JEAN JACQUES)
ROY (MANABENDRA NATH)
ROYCE (JOSIAH)
ROZANSKI (ZENON)
RUPPIN (ARTHUR)
RUSH (BENJAMIN)
RUSSELL (BERTRAND ARTHUR WILLIAM) 3rd Earl Russell
RUSSELL (ELIZABETH ANNE) Lady William Russell
RUSSELL (JOHN) 1st Earl Russell
RUSSELL (Lord WILLIAM)
SABREVOIS DE BLEURY (CLEMENT CHARLES)
SACCO (NICOLA)
SADE (DONATIEN ALPHONSE FRANÇOIS DE) Marquis
SALAN (RAOUL)
SALAZAR (ANTONIO DE OLIVEIRA)
SALCEDO (MANUEL MARIA DE)
SALOMON (WALTER HANS)
SAMUELSON (PAUL ANTHONY)
SANCHEZ CERRO (LUIS MIGUEL) President of Peru
SANCTIS (FRANCESCO DE)
SANDINO (AUGUSTO CÉSAR)
SARAGAT (GIUSEPPE)
SARKISOV (GRIGORII KHOSROVOVICH)
SARTRE (JEAN PAUL)
SAUCKE (KURT)
SAVINKOV (BORIS VIKTOROVICH)
SAY (JEAN BAPTISTE)
SCAVENIUS (ERIK)
SCHACHT (HORACE GREELEY HJALM
SCHEIDEMANN (PHILIPP)
SCHELER (MAX FERDINAND)
SCHELLING (FRIEDRICH WILHELM JOSEPH VO
SCHEU (FRIEDRICH)
SCHEURER (KARL)
SCHICK (ALLEN)
SCHINCKEL (MAXMILIAN HEINRICH VON)

BIOGRAPHY (cont'd)

SCHLEIERMACHER (FRIEDRICH DANIEL ERNST)

SCHMITT (CARL)

SCHNITZER (EDUARD) called Emin, Pasha

SCHOBER (JOHANNES)

SCHOENLANK (BRUNO)

SCHUECKING (WALTHER)

SCHUMACHER (KURT)

SCHUMAN (ROBERT)

SCHWEITZER (ALBERT)

ŚCIEGIENNY (PIOTR)

SCOTT (KATHERINE GRACE HEPBURNE)

SECONDAT (CHARLES LOUIS DE) Baron de Montesquieu

SEDAR SENGHOR (LEOPOLD)

SEDIN (MITROFAN KARPOVICH)

SEDOVA (NATAL'IA IVANOVNA)

SEIPEL (IGNAZ)

SELEME VARGAS (ANTONIO)

SELEZNEV (ARKHIP ANDREEVICH)

SENIOR (THOMAS GEORGE)

SERGEEV (FEDOR ANDREEVICH)

SERGENT (PIERRE)

SERVAN-SCHREIBER (JEAN JACQUES)

SETALVAD (MOTILAL CHIMANLAL)

SEYSS-INQUART (ARTHUR)

SEYSSEL (CLAUDE DE) Successively Bishop of Marseilles and Archbishop of Turin

SHAKHOVSKOI (VSEVOLOD NIKOLAEVICH) Prince

SHAUMIAN (STEPAN GEORGIEVICH)

SHAW (GEORGE BERNARD)

SHELEST (PETR EFIMOVICH)

SHINWELL (EMANUEL) Baron Shinwell

SHOTMAN (ALEKSANDR VASIL'EVICH)

SIEGMUND-SCHULTZE (FRIEDRICH)

ŠIK (OTA)

SIMKHOVITCH (MARY KINGSBURY)

SIMMEL (GEORG)

SIMON (JOHN ALLSEBROOK) 1st Viscount Simon

SIMONDE DE SISMONDI (JEAN CHARLES LEONARD)

SIMPSON (EDWARD) Unitarian

SIMPSON (Sir GEORGE)

SIMPSON (RICHARD)

SKINNER (BURRHUS FREDERIC)

SKOVORODA (HRYHORII SAVYCH)

SKVORTSOV-STEPANOV (IVAN IVANOVICH)

SLÁNSKÝ (RUDOLF)

SLASHCHEV-KRYMSKII (IAKOV ALEKSANDROVICH)

SLAVICH (VALERIAN VECHESLAVOVICH)

SLEPTSOV (VASILII ALEKSEEVICH)

SMIRNOV (DMITRII MIKHAILOVICH)

SMIT (ERASMUS)

SMITH (ADAM)

SNOW (CHARLES PERCY) Baron Snow

SOLARI (GIOELE)

SOLARI (LUIGI)

SOLOMON (GEORGII ALEKSANDROVICH)

SOLOMON (SAUL)

SOLOV'EV (VLADIMIR SERGEEVICH)

SOLZHENITSYN (ALEKSANDR ISAEVICH)

SONCINO FAMILY

SOREL (GEORGES)

SØRENSEN (POUL)

SOYINKA (WOLE)

SPANN (OTHMAR)

SPAVENTA (SILVIO)

SPENCE (THOMAS) Bookseller

SPIEKER (JOSEF)

SPINOZA (BENEDICTUS DE)

SPRETI (KARL VON) Graf

SPRINGER (AXEL)

SPRUENGLI-AMMANN (RUDOLF)

SPRUENGLI-BAUD (DAVID ROBERT)

SPRUENGLI-SCHIFFERLI (RUDOLF)

SRAFFA (PIERO)

STAEMPFLI (PAUL)

STAJIĆ (VASA)

STALIN (IOSIF VISSARIONOVICH)

STANLEY (Sir HENRY MORTON)

STARČEVIĆ (ANTE)

STARHEMBERG (ERNST RUEDIGER) Prince

STARSKY (MORRIS)

STEAD (WILLIAM THOMAS)

STEYN (MARTHINUS THEUNIS).

STILWELL (JOSEPH WARREN)

STOECKER (ADOLF)

STOKES (CARL BURTON)

STOLYPIN (PETR ARKAD'EVICH)

STRACHEY (EVELYN JOHN ST. LOE)

STREICHER (JULIUS)

STRESEMANN (GUSTAV)

STUBBE (HENRY)

STURZO (LUIGI)

SUGATHADASA (V. A.)

SUKARNO, President of Indonesia

SUKHE-BATOR (DAMDINY)

SUKIENNICKI (WIKTOR)

SUMNER (CHARLES)

SUN (CHING-LING)

SUNG (CHIAO-JEN)

SUNG FAMILY

SUTTNER (BERTHA FELICIE SOPHIE VON) Freifrau

SUVORIN (ALEKSEI SERGEEVICH)

SVERDLOV (IAKOV MIKHAILOVICH)

SVOBODA (LUDVÍK)

SWEENY (CHARLES)

SWING (PHILIP DAVID)

TAGANTSEV (NIKOLAI STEPANOVICH)

TAGORE (Sir RABINDRANATH)

TALLEYRAND-PERIGORD (CHARLES MAURICE DE) Prince

TANDON (PRAKASH)

TARLE (EVGENII VIKTOROVICH)

TARRY (ELLEN)

TAWNEY (RICHARD HENRY)

TAYLER (WILLIAM)

TAYLOR (HARRY BERNARD) Baron Taylor of Mansfield

TAYLOR (JOHN) Publisher

TEMPLE (HENRY JOHN) 3rd Viscount Palmerston

TENNERY (THOMAS DOUTHIT)

TENNYSON (ALFRED) 1st Baron Tennyson

TER-PETROSIAN (SIMON ARSHAKOVICH) called KAMO

THAELMANN (ERNST)

THEODŌRAKIS (MIKES)

THIRION (ANDRE)

THOMAS, Aquinas, Saint

THOREZ (MAURICE)

BIOGRAPHY (cont'd)

THURNEYSEN (JOHANN JAKOB)

TIJERINA (REIES)

TILLICH (PAUL JOHANNES OSKAR)

TILLON (CHARLES)

TIRPITZ (ALFRED VON)

TITO (JOSIP BROZ)

TODD (JUDITH)

TOENNIES (FERDINAND)

TOGLIATTI (PALMIRO)

TOLMER (ALEXANDER)

TOLSTOI (LEV NIKOLAEVICH) Graf

TOMILIN (SERGEI ARKAD'EVICH)

TOOKE (THOMAS)

TORRE (LISANDRO DE LA)

TORRES BODET (JAIME)

TORRES RESTREPO (CAMILO)

TORRIENTE Y BRAU (PABLO FELIX ALEJANDRO SALVADOR DE LA)

TOYNBEE (ARNOLD JOSEPH)

TREUTLER (KARL GEORG VON)

TREVELYAN (Sir CHARLES EDWARD)

TREVELYAN (HUMPHREY) Baron Trevelyan

TROFIMENKO (GRIGORII)

TROTSKII (LEV DAVYDOVICH)

TRUDEAU (PIERRE ELLIOTT)

TRUJILLO MOLINA (RAFAEL LEONIDAS)

TRUMAN (HARRY S.) President of the United States

TSENG (KUO-FAN)

TUBMAN (WILLIAM VACANARAT SHADRACH)

TURCIOS LIMA (LUIS AUGUSTO)

TURGENEV (NIKOLAI IVANOVICH)

TURNER (NAT)

TWINING (EDWARD FRANCIS) Baron Twining

TYLER (JOHN) President of the United States

UL'IANOV (ALEKSANDR IL'ICH)

UL'IANOV (IL'IA NIKOLAEVICH)

UL'IANOVA (MARIIA IL'INICHNA)

UNWIN (THOMAS FISHER)

UNWIN FAMILY

USPENSKII (NIKOLAI VASIL'EVICH)

USTINOV (S. M.)

VAKHITOV (MULLANUR MULLAZIANOVICH)

VALIKHANOV (CHOKAN CHINGISOVICH)

VALLESE (FELIPE)

VALLIERES (PIERRE)

VANDERVELDE (EMILE)

VANZETTI (BARTOLOMEO)

VARELA (FELIPE)

VARGAS (GETÚLIO)

VARSHER (TATIANA S.)

VASIL'CHIKOV (ALEKSANDR ILLARIONOVICH) Prince

VASTO (LANZA DEL)

VAUGHAN (HENRY HALFORD)

VAZQUEZ COBO CARRIZOSA (CAMILO)

VECKINCHUSEN (HILDEBRAND)

VELICHKINA (VERA MIKHAILOVNA)

VERNE (JULES)

VETLUGIN (A.) pseud.

VICO (GIAMBATTISTA)

VICTORIA, Queen of Great Britain and Ireland

VIERECK (GEORGE SYLVESTER)

VILLA (FRANCISCO)

VINOGRADOFF (Sir PAUL)

VISHNIAKOVA-AKIMOVA (VERA VLADIMIROVNA)

VITTE (SERGEI IUL'EVICH) Graf

VIVEKANANDA, Swami, pseud.

VIVIEN DE GOUBERT (ALEXANDRE FRANÇOIS AUGUSTE)

VLADIMIR I., Saint, Grand Duke of Kiev

VLASOV (ANDREI ANDREEVICH)

VO NGUYEN GIAP

VOLTAIRE (FRANÇOIS MARIE AROUET DE)

VON NEUMANN (JOHN)

VOZNESENSKII (NIKOLAI ALEKSEEVICH)

VRANGEL' (LIUDMILA S.) Baronessa

VRANGEL' (PETR NIKOLAEVICH) Baron

WALDECK (BENEDIKT FRANZ LEO)

WALLACE (HENRY AGARD)

WALLENBERG (RAOUL)

WALLENSTEIN (ALBRECHT WENZEL EUSEBIUS VON) Herzog von Friedland

WALLISCH (KOLOMAN)

WALRAS (LEON)

WANG (CHIEH)

WANG (CHING-WEI)

WARBURG (FREDRIC J.)

WARTENWEILER (FRITZ)

WASHINGTON (BOOKER TALIAFERRO)

WASHINGTON (GEORGE) President of the United States

WATSON (AARON)

WATSON (DAVID)

WATSON (JAMES)

WATT (Sir ALAN STEWART)

WAVELL (ARCHIBALD PERCIVAL) 1st Earl Wavell

WEBB (BEATRICE)

WEBB (SIDNEY) 1st Baron Passfield

WEBER (MAX)

WEBSTER (DANIEL)

WEHBERG (HANS)

WEISGAL (MEYER WOLFE)

WEISS (LOUISE)

WEISSBERG (ALEX)

WEIT (ERWIN)

WELLESLEY (ARTHUR) 1st Duke of Wellington

WELLS (HERBERT GEORGE)

WELTI (FRIEDRICH EMIL)

WENTWORTH FAMILY

WESEMANN (HANS)

WHITE (HORACE) 1834-1916

WHITE (JOHN CAMPBELL) Baron Overtoun

WHITMAN (WALT)

WHITSON (JOHN)

WICKSELL (JOHAN GUSTAF KNUT)

WIGG (GEORGE EDWARD CECIL) Baron Wigg

WILBERFORCE (SAMUEL) Successively Bishop of Oxford and of Winchester

WILLERT (Sir ARTHUR)

WILLIAM II, Emperor of Germany

WILLIAM IV., King of Great Britain and Ireland

WILLIAMS (ALBERT RHYS)

WILLIAMS (Sir GEORGE)

WILLIAMS (MARCIA)

WILSON (HAROLD)

WILSON (THOMAS WOODROW) President of the United States

WINGATE (ORDE CHARLES)

WINNACKER (KARL)

WITTGENSTEIN (LUDWIG)

390

BIOGRAPHY (cont'd)

WODZICKI (ROMAN)

WOHLGEMUTH (AUGUST)

WONG (CHIN-FOO)

WOOD (LEONARD)

WRIGHT (FRANCES)

YAMAGATA (ARITOMO)

YEATS (WILLIAM BUTLER)

YGLESIAS CASTRO (RAFAEL) President of Costa Rica

YUAN (SHIH-K'AI)

ZALOMOV (PETR ANDREEVICH)

ZAWADZKA-WETZ (ALICJA)

ZEHRER (HANS)

ZELIKSON-BOBROVSKAIA (TSETSILIIA SAMOILOVNA)

ZERNATTO (GUIDO)

ZEROMSKI (STEFAN)

ZHIVKOV (TODOR)

ZHLOBA (DMITRII PETROVICH)

ZHUKEEV (TAVALDY)

ZHUKOV (GEORGII KONSTANTINOVICH)

ZINOV'EV (GRIGORII EVSEEVICH)

ZIPF (GEORGE KINGSLEY)

ZLATOVRATSKII (NIKOLAI NIKOLAEVICH)

ZOLA (ÉMILE ÉDOUARD CHARLES ANTOINE)

ZUMAN (FRANTIŠEK)

COMMERCE AND INDUSTRY

General

ACCOUNTING

ACCOUNTING AND PRICE FLUCTUATIONS

ADVERTISING

APPLICATIONS FOR POSITIONS

APPRENTICES

ARBITRATION, INDUSTRIAL

AUDITING

BALANCE OF TRADE

BIG BUSINESS

BOOKKEEPING

BRAIN DRAIN

BUDGET IN BUSINESS

BUSINESS

BUSINESS AND POLITICS

BUSINESS CYCLES

BUSINESS EDUCATION

BUSINESS ETHICS

BUSINESS FORECASTING

BUSINESS INTELLIGENCE

BUSINESS NAMES

BUSINESS RECORDS

BUYING

CENTRAL AMERICAN COMMON MARKET

CENTRAL BUSINESS DISTRICTS

CHAIN STORES, VOLUNTARY

CHAMBERS OF COMMERCE

CHURCH AND INDUSTRY

COLONIAL COMPANIES

COMMERCE

COMMERCIAL ASSOCIATIONS

COMMERCIAL COURTS

COMMERCIAL DOCUMENTS

COMMERCIAL FINANCE COMPANIES

COMMERCIAL POLICY

COMMERCIAL PRODUCTS

COMMODITY CONTROL

COMMODITY EXCHANGES

COMMUNICATION IN MANAGEMENT

COMPANY TOWNS

CONSOLIDATION AND MERGER OF CORPORATIONS

CONSUMER PROTECTION

CONSUMERS

CONTRACTS

CONTRACTS, LETTING OF

COOPERATION

COOPERATIVE MARKETING OF FARM PRODUCE

COOPERATIVE SOCIETIES

CORPORATION REPORTS

CORPORATIONS

CORPORATIONS, AMERICAN

CORPORATIONS, BRITISH

CORPORATIONS, FOREIGN

CORPORATIONS, GOVERNMENT

CORPORATIONS, INTERNATIONAL

CORPORATIONS, PUBLIC

CORPORATIONS, SWEDISH

CORPORATIONS, SWISS

DANGEROUS GOODS

DEFENCE CONTRACTS

DEPRECIATION

DESIGN, INDUSTRIAL

DISCOUNT HOUSES (RETAIL TRADE)

DUMPING (COMMERCIAL POLICY)

DURABLE GOODS, CONSUMER

EAST-WEST TRADE (1945-

EFFICIENCY, INDUSTRIAL

EMPLOYEE OWNERSHIP

EMPLOYEES, DISMISSAL OF

EMPLOYEES, RATING OF

EMPLOYEES, REINSTATEMENT OF

EMPLOYEES, RELOCATION OF

EMPLOYEES, SUSPENSION OF

EMPLOYEES, TRAINING OF

EMPLOYEES' REPRESENTATION IN MANAGEMENT

EMPLOYERS' ASSOCIATIONS

EMPLOYMENT AGENCIES

EMPLOYMENT FORECASTING

EMPLOYMENT INTERVIEWING

EMPLOYMENT MANAGEMENT

ENVIRONMENTAL ENGINEERING

EUROPEAN COAL AND STEEL COMMUNITY

EUROPEAN ECONOMIC COMMUNITY

EUROPEAN FREE TRADE ASSOCIATION

EXECUTIVES, TRAINING OF

EXPORT CREDIT

EXPORT MARKETING

EXPORT SALES

COMMERCE AND INDUSTRY (cont'd)

FACTORIES	INTERNATIONAL CHAMBER OF COMMERCE	PERFORMANCE STANDARDS
FACTORY INSPECTION	INTERNATIONAL SUGAR ORGANIZATION	POSTERS
FACTORY MANAGEMENT	INTERSTATE COMMERCE	POWER RESOURCES
FACTORY SYSTEM	INVENTIONS	PRIORITIES, INDUSTRIAL
FIRMS	INVENTIONS, EMPLOYEES'	PRODUCT MANAGEMENT
FOOD PRICES	INVENTORIES, RETAIL	PRODUCTION CONTROL
FOREIGN TRADE PROMOTION	INVENTORY CONTROL	PRODUCTION MANAGEMENT
FOREIGN TRADE REGULATION	JOINT ADVENTURES	PRODUCTION PLANNING
FRANCHISES (RETAIL TRADE)	JOURNALISM, COMMERCIAL	PRODUCTIVITY
FUEL	LAND COMPANIES	PROFESSIONS
GENERAL STORES	LATIN AMERICAN FREE TRADE ASSOCIATION	PSYCHOLOGY, INDUSTRIAL
GOVERNMENT BUSINESS ENTERPRISES		PUBLIC CONTRACTS
GOVERNMENT MONOPOLIES	LICENCES	PUBLIC SERVICE
GOVERNMENT OWNERSHIP	MACHINERY IN INDUSTRY	PUBLIC UTILITIES
HANDICRAFT	MAIL ORDER BUSINESS	QUALITY CONTROL
IMPERIAL PREFERENCE	MANAGEMENT	RAW MATERIALS
IMPORT QUOTAS	MANAGEMENT GAMES	REBATES
INCENTIVES IN INDUSTRY	MANAGEMENT INFORMATION SYSTEMS	RECRUITING OF EMPLOYEES
INDUSTRIAL ACCIDENTS	MAN-MACHINE SYSTEMS	RESEARCH, INDUSTRIAL
INDUSTRIAL CAPACITY	MANUFACTURERS' RETAIL OUTLETS	RESEARCH AND DEVELOPMENT CONTRACTS
INDUSTRIAL DISTRICTS	MANUFACTURES	RETAIL TRADE
INDUSTRIAL EQUIPMENT	MARKET SURVEYS	SAFETY EDUCATION, INDUSTRIAL
INDUSTRIAL HYGIENE	MARKETING	SERVICE INDUSTRIES
INDUSTRIAL MANAGEMENT	MARKETING MANAGEMENT	SHOPPING
INDUSTRIAL MUSEUMS	MARKETING RESEARCH	SHOPPING CENTRES
INDUSTRIAL NOISE	MARKETS	SHOPPING HOURS
INDUSTRIAL ORGANIZATION	MARKS OF ORIGIN	SHOPPING MALLS
INDUSTRIAL PROCUREMENT	MATERIALS MANAGEMENT	SMALL BUSINESS
INDUSTRIAL PROJECT MANAGEMENT	MECHANICS' INSTITUTES	STANDARDIZATION
INDUSTRIAL PROMOTION	MEDICINE, INDUSTRIAL	STORE LOCATION
INDUSTRIAL PROPERTY	METHODS ENGINEERING	STORES, RETAIL
INDUSTRIAL RELATIONS	METRIC SYSTEM	SUBSIDIARY CORPORATIONS
INDUSTRIAL SAFETY	MILLS AND MILL WORK	SUBSTITUTE PRODUCTS
INDUSTRIAL STATISTICS	MINE INSPECTION	SUPERMARKETS
INDUSTRIAL SURVEYS	NEUTRAL TRADE WITH BELLIGERENTS	SUPERVISION OF EMPLOYEES
INDUSTRIALIZATION	NEW BUSINESS ENTERPRISES	TECHNICIANS IN INDUSTRY
INDUSTRIES, LOCATION OF	NEW PRODUCTS	TIME AND MOTION STUDY
INDUSTRIES, SIZE OF	OCCUPATIONS	TRADE-MARKS
INDUSTRY	OFFICE BUILDINGS	TRADE REGULATION
INDUSTRY AND EDUCATION	OFFICE EQUIPMENT AND SUPPLIES	UNITED NATIONS CONFERENCE ON TRADE AND DEVELOPMENT
INDUSTRY AND STATE	OFFICE PRACTICE	
INFORMATION THEORY IN MANAGEMENT	OFFICES	UNITED NATIONS INDUSTRIAL DEVELOPMENT ORGANIZATION
INSTALMENT PLAN	ORGANIZATION	
INTERINDUSTRY ECONOMICS	ORGANIZATION OF THE PETROLEUM EXPORTING COUNTRIES	VALUE ANALYSIS (COST CONTROL)
INTERNATIONAL BUSINESS ENTERPRISES		VOCATIONAL GUIDANCE
	PATENTS	VOCATIONAL INTERESTS

COMMERCE AND INDUSTRY (cont'd)

WAREHOUSES
WATER-POWER ELECTRIC PLANTS
WATER-SUPPLY, INDUSTRIAL
WELFARE WORK IN INDUSTRY
WHOLESALE TRADE
WOMEN IN COOPERATIVE SOCIETIES
WORK MEASUREMENT
WORKMEN'S COMPENSATION

Occupations and professions

ACCOUNTANTS
AEROPLANE INDUSTRY WORKERS
AGRICULTURAL LABOURERS
AGRICULTURAL LABOURERS, ITALIAN
AGRICULTURAL LABOURERS, MEXICAN
AIR PILOTS
AMBASSADORS
ANTHROPOLOGISTS
ANTHROPOLOGISTS, WHITE RUSSIAN
ARCHITECTS
ARTISANS
AUTOMOBILE INDUSTRY WORKERS
BANK EMPLOYEES
BANKERS
BOOKSELLERS AND BOOKSELLING
BUSINESSMEN
BUSINESSMEN, BRITISH
CABINET WORKERS
CAPITALISTS AND FINANCIERS
CHEMICAL WORKERS
CHEMISTS
CITY PLANNERS
CIVIL ENGINEERS
CLERKS
CLOCK AND WATCH MAKERS
CLOTHING WORKERS
COAL MINERS
CONSTRUCTION WORKERS
CONSULTING ENGINEERS
COOKERY AS A PROFESSION
COPPER MINERS
DENTAL ASSISTANTS

DENTAL TECHNICIANS
DENTISTS
DIPLOMATS, AUSTRALIAN
DIPLOMATS, BRITISH
DIPLOMATS, FRENCH
DIPLOMATS, RUSSIAN
DIPLOMATS, SWEDISH
DIRECTORS OF CORPORATIONS
DOCK WORKERS
ECONOMISTS
EDUCATORS, KAZAK
ELECTRIC INDUSTRY WORKERS
ELECTRICIANS
ELECTRONIC DATA PROCESSING PERSONNEL
ELECTRONIC INDUSTRY WORKERS
ENGINEERS
ENTERTAINERS
EXECUTIVES
FIREMEN
FISHERMEN
FORESTERS
FORWARDING MERCHANTS
FOUNDRYMEN
FRONTIER WORKERS
GLASS WORKERS
GOLD MINERS
HATTERS
HEALTH OFFICERS
HORSEMEN
HOSPITAL ADMINISTRATORS
IRON AND STEEL WORKERS
JOURNALISTS
JUDGES
LAWYERS
LIBRARIANS
MEDICAL PERSONNEL
MEN NURSES
MERCHANTS
MERCHANTS, AMERICAN
MERCHANTS, BRITISH
MERCHANTS, FOREIGN
MERCHANTS, FRENCH
MERCHANTS, GERMAN
MERCHANTS, MOROCCAN

METAL-WORKERS
MINERS
MINING ENGINEERS
MISSIONARIES, AMERICAN
MOTOR BUS DRIVERS
MOVING PICTURE ACTORS AND ACTRESSES
NEGRO PHYSICIANS
NEGROES AS BUSINESSMEN
PAINTERS, INDUSTRIAL
PETROLEUM WORKERS
PHARMACISTS
PHYSICIANS
PHYSICISTS
PRINTERS
PSYCHOLOGISTS
PUBLIC HEALTH PERSONNEL
RAILWAY CONSTRUCTION WORKERS
ROAD TRANSPORT WORKERS
SCIENCE AS A PROFESSION
SCIENCE TEACHERS
SEAMEN
SHIPBUILDING WORKERS
SHOEMAKERS
SHOP ASSISTANTS
SOCIAL WORK AS A PROFESSION
SOCIOLOGISTS
STONE CUTTERS
SUGAR WORKERS
SURVEYORS
TEACHERS
TEACHING AS A PROFESSION
TEXTILE WORKERS
TRAFFIC POLICE
TRANSPORT WORKERS
WEAVERS
WOMEN AS ARTISTS
WOMEN AS AUTHORS
WOMEN AS BANKERS
WOMEN AS FARMERS
WOMEN IN BUSINESS

COMMERCE AND INDUSTRY (cont'd)

Particular trades and industries

AEROPLANE INDUSTRY AND TRADE
AEROSPACE INDUSTRIES
AGGREGATES (BUILDING MATERIALS)
ALCOHOL
ALUMINIUM INDUSTRY AND TRADE
ART INDUSTRIES AND TRADE
ASBESTOS
ATOMIC ENERGY INDUSTRIES
ATOMIC POWER INDUSTRY
AUTOMOBILE INDUSTRY AND TRADE
BAKED PRODUCTS
BAKERS AND BAKERIES
BALL BEARINGS
BANANA TRADE
BANDAGES AND BANDAGING
BASKET MAKING
BEDDING
BICYCLE INDUSTRY
BISCUITS
BITUMEN
BOOK INDUSTRIES AND TRADE
BOOKBINDING
BOOKBINDING MACHINERY
BOOKSELLERS AND BOOKSELLING
BOOTS AND SHOES
BRANDY
BRASS INDUSTRY AND TRADE
BREAD
BREWING INDUSTRIES
BRICK TRADE
BRICKMAKING
BRIDGES
BRIDGES, IRON AND STEEL
BRIQUETTES (FUEL)
BROOM AND BRUSH INDUSTRY
BUILDING
BUILDING MATERIALS
BUILDING MATERIALS INDUSTRY
BUILDING RESEARCH
BUILDINGS
BUILDINGS, PREFABRICATED
BUILDING STONES

CALICO PRINTING
CANNING AND PRESERVING
CARGO HANDLING
CARPETS
CASHEW NUT INDUSTRY
CATERERS AND CATERING
CATGUT
CATTLE TRADE
CELLULOSE INDUSTRY
CEMENT
CEMENT INDUSTRIES
CERAMIC INDUSTRIES
CHEESE INDUSTRY
CHEMICAL INDUSTRIES
CHEMICALS
CIGARETTE MANUFACTURE AND TRADE
CITRUS FRUIT INDUSTRY
CIVIL ENGINEERING
CLAY INDUSTRIES
CLEANING COMPOUNDS
CLOCK AND WATCH MAKING
CLOCKS AND WATCHES
CLOTHING TRADE
COAL
COAL MINES AND MINING
COAL TRADE
COCOA TRADE
COFFEE TRADE
COMPUTER INDUSTRY
COMPUTERIZED TYPESETTING
COMPUTERS
CONCRETE
CONSTRUCTION EQUIPMENT
CONSTRUCTION INDUSTRY
COOPERS AND COOPERAGE
COPPER INDUSTRY AND TRADE
COPPER MINES AND MINING
COTTAGE INDUSTRIES
COTTON GINS AND GINNING
COTTON GROWING AND MANUFACTURE
COTTON TRADE
DIAMOND CUTTING INDUSTRY
DIAMOND MINES AND MINING
DIESEL MOTOR INDUSTRY
DISTILLING INDUSTRIES
DRUG TRADE (PHARMACEUTICAL)

EARTHWORK
ELECTRIC ENGINEERING
ELECTRIC INDUSTRIES
ELECTRIC LAMPS
ELECTRIC MACHINERY INDUSTRY
ELECTRIC MOTORS
ELECTRIC POWER DISTRIBUTION
ELECTRIC POWER PLANTS
ELECTRICITY SUPPLY
ELECTRONIC DATA PROCESSING
ELECTRONIC DATA PROCESSING IN RESEARCH
ELECTRONIC DIGITAL COMPUTERS
ELECTRONIC INDUSTRIES
ENGINEERING
FERTILIZER INDUSTRY
FIBRES, SYNTHETIC
FLOUR MILLS
FOOD
FOOD INDUSTRY AND TRADE
FOOD RESEARCH
FOOD SUPPLY
FORGING
FOUNDRIES
FRUIT TRADE
FUEL TRADE
FUR TRADE
FURNITURE
FURNITURE INDUSTRY AND TRADE
GAS, NATURAL
GAS COMPANIES
GAS MANUFACTURE AND WORKS
GLASS INDUSTRY AND TRADE
GOLD MINES AND MINING
GOLDSMITHERY
GRAIN TRADE
GROCERY TRADE
HAIRDRESSING
HAND WEAVING
HARDBOARD
HORSE-RACING
HOSIERY INDUSTRY
HOTELS, TAVERNS, ETC.
HOUSE CONSTRUCTION
HOUSEHOLD APPLIANCES
INSTRUMENT INDUSTRY
IRON INDUSTRY AND TRADE

COMMERCE AND INDUSTRY (cont'd)

IRON MINES AND MINING
JEWELLERY TRADE
KNIT GOODS
KNIT GOODS INDUSTRY
LEAD MINES AND MINING
LEATHER INDUSTRY AND TRADE
LIQUEFIED NATURAL GAS
LIQUOR TRAFFIC
LOOMS
MACHINE TOOLS
MACHINERY
MARINE ALGAE
MARKET GARDENING
MEAT INDUSTRY AND TRADE
MECHANICAL ENGINEERING
MERCURY
METAL TRADE
METALLURGICAL FURNACES
MICA
MILK, CONCENTRATED
MILK SUPPLY
MILK TRADE
MINERAL INDUSTRIES
MINES AND MINERAL RESOURCES
MINING CORPORATIONS
MINING CORPORATIONS, BRITISH
MINING INDUSTRY AND FINANCE
MOVING-PICTURE INDUSTRY
MUNITIONS
NAILS AND SPIKES
NON FERROUS METAL INDUSTRIES
NONMETALLIC MINERALS
NUCLEAR FUELS
NUCLEAR REACTORS
OIL INDUSTRIES
OPIUM TRADE

PAPER MAKING AND TRADE
PAPERBOARD INDUSTRY
PERIODICALS, PUBLISHING OF
PETROL
PETROLEUM
PETROLEUM CHEMICALS INDUSTRY
PETROLEUM CONSERVATION
PETROLEUM IN SUBMERGED LANDS
PETROLEUM INDUSTRY AND TRADE
PETROLEUM PRODUCTS
PETROLEUM REFINERIES
PHARMACY
PHOSPHATE INDUSTRY
PLASTICS INDUSTRY AND TRADE
PLYWOOD INDUSTRY
POLYETHYLENE
PORCELAIN
PORK INDUSTRY AND TRADE
PORT WINE
POTASH MINES AND MINING
POTTERY
PRINTING INDUSTRY
PRODUCE TRADE
PUBLISHERS AND PUBLISHING
PUMPING MACHINERY
QUARRIES AND QUARRYING
REAL ESTATE BUSINESS
ROLLING MILLS
RUBBER INDUSTRY AND TRADE
RUG AND CARPET INDUSTRY
RURAL ELECTRIFICATION
SALT INDUSTRY AND TRADE
SALT MINES AND MINING
SCRAP METAL INDUSTRY
SECOND HAND TRADE
SHERRY
SHIPBUILDING

SILK MANUFACTURE AND TRADE
SILVER MINES AND MINING
SLAUGHTERING AND SLAUGHTER-HOUSES
SODA INDUSTRY
SPINNING
STATIONERY TRADE
STEEL INDUSTRY AND TRADE
STORAGE AND MOVING TRADE
SUGAR TRADE
SYNTHETIC FABRICS
TABLE-CLOTHS
TANNING
TEA TRADE
TEXTILE FIBRES
TEXTILE FIBRES, SYNTHETIC
TEXTILE FINISHING
TEXTILE INDUSTRY AND FABRICS
TEXTILE MACHINERY
TIN INDUSTRY
TIN MINES AND MINING
TOBACCO MANUFACTURE AND TRADE
TOURIST CAMPS, HOSTELS, ETC
TOURISTS
TRACTOR INDUSTRY
TRAVEL AGENTS
TWINE
URANIUM MINES AND MINING
VEGETABLE TRADE
WEAVING
WELDING
WHISKY
WINE AND WINE MAKING
WIRE INDUSTRY
WOOD PULP INDUSTRY
WOOD-USING INDUSTRIES
WOOL TRADE AND INDUSTRY
WOOLLEN AND WORSTED MANUFACTURE

ECONOMICS

see also AGRICULTURE; COMMERCE AND INDUSTRY;
FINANCE; TRANSPORT

ABSENTEEISM (LABOUR)
AGE AND EMPLOYMENT
ALIEN LABOUR
ANDEAN GROUP
BONUS SYSTEM
BOYCOTT
BUSINESS CYCLES
BUSINESS FORECASTING
CAPITALISM
CHARTISM
CHRISTIANITY AND ECONOMICS
CHURCH AND ECONOMICS
CHURCH AND LABOUR
CIVIL SERVICE PENSIONS
COLLECTIVE BARGAINING
COLLECTIVE LABOUR AGREEMENTS
COLLECTIVISM
COMMUNISM
COMMUNITY DEVELOPMENT
COMPETITION
COMPETITION, INTERNATIONAL
COMPETITION, UNFAIR
CONSUMPTION (ECONOMICS)
CONTRACT LABOUR
CONVICT LABOUR
CO PARTNERSHIP
COST
COST AND STANDARD OF LIVING
COST EFFECTIVENESS
COSTS, INDUSTRIAL
COUNCIL FOR MUTUAL ECONOMIC ASSISTANCE
CRISES
DEPRECIATION
DIMINISHING RETURNS
DISABILITY EVALUATION
DISCRIMINATION IN EMPLOYMENT
DIVISION OF LABOUR
DOMESTIC ECONOMY
ECONOMIC ASSISTANCE
ECONOMIC ASSISTANCE, AMERICAN

ECONOMIC ASSISTANCE, AUSTRIAN
ECONOMIC ASSISTANCE, BRITISH
ECONOMIC ASSISTANCE, CANADIAN
ECONOMIC ASSISTANCE, COMMUNIST
ECONOMIC ASSISTANCE, DANISH
ECONOMIC ASSISTANCE, DOMESTIC
ECONOMIC ASSISTANCE, EUROPEAN
ECONOMIC ASSISTANCE, FRENCH
ECONOMIC ASSISTANCE, GERMAN
ECONOMIC ASSISTANCE, NEW ZEALAND
ECONOMIC ASSISTANCE, RUSSIAN
ECONOMIC ASSISTANCE, SWEDISH
ECONOMIC ASSISTANCE IN AFGHANISTAN
ECONOMIC ASSISTANCE IN AFRICA
ECONOMIC ASSISTANCE IN ASIA
ECONOMIC ASSISTANCE IN COLOMBIA
ECONOMIC ASSISTANCE IN GHANA
ECONOMIC ASSISTANCE IN INDONESIA
ECONOMIC ASSISTANCE IN LATIN AMERICA
ECONOMIC ASSISTANCE IN MALAWI
ECONOMIC ASSISTANCE IN PAKISTAN
ECONOMIC CONDITIONS
ECONOMIC COUNCILS
ECONOMIC DEVELOPMENT
ECONOMIC FORECASTING
ECONOMIC HISTORY
ECONOMIC INDICATORS
ECONOMIC LEGISLATION
ECONOMIC POLICY
ECONOMIC RESEARCH
ECONOMIC STABILIZATION
ECONOMIC SURVEYS
ECONOMIC ZONING
ECONOMICS
ECONOMICS, COMPARATIVE
ECONOMICS, MATHEMATICAL
ECONOMICS, PRIMITIVE
ECONOMISTS, AMERICAN
ECONOMISTS, DUTCH
ECONOMISTS, FRENCH

ECONOMISTS, GERMAN
ECONOMISTS, RUSSIAN
EIGHT-HOUR MOVEMENT
EMBLEMS
EMPLOYMENT (ECONOMIC THEORY)
ENTREPRENEUR
ENTROPY
EQUAL PAY FOR EQUAL WORK
EXCHANGE
EXTERNALITIES (ECONOMICS)
FAMILY ALLOWANCES
FREE CHOICE OF EMPLOYMENT
FREE TRADE AND PROTECTION
FULL EMPLOYMENT POLICIES
FUNDACION NACIONAL DE DESARROLLO
GENERAL STRIKE, BELGIUM, 1961
GENERAL STRIKE, SPAIN, 1917
GENERAL STRIKE, UNITED KINGDOM, 1926
GILD SOCIALISM
GILDS
GOVERNMENT MONOPOLIES
GOVERNMENT OWNERSHIP
GOVERNMENT PURCHASING
GOVERNMENT PURCHASING OF REAL PROPERTY
GOVERNMENT SPENDING POLICY
GROSS DOMESTIC PRODUCT
GROSS NATIONAL PRODUCT
HOME LABOUR
HOME OWNERSHIP
HOURS OF LABOUR
HOUSE BUYING
HOUSING
HOUSING, COOPERATIVE
HOUSING, RURAL
HOUSING SURVEYS
HUMAN CAPITAL
INDENTURED SERVANTS
INDEX NUMBERS (ECONOMICS)
INDUSTRIAL RELATIONS
INFORMATION THEORY IN ECONOMICS

ECONOMICS (cont'd)

INTEREST AND USURY
INTEREST INVENTORIES
INTERINDUSTRY ECONOMICS
INTERNATIONAL ECONOMIC INTEGRATION
INTERNATIONAL ECONOMIC RELATIONS
INTERNATIONAL LABOUR ORGANISATION
INTERNATIONAL LIQUIDITY
JOB ANALYSIS
JOB SATISFACTION
JOB VACANCIES
JOINT TENANCY
JOURNALISM, LABOUR
LABOUR AND LABOURING CLASSES
LABOUR BUREAUS
LABOUR CONTRACT
LABOUR COSTS
LABOUR DISCIPLINE
LABOUR DISPUTES
LABOUR ECONOMICS
LABOUR EXCHANGES
LABOUR INSPECTION
LABOUR MOBILITY
LABOUR SERVICE
LABOUR SUPPLY
LABOUR TURNOVER
LAISSEZ-FAIRE
LAND, NATIONALIZATION OF
LAND SUBDIVISION
LAND TENURE
LEAVE OF ABSENCE
LIQUIDITY (ECONOMICS)
MALTHUSIANISM
MARGINAL PRODUCTIVITY
MARGINAL UTILITY
MEDIATION AND CONCILIATION, INDUSTRIAL
MEDICAL CARE, COST OF
MEDICAL ECONOMICS
METERS
MIGRANT LABOUR
MILLIONAIRES
MIR
MONOPOLIES
MOTHERS' PENSIONS
NEGOTIATION
NON-WAGE PAYMENTS
OLIGOPOLIES
OPEN AND CLOSED SHOP

ORGANISATION FOR ECONOMIC CO-OPERATION AND DEVELOPMENT
OVERHEAD COSTS
OVERTIME
PART-TIME EMPLOYMENT
PENSION TRUSTS
PENSIONS
PHYSIOCRATS
PIECEWORK
PLANT SHUTDOWNS
POPULATION
PRESS MONOPOLIES
PRICE DISCRIMINATION
PRICE INDEXES
PRICE MAINTENANCE
PRICE REGULATION
PRICES
PRODUCTION (ECONOMIC THEORY)
PROFIT
PROFIT SHARING
PROLETARIAT
PROPERTY
PROTESTANTISM AND CAPITALISM
RATIONING, CONSUMER
REAL PROPERTY
REGIONALISM
RELIGION AND ECONOMICS
RENT
RENT (ECONOMIC THEORY)
RENT CONTROL
RENT STRIKES
RENT SUBSIDIES
RESTAURANTS, LUNCHROOMS, ETC.
RESTRAINT OF TRADE
RETRAINING, OCCUPATIONAL
RIGHT TO LABOUR
RISK
SALARIED EMPLOYEES
SEASONAL LABOUR
SEASONAL VARIATIONS (ECONOMICS)
SELF EMPLOYED
SERVICE, COMPULSORY NON-MILITARY
SHIFT SYSTEMS
SHOP STEWARDS
SICK LEAVE
SIT DOWN STRIKES
SKILLED LABOUR

SOCIALIST COMPETITION
SPACE IN ECONOMICS
STRIKES AND LOCKOUTS
SUBSIDIES
SUBSTITUTION (ECONOMICS)
SUPPLY AND DEMAND
SURVIVORS' BENEFITS
SYNDICALISM
TECHNICAL ASSISTANCE
TECHNICAL ASSISTANCE, AMERICAN
TECHNICAL ASSISTANCE, BRITISH
TECHNICAL ASSISTANCE, DANISH
TECHNICAL ASSISTANCE, DUTCH
TECHNICAL ASSISTANCE, FRENCH
TECHNICAL ASSISTANCE, JAPANESE
TECHNICAL ASSISTANCE, RUSSIAN
TECHNICAL ASSISTANCE IN AFRICA
TECHNICAL ASSISTANCE IN COMMUNIST COUNTRIES
TECHNICAL ASSISTANCE IN INDIA
TECHNICAL ASSISTANCE IN IRAN
TECHNICAL ASSISTANCE IN LATIN AMERICA
TECHNICAL ASSISTANCE IN MEXICO
TECHNICAL ASSISTANCE IN PAKISTAN
TECHNICAL ASSISTANCE IN SPAIN
TECHNICAL ASSISTANCE IN THE PHILIPPINE ISLANDS
TECHNICAL ASSISTANCE IN TURKEY
TRADE AND PROFESSIONAL ASSOCIATIONS
TRADE UNION EMBLEMS
TRADE UNIONS
TRADE UNIONS, CATHOLIC
TRADE UNIONS AND COMMUNISM
TRADE UNIONS AND FOREIGN POLICY
TRANSFER PRICING
TRUSTS, INDUSTRIAL
TIME AND MOTION STUDY
TIME AND ECONOMIC REACTIONS
UNDERDEVELOPED AREAS
UNEMPLOYED
UNEMPLOYMENT, TECHNOLOGICAL
UNITED NATIONS ECONOMIC COMMISSION FOR EUROPE
URBAN ECONOMICS
VALUE
WAGE PAYMENT SYSTEMS
WAGE-PRICE POLICY

ECONOMICS (cont'd)

WAGES	WEALTH	WORK
WAGES AND PRODUCTIVITY	WELFARE ECONOMICS	WORKS COUNCILS
WAR, COST OF	WOMEN IN TRADE UNIONS	

EDUCATION

General

ABILITY GROUPING IN EDUCATION
ACADEMIC ACHIEVEMENT
AFRICAN STUDIES
AGRICULTURAL EDUCATION
ASIAN STUDENTS IN THE UNITED STATES
ASIAN STUDIES
BUSINESS EDUCATION
CAMPUS PLANNING
CATHOLIC UNIVERSITIES AND COLLEGES
CHARITY SCHOOLS
CHINESE STUDIES
CHURCH AND COLLEGE IN THE UNITED STATES
CHURCH AND EDUCATION IN LATIN AMERICA
CHURCH AND EDUCATION IN NORTHERN IRELAND
COMMUNISM AND EDUCATION
COMMUNIST EDUCATION
COMMUNITY AND COLLEGE
COMMUNITY AND SCHOOL
COMPUTER ASSISTED INSTRUCTION
CONCEPT LEARNING
CORRESPONDENCE SCHOOLS AND COURSES
DEGREES, ACADEMIC
DISCRIMINATION IN EDUCATION
DISSERTATIONS, ACADEMIC
DROPOUTS
EDUCATION
EDUCATION, COMPARATIVE
EDUCATION, COMPULSORY
EDUCATION, COOPERATIVE
EDUCATION, ELEMENTARY
EDUCATION, HIGHER
EDUCATION, PRESCHOOL
EDUCATION, RURAL

EDUCATION, SECONDARY
EDUCATION, URBAN
EDUCATION AND CRIME
EDUCATION AND STATE
EDUCATION OF ADULTS
EDUCATION OF PRINCES
EDUCATION OF PRISONERS
EDUCATION OF WOMEN
EDUCATIONAL ANTHROPOLOGY
EDUCATIONAL ASSISTANCE
EDUCATIONAL ASSISTANCE, FRENCH
EDUCATIONAL ASSOCIATIONS
EDUCATIONAL BROADCASTING
EDUCATIONAL EQUALIZATION
EDUCATIONAL EXCHANGES
EDUCATIONAL INNOVATIONS
EDUCATIONAL LAW AND LEGISLATION
EDUCATIONAL PLANNING
EDUCATIONAL PSYCHOLOGY
EDUCATIONAL RESEARCH
EDUCATIONAL SOCIOLOGY
EDUCATIONAL STATISTICS
EDUCATIONAL TECHNOLOGY
EDUCATIONAL TESTS AND MEASUREMENTS
EVENING AND CONTINUATION SCHOOLS
EXAMINATIONS
FEDERAL AID TO HIGHER EDUCATION
FILMSTRIPS
FINNISH STUDENTS IN FRANCE
GIFTED CHILDREN
GRADING AND MARKING (STUDENTS)
GRADUATES
HEALTH EDUCATION
HIGH SCHOOLS
HIGHER EDUCATION AND STATE
HOME AND SCHOOL

HUMANITIES
ILLITERACY
INDUSTRY AND EDUCATION
INTELLECTUAL COOPERATION
INTELLECTUAL LIFE
INTELLECTUALS
INTERCULTURAL EDUCATION
INTERNATIONAL EDUCATION
INTERNATIONAL STUDENT CONFERENCE
INTERNATIONAL UNION OF STUDENTS
LATIN AMERICAN STUDENTS IN SPAIN
LATIN AMERICAN STUDIES
LEARNING AND SCHOLARSHIP
LIBRARY SCHOOLS AND TRAINING
MECHANICS' INSTITUTES
MEDICAL COLLEGES
MILITARY EDUCATION
MORAL EDUCATION
MOVING-PICTURES IN EDUCATION
MULTIPLE CHOICE EXAMINATIONS
NATIONALISM AND EDUCATION
NEGRO STUDENTS
NURSERY SCHOOLS
PERSONNEL SERVICE IN EDUCATION
PHYSICAL EDUCATION AND TRAINING
POLITICS AND EDUCATION
PRIVATE SCHOOLS
PROFESSIONAL EDUCATION
PROGRAMMED INSTRUCTION
PUBLIC SCHOOLS
PUBLIC SCHOOLS (ENDOWED)
RADIO IN EDUCATION
RAGGED SCHOOLS
READERS AND SPEAKERS
RELIGIOUS EDUCATION
RURAL SCHOOLS
SAFETY EDUCATION, INDUSTRIAL

EDUCATION (cont'd)

SCHOLARS
SCHOLARS, AMERICAN
SCHOLARS, RUSSIAN
SCHOLARSHIPS
SCHOLASTIC APTITUDE TEST
SCHOOL, CHOICE OF
SCHOOL ADMINISTRATORS
SCHOOL ATTENDANCE
SCHOOL BOARDS
SCHOOL BUILDINGS
SCHOOL CHILDREN
SCHOOL DISCIPLINE
SCHOOL DISTRICTS
SCHOOL EXCURSIONS
SCHOOL FACILITIES
SCHOOL INTEGRATION
SCHOOL MANAGEMENT AND ORGANIZATION
SCHOOLS
SCIENCE AND THE HUMANITIES
SEGREGATION IN EDUCATION
SEGREGATION IN HIGHER EDUCATION
SEX INSTRUCTION
SLAVIC STUDIES
SLOW LEARNING CHILDREN
SOCIAL WORK EDUCATION
SOCIALISM AND EDUCATION
STUDENT ACTIVITIES.
STUDENT EMPLOYMENT
STUDENT HOUSING
STUDENT PARTICIPATION IN ADMINISTRATION.
STUDENTS.
STUDENTS, FOREIGN
STUDENTS, INTERCHANGE OF
STUDENTS' SOCIETIES
STUDY, METHOD OF
TEACHER-STUDENT RELATIONSHIPS
TEACHERS, TRAINING OF
TEACHERS' COLLEGES

TEACHERS' UNIONS
TEACHING
TEACHING, FREEDOM OF
TEACHING MACHINES
TECHNICAL EDUCATION
TELEVISION IN ADULT EDUCATION
TELEVISION IN EDUCATION
TELEVISION IN TECHNICAL EDUCATION
TEXTBOOKS
UNITED NATIONS EDUCATIONAL, SCIENTIFIC AND CULTURAL ORGANIZATION
UNIVERSITIES AND COLLEGES
UNIVERSITY COOPERATION
VISUAL EDUCATION
VOCATIONAL EDUCATION
WEST INDIAN STUDENTS IN CANADA
WOMEN COLLEGE STUDENTS
WOMEN'S COLLEGES

Educational institutions

AMSTERDAM UNIVERSITY
ARIZONA STATE UNIVERSITY
BASEL UNIVERSITY
BENNINGTON COLLEGE
BERLIN FREE UNIVERSITY
BRANDEIS UNIVERSITY
BUCHAREST UNIVERSITY
CAMDEN SCHOOL FOR GIRLS
DUBLIN UNIVERSITY COLLEGE
ECOLE NORMALE SUPERIEURE
FORDHAM UNIVERSITY
FORT HARE UNIVERSITY
GLASGOW UNIVERSITY
GOETTINGEN UNIVERSITY
HARVARD UNIVERSITY
HEIDELBERG UNIVERSITY

IFE UNIVERSITY
ILLINOIS UNIVERSITY
INTER-AMERICAN INSTITUTE OF AGRICULTURAL SCIENCES
KAZAN' UNIVERSITY
KEELE UNIVERSITY
KISHINEV UNIVERSITY
KNEESWORTH HALL SCHOOL
KUMASI UNIVERSITY OF SCIENCE AND TECHNOLOGY
LENINGRAD UNIVERSITY
LONDON UNIVERSITY
MAGEE UNIVERSITY COLLEGE
MANNHEIM HANDELSHOCHSCHULE
MASSACHUSETTS INSTITUTE OF TECHNOLOGY
MESSINA UNIVERSITY
MONTEVIDEO UNIVERSITY
MOSCOW UNIVERSITY
MUENSTER UNIVERSITY
NEW UNIVERSITY OF ULSTER
OPEN UNIVERSITY
OXFORD UNIVERSITY
PRINCE OF WALES COLLEGE AND SCHOOL, ACHIMOTA
PUERTO RICO UNIVERSITY
QUEEN'S COLLEGE, LONDON
READING UNIVERSITY
RENSSELAER POLYTECHNIC INSTITUTE
RHODESIA UNIVERSITY
SIR GEORGE WILLIAMS UNIVERSITY
SUMMERHILL SCHOOL
SUSSEX UNIVERSITY
TORONTO UNIVERSITY
TSING HUA UNIVERSITY
TUNIS UNIVERSITY
UNIVERSITY OF THE SOUTH PACIFIC
VILNA UNIVERSITY
WISCONSIN UNIVERSITY
WROCŁAW UNIVERSITY
YALE UNIVERSITY

FINANCE

General

AGRICULTURAL COOPERATIVE CREDIT ASSOCIATIONS
AGRICULTURAL CREDIT
AMORTIZATION
ANNUITIES
ASSESSMENT
BALANCE OF PAYMENTS
BANK DEPOSITS
BANK MERGERS
BANK-NOTES
BANKRUPTCY
BANKS AND BANKING
BANKS AND BANKING, CENTRAL
BANKS AND BANKING, COOPERATIVE
BANKS AND BANKING, INTERNATIONAL
BILLS OF EXCHANGE
BIMETALLISM
BONDS
BOOKMAKING (BETTING)
BROKERS
BUDGET
BUDGET IN BUSINESS
BUILDING AND LOAN ASSOCIATIONS
BUSINESS TAX
CAPITAL
CAPITAL BUDGET
CAPITAL GAINS TAX
CAPITAL INVESTMENTS
CAPITAL LEVY
CHEQUES
COINAGE
COINS, MEDIEVAL
COMMERCIAL FINANCE COMPANIES
CONSUMER CREDIT
CONVERTIBILITY (MONEY)
CORPORATION RESERVES
COST ACCOUNTING
COUNTERFEITS AND COUNTERFEITERS
CREDIT

CUSTOMS ADMINISTRATION
CUSTOMS APPRAISAL
CUSTOMS CO-OPERATION COUNCIL
CUSTOMS UNIONS
DEBTS, EXTERNAL
DEBTS, PUBLIC
DEFICIT FINANCING
DEFLATION (FINANCE)
DENTAL FEES
DEVELOPMENT BANKS
DEVELOPMENT CREDIT CORPORATIONS
DISCOUNT
DIVIDENDS
DOLLAR
DUTY-FREE IMPORTATION OF SAMPLES
ESCALATOR CLAUSE
EURODOLLAR MARKET
EUROPEAN PAYMENTS UNION
EXPENDITURES, PUBLIC
EXPORT CREDIT
FEDERAL FUNDS MARKET (U.S.)
FEDERAL RESERVE BANKS
FEDERATIONS, FINANCIAL (SOCIAL SERVICE)
FEES, PROFESSIONAL
FINANCE
FINANCE, PERSONAL
FINANCE CHARGES
FINANCIAL INSTITUTIONS
FINANCIAL STATEMENTS
FLOW OF FUNDS
FOREIGN EXCHANGE
FORWARD EXCHANGE
FRENCH FRANC AREA
FRIENDLY SOCIETIES
FUND RAISING
GOLD
GOLD STANDARD
GOVERNMENT LENDING
GRANTS-IN-AID
GUARANTEED ANNUAL INCOME
INCOME

INCOME TAX
INCOME TAX, MUNICIPAL
INDUSTRIAL LOAN ASSOCIATIONS
INFLATION (FINANCE)
INHERITANCE AND TRANSFER TAX
INSURANCE
INSURANCE, ACCIDENT
INSURANCE, AGRICULTURAL
INSURANCE, ATOMIC HAZARDS
INSURANCE, AUTOMOBILE
INSURANCE, CREDIT
INSURANCE, CREMATION
INSURANCE, DEPOSIT
INSURANCE, DISABILITY
INSURANCE, EXPORT CREDIT
INSURANCE, FIRE
INSURANCE, GOVERNMENT
INSURANCE, HEALTH
INSURANCE, INDUSTRIAL
INSURANCE, LIABILITY
INSURANCE, LIFE
INSURANCE, MARINE
INSURANCE, MATERNITY
INSURANCE, SOCIAL
INSURANCE, UNEMPLOYMENT
INSURANCE COMPANIES
INSURANCE POLICIES
INSURANCE STOCKS
INTERGOVERNMENTAL FISCAL RELATIONS
INTERNAL REVENUE
INTERNATIONAL DEVELOPMENT ASSOCIATION
INTERNATIONAL FINANCE
INTERNATIONAL FINANCE CORPORATION
INTERNATIONAL MONETARY FUND
INVESTMENT OF PUBLIC FUNDS
INVESTMENT TAX CREDIT
INVESTMENT TRUSTS
INVESTMENTS
INVESTMENTS, AMERICAN
INVESTMENTS, BRITISH

FINANCE (cont'd)

INVESTMENTS, FOREIGN	RESERVES (ACCOUNTING)	TOLLS
INVESTMENTS, FRENCH	REVENUE	UNIVERSITY INVESTMENTS
INVESTMENTS, GERMAN	SALES TAX	VALUE-ADDED TAX
INVESTMENTS, ITALIAN	SAVING AND INVESTMENT	VEHICLES
INVESTMENTS, JAPANESE	SAVINGS BANKS	WALL STREET
INVESTMENTS, SWEDISH	SECURITIES	WOMEN AS BANKERS
INVESTMENTS, SWISS	SELECTIVE EMPLOYMENT TAX	
LAND GRANTS	SILVER	
LOANS	SINGLE TAX	### Banks, exchanges, etc.
LOANS, BRITISH	SMALL BUSINESS INVESTMENT COMPANIES	
LOANS, FOREIGN	SOCIAL SECURITY TAXES	BANCO CENTRAL DE NICARAGUA
LOANS, ITALIAN	SPECIAL DRAWING RIGHTS	BANCO CENTRAL DE VENEZUELA
LOANS, PERSONAL	SPECULATION	BANCO DE ESPAÑA
LOCAL FINANCE	STERLING AREA	BANCO DE PORTUGAL
MEDICAL FEES	STOCK COMPANIES	BANK OF ENGLAND
MINTS	STOCK EXCHANGE	BANK OF JAPAN
MONETARY UNIONS	STOCK OWNERSHIP	BANK OF SIERRA LEONE
MONEY	STOCKHOLDERS	BANQUE DE FRANCE
MORTGAGES	STOCKS	BANQUE NATIONALE SUISSE
NATIONAL INCOME	TARIFFS	CARIBBEAN DEVELOPMENT BANK
PAPER MONEY	TAX ADMINISTRATION	CENTRAL BANK OF NIGERIA
PAYMENT	TAX EVASION	DEUTSCHE BUNDESBANK
PROFITS TAX	TAX PLANNING	GOSUDARSTVENNYI BANK SSSR
PROGRAMME BUDGETING	TAXATION	INTER-AMERICAN DEVELOPMENT BANK
PROPERTY TAX	TAXATION, EXEMPTION FROM	INTERNATIONAL BANK FOR RECONSTRUCTION AND DEVELOPMENT
QUANTITY THEORY OF MONEY	TAXATION OF BONDS, SECURITIES, ETC.	NORGES BANK
REAL PROPERTY TAX	TAXES, FARMING OF	REICHSBANK
RESEARCH GRANTS	TOKENS	

GEOGRAPHY, GEOLOGY AND METEOROLOGY

General

	ATLASES	CROPS AND CLIMATE
	BOUNDARIES	DIFFUSION OF INNOVATIONS
	CARTOGRAPHY	DISCOVERIES (IN GEOGRAPHY)
AGRICULTURAL GEOGRAPHY	CENTRAL PLACES	DROUGHTS
AIR	CITIES AND TOWNS	EARTH SCIENCES
ANIMAL POPULATIONS	CLIMATIC CHANGES	EARTHQUAKES
ANTARCTIC REGIONS	COAST CHANGES	ECOLOGICAL RESEARCH
ANTHROPOGEOGRAPHY	COASTS	ECOLOGY
ARCTIC REGIONS	COMBINATIONS	ENVIRONMENTAL POLICY
ARID REGIONS	CONSERVATION OF NATURAL RESOURCES	EROSION
ATLANTIC, THE	CONTINENTAL DRIFT	EUROPEAN ECONOMIC COMMUNITY ASSOCIATED COUNTRIES
	CONTINENTAL SHELF	

GEOGRAPHY, GEOLOGY AND METEOROLOGY (cont'd)

EXPLORERS, RUSSIAN

EXPLORERS, SPANISH

FLOODS

FOG

GEOCHEMICAL PROSPECTING

GEOGRAPHERS, BRITISH

GEOGRAPHICAL DISTRIBUTION OF ANIMALS AND PLANTS

GEOGRAPHICAL RESEARCH

GEOGRAPHICAL SOCIETIES

GEOGRAPHY

GEOGRAPHY, ANCIENT

GEOGRAPHY, ECONOMIC

GEOGRAPHY, HISTORICAL

GEOGRAPHY, MATHEMATICAL

GEOGRAPHY, POLITICAL

GEOLOGY

GEOLOGY, ECONOMIC

GEOLOGY, STRATIGRAPHIC

GEOMORPHOLOGY

GEOPOLITICS

GLACIAL EPOCH

GLACIERS

GLACIOLOGY

GREEN BELTS

HEALTH RESORTS, WATERING PLACES, ETC.

HILL FARMING

HOMESITES

HYDROLOGY

ISLANDS

LAKES

LAND

LANDSCAPE

LANDSCAPE ARCHITECTURE

LANDSCAPE PROTECTION

LANDSLIDES

MAGNETIC ANOMALIES

MAPS

MARINE POLLUTION

MARINE RESOURCES

MARINE RESOURCES CONSERVATION

MARSHES

MEDICAL GEOGRAPHY

METEOROLOGY IN AERONAUTICS

MINES AND MINERAL RESOURCES

MOHAMMEDAN COUNTRIES

NAMES, GEOGRAPHICAL

NATIONAL PARKS AND RESERVES

NATIONAL TRUST FOR SCOTLAND

NATURAL AREAS

NATURAL RESOURCES

NATURE CONSERVATION

OASES

OCEAN

OCEAN BOTTOM

OCEANOGRAPHIC RESEARCH

OCEANOGRAPHY

OCEANOGRAPHY AND STATE

OIL POLLUTION OF RIVERS, HARBOURS, ETC

OPEN SPACES

PALAEONTOLOGY

PESTICIDES AND THE ENVIRONMENT

PHOTOGRAPHY, AERIAL

PHYSICAL GEOGRAPHY

POLLUTION

RADIOACTIVE FALLOUT

RADIOACTIVE POLLUTION

RADIOACTIVE WASTE DISPOSAL IN THE OCEAN

RAIN AND RAINFALL

RAIN MAKING

RECLAMATION OF LAND

RECREATION AREAS

REGIONAL PLANNING

REGIONALISM

RELIGION AND GEOGRAPHY

RESERVOIRS

RIVERS

ROCKS

SEDIMENTATION AND DEPOSITION

SLOPES (PHYSICAL GEOGRAPHY)

SOILS

SUBMARINE GEOLOGY

SUBSIDENCES (EARTH MOVEMENTS)

SURVEYING

TRAILER CAMPS

TROPICS

VOLUNTEER WORKERS IN CONSERVATION

VOYAGES AND TRAVELS

WATER

WATER, UNDERGROUND

WATER QUALITY MANAGEMENT

WATER RESOURCES DEVELOPMENT

WATER-STORAGE

WATER-SUPPLY

WEATHER

WEATHERING

WILD LIFE, CONSERVATION OF

ZONING

Rocks, minerals, etc.

BARIUM

FULLER'S EARTH

GRAVEL

GYPSUM

IRON ORES

LEAD

LIMESTONE

MANGANESE ORES

PHOSPHATE ROCK

SALT DEPOSITS

SAND

SAND, GLASS

SULPHUR

TIN

TUNGSTEN

Individual countires and places

Africa

AFRICA

AFRICA, CENTRAL

AFRICA, EAST

AFRICA, NORTH

AFRICA, SUBSAHARAN

AFRICA, WEST

AKOKOASO

AKUAPEM

ALGERIA

ANGOLA

GEOGRAPHY, GEOLOGY AND METEOROLOGY (cont'd)

ANKOLE
ARAB COUNTRIES
ASHANTI
ASWAN HIGH DAM
BAROTSELAND
BASOTHO-QWAQWA TERRITORY
BENIN
BLOEMFONTEIN
BOTSWANA
BRITISH EAST AFRICA
BUGANDA
BULAWAYO
BUNYORO
BURUNDI
BUSOGA
BUSSA, NIGERIA
CABORA BASSA DAM
CAMEROONS
CAMEROUN
CANARY ISLANDS
CAPE VERDE ISLANDS
CAPE OF GOOD HOPE
CAPE TOWN
CEUTA
CONGO
CONGO (BRAZZAVILLE)
CUNENE DAM
CYRENAICA
DAHOMEY
DAKAR METROPOLITAN AREA
DAR ES SALAAM
EAST LONDON
EGYPT
EQUATORIA (PROVINCE)
ERITREA
ETHIOPIA
FRENCH WEST AFRICA
GABON
GAMBIA
GERMAN EAST AFRICA
GHANA
GUINEA
IVORY COAST
IWO
JINJA

KARAMOJA
KARIBA DAM
KARROO
KAVANGO TERRITORIES
KENYA
KIMBERLEY
KITA
LAGOS
LESOTHO
LIBERIA
LIBYA
LOURENÇO MARQUES
MADAGASCAR
MADEIRA
MAFEKING
MALAWI
MALI EMPIRE
MANIEMA
MASCARENE ISLANDS
MAURITANIA
MAURITIUS
MEDJERDA VALLEY
MELILLA
MOROCCO
MOZAMBIQUE
NATAL
NIGER
NIGERIA
OMO RIVER
ONITSHA
ORANGE FREE STATE
PIETERMARITZBURG
PORT ELIZABETH
PORT-LYAUTEY
PORT NOLLOTH
PORTUGUESE GUINEA
PRETORIA
RHODESIA
RHODESIA AND NYASALAND, FEDERATION OF
SALISBURY, RHODESIA
SENEGAL
SEYCHELLES
SHABA
SIERRA LEONE
SOMALILAND

SOUTH AFRICA
SOUTH WEST AFRICA
SOWETO
SUDAN
SWAZILAND
TANZANIA
TOGO
TORO
TRANSKEIAN TERRITORIES
TRANSVAAL
TUGELA BASIN
TUNISIA
UGANDA
UPPER VOLTA
VOLTA RIVER
ZAIRE
ZAMBIA

America, Latin

AGUASCALIENTES
ALAGOAS
AMAZON VALLEY
AMERICA
AMERICA, LATIN
ANTIGUA
ANTIOQUIA
AREQUIPA (DEPARTMENT)
ARGENTINE REPUBLIC
AYACUCHO
BAHAMAS
BAHIA (STATE)
BARBADOS
BARINAS (STATE)
BOLIVIA
BRASILIA
BRAZIL
BRITISH HONDURAS
BRITISH VIRGIN ISLANDS
BUENOS AIRES (CITY)
CAGUAS
CARACAS
CARIBBEAN AREA

GEOGRAPHY, GEOLOGY AND METEOROLOGY (cont'd)

CAUCA VALLEY
CAYMAN ISLANDS
CEARÁ
CHAN KOM
CHANCAY VALLEY
CHANCHAMAYO
CHILE
CHIRIQUI (PROVINCE)
COCHABAMBA
COCHABAMBA (DEPARTMENT)
COJEDES
COLOMBIA
CORDOBA, ARGENTINE REPUBLIC (CITY)
COSTA RICA
CUBA
CUZCO (DEPARTMENT)
DOMINICAN REPUBLIC
DUTCH GUIANA
ECUADOR
ESPÍRITO SANTO (STATE, BRAZIL)
FALCON (STATE)
FRENCH GUIANA
FRENCH WEST INDIES
GUADALAJARA
GUADELOUPE
GUANABARA (STATE)
GUATEMALA
GUATEMALA (CITY)
GUYANA
HAITI
HAVANA
HONDURAS
IXTEPEJI
JALAPA, MEXICO
JAMAICA
JESUS MARIA (DISTRICT, PERU)
JUAZEIRO
LA PAZ
LEEWARD ISLANDS
LIMA
MARANHÃO
MEXICO
MEXICO CITY
MINAS GERAIS

MONAGAS (STATE)
MONTERREY
MONTEVIDEO
MONTSERRAT
MOXOTÓ VALLEY
NASSAU (BAHAMAS)
NETHERLANDS ANTILLES
NEW GRANADA (VICEROYALTY)
NEW PROVIDENCE ISLAND
NEW SPAIN (VICEROYALTY)
NICARAGUA
NUEVA ESPARTA
NUEVO LEON
OAXACA
OAXACA VALLEY
PANAMA
PARAGUAY
PARAIBA
PARATIA
PATAGONIA
PERNAMBUCO
PERU
PETROLINA
PISAC
PUERTO RICO
PUNO
RAVELO
RECIFE
RIO DE JANEIRO (CITY)
RIO DE JANEIRO (STATE)
RIO DE LA PLATA
RIO GRANDE DO NORTE
RIO GRANDE DO SUL
RIOBAMBA
RORAIMA
SABA
SAINT LUCIA
SALVADOR
SAN JUAN (PROVINCE OF THE ARGENTINE REPUBLIC)
SAN LUIS POTOSI
SANTA CATARINA (STATE)
SANTO DOMINGO
SÃO FRANCISCO VALLEY

SAO PAULO (CITY)
SAO PAULO (STATE)
SERGIPE
SOSUA
TABASCO
TAMBOPATA VALLEY, PERU
TIJUANA
TRES MARIAS
TRINIDAD AND TOBAGO
URUGUAY
VENEZUELA
VICOS, (PERU)
VIRGIN ISLANDS
WEST INDIES
ZINACANTAN

America, North

ALASKA
AMERICA
AMERICA, NORTH
AMHERST, NEW YORK
APPALACHIAN MOUNTAINS
ARIZONA
BAFFIN ISLAND
BATON ROUGE
BERMUDA
BEVERLY HILLS
BOSTON, MASSACHUSETTS
BOULDER DAM
BROWNSVILLE, TEXAS
BUFFALO
CAIRO, ILLINOIS
CALIFORNIA
CANADA
CAYUGA LAKE
CHICAGO
CLEVELAND
COE RIDGE
COLUMBIA RIVER
CONNECTICUT
DELAWARE
DETROIT

GEOGRAPHY, GEOLOGY AND METEOROLOGY (cont'd)

DETROIT METROPOLITAN AREA
EAST ST. LOUIS
ERIE, LAKE
FLORIDA
GEORGIA (UNITED STATES)
GREAT LAKES
GREENLAND
HALIFAX, NOVA SCOTIA
HARLEM
HOWARD COUNTY
ILLINOIS
JACKSONVILLE
JERSEY CITY
KANSAS
LOS ANGELES
LOUISIANA
MACKENZIE DELTA
MANITOBA
MARYLAND
MASSACHUSETTS
MICHIGAN
MILWAUKEE
MISSISSIPPI
MISSOURI
MONTREAL
NEW BRUNSWICK
NEW ENGLAND
NEW HARMONY
NEW HAVEN
NEW JERSEY
NEW YORK (CITY)
NEW YORK (STATE)
NEWFOUNDLAND
NORTH CAROLINA
NORTHWEST TERRITORIES
NOVA SCOTIA
OAKLAND, CALIFORNIA
OHIO
OMAHA
ONTARIO
ONTARIO, LAKE
ORLEANS, ISLAND OF
OTTAWA
PEACE RIVER
PEACE RIVER BASIN

PEMBINA RIVER BASIN
PENNSYLVANIA
PHILADELPHIA
PHOENIX, ARIZONA
PRINCETON
QUAD-CITY METROPOLITAN AREA
QUEBEC
QUEBEC (PROVINCE)
RHODE ISLAND
ST. JOHN, NEW BRUNSWICK
ST. LAWRENCE RIVER
SAN FRANCISCO
SAN JOSE METROPOLITAN AREA
SASKATCHEWAN
SOUTH SASKATCHEWAN RIVER
SPRINGFIELD, MASSACHUSETTS
STAMFORD
SYRACUSE (UNITED STATES)
TENNESSEE
TEXAS
TORONTO
UNITED STATES
VANCOUVER
VIRGINIA
WABASH VALLEY
WASHINGTON, D.C.
WINNIPEG
WISCONSIN
WISCONSIN RIVER
YUKON

Asia

ABKHAZIA
ABU DHABI
AFGHANISTAN
AL-KARAK
ALTAI (KRAI)
AMBOINA
AMRITSAR
AMUR (OBLAST')
ANDAMAN ISLANDS
ANDHRA PRADESH

ANTIOCH
ARAB COUNTRIES
ARABIA
ARMENIA
ASIA
ASIA, SOUTHEAST
BAHRAIN
BALI
BALUCHISTAN
BANGCHAN
BANGKOK
BANGLADESH
BATUMI
BEIRUT
BENGAL
BENGAL, WEST
BHUTAN
BIHAR
BOMBAY (CITY)
BORNEO
BRUNEI
BUKHARA
BURMA
BURYAT REPUBLIC
BURSA
CAGAYAN DE ORO
CALCUTTA
CAMBODIA
CHINA
CHUKOTKA
COMILLA
COORG
CYPRUS
DAGESTANSKIE OGNI
DELHI
DZHAMBUL (OBLAST')
EAST
EAST (FAR EAST)
EAST (NEAR EAST)
EREVAN
FAR EASTERN REPUBLIC
FRUNZE
GANGES, RIVER
GAZA STRIP
GEORGIA

GEOGRAPHY, GEOLOGY AND METEOROLOGY (cont'd)

GOA, DAMAN AND DIU
GORNOALTAISK (OBLAST')
GUJARAT
HALDIA
HARYANA
HONG KONG
INDIA
INDIAN OCEAN
INDOCHINA
INDONESIA
INDUS, RIVER
IRAN
IRAQ
IRKUTSK
IRKUTSK (OBLAST')
ISRAEL
JAMMU AND KASHMIR
JAPAN
JAVA
JERUSALEM
JEWISH AUTONOMOUS OBLAST'
JORDAN
KAMCHATKA
KARACHI
KARAKALPAK REPUBLIC
KAZAKSTAN
KEMEROVO (OBLAST')
KERALA
KHAKASIA
KHOREZM PEOPLE'S SOVIET REPUBLIC
KIANGSI
KIRGHIZIA
KITAKAMI RIVER
KODAIKANAL
KOMI-PERMIAK NATIONAL OKRUG
KOREA
KORYAK NATIONAL OKRUG
KRASNOYARSK
KUALA LUMPUR
KURGAN (OBLAST')
KUWAIT
LAOS
LEBANON
LESSER SUNDA ISLANDS
LEVANT
LYS'VA

MACAO
MALAYA
MALAYSIA
MANCHURIA
MANILA
MEKONG BASIN
MONGOLIA
MYSORE
NAKORN PATHOM
NEPAL
NICOBAR ISLANDS
NORTH-WEST FRONTIER PROVINCE
ORISSA
PAKISTAN
PALESTINE
PAMPANGA
PENANG
PERM' (OBLAST')
PERSIAN GULF
PHILIPPINE ISLANDS
PUNJAB
QATAR
RAJASTHAN
RANGOON
RUSSIA
SAKHALIN
SARAWAK
SHANGHAI
SIKKIM
SIBERIA
SINGAPORE
SOVIET CENTRAL ASIA
SOVIET FAR EAST
SOVIET NORTH
SRI LANKA
STEPPES
SUMATRA
SULU ISLANDS
SYRIA
T'AI-CHUNG
TAIMYR NATIONAL OKRUG
TAIWAN
TAJIKISTAN
TASHKENT
TBILISI

THAILAND
TIBET
TOKYO
TSELINOGRAD (OBLAST')
TURKESTAN
TURKEY
TURKMENISTAN
TUVA
TYUMEN' (OBLAST')
UNITED ARAB EMIRATES
UTTAR PRADESH
UZBEKISTAN
VIETNAM
YAKUTIA
YENAN

Australia and Oceania

ADELAIDE
AUCKLAND
AUSTRALIA
BIAK
BRISBANE
CANBERRA
D'ENTRECASTEAUX ISLANDS
DRUMMOYNE
DUNEDIN
FIJI ISLANDS
FREMANTLE
FRENCH POLYNESIA
GILBERT AND ELLICE ISLANDS COLONY
GLADSTONE, QUEENSLAND
HAMILTON, NEW ZEALAND
HAWAIIAN ISLANDS
MELANESIA
MELBOURNE
MICRONESIA
MONARO
NEW CALEDONIA
NEW GUINEA
NEW HEBRIDES
NEW SOUTH WALES
NEW ZEALAND

GEOGRAPHY, GEOLOGY AND METEOROLOGY (cont'd)

NOEMFOOR
NORTHERN TERRITORY
OCEANIA
PACIFIC, THE
PERTH, WESTERN AUSTRALIA
PITCAIRN ISLAND
POLYNESIA
QUEENSLAND
SAMOA
SOLOMON ISLANDS
SYDNEY
TAHITI
TASMANIA
TONGA
VICTORIA, AUSTRALIA
WAGGA WAGGA
WELLINGTON, NEW ZEALAND
WESTERN AUSTRALIA

Europe

AALST
AARGAU (CANTON)
ABRUZZI
ABRUZZI E MOLISE
AIX-EN-PROVENCE
ALBANIA
ALESSANDRIA (PROVINCE)
ALLENDORF
ALPES-MARITIMES
ALPS
ALSACE
ALSACE-LORRAINE
AMBERG
AMSTERDAM
ANDALUSIA
ANDORRA
ANGERS
ANJOU
ANTWERP
ANTWERP (PROVINCE)
APULIA
ARKHANGEL'SK

ARKHANGEL'SK (OBLAST')
ARTEMOVSK
ASTRAKHAN'
ASTURIAS
ATHENS
AUBE
AUBRAC
AUSTRIA
AUSTRIA-HUNGARY
AUVERGNE
AVESNELLES
AZERBAIJAN
AZORES
BADEN
BADEN-WUERTTEMBERG
BAGNOLS-SUR-CEZE
BAKU
BALKAN STATES
BALLINA
BALTIC, THE
BALTIC STATES
BARANYA
BARCELONA
BARI (PROVINCE)
BASEL (CITY)
BASEL (DIOCESE)
BASHKIR REPUBLIC
BASQUE PROVINCES
BAVARIA
BAYEUX
BAYREUTH
BECHHOFEN
BELGIUM
BELGOROD (OBLAST')
BELOMORSK
BERGEN
BERLIN
BERN (CANTON)
BERN (CITY)
BESSARABIA
BIAYSTOK
BIAŁYSTOK
BINCHE
BLACK SEA REGION
BOLOGNA

BOLOGNA (PROVINCE)
BOLZANO
BORDEAUX
BORGERHOUT
BRANDENBURG (PROVINCE)
BREMEN
BRESCIA (PROVINCE)
BRETTEN
BRIANSK (OBLAST')
BRITTANY
BRITTAS BAY
BRUNSWICK
BRUSSELS
BUDAPEST
BUKOVINA
BULGARIA
BURGENLAND
BYDGOSZCZ
BYDGOSZCZ (PROVINCE)
CAEN
CALABRIA
CALVADOS
CAMPANIA
CARBONIA
CARPI
CASSEL
CASTELVOLTURNO
CATALONIA
CAUCASUS
CHAMPAGNE
CHAMPSAUR
CHARLEROI
CHECHEN-INGUSH REPUBLIC
CHUVASH REPUBLIC
CLERMONT-FERRAND
COLOGNE
COPENHAGEN
CORK
CORSICA
COTTBUS
CRACOW
CRACOW (PROVINCE)
CRIMEA
CROATIA
CZECHOSLOVAKIA
DAGHESTAN

GEOGRAPHY, GEOLOGY AND METEOROLOGY (cont'd)

DANUBE VALLEY
DENMARK
DNEPROPETROVSK (OBLAST')
DOBRUDJA
DONETS BASIN
DORDOGNE
DORTMUND
DUBLIN
DUBLIN (COUNTY)
DUBROVNIK
DUESSELDORF
DUNKIRK
EAST FLANDERS
EAST PRUSSIA
EASTERN ROUMELIA
EITORF
EL PINAR
EMILIA-ROMAGNA
EMPOLI
EPERNAY
EPIRUS
ESTARREJA
ESTONIA
EUROPE
EUROPE, EASTERN
EUROPEAN ECONOMIC COMMUNITY COUNTRIES
EUROPEAN FREE TRADE ASSOCIATION COUNTRIES
FARO
FAROE ISLANDS
FERRARA
FERRARA (PROVINCE)
FINLAND
FLANDERS
FLORENCE
FRANCE
FRANCONIA
FRANKFURT-AM-MAIN
FRIBOURG
FRIESLAND
FRIULI
FRIULI- VENEZIA GIULIA
GALICIA (EASTERN EUROPE)
GALICIA (SPAIN)
GASCONY
GDANSK

GDAŃSK (PROVINCE)
GEISENHEIM
GELA
GENEVA (CANTON)
GENOA
GERMANY
GERMANY, EASTERN
GHENT
GIBRALTAR
GOERLITZ
GOETTINGEN
GOMEL'
GOR'KII
GOR'KII (OBLAST')
GOTHENBURG
GRAUBUENDEN
GRAZ
GREECE
GRENOBLE
HAGUE
HAINAUT
HALLE
HAMBURG
HANAU
HANOVER
HARDENBERG-NEVIGES
HERAULT
HESSE
HORSENS
HUNGARY
IRELAND (REPUBLIC)
ITALY
IVANOVO
IVANOVO (OBLAST')
IVREA
JURA
JURA (DEPARTMENT)
KABARDINO BALKARIAN REPUBLIC
KALININ (OBLAST')
KALMYK REPUBLIC
KARELIA
KARL-MARX-STADT
KATOWICE (PROVINCE)
KAZAN'
KHARKOV (OBLAST')

KHMEL'NITSKII (OBLAST')
KIEV
KIROVOGRAD (OBLAST')
KLAGENFURT
KOMI REPUBLIC
KOSTROMA (OBLAST')
KOSZALIN (PROVINCE)
KRONSTADT
KUBAN'
KUIBYSHEV (OBLAST')
KUNGUR
KURSK (OBLAST')
LANGENBERG
LANGHE
LANGUEDOC
LATVIA
LAZIO
LE HAVRE
LEIPZIG
LEMAN (DEPARTMENT, 1801-1815)
LENINGRAD
LENINGRAD (OBLAST')
LIECHTENSTEIN
LIMBURG (PROVINCE)
LIPETSK (OBLAST')
LITHUANIA
ŁÓDŹ
ŁÓDŹ (PROVINCE)
LOIRE (DEPARTMENT)
LOMBARDY
LORRAINE
LOWER AUSTRIA
LOWER SAXONY
LUBLIN (PROVINCE)
LUXEMBOURG
L'VOV (OBLAST')
LYONS
MACEDONIAN REPUBLIC
MADRID
MADRID (PROVINCE)
MALBORK
MALMÖ
MALTA
MANNHEIM
MANSFELD

GEOGRAPHY, GEOLOGY AND METEOROLOGY (cont'd)

MARBURG
MARCHE, LA
MARCHES
MARI REPUBLIC
MARSEILLES
MEDA
MEDITERRANEAN
MEMMINGEN
MEUSE, RIVER
MILAN (CITY)
MILAN (DUCHY)
MOGILEV
MOLDAVIA
MOLDAVIAN REPUBLIC
MONACO
MONTBRISON
MORDVINIAN REPUBLIC
MOSCOW
MOSCOW (OBLAST')
MOSELLE
MUENSTER
MUNICH
MURMANSK (OBLAST')
NAMUR
NAPLES
NENZING
NETHERLANDS
NEUCHÂTEL (CANTON)
NIJMEGEN
NIVELLES
NORRBOTTEN
NORTH OSSETIAN REPUBLIC
NORTH RHINE-WESTPHALIA
NORWAY
NOVGOROD (OBLAST')
NOVOROSSIISK
NOWY SACZ
NUREMBERG
ODESSA
OISE (DEPARTMENT)
OREL (OBLAST')
ORENBURG (OBLAST')
OSLO
PADERBORN

PALERMO
PARIS
PECS
PFORZHEIM
PIEDMONT
PIOMBINO
PISA
PISTICCI
PŁOCK
PO
PO VALLEY
POHJANMAA
POLAND
PORTUGAL
PORZ
PROVENCE
PRUSSIA
PSKOV (OBLAST')
PUTTERSHOEK
RANCIE
RAVENSBURG
REGGIO CALABRIA
REMSCHEID
RENNES
RENNES, AUDE
RHEIMS
RHINE
RHINE PROVINCE
RHINELAND-PALATINATE
RIETI (PROVINCE)
RHÔNE-ALPES
RHÔNE RIVER
RHÔNE VALLEY
ROANNE
ROME (CITY)
ROME (PROVINCE)
ROSTOV (OBLAST')
ROUMANIA
ROUSSILLON
RUHR
RUSSIA
RUSSIA (R.S.F.S.R.)
RUTHENIA
SAARLAND

SAINT-ETIENNE
SAINT-FONS
ST. GALL (CANTON)
SALERNO (PROVINCE)
SARDINIA
SASSARI (CITY)
SCANDICCI
SCANDINAVIA
SCHAUMBURG-LIPPE
SCHLESWIG-HOLSTEIN
SEDLABANKI ISLANDS
SERAING
SERBIA
SEVILLE
SICILY
SIEBELDINGEN
SIEGEN
SIEG-LAHN-DILL
SILESIA
SLOVAKIA
SLOVENIA
SÖDERALA
SPAIN
SPARTA
STAVROPOL' (KRAI)
STEINSTUECKEN
STOCKHOLM
STRALSUND
STRASBOURG
STRUMA
STUTTGART
STYRIA
SWEDEN
ŚWINIARY STARE
SWITZERLAND
TAGANROG
TAMBOV (OBLAST')
TATAR REPUBLIC
TEREK
THURGAU
TOULOUSE
TRANSYLVANIA
TRENTINO-ALTO ADIGE
TRIER
TULA (OBLAST')

GEOGRAPHY, GEOLOGY AND METEOROLOGY (cont'd)

TURIN	**United Kingdom**	DARTMOOR NATIONAL PARK
TUSCANY		DENBIGH
TYROL		DENBIGHSHIRE
UDMURT REPUBLIC	ABERDEEN	DERBY
UKRAINE	ALDERNEY	DERBYSHIRE
UKRAINE, WESTERN	ANDOVER	DEVONSHIRE
UMBRIA	ANGLESEY	DOVER
UPPER ADIGE	ASHFORD	DOWN (COUNTY)
URAL REGION	AYCLIFFE	DUDLEY
VAL D'ARDA	BANBURY	DURHAM (COUNTY)
VAL-DE-MARNE	BARNSBURY	DURHAM (DIOCESE)
VAL TIDONE	BARROW-IN-FURNESS	EALING
VALAIS	BELFAST	EAST ANGLIA
VALGAUDEMAR	BERKSHIRE	EDINBURGH
VÄSTERNORRLAND	BEWDLEY	EDMONTON, MIDDLESEX
VAUD (CANTON)	BILSTON	ENFIELD
VENICE	BIRKENHEAD	ENGLISH CHANNEL
VERCELLI (PROVINCE)	BIRMINGHAM	ESSEX
VIENNA	BLACKPOOL	EXETER
VLADIMIR (OBLAST')	BLACKWATER, RIVER	FIFE
VOLGA BASIN	BRACKNELL	FOREST OF DEAN
VORARLBERG	BRIDGNORTH	FOULNESS
VORONEZH (OBLAST')	BRISTOL	FRAMLINGHAM
VRIES	BRIXHAM	GLASGOW
WALLACHIA	BUCKINGHAMSHIRE	GLOUCESTER
WALLONIA	BUXTON	GUERNSEY
WARSAW	CAERNARVONSHIRE	HALESOWEN
WERTHEIM	CAITHNESS	HAMPSHIRE
WEST FLANDERS	CAMBRIDGE	HAVERHILL
WESTPHALIA	CAMDEN	HEMEL HEMPSTEAD
WHITE RUSSIA	CARDIFF	HEREFORDSHIRE
WOLFSBURG	CARLISLE	HERTFORDSHIRE
WUERTTEMBERG	CHELTENHAM	HILLINGDON
WUPPERTAL	CHESHIRE	HULL
YONNE	CHESTER	HUMBERSIDE
YUGOSLAVIA	CHESTER (DIOCESE)	IPSWICH
ZADRUGA	CHILTERN HILLS	IRELAND
ZAPOROZH'E (OBLAST')	CORNWALL	IRELAND, NORTHERN
ZARNOWIEC	COVENTRY	IRVINE
ŽEROVNICA	CREWE	ISLE OF MAN
ZHITOMIR (OBLAST')	CROYDON	ISLE OF WIGHT
ZLIN	CUMBERLAND	ISLINGTON
ZUERICH (CANTON)	CUMBERNAULD	JERSEY
ZUERICH (CITY)	DAGENHAM	KENSINGTON AND CHELSEA
	DARLINGTON	KENT
	DARTMOOR	

GEOGRAPHY, GEOLOGY AND METEOROLOGY (cont'd)

KETTERING	NEW WINDSOR	STEPNEY
KILDONAN, STRATH OF	NEWCASTLE-UPON-TYNE	STEVENAGE
KING'S LYNN	NORTH YORK MOORS NATIONAL PARK	STOURBRIDGE
LAMBETH	NORTHAMPTON	SUNDERLAND
LANCASHIRE	NORTHUMBERLAND	SUSSEX
LEEDS	NORWICH	SUTHERLAND
LEICESTER	NOTTINGHAM	SWINDON
LEICESTERSHIRE	NOTTINGHAMSHIRE	THAMES, RIVER
LINCOLNSHIRE	ORPINGTON	TORBAY
LITTLEHAMPTON	OXFORD	TRENT RIVER
LIVERPOOL	PEAK NATIONAL PARK	TYNESIDE
LONDON	POPLAR	TYRONE
LONDONDERRY	PORTSMOUTH	UNITED KINGDOM
LOSTWITHIEL	PURBECK, ISLE OF	WALES
MANCHESTER	RAWTENSTALL	WALSALL
MARYPORT	READING	WANDSWORTH
MEDWAY, RIVER	REDDITCH	WARRINGTON
MERSEYSIDE	ROXBURGH	WEARSIDE
MERTHYR TYDFIL	SALFORD	WEST HAM
MIDDLESEX	SCOTLAND	WESTMINSTER
MILTON KEYNES	SEVERN	WIGGINTON
MORECAMBE BAY	SHOREDITCH	WINCHESTER (DIOCESE)
NANTWICH	SHROPSHIRE	WORCESTER
NEAGH, LOUGH	SOUTHAMPTON	WORCESTERSHIRE
NELSON (LANCASHIRE)	SOUTHWARK	YORK
NEW FOREST	STAFFORDSHIRE	YORKSHIRE

HISTORY

<u>General</u>

	CIVIL WAR	GILDS
	CIVILIZATION	GOLD ARTICLES
	CIVILIZATION, ANCIENT	HISTORIANS
ALLIANCES	CIVILIZATION, CHRISTIAN	HISTORIANS, AMERICAN
ARCHAEOLOGY	CIVILIZATION, GREEK	HISTORIANS, BRITISH
ARCHAEOLOGY, INDUSTRIAL	CIVILIZATION, MEDIEVAL	HISTORIANS, CHINESE
ARCHIVES	CIVILIZATION, MODERN	HISTORIANS, GERMAN
BRITISH ACADEMY	CIVILIZATION, MOHAMMEDAN	HISTORIANS, MEXICAN
BUSINESS RECORDS	CIVILIZATION, OCCIDENTAL	HISTORIANS, RUSSIAN
CHRONOLOGY, HISTORICAL	COLONIAL COMPANIES	HISTORIANS, UKRAINIAN
CHURCH HISTORY	CONSTITUTIONAL HISTORY	HISTORICAL LIBRARIES
CHURCH RECORDS AND REGISTERS	DEATH	HISTORICAL RESEARCH
CITIES AND TOWNS, ANCIENT	EXCAVATIONS (ARCHAEOLOGY)	HISTORICAL SOCIETIES
CITIES AND TOWNS, MEDIEVAL	FUNERAL ORATIONS	HISTORIOGRAPHY

HISTORY (cont'd)

HISTORY

HISTORY, MODERN

HISTORY, UNIVERSAL

HOSPITALS, MEDIAEVAL

INQUISITION

LITERATURE AND HISTORY

MANUSCRIPTS

MEGALITHIC MONUMENTS

MIDDLE AGES

MONUMENTS

NINETEENTH CENTURY

PEASANT UPRISINGS

REFORMATION

RENAISSANCE

SERFDOM

SOCIAL HISTORY

TWENTIETH CENTURY

TWENTY-FIRST CENTURY

International (including wars)

BREST-LITOVSK, TREATY OF, MARCH 3, 1918 (RUSSIA)

BURMESE WAR, 1824-1826

BURMESE WAR, 1852

CHACO DISPUTE

CHINESE-JAPANESE WAR, 1937-1945

CRIMEAN WAR, 1853-1856

EUROPEAN WAR, 1914-1918

FOREIGN NEWS

FRANCO-GERMAN WAR, 1870-1871

GENEVA CONVENTIONS

GENEVA FOUR POWER CONFERENCE, JULY, 1955

GUERRILLAS

HUNDRED YEARS WAR, 1339-1453

INDO-SOVIET TREATY OF PEACE, FRIENDSHIP AND COOPERATION, 1971

ISRAEL-ARAB CONFLICT, 1948-

ISRAEL-ARAB WAR, 1948-1949

ISRAEL-ARAB WAR, 1967

ITALO-ABYSSINIAN WAR, 1935-1936

KOREAN WAR, 1950-1953

LEND-LEASE OPERATIONS (1941-1945)

LOCARNO CONFERENCE, 1925

LONDON NAVAL TREATY, 1930

MIDDLE EAST SUPPLY CENTRE

MONTREUX CONFERENCE

MUNICH FOUR POWER AGREEMENT, 1938

NEPALESE WAR, 1814-1816

NORTHERN SEVEN YEARS' WAR, 1563-1570

PARAGUAYAN WAR, 1865-1870

PEACE TREATIES

PEASANTS' WAR, 1524-1525

RAPALLO, TREATY OF, 1922

RECONSTRUCTION (1939-1951)

RUSSO-TURKISH WAR, 1877-1878

SCHLESWIG-HOLSTEIN WAR, 1848-1850

SERBO-BULGARIAN WAR, 1885

SOUTH AFRICAN WAR, 1899-1902

STRAITS QUESTION

THIRTY YEARS' WAR, 1618-1648

TRIANON, TREATY OF, JUNE 4, 1920 (HUNGARY)

VERSAILLES, TREATY OF, JUNE 28, 1919 (GERMANY)

VIETNAMESE WARS, 1945-

WARSAW, PACT OF, 1955

WORLD WAR, 1939-1945

African territories

CASABLANCA CONFERENCE, 1961

JAMESON'S RAID, 1895-1896

American territories

ALLIANCE FOR PROGRESS

CONFEDERATE STATES OF AMERICA

FREEDMEN IN KENTUCKY

FRIENDS IN THE UNITED STATES

FRONTIER AND PIONEER LIFE

GRUPO OBRA DE UNIFICACION

MONROE DOCTRINE

RECONSTRUCTION (UNITED STATES)

Asiatic territories

ARMENIAN QUESTION

EASTERN QUESTION (FAR EAST)

EASTERN QUESTION (NEAR EAST)

GOLDEN HORDE

HAGANAH

INDIA-PAKISTAN CONFLICT, 1965

INDIA-PAKISTAN CONFLICT, 1971

KASHMIR QUESTION

KOREAN RESISTANCE MOVEMENTS, 1905-1945

KOREAN REUNIFICATION QUESTION (1945-)

LONG MARCH, 1934-1935

SINO-INDIAN BORDER DISPUTE, 1957-

European territories

ALAND QUESTION

ALSACE-LORRAINE QUESTION

ANSCHLUSS MOVEMENT, 1918-1938

ANTINAZI MOVEMENT

BERLIN QUESTION (1945-

BYZANTINE EMPIRE

CIVILIZATION, GERMANIC

CIVILIZATION, HISPANIC

CONCERT OF EUROPE

CONCORDAT OF 1929 (ITALY)

CONGRESS OF VERONA

COSSACKS

COUNTER REFORMATION

DENAZIFICATION

EASTERN QUESTION (BALKAN)

ÉMIGRÉS

FEUDALISM

FLEMISH MOVEMENT

FRANKS

FRONDE

GENERAL STRIKE, BELGIUM, 1961

GENERAL STRIKE, SPAIN, 1917

GERMAN REUNIFICATION QUESTION (1949-)

HISTORY (cont'd)

GREECE, ANCIENT
HANSA TOWNS
HANSEATIC LEAGUE
HOLY ROMAN EMPIRE
ITALIAN QUESTION, 1848-1870
JACOBINS
JACQUERIE, 1358
KULTURKAMPF
MACEDONIAN QUESTION
MOSCOW TRIALS, 1930
MOSCOW TRIALS, 1931
MOSCOW TRIALS, 1936-1937
PAPAL STATES
POLISH QUESTION
RECONSTRUCTION (1914-1939)
RHINE, CONFEDERATION OF THE, 1806-1813
ROMAN QUESTION
ROME, ANCIENT
SAAR QUESTION
SANSCULOTTES
SCHLESWIG-HOLSTEIN QUESTION
SCHMALKALDIC LEAGUE, 1530-1547
TRENT, COUNCIL OF, 1545-1563
TRIBUNUS PLEBIS
UPPER SILESIAN QUESTION
VISIGOTHS

United Kingdom

ANGLO-SAXONS
CHARTISM
DOMESDAY BOOK
FORFEITURE
GENERAL STRIKE, UNITED KINGDOM, 1926
HEDGES
INCLOSURES
IRISH QUESTION
KETT'S REBELLION, 1549
LOLLARDS
LUDDITES
"MANCHESTER MASSACRE", 1819
MANORS
ORANGEMEN
PARISHES
TYLER'S INSURRECTION, 1381
WINDMILLS

Colonial companies

BRITISH NORTH BORNEO (CHARTERED) COMPANY
DANISH EAST INDIA COMPANY
EAST INDIA COMPANY
HUDSON'S BAY COMPANY
IMPERIAL BRITISH EAST AFRICA COMPANY
SPANISH COMPANY

LANGUAGE, LITERATURE AND THE ARTS

Language

AFRIKAANS LANGUAGE
AMBIGUITY
APHASIA
ARYAN LANGUAGES
BANTU LANGUAGES
BILINGUALISM
CANT
CELTIC LANGUAGES
CHINESE LANGUAGE
COLOUR
CONVERSATION
CREOLE DIALECTS
DYIRBAL LANGUAGE
ENGLISH LANGUAGE
ENGLISH LANGUAGE IN THE UNITED STATES
ENGLISH LANGUAGE IN TRINIDAD AND TOBAGO
FINNISH LANGAUGE
FLEMISH LANGUAGE
FRANDIC LANGUAGE
FRENCH LANGUAGE
FRENCH LANGUAGE IN CANADA
GENERATIVE GRAMMAR
GERMAN LANGUAGE
GERMAN LANGUAGE IN ITALY
GRAMMAR, COMPARATIVE AND GENERAL
GREEK LANGUAGE
ITALIAN LANGUAGE
LANGUAGE AND LANGUAGES
LANGUAGE DATA PROCESSING
LANGUAGES
LANGUAGES, MIXED
LANGUAGES, MODERN
LATIN LANGUAGE
LEXICOGRAPHY
LINGUISTIC ANALYSIS (LINGUISTICS)
LINGUISTIC CHANGE
LINGUISTIC RESEARCH
LINGUISTICS
MATHEMATICAL LINGUISTICS
MEANING
MOLDAVIAN LANGUAGE
NAMES
NEGRO-ENGLISH DIALECTS
NORWEGIAN LANGUAGE IN THE UNITED STATES
PHONETICS
PSYCHOLINGUISTICS
RUSSIAN LANGUAGE
RUSSIAN LANGUAGE IN ABKHAZIA
SEMANTICS, COMPARATIVE
SIGN LANGUAGE
SOCIOLINGUISTICS
SPANISH LANGUAGE
SPEECH
WRITING

LANGUAGE, LITERATURE AND THE ARTS (cont'd)

Literature

AFRICAN FICTION
AFRICAN LITERATURE
AFRICAN NEWSPAPERS
AFRICAN PERIODICALS
AMERICAN FICTION
AMERICAN LITERATURE
AMERICAN NEWSPAPERS
AMERICAN PERIODICALS
ANECDOTES
AUSTRALIAN LITERATURE
AUSTRALIAN NEWSPAPERS
AUTHORS, FRENCH
AUTHORS, GERMAN
AUTHORS, RUSSIAN
AUTHORS AND PUBLISHERS
AUTHORSHIP
AUTOBIOGRAPHY
AZERBAIJANI LITERATURE
BIOGRAPHY
CANADIAN PERIODICALS
CHAP BOOKS
CHILDREN'S LITERATURE
CHILDREN'S PERIODICALS, RUSSIAN
CHILDREN'S POETRY
COLONIES IN LITERATURE
COMMUNISM AND LITERATURE
COMMUNITY NEWSPAPERS
CREATION (LITERARY, ARTISTIC, ETC.)
CRIME AND THE PRESS
CRITICISM
CUBAN NEWSPAPERS
DANISH NEWSPAPERS
DEATH IN LITERATURE
ECONOMICS IN LITERATURE
EGYPT IN LITERATURE
ENGLISH FICTION
ENGLISH LITERATURE
ENGLISH NEWSPAPERS
ENGLISH PERIODICALS
FINNISH PERIODICALS
FRENCH FICTION
FRENCH LITERATURE

FRENCH NEWSPAPERS
GERMAN FICTION
GERMAN LITERATURE
GERMAN NEWSPAPERS
GERMAN PERIODICALS
GREEK NEWSPAPERS
HEROES IN LITERATURE
INDIAN PERIODICALS
IRISH LITERATURE
ISRAELI PERIODICALS
ITALIAN NEWSPAPERS
ITALIAN PERIODICALS
JEWS IN LITERATURE
JOURNALISM
LABOUR AND LABOURING CLASSES IN LITERATURE
LATIN AMERICAN LITERATURE
LATIN AMERICAN PERIODICALS
LEGENDS
LITERARY RESEARCH
LITERARY SOCIETIES
LITERATURE
LITERATURE, IMMORAL
LITERATURE AND HISTORY
LITERATURE AND SOCIETY
LITERATURE AND STATE
LITHUANIAN PERIODICALS
NATIONAL SOCIALISM IN LITERATURE
NEGRO LITERATURE
NEGRO PRESS
NEGROES IN LITERATURE
NEWSPRINT
NOVELISTS, MEXICAN
PERUVIAN LITERATURE
POETRY
POLISH LITERATURE
POLISH PERIODICALS
POLITICAL POETRY, ENGLISH
POLITICAL POETRY, GERMAN
POLITICAL POETRY, POLISH
POLITICAL SATIRE, CHINESE
POLITICAL SATIRE, ENGLISH
POLITICAL SATIRE, GERMAN
POLITICAL SATIRE, ITALIAN
POLITICAL SATIRE, POLISH
POLITICAL SCIENCE IN LITERATURE

POLITICS IN LITERATURE
PRESS
PRISON PERIODICALS
PRISONERS' WRITINGS, NEGRO
PROHIBITED BOOKS
REALISM IN LITERATURE
RELIGION IN LITERATURE
REPORTERS AND REPORTING
RUSSIAN ESSAYS
RUSSIAN LETTERS
RUSSIAN LITERATURE
RUSSIAN NEWSPAPERS
SATIRE, ENGLISH
SOCIAL PROBLEMS IN LITERATURE
SOCIALISM IN LITERATURE
SPANISH NEWSPAPERS
STATE ENCOURAGEMENT OF SCIENCE, LITERATURE AND ART
SWEDISH NEWSPAPERS
SYMBOLISM IN LITERATURE
UNDERGROUND LITERATURE
VIOLENCE IN LITERATURE
WOMEN AS AUTHORS
WOMEN'S PERIODICALS, ENGLISH
WOMEN'S PERIODICALS, FRENCH
WOMEN'S PERIODICALS, GERMAN

The Arts

ACTORS AND ACTING
AESTHETICS
ARCHITECTURE
ARCHITECTURE, DOMESTIC
ARCHITECTURE, MODERN
ARCHITECTURE, MODERN
ARCHITECTURE AND SOCIETY
ART
ART AND SOCIETY
ART AND WAR
ART PATRONAGE
ARTS, THE
ARTS, THE, AFRICAN
ARTS, THE, JAVANESE
ARTS AND SOCIETY, THE

LANGUAGE, LITERATURE AND THE ARTS (cont'd)

BALLET
BLACKLISTING OF ENTERTAINERS
BRITISH BROADCASTING CORPORATION
BRITISH COUNCIL
CARICATURES AND CARTOONS
CHINESE DRAMA
COMMUNISM AND ART
COMMUNISM AND THE ARTS
COMMUNIST AESTHETICS
CREATION (LITERARY, ARTISTIC, ETC.)
CULTURAL PROPERTY, PROTECTION OF
DANCING
DESIGN

FOLK ART
FOLK SONGS, AMERICAN
GRAPHIC ARTS
MODULAR COORDINATION (ARCHITECTURE)
MUSIC
MUSIC, POPULAR (SONGS, ETC.)
MUSIC AND SOCIETY
OPERA
OPERA, CHINESE.
PAINTING, CHINESE
POLITICAL BALLADS AND SONGS, AMERICAN
POLITICAL BALLADS AND SONGS, AUSTRIAN

POLITICAL BALLADS AND SONGS, ENGLISH
POLITICAL BALLADS AND SONGS, GERMAN
POLITICAL BALLADS AND SONGS, MEXICAN
POLITICAL BALLADS AND SONGS, SLAVIC
POPULAR CULTURE
STATE ENCOURAGEMENT OF SCIENCE, LITERATURE AND ART
SURREALISM
SYMBOLISM IN ART
THEATRE
WOMEN AS ARTISTS
WOOD ENGRAVINGS, ENGLISH

LAW (including INTERNATIONAL LAW)

General

ADVISORY OPINIONS
APPELLATE PROCEDURE
BAIL
COMMON LAW
CONFIDENTIAL COMMUNICATIONS
CONTEMPT OF COURT
COURT RECORDS
COURT RULES
COURTS
CROSS-EXAMINATION
CUSTOMARY LAW
DISSENTING OPINIONS
DUE PROCESS OF LAW
EQUALITY BEFORE THE LAW
ETHNOLOGICAL JURISPRUDENCE
EVIDENCE (LAW)
EVIDENCE, EXPERT
IDENTIFICATION
INTER-AMERICAN COUNCIL OF JURISTS
JUDGMENTS
JUDGEMENTS, DECLARATORY
JUDICIAL ASSISTANCE
JUDICIAL DISCRETION
JUDICIAL ERROR

JUDICIAL POWER
JUDICIAL PROCESS
JUDICIAL REVIEW
JURISDICTION
JURISPRUDENCE
JURY
JUSTICE
JUSTICE, ADMINISTRATION OF
JUSTICE AND POLITICS
JUSTICES OF THE PEACE
LACUNAE IN LAW
LAW
LAW, COMPARATIVE
LAW AND ETHICS
LAW ENFORCEMENT
LAW LIBRARIES
LAW REFORM
LAW REPORTING
LAW REPORTS, DIGESTS, ETC.
LEGAL AID
LEGAL CERTAINTY
LEGAL ETHICS
MISTAKE (LAW)
MOTIVE (LAW)
NATURAL LAW
NOTARIES
OBSCENITY (LAW)

PRE-TRIAL PROCEDURE
PROCEDURE (LAW)
RELIGION AND LAW
RESPONSIBILITY, LEGAL
RIGHT TO COUNSEL
RULE OF LAW
SEX AND LAW
SOCIAL LEGISLATION
SOCIOLOGICAL JURISPRUDENCE
TIME (LAW)
TRIAL PRACTICE
TRIALS
UNINCORPORATED SOCIETIES
WITNESSES
WRITS

Public law

ABUSE OF ADMINISTRATIVE POWER
ADMINISTRATIVE COURTS
ADMINISTRATIVE DISCRETION
ADMINISTRATIVE LAW
ADMINISTRATIVE REMEDIES
ADMINISTRATIVE RESPONSIBILITY
AGRICULTURAL LAWS AND LEGISLATION

LAW (including INTERNATIONAL LAW) (cont'd)

ALIENS
AMNESTY
APPORTIONMENT (ELECTION LAW)
ARREST
ASSEMBLY, RIGHT OF
BUILDING LAWS AND REGULATIONS
CHARITY LAWS AND LEGISLATION
COMPENSATION (LAW)
CONSTITUTIONAL COURTS
CONSTITUTIONAL LAW
DISALLOWANCE OF LEGISLATION
ECONOMIC LEGISLATION
EDUCATIONAL LAW AND LEGISLATION
ELECTION LAW
EMIGRATION AND IMMIGRATION LAW
EMINENT DOMAIN
ENVIRONMENTAL LAW
FIRE DEPARTMENTS
FIRE PREVENTION
FISHERY LAW AND LEGISLATION
FOOD LAW AND LEGISLATION
FORESTRY LAW AND LEGISLATION
GOVERNMENT LIABILITY
HABEAS CORPUS
IMPEACHMENTS
INDEPENDENT REGULATORY COMMISSIONS
INTERNAL REVENUE LAW
JUDICIAL REVIEW OF ADMINISTRATIVE ACTS
LEGISLATION
LEGISLATIVE BODIES
LEGISLATIVE POWER
LICENCE SYSTEM
LOCUS STANDI
MENTAL HEALTH LAWS
MILITARY LAW
MISCONDUCT IN OFFICE
MUNICIPAL CORPORATIONS
NARCOTIC LAWS
NAVAL LAW
POLITICAL CRIMES AND OFFENCES
POLITICAL QUESTIONS AND JUDICIAL POWER
POOR LAWS
PRESS LAW
PUBLIC INTEREST

PUBLIC LAW
RADIO
RAILWAY LAW
RECORDING AND REGISTRATION
REPEAL OF LEGISLATION
RESTITUTION
RESTITUTION AND INDEMNIFICATION CLAIMS (1933-   )
SERVITUDES
SUGAR LAWS AND LEGISLATION
TELEVISION
TRIALS (IMPEACHMENT)
ZONING LAW

Civil law and procedure

ACCIDENT LAW
ACTIONS AND DEFENCES
ADMINISTRATION OF ESTATES
ALIMONY
ATTACHMENT AND GARNISHMENT
BUILDING LEASES
CHARITABLE USES, TRUSTS AND FOUNDATIONS
CHARITY LAWS AND LEGISLATION
CIVIL LAW
CIVIL PROCEDURE
COMMUNITY PROPERTY
COMPENSATION (LAW)
CONSIDERATION (LAW)
CONTRACTS
CONTRACTS, AGRICULTURAL
CONVEYANCING
DAMAGES
DEBTOR AND CREDITOR
DESERTION AND NON-SUPPORT
DIVORCE
DOMESTIC RELATIONS
EQUITY
ESTATE PLANNING
EXECUTIONS (LAW)
EXECUTORS AND ADMINISTRATORS
GUARDIAN AND WARD
HUSBAND AND WIFE
ILLEGITIMACY

IMPOSSIBILITY OF PERFORMANCE
INHERITANCE AND SUCCESSION
INTERVENTION (CIVIL PROCEDURE)
JURISTIC PERSONS
LAND CHARGES (UNITED KINGDOM)
LAND TITLES
LANDLORD AND TENANT
LEASES
LEGITIME
LETTERS ROGATORY
LIABILITY FOR ANIMALS
LIBEL AND SLANDER
LIENS
LIMITATION OF ACTIONS
MARRIAGE LAW
NEGLIGENCE
NOISE CONTROL
NUISANCES
OBLIGATIONS (LAW)
PARENT AND CHILD (LAW)
PATERNITY
PERSONAL PROPERTY
PERSONS (LAW)
POSSESSORY ACTIONS
PRIVACY, RIGHT OF
PROBATE LAW AND PRACTICE
PROXIMATE CAUSE (LAW)
REAL PROPERTY
RECEIVERS
REMEDIES (LAW)
SECURITY (LAW)
SEPARATION (LAW)
SERVANTS
SET-OFF AND COUNTERCLAIM
SETTLEMENTS (LAW)
SUPPORT (DOMESTIC RELATIONS)
SURETYSHIP AND GUARANTY
TORTS
TRESPASS
TRUSTS AND TRUSTEES
UNBORN CHILDREN (LAW)
VENDORS AND PURCHASERS

LAW (including INTERNATIONAL LAW) (cont'd)

Commercial, Industrial and Labour Laws

ADVERTISING LAWS
AGENCY (LAW)
ARBITRATION AND AWARD
BANKING LAW
BREACH OF CONTRACT
BUILDING LAWS AND REGULATIONS
BUSINESS LAW
CLUBS
COMMERCIAL COURTS
COMMERCIAL CRIMES
COMMERCIAL LAW
COMMERCIAL TREATIES
CONCESSIONS
CONTRACTS
COPYRIGHT
CORN LAWS
CORPORATION LAW
CUSTOMS COURTS
DELIVERY OF GOODS (LAW)
DESIGN PROTECTION
ECONOMIC LEGISLATION
FACTORY LAWS AND LEGISLATION
HIRE
ILLEGAL CONTRACTS
INDUSTRIAL LAWS AND LEGISLATION
INSURANCE LAW
INTEREST (LAW)
LABOUR COURTS
LABOUR LAWS AND LEGISLATION
LAY DAYS
LIABILITY FOR MARINE ACCIDENTS
LIBERTY OF CONTRACT
LIMITED PARTNERSHIP
MASTER AND SERVANT
MINING LAW
NEGOTIABLE INSTRUMENTS
OIL AND GAS LEASES
PARTNERSHIP
PATENT LAWS AND LEGISLATION
PATENT LICENCES
PETROLEUM LAW AND LEGISLATION
QUALITY OF PRODUCTS

RECEIVERS
SALES
SUPPLEMENTARY EMPLOYMENT
TRADE MARKS
TRADE SECRETS
TRUCK SYSTEM

Criminal law and procedure

ARREST
ARSON
ASSAULT AND BATTERY
BREACH OF THE PEACE
CAPITAL PUNISHMENT
CLASSIFICATION OF CRIMES
COMPOUND OFFENCES
CONFESSION (LAW)
CONSPIRACY
COURTS- MARTIAL AND COURTS OF INQUIRY
CRIMINAL ATTEMPT
CRIMINAL COURTS
CRIMINAL INTENT
CRIMINAL INVESTIGATION
CRIMINAL JURISDICTION
CRIMINAL JUSTICE, ADMINISTRATION OF
CRIMINAL LAW
CRIMINAL LIABILITY
CRIMINAL PROCEDURE
DEFENCE (CRIMINAL PROCEDURE)
DRUNKENNESS (CRIMINAL LAW)
EMBEZZLEMENT
EVIDENCE, CRIMINAL
FINES (PENALTIES)
FIREARMS
GUILT (LAW)
HIJACKING OF AIRCRAFT
HOMICIDE
IMPRISONMENT
INDICTMENTS
INSANITY
JUDGMENTS, CRIMINAL
LARCENY
LIMITATION OF ACTIONS (CRIMINAL LAW)

OFFENCES AGAINST PROPERTY
OFFENCES AGAINST THE PERSON
PARDON
PAROLE
PERJURY
PRELIMINARY EXAMINATIONS (CRIMINAL PROCEDURE)
PRINCIPALS (CRIMINAL LAW)
PROSECUTION
PUBLIC DEFENDERS
PUBLIC PROSECUTORS
PUNISHMENT
REPARATION
ROBBERY
SENTENCES (CRIMINAL PROCEDURE)
SEX CRIMES
SHOPLIFTING
TRIALS (BLASPHEMY)
TRIALS (CONSPIRACY)
TRIALS (ESPIONAGE)
TRIALS (HERESY)
TRIALS (MILITARY OFFENCES)
TRIALS (MURDER)
TRIALS (OBSCENITY)
TRIALS (POLITICAL CRIMES AND OFFENCES)
TRIALS (SEDITION)
TRIALS (SEDITIOUS LIBEL)
TRIALS (SODOMY)
TRIALS (TREASON)

Ecclesiastic law

CANON LAW
ECCLESIASTICAL COURTS
ECCLESIASTICAL LAW

Foreign law

COURTS (MOHAMMEDAN LAW)
DOMESTIC RELATIONS (JEWISH LAW)
INHERITANCE AND SUCCESSION (JEWISH LAW)

LAW (including INTERNATIONAL LAW) (cont'd)

LAW, JEWISH

Legal history

FEUDAL COURTS
LAW, GREEK
LAW, VISIGOTHIC
MANORIAL COURTS
ROMAN DUTCH LAW
ROMAN LAW

Conflict of laws, civil and criminal

ALIEN PROPERTY
COPYRIGHT, INTERNATIONAL
DOMICILE
EXTRADITION
INTERNATIONAL LAW, PRIVATE
JUDGMENTS, FOREIGN
JURISDICTION, TERRITORIAL

International law

AGGRESSION (INTERNATIONAL LAW)
AIRSPACE (INTERNATIONAL LAW)

ANNEXATION (INTERNATIONAL LAW)
ARBITRATION, INTERNATIONAL
ARMISTICES
ASYLUM, RIGHT OF
ATOMIC WEAPONS (INTERNATIONAL LAW)
BELLIGERENCY
CIVIL PROCEDURE (INTERNATIONAL LAW)
CIVIL RIGHTS (INTERNATIONAL LAW)
CLAIMS
COLLISIONS AT SEA
COLONIES (INTERNATIONAL LAW)
CONTRABAND OF WAR
CONTRACTS (INTERNATIONAL LAW)
CONTRACTS, MARITIME
COURT OF JUSTICE OF THE EUROPEAN COMMUNITIES
CRIMES AGAINST HUMANITY, GERMAN
EMINENT DOMAIN (INTERNATIONAL LAW)
ESCALATOR CLAUSE
FAVOURED NATION CLAUSE
FREEDOM OF MOVEMENT (INTERNATIONAL LAW)
FREEDOM OF THE SEAS
GENERAL AGREEMENT ON TARIFFS AND TRADE
GENEVA CONVENTIONS
GOVERNMENT LIABILITY (INTERNATIONAL LAW)
HAGUE. INTERNATIONAL COURT OF JUSTICE
HAGUE. PERMANENT COURT OF INTERNATIONAL JUSTICE
IMMUNITIES OF FOREIGN STATES
INTERNATIONAL AND MUNICIPAL LAW
INTERNATIONAL COURTS

INTERNATIONAL LAW
INTERNATIONAL LAW COMMISSION
INTERVENTION (INTERNATIONAL LAW)
INVESTMENTS, FOREIGN (INTERNATIONAL LAW)
JURISDICTION (INTERNATIONAL LAW)
JURISTIC ACTS (INTERNATIONAL LAW)
LABOUR LAWS AND LEGISLATION, INTERNATIONAL
MARINE ACCIDENTS
MARITIME LAW
NORTH SEA
OCEAN BOTTOM
PASSPORTS
PERSONS (INTERNATIONAL LAW)
RECIPROCITY
RECOGNITION (INTERNATIONAL LAW)
RESPONSIBILITY, LEGAL (INTERNATIONAL LAW)
SANCTIONS (INTERNATIONAL LAW)
SELF DEFENCE (INTERNATIONAL LAW)
SPACE LAW
TERRITORIAL WATERS
TERRITORY, NATIONAL
TORTS (INTERNATIONAL LAW)
TRADE-MARKS (INTERNATIONAL LAW)
TREATIES
VIENNA CONVENTION ON THE LAW OF TREATIES
WAR (INTERNATIONAL LAW)
WAR, MARITIME (INTERNATIONAL LAW)

MATHEMATICS AND STATISTICS

ALGEBRA
ALGEBRA, ABSTRACT
ALGEBRA, BOOLEAN
ALGEBRAS, LINEAR
ALGORITHMS
ANALYSIS OF VARIANCE
ARITHMETIC
ASCOP (ELECTRONIC COMPUTER SYSTEM)
AXIOMATIC SET THEORY

AXIOMS
BAYESIAN STATISTICAL DECISION THEORY
BUSINESS MATHEMATICS
CASHFLO (COMPUTER PROGRAM)
CENSUS
CLUSTER ANALYSIS
COMPUTERS
CONTROL SYSTEMS
CONTROL THEORY

CONVERGENCE
CORRELATION (STATISTICS)
CRIMINAL STATISTICS
CRITICAL PATH ANALYSIS
DATA-TEXT (COMPUTER PROGRAMME LANGUAGE)
DATA TRANSMISSION SYSTEMS
DECIMAL SYSTEM
DEMOGRAPHY
DIFFERENTIAL GAMES

MATHEMATICS AND STATISTICS (cont'd)

- DIGITAL COMPUTER SIMULATION
- DISTRIBUTION (PROBABILITY THEORY)
- DYNAMIC PROGRAMMING
- ECONOMICS, MATHEMATICAL
- EDUCATIONAL STATISTICS
- ELECTRONIC DIGITAL COMPUTERS
- EQUATIONS
- EQUATIONS, SIMULTANEOUS
- ESTIMATION THEORY
- EXPERIMENTAL DESIGN
- FACTOR ANALYSIS
- FECUNDITY
- FORTRAN (COMPUTER PROGRAMME LANGUAGE)
- FREQUENCY CURVES
- FUNCTIONAL ANALYSIS
- FUNCTIONS
- GAMES, THEORY OF
- GAMES OF STRATEGY (MATHEMATICS)
- GEOMETRIC PROGRAMMING
- GEOMETRY
- GRAPH THEORY
- HARMONIC ANALYSIS
- HOMOLOGY THEORY
- INDUSTRIAL STATISTICS
- INTEGER PROGRAMMING
- INTEGRAL TRANSFORMS
- INTEGRALS
- INTEGRALS, STOCHASTIC
- KALMAN FILTERING
- LATENT STRUCTURE ANALYSIS
- LEAST SQUARES
- LINEAR PROGRAMMING
- MARKOV PROCESSES
- MATHEMATICAL ANALYSIS
- MATHEMATICAL LINGUISTICS
- MATHEMATICAL MODELS
- MATHEMATICAL OPTIMIZATION
- MATHEMATICAL PHYSICS
- MATHEMATICS
- MATRICES
- MEASURE THEORY
- MEDICAL STATISTICS
- METAMATHEMATICS
- MORTALITY
- MULTIVARIATE ANALYSIS
- NETWORK ANALYSIS (PLANNING)
- NONLINEAR PROGRAMMING
- NONLINEAR THEORIES
- NONPARAMETRIC STATISTICS
- NUMBERS, THEORY OF
- NUMERICAL TAXONOMY
- OPERATIONS RESEARCH
- ORDER STATISTICS.
- POLITICAL STATISTICS
- POLYNOMIALS
- POPULATION FORECASTING
- POPULATION GENETICS
- PROBABILITIES
- PROGRAMMING (ELECTRONIC COMPUTERS)
- PROGRAMMING (MATHEMATICS)
- PROGRAMMING LANGUAGES (ELECTRONIC COMPUTERS)
- QUEUING THEORY
- RANDOM WALKS (MATHEMATICS)
- RECURSIVE FUNCTIONS
- REGISTERS OF BIRTHS, ETC.
- REGRESSION ANALYSIS
- SAMPLING (STATISTICS)
- SIMULATION METHODS
- SOCIAL INDICATORS
- SOCIOMETRY
- STATISTICAL DECISION
- STATISTICS
- STOCHASTIC DIFFERENTIAL EQUATIONS
- STOCHASTIC PROCESSES
- STOCHASTIC PROGRAMMING
- SWITCHING THEORY
- SYSTEM ANALYSIS
- SYSTEM THEORY
- TIME SERIES ANALYSIS
- TOPOLOGY
- TRANSFORMATIONS (MATHEMATICS)
- VITAL STATISTICS
- WEIGHTS AND MEASURES

MILITARY AND NAVAL SCIENCE

- AERONAUTICS, MILITARY
- AIR POWER
- ARMAMENTS
- ARMED FORCES
- ARMIES
- ART AND WAR
- ATOMIC BOMB
- ATOMIC WARFARE
- ATOMIC WEAPONS
- BAC TSR 2 (TURBOJET FIGHTER PLANES)
- BALLISTIC MISSILES
- BIOLOGICAL WARFARE
- BRITISH LEGION
- CHEMICAL WARFARE
- CIVILIAN DEFENCE
- COMBAT
- DEFENCE CONTRACTS
- DEFENCES, NATIONAL
- DESERTION, MILITARY
- DETERRENCE (STRATEGY)
- EX-SERVICEMEN
- FIREARMS
- GUERRILLA WARFARE
- JEWS AS SOLDIERS
- LOGISTICS
- MAGINOT LINE
- MILITARISM
- MILITARY ART AND SCIENCE
- MILITARY ASSISTANCE, AMERICAN
- MILITARY ASSISTANCE, GERMAN
- MILITARY EDUCATION
- MILITARY ASSISTANCE, NORWEGIAN
- MILITARY GOVERNMENT
- MILITARY LAW
- MILITARY POLICY
- MILITARY RESEARCH

MILITARY AND NAVAL SCIENCE (cont'd)

MILITARY SERVICE, COMPULSORY	PENSIONS, MILITARY	PSYCHOLOGY, MILITARY
MINES, MILITARY	POLARIS (MISSILE)	SABOTAGE
MINES, SUBMARINE	POLITICS AND WAR	SEA POWER
MIRAGE (FIGHTER PLANES)	PRISONERS OF WAR, ALSATIAN	SOCIOLOGY, MILITARY
MUNITIONS	PRISONERS OF WAR, GERMAN	SOLDIERS
MUTINY	PRISONERS OF WAR, RUSSIAN	STRATEGY
NAPALM	PRISONERS OF WAR, YUGOSLAV	SUBMARINE WARFARE
NAVAL LAW	PRIVATEERING	WAR
NAVY-YARDS AND NAVAL STATIONS	PSYCHOLOGICAL WARFARE	

PHILOSOPHY AND RELIGION

Philosophy

	HELLENISM	NIHILISM (PHILOSOPHY)
	HERMENEUTICS	OBEDIENCE
	HUMANISM	ONTOLOGY
ANALYSIS (PHILOSOPHY)	HYPOCRISY	OPPOSITION, THEORY OF
BELIEF AND DOUBT	IDEALISM	OPTIMISM
BUSINESS ETHICS	IDENTITY	PHENOMENOLOGY
CAUSATION	IDEOLOGY	PHILOSOPHERS
CHRISTIAN ETHICS	IMMORTALITY	PHILOSOPHERS, AMERICAN
COMMUNIST ETHICS	INDIVIDUALISM	PHILOSOPHICAL ANTHROPOLOGY
CONDUCT OF LIFE	INDIVIDUALITY	PHILOSOPHY
CONSCIOUSNESS	INFINITE	PHILOSOPHY, AFRICAN
CREATION	JUDGMENT	PHILOSOPHY, AMERICAN
DECISION MAKING (ETHICS)	KNOWLEDGE, THEORY OF	PHILOSOPHY, ANCIENT
DEGENERATION	LAST WORDS	PHILOSOPHY, ARMENIAN
DIALECTIC	LAW AND ETHICS	PHILOSOPHY, CHINESE
EMPIRICISM	LEGAL ETHICS	PHILOSOPHY, FRENCH
ENLIGHTENMENT	LIFE	PHILOSOPHY, GERMAN
ETHICS	LOGIC	PHILOSOPHY, MEDIEVAL
ETHICS, AMERICAN	LOGIC, SYMBOLIC AND MATHEMATICAL	PHILOSOPHY, MODERN
ETHICS, GREEK	LOGICAL POSITIVISM	PHILOSOPHY, POLISH
ETHICS, JEWISH	MATERIALISM	PHILOSOPHY, PRIMITIVE
ETHICS, RUSSIAN	MATHEMATICAL PHYSICS	PHILOSOPHY, RUSSIAN
EVIDENCE	MATTER	PHILOSOPHY, SCANDINAVIAN
EXISTENTIALISM	MEANING	PHILOSOPHY, SCOTTISH
FAITH AND REASON	MEDICAL ETHICS	PHILOSOPHY, UKRAINIAN
FOLLY	METAPHYSICS	PHILOSOPHY, VENEZUELAN
FREE THOUGHT	METHODOLOGY	PHILOSOPHY, WHITE RUSSIAN
FREE WILL AND DETERMINISM	MIND AND BODY	PHILOSOPHY OF NATURE
GOOD AND EVIL	MODERATION	PLEASURE
GUILT	MONISM	POLITICAL ETHICS
HAPPINESS	MORAL EDUCATION	
	NEOPLATONISM	

PHILOSOPHY AND RELIGION (cont'd)

POSITIVISM

POWER (PHILOSOPHY)

PRACTICE (PHILOSOPHY)

PRAGMATISM

PROFESSIONAL ETHICS

PROGRESS

QUALITY (PHILOSOPHY)

RATIONALISM

REASON

SCIENCE AND ETHICS

SELF

SENSES AND SENSATION

SEXUAL ETHICS

SHAME

SOCIAL ETHICS

SOCIAL VALUES

SPACE AND TIME

STRUCTURE (PHILOSOPHY)

SUBJECTIVITY

SYMPATHY

THOUGHT AND THINKING

TIME

TRUTH

UNIVERSALS (PHILOSOPHY)

UTILITARIANISM

UTOPIAS

VISION

VISUAL PERCEPTION

WAR AND MORALS

WEALTH, ETHICS OF

WILL

WORTH

Religion

ALBIGENSES

ANABAPTISTS

ANCESTOR WORSHIP

ANTICHRIST

ANTICLERICALISM

ANTINOMIANISM

ATHANASIAN CREED

ATHEISM

AUTHORITY (RELIGION)

BAPTISTS

BENEDICTINES IN THE UNITED KINGDOM

BIBLE

BIBLE OLD TESTAMENT

BIBLE. NEW TESTAMENT

BIBLE AND SCIENCE

BLACK MUSLIM MOVEMENT

BLASPHEMY

BOGOMILES

BOLTON PRIORY

BRADLAUGH FELLOWSHIP

BUDDHA AND BUDDHISM

CAPUCHINS IN COLOMBIA

CATHOLIC ACTION

CATHOLIC CHURCH

CATHOLIC CHURCH IN AUSTRIA

CATHOLIC CHURCH IN CHINA

CATHOLIC CHURCH IN FRANCE

CATHOLIC CHURCH IN GERMANY

CATHOLIC CHURCH IN IRELAND

CATHOLIC CHURCH IN ITALY

CATHOLIC CHURCH IN LATIN AMERICA

CATHOLIC CHURCH IN MEXICO

CATHOLIC CHURCH IN MOZAMBIQUE

CATHOLIC CHURCH IN SPAIN

CATHOLIC CHURCH IN THE UNITED KINGDOM

CATHOLIC CHURCH IN THE UNITED STATES

CATHOLIC CHURCH IN YUGOSLAVIA

CATHOLIC UNIVERSITIES AND COLLEGES

CATHOLICS IN AUSTRALIA

CATHOLICS IN AUSTRIA

CATHOLICS IN BELGIUM

CATHOLICS IN CANADA

CATHOLICS IN GERMANY

CATHOLICS IN ITALY

CATHOLICS IN POLAND

CATHOLICS IN THE NETHERLANDS

CATHOLICS IN THE UNITED KINGDOM

CATHOLICS IN THE UNITED STATES

CATHOLICS IN VIETNAM

CELIBACY

CHASSIDISM

CHRISTIAN ETHICS

CHRISTIAN LIFE

CHRISTIAN SCIENCE

CHRISTIANITY

CHRISTIANITY AND ANTISEMITISM

CHRISTIANITY AND ECONOMICS

CHRISTIANITY AND INTERNATIONAL AFFAIRS

CHRISTIANITY AND OTHER RELIGIONS

CHRISTIANITY AND POLITICS

CHRISTIANS IN AFRICA

CHRISTIANS IN INDIA

CHRISTIANS IN RUSSIA

CHRISTIANS IN THE UNITED KINGDOM

CHRISTIANS IN WEST AFRICA

CHURCH

CHURCH AND COLLEGE IN THE UNITED STATES

CHURCH AND ECONOMICS

CHURCH AND EDUCATION IN LATIN AMERICA

CHURCH AND EDUCATION IN NORTHERN IRELAND

CHURCH AND INDUSTRY

CHURCH AND LABOUR

CHURCH AND RACE PROBLEMS

CHURCH AND SOCIAL PROBLEMS

CHURCH AND STATE

CHURCH AND STATE IN AUSTRIA

CHURCH AND STATE IN BOLIVIA

CHURCH AND STATE IN BRAZIL

CHURCH AND STATE IN EASTERN GERMANY

CHURCH AND STATE IN FRANCE

CHURCH AND STATE IN GERMANY

CHURCH AND STATE IN HUNGARY

CHURCH AND STATE IN ITALY

CHURCH AND STATE IN MADAGASCAR

CHURCH AND STATE IN MEXICO

CHURCH AND STATE IN POLAND

CHURCH AND STATE IN PORTUGAL

CHURCH AND STATE IN PRUSSIA

CHURCH AND STATE IN RUSSIA

CHURCH AND STATE IN SCANDINAVIA

CHURCH AND STATE IN SPAIN

CHURCH AND STATE IN THE NETHERLANDS

CHURCH AND STATE IN THE UKRAINE

CHURCH AND STATE IN THE UNITED KINGDOM

CHURCH AND STATE IN THE UNITED STATES

CHURCH AND STATE IN VENEZUELA

PHILOSOPHY AND RELIGION (cont'd)

CHURCH AND STATE IN YUGOSLAVIA
CHURCH AND UNDERDEVELOPED AREAS
CHURCH HISTORY
CHURCH OF ENGLAND
CHURCH OF ENGLAND IN AUSTRALIA
CHURCH OF IRELAND
CHURCH OF SCOTLAND
CHURCH RECORDS AND REGISTERS
CHURCH WORK
CHURCH WORK WITH YOUTH
CISTERCIANS IN POLAND
CITY MISSIONS
CLERGY
CLUNIACS
COMMUNISM AND CHRISTIANITY
COMMUNISM AND MOHAMMEDANISM
COMMUNISM AND RELIGION
CONFESSION
CONFUCIUS AND CONFUCIANISM
COUNCIL OF CHRISTIANS AND JEWS
COUNTER REFORMATION
CREATION
DEATH OF GOD THEOLOGY
DEISM
DEMONIAC POSSESSION
DEVIL
DISSENTERS, RELIGIOUS
DRUSES
ECSTASY
ECUMENICAL MOVEMENT
ENCYCLICALS, PAPAL
END OF THE WORLD
FAITH
FAITH AND REASON
FAITH CURE
FATHERS OF THE CHURCH
FIFTH MONARCHY MEN
FREE THOUGHT
FRIENDS, SOCIETY OF
FUNDAMENTALISM
FUNERAL RITES AND CEREMONIES
FUTURE LIFE
FUTURE PUNISHMENT
GLOSSOLALIA
GNOSTICISM

GOD
GOOD AND EVIL
GREAT AWAKENING
HALLUCINOGENIC DRUGS AND RELIGIOUS EXPERIENCE
HASHISH
HINDUISM
HOLY CROSS
HYMNS, ENGLISH
IMMORTALITY
JAINS
JEHOVAH'S WITNESSES
JESUITS IN LATIN AMERICA
JESUS CHRIST
JONAH
JUDAISM
JUDAISM AND STATE
KORAN
KULTURKAMPF
LIBERALISM (RELIGION)
LIBERTY OF CONSCIENCE
LOGOS
LORD'S PRAYER
LUTHERAN CHURCH
LUTHERAN CHURCH IN EASTERN GERMANY
LUTHERAN CHURCH IN GERMANY
LUTHERAN CHURCH IN ICELAND
LUTHERAN CHURCH IN TANZANIA
MAN (THEOLOGY)
MARRIAGE
MARRAIGE, MIXED
MARY, Virgin
MEDICINE AND RELIGION
MENNONITES
MENNONITES IN BRITISH HONDURAS
MENNONITES IN MEXICO
METHODIST CHURCH IN THE UNITED KINGDOM
MILLENIUM
MISSIONS
MISSIONS, BRITISH
MISSIONS, GERMAN
MISSIONS, SPANISH
MISSIONS, SWEDISH
MODERNISM
MOHAMMED, the Prophet
MOHAMMEDAN SECTS

MOHAMMEDANISM AND STATE
MOHAMMEDANS IN ABKHAZIA
MOHAMMEDANS IN AFRICA
MOHAMMEDANS IN BURMA
MOHAMMEDANS IN INDIA
MOHAMMEDANS IN INDONESIA
MOHAMMEDANS IN IRAN
MOHAMMEDANS IN NIGERIA
MOHAMMEDANS IN NORTH AFRICA
MOHAMMEDANS IN PAKISTAN
MOHAMMEDANS IN RUSSIA
MOHAMMEDANS IN SUMATRA
MOHAMMEDANS IN THE SUDAN
MONASTERIES
MONASTIC AND RELIGIOUS LIFE
MONASTICISM AND RELIGIOUS ORDER
MONASTICISM AND RELIGIOUS ORDERS, BUDDH
MORMONS AND MORMONISM
MOSES
MYSTICISM
MYTH
MYTHOLOGY
MYTHOLOGY, AUSTRALIAN (ABORIGINAL)
MYTHOLOGY, INDONESIAN
MYTHOLOGY, MELANESIAN
MYTHOLOGY, MICRONESIAN
NATIONALISM AND RELIGION
NATIVISTIC MOVEMENTS
NATURAL THEOLOGY
NEGRO CHURCHES
OPUS DEI.
ORTHODOX EASTERN CHURCH, RUSSI
PANTHEISM
PAPACY
PARISHES
PENTECOSTAL CHURCHES
PETERBOROUGH ABBEY
PILGRIMS AND PILGRIMAGES
POLISH NATIONAL CATHOLIC CHURCH OF AMERICA
POPES
PRAYER
PRIEST WORKERS
PRIESTS
PROTESTANT CHURCHES
PROTESTANTISM

PHILOSOPHY AND RELIGION (cont'd)

PROTESTANTISM AND CAPITALISM
PROTESTANTS IN THE UNITED STATES
PROVIDENCE AND GOVERNMENT OF GOD
PSYCHOLOGY, RELIGIOUS
PURITANS
RASKOLNIKS
RECONCILIATION
REFORMATION
RELIGION
RELIGION, PRIMITIVE
RELIGION AND ECONOMICS
RELIGION AND GEOGRAPHY
RELIGION AND LAW
RELIGION AND POLITICS
RELIGION AND SCIENCE
RELIGION AND SOCIOLOGY
RELIGION AND STATE
RELIGIONS
RELIGIOUS EDUCATION
RELIGIOUS LIBERTY

RELIGIOUS THOUGHT
REPENTANCE
REVELATION
REVOLUTION (THEOLOGY)
SACRIFICE
SCIENTOLOGY
SECTS
SECULARISM
SECULARIZATION
SECULARIZATION (THEOLOGY)
SERMON ON THE MOUNT
SEVENTH-DAY ADVENTISTS
SHAKERS
SHAMANISM
SOCIALISM, CHRISTIAN
SOCIALISM AND RELIGION
SOCIALISM AND THE CATHOLIC CHURCH
SOCIOLOGY, CHRISTIAN
SOKAGAKKAI

SONG OF SOLOMON
SOUL
SPIRITUALISM
SUNDAY
THEOLOGY, DUTCH REFORMED CHURCH
THEOSOPHY
TOLERATION
TRADE UNIONS, CATHOLIC
TREE OF LIFE
TRENT, COUNCIL OF, 1545-1563
UNITARIAN CHURCHES IN THE UNITED KINGDOM
UNITARIANISM
VATICAN COUNCIL, 1962-1965
WAR AND RELIGION
WHITE FATHERS
WOMEN AND RELIGION
YOUNG MEN'S CHRISTIAN ASSOCIATION
YOUNG WOMEN'S CHRISTIAN ASSOCIATION
ZIONIST CHURCHES (AFRICA)

POLITICAL SCIENCE, POLITICS AND GOVERNMENT

General

ADMINISTRATION
ADMINISTRATIVE ACTS
ADMINISTRATIVE AGENCIES
ADMINISTRATIVE AND POLITICAL DIVISIONS
ADMINISTRATIVE PROCEDURE
AERONAUTICS AND STATE
AGRICULTURE AND STATE
ALLEGIANCE
ANARCHISM AND ANARCHISTS
ANTICOMMUNIST MOVEMENTS
ANTISEMITISM
ARISTOCRACY
ARSON
ASSASSINATION
ASSEMBLY, RIGHT OF
ASYLUM, RIGHT OF
ATOMIC WEAPONS AND DISARMAMENT
AUTHORITARIANISM

AUTHORITY
AUTOMOBILES, GOVERNMENT
BALANCE OF POWER
BLACKLISTING OF ENTERTAINERS
BOROUGHS
BOUNDARIES
BRIBERY
BUREAUCRACY
BUSINESS AND POLITICS
CABINET MINISTERS
CABINET SYSTEM
CAMPAIGN FUNDS
CAMPAIGN MANAGEMENT
CENSORSHIP
CENSUS
CENTRE PARTIES
CHILDREN AND POLITICS
CHRISTIAN DEMOCRACY
CHRISTIANITY AND INTERNATIONAL AFFAIRS
CHRISTIANITY AND POLITICS
CHURCH AND STATE

CITIZENSHIP
CIVICS
CIVICS, BRITISH
CIVICS, CHINESE
CIVICS, DUTCH
CIVICS, GERMAN
CIVICS, ITALIAN
CIVICS, LATIN AMERICAN
CIVICS, POLISH
CIVICS, RUSSIAN
CIVIL RIGHTS
CIVIL RIGHTS WORKERS
CIVIL SERVICE
CIVIL SUPREMACY OVER THE MILITARY
COALITION GOVERNMENTS
COLONIES
COLONIES IN AFRICA
COLONIES IN SOUTHEAST ASIA
COLONIES IN THE PACIFIC
COLONIZATION

POLITICAL SCIENCE, POLITICS AND GOVERNMENT (cont'd)

- COMMISSIONS OF INQUIRY
- COMMITTEES
- COMMUNISM
- COMMUNISM AND ART
- COMMUNISM AND CHRISTIANITY
- COMMUNISM AND EDUCATION
- COMMUNISM AND FAMILY
- COMMUNISM AND LITERATURE
- COMMUNISM AND MOHAMMEDANISM
- COMMUNISM AND RELIGION
- COMMUNISM AND SOCIETY
- COMMUNISM AND THE ARTS
- COMMUNISM AND ZIONISM
- COMMUNIST PARTY PURGES
- COMMUNIST REVISIONISM
- COMMUNIST STATE
- COMMUNIST STRATEGY
- COMMUNISTIC SETTLEMENTS
- COMMUNITY LEADERSHIP
- COMMUNITY POWER
- CONCENTRATION CAMPS
- CONFLICT OF INTERESTS (PUBLIC OFFICE)
- CONGRESSES AND CONVENTIONS
- CONSCIENTIOUS OBJECTORS
- CONSERVATISM
- CONSTITUTIONAL HISTORY
- CONSTITUTIONS
- CORPORATE STATE
- CORRUPTION (IN POLITICS)
- COUNTERREVOLUTIONS
- COUPS D'ETAT
- CROWN LANDS
- DECENTRALIZATION IN GOVERNMENT
- DELEGATION OF POWERS
- DEMOCRACY
- DENAZIFICATION
- DEPORTATION
- DESPOTISM
- DICTATORS
- DICTATORSHIP OF THE PROLETARIAT
- DIPLOMACY
- DIPLOMATIC AND CONSULAR SERVICE
- DIPLOMATIC COURIERS
- DIPLOMATIC ETIQUETTE
- DIPLOMATIC PRIVILEGES AND IMMUNITIES
- DIPLOMATIC PROTECTION
- DIRECT ACTION
- DISARMAMENT
- DIVINE RIGHT OF KINGS
- EDUCATION AND STATE
- ELECTIONS
- ELITE
- EMIGRES
- EMPLOYEE MANAGEMENT RELATIONS IN GOVERNMENT
- EQUALITY
- ESPIONAGE
- ESPIONAGE, AMERICAN
- ESPIONAGE, GERMAN
- ESPIONAGE, PAKISTANI
- ESPIONAGE, RUSSIAN
- EUROPEAN COOPERATION
- EUROPEAN FEDERATION
- EXECUTIVE POWER
- EXECUTIVE PRIVILEGE (GOVERNMENT INFORMATION)
- EXPATRIATION
- FASCISM
- FEDERAL GOVERNMENT
- FREEDOM OF ASSOCIATION
- FREEDOM OF INFORMATION
- FUNCTIONAL REPRESENTATION
- GEOPOLITICS
- GILD SOCIALISM
- GOVERNMENT, COMPARATIVE
- GOVERNMENT, RESISTANCE TO
- GOVERNMENT AND THE PRESS
- GOVERNMENT INFORMATION
- GOVERNMENT PUBLICITY
- GUERRILLAS
- HEROIN
- HIGHER EDUCATION AND STATE
- HOME RULE
- HYSTERIA (SOCIAL PSYCHOLOGY)
- IMPEACHMENTS
- IMPERIALISM
- INDUSTRY AND STATE
- INSURGENCY
- INTELLIGENCE SERVICE
- INTERNAL SECURITY
- INTERNATIONAL AGENCIES
- INTERNATIONAL AGENCIES IN AFRICA
- INTERNATIONAL AGENCIES IN LATIN AMERICA
- INTERNATIONAL COOPERATION
- INTERNATIONAL OBLIGATIONS
- INTERNATIONAL OFFENCES
- INTERNATIONAL ORGANIZATION
- INTERNATIONAL RELATIONS
- INTERNATIONALISM
- INTERNATIONALIZED TERRITORIES
- INTERPELLATION
- JOURNALISM, SOCIALIST
- JUDAISM AND STATE
- JUSTICE AND POLITICS
- KIDNAPPING
- KINGS AND RULERS
- LEADERSHIP
- LEGISLATORS
- LEGITIMACY OF GOVERNMENTS
- LIBERALISM
- LIBERTY
- LIBERTY OF INFORMATION
- LIBERTY OF SPEECH
- LIBERTY OF THE PRESS
- LITERATURE AND STATE
- LOBBYING
- LOBBYISTS
- LOCAL GOVERNMENT
- LOCAL GOVERNMENT OFFICIALS AND EMPLOYEES
- MARXISM
- MEDIATION, INTERNATIONAL
- MESSIANISM, POLITICAL
- METROPOLITAN GOVERNMENT
- MILITARISM
- MILITARY GOVERNMENT
- MILITARY POLICY
- MILITARY SERVICE, COMPULSORY
- MINISTERIAL RESPONSIBILITY
- MINORITIES
- MOHAMMEDANISM AND STATE
- MONARCHY
- MUNICIPAL GOVERNMENT
- MUNICIPAL OWNERSHIP
- MUNICIPAL SERVICES
- NATIONALISM

POLITICAL SCIENCE, POLITICS AND GOVERNMENT (cont'd)

NATIONALISM AND EDUCATION
NATIONALISM AND RELIGION
NATURALIZATION
NEUTRAL TRADE WITH BELLIGERANTS
NEUTRALITY
NIHILISM
NOMINATIONS FOR OFFICE
OCEONOGRAPHY AND STATE
OFFICE PRACTICE IN GOVERNMENT
OFFICIAL SECRETS
OMBUDSMAN
OPPOSITION (POLITICAL SCIENCE)
ORGANIZATIONAL CHANGE
PACIFIC SETTLEMENT OF INTERNATIONAL DISPUTES
PACIFISM
PARTY DISCIPLINE
PASSIVE RESISTANCE
PATRIOTIC SOCIETIES
PATRIOTISM
PATRONAGE, POLITICAL
PEACE
PEACE SOCIETIES
PEACEFUL CHANGE (INTERNATIONAL RELATIONS)
PEASANT UPRISINGS
PLEBISCITE
POLICE, POLITICAL AND SECRET
POLICE, PRIVATE
POLICE QUESTIONING
POLITICAL CLUBS
POLITICAL CONVENTIONS
POLITICAL CRIMES AND OFFENCES
POLITICAL ETHICS
POLITICAL PARTICIPATION
POLITICAL PARTIES
POLITICAL POSTERS
POLITICAL PRISONERS
POLITICAL PSYCHOLOGY
POLITICAL RIGHTS
POLITICAL SCIENCE
POLITICAL SCIENCE RESEARCH
POLITICAL SOCIALIZATION
POLITICAL SOCIOLOGY
POLITICAL STATISTICS
POLITICS, PRACTICAL
POLITICS AND EDUCATION

POLITICS AND WAR
POLITICS IN MOVING PICTURES
POPULAR FRONTS
POPULATION TRANSFERS
POWER (SOCIAL SCIENCES)
PREFECTS (FRENCH GOVERNMENT)
PREFECTS (ITALIAN GOVERNMENT)
PREROGATIVE, ROYAL
PRESIDENTS
PRESS, COMMUNIST
PRESS AND POLITICS
PRESSURE GROUPS
PRIMARIES
PRIME MINISTERS
PROGRESSIVISM (U.S. POLITICS)
PROPAGANDA
PROPORTIONAL REPRESENTATION
PUBLIC RELATIONS AND POLITICS
PUGWASH CONFERENCE ON SCIENCE AND WORLD AFFAIRS
RADICALISM
RADIO IN POLITICS
RAILWAYS AND STATE
REFERENDUM
REFUGEES
REFUGEES, AMERICAN
REFUGEES, ARAB
REFUGEES, AUSTRIAN
REFUGEES, FRENCH
REFUGEES, GERMAN
REFUGEES, GREEK
REFUGEES, JEWISH
REFUGEES, LITHUANIAN
REFUGEES, POLISH
REFUGEES, RUSSIAN
REFUGEES, RWANDAN
REFUGEES, TIBETAN
REGIONALISM (INTERNATIONAL ORGANIZATION)
RELIGION AND POLITICS
RELIGION AND STATE
RELIGIOUS LIBERTY
REPATRIATION
REPRESENTATIVE GOVERNMENT AND REPRESENTATION
REVOLUTIONISTS
REVOLUTIONS

RIGHT AND LEFT (POLITICAL SCIENCE)
RIOTS
SCIENCE AND STATE
SECURITY, INTERNATIONAL
SECURITY CLASSIFICATION (GOVERNMENT DOCUMENTS)
SECRET SOCIETIES
SECULARIZATION
SEDITION
SELF DETERMINATION, NATIONAL
SEPARATION OF POWERS
SOCIAL SCIENCES AND STATE
SOCIALISM
SOCIALISM, CHRISTIAN
SOCIALISM AND AGRICULTURE
SOCIALISM AND EDUCATION
SOCIALISM AND RELIGION
SOCIALISM AND THE CATHOLIC CHURCH
SOCIALISM AND YOUTH
SOCIALISTS
SOVEREIGNTY
SOVEREIGNTY, VIOLATION OF
SOVIETS
STATE, THE
STATE GOVERNMENTS
STATE RIGHTS
STATE SUCCESSION
STATES, NEW
STATES, SIZE OF
STATES, SMALL
STATESMEN
SUBVERSIVE ACTIVITIES
SUFFRAGE
TECHNOLOGY AND STATE
TELEVISION IN POLITICS
TERRORISM
TORTURE
TOTALITARIANISM
TRADE UNIONS AND COMMUNISM
TRADE UNIONS AND FOREIGN POLICY
TREASON
TREATIES
TREATY-MAKING POWER
TRIBAL GOVERNMENT
TRUST TERRITORIES
VETO

POLITICAL SCIENCE, POLITICS AND GOVERNMENT (cont'd)

VOTERS, REGISTRATION OF
VOTING
VOTING, ABSENT
VOTING, COMPULSORY
WAR
WAR, DECLARATION OF
WAR AND EMERGENCY POWERS
WAR AND SOCIALISM
WOMEN AND PEACE
WOMEN AND SOCIALISM
WOMEN IN POLITICS
WOMEN IN PUBLIC LIFE
WOMEN'S LIBERATION MOVEMENT
WORLD POLITICS

Particular countries, nationalities, parties, organizations, etc.

ACCION REVOLUCIONARIA NACIONAL ECUATORIANA
ACTION FRANÇAISE
ALIANZA POPULAR REVOLUCIONARIA AMERICANA
ANTINAZI MOVEMENT
ARAB SOCIALIST UNION
ATLANTIC COMMUNITY
BAATH PARTY
BAYERISCHE VOLKSPARTEI
BLACK MUSLIM MOVEMENT
BLACK PANTHER PARTY
BLACK POWER
BUND
CARBONARI
CARIBBEAN ECONOMIC DEVELOPMENT CORPORATION
CARIBBEAN ORGANIZATION
CENTRAL TREATY ORGANIZATION
CHURCH AND STATE IN AUSTRIA
CHURCH AND STATE IN BOLIVIA
CHURCH AND STATE IN BRAZIL
CHURCH AND STATE IN EASTERN GERMANY
CHURCH AND STATE IN FRANCE
CHURCH AND STATE IN GERMANY
CHURCH AND STATE IN HUNGARY
CHURCH AND STATE IN ITALY

CHURCH AND STATE IN MADAGASCAR
CHURCH AND STATE IN MEXICO
CHURCH AND STATE IN POLAND
CHURCH AND STATE IN PORTUGAL
CHURCH AND STATE IN PRUSSIA
CHURCH AND STATE IN SCANDINAVIA
CHURCH AND STATE IN SPAIN
CHURCH AND STATE IN THE NETHERLANDS
CHURCH AND STATE IN THE UKRAINE
CHURCH AND STATE IN THE UNITED KINGDOM
CHURCH AND STATE IN THE UNITED STATES
CHURCH AND STATE IN VENEZUELA
CHURCH AND STATE IN YUGOSLAVIA
COMMUNIST COUNTRIES
COMMUNIST LEAGUE
COMMUNIST PARTIES
COMMUNIST PARTY
COMMUNISTS
COMMUNISTS, BRITISH
COMMUNISTS, BULGARIAN
COMMUNISTS, CAUCASIAN
COMMUNISTS, CHINESE
COMMUNISTS, FRENCH
COMMUNISTS, ITALIAN
COMMUNISTS, KIRGHIZ
COMMUNISTS, MONGOLIAN
COMMUNISTS, POLISH
COMMUNISTS, RUSSIAN
COMMUNISTS, UKRAINIAN
CONGRESS OF RACIAL EQUALITY
CONGRESS OF THE PEOPLES OF THE EAST, BAKU, 1920
CONSEIL DE L'ENTENTE
CONSERVATISM IN GERMANY
CONSERVATISM IN ITALY
CONSERVATISM IN SPAIN
CONSERVATISM IN THE UNITED KINGDOM
CONSERVATISM IN THE UNITED STATES
CONSERVATIVE PARTY (DENMARK)
CONSERVATIVE PARTY (UNITED KINGDOM)
CONVENTION DES INSTITUTIONS REPUBLICAINES
COUNCIL OF EUROPE
COUNTRY PARTY
DECEMBRISTS
DEMOCRATIC PARTY (NETHERLANDS)

DEMOCRATIC PARTY (UNITED STATES)
DEUTSCHE DEMOKRATISCHE PARTEI
DEUTSCHE VOLKSPARTEI
EAST AFRICA HIGH COMMISSION
EUROPEAN ATOMIC ENERGY COMMUNITY
EUROPEAN COAL AND STEEL COMMUNITY
EUROPEAN COMMISSION OF HUMAN RIGHTS
EUROPEAN COMMUNITIES
EUROPEAN CONVENTION ON HUMAN RIGHTS
EUROPEAN ECONOMIC COMMUNITY
EUROPEAN FREE TRADE ASSOCIATION
EUROPEAN PARLIAMENT
EUROPEAN PAYMENTS UNION
EUZKADI TA ASKATASUNA
FABIAN SOCIETY
FALANGE SOCIALISTA BOLIVIANA
FEDERAL PARTY
FEDERATION NATIONALE DES REPUBLICAINS INDEPENDANTS
FLEMISH MOVEMENT
FORTSCHRITTLICHE VOLKSPARTEI
FREE SOIL PARTY
FREIE DEMOKRATISCHE PARTEI
FRENTE DE LIBERACION NACIONAL
FRENTE NACIONAL (COLOMBIA)
FRONT DE LIBERATION DU QUEBEC
GARDA DE FIER
GROUPE D'ETUDE ET D'ACTION RADICAL-SOCIALISTE
GRUPO OBRA DE UNIFICACION
HAGANAH
HRVATSKA SELJAČKA STRANKA
INDEPENDENT PEASANT PARTY (POLAND)
INDIAN NATIONAL CONGRESS
INTERNATIONAL, THE
IRISH REPUBLICAN ARMY
JACOBINS
JANATA VIMUKHTI PERAMUNA
JEWISH AGENCY
JEWISH-ARAB RELATIONS
JEWISH QUESTION
KAMPAGNEN MOD ATOMVABEN
KUOMINTANG
LABOUR PARTY
LATIN AMERICAN FEDERATION
LEAGUE OF NATIONS

POLITICAL SCIENCE, POLITICS AND GOVERNMENT (cont'd)

LIBERAL-DEMOKRATISCHE PARTEI DEUTSCHLANDS
LIBERAL PARTY
LIBERALISM IN CANADA
LIBERALISM IN COLOMBIA
LIBERALISM IN EUROPE
LIBERALISM IN FRANCE
LIBERALISM IN GERMANY
LIBERALISM IN ITALY
LIBERALISM IN RUSSIA
LIBERALISM IN SPAIN
LIBERALISM IN THE UNITED KINGDOM
LIBERALISM IN THE UNITED STATES
LOTTA CONTINUA
LOYALTY-SECURITY PROGRAM, 1947-
MILITARY ASSISTANCE, AMERICAN
MILITARY ASSISTANCE, GERMAN
MILITARY ASSISTANCE, NORWEGIAN
MŁODA POLSKA
MONROE DOCTRINE
MOVIMENTO SOCIALE ITALIANO
MOVIMIENTO NACIONALISTA REVOLUCIONARIO
NARODOWY ZWIĄZEK ROBOTNICZY
NATIONAL PARTY (SOUTH AFRICA)
NATIONAL SOCIALISM
NATIONAL URBAN LEAGUE
NATIONALDEMOKRATISCHE PARTEI DEUTSCHLAND [BUNDESREPUBLIK]
NORTH ATLANTIC TREATY ORGANIZATION
OESTERREICHISCHE VOLKSPARTEI
ORGANISATION DE L'ARMÉE SECRÈTE
ORGANIZATION OF AFRICAN UNITY
ORGANIZATION OF AMERICAN STATES
PANAFRICANISM
PANAMERICAN TREATIES AND CONVENTIONS
PANAMERICANISM
PANGERMANISM
PANSLAVISM
PANTURANIANISM
PARTI SOCIALISTE UNIFIE
PARTIDO INDIO DE BOLIVIA
PARTIDO LIBERACION NACIONAL
PARTIDO NACIONAL DEMOCRATICO [MEXICO]
PARTIDO REVOLUCIONARIO INSTITUCIONAL
PARTIDO SOCIALISTA DE LA IZQUIERDA NACIONAL

PATHET LAO
PEOPLE'S ACTION PARTY
POLITICAL BALLADS AND SONGS, AMERICAN
POLITICAL BALLADS AND SONGS, AUSTRIAN
POLITICAL BALLADS AND SONGS, ENGLISH
POLITICAL BALLADS AND SONGS, GERMAN
POLITICAL BALLADS AND SONGS, MEXICAN
POLITICAL BALLADS AND SONGS, SLAVIC
POLITICAL POETRY, ENGLISH
POLITICAL POETRY, GERMANY
POLITICAL POETRY, POLISH
POLITICAL POSTERS, CUBAN
POLITICAL POSTERS, ENGLISH
POLITICAL POSTERS, FRENCH
POLITICAL SATIRE, CHINESE
POLITICAL SATIRE, ENGLISH
POLITICAL SATIRE, GERMAN
POLITICAL SATIRE, ITALIAN
POLITICAL SATIRE, POLISH
POPULISM IN NORWAY
POPULISM IN RUSSIA
POPULISM IN THE UKRAINE
POPULISM IN THE UNITED STATES
POPULISM IN WHITE RUSSIA
PROGRESSIVE LABOR PARTY
PROPAGANDA, AMERICAN
PROPAGANDA, ANTI-AMERICAN
PROPAGANDA, ANTI-COMMUNIST
PROPAGANDA, ARAB
PROPAGANDA, BRITISH
PROPAGANDA, CHINESE
PROPAGANDA, COMMUNIST
PROPAGANDA, CUBAN
PROPAGANDA, GERMAN
PROPAGANDA, POLISH
PROPAGANDA, RUSSIAN
RADICALISM IN AUSTRALIA
RADICALISM IN CANADA
RADICALISM IN FRANCE
RADICALISM IN GERMANY
RADICALISM IN ITALY
RADICALISM IN LATIN AMERICA
RADICALISM IN POLAND
RADICALISM IN RUSSIA

RADICALISM IN THE ARGENTINE REPUBLIC
RADICALISM IN THE NETHERLANDS
RADICALISM IN THE UKRAINE
RADICALISM IN THE UNITED KINGDOM
RADICALISM IN THE UNITED STATES
REFUGEES IN GERMANY
REFUGEES IN SWEDEN
REFUGEES IN SWITZERLAND
REFUGEES IN THAILAND
REFUGEES IN THE DOMINICAN REPUBLIC
REFUGEES IN THE UNITED KINGDOM
REFUGEES IN THE UNITED STATES
REPUBLICAN PARTY (ITALY)
REPUBLICAN PARTY (UNITED STATES)
REPUBLICANISM IN FRANCE
REVOLUTIONISTS, BULGARIAN
REVOLUTIONISTS, DANISH
REVOLUTIONISTS, GERMAN
REVOLUTIONISTS, INDIAN
REVOLUTIONISTS, RUSSIAN
ROYAL INSTITUTE OF PUBLIC ADMINISTRATION
SCOTTISH NATIONAL PARTY
SINN FEIN
SITUATIONIST INTERNATIONAL
SOCIAL DEMOCRATIC PARTY (DENMARK)
SOCIAL DEMOCRATIC PARTY (GERMANY)
SOCIAL DEMOCRATIC PARTY (ITALY)
SOCIAL DEMOCRATIC PARTY (LATVIA)
SOCIAL DEMOCRATIC PARTY (RUSSIA)
SOCIAL DEMOCRATIC PARTY (RUSSIA) (MENSHEVIKS)
SOCIAL DEMOCRATIC PARTY (SWITZERLAND)
SOCIALISM IN AFRICA
SOCIALISM IN ALGERIA
SOCIALISM IN ARAB COUNTRIES
SOCIALISM IN ASIA
SOCIALISM IN AUSTRIA
SOCIALISM IN AZERBAIJAN
SOCIALISM IN BELGIUM
SOCIALISM IN BULGARIA
SOCIALISM IN CANADA
SOCIALISM IN CHILE
SOCIALISM IN CUBA
SOCIALISM IN CZECHOSLOVAKIA
SOCIALISM IN DENMARK

POLITICAL SCIENCE, POLITICS AND GOVERNMENT (cont'd)

SOCIALISM IN EASTERN EUROPE
SOCIALISM IN EASTERN GERMANY
SOCIALISM IN EGYPT
SOCIALISM IN EUROPE
SOCIALISM IN FRANCE
SOCIALISM IN GERMANY
SOCIALISM IN GUYANA
SOCIALISM IN INDIA
SOCIALISM IN IRELAND
SOCIALISM IN ISRAEL
SOCIALISM IN ITALY
SOCIALISM IN KAZAKSTAN
SOCIALISM IN KIRGHIZIA
SOCIALISM IN LATIN AMERICA
SOCIALISM IN MACEDONIA
SOCIALISM IN NORWAY
SOCIALISM IN POLAND
SOCIALISM IN RUSSIA
SOCIALISM IN SENEGAL
SOCIALISM IN SERBIA
SOCIALISM IN SPAIN
SOCIALISM IN SUBSAHARAN AFRICA
SOCIALISM IN SWEDEN
SOCIALISM IN SWITZERLAND
SOCIALISM IN THE ARGENTINE REPUBLIC
SOCIALISM IN THE CAUCASUS

SOCIALISM IN THE NEAR EAST
SOCIALISM IN THE NETHERLANDS
SOCIALISM IN THE TATAR REPUBLIC
SOCIALISM IN THE UKRAINE
SOCIALISM IN THE UNITED KINGDOM
SOCIALISM IN THE UNITED STATES
SOCIALISM IN TURKESTAN
SOCIALISM IN WHITE RUSSIA
SOCIALIST PARTY (ARGENTINE REPUBLIC)
SOCIALIST PARTY (AUSTRIA)
SOCIALIST PARTY (CHILE)
SOCIALIST PARTY (FRANCE)
SOCIALIST PARTY (ITALY)
SOCIALIST PARTY (POLAND)
SOCIALIST REVOLUTIONARY PARTY (RUSSIA)
SOCIALIST WORKERS PARTY (UNITED STATES)
SOCIALISTS, BRITISH
SOCIALISTS, EUROPEAN
SOCIALISTS, GERMAN
SOLIDARITAT CATALANA
STATESMEN, AMERICAN
STATESMEN, ARAB
STATESMEN, AUSTRALIAN
STATESMEN, DANISH
STATESMEN, DOMINICAN
STATESMEN, GERMAN

STATESMEN, LATIN AMERICAN
STATESMEN, SPANISH
STRONNICTWO LUDOWE
SVENSKA FOLKPARTIET
TAMMANY HALL
TENNESSEE VALLEY AUTHORITY
ULSTER VOLUNTEER FORCE
UNIDAD POPULAR
UNION CIVICA RADICAL
UNION DES DEMOCRATES POUR LA REPUBLIQUE
UNION POUR LA NOUVELLE REPUBLIQUE
UNION PROGRESSISTE SENEGALAISE
UNITED NATIONS
UNITED NATIONS RELIEF AND WORKS AGENCY FOR PALESTINE REFUGEES IN THE NEAR EAST
UNITED SOUTH AFRICAN NATIONAL PARTY
UNIVERSAL DECLARATION OF HUMAN RIGHTS, 1948
WHIG PARTY (UNITED KINGDOM)
WHIG PARTY (UNITED STATES)
WILTON PARK
WORLD JEWISH CONGRESS
WORLD ZIONIST ORGANIZATION
YOUNG COMMUNIST INTERNATIONAL
YOUNG COMMUNIST LEAGUE
ZEMSTVOS
ZJEDNOCZONE STRONNICTWO LUDOWE

PSYCHOLOGY

ABILITY
ADOLESCENCE
AGGRESSIVENESS (PSYCHOLOGY)
AMBITION
ANIMALS, HABITS AND BEHAVIOUR OF
ANTIPATHIES AND PREJUDICES
ANXIETY
ATTITUDE (PSYCHOLOGY)
ATTITUDE CHANGE
BEHAVIOUR MODIFICATION
BEHAVIOUR THERAPY
BRAIN
CHILD GUIDANCE CLINICS

CHILD MENTAL HEALTH
CHILD PSYCHIATRY
CHILD STUDY
CHOICE (PSYCHOLOGY)
COGNITION
CONCEPT LEARNING
CONCEPTS
CONDITIONED RESPONSE
CONFLICT (PSYCHOLOGY)
CONFORMITY
CONTROL (PSYCHOLOGY)
CRIMINAL BEHAVIOUR, PREDICTION OF
CRIMINAL PSYCHOLOGY

DECISION MAKING
DEPENDENCY (PSYCHOLOGY)
DOGMATISM
EDUCATIONAL PSYCHOLOGY
EMOTIONS
EMPATHY
ETHNOPSYCHOLOGY
EXTRASENSORY PERCEPTION
FIGHTING (PSYCHOLOGY)
GENETIC PSYCHOLOGY
GIFTED CHILDREN
GRIEF
GROUP PSYCHOTHERAPY

PSYCHOLOGY (cont'd)

HABIT	OPERANT CONDITIONING	PSYCHOLOGY, MILITARY
HATE	ORIENTATION	PSYCHOLOGY, PATHOLOGICAL
HEALTH ATTITUDES	PERCEPTION	PSYCHOLOGY, PHYSIOLOGICAL
HEARING	PERSONALITY	PSYCHOLOGY, RELIGIOUS
HUMAN BEHAVIOUR	PERSONALITY, DISORDERS OF	PSYCHOMETRICS
HYPNOTISM	PERSONALITY TESTS	PSYCHOSES
HYSTERIA (SOCIAL PSYCHOLOGY)	PERSUASION (PSYCHOLOGY)	PSYCHOTHERAPY
IDENTIFICATION (PSYCHOLOGY)	POLITICAL PSYCHOLOGY	REASONING (PSYCHOLOGY)
IMAGINATION	PSYCHOLINGUISTICS	REINFORCEMENT (PSYCHOLOGY)
INFORMATION THEORY IN PSYCHOLOGY	PREDICTION (PSYCHOLOGY)	SCALE ANALYSIS (PSYCHOLOGY)
INTELLECT	PRISON PSYCHOLOGY	SCHIZOPHRENIA
INTELLIGENCE LEVELS	PROBLEM SOLVING	SCHIZOPHRENICS
INTERPERSONAL RELATIONS	PSYCHIATRIC RESEARCH	SELF RELIANCE
JESNESS INVENTORY	PSYCHIATRY	SEX (PSYCHOLOGY)
LEARNING, PSYCHOLOGY OF	PSYCHOANALYSIS	SHAME
MEMORY	PSYCHOBIOLOGY	SOCIAL PERCEPTION
MENTAL ILLNESS	PSYCHOLOGICAL RESEARCH	SOCIAL PSYCHOLOGY
MENTAL TESTS	PSYCHOLOGICAL WARFARE	TIME PERCEPTION
MOTIVATION (PSYCHOLOGY)	PSYCHOLOGY	TYPOLOGY (PSYCHOLOGY)
NEUROSES	PSYCHOLOGY, APPLIED	UNCERTAINTY
	PSYCHOLOGY, INDUSTRIAL	

PUBLIC HEALTH AND MEDICINE

ABORTION	CEREBROVASCULAR DISEASE	ENVIRONMENTAL HEALTH
ACCIDENTS	CHARITIES, MEDICAL	EPIDEMICS
AIR	CHILD MENTAL HEALTH	EPIDEMIOLOGY
ALCOHOLICS	CHILD PSYCHIATRY	EPILEPTICS
ALCOHOLISM	CHILDREN, DEAF	EUTHANASIA
AMERICAN MEDICAL ASSOCIATION	CHRONICALLY ILL	EX-SERVICEMEN, DISABLED
ANIMALS AS CARRIERS OF DISEASE	COMMUNICABLE DISEASES	FETUS
APHASIA	COMMUNITY MENTAL HEALTH SERVICES	FOLK MEDICINE
ASYLUMS	CONCEPTION	FOOD ADULTERATION AND INSPECT
AUTISM	CONTRACEPTIVES	FOOD CONSUMPTION
BANDAGES AND BANDAGING	DEAF	FOOD CONTAMINATION
BATHS, PUBLIC	DEATH	FRONTAL LOBOTOMY
BIRTH CONTROL	DENTAL CARE	GENETIC COUNSELLING
BIRTH CONTROL CLINICS	DENTAL FEES	GERIATRIC PSYCHIATRY
BLIND	DENTISTRY	GERIATRICS
BRAIN	DENTITION	HAEMODIALYSIS
CANCER	DIET	HANDICAPPED
CANCER RESEARCH	DISEASES	HANDICAPPED CHILDREN
CEMETERIES	DISPENSARIES	HEALTH ATTITUDES
CEREBRAL PALSY	DRUGS	HEALTH EDUCATION

PUBLIC HEALTH AND MEDICINE (cont'd)

- HEALTH RESORTS, WATERING PLACES, ETC.
- HEART
- HOME NURSING
- HOSPITAL CARE
- HOSPITALS
- HOSPITALS, MEDIAEVAL
- HOUSING AND HEALTH
- HUMAN CHROMOSOME ABNORMALITIES
- HYGIENE, PUBLIC
- INDUSTRIAL ACCIDENTS
- INDUSTRIAL HYGIENE
- INTRAUTERINE CONTRACEPTIVES
- KIDNEYS
- LAUNDRIES, PUBLIC
- LEPROSY
- MALNUTRITION
- MATERNAL AND INFANT WELFARE
- MEDICAL CARE
- MEDICAL CARE, COST
- MEDICAL CENTRES
- MEDICAL COLLEGES
- MEDICAL COOPERATION
- MEDICAL ECONOMICS
- MEDICAL ETHICS
- MEDICAL FEES
- MEDICAL GEOGRAPHY
- MEDICAL PARASITOLOGY
- MEDICAL RECORDS
- MEDICAL RESEARCH
- MEDICAL SOCIAL WORK
- MEDICAL STATISTICS
- MEDICINE
- MEDICINE, INDUSTRIAL
- MEDICINE, PRIMITIVE
- MEDICINE, STATE
- MEDICINE AND RELIGION

- MENTAL HEALTH LAWS
- MENTAL HYGIENE
- MENTAL ILLNESS
- MENTALLY HANDICAPPED
- MENTALLY HANDICAPPED CHILDREN
- MENTALLY ILL
- MIGRAINE
- MINE ACCIDENTS
- MORTALITY
- MOTOR ABILITY
- MOUTH
- NARCOTIC ADDICTS
- NARCOTIC HABIT
- NOISE
- NOISE POLLUTION
- NURSES AND NURSING
- NUTRITION
- NUTRITION SURVEYS
- OCCUPATIONAL DISEASES
- OIL POLLUTION OF RIVERS, HARBOURS, ETC.
- OPERATING ROOMS
- ORAL CONTRACEPTIVES
- PAIN
- PATHOLOGICAL LABORATORIES
- PELLAGRA
- PHARMACY
- PHYSICAL EDUCATION AND TRAINING
- PHYSICIAN AND PATIENT
- PHYSIOLOGY
- POISONS
- PREGNANCY
- PROTEIN METABOLISM
- PROTEINS
- PSYCHIATRIC CLINICS
- PSYCHIATRIC HOSPITALS
- PSYCHIATRIC NURSING
- PSYCHIATRY

- PSYCHOBIOLOGY
- PSYCHOLOGY, PATHOLOGICAL
- PSYCHOLOGY, PHYSIOLOGICAL
- PSYCHOSES
- PSYCHOTHERAPY
- RADIATION
- RED CROSS
- REFUSE AND REFUSE DISPOSAL
- REHABILITATION
- RESPIRATORY ORGANS
- ROAD ACCIDENTS
- SCHISTOSOMIASIS
- SICK
- SMOKING
- SOCIAL MEDICINE
- SOCIAL PSYCHIATRY
- SOCIALIST MEDICAL ASSOCIATION
- SPECTACLES
- SPEECH, DISORDERS OF
- SPEECH THERAPY
- STERILIZATION (BIRTH CONTROL)
- STILL-BIRTH
- STRESS (PHYSIOLOGY)
- SURGERY
- SURGICAL INSTRUMENTS AND APPARATUS
- THALIDOMIDE
- TOBACCO HABIT
- TUBERCULOSIS
- VACCINATION
- VEGETARIANISM
- VENEREAL DISEASES
- VOLUNTEER WORKERS IN HOSPITALS
- WASTE PRODUCTS
- WATER
- WATER QUALITY MANAGEMENT
- WORLD HEALTH ORGANIZATION

SCIENCE AND TECHNOLOGY

- AGRICULTURAL INNOVATIONS
- ALCHEMY
- ASTROLOGY
- ASTRONOMY
- ATOMIC ENERGY
- ATOMIC ENERGY RESEARCH
- ATOMIC POWER
- ATOMIC POWER PLANTS
- AUTOMATION
- BIBLE AND SCIENCE
- BIOLOGICAL CHEMISTRY
- BIOLOGICAL CONTROL SYSTEMS
- BIOLOGICAL RESEARCH
- BIOLOGICAL WARFARE
- BIOLOGY
- CHEMICAL AFFINITY
- CHEMICAL WARFARE
- CHEMISTRY, ORGANIC
- CIVIL ENGINEERING
- COMMUNICATION IN SCIENCE
- DIFFUSION OF INNOVATIONS
- EDUCATIONAL TECHNOLOGY
- EVOLUTION
- FIRE EXTINCTION
- FORECASTING
- GENETICS
- HUMAN BIOLOGY
- HUMAN ENGINEERING
- HYDRAULIC ENGINEERING
- INTERNATIONAL ATOMIC ENERGY AGENCY
- INVENTIONS
- JOURNALISM, TECHNICAL
- KUMASI UNIVERSITY OF SCIENCE AND TECHNOLOGY
- MASSACHUSETTS INSTITUTE OF TECHNOLOGY
- MOLECULES
- NEUTRON SOURCES
- NUMERICAL TAXONOMY
- OIL WELL DRILLING
- PHYSICS
- PUGWASH CONFERENCE ON SCIENCE AND WORLD AFFAIRS
- RADIATION
- RADIO
- RADIOACTIVE FALLOUT
- RADIOACTIVE POLLUTION
- RADIOISOTOPES
- RELATIVITY (PHYSICS)
- RELIGION AND SCIENCE
- RESEARCH
- ROYAL SOCIETY OF LONDON
- SALINE WATER CONVERSION
- SCIENCE
- SCIENCE AND CIVILIZATION
- SCIENCE AND ETHICS
- SCIENCE AND STATE
- SCIENCE AND THE HUMANITIES
- SCIENTIFIC SOCIETIES
- SCIENTISTS
- SCIENTISTS, AMERICAN
- SCIENTISTS, GERMAN
- SEMICONDUCTORS
- SEWAGE DISPOSAL
- SEWAGE SLUDGE
- SEWERAGE
- SPACE FLIGHT
- SPACE FLIGHT TO THE MOON
- SPACE SCIENCES
- STATE ENCOURAGEMENT OF SCIENCE LITERATURE AND ART
- TECHNOLOGICAL FORECASTING
- TECHNOLOGICAL INNOVATIONS
- TECHNOLOGISTS
- TECHNOLOGISTS, GERMAN
- TECHNOLOGY
- TECHNOLOGY AND CIVILIZATION
- TECHNOLOGY AND STATE
- TECHNOLOGY ASSESSMENT
- TECHNOLOGY TRANSFER
- UNEMPLOYMENT, TECHNOLOGICAL
- UNITED NATIONS EDUCATIONAL, SCIENTIFIC AND CULTURAL ORGANIZATION
- VIVISECTION
- WEIZMANN INSTITUTE OF SCIENCE
- ZOOLOGY

SOCIOLOGY, ANTHROPOLOGY AND ETHNOGRAPHY

General

- ABOLITIONISTS
- ACCULTURATION
- ADOPTION
- AGRICULTURAL COLONIES
- AGRICULTURE, PRIMITIVE
- ALCOHOLICS
- ALCOHOLISM
- ALCOHOLISM AND CRIME
- ALIENATION (SOCIAL PSYCHOLOGY)
- AMERICANIZATION
- ANCESTOR WORSHIP
- ANIMALS, TREATMENT OF
- ANOMY
- ANTHROPOLOGY
- ANTHROPOMETRY
- APARTMENT HOUSES
- AQUATIC SPORTS
- AQUATIC SPORTS FACILITIES
- ARCHITECTURE AND SOCIETY
- ARISTOCRACY
- ART AND SOCIETY

SOCIOLOGY, ANTHROPOLOGY AND ETHNOGRAPHY (cont'd)

ARTS, THE, AFRICAN
ARTS, THE, JAVANESE
ARTS AND SOCIETY, THE
ASSIMILATION (SOCIOLOGY)
ASSOCIATIONS, INSTITUTIONS, ETC.
ASTRONAUTICS AND CIVILIZATION
AUTOMOBILE THIEVES
BIRTH CONTROL
BLIND
BOOKMAKING (BETTING)
BOYS
BRAIN DRAIN
BREACH OF THE PEACE
BRIBERY
BRIGANDS AND ROBBERS
BRITISH ACADEMY
BRITISH BROADCASTING CORPORATION
BRITISH LEGION
CAMPING
CASTE
CATTLE STEALING
CELIBACY
CEMETERIES
CENTRAL PLACES
CHARITABLE BEQUESTS
CHARITIES
CHARITIES, MEDICAL
CHARITY ORGANIZATION
CHARITY SCHOOLS
CHILD GUIDANCE CLINICS
CHILD WELFARE
CHILDREN
CHILDREN, ADOPTED
CHILDREN, DEAF
CHILDREN AND POLITICS
CHILDREN IN FINLAND
CHILDREN IN NORTHERN IRELAND
CHILDREN IN RUSSIA
CHILDREN IN SUBSAHARAN AFRICA
CHILDREN IN SWITZERLAND
CHILDREN IN THE UNITED KINGDOM
CHILDREN IN THE UNITED STATES
CHILDREN OF IMMIGRANTS
CHURCH AND RACE PROBLEMS
CHURCH AND SOCIAL PROBLEMS

CHURCH WORK
CHURCH WORK WITH YOUTH
CITIES AND TOWNS
CITIZENS' ADVICE BUREAUX
COLLECTIVE SETTLEMENTS
COLLECTIVISM
COMMONS
COMMUNES (CHINA)
COMMUNICATION
COMMUNICATIONS RESEARCH
COMMUNISM AND FAMILY
COMMUNISM AND SOCIETY
COMMUNITY
COMMUNITY AND COLLEGE
COMMUNITY AND SCHOOL
COMMUNITY CENTRES
COMMUNITY DEVELOPMENT
COMMUNITY LIFE
COMMUNITY ORGANIZATION
COMPANY TOWNS
COMPONENTIAL ANALYSIS IN ANTHROPOLOGY
CONFLICT OF GENERATIONS
CONSTABLES
CONVICT LABOUR
COSTUME
COUNSELLING
COUNTRY HOMES
CREMATION
CRIME AND CRIMINALS
CRIME AND THE PRESS
CRIME PREVENTION
CRIMINAL ANTHROPOLOGY
CRIMINAL REGISTERS
CRIMINAL STATISTICS
CRUELTY TO CHILDREN
CULTURAL RELATIONS
CULTURAL RELATIVISM
CULTURE
CULTURE DIFFUSION
DACOITS
DANCING
DANDIES
DAY NURSERIES
DEAF
DELINQUENT GIRLS
DELINQUENT WOMEN

DELINQUENTS
DEMONSTRATIONS
DESERTION AND NON-SUPPORT
DETENTION OF PERSONS
DEVIANT BEHAVIOUR
DISASTER RELIEF
DISASTERS
DISCRIMINATION
DISCRIMINATION IN HOUSING
DISSENTERS
DIVORCE
DWELLINGS
EAST AND WEST
EDUCATION AND CRIME
EDUCATIONAL ANTHROPOLOGY
EDUCATIONAL SOCIOLOGY
ELITE
EMIGRATION AND IMMIGRATION
ENDOWMENTS
EQUALITY
ESCAPES
ESTATES (SOCIAL ORDERS)
ETHNOCENTRISM
ETHNOLOGICAL JURISPRUDENCE
ETHNOLOGY
ETIQUETTE
EUTHANASIA
EVALUATION RESEARCH (SOCIAL ACTION PROGRAMMES)
EVOLUTION
EX-CONVICTS, EMPLOYMENT OF
EX-SERVICEMEN
EX-SERVICEMEN, DISABLED
EXILES
FAMILY
FAMILY RESEARCH
FAMILY SIZE
FAMILY SOCIAL WORK
FASHION
FATHER SEPARATED CHILDREN
FATHERS
FECUNDITY
FESTIVALS
FOLK ART
FOLKLORE
FOLK LORE, ITALIAN

SOCIOLOGY, ANTHROPOLOGY AND ETHNOGRAPHY (cont'd)

FOLK LORE, SARDINIAN
FOLK LORE, SLAVIC
FOLK MEDICINE
FOOD HABITS
FOOD RELIEF
FOOD RELIEF, AMERICAN
FOSTER DAY CARE
FOSTER HOME CARE
FREEDMEN
FREEMASONS
FUNCTIONAL ANALYSIS (SOCIAL SCIENCES)
FUNERAL RITES AND CEREMONIES
GAMBLING
GAMES
GANGS
GARDEN CITIES
GAUCHOS
GAY LIBERATION MOVEMENT
GENETICS
GESTURE
GIRLS
GROUP COUNSELLING
GROUP RELATIONS TRAINING
HALFWAY HOUSES
HALLUCINOGENIC DRUGS
HANDICAPPED
HANDICAPPED CHILDREN
HARMONISTS
HEAD GEAR
HEROIN
HIPPIES
HISTORICAL SOCIOLOGY
HITCHHIKING
HOLIDAYS
HOME HELPS
HOMOSEXUALITY
HOOLIGANS
HOUSING
HOUSING AND HEALTH
HOUSING MANAGEMENT
HUMAN ECOLOGY
HUNTING
HUNTING, PRIMITIVE
HUSBAND AND WIFE
ILLEGITIMACY
INDIVIDUALISM

INDUSTRIAL SOCIOLOGY
INFANTICIDE
INFANTS
INITIATIONS (IN RELIGION, FOLK-LORE, ETC.)
INITIATIONS (INTO TRADES, SOCIETIES, ETC.)
INSANE, CRIMINAL AND DANGEROUS
INSANE, KILLING OF THE
INSANITY
INTERCULTURAL COMMUNICATION
INTERPERSONAL RELATIONS
INTERVIEWING
JAMAA MOVEMENT
JUNIOR REPUBLICS
JUVENILE DELINQUENCY
KIDNAPPING
KINGS AND RULERS (IN RELIGION, FOLKLORE, ETC.)
KINSHIP
KNOWLEDGE, SOCIOLOGY OF
LABOUR AND LABOURING CLASSES
LABOUR REST HOMES
LARCENY
LEISURE
LESBIANISM
LICENCE SYSTEM
LIQUOR PROBLEM
LITERATURE AND SOCIETY
LONELINESS
LOTTERIES
MAFIA
MAGIC
MAN
MARIHUANA
MARRIAGE
MARRIAGE GUIDANCE
MARRIED WOMEN
MASS MEDIA
MASS SOCIETY
MATERNAL AND INFANT WELFARE
MATERNAL DEPRIVATION
MATRILINEAL KINSHIP
MEDICAL SOCIAL WORK
MEDICINE, PRIMITIVE
MEETINGS
MENTALLY HANDICAPPED
MENTALLY HANDICAPPED CHILDREN

MENTALLY ILL
METROPOLITAN AREAS
MIDDLE CLASSES
MISCEGENATION
MOBILE HOME LIVING
MOLLY MAGUIRES
MOON (IN RELIGION, FOLK-LORE, ETC.)
MORAL CONDITIONS
MOTHER AND CHILD
MOTHERS
MOTORCYCLISTS
MOVING-PICTURE AUDIENCES
MOVING-PICTURES
MURDER
MUSIC AND SOCIETY
MYTH
MYTHOLOGY
MYTHOLOGY, AUSTRALIAN (ABORIGINAL)
MYTHOLOGY, INDONESIAN
MYTHOLOGY, MELANESIAN
MYTHOLOGY, MICRONESIAN
NARCOTIC ADDICTS
NARCOTIC HABIT
NARCOTICS, CONTROL OF
NARCOTICS AND YOUTH
NATIONAL CHARACTERISTICS
NATIONAL CHARACTERISTICS, AMERICAN
NATIONAL CHARACTERISTICS, FRENCH
NATIONAL CHARACTERISTICS, RUSSIAN
NATIONAL CHARACTERISTICS, URUGUAYAN
NATIONAL PARKS AND RESERVES
NATIVISTIC MOVEMENTS
NEWSREEL
NOMADS
NONVERBAL COMMUNICATION
OATHS
OCCUPATIONAL MOBILITY
OLD AGE
OLD AGE ASSISTANCE
OLD AGE HOMES
OLD AGE PENSIONS
OLYMPIC GAMES
OPIUM HABIT
ORAL TRADITION
ORPHANS AND ORPHAN ASYLUMS

SOCIOLOGY, ANTHROPOLOGY AND ETHNOGRAPHY (cont'd)

OUTDOOR RECREATION
PALAEONTOLOGY
PARENT AND CHILD
PARKS
PAROLE
PATRON AND CLIENT
PEASANTRY
PENAL COLONIES
PEONAGE
PERSONAL SPACE
PERSONALITY
PHILOSOPHICAL ANTHROPOLOGY
PHYSICAL EDUCATION AND TRAINING
PHYSICALLY HANDICAPPED
PIRATES
PLANNING
PLANTATION LIFE
PLAY
PLAY SCHOOLS
PLURALISM (SOCIAL SCIENCES)
POLICE
POLITICAL SOCIALIZATION
POLITICAL SOCIOLOGY
POLITICS IN MOVING PICTURES
POOR
POOR LAWS
POPULAR CULTURE
POPULATION GENETICS
POVERTY
POVERTY RESEARCH
POWER (SOCIAL SCIENCES)
PRESTIGE
PREVENTIVE DETENTION
PRIMATES
PRISONERS
PRISONS
PROBATION
PROBLEM CHILDREN
PROBLEM FAMILY
PROFESSIONS
PROGRESS
PROPAGANDA
PROSTITUTION
PSYCHIATRIC SOCIAL WORK
PUBLIC HOUSING
PUBLIC INSTITUTIONS

PUBLIC OPINION
PUBLIC OPINION POLLS.
PUBLIC RELATIONS
PUNISHMENT
QUESTIONNAIRES
RACE
RACE AWARENESS
RACE DISCRIMINATION
RACE PROBLEMS
RADIO PROGRAMMES
RANCH LIFE
RAPE
RECIDIVISTS
RECREATION
RECREATION RESEARCH
RED CROSS
REFORMATORIES
REFORMATORIES FOR WOMEN
REGIONAL PLANNING
REHABILITATION, RURAL
REHABILITATION CENTRES
REHABILITATION OF CRIMINALS
REHABILITATION OF JUVENILE DELINQUENTS
RELATIVITY
RELIGION, PRIMITIVE
RELIGION AND SOCIOLOGY
REMAND HOMES
RESIDENTIAL MOBILITY
RESPONSIBILITY
RETIREMENT
RIOTS
RITES AND CEREMONIES
ROLE CONFLICT
RURAL CONDITIONS
RURAL-URBAN MIGRATION
RURAL YOUTH
SCHIZOPHRENICS
SECRET SOCIETIES
SEGREGATION
SERFDOM
SEX
SEX CUSTOMS
SEX RESEARCH
SEX ROLE
SHAMANISM
SHUDRAS

SIGNS AND SIGN BOARDS
SINGLE PARENT FAMILY
SINGLE PEOPLE
SINGLE WOMEN
SLAVE-TRADE
SLAVERY
SLAVERY IN ANCIENT ROME
SLAVERY IN BRAZIL
SLAVERY IN CUBA
SLAVERY IN PANAMA
SLAVERY IN PUERTO RICO
SLAVERY IN THE BRITISH EMPIRE
SLAVERY IN THE DOMINICAN REPUBLIC
SLAVERY IN THE UNITED KINGDOM
SLAVERY IN THE UNITED STATES
SLAVERY IN THE WEST INDIES
SLAVERY IN VENEZUELA
SLOW-LEARNING CHILDREN
SLUMS
SMALL GROUPS
SMOKING
SOCCER
SOCIAL ACTION
SOCIAL ADJUSTMENT
SOCIAL CASE WORK
SOCIAL CHANGE
SOCIAL CLASSES
SOCIAL CONDITIONS
SOCIAL CONFLICT
SOCIAL CONTROL
SOCIAL CREDIT
SOCIAL ETHICS
SOCIAL GROUP WORK
SOCIAL GROUPS
SOCIAL HISTORY
SOCIAL INDICATORS
SOCIAL INTERACTION
SOCIAL ISOLATION
SOCIAL LEGISLATION
SOCIAL MOBILITY
SOCIAL MOVEMENTS
SOCIAL PARTICIPATION
SOCIAL POLICY
SOCIAL PROBLEMS
SOCIAL PSYCHIATRY
SOCIAL PSYCHOLOGY

SOCIOLOGY, ANTHROPOLOGY AND ETHNOGRAPHY (cont'd)

SOCIAL REFORMERS
SOCIAL ROLE
SOCIAL SCIENCE RESEARCH
SOCIAL SCIENCES
SOCIAL SCIENCES AND STATE
SOCIAL SERVICE
SOCIAL SETTLEMENTS
SOCIAL STABILITY
SOCIAL STATUS
SOCIAL SURVEYS
SOCIAL VALUES
SOCIAL WORK EDUCATION
SOCIAL WORK WITH CHILDREN
SOCIAL WORK WITH DELINQUENTS AND CRIMINALS
SOCIAL WORK WITH YOUTH
SOCIAL WORKERS
SOCIALISM
SOCIALISM AND YOUTH
SOCIALIZATION
SOCIALLY HANDICAPPED
SOCIALLY HANDICAPPED CHILDREN
SOCIETY, PRIMITIVE
SOCIOLINGUISTICS
SOCIOLOGICAL JURISPRUDENCE
SOCIOLOGICAL RESEARCH
SOCIOLOGY
SOCIOLOGY, CHRISTIAN
SOCIOLOGY, MILITARY
SOCIOLOGY, RURAL
SOCIOLOGY, URBAN
SOCIOMETRY
SOLDIERS
SOLIDARITY
SPORTS
SQUATTERS
STEALING
STREET SIGNS.
STRUCTURALISM.
SUBURBAN LIFE
SUBURBS
SUCCESS
SUICIDE
SUMMER HOMES
SWINDLERS AND SWINDLING
SYMBOLISM

TECHNOCRACY
TECHNOLOGY AND CIVILIZATION
TELEVISION AND CHILDREN
TELEVISION AUDIENCES
TELEVISION BROADCASTING
TELEVISION PROGRAMMES
TEMPERANCE
THALIDOMIDE
THEATRE AUDIENCES
TIME ALLOCATION
TIME ALLOCATION SURVEYS
TOBACCO HABIT
TORTURE
TRAILER CAMPS
TRAMPS
TRIBES AND TRIBAL SYSTEM
TWINS
UNDERDEVELOPED AREAS
UNITED NATIONS EDUCATIONAL, SCIENTIFIC AND CULTURAL ORGANIZATION
UNMARRIED FATHERS
UNMARRIED MOTHERS
UNTOUCHABLES
VENDETTA
VICTIMS OF CRIMES
VILLAGE COMMUNITIES
VILLAGES
VIOLENCE
VIOLENCE IN MASS MEDIA
VIOLENCE IN TELEVISION
VOCATIONAL REHABILITATION
WAR AND SOCIETY
WAR CRIMES
WAR CRIMINALS
WELFARE ECONOMICS
WITCHCRAFT
WOLF CHILDREN
WOMAN
WOMEN, NEGRO
WOMEN AND PEACE
WOMEN AND RELIGION
WOMEN AND SOCIALISM
WOMEN AS ARTISTS
WOMEN AS AUTHORS
WOMEN AS BANKERS
WOMEN AS FARMERS

WOMEN IN AFRICA
WOMEN IN ASIA
WOMEN IN BOLIVIA
WOMEN IN BUSINESS
WOMEN IN CANADA
WOMEN IN COOPERATIVE SOCIETIES
WOMEN IN DENMARK
WOMEN IN FRANCE
WOMEN IN GERMANY
WOMEN IN HUNGARY
WOMEN IN INDIA
WOMEN IN ITALY
WOMEN IN JAPAN
WOMEN IN KOREA
WOMEN IN NEW GUINEA
WOMEN IN NEW ZEALAND
WOMEN IN NIGER
WOMEN IN NORWAY
WOMEN IN POLITICS
WOMEN IN PUBLIC LIFE
WOMEN IN PUERTO RICO
WOMEN IN RUSSIA
WOMEN IN SWEDEN
WOMEN IN TAIWAN
WOMEN IN THE NETHERLANDS
WOMEN IN THE UNITED KINGDOM
WOMEN IN THE UNITED STATES
WOMEN IN TRADE UNIONS
WOMEN IN TURKEY
WOMEN'S LIBERATION MOVEMENT
WORKING MEN'S CLUBS
WORTH
YOUNG MEN'S CHRISTIAN ASSOCIATION
YOUNG WOMEN'S CHRISTIAN ASSOCIATION
YOUTH
YOUTH VOLUNTEER WORKERS IN DEVELOPING COUNTRIES
YOUTH VOLUNTEERS IN SOCIAL SERVICE

Particular races, tribes and nationalities

ABKHAZIANS
AFRICANS
AFRICANS IN ASIA
AFRICANS IN FRANCE

SOCIOLOGY, ANTHROPOLOGY AND ETHNOGRAPHY (cont'd)

AFRICANS IN INDIA	CAPAUKOOS	EUROPEANS IN CHINA
AFRICANS IN THE UNITED KINGDOM	CANAVESE	EWES (AFRICAN PEOPLE)
AKAMBAS	CARIB INDIANS	FAN (AFRICAN PEOPLE)
AMERICANS	CHILEANS IN THE UNITED STATES	FANTIS
AMERICANS IN CHINA	CHIMBUS	FINGOS
ANGLO-INDIANS	CHINESE IN CAMBODIA	FINNS IN RUSSIA
ANGLO-SAXONS	CHINESE IN FOREIGN COUNTRIES	FINNS IN SWEDEN
ARABS IN AFRICA	CHINESE IN INDONESIA	FRANKS
ARABS IN EAST AFRICA	CHINESE IN MALAYA	FRENCH CANADIANS
ARABS IN ISRAEL	CHINESE IN MALAYSIA	FRENCH IN FOREIGN COUNTRIES
ARABS IN PALESTINE	CHINESE IN SOUTHEAST ASIA	FRENCH IN GERMANY
ARABS IN THE SUDAN	CHINESE IN THE PHILIPPINE ISLANDS	FRENCH IN INDIA
ARAUCANIAN INDIANS	CHINESE IN THE UNITED STATES	FRENCH IN RUSSIA
ARMENIANS IN TURKEY	CHOCTAW INDIANS	FRENCH IN SENEGAL
ARYANS	CHONTAL INDIANS	FRENCH IN SOUTH AFRICA
ASHANTIS	COLOURED PEOPLE (SOUTH AFRICA)	FRENCH IN SPAIN
AUSTRALIAN ABORIGINES	COSSACKS	FRENCH IN SWITZERLAND
AUSTRALIANS	CREE INDIANS	FRENCH IN THE UNITED KINGDOM
AUSTRIANS IN FOREIGN COUNTRIES	CROATS IN THE UNITED STATES	FULAHS
AUSTRIANS IN YUGOSLAVIA	CZECHOSLOVAKS IN AUSTRIA	GAGAUZ
AYMARA INDIANS	CZECHOSLOVAKS IN RUSSIA	GERE (AFRICAN PEOPLE)
BAJAU (MALAY PEOPLE)	CZECHS IN THE UNITED STATES	GERMANS IN BRAZIL
BANABANS	DAGOMBA (AFRICAN PEOPLE)	GERMANS IN CZECHOSLOVAKIA
BANGWA (AFRICAN PEOPLE)	DANES IN RUSSIA	GERMANS IN EASTERN EUROPE
BANTUS	DARIBI	GERMANS IN ESTONIA
BANYANKOLE	DIOLAS	GERMANS IN FOREIGN COUNTRIES
BAOULÉ (AFRICAN PEOPLE)	DUNGANS	GERMANS IN HUNGARY
BARIBA	DUTCH IN INDONESIA	GERMANS IN LATIN AMERICA
BASQUES	DUTCH IN SOUTH AFRICA	GERMANS IN LATVIA
BENGALIS IN BANGLADESH	DUTCH IN THE CARIBBEAN AREA	GERMANS IN POLAND
BERBERS	EAST GERMANS	GERMANS IN ROUMANIA
BETSILEOS	EAST INDIANS IN EAST AFRICA	GERMANS IN RUSSIA
BIHARIS IN BANGLADESH	EAST INDIANS IN FOREIGN COUNTRIES	GERMANS IN SILESIA
BOMAGAI-ANGOIANG	EAST INDIANS IN GUYANA	GERMANS IN THE ARGENTINE REPUBLIC
BRITISH IN CHINA	EAST INDIANS IN HONG KONG	GERMANS IN THE BALTIC STATES
BRITISH IN EGYPT	EAST INDIANS IN ISRAEL	GERMANS IN THE CAUCASUS
BRITISH IN FOREIGN COUNTRIES	EAST INDIANS IN NATAL	GERMANS IN THE MOLDAVIAN REPUBLIC
BRITISH IN INDIA	EAST INDIANS IN THE FIJI ISLANDS	GERMANS IN THE NETHERLANDS
BRITISH IN IRELAND	EAST INDIANS IN THE UNITED KINGDOM	GERMANS IN THE UNITED KINGDOM
BRITISH IN NIGERIA	EAST INDIANS IN TRINIDAD	GERMANS IN THE UNITED STATES
BRITISH IN SOUTH AFRICA	EAST INDIANS IN TURKESTAN	GERMANS IN TRANSYLVANIA
BRITISH IN THE CARIBBEAN	EMBUS	GILYAKS
BRITISH IN THE WEST INDIES	ENGA (NEW GUINEA PEOPLE)	GIPSIES
BULGARIANS IN BESSARABIA	ESKIMOS	GIRYAMAS
BULGARIANS IN RUSSIA	ETA	GNAU
BURYATS	EUROPEANS IN AFRICA	GOANESE IN UGANDA

SOCIOLOGY, ANTHROPOLOGY AND ETHNOGRAPHY (cont'd)

GONJA (AFRICAN TRIBE)
GREEKS IN RUSSIA
GREEKS IN THE UNITED STATES
GUARAYO INDIANS
GUAYAQUI INDIANS
GUAYCURU INDIANS
GUAYMI INDIANS
GUENS
GURU (AFRICAN TRIBE)
HAUSAS
HINDUS
HUNGARIANS IN RUSSIA
HUNGARIANS IN THE UNITED KINGDOM
HUNGARIANS IN THE UNITED STATES
IBOS
IJO (AFRICAN PEOPLE)
ILOKANOS
INDIANS
INDIANS OF CENTRAL AMERICA
INDIANS OF MEXICO
INDIANS OF NORTH AMERICA
INDIANS OF SOUTH AMERICA
INDIANS OF THE WEST INDIES
IRISH IN THE UNITED KINGDOM
IRISH IN THE UNITED STATES
ITALIANS IN BELGIUM
ITALIANS IN GERMANY
ITALIANS IN THE UNITED STATES
JAPANESE
JAPANESE IN BRAZIL
JAPANESE IN CANADA
JAPANESE IN MICRONESIA
JAPANESE IN THE HAWAIIAN ISLANDS
JAPANESE IN THE UNITED STATES
JEWISH CHILDREN
JEWS
JEWS, LIBYAN
JEWS, NORTH AFRICAN
JEWS IN AUSTRIA
JEWS IN BULGARIA
JEWS IN CANADA
JEWS IN CHINA
JEWS IN CZECHOSLOVAKIA
JEWS IN EUROPE
JEWS IN FRANCE

JEWS IN GDAŃSK
JEWS IN GERMANY
JEWS IN IRELAND
JEWS IN ITALY
JEWS IN LATIN AMERICA
JEWS IN PALESTINE
JEWS IN POLAND
JEWS IN RUSSIA
JEWS IN THE NETHERLANDS
JEWS IN THE UKRAINE
JEWS IN THE UNITED KINGDOM
JEWS IN THE UNITED STATES
KAGURU (BANTU TRIBE)
KAIADILT (AUSTRALIAN TRIBE)
KALMYKS
KANURI
KARAKALPAKS
KAWELKA (NEW GUINEA TRIBE)
KAWIA INDIANS
KAZAKS
KAZAKS IN RUSSIA
KECHUA INDIANS
KIKUYUS
KIMBU (BANTU PEOPLE)
KIRGHIZ
KOMIS
KONGOS
KONSO (AFRICAN PEOPLE)
KPELLE
KU-KLUX-KLAN
KURDS
KURDS IN IRAQ
KURDS IN RUSSIA
LAPPS IN RUSSIA
LARDIL (AUSTRALIAN TRIBE)
LOZIS
MAHALIS
MAILU
MALAY RACE IN SINGAPORE
MALAY RACE IN SOUTH AFRICA
MANDINGO (AFRICAN PEOPLE)
MAORIS
MASHONA
MATABELE
MAYAS

MELANESIANS
MERU (AFRICAN TRIBE)
MEXICANS IN THE UNITED STATES
MIAO PEOPLE
MOHAVE INDIANS
MONGOLS
MORIORIS
MOSQUITO INDIANS
MOTILON INDIANS
MOURIDES
MUKTELE TRIBE
MULATTOES
MURLE (AFRICAN PEOPLE)
NANDIS
NAVAHO INDIANS
NEGRO CHILDREN
NEGRO RACE
NEGRO YOUTH
NEGROES
NEGROES IN AFRICA
NEGROES IN AMERICA
NEGROES IN FRANCE
NEGROES IN RHODESIA
NEGROES IN SOUTH AFRICA
NEGROES IN THE DOMINICAN REPUBLIC
NEGROES IN THE UNITED KINGDOM
NEGROES IN THE WEST INDIES
NEGROES IN TRINIDAD AND TOBAGO
NOGAIS
NORWEGIANS IN THE UNITED STATES
NUAULUS
NUERS
OSSETIANS
PAEZ INDIANS
PAKISTANIS IN EAST AFRICA
PAKISTANIS IN THE UNITED KINGDOM
PAMIR TAJIKS.
PATHANS
PATIDARS
PERUVIANS IN THE UNITED STATES
POLES IN BELGIUM
POLES IN FOREIGN COUNTRIES
POLES IN FRANCE
POLES IN GERMANY
POLES IN ISRAEL
POLES IN NEW ZEALAND

SOCIOLOGY, ANTHROPOLOGY AND ETHNOGRAPHY (cont'd)

POLES IN RUSSIA	**RUSSIANS IN YAKUTIA**	**TUVANS**
POLES IN THE UNITED STATES	**RUSSIANS IN YUGOSLAVIA**	**UIGURS**
POLYNESIANS	**SAMBURU**	**UMEDAS (NEW GUINEA PEOPLE)**
PORTUGUESE IN AFRICA	**SEMINOLE INDIANS**	**UZBEKS**
PORTUGUESE IN MOZAMBIQUE	**SCOTCH IN GERMANY**	**VIETNAMESE IN THAILAND**
PORTUGUESE IN SRI LANKA	**SIKHS**	**VISIGOTHS**
PORTUGUESE IN THE UNITED STATES	**SIRIONO INDIANS**	**WELSH IN LONDON**
PUERTO RICANS IN THE UNITED STATES	**SLAVS**	**WENDS**
RENDILI	**SOGAS**	WEST INDIANS IN THE UNITED KINGD
ROUMANIANS IN AUSTRIA	**SONINKE (AFRICAN PEOPLE)**	**WHITE RUSSIANS IN POLAND**
RUSSIANS IN BULGARIA	**SPANIARDS IN AMERICA**	**YAQUI INDIANS**
RUSSIANS IN CHINA	SPANIARDS IN EUROPE	YECUANA INDIANS
RUSSIANS IN FINLAND	SPANIARDS IN FRANCE	YORUBAS
RUSSIANS IN FOREIGN COUNTRIES	SPANIARDS IN MEXICO	YUGOSLAVS IN SPAIN
RUSSIANS IN FRANCE	SPANIARDS IN THE UNITED STATES	YUGOSLAVS IN THE UNITED STATES
RUSSIANS IN GERMANY	**SWEDES IN THE UNITED STATES**	**ZANDES**
RUSSIANS IN HUNGARY	**TATARS**	**ZAPOTEC INDIANS**
RUSSIANS IN ITALY	**THONGA TRIBE**	**ZARMA (AFRICAN PEOPLE)**
RUSSIANS IN KIRGHIZIA	**TIOS**	**ZULUS**
RUSSIANS IN NORTH AMERICA	**TOUCOULEURS**	

TRANSPORT AND COMMUNICATIONS

General		
	AUTOMOBILE OWNERSHIP	**FREIGHT AND FREIGHTAGE**
	AUTOMOBILE PARKING	**FREIGHTERS**
	AUTOMOBILES	**HARBOURS**
AERONAUTICAL RESEARCH	**AUTOMOBILES, GOVERNMENT**	**HIJACKING OF AIRCRAFT**
AERONAUTICS	**BARGES**	**HITCHHIKING**
AERONAUTICS, COMMERCIAL	**BRIDGES**	INLAND NAVIGATION
AERONAUTICS AND STATE	**BRIDGES, IRON AND STEEL**	INLAND WATER TRANSPORTATION
AEROPLANES	CANALS	INTERGOVERNMENTAL MARITIME CONSULTAT ORGANIZATION
AIR LINES	CANALS, INTEROCEANIC	INTERNATIONAL CIVIL AVIATION ORGANIZATIO
AIR LINES, LOCAL SERVICE	**CARRIERS**	**LIABILITY FOR MARINE ACCIDENTS**
AIR TRAFFIC CONTROL	CHOICE OF TRANSPORTATION	LOADING AND UNLOADING
AIR TRAVEL	CITY TRAFFIC	**LOCAL TRANSIT**
AIRPORT NOISE	**COASTWISE SHIPPING**	**LOCOMOTIVES**
AIRPORTS	**COLLISIONS AT SEA**	**MARINE ACCIDENTS**
ALLIED MARITIME TRANSPORT COUNCIL	COMMUNICATION AND TRAFFIC	**MERCHANT MARINE**
ARTIFICIAL SATELLITES IN TELECOMMUNICATION	COMMUNITY ANTENNA TELEVISION	METEREOLOGY IN AERONAUTICS
ASTRONAUTICS	COMMUTING	MOTOR BUS LINES
ASTRONAUTICS AND CIVILIZATION	CONCORDE (JET TRANSPORTS)	MOTOR BUSES
AUTOMOBILE DRIVERS	**DANGEROUS GOODS**	MOTOR-TRUCKS
AUTOMOBILE DRIVERS' LICENCES	**ELECTRIC RAILWAYS**	**MOTORCYCLES**
AUTOMOBILE DRIVERS' TESTS	**FERRIES**	ORIGIN AND DESTINATION TRAFFIC SURVEYS
	FOOTBRIDGES	

TRANSPORT AND COMMUNICATIONS (cont'd)

PHYSICAL DISTRIBUTION OF GOODS
PORT DISTRICTS
POSTAGE-STAMPS
POSTAL SERVICE
RADIO BROADCASTING
RADIO FREQUENCY ALLOCATION
RADIO STATIONS
RAILWAY TERMINALS
RAILWAYS
RAILWAYS, LOCAL AND LIGHT
RAILWAYS AND OTHER CARRIERS
RAILWAYS AND STATE
ROAD ACCIDENTS
ROAD CONSTRUCTION
ROAD SAFETY
ROADS
SEARCH AND RESCUE OPERATIONS
SHIPPING
SHIPPING CONFERENCES
SHIPS
STEAMBOAT LINES
SUBWAYS
SUPERSONIC TRANSPORT PLANES
TAXICABS
TELECOMMUNICATION
TELEGRAPH
TELEPHONE
TELEVISION
TOLL ROADS
TOLLS
TONNAGE
TRAFFIC ASSIGNMENT
TRAFFIC ENGINEERING
TRAFFIC ESTIMATION
TRAFFIC FLOW
TRAFFIC NOISE
TRAFFIC OFFENCES
TRAFFIC REGULATIONS
TRAFFIC SIGNS AND SIGNALS
TRAFFIC SURVEYS
TRAMWAYS
TRANSIT, INTERNATIONAL
TRANSPORT LIBRARIES
TRANSPORTATION
TRANSPORTATION, AUTOMOTIVE
TRANSPORTATION, PRIMITIVE
TRAVEL
TRAVEL TIME (TRAFFIC ENGINEERING)
TUGBOATS
UNDERGROUND RAILWAYS
UNITIZED CARGO SYSTEMS
URBAN TRANSPORTATION
VEHICLES
VERTICALLY RISING AEROPLANES
VOYAGES AND TRAVELS
WATERWAYS

Individual undertakings, etc.

ARROW (SHIP)
BOUNTY (SHIP)
BURMA-YUNNAN RAILWAY
CANADIAN PACIFIC RAILWAY
CHANNEL TUNNEL
CHARLES ET GEORGES (SHIP)
DERBY CANAL
FEDERAL STEAM NAVIGATION COMPANY
GRAND JUNCTION RAILWAY
GRAND UNION CANAL
HOLLAND AMERICA LINE
ISLE OF MAN RAILWAY
LONDON AND NORTH EASTERN RAILWAY
LONDON AND NORTH WESTERN RAILWAY
MANCHESTER SHIP CANAL
MEFKURE
NEW ZEALAND SHIPPING COMPANY
OLD UNION CANAL
PANAMA CANAL
ROYAL MILITARY CANAL

Ref

Z
7161
L84
v.31
1972-73

APR 13 1976